D0210299

The Norton Anthology

The Norton anthology of
world literature

DISCARD

JAN 06 2014

VOLUME E

DATE DUE

	SEP 2 5 2014		

The Norton Anthology
of World Literature

SECOND EDITION

Sarah Lawall, *General Editor*

PROFESSOR OF COMPARATIVE LITERATURE AND ADJUNCT PROFESSOR OF
FRENCH, UNIVERSITY OF MASSACHUSETTS, AMHERST

Maynard Mack, *General Editor Emeritus*

LATE OF YALE UNIVERSITY

VOLUME E

1800–1900

W · W · NORTON & COMPANY · *New York* · *London*

Editor: Peter J. Simon
Developmental Editor: Carol Flechner
Associate Managing Editor: Marian Johnson
Production Manager: Diane O'Connor
Editorial Assistant: Isobel T. Evans
Project Editors: Candace Levy, Vivien Reinart, Carol Walker, Will Rigby
Permissions Manager: Nancy Rodwan
Assistant Permissions Manager: Sandra Chin
Text Design: Antonina Krass
Art Research: Neil Ryder Hoos
Maps: Jacques Chazaud

The text of this book is composed in Fairfield Medium
with the display set in Bernhard Modern.
Composition by Binghamton Valley Composition.
Manufacturing by R. R. Donnelley & Sons.
Cover illustration: Francisco José de Goya y Lucientes, *The Water Carrier.* Museum of Fine
Arts, Budapest, Hungary. Photo by Erich Lessing / Art Resource, NY.

Library of Congress Cataloging-in-Publication Data

The Norton anthology of world literature / Sarah Lawall, general editor ; Maynard Mack,
general editor emeritus. — 2nd ed.
    p. cm.
    Rev. ed. of: The North anthology of world masterpieces.
    Includes bibliographical references and index.
    Contents: v. A. Beginnings to A.D. 100 — v. B. A.D. 100–1500 — v. C. 1500–1650 — v.
D. 1650–1800 — v. E. 1800–1900 — v. F. The twentieth century.
    ISBN 0-393-97764-1 (v. 1) — ISBN 0-393-97765-X (v. 2)
    1. Literature — Collections.   I. Lawall, Sarah N.   II. Mack, Maynard, 1909–   III. Norton
anthology of world masterpieces.

PN6014 .N66 2001
808.8 — dc21   2001030824

ISBN 0-393-97759-5 (pbk.)

W. W. Norton & Company, Inc., 500 Fifth Avenue, New York, NY 10110
www.wwnorton.com

W. W. Norton & Company Ltd., Castle House, 75/76 Wells Street, London W1T 3QT

3 4 5 6 7 8 9 0

Contents

Urdu Lyric Poetry in North India   1061

Realism, Naturalism, and Symbolism in Europe 1071

Preface

The first edition of the *Norton Anthology of World Literature* to appear in the twenty-first century offers many new works from around the world and a fresh new format that responds to contemporary needs. The global reach of this anthology encompasses important works from Asia and Africa, central Asia and India, the Near East, Europe, and North and South America—all presented in the light of their own literary traditions, as a shared heritage of generations of readers in many countries, and as part of a network of cultural and literary relationships whose scope is still being discovered. With this edition, we institute a shift in title that reflects the way the anthology has grown. The initial *Norton Anthology of World Masterpieces* (1956) aimed to present a broader "Western tradition of world literature" in contrast to previous anthologies confined to English and American works; it focused on the richness and diversity of Western literary tradition, as does the Seventh Edition of 1999. The present volume, which derives from the "Expanded" edition of 1995, contains almost all the texts of the Seventh Edition and also thousands of pages from works around the globe; it now logically assumes the broader title of "World Literature." In altering the current title to *The Norton Anthology of World Literature,* we do not abandon the anthology's focus on major works of literature or a belief that these works especially repay close study. It is their consummate artistry, their ability to express complex signifying structures, that gives access to multiple dimensions of meaning, meanings that are always rooted in a specific setting and cultural tradition but that further constitute, upon comparison, a thought-provoking set of perspectives on the varieties of human experience. Readers familiar with the anthology's two volumes, whose size increased proportionally with the abundance of new material, will welcome the new boxed format, in which each of the earlier volumes is separated into three slim and easily portable smaller books. Whether maintaining the chronological structure of the original boxed set or selecting a different configuration, you will be able to consult a new Web site, developed by Norton specifically for the world-literature anthologies and containing contextual information, audiovisual resources, exploratory analyses, and related material to illustrate and illuminate these compelling texts.

The six volumes represent six consecutive chronological periods from approximately 2500 B.C. to the present. Subsequently, and for pedagogical reasons, our structure is guided by the broad continuities of different cultural traditions and the literary or artistic periods they recognize for themselves. This means that chronology advises but does not dictate the order in which works appear. If Western tradition names a certain time slot "the Renaissance" or "the Enlightenment" (each term implying a shared set of beliefs), that designation has little relevance in other parts of the globe; similarly, "vernacular literature" does not have the same literary-historical status in all traditions; and "classical" periods come at different times in India, China, and Western Europe. We find that it is more useful to start from a tradition's own sense of itself and the specific shape it gives to the community memory embodied as art. Occasionally there are displacements of absolute chronology: Petrarch, for example, belongs chronologically with Boccaccio and Chaucer, and Rousseau is a contemporary of Voltaire. Each can be read as a new and dissonant voice within his own century, a foil and balance for accepted ideas, or he can be considered as part of a powerful new consciousness, along with those indebted to his thought and example. In the first and last volumes of the anthology, for different pedagogical purposes, we have chosen to present diverse cultural traditions together. The first section of the first volume, "The Invention of Writing and the Earliest Literatures," introduces students to the study of world literature with works from three different cultural traditions—Babylonian, Egyptian, Judaic—each among the oldest works that have come down to us in written form, each in its origins reaching well back into a preliterate past, yet directly accessible as an image of human experience and still provocative at the beginning of the twenty-first century. The last volume, *The Twentieth Century*, reminds us that separation in the modern world is no longer a possibility. Works in the twentieth century are demonstrably part of a new global consciousness, itself fostered by advances in communications, that experiences reality in terms of interrelationships, of boundaries asserted or transgressed, and of the creation of personal and social identity from the interplay of sameness and difference. As teachers, we have tried to structure an anthology that is usable, accessible, and engaging in the classroom—that clarifies patterns and relationships for your students, while leaving you free to organize selections from this wealth of material into the themes, genres, topics, and special emphases that best fit your needs.

Changes in this edition have taken several forms. Most visibly, there are many new selections to spark further combinations with works you have already been teaching and to suggest ways of extending your favorite themes with additional geographic, gendered, chronological, or cultural perspectives. Thus the volume on the twentieth-century adds five important Latin American authors who are pivotal figures in their own time and with an established international stature that, in a few cases, is just beginning to be recognized in the United States. In fiction, there is Juan Rulfo, whose landmark novel *Pedro Páramo* is at once an allegory of political power in modern Mexico and a magical narrative that introduced modernist techniques to Latin American fiction, and Clarice Lispector, the innovative Brazilian novelist and short-story writer who writes primarily about women's experience and is internationally known for her descriptions of psychological states of mind. In poetry, the vehicle for political and cultural revolution in so many European and Latin American countries, we introduce the Nicaraguan Rubén Darío, a charismatic diplomat-poet at home in Europe and Latin America who created the image of a Spanish cultural identity that included his own Indian ancestry and counteracted prevailing images of North American dominance. After Darío there is Alfonsina Storni, the Argentinian poet who was as well known in the 1920s and 1930s for her independent journal articles and her feminism as for the intensely personal poetry that assures her reputation today. Finally, the Nobel Prize winner and Chilean activist Pablo Neruda, who reinvigorated the concept of public poet and became the best-known Latin American poet of the twentieth century, is represented by selections from various periods and styles of his work—in particular, the epic vision of human history taken by many to be his crowning achievement, *The Heights of Macchu Picchu.* Works by all five authors add to our representation of Spanish and Latin American literature, but their importance is not limited to regional or cultural representation. Each functions within a broader framework that may be artistic convention; national, ethnic, or class identity; feminist or postcolonial perspectives; or a particular vision of human experience. Each resonates with other works throughout the volume and is an opportunity to enrich your world-literature syllabus with new comparisons and contrasts.

Many of the new selections draw attention to historical circumstances and the texture of everyday life. Biographical tales from records of the ancient Chinese historian Ssu-ma Ch'ien give a glimpse of contemporary attitudes and ideals, as does the dedicated historian's poignant *Letter in Reply to Jen An,* written after his official punishment by castration. Entries in Dorothy Wordsworth's *Grasmere Journals* express the very personal world of the intimate journal, and Virginia Woolf's passionate analysis of the woman writer's position, in *A Room of One's Own,* combines autobiography with essay and fiction. Still other texts focus on specific historical events or issues but employ fictional techniques for greater immediacy. There is a thin line between fiction and autobiography in Tadeusz Borowski's terrifying Holocaust story *Ladies and Gentlemen, to the Gas Chamber.* Nawal El Saadawi's chilling courtroom tale *In Camera* uses the victim's shifting and fragmented perspectives to evoke the harsh realities of twentieth-century political torture and repression. Zhang Ailing's novella of a difficult love, *Love in a Fallen City,* depicts the decline of traditional Chinese society and concludes with the Japanese bombing of Hong Kong in World War II, while Anita Desai's *The Rooftop Dwellers* follows the struggles of a single woman in Delhi to make a career for herself in the face of social disapproval and family pressure. African American realist author Richard Wright, describes an adolescent crisis related to specific social images of manliness in *The Man Who Was Almost a Man.* Yet there are always different ways of presenting historical circumstances and dealing with the questions they raise. A play from Renaissance Spain, Lope de Vega's *Fuente Ovejuna,* is a light romantic comedy that draws heavily on dramatic conventions for its humor; yet it is also set during a famous peasant uprising whose bloodshed, political repercussions, and torture of the entire citizenry are represented in the course of the play. Readers who follow historical and cultural themes throughout the anthology will find much provocative material in these diverse new selections.

In renewing this edition, we have taken several routes: introducing new authors (many previously mentioned); choosing an alternate work by the same author when it resonates with material in other sections or speaks strongly to current concerns; adding small sections to existing larger pieces in order to fill out a theme or narrative line, or to suggest connections with other texts; and grouping several works to bring out new strengths. Three stories by the African writer Bernard Dadié appear here for the first time, as do the romantic adventures of Ludovico Ariosto's epic parody *Orlando Furi-*

oso, an African tale by Doris Lessing—*The Old Chief Mshlanga*—and Alice Munro's complex evocation of childhood memories *Walker Brothers Cowboy.* Among the alternate works by existing authors, we present Gustave Flaubert's great realist novel *Madame Bovary,* James Joyce's Dublin tale *The Dead,* and William Faulkner's *The Bear,* the latter printed in its entirety to convey its full scope as a chronicle of the legacy of slavery in the American South. New plays include Bertolt Brecht's drama *The Good Woman of Setzuan* and William Shakespeare's *Othello* as well as *Hamlet;* each has its own special resonance in world literature. Derek Walcott is represented by a selection of his poetry, including excerpts from the modern epic *Omeros.* Five more magical tales are added to the *Thousand and One Nights* and three new essays from Montaigne, including his memorable *To the Reader.* Six new tales from Ovid (in a new translation by Allen Mandelbaum) round out a set of myths exploring different images of love and gender, themes that reappear in two of the best-known lays of Marie de France, *Lanval* and *Laüstic,* as well as in Boccaccio's famous "Pot of Basil" and the influential tale of patient Griselda and her tyrannical husband, all presented here. From Chaucer, there is the bawdy, popular *Wife of Bath's Tale,* and from the *Heptameron* of Marguerite de Navarre fresh tales of love and intrigue that emphasize the stereotyping of gender roles. To *The Cherry Orchard* by Anton Chekhov, we add his famous tale of uncertain love *The Lady with the Dog.* New selections from Books 4 and 8 of John Milton's *Paradise Lost* depict the drama of Satan's malevolent entry into Paradise, Adam and Eve's innocent conversation, and the angel's warning to Adam. Finally, the poignant tales of Abraham and Isaac and of Jacob and Esau (Genesis 22, 25, 27) are added to the Old Testament selections, as well as the glorious love poetry of the Song of Songs; and Matthew 13 [Why Jesus Teaches in Parables] is included among the selections from the New Testament.

Two founding works of early India, the *Rāmāyaṇa* and the *Mahābhārata,* are offered in greatly increased selections and with new and exceptionally accessible translations. Readers can now follow (in a new translation by Swami Venkatesananda) the trajectory of Rāma's exile and life in the forest, the kidnapping of his wife Sītā, and ensuing magical adventures up to the final combat between Rāma and the demon king Rāvaṇa. A lively narrative of the *Mahābhārata*'s civil war (in a new translation by C. V. Narasimhan) unfolds in sequential excerpts that include two sections of special interest to modern students: the insulted Draupadī's formal accusation of the rulers in the Assembly Hall and the tragic story of the heroic but ill-fated warrior Karṇa.

To increase our understanding of individual authors' achievement, we join to the Indian Rabindranath Tagore's story *Punishment* a selection of the Bengali poems with which he revolutionized literary style in his homeland, and to the Chinese Lu Xun's two tales, examples of his poetry from *Wild Grass.* Rousseau's *Confessions* gain historical and psychological depth through new passages that shed light on his early years and on the development of his political sympathies.

The epic poetry that acts as the conscience of a community—*The Iliad, The Mahābhārata,* the *Son-Jara,* among others—has long been represented in the anthology. It has been our practice, however, to minimize the presence of lyric poetry in translation, recognizing—as is so cogently argued in the

"Note on Translation," printed at the end of each volume—that the precise language and music of an original poem will never be identical with its translation and that short poems risk more of their substance in the transfer. Yet good translations often achieve a poetry of their own and occupy a pivotal position in a second literary history; thus the Egyptian love songs, the Chinese *Classic of Poetry* (*Book of Songs*), the biblical Song of Songs, and the lyrics of Sappho, Catullus, Petrarch, Rumi, and Baudelaire have all had influence far beyond the range of those who could read the original poems. Some poetry collections—like the Japanese *Man'yōshū* and *Kokinshū*—are recognized as an integral part of the society's cultural consciousness, and others—notably, the European Romantics—embody a sea change in artistic and cultural consciousness.

New to this edition is a series of poetry clusters that complement existing collections and represent a core of important and influential poetry in five different periods. You may decide to teach them as part of a spectrum of poetic expression or as reference points in a discussion of cultural consciousness. Thus a newly translated series of early hymns by the Tamil Śaiva saints exemplifies the early mystical poetry of India, while the multifarious vitality of medieval Europe is recaptured in poems by men and women from Arabic, Judaic, Welsh, Spanish, French, Provençal, Italian, English, and German traditions. Those who have taught English Romantic poetry will find both contrast and comparison in Continental poets from France, Italy, Germany, Spain, and Russia, many of whom possess lasting influence in nineteenth- and twentieth-century literature. Symbolism, whose insights into the relation of language and reality have permeated modern poetry and linguistic theory, is represented by the great nineteenth-century poets Charles Baudelaire, Stéphane Mallarmé, Paul Verlaine, and Arthur Rimbaud. Finally, a cluster of Dada-Surrealist poems that range from slashing, rebellious humor to ecstatic love introduces the free association and dreamlike structures of this visionary movement, whose influence extends around the world and has strong links to modern art and film.

How to choose, as you turn from the library before you to the inevitable constraint of available time? There is an embarrassment of riches, an inexhaustible series of options, to fit whatever course pattern you wish. Perhaps you have already decided to proceed by theme or genre, in chronological order or by a selected comparative principle; or you have favorite titles that work well in the classroom, and you seek to combine them with new pieces. Perhaps you want to create modules that compare ideas of national identity or of bicultural identity and shifting cultural paradigms, that survey images of gender in different times and places or that examine the place of memory in a range of texts. In each instance, you have only to pick and choose among a variety of works from different countries, languages, and cultural backgrounds. If you are teaching the course for the first time or wish to try something different, you may find what you are looking for in the sample syllabi of the *Instructor's Guide* or on the new Web site, which will also contain supporting material such as maps, time lines, and audio pronunciation glossaries, resource links, guides to section materials, various exercises and assignments, and a series of teaching modules related to specific works. Throughout, the editors (who are all practicing teachers) have selected and prepared texts that are significant in their own area of scholarly expertise, meaningful in the larger context of world literature, and, always, delightful, captivating and challenging to students.

Clearly one can parcel out the world in a variety of ways, most notably geopolitical, and there is no one map of world literature. In order to avoid parochialism, some scholars suggest that we should examine cultural activity in different countries at the same period of time. Others attempt to deconstruct prevailing literary assumptions (often selected from Western literary theory) by using history or cultural studies as a framework for examining texts as documents. "Global" literary studies project a different map that depends on one's geopolitical view of global interactions and of the energies involved in the creation and dissemination of literature. *The Norton Anthology of World Literature*, Second Edition, takes a different point of departure, focusing first of all on literary texts—artifacts, if you will, that have a special claim on our attention because they have been read over a great period of time and are cherished by a wide variety of readers. Once such texts have been proposed as objects of knowledge—and enjoyment, and illumination— they are available for any and all forms of analysis. Situating them inside larger forms of textuality—linguistic, historical, or cultural—is, after all, an inevitable part of the meaning-making process. It is the primary task of this anthology, however, to present them as multidimensional objects for discussion and then to let our readers choose when and where to extend the analysis.

From the beginning, the editors of *The Norton Anthology of World Literature* have always balanced the competing—and, we like to think, complementary—claims of teaching and scholarship, of the specialist's focused expertise and the generalist's broader perspectives. The founding editors set the example, which guides their successors. We welcome three new successor editors to this edition: William G. Thalmann, Professor of Classics at the University of Southern California; Lee Patterson, Professor of English at Yale University; and Heather James, Associate Professor of English at the University of Southern California. Two founding editors have assumed Emeritus status: Bernard M. W. Knox, eminent classical scholar and legendary teacher and lecturer; and P. M. Pasinetti, who combines the intellectual breadth of the Renaissance scholar with a novelist's creative intuition. We also pay tribute to the memory of Robert Lyons Danly, translator and astute scholar of Japanese literature, whose lively interventions have been missed since his untimely death in 1995. Finally, we salute the memory of Maynard Mack, General Editor and presiding genius from the first edition through the Expanded Edition of 1995. An Enlightenment scholar of much wisdom, humanity, and gracefully worn knowledge, and a firm believer in the role of great literature—world literature—in illuminating human nature, he was also unstintingly dedicated to this anthology as a teaching enterprise. To him, therefore, and on all counts, we dedicate the first millennial edition of the anthology.

Acknowledgments

Among our many critics, advisers, and friends, the following were of special help in providing suggestions and corrections: Joseph Barbarese (Rutgers University); Carol Clover (University of California, Berkeley); Patrick J. Cook (George Washington University); Janine Gerzanics (University of Southern California); Matthew Giancarlo (Yale University); Kevis Goodman (University of California at Berkeley); Roland Greene (University of Oregon); Dmitri Gutas (Yale University); John H. Hayes (Emory University); H. Mack Horton (University of California at Berkeley); Suzanne Keen (Washington and Lee University); Charles S. Kraszewski (King's College); Gregory F. Kuntz; Michelle Latiolais (University of California at Irvine); Sharon L. James (Bryn Mawr College); Ivan Marcus (Yale University); Timothy Martin (Rutgers University, Camden); William Naff (University of Massachusetts); Stanley Radosh (Our Lady of the Elms College); Fred C. Robinson (Yale University); John Rogers (Yale University); Robert Rothstein (University of Massachusetts); Lawrence Senelick (Boston University); Jack Shreve (Alleghany Community College); Frank Stringfellow (University of Miami); Nancy Vickers (Bryn Mawr College); and Jack Welch (Abilene Christian University).

We would also like to thank the following people who contributed to the planning of the Second Edition: Charles Adams, University of Arkansas; Dorothy S. Anderson, Salem State College; Roy Anker, Calvin College; John Apwah, County College of Morris; Doris Bargen, University of Massachusetts; Carol Barrett, Austin Community College, Northridge Campus; Michael Beard, University of North Dakota; Lysbeth Em Berkert, Northern State University; Marilyn Booth, University of Illinois; George Byers, Fairmont State College; Shirley Carnahan, University of Colorado; Ngwarsungu Chiwengo, Creighton University; Stephen Cooper, Troy State University; Bonita Cox, San Jose State University; Richard A. Cox, Abilene Christian University; Dorothy Deering, Purdue University; Donald Dickson, Texas A&M University; Alexander Dunlop, Auburn University; Janet Eber, County College of Morris; Angela Esterhammer, University of Western Ontario; Walter Evans, Augusta State University; Fidel Fajardo-Acosta, Creighton University; John C. Freeman, El Paso Community College, Valle Verde Campus; Barbara Gluck, Baruch College; Michael Grimwood, North Carolina State University; Rafey Habib, Rutgers University, Camden; John E. Hallwas, Western Illinois College; Jim Hauser, William Patterson College; Jack Hussey, Fairmont State College; Dane Johnson, San Francisco State University; Andrew Kelley, Jackson State Community College; Jane Kinney, Valdosta State University; Candace Knudson, Truman State University; Jameela Lares, University of Southern Mississippi; Thomas L. Long, Thomas Nelson Community College; Sara MacDonald, Sterling College; Linda Macri, University of Maryland; Rita Mayer, San Antonio College; Christopher Morris,

Norwich University; Deborah Nestor, Fairmont State College; John Netland, Calvin College; Kevin O'Brien, Chapman University; Mariannina Olcott, San Jose State University; Charles W. Pollard, Calvin College; Pilar Rotella, Chapman University; Rhonda Sandford, Fairmont State College; Daniel Schenker, University of Alabama at Huntsville; Robert Scotto, Baruch College; Carl Seiple, Kutztown University; Glenn Simshaw, Chemeketa Community College; Evan Lansing Smith, Midwestern State University; William H. Smith, Piedmont College; Floyd C. Stuart, Norwich University; Cathleen Tarp, Fairmont State College; Diane Thompson, Northern Virginia Community College; Sally Wheeler, Georgia Perimiter College; Jean Wilson, McMaster University; Susan Wood, University of Nevada, Las Vegas; Tom Wymer, Bowling Green State University.

Phonetic Equivalents

for use with the Pronouncing Glossaries preceding most
selections in this volume

a as in *cat*
ah as in *father*
ai as in *light*
ay as in *day*
aw as in *raw*
e as in *pet*
ee as in *street*
ehr as in *air*
er as in *bird*
eu as in *lurk*
g as in *good*
i as in *sit*
j as in *joke*
nh a nasal sound (as in French *vin, vẽ*)
o as in *pot*
oh as in *no*
oo as in *boot*
oy as in *toy*
or as in *bore*
ow as in *now*
s as in *mess*
ts as in *ants*
u as in *us*
zh as in *vision*

The Norton Anthology
of World Literature

SECOND EDITION

VOLUME E

1800–1900

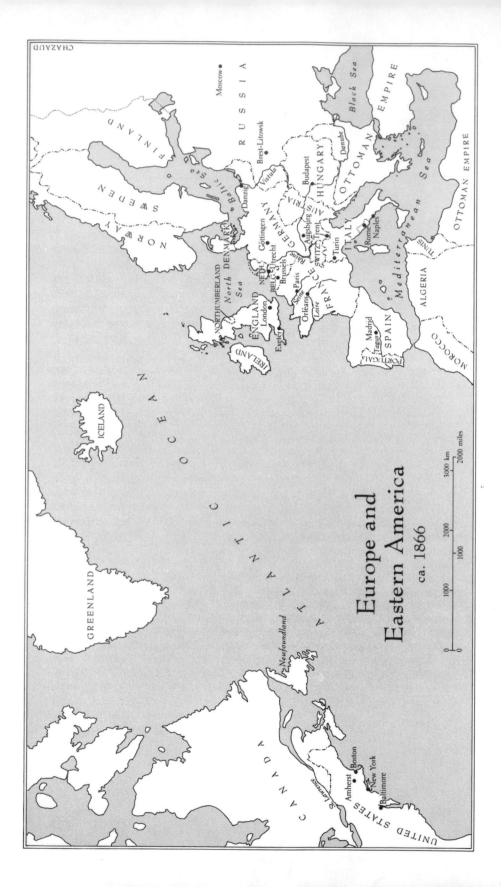

Europe and
Eastern America
ca. 1866

Revolution and Romanticism in Europe and America

"Bliss was it in that dawn to be alive, / But to be young was very heaven." William Wordsworth alludes here to his experience, at the age of seventeen, of the French Revolution. The possibility of referring to a national cataclysm in such terms suggests the remarkable shift in sensibility, in dominant assumptions, in intellectual preoccupations, that occurred late in the eighteenth century. We call the evidence of that shift "Romanticism"—a designation so grandly inclusive as to defy definition. If our terms for the late seventeenth and early eighteenth centuries ("Enlightenment," "Age of Reason") emphasize one aspect of the prevailing intellectual culture to the exclusion of others equally important, the label *Romanticism* refers to so many cultural manifestations that one can hardly pin it down. In general, it implies new emphases on imagination, on feeling, on the value of the primitive and untrammeled, and particularly a narrowing of outlook from the universal to the particular, from humankind or "man" (the subject of Pope's *Essay*) to nation or ethnic group, and from the stability of community to the "fulfillment" of the individual. Such shifts have important political and philosophic as well as literary implications.

In the writings of individuals, one finds lines of continuity between the late and early parts of the eighteenth century; but when it comes to generalizations, all the important truths appear to have reversed themselves. In the middle of the century, reason was the guide to certainty; at the century's end, *feeling* tested authenticity. Earlier, tradition still anchored experience; now, the ideal of joyous liberation implied rejection of traditional authority. Wisdom had long associated itself with maturity, even with old age; by the 1790s, William Blake hinted at the child's superior insight, and Wordsworth openly claimed for the infant holy wisdom inevitably lost in the process of aging. Johnson had valued experience as a vital path to knowledge; at the beginning of the nineteenth century, innocence—in its nature evanescent—provided a more generally treasured resource.

Cause and effect, in such massive shifts of perspective, can never be ascertained. The French Revolution derived from new ideas about the sacredness of the individual; it also helped generate such ideas. Without trying to distinguish causes from effects—indeed, with a strong suspicion that the period's striking phenomena constitute simultaneous causes and effects—one can specify a number of ways that the world appeared to change, as the eighteenth century approached the nineteenth, as well as ways that these changes both solidified themselves and evoked challenges later in the nineteenth century.

NEW AND OLD

The embattled farmers of Concord, Massachusetts, fired the shot heard round the world in 1775; fourteen years later, the Bastille fell. Both the American and the

French revolutions developed out of strong convictions about the innate rights of individual human beings—in other words, Protestantism in political form. Those who developed revolutionary theory glimpsed new human possibility. The hope of salvation lay in the overturning of established institutions. Swift, in *Gulliver's Travels,* had made a clear distinction between institutions as ideal constructions of human reason and their corruption in practice. Lawyers might be a money-grubbing, hypocritical lot; but the idea of law, of a social structure designed to ensure the provision of justice, has its own inherent power. The theory of revolution implied radical assault on virtually all social institutions. Fundamental hierarchies of government, notions of sovereignty and of aristocracy, inherited systems of distinction—all fell. Old conventions, once emblems of social and of literary stability, now exemplified the dead hand of the past. Only a few years before, the old, the inherited, and the traditional embodied truth, its power attested by its survival. But the revolutionaries felt themselves to be originators; the newness of what they proposed gave it the almost religious authority suggested by Wordsworth's allusions to "bliss" and "heaven."

The blessed state evoked by the new political thinkers embodied a sense of infinite possibility. Pope had written, in *Essay on Man,* "The bliss of Man (could Pride that blessing find) / Is not to act or think beyond mankind." By the century's end, people were doing their best to "think beyond mankind"—or, at any rate, beyond what had been considered normal limitations. Evidence of this effort abounds, in revolutionary sermons preached from pulpits even in England, in writings by such flamboyant defenders of human rights as Thomas Paine, in the development, even, of a political theory about women's social position. Mary Wollstonecraft was not the first to note the oppression of women; a century before her, Mary Astell had suggested the need for broader female education, and outcries on the subject emerged sporadically even earlier in the seventeenth century. But Wollstonecraft's *Vindication of the Rights of Woman* (1792) offered the first detailed argument that the ideal of fulfilled human possibility for men and for women demanded political acknowledgment of women's equality.

The very existence of such a work (which achieved a second edition in the year of its first publication) testifies to the atmosphere of political expectancy in which men and women could rethink "self-evident" principles. Replacing the ideal of hierarchy (what Dr. Johnson revered as "subordination"), for example, was the revolutionary notion of human brotherhood. Liberty, equality, and fraternity, the French proclaimed; the new American nation celebrated essentially the same ideals. In practice, though, *fraternity* turned out to involve the citizens specifically of France, or of the new United States. The emphasis on individual uniqueness extended itself to national uniqueness. In America particularly, ideas of national character and of national destiny developed almost talismanic force. Although peace generally prevailed among nations in the early nineteenth century, the developing distinctions dividing one country imaginatively from another foretold future danger.

New ideas with massive practical consequences included more than the political. In 1776, Adam Smith published *The Wealth of Nations,* a theory of laissez-faire economics presaging the enormous importance of money in subsequent history. Matters of exchange and acquisition, Smith argued, could be left to regulate themselves—a doctrine behind which still lurked unobtrusively the confidence, expressed in market terms, that Pope had expressed in religious ones: "All Chance, Direction, which thou canst not see, / All Discord, Harmony, not understood." As manufacturing and trade developed increasing financial vitality, however, their importance as financial resources in fact heightened discord, through growing nationalism. Early in the century, at the end of *Windsor Forest* (1713), Pope had recognized in Britain's trade a form of power. A century later, the acceleration of this power would have astonished Pope. No longer did agriculture provide England's central economic resource. New forms of manufacture provided new substance for trade, generated new fortunes, produced a new social class—a "middle class" with the influence of wealth and without the inherited system of responsibilities, restrictions, and decorums that had helped control aristocratic possessors of wealth in preceding generations. Aristocrats had used their money, on the whole, to enlarge and beautify their estates. The new money-holders developed new ideas about what money might do. Reinvested, it could support innovation in manufacture and trade. It could educate the children of the uneducated; it could buy them (as it had been doing for a century) husbands and wives from the aristocracy; it could help obviate ancient class distinctions. England's increasing economic ascendancy in the nineteenth century derived not only from new money but from the development of men willing and able to employ money ingeniously as power.

The enlarged possibilities of manufacture testified to practical applications of scientific research, another area of activity in which the new overwhelmingly replaced the old. In England and America especially, inventions multiplied: the steam engine, the spinning jenny, the cotton gin. Increasingly often, and in increasing numbers, men and women left their native rural environments to congregate in cities, where opportunities for relatively unskilled workers abounded—and where more and more people lived in congestion, poverty, and misery.

More vividly, perhaps, than ever before in history, the world was changing—was becoming, in fact, the world we ourselves assume, in which *mankind* as an ideal wanes, nations define themselves in psychic and military opposition to one another, money constitutes immediate power, science serves manufacture and hence commerce. From the beginning of these crucial changes, certain thinkers and writers realized the destructive possibilities inherent in every form of "progress." Blake, for example, glimpsed London's economic brutality and human wastefulness; his "revolutionary" impulses expressed themselves partly in resistance to the consequences of the new. That is to say, the new gave way to the newer, as it had not previously done on such a scale. No longer did the impulse to conserve past values express itself with the authority and power that Swift and Johnson had brought to the theme. As M. H. Abrams has written, "the Romantic period was eminently an age obsessed with the fact of violent change." Such change might provide ground for fear; it also supplied the substance for hope.

INDIVIDUALISM

Immanuel Kant (1724–1804), a German philosopher whose work influenced virtually all philosophers after him, questioned the power of reason to provide the most significant forms of knowledge—knowledge of the ultimately real. Feeling, on the other hand, might offer a guide. The individual will must engage itself in ethical struggle to locate and experience the good. Such followers of Kant as Johann Fichte (1762–1814) more clearly suggested an identification between will and what we call ego. The idea of the self took on ever greater importance, for philosophers and for poets, for political thinkers, autobiographers, and novelists.

To locate authority in the self rather than in society implies yet another radical break with the assumptions of the previous period. The idea of the self's importance is so familiar to us that it may be difficult to imagine the startling implications of the new focus. "I know the feelings of my heart, and I know men," Jean-Jacques Rousseau writes, at the beginning of his *Confessions*. "I am not made like any of those I have seen; I venture to believe that I am not made like any of those who are in existence." Samuel Johnson would have felt certain that a man who could write such words must be mad, like the astronomer in *Rasselas* who believes himself to control the weather. Yet faith in the absolute uniqueness of every consciousness became increasingly prevalent. Rousseau's significance for his period derives partly from the fact that his stress on the feelings of his heart and on his own specialness aroused recognition in his audience. No longer did the universality of human nature supply comfort to individuals; now they might seek reassurance instead in their uniqueness. It was the ultimate development of protestantism—to everyone his or her own church.

Not only could individuals now see themselves as unique but they could also understand themselves as *good*. In its earlier forms, Christianity had emphasized the fallen nature of the human soul. Every self, according to this view, contains the potential for violence and destructiveness. One must rely on God's grace for salvation, which cannot depend on human worth. At the secular level, human beings need institutions to provide the controls that save us from anarchy—from the evil latent in ourselves. Rousseau and his successors articulated the opposite position, stressing the essential goodness of human nature and the corresponding danger of institutional restraint. Repressiveness now became the fearful enemy, uniformity the menace. We may recognize the fear of external control today in the slogans of those celebrating the importance of "individual rights," and we still hear the older faith in institutions in the proponents of "law and order."

The new emphasis on the individual opened new possibilities for writers of poetry and prose alike. Even the grotesque and deviant became interesting. Victor Hugo could explore the psychology of Satan, for example: the angel cast out of heaven and falling through the abyss, undergoing a process of increasing horror, enduring the going out of light, but remaining defiant throughout his long ordeal. Unlike John Milton, who directed attention to cosmic drama on a large scale, Hugo concentrates his focus to create an impression of poignance as well as nightmare. In Russia, Alexander Pushkin investigated the psychology (as well as the social arrangements) of a group of people concerned only with money, generating a quite different sense of horror.

As these instances will suggest, stress on the individual implied revaluation of inner as opposed to outer experience. Previously, life in the public arena had been assumed to test human capacities and to provide meaningful forms of experience. After Rousseau, however, psychic experience could provide the proper measure of an individual's emotional capacity. To place value *there* opened the possibility of taking women as seriously as men, children as seriously as adults, "savages" as seriously as civilized beings. Indeed, women, children, and "primitive" peoples were often thought to exceed cultivated adult males in their capacity both to feel and to express their feelings spontaneously—although the social subordination of such groups continued unchanged.

Even before Rousseau, the novel of sensibility in England and on the Continent revealed interest in highly developed emotional responsiveness. Johann Wolfgang von Goethe's *The Sorrows of Young Werther* (1774) made its author famous and inspired a cult of introverted, melancholy young people. In England, Henry Mackenzie's *The Man of Feeling* (1771) associated intense emotion with benevolent action. By the latter part of the century, the Gothic novel had become an important form—a novelistic mode, often practiced by women, that typically placed a young woman at the center of the action. The heroines of such novels confront a kind of experience (usually involving at least apparent supernatural elements) for which their social training, that important resource of earlier heroines, provided no help; instead, quick intuitions and subtle feelings ensure their triumph over apparently insurmountable obstacles with no loss of feminine delicacy.

Given the view of feeling's centrality that replaced the earlier stress on passion's fruitful tension with reason, a broader spectrum of feeling drew literary attention. From its beginnings, the novel had tended to emphasize (usually in decorous terms) love between the sexes. Now romantic love became a central subject of poetry and drama as well. More surprising kinds of emotion also attracted notice. William Blake imagined a chimney sweep's emotional relation to the idea of heaven; Samuel Taylor Coleridge and Percy Bysshe Shelley made poetry of dejection; Alfred, Lord Tennyson, at the midpoint of the nineteenth century, wove his anxieties about the revelations of recent scientific inquiry into the texture of an elegiac poem. Rosalía de Castro wrote of the death of her child; Giacomo Leopardi could produce a lyric called *To Himself*, exploring his personal relation to large ideas; Friedrich Hölderlin, in Germany, like Wordsworth and Coleridge in England, used the making of poetry as a subject for thought and feeling alike. As these examples indicate, painful as well as pleasurable emotion interested readers and writers. The poet, Wordsworth said, is a man speaking to men; poetry originates in recollected emotion and recapitulates lost feeling. Lyric, not epic, typifies poetry for Wordsworth, who understands his genre as a form of emotional communication.

Wordsworth's definition ignores the fact that women, too (including his own sister, Dorothy), wrote poetry. Emily Brontë, Christina Rossetti, Rosalía de Castro, Anna Petrovna Bunina, Emily Dickinson—such women writing in different countries evoked intense passion in verse. In the Romantic novel, too, women excelled in the rendering of powerful feeling. The Brontë sisters, like George Eliot after them in England, like the equally passionate George Sand in France, wrote under male pseudonyms but established distinctively female visions of the struggle not only for love but also for freedom and power within a context of social restriction. Mary Shelley (daughter of Mary Wollstonecraft and wife of the poet Shelley) in her eloquent fable of creativity, *Frankenstein* (1818), epitomizes the peculiar intensity of much women's writing in this period.

As the nineteenth century wore on, hope for a new terrestrial Eden faded. The efflorescence of commerce and the innovations of science turned out to have negative as well as positive consequences. As the novels of Charles Dickens and William Thackeray insist, the new middle class frequently became the repository of moral mediocrity. The autocracy of money had effects more brutal than those of inherited privilege. Science, once the emblem of progress, began to generate theological confusion. Charles Darwin's *Origin of Species* (1859) stated clearly humanity's mean rather than transcendent origins: animal and plant species had evolved over the centuries, adapting themselves to their environment through the process of natural selection. Fossils found in rocks provided supporting evidence for this theory—an assertion troubling to many Christians because it contradicted the biblical account of creation. Eight years after Darwin's revolutionary work, Karl Marx published *Das Kapital*, with its dialectical theory of history and its vision of capitalism's eventual decay and of the working class inevitably triumphant. In the United States civil war raged from 1860 to 1865, its central issue states' rights, a topic that, of course, implicated the morality of slavery—that by-product of agricultural capitalism. Neither the making of money nor the effort to fathom natural law seemed merely reassuring.

In the face of history's threats—the menace of Marx's prophecy and of Darwin's biology, the chaos of civil war—to insist on the importance of private experience offered tentative security, a standing place, a temporary source of authority. The voices of blacks and, in increasing numbers, of women could now be heard: placing high value on the personal implied respecting all persons. The American Civil War made African Americans for the first time truly visible to the society that both contained and denied them. Slave narratives—sometimes wholly or partly fictionized, sometimes entirely authentic renditions of often horrifying experience—provided useful propaganda for the abolitionist cause, the ideology opposed to the institution of slavery. They also opened a new emotional universe. In their typical emphasis, for instance, on the salvationary force of reading and writing (for most slaves officially forbidden knowledge), these narratives illuminated a new area of the taken-for-granted, thus extending the enterprise of Romantic poetry.

The capacity for revelatory illumination belonged, according to the dominant nineteenth-century view, to imagination, a mysterious and virtually sacred power of individual consciousness. When Johnson, in *Rasselas*, suggested that all predominance of imagination over reason constituted a degree of insanity, he intended, to put it crudely, an antithesis of true and false. Imagination, the faculty of generating images, had no necessary anchor in the communal, historical experience that tested truth. For Wordsworth and Coleridge and those who came after them, imagination was a visionary and unifying force (a new incarnation of the seventeenth century's inner light or candle of the Lord) through which the gifted person discovered and communicated new truth. (Johnson, of course, would have denied the possibility of "new" truth.) As Coleridge wrote,

> from the soul itself must issue forth
> A light, a glory, a fair luminous cloud
> Enveloping the Earth.

Imagination derived from the soul, the aspect of human being that links the human with the eternal. Through it, men and women can transcend earthly limitations, can express high aspiration, can escape, and help one another escape, the dreariness of mortality without necessarily positing a life beyond the present one.

A corollary of the high value attached to creative imagination was a new concern with originality. The notion of "the genius," the man or woman so gifted as to operate by principles unknown to ordinary mortals, developed only in the late eighteenth century. Previously, a person *had* rather than *was a* genius: the term designated a particular tendency or gift (a genius for cooking, say) rather than a human being with vast creative power. Now the genius was revered for his or her extraordinary difference from others, idealized as a being set apart; and the literary or artistic products of genius, it could be assumed, would correspondingly differ from everything previously produced. Yet the writers of this movement also recorded their anxiety about the claim of specialness implicit in the idea of genius. Goethe's *Faust*, a rewriting of an old legend, emphasizes the danger inherent in the desire to do what no one had ever done, to be what no one had ever been.

Despite all reservations, though, newness now became as never before a measure of value. The language, the themes, the forms of the preceding century would no longer suffice. In the early eighteenth century, literary figures wishing to congratulate themselves and their contemporaries would compare their artistic situation to that of Rome under the benevolent patronage of Augustus Caesar. A hundred years later, the note of self-congratulation would express itself in the claim of an unprecedented situation, unprecedented kinds of accomplishment. John Keats in a letter characterized Wordsworth as representing "the egotistical sublime." Such sublimity—authority and grandeur emanating from a unique self still in touch with something beyond itself—was the nineteenth century's special achievement.

NATURE

Nature and nature's laws, the rationally ordered universe, provided the foundation for much early eighteenth-century thought. In the nineteenth century, nature's importance possibly increased—but *nature* now meant something new. *Wuthering Heights* (1847) creates a setting of windswept moors for its romantic lovers—both environment and metaphor of their love. Wordsworth could value a host of daffodils, or fog-enveloped hills, or an icy lake. Lamartine appealed to the landscape to embody the characteristics of his lost love. The physical reality of the natural world, in its varied abundance, became a matter of absorbing interest for poets and novelists. Nature provided an alternative to the human, a possibility for imaginative as well as literal escape. Its imagery—flowers, clouds, ocean—became the common poetic stock. Workers still hastened from the country to the city, because the city housed possibilities of wealth; yet educated men and women increasingly declared their nostalgia for rural or sylvan landscapes embodying peace and beauty.

Nature, in the nineteenth-century mind, however, did not consist only in physical details. It also implied a totality, an enveloping whole greater than the sum of its parts, a vast unifying spirit. Wordsworth evokes

> a sense sublime
> Of something far more deeply interfused,
> Whose dwelling is the light of setting suns,
> And the round ocean and the living air,
> And the blue sky, and in the mind of man:
> A motion and a spirit, that impels
> All thinking things, all objects of all thought,
> And rolls through all things.

Coleridge and Shelley hint similar visions, vague yet comforting. The unifying whole, as Wordsworth's language suggests, depends less on rational system than on emotional association. Human beings link themselves with the infinite by what Wordsworth elsewhere terms "wise passiveness," the capacity to submit to feeling and be led by it to transcendence. Natural detail, too, acquires value by evoking and symbolizing emotion. Nature belongs to the realm of the nonrational, the superrational. It can be linked, as it is for Anna Petrovna Bunina, with a sense of misery and pain, or it can evoke, as it does for Dorothy Wordsworth, possibilities of utter joy and transcendence.

The idea of the natural can also imply the uncivilized, or precivilized. Philosophers have differed dramatically in their hypotheses about what humankind was like in its "natural" state. Thomas Hobbes, in the seventeenth century, argued that the natural human condition was one of conflict. Society developed to curb the violent impulses human beings would manifest without its restraint. The prevailing nineteenth-century view, on the other hand, made civilization the agent of corruption. Rousseau expounded the crippling effect of institutions. The child raised with the greatest possible freedom, he maintained, would develop in more admirable ways than one subjected to system. By the second half of the eighteenth century, a French novelist could contrast the decadent life of Europe unfavorably with existence on an unspoiled island (Bernardin de Saint-Pierre, *Paul and Virginia,* 1788); Thomas Chatterton, before committing suicide in 1770 at the age of eighteen, wrote poems rich in nostalgia for a more primitive stage of social development that he tried to pass off as medieval works; the forged Ossian poems (1760–63) of James Macpherson, purportedly ancient texts, attracted a large and enthusiastic audience. New interest manifested itself in ballads, poetic survivals of the primitive; Romantic poets imitated the form. The interest in a simpler past, a simpler life, continued throughout the nineteenth century: in Victorian England, Tennyson recast Arthurian legend in modern verse; the Pre-Raphaelites evoked the medieval in visual and verbal arts.

The revolutionary fervor of the late eighteenth century had generated a vision of infinite human possibility, political and personal. The escapist implications of the increasing emphasis on nature, the primitive, the uncomplicated past, suggest, however, a sense of alienation. Blake, Wordsworth, Shelley, all wrote poems of social protest. "Society" would not help the individual work out his or her salvation; on the contrary, it embodied forces opposed to individual development. Indeed, the word *society* had come to embody the impulses that desecrated nature and oppressed the poor in the interests of industry and "progress." Melancholy marked the Romantic hero (Lord Byron in his poetic self-manifestations; Heathcliff in fiction, for example) and tinged nineteenth-century poetry and fiction. The satiric spirit—that spirit of social reform—was in abeyance. Hope lay in the individual's separation from, not participation in, society. In the woods and mountains, one might feel free.

The Waste Land (1922), T. S. Eliot's twentieth-century epic, contains the line "In the mountains, there you feel free," a line given complex ironic overtones by its context. Its occurrence, however, may remind us how powerfully ideas that came into currency in the late eighteenth and early nineteenth centuries survive into our own time. The world of the Romantic period specifically prefigures our own, despite all the differences dividing the two cultures. We have developed more fully important Romantic tendencies: stress on the sacredness of the individual, suspicion of social institutions, belief in expressed feeling as the sign of authenticity, nostalgia for simpler ways of being, faith in genius, valuing of originality and imagination, an ambivalent relation to science. Although Wordsworth and Dickinson and Melville employ vocabularies and use references partly strange to us, they speak directly to the preoccupations of our time. By attending closely to them, we may learn more about ourselves: not only in the common humanity that we share with all our predecessors but in our special historical situation as both direct heirs of nineteenth-century assumptions and rebels against them. Chronology provides little guide to the Romantic period. Jean-Jacques Rousseau, the first writer included in this section, died before Gustavo Bécquer was born. The Romantic movement, as subsequent critics have defined it, extends from the late eighteenth to the late nineteenth century, but it is overlapped throughout by other sets of literary and philosophic assumptions.

FURTHER READING

Useful introductions to the Romantic period include L. Furst, *Romanticism in Perspective: A Comparative Study of Aspects of the Romantic Movements in England, France, and Germany* (1979); R. F. Gleckner and G. E. Enscoe, eds., *Romanticism: Points of View* (1962), a collection of essays by various contributors; Charles Larmore, *The Romantic Legacy* (1996); and M. Cranston, *The Romantic Movement* (1994). On French Romanticism, see P. T. Comeau, *Diehards and Innovators: The French Romantic Struggle, 1800–1830* (1988); on Germany, T. Ziolkowski, *German Romanticism and Its Institutions* (1990); on English and American developments, B. Taylor, R. Bain, and M. H. Abrams, *The Cast of Consciousness: Concepts of the Mind in British and American Romanticism* (1987); on the English and German situation, C. Jacobs, *Uncontainable Romanticism* (1989). Useful for the English scene is K. Everest, *English Romantic Poetry: An Introduction to the Historical Context and the Literary Scene* (1990). For a general historical introduction to the European situation, see J. Talmon, *Romanticism and Revolt: Europe 1815–1848* (1967).

TIME LINE

TEXTS	CONTEXTS
1781–1788 Jean-Jacques Rousseau, *Confessions*	**1781** Immanuel Kant, *Critique of Pure Reason*
	1787 Wolfgang Amadeus Mozart's *Don Giovanni* is first performed
	1789 The National Assembly in France issues its charter, *Declaration of the Rights of Man*
1794 William Blake, ***Songs of Innocence and of Experience***	
1798 William Wordsworth and Samuel Taylor Coleridge, ***Lyrical Ballads*** • Dorothy Wordsworth begins her journals	
1800 Novalis, ***Hymns to the Night***	
	1801 United Kingdom of Great Britain (England and Scotland) and Ireland established
1802 Coleridge, ***Dejection: An Ode***	
	1803 President Thomas Jefferson purchases French "Louisiana"
	1804 Napoleon crowned emperor of France
1806 First published lyrics by Anna Petrovna Bunina	
1808 Johann Wolfgang von Goethe, ***Faust, Part I*** (*Part II,* 1832)	
1812–1870 Charles Dickens, English novelist	
	1815 Battle of Waterloo, ending Napoleon's career
1816 Coleridge, ***Kubla Khan*** • John Keats, ***On First Looking into Chapman's Homer***	
1818–1820 Lyrics by Percy Bysshe Shelley and John Keats	
1820 Alphonse de Lamartine, ***Poetic Meditations,*** his first collection of poems	
1824 Giacomo Leopardi, ***Canzoni,*** his first collection of poems	
1827 Heinrich Heine, ***Book of Songs***	
1828 Victor Hugo, ***Odes and Ballads***	
	1831 First preparation of chloroform inaugurates a new medical era
1834 Alexander Sergeyevich Pushkin, ***The Queen of Spades***	

Boldface titles indicate works in the anthology.

TIME LINE

TEXTS	CONTEXTS
	1837 Victoria crowned queen of the United Kingdom • Electric telegraph patented
1842 Alfred, Lord Tennyson, *Ulysses*	
1845 Frederick Douglass, *Narrative of the Life of Frederick Douglass, An American Slave*	
1847 Charlotte Brontë, *Jane Eyre* • Emily Brontë, *Wuthering Heights*	
	1848 Karl Marx and Friedrich Engels, *Communist Manifesto* • Revolutions in France, Italy, Austria, Prague • Gold discovered in California
1850 Alfred, Lord Tennyson, *In Memoriam A. H. H.*	
1842–1855 Robert Browning writes poems, including *"Childe Roland to the Dark Tower Came"*	
	1854 Electric lightbulb invented
1855 Walt Whitman, *Song of Myself*	
	1859 Charles Darwin's *Origin of Species*, presenting his theory of evolution
	1861 Serfs emancipated in Russia • Beginning of American Civil War
	1863 Emancipation Proclamation frees slaves in the Confederate States of America
	1864 Louis Pasteur, who formulated germ theory of infection, invents pasteurization
	1865 American Civil War ends • President Abraham Lincoln assassinated • Thirteenth amendment emancipates all slaves in the United States
	1867 Karl Marx, *Capital*
	1874 First Impressionist Exhibition, Paris
	1876 Alexander Graham Bell invents the telephone
1884 Rosalía de Castro, *Beside the River Sar*	
1890 Emily Dickinson, *Poems*, published posthumously	
1891 Herman Melville leaves manuscript of *Billy Budd, Sailor* at his death; not published until 1924	
	1894 X rays discovered by Bavarian physicist Wilhelm Röntgen

JEAN-JACQUES ROUSSEAU
1712–1778

It would be difficult to overstate the historical importance of Jean-Jacques Rousseau's *Confessions* (composed between 1765 and 1770, published 1781–88), which inaugurated a new form of autobiography and suggested new ways of thinking about the self and its relation to other selves. Even for readers two centuries after its first publication, the book's sheer audacity compels attention, demanding that we rethink easy assumptions about important and trivial, right and wrong.

The facts of Rousseau's life are not altogether clear, partly because the *Confessions,* despite its claim of absolute truthfulness, sometimes appears more concerned to create a self-justifying story than to confine itself strictly to actuality. The son of a Geneva watchmaker, Rousseau left home in his teens and lived for some time with Françoise-Louise de Warens, his protector and eventually his mistress, the "mamma" of the *Confessions.* He worked at many occupations, from secretary to government official (under the king of Sardinia). In Paris, where he settled in 1745, he lived with Thérèse le Vasseur; he claims she bore him five children, all consigned to an orphanage, but the claim has never been substantiated (or, for that matter, disproved). At various times his controversial writing forced Rousseau to leave France, usually for Switzerland; in 1766 he went to England as the guest of the philosopher David Hume. He was allowed to return to Paris in 1770 only on condition that he write nothing against the government or the Church.

Rousseau's social ideas, elaborated in his didactic novels *Julie: or, the New Eloise* (1761) and *Émile* (1762) as well as in his autobiographical writings and political treatises (for example, *The Social Contract,* 1762), stirred much contemporary discussion. He believed in the destructiveness of institutions, the gradual corruption of humankind throughout history, the importance of nature and of feeling in individual development and consequently in society. As he writes in *Émile,* "I hate books; they only teach us to talk about things we know nothing about." He proposes to teach children by immersing them first in the natural, then in the human world, preventing the corruption of their bodies and their feelings. For a time he was a music teacher, and he published several works on music, including a dictionary, and composed a comic opera called *The Village Soothsayer* (1752).

The *Confessions* presents its subject as a man (and boy) striving always to express natural impulses and recurrently frustrated by society's demands and assumptions. The central figure described here rather resembles Candide in his naïveté and good feeling. Experience chastens him less than it does Candide, however, although he reports many psychic hard knocks. For Voltaire's didactic purposes, his character's experience was more important than his personality; for Rousseau, his own nature has much more significance than anything that happens to him. His account of that nature becomes ever more complicated as the *Confessions* continue and the writer concerns himself increasingly with the problem of his relation to society at large. His sense of alienation alternates with wistful longing for inclusion as he delineates the dilemmas of the extraordinary individual in a world full of people primarily concerned to accrete wealth and power.

To read even a few pages of the work reveals how completely Rousseau exemplifies several of his period's dominant values. He describes himself as a being of powerful passions but confused ideas, he makes feeling the guide of conduct, he glorifies imagination and romantic love, he believes the common people morally superior to the upper classes. The emphasis on imagination and passion for him seems not a matter of ideology but of experience: life presents itself to him in this way. The fact emphasizes the degree to which the movement we call Romanticism involved genuine revision. Everything looked different in the late eighteenth century, everything demanded categories changed from those previously accepted without question. The new way of looking at the world that characterizes the Romantic movement, inasmuch as it implies valuing the inner life of emotion and fancy for its own sake (not for the sake of any insight it might provide), always includes the danger of narcissism, a kind of concentration on the self that shuts out awareness of the reality and integrity of others. Rousseau, in the *Confessions*, vividly expresses the narcissistic side of Romanticism.

Implicit in Rousseau's ways of understanding himself and his life are new moral assumptions as well. Honesty of a particular kind becomes the highest value; however disreputable his behavior, Rousseau can feel comfortable about it because he reports it accurately. What Johnson or Pope would see as self-indulgence, care exclusively for one's own pleasure, seems acceptable to Rousseau because of the minute, exacting attention devoted to it. The autobiographer examines each nuance of his own happiness, as if to know it fully constituted moral achievement. To take the self this seriously as subject—not in relation to a progress of education or of salvation, merely in its moment-to-moment being—implies belief in self-knowledge (knowledge of feeling, thought, action) as a high moral achievement. This is not the slowly achieved, arduous discipline recommended by Socrates but a somewhat more indulgent form of self-contemplation. To connect it, as Rousseau does, with morality conveys the view that self-absorption without self-judgment provides valuable and sufficient insight.

In his presentation of self, Rousseau contrasts vividly with his great predecessor, Montaigne. Rousseau insists on his uniqueness: "I am not made like any of those I have seen; I venture to believe that I am not made like any of those who are in existence." He presents himself for the reader's contemplation as a remarkable phenomenon. Montaigne, on the other hand, reminds us constantly of what author and reader (and humankind in general) have in common. "Not only does the wind of accidents stir me according to its blowing, but I am also stirred and troubled by the instability of my attitude; and he who examines himself closely will seldom find himself twice in the same state." The movement within the sentence from *I* to the universalizing *he* characterizes a more outward-looking mode.

It must be said, however, that the intensity of Rousseau's self-concentration makes his subject compelling for others as well. However distasteful one might find his obsessive focus, it is difficult to stop reading. The writer hints   makes us believe—that he will reveal all secrets about himself; and learning such secrets, despite Rousseau's insistence on his own uniqueness, tells us of human weakness, inconsistency, power, scope—tells us, therefore, something of ourselves.

F. C. Green, *Jean-Jacques Rousseau: A Critical Study of His Life and Writings* (1955), provides biography and criticism. Thomas McFarland, *Romanticism and the Heritage of Rousseau* (1995), examines the relation of Rousseau's assumptions to those of the Romantic movement. A thorough evaluation of Rousseau's achievement is L. G. Crocker, *Jean-Jacques Rousseau: A New Interpretative Analysis of His Works* (1973). More directly focused on the *Confessions* is H. Williams, *Rousseau and Romantic Autobiography* (1983). More recent studies include C. Kelly, *Rousseau's Exemplary Life: The Confessions as Political Philosophy* (1987); J. Starobinski, *Jean-Jacques Rousseau: Transparency and Obstruction* (1988); C. A. Beaudry, *The Role of the Reader in Rousseau's Confessions* (1991); E. de Mijolla, *Autobiographical Quests: Augustine, Montaigne, Rousseau, and Wordsworth* (1994); M. Morgenstern, *Rousseau and the Politics of Ambiguity* (1996); and J. Olney, *Memory and Narrative: The Weave of Life-Writing* (1998). A collection of essays by various authors is H. Bloom, ed., *Jean-Jacques Rousseau* (1988).

From Confessions

Part I

BOOK I

[*The Years 1712–1719*]

I am commencing an undertaking, hitherto without precedent, and which will never find an imitator. I desire to set before my fellows the likeness of a man in all the truth of nature, and that man myself.

Myself alone! I know the feelings of my heart, and I know men. I am not made like any of those I have seen; I venture to believe that I am not made like any of those who are in existence. If I am not better, at least I am different. Whether Nature has acted rightly or wrongly in destroying the mould in which she cast me, can only be decided after I have been read.

Let the trumpet of the Day of Judgment sound when it will, I will present myself before the Sovereign Judge with this book in my hand. I will say boldly: "This is what I have done, what I have thought, what I was. I have told the good and the bad with equal frankness. I have neither omitted anything bad, nor interpolated anything good. If I have occasionally made use of some immaterial embellishments, this has only been in order to fill a gap caused by lack of memory. I may have assumed the truth of that which I knew might have been true, never of that which I knew to be false. I have shown myself as I was: mean and contemptible, good, high-minded and sublime, according as I was one or the other. I have unveiled my inmost self even as Thou hast seen it, O Eternal Being. Gather round me the countless host of my fellow-men; let them hear my confessions, lament for my unworthiness, and blush for my imperfections. Then let each of them in turn reveal, with the same frankness, the secrets of his heart at the foot of the Throne, and say, if he dare, '*I was better than that man!*' "

I was born at Geneva, in the year 1712, and was the son of Isaac Rousseau and Susanne Bernard, citizens. The distribution of a very moderate inheritance amongst fifteen children had reduced my father's portion almost to nothing; and his only means of livelihood was his trade of watchmaker, in which he was really very clever. My mother, a daughter of the Protestant minister Bernard, was better off. She was clever and beautiful, and my father had found difficulty in obtaining her hand. Their affection for each other had commenced almost as soon as they were born. When only eight years old, they walked every evening upon the Treille;[1] at ten, they were inseparable. Sympathy and union of soul strengthened in them the feeling produced by intimacy. Both, naturally full of tender sensibility, only waited for the moment when they should find the same disposition in another—or, rather, this moment waited for them, and each abandoned their heart to the first which opened to receive it. Destiny, which appeared to oppose their passion, only encouraged it. The young lover, unable to obtain possession of his mistress, was consumed by grief. She advised him to travel, and endeavour to forget her. He travelled, but without result, and returned more in love than ever. He found her whom he loved still faithful and true. After this trial of affection, nothing was left for them but to love each other all their lives. This they swore to do, and Heaven blessed their oath. * * *

My father, after the birth of my only brother, set out for Constantinople, whither he was summoned to undertake the post of watchmaker to the Sultan. During his absence, my mother's beauty, intellect and talents gained for her the devotion of numerous admirers. M. de la Closure, the French Resident, was one of the most eager to offer his. His passion must have been great, for, thirty years later, I saw him greatly affected when speaking to me of her. To enable her to resist such advances, my mother had more than her virtue: she loved her husband tenderly. She pressed him to return; he left all, and returned. I was the unhappy fruit of this return. Ten months later I was born, a weak and ailing child; I cost my mother her life, and my birth was the first of my misfortunes.

I have never heard how my father bore this loss, but I know that he was inconsolable. He believed that he saw his wife again in me, without being able to forget that it was I who had robbed him of her; he never embraced me without my perceiving, by his sighs and the convulsive manner in which he clasped me to his breast, that a bitter regret was mingled with his caresses, which were on that account only the more tender. When he said to me, "Jean Jacques, let us talk of your mother," I used to answer, "Well, then, my father, we will weep!"—and this word alone was sufficient to move him to tears. "Ah!" said he, with a sigh, "give her back to me, console me for her loss, fill the void which she has left in my soul. Should I love you as I do, if you were only my son?" Forty years after he had lost her, he died in the arms of a second wife, but the name of the first was on his lips and her image at the bottom of his heart.

Such were the authors of my existence. Of all the gifts which Heaven had bestowed upon them, a sensitive heart is the only one they bequeathed to me; it had been the source of their happiness, but for me it proved the source of all the misfortunes of my life.

I was brought into the world in an almost dying condition; little hope was entertained of saving my life. I carried within me the germs of a complaint which the course of time has strengthened, and which at times allows me a respite only to make me suffer more cruelly in another manner. One of my father's sisters, an amiable and virtuous young woman, took such care of me that she saved my life. At this moment, while I am writing, she is still alive, at the age of eighty, nursing a husband younger than herself, but exhausted

---

1. A fashionable promenade in Geneva.

by excessive drinking. Dear aunt, I forgive you for having preserved my life; and I deeply regret that, at the end of your days, I am unable to repay the tender care which you lavished upon me at the beginning of my own.[2] My dear old nurse Jacqueline is also still alive, healthy and robust. The hands which opened my eyes at my birth will be able to close them for me at my death.

I felt before I thought: this is the common lot of humanity. I experienced it more than others. I do not know what I did until I was five or six years old. I do not know how I learned to read; I only remember my earliest reading, and the effect it had upon me; from that time I date my uninterrupted self-consciousness. My mother had left some romances behind her, which my father and I began to read after supper. At first it was only a question of practising me in reading by the aid of amusing books; but soon the interest became so lively, that we used to read in turns without stopping, and spent whole nights in this occupation. We were unable to leave off until the volume was finished. Sometimes, my father, hearing the swallows begin to twitter in the early morning, would say, quite ashamed, "Let us go to bed; I am more of a child than yourself."

In a short time I acquired, by this dangerous method, not only extreme facility in reading and understanding what I read, but a knowledge of the passions that was unique in a child of my age. I had no idea of things in themselves, although all the feelings of actual life were already known to me. I had conceived nothing, but felt everything. These confused emotions which I felt one after the other, certainly did not warp the reasoning powers which I did not as yet possess; but they shaped them in me of a peculiar stamp, and gave me odd and romantic notions of human life, of which experience and reflection have never been able wholly to cure me. * * *

I had a brother seven years older than myself, who was learning my father's trade. The excessive affection which was lavished upon myself caused him to be somewhat neglected, which treatment I cannot approve of. His education felt the consequences of this neglect. He took to evil courses before he was old enough to be a regular profligate. He was put with another master, from whom he was continually running away, as he had done from home. I hardly ever saw him; I can scarcely say that I knew him; but I never ceased to love him tenderly, and he loved me as much as a vagabond can love anything. I remember that, on one occasion, when my father was chastising him harshly and in anger, I threw myself impetuously between them and embraced him closely. In this manner I covered his body with mine, and received the blows which were aimed at him; I so obstinately maintained my position that at last my father was obliged to leave off, being either disarmed by my cries and tears, or afraid of hurting me more than him. At last, my brother turned out so badly that he ran away and disappeared altogether. Some time afterwards we heard that he was in Germany. He never once wrote to us. From that time nothing more has been heard of him, and thus I have remained an only son.

---

2. The name of this aunt was Madame Gonceru. In March 1767, Rousseau settled upon her an income of one hundred livres and, even in the time of his greatest distress, always paid it with scrupulous exactitude.

If this poor boy was carelessly brought up, this was not the case with his brother; the children of kings could not be more carefully looked after than I was during my early years—worshipped by all around me, and, which is far less common, treated as a beloved, never as a spoiled child. Till I left my father's house, I was never once allowed to run about the streets by myself with the other children; in my case no one ever had to satisfy or check any of those fantastic whims which are attributed to Nature, but are all in reality the result of education. I had the faults of my age: I was a chatterbox, a glutton, and, sometimes, a liar. I would have stolen fruits, bonbons, or eatables; but I have never found pleasure in doing harm or damage, in accusing others, or in tormenting poor dumb animals. I remember, however, that I once made water in a sauce-pan belonging to one of our neighbours, Madame Clot, while she was at church. I declare that, even now, the recollection of this makes me laugh, because Madame Clot, a good woman in other respects, was the most confirmed old grumbler I have ever known. Such is the brief and true story of all my childish offences.

How could I become wicked, when I had nothing but examples of gentleness before my eyes, and none around me but the best people in the world? My father, my aunt, my nurse, my relations, our friends, our neighbours, all who surrounded me, did not, it is true, obey me, but they loved me; and I loved them in return. My wishes were so little excited and so little opposed, that it did not occur to me to have any. I can swear that, until I served under a master, I never knew what a fancy was. Except during the time I spent in reading or writing in my father's company, or when my nurse took me for a walk, I was always with my aunt, sitting or standing by her side, watching her at her embroidery or listening to her singing; and I was content. Her cheerfulness, her gentleness and her pleasant face have stamped so deep and lively an impression on my mind that I can still see her manner, look, and attitude; I remember her affectionate language: I could describe what clothes she wore and how her head was dressed, not forgetting the two little curls of black hair on her temples, which she wore in accordance with the fashion of the time.

I am convinced that it is to her I owe the taste, or rather passion, for music, which only became fully developed in me a long time afterwards. She knew a prodigious number of tunes and songs which she used to sing in a very thin, gentle voice. This excellent woman's cheerfulness of soul banished dreaminess and melancholy from herself and all around her. The attraction which her singing possessed for me was so great, that not only have several of her songs always remained in my memory, but even now, when I have lost her, and as I grow older, many of them, totally forgotten since the days of my childhood, return to my mind with inexpressible charm. Would anyone believe that I, an old dotard, eaten up by cares and troubles, sometimes find myself weeping like a child, when I mumble one of those little airs in a voice already broken and trembling? * * *

I remained under the care of my uncle Bernard, who was at the time employed upon the fortifications of Geneva. His eldest daughter was dead, but he had a son of the same age as myself. We were sent together to Bossey, to board with the Protestant minister Lambercier, in order to learn, together with Latin, all the sorry trash which is included under the name of education.

Two years spent in the village in some degree softened my Roman roughness and made me a child again. At Geneva, where no tasks were imposed upon me, I loved reading and study, which were almost my only amusements; at Bossey, my tasks made me love the games which formed a break in them. The country was so new to me, that my enjoyment of it never palled. I conceived so lively an affection for it, that it has never since died out. The remembrance of the happy days I have spent there filled me with regretful longing for its pleasures, at all periods of my life, until the day which has brought me back to it. M. Lambercier was a very intelligent person, who, without neglecting our education, never imposed excessive tasks upon us. The fact that, in spite of my dislike to restraint, I have never recalled my hours of study with any feeling of disgust—and also that, even if I did not learn much from him, I learnt without difficulty what I did learn and never forgot it—is sufficient proof that his system of instruction was a good one.
* * *

As Mademoiselle Lambercier had the affection of a mother for us, she also exercised the authority of one, and sometimes carried it so far as to inflict upon us the punishment of children when we had deserved it. For some time she was content with threats, and this threat of a punishment that was quite new to me appeared very terrible; but, after it had been carried out, I found the reality less terrible than the expectation; and, what was still more strange, this chastisement made me still more devoted to her who had inflicted it. It needed all the strength of this devotion and all my natural docility to keep myself from doing something which would have deservedly brought upon me a repetition of it; for I had found in the pain, even in the disgrace, a mixture of sensuality which had left me less afraid than desirous of experiencing it again from the same hand. * * *

Who would believe that this childish punishment, inflicted upon me when only eight years old by a young woman of thirty, disposed of my tastes, my desires, my passions, and my own self for the remainder of my life, and that in a manner exactly contrary to that which should have been the natural result? When my feelings were once inflamed, my desires so went astray that, limited to what I had already felt, they did not trouble themselves to look for anything else. In spite of my hot blood, which has been inflamed with sensuality almost from my birth, I kept myself free from every taint until the age when the coldest and most sluggish temperaments begin to develop. In torments for a long time, without knowing why, I devoured with burning glances all the pretty women I met; my imagination unceasingly recalled them to me, only to make use of them in my own fashion, and to make of them so many Mlles Lambercier.

* * * Thus I have spent my life in idle longing, without saying a word, in the presence of those whom I loved most. Too bashful to declare my taste, I at least satisfied it in situations which had reference to it and kept up the idea of it. To lie at the feet of an imperious mistress, to obey her commands, to ask her forgiveness—this was for me a sweet enjoyment; and, the more my lively imagination heated my blood, the more I presented the appearance of a bashful lover. It may be easily imagined that this manner of making love does not lead to very speedy results, and is not very dangerous to the virtue of those who are its object. For this reason I have rarely possessed, but have none the less enjoyed myself in my own way—that is to say, in imagination.

Thus it has happened that my senses, in harmony with my timid disposition and my romantic spirit, have kept my sentiments pure and my morals blameless, owing to the very tastes which, combined with a little more impudence, might have plunged me into the most brutal sensuality. * * *

I am a man of very strong passions, and, while I am stirred by them, nothing can equal my impetuosity; I forget all discretion, all feelings of respect, fear and decency; I am cynical, impudent, violent and fearless; no feeling of shame keeps me back, no danger frightens me; with the exception of the single object which occupies my thoughts, the universe is nothing to me. But all this lasts only for a moment, and the following moment plunges me into complete annihilation. In my calmer moments I am indolence and timidity itself; everything frightens and discourages me; a fly, buzzing past, alarms me; a word which I have to say, a gesture which I have to make, terrifies my idleness; fear and shame overpower me to such an extent that I would gladly hide myself from the sight of my fellow-creatures. If I have to act, I do not know what to do; if I have to speak, I do not know what to say; if anyone looks at me, I am put out of countenance. When I am strongly moved I sometimes know how to find the right words, but in ordinary conversation I can find absolutely nothing, and my condition is unbearable for the simple reason that I am obliged to speak.

Add to this, that none of my prevailing tastes centre in things that can be bought. I want nothing but unadulterated pleasures, and money poisons all. For instance, I am fond of the pleasures of the table; but, as I cannot endure either the constraint of good society or the drunkenness of the tavern, I can only enjoy them with a friend; alone, I cannot do so, for my imagination then occupies itself with other things, and eating affords me no pleasure. If my heated blood longs for women, my excited heart longs still more for affection. Women who could be bought for money would lose for me all their charms; I even doubt whether it would be in me to make use of them. I find it the same with all pleasures within my reach; unless they cost me nothing, I find them insipid. I only love those enjoyments which belong to no one but the first man who knows how to enjoy them.

* * * I worship freedom; I abhor restraint, trouble, dependence. As long as the money in my purse lasts, it assures my independence; it relieves me of the trouble of finding expedients to replenish it, a necessity which always inspired me with dread; but the fear of seeing it exhausted makes me hoard it carefully. The money which a man possesses is the instrument of freedom; that which we eagerly pursue is the instrument of slavery. Therefore I hold fast to that which I have, and desire nothing.

My disinterestedness is, therefore, nothing but idleness; the pleasure of possession is not worth the trouble of acquisition. In like manner, my extravagance is nothing but idleness; when the opportunity of spending agreeably presents itself, it cannot be too profitably employed. Money tempts me less than things, because between money and the possession of the desired object there is always an intermediary, whereas between the thing itself and the enjoyment of it there is none. If I see the thing, it tempts me; if I only see the means of gaining possession of it, it does not. For this reason I have committed thefts, and even now I sometimes pilfer trifles which tempt me, and which I prefer to take rather than to ask for; but neither when a child nor a grown-up man do I ever remember to have robbed anyone of a farthing, except on one occasion, fifteen years ago, when I stole seven *livres* ten *sous*.

*　　*　　*

BOOK II

[*The Years 1728–1731*]

* * * I have drawn the great moral lesson, perhaps the only one of any practical value, to avoid those situations of life which bring our duties into conflict with our interests, and which show us our own advantage in the misfortunes of others; for it is certain that, in such situations, however sincere our love of virtue, we must, sooner or later, inevitably grow weak without perceiving it, and become unjust and wicked in act, without having ceased to be just and good in our hearts.

This principle, deeply imprinted on the bottom of my heart, which, although somewhat late, in practice guided my whole conduct, is one of those which have caused me to appear a very strange and foolish creature in the eyes of the world, and, above all, amongst my acquaintances. I have been reproached with wanting to pose as an original, and different from others. In reality, I have never troubled about acting like other people or differently from them. I sincerely desired to do what was right. I withdrew, as far as it lay in my power, from situations which opposed my interests to those of others, and might, consequently, inspire me with a secret, though involuntary, desire of injuring them.

* * * I loved too sincerely, too completely, I venture to say, to be able to be happy easily. Never have passions been at once more lively and purer than mine; never has love been tenderer, truer, more disinterested. I would have sacrificed my happiness a thousand times for that of the person whom I loved; her reputation was dearer to me than my life, and I would never have wished to endanger her repose for a single moment for all the pleasures of enjoyment. This feeling has made me employ such carefulness, such secrecy, and such precaution in my undertakings, that none of them have ever been successful. My want of success with women has always been caused by my excessive love for them.

*　　*　　*

BOOK III

[*The Years 1731–1732*]

* * * I only felt the full strength of my attachment when I no longer saw her.[3] When I saw her, I was only content; but, during her absence, my restlessness became painful. The need of living with her caused me outbreaks of tenderness which often ended in tears. I shall never forget how, on the day of a great festival, while she was at vespers, I went for a walk outside the town, my heart full of her image and a burning desire to spend my life with her. I had sense enough to see that at present this was impossible, and that the happiness which I enjoyed so deeply could only be short. This gave to my reflections a tinge of melancholy, about which, however, there was noth-

3. Rousseau refers here to Françoise-Louise de Warens, whom he also calls "mamma."

ing gloomy, and which was tempered by flattering hopes. The sound of the bells, which always singularly affects me, the song of the birds, the beauty of the daylight, the enchanting landscape, the scattered country dwellings in which my fancy placed our common home—all these produced upon me an impression so vivid, tender, melancholy and touching, that I saw myself transported, as it were, in ecstasy, into that happy time and place, wherein my heart, possessing all the happiness it could desire, tasted it with inexpressible rapture, without even a thought of sensual pleasure. I never remember to have plunged into the future with greater force and illusion than on that occasion; and what has struck me most in the recollection of this dream after it had been realised, is that I have found things again exactly as I had imagined them. If ever the dream of a man awake resembled a prophetic vision, it was assuredly that dream of mine. I was only deceived in the imaginary duration; for the days, the years, and our whole life were spent in serene and undisturbed tranquillity, whereas in reality it lasted only for a moment. Alas! my most lasting happiness belongs to a dream, the fulfilment of which was almost immediately followed by the awakening. * * *

Two things, almost incompatible, are united in me in a manner which I am unable to understand: a very ardent temperament, lively and tumultuous passions, and, at the same time, slowly developed and confused ideas, which never present themselves until it is too late. One might say that my heart and my mind do not belong to the same person. Feeling takes possession of my soul more rapidly than a flash of lightning; but, instead of illuminating, inflames and dazzles me. I feel everything and see nothing. I am carried away by my passions, but stupid; in order to think, I must be cool. The astonishing thing is that, notwithstanding, I exhibit tolerably sound judgment, penetration, even finesse, if I am not hurried; with sufficient leisure I can compose excellent impromptus; but I have never said or done anything worthy of notice on the spur of the moment. I could carry on a very clever conversation through the post, as the Spaniards are said to carry on a game of chess. When I read of that Duke of Savoy, who turned round on his journey, in order to cry, "At your throat, Parisian huckster," I said, "There you have myself!"

This sluggishness of thought, combined with such liveliness of feeling, not only enters into my conversation, but I feel it even when alone and at work. My ideas arrange themselves in my head with almost incredible difficulty; they circulate in it with uncertain sound, and ferment till they excite and heat me, and make my heart beat fast; and, in the midst of this excitement, I see nothing clearly and am unable to write a single word—I am obliged to wait. Imperceptibly this great agitation subsides, the confusion clears up, everything takes its proper place, but slowly, and only after a period of long and confused agitation.

*   *   *

Hence comes the extreme difficulty which I find in writing. My manuscripts, scratched, smeared, muddled and almost illegible, bear witness to the trouble they have cost me. There is not one of them which I have not been obliged to copy four or five times before I could give it to the printer. I have never been able to produce anything, pen in hand, in front of my table and paper; it is during a walk, in the midst of rocks and forests, at night in my bed while lying awake, that I write in my brain; one may judge how slowly, especially in the case of a man utterly without verbal memory and who has never been able to learn six lines by heart in his life. Many of my periods have been turned and turned again five or six nights in my head before they were fit to be set down on paper. This, also, is the reason why I succeed better in works which require labour than in those which require to be written with a certain lightness of style, such as letters—a style of which I have never been able to properly catch the tone, so that such occupation is a perfect torture to me. I cannot write a letter on the most trifling subject, which does not cost me hours of fatigue; or, if I try to write down immediately what occurs to me, I know neither how to begin nor how to end; my letter is a long and confused mass of verbosity, and, when it is read, my meaning is difficult to make out.

Not only is it painful for me to put my ideas into shape: I also find a difficulty in grasping them. I have studied mankind, and believe that I am a fairly shrewd observer; nevertheless, I cannot see clearly anything of all that I perceive; I only see clearly what I remember, and only show intelligence in my recollections. Of all that is said, of all that is done, of all that goes on in my presence, I feel nothing, I see through nothing. The outward sign is the only thing that strikes me. But, later, all comes back to me; I recall place, time, manner, look, gesture, and circumstances: nothing escapes me. Then, from what people have said or done, I discover what they have thought; and I am rarely mistaken.

*   *   *

BOOK IV

[*The Years 1731–1732*]

* * * I returned, not to Nyon, but to Lausanne.[4] I wanted to sate myself with the sight of this beautiful lake, which is there seen in its greatest extent. Few of the secret motives which have determined me to act have been more rational. Things seen at a distance are rarely powerful enough to make me act. The uncertainty of the future has always made me look upon plans, which need considerable time to carry them out, as decoys for fools. I indulge in hopes like others, provided it costs me nothing to support them; but if they require continued attention, I have done with it. The least trifling pleasure which is within my reach tempts me more than the joys of Paradise. However, I make an exception of the pleasure which is followed by pain; this has no temptation for me, because I love only pure enjoyments, and these a man never has when he knows that he is preparing for himself repentance and regret.

It was very necessary for me to reach some place, the nearer the better; for, having lost my way, I found myself in the evening at Moudon, where I spent the little money I had left, except ten kreutzers, which went the next day for dinner; and, in the evening, when I reached a little village near Lausanne, I entered an inn without a sou to pay for my bed, and not knowing what to do. Being very hungry, I put a good face upon the matter, and called

4. In southwest Switzerland, the capital of Vaud, which is situated between the Lake of Geneva, the Jura mountains, and the Bernese Alps.

for supper, as if I had been quite able to pay for it. I went to bed without thinking of anything, and slept soundly; and, after I had breakfasted in the morning and reckoned with my host, I wanted to leave him my waistcoat as security for the seven *batz*, which was the amount of my bill. This good fellow refused it; he said that, thanks to heaven, he had never stripped anyone; that he did not mean to begin for the sake of seven *batz*; that I could keep my waistcoat and pay him when I could. I was touched by his kindness, but less than I ought to have been, and less than I have been since, when I have thought of it again. I soon sent him his money, with thanks, by a messenger whom I could trust; but, fifteen years afterwards, returning from Italy by way of Lausanne, I sincerely regretted to find that I had forgotten the name of the landlord and of the inn. I should certainly have gone to see him; it would have been a real pleasure to me to remind him of his act of charity, and to prove to him that it had not been ill-applied. The simple and unpretentious kindness of this worthy man appears to me more deserving of gratitude than services, doubtless more important, but rendered with greater ostentation.

When approaching Lausanne, I mused upon the straits in which I found myself, and thought how I might extricate myself without betraying my distress to my step-mother; and, in this pilgrimage on foot, I compared myself to my friend Venture on his arrival at Annecy. I was so heated with this idea that, without reflecting that I possessed neither his charm of manner nor his accomplishments, I took it into my head to play the little Venture at Lausanne, to give lessons in music which I did not understand, and to say that I came from Paris, where I had never been. As there was no choir-school, in which I could have offered to assist, and as, besides, I was not such a fool as to venture amongst those who were acquainted with the art, I commenced to carry out my fine project by making inquiries for a small inn where I could live well and cheaply. I was recommended to a certain M. Perrotet, who took boarders. This Perrotet proved to be the best fellow in the world, and gave me a most hearty reception. I told him my petty lies, as I had prepared them. He promised to speak about me, and try to get me some pupils, and said that he would not ask me for any money until I had earned some. His charge for board was five "white crowns," little enough, everything considered, for the accommodation, but a great deal for me. He advised me only to put myself on half-board at first; this meant some good soup, and nothing else, for dinner, but a good supper later. I agreed. Poor Perrotet let me have all this without payment, and with the best heart in the world, and spared no pains to be of use to me.

Why is it that, having found so many good people in my youth, I find so few in my later years? Is their race extinct? No; but the class in which I am obliged to look for them now, is no longer the same as that in which I found them. Among the people, where great passions only speak at intervals, the sentiments of nature make themselves more frequently heard; in the higher ranks they are absolutely stifled, and, under the mask of sentiment, it is only interest or vanity that speaks.

* * * Whenever I approach the Canton⁵ of Vaud, I am conscious of an impression in which the remembrance of Madame de Warens, who was born there, of my father who lived there, of Mademoiselle de Vulson who enjoyed

---

5. Roughly equivalent to a state.

the first fruits of my youthful love, of several pleasure trips which I made there when a child and, I believe, some other exciting cause, more mysterious and more powerful than all this, is combined. When the burning desire of this happy and peaceful life, which flees from me and for which I was born, inflames my imagination, it is always the Canton of Vaud, near the lake, in the midst of enchanting scenery, to which it draws me. I feel that I must have an orchard on the shore of this lake and no other, that I must have a loyal friend, a loving wife, a cow, and a little boat. I shall never enjoy perfect happiness on earth until I have all that. I laugh at the simplicity with which I have several times visited this country merely in search of this imaginary happiness. I was always surprised to find its inhabitants, especially the women, of quite a different character from that which I expected. How contradictory it appeared to me! The country and its inhabitants have never seemed to me made for each other.

During this journey to Vévay,[6] walking along the beautiful shore, I abandoned myself to the sweetest melancholy. My heart eagerly flung itself into a thousand innocent raptures; I was filled with emotion, I sighed and wept like a child. How often have I stopped to weep to my heart's content, and, sitting on a large stone, amused myself with looking at my tears falling into the water! * * *

How greatly did the entrance into Paris belie the idea I had formed of it! The external decorations of Turin,[7] the beauty of its streets, the symmetry and regularity of the houses, had made me look for something quite different in Paris. I had imagined to myself a city of most imposing aspect, as beautiful as it was large, where nothing was to be seen but splendid streets and palaces of gold and marble. Entering by the suburb of St. Marceau, I saw nothing but dirty and stinking little streets, ugly black houses, a general air of slovenliness and poverty, beggars, carters, menders of old clothes, criers of decoctions and old hats. All this, from the outset, struck me so forcibly, that all the real magnificence I have since seen in Paris has been unable to destroy this first impression, and I have always retained a secret dislike against residence in this capital. I may say that the whole time, during which I afterwards lived there, was employed solely in trying to find means to enable me to live away from it.

Such is the fruit of a too lively imagination, which exaggerates beyond human exaggeration, and is always ready to see more than it has been told to expect. I had heard Paris so much praised, that I had represented it to myself as the ancient Babylon,[8] where, if I had ever visited it, I should, perhaps, have found as much to take off from the picture which I had drawn of it. The same thing happened to me at the Opera, whither I hastened to go the day after my arrival. The same thing happened to me later at Versailles;[9] and again, when I saw the sea for the first time; and the same thing will always happen to me, when I see anything which has been too loudly announced; for it is impossible for men, and difficult for Nature herself, to surpass the exuberance of my imagination.

* * * The sight of the country, a succession of pleasant views, the open air, a good appetite, the sound health which walking gives me, the free life

---

6. Resort town in Vaud, on the Lake of Geneva. 7. City in northwest Italy. 8. City in ancient Mesopotamia, noted for extreme luxury. 9. Town southwest of Paris containing the splendid palace built for Louis XIV.

of the inns, the absence of all that makes me conscious of my dependent position, of all that reminds me of my condition—all this sets my soul free, gives me greater boldness of thought, throws me, so to speak, into the immensity of things, so that I can combine, select, and appropriate them at pleasure, without fear or restraint. I dispose of Nature in its entirety as its lord and master; my heart, roaming from object to object, mingles and identifies itself with those which soothe it, wraps itself up in charming fancies, and is intoxicated with delicious sensations. If, in order to render them permanent, I amuse myself by describing them by myself, what vigorous outlines, what fresh colouring, what power of expression I give them!

* * * At night I lay in the open air, and, stretched on the ground or on a bench, slept as calmly as upon a bed of roses. I remember, especially, that I spent a delightful night outside the city, on a road which ran by the side of the Rhône or Saône,[1] I do not remember which. Raised gardens, with terraces, bordered the other side of the road. It had been very hot during the day; the evening was delightful; the dew moistened the parched grass; the night was calm, without a breath of wind; the air was fresh, without being cold; the sun, having gone down, had left in the sky red vapours, the reflection of which cast a rose-red tint upon the water; the trees on the terraces were full of nightingales answering one another. I walked on in a kind of ecstasy, abandoning my heart and senses to the enjoyment of all, only regretting, with a sigh, that I was obliged to enjoy it alone. Absorbed in my delightful reverie, I continued my walk late into the night, without noticing that I was tired. At last, I noticed it. I threw myself with a feeling of delight upon the shelf of a sort of niche or false door let into a terrace wall; the canopy of my bed was formed by the tops of trees; a nightingale was perched just over my head, and lulled me to sleep with his song; my slumbers were sweet, my awaking was still sweeter. * * *

In relating my journeys, as in making them, I do not know how to stop. My heart beat with joy when I drew near to my dear mamma, but I walked no faster. I like to walk at my ease, and to stop when I like. A wandering life is what I want. To walk through a beautiful country in fine weather, without being obliged to hurry, and with a pleasant prospect at the end, is of all kinds of life the one most suited to my taste. My idea of a beautiful country is already known. No flat country, however beautiful, has ever seemed so to my eyes. I must have mountain torrents, rocks, firs, dark forests, mountains, steep roads to climb or descend, precipices at my side to frighten me. * * *

These lengthy details of my early youth will naturally have seemed puerile, and I regret it; although born a man in certain respects, I long remained a child, and in many respects I am one still. I have never promised to introduce a great character to the public; I have promised to describe myself as I am; and, in order to know me in my riper years, it is necessary to have known me well in my youth. Since, as a rule, objects make less impression upon me than the remembrance of them, and since all my ideas assume the form of the representations of objects in my mind, the first traits which have stamped themselves upon my mind have remained, and those which have since imprinted themselves there have rather combined with them than obliterated them. There is a certain sequence of mental conditions and ideas, which

---

1. French rivers that join courses at Lyons.

exercises an influence upon those which follow them, with which it is necessary to be acquainted, in order to pass a correct judgment upon the latter. I endeavour in all cases to develop the first causes, in order to make the concatenation of effects felt. I should like to be able to make my soul to a certain extent transparent to the eyes of the reader; and, with this object, I endeavour to show it to him from all points of view, to exhibit it to him in every aspect, and to contrive that none of its movements shall escape his notice, so that he may be able by himself to judge of the principles that produce them.

If I made myself responsible for the result, and said to him. Such is my character, he might think that, if I am not deceiving him, I am at least deceiving myself. But, in simply detailing to him everything that has happened to me, all my acts, thoughts, and feelings, I cannot mislead him, except wilfully, and even if I wished to do so, I should not find it easy. It is his business to collect these scattered elements, and to determine the being which is composed of them; the result must be his work; and if he is mistaken, all the fault will be his. But for this purpose it is not sufficient that my narrative should be true; it must also be exact. It is not for me to judge of the importance of facts; it is my duty to mention them all, and to leave him to select them. This is what I have hitherto aimed at with all my best endeavours, and in the sequel I will not depart from it. But the recollections of middle-age are always less vivid than those of early youth. I have begun by making the best possible use of the latter. If the former return to me with the same freshness, impatient readers will, perhaps, grow tired; but I myself shall not be dissatisfied with my work. I have only one thing to fear in this undertaking; not that I may say too much or what is not true, but that I may not say all, and may conceal the truth.

BOOK V

[The Years 1732–1736]

* * * It is sometimes said that the sword wears out the scabbard. That is my history. My passions have made me live, and my passions have killed me. What passions? will be asked. Trifles, the most childish things in the world, which, however, excited me as much as if the possession of Helen or the throne of the universe had been at stake. In the first place—women. When I possessed one, my senses were calm; my heart, never. The needs of love devoured me in the midst of enjoyment; I had a tender mother, a dear friend; but I needed a mistress. I imagined one in her place; I represented her to myself in a thousand forms, in order to deceive myself. If I had thought that I held mamma in my arms when I embraced her, these embraces would have been no less lively, but all my desires would have been extinguished; I should have sobbed from affection, but I should never have felt any enjoyment. Enjoyment! Does this ever fall to the lot of man? If I had ever, a single time in my life, tasted all the delights of love in their fulness, I do not believe that my frail existence could have endured it; I should have died on the spot.

Thus I was burning with love, without an object; and it is this state, perhaps, that is most exhausting. I was restless, tormented by the hopeless condition of poor mamma's affairs, and her imprudent conduct, which were bound to ruin her completely at no distant date. My cruel imagination, which always anticipates misfortunes, exhibited this particular one to me continually, in all its extent and in all its results. I already saw myself compelled by want to separate from her to whom I had devoted my life, and without whom I could not enjoy it. Thus my soul was ever in a state of agitation; I was devoured alternately by desires and fears.

*   *   *

BOOK VI

[The Year 1736]

* * * At this period commences the brief happiness of my life; here approach the peaceful, but rapid moments which have given me the right to say, *I have lived.* Precious and regretted moments! Begin again for me your delightful course; and, if it be possible, pass more slowly in succession through my memory, than you did in your fugitive reality. What can I do, to prolong, as I should like, this touching and simple narrative, to repeat the same things over and over again, without wearying my readers by such repetition, any more than I was wearied of them myself, when I recommenced the life again and again? If all this consisted of facts, actions, and words, I could describe, and in a manner, give an idea of them; but how is it possible to describe what was neither said nor done, nor even thought, but enjoyed and felt, without being able to assign any other reason for my happiness than this simple feeling? I got up at sunrise, and was happy; I walked, and was happy; I saw mamma, and was happy; I left her, and was happy; I roamed the forests and hills, I wandered in the valleys, I read, I did nothing, I worked in the garden, I picked the fruit, I helped in the work of the house, and happiness followed me everywhere—happiness, which could not be referred to any definite object, but dwelt entirely within myself, and which never left me for a single instant. * * *

I should much like to know, whether the same childish ideas ever enter the hearts of other men as sometimes enter mine. In the midst of my studies, in the course of a life as blameless as a man could have led, the fear of hell still frequently troubled me. I asked myself: "In what state am I? If I were to die this moment, should I be damned?" According to my Jansenists,[2] there was no doubt about the matter; but, according to my conscience, I thought differently. Always fearful, and a prey to cruel uncertainty, I had recourse to the most laughable expedients to escape from it, for which I would unhesitatingly have anyone locked up as a madman if I saw him doing as I did. One day, while musing upon this melancholy subject, I mechanically amused myself by throwing stones against the trunks of trees with my usual good aim, that is to say, without hardly hitting one. While engaged in this useful exercise, it occurred to me to draw a prognostic from it to calm my anxiety. I said to myself: "I will throw this stone at the tree opposite; if I hit it, I am saved; if I miss it, I am damned." While speaking, I threw my stone with a trembling hand and a terrible palpitation of the heart, but with so successful an aim that it hit the tree right in the middle, which, to tell the truth, was no very difficult feat, for I had been careful to choose a tree with a thick

---

2. A sect of strict Catholics, named for Cornelis Jansen (1585–1638). Voltaire mentions them in *Candide*, chaps. 21 and 22.

trunk close at hand. From that time I have never had any doubt about my salvation! When I recall this characteristic incident, I do not know whether to laugh or cry at myself. You great men, who are most certainly laughing, may congratulate yourselves; but do not mock my wretchedness, for I swear to you that I feel it deeply. * * *

JOHANN WOLFGANG VON GOETHE
1749–1832

Recasting the ancient legend of Faust, Johann Wolfgang von Goethe created a powerful symbol of the Romantic imagination in all its aspiration and anxiety. Faust himself, central character of the epic drama, emerges as a Romantic hero, ever testing the limits of possibility. Yet to achieve his ends he must make a contract with the Devil: as if to say that giving full scope to imagination necessarily partakes of sin.

Goethe's *Faust* (Part I, 1808; Part II, 1832) constituted the crowning masterpiece of a life rich in achievement. Goethe exemplifies the nineteenth-century meaning of *genius*. Accomplished as poet, dramatist, novelist, and autobiographer, he also practiced law, served as a diplomat, and pursued scientific research. He had a happy childhood in Frankfurt, after which he studied law at Leipzig and then at Strasbourg, where in 1770–71 he met Gottfried Herder, leader of a new literary movement called the Sturm und Drang (Storm and Stress) movement. Participants in this movement emphasized the importance of revolt against established standards; they interested Goethe in such newly discovered forms as the folk song and in the literary vitality of Shakespeare, as opposed to more formally constricted writers.

During the brief period when he practiced law, after an unhappy love affair, Goethe wrote *The Sorrows of Young Werther* (1774), a novel of immense influence in establishing the image of the introspective, self-pitying, melancholy Romantic hero. In 1775 he accepted an invitation to the court of Charles Augustus, duke of Saxe-Weimar. He remained in Weimar for the rest of his life, for ten years serving the duke as chief minister. A trip to Italy from 1786 to 1788 aroused his interest in classic sources. He wrote dramas based on classic texts, most notably *Iphigenia* (1787); novels (for example, *Elective Affinities*, 1809) that pointed the way to the psychological novel; lyric poetry; and an important autobiography, *Poetry and Truth* (1811–33). He also did significant work in botany and physiology. Increasingly famous, he became in his own lifetime a legendary figure; all Europe flocked to Weimar to visit him.

The legend of Dr. Faustus (the real Johannes Faustus, a scholar, lived from 1480 to 1540), in most versions a seeker after forbidden knowledge, had attracted other writers before Goethe. The most important previous literary embodiment of the tale was Christopher Marlowe's *Doctor Faustus* (ca. 1588), a drama ending in its protagonist's damnation as a result of his search for illegitimate power through learning. Goethe's Faust meets no such fate. Pursuing not knowledge but experience, he embodies the ideal of limitless aspiration in all its glamour and danger. His contract with Mephistopheles provides that he will die at the moment he declares himself satisfied, content to rest in the present; he stakes his life and his salvation on his capacity ever to yearn for something beyond.

In Part I of Goethe's play, the protagonist's vision of the impossible locates itself specifically in the figure of Margaret (in German, *Margarete* or its diminutive, *Gretchen*), the simple, innocent girl whom he possesses physically but with whom he can never attain total union. In a speech epitomizing Romantic attitudes toward nature and toward emotion (especially the emotion of romantic love), Faust responds to his beloved's question "Do you believe in God?"

> Does not the heaven vault above?
> Is the earth not firmly based down here?
> And do not, friendly,
> Eternal stars arise?
> Do we not look into each other's eyes,
> And all in you is surging
> To your head and heart,
> And weaves in timeless mystery,
> Unseeable, yet seen, around you?
> Then let it fill your heart entirely,
> And when your rapture in this feeling is complete,
> Call it then as you will,
> Call it bliss! heart! love! God!
> I do not have a name
> For this. Feeling is all.

The notion of *bliss,* for Pope associated with respect for limitation, for Wordsworth connected with revolutionary vision, here designates an unnameable feeling, derived from experience of nature and of romantic love, possibly identical with God, but valued partly for its very vagueness.

Modern readers may feel that Faust bullies Margaret, allowing her no reality except as instrument for his desires. In a poignant moment early in the play, interrupting Faust's rhapsody about her "meekness" and "humility," Margaret suggests, "If you should think of me one moment only . . ." Faust seems incapable of any such awareness, too busy inventing his loved one to see her as she is. He dramatically represents the "egotistical sublime," with a kind of imaginative grandeur inseparable from his utter absorption in the wonder of his own being, his own experience.

Yet the action of Part I turns on Faust's development of just that consciousness of another's reality that seemed impossible for him, and Margaret is the agent of his development. In the great final scene—Margaret in prison, intermittently mad, condemned to death for murdering her illegitimate child by Faust—the woman again appeals to the man to think about her, to *know* her: "Do you know, my love, *whom* you are setting free?" Her anguish, his responsibility for it, force themselves on Faust. He wishes he had never been born: his lust for experience has resulted in this terrible culpability, this agonizing loss. At the final moment of separation, with Margaret's spiritual redemption proclaimed from above, Faust implicitly acknowledges the full reality of the woman he has lost and thus, even though he departs with Mephistopheles, distinguishes himself from his Satanic mentor. Mephistopheles in his nature cannot grasp a reality utterly apart from his own; he can recognize only what belongs to him. Faust, at least fleetingly, realizes the otherness of the woman and the value of what he has lost.

Mephistopheles, at the outset witty and powerful in his own imagination, gradually reveals his limitations. In the *Prologue in Heaven,* the Devil seems energetic, perceptive, enterprising, fearless: as the Lord says, a "joker," apparently more playful than malign. His bargain with the Lord turns on his belief in the essentially "beastly" nature of humankind: like Gulliver's Houyhnhnm master, he emphasizes the human misuse of reason. Although the scene is modeled on the interchange between God and Satan in the Book of Job, it differs significantly in that the Lord gives an explicit reason for allowing the Tempter to function. "Man errs as long as he will," He says, but He adds that Mephistopheles's value is in prodding humanity into action. The introductory scene thus suggests that Mephistopheles will function as an agent of salvation rather than damnation. The Devil's subsequent exchanges with Faust, in Mephistopheles's mind predicated on his own superior knowledge and comprehension, gradually make one realize that the man in significant respects knows more than does the Devil. Mephistopheles, for example, can understand Faust's desire for Margaret only in sexual terms. His witty cynicism seems more and more inadequate to the actual situation. By the end of Part I, Faust's suffering has enlarged him; but from the beginning, his capacity for sympathy marks his potential superiority to the Devil.

The *Walpurgis Night* section, with the *Walpurgis Night's Dream*, marks a stage in Faust's education and an extreme moment in the play's dramatic structure. Goethe here allows himself to indulge in unrestrained fantasy—grotesque, obscene, comic, with an explosion of satiric energy in the dream. The shifting tone and reference of these passages embody ways in which the diabolic might be thought to operate in human terms. While Margaret suffers the consequences of her sin, Faust experiences the ambiguous freedom of the imagination, always at the edge of horror.

The pattern of Faust's moral development in Part I prepares the reader for a nontragic denouement to the drama as a whole. In Part II, which he worked on for some thirty years, completing it only the year before his death, Goethe moves from the individual to the social. Faust marries Helen of Troy, who gives birth to Euphorion, symbol of new humanity. He turns soldier to save a kingdom; he reclaims land from the sea; finally he rests contented in a vision of happy community generated by the industry of humankind. Mephistopheles thinks this his moment of victory: now Faust has declared himself satisfied. But since his satisfaction depends still on aspiration, on a dream of the future, the angels rescue him at last and take him to heaven.

One cannot read *Faust* with twenty-first-century expectations of what a play should be like. This is above all *poetic* drama, to be read with pleasure in the richness of its language, the fertility and daring of its imagination. Although its cast of characters natural and supernatural and its sequence of supernaturally generated events are far from "realistic," it addresses problems still very much with us. How can individual ambition and desire be reconciled with responsibility to others? Does a powerful imagination—an artist's, say, or a scientist's—justify its possessor in ignoring social obligations? Goethe investigates such perplexing issues in symbolic terms, drawing his readers into personal involvement by playing on their emotions even as he questions the proper functions and limitations of commitment to desire—that form of emotional energy that leads to the greatest human achievements, but involves the constant danger of debilitating narcissism.

E. Ludwig, *Goethe, the History of a Man, 1749–1832* (1928), is a solid biography. A biography that also contextualizes Goethe is N. Boyle, *Goethe: The Poet and the Age* (1991). Also useful are V. Lange, ed., *Goethe: A Collection of Critical Essays* (1960), and the essays contained in the critical edition of W. Arndt and C. Hamlin, eds., *Faust* (1976). See also H. Hatfield, *Goethe: A Critical Introduction* (1963); M. Bidney, *Blake and Goethe* (1988); and specifically for *Faust*, L. Dieckmann, *Goethe's Faust: A Critical Reading* (1972). Good introductions to *Faust* include C. Hamlin, ed., *Faust: A Tragedy*, a Norton Critical Edition (2000); and J. K. Brown, *Faust: Theater of the World* (1992). An important recent study is J. Simpson, *Goethe and Patriarchy: Faust and the Fates of Desire* (1998).

PRONOUNCING GLOSSARY

The following list uses common English syllables and stress accents to provide rough equivalents of selected words whose pronunciation may be unfamiliar to the general reader.

Altmayer: *ahlt'-maier*

Auerbach: *aw'-er-bahk*

Elend: *ay'-lend*

encheirisis naturae: *en-kai-ray'-sis nah-tu'-rai*

Euphorion: *oy-foh'-ree-on*

Faust: *fowst*

Goethe: *gur'te*

Leipzig: *laip'-zig*

Proktophantasmist: *prohk-toh-fan-tas'-mist*

Schierke: *sheer'ke*

Sturm und Drang: *shturm unt drahng*

Te Deum: *tay day'-um*

Wagner: *vahg'-ner*

Walpurgis: *vahl-poor'-gis*

Werther: *vayr'-ter*

Zenien: *tsay'-nee-en*

Faust[1]

Prologue in Heaven[2]

[*The* LORD, *the* HEAVENLY HOSTS. *Later,* MEPHISTOPHELES.[3] *The three* ARCHANGELS *step forward.*]

RAPHAEL   The sun intones, in ancient tourney
  With brother spheres, a rival air;
  And his predestinated journey,
  He closes with a thundrous blare.
  His sight, as none can comprehend it,   5
  Gives strength to angels; the array
  Of works, unfathomably splendid,
  Is glorious as on the first day.
GABRIEL   Unfathomably swiftly speeded,
  Earth's pomp revolves in whirling flight,   10
  As Eden's brightness is succeeded
  By deep and dread-inspiring night;
  In mighty torrents foams the ocean
  Against the rocks with roaring song—
  In ever-speeding spheric motion,   15
  Both rock and sea are swept along.
MICHAEL   And rival tempests roar and ravage
  From sea to land, from land to sea,
  And, raging, form a chain of savage,
  Deeply destructive energy.   20
  There flames a flashing devastation
  To clear the thunder's crashing way;
  Yet, Lord, thy herald's admiration
  Is for the mildness of thy day.
THE THREE   The sight, as none can comprehend it,   25
  Gives strength to angels; thy array
  Of works, unfathomably splendid
  Is glorious as on the first day.
MEPHISTOPHELES   Since you, oh Lord, have once again drawn near,
  And ask how we have been, and are so genial,   30

---

1. Translated by Walter Kaufmann.   2. The scene is patterned on Job 1.6–12 and 2.1–6.   3. The origin of the name remains debatable. It may come from Hebrew, Persian, or Greek, with such meanings as "destroyer-liar," "no friend of Faust," and "no friend of light."

And since you used to like to see me here,
You see me, too, as if I were a menial.
I cannot speak as nobly as your staff,
Though by this circle here I shall be spurned:
My pathos would be sure to make you laugh,   35
Were laughing not a habit you've unlearned.
Of suns and worlds I know nothing to say;
I only see how men live in dismay.
The small god of the world will never change his ways
And is as whimsical—as on the first of days.   40
His life might be a bit more fun,
Had you not given him that spark of heaven's sun;
He calls it reason and employs it, resolute
To be more brutish than is any brute.
He seems to me, if you don't mind, Your Grace,   45
Like a cicada of the long-legged race,
That always flies, and, flying, springs,
And in the grass the same old ditty sings;
If only it were grass he could repose in!
There is no trash he will not poke his nose in.   50

THE LORD   Can you not speak but to abuse?
    Do you come only to accuse?
    Does nothing on the earth seem to you right?

MEPHISTOPHELES   No, Lord. I find it still a rather sorry sight.
    Man moves me to compassion, so wretched is his plight.   55
    I have no wish to cause him further woe.

THE LORD   Do you know Faust?

MEPHISTOPHELES   The doctor?[4]

THE LORD   Aye, my servant.

MEPHISTOPHELES   Lo!
    He serves you[5] most peculiarly, I think.
    Not earthly are the poor fool's meat and drink.
    His spirit's ferment drives him far,   60
    And he half knows how foolish is his quest:
    From heaven he demands the fairest star,
    And from the earth all joys that he thinks best;
    And all that's near and all that's far
    Cannot soothe the upheaval in his breast.   65

THE LORD   Though now he serves me but confusedly,
    I shall soon lead him where the vapor clears.
    The gardener knows, however small the tree,
    That bloom and fruit adorn its later years.

MEPHISTOPHELES   What will you bet? You'll lose him yet to me, 70
    If you will graciously connive
    That I may lead him carefully.

THE LORD   As long as he may be alive,

---

4. Of philosophy.   5. In the German text, Mephistopheles shifts from *ihr* to *du*, indicating his lack of respect for God.

So long you shall not be prevented.
Man errs as long as he will strive.   75
MEPHISTOPHELES   Be thanked for that; I've never been contented
To waste my time upon the dead.
I far prefer full cheeks, a youthful curly-head.
When corpses come, I have just left the house—
I feel as does the cat about the mouse.   80
THE LORD   Enough—I grant that you may try to clasp him,
Withdraw this spirit from his primal source
And lead him down, if you can grasp him,
Upon your own abysmal course—
And stand abashed when you have to attest: 85
A good man in his darkling aspiration
Remembers the right road throughout his quest.
MEPHISTOPHELES   Enough—he will soon reach his station;
About my bet I have no hesitation,
And when I win, concede your stake   90
And let me triumph with a swelling breast:
Dust he shall eat, and that with zest,
As my relation does, the famous snake.
THE LORD   Appear quite free on that day, too;
I never hated those who were like you: 95
Of all the spirits that negate,
The knavish jester gives me least to do.
For man's activity can easily abate,
He soon prefers uninterrupted rest;
To give him this companion hence seems best   100
Who roils and must as Devil help create.
But you, God's rightful sons, give voice
To all the beauty in which you rejoice;
And that which ever works and lives and grows
Enfold you with fair bonds that love has wrought,   105
And what in wavering apparition flows
That fortify with everlasting thought.
          [*The heavens close, the* ARCHANGELS *disperse.*]
MEPHISTOPHELES [*Alone.*]   I like to see the Old Man now and then
And try to be not too uncivil.
It's charming in a noble squire when   110
He speaks humanely with the very Devil.

The First Part of the Tragedy

NIGHT

[*In a high-vaulted, narrow Gothic den,* FAUST, *restless in his arm-chair at the desk.*]
FAUST   I have, alas, studied philosophy,
Jurisprudence and medicine, too,

And, worst of all, theology
With keen endeavor, through and through—
And here I am, for all my lore,   5
The wretched fool I was before.
Called Master of Arts, and Doctor to boot,
For ten years almost I confute
And up and down, wherever it goes,
I drag my students by the nose—   10
And see that for all our science and art
We can know nothing. It burns my heart.
Of course, I am smarter than all the shysters,
The doctors, and teachers, and scribes, and Christers;
No scruple nor doubt could make me ill,   15
I am not afraid of the Devil or hell—
But therefore I also lack all delight,
Do not fancy that I know anything right,
Do not fancy that I could teach or assert
What would better mankind or what might convert.   20
I also have neither money nor treasures,
Nor worldly honors or earthly pleasures;
No dog would want to live longer this way!
Hence I have yielded to magic to see
Whether the spirit's mouth and might   25
Would bring some mysteries to light,
That I need not with work and woe
Go on to say what I don't know;
That I might see what secret force
Hides in the world and rules its course.   30
Envisage the creative blazes
Instead of rummaging in phrases.

Full lunar light, that you might stare
The last time now on my despair!
How often I've been waking here   35
At my old desk till you appeared,
And over papers, notes, and books
I caught, my gloomy friend, your looks.
Oh, that up on a mountain height
I could walk in your lovely light   40
And float with spirits round caves and trees,
Weave in your twilight through the leas,
Cast dusty knowledge overboard,
And bathe in dew until restored.

Still this old dungeon, still a mole!   45
Cursed be this moldy walled-in hole
Where heaven's lovely light must pass,
And lose its luster, through stained glass.
Confined with books, and every tome
Is gnawed by worms, covered with dust,   50

And on the walls, up to the dome,
A smoky paper, spots of rust;
Enclosed by tubes and jars that breed
More dust, by instruments and soot,
Ancestral furniture to boot— 55
That is your world! A world indeed!

And need you ask why in your breast
Your cramped heart throbs so anxiously?
Life's every stirring is oppressed
By an unfathomed agony? 60
Instead of living nature which
God made man for with holy breath,
Must[6] stifles you, and every niche
Holds skulls and skeletons and death.

Flee! Out into the open land! 65
And this book full of mystery,
Written in Nostradamus'[7] hand—
Is it not ample company?
Stars' orbits you will know; and bold,
You learn what nature has to teach; 70
Your soul is freed, and you behold
The spirits' words, the spirits' speech.
Though dry reflection might expound
These holy symbols, it is dreary:
You float, oh spirits, all around; 75
Respond to me, if you can hear me.
    [*He opens the book and sees the symbol of the macrocosm.*[8]]
What jubilation bursts out of this sight
Into my senses—now I feel it flowing,
Youthful, a sacred fountain of delight,
Through every nerve, my veins are glowing. 80
Was it a god that made these symbols be
That soothe my feverish unrest,
Filling with joy my anxious breast,
And with mysterious potency
Make nature's hidden powers around me, manifest? 85

Am I a god? Light grows this page—
In these pure lines my eye can see
Creative nature spread in front of me.
But now I grasp the meaning of the sage:
"The realm of spirits is not far away; 90
Your mind is closed, your heart is dead.
Rise, student, bathe without dismay
In heaven's dawn your mortal head."

---

6. Mustiness, mold.   7. Latin name of the French astrologer and physician Michel de Notredame (1503–1566). His collection of rhymed prophecies, *The Centuries*, appeared in 1555.   8. The great world (literal trans.); the universe as a whole. It represents the ordered, harmonious universe in its totality.

[He contemplates the symbol.]
All weaves itself into the whole,
Each living in the other's soul.   95
How heaven's powers climb up and descend.
Passing the golden pails from hand to hand!
Bliss-scented, they are winging
Through the sky and earth—their singing
Is ringing through the world.   100

What play! Yet but a play, however vast!
Where, boundless nature, can I hold you fast?
And where you breasts? Wells that sustain
All life—the heaven and the earth are nursed.
The wilted breast craves you in thirst—   105
You well, you still—and I languish in vain?
      *[In disgust, he turns some pages and beholds the symbol of the earth
      spirit.⁹]*
How different is the power of this sign!
You, spirit of the earth, seem close to mine:
I look and feel my powers growing,
As if I'd drunk new wine I'm glowing,   110
I feel a sudden courage, and should dare
To plunge into the world, to bear
All earthly grief, all earthly joy—compare
With gales my strength, face shipwreck without care.
Now there are clouds above—   115
The moon conceals her light—
The lamp dies down.
It steams. Red light rays dash
About my head—a chill
Blows from the vaulting dome   120
And seizes me.
I feel you near me, spirit I implored.
Reveal yourself!
Oh, how my heart is gored
By never felt urges,   125
And my whole body surges—
My heart is yours; yours, too, am I.
You must. You must. Though I should have to die.
      *[He seizes the book and mysteriously pronounces the symbol of the
      spirit. A reddish flame flashes, and the* SPIRIT *appears in the flame.]*
SPIRIT   Who calls me?
FAUST *[Turning away.]*
                        Vision of fright!   130
SPIRIT   With all your might you drew me near
   You have been sucking at my sphere,
   And now—
FAUST   I cannot bear your sight!

---

9. This figure seems to be a symbol for the energy of terrestrial nature—neither good nor bad, merely powerful.

SPIRIT   You have implored me to appear,
    Make known my voice, reveal my face;   135
    Your soul's entreaty won my grace:
    Here I am! What abject fear
    Grasps you, oh superman! Where is the soul's impassioned
    Call? And where the breast that even now had fashioned
    A world to bear and nurse within—that trembled thus,   140
    Swollen with joy that it resembled us?
    Where are you, Faust, whose voice pierced my domain,
    Who surged against me with his might and main?
    Could it be you who at my breath's slight shiver
    Are to the depths of life aquiver,   145
    A miserably writhing worm?
FAUST   Should I, phantom of fire, fly?
    It's I, it's Faust; your peer am I!
SPIRIT   In the floods of life and creative storm
    To and fro I wave.   150
    Weave eternally.
    And birth and grave,
    An eternal sea,
    A changeful strife,
    A glowing life: 155
    At the roaring loom of the ages I plod
    And fashion the life-giving garment of God.
FAUST   You that traverse worlds without end,
    Sedulous spirit, I feel close to you.
SPIRIT   Peer of the spirit that you comprehend   160
    Not mine! [*Vanishes.*]
FAUST [*Collapsing.*]   Not yours?
    Whose then?
    I, image of the godhead!
    And not even yours!   165
       [*A knock.*]
    O death! My famulus[1]—I know it well.
    My fairest happiness destroyed!
    This wealth of visions I enjoyed
    The dreary creeper must dispel!
       [WAGNER *enters in a dressing gown and night cap, a light in his*
       hand. FAUST *turns away in disgust.*]
WAGNER   Forgive! I hear your declamation;   170
    Surely, you read a Grecian tragedy?
    I'd profit from some work in this vocation,
    These days it can be used effectively.
    I have been told three times at least
    That a comedian could instruct a priest.   175
FAUST   Yes, when the priest is a comedian for all his Te Deum.[2]
    As happens more often than one would own.
WAGNER   Ah, when one is confined to one's museum

1. Assistant to a medieval scholar.   **2.** A chant of praise to God.

And sees, the world on holidays alone,
But from a distance, only on occasion,   180
How can one guide it by persuasion?
FAUST   What you don't feel, you will not grasp by art,
Unless it wells out of your soul
And with sheer pleasure takes control,
Compelling every listener's heart.   185
But sit—and sit, and patch and knead,
Cook a ragout, reheat your hashes,
Blow at the sparks and try to breed
A fire out of piles of ashes!
Children and apes may think it great,   190
If that should titillate your gum,
But from heart to heart you will never create.
If from your heart it does not come.
WAGNER   Yet much depends on the delivery;
I still lack much; don't you agree?   195
FAUST   Oh, let him look for honest gain!
Let him not be a noisy fool!
All that makes sense you can explain
Without the tricks of any school.
If you have anything to say,   200
Why juggle words for a display?
Your glittering rhet'ric, subtly disciplined,
Which for mankind thin paper garlands weaves,
Is as unwholesome as the foggy wind
That blows in autumn through the wilted leaves.   205
WAGNER   Oh God, art is forever
And our life is brief.
I fear that with my critical endeavor
My head and heart may come to grief.
How hard the scholars' means are to array   210
With which one works up to the source;
Before we have traversed but half the course,
We wretched devils pass away.
FAUST   Parchment—is that the sacred fount
From which you drink to still your thirst forever?   215
If your refreshment does not mount.
From your own soul, you gain it never.
WAGNER   Forgive! It does seem so sublime,
Entering into the spirit of the time
To see what wise men, who lived long ago, believed,   220
Till we at last have all the highest aims achieved.
FAUST   Up to the stars—achieved indeed!
My friend, the times that antecede
Our own are books safely protected
By seven seals.[3] What spirit of the time you call,   225
Is but the scholars' spirit, after all,
In which times past are now reflected.

3. Revelation 5.1.

In truth, it often is pathetic,
And when one sees it, one would run away:
A garbage pail, perhaps a storage attic,   230
At best a pompous moralistic play
With wonderfully edifying quips,
Most suitable to come from puppets' lips.
WAGNER   And yet the world! Man's heart and spirit! Oh,
That everybody knew part of the same!   235
FAUST   The things that people claim to know!
Who dares to call the child by its true name?
The few that saw something like this and, starry-eyed
But foolishly, with glowing hearts averred
Their feelings and their visions before the common herd   240
Have at all times been burned and crucified.
I beg you, friend, it is deep in the night;
We must break off this interview.
WAGNER   Our conversation was so erudite,
I should have liked to stay awake with you.   245
Yet Easter comes tomorrow; then permit
That I may question you a bit.
Most zealously I've studied matters great and small;
Though I know much, I should like to know all.
            [Exit.]
FAUST [Alone.]   Hope never seems to leave those who affirm,   250
The shallow minds that stick to must and mold—
They dig with greedy hands for gold
And yet are happy if they find a worm.
Dare such a human voice be sounded
Where I was even now surrounded   255
By spirits' might? And yet I thank you just this once,
You, of all creatures the most wretched dunce.
You tore me from despair that had surpassed
My mind and threatened to destroy my sense.
Alas, the apparition was so vast   260
That I felt dwarfed in impotence.

I, image of the godhead, that began
To dream eternal truth was within reach,
Exulting on the heavens' brilliant beach
As if I had stripped off the mortal man;   265
I, more than cherub, whose unbounded might
Seemed even then to flow through nature's veins,
Shared the creative joys of God's domains—
Presumptuous hope for which I pay in pains:
One word of thunder swept me from my height.   270

I may no longer claim to be your peer:
I had the power to attract you here,
But to retain you lacked the might.
In that moment of bliss, alack,
In which I felt so small, so great,   275
You, cruel one, have pushed me back

Into uncertain human fate.
Who teaches me? What should I shun?
Should I give in to that obsession?
Not our sufferings only, the deeds that we have done   280
Inhibit our life's progression.

Whatever noblest things the mind received,
More and more foreign matter spoils the theme;
And when the good of this world is achieved,
What's better seems an idle dream.   285
That gave us our life, the noblest urges
Are petrified in the earth's vulgar surges.

Where fantasy once rose in glorious flight,
Hopeful and bold to capture the sublime,
It is content now with a narrow site,   290
Since joy on joy crashed on the rocks of time.
Deep in the heart there dwells relentless care
And secretly infects us with despair;
Restless, she sways and poisons peace and joy
She always finds new masks she can employ: 295
She may appear as house and home, as child and wife,
As fire, water, poison, knife—
What does not strike, still makes you quail,
And what you never lose, for that you always wail.

I am not like the gods! That was a painful thrust;   300
I'm like the worm that burrows in the dust,
Who, as he makes of dust his meager meal,
Is crushed and buried by a wanderer's heel.
Is it not dust that stares from every rack
And narrows down this vaulting den?   305
This moths' world full of bric-a-brac
In which I live as in a pen?
Here I should find for what I care?
Should I read in a thousand books, maybe,
That men have always suffered everywhere,   310
Though now and then some man lived happily?—
Why, hollow skull, do you grin like a faun?
Save that your brain, like mine, once in dismay
Searched for light day, but foundered in the heavy dawn
And, craving truth, went wretchedly astray.   315
You instruments, of course, can scorn and tease
With rollers, handles, cogs, and wheels:
I found the gate, you were to be the keys;
Although your webs are subtle, you cannot break the seals.
Mysterious in the light of day,   320
Nature, in veils, will not let us perceive her,
And what she is unwilling to betray,
You cannot wrest from her with thumbscrews, wheel, or lever.

You ancient tools that rest upon the rack,
Unused by me, but used once by my sire,[4]   325
You ancient scroll that slowly has turned black
As my lamp on this desk gave off its smoky fire—

Far better had I squandered all of my wretched share
Than groan under this wretched load and thus address it!
What from your fathers you received as heir,   330
Acquire if you would possess it.
What is not used is but a load to bear;
But if today creates it, we can use and bless it.

Yet why does this place over there attract my sight?
Why is that bottle as a magnet to my eyes?   335
Why does the world seem suddenly so bright,
As when in nightly woods one sees the moon arise?
I welcome you, incomparable potion,
Which from your place I fetch now with devotion:
In you I honor human wit and art.   340
You essence from all slumber-bringing flowers,
You extract of all subtly fatal powers,
Bare to your master your enticing heart!
I look upon you, soothed are all my pains,
I seize you now, and all my striving wanes,   345
The spirit's tidal wave now ebbs away.
Slowly I float into the open sea,
The waves beneath me now seem gay and free,
To other shores beckons another day.
A fiery chariot floats on airy pinions   350
Cleaving the ether—tarry and descend!
Uncharted orbits call me, new dominions
Of sheer creation, active without end.
This higher life, joys that no mortal won!
You merit this—but now a worm, despairing?   355
Upon the mild light of the earthly sun
Turn, bold, your back! And with undaunted daring
Tear open the eternal portals
Past which all creatures slink in silent dread.
The time has come to prove by deeds that mortals   360
Have as much dignity as any god,
And not to tremble at that murky cave
Where fantasy condemns itself to dwell
In agony. The passage brave
Whose narrow mouth is lit by all the flames of hell;   365
And take this step with cheerful resolution,
Though it involve the risk of utter dissolution.

Now you come down to me, pure crystal vase,
Emerge again out of your ancient case
Of which for many years I did not think.   370

---

4. Later we find that Faust's father was a doctor of medicine.

You glistened at my father's joyous feasts
And cheered the solemn-looking guests,
When you were passed around for all to drink.
The many pictures, glistening in the light,
The drinker's duty rhyming to explain them,[5]   375
To scan your depths and in one draught to drain them,
Bring back to mind many a youthful night.
There is no friend now to fulfill this duty,
Nor shall I exercise my wit upon your beauty.
Here is a juice that fast makes drunk and mute;   380
With its brown flood it fills this crystal bowl,
I brewed it and shall drink it whole
And offer this last drink with all my soul
Unto the morning as a festive high salute. [*He puts the bowl to his lips.*]
  [*Chime of bells and choral song.*]
CHOIR OF ANGELS Christ is arisen.   385
  Hail the meek-spirited
  Whom the ill-merited,
  Creeping, inherited
  Faults held in prison.
FAUST What deeply humming strokes, what brilliant tone   390
 Draws from my lips the crystal bowl with power?
 Has the time come, deep bells, when you make known
 The Easter holiday's first holy hour?
 Is this already, choirs, the sweet consoling hymn
 That was first sung around his tomb by cherubim,   395
 Confirming the new covenant?
CHOIR OF WOMEN With myrrh, when bereaved,
  We had adorned him;
  We that believed
  Laid down and mourned him.   400
  Linen we twined
  Round the adored—
  Returning, we cannot find
  Christ, our Lord.
CHOIR OF ANGELS Christ is arisen.   405
  Blessed be the glorious
  One who victorious
  Over laborious
  Trials has risen.
FAUST Why would you, heaven's tones, compel   410
 Me gently to rise from my dust?
 Resound where tenderhearted people dwell:
 Although I hear the message, I lack all faith or trust;
 And faith's favorite child is miracle.
 For those far spheres I should not dare to strive,   415
 From which these tidings come to me;
 And yet these chords, which I have known since infancy:

---

5. Faust here alludes to the drinking of toasts. The maker of a toast often produced impromptu rhymes.

Call me now, too, back into life.
Once heaven's love rushed at me as a kiss
In the grave silence of the Sabbath day,   420
The rich tones of the bells, it seemed, had much to say,
And every prayer brought impassioned bliss.
An unbelievably sweet yearning
Drove me to roam through wood and lea,
Crying, and as my eyes were burning,   425
I felt a new world grow in me.
This song proclaimed the spring feast's free delight, appealing
To the gay games of youth—they plead:
Now memory entices me with childlike feeling
Back from the last, most solemn deed.   430
Sound on, oh hymns of heaven, sweet and mild!
My tears are flowing; earth, take back your child!
CHOIR OF DISCIPLES   Has the o'ervaulted one
      Burst from his prison,
      The living-exalted one   435
      Gloriously risen,
      Is in this joyous birth
      Zest for creation near—
      Oh, on the breast of earth
      We are to suffer here.   440
      He left his own
      Pining in sadness;
      Alas, we bemoan,
      Master, your gladness.
CHOIR OF ANGELS   Christ is arisen   445
      Out of corruption's womb.
      Leave behind prison,
      Fetters and gloom!
      Those who proceed for him,
      Lovingly bleed for him,   450
      Brotherly feed for him,
      Travel and plead for him,
      And to bliss lead for him,
      For you the Master is near,
      For you he is here.   455

BEFORE THE CITY GATE

[*People of all kinds are walking out.*]
SOME APPRENTICES   Why do you go that way?
OTHERS   We are going to Hunter's Lodge today.
THE FIRST   But we would rather go to the mill.
AN APPRENTICE   Go to the River Inn, that's my advice.
ANOTHER   I think, the way there isn't nice.   5
THE OTHERS   Where are you going?
A THIRD ONE   Up the hill.
A FOURTH ONE   Burgdorf would be much better. Let's go there with the
    rest:

The girls there are stunning, their beer is the best,
And it's first-class, too, for a fight.
A FIFTH ONE   You are indeed a peppy bird,   10
Twice spanked, you're itching for the third.
Let's not, the place is really a fright.
SERVANT GIRL   No, no! I'll go back to the town again.
ANOTHER   We'll find him at the poplars, I'm certain it is true.
THE FIRST   What's that to me? Is it not plain,   15
He'll walk and dance only with you?
He thinks, you are the only one.
And why should I care for your fun?
THE OTHER ONE   He will not be alone. He said,
Today he'd bring the curly-head.   20
STUDENT   Just see those wenches over there!
Come, brother, let us help the pair.
A good strong beer, a smarting pipe,
And a maid, nicely dressed—that is my type!
CITIZEN'S DAUGHTER   Look there and see those handsome blades!   25
I think it is a crying shame:
They could have any girl that meets with their acclaim,
And chase after these silly maids.
SECOND STUDENT [*To the* FIRST.]   Don't go so fast; behind us are two more,
And they are dressed at least as neatly.   30
I know one girl, she lives next door,
And she bewitches me completely.
The way they walk, they seem demure,
But won't mind company, I'm sure.
THE FIRST   No, brother, I don't like those coy addresses.   35
Come on, before we lose the wilder prey.
The hand that wields the broom on Saturday
Will, comes the Sunday, give the best caresses.
CITIZEN   No, the new mayor is no good, that's what I say.
Since he's in, he's fresher by the day.   40
What has he done for our city?
Things just get worse; it is a pity!
We must obey, he thinks he's clever,
And we pay taxes more than ever.
BEGGAR [*Sings.*]   Good gentlemen and ladies fair,   45
So red of cheek, so rich in dress,
Be pleased to look on my despair,
To see and lighten my distress.
Let me not grind here, vainly waiting!
For only those who give are gay,   50
And when all men are celebrating,
Then I should have my harvest day.
ANOTHER CITIZEN   On Sun- and holidays, there is no better fun,
Than chattering of wars and warlike fray,
When off in Turkey, far away,   55
One people beats the other one.
We stand at the window, drink a wine that is light,

Watch the boats glide down the river, see the foam,
And cheerfully go back at night,
Grateful that we have peace at home.   60
THIRD CITIZEN   Yes, neighbor, that is nicely said.
Let them crack skulls, and wound, and maim,
Let all the world stand on its head;
But here, at home, all should remain the same.
OLD WOMAN [*To the* CITIZEN'S DAUGHTERS.]
Ah, how dressed up! So pretty and so young!   65
Who would not stop to stare at you?
Don't be puffed up, I'll hold my tongue.
I know your wish, and how to get it, too.
CITIZEN'S DAUGHTER   Come quickly, Agatha! I take good heed
Not to be seen with witches; it's unwise.—   70
Though on St. Andrew's Night[6] she brought indeed
My future lover right before my eyes.
THE OTHER ONE   She showed me mine, but in a crystal ball
With other soldiers, bold and tall;
I have been looking ever since,   75
But so far haven't found my prince.
SOLDIERS   Castles with lofty
        Towers and banners,
        Maidens with haughty,
        Disdainful manners   80
        I want to capture.
        Fair is the dare,
        Splendid the pay.
        And we let trumpets
        Do our wooing,   85
        For our pleasures
        And our undoing.
        Life is all storming,
        Life is all splendor,
        Maidens and castles   90
        Have to surrender.
        Fair is the dare,
        Splendid the pay.
        And then the soldiers
        March on away.   95
        [FAUST *and* WAGNER.]
FAUST   Released from the ice are river and creek,
Warmed by the spring's fair quickening eye;
The valley is green with hope and joy;
The hoary winter has grown so weak
He has withdrawn to the rugged mountains.   100
From there he sends, but only in flight,

---

6. St. Andrew's Eve, November 29, the traditional time for young girls to consult fortune-tellers about their future lovers or husbands.

Impotent showers of icy hail
That streak across the greening vale;
But the sun will not suffer the white;
Everywhere stirs what develops and grows,   105
All he would quicken with color that glows;
Flowers are lacking, blue, yellow, and red,
But he takes dressed-up people instead.
Turn around now and look down
From the heights back to the town.   110
Out of the hollow gloomy gate
Surges and scatters a motley horde.
All seek sunshine. They celebrate
The resurrection of the Lord.
For they themselves are resurrected   115
From lowly houses, musty as stables,
From trades to which they are subjected,
From the pressure of roofs and gables,
From the stifling and narrow alleys,
From the churches' reverent night   120
They have emerged into the light.
Look there! Look, how the crowd now sallies
Gracefully into the gardens and leas,
How on the river, all through the valley,
Frolicsome floating boats one sees,   125
And, overloaded beyond its fill,
This last barge now is swimming away.
From the far pathways of the hill
We can still see how their clothes are gay.
I hear the village uproar rise;   130
Here is the people's paradise,
And great and small shout joyously:
Here I am human, may enjoy humanity.
WAGNER   To take a walk with you, good sir,
Is a great honor and reward,   135
But I myself should never so far err,
For the uncouth I always have abhorred.
This fiddling, bowling, loud delight—
I hate these noises of the throng;
They rage as if plagued by an evil sprite   140
And call it joy and call it song.
          [PEASANTS *under the linden tree. Dance and Song.*]
          The shepherd wished to dance and dressed
          With ribbons, wreath, and motley vest,
          He was a dandy beau.
          Around the linden, lass and lad.   145
          Were crowding, dancing round like mad.
          Hurrah! Hurrah!
          Hurrah! Hi-diddle-dee!
          Thus went the fiddle bow.

He pressed into the dancing whirl   150
His elbow bumped a pretty girl,
And he stepped on her toe.
The lively wench, she turned and said:
"You seem to be a dunderhead!"
Hurrah! Hurrah!   155
Hurrah! Hi-diddle-dee!
Don't treat a poor girl so.

The circle whirled in dancing flight,
Now they danced left, now they danced right,
The skirts flow high and low.   160
Their cheeks were flushed and they grew warm
And rested, panting, arm in arm.
Hurrah! Hurrah!
Hurrah! Hi-diddle-dee!
With waists and elbows so.   165

Please do not make so free with me!
For many fool their bride-to-be
And lie, as you well know.
And yet he coaxed the girl aside,
And from the linden, far and wide: 170
Hurrah! Hurrah!
Hurrah! Hi-diddle-dee!
Clamor and fiddle bow.

OLD PEASANT   Dear doctor, it is good of you
That you don't spurn us on this day   175
But find into this swarming throng,
Though a great scholar, still your way.
So please accept the finest mug;
With a good drink it has been filled,
I offer it and wish aloud: 180
Not only may your thirst be stilled;
As many drops as it conveys
Ought to be added to your days.

FAUST   I take the bumper and I, too,
Thank and wish health to all of you.   185
     [*The people gather around in a circle.*]

OLD PEASANT   Indeed, it is most kind of you
That you appear this happy day;
When evil days came in the past,
You always helped in every way.
And many stand here, still alive,   190
Whom your good father toiled to wrest
From the hot fever's burning rage
When he prevailed over the pest.[7]

---

7. Pestilence or plague.

And you, a young man at that time,
Made to the sick your daily round.   195
While many corpses were brought out,
You always emerged safe and sound,
And took these trials in your stride:
The Helper helped the helper here.
ALL   Health to the man so often tried!   200
    May he yet help for many a year!
FAUST   Bow down before Him, all of you,
    Who teaches help and sends help, too. [*He walks on with* WAGNER.]
WAGNER   Oh, what a feeling you must have, great man,
    When crowds revere you like a mighty lord.   205
    Oh, blessed are all those who can
    Employ their gifts for such reward.
    The father shows you to his son,
    They ask what gives and come and run,
    The fiddle stops, the dance is done.   210
    You walk, they stand in rows to see,
    Into the air their caps will fly—
    A little more, and they would bend their knee
    As if the Holy Host[8] went by.
FAUST   Now just a few more steps uphill to the big stone,   215
    From our wandering we can rest up there.
    I often sat there, thoughtful and alone,
    And vexed myself with fasting and with prayer.
    In hope still rich, with faith still blessed,
    I thought entreaties, tears, and sighs   220
    Would force the Master of the Skies
    To put an end to the long pest.
    The crowd's applause now sounds like caustic fun.
    I only wish you could read in my heart
    How little father and son   225
    Deserve such fame for their poor art.
    My father was obscure, if quite genteel,
    And pondered over nature and every sacred sphere
    In his own cranky way, though quite sincere,
    With ardent, though with wayward, zeal.   230
    And with proficient devotees,
    In his black kitchen he would fuse
    After unending recipes,
    Locked in, the most contrary brews.
    They made red lions, a bold wooer came,   235
    In tepid baths was mated to a lily;
    And then the pair was vexed with a wide-open flame
    From one bride chamber to another, willy-nilly.
    And when the queen appeared, all pied,
    Within the glass after a spell,   240
    The medicine was there, and though the patients died,

---

8. The Eucharist, the consecrated bread and wine of the Sacrament.

Nobody questioned: who got well?[9]
And thus we raged fanatically
In these same mountains, in this valley,
With hellish juice worse than the pest.   245
Though thousands died from poison that I myself would give,
Yes, though they perished, I must live
To hear the shameless killers blessed.
WAGNER   I cannot see why you are grieved.
What more can honest people do   250
Than be conscientious and pursue
With diligence the art that they received?
If you respect your father as a youth,
You'll learn from him what you desire;
If as a man you add your share of truth   255
To ancient lore, your son can go still higher.
FAUST   Oh, happy who still hopes to rise
Out of this sea of errors and false views!
What one does *not* know, one could utilize,
And what one knows one cannot use.   260
But let the beauty offered by this hour
Not be destroyed by our spleen!
See how, touched by the sunset's parting power,
The huts are glowing in the green.
The sun moves on, the day has had its round;   265
He hastens on, new life greets his salute.
Oh,[1] that no wings lift me above the ground
To strive and strive in his pursuit!
In the eternal evening light
The quiet world would lie below   270
With every valley tranquil, on fire every height,
The silver stream to golden rivers flow.
Nor could the mountain with its savage guise
And all its gorges check my godlike ways;
Already ocean with its glistening bays   275
Spreads out before astonished eyes.
At last the god sinks down, I seem forsaken;
But I feel new unrest awaken
And hurry hence to drink his deathless light,
The day before me, and behind me night,   280
The billows under me, and over me the sky.
A lovely dream, while he makes his escape.
The spirit's wings will not change our shape:
Our body grows no wings and cannot fly.
Yet it is innate in our race   285
That our feelings surge in us and long
When over us, lost in the azure space
The lark trills out her glorious song;

---

9. This confusing sequence evokes a kind of medicine closely allied to magic and inappropriate to the
needs of the ill people seeking help.   1. Alas.

When over crags where fir trees quake
In icy winds, the eagle soars, 290
And over plains and over lakes
The crane returns to homeward shores.

WAGNER I, too, have spells of eccentricity,
But such unrest has never come to me.
One soon grows sick of forest, field, and brook, 295
And I shall never envy birds their wings.
Far greater are the joys the spirit brings—
From page to page, from book to book.
Thus winter nights grow fair and warm the soul;
Yes, blissful life suffuses every limb, 300
And when one opens up an ancient parchment scroll,
The very heavens will descend on him.

FAUST You are aware of only one unrest;
Oh, never learn to know the other!
Two souls, alas, are dwelling in my breast, 305
And one is striving to forsake its brother.
Unto the world in grossly loving zest,
With clinging tendrils, one adheres;
The other rises forcibly in quest
Of rarefied ancestral spheres. 310
If there be spirits in the air
That hold their sway between the earth and sky,
Descend out of the golden vapors there
And sweep me into iridescent life.
Oh, came a magic cloak into my hands 315
To carry me to distant lands,
I should not trade it for the choicest gown,
Nor for the cloak and garments of the crown.

WAGNER Do not invoke the well-known throng that flow
Through mists above and spread out in the haze, 320
Concocting danger in a thousand ways
For man wherever he may go.
From the far north the spirits' deadly fangs
Bear down on you with arrow-pointed tongues;
And from the east they come with withering pangs 325
And nourish themselves from your lungs.
The midday sends out of the desert those
Who pile heat upon heat upon your crown,
While evening brings the throng that spells repose—
And then lets you, and fields and meadows, drown. 330
They gladly listen, but are skilled in harm,
Gladly obey, because they like deceit;
As if from heaven sent, they please and charm,
Whispering like angels when they cheat.
But let us go! The air has cooled, the world 335
Turned gray, mists are unfurled.
When evening comes one values home,
Why do you stand amazed? What holds your eyes?
What in the twilight merits such surprise?

FAUST   See that black dog through grain and stubble roam?   340
WAGNER   I noticed him way back, but cared not in the least.
FAUST   Look well! For what would *you* take this strange beast?
WAGNER   Why, for a poodle fretting doggedly
　　As it pursues the tracks left by its master.
FAUST   It spirals all around us, as you see,   345
　　And it approaches, fast and faster.
　　And if I do not err, a fiery eddy
　　Whirls after it and marks the trail.
WAGNER   I see the poodle, as I said already;
　　As for the rest, your eyesight seems to fail.   350
FAUST   It seems to me that he winds magic snares
　　Around our feet, a bond of future dangers.
WAGNER   He jumps around, unsure, and our presence scares
　　The dog who seeks his master, and finds instead two strangers.
FAUST   The spiral narrows, he is near!   355
WAGNER   You see, a dog and not a ghost is here.
　　He growls, lies on his belly, thus he waits,
　　He wags his tail: all canine traits.
FAUST   Come here and walk along with us!
WAGNER   He's poodlishly ridiculous.   360
　　You stand and rest, and he waits, too;
　　You speak to him, and he would climb on you;
　　Lose something, he will bring it back again,
　　Jump in the lake to get your cane.
FAUST   You seem quite right, I find, for all his skill,   365
　　No trace of any spirit: all is drill.
WAGNER   By dogs that are expertly trained
　　The wisest man is entertained.
　　He quite deserves your favor: it is prudent
　　To cultivate the students' noble student.   370
　　　[*They pass through the City Gate.*]

STUDY

FAUST [*Entering with the poodle.*]   The fields and meadows I have fled
　　As night enshrouds them and the lakes;
　　With apprehensive, holy dread
　　The better soul in us awakes.
　　Wild passions have succumbed to sleep,   5
　　All vehement exertions bow;
　　The love of man stirs in us deep,
　　The love of God is stirring now.

Be quiet, poodle! Stop running around!
Why do you snuffle at the sill like that?   10
Lie down behind the stove—not on the ground:
Take my best cushion for a mat.
As you amused us on our way
With running and jumping and did your best,
Let me look after you and say: 15
Be quiet, please, and be my guest.

When in our narrow den
The friendly lamp glows on the shelf,
Then light pervades our breast again
And fills the heart that knows itself.   20
Reason again begins to speak,
Hope blooms again with ancient force,
One longs for life and one would seek
Its rivers and, alas, its source.

Stop snarling poodle! For the sacred strain   25
To which my soul is now submitting
Beastly sounds are hardly fitting.
We are accustomed to see *men* disdain
What they don't grasp;
When it gives trouble, they profane   30
Even the beautiful and the good.
Do dogs, too, snarl at what's not understood?

Even now, however, though I tried my best,
Contentment flows no longer through my breast.
Why does the river rest so soon, and dry up, and   35
Leave us to languish in the sand?
How well I know frustration!
This want, however, we can overwhelm:
We turn to the supernatural realm,
We long for the light of revelation   40
Which is nowhere more magnificent
Than in our New Testament.
I would for once like to determine—
Because I am sincerely perplexed—
How the sacred original text[2]   45
Could be translated into my beloved German.

[*He opens a tome and begins.*]
It says: "In the beginning was the *Word*."[3]
Already I am stopped. It seems absurd.
The *Word* does not deserve the highest prize,
I must translate it otherwise   50
If I am well inspired and not blind.
It says: In the beginning was the *Mind*.
Ponder that first line, wait and see,
Lest you should write too hastily.
Is mind the all-creating source?   55
It ought to say: In the beginning there was *Force*.
Yet something warns me as I grasp the pen,
That my translation must be changed again.
The spirit helps me. Now it is exact.
I write: In the beginning was the *Act*.   60

If I am to share my room with you,
Poodle, stop moaning so!

2. I.e., the Greek.   3. John 1.1.

And stop your bellow,
For such a noisy, whiny fellow
I do not like to have around.   65
One of us, black hound,
Will have to give ground.
With reluctance I change my mind:
The door is open, you are not confined.
But what must I see!   70
Can that happen naturally?
Is it a shadow? Am I open-eyed?
How grows my poodle long and wide!
He reaches up like rising fog—
This is no longer the shape of a dog!   75
Oh, what a specter I brought home!
A hippopotamus of foam,
With fiery eyes; how his teeth shine!
You are as good as mine:
For such a semi-hellish brow   80
The Key of Solomon[4] will do.
SPIRITS [*In the corridor.*]   One has been caught inside.
            Do not follow him! Abide!
            As a fox in a snare,
            Hell's old lynx is caught in there.   85
            But give heed!
            Float up high, float down low,
            To and fro,
            And he tries, and he is freed.
            Can you avail him?   90
            Then do not fail him!
            For you must not forget,
            We are in his debt.
FAUST   Countering the beast, I might well
    First use the fourfold spell: 95

            Salamander shall broil,
            Undene shall grieve,
            Sylphe shall leave,
            Kobold[5] shall toil.

Whoever ignores   100
The elements' cores,
Their energy
And quality,
Cannot command
In the spirits' land.   105

            Disappear flashing,
            Salamander!
            Flow together, splashing,

---

4. The *Clavicula Salomonis*, a standard work used by magicians for conjuring. In many medieval legends, Solomon was noted as a great magician.   **5.** A spirit of the earth. *Salamander:* spirit of fire. *Undene:* or undine, spirit of water. *Sylphe:* or sylph, spirit of air.

Undene!
Glow in meteoric beauty,   110
Sylphe!
Do your domestic duty,
Incubus! Incubus!
Step forward and finish thus.

None of the four   115
Is this beast's core.
It lies quite calmly there and beams;
I have not hurt it yet, it seems.
Now listen well
To a stronger spell.   120

If you should be
Hell's progeny,
Then see this symbol
Before which tremble
The cohorts of Hell!   125

Already it bristles and starts to swell.

Spirit of shame,
Can you read the name
Of the Uncreated,
Defying expression,   130
With whom the heavens are sated,
Who was pierced in transgression?

Behind the stove it swells
As an elephant under my spells;
It fills the whole room and quakes,   135
It would turn into mist and fleet.
Stop now before the ceiling breaks!
Lie down at your master's feet!

You see, I do not threaten in vain:
With holy flames I cause you pain.   140
Do not require
The threefold glowing fire!6
Do not require
My art in its full measure!

MEPHISTOPHELES [*Steps forward from behind the stove, dressed as a traveling
scholar, while the mist clears away.*]
  Why all the noise? Good sir, what is your pleasure?   145
FAUST   Then this was our poodle's core!
  Simply a traveling scholar? The *casus*7 makes me laugh.
MEPHISTOPHELES   Profound respects to you and to your lore:
  You made me sweat with all your chaff.
FAUST   What is your name?

6. Perhaps the Trinity or a triangle with divergent rays.   7. Occurrence.

MEPHISTOPHELES   This question seems minute   150
   For one who thinks the word so beggarly,
   Who holds what seems in disrepute,
   And craves only reality.[8]
FAUST   Your real being no less than your fame
   Is often shown, sirs, by your name,   155
   Which is not hard to analyze
   When one calls you the Liar, Destroyer, God of Flies.[9]
   Enough, who are you then?
MEPHISTOPHELES   Part of that force which would
   Do evil evermore, and yet creates the good.
FAUST   What is it that this puzzle indicates?   160
MEPHISTOPHELES   I am the spirit that negates.
   And rightly so, for all that comes to be
   Deserves to perish wretchedly;
   'Twere better nothing would begin.
   Thus everything that your terms, sin,   165
   Destruction, evil represent—
   That is my proper element.
FAUST   You call yourself a part, yet whole make your debut?
MEPHISTOPHELES   The modest truth I speak to you.
   While man, this tiny world of fools, is droll   170
   Enough to think himself a whole,
   I am part of the part that once was everything,
   Part of the darkness which gave birth to light,
   That haughty light which envies mother night
   Her ancient rank and place and would be king—   175
   Yet it does not succeed: however it contend,
   It sticks to bodies in the end.
   It streams from bodies, it lends bodies beauty,
   A body won't let it progress;
   So it will not take long, I guess,   180
   And with the bodies it will perish, too.
FAUST   I understand your noble duty:
   Too weak for great destruction, you
   Attempt it on a minor scale.
MEPHISTOPHELES   And I admit it is of slight avail.   185
   What stands opposed to our Nought,
   The some, your wretched world—for aught
   That I have so far undertaken,
   It stands unruffled and unshaken:
   With billows, fires, storms, commotion,   190
   Calm, after all, remain both land and ocean.
   And that accursed lot, the brood of beasts and men,
   One cannot hurt them anyhow.
   How many have I buried now!
   Yet always fresh new blood will circulate again.   195

---

8. Mephistopheles refers to Faust's substitution of *Act* for *Word* in the passage from John (see line 60).
9. An almost literal translation of the name of the Philistine deity Beelzebub.

Thus it goes on—I could rage in despair!
From water, earth, and even air,
A thousand seeds have ever grown
In warmth and cold and drought and mire!
If I had not reserved myself the fire,   200
I should have nothing of my own.
FAUST   And thus, I see, you would resist
The ever-live creative power
By clenching your cold devil's fist
Resentfully—in vain you glower.   205
Try something new and unrelated,
Oh you peculiar son of chaos!
MEPHISTOPHELES   Perchance your reasoning might sway us—
The next few times we may debate it.
But for the present, may I go?   210
FAUST   I cannot see why you inquire.
Now that we met, you ought to know
That you may call as you desire.
Here is the window, here the door,
A chimney there, if that's preferred.   215
MEPHISTOPHELES   I cannot leave you that way, I deplore:
By a small obstacle I am deterred:
The witch's foot on your threshold, see—
FAUST   The pentagram[1] distresses you?
Then, son of hell, explain to me: 220
How could you enter here without ado?
And how was such a spirit cheated?
MEPHISTOPHELES   Behold it well: It is not quite completed;
One angle—that which points outside—
Is open just a little bit.   225
FAUST: That was indeed a lucky hit.
I caught you and you must abide.
How wonderful, and yet how queer!
MEPHISTOPHELES   The poodle never noticed, when he first jumped in
    here,
But now it is a different case;   230
The Devil cannot leave this place.
FAUST   The window's there. Are you in awe?
MEPHISTOPHELES   The devils and the demons have a law:
Where they slipped in, they always must withdraw.
The first time we are free, the second time constrained.   235
FAUST   For hell, too, laws have been ordained?
Superb! Then one should surely make a pact,
And one of you might enter my employ.
MEPHISTOPHELES   What we would promise you, you would enjoy,
And none of it we would subtract.   240
But that we should not hurry so,
And we shall talk about it soon;

1. A magic five-pointed star designed to keep away evil spirits.

For now I ask the single boon
That you permit me now to go.
FAUST   For just a moment stay with me   245
And let me have some happy news.
MEPHISTOPHELES   Not now. I'll come back presently,
Then you may ask me what you choose.
FAUST   You were not caught by my device
When you were snared like this tonight.   250
Who holds the Devil, hold him tight!
He can't expect to catch him twice.
MEPHISTOPHELES   If you prefer it, I shall stay
With you, and I shall not depart,
Upon condition that I may   255
Amuse you with some samples of my art.
FAUST   Go right ahead, you are quite free—
Provided it is nice to see.
MEPHISTOPHELES   Right in this hour you will obtain
More for your senses than you gain   260
In a whole year's monotony.
What tender spirits now will sing,
The lovely pictures that they bring
Are not mere magic for the eye:
They will delight your sense of smell,   265
Be pleasing to your taste as well,
Excite your touch, and give you joy.
No preparation needs my art,
We are together, let us start.
SPIRITS   Vanish, you darkling   270
    Arches above him.
    Friendlier beaming,
    Sky should be gleaming
    Down upon us.
    Ah, that the darkling   275
    Clouds had departed!
    Stars now are sparkling,
    More tenderhearted
    Suns shine on us.
    Spirits aerial,   280
    Fair and ethereal,
    Wavering and bending,
    Sail by like swallows.
    Yearning unending
    Sees them and follows,   285
    Garments are flowing,
    Ribbons are blowing,
    Covering the glowing
    Land and the bower
    Where, in the hedges,   290
    Thinking and dreaming,
    Lovers make pledges.

Bower on bower.
Tendrils are streaming;
Heavy grapes shower   295
Their sweet excesses
Into the presses;
In streams are flowing
Wines that are glowing,
Foam, effervescent,   300
Through iridescent
Gems; they are storming
Down from the mountains;
Lakes they are forming,
Beautiful fountains   305
Where hills are ending,
Birds are descending,
Drink and fly onward,
Fly ever sunward,
Fly from the highlands   310
Toward the ocean
Where brilliant islands
Sway in soft motion.
Jubilant choirs
Soothe all desires,   315
And are entrancing
Those who are dancing
Like whirling satyrs,
But the throng scatters.
Some now are scaling   320
Over the mountains,
Others are sailing
Toward the fountains,
Others are soaring,
All life adoring,   325
All crave the far-off
Love-spending star of
Rapturous bliss.

MEPHISTOPHELES   He sleeps. I thank you, airy, tender throng.
    You made him slumber with your song.   330
    A splendid concert. I appreciate this.
    You are not yet the man to hold the Devil fast.
    Go, dazzle him with dream shapes, sweet and vast,
    Plunge him into an ocean of untruth.
    But now, to break the threshold's spell at last,   335
    I have to get a rat's sharp tooth.
    I need no conjuring today,
    One's rustling over there and will come right away.
    The lord of rats, the lord of mice,
    Of flies and frogs, bedbugs and lice,   340
    Bids you to dare now to appear
    To gnaw upon this threshold here,

Where he is dabbing it with oil.
Ah, there you come. Begin your toil.
The point that stopped me like a magic hedge   345
Is way up front, right on the edge.
Just one more bite, and that will do.
Now, Faustus, sleep and dream, till I come back to you.
FAUST [*Awakening.*]   Betrayed again? Fooled by a scheme?
Should spirits' wealth so suddenly decay   350
That I behold the Devil in a dream,
And that a poodle jumps away?

STUDY

[FAUST, MEPHISTOPHELES.]
FAUST   A knock? Come in! Who comes to plague me now?
MEPHISTOPHELES   It's I.
FAUST   Come in!
MEPHISTOPHELES   You have to say it thrice.
FAUST   Come in, then.
MEPHISTOPHELES   Now you're nice.
We should get along well, I vow.
To chase your spleen away, allow   5
That I appear a noble squire:[2]
Look at my red and gold attire,
A little cloak of silk brocade,
The rooster's feather in my hat,
And the long, nicely pointed blade—   10
And now it is my counsel that
You, too, should be like this arrayed;
Then you would feel released and free,
And you would find what life can be.
FAUST   I shall not cease to feel in all attires,   15
The pains of our narrow earthly day.
I am too old to be content to play,
Too young to be without desire.
What wonders could the world reveal?
You must renounce! You ought to yield!   20
That is the never-ending drone
Which we must, our life long, hear,
Which, hoarsely, all our hours intone
And grind into our weary ears.
Frightened I waken to the dismal dawn,   25
Wish I had tears to drown the sun
And check the day that soon will scorn
My every wish—fulfill not one.
If I but think of any pleasure,
Bright critic day is sure to chide it,   30
And if my heart creates itself a treasure,

2. In the popular plays based on the Faust legend, the Devil often appeared as a monk when the play
catered to a Protestant audience and as a noble squire when the audience was predominantly Catholic.

A thousand mocking masks deride it.
When night descends at last, I shall recline
But anxiously upon my bed;
Though all is still, no rest is mine   35
As dreams enmesh my mind in dread.
The god that dwells within my heart
Can stir my depths, I cannot hide—
Rules all my powers with relentless art,
But cannot move the world outside;   40
And thus existence is for me a weight,
Death is desirable, and life I hate.

MEPHISTOPHELES   And yet when death approaches, the welcome is not
    great.

FAUST   Oh, blessed whom, as victory advances,
He lends the blood-drenched laurel's grace,   45
Who, after wildly whirling dances,
Receives him in a girl's embrace!
Oh, that before the lofty spirit's power
I might have fallen to the ground, unsouled!

MEPHISTOPHELES   And yet someone, in that same nightly hour   50
    Refused to drain a certain bowl.

FAUST   You seem to eavesdrop quite proficiently.

MEPHISTOPHELES   Omniscient I am not, but there is much I see.

FAUST   As in that terrifying reeling
I heard the sweet familiar chimes   55
That duped the traces of my childhood feeling
With echoes of more joyous times,
I now curse all that would enamor
The human soul with lures and lies,
Enticing it with flattering glamour   60
To live on in this cave of sighs.
Cursed above all our high esteem,
The spirit's smug self-confidence,
Cursed be illusion, fraud, and dream
That flatter our guileless sense!   65
Cursed be the pleasing make-believe
Of fame and long posthumous life!
Cursed be possessions that deceive,
As slave and plough, and child and wife!
Cursed, too, be Mammon[3] when with treasures   70
He spurs us on to daring feats,
Or lures us into slothful pleasures
With sumptuous cushions and smooth sheets!
A curse on wine that mocks our thirst!
A curse on love's last consummations!   75
A curse on hope! Faith, too, be cursed!
And cursed above all else be patience!

---

3. The Aramaic word for "riches," used in the New Testament. Medieval writers interpreted the word as
a proper noun, the name of the Devil, as representing covetousness or avarice.

CHOIR OF SPIRITS [*Invisible.*]   Alas!
    You have shattered
    The beautiful world   80
    With brazen fist;
    It falls, it is scattered—
    By a demigod destroyed.
    We are trailing
    The ruins into the void   85
    And wailing
    Over beauty undone
    And ended.
    Earth's mighty son,
    More splendid   90
    Rebuild it, you that are strong,
    Build it again within!
    And begin
    A new life, a new way,
    Lucid and gay,   95
    And play
    New songs.
MEPHISTOPHELES   These are the small
    Ones of my thralls.
    Hear how precociously they plead   100
    For pleasure and deed!
    To worldly strife
    From your lonely life
    Which dries up sap and sense,
    They would lure you hence.   105

Stop playing with your melancholy
That, like a vulture, ravages your breast;
The worst of company still cures this folly,
For you are human with the rest.
Yet that is surely not to say   110
That you should join the herd you hate.
I'm not one of the great,
But if you want to make your way
Through the world with me united,
I should surely be delighted   115
To be yours, as of now,
Your companion, if you allow;
And if you like the way I behave,
I shall be your servant, or your slave.
FAUST   And in return, what do you hope to take?   120
MEPHISTOPHELES   There's so much time—so why insist?
FAUST   No, no! The Devil is an egoist
And would not just for heaven's sake
Turn into a philanthropist.
Make your conditions very clear;   125
Where such a servant lives, danger is near.

MEPHISTOPHELES   *Here* you shall be the master, I be bond,
  And at your nod I'll work incessantly;
  But when we meet again *beyond,*
  Then you shall do the same for me.   130
FAUST   Of the beyond I have no thought;
  When you reduce this world to nought,
  The other one may have its turn.
  My joys come from this earth, and there,
  That sun has burnt on my despair: 135
  Once I have left those, I don't care:
  What happens is of no concern.
  I do not even wish to hear
  Whether beyond they hate and love,
  And whether in that other sphere   140
  One realm's below and one above.
MEPHISTOPHELES   So minded, dare it cheerfully.
  Commit yourself and you shall see
  My arts with joy. I'll give you more
  Than any man has seen before.   145
FAUST   What would you, wretched Devil, offer?
  Was ever a man's spirit in its noble striving
  Grasped by your like, devilish scoffer?
  But have you food that is not satisfying,
  Red gold that rolls off without rest,   150
  Quicksilver-like, over your skin—
  A game in which no man can win—
  A girl who, lying at my breast,
  Ogles already to entice my neighbor,
  And honor—that perhaps seems best—   155
  Though like a comet it will turn to vapor?
  Show me fruit that, before we pluck them, rot,
  And trees whose foliage every day makes new!
MEPHISTOPHELES   Such a commission scares me not,
  With such things I can wait on you.   160
  But, worthy friend, the time comes when we would
  Recline in peace and feast on something good.
FAUST   If ever I recline, calmed, on a bed of sloth,
  You may destroy me then and there.
  If ever flattering you should wile me   165
  That in myself I find delight,
  If with enjoyment you beguile me,
  Then break on me, eternal night!
  This bet I offer.
MEPHISTOPHELES I accept it.
FAUST   Right.
  If to the moment I should say: 170
  Abide, you are so fair—
  Put me in fetters on that day,
  I *wish* to perish then, I swear.
  Then let the death bell ever toll,

Your service done, you shall be free,   175
The clock may stop, the hand may fall,
As time comes to an end for me.
MEPHISTOPHELES   Consider it, for we shall not forget it.
FAUST   That is a right you need not waive.
I did not boast, and I shall not regret it.   180
As I grow stagnant I shall be a slave,
Whether or not to anyone indebted.
MEPHISTOPHELES   At the doctor's banquet[4] tonight I shall do
My duties as a servant without fail.
But for life's sake, or death's—just one detail: 185
Could you give me a line or two?
FAUST   You pedant need it black on white?
Are man and a man's word indeed new to your sight?
Is not my spoken word sufficient warrant
When it commits my life eternally?   190
Does not the world rush on in every torrent,
And a mere promise should hold me?
Yet this illusion our heart inherits,
And who would want to shirk his debt?
Blessed who counts loyalty among his merits.   195
No sacrifice will he regret.
And yet a parchment, signed and sealed, is an abhorrent
Specter that haunts us, and it makes us fret.
The word dies when we seize the pen,
And wax and leather lord it then.   200
What, evil spirit, do you ask?
Paper or parchment, stone or brass?
Should I use chisel, style, or quill?
It is completely up to you.
MEPHISTOPHELES   Why get so hot and overdo   205
Your rhetoric? Why must you shrill?
Use any sheet, it is the same;
And with a drop of blood you sign your name.
FAUST   If you are sure you like this game,
Let it be done to humor you.   210
MEPHISTOPHELES   Blood is a very special juice.
FAUST   You need not fear that someday I retract.
That all my striving I unloose
Is the whole purpose of the pact.
Oh, I was puffed up all too boldly,   215
At your rank only is my place.
The lofty spirit spurned me coldly,
And nature hides from me her face.
Torn is the subtle thread of thought,
I loathe the knowledge I once sought.   220
In sensuality's abysmal land
Let our passions drink their fill!

4. The dinner given by a successful candidate for a Ph.D. degree.

In magic veils, not pierced by skill,
Let every wonder be at hand!
Plunge into time's whirl that dazes my sense,   225
Into the torrent of events!
And let enjoyment, distress,
Annoyance and success
Succeed each other as best they can;
For restless activity proves a man.   230
MEPHISTOPHELES   You are not bound by goal or measure.
If you would nibble everything
Or snatch up something on the wing,
You're welcome to what gives you pleasure.
But help yourself and don't be coy!   235
FAUST   Do you not hear, I have no thought of joy!
The reeling whirl I seek, the most painful excess,
Enamored hate and quickening distress.
Cured from the craving to know all, my mind
Shall not henceforth be closed to any pain,   240
And what is portioned out to all mankind,
I shall enjoy deep in my self, contain
Within my spirit summit and abyss,
Pile on my breast their agony and bliss,
And thus let my own self grow into theirs, unfettered,   245
Till as they are, at last I, too, am shattered.
MEPHISTOPHELES   Believe me who for many a thousand year
Has chewed this cud and never rested,
That from the cradle to the bier
The ancient leaven cannot be digested.   250
Trust one like me, this whole array
Is for a God—there's no contender:
He dwells in his eternal splendor,
To darkness we had to surrender,
And you need night as well as day.   255
FAUST   And yet it is my will.
MEPHISTOPHELES   It does sound bold.
But I'm afraid, though you are clever,
Time is too brief, though art's forever.
Perhaps you're willing to be told.
Why don't you find yourself a poet,   260
And let the gentleman ransack his dreams:
And when he finds a noble trait, let him bestow it
Upon your worthy head in reams and reams:
The lion's daring,
The swiftness of the hind,   265
The northerner's forbearing
And the Italian's fiery mind,
Let him resolve the mystery
How craft can be combined with magnanimity,
Or how a passion-crazed young man   270
Might fall in love after a plan.

If there were such a man, I'd like to meet him,
As Mr. Microcosm I would greet him.
FAUST   Alas, what am I, if I can
   Not reach for mankind's crown which merely mocks   275
   Our senses' craving like a star?
MEPHISTOPHELES   You're in the end—just what you are!
   Put wigs on with a million locks
   And put your foot on ell-high socks,
   You still remain just what you are.   280
FAUST   I feel, I gathered up and piled up high
   In vain the treasures of the human mind:
   When I sit down at last, I cannot find
   New strength within—it is all dry.
   My stature has not grown a whit,   285
   No closer to the Infinite.
MEPHISTOPHELES   Well, my good sir, to put it crudely,
   You see matters just as they lie;
   We have to look at them more shrewdly,
   Or all life's pleasures pass us by.   290
   Your hands and feet—indeed that's trite—
   And head and seat are yours alone;
   Yet all in which I find delight,
   Should they be less my own?
   Suppose I buy myself six steeds: 295
   I buy their strength; while I recline
   I dash along at whirlwind speeds,
   For their two dozen legs are mine.
   Come on! Let your reflections rest
   And plunge into the world with zest!   300
   I say, the man that speculates
   Is like a beast that in the sand,
   Led by an evil spirit, round and round gyrates,
   And all about lies gorgeous pasture land.
FAUST   How shall we set about it?
MEPHISTOPHELES   Simply leave.   305
   What torture room is this? What site of grief?
   Is this the noble life of prudence—
   You bore yourself and bore your students?
   Oh, let your neighbor, Mr. Paunch, live so!
   Why work hard threshing straw, when it annoys?   310
   The best that you could ever know
   You may not tell the little boys.
   Right now I hear one in the aisle.
FAUST   I simply cannot face the lad.
MEPHISTOPHELES   The poor chap waited quite a while,   315
   I do not want him to leave sad.
   Give me your cap and gown. Not bad! [*He dresses himself up.*]
   This mask ought to look exquisite!
   Now you can leave things to my wit.
   Some fifteen minutes should be all I need;   320
   Meanwhile get ready for our trip, and speed!

[*Exit* FAUST.]

MEPHISTOPHELES [*In* FAUST's *long robe.*]

Have but contempt for reason and for science,
Man's noblest force spurn with defiance,
Subscribe to magic and illusion,
The Lord of Lies aids your confusion,   325
And, pact or no, I hold you tight.—
The spirit which he has received from fate
Sweeps ever onward with unbridled might,
Its hasty striving is so great
It leaps over the earth's delights.   330
Through life I'll drag him at a rate,
Through shallow triviality,
That he shall writhe and suffocate;
And his insatiability,
With greedy lips, shall see the choicest plate   335
And ask in vain for all that he would cherish—
And were he not the Devil's mate
And had not signed, he still must perish.

[*A* STUDENT *enters.*]

STUDENT   I have arrived quite recently
And come, full of humility,   340
To meet that giant intellect
Whom all refer to with respect.

MEPHISTOPHELES   This is a charming pleasantry.
A man as others are, you see.—
Have you already called elsewhere?   345

STUDENT   I pray you, take me in your care.
I am, believe me, quite sincere,
Have some odd cash and lots of cheer;
My mother scarcely let me go,
But there is much I hope to know.   350

MEPHISTOPHELES   This is just the place for you to stay.

STUDENT   To be frank, I should like to run away.
I cannot say I like these walls,
These gloomy rooms and somber halls.
It seems so narrow, and I see   355
No patch of green, no single tree;
And in the auditorium
My hearing, sight, and thought grow numb.

MEPHISTOPHELES   That is a question of mere habit.
The child, offered the mother's breast,   360
Will not in the beginning grab it;
But soon it clings to it with zest.
And thus at wisdom's copious breasts
You'll drink each day with greater zest.

STUDENT   I'll hang around her neck, enraptured;   365
But tell me first: how is she captured?

MEPHISTOPHELES   Before we get into my views—
What Department do you choose?

STUDENT   I should like to be erudite,
 And from the earth to heaven's height   370
 Know every law and every action:
 Nature and science is what I need.
MEPHISTOPHELES   That is the way; you just proceed
 And scrupulously shun distraction.
STUDENT   Body and soul, I am a devotee;   375
 Though, naturally, everybody prays
 For some free time and liberty
 On pleasant summer holidays.
MEPHISTOPHELES   Use well your time, so swiftly it runs on!
 Be orderly, and time is won!   380
 My friend, I shall be pedagogic,
 And say you ought to start with Logic.
 For thus your mind is trained and braced,
 In Spanish boots it will be laced,
 That on the road of thought maybe   385
 It henceforth creep more thoughtfully,
 And does not crisscross here and there,
 Will-o'-the-wisping through the air.
 Days will be spent to let you know
 That what you once did at one blow,   390
 Like eating and drinking so easy and free,
 Can only be done with One, Two, Three.
 Yet the web of thought has no such creases
 And is more like a weaver's masterpieces:
 One step, a thousand threads arise,   395
 Hither and thither shoots each shuttle,
 The threads flow on, unseen and subtle,
 Each blow effects a thousand ties.
 The philosopher comes with analysis
 And proves it had to be like this: 400
 The first was so, the second so,
 And hence the third and fourth was so,
 And were not the first and the second here,
 Then the third and fourth could never appear.
 That is what all the students believe,   405
 But they have never learned to weave.
 Who would study and describe the living, starts
 By driving the spirit out of the parts:
 In the palm of his hand he holds all the sections,
 Lacks nothing, except the spirit's connections.   410
 Enchcirisis naturae[5] the chemists baptize it,
 Mock themselves and don't realize it.
STUDENT   I did not quite get everything.
MEPHISTOPHELES   That will improve with studying:
 You will reduce things by and by   415

---

5. The natural process by which substances are united into a living organism—a name for an action no one understands.

And also learn to classify.
STUDENT   I feel so dazed by all you said
As if a mill went around in my head.
MEPHISTOPHELES   Then, without further circumvention,
Give metaphysics your attention.   420
There seek profoundly to attain
What does not fit the human brain;
Whether you do or do not understand,
An impressive word is always at hand.
But now during your first half-year,   425
Keep above all our order here.
Five hours a day, you understand,
And when the bell peals, be on hand.
Before you come, you must prepare,
Read every paragraph with care,   430
Lest you, forbid, should overlook
That all he says is in the book.
But write down everything, engrossed
As if you took dictation from the Holy Ghost.
STUDENT   Don't say that twice—I understood: 435
I see how useful it's to write,
For what we possess black on white
We can take home and keep for good.
MEPHISTOPHELES   But choose a field of concentration!
STUDENT   I have no hankering for jurisprudence.   440
MEPHISTOPHELES   For that I cannot blame the students,
I know this science is a blight.
The laws and statutes of a nation
Are an inherited disease,
From generation unto generation   445
And place to place they drag on by degrees.
Wisdom becomes nonsense; kindness, oppression:
To be a grandson is a curse.
The right that is innate in us
Is not discussed by the profession.   450
STUDENT   My scorn is heightened by your speech.
Happy the man that you would teach!
I almost think theology would pay.
MEPHISTOPHELES   I should not wish to lead you astray.
When it comes to this discipline,   455
The way is hard to find, wrong roads abound,
And lots of hidden poison lies around
Which one can scarcely tell from medicine.
Here, too, it would be best you heard
One only and staked all upon your master's word.   460
Yes, stick to words at any rate;
There never was a surer gate
Into the temple, Certainty.
STUDENT   Yet some idea there must be.
MEPHISTOPHELES   All right. But do not plague yourself too
      anxiously;   465

For just where no ideas are
The proper word is never far.
With words a dispute can be won,
With words a system can be spun,
In words one can believe unshaken,   470
And from a word no tittle can be taken.
STUDENT   Forgive, I hold you up with many questions,
But there is one more thing I'd like to see.
Regarding medicine, maybe,
You have some powerful suggestions?   475
Three years go by so very fast,
And, God, the field is all too vast.
If but a little hint is shown,
One can attempt to find one's way.
MEPHISTOPHELES [*Aside.*]   I'm sick of this pedantic tone.   480
The Devil now again I'll play.
[*Aloud.*] The spirit of medicine is easy to know:
Through the macro- and microcosm you breeze,
And in the end you let it go
As God may please.   485
In vain you roam about to study science,
For each learns only what he can;
Who places on the moment his reliance,
He is the proper man.
You are quite handsome, have good sense,   490
And no doubt, you have courage, too,
And if you have self-confidence,
Then others will confide in you.
And give the women special care;
Their everlasting sighs and groans   495
In thousand tones
Are cured at *one* point everywhere.
And if you seem halfway discreet,
They will be lying at your feet.
First your degree inspires trust,   500
As if your art had scarcely any peers;
Right at the start, remove her clothes and touch her bust,
Things for which others wait for years and years.
Learn well the little pulse to squeeze,
And with a knowing, fiery glance you seize   505
Her freely round her slender waist
To see how tightly she is laced.
STUDENT   That looks much better, sir. For one sees how and where.
MEPHISTOPHELES   Gray, my dear friend, is every theory,
And green alone life's golden tree.   510
STUDENT   All this seems like a dream, I swear.
Could I impose on you sometime again
And drink more words of wisdom then?
MEPHISTOPHELES   What I can give you, you shall get.
STUDENT   Alas, I cannot go quite yet: 515
My album I must give to you;

Please, sir, show me this favor, too.
MEPHISTOPHELES   All right. [*He writes and returns it.*]
STUDENT [*Reads.*]   Eritis sicut Deus, scientes bonum et malum.[6] [*Closes
  the book reverently and takes his leave.*]
MEPHISTOPHELES   Follow the ancient text and my relation, the
      snake;   520
  Your very likeness to God will yet make you quiver and quake.
          [FAUST *enters.*]
FAUST   Where are we heading now?
MEPHISTOPHELES   Wherever you may please.
  We'll see the small world, then the larger one.
  You will reap profit and have fun
  As you sweep through this course with ease.   525
FAUST   With my long beard I hardly may
  Live in this free and easy way.
  The whole endeavor seems so futile;
  I always felt the world was strange and brutal.
  With others, I feel small and harassed,   530
  And I shall always be embarrassed.
MEPHISTOPHELES   Good friend, you will become less sensitive:
  Self-confidence will teach you how to live.
FAUST   How shall we get away from here?
  Where are your carriage, groom and steed?   535
MEPHISTOPHELES   I rather travel through the air:
  We spread this cloak—that's all we need
  But on this somewhat daring flight,
  Be sure to keep your luggage light.
  A little fiery air, which I plan to prepare,   540
  Will raise us swiftly off the earth;
  Without ballast we'll go up fast—
  Congratulations, friend, on your rebirth!

AUERBACH'S KELLER IN LEIPZIG

          [*Jolly fellows' drinking bout.*]
FROSCH   Will no one drink and no one laugh?
  I'll teach you not to look so wry.
  Today you look like sodden chaff
  And usually blaze to the sky
BRANDER   It's all your fault; you make me sick: 5
  No joke, and not a single dirty trick.
FROSCH [*Pours a glass of wine over* BRANDER's *head.*]
  There you have both.
BRANDER   You filthy pig!
FROSCH   You said I shouldn't be a prig.
SIEBEL   Let those who fight, stop or get out!
  With all your lungs sing chorus, swill, and shout!   10
  Come! Holla-ho!
ALTMAYER   Now this is where I quit.

---

6. A slight alteration of the serpent's words to Eve in Genesis: "Ye shall be as God, knowing good and evil"
(Latin).

Get me some cotton or my ears will split.
SIEBEL When the vault echoes and the place
  Is quaking, then you can enjoy a bass.
FROSCH Quite right! Throw out who fusses because he is lampooned! 15
  A! tara lara da!
ALTMAYER A! tara lara da!
FROSCH The throats seem to be tuned.
     [*Sings.*] Dear Holy Roman Empire,
     What holds you still together? 20
BRANDER A nasty song! It reeks of politics!
  A wretched song! Thank God in daily prayer,
  That the old Empire isn't your affair!
  At least I think it is much to be grateful for
  That I'm not Emperor nor Chancellor. 25
  And yet we, too, need someone to respect—
  I say, a Pope let us elect.
  You know the part that elevates
  And thereby proves the man who rates.
FROSCH [*Sings.*] Oh, Dame Nightingale, arise! 30
     Bring my sweet love ten thousand sighs!
SIEBEL No sighs for your sweet love! I will not have such mush.
FROSCH A sigh and kiss for her! You cannot make me blush.
     [*Sings.*] Ope the latch in silent night!
     Ope the latch, your love invite! 35
     Shut the latch, there is the dawn!
SIEBEL Go, sing and sing and sing, pay compliments and fawn!
  The time will come when I shall laugh:
  She led me by the nose, and you are the next calf.
  Her lover should be some mischievous gnome! 40
  He'd meet her at a crossroads and make light,
  And an old billy goat that's racing home
  From Blocksberg could still bleat to her "Good night!"
  A decent lad of real flesh and blood
  Is far too good to be her stud. 45
  I'll stand no sighs, you silly ass,
  But throw rocks through her window glass.
BRANDER [*Pounding on the table.*]
  Look here! Look here! Listen to me!
  My friends, confess I know what's right;
  There are lovers here, and you'll agree 50
  That it's only civility
  That I should try to honor them tonight.
  Watch out! This song's the latest fashion.
  And join in the refrain with passion!
  [*Sings.*] A cellar once contained a rat 55
     That couldn't have been uncouther,
     Lived on grease and butter and grew fat—
     Just like old Doctor Luther.[7]

---

7. Martin Luther (1483–1546), German leader of the Protestant Reformation, hence an object of distaste for Catholics.

        The cook put poison in his food,
        Then he felt cramped and just as stewed,   60
        As if love gnawed his vitals.
CHORUS [*Jubilant.*]   As if love gnawed his vitals.
BRANDER   He dashed around, he dashed outdoors,
        Sought puddles and swilled rain,
        He clawed and scratched up walls and floors,   65
        But his frenzy was in vain;
        He jumped up in a frightful huff,
        But soon the poor beast had enough,
        As if love gnawed his vitals.
CHORUS   As if love gnawed his vitals.   70
BRANDER   At last he rushed in open day
        Into the kitchen, crazed with fear,
        Dropped near the stove and writhed and lay,
        And puffed out his career.
        The poisoner only laughed: I hope   75
        He's at the end now of his rope,
        As if love gnawed his vitals.
CHORUS   As if love gnawed his vitals.
SIEBEL   How pleased these stupid chaps are! That's,
   I think, indeed a proper art   80
   To put out poison for poor rats.
BRANDER   I see, you'd like to take their part.
ALTMAYER   Potbelly with his shiny top!
   His ill luck makes him mild and tame.
   He sees the bloated rat go flop—   85
   And sees himself: they look the same.
      [FAUST *and* MEPHISTOPHELES *enter.*]
MEPHISTOPHELES   Above all else, it seems to me,
   You need some jolly company
   To see life can be fun—to say the least:
   The people here make every day a feast.   90
   With little wit and boisterous noise,
   They dance and circle in their narrow trails
   Like kittens playing with their tails.
   When hangovers don't vex these boys,
   And while their credit's holding out,   95
   They have no cares and drink and shout.
BRANDER   Those two are travelers, I swear.
   I tell it right off by the way they stare.
   They have been here at most an hour.
FROSCH   No doubt about it. Leipzig is a flower,   100
   It is a little Paris and educates its people.
SIEBEL   What may they be? Who knows the truth?
FROSCH   Leave it to me! A drink that interposes—
   And I'll pull like a baby tooth
   The worms they hide, out of these fellows' noses.   105
   They seem to be of noble ancestry,
   For they look proud and act disdainfully.

BRANDER   They are mere quacks and born in squalor.
ALTMAYER   Maybe.
FROSCH   Watch out! We shall commence.
MEPHISTOPHELES *[To* FAUST.]   The Devil people never sense,   110
    Though he may hold them by the collar.
FAUST   Good evening, gentlemen.
SIEBEL   Thank you, to you the same.
    [*Softly, looking at* MEPHISTOPHELES *from the side.*]
    Look at his foot. Why is it lame?[8]
MEPHISTOPHELES   We'll join you, if you grant the liberty.
    The drinks they have are poor, their wine not very mellow,   115
    So we'll enjoy your company.
ALTMAYER   You seem a most fastidious fellow.
FROSCH   Did you leave Rippach rather late and walk?
    And did you first have dinner with Master Jackass there?
MEPHISTOPHELES   Tonight we had no time to spare.   120
    Last time, however, we had quite a talk.
    He had a lot to say of his relations
    And asked us to send each his warmest salutations. [*He bows to* FROSCH.]
ALTMAYER [*Softly.*]   You got it! He's all right.
SIEBEL   A pretty repartee!
FROSCH   I'll get him yet. Just wait and see.   125
MEPHISTOPHELES   Just now we heard, if I'm not wrong,
    Some voices singing without fault.
    Indeed this seems a place for song;
    No doubt, it echoes from the vault.
FROSCH   Are you perchance a virtuoso?   130
MEPHISTOPHELES   Oh no, the will is great, the power only so-so.
ALTMAYER   Give us a song!
MEPHISTOPHELES   As many as you please.
SIEBEL   But let us have a brand-new strain!
MEPHISTOPHELES   We have just recently returned from Spain,
    The beauteous land of wine and melodies.   135
        [*Sings.*] A king lived long ago
        Who had a giant flea—
FROSCH   Hear, hear! A flea! That's what I call a jest.
    A flea's a mighty pretty guest.
MEPHISTOPHELES [*Sings.*]   A king lived long ago   140
        Who had a giant flea,
        He loved him just as though
        He were his son and heir.
        He sent his tailor a note
        And offered the tailor riches   145
        If he would measure a coat
        And also take measure for breeches.
BRANDER   Be sure to tell the tailor, if he twinkles,
    That he must take fastidious measure;
    He'll lose his head, not just the treasure,   150

---

8. By tradition, the Devil had a cloven foot, split like a sheep's hoof.

    If in the breeches there are wrinkles.

MEPHISTOPHELES   He was in silk arrayed,
      In velvet he was dressed,
      Had ribbons and brocade,
      A cross upon his chest   155
      A fancy star, great fame—
      A minister, in short;
      And all his kin became
      Lords at the royal court.
      The other lords grew lean   160
      And suffered with their wives,
      The royal maid and the queen
      Were all but eaten alive,
      But weren't allowed to swat them
      And could not even scratch,   165
      While we can swat and blot them
      And kill the ones we catch.

CHORUS [Jubilant.]   While we can swat and blot them
      And kill the ones we catch.

FROSCH   Bravo! Bravo! That was a treat!   170

SIEBEL   That is the end all fleas should meet.

BRANDER   Point your fingers and catch 'em fine!

ALTMAYER   Long live our freedom! And long live wine!

MEPHISTOPHELES   When freedom is the toast, my own voice I should
    add,
   Were your forsaken wines only not quite so bad.[9]   175

SIEBEL   You better mind your language, lad.

MEPHISTOPHELES   I only fear the landlord might protest,
   Else I should give each honored guest
   From our cellar a good glass.

SIEBEL   Let's go! The landlord is an ass.   180

FROSCH   If you provide good drinks, you shall be eulogized;
   But let your samples be good-sized.
   When I'm to judge, I'm telling him,
   I want my snout full to the brim.

ALTMAYER [Softly.]   They're from the Rhineland, I presume.   185

MEPHISTOPHELES   Bring me a gimlet.

BRANDER   What could that be for?
   You couldn't have the casks in the next room?

ALTMAYER   The landlord keeps his tools right there behind the door.

MEPHISTOPHELES [Takes the gimlet. To FROSCH.]
   What would you like? Something that's cool?

FROSCH   What do you mean? You got a lot of booze?   190

MEPHISTOPHELES   I let each have what he may choose.

ALTMAYER [To FROSCH.]   Oho! You lick your chops and start to drool.

FROSCH   If it is up to me, I'll have a Rhenish brand:
   There's nothing that competes with our fatherland.

MEPHISTOPHELES [Boring a hole near the edge of the table where FROSCH
   sits.]   Now let us have some wax to make a cork that sticks.   195

---

9. Cursed.

ALTMAYER   Oh, is it merely parlor tricks?
MEPHISTOPHELES [*To* BRANDER.]   And you?
BRANDER   I want a good champagne—
  Heady; I do not like it plain.
    [MEPHISTOPHELES *bores; meanwhile someone else has made the wax*
    stoppers and plugged the holes.]
BRANDER   Not all that's foreign can be banned,
  For what is far is often fine.   200
  A Frenchman is a thing no German man can stand,
  And yet we like to drink their wine.
SIEBEL [*As* MEPHISTOPHELES *approaches his place.*]
  I must confess, I think the dry tastes bad,
  The sweet alone is exquisite.
MEPHISTOPHELES [*Boring.*]   Tokay[1] will flow for you, my lad.   205
ALTMAYER   I think, you might as well admit,
  Good gentlemen, that these are simply jests.
MEPHISTOPHELES   Tut, tut! With such distinguished guests
  That would be quite a lot to dare.
  So don't be modest, and declare   210
  What kind of wine you would prefer.
ALTMAYER   I like them all, so I don't care.
    [*After all the holes have been bored and plugged.*]
MEPHISTOPHELES [*With strange gestures.*]   The grape the vine adorns,
      The billy goat sports horns;
      The wine is juicy, vines are wood,   215
      The wooden table gives wine as good,
      Profound insight! Now you perceive
      A miracle; only believe!
  Now pull the stoppers and have fun!
ALL [*As they pull out the stoppers and the wine each asked for flows into his*
    glass.]   A gorgeous well for everyone!   220
MEPHISTOPHELES   Be very careful lest it overrun!
    [*They drink several times.*]
ALL [*Sing.*]   We feel gigantically well,
      Just like five hundred sows.
MEPHISTOPHELES   Look there how well men are when they are free.
FAUST   I should like to get out of here.   225
MEPHISTOPHELES   First watch how their bestiality
  Will in full splendor soon appear.
SIEBEL [*Drinks carelessly and spills his wine on the floor where it turns into*
    a flame.]   Help! Fire! Help! Hell blew a vent!
MEPHISTOPHELES [*Conjuring the flame.*]   Be quiet, friendly element!
    [*To the fellow.*] For this time it was only a drop of purgatory. 230
SIEBEL   You'll pay for it, and you can save your story!
  What do you think we are, my friend?
FROSCH   Don't dare do that a second time, you hear!
ALTMAYER   Just let him leave in silence; that is what I say, gents!
SIEBEL   You have the brazen impudence   235
  To do your hocus-pocus here?

---

1. A sweet Hungarian wine.

MEPHISTOPHELES   Be still, old barrel!
SIEBEL   Broomstick, you!
   Will you insult us? Mind your prose!
BRANDER   Just wait and see, there will be blows.
ALTMAYER [*Pulls a stopper out of the table and fire leaps at him.*]
   I burn! I burn!
SIEBEL   It's magic, as I said.   240
   He is an outlaw. Strike him dead!
      [*They draw their knives and advance on* MEPHISTOPHELES.]
MEPHISTOPHELES [*With solemn gestures.*]
      False images prepare
      Mirages in the air.
      Be here and there!
      [*They stand amazed and stare at each other.*]
ALTMAYER   Where am I? What a gorgeous land!   245
FROSCH   And vineyards! Am I mad?
SIEBEL   And grapes right by my hand!
BRANDER   See in the leaves that purple shape?
   I never saw that big a grape!
      [*Grabs* SIEBEL'*s nose. They all do it to each other and raise their*
      knives.]
MEPHISTOPHELES   [*As above.*] Fall from their eyes, illusion's band!
   Remember how the Devil joked.   250
      [*He disappears with* FAUST, *the revelers separate.*]
SIEBEL   What's that?
ALTMAYER   Hah?
FROSCH   Your nose I stroked?
BRANDER   [*To* SIEBEL.] And yours is in my hand!
ALTMAYER   The shock is more than I can bear.
   I think I'll faint. Get me a chair!
FROSCH   What was all this? Who understands?   255
SIEBEL   Where is the scoundrel? I'm so sore,
   If I could only get my hands—
ALTMAYER   I saw him whiz right through the cellar door,
   Riding a flying barrel. Zounds,
   The fright weighs on me like a thousand pounds.   260
[*Turning toward the table.*]   Do you suppose the wine still flows?
SIEBEL   That was a fraud! You're asinine!
FROSCH   I surely thought that I drank wine.
BRANDER   But what about the grapes, I say.
ALTMAYER   Who says there are no miracles today!   265

WITCH'S KITCHEN

[*On a low stove, a large caldron stands over the fire. In the steam that rises from it, one can see several shapes. A longtailed* FEMALE MONKEY *sits near the caldron, skims it, and sees to it that it does not overflow. The* MALE MONKEY *with the little ones sits next to her and warms himself. Walls and ceiling are decorated with the queerest implements of witchcraft.* FAUST *and* MEPHISTOPHELES *enter.*]

FAUST　How I detest this crazy sorcery!
　　I should get well, you promise me,
　　In this mad frenzy of a mess?
　　Do I need the advice of hag fakirs?
　　And should this quackish sordidness　　　　　　5
　　Reduce my age by thirty years?
　　I'm lost if that's all you could find.
　　My hope is drowned in sudden qualm.
　　Has neither nature nor some noble mind
　　Invented or contrived a wholesome balm?　　　10
MEPHISTOPHELES　My friend, that was nice oratory!
　　Indeed, to make you young there is one way that's apter;
　　But, I regret, that is another story
　　And forms quite an amazing chapter.
FAUST　I want to know it.
MEPHISTOPHELES　　　All right, you need no sorcery　　15
　　And no physician and no dough.
　　Just go into the fields and see
　　What fun it is to dig and hoe;
　　Live simply and keep all your thoughts
　　On a few simple objects glued;　　　　　　　　20
　　Restrict yourself and eat the plainest food;
　　Live with the beasts, a beast: it is no thievery
　　To dress the fields you work, with your own dung.
　　That is the surest remedy:
　　At eighty, you would still be young.　　　　　　25
FAUST　I am not used to that and can't, I am afraid,
　　Start now to work with hoe and spade.
　　For me a narrow life like that's too small.
MEPHISTOPHELES　We need the witch then after all.
FAUST　Why just the hag with all her grime!　　　30
　　Could you not brew it—with *your* head!
MEPHISTOPHELES　A splendid way to waste my time!
　　A thousand bridges I could build instead.[2]
　　Science is not enough, nor art;
　　In this work patience plays a part.　　　　　　35
　　A quiet spirit plods and plods at length;
　　Nothing but time can give the brew its strength.
　　With all the things that go into it,
　　It's sickening just to *see* them do it.
　　The Devil taught them, true enough　　　　　　40
　　But he himself can't make the stuff.
　　　　[*He sees the* ANIMALS.]
　　Just see how delicate they look!
　　This is the maid, and that the cook.
　　[*To the* ANIMALS.] It seems the lady isn't home?
ANIMALS　She went to roam　　　　　　　　　　45

---

2. According to folk legend, the Devil built bridges at the request of human beings. As a reward, he caught either the first or the thirteenth soul to cross each new bridge.

Away from home,
Right through the chimney in the dome.
MEPHISTOPHELES   And how long will she walk the street?
ANIMALS   As long as we warm our feet.
MEPHISTOPHELES [*To* FAUST.]   How do you like this dainty pair?   50
FAUST   They are inane beyond comparison.
MEPHISTOPHELES   A conversation like this one
  Is just the sort of thing for which I care.
  [*To the* ANIMALS.] Now tell me, you accursed group,
  Why do you stir that steaming mess?   55
ANIMALS   We cook a watery beggars' soup.
MEPHISTOPHELES   You should do a brisk business.
MALE MONKEY [*Approaches* MEPHISTOPHELES *and fawns.*]
      Oh please throw the dice
      And lose, and be nice
      And let me get wealthy!   60
      We are in the ditch,
      And if I were rich,
      Then I might be healthy.
MEPHISTOPHELES   How happy every monkey thinks he'd be,
  If he could play the lottery.   65
      [*Meanwhile the monkey youngsters have been playing with a large*
      ball, and now they roll it forward.]
MALE MONKEY   The world and ball
      Both rise and fall
      And roll and wallow;
      It sounds like glass,
      It bursts, alas,   70
      The inside's hollow.
      Here it is light,
      There still more bright,
      Life's mine to swallow!
      Dear son, I say,   75
      Please keep away!
      You'll die first.
      It's made of clay
      It will burst.
MEPHISTOPHELES   The sieve there, chief—?   80
MALE MONKEY [*Gets it down.*]   If you were a thief,
      I'd be wise to you.
      [*He runs to the* FEMALE MONKEY *and lets her see through it.*]
      Look through, be brief!
      You know the thief,
      But may not say *who*?   85
MEPHISTOPHELES [*Approaching the fire.*]   And here this pot?
BOTH BIG MONKEYS   The half-witted sot!
      Does not know the pot,
      Does not know the kettle!
MEPHISTOPHELES   You impolite beast!   90
MALE MONKEY   Take this brush at least

And sit down and settle!
[He makes MEPHISTOPHELES *sit down.*]
FAUST [*Who has been standing before a mirror all this time, now stepping*
close to it, now back.] What blissful image is revealed
To me behind this magic glass!
Lend me your swiftest pinions, love, that I might pass   95
From here to her transfigured field!
When I don't stay right on this spot, but, pining,
Dare to step forward and go near
Mists cloud her shape and let it disappear.
The fairest image of a woman!   100
Indeed, could woman be so fair?
Or is this body which I see reclining
Heaven's quintessence from another sphere?
Is so much beauty found on earth?
MEPHISTOPHELES   Well, if a god works hard for six whole days, my
    friend,   105
And then says bravo in the end,
It ought to have a little worth.
For now, stare to your heart's content!
I could track down for you just such a sweet—
What bliss it would be to get her consent,   110
To marry her and be replete.
    [FAUST *gazes into the mirror all the time.* MEPHISTOPHELES, *stretch-*
    ing in the armchair and playing with the brush, goes on speaking.]
I sit here like the king upon his throne:
The scepter I hold here, I lack the crown alone.
ANIMALS [*Who have so far moved around in quaint confusion, bring a crown*
    to MEPHISTOPHELES, *clamoring loudly.*]   Oh, please be so good.
    With sweat and with blood   115
    This crown here to lime!
    [*They handle the crown clumsily and break it into two pieces with*
    which they jump around.]
    It's done, let it be!
    We chatter and see,
    We listen and rhyme—
FAUST [*At the mirror.*]   Alas, I think I'll lose my wits.   120
MEPHISTOPHELES [*Pointing toward the* ANIMALS.]
    I fear that my head, too, begins to reel.
ANIMALS   And if we score hits
    And everything fits,
    It's thoughts that we feel.
FAUST [*As above.*]   My heart and soul are catching fire,   125
    Please let us go away from here!
MEPHISTOPHELES [*In the same position as above.*]
    The one thing one has to admire
    Is that their poetry is quite sincere.
    [*The caldron which the* FEMALE MONKEY *has neglected begins to*
    run over, and a huge flame blazes up through the chimney. The
    WITCH *scoots down through the flame with a dreadful clamor.*]

WITCH   Ow! Ow! Ow! Ow!
   You damned old beast! You cursed old sow!   130
   You leave the kettle and singe the frau.
   You cursed old beast! [*Sees* FAUST *and* MEPHISTOPHELES.]
       What goes on here?
       Why are you here?
       Who are you two?   135
       Who sneaked inside?
       Come, fiery tide!
       Their bones be fried!
      [*She plunges the skimming spoon into the caldron and spatters
      flames at* FAUST, MEPHISTOPHELES, *and the* ANIMALS. *The* ANIMALS
      whine.*]
MEPHISTOPHELES [*Reversing the brush he holds in his hand, and striking
   into the glasses and pots.*]
       In two! In two!
       There lies the brew.   140
       There lies the glass.
       A joke, my lass,
       The beat, you ass,
       For melodies from you.
      [*As the* WITCH *retreats in wrath and horror.*]
   You know me now? You skeleton! You shrew!   145
   You know your master and your lord?
   What holds me? I could strike at you
   And shatter you and your foul monkey horde.
   Does not the scarlet coat reveal His Grace?
   Do you not know the rooster's feather, ma'am?   150
   Did I perchance conceal my face?
   Or must I tell you who I am?
WITCH   Forgive the uncouth greeting, though
   You have no cloven feet, you know.
   And your two ravens, where are they?   155
MEPHISTOPHELES   For just this once you may get by,
   For it has been some time, I don't deny,
   Since I have come your way,
   And culture which licks out at every stew
   Extends now to the Devil, too: 160
   Gone is the Nordic phantom that former ages saw;
   You see no horns, no tail or claw.
   And as regards the foot with which I can't dispense,
   That does not look the least bit suave;
   Like other young men nowadays, I hence   165
   Prefer to pad my calves.
WITCH [*Dancing.*]   I'll lose my wits, I'll lose my brain
   Since Squire Satan has come back again.
MEPHISTOPHELES   That name is out, hag! Is that plain?
WITCH   But why? It never gave you pain!   170
MEPHISTOPHELES   It's dated, called a fable; men are clever,
   But they are just as badly off as ever:

The Evil One is gone, the evil ones remain.
You call me baron, hag, and you look out:
I am a cavalier with cavalierly charms,   175
And my nobility don't dare to doubt!
Look here and you will see my coat of arms!
          [*He makes an indecent gesture.*]
WITCH [*Laughs immoderately.*]   Ha! Ha! That is your manner, sir!
You are a jester as you always were.
MEPHISTOPHELES [*To* FAUST.]   My friend, mark this, but don't repeat
          it: 180
This is the way a witch likes to be treated.
WITCH   Now tell me why you came in here.
MEPHISTOPHELES   A good glass of the famous juice, my dear!
But I must have the oldest kind:
Its strength increases with each year.   185
WITCH   I got a bottle on this shelf
From which I like to nip myself;
By now it doesn't even stink.
I'll give you some, it has the power.
[*Softly.*] But if, quite unprepared, this man should have a drink,   190
He could, as you know well, not live another hour.
MEPHISTOPHELES   He is a friend of mine, and he will take it well
The best you have is not too good for him.
Now draw your circle, say your spell,
And fill a bumper to the brim.   195
          [*The* WITCH *draws a circle with curious gestures and puts quaint
          objects into it, while the glasses begin to tinkle, the caldrons begin
          to resound and they make music. In the end, she gets a big book and
          puts the* MONKEYS *into the circle, and they serve her as a desk and
          have to hold a torch for her. She motions* FAUST *to step up.*]
FAUST [*To* MEPHISTOPHELES.]   No, tell me why these crazy antics?
The mad ado, the gestures that are frantic,
The most insipid cheat—this stuff
I've known and hated long enough.
MEPHISTOPHELES   Relax! It's fun—a little play;   200
Don't be so serious, so sedate!
Such hocus-pocus is a doctor's way,
Of making sure the juice will operate.
          [*He makes* FAUST *step into the circle.*]
WITCH [*Begins to recite from the book with great emphasis.*]
          This you must know!
          From one make ten,   205
          And two let go,
          Take three again,
          Then you'll be rich.
          The four you fix.
          From five and six,   210
          Thus says the witch,
          Make seven and eight,
          That does the trick;

And nine is one,
And ten is none.   215
That is the witch's arithmetic.
FAUST   It seems to me the old hag runs a fever.
MEPHISTOPHELES   You'll hear much more before we leave her.
I know, it sounds like that for many pages.
I lost much time on this accursed affliction   220
Because a perfect contradiction
Intrigues not only fools but also sages.
This art is old and new, forsooth:
It was the custom in all ages
To spread illusion and not truth   225
With Three in One and One in Three.[3]
They teach it twittering like birds;
With fools there is no intervening.
Men usually believe, if only they hear words,
That there must also be some sort of meaning.   230
WITCH [Continues.]   The lofty prize
        Of science lies
        Concealed today as ever.
        Who has no thought,
        To him it's brought   235
        To own without endeavor.
FAUST   What nonsense does she put before us?
My head aches from her stupidness.
It seems as if I heard a chorus
Of many thousand fools, no less.   240
MEPHISTOPHELES   Excellent sybil, that is quite enough!
Now pour the drink—just put the stuff
Into this bowl here. Fill it, sybil, pour;
My friend is safe from any injuries:
He has a number of degrees   245
And has had many drinks before.
        [The WITCH pours the drink into a bowl with many ceremonies; as
        FAUST puts it to his lips, a small flame spurts up.]
MEPHISTOPHELES   What is the matter? Hold it level!
Drink fast and it will warm you up.
You are familiar with the Devil,
And shudder at a fiery cup?   250
        [The WITCH breaks the circle. FAUST steps out.]
MEPHISTOPHELES   Come on! Let's go! You must not rest.
WITCH   And may this gulp give great delight!
MEPHISTOPHELES [To the WITCH.]   If there is anything that you request,
Just let me know the next Walpurgis Night.[4]
WITCH   Here is a song; just sing it now and then,   255
And you will feel a queer effect indeed.
MEPHISTOPHELES [To FAUST.]   Come quickly now before you tire,

---

3. The Christian doctrine of the Trinity.   4. May Day Eve (April 30), when witches are supposed to assemble on the Brocken, a peak in the Harz Mountains, which are in central Germany.

And let me lead while you perspire
So that the force can work out through your skin.
I'll teach you later on to value noble leisure,   260
And soon you will perceive the most delightful pleasure,
As Cupid starts to stir and dance like jumping jinn.[5]
FAUST   One last look at the mirror where I stood!
So beauteous was that woman's form!
MEPHISTOPHELES   No! No! The paragon of womanhood   265
You shall soon see alive and warm.
[*Softly.*] You'll soon find with this potion's aid,
Helen of Troy in every maid.

STREET

[FAUST. MARGARET *passing by.*]
FAUST   Fair lady, may I be so free
To offer my arm and company?
MARGARET   I'm neither a lady nor am I fair,
And can go home without your care.
[*She frees herself and exits.*]
FAUST   By heaven, this young girl is fair!   5
Her like I don't know anywhere.
She is so virtuous and pure,
But somewhat pert and not demure.
The glow of her cheeks and her lips so red
I shall not forget until I am dead.   10
Her downcast eyes, shy and yet smart,
Are stamped forever on my heart;
Her curtness and her brevity
Was sheer enchanting ecstasy!
[MEPHISTOPHELES *enters.*]
FAUST   Get me that girl, and don't ask why!   15
MEPHISTOPHELES   Which one?
FAUST   She only just went by.
MEPHISTOPHELES   That one! She saw her priest just now,
And he pronounced her free of sin.
I stood right there and listened in.
She's so completely blemishless   20
That there was nothing to confess.
Over her I don't have any power.
FAUST   She is well past her fourteenth year.
MEPHISTOPHELES   Look at the gay Lothario[6] here!
He would like to have every flower,   25
And thinks each prize or pretty trick
Just waits around for him to pick;
But sometimes that just doesn't go.
FAUST   My Very Reverend Holy Joe,

---

5. A supernatural being that can take human or animal form.   6. The seducer in Nicholas Rowe's play *The Fair Penitent* (1703); hence, figuratively, any seducer. The German reads *Hans Liederlich,* meaning a profligate, since *liederlich* means "careless" or "dissolute."

Leave me in peace with law and right!   30
  I tell you, if you don't comply,
  And this sweet young blood doesn't lie
  Between my arms this very night,
  At midnight we'll have parted ways.
MEPHISTOPHELES   Think of the limits of my might.   35
  I need at least some fourteen days
  To find a handy evening.
FAUST   If I had peace for seven hours,
  I should not need the Devil's powers
  To seduce such a little thing.   40
MEPHISTOPHELES   You speak just like a Frenchman. Wait
  I beg you, and don't be annoyed:
  What have you got when it's enjoyed?
  The fun is not nearly so great
  As when you bit by bit imbibe it,   45
  And first resort to playful folly
  To knead and to prepare your dolly,
  The way some Gallic tales describe it.
FAUST   I've appetite without all that.
MEPHISTOPHELES   Now without jokes or tit-for-tat: 50
  I tell you, with this fair young child
  We simply can't be fast or wild.
  We'd waste our time storming and running;
  We have to have recourse to cunning.
FAUST   Get something from the angel's nest!   55
  Or lead me to her place of rest!
  Get me a kerchief from her breast,
  A garter from my darling's knee.
MEPHISTOPHELES   Just so you see, it touches me
  And I would soothe your agony,   60
  Let us not linger here and thus delay:
  I'll take you to her room today.
FAUST   And shall I see her? Have her?
MEPHISTOPHELES   No.
  To one of her neighbors she has to go.
  But meanwhile you may at your leisure   65
  Relish the hopes of future pleasure,
  Till you are sated with her atmosphere.
FAUST   Can we go now?
MEPHISTOPHELES   It's early yet, I fear.
FAUST   Get me a present for the dear!
      [*Exit.*]
MEPHISTOPHELES   A present right away? Good! He will be a hit.   70
  There's many a nice place I know
  With treasures buried long ago;
  I better look around a bit.
      [*Exit.*]

EVENING

[*A small neat room.*]
MARGARET [*Braiding and binding her hair.*]
  I should give much if I could say
  Who was that gentleman today.
  He looked quite gallant, certainly,
  And is of noble family;
  That much even his forehead told—   5
  How else could he have been so bold?
    [*Exit. Enter* MEPHISTOPHELES, FAUST.]
MEPHISTOPHELES   Come in, but very quietly!
FAUST [*After a short silence.*]   I beg you, leave and let me be!
MEPHISTOPHELES [*Sniffing around.*]   She's neater than a lot of girls I see.
    [*Exit.*]
FAUST [*Looking up and around.*]   Sweet light of dusk, guest from above   10
  That fills this shrine, be welcome you!
  Seize now my heart, sweet agony of love
  That languishes and feeds on hope's clear dew!
  What sense of calm embraces me,
  Of order and complete content!   15
  What bounty in this poverty!
  And in this prison, ah, what ravishment!
    [*He throws himself into the leather armchair by the bed.*]
  Welcome me now, as former ages rested
  Within your open arms in grief and joy!
  How often was this fathers' throne contested   20
  By eager children, prized by girl and boy!
  And here, perhaps, her full cheeks flushed with bliss,
  My darling, grateful for a Christmas toy,
  Pressed on her grandsire's withered hand a kiss.
  I feel your spirit, lovely maid,   25
  Of ordered bounty breathing here
  Which, motherly, comes daily to your aid
  To teach you how a rug is best on tables laid
  And how the sand should on the floor appear.[7]
  Oh godlike hand, to you it's given   30
  To make a cottage, a kingdom of heaven.
  And here!
    [*He lifts a bed curtain.*]
        What raptured shudder makes me stir?
  How I should love to be immured
  Where in light dreams nature matured
  The angel that's innate in her,   35
  Here lay the child, developed slowly,
  Her tender breast with warm life fraught,
  And here, through weaving pure and holy,
  The image of the gods was wrought.

---

7. Floors were sprinkled with sand after cleaning.

And you! Alas, what brought you here?   40
I feel so deeply moved, so queer!
What do you seek? Why is your heart so sore?
Poor Faust! I do not know you any more.

Do magic smells surround me here?
Immediate pleasure was my bent,   45
But now—in dreams of love I'm all but spent.
Are we mere puppets of the atmosphere?

If she returned this instant from her call,
How for your mean transgression you would pay!
The haughty lad would be so small,   50
Lie at her feet and melt away.
MEPHISTOPHELES [*Entering.*]   Let's go! I see her in the lane!
FAUST   Away! I'll never come again.
MEPHISTOPHELES   Here is a fairly decent case,
    I picked it up some other place.   55
    Just leave it in the chest up there.
    She'll go out of her mind, I swear;
    For I put things in it, good sir,
    To win a better one than her.
    But child is child and play is play.   60
FAUST   I don't know—should I?
MEPHISTOPHELES   Why delay?
    You do not hope to save your jewel?
    Or I'll give your lust this advice:
    Don't waste fair daytime like this twice,
    Nor my exertions: it is cruel.   65
    It is not simple greed, I hope!
    I scratch my head, I fret and mope—
        [*He puts the case into the chest and locks it again.*]
    Away! Let's go!—
    It's just to make the child fulfill
    Your heart's desire and your will;   70
    And you stand and frown
    As if you had to lecture in cap and gown—
    As if in gray there stood in front of you
    Physics and Metaphysics, too.
    Away!
        [*Exeunt.*]
MARGARET [*With a lamp.*]   It seems so close, so sultry now,   75
    [*She opens the window.*]
And yet outside it's not so warm.
I feel so strange, I don't know how—
I wish my mother would come home.
A shudder grips my body, I feel chilly—
How fearful I am and how silly!   80
    [*She begins to sing as she undresses.*]
    In Thule[8] there was a king,

---

8. The fabled *ultima Thule* of Latin literature—those distant lands just beyond the reach of every explorer. Goethe wrote the ballad in 1774; it was published in 1782 and set to music by several composers.

Faithful unto the grave,
To whom his mistress, dying,
A golden goblet gave.

Nothing he held more dear.   85
At every meal he used it;
His eyes would fill with tears
As often as he mused it.

And when he came to dying,
The towns in his realm he told.   90
Naught to his heir denying,
Except the goblet of gold.

He dined at evenfall
With all his chivalry
In the ancestral hall   95
In the castle by the sea.

The old man rose at last
And drank life's sunset glow.
And the sacred goblet he cast
Into the flood below.   100

He saw it plunging, drinking.
And sinking into the sea;
His eyes were also sinking,
And nevermore drank he.
    [*She opens the chest to put away her clothes and sees the case.*]
How did this lovely case get in my chest?   105
I locked it after I got dressed.
It certainly seems strange. And what might be in there?
It might be a security
Left for a loan in Mother's care.
There is a ribbon with a key;   110
I think I'll open it and see.
What is that? God in heaven! There—
I never saw such fine array!
These jewels! Why a lord's lady could wear
These on the highest holiday.   115
How would this necklace look on me?
Who owns all this? It is so fine.
    [*She adorns herself and steps before the mirror.*]
If those earrings were only mine!
One looks quite different right away.
What good is beauty, even youth?   120
All that may be quite good and fair,
But does it get you anywhere?
Their praise is half pity, you can be sure.
For gold contend,
On gold depend   125
All things. Woe to us poor!

PROMENADE

[FAUST *walking up and down, lost in thought.* MEPHISTOPHELES
enters.]

MEPHISTOPHELES   By the pangs of despised love! By the elements of hell!
I wish I knew something worse to curse by it as well!
FAUST   What ails you? Steady now, keep level!
I never saw a face like yours today.
MEPHISTOPHELES   I'd wish the Devil took me straightaway,   5
If I myself were not a devil.
FAUST   Has something in your head gone bad?
It sure becomes you raving like one mad.
MEPHISTOPHELES   Just think, the jewels got for Margaret—
A dirty priest took the whole set.   10
The mother gets to see the stuff
And starts to shudder, sure enough:
She has a nose to smell things out—
In prayerbooks she keeps her snout—
A whiff of anything makes plain   15
Whether it's holy or profane.
She sniffed the jewelry like a rat
And knew no blessings came with that.
My child, she cried, ill-gotten wealth
Will soil your soul and spoil your health.   20
We'll give it to the Mother of the Lord
And later get a heavenly reward.
Poor Margaret went into a pout;
She thought: a gift horse![9] and, no doubt,
Who[1] brought it here so carefully   25
Could not be godless, certainly.
The mother called a priest at once,
He saw the gems and was no dunce;
He drooled and then said: Without question,
Your instinct is quite genuine,   30
Who overcomes himself will win.
The Church has a superb digestion,
Whole countries she has gobbled up,
But never is too full to sup;
The Church alone has the good health   35
For stomaching ill-gotten wealth.
FAUST   Why, everybody does: a Jew
And any king can do it, too.
MEPHISTOPHELES   So he picked up a clasp, necklace, and rings,
Like toadstools or some worthless things,   40
And did not thank them more nor less
Than as if it were nuts or some such mess,
And he promised them plenty after they died—
And they were duly edified.

---

9. Like the wooden horse in which Greek soldiers entered Troy to capture it; an emblem of treachery.
1. Whoever.

FAUST   And Gretchen?[2]
MEPHISTOPHELES   She, of course, feels blue,   45
   She sits and doesn't know what to do,
   Thinks day and night of every gem—
   Still more of him who furnished them.
FAUST   My darling's grief distresses me.
   Go, get her some new jewelry.   50
   The first one was a trifling loss.
MEPHISTOPHELES   Oh sure, it's child's play for you, boss.
FAUST   Just fix it all to suit my will;
   Try on the neighbor, too, your skill.
   Don't, Devil, act like sluggish paste!   55
   Get some new jewels and make haste!
MEPHISTOPHELES   Yes, gracious lord, it is a pleasure.
      [FAUST *exits.*]
MEPHISTOPHELES   A fool in love just doesn't care
   And, just to sweeten darling's leisure,
   He'd make sun, moon, and stars into thin air.   60
      [*Exit.*]

THE NEIGHBOR'S HOUSE

MARTHA [*Alone.*]   May God forgive my husband! He
   Was certainly not good to me.
   He went into the world to roam
   And left me on the straw at home.
   God knows that I have never crossed him,   5
   And loved him dearly; yet I lost him.
   [*She cries.*] Perhaps—the thought kills me—he died!—
   If it were only certified!
      [MARGARET *enters.*]
MARGARET   Dame Martha!
MARTHA   Gretchen, what could it be?
MARGARET   My legs feel faint, though not with pain: 10
   I found another case, again
   Right in my press,[3] of ebony,
   With things more precious all around
   Than was the first case that I found.
MARTHA   You must not show them to your mother,   15
   She'd tell the priest as with the other.
MARGARET   Oh look at it! Oh see! Please do!
MARTHA [*Adorns her.*]   You lucky, lucky creature, you!
MARGARET   Unfortunately, it's not meet
   To wear them in the church or street.   20
MARTHA   Just come here often to see me,
   Put on the jewels secretly,
   Walk up and down an hour before the mirror here,
   And we shall have a good time, dear.

---

2. Diminutive of the German *Margarete*. She is given this name through much of the play.   3. A type of cupboard in which pressed linens were stored.

Then chances come, perhaps a holiday,   25
When we can bit by bit, gem after gem display,
A necklace first, than a pearl in your ear;
Your mother—we can fool her, or she may never hear.
MARGARET   Who brought the cases and has not appeared?
It certainly seems very weird.   30
        [A knock.]
Oh God, my mother—is it her?
MARTHA [Peeping through the curtain.]   It is a stranger—come in, sir!
        [MEPHISTOPHELES enters.]
MEPHISTOPHELES   I'll come right in and be so free,
If the ladies will grant me the liberty.
        [Steps back respectfully as he sees MARGARET.]
To Martha Schwerdtlein I wished to speak.   35
MARTHA   It's I. What does your honor seek?
MEPHISTOPHELES [Softly to her.]   I know you now, that satisfies me,
You have very elegant company;
Forgive my intrusion; I shall come back soon—
If you don't mind, this afternoon.   40
MARTHA [Loud.]   Oh goodness gracious! Did you hear?
He thinks you are a lady, dear!
MARGARET   I'm nothing but a poor young maid;
You are much too kind, I am afraid;
The gems and jewels are not my own.   45
MEPHISTOPHELES   It is not the jewelry alone!
Your noble eyes—indeed, it is your whole way!
How glad I am that I may stay!
MARTHA   What is your errand? Please, good sir—
MEPHISTOPHELES   I wish I had better news for her!   50
And don't get cross with your poor guest:
Your husband is dead and sends his best.
MARTHA   Is dead? The faithful heart! Oh dear!
My husband is dead! I shall faint right here.
MARGARET   Oh my dear woman! Don't despair!   55
MEPHISTOPHELES   Let me relate the sad affair.
MARGARET   I should sooner never be a bride:
The grief would kill me if he died.
MEPHISTOPHELES   Joy needs woe, woe requires joy.
MARTHA   Tell me of the end of my sweet boy.   60
MEPHISTOPHELES   In Padua, in Italy,
He is buried in St. Anthony
In ground that has been duly blessed
For such cool, everlasting rest.
MARTHA   Surely, there is something more you bring.   65
MEPHISTOPHELES   One solemn and sincere request:
For his poor soul they should three hundred masses sing.
That's all, my purse is empty, though not of course my breast.
MARTHA   What? Not a gem? No work of art?
I am sure, deep in his bag the poorest wanderer   70
Keeps some remembrance that gives pleasure,

And sooner starves than yields this treasure.
MEPHISTOPHELES   Madam, don't doubt it breaks my heart.
   And you may rest assured, he was no squanderer.
   He knew his errors well, and he repented,   75
   Though his ill fortune was the thing he most lamented.
MARGARET   That men are so unfortunate and poor!
   I'll say some Requiems, and for his soul I'll pray.
MEPHISTOPHELES   You would deserve a marriage right away,
   For you are charming, I am sure.   80
MARGARET   Oh no! I must wait to be wed.
MEPHISTOPHELES   If not a husband, have a lover instead.
   It is one of heaven's greatest charms
   To hold such a sweetheart in one's arms.
MARGARET   That is not the custom around here.   85
MEPHISTOPHELES   Custom or not, it's done, my dear.
MARTHA   Please tell me more!
MEPHISTOPHELES   I stood beside the bed he died on;
   It was superior to manure,
   Of rotted straw, and yet he died a Christian, pure,
   And found that there was more on his unsettled score.   90
   "I'm hateful," he cried; "wicked was my life,
   As I forsook my trade and also left my wife.
   To think of it now makes me die.
   If only she forgave me even so!"
MARTHA [*Weeping.*]   The darling! I forgave him long ago.   95
MEPHISTOPHELES   "And yet, God knows, she was far worse than I."
MARTHA   He lied—alas, lied at the brink of death!
MEPHISTOPHELES   Surely, he made up things with dying breath,
   If ever I saw death before.
   "To pass the time, I could not look around," he said;   100
   "First she got children, then they needed bread—
   When I say bread, I mean much more—
   And she never gave peace for me to eat my share."
MARTHA   Did he forget my love, my faithfulness and care
   And how I slaved both day and night?   105
MEPHISTOPHELES   Oh no, he thought of that with all his might;
   He said: "When we left Malta for another trip,
   I prayed for wife and children fervently,
   So heaven showed good grace to me.
   And our boat soon caught a Turkish ship   110
   That had the mighty sultan's gold on it.
   Then fortitude got its reward,
   And I myself was given, as was fit,
   My share of the great sultan's hoard."
MARTHA   Oh how? Oh where? Might it be buried now?   115
MEPHISTOPHELES   The winds have scattered it, and who knows how?
   A pretty girl in Naples, sweet and slim,
   Cared for him when he was without a friend
   And did so many deeds of love for him
   That he could feel it till his blessed end.   120

MARTHA   The rogue! He robbed children and wife!
  No misery, no lack of bread
  Could keep him from his shameful life!
MEPHISTOPHELES   You see! For that he now is dead.
  If I were in your place, I'd pause   125
  To mourn him for a year, as meet,
  And meanwhile I would try to find another sweet.
MARTHA   Oh God, the way my first one was
  I'll hardly find another to be mine!
  How could there be a little fool that's fonder?   130
  Only he liked so very much to wander,
  And foreign women, and foreign wine,
  And that damned shooting of the dice.
MEPHISTOPHELES   Well, well! It could have been quite nice,
  Had he been willing to ignore   135
  As many faults in you, or more.
  On such terms, I myself would woo
  And willingly change rings with you.
MARTHA   The gentleman is pleased to jest.
MEPHISTOPHELES [*Aside.*]   I better get away from here;   140
  She'd keep the Devil to his word, I fear.
  [*To* GRETCHEN.] And how is your heart? Still at rest?
MARGARET   What do you mean, good sir?
MEPHISTOPHELES [*Aside.*]   You good, innocent child!
  [*Aloud.*] Good-by, fair ladies!
MARGARET   Good-by.
MARTHA   Oh, not so fast and wild!   145
  I'd like to have it certified
  That my sweetheart was buried, and when and where he died.
  I always hate to see things done obliquely
  And want to read his death in our weekly.
MEPHISTOPHELES   Yes, lady, what is testified by two   150
  Is everywhere known to be true;
  And I happen to have a splendid mate
  Whom I'll take along to the magistrate.
  I'll bring him here.
MARTHA   Indeed, please do!
MEPHISTOPHELES   And will this maiden be here, too?   155
  A gallant lad! Has traveled much with me
  And shows young ladies all courtesy.
MARGARET   I would have to blush before him, poor thing.[4]
MEPHISTOPHELES   Not even before a king!
MARTHA   Behind the house, in my garden, then,   160
  Tonight we shall expect the gentlemen.

STREET

[FAUST. MEPHISTOPHELES.]
FAUST   How is it? Well? Can it be soon?

---

4. Referring to herself, not to Faust.

MEPHISTOPHELES   Oh bravo! Now you are on fire?
   Soon Gretchen will still your desire.
   At Martha's you may see her later this afternoon:
   That woman seems expressly made   5
   To ply the pimps' and gypsies' trade.
FAUST   Oh good!
MEPHISTOPHELES   But something's wanted from us, too.
FAUST   One good turn makes another due.
MEPHISTOPHELES   We merely have to go and testify   10
   That the remains of her dear husband lie
   In Padua where Anthony once sat.
FAUST   Now we shall have to go there. Now that was smart of you!
MEPHISTOPHELES   Sancta simplicitas![5] Who ever thought of that?
   Just testify, and hang whether it's true!   15
FAUST   If you know nothing better, this plan has fallen through.
MEPHISTOPHELES   Oh, holy man! You are no less!
   Is this the first time in your life that you
   Have testified what is not true?
   Of God and all the world, and every single part,   20
   Of man and all that stirs inside his head and heart
   You gave your definitions with power and finesse.
   With brazen cheek and haughty breath.
   And if you stop to think, I guess,
   You know as much of that, you must confess,   25
   As you know now of Mr. Schwerdtlein's death.
FAUST   You are and you remain a sophist and a liar.
MEPHISTOPHELES   Yes, if one's knowledge were not just a little higher.
   Tomorrow, won't you, pure as air,
   Deceive poor Gretchen and declare   30
   Your soul's profoundest love, and swear?
FAUST   With all my heart.
MEPHISTOPHELES   Good and fair!
   Then faithfulness and love eternal
   And the super-almighty urge supernal—
   Will that come from your heart as well?   35
FAUST   Leave off! It will. —When, lost in feeling,
   For this urge, for this surge
   I seek a name, find none, and, reeling
   All through the world with all my senses gasping,
   At all the noblest words I'm grasping   40
   And call this blaze in which I flame,
   Infinite, eternal eternally—
   Is that a game or devilish jugglery?
MEPHISTOPHELES   I am still right.
FAUST   Listen to me,
   I beg of you, and don't wear out my lung: 45
   Whoever would be right and only has a tongue,
   Always will be.

5. Holy simplicity (Latin).

Come on! I'm sick of prating, spare your voice,
For you are right because I have no choice.

GARDEN

[MARGARET *on* FAUST's *arm,* MARTHA *with* MEPHISTOPHELES, *walking up and down.*]

MARGARET   I feel it well, good sir, you're only kind to me:
You condescend—and you abash.
It is the traveler's courtesy
To put up graciously with trash.
I know too well, my poor talk never can   5
Give pleasure to a traveled gentleman.
FAUST   One glance from you, one word gives far more pleasure
Than all the wisdom of this world. [*He kisses her hand.*]
MARGARET   Don't incommode yourself! How could you kiss it? You?
It is so ugly, is so rough.   10
But all the things that I have had to do!
For Mother I can't do enough.
          [*They pass.*]
MARTHA   And you, sir, travel all the time, you say?
MEPHISTOPHELES   Alas, our trade and duty keeps us going!
Though when one leaves the tears may well be flowing,   15
One never is allowed to stay.
MARTHA   While it may do in younger years
To sweep around the world, feel free and suave,
There is the time when old age nears,
And then to creep alone, a bachelor, to one's grave.   20
That's something everybody fears.
MEPHISTOPHELES   With dread I see it far away.
MARTHA   Then, my dear sir, consider while you may.
          [*They pass.*]
MARGARET   Yes, out of sight is out of mind.
You are polite, you can't deny,   25
And often you have friends and find
That they are cleverer than I.
FAUST   Oh dearest, trust me, what's called clever on this earth
Is often vain and rash rather than clever.
MARGARET   What?
FAUST   Oh, that the innocent and simple never   30
Appreciate themselves and their own worth!
That meekness and humility, supreme
Among the gifts of loving, lavish nature—
MARGARET   If you should think of me one moment only,
I shall have time enough to think of you and dream.   35
FAUST   Are you so often lonely?
MARGARET   Yes; while our household is quite small,
You see, I have to do it all.
We have no maid, so I must cook, and sweep, and knit.
And sew, and run early and late;   40
And mother is in all of it

So accurate!
Not that it's necessary; our need is not so great.
We could afford much more than many another:
My father left a tidy sum to mother,   45
A house and garden near the city gate.
But now my days are rather plain:
A soldier is my brother,
My little sister dead.
Sore was, while she was living, the troubled life I led;   50
But I would gladly go through all of it again:
She was so dear to me.
FAUST   An angel, if like you.
MARGARET   I brought her up, and she adored me, too.
She was born only after father's death;
Mother seemed near her dying breath,   55
As stricken as she then would lie,
Though she got well again quite slowly, by and by.
She was so sickly and so slight,
She could not nurse the little mite;
So I would tend her all alone,   60
With milk and water; she became my own.
Upon my arms and in my lap
She first grew friendly, tumbled, and grew up.
FAUST   You must have felt the purest happiness.
MARGARET   But also many hours of distress.   65
The baby's cradle stood at night
Beside my bed, and if she stirred I'd wake,
I slept so light.
Now I would have to feed her, now I'd take
Her into my bed, now I'd rise   70
And dandling pace the room to calm the baby's cries.
And I would wash before the sun would rise,
Fret in the market and over the kitchen flame,
Tomorrow as today, always the same.
One's spirits, sir, are not always the best,   75
But one can relish meals and relish rest.
          [They pass.]
MARTHA   Poor woman has indeed a wretched fate:
A bachelor is not easy to convert.
MEPHISTOPHELES   For one like you the job is not too great;
You might convince me if you are alert.   80
MARTHA   Be frank, dear sir, so far you have not found?
Has not your heart in some way yet been bound?
MEPHISTOPHELES   A hearth one owns and a good wife, we're told,
Are worth as much as pearls and gold.
MARTHA   I mean, have you not ever had a passion?   85
MEPHISTOPHELES   I always was received in the most friendly fashion.
MARTHA   Would say: weren't you ever in earnest in your breast?
MEPHISTOPHELES   With women one should never presume to speak in
     jest.
MARTHA   Oh, you don't understand.

MEPHISTOPHELES   I'm sorry I'm so blind!
  But I do understand—that you are very kind.   90
      [*They pass.*]
FAUST   Oh little angel, you did recognize
  Me as I came into the garden?
MARGARET   Did you not notice? I cast down my eyes.
FAUST   My liberty you're then prepared to pardon?
  What insolence presumed to say   95
  As you left church the other day?
MARGARET   I was upset, I did not know such daring
  And no one could have spoken ill of me.
  I thought that something in my bearing
  Must have seemed shameless and unmaidenly.   100
  He seemed to have the sudden feeling
  That this wench could be had without much dealing.
  Let me confess, I didn't know that there
  Were other feelings stirring in me, and they grew;
  But I was angry with myself, I swear,   105
  That I could not get angrier with you.
FAUST   Sweet darling!
MARGARET   Let me do this! [*She plucks a daisy and pulls out the*
  petals one by one.]
FAUST   A nosegay? Or what shall it be?
MARGARET
  No, it is just a game.
FAUST   What?
MARGARET   Go, you will laugh at me. [*She pulls out petals*
  and murmurs.]
FAUST
  What do you murmur?
MARGARET [*Half aloud.*]   He loves me—loves me not.
FAUST   You gentle countenance of heaven!   110
MARGARET [*Continues.*]   Loves me—not—loves me—not—
  [*Tearing out the last leaf, in utter joy.*]
  He loves me.
FAUST   Yes, my child. Let this sweet flower's word
  Be as a god's word to you. He loves you.
  Do you know what this means? He loves you. [*He takes both her hands.*]
MARGARET   My skin creeps.   115
FAUST   Oh, shudder not! But let this glance,
  And let this clasp of hands tell you
  What is unspeakable:
  To yield oneself entirely and feel
  A rapture which must be eternal.   120
  Eternal! For its end would be despair.
  No, no end! No end!
      [MARGARET *clasps his hands, frees herself, and runs away. He stands*
      for a moment, lost in thought; then he follows her.]
MARTHA [*Entering.*]   The night draws near.
MEPHISTOPHELES   Yes, and we want to go.

MARTHA   I should ask you to tarry even so,
But this place simply is too bad: 125
It is as if nobody had
Work or labor
Except to spy all day long on his neighbor,
And one gets talked about, whatever life one leads.
And our couple?
MEPHISTOPHELES   Up that path I heard them whirr—   130
Frolicking butterflies.
MARTHA   He is taking to her.
MEPHISTOPHELES   And she to him. That's how the world proceeds.

A GARDEN BOWER

[MARGARET *leaps into it, hides behind the door, puts the tip of one
finger to her lips, and peeks through the crack.*]
MARGARET   He comes.
FAUST [*Entering.*]   Oh rogue, you're teasing me.
Now I see. [*He kisses her.*]
MARGARET [*Seizing him and returning the kiss.*]
Dearest man! I love you from my heart.
[MEPHISTOPHELES *knocks.*]
FAUST [*Stamping his foot.*]
Who's there?
MEPHISTOPHELES   A friend.
FAUST   A beast!
MEPHISTOPHELES   The time has come to part.
MARTHA [*Entering.*]
Yes, it is late, good sir.
FAUST   May I not take you home?   5
MARGARET   My mother would—Farewell!
FAUST   Must I leave then?
Farewell.
MARTHA   Adieu.
MARGARET   Come soon again!
[FAUST *and* MEPHISTOPHELES *exeunt.*]
MARGARET   Dear God, the things he thought and said!
How much goes on in a man's head!
Abashed, I merely acquiesce   10
And cannot answer, except Yes!
I am a poor, dumb child and cannot see
What such a man could find in me.
[*Exit.*]

WOOD AND CAVE

FAUST [*Alone.*]   Exalted spirit, all you gave me, all
That I have asked. And it was not in vain
That amid flames you turned your face toward me.
You gave me royal nature as my own dominion,
Strength to experience her, enjoy her. Not   5

The cold amazement of a visit only
You granted me, but let me penetrate
Into her heart as into a close friend's.
You lead the hosts of all that is alive
Before my eyes, teach me to know my brothers   10
In quiet bushes and in air and water.
And when the storm roars in the wood and creaks,
The giant fir tree, falling, hits and smashes
The neighbor branches and the neighbor trunks,
And from its hollow thud the mountain thunders,   15
Then you lead me to this safe cave and show
Me to myself, and all the most profound
And secret wonders of my breast are opened.
And when before my eyes the pure moon rises
And passes soothingly, there float to me   20
From rocky cliffs and out of dewy bushes
The silver shapes of a forgotten age,
And soften meditation's somber joy.
Alas, that man is granted nothing perfect
I now experience. With this happiness   25
Which brings me close and closer to the gods,
You gave me the companion whom I can
Forego no more, though with cold impudence
He makes me small in my own eyes and changes
Your gifts to nothing with a few words' breath.   30
He kindles in my breast a savage fire
And keeps me thirsting after that fair image.
Thus I reel from desire to enjoyment,
And in enjoyment languish for desire.
MEPHISTOPHELES [*Enters.*]   Have you not led this life quite long
    enough?   35
How can it keep amusing you?
It may be well for once to try such stuff
But then one turns to something new.
FAUST   I wish that you had more to do
And would not come to pester me.   40
MEPHISTOPHELES   All right. I gladly say adieu—
You should not say that seriously.
A chap like you, unpleasant, mad, and cross,
Would hardly be a serious loss.
All day long one can work and slave away.   45
And what he likes and what might cause dismay,
It simply isn't possible to say.
FAUST   That is indeed the proper tone!
He wants my thanks for being such a pest.
MEPHISTOPHELES   If I had left you wretch alone,   50
Would you then live with greater zest?
Was it not I that helped you to disown,
And partly cured, your feverish unrest

Yes, but⁶ for me, the earthly zone
Would long be minus one poor guest.   55
And now, why must you sit like an old owl
In caves and rocky clefts, and scowl?
From soggy moss and dripping stones you lap your food
Just like a toad, and sit and brood.
A fair, sweet way to pass the time!   60
Still steeped in your doctoral slime!
FAUST   How this sojourn in the wilderness
Renews my vital force, you cannot guess.
And if you apprehended this,
You would be Devil enough, to envy me my bliss.   65
MEPHISTOPHELES   A supernatural delight!
To lie on mountains in the dew and night,
Embracing earth and sky in raptured reeling,
To swell into a god—in one's own feeling—
To probe earth's marrow with vague divination,   70
Sense in your breast the whole work of creation,
With haughty strength enjoy, I know not what,
Then overflow into all things with love so hot,
Gone is all earthly inhibition,
And then the noble intuition— [*With a gesture.*]   75
Of—need I say of what emission?
FAUST   Shame!
MEPHISTOPHELES   That does not meet with your acclaim;
You have the right to cry indignant: shame!
One may not tell chaste ears what, beyond doubt,
The chastest heart could never do without.   80
And, once for all, I don't grudge you the pleasure
Of little self-deceptions at your leisure;
But it can't last indefinitely.
Already you are spent again,
And soon you will be rent again,   85
By madness and anxiety.
Enough of that. Your darling is distraught,
Sits inside, glum and in despair,
She can't put you out of her mind and thought
And loves you more than she can bear.   90
At first your raging love was past control,
As brooks that overflow when filled with melted snow;
You poured it out into her soul,
But now your little brook is low.
Instead of posing in the wood,   95
It seems to me it might be good
If for her love our noble lord
Gave the poor monkey some reward.
Time seems to her intolerably long;

6. Were it not.

She stands at her window and sees the clouds in the sky   100
Drift over the city wall and go by.
Were I a little bird! thus goes her song
For days and half the night long.
Once she may be cheerful, most of the time sad,
Once she has spent her tears,   105
Then she is calm, it appears,
And always loves you like mad.

FAUST   Serpent! Snake!

MEPHISTOPHELES [*Aside.*]   If only I catch the rake!

FAUST   Damnable fiend! Get yourself hence,   110
And do not name the beautiful maid!
Let not the lust for her sweet limbs invade
And ravish once again my frenzied sense!

MEPHISTOPHELES   What do you mean? She thinks you've run away:
And it is half-true, I must say.   115

FAUST   I am near her, however far I be,
She'll never be forgotten and ignored;
Indeed, I am consumed with jealousy
That her lips touch the body of the Lord.[7]

MEPHISTOPHELES   I'm jealous of my friend when she exposes   120
The pair of twins that feed among the roses.[8]

FAUST   Begone, pander!

MEPHISTOPHELES   Fine! Your wrath amuses me.
The God who fashioned man and maid
Was quick to recognize the noblest trade,
And procured opportunity.   125
Go on! It is a woeful pain!
You're to embrace your love again,
Not sink into the tomb.

FAUST   What are the joys of heaven in her arms?   130
Let me embrace her, feel her charms—
Do I not always sense her doom?
Am I not fugitive? without a home?
Inhuman, without aim or rest,
As, like the cataract, from rock to rock I foam,   135
Raging with passion, toward the abyss?
And nearby, she—with childlike blunt desires
Inside her cottage on the Alpine leas,
And everything that she requires
Was in her own small world at ease.   140
And I, whom the gods hate and mock,
Was not satisfied
That I seized the rock
And smashed the mountainside.
Her—her peace I had to undermine.   145
You, hell, desired this sacrifice upon your shrine.

7. When the bread of Communion miraculously turns into the body of Christ.   8. Cf. Song of Solomon 4.5: "Thy two breasts are like two young roes that are twins, which feed among the lilies."

Help, Devil, shorten this time of dread.
What must be done, come let it be.
Let then her fate come shattering on my head,
And let her perish now with me.   150
MEPHISTOPHELES   How now it boils again and how you shout.
Go in and comfort her, you dunce.
Where such a little head sees no way out,
He thinks the end must come at once.
Long live who holds out undeterred!   155
At other times you have the Devil's airs.
In all the world there's nothing more absurd
Than is a Devil who despairs.

GRETCHEN'S ROOM

GRETCHEN [*At the spinning wheel, alone.*]
        My peace is gone,
        My heart is sore;
        I find it never
        And nevermore.

        Where him I not have   5
        There is my grave.
        This world is all
        Turned into gall.

        And my poor head
        Is quite insane,   10
        And my poor mind
        Is rent with pain.

        My peace is gone,
        My heart is sore;
        I find it never   15
        And nevermore.

        For him only I look
        From my window seat,
        For him only I go
        Out into the street.   20

        His lofty gait,
        His noble guise,
        The smile of his mouth,
        The force of his eyes,

        And his words' flow—   25
        Enchanting bliss—
        The touch of his hand,
        And, oh, his kiss.

        My peace is gone,
        My heart is sore;   30

I find it never
And nevermore.

My bosom surges
For him alone,
Oh that I could clasp him   35
And hold him so,

And kiss him
To my heart's content,
Till in his kisses
I were spent.   40

MARTHA'S GARDEN

[MARGARET. FAUST.]

MARGARET Promise me, Heinrich.[9]
FAUST   Whatever I can.
MARGARET How is it with your religion, please admit—
   You certainly are a very good man,
   But I believe you don't think much of it.
FAUST Leave that, my child. I love you, do not fear   5
   And would give all for those whom I hold dear,
   Would not rob anyone of church or creed.
MARGARET That is not enough, it is faith we need.
FAUST Do we?
MARGARET   Oh that I had some influence!
   You don't respect the holy sacraments.   10
FAUST I do respect them.
MARGARET   But without desire.
   The mass and confession you do not require.
   Do you believe in God?
FAUST   My darling who may say
   I believe in God?
   Ask priests and sages, their reply   15
   Looks like sneers that mock and prod
   The one who asked the question.
MARGARET   Then you deny him there?
FAUST Do not mistake me, you who are so fair.
   Him—who may name?
   And who proclaim: 20
   I believe in him?
   Who may feel,
   Who dare reveal
   In words: I believe him not?
   The All-Embracing,   25
   The All-Sustaining,
   Does he not embrace and sustain
   You, me, himself?

9. Faust. In the legend, Faust's name was generally Johann (John). Goethe changed it to Heinrich (Henry).

Does not the heaven vault above?
Is the earth not firmly based down here?   30
And do not, friendly,
Eternal stars rise?
Do we not look into each other's eyes,
And all in you is surging
To your head and heart,   35
And weaves in timeless mystery,
Unseeable, yet seen, around you?
Then let it fill your heart entirely,
And when your rapture in this feeling is complete,
Call it then as you will,   40
Call it bliss! heart! love! God!
I do not have a name
For this. Feeling is all;
Names are but sound and smoke
Befogging heaven's blazes.   45
MARGARET   Those are very fair and noble phrases;
  The priest says something, too, like what you spoke—
  Only his words are not quite so—
FAUST   Wherever you go,
  All hearts under the heavenly day   50
  Say it, each in its own way;
  Why not I in mine?
MARGARET   When one listens to you, one might incline
  To let it pass—but I can't agree,
  For you have no Christianity.   55
FAUST   Dear child!
MARGARET   It has long been a grief to me
  To see you in such company.
FAUST   Why?
MARGARET   The man that goes around with you
  Seems hateful to me through and through: 60
  In all my life there's not a thing
  That gave my heart as sharp a sting
  As his repulsive eyes.
FAUST   Sweet doll, don't fear him anywise.
MARGARET   His presence makes me feel quite ill.   65
  I bear all other men good will;
  But just as to see you I languish,
  This man fills me with secret anguish;
  He seems a knave one should not trust.
  May God forgive me if I am unjust.   70
FAUST   There must be queer birds, too, you know.
MARGARET   But why live with them even so?
  Whenever he comes in,
  He always wears a mocking grin
  And looks half threatening: 75
  One sees, he has no sympathy for anything;
  It is written on his very face

That he thinks love is a disgrace.
In your arm I feel good and free,
Warm and abandoned as can be;   80
Alas, my heart and feelings are choked when he comes, too.
FAUST   Oh, you foreboding angel, you.
MARGARET   It makes my heart so sore
  That, when he only comes our way,
  I feel I do not love you any more;   85
  And where he is, I cannot pray.
  It eats into my heart. Oh you,
  Dear Heinrich, must feel that way, too.
FAUST   That is just your antipathy.
MARGARET   I must go.
FAUST   Will there never be   90
  At your sweet bosom one hour of rest
  When soul touches on soul and breast on breast?
MARGARET   Had I my own room when I sleep,
  I should not bolt the door tonight;
  But Mother's slumber is not deep,   95
  And if she found us thus—oh fright,
  Right then and there I should drop dead.
FAUST   My angel, if that's what you dread,
  Here is a bottle. Merely shake
  Three drops into her cup,   100
  And she won't easily wake up.
MARGARET   What should I not do for your sake?
  It will not harm her if one tries it?
FAUST   Dear, if it would, would I advise it?
MARGARET   When I but look at you, I thrill,   105
  I don't know why, my dear, to do your will;
  I have already done so much for you
  That hardly anything seems left to do.
      [*Exit. Enter* MEPHISTOPHELES.]
MEPHISTOPHELES   The monkey! Is she gone?
FAUST   You spied?
MEPHISTOPHELES   Are you surprised?
  I listened and I understood   110
  Our learned doctor just was catechized.
  I hope that it may do you good.
  The girls are quite concerned to be apprised
  If one is pious and obeys tradition.
  If yes, they trust they can rely on his submission.   115
FAUST   You monster will not see nor own
  That this sweet soul, in loyalty,
  Full of her own creed
  Which alone,
  She trusts, can bring salvation, lives in agony   120
  To think her lover lost, however she may plead.
MEPHISTOPHELES   You supersensual, sensual wooer,
  A maiden leads you by the nose.
FAUST   You freak of filth and fire! Evildoer!

MEPHISTOPHELES   And what a knowledge of physiognomy she shows. 125
  She feels, she knows not what, whenever I'm about;
  She finds a hidden meaning in my eyes:
  I am a demon, beyond doubt,
  Perhaps the Devil, that is her surmise.
  Well, tonight—?
FAUST   What's that to you?   130
MEPHISTOPHELES   I have my pleasure in it, too.

AT THE WELL

[GRETCHEN *and* LIESCHEN *with jugs.*]
LIESCHEN   Of Barbara you haven't heard?
GRETCHEN   I rarely see people—no, not a word.
LIESCHEN   Well, Sibyl just told me in front of the school:
  That girl has at last been made a fool.
  That comes from having airs.
GRETCHEN   How so?
LIESCHEN   It stinks!   5
  She is feeding two when she eats and drinks.
GRETCHEN   Oh!
LIESCHEN   At last she has got what was coming to her.
  She stuck to that fellow like a burr.
  That was some prancing,   10
  In the village, and dancing,
  She was always the first in line;
  And he flirted with her over pastries and wine;
  And she thought that she looked divine—
  But had no honor, no thought of her name,   15
  And took his presents without any shame.
  The way they slobbered and carried on;
  But now the little flower is gone.
GRETCHEN   Poor thing!
LIESCHEN   That you don't say!
  When girls like us would be spinning away,   20
  And mother kept us at home every night,
  She was with her lover in sweet delight
  On the bench by the door, in dark alleys they were,
  And the time was never too long for her.
  Now let her crouch and let her bend down   25
  And do penance in a sinner's gown!
GRETCHEN   He will surely take her to be his wife.
LIESCHEN   He would be a fool! A handsome boy
  Will elsewhere find more air and joy.
  He's already gone.
GRETCHEN   That is not fair!   30
LIESCHEN   And if she gets him, let her beware:
  Her veil the boys will throw to the floor,
  And we shall strew chaff in front of her door.[1]

---

1. In Germany this treatment was reserved for young women who had sexual relations before marriage.

[*Exit.*]

GRETCHEN [*Going home.*]   How I once used to scold along
  When some poor woman had done wrong.   35
  How for another person's shame
  I found not words enough of blame.
  How black it seemed—I made it blacker still,
  And yet not black enough to suit my will.
  I blessed myself, would boast and grin—   40
  And now myself am caught in sin.
  Yet—everything that brought me here,
  God, was so good, oh, was so dear.

CITY WALL

    [*In a niche in the wall, an image of the Mater Dolorosa.*[2] *Ewers with
    flowers in front of it.*]

GRETCHEN [*Puts fresh flowers into the ewers.*]
      Incline,
      Mother of pain,
      Your face in grace to my despair.

      A sword in your heart,
      With pain rent apart,   5
      Up to your son's dread death you stare.

      On the Father your eyes,
      You send up sighs
      For your and your son's despair.

      Who knows   10
      My woes—
      Despair in every bone!

      How my heart is full of anguish,
      How I tremble, how I languish,
      Know but you, and you alone.   15

      Wherever I may go,
      What woe, what woe, what woe
      Is in my bosom aching!

      Scarcely alone am I,
      I cry, I cry, I cry;   20
      My heart in me is breaking.

      The pots in front of my window
      I watered with tears as the dew,
      When early in the morning
      I broke these flowers for you.   25

      When bright into my room
      The sun his first rays shed,

---

2. Sorrowful mother (Latin; literal trans.); i.e., the Virgin Mary.

I sat in utter gloom
Already on my bed.

Help! Rescue me from shame and death!   30
Incline,
Mother of pain,
Your face in grace to my despair.

NIGHT

[*Street in front of* GRETCHEN's *door.*]
VALENTINE [*Soldier,* GRETCHEN's *brother.*]
  When I would sit at a drinking bout
  Where all had much to brag about,
  And many fellows raised their voice
  To praise the maidens of their choice,
  Glass after glass was drained with toasting,   5
  I listened smugly to their boasting,
  My elbow propped up on the table,
  And sneered at fable after fable.
  I'd stroke my beard and smile and say,
  Holding my bumper in my hand: 10
  Each may be nice in her own way,
  But is there one in the whole land
  Like sister Gretchen to outdo her,
  Hear, hear! Clink! Clink! it went around;
  And some would cry: It's true, yes sir,   15
  There is no other girl like her!
  The braggarts sat without a sound.
  And *now*—I could tear out my hair
  And dash my brain out in despair!
  His nose turned up, a scamp can face me,   20
  With taunts and sneers he can disgrace me;
  And I should I sit, like one in debt,
  Each chance remark should make me sweat!
  I'd like to grab them all and maul them,
  But liars I could never call them.   25

  What's coming there? What sneaks in view?
  If I mistake not, there are two.
  If it is he, I'll spare him not,
  He shall not living leave this spot.
    [FAUST *and* MEPHISTOPHELES *enter.*]
FAUST How from the window of that sacristy   30
  The light of the eternal lamp is glimmering,
  And weak and weaker sideward shimmering,
  As night engulfs it like the sea.
  My heart feels like this nightly street.
MEPHISTOPHELES And I feel like a cat in heat,   35
  That creeps around a fire escape
  Pressing against the wall its shape.

I feel quite virtuous, I confess,
A little thievish lust, a little rammishness.
Thus I feel spooking through each vein   40
The wonderful Walpurgis Night.
In two days it will come again,
And waking then is pure delight.
FAUST   And will the treasure that gleams over there
Rise in the meantime up into the air?   45
MEPHISTOPHELES   Quite soon you may enjoy the pleasure
Of taking from the pot the treasure.
The other day I took a squint
And saw fine lion dollars in't.
FAUST   Not any jewelry, not a ring   50
To adorn my beloved girl?
MEPHISTOPHELES   I did see something like a string,
Or something like it, made of pearl.
FAUST   Oh, that is fine, for it's unpleasant
To visit her without a present.   55
MEPHISTOPHELES   It should not cause you such distress
When you have gratis such success.
Now that the sky gleams with its starry throng,
Prepare to hear a work of art:
I shall sing her a moral song   60
To take no chance we fool her heart.
[*Sings to the cither.*³]
      It's scarcely day,
      Oh, Katie, say,
      Why do you stay
      Before your lover's door?   65
      Leave now, leave now!
      For in you'll go
      A maid, I know,
      Come out a maid no more.

      You ought to shun   70
      That kind of fun;
      Once it is done,
      Good night, you poor, poor thing.
      For your own sake
      You should not make   75
      Love to a rake
      Unless you have the ring.⁴
VALENTINE [*Comes forward.*]   Whom would you lure? God's element!
Rat-catching piper! Oh, perdition!
The Devil take your instrument!   80
The Devil then take the musician!
MEPHISTOPHELES   The cither is all smashed. It is beyond repair.
VALENTINE   Now let's try splitting skulls. Beware!

---

3. Or zither, a stringed instrument.   4. Lines 63–78 are adapted by Goethe from Shakespeare's *Hamlet*
4.5.

MEPHISTOPHELES [*To* FAUST.]   Don't withdraw, doctor! Quick, don't
    tarry!
  Stick close to me, I'll lead the way.   85
  Unsheathe your toothpick, don't delay;
  Thrust out at him, and I shall parry.
VALENTINE   Then parry that!
MEPHISTOPHELES   Of course.
VALENTINE   And that.
MEPHISTOPHELES   All right.
VALENTINE   I think the Devil must be in this fight.
  What could that be? My hand is getting lame.   90
MEPHISTOPHELES [*To* FAUST.]   Thrust home!
VALENTINE [*Falls.*]   Oh God!
MEPHISTOPHELES   The rogue is tame.
  Now hurry hence, for we must disappear:
  A murderous clamor rises instantly,
  And while the police does not trouble me,   95
  The blood ban is a thing I fear.
MARTHA [*At a window.*]   Come out! Come out!
GRETCHEN [*At a window.*]   Quick! Bring a light.
MARTHA [*As above.*]   They swear and scuffle, yell and fight.
PEOPLE   There is one dead already, see.   100
MARTHA [*Coming out.*]   The murderers—where did they run?
GRETCHEN [*Coming out.*]   Who lies there?
PEOPLE   Your own mother's son.
GRETCHEN   Almighty God! What misery!
VALENTINE   I'm dying. That is quickly said,
  And still more quickly done.   105
  Why do you women wail in dread?
  Come here, listen to me.
     [*All gather around him.*]
  My Gretchen, you are still quite green,
  Not nearly smart enough or keen,
  You do not do things right.   110
  In confidence, I should say more:
  Since after all you are a whore,
  Be one with all your might.
GRETCHEN   My brother! God! What frightful shame!
VALENTINE   Leave the Lord God out of this game.   115
  What has been done, alas, is done,
  And as it must, it now will run.
  You started secretly with one,
  Soon more will come to join the fun,
  And once a dozen lays you down,   120
  You might as well invite the town.

  When shame is born and first appears,
  It is an underhand delight,
  And one drags the veil of night
  Over her head and ears;   125

One is tempted to put her away.
But as she grows, she gets more bold,
Walks naked even in the day,
Though hardly fairer to behold.
The more repulsive grows her sight,   130
The more she seeks day's brilliant light.

The time I even now discern
When honest citizens will turn,
Harlot, away from you and freeze
As from a corpse that breeds disease.   135
Your heart will flinch, your heart will falter
When they will look you in the face.
You'll wear no gold, you'll wear no lace,
Nor in the church come near the altar.
You will no longer show your skill   140
At dances, donning bow and frill,
But in dark corners on the side
With beggars and cripples you'll seek to hide;
And even if God should at last forgive,
Be cursed as long as you may live!   145
MARTHA   Ask God to show your own soul grace.
    Don't make it with blasphemies still more base.
VALENTINE   That I could lay my hands on you,
    You shriveled, pimping bugaboo,
    Then, I hope, I might truly win   150
    Forgiveness for my every sin.
GRETCHEN   My brother! This is agony!
VALENTINE   I tell you, do not bawl at me.
    When you threw honor overboard,
    You pierced my heart more than the sword.   155
    Now I shall cross death's sleeping span
    To God, a soldier and an honest man.
        [*Dies.*]

CATHEDRAL

[*Service, Organ, and Singing.* GRETCHEN *among many people.* EVIL
    SPIRIT *behind* GRETCHEN.]
EVIL SPIRIT   How different you felt, Gretchen,
    When in innocence
    You came before this altar;
    And from the well-worn little book
    You prattled prayers,   5
    Half childish games,
    Half God in your heart!
    Gretchen!
    Where are your thoughts?
    And in your heart   10
    What misdeed?
    Do you pray for your mother's soul that went

Because of you from sleep to lasting, lasting pain?
Upon your threshold, whose blood?
And underneath your heart, 15
Does it not stir and swell,
Frightened and frightening you
With its foreboding presence?

GRETCHEN   Oh! Oh!
That I were rid of all the thoughts 20
Which waver in me to and fro
Against me!

CHOIR   *Dies irae, dies illa*
       Solvet saeclum in favilla.[5]
       [*Sound of the organ.*]

EVIL SPIRIT   Wrath grips you. 25
The great trumpet sounds.
The graves are quaking.
And your heart,
Resurrected
From ashen calm 30
To flaming tortures,
Flares up.

GRETCHEN   Would I were far!
I feel as if the organ had
Taken my breath, 35
As if the song
Dissolved my heart!

CHOIR   *Judex ergo cum sedebit,*
       Quidquid latet adparebit,
       Nil inultum remanebit.[6] 40

GRETCHEN   I feel so close.
The stony pillars
Imprison me.
The vault above
Presses on me.—Air! 45

EVIL SPIRIT   Hide yourself. Sin and shame
Do not stay hidden.
Air? Light?
Woe unto you!

CHOIR   *Quid sum miser tunc dicturus?* 50
       Quem patronum rogaturus?
       Cum vix justus sit securus.[7]

EVIL SPIRIT   The transfigured turn
Their countenance from you.
To hold out their hands to you 55
Makes the pure shudder.
Woe!

---

5. Day of wrath, that day that dissolves the world into ashes (Latin). The choir sings a famous 13th-century hymn by Thomas Celano.   6. When the judge shall be seated, what is hidden shall appear, nothing shall remain unavenged (Latin).   7. What shall I say in my wretchedness? To whom shall I appeal when scarcely the righteous man is safe (Latin).

CHOIR   *Quid sum miser tunc dicturus?*
GRETCHEN   Neighbor! Your smelling salts! [*She faints.*]

WALPURGIS NIGHT

[*Harz Mountains. Region of Schierke and Elend.* FAUST *and* MEPHISTOPHELES.]

MEPHISTOPHELES   How would you like a broomstick now to fly?
  I wish I had a billy goat that's tough.
  For on this road we still have to climb high.
FAUST   As long as I feel fresh, and while my legs are spry,
  This knotted staff seems good enough.   5
  Why should we shun each stumbling block?
  To creep first through the valleys' lovely maze,
  And then to scale this wall of rock
  From which the torrent foams in silver haze—
  There is the zest that spices our ways.   10
  Around the birches weaves the spring,
  Even the fir tree feels its spell:
  Should it not stir in our limbs as well?
MEPHISTOPHELES   Of all that I don't feel a thing.
  In me the winter is still brisk,   15
  I wish my path were graced with frost and snow.
  How wretchedly the moon's imperfect disk
  Arises now with its red, tardy glow,
  And is so dim that one could bump one's head
  At every step against a rock or tree!   20
  Let's use a will-o'-the-wisp[8] instead!
  I see one there that burns quite merrily.
  Hello there! Would you come and join us, friend?
  Why blaze away to no good end?
  Please be so kind and show us up the hill!   25
WILL-O'-THE-WISP   I hope my deep respect will help me force
  My generally flighty will;
  For zigzag is the rule in our course.
MEPHISTOPHELES   Hear! Hear! It's man you like to imitate!
  Now, in the Devil's name, go straight—   30
  Or I shall blow your flickering life span out.
WILL-O'-THE-WISP   You are the master of the house, no doubt,
  And I shall try to serve you nicely.
  But don't forget, the mountain is magic-mad today,
  And if Will-o'-the-wisp must guide you on your way,   35
  You must not take things too precisely.
FAUST, MEPHISTOPHELES, AND WILL-O'-THE-WISP [*In alternating song.*]
      In the sphere of dream and spell
      We have entered now indeed.
      Have some pride and guide us well
      That we get ahead with speed   40
      In the vast deserted spaces!

---

8. *Ignis fatuus,* a wavering light formed by marsh gas. In German folklore thought to lead travelers to their destruction.

See the trees behind the trees,
See how swiftly they change places,
And the cliffs that bow with ease,
Craggy noses, long and short,   45
How they snore and how they snort!

Through the stones and through the leas
Tumble brooks of every sort.
Is it splash or melodies?
Is it love that wails and prays,   50
Voices of those heavenly days?
What we hope and what we love!
Echoes and dim memories
Of forgotten times come back.

Oo-hoo! Shoo-hoo! Thus they squawk,   55
Screech owl, plover, and the hawk;
Did they all stay up above?
Are those salamanders crawling?
Bellies bloated, long legs sprawling!
And the roots, as serpents, coil   60
From the rocks through sandy soil,
With their eerie bonds would scare us,
Block our path and then ensnare us;
Hungry as a starving leech,
Their strong polyp's tendrils reach   65
For the wanderer. And in swarms
Mice of myriad hues and forms
Storm through moss and heath and lea.
And a host of fireflies
Throng about and improvise   70
The most maddening company.

Tell me: do we now stand still,
Or do we go up the hill?
Everything now seems to mill,
Rocks and trees and faces blend,   75
Will-o'-the-wisps grow and extend
And inflate themselves at will.
MEPHISTOPHELES   Grip my coat and hold on tight!
  Here is such a central height
  Where one sees, and it amazes,   80
  In the mountain, Mammon's blazes.[9]
FAUST   How queer glimmers a dawnlike sheen
  Faintly beneath this precipice,
  And plays into the dark ravine
  Of the near bottomless abyss.   85
  Here mists arise, there vapors spread,
  And here it gleams deep in the mountain,

9. Mammon is imagined as leading a group of fallen angels in digging out gold and gems from the ground of hell, presumably for Satan's palace, as described in Milton's *Paradise Lost* I.678ff.

Then creeps along, a tender thread,
And gushes up, a glistening fountain.

Here it is winding in a tangle,   90
With myriad veins the gorges blaze,
And here in this congested angle
A single stream shines through the haze.
There sparks are flying at our right,
As plentiful as golden sand.   95
But look! In its entire height
The rock becomes a firebrand.

MEPHISTOPHELES   Sir Mammon never spares the light
To hold the feast in proper fashion.
How lucky that you saw this sight!   100
I hear the guests approach in wanton passion.

FAUST   The tempests lash the air and rave,
And with gigantic blows they hit my shoulders.

MEPHISTOPHELES   You have to clutch the ribs of those big hoary boulders,
Or they will hurtle you to that abysmal grave.   105
A fog blinds the night with its hood.
Do you hear the crashes in the wood?
Frightened, the owls are scattered.
Hear how the pillars
Of ever green castles are shattered.   110
Quaking and breaking of branches!
The trunks' overpowering groaning!
The roots' creaking and moaning!
In a frightfully tangled fall
They crash over each other, one and all,   115
And through the ruin-covered abysses
The frenzied air howls and hisses.
Do you hear voices up high?
In the distance and nearby?
The whole mountain is afire   120
With a furious magic choir.

WITCHES' CHORUS   The witches ride to Blocksberg's top,
The stubble is yellow, and green the crop.
They gather on the mountainside,
Sir Urian[1] comes to preside.   125
We are riding over crag and brink,
The witches fart, the billy goats stink.

VOICE   Old Baubo[2] comes alone right now,
She is riding on a mother sow.

CHORUS   Give honor to whom honor's due!   130
Dame Baubo, lead our retinue!
A real swine and mother, too,
The witches' crew will follow you.

VOICE   Which way did you come?

---

1. A name for the Devil.   2. In Greek mythology, the nurse of Demeter, noted for her obscenity and bestiality.

VOICE   By the Ilsenstone.
  I peeped at the owl who was roosting alone.   135
  Did she ever make eyes!
VOICE   Oh, go to hell!
  Why ride so pell-mell?
VOICE   See how she has flayed me!
  The wounds she made me!
WITCHES' CHORUS   The way is wide, the way is long;   140
      Just see the frantic pushing throng!
      The broomstick pokes, the pitchfork thrusts
      The infant chokes, the mother bursts.
WIZARDS' HALF CHORUS   Slow as the snail's is our pace,
      The women are ahead and race;   145
      When it goes to the Devil's place,
      By a thousand steps they win the race.
OTHER HALF   If that is so, we do not mind it:
      With a thousand steps the women find it;
      But though they rush, we do not care: 150
      With one big jump the men get there.
VOICE [*Above.*]   Come on, come on from Rocky Lake!
VOICES [*From below.*]   We'd like to join you and partake.
  We wash, but though we are quite clean,
  We're barren as we've always been.   155
BOTH CHORUSES   The wind is hushed, the star takes flight,
      The dreary moon conceals her light.
      As it whirls by, the wizards' choir
      Scatters a myriad sparks of fire.
VOICE [*From below.*]   Halt, please! Halt, ho!   160
VOICE [*From above.*]   Who calls out of the cleft below?
VOICE [*Below.*]   Take me along! Take me along!
  I've been climbing for three hundred years,
  And yet the peak I cannot find.
  But I would like to join my kind.   165
BOTH CHORUSES   The stick and broom can make you float,
      So can pitchfork and billy goat;
      Who cannot rise today to soar,
      That man is doomed for evermore.
HALF-WITCH [*Below.*]   I move and move and try and try;   170
  How did the others get so high?
  At home I'm restless through and through,
  And now shall miss my chance here, too.
WITCHES' CHORUS   The salve gives courage to the witch,
      For sails we use a rag and switch,   175
      A tub's a ship, if you know how;
      If you would ever fly, fly now!
BOTH CHORUSES   We near the peak, we fly around,
      Now sweep down low over the ground,
      And cover up the heath's vast regions   180
      With witches' swarms and wizards' legions.
      [*They alight.*]

MEPHISTOPHELES   They throng and push, they rush and clatter.
  They hiss and whirl, they pull and chatter.
  It glistens, sparks, and stinks and flares;
  Those are indeed the witches' airs!   185
  Stay close to me, or we'll be solitaires!
  Where are you?
FAUST [*Far away.*]   Here.
MEPHISTOPHELES   So far? Almost a loss!
  Then I must show them who is boss.
  Back! Squire Nick is coming! Back, sweet rabble! Slump!
  Here, Doctor, take a hold! And now in one big jump   190
  Let's leave behind this noisy crowd;
  Even for me it's much too loud.
  On that side is a light with quite a special flare,
  Let's penetrate the bushes' shroud;
  Come, come! Now let us slink in there!   195
FAUST   Spirit of Contradiction! Go on! I'll follow him.
  I must say, it's exceptionally bright
  To wander to the Blocksberg in the Walpurgis Night,
  To isolate ourselves to follow out some whim.
MEPHISTOPHELES   You see that multicolored flare?   200
  A cheerful club is meeting there:
  In small groups one is not alone.
FAUST   I'd rather be up there: around that stone
  The fires blaze, they have begun;
  The crowds throng to the Evil One   205
  Where many riddles must be solved.
MEPHISTOPHELES   But many new ones are evolved.
  Leave the great world, let it run riot,
  And let us stay where it is quiet.
  It's something that has long been done,   210
  To fashion little worlds within the bigger one.
  I see young witches there, completely nude,
  And old ones who are veiled as shrewdly.
  Just for my sake, don't treat them rudely;
  It's little effort and great fun!   215
  There are some instruments that grind and grit.
  Damnable noise! One must get used to it.
  Come on! Come on! Please do not fret!
  I'll lead the way and take you to this place,
  And you will be quite grateful yet!   220
  What do you say? There isn't enough space?
  Just look! You barely see the other end.
  A hundred fires in a row, my friend!
  They dance, they chat, they cook, they drink, they court;
  Now you just tell me where there's better sport!   225
FAUST   When you will introduce us at this revel,
  Will you appear a sorcerer or devil?
MEPHISTOPHELES   I generally travel, without showing my station,

But on a gala day one shows one's decoration.
I have no garter[3] I could show,   230
But here the cloven foot is honored, as you know.
Do you perceive that snail? It comes, though it seems stiff;
For with its eager, groping face
It knows me with a single whiff.
Though I'd conceal myself, they'd know me in this place.   235
Come on! From flame to flame we'll make our tour,
I am the go-between, and you the wooer.
       [*To some who sit around dying embers.*]
Old gentlemen, why tarry outside? Enter!
I'd praise you if I found you in the center,
Engulfed by youthful waves and foam;   240
You are alone enough when you are home.
GENERAL   Who ever thought nations were true,
    Though you have served them with your hands and tongue;
    For people will, as women do,
    Reserve their greatest favors for the young.   245
STATESMAN   Now they are far from what is sage;
    The old ones should be kept in awe;
    For, truly, when our word was law,
    Then was indeed the golden age.
PARVENU   We, too, had surely ample wits,   250
    And often did things that we shouldn't;
    But now things are reversed and go to bits,
    Just when we changed our mind and wished they wouldn't.
AUTHOR   Today, who even looks at any book
    That makes some sense and is mature?   255
    And our younger generation—look,
    You never saw one that was so cocksure.
MEPHISTOPHELES [*Who suddenly appears very old.*]
    I think the Judgment Day must soon draw nigh,
    For this is the last time I can attend this shrine;
    And as my little cask runs dry,   260
    The world is certain to decline.
HUCKSTER-WITCH   Please, gentlemen, don't pass like that!
    Don't miss this opportunity!
    Look at my goods attentively:
    There is a lot to marvel at.   265
    And my shop has a special charm—
    You will not find its peer on earth:
    All that I sell has once done harm
    To man and world and what has worth.
    There is no dagger here which has not gored;   270
    No golden cup from which, to end a youthful life,
    A fatal poison was not poured;
    No gems that did not help to win another's wife;

---

3. I.e., he has no decoration of nobility, such as the Order of the Garter.

No sword but broke the peace with sly attack,
By stabbing, for example, a rival in the back.   275
MEPHISTOPHELES   Dear cousin, that's no good in times like these!
What's done is done; what's done is trite.
You better switch to novelties,
For novelties alone excite.
FAUST   I must not lose my head, I swear;   280
For this is what I call a fair.
MEPHISTOPHELES   This eddy whirls to get above,
And you are shoved, though you may think you shove.
FAUST   And who is that?
MEPHISTOPHELES   That little madam?
That's Lilith.[4]
FAUST   Lilith?
MEPHISTOPHELES   The first wife of Adam.   285
Watch out and shun her captivating tresses:
She likes to use her never-equaled hair
To lure a youth into her luscious lair,
And he won't lightly leave her lewd caresses.
FAUST   There two sit, one is young, one old;   290
They certainly have jumped and trolled!
MEPHISTOPHELES   They did not come here for a rest.
There is another dance. Come, let us do our best.
FAUST [*Dancing with the young one.*]
             A pretty dream once came to me
             In which I saw an apple tree;   295
             Two pretty apples gleamed on it,
             They lured me, and I climbed a bit.
THE FAIR ONE   You find the little apples nice
             Since first they grew in Paradise.
             And I am happy telling you   300
             That they grow in my garden, too.
MEPHISTOPHELES [*With the old one.*]
             A wanton dream once came to me
             In which I saw a cloven tree.
             It had the most tremendous hole;
             Though it was big, it pleased my soul.   305
THE OLD ONE   I greet you with profound delight,
             My gentle, cloven-footed knight!
             Provide the proper grafting-twig,
             If you don't mind the hole so big.
PROKTOPHANTASMIST[5]   Damnable folk! How dare you make such fuss! 310
Have we not often proved to you
That tales of walking ghosts cannot be true?
And now you dance just like the rest of us!

---

4. According to rabbinical legend, Adam's first wife; the *female* mentioned in Genesis 1.27: "So God created man in his own image, in the image of God created he him; male and female created he them." After Eve was created, Lilith became a ghost who seduced men and inflicted evil on children.   5. A German coinage meaning "Rump-ghostler." The figure caricatures Friedrich Nicolai (1733–1811), who opposed modern movements in German thought and literature and had parodied Goethe's *The Sorrows of Young Werther* (1774).

THE FAIR ONE [*Dancing.*]   What does he want at our fair?
FAUST [*Dancing.*]   Oh, he! You find him everywhere.   315
  What others dance, he must assess;
  No step has really occurred, unless
  His chatter has been duly said.
  And what annoys him most, is when we get ahead.
  If you would turn in circles, in endless repetition,   320
  As he does all the time in his old mill,
  Perhaps he would not take it ill,
  Especially if you would first get his permission.
PROKTOPHANTASMIST   You still are there! Oh no! That's without precedent.
  Please go! Have we not brought enlightenment?   325
  By our rules these devils are not daunted;
  We are so smart, but Tegel[6] is still haunted.
  To sweep illusion out, my energies were spent,
  But things never get clean; that's without precedent.
THE FAIR ONE   Why don't you stop annoying us and quit!   330
PROKTOPHANTASMIST   I tell you spirits to your face,
  The spirit's despotism's a disgrace:
  My spirit can't make rules for it.
     [*The dancing goes on.*]
  Today there's nothing I can do;
  But traveling is always fun,   335
  And I still hope, before my final step is done,
  I'll ban the devils, and the poets, too.
MEPHISTOPHELES   He'll sit down in a puddle and unbend:
  That is how his condition is improved;
  For when the leeches prosper on his fat rear end,[7]   340
  The spirits and his spirit are removed.
     [*To* FAUST, *who has left the dance.*]
  Why did you let that pretty woman go
  Who sang so nicely while you danced?
FAUST   She sang, and suddenly there pranced
  Out of her mouth a little mouse, all red.   345
MEPHISTOPHELES   That is a trifle and no cause for dread!
  Who cares? At least it was not gray.
  Why bother on this glorious lovers' day?
FAUST   Then I saw—
MEPHISTOPHELES   What?
FAUST   Mephisto, do you see
  That pale, beautiful child, alone there on the heather?   350
  She moves slowly but steadily,
  She seems to walk with her feet chained together.
  I must confess that she, forbid,
  Looks much as my good Gretchen did.
MEPHISTOPHELES   That does nobody good; leave it alone!   355
  It is a magic image, a lifeless apparition.

6. A town near Berlin, where ghosts had been reported.   7. Nicolai claimed that he had been bothered by ghosts but had repelled them by applying leeches to his rump.

Encounters are fraught with perdition;
Its icy stare turns human blood to stone
In truth, it almost petrifies;
You know the story of Medusa's[8] eyes.   360
FAUST   Those are the eyes of one that's dead I see,
No loving hand closed them to rest.
That is the breast that Gretchen offered me,
And that is the sweet body I possessed.
MEPHISTOPHELES   That is just sorcery; you're easily deceived!   365
All think she is their sweetheart and are grieved.
FAUST   What rapture! Oh, what agony!
I cannot leave her, cannot flee.
How strange, a narrow ruby band should deck,
The sole adornment, her sweet neck,   370
No wider than a knife's thin blade.
MEPHISTOPHELES   I see it, too; it is quite so.
Her head under her arm she can parade,
Since Perseus lopped it off, you know.—
Illusion holds you captive still.   375
Come, let us climb that little hill,
The Prater's[9] not so full of glee;
And if they're not bewitching me,
There is a theatre I see.
What will it be?
SERVIBILIS   They'll resume instantly.   380
We'll have the seventh play, a brand-new hit;
We do not think, so many are exacting.
An amateur has written it,
And amateurs do all the acting.
Forgive, good sirs, if now I leave you;   385
It amateurs me to draw up the curtain.
MEPHISTOPHELES   When it's on Blocksberg I perceive you,
I'm glad; for that's where you belong for certain.

WALPURGIS NIGHT'S DREAM OR THE GOLDEN WEDDING OF OBERON AND TITANIA

Intermezzo[1]

STAGE MANAGER   This time we can keep quite still,
        Mieding's[2] progeny;
        Misty vale and hoary hill,
        That's our scenery.
HERALD   To make a golden wedding day   5
        Takes fifty years to the letter;
        But when their quarrels pass away,
        That gold I like much better.

---

8. The Gorgon with hair of serpents and a glance that turned people to stone.   9. A famous park in Vienna.   1. Brief interlude. Oberon and Titania are king and queen of the fairies.   2. Johann Martin Mieding (d. 1782), a master carpenter and scene builder in the Weimar theater.

OBERON   If you spirits can be seen,
  Show yourselves tonight;   10
  Fairy king and fairy queen
  Now will reunite.

PUCK[3]   Puck is coming, turns about,
  And drags his feet to dance;
  Hundreds come behind and shout   15
  And join with him and prance.

ARIEL[4]   Ariel stirs up a song,
  A heavenly pure air;
  Many gargoyles come along,
  And many who are fair.   20

OBERON   You would get along, dear couple?
  Learn from us the art;
  If you want to keep love supple,
  You only have to part.

TITANIA   He is sulky, sullen she,   25
  Grab them, upon my soul;
  Take her to the Southern Sea,
  And him up to the pole.

ORCHESTRA TUTTI [*Fortissimo.*]   Snout of Fly, Mosquito Nose,
  With family additions,   30
  Frog O'Leaves and Crick't O'Grass,
  Those are the musicians.

SOLO   Now the bagpipe's joining in,
  A soap bubble it blows;
  Hear the snicker-snacking din   35
  Come through his blunted nose.

SPIRIT IN PROCESS OF FORMATION   Spider feet, belly of toad,
  And little wings, he'll grow 'em;
  There is no animal like that,
  But it's a little poem.   40

A LITTLE COUPLE   Mighty leaps and nimble feet,
  Through honey scent up high;
  While you bounce enough, my sweet,
  Still you cannot fly.

INQUISITIVE TRAVELER   Is that not mummery right there? 45
  Can that be what I see?
  Oberon who is so fair
  Amid this company!

ORTHODOX   No claws or tail or satyr's fleece!
  And yet you cannot cavil: 50
  Just like the gods of ancient Greece,
  He, too, must be a devil.

NORDIC ARTIST   What I do in the local clime,
  Are sketches of this tourney;
  But I prepare, while it is time,   55
  For my Italian journey.

---

3. A mischievous spirit. 4. A helpful sprite.

PURIST   Bad luck brought me to these regions:
  They could not be much louder;
  And in the bawdy witches' legions
  Two only have used powder.   60

YOUNG WITCH   White powder, just like dresses, serves
  Old hags who are out of luck;
  I want to show my luscious curves,
  Ride naked on my buck.

MATRON   Our manners, dear, are far too neat   65
  To argue and to scold;
  I only hope that young and sweet,
  Just as you are, you mold.

CONDUCTOR   Snout of Fly, Mosquito Nose,
  Leave off the naked sweet;
  Frog O'Leaves and Crick't O'Grass   70
  Get back into the beat!

WEATHERCOCK [*To one side.*]   The most exquisite company!
  Each girl should be a bride;
  The bachelors, grooms; for one can see
  How well they are allied.   75

WEATHERCOCK [*To the other side.*]   The earth should open up and gape
  To swallow this young revel,
  Or I will make a swift escape
  To hell to see the Devil.   80

XENIEN[5]   We appear as insects here,
  Each with a little stinger,
  That we may fittingly revere
  Satan, our sire and singer.

HENNINGS[6]   Look at their thronging legions play, 85
  Naïve, with little art;
  The next thing they will dare to say
  Is that they're good at heart.

MUSAGET[7]   To dwell among the witches' folk
  Seems quite a lot of fun;   90
  They are the ones I should invoke,
  Not Muses, as I've done.

CI-DEVANT GENIUS OF THE AGE[8]   Choose your friends well and you
   will zoom,
  Join in and do not pass us!
  Blocksberg has almost as much room 95
  As Germany's Parnassus.[9]

INQUISITIVE TRAVELER   Say, who is that haughty man
  Who walks as if he sits?
  He sniffs and snuffles as best he can:
  "He smells out Jesuits."   100

---

5. Literally, polemical verses written by Goethe and Friedrich von Schiller (1739–1805). The characters here are versions of Goethe himself. 6. August Adolf von Hennings (1746–1826), publisher of a journal called *Genius of the Age* that had attacked Schiller. 7. The title of a collection of Hennings's poetry. 8. I.e., "Former Genius of the Age"; probably alludes to the journal's change of title in 1800 to *Genius of the 19th Century.* 9. A mountain sacred to Apollo and the Muses; hence figuratively the locale of poetic excellence.

CRANE   I like to fish where it is clear,
      Also in muddy brew;
      That's why the pious man is here
      To mix with devils, too.

CHILD OF THE WORLD   The pious need no fancy prop,   105
      All vehicles seem sound:
      Even up here on Blocksberg's top
      Conventicles abound.

DANCERS   It seems, another choir succeeds,
      I hear the drums resuming.   110
      "That dull sound comes out of the reeds,
      It is the bitterns' booming."

BALLET MASTER   How each picks up his legs and toddles,
      And comes by hook or crook!
      The stooped one jumps, the plump one waddles: 115
      They don't know how they look!

FIDDLER   They hate each other, wretched rabble,
      And each would kill the choir;
      They're harmonized by bagpipe babble,
      As beasts by Orpheus' lyre.[1]   120

DOGMATIST   I am undaunted and resist
      Both skeptic and critique;
      The Devil simply must exist,
      Else *what* would he be? Speak!

IDEALIST   Imagination is in me   125
      Today far too despotic;
      If I am everything I see,
      Then I must be idiotic.

REALIST   The spirits' element is vexing,
      I wish it weren't there;   130
      I never saw what's so perplexing,
      It drives me to despair.

SUPERNATURALIST   I am delighted by this whir,
      And glad that they persist;
      For from the devils I infer,   135
      Good spirits, too, exist.

SKEPTIC   They follow little flames about,
      And think they're near the treasure;
      Devil alliterates with doubt
      So I am here with pleasure.   140

CONDUCTOR   Snout of Fly, Mosquito Nose,
      Damnable amateurs!
      Frog O'Leaves and Crick't O'Grass
      You are musicians, sirs!

ADEPTS   Sansouci,[2] that is the name   145
      Of our whole caboodle;
      Walking meets with ill acclaim,

---

1. In Greek mythology, Orpheus's music was said to have the power to quiet wild animals.   **2.** Without care or unhappiness (French).

So we move on our noodle.

NE'ER-DO-WELLS   We used to be good hangers-on
And sponged good wine and meat;   150
We danced till our shoes were gone,
And now walk on bare feet.

WILL-O'-THE-WISPS   We come out of the swamps where we
Were born without a penny;
But now we join the revelry,   155
As elegant as any.

SHOOTING STAR   I shot down from starry height
With brilliant, fiery charm;
But I lie in the grass tonight:
Who'll proffer me his arm?   160

MASSIVE MOB   All around, give way! Give way!
Trample down the grass!
Spirits come, and sometimes they
Form a heavy mass.

PUCK   Please don't walk like elephants,   165
And do not be so rough;
Let no one be as plump as Puck,
For he is plump enough.

ARIEL   If nature gave with lavish grace,
Or Spirit, wings and will,   170
Follow in my airy trace
Up to the roses' hill!

ORCHESTRA [*Pianissimo.*]   Floating clouds and wreaths of fog
Dawn has quickly banished;
Breeze in leaves, wind in the bog,   175
And everything has vanished.

DISMAL DAY

[*Field.* FAUST. MEPHISTOPHELES.]

FAUST   In misery! Despairing! Long lost wretchedly on the earth, and
now imprisoned! As a felon locked up in a dungeon with horrible
torments, the fair ill-fated creature! It's come to that! To that!—
Treacherous, despicable Spirit—and that you have kept from me!—
Keep standing there, stand! Roll your devilish eyes wrathfully   5
in your face! Stand and defy me with your intolerable presence!
Imprisoned! In irreparable misery! Handed over to evil spirits and
judging, unfeeling mankind! And meanwhile you soothe me with
insipid diversions; hide her growing grief from me, and let her perish
helplessly!   10

MEPHISTOPHELES   She's not the first one.

FAUST   Dog! Abominable monster!—Change him, oh infinite spirit!
Change back this worm into his dogshape, as he used to amuse
himself in the night when he trotted along before me, rolled in front
of the feet of the harmless wanderer and, when he stumbled, clung   15
to his shoulders. Change him again to his favorite form that he may
crawl on his belly in the sand before me and I may trample on him

with my feet, the caitiff!—Not the first one!—Grief! Grief! past what
a human soul can grasp, that more than one creature has sunk into
the depth of this misery, that the first one did not enough for   20
the guilt of all the others, writhing in the agony of death before the
eyes of the everforgiving one! The misery of this one woman surges
through my heart and marrow, and you grin imperturbed over the
fate of thousands!

MEPHISTOPHELES   Now we're once again at our wit's end where your   25
human minds snap. Why do you seek fellowship with us if you can't
go through with it? You would fly, but get dizzy? Did we impose on
you, or you on us?

FAUST   Don't bare your greedy teeth at me like that! It sickens me!—
Great, magnificent spirit that deigned to appear to me, that know   30
my heart and soul—why forge me to this monster who gorges himself
on harm, and on corruption—feasts.

MEPHISTOPHELES   Have you finished?

FAUST   Save her! or woe unto you! The most hideous curse upon you
for millenniums!   35

MEPHISTOPHELES   I cannot loosen the avenger's bonds, nor open his
bolts.—Save her!—Who was it that plunged her into ruin? I or you?
[FAUST *looks around furiously.*] Are you reaching for thunder? Well
that it was not given to you wretched mortals! Shattering those who
answer innocently, is the tyrant's way of easing his embarrassment.   40

FAUST   Take me there! She shall be freed!

MEPHISTOPHELES   And the dangers you risk? Know that blood-guilt
from your hand still lies on the town. Over the slain man's site avenging spirits hover, waiting for the returning murderer.

FAUST   That, too, from you? A world's murder and death upon you,   45
monster! Guide me to her, I say, and free her!

MEPHISTOPHELES   I shall guide you; hear what I can do. Do I have all
the power in the heaven and on the earth? I shall make the jailer's
senses foggy, and you may get the keys and lead her out with human
hands. I shall stand guard, magic horses shall be prepared, and   50
I shall carry you away. That I can do.

FAUST   Up and away!

NIGHT, OPEN FIELD

[FAUST *and* MEPHISTOPHELES, *storming along on black horses.*]

FAUST   What are they weaving around the Ravenstone?

MEPHISTOPHELES   I do not know what they do and brew.

FAUST   Floating to, floating fro, bowing and bending.

MEPHISTOPHELES   A witches' guild.

FAUST   They strew and dedicate.   5

MEPHISTOPHELES   Go by! Go by!

DUNGEON

FAUST [*With a bunch of keys and a lamp before a small iron gate.*]
A long unwonted shudder grips,
Mankind's entire grief grips me.

She's here, behind this wall that drips,
And all her crime was a fond fantasy.
You hesitate to go in?
You dread to see her again?   5
On! Your wavering waves on death's decree. [*He seizes the lock.*]
 [*Song from within.*]
GRETCHEN My mother, the whore,
 Who has murdered me—
 My father, the rogue,
 Who has eaten me—   10
 My little sister alone
 Picked up every bone,
 In a cool place she put them away;
 Into a fair bird I now have grown;   15
 Fly away, fly away!
FAUST [*Unlocking.*] She does not dream how her lover at the door
 Hears the clanking chains and the rustling straw. [*Enters.*]
MARGARET [*Hiding on her pallet.*] Oh! Oh! They come. Death's bitterness!
FAUST [*Softly.*] Still! Still! I come to set you free.   20
MARGARET [*Groveling toward his feet.*] If you are human, pity my distress.
FAUST You'll awaken the guards. Speak quietly.
 [*He seizes the chains to unlock them.*]
MARGARET [*On her knees.*] Who, hangman, could give
 You over me this might?
 You come for me in the middle of the night.   25
 Have pity on me, let me live!
 Is it not time when the morning chimes have rung?
  [*She gets up.*]
 I am still so young, so very young.
 And must already die.
 I was beautiful, too, and that was why.   30
 Near was the friend, now he is away.
 Torn lies the wreath, the flowers decay.
 Do not grip me so brutally. What shall I do?
 Spare me. What have I done to you?
 Let me not in vain implore.   35
 After all, I have never seen you before.
FAUST After such grief, can I live any more?
MARGARET Now I am entirely in your might.
 Only let me nurse the baby again.
 I fondled it all through the night;   40
 They took it from me to give me pain,
 And now they say I put it away.
 And I shall never again be gay.
 They sing songs about me. The people are wicked.
 An ancient fairy tale ends that way,   45
 Who made them pick it?
FAUST [*Casts himself down.*] One loving you lies at your feet
 To end your bondage. Listen, sweet!

MARGARET [*Casts herself down beside him.*]
  Ah, let us kneel, send to the saints our prayers!
  See, underneath these stairs,   50
  Underneath the sill
  There seethes hell.
  The Devil
  Makes a thundering noise
  With his angry revel.   55
FAUST [*Loud.*]   Gretchen! Gretchen!
MARGARET [*Attentively.*]   That was my lover's voice!
      [*She jumps up. The chains drop off.*]
  Where is he? I heard him call. I am free.
  No one shall hinder me.
  To his neck I shall fly,   60
  On his bosom lie.
  He called Gretchen. He stood on the sill.
  Amid the wailing and howling of hell,
  Through the angry and devilish jeers
  The sweet and loving tone touched my ears.   65
FAUST   It is I.
MARGARET   It is you. Oh, do say it again. [*She seizes him.*]
  It is he. It is he. Where, then, is all my pain?
  Where the fear of the dungeon? the chain?
  It is you. Come to save me.   70
  I am saved!
  Now I see the road again, too,
  Where, for the first time, I laid eyes on you—
  And the garden and the gate
  Where I and Martha stand and wait.   75
FAUST [*Striving away.*]   Come on! Come on!
MARGARET   O Stay!
  Because I am so happy where you are staying. [*Caresses him.*]
FAUST   Do not delay.
  If you keep on delaying,   80
  We shall have to pay dearly therefor.
MARGARET   What? You cannot kiss any more?
  My friend, you were not gone longer than this—
  And forgot how to kiss?
  Why, at your neck, do I feel such dread,   85
  When once from your eyes and from what you said
  A whole heaven surged down to fill me,
  And you would kiss me as if you wanted to kill me?
  Kiss me!
  Else I'll kiss you. [*She embraces him.*]   90
  Oh, grief! Your lips are cold,
  Are mute.
  Where
  Is your loving air?
  Who took it from me? [*She turns away from him.*]   95

FAUST   Come, follow me, dearest, and be bold!
 I shall caress you a thousandfold;
  Only follow me! That is all I plead.
MARGARET [*Turning toward him.*]   And is it you? Is it you indeed?
FAUST   It is I. Come along!   100
MARGARET   You take off the chain,
 And take me into your lap again.
  How is it that you do not shrink from me?—
  Do you know at all, my friend, whom you make free?
FAUST   Come! Come! Soon dawns the light of day.   105
MARGARET   I've put my mother away,
 I've drowned my child, don't you see?
  Was it not given to you and to me?
  You, too—it is you! Could it merely seem?
  Give me your hand! It is no dream.   110
  Your dear hand!—But alas, it is wet.
  Wipe it off! There is yet
  Blood on this one.
  Oh God! What have you done!
  Sheathe your sword;   115
  I am begging you.
FAUST   Let the past be forever past—oh Lord,
 You will kill me, too.
MARGARET   Oh no, you must outlive us!
 I'll describe the graves you should give us.   120
 Care for them and sorrow
 Tomorrow:
 Give the best place to my mother,
 And next to her lay my brother;
 Me, a little aside,   125
 Only don't make the space too wide!
 And the little one at my right breast.
 Nobody else will lie by my side.—
 Oh, to lie with you and to hide
 In your arms, what happiness!   130
 Now it is more than I can do;
 I feel, I must force myself on you,
 And you, it seems, push back my caress;
 And yet it is you, and look so pure, so devout.
FAUST   If you feel, it is I, come out!   135
MARGARET   Out where?
FAUST   Into the open.
MARGARET   If the grave is there,
 If death awaits us, then come!
 From here to the bed of eternal rest,   140
 And not a step beyond—no!
 You are leaving now? Oh, Heinrich, that I could go!
FAUST   You can! If only you would! Open stands the door.
MARGARET   I may not go; for me there is no hope any more.
 What good to flee? They lie in wait for me.   145

To have to go begging is misery,
And to have a bad conscience, too.
It is misery to stray far and forsaken,
And, anyhow, I would be taken.

FAUST   I shall stay with you.   150

MARGARET   Quick! Quick! I pray.
Save your poor child.
On! Follow the way
Along the brook,
Over the bridge,   155
Into the wood,
To the left where the planks stick
Out of the pond.
Seize it—oh, quick!
It wants to rise,   160
It is still struggling.
Save! Save!

FAUST   Can you not see,
It takes *one* step, and you are free.

MARGARET   If only we were past the hill!   165
My mother sits there on a stone,
My scalp is creeping with dread!
My mother sits there on a stone
And wags and wags her head;
She becks not, she nods not, her head is heavy and sore,   170
She has slept so long, she awakes no more.
She slept that we might embrace.
Those were the days of grace.

FAUST   In vain is my pleading, in vain what I say;
What can I do but bear you away?   175

MARGARET   Leave me! No, I shall suffer no force!
Do not grip me so murderously!
After all, I did everything else you asked.

FAUST   The day dawns. Dearest! Dearest!

MARGARET   Day. Yes, day is coming. The last day breaks;   180
It was to be my wedding day.
Tell no one that you have already been with Gretchen.
My veil! Oh pain!
It just happened that way.
We shall meet again,   185
But not dance that day.
The crowd is pushing, no word is spoken.
The alleys below
And the streets overflow.
The bell is tolling, the wand is broken.   190
How they tie and grab me, now one delivers
Me to the block and gives the sign,
And for every neck quivers
The blade that quivers for mine.
Mute lies the world as a grave.   195

FAUST   That I had never been born!
MEPHISTOPHELES [*Appears outside.*]   Up! Or you are lost.
  Prating and waiting and pointless wavering.
  My horses are quavering,
  Over the sky creeps the dawn.   200
MARGARET   What did the darkness spawn?
  He! He! Send him away!
  What does he want in this holy place?
  He wants me!
FAUST   You shall live.
MARGARET   Judgment of God! I give   205
  Myself to you.
MEPHISTOPHELES [*To* FAUST.]   Come! Come! I shall abandon you with
  her.
MARGARET   Thine I am, father. Save me!
  You angels, hosts of heaven, stir,
  Encamp about me, be my guard.   210
  Heinrich! I quail at thee.
MEPHISTOPHELES   She is judged.
VOICE [*From above.*]   Is saved.
MEPHISTOPHELES [*To* FAUST.]   Hither to me! [*Disappears with*
  FAUST.]
VOICE [*From within, fading away.*]   Heinrich! Heinrich!

WILLIAM BLAKE
1757–1827

Few works so ostentatiously "simple" as William Blake's *Songs of Innocence and of Experience* (1794) can ever have aroused such critical perplexity. Employing uncomplicated vocabulary and, often, variants of traditional ballad structure; describing the experience usually of naive subjects; supplying no obvious intellectual substance, these short lyrics have long fascinated and baffled their readers.

With no formal education, Blake, son of a London hosier, was at the age of fourteen apprenticed to the engraver James Basire. He developed both as painter and as engraver, partly influenced by the painter Henry Fuseli and the sculptor John Flaxman, both his friends, but remaining always highly individual in style and technique. An acknowledged mystic, he saw visions from the age of four: trees filled with angels, God looking at him through the window. His highly personal view of a world penetrated by the divine helped to form both his visual and his verbal art. In 1800, Blake moved from London to Felpham, where the poet William Hayley was his patron. He returned to London in 1803 and remained there for the rest of his life, married but childless, engaged in writing, printing, and engraving.

Blake felt a close relation between the visual and the verbal; he illustrated the works of many poets, notably Milton and Dante. His first book, *Poetical Sketches* (1783), was conventionally published, but he produced all of his subsequent books himself, combining pictorial engravings with lettering, striking off only a few copies of each work by hand. Gradually, in increasingly long poems, he developed an elaborate private mythology, with important figures appearing in one work after another. His major mythic poems include *The Marriage of Heaven and Hell* (1793), *America* (1793), *The Book of Los* (1795), *Milton* (1804), *Jerusalem* (1804), and *The Four Zoas* (which he never completed).

As his short poem *Mock On, Mock On, Voltaire, Rousseau* testifies, Blake was bitterly opposed to what he thought the destructive and repressive rationalism of the eighteenth century. Voltaire and Rousseau might have been surprised to find themselves thus associated; they belong together, in Blake's view, because both implicitly oppose not only orthodox Christianity but the more private variety of revealed religion so vital to Blake himself. Although, like his contemporaries, Blake idealizes imagination and emotion and believes in the sacredness of the individual, he entirely avoids the "egotistical sublime," neither speaking directly of himself in his poetry, as Wordsworth did, nor, like Goethe, creating self-absorbed characters. In his short lyrics he adopts many different voices; the difficulties of interpretation stem partly from this fact. He insistently deals with metaphysical questions about our place in the universe and with social questions about the nature of human responsibility.

In *Songs of Innocence*, the speaker is often a child: asking questions of a lamb, meditating on his own blackness, describing the experience of a chimney sweep. Ostensibly these children in their innocence feel no anger or bitterness at the realities of the world in which they find themselves. The "little black boy" ensures himself a future when the "little English boy" will resemble him and love him; the child addressing the lamb evokes a realm of pure delight; the chimney sweep comforts himself with conventional morality and with a companion's dream. When an adult observer watches children, as in *Holy Thursday*, he too sees a benign arrangement, in which children are "flowers of London town," supervised by "agèd men, wise guardians of the poor." In the *Introduction* to the volume, the adult speaker receives empowering advice from a child, who instructs him to write. Everything is for the best in this best of all possible worlds.

But not quite. Disturbing undertones reverberate through even the most "innocent" of these songs. Innocence is, after all, by definition a state automatically lost through experience and never possible to regain. If the children evoked by the text still possess their innocence, the adult reader does not. *The Little Black Boy* suggests the kind of ambiguity evoked by the conjunction between innocent speaker and experienced reader. The poem opens with a situation that the speaker does not entirely understand—but one likely to be painfully familiar to the reader. "White as an angel is the English child: / But I am black as if bereaved of light": the child's similes indicate how completely he has incorporated the value judgments of his society, in which white suggests everything good and black means deficiency and deprivation. In this context, the mother's teaching, a comforting myth, becomes comprehensible as a way of dealing with her child's bewilderment and anxiety about his difference. At the end of the poem, the boy extends his mother's story into a prophetic vision in which black means protective power ("I'll shade him from the heat till he can bear / To lean in joy upon our father's knee"), and difference disappears into likeness, hostility into love. The vision evokes an ideal situation located in an imagined afterlife; it has only an antithetical connection to present actuality. Its emphatic divergence from real social conditions creates the subterranean disturbance characteristic of Blake's lyrics, the disturbance that calls attention to the serious social criticism implicit even in lyrics that may appear sweet to the point of blandness.

For all Blake's dislike of the earlier eighteenth century, he shares with his forebears one important assumption: his poetry, too, instructs as well as pleases. The innocent chimney sweep evokes parental death and betrayal, horrifying working conditions (soot and nakedness, darkness and shaved heads), and compensatory dreams. He never complains, but when he ends with the tag "So if all do their duty, they need not fear harm," it generates moral shock. The discrepancy between the child's purity and his brutal exploitation indicts the society that allows such things. Innocence may be its own protection, these poems suggest, but that fact does not obviate social guilt.

If the *Songs of Innocence,* for all their atmosphere of brightness, cheer, and peace, convey outrage at the ways that social institutions harm those they should protect, the *Songs of Experience* more directly evoke a world worn, constricted, burdened with misery created by human beings. Now a new version of *The Chimney Sweeper* openly states what the earlier poem suggested:

> "And because I am happy, & dance & sing,
> They think they have done me no injury,
> And are gone to praise God & his Priest & King,
> Who make up a heaven of our misery."

The child understands the protective self-blinding of adults.

London in its sixteen lines sums up many of the collection's implications. Like most of the *Songs of Experience, London* presents an adult speaker, a wanderer through the city, who finds wherever he goes, in every face, "Marks of weakness, marks of woe." The city is the repository of suffering: men and infants and chimney sweepers cry; soldiers sigh; harlots curse. All are victims of corrupt institutions: blackening Church, bloody palace. Marriage and death interpenetrate; the curses of illness and corruption pass through the generations. The speaker reports only what he sees and hears, without commentary. He evokes a society in dreadful decay, and he conveys his despairing rage at a situation he cannot remedy.

Blake's lyrics, in their mixture of the visionary and the observational, strike notes far different from those of satire. Like the visionary observations of Swift and Voltaire, though, they insist on the connection between literature and life. Literature has transformative capacity, but it works with the raw material of actual experience. And its visions have the power to insist on the necessity of change.

Blake has provided material for an enormous outpouring of critical work. Particularly useful for the student are the collections of critical essays, N. Frye, ed., *Blake* (1966), and H. Adams, ed., *Critical Essays on William Blake* (1991). Valuable longer studies include M. Schorer, *William Blake: The Politics of Vision* (1946); H. Adams, *William Blake: A Reading of the Shorter Poems* (1963); E. D. Hirsch, *Innocence and Experience* (1969); D. G. Gilham, *William Blake* (1973); and S. Gardner, *Blake's Innocence and Experience Retraced* (1986). H. Bloom, ed., *William Blake* (1985), provides a useful compendium of criticism; N. Hilton, ed., *Essential Articles for the Study of William Blake* (1986), is more wide ranging. A valuable general study is E. Larrissy, *William Blake* (1985). Specifically focused on the *Songs of Innocence and Experience* are the essays by various writers in M. D. Paley, ed., *Twentieth Century Interpretations of Songs of Innocence and of Experience* (1969) and S. Gardner, *The Tyger, the Lamb, and the Terrible Desart: Songs of Innocence and of Experience in Its Times and Circumstance, Including Facsimiles of Two Copies* (1998).

SONGS OF INNOCENCE AND OF EXPERIENCE

SHEWING THE TWO CONTRARY STATES OF THE HUMAN SOUL

From *Songs of Innocence*[1]

Introduction

Piping down the valleys wild
Piping songs of pleasant glee

---

1. The text for all of Blake's works is edited by David V. Erdman and Harold Bloom. *Songs of Innocence* (1789) was later combined with *Songs of Experience* (1794), and the poems were etched and accompanied by Blake's illustrations, the process accomplished by copper engravings stamped on paper, then colored by hand.

On a cloud I saw a child,
And he laughing said to me,

"Pipe a song about a Lamb";   5
So I piped with merry chear;
"Piper pipe that song again"—
So I piped, he wept to hear.

"Drop thy pipe thy happy pipe
Sing thy songs of happy chear";   10
So I sung the same again
While he wept with joy to hear.

"Piper sit thee down and write
In a book that all may read"—
So he vanished from my sight.   15
And I plucked a hollow reed,

And I made a rural pen,
And I stained the water clear,
And I wrote my happy songs
Every child may joy to hear.   20

The Lamb

Little Lamb, who made thee?
  Dost thou know who made thee?
Gave thee life & bid thee feed,
By the stream & o'er the mead;
Gave thee clothing of delight,   5
Softest clothing wooly bright;
Gave thee such a tender voice,
Making all the vales rejoice!
  Little Lamb who made thee?
  Dost thou know who made thee?   10

Little Lamb I'll tell thee,
  Little Lamb I'll tell thee!
He is callèd by thy name,
For he calls himself a Lamb:
He is meek & he is mild,   15
He became a little child:
I a child & thou a lamb,
We are callèd by his name.[1]
  Little Lamb God bless thee.
  Little Lamb God bless thee.   20

The Little Black Boy

My mother bore me in the southern wild,
And I am black, but O! my soul is white;

1. Christians use the name of Christ to designate themselves.

784 / William Blake

White as an angel is the English child:
But I am black as if bereaved of light.

My mother taught me underneath a tree,
And sitting down before the heat of day,
She took me on her lap and kissèd me,
And pointing to the east, began to say:

"Look on the rising sun: there God does live,
And gives his light, and gives his heat away;
And flowers and trees and beasts and men receive
Comfort in morning, joy in the noon day.

"And we are put on earth a little space,
That we may learn to bear the beams of love,
And these black bodies and this sun-burnt face
Is but a cloud, and like a shady grove.

"For when our souls have learned the heat to bear,
The cloud will vanish; we shall hear his voice,
Saying: 'Come out from the grove, my love & care,
And round my golden tent like lambs rejoice.' "

Thus did my mother say, and kissèd me;
And thus I say to little English boy:
When I from black and he from white cloud free,
And round the tent of God like lambs we joy,

I'll shade him from the heat till he can bear
To lean in joy upon our father's knee;
And then I'll stand and stroke his silver hair,
And be like him, and he will then love me.

Holy Thursday[1]

'Twas on a Holy Thursday, their innocent faces clean,
The children walking two & two, in red & blue & green,[2]
Grey headed beadles[3] walked before with wands as white as snow,
Till into the high dome of Paul's they like Thames' waters flow.

O what a multitude they seemed, these flowers of London town!
Seated in companies they sit with radiance all their own.
The hum of multitudes was there, but multitudes of lambs,
Thousands of little boys & girls raising their innocent hands.

Now like a mighty wind they raise to heaven the voice of song,
Or like harmonious thunderings the seats of heaven among.
Beneath them sit the agèd men, wise guardians[4] of the poor;
Then cherish pity, lest you drive an angel from your door.[5]

---

1. Ascension Day, forty days after Easter, when children from charity schools were marched to St. Paul's Cathedral.   2. Each school had its own distinctive uniform.   3. Ushers and minor functionaries, whose job was to maintain order.   4. The governors of the charity schools.   5. See Hebrews 13.2: "Be not forgetful to entertain strangers: for thereby some have entertained angels unawares."

The Chimney Sweeper

When my mother died I was very young,
And my father sold me[1] while yet my tongue
Could scarcely cry " 'weep![2] 'weep! 'weep! 'weep!"
So your chimneys I sweep & in soot I sleep.

There's little Tom Dacre, who cried when his head   5
That curled like a lamb's back, was shaved, so I said,
"Hush, Tom! never mind it, for when your head's bare,
You know that the soot cannot spoil your white hair."

And so he was quiet, & that very night,
As Tom was a-sleeping he had such a sight!   10
That thousands of sweepers, Dick, Joe, Ned, & Jack,
Were all of them locked up in coffins of black;

And by came an Angel who had a bright key,
And he opened the coffins & set them all free;
Then down a green plain, leaping, laughing they run,   15
And wash in a river and shine in the Sun;

Then naked[3] & white, all their bags left behind,
They rise upon clouds, and sport in the wind.
And the Angel told Tom, if he'd be a good boy,
He'd have God for his father & never want joy.   20

And so Tom awoke; and we rose in the dark
And got with our bags & our brushes to work.
Tho' the morning was cold, Tom was happy & warm;
So if all do their duty, they need not fear harm.

From *Songs of Experience*

Introduction

Hear the voice of the Bard!
Who Present, Past, & Future sees;
Whose ears have heard
The Holy Word
That walked among the ancient trees;[1]   5

Calling the lapsèd Soul
And weeping in the evening dew;[2]
That might control
The starry pole,
And fallen, fallen light renew!   10

1. It was common practice in Blake's day for fathers to sell, or indenture, their children to become chimney sweeps. The average age at which such children began working was six or seven; they were generally employed for seven years, until they were too big to ascend the chimneys.   2. The child's lisping effort to say "sweep," as he walks the streets looking for work.   3. They climbed up the chimneys naked.
1. Genesis 3.8: "And [Adam and Eve] heard the voice of the Lord God walking in the garden in the cool of the day."   2. Blake's ambiguous use of pronouns makes for interpretative difficulties. It would seem that *The Holy Word* (Jehovah, a name for God in the Old Testament) calls *the lapsèd Soul*, and weeps— not the Bard.

"O Earth, O Earth, return!
Arise from out the dewy grass;
Night is worn,
And the morn
Rises from the slumberous mass.   15

"Turn away no more;
Why wilt thou turn away?
The starry floor
The watery shore
Is given thee till the break of day."   20

Earth's Answer

Earth raised up her head,
From the darkness dread & drear.
Her light fled:
Stony dread!
And her locks covered with grey despair.   5

"Prisoned on watery shore
Starry Jealousy does keep my den,
Cold and hoar
Weeping o'er
I hear the Father[1] of the ancient men.   10

"Selfish father of men,
Cruel, jealous, selfish fear!
Can delight
Chained in night
The virgins of youth and morning bear?   15

"Does spring hide its joy
When buds and blossoms grow?
Does the sower
Sow by night,
Or the plowman in darkness plow?   20

"Break this heavy chain
That does freeze my bones around;
Selfish! vain!
Eternal bane!
That free Love with bondage bound."   25

The Tyger

Tyger! Tyger! burning bright
In the forests of the night,

---

1. In Blake's later prophetic works, one of the four Zoas, representing the four chief faculties of humankind, is Urizen. In general, he stands for the orthodox conception of the Divine Creator, sometimes Jehovah in the Old Testament, often the God conceived by Newton and Locke—in all instances a tyrant associated with excessive rationalism and sexual repression, and the opponent of the imagination and creativity. This may be "the Holy Word" in line 4 of *Introduction* (p. 785).

What immortal hand or eye
Could frame thy fearful symmetry?

In what distant deeps or skies   5
Burnt the fire of thine eyes?
On what wings dare he aspire?
What the hand dare seize the fire?

And what shoulder, & what art,
Could twist the sinews of thy heart?   10
And when thy heart began to beat,
What dread hand? & what dread feet?

What the hammer? what the chain?
In what furnace was thy brain?
What the anvil? what dread grasp   15
Dare its deadly terrors clasp?

When the stars threw down their spears,
And watered heaven with their tears,
Did he smile his work to see?
Did he who made the Lamb make thee?   20

Tyger! Tyger! burning bright
In the forests of the night,
What immortal hand or eye
Dare frame thy fearful symmetry?

The Sick Rose

O Rose, thou art sick.
The invisible worm
That flies in the night
In the howling storm

Has found out thy bed   5
Of crimson joy,
And his dark secret love
Does thy life destroy.

London

I wander thro' each chartered¹ street,
Near where the chartered Thames does flow,
And mark in every face I meet
Marks of weakness, marks of woe.

In every cry of every Man,   5
In every Infant's cry of fear,
In every voice, in every ban,
The mind-forged manacles I hear:

---

1. Hired (literally). Blake implies that the streets and the river are controlled by commercial interests.

How the Chimney-sweeper's cry
Every blackening Church appalls;[2]   10
And the hapless Soldier's sigh
Runs in blood down Palace walls.

But most thro' midnight streets I hear
How the youthful Harlot's curse
Blasts the new-born Infant's tear,[3]   15
And blights with plagues the Marriage hearse.

The Chimney Sweeper

A little black thing among the snow
Crying " 'weep, 'weep," in notes of woe!
"Where are thy father & mother? say?"
"They are both gone up to the church to pray.

"Because I was happy upon the heath,   5
And smiled among the winter's snow;
They clothèd me in the clothes of death,
And taught me to sing the notes of woe.

"And because I am happy, & dance & sing,
They think they have done me no injury,   10
And are gone to praise God & his Priest & King,
Who make up a heaven of our misery."

Mock On, Mock On, Voltaire, Rousseau

Mock on, Mock on, Voltaire, Rousseau;
Mock on, Mock on, 'tis all in vain.
You throw the sand against the wind,
And the wind blows it back again.

And every sand becomes a Gem   5
Reflected in the beams divine;
Blown back, they blind the mocking Eye,
But still in Israel's paths they shine.

The Atoms of Democritus[1]
And Newton's Particles of light[2]   10
Are sands upon the Red sea shore,
Where Israel's tents do shine so bright.

---

2. Makes white (literally), punning also on *appall* (to dismay) and *pall* (the cloth covering a corpse or bier).
3. The harlot infects the parents with venereal disease, and thus the infant is inflicted with neonatal blindness.   1. Greek philosopher (460?–362? B.C.), who advanced a theory that all things are merely patterns of atoms.   2. Sir Isaac Newton's (1642–1727) corpuscular theory of light. For Blake, both men were condemned as materialists.

And Did Those Feet

And did those feet in ancient time
Walk upon England's mountains green?[1]
And was the holy Lamb of God
On England's pleasant pastures seen?

And did the Countenance Divine   5
Shine forth upon our clouded hills?
And was Jerusalem builded here,
Among those dark Satanic Mills?[2]

Bring me my Bow of burning gold:
Bring me my Arrows of desire: 10
Bring me my Spear: O clouds unfold!
Bring me my Chariot of fire!

I will not cease from Mental Fight,
Nor shall my Sword sleep in my hand,
Till we have built Jerusalem   15
In England's green & pleasant Land.

1. A reference to an ancient legend that Jesus came to England with Joseph of Arimathea.   2. Possibly industrial England, but *mills* also meant for Blake 18th-century arid, mechanistic philosophy.

WILLIAM WORDSWORTH
1770–1850

William Wordsworth both proclaimed and embodied the *newness* of the Romantic movement. In his preface to the second edition of *Lyrical Ballads* (1800), a collection of poems by him and his friend Samuel Taylor Coleridge, he announced the advent of a poetic revolution. Like other revolutionaries, Wordsworth and Coleridge created their identities by rebelling against and travestying their predecessors. Now no longer would poets write in "dead" forms; now they had discovered a "new" direction, "new" subject matter; now poetry could at last serve as an important form of human communication. Reading Wordsworth's poems with the excitement of that revolution long past, we can still feel the power of his desire to communicate. The human heart is his subject; he writes, in particular, of growth and of memory and of the perplexities inherent in the human condition.

Born at Cockermouth, Cumberland, to the family of an attorney, Wordsworth attended St. John's College, Cambridge, from 1787 to 1791. The next year, early in the French Revolution, he spent in France, where he met Annette Vallon and had a daughter by her. In 1795, Wordsworth met Coleridge; two years later, Wordsworth and his sister, Dorothy, moved to Alfoxden, near Coleridge's home in Nether Stowey, in the county of Somerset. There the two men conceived the idea of collaboration; in 1798, the first edition of their *Lyrical Ballads* appeared, anonymously. The next year, Wordsworth and his sister settled in the Lake District of northwest England. In 1802, the poet married Mary Hutchinson, with whom he had five children. He received the sinecure of stamp distributor in 1813 and in 1843 succeeded Robert

Southey as England's poet laureate, having long since abandoned the political radicalism of his youth.

Wordsworth wrote little prose, except for the famous preface of 1800 and another preface in 1815; his accomplishment was almost entirely poetic. His early work employed conventional eighteenth-century techniques, but *Lyrical Ballads* marked a new direction: an effort to employ simple language and to reveal the high significance of simple themes, the transcendent importance of the everyday. Between 1798 and 1805 he composed his nineteenth-century version of an epic, *The Prelude*, an account of the development of a poet's mind—his own. His subsequent work included odes, sonnets, and many poems written to mark specific occasions.

It would be difficult to overestimate the extent of Wordsworth's historical and poetic importance. In *The Prelude*, not published until 1850, he not only made powerful poetry out of his own experience but also specified a way of valuing experience:

> There are in our existence spots of time,
> That with distinct pre-eminence retain
> A renovating virtue, whence, depressed
> By false opinion and contentious thought,
> Or aught of heavier or more deadly weight,
> In trivial occupations, and the round
> Of ordinary intercourse, our minds
> Are nourished and invisibly repaired;
> A virtue, by which pleasure is enhanced,
> That penetrates, enables us to mount
> When high, more high, and lifts us up when fallen.

To take seriously the moment, this passage suggests, enables us to resist the dulling force of everyday life ("trivial occupations") and provides the means of personal salvation.

Wordsworth often uses religious language (a religious reference is hinted in the idea of being lifted up when fallen) to insist on the importance of his doctrine. He inaugurated an attempt—lasting far into the century—to establish and sustain a secular religion to substitute for Christian faith. The attempt was, even for Wordsworth, only intermittently successful. *The Prelude* records experiences of persuasive visionary intensity, as when the poet speaks of seeing a shepherd in the distance:

> Or him have I descried in distant sky,
> A solitary object and sublime,
> Above all height! like an aerial cross
> Stationed alone upon a spiry rock
> Of the Chartreuse, for worship.

But such "spots of time" exist in isolation; it is difficult to maintain a saving faith on their basis.

The two long poems printed here treat the problem of discovering and sustaining faith. *Lines Composed a Few Miles Above Tintern Abbey*, first published in *Lyrical Ballads*, and *Ode on Intimations of Immortality*, published in 1807 but written between 1802 and 1806, share a preoccupation with loss and with the saving power of memory. Both speak of personal experience, although the ode, a more formal poem, also generalizes to a hypothetical "we." Both insist that nature—the external world experienced through the senses and the containing pattern assumed beyond that world—offers the possibility of wisdom to combat the pain inherent in human growth.

But it would be a mistake to assume that the poems exist to promulgate a doctrine of natural salvation, although some readers have considered their "pantheism" (the belief that God pervades every part of His created universe) their most important aspect. Both poems evoke an intellectual and emotional process, not a conclusion; they sketch dramas of human development.

In *Tintern Abbey*, the speaker conveys his relief at returning to a sylvan scene that has been important to him in memory. His recollections of this natural beauty, he says, have helped sustain him in the confusion and weariness of city life; he thinks they may also have encouraged him toward goodness and serenity. But this second suggestion, that memories of nature have a moral effect, is only hypothetical, qualified in the text by such words and phrases as "I trust" and "perhaps." Indeed, the poem's next section opens with explicit statement that this may "Be but a vain belief." True or false, though, the belief comforts the speaker, who then recalls his more direct relation with nature in the past, when "The sounding cataract / Haunted me like a passion." He hopes, but cannot quite be sure, that his present awareness of "the still, sad music of humanity" and of the great "presence" that infuses nature compensates for what he has sacrificed in losing the immediacy of youthful experience.

The last section of *Tintern Abbey* emphasizes still more that the speaker is struggling with depression over his sense of loss; he observes that the presence of his "dearest Friend," his sister, would protect his "genial spirits" from decay even without his faith in what he has learned. That sister now becomes the focus for his thoughts about nature; he imagines her growth as like his own, but perfected, and her power of memory as able to contain not only the beauties of the landscape but his presence as part of that landscape. The poem thus resolves itself with emphasis on a human relationship, between the man and his sister, as well as on the importance of nature. Its emotional power derives partly from its evocation of the *need* to believe in nature as a form of salvation and of the process of development through which that need manifests itself.

At about the same time that he wrote the *Ode on Intimations of Immortality*, Wordsworth composed his sonnet *The World Is Too Much with Us*:

> . . . we lay waste our powers
> Little we see in Nature that is ours;
> . . . we are out of tune.

Despite the rhapsodic tone that dominates the ode, it too reveals itself as a hard-won act of faith, an effort to combat the view of the present world conveyed in the sonnet.

The ode opens with insistence on loss: "The things which I have seen I now can see no more." The speaker feels grief; he tries to deny it, because it seems at odds with the harmony and joy of the natural world. Yet the effort fails: even natural beauty speaks to him of what he no longer possesses. Stanzas V through VIII emphasize the association of infancy with natural communion and the inevitable deprivation attending growth. In stanza IX, the speaker attempts to value what still remains to him: it's all he has, he's grateful for it. In the concluding stanzas, however, he arrives at a new revelation: now nature acquires value not as a form of unmixed ecstasy, but in connection with the experience of human suffering:

> Though nothing can bring back the hour
> Of splendour in the grass, of glory in the flower;
>   We will grieve not, rather find
>   Strength in what remains behind; . . .
>   In the soothing thoughts that spring
>   Out of human suffering . . .

It is "the human heart by which we live" that finally enables the poet to experience the wonder of a flower, now become the source of "Thoughts that do often lie too deep for tears."

The view that the processes of maturing involve giving up a kind of wisdom accessible only to children belongs particularly to the Romantic period, but most people at least occasionally feel that in growing up they have left behind something they would rather keep. Wordsworth's poetic expression of the effort to come to terms with such feelings may remind his readers of barely noticed aspects of their own experience.

G. M. Harper, *Wordsworth* (1916–1929), remains the standard biography. More recent biographical studies include J. L. Mahoney, *William Wordsworth: A Poetic Life* (1997), and K. R. Johnston, *The Hidden Wordsworth: Poet, Lover, Rebel, Spy* (1998), which incorporates important readings of Wordsworth's poetry as well as new biographical data. Significant critical works are G. Hartman, *Wordsworth's Poetry* (1964); A. Bewell, *Wordsworth and the Enlightenment: Nature, Man, and Society in the Experimental Poetry* (1989); J. W. Page, *Wordsworth and the Cultivation of Women* (1994); R. E. Matlak, *The Poetry of Relationship: The Wordsworths and Coleridge, 1797–1800* (1997); and Y. Liu, *Poetics and Politics: The Revolutions of Wordsworth* (1999). A useful collection of critical essays is G. Gilpin, ed., *Critical Essays on William Wordsworth* (1990).

PRONOUNCING GLOSSARY

The following list uses common English syllables and stress accents to provide rough equivalents of selected words whose pronunciation may be unfamiliar to the general reader.

Proteus: *proh'-tee-us*   Triton: *try'-tun*

[POEMS]

Lines Composed a Few Miles Above Tintern Abbey

On Revisiting the Banks of the Wye During a Tour, July 13, 1798

Five years have past; five summers, with the length
Of five long winters! and again I hear
These waters, rolling from their mountain-springs
With a soft inland murmur.—Once again
Do I behold these steep and lofty cliffs,   5
That on a wild secluded scene impress
Thoughts of more deep seclusion; and connect
The landscape with the quiet of the sky.
The day is come when I again repose
Here, under this dark sycamore, and view   10
These plots of cottage-ground, these orchard-tufts,
Which at this season, with their unripe fruits,
Are clad in one green hue, and lose themselves
'Mid groves and copses. Once again I see
These hedge-rows, hardly hedge-rows, little lines   15
Of sportive wood run wild: these pastoral farms,
Green to the very door; and wreaths of smoke
Sent up, in silence, from among the trees!
With some uncertain notice, as might seem
Of vagrant dwellers in the houseless woods,   20
Or of some Hermit's cave, where by his fire
The Hermit sits alone.

                These beauteous forms,
Through a long absence, have not been to me
As is a landscape to a blind man's eye:
But oft, in lonely rooms, and 'mid the din   25
Of towns and cities, I have owed to them,
In hours of weariness, sensations sweet,

Felt in the blood, and felt along the heart;
And passing even into my purer mind,
With tranquil restoration:—feelings too   30
Of unremembered pleasure: such, perhaps,
As have no slight or trivial influence
On that best portion of a good man's life,
His little, nameless, unremembered, acts
Of kindness and of love. Nor less, I trust,   35
To them I may have owed another gift,
Of aspect more sublime; that blessèd mood,
In which the burthen of the mystery,
In which the heavy and the weary weight
Of all this unintelligible world,   40
Is lightened:—that serene and blessèd mood,
In which the affections gently lead us on,—
Until, the breath of this corporeal frame
And even the motion of our human blood
Almost suspended, we are laid asleep   45
In body, and become a living soul:
While with an eye made quiet by the power
Of harmony, and the deep power of joy,
We see into the life of things.

                    If this
Be but a vain belief, yet, oh! how oft—   50
In darkness and amid the many shapes
Of joyless daylight; when the fretful stir
Unprofitable, and the fever of the world,
Have hung upon the beatings of my heart—
How oft, in spirit, have I turned to thee,   55
O sylvan Wye! thou wanderer thro' the woods,
How often has my spirit turned to thee!

    And now, with gleams of half-extinguished thought,
With many recognitions dim and faint,
And somewhat of a sad perplexity,   60
The picture of the mind revives again:
While here I stand, not only with the sense
Of present pleasure, but with pleasing thoughts
That in this moment there is life and food
For future years. And so I dare to hope,   65
Though changed, no doubt, from what I was when first
I came among these hills; when like a roe
I bounded o'er the mountains, by the sides
Of the deep rivers, and the lonely streams,
Wherever nature led: more like a man   70
Flying from something that he dreads, than one
Who sought the thing he loved. For nature then
(The coarser pleasures of my boyish days,
And their glad animal movements all gone by)
To me was all in all.—I cannot paint   75
What then I was. The sounding cataract
Haunted me like a passion: the tall rock,

The mountain, and the deep and gloomy wood,
Their colours and their forms, were then to me
An appetite; a feeling and a love,   80
That had no need of a remoter charm,
By thought supplied, nor any interest
Unborrowed from the eye.—That time is past,
And all its aching joys are now no more,
And all its dizzy raptures. Not for this   85
Faint I, nor mourn nor murmur; other gifts
Have followed; for such loss, I would believe,
Abundant recompense. For I have learned
To look on nature, not as in the hour
Of thoughtless youth; but hearing oftentimes   90
The still, sad music of humanity,
Nor harsh nor grating, though of ample power
To chasten and subdue. And I have felt
A presence that disturbs me with the joy
Of elevated thoughts; a sense sublime   95
Of something far more deeply interfused,
Whose dwelling is the light of setting suns,
And the round ocean and the living air,
And the blue sky, and in the mind of man:
A motion and a spirit, that impels   100
All thinking things, all objects of all thought,
And rolls through all things. Therefore am I still
A lover of the meadows and the woods,
And mountains; and of all that we behold
From this green earth; of all the mighty world   105
Of eye, and ear,—both what they half create,
And what perceive; well pleased to recognise
In nature and the language of the sense,
The anchor of my purest thoughts, the nurse,
The guide, the guardian of my heart, and soul   110
Of all my moral being.

                            Nor perchance,
If I were not thus taught, should I the more
Suffer my genial[1] spirits to decay:
For thou art with me here upon the banks
Of this fair river; thou my dearest Friend,   115
My dear, dear Friend; and in thy voice I catch
The language of my former heart, and read
My former pleasures in the shooting lights
Of thy wild eyes. Oh! yet a little while
May I behold in thee what I was once,   120
My dear, dear Sister! and this prayer I make,
Knowing that Nature never did betray
The heart that loved her; 'tis her privilege,
Through all the years of this our life, to lead
From joy to joy: for she can so inform   125

1. Generative, creative.

The mind that is within us, so impress
With quietness and beauty, and so feed
With lofty thoughts, that neither evil tongues,
Rash judgments, nor the sneers of selfish men,
Nor greetings where no kindness is, nor all   130
The dreary intercourse of daily life,
Shall e'er prevail against us, or disturb
Our cheerful faith, that all which we behold
Is full of blessings. Therefore let the moon
Shine on thee in thy solitary walk;   135
And let the misty mountain-winds be free
To blow against thee: and, in after years,
When these wild ecstasies shall be matured
Into a sober pleasure; when thy mind
Shall be a mansion for all lovely forms,   140
Thy memory be as a dwelling-place
For all sweet sounds and harmonies; oh! then,
If solitude, or fear, or pain, or grief
Should be thy portion, with what healing thoughts
Of tender joy wilt thou remember me,   145
And these my exhortations! Nor, perchance—
If I should be where I no more can hear
Thy voice, nor catch from thy wild eyes these gleams
Of past existence—wilt thou then forget
That on the banks of this delightful stream   150
We stood together; and that I, so long
A worshipper of Nature, hither came
Unwearied in that service; rather say
With warmer love—oh! with far deeper zeal
Of holier love. Nor wilt thou then forget   155
That after many wanderings, many years
Of absence, these steep woods and lofty cliffs,
And this green pastoral landscape, were to me
More dear, both for themselves and for thy sake!

Ode on Intimations of Immortality

From Recollections of Early Childhood

> The Child is father of the Man;
> And I could wish my days to be
> Bound each to each by natural piety.

I

There was a time when meadow, grove, and stream,
The earth, and every common sight,
        To me did seem
        Apparelled in celestial light,
The glory and the freshness of a dream.   5
It is not now as it hath been of yore;—

Turn wheresoe'er I may,
    By night or day,
The things which I have seen I now can see no more.

II

The Rainbow comes and goes,   10
And lovely is the Rose;
The Moon doth with delight
Look round her when the heavens are bare,
    Waters on a starry night
    Are beautiful and fair;   15
The sunshine is a glorious birth;
But yet I know, where'er I go,
That there hath past away a glory from the earth.

III

Now, while the birds thus sing a joyous song,
    And while the young lambs bound   20
        As to the tabor's sound,
To me alone there came a thought of grief:
A timely utterance gave that thought relief,
    And I again am strong:
The cataracts blow their trumpets from the steep;   25
No more shall grief of mine the season wrong;
I hear the Echoes through the mountains throng,
The Winds come to me from the fields of sleep,
    And all the earth is gay;
        Land and sea   30
    Give themselves up to jollity,
        And with the heart of May
Doth every Beast keep holiday;—
        Thou Child of Joy,
Shout round me, let me hear thy shouts, thou happy   35
    Shepherd-boy!

IV

Ye blessèd Creatures, I have heard the call
    Ye to each other make; I see
The heavens laugh with you in your jubilee;
    My heart is at your festival,   40
    My head hath its coronal,
The fulness of your bliss, I feel—I feel it all.
        Oh evil day! if I were sullen
        While Earth herself is adorning,
            This sweet May-morning,   45
        And the Children are culling
            On every side,
    In a thousand valleys far and wide,
    Fresh flowers; while the sun shines warm,

And the Babe leaps up on his Mother's arm:— 50
   I hear, I hear, with joy I hear!
   —But there's a Tree, of many, one,
A single Field which I have looked upon,
Both of them speak of something that is gone:
     The Pansy at my feet 55
     Doth the same tale repeat:
Whither is fled the visionary gleam?
Where is it now, the glory and the dream?

V

Our birth is but a sleep and a forgetting:
The Soul that rises with us, our life's Star, 60
   Hath had elsewhere its setting,
     And cometh from afar:
   Not in entire forgetfulness,
   And not in utter nakedness,
But trailing clouds of glory do we come 65
   From God, who is our home:
Heaven lies about us in our infancy!
Shades of the prison-house begin to close
   Upon the growing Boy,
But He beholds the light, and whence it flows, 70
   He sees it in his joy;
The Youth, who daily farther from the east
   Must travel, still is Nature's Priest,
   And by the vision splendid
   Is on his way attended; 75
At length the Man perceives it die away,
And fade into the light of common day.

VI

Earth fills her lap with pleasures of her own;
Yearnings she hath in her own natural kind,
And, even with something of a Mother's mind, 80
   And no unworthy aim,
   The homely Nurse doth all she can
To make her Foster-child, her Inmate, Man,
   Forget the glories he hath known,
And that imperial palace whence he came. 85

VII

Behold the Child among his new-born blisses,
A six years' Darling of a pigmy size!
See, where 'mid work of his own hand he lies,
Fretted by sallies of his mother's kisses,
With light upon him from his father's eyes! 90
See, at his feet, some little plan or chart,
Some fragment from his dream of human life,

Shaped by himself with newly-learnèd art;
  A wedding or a festival,
  A mourning or a funeral;   95
    And this hath now his heart,
And unto this he frames his song:
    Then will he fit his tongue
To dialogues of business, love, or strife;
  But it will not be long   100
  Ere this be thrown aside,
  And with new joy and pride
The little Actor cons another part;
Filling from time to time his "humorous stage"
With all the Persons, down to palsied Age,   105
That Life brings with her in her equipage;
    As if his whole vocation
    Were endless imitation.

               VIII

Thou, whose exterior semblance doth belie
    Thy Soul's immensity;   110
Thou best Philosopher, who yet dost keep
Thy heritage, thou Eye among the blind,
That, deaf and silent, read'st the eternal deep,
Haunted for ever by the eternal mind,—
    Mighty Prophet! Seer blest!   115
    On whom those truths do rest,
Which we are toiling all our lives to find,
In darkness lost, the darkness of the grave;
Thou, over whom thy Immortality
Broods like the Day, a Master o'er a Slave,   120
A Presence which is not to be put by;
      [To whom the grave
Is but a lonely bed without the sense or sight
    Of day or the warm light,
A place of thought where we in waiting lie;][1]   125
Thou little Child, yet glorious in the might
Of heaven-born freedom on thy being's height,
Why with such earnest pains dost thou provoke
The years to bring the inevitable yoke,
Thus blindly with thy blessedness at strife?   130
Full soon thy Soul shall have her earthly freight,
And custom lie upon thee with a weight,
Heavy as frost, and deep almost as life!

               IX

    O joy! that in our embers
    Is something that doth live,   135

---

1. The lines within brackets were included in the *Ode* in the 1807 and 1815 editions of Wordsworth's poems but were omitted in the 1820 and subsequent editions, as a result of Coleridge's severe censure of them.

That nature yet remembers
    What was so fugitive!
The thought of our past years in me doth breed
Perpetual benediction: not indeed
For that which is most worthy to be blest;   140
Delight and liberty, the simple creed
Of Childhood, whether busy or at rest,
With new-fledged hope still fluttering in his breast—
    Not for these I raise
    The song of thanks and praise;   145
  But for those obstinate questionings
  Of sense and outward things,
  Fallings from us, vanishings;
  Blank misgivings of a Creature
Moving about in worlds not realized,   150
High instincts before which our mortal Nature
Did tremble like a guilty Thing surprised:
    But for those first affections,
    Those shadowy recollections,
  Which, be they what they may,   155
Are yet the fountain-light of all our day,
Are yet a master-light of all our seeing;
  Uphold us, cherish, and have power to make
Our noisy years seem moments in the being
Of the eternal Silence: truths that wake,   160
    To perish never;
Which neither listlessness, nor mad endeavour,
    Nor Man nor Boy,
Nor all that is at enmity with joy,
Can utterly abolish or destroy!   165
  Hence in a season of calm weather
    Though inland far we be,
Our Souls have sight of that immortal sea
    Which brought us hither,
  Can in a moment travel thither,   170
And see the Children sport upon the shore,
And hear the mighty waters rolling evermore.

X

Then sing, ye Birds, sing, sing a joyous song!
    And let the young Lambs bound
    As to the tabor's sound!   175
We in thought will join your throng,
    Ye that pipe and ye that play,
    Ye that through your hearts to-day
    Feel the gladness of the May!
What though the radiance which was once so bright   180
Be now for ever taken from my sight,
  Though nothing can bring back the hour
Of splendour in the grass, of glory in the flower;
    We will grieve not, rather find

Strength in what remains behind; 185
In the primal sympathy
Which having been must ever be;
In the soothing thoughts that spring
Out of human suffering;
In the faith that looks through death, 190
In years that bring the philosophic mind.

XI

And O, ye Fountains, Meadows, Hills, and Groves,
Forebode not any severing of our loves!
Yet in my heart of hearts I feel your might;
I only have relinquished one delight 195
To live beneath your more habitual sway.
I love the Brooks which down their channels fret,
Even more than when I tripped lightly as they;
The innocent brightness of a new-born Day
    Is lovely yet; 200
The Clouds that gather round the setting sun
Do take a sober colouring from an eye
That hath kept watch o'er man's mortality;
Another race hath been, and other palms are won.
Thanks to the human heart by which we live, 205
Thanks to its tenderness, its joys, and fears,
To me the meanest flower that blows can give
Thoughts that do often lie too deep for tears.

Composed upon Westminster Bridge,
September 3, 1802

Earth has not anything to show more fair:
Dull would he be of soul who could pass by
A sight so touching in its majesty;
This City now doth, like a garment, wear
The beauty of the morning; silent, bare, 5
Ships, towers, domes, theatres, and temples lie
Open unto the fields, and to the sky;
All bright and glittering in the smokeless air.
Never did sun more beautifully steep
In his first splendour, valley, rock, or hill; 10
Ne'er saw I, never felt, a calm so deep!
The river glideth at his own sweet will:
Dear God! the very houses seem asleep;
And all that mighty heart is lying still!

The World Is Too Much with Us

The world is too much with us; late and soon,
Getting and spending, we lay waste our powers:

Little we see in Nature that is ours;
We have given our hearts away, a sordid boon![1]
This Sea that bares her bosom to the moon, 5
The winds that will be howling at all hours,
And are up-gathered now like sleeping flowers;
For this, for everything, we are out of tune;
It moves us not.—Great God! I'd rather be
A Pagan suckled in a creed outworn; 10
So might I, standing on this pleasant lea,
Have glimpses that would make me less forlorn;
Have sight of Proteus[2] rising from the sea;
Or hear old Triton[3] blow his wreathèd horn.

---

1. Gift. *Sordid:* refers to the act of giving the heart away.　　2. An old man of the sea who, in the *Odyssey*, could assume a variety of shapes.　　3. A sea deity, usually represented as blowing on a conch shell.

DOROTHY WORDSWORTH
1771–1855

The era inaugurated by Jean-Jacques Rousseau encouraged self-reflection and the development of a highly articulated language of feeling. Among the writers about themselves who flourished during the period of Romanticism, Dorothy Wordsworth occupies a unique position. Her voluminous journals include relatively little open discussion of her personal feelings. Instead, she perfects a technique of indirect self-revelation through intense concentration on details of the world outside her.

In her youth, Dorothy Wordsworth was separated from her four brothers after the death of their mother when Dorothy was seven years old. In 1795, however, her brother William was lent a house in Dorset, where she joined him, acting as homemaker. From that time on, she lived with William, even after he married in 1802. Like William, she became close to Samuel Taylor Coleridge, and she accompanied the two men to Germany in 1798–99. As the journals reveal, she led a quiet domestic life. After a serious illness in 1829, she was an invalid for the rest of her life.

The Grasmere Journals, from which the selections printed here are taken, record the texture of Dorothy's daily existence with William at Dove Cottage, Grasmere, in the English Lake District. The two of them had moved there in 1799, taking pleasure in the first home they had owned. They lived close to Grasmere Lake, in a landscape of hills, mountains, woods, and water of striking beauty, through which they walked almost every day. They also created a garden, transplanting plants from the wild. William wrote poems; Dorothy copied them out for him. She made bread and pies, sewed, read aloud and to herself. She enjoyed her association with their neighbors, as well as the more intense friendship with Coleridge and with the Hutchinson sisters—Mary, whom William married, and Sara, with whom Coleridge, already married and the father of two sons, fell disastrously in love. The journals report these facts in considerable detail.

But they do far more. Wordsworth responded to what she saw with the eye of a poet. She noted the precise aspects of flowers; the names of birds; and the look of the clouds on a summer day, of the fleece on sheep, of the moon in its varying appearances. Seldom does she write in any detail directly of her own emotions. The characteristic sequence of the *Journals* printed here includes only one moment of sharp, open self-revelation: "I shall be beloved—I want no more." Unlike Rousseau, Wordsworth does not appear to consider herself remarkable. But she uses the minute particulars of what she sees as an indirect means of expressing feeling, and the *Journals* convey an emotional life of subtle complexity. Thus she describes crows flying: "We watched the crows at a little distance from us become white as silver as they flew in the sunshine, and when they went still further they looked like shapes of water passing over the green fields." The precision of the observation and the brilliance of the image ("shapes of water") express the passion of the watcher, for whom powerful meaning inheres in the natural world.

Consciously, Dorothy wrote her journals, as she did so much else, for the sake of her brother. William read them and used them as data for his poetry. Dorothy writes of daffodils that they "tossed and reeled and danced and seemed as if they verily laughed with the wind." William, two years later, describes "a jocund company" of daffodils in *I Wandered Lonely as a Cloud*:

> Ten thousand saw I at a glance,
> Tossing their heads in sprightly dance.

Dorothy had provided him with raw material. But the power of her writing does not depend on her brother's conversion of it to verse. In its own right, it expresses a subtle and compelling sensibility.

The *Journals* make no ostentatious claim of profundity, but they evoke a consistent vision of unity between inanimate and animate nature, including humankind. One of Wordsworth's characteristic rhetorical devices is the sentence composed largely of miscellaneous nouns, their conjunction evoking a sense of pattern created by the observer but also inherent in the universe. For example: "Lasses spreading dung, a dog's barking now and then, cocks crowing, birds twittering, the snow in patches at the top of the highest hills, yellow palms, purple and green twigs on the birches, ashes with their glittering spikes quite bare." Utterly unpretentious, the lucid prose brings the world alive.

Little effort has been made here to annotate the names of local people and places in the anthologized selections. They have scanty importance for a modern reader, except through what Wordsworth has made of them.

The source of the text is Dorothy Wordsworth, *The Grasmere Journals*, ed. Pamela Woolf (1991).

Recent biographies of Dorothy Wordsworth include R. Gittings and J. Manton, *Dorothy Wordsworth* (1985), and E. Gunn, *A Passion for the Particular: Dorothy Wordsworth: A Portrait* (1981). A useful study placing Dorothy and William Wordsworth in political and intellectual context is A. M. Ellis, *Rebels and Conservatives: Dorothy and William Wordsworth and Their Circle* (1967). Also useful are S. Manley, *Dorothy and William Wordsworth: The Heart of a Circle of Friends* (1974), and, especially, S. M. Levin, *Dorothy Wordsworth and Romanticism* (1987).

PRONOUNCING GLOSSARY

The following list uses common English syllables and stress accents to provide rough equivalents of selected words whose pronunciation may be unfamiliar to the general reader.

Eusemere: *yooz'-meer*   Loughrigg: *luf'-rig*

Grasmere: *gras'-meer*   Wytheburn: *waith'-burn*

From The Grasmere Journals

[This selection from the *Journals* begins
in mid-April 1802.]

Wednesday 14th

William did not rise till dinner time. I walked with Mrs. C. I was ill out of
spirits—disheartened. Wm and I took a long walk in the rain.

Thursday 15th

It was a threatening misty morning—but mild. We set off after dinner from
Eusemere—Mrs. Clarkson went a short way with us but turned back. The
wind was furious and we thought we must have returned. We first rested in
the large boat-house, then under a furze bush opposite Mr. Clarkson's, saw
the plough going in the field. The wind seized our breath; the lake was rough.
There was a boat by itself floating in the middle of the bay below Water
Millock—We rested again in the Water Millock lane. The hawthorns are
black and green, the birches here and there greenish but there is yet more
of purple to be seen on the twigs. We got over into a field to avoid some
cows—people working, a few primroses by the roadside, woodsorrel flowers,
the anemone, scentless violets, strawberries, and that starry yellow flower
which Mrs. C calls pile wort.[1] When we were in the woods beyond Gowbarrow park we saw a few daffodils close to the water side, we fancied that the
lake had floated the seeds ashore and that the little colony had so sprung
up—But as we went along there were more and yet more and at last under
the boughs of the trees, we saw that there was a long belt of them along the
shore, about the breadth of a country turnpike road. I never saw daffodils so
beautiful; they grew among the mossy stones about and about them, some
rested their heads upon these stones as on a pillow for weariness and the
rest tossed and reeled and danced and seemed as if they verily laughed with
the wind that blew upon them over the lake, they looked so gay, ever glancing, ever changing. This wind blew directly over the lake to them. There was
here and there a little knot and a few stragglers a few yards higher up but
they were so few as not to disturb the simplicity and unity and life of that
one busy highway—We rested again and again. The bays were stormy and
we heard the waves at different distances and in the middle of the water like
the sea—Rain came on, we were wet when we reached Luffs' but we called
in. Luckily all was chearless and gloomy so we faced the storm—we *must*
have been wet if we had waited—put on dry clothes at Dobson's. I was very
kindly treated by a young woman, the landlady looked sour but it is her way.
She gave us a goodish supper, excellent ham and potatoes. We paid 7/2 when
we came away. William was sitting by a bright fire when I came downstairs.
He soon made his way to the library piled up in a corner of the window. He
brought out a volume of Enfield's Speaker, another miscellany, and an odd
volume of Congreve's[3] plays. We had a glass of warm rum and water—we

---

1. I.e., the lesser celandine. 2. Seven shillings, approximately $28. In a subsequent note, Wordsworth
wrote that they had paid one shilling more than they should have, 3. William Congreve (1670–1729),
Restoration dramatist, best known for his witty comedies. *Speaker: The Speaker; or, Miscellaneous Pieces
Selected from the Best English Writers, and Disposed Under Proper Heads, for the Improvement of Youth in
Reading and Speaking* (1778), compiled by William Enfield.

enjoyed ourselves and wished for Mary.[4] It rained and blew when we went to bed. N.B. deer in Gowbarrow park like to skeletons.

Friday 16th April (Good Friday)

When I undrew my curtains in the morning, I was much affected by the beauty of the prospect and the change. The sun shone, the wind had passed away, the hills looked chearful. The river was very bright as it flowed into the lake. The church rises up behind a little knot of rocks, the steeple not so high as an ordinary three story house. Bees, in a row in the garden under the wall. After Wm had shaved we set forward. The valley is at first broken by little rocky woody knolls that make retiring places, fairy valleys in the vale, the river winds along under these hills travelling not in a bustle but not slowly to the lake. We saw a fisherman in the flat meadow on the other side of the water; he came towards us and threw his line over the two-arched bridge. It is a bridge of a heavy construction, almost bending inwards in the middle, but it is grey and there is a look of ancientry in the architecture of it that pleased me. As we go on the vale opens out more into one vale with somewhat of a cradle bed. Cottages with groups of trees on the side of the hills. We passed a pair of twin children two years old—and sate on the next bridge which we crossed, a single arch, we rested again upon the turf and looked at the same bridge—we observed arches in the water occasioned by the large stones sending it down in two streams—a sheep came plunging through the river, stumbled up the bank and passed close to us, it had been frightened by an insignificant little dog on the other side, its fleece dropped a glittering shower under its belly—primroses by the roadside, pile wort that shone like stars of gold in the sun, violets, strawberries, retired and half buried among the grass. When we came to the foot of Brothers' Water I left William sitting on the bridge and went along the path on the right side of the lake through the wood—I was delighted with what I saw—the water under the boughs of the bare old trees, the simplicity of the mountains and the exquisite beauty of the path. There was one grey cottage. I repeated "The Glowworm"[5] as I walked along—I hung over the gate, and thought I could have stayed for ever. When I returned I found William writing a poem descriptive of the sights and sounds we saw and heard. There was the gentle flowing of the stream, the glittering lively lake, green fields without a living creature to be seen on them, behind us, a flat pasture with forty-two cattle feeding, to our left the road leading to the hamlet, no smoke there, the sun shone on the bare roofs. The people were at work ploughing, harrowing and sowing— lasses spreading dung, a dog's barking now and then, cocks crowing, birds twittering, the snow in patches at the top of the highest hills, yellow palms, purple and green twigs on the birches, ashes[6] with their glittering spikes quite bare. The hawthorn a bright green with black stems under, the oak and the moss of the oak glossy. We then went on, passed two sisters at work, *they first passed us*, one with two pitch forks in her hand. The other had a spade. We had some talk with them. They laughed aloud after we were gone, perhaps half in wantonness, half boldness. William finished his poem before we

---

4. Mary Hutchinson (1770–1859), whom William later married.   5. *Among All Lovely Things My Love Had Been*.   6. I.e., ash trees.

got to the foot of Kirkstone. There were hundreds of cattle in the vale. There we ate our dinner. The walk up Kirkstone was very interesting. The becks[7] among the rocks were all alive—Wm showed me the little mossy streamlet which he had before loved when he saw its bright green track in the snow. The view above Ambleside, very beautiful. There we sate and looked down on the green vale. We watched the crows at a little distance from us become white as silver as they flew in the sunshine, and when they went still further they looked like shapes of water passing over the green fields. The whitening of Ambleside Church is a great deduction from the beauty of it seen from this point. We called at the Luffs', the Boddingtons there, did not go in and went round by the fields. I pulled off, my stockings intending to wade the beck but I was obliged to put them on and we climbed over the wall at the bridge. The post[8] passed us. No letters! Rydale Lake was in its own evening brightness, the islands and points distinct. Jane Ashburner came up to us when we were sitting upon the wall—we rode in her cart to Tom Dawson's— all well. The garden looked pretty in the half moonlight half daylight. As we went up the vale of Brothers' Water more and more cattle feeding, one hundred of them.

Saturday 17th

A mild warm rain. We sate in the garden all the morning. William dug a little. I transplanted a honey suckle. The lake was still, the sheep on the island reflected in the water, like the grey deer we saw in Gowbarrow park. We walked after tea by moonlight. I had been in bed in the afternoon and William had slept in his chair. We walked towards Rydale first then back- wards and forwards below Mr. Olliff's. The village was beautiful in the moon- light—Helm Crag we observed very distinct. The dead hedge round Benson's field bound together at the top by an interlacing of ash sticks which made a chain of silver when we faced the moon—a letter from C, and also from S. H.[9] I saw a robin chacing a scarlet butterfly this morning.

Sunday 18th

I lay in bed late. Again a mild grey morning with rising vapours we sate in the orchard—William wrote the poem on the robin and the butterfly. I went to drink tea at Luff's but as we did not dine till six o'clock it was late. It was mist and small[1] rain all the way but very pleasant. William met me at Rydale—Aggy[2] accompanied me thither. We sate up late. He met me with the conclusion of the poem of the robin.[3] I read it to him in bed. We left out some lines.

Monday 19th

A mild rain, very warm. Wm worked in the garden, I made pies and bread. After dinner the mist cleared away and sun shone. William walked to Luff's.

7. Creeks, small streams.   8. Mailman.   9. Sara Hutchinson, sister of Mary. C: Samuel Taylor Cole- ridge (1772–1834), the Wordsworths' fellow poet and close friend.   1. Light.   2. Agnes Fisher, a friend.   3. *The Redbreast and the Butterfly*.

I was not very well and went to bed. Wm came home pale and tired. I could not rest when I got to bed.

Tuesday 20th

A beautiful morning, the sun shone—William wrote a conclusion to the poem of the butterfly, "I've watch'd you now a full half-hour." I was quite out of spirits and went into the orchard—When I came in he had finished the poem. We sate in the orchard after dinner, it was a beautiful afternoon. The sun shone upon the level fields and they grew greener beneath the eye— houses, village all chearful, people at work. We sate in the orchard and repeated "The Glowworm" and other poems. Just when William came to a well or a trough which there is in Lord Darlington's Park he began to write that poem of the glow-worm, not being able to ride⁴ upon the long trot— interrupted in going through the Town of Staindrop. Finished it about two miles and a half beyond Staindrop—he did not feel the jogging of the horse while he was writing but when he had done he felt the effect of it and his fingers were cold with his gloves. His horse fell with him on the other side of St. Helen's, Auckland.—So much for "The Glowworm": It was written coming from Middleham on Monday, April 12th, 1802. On Tuesday 20th when we were sitting after tea Coleridge came to the door. I started Wm with my voice—C came up palish but I afterwards found he looked well. William was not well and I was in low spirits.

Wednesday 21st

William and I sauntered a little in the garden. Coleridge came to us and repeated the verses he wrote to Sara—I was affected with them and was on the whole, not being well, in miserable spirits. The sunshine—the green fields and the fair sky made me sadder; even the little happy sporting lambs seemed but sorrowful to me. The pile wort spread out on the grass a thousand shining stars, the primroses were there and the remains of a few daffodils. The well which we cleaned out last night is still but a little muddy pond, though full of water. I went to bed after dinner, could not sleep, went to bed again. Read Ferguson's life⁵ and a poem or two—fell asleep for five minutes and awoke better. We got tea. Sate comfortably in the evening. I went to bed early.

Thursday 22nd

A fine mild morning—we walked into Easedale. The sun shone. Coleridge talked of his plan of sowing the laburnum in the woods—The waters were high for there had been a great quantity of rain in the night. I was tired and sate under the shade of a holly tree that grows upon a rock—I sate there and looked down the stream. I then went to the single holly behind that single rock in the field and sate upon the grass till they came from the waterfall. I saw them there and heard Wm flinging stones into the river whose roaring

---

4. A mistake for "write." William could write only when the horse was walking.   5. David Irving, *Poetical Works of Robert Fergusson with the Life of the Author* (1800).

was loud even where I was. When they returned William was repeating the poem "I have thoughts that are fed by the Sun."[6] It had been called to his mind by the dying away of the stunning of the waterfall when he came behind a stone. When we had got into the vale a heavy rain came on. We saw a family of little children sheltering themselves under a wall before the rain came on, they sate in a row making a canopy for each other of their clothes. The servant lass was planting potatoes near them. Coleridge changed his clothes—we were all wet—Wilkinson[7] came in while we were at dinner. Coleridge and I after dinner drank black currants and water.

Friday 23rd April 1802

It being a beautiful morning we set off at eleven o'clock intending to stay out of doors all the morning. We went towards Rydale and before we got to Tom Dawson's we determined to go under Nab Scar.[8] Thither we went. The sun shone and we were lazy. Coleridge pitched upon several places to sit down upon but we could not be all of one mind respecting sun and shade so we pushed on to the foot of the scar. It was very grand when we looked up, very stony, here and there a budding tree. William observed that the umbrella yew tree that breasts the wind had lost its character as a tree and had become something like to solid wood. Coleridge and I pushed on before. We left William sitting on the stones feasting with silence—and C and I sate down upon a rock seat—a couch it might be under the bower of William's eglantine, Andrew's broom.[9] He was below us and we could see him—he came to us and repeated his poems while we sate beside him upon the ground. He had made himself a seat in the crumbly ground. After we had lingered long looking into the vales—Ambleside vale with the copses, the village under the hill and the green fields—Rydale with a lake all alive and glittering yet but little stirred by breezes, and our own dear Grasmere first making a little round lake of nature's own with never a house never a green field—but the copses and the bare hills, enclosing it and the river flowing out of it. Above rose the Coniston Fells in their own shape and colour—not man's hills but all for themselves, the sky and the clouds and a few wild creatures. C went to search for something new. We saw him climbing up towards a rock, he called us and we found him in a bower, the sweetest that was ever seen—the rock on one side is very high and all covered with ivy which hung loosely about and bore bunches of brown berries. On the other side it was higher than my head. We looked down upon the Ambleside vale that seemed to wind away from us, the village *lying* under the hill. The fir tree island was reflected beautifully—we now first saw that the trees are planted in rows. About this bower there is mountain ash, common ash, yew tree, ivy, holly, hawthorn, mosses and flowers, and a carpet of moss—Above at the top of the rock there is another spot—it is scarce a bower, a little parlour, one not *enclosed* by walls but shaped out for a resting place by the rocks and the ground rising about it. It had a sweet moss carpet—We

6. A poem that William had recently written; he never published it.   7. Probably the Reverend Joseph Wilkinson (1764–1831).   8. Rock or crag (obsolete). Nab Scar was a large local crag.   9. Allusion to two of William's poems from 1800. In *The Waterfall and the Eglantine*, an eglantine grows too close to a waterfall and is swept away in the wintertime. In *The Oak and the Broom*, narrated by the shepherd Andrew, an oak is struck by lightning in a storm while the smaller, carefree broom plant survives.

resolved to go and plant flowers in both these places tomorrow. We wished for Mary and Sara. Dined late. After dinner Wm and I worked in the garden. C read. A letter from Sara.

Saturday 24th

A very wet day. William called me out to see a waterfall behind the barberry tree—We walked in the evening to Rydale—Coleridge and I lingered behind—C stopped up the little runner[1] by the road side to make a lake. We all stood to look at Glowworm Rock—a primrose that grew there and just looked out on the road from its own sheltered bower. The clouds moved as William observed in one regular body like a multitude in motion, a sky all clouds over, not one cloud. On our return it broke a little out and we saw here and there a star. One appeared but for a moment in a lake—pale blue sky.

Sunday 25th April

After breakfast we set off with Coleridge towards Keswick. Wilkinson over-took us near the Potters' and interrupted our discourse. C got into a gig with Mr. Beck,[2] and drove away from us. A shower came on but it was soon over—we spent the morning in the orchard. Read the Prothalamium[3] of Spenser—walked backwards and forwards. Mr. Simpson[4] drank tea with us. I was not well before tea. Mr. S sent us some quills by Molly Ashburner and his brother's book.[5] The Luffs called at the door.

Monday 26th

I copied Wm's poems for Coleridge. Letters from Peggy[6] and Mary H—wrote to Peggy and Coleridge. A terrible rain and wind all day. Went to bed at twelve o'clock.

Tuesday 27th

A fine morning. Mrs. Luff called. I walked with her to the boat-house—William met me at the top of the hill with his fishing-rod in his hand. I turned with him and we sate on the hill looking to Rydale. I left him intending to join him but he came home, and said his line would not stand the pulling—he had had several bites. He sate in the orchard, I made bread. Miss Simpson called. I walked with her to Goans. When I came back I found that he and John Fisher had cleaned out the well—John had sodden[7] about the bee-stand. In the evening Wm began to write "The Tinker."[8] We had a letter and verses from Coleridge.

1. Rivulet.   2. Probably James Beck, a local gentleman.   3. A poem celebrating an aristocratic marriage (1596), by Edmund Spenser (1522–1599).   4. Probably Bartholomew Simpson, an old man at this time.   5. *Science Revived; or, The Vision of Alfred: A Poem in Eight Books* (1802), by the Reverend Joseph Simpson.   6. Once a servant of the Wordsworths; her last name is unknown.   7. Laid sod. 8. Unpublished.

Wednesday 28th April

A fine sunny but coldish morning. I copied the Prioress's tale.[9] Wm was in the orchard—I went to him—he worked away at his poem, though he was ill and tired—I happened to say that when I was a child I would not have pulled a strawberry blossom. I left him and wrote out the Manciple's Tale.[1] At dinner-time he came in with the poem of "Children gathering flowers"[2]— but it was not quite finished and it kept him long off his dinner. It is now done, he is working at "The Tinker," he promised me he would get his tea and do no more but I have got mine an hour and a quarter and he has scarcely begun his. I am not quite well—We have let the bright sun go down without walking—now a heavy shower comes on and I guess we shall not walk at all—I wrote a few lines to Coleridge. Then we walked backwards and forwards between our house and Olliff's. We talked about T Hutchinson and Bell Addison.[3] William left me sitting on a stone. When we came in we corrected the Chaucers but I could not finish them tonight, went to bed.

Thursday 29th

A beautiful morning. The sun shone and all was pleasant. We sent off our parcel to Coleridge by the waggon. Mr. Simpson heard the cuckow today. Before we went out, after I had written down "The Tinker" which William finished this morning, Luff called. He was very lame, limped into the kitchen—he came on a little pony. We then went to Johns Grove, sate a while at first. Afterwards William lay, and I lay in the trench under the fence—he with his eyes shut and listening to the waterfalls and the birds. There was no one waterfall above another—it was a sound of waters in the air—the voice of the air. William heard me breathing and rustling now and then but we both lay still, and unseen by one another—he thought that it would be as sweet thus to lie so in the grave, to hear the *peaceful* sounds of the earth and just to know that one's dear friends were near. The lake was still; there was a boat out. Silver how reflected with delicate purple and yellowish hues as I have seen spar[4]—Lambs on the island and running races together by the half dozen in the round field near us. The copses green*ish*, hawthorn green.—Came home to dinner then went to Mr. Simpson. We rested a long time under a wall. Sheep and lambs were in the field—cottages smoking. As I lay down on the grass, I observed the glittering silver line on the ridges of the backs of the sheep, owing to their situation respecting the sun—which made them look beautiful but with something of strangeness, like animals of another kind—as if belonging to a more splendid world. Met old Mr. S at the door   Mrs. S poorly—I got mullens and pansies—I was sick and ill[5] and obliged to come home soon. We went to bed immediately—I slept up stairs. The air coldish where it was felt somewhat frosty.

9. William had translated Geoffrey Chaucer's tale into modern English.   1. Another of Chaucer's *Canterbury Tales* that William had translated.   2. Later published as *Foresight*.   3. Isabella Addison (1784–1807), who married the Hutchinsons' cousin John Monkhouse. Tom Hutchinson (1773–1849), brother of Sara and Mary.   4. A crystalline mineral that shines in the sun.   5. Nauseated and generally did not feel well. *Mullens*: plants of the snapdragon family.

Friday April 30th

We came into the orchard directly after breakfast, and sate there. The lake was calm—the sky cloudy. We saw two fishermen by the lake side. William began to write the poem of the Celandine.[6] I wrote to Mary H—sitting on the fur gown. Walked backwards and forwards with William—he repeated his poem to me—then he got to work again and would not give over[7]—he had not finished his dinner till five o'clock. After dinner we took up the fur gowns into The Hollins[8] above. We found a sweet seat and thither we will often go. We spread the gown, put on each a cloak and there we lay—William fell asleep—he had a bad head ache owing to his having been disturbed the night before with reading C's letter which Fletcher had brought to the door— I did not sleep but I lay with half shut eyes, looking at the prospect as in a vision almost I was so resigned to it—Loughrigg Fell was the most distant hill, then came the lake slipping in between the copses and above the copse the round swelling field, nearer to me a wild intermixture of rocks, trees, and slacks[9] of grassy ground.—When we turned the corner of our little shelter we saw the church and the whole vale. It is a blessed place. The birds were about us on all sides—skobbys,[1] robins, bullfinches. Crows now and then flew over our heads as we were warned by the sound of the beating of the air above. We stayed till the light of day was going and the little birds had begun to settle their singing—But there was a thrush not far off that seemed to sing louder and clearer than the thrushes had sung when it was quite day. We came in at eight o'clock, got tea. Wrote to Coleridge, and I wrote to Mrs. Clarkson[2] part of a letter. We went to bed at twenty minutes past eleven with prayers that Wm might sleep well.

Saturday May 1st

Rose not till half past eight—a heavenly morning—as soon as breakfast was over we went into the garden and sowed the scarlet beans about the house. It was a clear sky, a heavenly morning. I sowed the flowers. William helped me. We then went and sate in the orchard till dinnertime, it was very hot. William wrote "The Celandine." We planned a shed, for the sun was too much for us. After dinner we went again to our old resting place in the Hollins under the rock. We first lay under a holly where we saw nothing but the holly tree and a budding elm mossed with[3] and the sky above our heads. But that holly tree had a beauty about it more than its own, knowing as we did where we were. When the sun had got low enough we went to the rock shade—Oh the overwhelming beauty of the vale below—greener than green. Two ravens flew high high in the sky and the sun shone upon their bellys and their wings long after there was none of his light to be seen but a little space on the top of Loughrigg Fell. We went down to tea at eight o'clock— had lost the poem[4] and returned after tea. The landscape was fading, sheep and lambs quiet among the rocks. We walked towards King's[5] and backwards

6. *To the Lesser Celandine.*   7. Stop.   8. A wood full of holly trees near the Wordsworths' house. 9. Hollows, dips in the ground.   1. Or scobbies, a north country name for chaffinches, which are small birds.   2. Catherine Clarkson (1772–1856), a close neighbor and friend.   3. A word has apparently been left out here.   4. Not the one William had been writing in the morning but the idea for a second poem on the celandine: *Pleasures newly found are sweet.* The idea returned to him in the evening. 5. Thomas King (1772–1831), who had a house in Grasmere, not far away.

and forwards. The sky was perfectly cloudless. N.B. is it often so? three solitary stars in the middle of the blue vault, one or two on the points of the high hills. Wm wrote "The Celandine" second part tonight. Heard the cuckow today this first of May.

Sunday 2nd May

Again a heavenly morning—Letter from Coleridge.

SAMUEL TAYLOR COLERIDGE
1772–1834

For Samuel Taylor Coleridge, the mystery of the imagination provided the most compelling and perplexing of subjects. In prose and in verse, by reasoned discussion and by poetic symbol making, he explored the subject, affirming imagination's virtually divine status as a creative power and suggesting his own emotional dependence on it.

Son of an English clergyman, Coleridge attended Jesus College, Cambridge, from 1791 to 1793. In 1795, he married Sara Fricker; the same year he met Wordsworth and began the fruitful collaboration leading to *Lyrical Ballads*. In 1810, his period of greatest poetic creativity already over, he separated from his wife; subsequently, he became increasingly addicted to opium. Known for his brilliant conversation, he spent much time talking and lecturing as well as writing.

The most intellectual of the English Romantics, Coleridge, after an early trip to Germany, was strongly influenced by the German Idealist philosophers, notably Immanuel Kant and Johann Fichte. His best-known critical work, *Biographia Literaria* (1817), in which he develops most fully and explicitly his theory of imagination, contains many borrowings from German sources. His output of poetry was relatively small. In some of his most important poems (such as *The Rime of the Ancient Mariner*), he tries to incorporate the supernatural into essentially psychological narrative. He was also much interested in the native English ballad tradition, which on occasion influenced his choice of stanzaic form and meter.

Like other Romantic poets, Coleridge was fascinated by the aeolian harp (it figures in the first stanza of *Dejection: An Ode*), an instrument that makes music without human intervention, by the action of wind on its strings. *Kubla Khan*, a poem recording (according to Coleridge's prefatory note) what the writer remembered of a dream stimulated by opium, makes up a kind of poetic equivalent for the aeolian harp: a work for which its author disclaims conscious responsibility. It simply came to his mind, he says, to be broken off when he was interrupted by a person from Porlock. The poem, therefore, makes no claim to rational coherence, but it has always invited exegesis. Evoking a lush and splendid setting, it yet contains ominous suggestions: the ruler who presides over the magnificence of landscape ("deep romantic chasm," river, caves, incense-bearing trees) and building, hears "Ancestral voices prophesying war." The theme of mingled beauty and danger intensifies as the poem focuses on the figure of a singer, a "damsel with a dulcimer," whose power the poem's speaker wishes to "revive" within himself. Then he could re-create the vision of Kubla Khan's domain, and people would respond to him with "holy dread," recognizing his association with the magic, the sacred, the dangerous, the unpredictable and uncontrollable power of imagination. Thus the singer becomes an image for the poet, and we are reminded that the uncannily evocative scene of the poem's opening section itself issues from the poetic imagination, which creates for its possessor and for his readers a new version of reality, closer to the heart's desire than our workaday world, but not without danger—including the danger of becoming lost in it.

In *Dejection: An Ode,* Coleridge concerns himself with the same theme in more extended personal terms. Paradoxically, this poem—mourning his loss of creative imagination—demonstrates the active presence of that quality whose absence it deplores, as it creates out of the dullness of depression a rich emotional and psychological texture. Like Wordsworth's *Ode on Intimations of Immortality, Dejection* confronts the speaker's sense of diminishing power. He has lost the "joy" that he considers associated with the spontaneity of youth. More emphatically than Wordsworth, Coleridge attributes even the beauty of nature to the human imagination:

> O Lady! we receive but what we give,
> And in our life alone does Nature live: . . .
> Ah! from the soul itself must issue forth
> A light, a glory, a fair luminous cloud
> Enveloping the Earth—

One cannot hope for inspiration from nature, cannot expect to receive from without that reassurance and pleasure whose sources are within. As the poem develops, it demonstrates the operation of imagination on the external world by hearing meaning—meaning related to human action and suffering—in the sound of wind and storm. The imaginative activity provides its own solace; although the speaker never ceases to assert his dejection, he, like Wordsworth, is enabled finally to displace his vision of joy, harmony, and peace onto the figure of a woman who will embody all that he now feels impossible for himself.

In its emphasis on the "shaping spirit of Imagination," that presiding power of Romantic poetry, *Dejection* makes a strong statement of Coleridge's central concern. By its capacity to evoke emotional complexity—longing for what is lost, resentment at its passing, struggle to repossess what is mourned—and to demonstrate the patterns in which the mind deals with its own problems, it exemplifies the subtlety and the force of his poetic achievement.

There are two important recent biographies: R. Holmes, *Coleridge: Early Visions* (1989), the first part of a projected two-part biography; and R. Ashton, *The Life of Samuel Taylor Coleridge: A Critical Biography* (1996). J. L. Lowes, *The Road to Xanadu* (1927), provides a fascinating study of the sources of *Kubla Khan.* For criticism, see also J. Cornwell, *Coleridge* (1973); J. Beer, *Coleridge's Poetic Intelligence* (1975); G. Davidson, *Coleridge's Career* (1990); and D. Suttana, ed., *New Approaches to Coleridge: Biographical and Critical Essays* (1981). Useful works that treat Coleridge in conjunction with Wordsworth are G. W. Ruoff, *Wordsworth and Coleridge* (1989); P. Magnuson, *Coleridge and Wordsworth* (1988); J. Ellison, *Delicate Subjects: Romanticism, Gender, and the Ethics of Understanding* (1990); R. Hewitt, *The Possibilities of Society: Wordsworth, Coleridge, and the Sociological Viewpoint of English Romanticism* (1997); and C. J. Rzepka, *The Self as Mind: Vision and Identity in Wordsworth, Coleridge, and Keats* (1986).

PRONOUNCING GLOSSARY

The following list uses common English syllables and stress accents to provide rough equivalents of selected words whose pronunciation may be unfamiliar to the general reader.

Aeolian: *ee-oh'-lee-an*   Xanadu: *zan'-a-doo*

Purchas: *pur'-chus*

[POEMS]

Kubla Khan

Or, a Vision in a Dream. A Fragment

The following fragment is here published at the request of a poet of great and deserved celebrity [Lord Byron], and, as far as the Author's own opinions are concerned, rather as a psychological curiosity, than on the ground of any supposed *poetic* merits.

In the summer of the year 1797, the Author, then in ill health, had retired to a lonely farm-house between Porlock and Linton, on the Exmoor confines of Somerset and Devonshire.[1] In consequence of a slight indisposition, an anodyne had been prescribed, from the effects of which he fell asleep in his chair at the moment that he was reading the following sentence, or words of the same substance, in "Purchas's Pilgrimage":[2] "Here the Khan Kubla commanded a palace to be built, and a stately garden thereunto. And thus ten miles of fertile ground were inclosed with a wall." The Author continued for about three hours in a profound sleep, at least of the external senses, during which time he has the most vivid confidence, that he could not have composed less than from two to three hundred lines; if that indeed can be called composition in which all the images rose up before him as *things,* with a parallel production of the correspondent expressions, without any sensation or consciousness of effort.[3] On awaking he appeared to himself to have a distinct recollection of the whole, and taking his pen, ink, and paper, instantly and eagerly wrote down the lines that are here preserved. At this moment he was unfortunately called out by a person on business from Porlock, and detained by him above an hour, and on his return to his room, found, to his no small surprise and mortification, that though he still retained some vague and dim recollection of the general purport of the vision, yet, with the exception of some eight or ten scattered lines and images, all the rest had passed away like the images on the surface of a stream into which a stone has been cast, but, alas! without the after restoration of the latter!

Then all the charm

Is broken—all that phantom-world so fair
Vanishes, and a thousand circlets spread,
And each mis-shape[s] the other. Stay awhile,
Poor youth! who scarcely dar'st lift up thine eyes—
The stream will soon renew its smoothness, soon
The visions will return! And lo, he stays,
And soon the fragments dim of lovely forms

---

1. A high moorland shared by the two southwestern counties in England.   2. Samuel Purchas (1575?–1626) published *Purchas his Pilgrimage, or Relations of the World and the Religions observed in all Ages* in 1613. The passage in Purchas is slightly different: "In Xamdu did Cublai Can build a stately Palace, encompassing sixteene miles of plaine ground with a wall, wherein are fertile meddowes, pleasant Springs, delightfull Streames, and all sorts of beasts of chase and game, and in the middest thereof a sumptuous house of pleasure, which may be removed from place to place" (book 4, chap. 13).   3. Coleridge's statement that he dreamed the poem and wrote down what he could later remember verbatim has been queried, most recently by medical opinion. The belief that opium produces special dreams, or even any dreams at all, seems to lack confirmation.

Come trembling back, unite, and now once more
The pool becomes a mirror.[4]

Yet from the still surviving recollections in his mind, the Author has frequently purposed to finish for himself what had been originally, as it were, given to him. Σαμερον αδιον ασω:[5] but the to-morrow is yet to come. . . .

In Xanadu did Kubla Khan[6]
A stately pleasure-dome decree:
Where Alph,[7] the sacred river, ran
Through caverns measureless to man
    Down to a sunless sea.   5
So twice five miles of fertile ground
With walls and towers were girdled round:
And there were gardens bright with sinuous rills,
Where blossomed many an incense-bearing tree;
And here were forests ancient as the hills,   10
Enfolding sunny spots of greenery.

But oh! that deep romantic chasm which slanted
Down the green hill athwart a cedarn cover!
A savage place! as holy and enchanted
As e'er beneath a waning moon was haunted   15
By woman wailing for her demon-lover!
And from this chasm, with ceaseless turmoil seething,
As if this earth in fast thick pants were breathing,
A mighty fountain momently was forced:
Amid whose swift half-intermitted burst   20
Huge fragments vaulted like rebounding hail,
Or chaffy grain beneath the thresher's flail:
And 'mid these dancing rocks at once and ever
It flung up momently the sacred river.
Five miles meandering with a mazy motion   25
Through wood and dale the sacred river ran,
Then reached the caverns measureless to man,
And sank in tumult to a lifeless ocean:
And 'mid this tumult Kubla heard from far
Ancestral voices prophesying war!   30
    The shadow of the dome of pleasure
    Floated midway on the waves;
    Where was heard the mingled measure
    From the fountain and the caves.
It was a miracle of rare device,   35
A sunny pleasure-dome with caves of ice!
    A damsel with a dulcimer
    In a vision once I saw:
    It was an Abyssinian maid,
    And on her dulcimer she played,   40

4. From Coleridge's poem *The Picture; or, The Lover's Resolution*, lines 91–100.   5. A misquotation from Theocritus's *Idylls* 1.145: "I'll sing a sweeter song later" (Greek).   6. Mongol emperor (1215?–1294), visited by Marco Polo.   7. J. L. Lowes, in *The Road to Xanadu* (1927), thinks that Coleridge may have had in mind the river Alpheus—linked with the Nile—mentioned by Virgil.

Singing of Mount Abora.[8]
Could I revive within me
Her symphony and song,
    To such a deep delight 'twould win me,
That with music loud and long,   45
I would build that dome in air,
That sunny dome! those caves of ice!
And all who heard should see them there,
And all should cry, Beware! Beware!
His flashing eyes, his floating hair!   50
Weave a circle round him thrice,
And close your eyes with holy dread,
For he on honey-dew hath fed,
And drunk the milk of Paradise.

Dejection: An Ode

Late, late yestreen I saw the new Moon,
With the old Moon in her arms;
And I fear, I fear, my Master dear!
We shall have a deadly storm.
                    Ballad of Sir Patrick Spence

I

Well! If the Bard was weather-wise, who made
    The grand old ballad of Sir Patrick Spence,
    This night, so tranquil now, will not go hence
Unroused by winds, that ply a busier trade
Than those which mould yon cloud in lazy flakes,   5
Or the dull sobbing draft, that moans and rakes
Upon the strings of this Aeolian lute,[1]
    Which better far were mute.
    For lo! the New-moon winter-bright!
    And overspread with phantom light,   10
    (With swimming phantom light o'erspread
    But rimmed and circled by a silver thread)
I see the old Moon in her lap, foretelling
    The coming-on of rain and squally blast.
And oh! that even now the gust were swelling,   15
    And the slant night-shower driving loud and fast!
Those sounds which oft have raised me, whilst they awed,
    And sent my soul abroad,
Might now perhaps their wonted impulse give,
Might startle this dull pain, and make it move and live!   20

---

8. Lowes argues that this may have been "Mt. Amara," mentioned by Milton in *Paradise Lost* (4.28), or Amhara in Samuel Johnson's *Rasselas*.   1. A frame fitted with strings or wires that produce musical tones when the wind hits them. Named after Aeolus, god of the winds.

II

A grief without a pang, void, dark, and drear,
  A stifled, drowsy, unimpassioned grief,
  Which finds no natural outlet, no relief,
    In word, or sigh, or tear—
O Lady! in this wan and heartless mood,   25
To other thoughts by yonder throstle[2] woo'd,
  All this long eve, so balmy and serene,
Have I been gazing on the western sky,
  And its peculiar tint of yellow green:
And still I gaze—and with how blank an eye!   30
And those thin clouds above, in flakes and bars,
That give away their motion to the stars;
Those stars, that glide behind them or between,
Now sparkling, now bedimmed, but always seen:
Yon crescent Moon, as fixed as if it grew   35
In its own cloudless, starless lake of blue;
I see them all so excellently fair,
I see, not feel, how beautiful they are!

III

  My genial spirits[3] fail;
    And what can these avail   40
To lift the smothering weight from off my breast?
    It were a vain endeavour,
    Though I should gaze forever
On that green light that lingers in the west:
I may not hope from outward forms to win   45
The passion and the life, whose fountains are within.

IV

O Lady! we receive but what we give,
And in our life alone does Nature live:
Ours is her wedding garment, ours her shroud!
  And would we aught behold of higher worth,   50
Than that inanimate cold world allowed
To the poor loveless ever-anxious crowd,
  Ah! from the soul itself must issue forth
A light, a glory, a fair luminous cloud
    Enveloping the Earth—   55
And from the soul itself must there be sent
  A sweet and potent voice, of its own birth,
Of all sweet sounds the life and element!

V

O pure of heart! thou need'st not ask of me
What this strong music in the soul may be!   60

---

2. The song thrush.   3. Generative spirits; creativity. This poem was written soon after Wordsworth had composed the first four stanzas of the *Ode on Intimations of Immortality,* and the themes are similar.

What, and wherein it doth exist,
This light, this glory, this fair luminous mist,
This beautiful and beauty-making power.
   Joy, virtuous Lady! Joy that ne'er was given,
Save to the pure, and in their purest hour,   65
Life, and Life's effluence, cloud at once and shower,
Joy, Lady! is the spirit and the power,
Which wedding Nature to us gives in dower
    A new Earth and new Heaven,
Undreamt of by the sensual and the proud—   70
Joy is the sweet voice, Joy the luminous cloud—
    We in ourselves rejoice!
And thence flows all that charms or ear or sight,
   All melodies the echoes of that voice,
All colours a suffusion from that light.   75

VI

There was a time when, though my path was rough,
   This joy within me dallied with distress,
And all misfortunes were but as the stuff
   Whence Fancy made me dreams of happiness:
For hope grew round me, like the twining vine,   80
And fruits, and foliage, not my own, seemed mine.
But now afflictions bow me down to earth:
Nor care I that they rob me of my mirth;
   But oh! each visitation[4]
Suspends what nature gave me at my birth,   85
   My shaping spirit of Imagination.[5]
For not to think of what I needs must feel,
   But to be still and patient, all I can;
And haply by abstruse research to steal
   From my own nature all the natural man—   90
   This was my sole resource, my only plan:
Till that which suits a part infects the whole,
And now is almost grown the habit of my soul.

VII

Hence, viper thoughts, that coil around my mind,
   Reality's dark dream!   95
I turn from you, and listen to the wind,
   Which long has raved unnoticed. What a scream
Of agony by torture lengthened out
That lute sent forth! Thou Wind that rav'st without,
   Bare crag, or mountain-tairn,[6] or blasted tree,   100
Or pine-grove whither woodman never clomb,
Or lonely house, long held the witches' home,

---

4. Of the *misfortunes* (line 78) and *afflictions* (line 82).   5. Coleridge made much of the distinction between *Fancy* (line 79) and *Imagination*. Fancy makes pleasant combinations of images; Imagination is a higher faculty of the mind that combines images in such a way that they create a higher reality, a poetic "truth" more valid than that which is perceived by the ordinary senses.   6. Or tarn; small mountain lake.

Methinks were fitter instruments for thee,
Mad Lutanist![7] who in this month of showers,
Of dark-brown gardens, and of peeping flowers,   105
Mak'st Devils' yule[8] with worse than wintry song,
The blossoms, buds, and timorous leaves among.
　　Thou Actor, perfect in all tragic sounds!
Thou mighty Poet, e'en to frenzy bold!
　　　What tell'st thou now about?   110
　　　'Tis of the rushing of an host in rout,
　With groans, of trampled men, with smarting wounds—
At once they groan with pain, and shudder with the cold!
But hush! there is a pause of deepest silence!
　　　And all that noise, as of a rushing crowd,   115
With groans, and tremulous shudderings—all is over—
　　It tells another tale,[9] with sounds less deep and loud!
　　　　A tale of less affright,
　　　　And tempered with delight,
As Otway's self[1] had framed the tender lay,—   120
　　　'Tis of a little child
　　　Upon a lonesome wild,
Not far from home, but she hath lost her way:
And now moans low in bitter grief and fear,
And now screams loud, and hopes to make her mother hear.   125

VIII

'Tis midnight, but small thoughts have I of sleep.
Full seldom may my friend such vigils keep!
Visit her, gentle Sleep! with wings of healing,
　And may this storm be but a mountain birth,
May all the stars hang bright above her dwelling,   130
　　Silent as though they watched the sleeping Earth!
　　　With light heart may she rise,
　　　Gay fancy, cheerful eyes,
　Joy lift her spirit, joy attune her voice;
To her may all things live, from pole to pole,   135
Their life the eddying of her living soul!
　　O simple spirit, guided from above,
Dear Lady! friend devoutest of my choice,
Thus mayest thou ever, evermore rejoice.

---

7. The storm wind in line 99.　**8.** Originally, a heathen feast.　**9.** The story of Wordsworth's *Lucy Gray*.　**1.** Originally, "William's," referring to Wordsworth. *As:* as if. Thomas Otway (1652–1685), a tragic dramatist, admired for his mastery of pathos.

PERCY BYSSHE SHELLEY
1792–1822

A longing for alternatives to things as they are dominates much of Shelley's poetry. Whether he writes of his own dejection, of the energizing force of the west wind, or of the political situation of England, he writes often from conviction that matters could and should be better.

Son of a country squire in Sussex, Shelley led a privileged early life, attending Eton and Oxford. He was, however, expelled from Oxford after a single year, for writing a work called *The Necessity of Atheism*: already he had begun to defy convention. He dramatized his defiance yet more forcefully in 1814, when, after three years of marriage (and two children) with Harriet Westbrook, he eloped with Mary Wollstonecraft Godwin, daughter of two advanced social thinkers. Harriet committed suicide; the lovers married and had several children. Shelley was on friendly terms with other important Romantic writers; in Italy, where he moved in 1818, he associated closely with Byron. He was drowned while sailing off the Italian coast.

Productive as a poet, Shelley mastered tones ranging from the satiric to the prophetic. His most important works include *Prometheus Unbound* (1820), a philosophic-visionary-revolutionary expansion of a classical theme; *Epipsychidon* (1821), a defense of free love; and the elegy *Adonais* (1821), for the death of Keats. He also wrote a verse play having to do with the incest of a father and daughter, *The Cenci* (1819).

At the end of his essay *A Defence of Poetry*, posthumously published in 1840, Shelley insists on poetry's necessary connection with the future. Poets, he says, are "the mirrors of the gigantic shadows which futurity casts upon the present . . . : the influence which is moved not but moves. Poets are the unacknowledged legislators of the World." His own lyrics corroborate such grandiose claims by insistently establishing images of the possible. The sonnet *England in 1819,* for example, after twelve lines of nouns and noun clauses about the political and social horrors of the current English situation, concludes that all these phenomena "Are graves from which a glorious Phantom may / Burst, to illumine our tempestuous day." The possibility—never the certainty—of good coming from evil always exists.

Like Coleridge, Shelley writes about his own dejection, interspersing penetrating images of natural beauty with detailed presentation of his painful psychic state. In the poem called *Stanzas Written in Dejection,* the speaker dreams of death as a kind of mild fulfillment, a reabsorption into nature. The ending of the poem, however, has less dismal implications. Finally, the speaker compares himself with the dying day as a presence in memory. Men do not love him, but would regret his passing; the day, which he has enjoyed, will linger "like joy in Memory." The comparison, which at first appears to sustain the mood of self-pity, also transcends that self-perpetuating emotion: it reminds the speaker of the capacity for enjoyment that he retains even in his bleakest mood. While he fancies his own easeful death, he still takes pleasure in the scene around him; that pleasure remains a lasting element in memory.

Ode to the West Wind makes a particularly emphatic statement of the good-from-evil theme. Images of violence and sinister power ("Thou, from whose unseen presence the leaves dead / Are driven, like ghosts from an enchanter fleeing") dominate the early part of the poem. The third section creates an atmosphere of luxurious beauty but ends with the depths of the sea growing suddenly "grey with fear" at the wind's advent. In the next section, however, the speaker places himself in relation with the natural force he has described, begging to be lifted, to "share / The impulse of thy strength." Finally, in imagination, the poet becomes the "lyre" (in effect, Coleridge's aeolian harp) of the wind, now revealed as a force of inspiration and change, which enables him to function as "The trumpet of a prophecy!" *Defence of Poetry* describes poets as "the trumpets which sing to battle"; in *Ode to the West Wind*, Shelley suggests that they acquire such inspirational capacity by imaginative union with nature and, particularly, as in the west wind blowing away the remnants of the past year, with the forces of regeneration and reform.

E. Blunden, *Shelley: A Life Story* (1946), provides a useful biography. A critically oriented biography is P. Hodgart, *A Preface to Shelley* (1985). For criticism, see C. Baker, *Shelley's Major Poetry: The Fabric of a Vision* (1948); E. Wasserman, *Shelley* (1971); R. Holmes, *Shelley: The Pursuit* (1974); J. Hall, *The Transforming Image: A Study of Shelley's Major Poetry* (1980); S. M. Sperry, *Shelley's Major Verse* (1989); W. A. Ulmer, *Shellyan Eros: The Rhetoric of Romantic Love* (1990); S. Haines, *Shelley's Poetry: The Divided Self* (1997); and K. Wheatley, *Shelley and His Readers: Beyond Paranoid Politics* (1999).

PRONOUNCING GLOSSARY

The following list uses common English syllables and stress accents to provide rough equivalents of selected words whose pronunciation may be unfamiliar to the general reader.

Baiæ: *by'-ee*   Mænad: *mee'-nad*

[Poems]

Stanzas Written in Dejection— December 1818, Near Naples

The Sun is warm, the sky is clear,
The waves are dancing fast and bright,
Blue isles and snowy mountains wear
The purple noon's transparent might,
The breath of the moist earth is light   5
Around its unexpanded buds;
Like many a voice of one delight,
The winds, the birds, the Ocean-floods,
The City's voice, itself is soft like Solitude's.

I see the Deep's untrampled floor   10
With green and purple seaweeds strown;
I see the waves upon the shore
Like light dissolved in star-showers, thrown;
I sit upon the sands alone;
The lightning of the noontide Ocean   15
Is flashing round me, and a tone
Arises from its measured motion,
How sweet! did any heart now share in my emotion.

Alas, I have nor hope nor health
Nor peace within nor calm around,   20
Nor that content surpassing wealth
The sage in meditation found,
And walked with inward glory crowned;
Nor fame nor power nor love nor leisure—

Others I see whom these surround,   25
Smiling they live and call life pleasure:
To me that cup has been dealt in another measure.

Yet now despair itself is mild,
Even as the winds and waters are;
I could lie down like a tired child   30
And weep away the life of care
Which I have borne and yet must bear
Till Death like Sleep might steal on me,
And I might feel in the warm air
My cheek grow cold, and hear the Sea   35
Breathe o'er my dying brain its last monotony.

Some might lament that I were cold,
As I, when this sweet day is gone,
Which my lost heart, too soon grown old,
Insults with this untimely moan—   40
They might lament,—for I am one
Whom men love not, and yet regret;
Unlike this day, which, when the Sun
Shall on its stainless glory set,
Will linger though enjoyed, like joy in Memory yet.   45

England in 1819

An old, mad, blind, despised, and dying King;[1]
Princes,[2] the dregs of their dull race, who flow
Through public scorn,—mud from a muddy spring;
Rulers who neither see nor feel nor know,
But leechlike to their fainting country cling   5
Till they drop, blind in blood, without a blow.
A people starved and stabbed in th' untilled field;
An army, whom liberticide and prey
Makes as a two-edged sword to all who wield;
Golden and sanguine[3] laws which tempt and slay;   10
Religion Christless, Godless—a book sealed;
A senate, Time's worst statute,[4] unrepealed—
Are graves from which a glorious Phantom may
Burst, to illumine our tempestuous day.

Ode to the West Wind

I

O wild West Wind, thou breath of Autumn's being,
Thou, from whose unseen presence the leaves dead
Are driven, like ghosts from an enchanter fleeing,

---

1. George III (1738–1820).   2. The king's sons, including the prince regent, whose dissolute behavior gave rise to public scandals.   3. Bloody, causing bloodshed. *Golden:* bought. The laws favor the rich and powerful.   4. The law by which the civil liberties of Roman Catholics and dissenters from the state religion (Anglicanism) were restricted.

Yellow, and black, and pale, and hectic red,
Pestilence-stricken multitudes: O Thou, 5
Who chariotest to their dark wintry bed

The winged seeds, where they lie cold and low,
Each like a corpse within its grave, until
Thine azure sister of the Spring shall blow

Her clarion o'er the dreaming earth, and fill 10
(Driving sweet buds like flocks to feed in air)
With living hues and odours plain and hill:

Wild Spirit, which art moving everywhere;
Destroyer and Preserver; hear, O hear!

II

Thou on whose stream,'mid the steep sky's commotion, 15
Loose clouds like Earth's decaying leaves are shed,
Shook from the tangled boughs of Heaven and Ocean,

Angels of rain and lightning; there are spread
On the blue surface of thine aery surge,
Like the bright hair uplifted from the head 20

Of some fierce Mænad,[1] even from the dim verge
Of the horizon to the zenith's height,
The locks of the approaching storm. Thou Dirge

Of the dying year, to which this closing night
Will be the dome of a vast sepulchre, 25
Vaulted with all thy congregated might

Of vapors, from whose solid atmosphere
Black rain and fire and hail will burst: O hear!

III

Thou who didst waken from his summer dreams
The blue Mediterranean, where he lay, 30
Lulled by the coil of his crystalline streams,

Beside a pumice isle in Baiæ's bay,[2]
And saw in sleep old palaces and towers
Quivering within the wave's intenser day,

All overgrown with azure moss and flowers 35
So sweet, the sense faints picturing them! Thou
For whose path the Atlantic's level powers

Cleave themselves into chasms, while far below
The sea-blooms and the oozy woods which wear
The sapless foliage of the ocean, know 40

1. Ecstatic female worshiper of Bacchus, Greek god of wine. 2. West of Naples; the Roman emperors built villas there.

Thy voice, and suddenly grow grey with fear,
And tremble and despoil themselves: O hear!

IV

If I were a dead leaf thou mightest bear;
If I were a swift cloud to fly with thee;
A wave to pant beneath thy power, and share   45

The impulse of thy strength, only less free
Than thou, O Uncontrollable! If even
I were as in my boyhood, and could be

The comrade of thy wanderings over Heaven,
As then, when to outstrip thy skiey speed   50
Scarce seemed a vision; I would ne'er have striven

As thus with thee in prayer in my sore need.
Oh! lift me as a wave, a leaf, a cloud!
I fall upon the thorns of life! I bleed!

A heavy weight of hours has chained and bowed   55
One too like thee: tameless, and swift, and proud.

V

Make me thy lyre,[3] even as the forest is:
What if my leaves are falling like its own!
The tumult of thy mighty harmonies

Will take from both a deep, autumnal tone,   60
Sweet though in sadness. Be thou, Spirit fierce,
My spirit! Be thou me, impetuous one!

Drive my dead thoughts over the universe
Like withered leaves to quicken a new birth!
And, by the incantation of this verse,   65

Scatter, as from an unextinguished hearth
Ashes and sparks, my words among mankind!
Be through my lips to unawakened Earth

The trumpet of a prophecy! O Wind,
If Winter comes, can Spring be far behind?   70

A Defence of Poetry

[Conclusion]

* * * Poetry is the record of the best and happiest moments of the happiest
and best minds. We are aware of evanescent visitations of thought and feeling sometimes associated with place or person, sometimes regarding our own

---

3. Ancient harp. The allusion is also to the aeolian harp, an instrument played by the wind and a frequent
image for the poet played by inspiration.

mind alone, and always arising unforeseen and departing unbidden, but elevating and delightful beyond all expression: so that even in the desire and the regret they leave, there cannot but be pleasure, participating as it does in the nature of its object. It is as it were the interpenetration of a diviner nature through our own; but its footsteps are like those of a wind over a sea, which the coming calm erases, and whose traces remain only as on the wrinkled sand which paves it. These and corresponding conditions of being are experienced principally by those of the most delicate sensibility and the most enlarged imagination; and the state of mind produced by them is at war with every base desire. The enthusiasm of virtue, love, patriotism, and friendship is essentially linked with these emotions, and whilst they last, self appears as what it is, an atom to a Universe. Poets are not only subject to these experiences as spirits of the most refined organization, but they can colour all that they combine with the evanescent hues of this ethereal world; a word, or a trait in the representation of a scene or a passion, will touch the enchanted chord, and reanimate, in those who have ever experienced these emotions, the sleeping, the cold, the buried image of the past. Poetry thus makes immortal all that is best and most beautiful in the world; it arrests the vanishing apparitions which haunt the interlunations of life, and veiling them or[1] in language or in form sends them forth among mankind, bearing sweet news of kindred joy to those with whom their sisters abide—abide, because there is no portal of expression from the caverns of the spirit which they inhabit into the universe of things. Poetry redeems from decay the visitations of the divinity in man.

* * *

The first part of these remarks has related to Poetry in its elements and principles; and it has been shown, as well as the narrow limits assigned them would permit, that what is called poetry, in a restricted sense, has a common source with all other forms of order and of beauty according to which the materials of human life are susceptible of being arranged, and which is poetry in an universal sense.

The second part[2] will have for its object an application of these principles to the present state of the cultivation of Poetry, and a defence of the attempt to idealize the modern forms of manners and opinion, and compel them into a subordination to the imaginative and creative faculty. For the literature of England, an energetic development of which has ever preceded or accompanied a great and free development of the national will, has arisen as it were from a new birth. In spite of the low-thoughted envy which would undervalue contemporary merit, our own will be a memorable age in intellectual achievements, and we live among such philosophers and poets as surpass beyond comparison any who have appeared since the last national struggle for civil and religious liberty.[3] The most unfailing herald, companion, and follower of the awakening of a great people to work a beneficial change in opinion or institution, is Poetry. At such periods there is an accumulation of the power of communicating and receiving intense and impassioned conceptions respecting man and nature. The persons in whom this power resides, may

1. Either. *Interlunations:* dark periods between the old and new moon.   2. The second part was never written.   3. The English Civil War. The great poet of that age was Milton.

often, as far as regards many portions of their nature, have little apparent correspondence with that spirit of good of which they are the ministers. But even whilst they deny and abjure, they are yet compelled to serve, the Power which is seated upon the throne of their own soul. It is impossible to read the compositions of the most celebrated writers of the present day without being startled with the electric life which burns within their words. They measure the circumference and sound the depths of human nature with a comprehensive and all-penetrating spirit, and they are themselves perhaps the most sincerely astonished at its manifestations, for it is less their spirit than the spirit of the age. Poets are the hierophants[4] of an unapprehended inspiration, the mirrors of the gigantic shadows which futurity casts upon the present, the words which express what they understand not; the trumpets which sing to battle, and feel not what they inspire: the influence which is moved not, but moves. Poets are the unacknowledged legislators of the World.

4. Interpreters, as priests who interpret sacred mysteries.

JOHN KEATS
1795–1821

A poet "half in love with easeful Death," to quote a line from his *Ode to a Nightingale*, John Keats expressed with compelling intensity the Romantic longing for the unattainable, a concept that he defined in ways very different from Goethe's. In a series of brilliant lyrics, he explored subtle links between the passion for absolute beauty, which provides an imagined alternative to the everyday world's sordidness and disappointment, and the desire to melt into extinction, another form of that alternative.

At the age of sixteen, Keats was apprenticed to a druggist and surgeon; in 1816, he was licensed as an apothecary—but almost immediately abandoned medicine for poetry. Son of a hostler (a groom for horses) at a London inn, he had earlier attended school at Enfield, where he manifested an interest in literature encouraged by his friend Charles Cowden Clarke, the headmaster's son. Through Leigh Hunt, a leading political radical, poet, and critic, whose literary circle he joined in 1816, Keats came to know Shelley, William Hazlitt, and Charles Lamb, important members of the Romantic movement. He had a brief love affair with Fanny Brawne, to whom he became engaged in 1819; the next year he went to Italy, seeking a cure for his tuberculosis, only to die in Rome.

Although his first book, *Poems* (1817), met with some critical success, the long mythological poem *Endymion*, which he published a year later, became an object of attack by conservative literary reviews (*Blackwood's* and the *Quarterly*). Shelley, in his elegy for Keats (*Adonais*, 1821), encouraged the myth that the harsh reviews caused the poet's death. In fact, Keats lived long enough to publish his most important volume—written scarcely five years after he first tried his hand at poetry—*Lamia, Isabella, The Eve of St. Agnes, and Other Poems* (1820), which won critical applause and contained most of the poems for which he is remembered today.

Some of Keats's greatest works return to a form popular in the eighteenth century: the ode addressed to an abstraction (for example, melancholy) or another nonhuman object (for example, a nightingale or an urn). Although the basic literary device seems highly artificial, Keats uses it powerfully to express his characteristic sense of beauty so intensely experienced that it almost corresponds to pain.

> My heart aches, and a drowsy numbness pains
> My sense, as though of hemlock I had drunk . . .
> 'Tis not through envy of thy happy lot,
> But being too happy in thy happiness. . . .

Ode on Melancholy, in its sharp contrast to Coleridge's and Shelley's poems on dejection as well as to seventeenth- and eighteenth-century evocations of melancholy, illustrates particularly well Keats's special exemplification of the Romantic sensibility. In the first stanza, the speaker explicitly rejects traditional concomitants of melancholy—yew, the death-moth, the owl—because such associations suggest a kind of passivity or inertia that might "drown the wakeful anguish of the soul," interfering with the immediate and intense experience of melancholy that he actively seeks. Instead, he advocates trying to live as completely as possible in the immediacy of emotion. Melancholy, he continues, dwells with beauty and joy and pleasure, all in their nature evanescent. To fully feel the wonder of beauty or happiness implies awareness that it will soon vanish. Only those capable of active participation in their own positive emotions can hope to know melancholy; paradoxically, the result of energetic commitment to the life of feeling is the utter submission to melancholy's power: one can hope to "be among her cloudy trophies hung."

Prose summary of such an argument risks sounding ridiculous or incomprehensible, for Keats's emotional logic inheres in the imagery and the music of his poems, which exert their own compelling force. Without any previous belief in the desirability of melancholy as an emotion, the reader, absorbed into a rich sequence of images, feels swept into an experience comparable to that which the poem endorses. The ode generates its own sense of beauty and of melancholy and of the close relation between the two. Its brilliantly evocative specificity of physical reference always suggests more than is directly said, more than paraphrase can encompass:

> Aye, in the very temple of Delight
> Veiled Melancholy has her sovereign shrine,
> Though seen of none save him whose strenuous tongue
> Can burst Joy's grape against his palate fine . . .

Everyone can recall the sensuous pleasure of a grape releasing its juice into the mouth, but it would be difficult to elucidate the full implications of the "strenuous tongue" or of "Joy's grape." Keat's great poetic gift manifests itself most unmistakably in his extraordinary power of suggestion—not only in the odes, but in the ballad-imitation, *La Belle Dame sans Merci,* with its haunting, half-told story, and in the understated sonnets, asserting the speaker's feeling but always hinting more emotion than they directly affirm.

A first-rate critical biography is A. Ward, *John Keats: The Making of a Poet* (1963). Also useful are W. J. Bate, *John Keats* (1963); S. Coote, *John Keats: A Life* (1995); T. Hilton, *Keats and His World* (1971); C. T. Watts, *A Preface to Keats* (1985); J. Barnard, *John Keats* (1987); H. Bloom, ed., *The Odes of Keats* (1987), a collection of essays; and H. De Almeida, *Critical Essays on John Keats* (1990). Recent critical works include K. Alwes, *Imagination Transformed: The Evolution of the Female Character in Keats's Poetry* (1993), and K. D. White, *John Keats and the Loss of Romantic Innocence* (1996).

PRONOUNCING GLOSSARY

The following list uses common English syllables and stress accents to provide rough equivalents of selected words whose pronounciation may be unfamiliar to the general reader.

Arcady: *ahr'-kah-dee*

Darien: *day'-ree-en*

Hippocrene: *hip'-oh-kreen*

La Belle Dame sans Merci: *lah bel dahm*
    sahnh mayr-see'

Lethe: *lee'-thee*

Proserpine: *pro'-ser-pain*

Provençal: *proh-vahn-sahl'*

Tempe: *tem'-pee*

[Poems]

On First Looking into Chapman's Homer[1]

Much have I traveled in the realms of gold,
    And many goodly states and kingdoms seen;
    Round many western islands have I been
Which bards in fealty to Apollo[2] hold.
Oft of one wide expanse had I been told   5
    That deep-browed Homer ruled as his demesne;[3]
    Yet did I never breathe its pure serene
Till I heard Chapman speak out loud and bold:
Then felt I like some watcher of the skies
    When a new planet swims into his ken;   10
Or like stout Cortez[4] when with eagle eyes
    He stared at the Pacific—and all his men
Looked at each other with a wild surmise—
    Silent, upon a peak in Darien.

Bright Star

Bright star, would I were steadfast as thou art—
    Not in lone splendor hung aloft the night,
And watching, with eternal lids apart,
    Like nature's patient, sleepless Eremite,[1]
The moving waters at their priestlike task   5
    Of pure ablution round earth's human shores,
Or gazing on the new soft fallen mask
    Of snow upon the mountains and the moors—
No—yet still steadfast, still unchangeable,
    Pillowed upon my fair love's ripening breast,   10
To feel forever its soft fall and swell,
    Awake forever in a sweet unrest,
Still, still to hear her tender-taken breath,
And so live ever—or else swoon to death.

1. Keat's friend and former teacher Charles Cowden Clarke had introduced Keats to George Chapman's translations of the *Iliad* (1611) and the *Odyssey* (1616) the night before this poem was written.   2. God of poetic inspiration.   3. Realm, kingdom.   4. In fact, Vasco Núñez de Balboa (ca. 1475–1519), Spanish conquistador, not Hernando Cortés (1485–1547), another Spaniard, was the European explorer who first saw the Pacific from Darien, Panama.   1. Hermit.

La Belle Dame sans Merci[1]

I

O what can ail thee, knight at arms,
  Alone and palely loitering?
The sedge has withered from the lake
  And no birds sing!

II

O what can ail thee, knight at arms,   5
  So haggard, and so woebegone?
The squirrel's granary is full
  And the harvest's done.

III

I see a lily on thy brow
  With anguish moist and fever dew,   10
And on thy cheeks a fading rose
  Fast withereth too.

IV

I met a lady in the meads,[2]
  Full beautiful, a faery's child,
Her hair was long, her foot was light   15
  And her eyes were wild.

V

I made a garland for her head,
  And bracelets too, and fragrant zone;[3]
She looked at me as she did love
  And made sweet moan.   20

VI

I set her on my pacing steed
  And nothing else saw all day long,
For sidelong would she bend and sing
  A faery's song.

VII

She found me roots of relish sweet,   25
  And honey wild, and manna[4] dew,
And sure in language strange she said
  "I love thee true."

---

1. The beautiful lady without pity (French); from a medieval poem by Alain Chartier. **2.** Meadows. Here the knight answers the question asked in lines 5–6. **3.** Girdle. **4.** The supernatural substance with which God fed the children of Israel in the wilderness (Exodus 16 and Joshua 5.12).

VIII

She took me to her elfin grot[5]
   And there she wept and sighed full sore,[6]   30
And there I shut her wild wild eyes
   With kisses four.

IX

And there she lullèd me asleep,
   And there I dreamed, ah woe betide!
The latest[7] dream I ever dreamt   35
   On the cold hill's side.

X

I saw pale kings, and princes too,
   Pale warriors, death-pale were they all;
They cried, "La belle dame sans merci
   Thee hath in thrall!'[8]   40

XI

I saw their starved lips in the gloam[9]
   With horrid warning gapèd wide,
And I awoke, and found me here
   On the cold hill's side.

XII

And this is why I sojourn here,   45
   Alone and palely loitering;
Though the sedge withered from the lake
   And no birds sing.

Ode on a Grecian Urn

I

Thou still unravished bride of quietness,
   Thou foster-child of silence and slow time,
Sylvan historian, who canst thus express
   A flowery tale more sweetly than our rhyme:
What leaf-fringed legend haunts about thy shape   5
   Of deities or mortals, or of both,
      In Tempe or the dales of Arcady?[1]
   What men or gods are these? What maidens loth?
What mad pursuit? What struggle to escape?
      What pipes and timbrels? What wild ecstasy?   10

---

5. Cavern.   6. With great grief.   7. Last.   8. Bondage.   9. Twilight.   1. A mountainous region in the Peloponnese, traditionally regarded as the place of ideal rustic, bucolic contentment. *Tempe:* a valley in Thessaly between Mount Olympus and Mount Ossa.

II

Heard melodies are sweet, but those unheard
  Are sweeter; therefore, ye soft pipes, play on;
Not to the sensual ear, but, more endeared,
  Pipe to the spirit ditties of no tone:
Fair youth, beneath the trees, thou canst not leave   15
  Thy song, nor ever can those trees be bare;
    Bold lover, never, never canst thou kiss,
Though winning near the goal—yet, do not grieve;
    She cannot fade, though thou hast not thy bliss,
For ever wilt thou love, and she be fair!   20

III

Ah, happy, happy boughs! that cannot shed
  Your leaves, nor ever bid the Spring adieu;
And, happy melodist, unwearièd,
  For ever piping songs for ever new;
More happy love! more happy, happy love!   25
  For ever warm and still to be enjoyed,
    For ever panting, and for ever young;
All breathing human passion far above,
    That leaves a heart high-sorrowful and cloyed,
    A burning forehead, and a parching tongue.   30

IV

Who are these coming to the sacrifice?
  To what green altar, O mysterious priest,
Lead'st thou that heifer lowing at the skies,
  And all her silken flanks with garlands drest?
What little town by river or sea shore,   35
  Or mountain-built with peaceful citadel,
    Is emptied of this folk, this pious morn?
And, little town, thy streets for evermore
  Will silent be; and not a soul to tell
    Why thou art desolate, can e'er return.   40

V

O Attic shape! Fair attitude! with brede[2]
  Of marble men and maidens overwrought,
With forest branches and the trodden weed;
  Thou, silent form, dost tease us out of thought
As doth eternity: Cold Pastoral!   45
  When old age shall this generation waste,
    Thou shalt remain, in midst of other woe
Than ours, a friend to man, to whom thou say'st,
  "Beauty is truth, truth beauty,"—that is all
    Ye know on earth, and all ye need to know.   50

---

2. Pattern. *Attic:* classical (literally, Athenian).

Ode to a Nightingale

I

My heart aches, and a drowsy numbness pains
  My sense, as though of hemlock I had drunk,
Or emptied some dull opiate to the drains
  One minute past, and Lethe-wards[1] had sunk:
'Tis not through envy of thy happy lot,   5
  But being too happy in thy happiness,
    That thou, light-winged Dryad[2] of the trees,
      In some melodious plot
Of beechen green, and shadows numberless,
    Singest of summer in full-throated ease.   10

II

O for a draught of vintage! that hath been
  Cooled a long age in the deep-delvèd earth,
Tasting of Flora[3] and the country green,
  Dance, and Provençal[4] song, and sunburnt mirth!
O for a beaker full of the warm South!   15
  Full of the true, the blushful Hippocrene,[5]
    With beaded bubbles winking at the brim,
      And purple-stainèd mouth;
That I might drink, and leave the world unseen,
  And with thee fade away into the forest dim: 20

III

Fade far away, dissolve, and quite forget
  What thou among the leaves hast never known,
The weariness, the fever, and the fret
  Here, where men sit and hear each other groan;
Where palsy shakes a few, sad, last gray hairs,   25
  Where youth grows pale, and spectre-thin, and dies;
    Where but to think is to be full of sorrow
      And leaden-eyed despairs;
Where beauty cannot keep her lustrous eyes,
  Or new love pine at them beyond tomorrow.   30

IV

Away! away! for I will fly to thee,
  Not charioted by Bacchus and his pards,[6]
But on the viewless wings of Poesy,
  Though the dull brain perplexes and retards:
Already with thee! tender is the night,   35

1. I.e., toward Lethe, the river of forgetfulness in Greek mythology. 2. Wood nymph. 3. The goddess of flowers and spring; here, flowers. 4. From Provence, the district in France associated with the troubadours. 5. The fountain on Mount Helicon, in Greece, sacred to the muse of poetry. 6. Leopards. Bacchus (Dionysus) was traditionally supposed to be accompanied by leopards, lions, goats, and so on.

And haply[7] the Queen-Moon is on her throne,
    Clustered around by all her starry Fays;[8]
        But here there is no light,
    Save what from heaven is with the breezes blown
        Through verdurous glooms and winding mossy ways.   40

V

I cannot see what flowers are at my feet,
    Nor what soft incense hangs upon the boughs,
But, in embalmèd darkness, guess each sweet
    Wherewith the seasonable month endows
The grass, the thicket, and the fruit-tree wild;   45
    White hawthorn, and the pastoral eglantine;
        Fast-fading violets covered up in leaves;
            And mid-May's eldest child,
The coming musk-rose, full of dewy wine,
        The murmurous haunt of flies on summer eves.   50

VI

Darkling[9] I listen; and for many a time
    I have been half in love with easeful Death,
Called him soft names in many a musèd rhyme,
    To take into the air my quiet breath;
Now more than ever seems it rich to die,   55
    To cease upon the midnight with no pain,
        While thou art pouring forth thy soul abroad
            In such an ecstasy!
Still wouldst thou sing, and I have ears in vain—
    To thy high requiem become a sod.[1]   60

VII

Thou wast not born for death, immortal Bird!
    No hungry generations tread thee down;
The voice I hear this passing night was heard
    In ancient days by emperor and clown:
Perhaps the self-same song that found a path   65
    Through the sad heart of Ruth, when, sick for home,
        She stood in tears amid the alien corn;[2]
            The same that ofttimes hath
Charmed magic casements, opening on the foam
    Of perilous seas, in faery lands forlorn.   70

VIII

Forlorn! the very word is like a bell
    To toll me back from thee to my sole self!
Adieu! the fancy cannot cheat so well
    As she is famed to do, deceiving elf.

---

7. Perhaps.   8. Fairies.   9. In the dark.   1. I.e., like dirt, unable to hear.   2. See the Book of Ruth. After her Ephrathite husband died, she returned to his native land with her mother-in-law.

Adieu! adieu! thy plaintive anthem fades 75
  Past the near meadows, over the still stream,
    Up the hill-side; and now 'tis buried deep
      In the next valley-glades:
Was it a vision, or a waking dream?
  Fled is that music:—do I wake or sleep? 80

Ode on Melancholy

I

No, no, go not to Lethe,[1] neither twist
  Wolfsbane, tight-rooted, for its poisonous wine;
Nor suffer thy pale forehead to be kissed
  By nightshade, ruby grape of Proserpine;[2]
Make not your rosary of yew-berries,[3] 5
  Nor let the beetle, nor the death-moth[4] be
    Your mournful Psyche,[5] nor the downy owl
A partner in your sorrow's mysteries;
  For shade to shade will come too drowsily,
    And drown the wakeful anguish of the soul. 10

II

But when the melancholy fit shall fall
  Sudden from heaven like a weeping cloud,
That fosters the droop-headed flowers all,
  And hides the green hill in an April shroud;
Then glut thy sorrow on a morning rose, 15
  Or on the rainbow of the salt sand-wave,
    Or on the wealth of globèd peonies;
Or if thy mistress some rich anger shows,
  Imprison her soft hand, and let her rave,
    And feed deep, deep upon her peerless eyes. 20

III

She[6] dwells with Beauty—Beauty that must die;
  And Joy, whose hand is ever at his lips
Bidding adieu; and aching Pleasure nigh,
  Turning to Poison while the bee-mouth sips:
Aye, in the very temple of Delight 25
  Veiled Melancholy has her sovereign shrine,
    Though seen of none save him whose strenuous tongue
Can burst Joy's grape against his palate fine;
  His soul shall taste the sadness of her might,
    And be among her cloudy trophies hung.[7] 30

1. The river of forgetfulness in Hades.   2. Wife of Pluto, queen of the underworld.   3. Wolfsbane, nightshade, and yew berries are all poisonous.   4. The death's-head moth has markings that resemble a skull. The scarab beetle, depicted in Egyptian tombs, was an emblem of death.   5. The soul, portrayed by the Greeks as a butterfly.   6. Melancholy.   7. The Greeks placed war trophies in their temples to commemorate victories.

To Autumn

I

Season of mists and mellow fruitfulness,
   Close bosom-friend of the maturing sun;
Conspiring with him how to load and bless
   With fruit the vines that round the thatch-eaves run;
To bend with apples the mossed cottage-trees,   5
   And fill all fruit with ripeness to the core;
     To swell the gourd, and plump the hazel shells
With a sweet kernel; to set budding more,
   And still more, later flowers for the bees,
   Until they think warm days will never cease,   10
     For Summer has o'er-brimmed their clammy cells.

II

Who hath not seen thee oft amid thy store?
   Sometimes whoever seeks abroad may find
Thee sitting careless on a granary floor,
   Thy hair soft-lifted by the winnowing wind;   15
Or on a half-reaped furrow sound asleep,
   Drowsed with the fume of poppies, while thy hook
     Spares the next swath and all its twinèd flowers:
And sometimes like a gleaner thou dost keep
   Steady thy laden head across a brook;   20
   Or by a cyder-press, with patient look,
     Thou watchest the last oozings hours by hours.

III

Where are the songs of Spring? Ay, where are they?
   Think not of them, thou hast thy music too,—
While barrèd clouds bloom the soft-dying day,   25
   And touch the stubble-plains with rosy hue;
Then in a wailful choir the small gnats mourn
   Among the river sallows,[1] borne aloft
     Or sinking as the light wind lives or dies;
And full-grown lambs loud bleat from hilly bourn;   30
   Hedge-crickets sing; and now with treble soft
   The red-breast whistles from a garden-croft;
     And gathering swallows twitter in the skies.

1. Willows.

CONTINENTAL ROMANTIC LYRICS: A SELECTION

This group of poems from five European countries exemplifies both the scope and the consistency of the Romantic imagination. Like their English counterparts, the writers represented here concern themselves with time, death, nature, and love and with the connections among these vast subjects. They express emotions ranging from extreme depression to exhilaration. As one can see even in translation, these poets explore a broad spectrum of metrical possibilities. Although they write mainly in the first person, they consistently meditate, explicitly or implicitly, the links between the self and the world—both the natural world and that composed of other people (including, in Heinrich Heine's *Silesian Weavers,* the political realm). In their insistence on feeling's importance and complexity, its capacity to guide the individual toward profound insight, they reveal why it is that Romantic poetry continues to communicate directly with readers living long after the era of its writing.

This poetry characteristically reveals a spiritual dimension even when its ostensible concerns appear relatively trivial. Thus Rosalía de Castro, feeling the heat of a summer day, finds herself aware of "the anguish of the soul," and Friedrich Hölderlin, also contemplating a summer scene, perceives the water into which swans dip their heads as "holy." Often, though, the poets directly confront metaphysical issues. Like Wordsworth, they may feel themselves united with the natural universe (see, for example, Gustavo Adolfo Bécquer's *Nameless Spirit).* But they also explore the emotional reverberations of Christianity. The German poet known as Novalis (born Friedrich von Hardenberg) unites his preoccupation with time and his sense of loss with his Christian convictions, imagining Jesus not only as the type of perfection but as the representative of vanished serenity and nobility of spirit. Victor Hugo, employing the lyric impulse to illuminate a narrative plot, evokes the almost inconceivable emotional experience of Satan falling from heaven to hell. Whether writing openly or covertly of religious feeling, Romantic poets consciously and often triumphantly stretch the limits of the expressible.

Particularly striking in this group of selections, as in the entire body of Romantic lyrics, is the complex symbolic use made of material from the natural world. Anna Petrovna Bunina, for instance, an early nineteenth-century Russian poet, begins *From the Seashore* with a scene of calm natural beauty—quiet sea, shining sky, birds in their nests. The poem then mutates into an equally peaceful domestic scene, only to return to a new figuration of the sea, invoked now as a prospective grave. The shift calls attention to the way that human beings attach meanings to nature in accord with mutable psychic conditions.

The French poet Alphonse de Lamartine, in his long lyric, *The Lake,* explores the assignment of meaning to nature yet more fully, using his memory of an idyllic summer evening in a boat with his beloved to reflect on the ineluctable passing of time. Now the woman he loves is dying. In the earlier time, she spoke to him about the need to live intensely, given the flight of the moments, using the boat trip as a metaphor:

> "We have no port, time itself has no shore;
> It glides by, and we pass away."

Now, the speaker can only hope that the beauty of the lake and its surroundings will survive as a symbol of their love, possessing a kind of permanence that human beings cannot attain.

Yet more mysterious are the allusions to nature in Heine's lyrics, which rely on subtle suggestion rather than overt statement. Writing, for instance, of a pine tree in the north that dreams during the winter of a faraway palm tree, he evokes the omnipresence of human longing without ever mentioning the human. "Death is like the long cool night," he writes in another poem, without explaining, but his allusion to young nightingales singing in the trees captures a sense of death as beautiful, remote, and haunting.

These lyricists value the inexpressibility of powerful feeling. At the same time, they set themselves the impossible task of communicating precisely what defies expression. The sheer musicality of their verse helps to convey emotion, as they create powerful (and often untranslatable) verbal melodies through the rhythms of their stanzaic forms and the varied movement of their lines. By strategies of indirection, they often succeed in persuading their readers that lyric verse can after all convey the kinds of feeling that most of us lock within ourselves. The poems collected here investigate experience both commonplace and extraordinary; interrogate the universe; but most important, explore and imagine the depths of human emotion.

FRIEDRICH HÖLDERLIN
1770–1843

Important partly for his capacity to combine classical and Romantic sensibility, the German poet Friedrich Hölderlin (*freed'-rick hul'der-lin*) wrote his considerable body of lyric verse early in his life, before becoming incurably schizophrenic at the age of thirty-six. He had prepared himself for the ministry but decided that he was unsuited for such a vocation and found work—not very successfully—as a tutor. In his lyrics, which have become celebrated only in the twentieth century, he records and evokes intensities of personal feeling, with particular emphasis, as the selections printed here reveal, on what it means for human beings to live in time.

The poems are translated by Christopher Middleton, who successfully evokes Hölderlin's range of tones and meters.

A valuable biographical and critical study is L. S. Salzberger, *Hölderlin* (1952). Also useful is E. L. Stahl, *Hölderlin's Symbolism* (1945). More recent critical works include E. Mason and others, *Hölderlin and Goethe* (1975); R. Unger, *Hölderlin's Major Poetry: The Dialectics of Unity* (1976); and A. Del Caro, *Hölderlin: The Poetics of Being* (1991).

The Half of Life

With yellow pears the country,
Brimming with wild roses,
Hangs into the lake,
You gracious swans,
And drunk with kisses   5
Your heads you dip
Into the holy lucid water.

Where, ah where shall I find,
When winter comes, the flowers,
And where the sunshine   10
And shadows of the earth?
Walls stand
Speechless and cold, in the wind
The weathervanes clatter.

Hyperion's[1] Song of Fate

You walk up there in the light
  On floors like velvet, blissful spirits.
    Shining winds divine
      Touch you lightly
        As a harper touches holy   5
          Strings with her fingers.

Fateless as babes asleep
  They breathe, the celestials.
    Chastely kept
      In a simple bud,   10
        For them the spirit
          Flowers eternal,
            And in bliss their eyes
              Gaze in eternal
                Calm clarity.   15

But to us it is given
  To find no resting place,
    We faint, we fall,
      Suffering, human,
        Blindly from one   20
          To the next moment
           Like water flung
            From rock to rock down
              Long years into uncertainty.

Brevity

Why make it so short? Have you lost your old liking
For song? Why, in days of hope, when young,
  You sang and sang,
    There scarce was an end of it.

My song is short as my luck was. Who'd go   5
  Gaily swimming at sundown? It's gone, earth's cold,
    And the annoying nightbird
      Flits, close, blocking your vision.

To the Fates

Grant me a single summer, you lords of all,
  A single autumn, for the fullgrown song,

---

1. In Greek mythology, a Titan, father of Aurora, goddess of dawn.

So that, with such sweet playing sated,
Then my heart may die more willing.

The soul, in life robbed of its godly right,   5
Rests not, even in Orcus[1] down below;
Yet should I once achieve my heart's
First holy concern, the poem,

Welcome then, O stillness of the shadow world!
Even if down I go without my   10
Music, I shall be satisfied; once
Like gods I shall have lived, more I need not.

1. Hades.

NOVALIS (FRIEDRICH VON HARDENBERG)
1772–1801

Born into a family of the German nobility, Friedrich von Hardenberg assumed the pseudonym Novalis on the basis of his family's earlier use of the name "de Novali." He studied first law, then mining, and ended his career as a mine inspector at a saltworks. His achievement as poet and philosopher, however, despite his short life (he died of tuberculosis), powerfully influenced later Romantic thought. *Hymns to the Night*, from which the selection printed here is taken, expressed his grief over the death, also from tuberculosis, of the young girl to whom he had been engaged. In the hymns, Novalis insists that death provides the entrance into a higher life, and he anticipates his eventual union with his fiancée and with the universe as a whole.

The translator is Charles E. Passage, who attempts to convey Novalis's characteristic combination of mystical and sentimental feeling.

Useful studies of Novalis include J. Neubauer, *Novalis* (1980), a biographical and critical introduction; M. C. Massey, *Feminine Soul: The Fate of an Ideal Author* (1985); K. Pfefferkorn, *Novalis: A Romantic's Theory of Language and Poetry* (1988); and W. A. O'Brien, *Novalis: Signs of Revolution* (1995). Novalis is also treated in M. R. Strand, *I/You: Paradoxical Constructions of Self and Other in Early German Romanticism* (1998).

PRONOUNCING GLOSSARY

The following list uses common English syllables and stress accents to provide rough equivalents of selected words whose pronunciation may be unfamiliar to the general reader.

Friedrich von Hardenberg: *freed'-rick fon hahr'-den-berg*

Novalis: *noh-vahl'-is*

Yearning for Death

Down now into the dark earth's womb,
From Light's domain away!
Wild rage of grief and pangs of gloom

Mark glad departure's day.
In narrow barque[1] we swiftly ply   5
To land along the shores of sky.
Praised be the everlasting Night,
Praised be eternal slumber!
Day's heat has withered us, and blight
Of sorrows without number.   10
For alien lands we no more yearn,
To our Father's house we would return.

In this world what can us betide
Our love and constancy?
When old things have been put aside   15
What use can new things be?
O! lonely stands and all undone
Whoever loves the times foregone.

The times foregone, when in bright dance
High spirits flamed, and when   20
The Father's hand and countenance
Were still in mankind's ken,
And nobly, simply, many bore
The lofty image that he bore.

The times foregone, when full-bloom-blowing   25
Primaeval races throve,
And children toward God's kingdom going
For death and torment strove;
And when, though life and pleasure spoke,
Yet many hearts, for loving, broke.   30

Those times, when God himself revealed
Himself with youthful ardor,
And with love's strength his sweet life sealed
In young death as a martyr,
Refusing not the smart and pain,   35
That it might be our dearer gain.

We see them now, with anxious yearning,
Shrouded in dark of night;
In temporal life our hot thirst's burning
Will not be slaked outright;   40
Unto our homeland we must go
That we that holy time may know.

What holds up our return? To rest
Our loved ones are long laid.
At their graves closes our lives' quest,   45
Sad are we and afraid.

1. Boat.

There is no more for us to seek,
The heart is sated, the world is bleak.

A mystic shudder, sweet, unbounded,
Now courses through our marrow;   50
Methinks from the far distance sounded
An echo of our sorrow.
Perhaps our loved ones likewise longing
Have wafted us this sigh of longing.

Down to the sweet bride[2] come away,   55
To Jesus whom we love!
Good cheer! The evening dawn shows gray
On them who grieve and love.
Dream bursts our bonds and sinks us free
To our Father's arms eternally.   60

2. Jesus, as the bride of humankind.

ANNA PETROVNA BUNINA
1774–1829

One of the first woman poets to be published in Russia, Anna Petrovna Bunina (*ah'-na pet-rohv'-na boo-nee'-na*) insisted, in the face of her parents' disapproval, on pursuing a literary career and on developing her intellectual capacities. She had inherited a small amount of money, which made it possible for her initially to hire tutors and to spend her time writing, demonstrating a gift for lyric verse that drew on details of the natural world as a means for expressing personal feeling. After she began publishing poetry (in 1806), she acquired literary supporters who tried to ease her financial and physical circumstances when she developed cancer in 1815. She died of the disease.

In the poem printed here, Bunina begins with a deceptively calm natural scene, lovingly evoking the appearance and mood of the sea just after sunset. The poem gradually builds intensity as it turns to the experience of human misery, ending with an appeal to the sea to abandon its calm to better respond to the speaker's mood. Like many other Romantic lyrics, the poem draws on the idea of harmony between humanity and nature—but only to declare the insufficiency of nature to the personal anguish in which "Poison flows / In my veins."

Pamela Perkins translated this selection.

Nothing has yet been written in English about Bunina.

From the Seashore

The bright sea
Flowed from the sky,
In quiet the waves
Lap along the shore,

Brief ripples   5
Faintly tremble.

The sun's gone down,
There is no moon,
In the scarlet glow
The west is shining,   10
Birds in their nests,
Flocks in the tree-crests.

Everything suddenly fell silent,
Everything in its place.
In the room it is quiet,   15
There is no rustle;
The children are nestled
Modestly in the corners.

Lina touched
The strings of the harp;   20
The golden harp
Gave voice;
Sounds in harmony
Sing with Lina.

In a rose flame   25
The hearth gives light;
The bright fire
Leaps along the coals;
The smoke dark-silver
Curls in a column.   30

The fierce flame
scorches the soul;
The heart languishes,
Everything has withered;
Poison flows   35
In my veins.

Tears ran dry
In troubled eyes,
Sighs stopped
The chest from heaving,   40
Speech dies down
On cold lips.

Sea, start to churn!
Be a grave for me!
Golden harp,   45
Strike like thunder!
Fire, flow,
Warm this poor woman!

ALPHONSE DE LAMARTINE
1790–1869

Celebrated among the French Romantics for his "poetry of the soul," lyric meditations that united passion, philosophy, and religious humanism, Alphonse de Lamartine was also a novelist and statesman who served in various diplomatic and elected positions before retiring in disgust at Louis Napoleon's coup d'état in 1851. His father was an aristocrat who had narrowly escaped the guillotine in the French Revolution; he himself had early royalist sympathies but became a liberal and a prominent opposition figure in the revolution of 1848, even holding a top position in the short-lived provisional government.

Poetry, Lamartine said, echoes our deepest intuitions and intelligence: it is a sincere expression of the whole human being. He boasted that he had "brought poetry down from Parnassus" and taught it to express human emotions. Much of his own poetry draws on personal life, and *The Lake,* whose lyrical passion inspired a generation of French romantics, recalls a brief but intense love affair between the poet and a young married woman, Julie Charles. Meeting one summer when both were at a health resort on Lake Bourget in the French Alps, they separated over the winter but promised to meet again the next year. When the poet returned to the lake, however, Julie was already dying and he found himself alone. *The Lake* is Lamartine's elegy to his lost love, a melodious complaint that moves from the intimate situation of two lovers to a meditation on nature and time.

Andrea Moorhead's remarkably faithful translation suggests Lamartine's lyrical yet philosophical voice.

The standard biography of Lamartine is H. R. Whitehouse, *The Life of Lamartine* (1918; reprinted 1969). More specialized is W. Fortescue, *Alphonse de Lamartine: A Political Biography* (1983). C. M. Lombard, *Lamartine* (1973), provides a general introduction. Critical works include M. E. Birkett, *Lamartine and the Poetics of Landscape* (1982), and D. Hillery, ed., *Lamartine: The "Méditations poétiques"* (1993).

PRONOUNCING GLOSSARY

The following list uses common English syllables and stress accents to provide rough equivalents of selected words whose pronunciation may be unfamiliar to the general reader.

Bourget: *boor-zhay'*   Lamartine: *lah-mahr-teen'*

The Lake

And thus, forever driven towards new shores,
Swept into eternal night without return,
Will we never, for even one day, drop anchor
    On time's vast ocean?
O lake! Only a year has now gone by,[1]   5
And to these dear waves she would have seen again,
Look! I'm returning alone to rest on the very work
    Where you last saw her rest!

Then as now, you rumbled under these great rocks;
Then as now, you broke against their torn flanks;   10

1. They met in October 1816; it is now August 1817.

The wind hurling the foam from your waves
  Onto her adored feet.

One evening, you recall? We drifted in silence;
Far off on the water and under the stars hearing
Only the rhythmic sound of oars striking   15
  Your melodious waves.

Suddenly strains unknown on earth
Echoed from the enchanted shore;
The water paid heed, and the voice so dear
  To me spoke these words: 20

"O time, suspend your flight! and you, blessed hours,
  Suspend your swift passage.
Allow us to savor the fleeting delights
  Of our most happy days!

So many wretched people beseech you: 25
  Flow, flow quickly for them;
Take away the cares devouring them;
  Overlook the happy.

But I ask in vain for just a few more moments,
  Time escaping me flees;   30
While I beg the night: 'Slow down,' already
  It fades into the dawn.

Then let us love, let us love! And the fleeting hours
  Let us hasten to enjoy.
We have no port, time itself has no shore;   35
  It glides by, and we pass away."

Jealous time, will these moments of such intoxication,
Love flooding us with overwhelming bliss,
Fly past us with the same speed
  As dark and painful days?   40

What! will we not keep at least the trace of them?
What! They are gone forever? Totally lost?
This time that gave them and is obliterating them,
  Will it never return them to us?

Eternity, nothingness, past, somber abysses,   45
What are you doing with the days you swallow up?
Speak: will you ever give back the sublime bliss
  You stole from us?

O lake! silent rocks! shaded grottoes! dark forest!
You whom time can spare or even rejuvenate,   50
Preserve, noble nature, preserve from this night
  At least the memory!

May it live in your peace, may it be in your storms,
Beautiful lake, and in the light of your glad slopes,
And in these tall dark firs and in these savage rocks,   55
   Overhanging your waves.

May it be in the trembling zephyr passing by,
In the endless sounds that carry from shore to shore
In the silver faced star[2] that whitens your surface
   With its softened brilliance.   60

May the moaning wind and sighing reed,
May the delicate scent of your fragrant breeze,
May everything that we hear and see and breathe,
   Awaken the memory of—their love!

2. The moon.

HEINRICH HEINE
1797–1856

Born in Germany of Jewish parents, Heinrich Heine is most famous as a lyric poet, although he also composed drama, narrative poetry, political commentary, and literary criticism. As *The Silesian Weavers* suggests, he had strong revolutionary sympathies, which drew him to Paris in 1831. There he died, after a prolonged illness.

Simple diction and frequent reliance on the metrical patterns of traditional ballads characterize many of Heine's lyrics, which have frequently been set to music. Naive though the lyrics often seem, they have dark undertones. When Heine openly confronts political actualities, one ground for his despair becomes apparent: he sees German society as divided between the uncaring and tyrannical rich and the profoundly oppressed poor, and he finds the structure of social inequity intolerable.

Hal Draper translated the selections printed here.

The best biography of Heine is J. L. Sammons, *Heinrich Heine: A Modern Biography* (1979). H. Spencer's volume in the Twayne series, *Heinrich Heine* (1982), provides a useful introduction to the poet and his work. Other critical studies include U. Franklin, *Exiles and Ironists* (1988); D. L. Justis, *The Feminine in Heine's Life and Oeuvre: Self and Other* (1977); and R. F. Cook, *By the Rivers of Babylon: Heinrich Heine's Late Songs and Reflections* (1998).

PRONOUNCING GLOSSARY

The following list uses common English syllables and stress accents to provide rough equivalents of selected words whose pronunciation may be unfamiliar to the general reader.

Heinrich Heine: *hain'-rik hai'-ne*   Silesian: *sai-lee'-zhahn*

[A pine is standing lonely]

A pine is standing lonely
In the North on a bare plateau.

He sleeps; a bright white blanket
Enshrouds him in ice and snow.

He's dreaming of a palm tree   5
Far away in the Eastern land
Lonely and silently mourning
On a sunburnt rocky strand.

[A young man loves a maiden]

A young man loves a maiden
Who chooses another instead;
This other loves still another
And these two haply wed.

The maiden out of anger   5
Marries, with no regard,
The first good man she runs into—
The young lad takes it hard.

It is so old a story,
Yet somehow always new;   10
And he that has just lived it,
It breaks his heart in two.

[Ah, death is like the long cool night]

Ah, death is like the long cool night,
    And life is like the sultry day.
        Dusk falls now; I grow sleepy;
The day makes me tired of light.

Over my bed there's a tree that gleams—   5
    Young nightingales are singing there,
        Of love, love only, singing—
I hear it even in dreams.

The Silesian Weavers[1]

In somber eyes no tears of grieving;
Grinding their teeth, they sit at their weaving;
"O Germany, at your shroud we sit,
We're weaving a threefold curse in it—
    We're weaving, we're weaving!   5

1. Silesia was a province of the kingdom of Prussia in northeast Germany. This poem was occasioned by violent uprisings of weavers protesting intolerable working conditions during June 1844.

"A curse on the god we prayed to, kneeling
With cold in our bones, with hunger reeling;
We waited and hoped, in vain persevered,
He scorned us and duped us, mocked and jeered—
    We're weaving, we're weaving!   10

"A curse on the king[2] of the rich man's nation
Who hardens his heart at our supplication,
Who wrings the last penny out of our hides
And lets us be shot like dogs besides—
    We're weaving, we're weaving!   15

"A curse on this false fatherland, teeming
With nothing but shame and dirty scheming,
Where every flower is crushed in a day,
Where worms are regaled on rot and decay—
    We're weaving, we're weaving!   20

"The shuttle flies, the loom creaks loud,
Night and day we weave your shroud—
Old Germany, at your shroud we sit,
We're weaving a threefold curse in it,
    We're weaving, we're weaving!"   25

2. Friedrich Wilhelm IV (1795–1861). Heine's poem is prophetic: in 1848 the king, though not deposed, was forced by revolution to grant a constitution to Prussia.

GIACOMO LEOPARDI
1798–1837

The product of a rigid upbringing by aristocratic parents, the Italian Giacomo Leopardi (*jah'-koh-moh lay-oh-pahr'-dee*) grew to adulthood plagued by many ailments, a hunchback close to blindness. But his intellectual powers were highly developed, and he soon developed a fine reputation as scholar, poet, and translator. His poetry characteristically expresses a poignant sensitivity to the beauty and promise of everyday life, as well as despair at its inevitable destruction with the passage of time. Only the poetic imagination, which allows Leopardi to grasp and transcend his own mortality, offers an escape: "And sweet to me the foundering in this sea [of eternity]," he writes in *The Infinite*.

Ottavio M. Casale translated the selections printed here, skillfully conveying the rhythms of Leopardi's free verse.

The best biography of Leopardi is I. Origo, *Leopardi: A Biography* (1935). G. P. Barricelli, *Giacomo Leopardi* (1986), provides a good general introduction. For critical insight, see the commentary in O. M. Casale, *A Leopardi Reader* (1981); J. P. Barricelli, *Giacomo Leopardi* (1986); and D. Bini, *A Fragrance from the Desert: Poetry and Philosophy in Giacomo Leopardi* (1983).

The Infinite

This lonely hill has always been so dear
To me, and dear the hedge which hides away
The reaches of the sky. But sitting here
And wondering, I fashion in my mind
The endless spaces far beyond, the more   5
Than human silences, and deepest peace;
So that the heart is on the edge of fear.
And when I hear the wind come blowing through
The trees, I pit its voice against that boundless
Silence and summon up eternity,   10
And the dead seasons, and the present one,
Alive with all its sound. And thus it is
In this immensity my thought is drowned:
And sweet to me the foundering in this sea.

To Himself

Now you may rest forever,
My tired heart. The last illusion is dead
That I believed eternal. Dead. I can
So clearly see—not only hope is gone
But the desire to be deceived as well.   5
Rest, rest forever.
You have beaten long enough. Nothing is worth
Your smallest motion, nor the earth your sighs.
This life is bitterness
And vacuum, nothing else. The world is mud.   10
From now on calm yourself.
Despair for the last time. The only gift
Fate gave our kind was death. Henceforth, heap scorn
Upon yourself, Nature, the ugly force
That, hidden, orders universal ruin,   15
And the boundless emptiness of everything.

To Sylvia

Sylvia. Do you remember still
The moments of your mortal lifetime here,
When such a loveliness
Shone in the elusive laughter of your eyes,
And you, contemplative and gay, climbed toward   5
The summit of your youth?

The tranquil chambers held,
The paths re-echoed, your perpetual song,
When at your woman's tasks

You sat, content to concentrate upon   10
The future beckoning within your mind.
It was the fragrant May,
And thus you passed your time.

   I often used to leave
The dear, belabored pages which consumed   15
So much of me and of my youth, and from
Ancestral balconies
Would lean to hear the music of your voice,
Your fingers humming through
The intricacies of the weaving work.   20
And I would gaze upon
The blue surrounding sky,
The paths and gardens golden in the sun,
And there the far-off sea, and here the mountain.
No human tongue can tell   25
What I felt then within my brimming heart.

   What tendernesses then,
What hopes, what hearts were ours, O Sylvia mine!
How large a thing seemed life, and destiny!
When I recall those bright anticipations,   30
Bitterness invades,
And I turn once again to mourn my lot.
O Nature, Nature, why
Do you not keep the promises you gave?
Why trick the children so?   35

   Before the winter struck the summer grass,
You died, my gentle girl,
Besieged by hidden illness and possessed.
You never saw the flowering of your years.
Your heart was never melted by the praise   40
Of your dark hair, your shy,
Enamoured eyes. Nor did you with your friends
Conspire on holidays to talk of love.

   The expectation failed
As soon for me, and fate denied my youth.   45
Ah how gone by, gone by,
You dear companion of my dawning time,
The hope that I lament!
Is this the world we knew? And these the joys
The love, the labors, happenings we shared?   50
And this the destiny
Of human beings? My poor one, when
The truth rose up, you fell,
And from afar you pointed me the way
To coldest death and the stark sepulchre.   55

The Village Saturday

The sun is falling as the peasant girl
Returns from the open fields,
Bearing a swathe of grass and in her hand
Her customary bunch of violets
And roses which will grace   5
Her hair and breast the coming holiday.
And, spinning, the old woman sits upon
The steps among her neighbors,
Their faces turned against the dying light;
And she tells tales of her green days, when she   10
Adorned her body for the holidays
And, slenderly robust,
Would dance the night away
Among the companions of her lovely prime.
The very air seems now to deepen, the sky   15
Turns darker blue. Down from the hills and roofs
Returning shadows fall
At the whitening of the moon.

    Now bells declare the time
Is near, the festive day,   20
The hour of heart's renewal.
The shouting lads invade
The village square in troops,
Leaping now here, now there,
Making such happy chatter.   25
Meanwhile the whistling laborer comes back
To take his meager meal
And ruminate about his day of rest.

    And then, when every other lamp is out
And other sounds are stilled—   30
Listen—a pounding hammer and a saw:
It is the carpenter,
Awake and hurrying by lanternlight
Inside his shuttered shop
To end his task before the morning breaks.   35

    Of all the seven days this is the one
Most cherished, full of joy and expectation.
The passing hours will bring tomorrow soon,
And tedium and sadness,
When each shall turn inside   40
His mind to his habitual travail.

    O playful little boy,
Your flowering time is like a day of grace,
So brightly blue,
Anticipating the great feast of life.   45
My child, enjoy the season.

> I will not tell you more; but if the day
> Seems slow in coming, do not grieve too much.

VICTOR HUGO
1802–1885

Celebrated as poet, dramatist, and novelist, Victor Hugo was a towering figure in his generation of French literary figures. He wrote in virtually every available genre and explored an enormous range of subject and feeling, helping throughout to articulate the principles of Romanticism. His various political allegiances determined some of his actions: for twenty years he exiled himself to the island of Guernsey (a possession of the British Crown), believing his life in danger after President Louis Napoleon seized power. Always, though, he devoted himself to writing. *Et nox facta est*, printed here, is the first section of the epic *The End of Satan* and depicts the fallen angel's defiant plunge from heaven. Hugo's portrait of Satan demonstrates both psychological acuity and powerful identification with the figure of a rebel. The poem makes one feel both the terror and the ugliness of Satan's nay-saying and the splendor of his refusal.

The translator is Mary Ann Caws, who has evoked the dignity and the intensity of Hugo's verse.

L. M. Porter, *Victor Hugo* (1998), provides a valuable introduction. Other useful critical treatments include W. N. Greenberg, *The Power of Rhetoric: Hugo's Metaphor and Poetics* (1985); H. Bloom, ed., *Victor Hugo* (1988), a collection of critical essays; and S. Guerlac, *The Impersonal Sublime* (1990). Hugo is also treated in E. S. Burt, *Poetry's Appeal: Nineteenth-Century French Lyric and the Political Space* (1999).

PRONOUNCING GLOSSARY

The following list uses common English syllables and stress accents to provide rough equivalents of selected words whose pronunciation may be unfamiliar to the general reader.

Barabbas: *bu-rab'-us*　　　　　　　　Victor Hugo: *vik-tor' yoo-goh*

Et nox facta est[1]

I

He[2] had been falling in the abyss some four thousand years.

> Never had he yet managed to grasp a peak,
> Nor lift even once his towering forehead.
> He sank deeper in the dark and the mist, aghast,
> Alone, and behind him, in the eternal nights,　　　　　5
> His wing feathers fell more slowly still.
> He fell dumbfounded, grim, and silent,
> Sad, his mouth open and his feet towards the heavens,

---

1. Written as part of *The End of Satan*, an epic poem never completed. The Latin title (And there was night) contrasts with the biblical "And there was light" (Genesis 1.3).　　2. Satan, formerly the rebellious Archangel Lucifer, thrown out of heaven by God (Revelation 12.7–9 and Isaiah 14.12).

The horror of the chasm imprinted on his livid face.
He cried: "Death!" his fists stretched out in the empty dark.   10
Later this word was man and was named Cain.[3]

He was falling. A rock struck his hand quite suddenly;
He held on to it, as a dead man holds on to his tomb,
And stopped. Someone, from on high, cried out to him: "Fall!
The suns will go out around you, accursed!"   15
And the voice was lost in the immensity of horror.
And pale, he looked toward the eternal dawn.
The suns were far off, but shone still.
Satan raised his head and spoke, his arms in the air:
"You lie!" This word was later the soul of Judas.[4]   20

Like the gods of bronze erect upon their pilasters,
He waited a thousand years, eyes fixed upon the stars.
The suns were far off, but were still shining.
The thunder then rumbled in the skies unhearing, cold.
Satan laughed, and spat towards the thunder.   25
Filled by the visionary shadow, the immensity
Shivered. This spitting out was later Barabbas.[5]

A passing breath made him fall lower still.

II

The fall of the damned one began once again.—Terrible,
Somber, and pierced with holes luminous as a sieve,   30
The sky full of suns withdrew, brightness
Trembled, and in the night the great fallen one,
Naked, sinister, and pulled by the weight of his crime,
Fell, and his head wedging the abyss apart.
Lower! Lower, and still lower! Everything presently   35
Fled from him; no obstacle to seize in passing,
No mountain, no crumbling rock, no stone,
Nothing, shadow! and from fright he closed his eyes.

And when they opened, three suns only
Shone, and shadow had eaten away the firmament.   40
All the other suns had perished.

III

A rock
Emerged from blackest mist like some arm approaching.
He grasped it, and his feet touched summits.

Then the dreadful being called Never
Dreamed. His forehead sank between his guilty hands.   45

---

3. The first murderer, son of Adam and brother of Abel, the victim (Genesis 4.1–15).   4. Judas Iscariot, the apostle who betrayed Jesus (Matthew 26.47–50, 27.3–5).   5. The condemned criminal who was freed instead of Jesus (Mark 15.6–15).

The three suns, far off, like three great eyes,
Watched him, and he watched them not.
Space resembled our earthly plains,
At evening, when the horizon sinking, retreating,
Blackens under the white eyes of the ghostly twilight.   50
Long rays entwined the feet of the great exile.
Behind him his shadow filled the infinite.
The peaks of chaos mingled in themselves.
In an instant he felt some horrendous growth of wings;
He felt himself become a monster, and that the angel in him   55
Was dying, and the rebel then knew regret.
He felt his shoulder, so bright before,[6]
Quiver in the hideous cold of membraned wing,
And folding his arms with his head lifted high,
This bandit, as if grown greater through affront,   60
Alone in these depths that only ruin inhabits,
Looked steadily at the shadow's cave.
The noiseless darkness grew in the nothingness.
Obscure opacity closed off the gaping sky;
And making beyond the last promontory   65
A triple crack in the black pane,
The three suns mingled their three lights.
You would have thought them three wheels of a chariot of fire,
Broken after some battle in the high firmament.
Like prows, the mountains from the mist emerged.   70
"So," cried Satan, "so be it! still I can see!
He shall have the blue sky, the black sky is mine.
Does he think I will come weeping to his door?
I hate him. Three suns suffice. What do I care?
I hate the day, the blueness, fragrance and the light."   75

Suddenly he shivered; there remained only one.

IV

The abyss was fading. Nothing kept its shape.
Darkness seemed to swell its giant wave.
Something nameless and submerged, something
That is no longer, takes its leave, falls silent;   80
And no one could have said, in this deep horror,
If this frightful remnant of a mystery or a world,
Like the vague mist where the dream takes flight,
Was called shipwreck or was called night;
And the archangel felt himself become a phantom.   85
He shouted: "Hell!" This word later made Sodom.[7]

And the voice repeated slowly on his forehead:
"Accursed! all about you the stars will go dark."

And already the sun was only a star.

---

6. Satan's previous name, Lucifer, means "Light Bearer."   7. Biblical city, with Gomorrah a symbol of
corruption and decadence. Both were destroyed by God (Genesis 18.20–19.28).

V

And all disappeared slowly under a veil.   90
Then the archangel quaked; Satan learned to shiver.
Toward the star trembling livid on the horizon
He hurled himself, leaping from peak to peak.
Then, although with horror at the wings of a beast,
Although it was the clothing of emprisonment,   95
Like a bird going from bush to bush,
Horrendous he took his flight from mount to mount,
And this convict began running in his cell.

He ran, he flew, he shouted: "Star of gold! Brother!
Wait for me! I'm running! Don't go out yet!   100
Don't leave me alone!"

                        Thus the monster
Crossed the first lakes of the dead immensity,
Former chaos, emptied and already stagnant,
And into the lugubrious depths he plunged.

Now the star was only a spark.   105

He went down further in universal shadow,
Sank further, cast himself wallowing in the night,
Climbed the filthy mountains, their damp gleaming front,
Whose base is unsteady in the cesspool deeps,
And trembling stared before him.

                        The spark   110
Was only a red dot in the depth of the dark abyss.

VI

As between two battlements the archer leans
On the wall, when twilight has reached his keep,
Wild he leaned from the mountain top,
And upon the star, hoping to arouse its flame,   115
He started to blow as upon some ember.
And anguish caused his fierce nostrils to swell.
The breath rushing from his chest
Is now upon earth and called hurricane.

With his breath a great noise stirred the shadow, an ocean   120
No being dwells in and no fires illumine.
The mountains found nearby took their flight,
The monstrous chaos full of fright arose
And began to shriek: Jehovah Jehovah!
The infinite opened, rent apart like a cloth,   125
But nothing moved in the lugubrious star;
And the damned one, crying: "Don't go out yet! I'll go on!
I'll get there!" resumed again his desperate flight.
And the glaciers mingled with the nights resembling them

Turned on their backs like frightened beasts,   130
And the black tornadoes and the hideous chasms
Bent in terror, while above them,
Flying toward the star like some arrow to the goal,
There passed, wild and haggard, this terrible supplicant.

And ever since it has seen this frightening flight,   135
This bitter abyss, aghast like a fleeing man
Retains forever the horror and the craze,
So monstrous was it to see, in the shadow immense,
Opening his atrocious wing far from the heavens,
This bat flying from his eternal prison!   140

VII

He flew for ten thousand years.

For ten thousand years,
Stretching forth his livid neck and his frenzied hands,
He flew without finding a peak on which to rest.
The star seemed sometimes to fade and to go out,   145
And the horror of the tomb caused the angel to shiver;
Then a pale brightness, vague, strange, uncertain,
Reappeared: and in joy, he cried: "Onward!"
Around him hovered the north wind birds.
He was flying. The infinite never ceases to start again.   150
His flight circled immense in that sea.
The night watched his horrible talons fleeing.
As a cloud feels its whirlwinds fall,
He felt his strength crumble in the chasm.
The winter murmured: tremble! and the shadow said: suffer!   155

Finally he perceived a black peak far off
Which a fearsome reflection in the shadow inflamed.
Satan, like a swimmer in his effort supreme,
Stretched out his wing, with claws and bald, and specter-pale,
Panting, broken, tired, and smoking with sweat,   160
He sank down on the edge of the abrupt descent.[8]

VIII

There was the sun dying in the abyss.
The star, in the deepest fog had no air to revive it,
Grew cold, dim, and was slowly destroyed.
Its sinister round was seen in the night;   165
And in this somber silence its fiery ulcers were seen
Subsiding under a leprosy of dark.
Coal of a world put out! torch blown out by God!
Its crevices still showed a trace of fire,
As if the soul could be seen through holes in the skull.   170
At the center there quivered and flickered a flame

---

8. Literally, escarpment, the steep wall before a fortification or cliff.

Now and then licking the outermost edge,
And from each crater flashes came
Shivering like flaming swords,
And fading noiselessly as dreams.   175
The star was almost black. The archangel was tired
Beyond voice or breath, a pity to see.
And the star in death throes under his savage glance,
Was dying, doing battle. With its somber apertures
Into the cold darkness it spewed now and again   180
Burning streams, crimson lumps, and smoking hills,
Rocks foaming with initial brightness:
As if this giant of life and light
Engulfed by the mist where all is fading,
Had refused to die without insulting the night   185
And spitting its lava in the shadow's face.
About it time and space and number,
Form, and noise expired, making
The forbidding and black oneness of void.
Then the specter Nothing[9] raised its head from the abyss.   190

Suddenly, from the heart of the star, a jet of sulphur
Sharp, clamorous like one dying in delirium,
Burst sudden, shining, splendid with surprise,
And lighting from far a thousand deathly forms,
Massive, pierced to the shadow's depths   195
The monstrous porches of endless deep.
Night and immensity formed
Their angels. Satan, wild and out of breath,
His vision dazzled and full of this flashing,
Beat with his wing, opened his hands and then shivered   200
And cried: "Despair! see it growing pale!"

The archangel understood, as does the mast in its sinking,
That he was the drowned man of the shadows' flood;
He furled once more his wing with its granite nails,
And wrung his hands. And the star went out.   205

IX

Now, near the skies, at chasm's edge where nothing changes,
One feather escaped from the archangel's wing
Remained and quivered, pure and white.
The angel on whose forehead the dazzling dawn is born
Saw and grasped it, observing the sublime sky: 210
"Lord, must it too fall into the abyss?"
God turned about, absorbed in being and in Life,
And said "Do not discard what has not fallen."[1]

*   *   *

9. Satan.   1. In the second part of *The End of Satan*—*Satan's Feather*—the feather is brought to life by a divine glance and becomes the female spirit Liberty. She wins God's permission to plunge into hell in an attempt to redeem her father (part 3), and in part 4 the repentant Archangel is released and re-created as Lucifer.

Black caves of the past, porches of time passed
With no date and no radiance, somber, unmeasured,   215
Cycles previous to man, chaos, heavens,
World terrible and rich in prodigious beings,
Oh fearful fog where the preadamites
Appeared, standing in limitless shadow.
Who could fathom you, oh chasms, oh unknown times.   220
The thinker barefoot like the poor,
Through respect for the One unseen, the sage,
Digs in the depths of origin and age,
Fathoms and seeks beyond the colossi,[2] further
Than the facts witnessed by the present sky,   225
Reaches with pale visage suspected things,
And finds, lifting the darkness of years
And the layers of days, worlds, voids,
Gigantic centuries dead beneath giants of centuries.
And thus the wise man dreams in the deep of the night   230
His face illumined by glints of the abyss.

2. Giants of preadamic time.

GUSTAVO ADOLFO BÉCQUER
1836–1870

Although his major literary reputation developed only after his death, Gustavo Adolfo Bécquer (*goo-stah'-voh ah-dol'-foh beh-hay'*), a pseudonym for Gustavo Adolfo Domínguez Bastida, is now generally considered the most important of the Spanish Romantic poets. Born in Seville, he was orphaned at the age of nine. He made his living—supporting a wife and two sons—by various means (government official, translator, journalist), but he always thought of himself as a writer, producing not only poetry but prose fiction and nonfiction. His early death resulted from tuberculosis.

Bécquer's poetry often attempts to express the ineffable, to convey his sense of spiritual exhilaration in the natural world. But the poet relies most often on simple, direct diction, in an attempt to familiarize grand ideas.

The selections printed here were translated by Bruce Phenix, who attempts both to offer as literal a rendition as possible of Bécquer's meaning and to convey the rhythm and movement of the Spanish text. The poems here included come from *Rimas*, a collection of Bécquer's verse in which individual poems are assigned only numbers, not titles. First lines have been used as titles in this anthology.

Although Bécquer has been the subject of much literary analysis in Spanish, little has been written about him in English. One useful study is E. L. King, *Gustavo Adolfo Bécquer: From Painter to Poet* (1953). A special issue of *Revista de Estudios Hispanicos* (1970) contains articles on Becquer in both Spanish and English.

[I know a strange, gigantic hymn]

I know a strange, gigantic hymn
that heralds a dawn in the night of the soul,

and these pages are cadences of this hymn
that the air carries abroad in the shadows.

    I should like to write it, subduing   5
the rebel against man, impoverished language,
in words that were at the same time
sighs and laughs, colours and notes.

    But in vain is the struggle; for there is no cipher
capable of containing it, and scarcely, oh beautiful one!   10
holding your hands in mine,
could I sing it, by ear, to you alone.

[Nameless spirit]

    Nameless spirit,
indefinable essence,
I live with the formless
life of idea.

    I swim in the void,   5
I quiver in the bonfire of the sun,
I palpitate among the shadows
and I float with the mists.

    I am the gold braid
of the distant star;   10
I am the lukewarm, serene light
of the high moon.

    I am the burning cloud
that undulates in the west:
I am the luminous wake   15
of the wandering star.

    I am snow on the peaks,
I am fire on the sands,
a blue wave on the seas,
and foam on the shores.   20

    I am a note in the lute,
perfume in the violet,
a fleeting flame in the tombs,
and ivy in the ruins.

    I deafen in the torrent,   25
and I hiss in the lightning,
and I blind in the flash,
and I roar in the storm.

    I laugh in the hills,
I whisper in the tall grass,   30

I sigh in the pure wave,
and I weep in the dead leaf.

I undulate with the atoms
of the smoke that rises,
and slowly goes up to the sky   35
in an immense spiral.

I, on the gilded threads
that the insects hang,
swing between the trees
in the fiery noonday heat.   40

I run after the nymphs
who in the cool stream
of the crystalline brook
frolic naked.

I, in forests of corals   45
carpeted by white pearls,
pursue in the ocean
the swift naiads.

I, in the hollow caverns
where the sun never penetrates,   50
mingling with the gnomes
observe their riches.

I look for the now obliterated
traces of the centuries,
and I know of those empires   55
of which not even the name is left.

I follow in rapid giddiness
the worlds that revolve,
and my pupil[1] embraces
the whole of creation.   60

I know of those regions
both where no noise reaches,
and where formless stars
wait for the breath of life.

I am the bridge that crosses   65
over the abyss,
I am the unknown ladder
that joins Heaven to the Earth.

I am the invisible
ring that fastens   70

1. Eye.

the world of form
to the world of idea.

I, in short, am that spirit,
unfamiliar essence,
mysterious perfume,   75
of which the poet is the vessel.

ROSALÍA DE CASTRO
1837–1885

An illegitimate child of a priest, who, of course, could not recognize her, the Spanish
writer Rosalía de Castro (*roh-za-lee'-a day kahs'-troh*) frequently expresses in her verse
a sense of despair that may, critics have speculated, derive from the ambiguities of
her birth. She began writing poetry as a child and published her first volume at the
age of twenty. A year later, she married, subsequently giving birth to seven children.
She died of cancer.

Beside the River Sar (1884), from which the selections printed here come, was the
last volume published in de Castro's lifetime. Predominantly melancholy in tone, the
poems express spiritual questioning, sorrow, and intense responsiveness to the environment. They are characteristically modest in tone (note, for example, *As I Composed This
Little Book*). At times they reveal the author's intimate reactions to her own experience,
as in *Mild Was the Air*, a lyric about the death of one of her infant children.

These poems were translated by S. Griswold Morley.

De Castro is the subject of a volume in the Twayne series: K. Kulp-Hill, *Rosalía de
Castro* (1977).

[As I composed this little book]

As I composed this little book, I thought:
Although my songs may never bring me fame,
    Simple they are and brief,
And may achieve, perhaps, my longed-for aim.
For they can be sure-fixed in memory   5
As are the prayers and rituals of belief,
Fervent though short, we learned in infancy.
Those we do not forget, in spite of grief
And time and distance and the destroying flame
Of passion. That is why my songs are brief   10
And simple,—though they may not bring me fame.

[Mild was the air]

Mild was the air
And still the day;

The rain fell gently
With never a stay.
I hushed my sobs
And softly wept;—   5
My child was dying
As he slept.
He left this world, and peace was in his heart;
I watched his going, and mine was torn apart!   10

Throw earth upon the unburied body . . . earth!
Before corruption fastens on his flesh!
Be calm; the grave is covered now. Quite soon
Up from the newly broken clods the grass
Will push; it will be green and fresh.   15

What are you seeking, you of the roving glance
And cloudy thought, prowling about that tomb?
With what is there to dust returning, fret
Not yourself. He'll not offend you more
Or love you more, who rests within that room.   20

Oh, never, never more! Can it be true
That all is ended now forever? No,
Surely immensity can have no end,
Eternity can never cease to flow.

You have left me forever; but my soul   25
Yearns with the eagerness of love to greet
My darling. You will come, or I shall go,
    Whither we twain can meet.

Within my body something of you remains
    That cannot die,   30
And God, because He is just and because He is good,
    Will never try
To take it from me. Somewhere—on earth, in Heaven,
Beyond all sounded space—you will find me,
I shall find you. For certainly I know   35
Immensity can never have an end,
Eternity can never cease to flow.

But . . . he is gone, gone never to return!
Ay, that is true. To man, guest of a day
In this our world, nothing eternal is.   40
Within its circle he is born and lives and dies,
As every creature is born and lives and dies;
    It is the earthly way.

[A glowworm scatters flashes through the moss]

A glowworm scatters flashes through the moss;
A star gleams in its high remote domain.

Abyss above, and in the depths abyss:
What things come to an end and what remain?
   Man's thought—we call it science!—peers and pries   5
Into the soundless dark. But it is vain:
When all is done, we still are ignorant
Of what things reach an end, and what remain.

   Kneeling before an image rudely carved,
I sink my spirit in the Infinite,   10
And—is it impious?—I vacillate
And tremble, questioning Heaven and Hell of it.

   My Deity, shattered in a thousand bits,
Has fallen to chasms where I cannot see.
I rush to seek Him, and my groping meets   15
A solitary vast vacuity.

   When lo! from their lofty marble niches,
Angels gazed down in sorrow; and in my ears
Murmured a gentle voice: "Unhappy soul,
   Take hope; pour out thy tears   20
Before the feet of the Most High;
But well remember this: No insolent cry
   To Heaven makes its way
From one whose heart adores material things,
Who makes an idol out of Adam's clay."   25

[The feet of Spring are on the stair]

   The feet of Spring are on the stair;
Her breath is sweet and warm and rare;
Beneath the soil in amorous heat
Seeds are astir with restless beat,
And atoms drifting in the air,   5
Afloat and silent, pair by pair,
   Kiss as they meet.

   Youth's blood is eager, youth's heart is hot,
Its courage leaps, its bold mad thought
Believes that man—oh, dreams of youth!—   10
Is, like the gods, immortal. What
If dreams are lies? This much is truth:
Unblest are they who dreamless draw their breath,
And fortunate who in a dream find death.

   How swift the passage of each thing   15
     In our sad world!
By a wild giant, quivering
     Our lives are whirled!
Yesterday bud, today a rose,
And then the sun-scorched blossom goes   20
     As Summer masters Spring.

[Candescent[1] lies the air]

Candescent lies the air.
A fox explores the unfrequented road.
  The brook which cleanly flowed
As crystal, turns now noisome, where
  A pine, motionless, misses   5
The breeze and its inconstant kisses.

  A stifling silence quells the countryside.
    Only the insect's drone,
    Persistent, shrilling
Over the breathless landscape, filling   10
The shadows moist and wide,
Like a low death-rattle, makes a monotone.

  In summer, to the fighter worn and dull,
    The midmost hour of day
    Is best called night.   15
    Then more than ever weigh
Upon him the unconquerable might
Of matter, and the anguish of the soul.

  Return, return, ye chill wild nights of winter,
Our well-tried friends of a not distant time!   20
Give us again your nipping frost and rime,
To cool the blood inflamed by sorry summer,
Insufferable with its flaming rays—
Yes, sorry! though it bring the fruited wheat!

[The ailing woman felt her forces ebb]

The ailing woman felt her forces ebb
With summer, and knew her time was imminent.
    "In autumn I shall die,"
She thought, half-melancholy, half-content,
"And I shall feel the leaves, that will be dead   5
Like me, drop on the grave in which I lie."

  Not even Death would do her so much pleasure.
    Cruel to her he too,
In winter spared her life, and when anew
The earth was being born in blossoming,   10
Slew her by inches to the joyous hymns
    Of fair and merry spring!

1. Glowing or dazzling as from great heat.

ALEXANDER SERGEYEVICH PUSHKIN
1799–1837

In his best-known story, *The Queen of Spades,* Alexander Pushkin combines familiar elements of Romantic fiction—the penniless young woman; the ambitious, passionate young man; the decayed beauty; the ghost—in a tale with intense ironic overtones, a tale later a favorite of the great Russian novelist Fyodor Dostoevsky. Pushkin's own life story sounds like a Romantic novel. Born into an aristocratic Russian family, neglected by his parents, he early began an extensive amatory and poetic career, publishing his first poem at the age of fifteen and becoming notorious about the same time for his many erotic involvements. At eighteen he graduated from a distinguished boarding school and accepted appointment in the Foreign Service; six years later, the various instances of his defiance of authority resulted in expulsion from the service and confinement, under police surveillance, on a paternal estate. After the death of Tsar Alexander I and the abortive military uprising that followed (an uprising involving several of Pushkin's friends, five of whom were subsequently hanged), Pushkin—by then a well-known poet—was befriended (1826) by the new tsar, Nicholas. He moved back to Moscow, then to Petersburg, leading a moneyed and relatively carefree life. In 1831, however, he married a nineteen-year-old woman, whose apparently flirtatious behavior embittered his subsequent life. He died after a duel with his wife's putative lover.

Producing short lyrics, narrative poems, a great novel in verse (*Eugene Onegin*), lyrical drama (notably *Boris Gudonov*), versified folk tales, and prose fiction, Pushkin established himself as one of Russia's greatest writers. His interest in his nation's past, his tendency to challenge authority, his fascination with the character and situation of strong individuals: such obsessive concerns link his work with that of his Romantic contemporaries elsewhere in Europe. Goethe, Byron, and early nineteenth-century French novelists had a marked influence on him. He retained also, however, the kind of clarity, discipline, and ironic distance more often associated with the literature of the preceding century.

The treatment of love and sexuality in *The Queen of Spades* exemplifies the complexity of Pushkin's approach. First of all we hear the story of the "Muscovite Venus," the beautiful young gambler who pays her debts by learning the secret of three infallible cards. Then we encounter a young woman suffering in her dependent position and longing for a "deliverer." Hermann, the immediate object of Lisaveta's dreams, has his own sexual fantasies: himself a young man, he imagines becoming the lover of the eighty-seven-year-old countess. At this point, if not before, the reader begins to realize that something's wrong here: this is not the kind of romantic tale we're used to. Describing Hermann's first glimpse of Lisaveta, Pushkin writes, "Hermann saw a small, fresh face and a pair of dark eyes. That moment decided his fate." A Romantic cliché—except that the young man sees Lisaveta not as an object of devotion but as a means to an end. He sends her a love letter, copied word for word from a German novel. His rapidly developing passion focuses on financial, not erotic, gain.

Lisaveta's character remains somewhat more ambiguous. The narrator invokes sympathy for her plight, at the mercy of a tyrannical employer who makes endless irrational demands and who never pays her. Her situation prohibits her from enjoying the kinds of amorous gratification other young women can expect. We can understand, therefore, why her dreams should concentrate specifically on a deliverer. Like Hermann, although far less unscrupulous, she may indulge in intrigues as a means to an end—in her case, not money but liberty.

The Queen of Spades contains no completely attractive characters. If Lisaveta's victimization arouses compassion, her lack of moral force or determination may also provoke irritation. Hermann's will to succeed, on the other hand, makes him a potential hero; but his obsession with money and his mean-spirited expediency alienate most readers. The countess, old and approaching death, uses the power of her money and rank with utter disregard for the needs or feelings of others. Even such a minor figure as the countess's grandson, Tomsky, playing with Lisaveta's feelings, going through his ritualized flirtation with Princess Polina, seems thoroughly contaminated by the values of the world he inhabits.

Indeed, those values provide the central subject of this tale. Pushkin employs conventions of the kind of ghost story common in folk tales to convey serious criticism of a social structure corrupted by universal concentration on money. Gambling provides not only the chief male activity but also the central metaphor of the story. Everyone is out for what he or she can get. The countess, whose days at the card table are past, uses her money to buy subservience; Lisaveta is willing to risk her reputation, maybe even her chastity, for the possibility of escaping servitude; Hermann frightens someone to death in an effort to make his fortune; Tomsky plays elaborate social games of advance and retreat, trying to get his princess. The queen of spades is a conventional symbol of death; the kind of death most important in Pushkin's story is not literal—not the countess's demise—but figurative: it is the spiritual death suffered by the other characters, over whose world the countess/queen of spades metaphorically presides.

The "Conclusion" of *The Queen of Spades*, a deadpan summary of the characters' future careers, epitomizes the story's central concerns. Hermann's madness dramatizes the financial obsession he has displayed from the beginning; Lisaveta's marriage, to an anonymous "very agreeable young man" with a good position "somewhere," emphasizes the degree to which she has always wished for marriage as rescue, not as attachment to a particular beloved other. In her married state, Lisaveta, ironically, "is bringing up a poor relative," recapitulating the structure of exploitation from which she herself suffered. Tomsky, relatively unimportant to the plot line, supplies the subject for the story's concluding sentence: his promotion and his "good" marriage remind us that everyone in the society here described seeks personal advantage at all costs. Hermann has simply paid the cost in the most dramatic way.

Henri Troyat, *Pushkin* (1971), is an excellent biography. For biography and criticism, the student might also consult Walter Arndt, *Pushkin Threefold: Narrative, Lyric, Polemic and Ribald Verse* (1972); John Bayley, *Pushkin: A Comparative Commentary* (1971); P. Debreczeny, *The Other Pushkin: A Study of Alexander Pushkin's Prose* (1983); W. M. Todd III, *Fiction and Society in the Age of Pushkin: Ideology, Institutions, and Narrative* (1986); P. Debreczeny, *Social Functions of Literature: Alexander Pushkin and Russian Culture* (1997); B. Cooke, *Pushkin and the Creative Process* (1998); and S. Evdokimova, *Pushkin's Historical Imagination* (1999).

PRONOUNCING GLOSSARY

The following list uses common English syllables and stress accents to provide rough equivalents of selected words whose pronunciation may be unfamiliar to the general reader.

Chekalinsky: *chek-a-lin'-skee*

Eletskaya: *el-et-skai'-yah*

Fedotovna: *fed-ot'-ohv-nah*

Ilyitch: *il'-yich*

Lisaveta Ivanovna: *lee-zah-vet'-ah ee-vahn'-ohv-nah*

Richelieu: *ree'-sha-lyeuh*

St-Germain: *sanh-zher-manhb'*

The Queen of Spades[1]

CHAPTER ONE

And on rainy days
They gathered
Often;
Their stakes—God help them!—
Wavered from fifty
To a hundred,
And they won
And marked up their winnings
With chalk.
Thus on rainy days
Were they
Busy.[2]

There was a card party one day in the rooms of Narumov, an officer of the Horse Guards. The long winter evening slipped by unnoticed; it was five o'clock in the morning before the assembly sat down to supper. Those who had won ate with a big appetite; the others sat distractedly before their empty plates. But champagne was brought in, the conversation became more lively, and everyone took a part in it.

"And how did you get on, Surin?" asked the host.

"As usual, I lost. I must confess, I have no luck: I never vary my stake, never get heated, never lose my head, and yet I always lose!"

"And weren't you tempted even once to back[3] on a series . . . ? Your strength of mind astonishes me."

"What about Hermann then," said one of the guests, pointing at the young Engineer.[4] "He's never held a card in his hand, never doubled a single stake in his life, and yet he sits up until five in the morning watching us play."

"The game fascinates me," said Hermann, "but I am not in the position to sacrifice the essentials of life in the hope of acquiring the luxuries."

"Hermann's a German: he's cautious—that's all," Tomsky observed. "But if there's one person I can't understand, it's my grandmother, the Countess Anna Fedotovna."

"How? Why?" the guests inquired noisily.

"I can't understand why it is," Tomsky continued, "that my grandmother doesn't gamble."

"But what's so astonishing about an old lady of eighty not gambling?" asked Narumov.

"Then you don't know . . . ?"

"No, indeed; I know nothing."

"Oh well, listen then:

"You must know that about sixty years ago my grandmother went to Paris, where she made something of a hit. People used to chase after her to catch a glimpse of *la vénus moscovite*; Richelieu[5] paid court to her, and my grandmother vouches that he almost shot himself on account of her cruelty. At

---

1. Translated by Gillon R. Aitken.   2. Like most of the chapter epigraphs, this was presumably written by Pushkin himself.   3. Bet.   4. A member of the Corps of Engineers, concerned with fortifications.
5. Louis-François-Arnand de Vignerod du Plessis, duc de Richelieu (1696–1788), French aristocrat renowned throughout the 18th century for both his military and his sexual exploits. *La vénus moscovite*: the Venus of Moscow (French). Venus was the goddess of love.

that time ladies used to play faro.[6] On one occasion at the Court, my grandmother lost a very great deal of money on credit to the Duke of Orleans. Returning home, she removed the patches[7] from her face, took off her hooped petticoat, announced her loss to my grandfather and ordered him to pay back the money. My late grandfather, as far as I can remember, was a sort of lackey to my grandmother. He feared her like fire; on hearing of such a disgraceful loss, however, he completely lost his temper; he produced his accounts, showed her that she had spent half a million francs in six months, pointed out that neither their Moscow nor their Saratov estates were in Paris, and refused point-blank to pay the debt. My grandmother gave him a box on the ear and went off to sleep on her own as an indication of her displeasure. In the hope that this domestic infliction would have had some effect on him, she sent for her husband the next day; she found him unshakeable. For the first time in her life she approached him with argument and explanation, thinking that she could bring him to reason by pointing out that there are debts and debts, that there is a big difference between a Prince and a coachmaker. But my grandfather remained adamant, and flatly refused to discuss the subject any further. My grandmother did not know what to do. A little while before, she had become acquainted with a very remarkable man. You have heard of Count St-Germain,[8] about whom so many marvellous stories are related. You know that he held himself out to be the Wandering Jew, and the inventor of the elixir of life, the philosopher's stone and so forth. Some ridiculed him as a charlatan and in his memoirs Casanova declares that he was a spy. However, St-Germain, in spite of the mystery which surrounded him, was a person of venerable appearance and much in demand in society. My grandmother is still quite infatuated with him and becomes quite angry if anyone speaks of him with disrespect. My grandmother knew that he had large sums of money at his disposal. She decided to have recourse to him, and wrote asking him to visit her without delay. The eccentric old man at once called on her and found her in a state of terrible grief. She depicted her husband's barbarity in the blackest light, and ended by saying that she pinned all her hopes on his friendship and kindness.

"St-Germain reflected. 'I could let you have this sum,' he said, 'but I know that you would not be at peace while in my debt, and I have no wish to bring fresh troubles upon your head. There is another solution—you can win back the money."

" 'But, my dear Count," my grandmother replied, 'I tell you—we have no money at all.'

" 'In this case money is not essential,' St-Germain replied. 'Be good enough to hear me out."

"And at this point he revealed to her the secret for which any one of us here would give a very great deal . . ."

The young gamblers listened with still great attention. Tomsky lit his pipe, drew on it and continued:

"That same evening my grandmother went to Versailles, *au jeu de la Reine.*[9] The Duke of Orleans kept the bank; inventing some small tale, my grandmother lightly excused herself for not having brought her debt,

6. A card game much used for gambling.   7. I.e., beauty patches, artificial "beauty marks" made of black silk or court plaster and worn on the face or neck.   8. Celebrated adventurer (ca. 1710–1784?) who frequented the French, German, and Russian courts.   9. To the queen's game (French).

and began to play against him. She chose three cards and played them one after the other: all three won and my grandmother recouped herself completely."

"Pure luck!" said one of the guests.

"A fairy-tale," observed Hermann.

"Perhaps the cards were marked!" said a third.

"I don't think so," Tomsky replied gravely.

"What!" cried Narumov. "You have a grandmother who can guess three cards in succession, and you haven't yet contrived to learn her secret."

"No, not much hope of that!" replied Tomsky. "She had four sons, including my father; all four were desperate gamblers, and yet she did not reveal her secret to a single one of them, although it would have been a good thing if she had told them—told me, even. But this is what I heard from my uncle, Count Ivan Ilyitch, and he gave me his word for its truth. The late Chaplitsky—the same who died a pauper after squandering millions—in his youth once lost nearly 300,000 roubles—to Zoritch, if I remember rightly. He was in despair. My grandmother, who was most strict in her attitude towards the extravagances of young men, for some reason took pity on Chaplitsky. She told him the three cards on condition that he played them in order; and at the same time she exacted his solemn promise that he would never play again as long as he lived. Chaplitsky appeared before his victor; they sat down to play. On the first card Chaplitsky staked 50,000 roubles and won straight off; he doubled his stake, redoubled—and won back more than he had lost. . . .

"But it's time to go to bed; it's already a quarter to six."

Indeed, the day was already beginning to break. The young men drained their glasses and dispersed.

CHAPTER TWO

"Il paraît que monsieur est décidément pour les suivantes."
"Que voulez-vous, madame? Elles sont plus fraîches."
FASHIONABLE CONVERSATION

The old Countess * * *[1] was seated before the looking-glass in her dressing-room. Three lady's maids stood by her. One held a jar of rouge, another a box of hairpins, and the third a tall bonnet with flame-coloured ribbons. The Countess no longer had the slightest pretensions to beauty, which had long since faded from her face, but she still preserved all the habits of her youth, paid strict regard to the fashions of the seventies, and devoted to her dress the same time and attention as she had done sixty years before. At an embroidery frame by the window sat a young lady, her ward.

"Good morning, *grand'maman!*" said a young officer as he entered the room. "*Bonjour, mademoiselle Lise. Grand'maman,*[2] I have a request to make of you."

"What is it, Paul?"

---

1. Asterisks in this selection are the author's and are intended to suggest that the proper name of an actual person has been omitted. The epigram can be translated as: "It appears that the gentleman is decidedly in favor of servant girls." "What would you have me do, Madam? They are fresher [than upper-class women]" (French). 2. Russian aristocrats often spoke French. Lisaveta is here called by the French name Lise, and Pavel, Paul.

"I want you to let me introduce one of my friends to you, and to allow me to bring him to the ball on Friday."

"Bring him straight to the ball and introduce him to me there. Were you at * * *'s yesterday?"

"Of course. It was very gay; we danced until five in the morning. How charming Eletskaya was!"

"But, my dear, what's charming about her? Isn't she like her grandmother, the Princess Darya Petrovna . . . ? By the way, I dare say she's grown very old now, the Princess Darya Petrovna?"

"What do you mean, 'grown old'?" asked Tomsky thoughtlessly. "She's been dead for seven years."

The young lady raised her head and made a sign to the young man. He remembered then that the death of any of her contemporaries was kept secret from the old Countess, and he bit his lip. But the Countess heard the news, previously unknown to her, with the greatest indifference.

"Dead!" she said. "And I didn't know it. We were maids of honour together, and when we were presented, the Empress . . ."

And for the hundredth time the Countess related the anecdote to her grandson.

"Come, Paul," she said when she had finished her story, "help me to stand up. Lisanka, where's my snuff-box?"

And with her three maids the Countess went behind a screen to complete her dress. Tomsky was left alone with the young lady.

"Whom do you wish to introduce?" Lisaveta Ivanovna asked softly.

"Narumov. Do you know him?"

"No. Is he a soldier or a civilian?"

"A soldier."

"An Engineer?"

"No, he's in the Cavalry. What made you think he was an Engineer?"

The young lady smiled but made no reply.

"Paul!" cried the Countess from behind the screen. "Bring along a new novel with you some time, will you, only please not one of those modern ones."

"What do you mean, *grand'maman?*"

"I mean not the sort of novel in which the hero strangles either of his parents or in which someone is drowned.[3] I have a great horror of drowned people."

"Such novels don't exist nowadays. Wouldn't you like a Russian one?"

"Are there such things? Send me one, my dear, please send me one."

"Will you excuse me now, *grand'maman,* I'm in a hurry. Good-bye, Lisaveta Ivanovna. What made you think that Narumov was in the Engineers?"

And Tomsky left the dressing-room.

Lisaveta Ivanovna was left on her own; she put aside her work and began to look out of the window. Presently a young officer appeared from behind the corner house on the other side of the street. A flush spread over her cheeks; she took up her work again and lowered her head over the frame. At this moment, the Countess returned, fully dressed.

---

3. Novels of the sort the countess does not wish to read were typical of the then current decadent movement in French literature.

"Order the carriage, Lisanka," she said, "and we'll go for a drive."

Lisanka got up from behind her frame and began to put away her work.

"What's the matter with you, my child? Are you deaf?" shouted the Countess. "Order the carriage this minute."

"I'll do so at once," the young lady replied softly and hastened into the ante-room.

A servant entered the room and handed the Countess some books from the Prince Pavel Alexandrovitch.

"Good, thank him," said the Countess. "Lisanka, Lisanka, where are you running to?"

"To get dressed."

"Plenty of time for that, my dear. Sit down. Open the first volume and read to me."

The young lady took up the book and read a few lines.

"Louder!" said the Countess. "What's the matter with you, my child? Have you lost your voice, or what . . . ? Wait . . . move that footstool up to me . . . nearer . . . that's right!"

Lisaveta Ivanovna read a further two pages. The Countess yawned.

"Put the book down," she said; "what rubbish! Have it returned to Prince Pavel with my thanks. . . . But where is the carriage?"

"The carriage is ready," said Lisaveta Ivanovna, looking out into the street.

"Then why aren't you dressed?" asked the Countess. "I'm always having to wait for you—it's intolerable, my dear!"

Lisa ran up to her room. Not two minutes elapsed before the Countess began to ring with all her might. The three lady's maids came running in through one door and the valet through another.

"Why don't you come when you're called?" the Countess asked them. "Tell Lisaveta Ivanovna that I'm waiting for her."

Lisaveta Ivanovna entered the room wearing her hat and cloak.

"At last, my child!" said the Countess. "But what clothes you're wearing . . . ! Whom are you hoping to catch? What's the weather like? It seems windy."

"There's not a breath of wind, your Ladyship," replied the valet.

"You never know what you're talking about! Open that small window. There; as I thought: windy and bitterly cold. Unharness the horses. Lisaveta, we're not going out—there was no need to dress up like that."

"And this is my life," thought Lisaveta Ivanovna.

And indeed Lisaveta Ivanovna was a most unfortunate creature. As Dante says: "You shall learn the salt taste of another's bread, and the hard path up and down his stairs";[4] and who better to know the bitterness of dependence than the poor ward of a well-born old lady? The Countess * * * was far from being wicked, but she had the capriciousness of a woman who has been spoiled by the world, and the miserliness and cold-hearted egotism of all old people who have done with loving and whose thoughts lie with the past. She took part in all the vanities of the *haut-monde*;[5] she dragged herself to balls, where she sat in a corner, rouged and dressed in old-fashioned style, like some misshapen but essential ornament of the ball-room; on arrival, the guests would approach her with low bows,

4. *Paradiso* 17.59.   5. High society (French).

as if in accordance with an established rite, but after that, they would pay no further attention to her. She received the whole town at her house, and although no longer able to recognise the faces of her guests, she observed the strictest etiquette. Her numerous servants, grown fat and grey in her hall and servants' room, did exactly as they pleased, vying with one another in stealing from the dying old lady. Lisaveta Ivanovna was the household martyr. She poured out the tea, and was reprimanded for putting in too much sugar; she read novels aloud, and was held guilty of all the faults of the authors; she accompanied the Countess on her walks, and was made responsible for the state of the weather and the pavement. There was a salary attached to her position, but it was never paid; meanwhile, it was demanded of her to be dressed like everybody else—that is, like the very few who could afford to dress well. In society she played the most pitiable role. Everybody knew her, but nobody took any notice of her; at balls she danced only when there was a partner short, and ladies only took her arm when they needed to go to the dressing-room to make some adjustment to their dress. She was proud and felt her position keenly, and looked around her in impatient expectation of a deliverer; but the young men, calculating in their flightiness, did not honour her with their attention, despite the fact that Lisaveta Ivanovna was a hundred times prettier than the cold, arrogant but more eligible young ladies on whom they danced attendance. Many a time did she creep softly away from the bright but wearisome drawing-room to go and cry in her own poor room, where stood a papered screen, a chest of drawers, a small looking-glass and a painted bedstead, and where a tallow candle burned dimly in its copper candle-stick.

One day—two days after the evening described at the beginning of this story, and about a week previous to the events just recorded—Lisaveta Ivanovna was sitting at her embroidery frame by the window, when, happening to glance out into the street, she saw a young Engineer, standing motionless with his eyes fixed upon her window. She lowered her head and continued with her work; five minutes later she looked out again—the young officer was still standing in the same place. Not being in the habit of flirting with passing officers, she ceased to look out of the window, and sewed for about two hours without raising her head. Dinner was announced. She got up and began to put away her frame, and, glancing casually out into the street, she saw the officer again. She was considerably puzzled by this. After dinner, she approached the window with a feeling of some disquiet, but the officer was no longer outside, and she thought no more of him.

Two days later, while preparing to enter the carriage with the Countess, she saw him again. He was standing just by the front-door, his face concealed by a beaver collar; his dark eyes shone from beneath his cap. Without knowing why, Lisaveta Ivanovna felt afraid, and an unaccountable trembling came over her as she sat down in the carriage.

On her return home, she hastened to the window—the officer was standing in the same place as before, his eyes fixed upon her; she drew back, tormented by curiosity and agitated by a feeling that was quite new to her.

Since then, not a day had passed without the young man appearing at the customary hour beneath the windows of their house. A sort of mute acquaintance grew up between them. At work in her seat, she used to feel him approaching, and would raise her head to look at him—for longer and longer each day. The young man seemed to be grateful to her for this: she saw, with the sharp eye of youth, how a sudden flush would spread across his pale cheeks on each occasion that their glances met. After a week she smiled at him. . . .

When Tomsky asked leave of the Countess to introduce one of his friends to her; the poor girl's heart beat fast. But on learning that Narumov was in the Horse Guards, and not in the Engineers, she was sorry that, by an indiscreet question, she had betrayed her secret to the light-hearted Tomsky.

Hermann was the son of a Russianised German, from whom he had inherited a small amount of money. Being firmly convinced of the necessity of ensuring his independence, Hermann did not draw on the income that this yielded, but lived on his pay, forbidding himself the slightest extravagance. Moreover, he was secretive and ambitious, and his companions rarely had occasion to laugh at his excessive thrift. He had strong passions and a fiery imagination, but his tenacity of spirit saved him from the usual errors of youth. Thus, for example, although at heart a gambler, he never took a card in his hand, for he reckoned that his position did not allow him (as he put it) "to sacrifice the essentials of life in the hope of acquiring the luxuries"—and meanwhile, he would sit up at the card table for whole nights at a time, and follow the different turns of the game with feverish anxiety.

The story of the three cards had made a strong impression on his imagination, and he could think of nothing else all night.

"What if the old Countess should reveal her secret to me?" he thought the following evening as he wandered through the streets of Petersburg. "What if she should tell me the names of those three winning cards? Why not try my luck . . . ? Become introduced to her, try to win her favour, perhaps become her lover . . . ? But all that demands time, and she's eighty-seven; she might die in a week, in two days . . . ! And the story itself . . . ? Can one really believe it . . . ? No! Economy, moderation and industry; these are my three winning cards, these will treble my capital, increase it sevenfold, and earn for me ease and independence!"

Reasoning thus, he found himself in one of the principal streets of Petersburg, before a house of old-fashioned architecture. The street was crowded with vehicles; one after another, carriages rolled up to the lighted entrance. From them there emerged, now the shapely little foot of some beautiful young woman, now a rattling jack-boot, now the striped stocking and elegant shoe of a diplomat. Furs and capes flitted past the majestic hall-porter. Hermann stopped.

"Whose house is this?" he asked the watchman at the corner.

"The Countess * * *'s," the watchman replied.

Hermann started. His imagination was again fired by the amazing story of the three cards. He began to walk around near the house, thinking of its owner and her mysterious faculty. It was late when he returned to his humble rooms; for a long time he could not sleep; and when at last he did drop off, cards, a green table,[6] heaps of banknotes and piles of golden coins appeared to him in his dreams. He played one card after the other, doubled his stake decisively, won unceasingly, and raked in the golden coins and stuffed his

---

6. Tables on which gambling took place were typically covered with green baize.

pockets with the banknotes. Waking up late, he sighed at the loss of his imaginary fortune, again went out to wander about the town and again found himself outside the house of the Countess * * *. Some unknown power seemed to have attracted him to it. He stopped and began to look at the windows. At one he saw a head with long black hair, probably bent down over a book or a piece of work. The head was raised. Hermann saw a small, fresh face and a pair of dark eyes. That moment decided his fate.

CHAPTER THREE

*Vous m'écrivez, mon ange, des lettres de
quatre pages plus vite que je ne puis
les lire.*[7]

CORRESPONDENCE

Scarcely had Lisaveta Ivanovna taken off her hat and cloak when the Countess sent for her and again ordered her to have the horses harnessed. They went out to take their seats in the carriage. At the same moment as the old lady was being helped through the carriage doors by two footmen, Lisaveta Ivanovna saw her Engineer standing close by the wheel; he seized her hand; before she could recover from her fright, the young man had disappeared—leaving a letter in her hand. She hid it in her glove and throughout the whole of the drive neither heard nor saw a thing. As was her custom when riding in her carriage, the Countess kept up a ceaseless flow of questions: "Who was it who met us just now? What's this bridge called? What's written on that signboard?" This time Lisaveta Ivanovna's answers were so vague and inappropriate that the Countess became angry.

"What's the matter with you, my child? Are you in a trance or something? Don't you hear me or understand what I'm saying . . . ? Heaven be thanked that I'm still sane enough to speak clearly."

Lisaveta Ivanovna did not listen to her. On returning home, she ran up to her room and drew the letter out of her glove; it was unsealed. Lisaveta Ivanovna read it through. The letter contained a confession of love; it was tender, respectful and taken word for word from a German novel. But Lisaveta Ivanovna had no knowledge of German and was most pleased by it.

Nevertheless, the letter made her feel extremely uneasy. For the first time in her life she was entering into a secret and confidential relationship with a young man. His audacity shocked her. She reproached herself for her imprudent behaviour, and did not know what to do. Should she stop sitting at the window and by a show of indifference cool off the young man's desire for further acquaintance? Should she send the letter back to him? Or answer it with cold-hearted finality? There was nobody to whom she could turn for advice: she had no friend or preceptress. Lisaveta Ivanovna resolved to answer the letter.

She sat down at her small writing-table, took a pen and some paper, and lost herself in thought. Several times she began her letter—and then tore it up; her manner of expression seemed to her to be either too condescending or too heartless. At last she succeeded in writing a few lines that satisfied her:

7. My angel, you write me four-page-long letters faster than I can read them (French).

I am sure that your intentions are honourable, and that you did not wish to offend me by your rash behaviour, but our acquaintance must not begin in this way. I return your letter to you and hope that in the future I shall have no cause to complain of undeserved disrespect.

The next day, as soon as she saw Hermann approach, Lisaveta Ivanovna rose from behind her frame, went into the ante-room, opened a small window, and threw her letter into the street, trusting to the agility of the young officer to pick it up. Hermann ran forward, took hold of the letter and went into a confectioner's shop. Breaking the seal of the envelope, he found his own letter and Lisaveta Ivanovna's answer. It was as he had expected, and he returned home, deeply preoccupied with his intrigue.

Three days afterwards, a bright-eyed young girl brought Lisaveta Ivanovna a letter from a milliner's shop. Lisaveta Ivanovna opened it uneasily, envisaging a demand for money, but she suddenly recognised Hermann's handwriting.

"You have made a mistake, my dear," she said; "this letter is not for me."

"Oh, but it is!" the girl answered cheekily and without concealing a sly smile. "Read it."

Lisaveta Ivanovna ran her eyes over the note. Hermann demanded a meeting.

"It cannot be," said Lisaveta Ivanovna, frightened at the haste of his demand and the way in which it was made: "this is certainly not for me."

And she tore the letter up into tiny pieces.

"If the letter wasn't for you, why did you tear it up?" asked the girl. "I would have returned it to the person who sent it."

"Please, my dear," Lisaveta Ivanovna said, flushing at the remark, "don't bring me any more letters in the future. And tell the person who sent you that he should be ashamed of . . ."

But Hermann was not put off. By some means or other, he sent a letter to Lisaveta Ivanovna every day. The letters were no longer translated from the German. Hermann wrote them inspired by passion, and used a language true to his character; these letters were the expression of his obsessive desires and the disorder of his unfettered imagination. Lisaveta Ivanovna no longer thought of returning them to him: she revelled in them, began to answer them, and with each day, her replies became longer and more tender. Finally, she threw out of the window the following letter:

This evening there is a ball at the * * * Embassy. The Countess will be there. We will stay until about two o'clock. Here is your chance to see me alone. As soon as the Countess has left the house, the servants will probably go to their quarters—with the exception of the hall-porter, who normally goes out to his closet anyway. Come at half-past eleven. Walk straight upstairs. If you meet anybody in the ante-room, ask whether the Countess is at home. You will be told 'No'—and there will be nothing you can do but go away. But it is unlikely that you will meet anybody. The lady's maids sit by themselves, all in the one room. On leaving the hall, turn to the left and walk straight on until you come to the Countess' bedroom. In the bedroom, behind a screen, you will see two small doors: the one on the right leads into the study, which the Countess never goes into; the one on

*the left leads into a corridor and thence to a narrow winding staircase: this
staircase leads to my bedroom.*

Hermann quivered like a tiger as he awaited the appointed hour. He was
already outside the Countess' house at ten o'clock. The weather was terrible;
the wind howled, and a wet snow fell in large flakes upon the deserted streets,
where the lamps shone dimly. Occasionally a passing cab-driver leaned forward over his scrawny nag, on the look-out for a late passenger. Feeling
neither wind nor snow, Hermann waited, dressed only in his frock-coat. At
last the Countess' carriage was brought round. Hermann saw two footmen
carry out in their arms the bent old lady, wrapped in a sable fur, and immediately following her, the figure of Lisaveta Ivanovna, clad in a light cloak,
and with her head adorned with fresh flowers. The doors were slammed and
the carriage rolled heavily away along the soft snow. The hall-porter closed
the front door. The windows became dark. Hermann began to walk about
near the deserted house; he went up to a lamp and looked at his watch; it
was twenty minutes past eleven. He remained beneath the lamp; his eyes
fixed upon the hands of his watch, waiting for the remaining minutes to pass.
At exactly half-past eleven, Hermann ascended the steps of the Countess'
house and reached the brightly-lit porch. The hall-porter was not there. Hermann ran up the stairs, opened the door into the ante-room and saw a servant
asleep by the lamp in a soiled antique armchair. With a light, firm tread
Hermann stepped past him. The drawing-room and reception-room were in
darkness, but the lamp in the ante-room sent through a feeble light. Hermann passed through into the bedroom. Before an icon-case, filled with old-
fashioned images,[8] glowed a gold sanctuary lamp. Faded brocade armchairs
and dull gilt divans with soft cushions were ranged in sad symmetry around
the room, the walls of which were hung with Chinese silk. Two portraits,
painted in Paris by Madame Lebrun,[9] were hung from one of the walls. One
of these featured a plump, red-faced man of about forty, in a light-green
uniform and with a star pinned to his breast; the other—a beautiful young
woman with an aquiline nose and powdered hair, brushed back at the temples and adorned with a rose. In the corners of the room stood porcelain
shepherdesses, table clocks from the workshop of the celebrated Leroy, little
boxes, roulettes,[1] fans and the various lady's playthings which had been popular at the end of the last century, when the Montgolfiers' balloon and
Mesmer's magnetism[2] were invented. Hermann went behind the screen,
where stood a small iron bedstead; on the right was the door leading to the
study; on the left the one which led to the corridor. Hermann opened the
latter, and saw the narrow, winding staircase which led to the poor ward's
room. . . . But he turned back and stepped into the dark study.

The time passed slowly. Everything was quiet. The clock in the drawing-
room struck twelve; one by one the clocks in all the other rooms sounded
the same hour, and then all was quiet again. Hermann stood leaning against
the cold stove. He was calm; his heart beat evenly, like that of a man who

---

8. I.e., religious images.   9. Marie-Louise-Élisabeth Vigée-Lebrun (1755–1842), French portrait
painter, particularly of the aristocracy and royalty.   1. Little balls; or possibly portable devices for playing
the gambling game of roulette. Julien Leroy (1686–1759), famous French clockmaker.   2. Franz Anton
Mesmer (1734–1815) argued that a person can transmit personal force to others in the form of "animal
magnetism." Joseph-Michel (1740–1810) and Jacques-Etienne (1745–1799) Montgolfier, French brothers,
helped develop the hot-air balloon and conducted the first untethered flights.

has decided upon some dangerous but necessary action. One o'clock sounded; two o'clock; he heard the distant rattle of the carriage. He was seized by an involuntary agitation. The carriage drew near and stopped. He heard the sound of the carriage-steps being let down. The house suddenly came alive. Servants ran here and there, voices echoed through the house and the rooms were lit. Three old maid-servants hastened into the bedroom, followed by the Countess, who, tired to death, lowered herself into a Voltairean armchair.[3] Hermann peeped through a crack. Lisaveta Ivanovna went past him. Hermann heard her hurried steps as she went up the narrow staircase. In his heart there echoed something like the voice of conscience, but it grew silent, and his heart once more turned to stone.

The Countess began to undress before the looking-glass. Her rose-bedecked cap was unfastened; her powdered wig was removed from her grey, closely-cropped hair. Pins fell in showers around her. Her yellow dress, embroidered with silver, fell at her swollen feet. Hermann witnessed all the loathsome mysteries of her dress; at last the Countess stood in her dressing-gown and night-cap; in this attire, more suitable to her age, she seemed less hideous and revolting.

Like most old people, the Countess suffered from insomnia. Having undressed, she sat down by the window in the Voltairean armchair and dismissed her maidservants. The candles were carried out; once again the room was lit by a single sanctuary lamp. Looking quite yellow, the Countess sat rocking to and fro in her chair, her flabby lips moving. Her dim eyes reflected a complete absence of thought and, looking at her, one would have thought that the awful old woman's rocking came not of her own volition, but by the action of some hidden galvanism.

Suddenly, an indescribable change came over her death-like face. Her lips ceased to move, her eyes came to life: before the Countess stood an unknown man.

"Don't be alarmed, for God's sake, don't be alarmed," he said in a clear, low voice. "I have no intention of harming you; I have come to beseech a favour of you."

The old woman looked at him in silence, as if she had not heard him. Hermann imagined that she was deaf, and bending right down over her ear, he repeated what he had said. The old woman kept silent as before.

"You can ensure the happiness of my life," Hermann continued, "and it will cost you nothing: I know that you can guess three cards in succession. . . . "

Hermann stopped. The Countess appeared to understand what was demanded of her; she seemed to be seeking words for her reply.

"It was a joke," she said at last. "I swear to you, it was a joke."

"There's no joking about it," Hermann retorted angrily. "Remember Chaplitsky whom you helped to win."

The Countess was visibly disconcerted, and her features expressed strong emotion; but she quickly resumed her former impassivity.

"Can you name these three winning cards?" Hermann continued.

The Countess was silent. Hermann went on:

"For whom do you keep your secret? For your grandsons? They are rich

3. A large armchair with a high back.

and they can do without it; they don't know the value of money. Your three cards will not help a spendthrift. He who cannot keep his paternal inheritance will die in want, even if he has the devil at his side. I am not a spendthrift; I know the value of money. Your three cards will not be lost on me. Come . . . !"

He stopped and awaited her answer with trepidation. The Countess was silent. Hermann fell upon his knees.

"If your heart has ever known the feeling of love," he said, "if you remember its ecstasies, if you ever smiled at the wailing of your new-born son, if ever any human feeling has run through your breast, I entreat you by the feelings of a wife, a lover, a mother, by everything that is sacred in life, not to deny my request! Reveal your secret to me! What is it to you . . . ? Perhaps it is bound up with some dreadful sin, with the loss of eternal bliss, with some contract made with the devil . . . Consider: you are old; you have not long to live—I am prepared to take your sins on my own soul. Only reveal to me your secret. Realise that the happiness of a man is in your hands, that not only I, but my children, my grandchildren, my great-grandchildren will bless your memory and will revere it as something sacred. . . . "

The old woman answered not a word.

Hermann stood up.

"You old witch!" he said, clenching his teeth. "I'll force you to answer. . . . "

With these words he drew a pistol from his pocket. At the sight of the pistol, the Countess, for the second time, exhibited signs of strong emotion. She shook her head and raising her hand as though to shield herself from the shot, she rolled over on her back and remained motionless.

"Stop this childish behaviour now," Hermann said, taking her hand. "I ask you for the last time: will you name your three cards or won't you?"

The Countess made no reply. Hermann saw that she was dead.

CHAPTER FOUR

7 Mai 18* *
Homme sans moeurs et sans religion![4]
CORRESPONDENCE

Still in her ball dress, Lisaveta Ivanovna sat in her room, lost in thought. On her arrival home, she had quickly dismissed the sleepy maid who had reluctantly offered her services, had said that she would undress herself, and with a tremulous heart had gone up to her room, expecting to find Hermann there and yet hoping not to find him. Her first glance assured her of his absence and she thanked her fate for the obstacle that had prevented their meeting. She sat down, without undressing, and began to recall all the circumstances which had lured her so far in so short a time. It was not three weeks since she had first seen the young man from the window—and yet she was already in correspondence with him, and already he had managed to persuade her to grant him a nocturnal meeting! She knew his name only because some of his letters had been signed; she had never spoken to him, nor heard his voice, nor heard anything about him . . . until that very evening. Strange thing! That very evening, Tomsky, vexed with the Princess Polina * * * for not flirting with him as she

4. A man without morals and without religion! (French).

usually did, had wished to revenge himself by a show of indifference: he had therefore summoned Lisaveta Ivanovna and together they had danced an endless mazurka. All the time they were dancing, he had teased her about her partiality to officers of the Engineers, had assured her that he knew far more than she would have supposed possible, and indeed, some of his jests were so successfully aimed that on several occasions Lisaveta Ivanovna had thought that her secret was known to him.

"From whom have you discovered all this?" she asked, laughing.

"From a friend of the person whom you know so well," Tomsky answered; "from a most remarkable man!"

"Who is this remarkable man?"

"He is called Hermann."

Lisaveta made no reply, but her hands and feet turned quite numb.

"This Hermann," Tomsky continued, "is a truly romantic figure: he has the profile of a Napoleon, and the soul of a Mephistopheles. I should think that he has at least three crimes on his conscience. . . . How pale you have turned. . . . !"

"I have a headache. . . . What did this Hermann—or whatever his name is—tell you?"

"Hermann is most displeased with his friend: he says that he would act quite differently in his place . . . I even think that Hermann himself has designs on you; at any rate he listens to the exclamations of his enamoured friend with anything but indifference."

"But where has he seen me?"

"At church, perhaps; on a walk—God only knows! Perhaps in your room, whilst you were asleep: he's quite capable of it . . ."

Three ladies approaching him with the question: *"oublie ou regret?"*[5] interrupted the conversation which had become so agonisingly interesting to Lisaveta Ivanovna.

The lady chosen by Tomsky was the Princess Polina * * * herself. She succeeded in clearing up the misunderstanding between them during the many turns and movements of the dance, after which he conducted her to her chair. Tomsky returned to his own place. He no longer had any thoughts for Hermann or Lisaveta Ivanovna, who desperately wanted to renew her interrupted conversation; but the mazurka came to an end and shortly afterwards the old Countess left.

Tomsky's words were nothing but ball-room chatter, but they made a deep impression upon the mind of the young dreamer. The portrait, sketched by Tomsky, resembled the image she herself had formed of Hermann, and thanks to the latest romantic novels, Hermann's quite commonplace face took on attributes that both frightened and captivated her imagination. Now she sat, her uncovered arms crossed, her head, still adorned with flowers, bent over her bare shoulders. . . . Suddenly the door opened, and Hermann entered. She shuddered.

"Where have you been?" she asked in a frightened whisper.

"In the old Countess' bedroom," Hermann answered: "I have just left it. The Countess is dead."

---

5. The ladies cut in, offering the man a choice: *oublie* (forgetting) or *regret*. He does not know which lady is which. He chooses correctly the one with whom he wants to dance.

"Good God! What are you saying?"

"And it seems," Hermann continued, "that I am the cause of her death."

Lisaveta Ivanovna looked at him, and the words of Tomsky echoed in her mind: "he has at least three crimes on his conscience"! Hermann sat down beside her on the window sill and told her everything.

Lisaveta Ivanovna listened to him with horror. So those passionate letters, those ardent demands, the whole impertinent and obstinate pursuit—all that was not love! Money—that was what his soul craved for! It was not she who could satisfy his desire and make him happy! The poor ward had been nothing but the unknowing assistant of a brigand, of the murderer of her aged benefactress! . . . She wept bitterly, in an agony of belated repentance. Hermann looked at her in silence; his heart was also tormented; but neither the tears of the poor girl nor the astounding charm of her grief disturbed his hardened soul. He felt no remorse at the thought of the dead old lady. He felt dismay for only one thing: the irretrievable loss of the secret upon which he had relied for enrichment.

"You are a monster!" Lisaveta Ivanovna said at last.

"I did not wish for her death," Hermann answered. "My pistol wasn't loaded."

They were silent.

The day began to break. Lisaveta Ivanovna extinguished the flickering candle. A pale light lit up her room. She wiped her tear-stained eyes and raised them to Hermann: he sat by the window, his arms folded and with a grim frown on his face. In this position he bore an astonishing resemblance to a portrait of Napoleon. Even Lisaveta Ivanovna was struck by the likeness.

"How am I going to get you out of the house?" Lisaveta Ivanovna said at last. "I had thought of leading you along the secret staircase, but that would mean going past the Countess' bedroom, and I am afraid."

"Tell me how to find this secret staircase; I'll go on my own."

Lisaveta Ivanovna stood up, took a key from her chest of drawers, handed it to Hermann, and gave him detailed instructions. Hermann pressed her cold, unresponsive hand, kissed her bowed head and left.

He descended the winding staircase and once more entered the Countess' bedroom. The dead old lady sat as if turned to stone; her face expressed a deep calm. Hermann stopped before her and gazed at her for a long time, as if wishing to assure himself of the dreadful truth; finally, he went into the study, felt for the door behind the silk wall hangings, and, agitated by strange feelings, he began to descend the dark staircase.

"Along this very staircase," he thought, "perhaps at this same hour sixty years ago, in an embroidered coat, his hair dressed *à l'oiseau royal,*[6] his three-cornered hat pressed to his heart, there may have crept into this very bedroom a young and happy man now long since turned to dust in his grave—and to-day the aged heart of his mistress ceased to beat."

At the bottom of the staircase Hermann found a door, which he opened with the key Lisaveta Ivanovna had given him, and he found himself in a corridor which led into the street.

---

6. In the style of the royal bird (French, literal trans.); an antiquated and elaborate hairstyle.

CHAPTER FIVE

*That evening there appeared before me
the figure of the late Baroness von V* *.
She was all in white and she said to me:
"How are you, Mr. Councillor!"*
                                        SWEDENBORG[7]

Three days after the fateful night, at nine o'clock in the morning, Hermann set out for the * * * monastery, where a funeral service for the dead Countess was going to be held. Although unrepentant, he could not altogether silence the voice of conscience, which kept on repeating: "You are the murderer of the old woman!" Having little true religious belief, he was extremely superstitious. He believed that the dead Countess could exercise a harmful influence on his life, and he had therefore resolved to be present at the funeral, in order to ask her forgiveness.

The church was full. Hermann could scarcely make his way through the crowd of people. The coffin stood on a rich catafalque beneath a velvet canopy. Within it lay the dead woman, her arms folded upon her chest, and dressed in a white satin robe, with a lace cap on her head. Around her stood the members of her household: servants in black coats, with armorial ribbons upon their shoulders and candles in their hands; the relatives—children, grandchildren, great-grandchildren—in deep mourning. Nobody cried; tears would have been *une affectation.* The Countess was so old that her death could have surprised nobody, and her relatives had long considered her as having outlived herself. A young bishop pronounced the funeral sermon. In simple, moving words, he described the peaceful end of the righteous woman, who for many years had been in quiet and touching preparation for a Christian end. "The angel of death found her," the speaker said, "waiting for the midnight bridegroom, vigilant in godly meditation." The service was completed with sad decorum. The relatives were the first to take leave of the body. Then the numerous guests went up to pay final homage to her who had so long participated in their frivolous amusements. They were followed by all the members of the Countess' household, the last of whom was an old housekeeper of the same age as the Countess. She was supported by two young girls who led her up to the coffin. She had not the strength to bow down to the ground—and merely shed a few tears as she kissed the cold hand of her mistress. After that, Hermann decided to approach the coffin. He knelt down and for several minutes lay on the cold floor, which was strewn with fir branches; at last he got up, as pale as the dead woman herself; he went up the steps of the catafalque and bent his head over the body of the Countess. . . . At that very moment it seemed to him that the dead woman gave him a mocking glance, and winked at him. Hermann, hurriedly stepping back, missed his footing, and crashed on his back against the ground. He was helped to his feet. At the same moment, Lisaveta Ivanovna was carried out in a faint to the porch of the church. These events disturbed the solemnity of the gloomy ceremony for a few moments. A subdued murmur rose among the congregation, and a tall, thin chamberlain, a near relative of the dead woman, whispered in the ear of an Englishman standing

---

7. Emmanuel Swedenborg (1688–1772), Swedish theologian, believed that he had several experiences of divine revelation, some involving appearances to him of the dead.

by him that the young officer was the Countess' illegitimate son, to which the Englishman replied coldly: "Oh?"

For the whole of that day Hermann was exceedingly troubled. He went to a secluded inn for dinner and, contrary to his usual custom and in the hope of silencing his inward agitation, he drank heavily. But the wine fired his imagination still more. Returning home, he threw himself on to his bed without undressing, and fell into a heavy sleep.

It was already night when he awoke: the moon lit up his room. He glanced at his watch; it was a quarter to three. He found he could not go back to sleep; he sat down on his bed and thought about the funeral of the old Countess.

At that moment somebody in the street glanced in at his window, and immediately went away again. Hermann paid no attention to the incident. A minute or so later, he heard the door into the front room being opened. Hermann imagined that it was his orderly, drunk as usual, returning from some nocturnal outing. But he heard unfamiliar footsteps and the soft shuffling of slippers. The door opened: a woman in a white dress entered. Hermann mistook her for his old wet-nurse and wondered what could have brought her out at that time of the night. But the woman in white glided across the room and suddenly appeared before him—and Hermann recognised the Countess!

"I have come to you against my will," she said in a firm voice, "but I have been ordered to fulfill your request. Three, seven, ace, played in that order, will win for you, but only on condition that you play not more than one card in twenty-four hours, and that you never play again for the rest of your life. I'll forgive you my death if you marry my ward, Lisaveta Ivanovna. . . . "

With these words, she turned round quietly, walked towards the door and disappeared, her slippers shuffling. Herman heard the door in the hall bang, and again saw somebody look in at him through the window.

For a long time Hermann could not collect his senses. He went out into the next room. His orderly was lying asleep on the floor; Hermann could scarcely wake him. The orderly was, as usual, drunk, and it was impossible to get any sense out of him. The door into the hall was locked. Hermann returned to his room, lit a candle, and recorded the details of his vision.

CHAPTER SIX

> *"Attendez!"*[8]
> *"How dare you say to me: 'Attendez'?"*
> *"Your Excellency, I said: 'Attendez, sir'!"*

Two fixed ideas can no more exist in one mind than, in the physical sense, two bodies can occupy one and the same place. "Three, seven, ace" soon eclipsed from Hermann's mind the form of the dead old lady. "Three, seven, ace" never left his thoughts, were constantly on his lips. At the sight of a young girl, he would say: "How shapely she is! Just like the three of hearts." When asked the time, he would reply: "About seven." Every pot-bellied man he saw reminded him of an ace. "Three, seven, ace," assuming all possible

---

8. Wait! (French). Attendants at the gaming table called *Attendez* to indicate the end of the period to place bets.

shapes, persecuted him in his sleep: the three bloomed before him in the shape of some luxuriant flower, the seven took on the appearance of a Gothic gateway, the ace—of an enormous spider. To the exclusion of all others, one thought alone occupied his mind—making use of the secret which had cost him so much. He began to think of retirement and of travel. He wanted to try his luck in the public gaming-houses of Paris. Chance spared him the trouble.

There was in Moscow a society of rich gamblers, presided over by the celebrated Chekalinsky, a man whose whole life had been spent at the card-table, and who had amassed millions long ago, accepting his winnings in the form of promissory notes and paying his losses with ready money. His long experience had earned him the confidence of his companions, and his open house, his famous cook and his friendliness and gaiety had won him great public respect. He arrived in Petersburg. The younger generation flocked to his house, forgetting balls for cards, and preferring the enticements of faro to the fascinations of courtship. Narumov took Hermann to meet him.

They passed through a succession of magnificent rooms, full of polite and attentive waiters. Several generals and privy councillors were playing whist; young men, sprawled out on brocade divans, were eating ices and smoking their pipes. In the drawing-room, seated at the head of a long table, around which were crowded about twenty players, the host kept bank. He was a most respectable-looking man of about sixty; his head was covered with silvery grey hair, and his full, fresh face expressed good nature; his eyes, enlivened by a perpetual smile, shone brightly. Narumov introduced Hermann to him. Chekalinsky shook his hand warmly, requested him not to stand on ceremony, and went on dealing.

The game lasted a long time. More than thirty cards lay on the table. Chekalinsky paused after each round in order to give the players time to arrange their cards, wrote down their losses, listened politely to their demands, and more politely still allowed them to retract any stake accidentally left on the table. At last the game finished. Chekalinsky shuffled the cards and prepared to deal again.

"Allow me to place a stake," Hermann said, stretching out his hand from behind a fat gentleman who was punting[9] there.

Chekalinsky smiled and nodded silently, as a sign of his consent. Narumov laughingly congratulated Hermann on forswearing a longstanding principle and wished him a lucky beginning.

"I've staked," Hermann said, as he chalked up the amount, which was very considerable, on the back of his card.

"How much is it?" asked the banker, screwing up his eyes. "Forgive me, but I can't make it out."

"47,000 roubles," Hermann replied.

At these words every head in the room turned, and all eyes were fixed on Hermann.

"He's gone out of his mind!" Narumov thought.

"Allow me to observe to you," Chekalinsky said with his invariable smile, "that your stake is extremely high: nobody here has ever put more than 275 roubles on any single card."

9. Betting against the dealer.

"What of it?" retorted Hermann. "Do you take me or not?"

Chekalinsky, bowing, humbly accepted the stake.

"However, I would like to say," he said, "that, being judged worthy of the confidence of my friends, I can only bank against ready money. For my own part, of course, I am sure that your word is enough, but for the sake of the order of the game and of the accounts, I must ask you to place your money on the card."

Hermann drew a banknote from his pocket and handed it to Chekalinsky who, giving it a cursory glance, put it on Hermann's card.

He began to deal. On the right a nine turned up, on the left a three.[1]

"The three wins," said Hermann, showing his card.

A murmur arose among the players. Chekalinsky frowned, but instantly the smile returned to his face.

"Do you wish to take the money now?" he asked Hermann.

"If you would be so kind."

Chekalinsky drew a number of banknotes from his pocket and settled up immediately. Hermann took up his money and left the table. Narumov was too astounded even to think. Hermann drank a glass of lemonade and went home.

The next evening he again appeared at Chekalinsky's. The host was dealing. Hermann walked up to the table; the players already there immediately gave way to him. Chekalinsky bowed graciously.

Hermann waited for the next deal, took a card and placed on it his 47,000 roubles together with the winnings of the previous evening.

Chekalinsky began to deal. A knave turned up on the right, a seven on the left.

Hermann showed his seven.

There was a general cry of surprise, and Chekalinsky was clearly disconcerted. He counted out 94,000 roubles and handed them to Hermann, who pocketed them coolly and immediately withdrew.

The following evening Hermann again appeared at the table. Everyone was expecting him; the generals and privy councillors abandoned their whist in order to watch such unusual play. The young officers jumped up from their divans; all the waiters gathered in the drawing-room. Hermann was surrounded by a crowd of people. The other players held back their cards, impatient to see how Hermann would get on. Hermann stood at the table and prepared to play alone against the pale but still smiling Chekalinsky. Each unsealed a pack of cards. Chekalinsky shuffled. Hermann drew and placed his card, covering it with a heap of banknotes. It was like a duel. A deep silence reigned all around.

His hands shaking, Chekalinsky began to deal. On the right lay a queen, on the left an ace.

"The ace wins," said Hermann and showed his card.

"Your queen has lost," Chekalinsky said kindly.

Hermann started: indeed, instead of an ace, before him lay the queen of spades. He could not believe his eyes, could not understand how he could have slipped up.

---

1. Bets in faro are made on the positions of cards. A player selects a card and places it facedown in front of him or her; if the card turns up on the dealer's left, the player wins; if on the right, the dealer wins.

At that moment it seemed to him that the queen of spades winked at him and smiled. He was struck by an unusual likeness . . .

"The old woman!" he shouted in terror.

Chekalinsky gathered up his winnings. Hermann stood motionless. When he left the table, people began to converse noisily.

"Famously punted!" the players said.

Chekalinsky shuffled the cards afresh; play went on as usual.

CONCLUSION

Hermann went mad. He is now installed in Room 17 at the Obukhov Hospital; he answers no questions, but merely mutters with unusual rapidity: "Three, seven, ace! Three, seven, queen!"

Lisaveta Ivanovna has married a very agreeable young man, who has a good position in the service somewhere; he is the son of the former steward of the old Countess. Lisaveta Ivanovna is bringing up a poor relative.

Tomsky has been promoted to the rank of Captain, and is going to marry Princess Polina.

ALFRED, LORD TENNYSON
1809–1892

Tennyson's poetry expresses a conflict—characteristic of his historical period but also of human experience generally—between the tendency to despair and the desire to hope. Hope locates itself, for Tennyson, in the human capacity to struggle toward future goals and, on occasion, in religious faith. Mortality causes despair: the death of others, the inevitable sense of increasing weakness as one ages, the scientific discovery that whole species have disappeared in the world's history. It is Tennyson's ability to remind us of both contradictory emotions, and of the degree to which they inevitably coexist and alternate, that makes his poetry compelling.

The poet's pervasive melancholy came partly from experience. Son of an Anglican clergyman, he spent four unhappy years in school before his father consented to allow him to be tutored at home. He attended Trinity College, Cambridge, where, with his friend Arthur Hallam, he belonged to an undergraduate society called The Apostles, whose members discussed contemporary social, religious, scientific, and literary issues. The friendship with Hallam retained its intensity after his undergraduate years; by 1830, Hallam had become engaged to Tennyson's sister. Three years later, however, at the age of twenty-two, Hallam died suddenly in Vienna. The loss acutely affected Tennyson, who during the next seventeen years gradually composed the long elegiac poem In Memoriam A. H. H. to record the profound emotional and intellectual effects on him of his friend's death.

In 1836, Tennyson became engaged to Emily Sellwood, but largely because of financial difficulties, he did not marry her until 1850, the year in which, after the publication of In Memoriam, he was made poet laureate. Five years earlier, he had received a pension. He lived quietly for the rest of his life, increasingly famous; in 1884, he was created first Baron Tennyson.

Tennyson's earliest independent collections of poems (1830 and 1833; he had published a collaborative volume with his brother in 1827) were the target of fierce critical attack, another cause for melancholy. He published nothing more until 1842, when a collection called simply *Poems* met great critical success. Subsequently revered as a kind of national spokesman, Tennyson won popularity particularly with *The Princess* (1847, revised 1855), *Maud* (1855), and *The Idylls of the King* (1859, 1885), a retelling of the legends of King Arthur.

In *Ulysses* (1842), Tennyson, imagining the situation of the Greek hero after his return to domestic peace, evokes the excitement and moral grandeur of the human capacity for aspiration.

> that which we are, we are;
> One equal temper of heroic hearts,
> Made weak by time and fate, but strong in will
> To strive, to seek, to find, and not to yield.

In another meditation on classic themes, *Tithonus* (published in 1860, written in 1833), he puts the other side of the case. "The woods decay, the woods decay and fall," the poem begins; its imagined speaker, a man who has been granted immortality at his own request, wishes to return the gift. "Why should a man desire in any way / To vary from the kindly race of men?" Ulysses insists on the specialness of his sort of man; Tithonus knows the burden of specialness. In conjunction, the two poems call attention to the fact that neither the Enlightenment nor the early Romantic view of experience seems entirely adequate to this poet. Tithonus's desire to share the common fate of humankind throbs with melancholy; he feels that fate as doom, although he equally experiences his exemption from it as doom. Ulysses' condescension to his prudent son ("Most blameless is he. . . . / He works his work, I mine") underlines the sense of desperation in his insistent striving. No alternative form of action or commitment satisfies the imagination.

In Memoriam, Tennyson's most ambitious work, suggests reasons for the poet's inability to imagine fulfillment. The problem is not merely temperament, but the effect on his consciousness of intellectual and social actuality as well as the loss and the possibility of loss made palpable to him by Hallam's death.

> Are God and Nature then at strife,
>   That Nature lends such evil dreams?
>   So careful of the type she seems,
> So careless of the single life.

That stanza comes from number 55 of the 125 linked poems that make up the whole. The next in the series begins,

> "So careful of the type?" but no, . . .
>   She [Nature] cries, "A thousand types are gone;
>   I care for nothing, all shall go."

Reality offers not the slightest assurance of survival; contemporary scientists, studying fossils, had revealed the extinction of entire species. "Man, [Nature's] last work, who seemed so fair, / Such splendid purpose in his eyes"—with a Ulysses' capacity for fine imaginings—even man, humankind in general, may face extinction (a possibility that today looks ever more compelling). The poem concludes with the faintest possible religious hope:

> O life as futile, then, as frail!
>   O for thy voice to soothe and bless!
>   What hope of answer, or redress?
> Behind the veil, behind the veil.

By the end of the entire sequence, the poet has arrived at a more affirmative vision; he claims to have discovered God through his own pain and through the processes of feeling, which he asserts as more revelatory than those of logic. Indeed, *In Memoriam* persuasively evokes the slow reconciliation of mourning, giving its readers vicarious experience of the despair, the false starts, the inconsistencies of grief. The poem's power, however, derives not only from its record of personal emotional experience but from its demonstration, its embodiment, of how the intellectual and the emotional intertwine. The private loss of a friend assimilates itself to a more general loss of faith and certainty characteristic of the Victorian period. The determination to strive, to seek, to find, and not to yield generated scientific discovery, industrial and mercantile development. As early as 1850, though, such achievements threatened established social and theological orders. Tennyson re-creates for us what such threats felt like to those actually experiencing them. He writes an elegy not only for Arthur Hallam but for the larger losses of his moment in history.

For useful biography, see L. Ormond, *Alfred Tennyson: A Literary Life* (1993). Important criticism includes J. Buckley, *Tennyson: The Growth of a Poet* (1961); C. Ricks, *Tennyson* (1972); H. F. Tucker, *Tennyson and the Doom of Romanticism* (1988); and H. Tucker, ed., *Critical Essays on Alfred, Lord Tennyson* (1993). A valuable general guide is F. B. Pinion, *Tennyson Companion: Life and Works* (1984). For a useful introduction to the poet's life and works, see W. D. Shaw, *Alfred Lord Tennyson* (1996). Valuable perspective on *In Memoriam* in particular is provided by C. Graham, *Ideologies of Epic: Nation, Empire, and Victorian Epic Poetry* (1998).

PRONOUNCING GLOSSARY

The following list uses common English syllables and stress accents to provide rough equivalents of selected words whose pronunciation may be unfamiliar to the general reader.

Aeonian: *ay-ohn'-ee-an*   Hyades: *hai'-u-deez*

Arcady: *ahr'-kah-dee*   Telemachus: *tel-em'-u-kus*

Argive: *ahr-gaive*   Tithonus: *ti-thoh'-nus*

[POEMS]

Ulysses

It little profits that an idle king,
By this still hearth, among these barren crags,
Matched with an agèd wife, I mete and dole
Unequal laws unto a savage race,
That hoard, and sleep, and feed, and know not me.   5
    I cannot rest from travel; I will drink
Life to the lees. All times I have enjoyed
Greatly, have suffered greatly, both with those
That loved me, and alone; on shore, and when
Through scudding drifts the rainy Hyades[1]   10
Vexed the dim sea. I am become a name,
For always roaming with a hungry heart
Much have I seen and known,—cities of men
And manners, climates, councils, governments,
Myself not least, but honored of them all,—   15

---

1. A cluster of seven stars in the constellation of Taurus. The ancients supposed that when Hyades rose with the sun, rainy weather would follow.

And drunk delight of battle with my peers,
Far on the ringing plains of windy Troy.
I am a part of all that I have met;
Yet all experience is an arch wherethrough
Gleams that untravelled world whose margin fades   20
Forever and forever when I move.
How dull it is to pause, to make an end,
To rust unburnished, not to shine in use!
As though to breathe were life! Life piled on life
Were all too little, and of one to me   25
Little remains; but every hour is saved
From that eternal silence, something more,
A bringer of new things; and vile it were
For some three suns to store and hoard myself,
And this gray spirit yearning in desire   30
To follow knowledge like a sinking star,
Beyond the utmost bound of human thought.
    This is my son, mine own Telemachus,
To whom I leave the scepter and the isle²—
Well-loved of me, discerning to fulfill   35
This labor, by slow prudence to make mild
A rugged people, and through soft degrees
Subdue them to the useful and the good.
Most blameless is he, centered in the sphere
Of common duties, decent not to fail   40
In offices of tenderness, and pay
Meet adoration to my household gods,
When I am gone. He works his work, I mine.
    There lies the port; the vessel puffs her sail;
There gloom the dark, broad seas. My mariners,   45
Souls that have toiled, and wrought, and thought with me—
That ever with a frolic welcome took
The thunder and the sunshine, and opposed
Free hearts, free foreheads—you and I are old;
Old age hath yet his honor and his toil;   50
Death closes all. But something ere the end,
Some work of noble note, may yet be done,
Not unbecoming men that strove with gods.
The lights begin to twinkle from the rocks;
The long day wanes; the slow moon climbs; the deep   55
Moans round with many voices. Come, my friends,
'Tis not too late to seek a newer world.
Push off, and sitting well in order smite
The sounding furrows; for my purpose holds
To sail beyond the sunset, and the baths   60
Of all the western stars, until I die.
It may be that the gulfs will wash us down;
It may be we shall touch the Happy Isles,³
And see the great Achilles,⁴ whom we knew.

2. Ithaca.   3. In Greek myth, the abode of the warriors after death.   4. Comrade-in-arms of Ulysses
at Troy.

Though much is taken, much abides; and though   65
We are not now that strength which in old days
Moved earth and heaven, that which we are, we are;
One equal temper of heroic hearts,
Made weak by time and fate, but strong in will
To strive, to seek, to find, and not to yield.   70

Tithonus[1]

The woods decay, the woods decay and fall,
The vapors weep their burthen to the ground,
Man comes and tills the field and lies beneath,
And after many a summer dies the swan.
Me only cruel immortality[2]   5
Consumes; I wither slowly in thine arms,
Here at the quiet limit of the world,
A white-haired shadow roaming like a dream
The ever-silent spaces of the East,
Far-folded mists, and gleaming halls of morn.   10
    Alas! for this gray shadow, once a man—
So glorious in his beauty and thy choice,
Who madest him thy chosen, that he seemed
To his great heart none other than a God!
I asked thee, "Give me immortality."   15
Then didst thou grant mine asking with a smile,
Like wealthy men who care not how they give.
But thy strong Hours[3] indignant worked their wills,
And beat me down and marred and wasted me,
And though they could not end me, left me maimed   20
To dwell in presence of immortal youth,
Immortal age beside immortal youth,
And all I was in ashes. Can thy love,
Thy beauty, make amends, though even now,
Close over us, the silver star,[4] thy guide,   25
Shines in those tremulous eyes that fill with tears
To hear me? Let me go; take back thy gift.
Why should a man desire in any way
To vary from the kindly race of men,
Or pass beyond the goal of ordinance   30
Where all should pause, as is most meet[5] for all?
    A soft air fans the cloud apart; there comes
A glimpse of that dark world where I was born.
Once more the old mysterious glimmer steals
From thy pure brows, and from thy shoulders pure,   35
And bosom beating with a heart renewed.
Thy cheek begins to redden through the gloom,
Thy sweet eyes brighten slowly close to mine,

---

1. A prince of Troy loved by Aurora, goddess of dawn, in whose palace he is depicted as living.   2. From Zeus, Aurora obtained for Tithonus the gift of immortality but not of eternal youth.   3. Or Horae, goddesses of the seasons and of growth and decay.   4. The morning star that precedes the dawn.
5. Suitable.

Ere yet they blind the stars, and the wild team[6]
Which love thee, yearning for thy yoke, arise, 40
And shake the darkness from their loosened manes,
And beat the twilight into flakes of fire.
　Lo! ever thus thou growest beautiful
In silence, then before thine answer given
Departest, and thy tears are on my cheek. 45
　Why wilt thou ever scare me with thy tears,
And make me tremble lest a saying learnt,
In days far-off, on that dark earth, be true?
"The Gods themselves cannot recall their gifts."
　Ay me! ay me! with what another heart 50
In days far-off, and with what other eyes
I used to watch—if I be he that watched—
The lucid outline forming round thee; saw
The dim curls kindle into sunny rings;
Changed with thy mystic change, and felt my blood 55
Glow with the glow that slowly crimsoned all
Thy presence and thy portals, while I lay,
Mouth, forehead, eyelids, growing dewy-warm
With kisses balmier than half-opening buds
Of April, and could hear the lips that kissed 60
Whispering I knew not what of wild and sweet,
Like that strange song I heard Apollo[7] sing,
While Ilion like a mist rose into towers.[8]
　Yet hold me not forever in thine East;
How can my nature longer mix with thine? 65
Coldly thy rosy shadows bathe me, cold
Are all thy lights, and cold my wrinkled feet
Upon thy glimmering thresholds, when the steam
Floats up from those dim fields about the homes
Of happy men that have the power to die, 70
And grassy barrows[9] of the happier dead.
Release me, and restore me to the ground.
Thou seest all things, thou wilt see my grave;
Thou wilt renew thy beauty morn by morn,
I earth in earth forget these empty courts, 75
And thee returning on thy silver wheels.

From *In Memoriam A. H. H.*

Obit. MDCCCXXXIII

[Prologue]

Strong Son of God, immortal Love,[1]
　Whom we, that have not seen thy face,

---

6. Of supernatural horses; they draw Aurora's chariot into the sky at dawn.　7. God of music and patron of Troy.　8. According to legend, the walls of Troy (Ilion) were raised by the sound of Apollo's song. 9. Burial mounds.　1. 1 John 4.8: "He that loveth not knoweth not God; for God is love." 1 John 4.15: "Whosoever shall confess that Jesus is the Son of God, God dwelleth in him, and he in God."

By faith, and faith alone, embrace,
    Believing where we cannot prove;

Thine are these orbs of light and shade;[2]   5
    Thou madest Life in man and brute;
    Thou madest Death; and lo, thy foot
Is on the skull which thou hast made.[3]

Thou wilt not leave us in the dust:
    Thou madest man, he knows not why,   10
    He thinks he was not made to die;
And thou hast made him: thou art just.

Thou seemest human and divine,
    The highest, holiest manhood, thou.
    Our wills are ours, we know not how;   15
Our wills are ours, to make them thine.

Our little systems have their day;
    They have their day and cease to be;[4]
    They are but broken lights of thee,[5]
And thou, O Lord, art more than they.   20

We have but faith: we cannot know,
    For knowledge is of things we see;
    And yet we trust it comes from thee,
A beam in darkness: let it grow.

Let knowledge grow from more to more,   25
    But more of reverence in us dwell;
    That mind and soul, according well,
May make one music as before,

But vaster. We are fools and slight;
    We mock thee when we do not fear: 30
    But help thy foolish ones to bear;
Help thy vain worlds to bear thy light.

Forgive what seemed my sin in me,
    What seemed my worth since I began;
    For merit lives from man to man,   35
And not from man, O Lord, to thee.

Forgive my grief for one removed,
    Thy creature, whom I found so fair.
    I trust he lives in thee, and there
I find him worthier to be loved.   40

---

2. I.e., the Earth and the planets, part of each of which is sunlit, the rest in shadow.   3. I.e., Jesus crushes Death underfoot, a common motif in painting and sculpture.   4. Transient theological and philosophical systems, contrasted with the enduring systems of the stars.   5. Refracted, as by a prism.

Forgive these wild and wandering cries,
　　Confusions of a wasted[6] youth;
　　Forgive them where they fail in truth,
And in thy wisdom make me wise.

1

I held it truth, with him[7] who sings
　　To one clear harp in divers[8] tones,
　　That men may rise on stepping-stones
Of their dead selves to higher things.

But who shall so forecast the years   5
　　And find in loss a gain to match?
　　Or reach a hand through time to catch
The far-off interest of tears?

Let Love clasp Grief lest both be drowned,
　　Let darkness keep her raven gloss.   10
　　Ah, sweeter to be drunk with loss,
To dance with Death, to beat the ground,

Than that the victor Hours[9] should scorn
　　The long result of love, and boast,
　　"Behold the man that loved and lost,   15
But all he was is overworn."[1]

2

Old yew,[2] which graspest at the stones
　　That name the underlying dead,
　　Thy fibers net the dreamless head,
Thy roots are wrapped about the bones.

The seasons bring the flower again,   5
　　And bring the firstling[3] to the flock;
　　And in the dusk of thee the clock
Beats out the little lives of men.

O, not for thee the glow, the bloom,
　　Who changest not in any gale,   10
　　Nor branding summer suns avail
To touch thy thousand years of gloom;

And gazing on thee, sullen tree,
　　Sick for thy stubborn hardihood,

6. Laid waste (by Hallam's loss).　　7. Goethe, who in the second part of *Faust* and elsewhere voices his conception of spiritual progress through the outgrowing of one's former selves.　　8. Various.　　9. Or Horae, goddesses of the seasons and of growth and decay.　　1. Worn out, exhausted.　　2. Evergreen capable of reaching great age. It is often planted in graveyards as a symbol of immortality.　　3. Firstborn.

I seem to fail from out my blood   15
And grow incorporate into thee.

3

O Sorrow, cruel fellowship,
    O Priestess in the vaults of Death,
    O sweet and bitter in a breath,
What whispers from thy lying lip?

"The stars," she whispers, "blindly run;   5
    A web is woven across the sky;
    From out waste places comes a cry,
And murmurs from the dying sun;

"And all the phantom, Nature, stands—
    With all the music in her tone,   10
    A hollow echo of my own,—
A hollow form with empty hands."

And shall I take a thing so blind,
    Embrace her as my natural good;
    Or crush her, like a vice of blood,   15
Upon the threshold of the mind?

                    *   *   *

5

I sometimes hold it half a sin
    To put in words the grief I feel;
    For words, like Nature, half reveal
And half conceal the Soul within.

But, for the unquiet heart and brain,   5
    A use in measured language lies;
    The sad mechanic exercise,
Like dull narcotics, numbing pain.

In words, like weeds,[4] I'll wrap me o'er,
    Like coarsest clothes against the cold;   10
    But that large grief which these enfold
Is given in outline and no more.

                    *   *   *

---

4. Garments (with allusion to mourning garments).

7

Dark house,[5] by which once more I stand
   Here in the long unlovely street,
   Doors, where my heart was used to beat
So quickly, waiting for a hand,

A hand that can be clasped no more—   5
   Behold me, for I cannot sleep,
   And like a guilty thing I creep
At earliest morning to the door.

He is not here; but far away
   The noise of life begins again,   10
   And ghastly through the drizzling rain
On the bald street breaks the blank day.

*   *   *

10

I hear the noise about thy keel;[6]
   I hear the bell struck in the night;
   I see the cabin-window bright;
I see the sailor at the wheel.

Thou bring'st the sailor to his wife,   5
   And traveled men from foreign lands;
   And letters unto trembling hands;
And, thy dark freight, a vanished life.

So bring him; we have idle dreams;
   This look of quiet flatters thus   10
   Our home-bred fancies. O, to us,
The fools of habit, sweeter seems

To rest beneath the clover sod,
   That takes the sunshine and the rains,
   Or where the kneeling hamlet drains   15
The chalice of the grapes of God;[7]

Than if with thee the roaring wells
   Should gulf him fathom-deep in brine,
   And hands so often clasped in mine,
Should toss with tangle[8] and with shells.   20

5. The Hallam family residence.   6. Of the ship bringing Hallam's body back from Vienna.   7. This stanza mentions alternate modes of burial: in the churchyard or under the chancel where worshipers kneel for the Sacrament.   8. Seaweed.

11

Calm is the morn without a sound,
  Calm as to suit a calmer grief,
  And only through the faded leaf
The chestnut pattering to the ground;[9]

Calm and deep peace on this high wold,[1]   5
  And on these dews that drench the furze,
  And all the silvery gossamers
That twinkle into green and gold;

Calm and still light on yon great plain
  That sweeps with all its autumn bowers,   10
  And crowded farms and lessening towers,
To mingle with the bounding main;

Calm and deep peace in this wide air,
  These leaves that redden to the fall,
  And in my heart, if calm at all,   15
If any calm, a calm despair;

Calm on the seas, and silver sleep,
  And waves that sway themselves in rest,
  And dead calm in that noble breast
Which heaves but with the heaving deep.   20

        *   *   *

15

Tonight the winds begin to rise
  And roar from yonder dropping day;
  The last red leaf is whirled away,
The rooks[2] are blown about the skies;

The forest cracked, the waters curled,   5
  The cattle huddled on the lea;[3]
  And wildly dashed on tower and tree
The sunbeam strikes along the world:

And but for fancies, which aver
  That all thy motions gently pass   10
  Athwart a plane of molten glass,
I scarce could brook the strain and stir

9. The time is September, when Hallam's body is still en route.   1. Open uplands; i.e., Tennyson is at his home in Somersby, Lincolnshire.   2. European crowlike birds.   3. Pasture.

That makes the barren branches loud;
  And but for fear it is not so,
  The wild unrest that lives in woe   15
Would dote and pore on yonder cloud[4]

That rises upward always higher,
  And onward drags a laboring breast,
  And topples round the dreary west,
A looming bastion fringed with fire.   20

16

What words are these have fall'n from me?
  Can calm despair and wild unrest
  Be tenants of a single breast,
Or Sorrow such a changeling be?

Or doth she only seem to take   5
  The touch of change in calm or storm,
  But knows no more of transient form
In her deep self, than some dead lake

That holds the shadow of a lark
  Hung in the shadow of a heaven?   10
  Or has the shock, so harshly given,
Confused me like the unhappy bark[5]

That strikes by night a craggy shelf,
  And staggers blindly ere she sink?
  And stunned me from my power to think   15
And all my knowledge of myself;

And made me that delirious man
  Whose fancy fuses old and new,
  And flashes into false and true,
And mingles all without a plan?   20

          *   *   *

19

The Danube to the Severn[6] gave
  The darkened heart that beat no more;

---

4. In the midst of a gathering storm, the poet's imagination soothes him with the fancy that Hallam's ship moves gently toward England on a glass-calm sea. Only a fear that this fancy may delude him (and Hallam's crossing be really in danger) prevents the stormy unrest within him from romantically luxuriating in the stormy sunset all around him.   5. Ship.   6. The church at Clevedon, Somerset, where Hallam was buried, is on the Severn. Vienna, where he died, is on the Danube.

They laid him by the pleasant shore,
And in the hearing of the wave.[7]

There twice a day the Severn fills;   5
    The salt sea-water passes by,
    And hushes half the babbling Wye,[8]
And makes a silence in the hills.

The Wye is hushed nor moved along,
    And hushed my deepest grief of all,   10
    When filled with tears that cannot fall,
I brim with sorrow drowning song.

The tide flows down, the wave again
    Is vocal in its wooded walls;
    My deeper anguish also falls,   15
And I can speak a little then.

                    *   *   *

21

I sing to him that rests below,
    And, since the grasses round me wave,
    I take the grasses of the grave,
And make them pipes[9] whereon to blow.

The traveler hears me now and then,   5
    And sometimes harshly will he speak:
    "This fellow would make weakness weak,
And melt the waxen hearts of men."

Another answers: "Let him be,
    He loves to make parade of pain,   10
    That with his piping he may gain
The praise that comes to constancy."

A third is wroth:[1] "Is this an hour
    For private sorrow's barren song,
    When more and more the people throng   15
The chairs and thrones of civil power?

"A time to sicken and to swoon,
    When Science reaches forth her arms

---

7. Tennyson was not present at the funeral and did not learn until years later that Hallam had been buried in the church, not in the graveyard by the river.   8. The tides reach far up the Bristol Channel into the Severn and the Wye, its tributary.   9. Alluding to the pipes of mourning shepherds in pastoral elegy, the genre to which *In Memoriam* in part belongs.   1. Very angry.

To feel from world to world, and charms
Her secret from the latest moon?"[2]   20

Behold, ye speak an idle thing;
    Ye never knew the sacred dust.
    I do but sing because I must,
And pipe but as the linnets sing;

And one is glad; her note is gay,   25
    For now her little ones have ranged;
    And one is sad; her note is changed,
Because her brood is stolen away.

22

The path by which we twain did go,
    Which led by tracts that pleased us well,
    Through four sweet years arose and fell,
From flower to flower, from snow to snow;

And we with singing cheered the way,   5
    And, crowned with all the season lent,
    From April on to April went,
And glad at heart from May to May.

But where the path we walked began
    To slant the fifth autumnal slope,   10
    As we descended following Hope,
There sat the Shadow feared of man;

Who broke our fair companionship,
    And spread his mantle dark and cold,
    And wrapt thee formless in the fold,   15
And dulled the murmur on thy lip,

And bore thee where I could not see
    Nor follow, though I walk in haste,
    And think that somewhere in the waste[3]
The Shadow sits and waits for me.   20

23

Now, sometimes in my sorrow shut,
    Or breaking into song by fits,
    Alone, alone, to where he sits,
The Shadow cloaked from head to foot,

---

2. From 1846 to 1848, astronomers discovered the planet Neptune and one of its moons, some of the satellites of Uranus, and the eighth moon of Saturn.   3. Wasteland.

Who keeps the keys of all the creeds,   5
　　I wander, often falling lame,
　　And looking back to whence I came,
Or on to where the pathway leads;

And cry, How changed from where it ran
　　Through lands where not a leaf was dumb,   10
　　But all the lavish hills would hum
The murmur of a happy Pan;[4]

When each by turns was guide to each,
　　And Fancy light from Fancy caught,
　　And Thought leapt out to wed with Thought   15
Ere Thought could wed itself with Speech;

And all we met was fair and good,
　　And all was good that Time could bring,
　　And all the secret of the Spring
Moved in the chambers of the blood;   20

And many an old philosophy
　　On Argive heights divinely sang,
　　And round us all the thicket rang
To many a flute of Arcady.[5]

　　　　　　*　　　*　　　*

27

　　I envy not in any moods
　　　　The captive void of noble rage,
　　　　The linnet born within the cage,
　　That never knew the summer woods;

　　I envy not the beast that takes   5
　　　　His license in the field of time,
　　　　Unfettered by the sense of crime,
　　To whom a conscience never wakes;

　　Nor, what may count itself as blest,
　　　　The heart that never plighted troth[6]   10
　　　　But stagnates in the weeds of sloth;
　　Nor any want-begotten rest.[7]

4. God of flocks and shepherds, and hence of pastoral poetry.　**5.** I.e., they were like shepherds on the hills of Greece when what is now "old philosophy" was brand new or on the plains of Arcady (home of pastoral poetry) when pastoral poetry was young.　**6.** Became engaged to be married.　**7.** I.e., any rest that comes from a lack or deficiency—specifically, from a failure to be fully human, a state that would entail vulnerability.

I hold it true, whate'er befall;
   I feel it, when I sorrow most;
   'Tis better to have loved and lost   15
Than never to have loved at all.

28

The time draws near the birth of Christ.
   The moon is hid, the night is still;
   The Christmas bells from hill to hill
Answer each other in the mist.

Four voices of four hamlets round,   5
   From far and near, on mead and moor,
   Swell out and fail, as if a door
Were shut between me and the sound;

Each voice four changes on the wind,
   That now dilate, and now decrease,   10
   Peace and goodwill, goodwill and peace,
Peace and goodwill, to all mankind.

This year I slept and woke with pain,
   I almost wished no more to wake,
   And that my hold on life would break   15
Before I heard those bells again;

But they my troubled spirit rule,
   For they controlled me when a boy;
   They bring me sorrow touched with joy,
The merry, merry bells of Yule.   20

        *   *   *

50

Be near me when my light is low,
   When the blood creeps, and the nerves prick
   And tingle; and the heart is sick,
And all the wheels of being slow.

Be near me when the sensuous frame   5
   Is racked with pangs that conquer trust;
   And Time, a maniac scattering dust,[8]
And Life, a Fury slinging flame.[9]

8. I.e., the dust from which life comes and to which it returns.   9. The Furies, avenging deities of Greek myth, carry torches.

Be near me when my faith is dry,
  And men the flies of latter spring,   10
  That lay their eggs, and sting and sing
And weave their petty cells and die.

Be near me when I fade away,
  To point the term of human strife,
  And on the low dark verge of life   15
The twilight of eternal day.

          *   *   *

54

O, yet we trust that somehow good
  Will be the final goal of ill,
  To pangs of nature, sins of will,
Defects of doubt, and taints of blood;

That nothing walks with aimless feet;   5
  That not one life shall be destroyed,
  Or cast as rubbish to the void,
When God hath made the pile complete;

That not a worm is cloven in vain;
  That not a moth with vain desire   10
  Is shriveled in a fruitless fire,
Or but subserves another's gain.

Behold, we know not anything;
  I can but trust that good shall fall
  At last—far off—at last, to all,   15
And every winter change to spring.

So runs my dream; but what am I?
  An infant crying in the night;
  An infant crying for the light,
And with no language but a cry.   20

55

The wish, that of the living whole
  No life may fail beyond the grave,
  Derives it not from what we have
The likest God within the soul?

Are God and Nature then at strife,   5
  That Nature lends such evil dreams?

So careful of the type[1] she seems,
So careless of the single life,[2]

That I, considering everywhere
   Her secret meaning in her deeds
   And finding that of fifty seeds   10
She often brings but one to bear,

I falter where I firmly trod,
   And falling with my weight of cares
   Upon the great world's altar-stairs   15
That slope through darkness up to God,

I stretch lame hands of faith, and grope,
   And gather dust and chaff, and call
   To what I feel is Lord of all,
And faintly trust the larger hope.   20

56

"So careful of the type?" but no.
   From scarpèd[3] cliff and quarried stone
   She cries, "A thousand types are gone;[4]
I care for nothing, all shall go.

"Thou makest thine appeal to me: 5
   I bring to life, I bring to death;
   The spirit does but mean the breath:
I know no more." And he, shall he,

Man, her last work, who seemed so fair,
   Such splendid purpose in his eyes,
   Who rolled the psalm to wintry skies,   10
Who built him fanes[5] of fruitless prayer,

Who trusted God was love indeed
   And love Creation's final law—
   Though Nature, red in tooth and claw   15
With ravin,[6] shrieked against his creed—

Who loved, who suffered countless ills,
   Who battled for the True, the Just,
   Be blown about the desert dust,
Or sealed within the iron hills?   20

---

1. Species.   2. The significance of nature's prodigality and destructiveness was widely debated during Tennyson's lifetime.   3. Shorn away vertically to expose the rock strata of different ages.   4. That whole species had disappeared, not merely individuals, had become evident from Charles Lyell's researchers, published in his *Principles of Geology* (1830–33) and *Elements of Geology* (1838).   5. Temples. 6. Prey.

No more? A monster then, a dream,
   A discord. Dragons of the prime,[7]
   That tear each other in their slime,
Were mellow music matched with him.

O life as futile, then, as frail!   25
   O for thy[8] voice to soothe and bless!
   What hope of answer, or redress?
Behind the veil,[9] behind the veil.

      *   *   *

78

Again at Christmas did we weave
   The holly round the Christmas hearth;
   The silent snow possessed the earth,
And calmly fell our Christmas-eve:

The yule-clog[1] sparkled keen with frost,   5
   No wing of wind the region swept,
   But over all things brooding slept
The quiet sense of something lost.

As in the winters left behind,
   Again our ancient games had place,   10
   The mimic picture's[2] breathing grace,
And dance and song and hoodman-blind.[3]

Who showed a token of distress?
   No single tear, no mark of pain:
   O sorrow, then can sorrow wane?   15
O grief, can grief be changed to less?

O last regret, regret can die!
   No—mixed with all this mystic frame,
   Her deep relations are the same,
But with long use her tears are dry.   20

      *   *   *

95

By night we lingered on the lawn,
   For underfoot the herb was dry;

7. Prehistoric creatures.   8. Hallam's.   9. Death.   1. Yule log.   2. The game may be charades.
3. Blindman's buff.

And genial warmth; and o'er the sky
The silvery haze of summer drawn;

And calm that let the tapers burn   5
Unwavering; not a cricket chirred;
The brook alone far-off was heard,
And on the board the fluttering urn.[4]

And bats went round in fragrant skies,
And wheeled or lit the filmy shapes   10
That haunt the dusk, with ermine capes
And woolly breasts and beaded eyes;

While now we sang old songs that pealed
From knoll to knoll, where, couched at ease,
The white kine[5] glimmered, and the trees   15
Laid their dark arms about the field.

But when those others, one by one,
Withdrew themselves from me and night,
And in the house light after light
Went out, and I was all alone,   20

A hunger seized my heart; I read
Of that glad year which once had been,
In those fall'n leaves which kept their green,
The noble letters of the dead.

And strangely on the silence broke   25
The silent-speaking words, and strange
Was love's dumb cry defying change
To test his worth; and strangely spoke

The faith, the vigor, bold to dwell
On doubts that drive the coward back,   30
And keen through wordy snares to track
Suggestion to her inmost cell.

So word by word, and line by line,
The dead man touched me from the past,
And all at once it seemed at last   35
The living soul was flashed on mine,

And mine in this was wound, and whirled
About empyreal[6] heights of thought,
And came on that which is, and caught
The deep pulsations of the world,   40

4. Boiling tea urn. *Board*: table.   5. Cattle.   6. Sublime.

Æonian[7] music measuring out
    The steps of Time—the shocks of Chance—
    The blows of Death. At length my trance
Was canceled, stricken through with doubt.

Vague words! but ah, how hard to frame   45
    In matter-molded forms of speech,
    Or even for intellect to reach
Through memory that which I became;

Till now the doubtful dusk revealed
    The knolls once more where, couched at ease,   50
    The white kine glimmered, and the trees
Laid their dark arms about the field;

And sucked from out the distant gloom
    A breeze began to tremble o'er
    The large leaves of the sycamore,   55
And fluctuate all the still perfume,

And gathering freshlier overhead,
    Rocked the full-foliaged elms, and swung
    The heavy-folded rose, and flung
The lilies to and fro, and said,   60

"The dawn, the dawn," and died away;
    And East and West, without a breath,
    Mixt their dim lights, like life and death,
To broaden into boundless day.

           ✻   ✻   ✻

106

Ring out, wild bells, to the wild sky,
    The flying cloud, the frosty light:
    The year is dying in the night;
Ring out, wild bells, and let him die.

Ring out the old, ring in the new,   5
    Ring, happy bells, across the snow:
    The year is going, let him go;
Ring out the false, ring in the true.

Ring out the grief that saps the mind,
    For those that here we see no more;   10
    Ring out the feud of rich and poor,
Ring in redress to all mankind.

7. Age-old.

Ring out a slowly dying cause,
  And ancient forms of party strife;
  Ring in the nobler modes of life,   15
With sweeter manners, purer laws.

Ring out the want, the care, the sin,
  The faithless coldness of the times;
  Ring out, ring out my mournful rhymes,
But ring the fuller minstrel in.   20

Ring out false pride in place and blood,
  The civic slander and the spite;
  Ring in the love of truth and right,
Ring in the common love of good.

Ring out old shapes of foul disease;   25
  Ring out the narrowing lust of gold;
  Ring out the thousand wars of old,
Ring in the thousand years of peace.[8]

Ring in the valiant man and free,
  The larger heart, the kindlier hand;   30
  Ring out the darkness of the land,
Ring in the Christ that is to be.

                  *   *   *

118

Contèmplate all this work of Time,
  The giant laboring in his youth;
  Nor dream of human love and truth,
As dying Nature's earth and lime;[9]

But trust that those we call the dead   5
  Are breathers of an ampler day
  For ever nobler ends. They say,
The solid earth whereon we tread

In tracts of fluent heat began,
  And grew to seeming-random forms,   10
  The seeming prey of cyclic storms,
Till at the last arose the man;

Who throve and branched from clime to clime,
  The herald of a higher race,

---

8. The poet has in mind Revelation 20, where it is said that Satan will be bound in chains for a thousand years, during which time the martyrs will be "priest of God and of Christ, and shall reign with him."
9. The products of the decay of flesh and bone.

And of himself in higher place,   15
If so he type[1] this work of time

Within himself, from more to more;
    Or, crowned with attributes of woe
    Like glories, move his course, and show
That life is not as idle ore,   20

But iron dug from central gloom,
    And heated hot with burning fears,
    And dipped in baths of hissing tears,
And battered with the shocks of doom

To shape and use. Arise and fly   25
    The reeling Faun, the sensual feast;
    Move upward, working out the beast,
And let the ape and tiger die.

                    *   *   *

124

That which we dare invoke to bless;
    Our dearest faith; our ghastliest doubt;
    He, They, One, All;[2] within, without;
The Power in darkness whom we guess,—

I found Him not in world or sun,   5
    Or eagle's wing, or insect's eye,
    Nor through the questions men may try,
The petty cobwebs we have spun.

If e'er when faith had fallen asleep,
    I heard a voice, "believe no more,"   10
    And heard an ever-breaking shore
That tumbled in the Godless deep,

A warmth within the breast would melt
    The freezing reason's colder part,
    And like a man in wrath the heart   15
Stood up and answered, "I have felt."

No, like a child in doubt and fear:
    But that blind clamor made me wise;
    Then was I as a child that cries,
But, crying, knows his father near;   20

---

1. Copy, emulate.   2. Christ, as part of the Trinity, seen as three elements and as indivisible.

And what I am beheld again
  What is, and no man understands;
  And out of darkness came the hands
That reach through nature, molding men.

[Epilogue]³

*   *   *

Today the grave is bright for me,
  For them⁴ the light of life increased,
  Who stay to share the morning feast,
Who rest tonight beside the sea.

Let all my genial spirits advance   5
  To meet and greet a whiter⁵ sun;
  My drooping memory will not shun
The foaming grape⁶ of eastern France.

It circles round, and fancy plays,
  And hearts are warmed and faces bloom,   10
  As drinking health to bride and groom
We wish them store of happy days.

Nor count me all to blame if I
  Conjecture of a stiller guest,
  Perchance, perchance, among the rest,   15
And, though in silence, wishing joy.

But they must go, the time draws on,
  And those white-favored⁷ horses wait;
  They rise, but linger; it is late;
Farewell, we kiss, and they are gone.   20

A shade falls on us like the dark
  From little cloudlets on the grass,
  But sweeps away as out we pass
To range the woods, to roam the park,

Discussing how their courtship grew,   25
  And talk of others that are wed,
  And how she looked, and what he said,
And back we come at fall of dew.

Again the feast, the speech, the glee,
  The shade of passing thought, the wealth   30
  Of words and wit, the double health,
The crowning cup, the three-times-three,⁸

---

3. The Epilogue celebrates the wedding of Tennyson's sister Cecilia to his friend Edmund Lushington (October 10, 1842) and brings the poem of mourning full circle to its conclusion in a marriage and in the prospect of a new birth.   4. The new husband and wife.   5. More joyous and hopeful because of the marriage.   6. Champagne.   7. Wearing white ribbons for the wedding.   8. Rousing cheers.

And last the dance;—till I retire.
    Dumb is that tower[9] which spake so loud,
    And high in heaven the streaming cloud,   35
And on the downs a rising fire:

And rise, O moon, from yonder down,
    Till over down and over dale
    All night the shining vapor sail
And pass the silent-lighted town,   40

The white-faced halls, the glancing rills,
    And catch at every mountain head,
    And o'er the friths[1] that branch and spread
Their sleeping silver through the hills;

And touch with shade the bridal doors,   45
    With tender gloom the roof, the wall;
    And breaking let the splendor fall
To spangle all the happy shores

By which they rest, and ocean sounds,
    And, star and system rolling past,   50
    A soul shall draw from out the vast
And strike his being into bounds,

And, moved through life of lower phase,
    Result in man, be born and think,
    And act and love, a closer link   55
Betwixt us and the crowning race

Of those that, eye to eye, shall look
    On knowledge; under whose command
    Is Earth and Earth's, and in their hand
Is Nature like an open book;   60

No longer half-akin to brute,
    For all we thought and loved and did,
    And hoped, and suffered, is but seed
Of what in them is flower and fruit;

Whereof the man that with me trod   65
    This planet was a noble type
    Appearing ere the times were ripe,
That friend of mine who lives in God,

That God, which ever lives and loves,
    One God, one law, one element,   70
    And one far-off divine event,
To which the whole creation moves.

9. The church tower where wedding bells recently rang.   1. Narrow bays of the sea.

ROBERT BROWNING
1812–1889

The pleasure of reading Robert Browning's dramatic monologues—the poems for which he is best known—involves the delight of encountering a vividly realized personality but is also, often, the kind of enjoyment one gets from detective fiction. An imaginary speaker utters words designed to generate a specific effect; from these words, typically, one can deduce a story never actually told. The poet allows us the enjoyment of figuring out what has really happened as well as more familiar poetic pleasures.

Browning was the son of a bank clerk who later became a prosperous banker. After attending the University of London, he traveled on the Continent. Back in England, he became friendly with other important Victorian literary figures: Charles Dickens, Thomas Carlyle, and Leigh Hunt, for example. His romance with the semi-invalid Elizabeth Barrett, also a poet, led to marriage in 1846; the two lived mainly in Italy for the remaining fifteen years of her life. Although Browning returned to England after his wife's death, he made frequent visits to the Continent and died in Venice.

Browning wrote verse plays and introspective Shelleyan lyrics, but his most popular poems have always been the dramatic monologues, originally included in such volumes as *Bells and Pomegranates* (1841–46), *Men and Women* (1855), and *Dramatis Personae* (1864). His most ambitious work was *The Ring and the Book* (1868–69), a linked series of blank verse dramatic monologues based on a Renaissance murder trial. In this long poem, in the course of which several people report the same events from very different points of view, Browning most clearly concentrates on the problem implicit in all his monologues, that of perspective. The nature of a story depends on who tells it: Browning's verse insistently reminds us of this fact.

My Last Duchess (1842), probably Browning's best-known and most popular monologue, in fifty-six lines exemplifies the characteristic technique. The speaker, a duke, prefers his wife's portrait to her corporeal existence, having put an end to her life because he found her gaiety and spiritual generosity offensive to his aristocratic pride. He explains his attitude to an envoy with whom he is negotiating for a new bride, with no awareness that his story reflects badly on himself. The pleasure of reading the poem derives largely from experiencing simultaneous communications: the story the duke thinks he tells, of offended dignity, and the story he really tells, of narcissistic self-indulgence.

The Bishop Orders His Tomb at Saint Praxed's Church (1845) invites more complicated responses to the personality it evokes. The imagined sixteenth-century bishop reveals his lack of real allegiance to the Church he nominally serves. He has violated his vows of celibacy, having had at least one mistress and several children. He feels powerful competitive impulses, as well as rage and envy, toward his predecessor as bishop. Even on his deathbed, he remains utterly absorbed in the things of this world: the lump of lapis lazuli he has buried, the splendor of the marble he imagines for his tomb. The mass itself exists in his memory and imagination only as a sensuous experience:

> And then how I shall lie through centuries,
> And hear the blessed mutter of the mass,
> And see God made and eaten all day long,
> And feel the steady candle-flame, and taste
> Good strong thick stupefying incense-smoke!

If one wished to summarize this bishop in abstract terms, one might allude to "the corruption of the Church." Indeed, he exemplifies such corruption in many different ways, by what he fails to say as well as by what he says. "And thence ye may perceive the world's a dream": occasionally such tag lines erupt in his speech, but his lack of real religious feeling is all too apparent. He imagines himself lying in his tomb in his church through eternity; he does not think of an afterlife in heaven—or, for that matter, in hell, perhaps his more likely destination. Browning, however, implicitly insists on the difference between people and abstractions. To sum up this bishop in terms of ecclesiastical corruption would leave out the fact of his enormous vitality, a vitality that informs the entire poem. The dramatic monologue makes the bishop's feeling come alive, makes the reader sympathetically understand his reluctance to leave behind beauty he has valued all his life.

Browning uses the superficially remote situation he has evoked to reiterate the great Romantic theme—we have encountered it most vividly in Wordsworth and in Keats—of the poignance and the inevitability of loss. Instead of considering the problem of loss in autobiographical terms, he enters imaginatively into the experience of an invented character.

> She, men would have to be your mother once,
> Old Gandolf envied me, so fair she was!
> What's done is done, and she is dead beside,
> Dead long ago, and I am Bishop since,
> And as she died so must we die ourselves.

The dying man's emotions recapitulate a feeling we have all had: the sadness of memory, even memory of happy experiences (in this case, love of a woman and triumph over an enemy), when it tells us of what is irretrievably gone. The bishop holds on still to what he knows he must lose. His speech, as Browning captures it, expresses in its rhythms and its idiom the enduring vigor of his personality, even on the edge of death.

> Ah, ye hope
> To revel down my villas while I gasp
> Bricked o'er with beggar's mouldy travertine
> Which Gandolf from his tomb-top chuckles at!

This is not a man who has given up: he insists on the preoccupations of his life as he faces his death. The poem, demanding no judgment of the bishop, suggests, rather, the inadequacy of judgment as a reaction to the multiplicity of any single human being.

Browning's greatest gift as a poet is his capacity to convey an energetic sense of pleasure in the reality of experience. "Grow old along with me, / The best is yet to be," urges a character in one of his poems. But he also recognizes the cost of such intense living as that the bishop enjoys, since all human existence involves loss. The tonal complexity of *The Bishop Orders His Tomb* suggests the kind of richness typical of the Victorian period, with its faith and hope in the possibilities of human accomplishment mingled with doubt about what it all means in the end.

"*Childe Roland to the Dark Tower Came*" (1855), on the other hand, supplies little faith or hope. A nightmare vision that lends itself to no ready rational explanation, the poem narrates, in the first person, the experience of a quester who understands neither the purpose nor the meaning of his quest. (Nor can the reader deduce purpose or meaning.) The speaker finds himself in a landscape of despair; he remembers the failures of those who have preceded him. Increasingly conscious of loss and failure, he yet finally blows on his horn a call of challenge, not knowing what he challenges or why. The affirmation implicit in that final challenge promises no cheerful outcome. It constitutes a kind of existential defiance of impossibility. The poem's peculiar appeal for twenty-first-century readers depends on its acknowledgment of the kind of dark consciousness that can afflict anyone. Browning here explains nothing away. Indeed, he explains nothing at all.

A useful biography of Browning is C. Ryals, *The Life of Robert Browning: A Critical Biography* (1993). W. C. De Vane, *A Browning Handbook* (1935), provides indispensable guidance. Valuable criticism includes I. Jack, *Browning's Major Poetry* (1973); L. Erickson, *Robert Browning: His Poetry and His Audiences* (1984); J. Woolford, *Browning, the Revisionary* (1988); R. Adams, ed., *Robert Browning* (1997), a collection of essays; and E. Loehndorf, *The Master's Voices: Robert Browning, the Dramatic Monologue, and Modern Poetry* (1997). Valuable perspective on Browning is offered in D. Mermin, *The Audience in the Poem: Five Victorian Poets* (1983).

PRONOUNCING GLOSSARY

The following list uses common English syllables and stress accents to provide rough equivalents of selected words whose pronunciation may be unfamiliar to the general reader.

Apollyon: *a-pol'-yon*

Elucescebat: *ay-loo-say-say'-but*

Frascati: *frah-skah'-tee*

Tophet: *toh'-fet*

[POEMS]

My Last Duchess

Ferrara

That's my last Duchess painted on the wall,
Looking as if she were alive. I call
That piece a wonder, now: Frà Pandolf's hands
Worked busily a day, and there she stands.
Will't please you sit and look at her? I said   5
'Frà Pandolf' by design, for never read
Strangers like you that pictured countenance,
The depth and passion of its earnest glance,
But to myself they turned (since none puts by
The curtain I have drawn for you, but I)   10
And seemed as they would ask me, if they durst,
How such a glance came there; so, not the first
Are you to turn and ask thus. Sir,'twas not
Her husband's presence only, called that spot
Of joy into the Duchess' cheek: perhaps   15
Frà Pandolf chanced to say 'Her mantle laps
Over my lady's wrist too much,' or 'Paint
Must never hope to reproduce the faint
Half-flush that dies along her throat:' such stuff
Was courtesy, she thought, and cause enough   20
For calling up that spot of joy. She had
A heart—how shall I say?—too soon made glad,
Too easily impressed; she liked whate'er
She looked on, and her looks went everywhere.
Sir,'twas all one! My favour at her breast,   25
The dropping of the daylight in the West,
The bough of cherries some officious fool
Broke in the orchard for her, the white mule
She rode with round the terrace—all and each
Would draw from her alike the approving speech,   30
Or blush, at least. She thanked men,—good! but thanked
Somehow—I know not how—as if she ranked
My gift of a nine-hundred-years-old name
With anybody's gift. Who'd stoop to blame

This sort of trifling? Even had you skill 35
In speech—(which I have not)—to make your will
Quite clear to such an one, and say, 'Just this
Or that in you disgusts me; here you miss,
Or there exceed the mark'—and if she let
Herself be lessoned so, nor plainly set 40
Her wits to yours, forsooth, and make excuse,
—E'en then would be some stooping; and I choose
Never to stoop. Oh sir, she smiled, no doubt,
Whene'er I passed her; but who passed without
Much the same smile? This grew; I gave commands; 45
Then all smiles stopped together. There she stands
As if alive. Will't please you rise? We'll meet
The company below, then. I repeat,
The Count your master's known munificence
Is ample warrant that no just pretence 50
Of mine for dowry will be disallowed;
Though his fair daughter's self, as I avowed
At starting, is my object. Nay, we'll go
Together down, sir. Notice Neptune, though,
Taming a sea-horse, thought a rarity, 55
Which Clause of Innsbruck cast in bronze for me!

The Bishop Orders His Tomb at Saint Praxed's Church[1]

Rome, 15—

Vanity, saith the preacher, vanity![2]
Draw round my bed: is Anselm keeping back?
Nephews—sons mine . . . ah God, I know not! Well—
She, men would have to be your mother once,
Old Gandolf[3] envied me, so fair she was! 5
What's done is done, and she is dead beside,
Dead long ago, and I am Bishop since,
And as she died so must we die ourselves,
And thence ye may perceive the world's a dream.
Life, how and what is it? As here I lie 10
In this state-chamber, dying by degrees,
Hours and long hours in the dead night, I ask
"Do I live, am I dead?" Peace, peace seems all.
Saint Praxed's ever was the church for peace;
And so, about this tomb of mine. I fought 15
With tooth and nail to save my niche, ye know:
   Old Gandolf cozened me, despite my care;
Shrewd was that snatch from out the corner south
He graced his carrion with, God curse the same!
Yet still my niche is not so cramped but thence 20

1. The bishop, his tomb, and the character Gandolf are all fictional. Saint Praxed's church, seen by Browning in 1844, is named after a 2nd-century Roman virgin. 2. Ecclesiastes 1.2. 3. The bishop's predecessor.

One sees the pulpit o' the epistle-side,[4]
And somewhat of the choir, those silent seats,
And up into the aery dome where live
The angels, and a sunbeam's sure to lurk:
And I shall fill my slab of basalt there,   25
And 'neath my tabernacle[5] take my rest,
With those nine columns round me, two and two,
The odd one at my feet where Anselm stands:
Peach-blossom marble all, the rare, the ripe
As fresh-poured red wine of a mighty pulse.   30
—Old Gandolf with his paltry onion-stone,[6]
Put me where I may look at him! True peach,
Rosy and flawless: how I earned the prize!
Draw close: that conflagration of my church
—What then? So much was saved if aught were missed!   35
My sons, ye would not be my death? Go dig
The white-grape vineyard where the oil-press stood,
Drop water gently till the surface sink,
And if ye find . . . Ah God, I know not, I! . . .
Bedded in store of rotten fig-leaves soft,   40
And corded up in a tight olive-frail,[7]
Some lump, ah God, of lapis lazuli,[8]
Big as a Jew's head cut off at the nape,
Blue as a vein o'er the Madonna's breast . . .
Sons, all have I bequeathed you, villas, all,   45
That brave Frascati[9] villa with its bath,
So, let the blue lump poise between my knees,
Like God the Father's globe on both his hands
Ye worship in the Jesu Church[1] so gay,
For Gandolf shall not choose but see and burst!   50
Swift as a weaver's shuttle[2] fleet our years:
Man goeth to the grave, and where is he?
Did I say basalt for my slab, sons? Black—
'Twas ever antique-black[3] I meant! How else
Shall ye contrast my frieze to come beneath?   55
The bas-relief in bronze ye promised me,
Those Pans and Nymphs ye wot[4] of, and perchance
Some tripod, thyrsus,[5] with a vase or so,
The Saviour at his sermon on the mount,
Saint Praxed in a glory, and one Pan   60
Ready to twitch the Nymph's last garment off,
And Moses with the tables[6] . . . but I know
Ye mark me not! What do they whisper thee,
Child of my bowels, Anselm? Ah, ye hope
To revel down my villas while I gasp   65

4. I.e., the right side as the congregation faces the altar, from which during the service some portion of Saint Paul's Epistles is read. 5. Here, the canopy over his tomb. 6. A lesser grade of green marble. 7. Basket made of rushes, for figs, raisins, olives, and so on. 8. A bright blue semiprecious stone. 9. A wealthy Roman suburb. 1. The principal Jesuit church in Rome. 2. Job 7.6. 3. A grade of good marble. 4. Know. Pans and nymphs were Greek nature deities. 5. A staff tipped with a pine-cone, associated with the Greek god Bacchus. 6. The stone tablets on which the Ten Commandments were inscribed.

Bricked o'er with beggar's mouldy travertine[7]
Which Gandolf from his tomb-top chuckles at!
Nay, boys, ye love me—all of jasper,[8] then!
'Tis jasper ye stand pledged to, lest I grieve.
My bath must needs be left behind, alas!   70
One block, pure green as a pistachio-nut,
There's plenty jasper somewhere in the world—
And have I not Saint Praxed's ear to pray
Horses for ye, and brown Greek manuscripts,
And mistresses with great smooth marbly limbs?   75
—That's if ye carve my epitaph aright,
Choice Latin, picked phrase, Tully's[9] every word,
No gaudy ware like Gandolf's second line—
Tully, my masters? Ulpian[1] serves his need!
And then how I shall lie through centuries,   80
And hear the blessed mutter of the mass,
And see God made and eaten[2] all day long,
And feel the steady candle-flame, and taste
Good strong thick stupefying incense-smoke!
For as I lie here, hours of the dead night,   85
Dying in state and by such slow degrees,
I fold my arms as if they clasped a crook,[3]
And stretch my feet forth straight as stone can point,
And let the bedclothes, for a mortcloth,[4] drop
Into great laps and folds of sculptor's-work: 90
And as yon tapers dwindle, and strange thoughts
Grow, with a certain humming in my ears,
About the life before I lived this life,
And this life too, popes, cardinals, and priests,
Saint Praxed at his[5] sermon on the mount,   95
Your tall pale mother with her talking eyes,
And new-found agate urns as fresh as day,
And marble's language, Latin pure, discreet,
—Aha, Elucescebat[6] quoth our friend?
No Tully, said I, Ulpian at the best!   100
Evil and brief hath been my pilgrimage.
All lapis, all, sons! Else I give the Pope
My villas! Will ye ever eat my heart?
Ever your eyes were as a lizard's quick,
They glitter like your mother's for my soul,   105
Or ye would heighten my impoverished frieze,
Piece out its starved design, and fill my vase
With grapes, and add a vizor and a Term,[7]
And to the tripod ye would tie a lynx
That in his struggle throws the thyrsus down,   110

7. A cheap, flaky Italian building stone.   8. Reddish quartz.   9. Marcus Tullius Cicero (106–43 B.C.), Roman writer and master of Latin prose style.   1. Ulpianus Domitius (A.D. 170–228), lawyer, secretary to Emperor Alexander Severus, writer of nonclassical Latin.   2. A reference to the Sacrament of Communion.   3. The bishop's crosier.   4. Funeral pall or winding sheet.   5. Roger Cruik interprets the drowsy bishop as conflating the two allusions of lines 59–60, to Christ's Sermon on the Mount and to the (female) St. Prassede.   6. "He was illustrious," or "famous." In classical Latin the word would be *elucebat*. *Elucescebat* is an example of the less elegant Latin associated with Ulpian's era.   7. A pillar bearing a statue or a bust. *Vizor*: a masked figure.

To comfort me on my entablature
Whereon I am to lie till I must ask
'Do I live, am I dead?' There, leave me, there!
For ye have stabbed me with ingratitude
To death—ye wish it—God, ye wish it! Stone—   115
Gritstone,[8] a-crumble! Clammy squares which sweat
As if the corpse they keep were oozing through—
And no more lapis to delight the world!
Well go! I bless ye. Fewer tapers there,
But in a row: and, going, turn your backs   120
—Ay, like departing altar-ministrants,
And leave me in my church, the church for peace,
That I may watch at leisure if he leers—
Old Gandolf, at me, from his onion-stone,
As still he envied me, so fair she was!   125

"Childe Roland to the Dark Tower Came"

(*See Edgar's Song in* Lear)[1]

I

My first thought was, he lied in every word,
    That hoary cripple, with malicious eye
    Askance to watch the working of his lie
On mine, and mouth scarce able to afford
Suppression of the glee, that pursed and scored   5
    Its edge, at one more victim gained thereby.

II

What else should he be set for, with his staff?
    What, save to waylay with his lies, ensnare
    All travellers who might find him posted there,
And ask the road? I guessed what skull-like laugh   10
Would break, what crutch 'gin[2] write my epitaph
    For pastime in the dusty thoroughfare,

III

If at his counsel I should turn aside
    Into that ominous tract which, all agree,
    Hides the Dark Tower. Yet acquiescingly   15
I did turn as he pointed: neither pride
Nor hope rekindling at the end descried,
    So much as gladness that some end might be.

IV

For, what with my whole world-wide wandering,
    What with my search drawn out through years, my hope   20
    Dwindled into a ghost not fit to cope

---

8. Sandstone, a cheap substitute for marble.   **1.** Shakespeare's *King Lear* 3.4.173.   **2.** Begin to.

With that obstreperous joy success would bring,—
I hardly tried now to rebuke the spring
 My heart made, finding failure in its scope.

V

As when a sick man very near to death   25
 Seems dead indeed, and feels begin and end
 The tears and takes the farewell of each friend,
And hears one bid the other go, draw breath
Freelier outside, ("since all is o'er," he saith,
 "And the blow fallen no grieving can amend");   30

VI

While some discuss if near the other graves
 Be room enough for this, and when a day
 Suits best for carrying the corpse away,
With care about the banners, scarves and staves:
And still the man hears all, and only craves   35
 He may not shame such tender love and stay.

VII

Thus, I had so long suffered in this quest,
 Heard failure prophesied so oft, been writ
 So many times among "The Band"—to wit,
The knights who to the Dark Tower's search addressed   40
Their steps—that just to fail as they, seemed best,
 And all the doubt was now—should I be fit?

VIII

So, quiet as despair, I turned from him,
 That hateful cripple, out of his highway
 Into the path he pointed. All the day   45
Had been a dreary one at best, and dim
Was settling to its close, yet shot one grim
 Red leer to see the plain catch its estray.[3]

IX

For mark! no sooner was I fairly found
 Pledged to the plain, after a pace or two,   50
 Than, pausing to throw backward a last view
O'er the safe road,'twas gone; grey plain all round:
Nothing but plain to the horizon's bound.
 I might go on; nought else remained to do.

X

So, on I went. I think I never saw   55
 Such starved ignoble nature; nothing throve:

---

3. In law, a stray and unclaimed domestic animal.

For flowers—as well expect a cedar grove!
But cockle, spurge, according to their law
Might propagate their kind, with none to awe,
    You'd think; a burr had been a treasure-trove.   60

XI

No! penury, inertness and grimace,
    In some strange sort, were the land's portion. "See
    Or shut your eyes," said Nature peevishly,
"It nothing skills: I cannot help my case:
'Tis the Last Judgment's fire must cure this place,   65
    Calcine its clods and set my prisoners free."

XII

If there pushed any ragged thistle-stalk
    Above its mates, the head was chopped; the bents[4]
    Were jealous else. What made those holes and rents
In the dock's[5] harsh swarth leaves, bruised as to baulk   70
All hope of greenness? 'tis a brute must walk
    Pashing their life out, with a brute's intents.

XIII

As for the grass, it grew as scant as hair
    In leprosy; thin dry blades pricked the mud
    Which underneath looked kneaded up with blood.   75
One stiff blind horse, his every bone a-stare,
Stood stupefied, however he came there:
    Thrust out past service from the devil's stud!

XIV

Alive? he might be dead for aught I know,
    With that red gaunt and colloped[6] neck a-strain,   80
    And shut eyes underneath the rusty mane;
Seldom went such grotesqueness with such woe;
I never saw a brute I hated so;
    He must be wicked to deserve such pain.

XV

I shut my eyes and turned them on my heart.   85
    As a man calls for wine before he fights,
    I asked one draught of earlier, happier sights,
Ere fitly I could hope to play my part.
Think first, fight afterwards—the soldier's art:
    One taste of the old time sets all to rights.   90

XVI

Not it! I fancied Cuthbert's reddening face
    Beneath its garniture of curly gold,

---

4. Coarse grasses.   5. Any of several coarse weeds of the buckwheat family.   6. Ridged.

Dear fellow, till I almost felt him fold
An arm in mine to fix me to the place,
That way he used. Alas, one night's disgrace!   95
    Out went my heart's new fire and left it cold.

XVII

Giles then, the soul of honour—there he stands
    Frank as ten years ago when knighted first.
    What honest men should dare (he said) he durst.
Good—but the scene shifts—faugh! what hangman-hands   100
Pin to his breast a parchment?[7] his own bands
    Read it. Poor traitor, spit upon and curst!

XVIII

Better this present than a past like that;
    Back therefore to my darkening path again!
    No sound, no sight as far as eye could strain.   105
Will the night send a howlet[8] or a bat?
I asked: when something on the dismal flat
    Came to arrest my thoughts and change their train.

XIX

A sudden little river crossed my path
    As unexpected as a serpent comes.   110
    No sluggish tide congenial to the glooms;
This, as it frothed by, might have been a bath
For the fiend's glowing hoof—to see the wrath
    Of its black eddy bespate[9] with flakes and spumes.

XX

So petty yet so spiteful! All along,   115
    Low scrubby alders kneeled down over it;
    Drenched willows flung them headlong in a fit
Of mute despair, a suicidal throng:
The river which had done them all the wrong,
    Whate'er that was, rolled by, deterred no whit.   120

XXI

Which, while I forded,—good saints, how I feared
    To set my foot upon a dead man's cheek,
    Each step, or feel the spear I thrust to seek
For hollows, tangled in his hair or beard!
—It may have been a water-rat I speared,   125
    But, ugh! it sounded like a baby's shriek.

XXII

Glad was I when I reached the other bank.
    Now for a better country. Vain presage!

7. Containing an account of the crime for which he is condemned.   8. Owl.   9. Spattered.

Who were the strugglers, what war did they wage,
Whose savage trample thus could pad the dank   130
Soil to a plash? Toads in a poisoned tank,
   Or wild cats in a red-hot iron cage—

XXIII

The fight must so have seemed in that fell[1] cirque.
   What penned them there, with all the plain to choose?
   No foot-print leading to the horrid mews,   135
None out of it. Mad brewage set to work
Their brains, no doubt, like galley-slaves the Turk
   Pits for his pastime, Christians against Jews.

XXIV

And more than that—a furlong on—why, there!
   What bad use was that engine for, that wheel,   140
   Or brake, not wheel—that harrow fit to reel
Men's bodies out like silk? with all the air
Of Tophet's[2] tool, on earth left unaware,
   Or brought to sharpen its rusty teeth of steel.

XXV

Then came a bit of stubbed ground, once a wood,   145
   Next a marsh, it would seem, and now mere earth
   Desperate and done with; (so a fool finds mirth,
Makes a thing and then mars it, till his mood
Changes and off he goes!) within a rood[3]—
   Bog, clay and rubble, sand and stark black dearth.   150

XXVI

Now blotches rankling, coloured gray and grim,
   Now patches where some leanness of the soul's
   Broke into moss or substances like boils;
Then came some palsied oak, a cleft in him
Like a distorted mouth that splits its rim   155
   Gaping at death, and dies while it recoils.

XXVII

And just as far as ever from the end!
   Nought in the distance but the evening, nought
   To point my footstep further! At the thought,
A great black bird. Apollyon's[4] bosom-friend,   160
Sailed past, nor beat his wide wing dragon-penned[5]
   That brushed my cap—perchance the guide I sought.

1. Cruel, terrible. 2. Hell (Hebrew). 3. Quarter acre (forty square rods). 4. "The angel of the bottomless pit" (Revelation 9.11). 5. Dragon-winged.

XXVIII

For, looking up, aware I somehow grew,
   'Spite of the dusk, the plain had given place
   All round to mountains—with such name to grace   165
Mere ugly heights and heaps now stolen in view
How thus they had surprised me,—solve it, you![6]
   How to get from them was no clearer case.

XXIX

Yet half I seemed to recognize some trick
   Of mischief happened to me, God knows when—   170
   In a bad dream perhaps. Here ended, then,
Progress this way. When, in the very nick
Of giving up, one time more, came a click
   As when a trap shuts—you're inside the den!

XXX

Burningly it came on me all at once,   175
   This was the place! those two hills on the right,
   Crouched like two bulls locked horn in horn in fight;
While to the left, a tall scalped mountain . . . Dunce,
Dotard, a-dozing at the very nonce,[7]
   After a life spent training for the sight!   180

XXXI

What in the midst lay but the Tower itself?
   The round squat turret, blind as the fool's heart,
   Built of brown stone, without a counterpart
In the whole world. The tempest's mocking elf
Points[8] to the shipman thus the unseen shelf   185
   He strikes on, only when the timbers start.

XXXII

Not see? because of night perhaps?—why, day
   Came back again for that! before it left,
   The dying sunset kindled through a cleft:
The hills, like giants at a hunting, lay,   190
Chin upon hand, to see the game at bay,—
   "Now stab and end the creature—to the heft!"

XXXIII

Not hear? when noise was everywhere! it tolled
   Increasing like a bell. Names in my ears
   Of all the lost adventurers my peers,—   195
How such a one was strong, and such was bold,

6. The speaker addresses an imaginary listener—or the reader of the poem.   7. Occasion.   8. Points out.

And such was fortunate, yet each of old
   Lost, lost! one moment knelled the woe of years.

XXXIV

There they stood, ranged along the hill-sides, met
   To view the last of me, a living frame   200
   For one more picture! in a sheet of flame
I saw them and I knew them all. And yet
Dauntless the slug-horn[9] to my lips I set,
   And blew. *"Childe Roland to the Dark Tower came."*

9. Trumpet; the word was apparently invented by the poet Thomas Chatterton (1752–1770).

FREDERICK DOUGLASS
1818?–1895

The *Narrative of the Life of Frederick Douglass, An American Slave* (1845) powerfully details the struggle for identity of a black man who, in the mid-nineteenth century, came to realize his own exclusion from the American myth of liberty and justice for all. His autobiographical record epitomizes the experience of many pre–Civil War slaves, but in its narrative skill it also suggests how the writer's effort to achieve selfhood and freedom partakes of a more nearly universal pattern, incident to men and women of whatever color.

Virtually everything that is known of Douglass's early life comes from the *Narrative* itself, which ends half a century before his death. The book became an immediate best-seller but also a subject of controversy when accusations of fraud (promptly refuted) were made against it by a man who claimed to have known Douglass as a slave and to know him incapable of writing such a book. Because the autobiography's publication endangered its author, who might have been returned to slavery, Douglass subsequently went to Great Britain for two years of highly successful lecture appearances. At the end of 1846, two Englishwomen purchased his freedom from his old master, Hugh Auld, and Douglass returned to the United States in March 1847. He then began a journalistic career, writing and publishing a series of newspapers and making himself a leader of his people who continued to locate and to proclaim the injustices to which blacks were subject. Late in his life, he held a number of diplomatic posts, including minister resident and consul general to the Republic of Haiti and chargé d'affaires for Santo Domingo. He died in Washington, D.C., and was buried in Rochester, New York.

Douglass gradually enlarged and elaborated his *Narrative*, which exists in three subsequent versions: *My Bondage and My Freedom* (1855) and two different editions of *Life and Times of Frederick Douglass* (1881, 1892). The earliest, shortest form has the greatest narrative integrity and clarity. For literary as well as historical reasons (its status as an important document in the abolitionist crusade), it merits reprinting. It belongs to a genre familiar in its time: thousands of slave narratives were published in America—and in many cases translated into European languages—between the end of the eighteenth century and the beginning of the American Civil War. They won a large, enthusiastic readership; by making the horrors of slavery emotionally immediate, they intensified abolitionist sentiment. From the first publication of Douglass's work, it was acknowledged as unusually forceful by virtue of its rhetorical control and its narrative skill.

Douglass casts his autobiography as an account of self-discovery. The contrast between the openings of the *Narrative* and of Rousseau's *Confessions* is instructive. Rousseau begins by proclaiming that he differs importantly from everyone else in his unique and early established personality and character. Douglass, on the other hand, starts by reporting what he does *not* know of himself. He must guess his own age, he doesn't know his birthday, he has only rumor to tell him his father's identity. Although he knows his mother, he spends virtually no time with her; she comes to him and leaves him in the dark. Most children develop their sense of who they are by precisely the clues missing in Douglass's experience: age, parentage, such ritual occasions as birthdays. Douglass has only a generic identity: slave. Like other slave children, he wears nothing but a shirt—not the trousers that would symbolize his maleness, not shoes to protect his feet, nothing to differentiate him from others of his kind. Like the other children, he eats cornmeal mush from a trough on the floor, thus, as he notes, treated like a pig and reduced to animality. Everything in Douglass's experience denies his individuality and declares his lack of particularized identity.

The narrative constructed by a man who has finally, arduously, discovered his selfhood recapitulates the process of that discovery: a process with language at its heart. The book ends with its author claiming his name: "I subscribe myself, FREDERICK DOUGLASS." The name itself is a triumph, not his father's or his mother's but the freshly bestowed name of his freedom. The author has won with difficulty the power to subscribe himself, to sign his name, for it involves the capacity to read and write as well as the claim to a name. Each step of the winning—learning to read, learning to write, acquiring a name—involves painful self-testing, but the *word* proves for Douglass literally a means to salvation.

Douglass believes his arrival in Baltimore, to serve the Aulds, a sign of Providential intervention: in Baltimore he learns to read. Mrs. Auld, wife of his master, begins to teach the boy the alphabet; her husband warns her to desist. Reading, he says, "would forever unfit him to be a slave." Douglass comments: "It was a new and special revelation, explaining dark and mysterious things, with which my youthful understanding had struggled, but struggled in vain." The word *revelation* has almost religious force: the child's vision of reading as the key to freedom saves his soul. From this point on in his story—and he is only about eight years old at the time—words lead Douglass to succeeding revelations. He defies all efforts to shut him up "in mental darkness." From little white street urchins he acquires the sustaining "bread of knowledge." At the age of twelve or thereabouts, he reads a book called *The Columbian Orator*, which contains forceful antislavery arguments, and is thus enabled for the first time to utter his thoughts. Without the authority of the written word, the contact through it with other minds, he could not know how to articulate what he thinks, could hardly know what it is he thinks. He puzzles over the word *abolitionist*, hearing but not understanding it. When he figures out its meaning, he has passed another milestone. A slave's thoughts must be free, this account suggests, before he can hope for meaningful freedom of body; and freedom of thought comes only through knowledge of the word.

We know that the writer successfully achieves freedom, but he makes gripping drama out of the gradual reporting of how he does so. First he must painfully learn to write, another step toward taking possession of language. For his first, agonizingly abortive attempt at escape, he writes passes for himself and his friends, briefly preempting the glory of being his own master. Subjected subsequently to more brutalized conditions, he sustains himself by making an imaginary speech, in what he remembers as elaborate literary language, to the fleet of ships he sees on Chesapeake Bay, images of freedom. He defies his brutal overseer, claims his manhood, teaches fellow slaves to read; finally, as though by magic, he escapes. (He withholds details of the escape to protect others; the effect of this suppression on the narrative is to suggest that the escape occurs almost as the inevitable, natural culmination of the process of self-discovery.) A friendly white man gives him a new name. And finally Douglass discovers his own voice and his own words: the *Narrative* concludes with his assuming the role of orator on behalf of his people.

Despite its emphasis on the power of language, the autobiography reminds us also that language cannot express everything. Rousseau exhaustively explores his own feelings; Douglass recurrently comments on the inexpressibility of his deepest feelings. At the end of Chapter I, Frederick, a small child, watches his aunt whipped until she is covered with blood. "It was a most terrible spectacle. I wish I could commit to paper the feelings with which I beheld it." His feelings exceed the possibility of verbal representation. Other episodes of comparable brutality elicit the same response: the narrator feels more than he can say. The reader is recurrently reminded that the horrible reality to which Douglass's words refer is in fact a reality beyond words.

Douglass's development of identity, his ultimate subscription of his new name as the sign of his self, leads to no claim of uniqueness. On the contrary, the identity he claims is partly *communal*. "Sincerely and earnestly hoping that this little book may do something toward throwing light on the American slave system, and hastening the glad day of deliverance to the millions of my brethren in bonds—faithfully relying upon the power of truth, love, and justice, for success in my humble efforts—and solemnly pledging my self anew to the sacred cause,—I subscribe myself, FREDERICK DOUGLASS." The "little book" exists not to establish Douglass's difference but to declare his unity. Now he possesses his own name, his own differentiating clothes, his own wife, his own self-defined occupation; but as much as when he was a half-naked child gobbling mush with the others, he feels part of a group. His love for fellow slaves, a recurrent theme of his story, provides the foundation for his identity—not, like Rousseau, emotionally isolated, but part of a sustaining community.

His language, both in the final paragraph just quoted and elsewhere, suggests that he partakes also of an even wider community. He evokes "truth" and "justice," proclaimed ideals of the American nation. He quotes John Greenleaf Whittier, "the slaves' poet," to express feelings he finds it hard to state for himself. Everywhere his prose rings with biblical rhythms and allusions. Frederick Douglass is not only a slave, not only an ex-slave; he is a literary man, an American, a Christian, claiming, relying on, and valuing these larger forms of communion as well as his union with his race— and implicitly demanding that others who call themselves Americans or Christians acknowledge his participation with them and accept the responsibility such acknowledgment implies.

An illuminating biography of Douglass, which elaborates on the information of the *Narrative,* is N. Huggins, *Slave and Citizen: The Life of Frederick Douglass* (1980). A biography placing Douglass in the context of the nineteenth-century antislavery movement is W. S. McFeely, *Frederick Douglass* (1991). For critical approaches, see W. E. Martin, *The Mind of Frederick Douglass* (1984); H. Bloom, ed., *Frederick Douglass's Narrative of the Life of Frederick Douglass* (1988), a collection of essays; W. L. Andrews, ed., *Critical Essays on Frederick Douglass* (1991); E. J. Sundquist, ed., *Frederick Douglass: New Literary and Historical Essays* (1991); and W. B. Rogers, *"We Are All Together Now": Frederick Douglass, William Lloyd Garrison, and the Prophetic Tradition* (1995). Intended for teachers, but useful as well to students, is J. C. Hall, ed., *Approaches to Teaching Narrative of the Life of Frederick Douglass* (1999).

Narrative of the Life of Frederick Douglass, An American Slave[1]

CHAPTER I

I was born in Tuckahoe, near Hillsborough, and about twelve miles from Easton, in Talbot county, Maryland. I have no accurate knowledge of my age, never having seen any authentic record containing it. By far the larger part of the slaves know as little of their ages as horses know of theirs, and it is the wish of most masters within my knowledge to keep their slaves thus ignorant. I do not remember to have ever met a slave who could tell of his birthday. They seldom come nearer to it than planting-time, harvest-time, cherry-time, spring-time, or fall-time. A want of information concerning my own was a source of unhappiness to me even during childhood. The white children could tell their ages. I could not tell why I ought to be deprived of the same privilege. I was not allowed to make any inquiries of my master concerning it. He deemed all such inquiries on the part of a slave improper and impertinent, and evidence of a restless spirit. The nearest estimate I can give makes me now between twenty-seven and twenty-eight years of age. I come to this, from hearing my master say, some time during 1835, I was about seventeen years old.

My mother was named Harriet Bailey. She was the daughter of Isaac and Betsey Bailey, both colored, and quite dark. My mother was of a darker complexion than either my grandmother or grandfather.

My father was a white man. He was admitted to be such by all I ever heard speak of my parentage. The opinion was also whispered that my master was my father; but of the correctness of this opinion, I know nothing; the means of knowing was withheld from me. My mother and I were separated when I was but an infant—before I knew her as my mother. It is a common custom, in the part of Maryland from which I ran away, to part children from their mothers at a very early age. Frequently, before the child has reached its twelfth month, its mother is taken from it, and hired out on some farm a considerable distance off, and the child is placed under the care of an old woman, too old for field labor. For what this separation is done, I do not know, unless it be to hinder the development of the child's affection toward its mother, and to blunt and destroy the natural affection of the mother for the child. This is the inevitable result.

I never saw my mother, to know her as such, more than four or five times in my life; and each of those times was very short in duration, and at night. She was hired by a Mr. Stewart, who lived about twelve miles from my home. She made her journeys to see me in the night, travelling the whole distance on foot, after the performance of her day's work. She was a field hand, and a whipping is the penalty of not being in the field at sunrise, unless a slave has special permission from his or her master to the contrary—a permission which they seldom get, and one that gives to him that gives it the proud name of being a kind master. I do not recollect of ever seeing my mother by the light of day. She was with me in the night. She would lie down with me, and get me to sleep, but long before I waked she was gone. Very little com-

---

1. The text, printed in its entirety, is that of the first American edition, published by the Massachusetts Anti-Slavery Society in Boston in 1845.

munication ever took place between us. Death soon ended what little we could have while she lived, and with it her hardships and suffering. She died when I was about seven years old, on one of my master's farms, near Lee's Mill. I was not allowed to be present during her illness, at her death, or burial. She was gone long before I knew anything about it. Never having enjoyed, to any considerable extent, her soothing presence, her tender and watchful care, I received the tidings of her death with much the same emotions I should have probably felt at the death of a stranger.

Called thus suddenly away, she left me without the slightest intimation of who my father was. The whisper that my master was my father, may or may not be true; and, true or false, it is of but little consequence to my purpose whilst the fact remains, in all its glaring odiousness, that slaveholders have ordained, and by law established, that the children of slave women shall in all cases follow the condition of their mothers; and this is done too obviously to administer to their own lusts, and make a gratification of their wicked desires profitable as well as pleasurable; for by this cunning arrangement, the slaveholder, in cases not a few, sustains to his slaves the double relation of master and father.

I know of such cases; and it is worthy of remark that such slaves invariably suffer greater hardships, and have more to contend with, than others. They are, in the first place, a constant offence to their mistress. She is ever disposed to find fault with them; they can seldom do any thing to please her; she is never better pleased than when she sees them under the lash, especially when she suspects her husband of showing to his mulatto children favors which he withholds from his black slaves. The master is frequently compelled to sell this class of his slaves, out of deference to the feelings of his white wife; and, cruel as the deed may strike any one to be, for a man to sell his own children to human flesh-mongers, it is often the dictate of humanity for him to do so; for, unless he does this, he must not only whip them himself, but must stand by and see one white son tie up his brother, of but few shades darker complexion than himself, and ply the gory lash to his naked back; and if he lisp one word of disapproval, it is set down to his parental partiality, and only makes a bad matter worse, both for himself and the slave whom he would protect and defend.

Every year brings with it multitudes of this class of slaves. It was doubtless in consequence of a knowledge of this fact, that one great statesman of the south predicted the downfall of slavery by the inevitable laws of population. Whether this prophecy is ever fulfilled or not, it is nevertheless plain that a very different-looking class of people are springing up at the south, and are now held in slavery, from those originally brought to this country from Africa; and if their increase will do no other good, it will do away the force of the argument, that God cursed Ham,[2] and therefore American slavery is right. If the lineal descendants of Ham are alone to be scripturally enslaved, it is certain that slavery at the south must soon become unscriptural; for thousands are ushered into the world, annually, who, like myself, owe their existence to white fathers, and those fathers most frequently their own masters.

2. It was thought that Noah cursed his second son, Ham, for mocking him; that black skin resulted from the curse; and that all black people descended from Ham. In fact, according to Genesis 9.20–27 and 10.6–14, Noah cursed not Ham but Ham's son Canaan, while Ham's son Cush was black.

I have had two masters. My first master's name was Anthony. I do not remember his first name. He was generally called Captain Anthony—a title which, I presume, he acquired by sailing a craft on the Chesapeake Bay. He was not considered a rich slaveholder. He owned two or three farms, and about thirty slaves. His farms and slaves were under the care of an overseer. The overseer's name was Plummer. Mr. Plummer was a miserable drunkard, a profane swearer, and a savage monster. He always went armed with a cowskin and a heavy cudgel. I have known him to cut and slash the women's heads so horribly, that even master would be enraged at his cruelty, and would threaten to whip him if he did not mind himself. Master, however, was not a humane slaveholder. It required extraordinary barbarity on the part of an overseer to affect him. He was a cruel man, hardened by a long life of slaveholding. He would at times seem to take great pleasure in whipping a slave. I have often been awakened at the dawn of day by the most heart-rending shrieks of an own aunt of mine, whom he used to tie up to a joist, and whip upon her naked back till she was literally covered with blood. No words, no tears, no prayers, from his gory victim, seemed to move his iron heart from its bloody purpose. The louder she screamed, the harder he whipped; and where the blood ran fastest, there he whipped longest. He would whip her to make her scream, and whip her to make her hush; and not until overcome by fatigue, would he cease to swing the blood-clotted cowskin. I remember the first time I ever witnessed this horrible exhibition. I was quite a child, but I well remember it. I never shall forget it whilst I remember any thing. It was the first of a long series of such outrages, of which I was doomed to be a witness and a participant. It struck me with awful force. It was the blood-stained gate, the entrance to the hell of slavery, through which I was about to pass. It was a most terrible spectacle. I wish I could commit to paper the feelings with which I beheld it.

This occurrence took place very soon after I went to live with my old master, and under the following circumstances. Aunt Hester went out one night,—where or for what I do not know,—and happened to be absent when my master desired her presence. He had ordered her not to go out evenings, and warned her that she must never let him catch her in company with a young man, who was paying attention to her, belonging to Colonel Lloyd. The young man's name was Ned Roberts, generally called Lloyd's Ned. Why master was so careful of her, may be safely left to conjecture. She was a woman of noble form, and of graceful proportions, having very few equals, and fewer superiors, in personal appearance, among the colored or white women of our neighborhood.

Aunt Hester had not only disobeyed his orders in going out, but had been found in company with Lloyd's Ned; which circumstance, I found, from what he said while whipping her, was the chief offence. Had he been a man of pure morals himself, he might have been thought interested in protecting the innocence of my aunt; but those who knew him will not suspect him of any such virtue. Before he commenced whipping Aunt Hester, he took her into the kitchen, and stripped her from neck to waist, leaving her neck, shoulders, and back, entirely naked. He then told her to cross her hands, calling her at the same time a d—d b—h. After crossing her hands, he tied them with a strong rope, and led her to a stool under a large hook in the joist, put in for the purpose. He made her get upon the stool, and tied her hands to the hook. She now stood fair for his infernal purpose. Her arms were stretched up at their full length, so that she stood upon the ends of her toes. He then said to her, "Now, you d—d b—h, I'll learn you how to disobey my orders!" and after rolling up his sleeves, he commenced to lay on the heavy cowskin, and soon the warm, red blood (amid heart-rending shrieks from her, and horrid oaths from him) came dripping to the floor. I was so terrified and horror-stricken at the sight, that I hid myself in a closet, and dared not venture out till long after the bloody transaction was over. I expected it would be my turn next. It was all new to me. I had never seen any thing like it before. I had always lived with my grandmother on the outskirts of the plantation, where she was put to raise the children of the younger women. I had therefore been, until now, out of the way of the bloody scenes that often occurred on the plantation.

CHAPTER II

My master's family consisted of two sons, Andrew and Richard; one daughter, Lucretia, and her husband, Captain Thomas Auld. They lived in one house, upon the home plantation of Colonel Edward Lloyd. My master was Colonel Lloyd's clerk and superintendent. He was what might be called the overseer of the overseers. I spent two years of childhood on this plantation in my old master's family. It was here that I witnessed the bloody transaction recorded in the first chapter; and as I received my first impressions of slavery on this plantation, I will give some description of it, and of slavery as it there existed. The plantation is about twelve miles north of Easton, in Talbot county, and is situated on the border of Miles River. The principal products raised upon it were tobacco, corn, and wheat. These were raised in great abundance; so that, with the products of this and the other farms belonging to him, he was able to keep in almost constant employment a large sloop, in carrying them to market at Baltimore. This sloop was named *Sally Lloyd*, in honor of one of the colonel's daughters. My master's son-in-law, Captain Auld, was master of the vessel; she was otherwise manned by the colonel's own slaves. Their names were Peter, Isaac, Rich, and Jake. These were esteemed very highly by the other slaves, and looked upon as the privileged ones of the plantation; for it was no small affair, in the eyes of the slaves, to be allowed to see Baltimore.

Colonel Lloyd kept from three to four hundred slaves on his home plantation, and owned a large number more on the neighboring farms belonging to him. The names of the farms nearest to the home plantation were Wye Town and New Design. "Wye Town" was under the overseership of a man named Noah Willis. New Design was under the overseership of a Mr. Townsend. The overseers of these, and all the rest of the farms, numbering over twenty, received advice and direction from the managers of the home plantation. This was the great business place. It was the seat of government for the whole twenty farms. All disputes among the overseers were settled here. If a slave was convicted of any high misdemeanor, became unmanageable, or evinced a determination to run away, he was brought immediately here, severely whipped, put on board the sloop, carried to Baltimore, and sold to Austin Woolfolk, or some other slave-trader, as a warning to the slaves remaining.

Here, too, the slaves of all the other farms received their monthly allow-ance of food, and their yearly clothing. The men and women slaves received, as their monthly allowance of food, eight pounds of pork, or its equivalent in fish, and one bushel of corn meal. Their yearly clothing consisted of two coarse linen shirts, one pair of linen trousers, like the shirts, one jacket, one pair of trousers for winter, made of coarse negro cloth, one pair of stockings, and one pair of shoes; the whole of which could not have cost more than seven dollars. The allowance of the slave children was given to their mothers, or the old women having the care of them. The children unable to work in the field had neither shoes, stockings, jackets, nor trousers, given to them; their clothing consisted of two coarse linen shirts per year. When these failed them, they went naked until the next allowance-day. Children from seven to ten years old, of both sexes, almost naked, might be seen at all seasons of the year.

There were no beds given the slaves, unless one coarse blanket be consid-ered such, and none but the men and women had these. This, however, is not considered a very great privation. They find less difficulty from the want of beds, than from the want of time to sleep; for when their day's work in the field is done, the most of them having their washing, mending, and cook-ing to do, and having few or none of the ordinary facilities for doing either of these, very many of their sleeping hours are consumed in preparing for the field the coming day; and when this is done, old and young, male and female, married and single, drop down side by side, on one common bed,— the cold, damp floor,—each covering himself or herself with their miserable blankets; and here they sleep till they are summoned to the field by the driver's horn. At the sound of this, all must rise, and be off to the field. There must be no halting; every one must be at his or her post; and woe betides them who hear not this morning summons to the field; for if they are not awakened by the sense of hearing, they are by the sense of feeling: no age nor sex finds any favor. Mr. Severe, the overseer, used to stand by the door of the quarter, armed with a large hickory stick and heavy cowskin, ready to whip any one who was so unfortunate as not to hear, or, from any other cause, was prevented from being ready to start for the field at the sound of the horn.

Mr. Severe was rightly named: he was a cruel man. I have seen him whip a woman, causing the blood to run half an hour at the time; and this, too, in the midst of her crying children, pleading for their mother's release. He seemed to take pleasure in manifesting his fiendish barbarity. Added to his cruelty, he was a profane swearer. It was enough to chill the blood and stiffen the hair of an ordinary man to hear him talk. Scarce a sentence escaped him but that was commenced or concluded by some horrid oath. The field was the place to witness his cruelty and profanity. His presence made it both the field of blood and of blasphemy. From the rising till the going down of the sun, he was cursing, raving, cutting, and slashing among the slaves of the field, in the most frightful manner. His career was short. He died very soon after I went to Colonel Lloyd's; and he died as he lived, uttering, with his dying groans, bitter curses and horrid oaths. His death was regarded by the slaves as the result of a merciful providence.

Mr. Severe's place was filled by a Mr. Hopkins. He was a very different man. He was less cruel, less profane, and made less noise, than Mr. Severe.

His course was characterized by no extraordinary demonstrations of cruelty. He whipped, but seemed to take no pleasure in it. He was called by the slaves a good overseer.

The home plantation of Colonel Lloyd wore the appearance of a country village. All the mechanical operations for all the farms were performed here. The shoemaking and mending, the blacksmithing, cartwrighting, coopering, weaving, and grain-grinding, were all performed by the slaves on the home plantation. The whole place wore a business-like aspect very unlike the neighboring farms. The number of houses, too, conspired to give it advantage over the neighboring farms. It was called by the slaves the *Great House Farm.* Few privileges were esteemed higher, by the slaves of the out-farms, than that of being selected to do errands at the Great House Farm. It was associated in their minds with greatness. A representative could not be prouder of his election to a seat in the American Congress, than a slave on one of the out-farms would be of his election to do errands at the Great House Farm. They regarded it as evidence of great confidence reposed in them by their overseers; and it was on this account, as well as a constant desire to be out of the field from under the driver's lash, that they esteemed it a high privilege, one worth careful living for. He was called the smartest and most trusty fellow, who had this honor conferred upon him the most frequently. The competitors for this office sought as diligently to please their overseers, as the office-seekers in the political parties seek to please and deceive the people. The same traits of character might be seen in Colonel Lloyd's slaves, as are seen in the slaves of the political parties.

The slaves selected to go to the Great House Farm, for the monthly allowance for themselves and their fellow-slaves, were peculiarly enthusiastic. While on their way, they would make the dense old woods, for miles around, reverberate with their wild songs, revealing at once the highest joy and the deepest sadness. They would compose and sing as they went along, consulting neither time nor tune. The thought that came up, came out—if not in the word, in the sound;—and as frequently in the one as in the other. They would sometimes sing the most pathetic sentiment in the most rapturous tone, and the most rapturous sentiment in the most pathetic tone. Into all of their songs they would manage to weave something of the Great House Farm. Especially would they do this, when leaving home. They would then sing most exultingly the following words:—

> "I am going away to the Great House Farm!
> O, yea! O, yea! O!"

This they would sing, as a chorus, to words which to many would seem unmeaning jargon, but which, nevertheless, were full of meaning to themselves. I have sometimes thought that the mere hearing of those songs would do more to impress some minds with the horrible character of slavery, than the reading of whole volumes of philosophy on the subject could do.

I did not, when a slave, understand the deep meaning of those rude and apparently incoherent songs. I was myself within the circle; so that I neither saw nor heard as those without might see and hear. They told a tale of woe which was then altogether beyond my feeble comprehension; they were tones loud, long, and deep; they breathed the prayer and complaint of souls boiling over with the bitterest anguish. Every tone was a testimony against slavery, and a prayer to God for deliverance from chains. The hearing of those wild notes always depressed my spirit, and filled me with ineffable sadness. I have frequently found myself in tears while hearing them. The mere recurrence to those songs, even now, afflicts me; and while I am writing these lines, an expression of feeling has already found its way down my cheek. To those songs I trace my first glimmering conception of the dehumanizing character of slavery. I can never get rid of that conception. Those songs still follow me, to deepen my hatred of slavery, and quicken my sympathies for my brethren in bonds. If any one wishes to be impressed with the soul-killing effects of slavery, let him go to Colonel Lloyd's plantation, and, on allowance-day, place himself in the deep pine woods, and there let him, in silence, analyze the sounds that shall pass through the chambers of his soul,—and if he is not thus impressed, it will only be because "there is no flesh in his obdurate heart."

I have often been utterly astonished, since I came to the north, to find persons who could speak of the singing, among slaves, as evidence of their contentment and happiness. It is impossible to conceive of a greater mistake. Slaves sing most when they are most unhappy. The songs of the slave represent the sorrows of his heart; and he is relieved by them, only as an aching heart is relieved by its tears. At least, such is my experience. I have often sung to drown my sorrow, but seldom to express my happiness. Crying for joy, and singing for joy, were alike uncommon to me while in the jaws of slavery. The singing of a man cast away upon a desolate island might be as appropriately considered as evidence of contentment and happiness, as the singing of a slave; the songs of the one and of the other are prompted by the same emotion.

CHAPTER III

Colonel Lloyd kept a large and finely cultivated garden, which afforded almost constant employment for four men, besides the chief gardener, (Mr. M'Durmond). This garden was probably the greatest attraction of the place. During the summer months, people came from far and near—from Baltimore, Easton, and Annapolis—to see it. It abounded in fruits of almost every description, from the hardy apple of the north to the delicate orange of the south. This garden was not the least source of trouble on the plantation. Its excellent fruit was quite a temptation to the hungry swarms of boys, as well as the older slaves, belonging to the colonel, few of whom had the virtue or the vice to resist it. Scarcely a day passed, during the summer, but that some slave had to take the lash for stealing fruit. The colonel had to resort to all kinds of stratagems to keep his slaves out of the garden. The last and most successful one was that of tarring his fence all around; after which, if a slave was caught with tar upon his person, it was deemed sufficient proof that he had either been into the garden, or had tried to get in. In either case, he was severely whipped by the chief gardener. This plan worked well; the slaves became as fearful of tar as of the lash. They seemed to realize the impossibility of touching *tar* without being defiled.[3]

The colonel also kept a splendid riding equipage. His stable and carriage-

3. Compare the proverb "He who touches pitch shall be defiled."

house presented the appearance of some of our large city livery establish-ments. His horses were of the finest form and noblest blood. His carriage-house contained three splendid coaches, three or four gigs, besides dearborns and barouches[4] of the most fashionable style.

This establishment was under the care of two slaves—old Barney and young Barney—father and son. To attend to this establishment was their sole work. But it was by no means an easy employment; for in nothing was Colonel Lloyd more particular than in the management of his horses. The slightest inattention to these was unpardonable, and was visited upon those, under whose care they were placed, with the severest punishment; no excuse could shield them, if the colonel only suspected any want of attention to his horses—a supposition which he frequently indulged, and one which, of course, made the office of old and young Barney a very trying one. They never knew when they were safe from punishment. They were frequently whipped when least deserving, and escaped whipping when most deserving it. Every thing depended upon the looks of the horses, and the state of Colonel Lloyd's own mind when his horses were brought to him for use. If a horse did not move fast enough, or hold his head high enough, it was owing to some fault of his keepers. It was painful to stand near the stable-door, and hear the various complaints against the keepers when a horse was taken out for use. "This horse has not had proper attention. He has not been suffi-ciently rubbed and curried, or he has not been properly fed; his food was too wet or too dry; he got it too soon or too late; he was too hot or too cold; he had too much hay, and not enough of grain; or he had too much grain, and not enough of hay; instead of old Barney's attending to the horse, he had very improperly left it to his son." To all these complaints, no matter how unjust, the slave must answer never a word. Colonel Lloyd could not brook any contradiction from a slave. When he spoke, a slave must stand, listen, and tremble; and such was literally the case. I have seen Colonel Lloyd make old Barney, a man between fifty and sixty years of age, uncover his bald head, kneel down upon the cold, damp ground, and receive upon his naked and toil-worn shoulders more than thirty lashes at the time. Colonel Lloyd had three sons—Edward, Murray, and Daniel,—and three sons-in-law, Mr. Win-der, Mr. Nicholson, and Mr. Lowndes. All of these lived at the Great House Farm, and enjoyed the luxury of whipping the servants when they pleased, from old Barney down to William Wilkes, the coach-driver. I have seen Win-der make one of the house-servants stand off from him a suitable distance to be touched with the end of his whip, and at every stroke raise great ridges upon his back.

To describe the wealth of Colonel Lloyd would be almost equal to describ-ing the riches of Job.[5] He kept from ten to fifteen house-servants. He was said to own a thousand slaves, and I think this estimate quite within the truth. Colonel Lloyd owned so many that he did not know them when he saw them; nor did all the slaves of the out-farms know him. It is reported of him, that, while riding along the road one day, he met a colored man, and

4. Light four-wheeled carriages (*dearborns*) and carriages with a front seat for the driver and two facing back seats for couples (*barouches*).   5. Job 1.3: "His substance also was seven thousand sheep, and three thousand camels, and five hundred yoke of oxen, and five hundred she asses, and a very great household; so that this man was the greatest of all the men of the east."

addressed him in the usual manner of speaking to colored people on the public highways of the south: "Well, boy, whom do you belong to?" "To Colonel Lloyd," replied the slave. "Well, does the colonel treat you well?" "No, sir," was the ready reply. "What, does he work you too hard?" "Yes, sir." "Well, don't he give you enough to eat?" "Yes, sir, he gives me enough, such as it is."

The colonel, after ascertaining where the slave belonged, rode on; the man also went on about his business, not dreaming that he had been conversing with his master. He thought, said, and heard nothing more of the matter, until two or three weeks afterwards. The poor man was then informed by his overseer that, for having found fault with his master, he was now to be sold to a Georgia trader. He was immediately chained and handcuffed; and thus, without a moment's warning, he was snatched away, and forever sundered, from his family and friends, by a hand more unrelenting than death. This is the penalty of telling the truth, of telling the simple truth, in answer to a series of plain questions.

It is partly in consequence of such facts, that slaves, when inquired of as to their condition and the character of their masters, almost universally say they are contented, and that their masters are kind. The slaveholders have been known to send in spies among their slaves, to ascertain their views and feelings in regard to their condition. The frequency of this has had the effect to establish among the slaves the maxim, that a still tongue makes a wise head. They suppress the truth rather than take the consequences of telling it, and in so doing prove themselves a part of the human family. If they have any thing to say of their masters, it is generally in their masters' favor, especially when speaking to an untried man. I have been frequently asked, when a slave, if I had a kind master, and do not remember ever to have given a negative answer; nor did I, in pursuing this course, consider myself as uttering what was absolutely false; for I always measured the kindness of my master by the standard of kindness set up among slaveholders around us. Moreover, slaves are like other people, and imbibe prejudices quite common to others. They think their own better than that of others. Many, under the influence of this prejudice, think their own masters are better than the masters of other slaves; and this, too, in some cases, when the very reverse is true. Indeed, it is not uncommon for slaves even to fall out and quarrel among themselves about the relative goodness of their masters, each contending for the superior goodness of his own over that of the others. At the very same time, they mutually execrate their masters when viewed separately. It was so on our plantation. When Colonel Lloyd's slaves met the slaves of Jacob Jepson, they seldom parted without a quarrel about their masters; Colonel Lloyd's slaves contending that he was the richest, and Mr. Jepson's slaves that he was the smartest, and most of a man. Colonel Lloyd's slaves would boast his ability to buy and sell Jacob Jepson. Mr. Jepson's slaves would boast his ability to whip Colonel Lloyd. These quarrels would almost always end in a fight between the parties, and those that whipped were supposed to have gained the point at issue. They seemed to think that the greatness of their masters was transferable to themselves. It was considered as being bad enough to be a slave; but to be a poor man's slave was deemed a disgrace indeed!

CHAPTER IV

Mr. Hopkins remained but a short time in the office of overseer. Why his career was so short, I do not know, but suppose he lacked the necessary severity to suit Colonel Lloyd. Mr. Hopkins was succeeded by Mr. Austin Gore, a man possessing, in an eminent degree, all those traits of character indispensable to what is called a first-rate overseer. Mr. Gore had served Colonel Lloyd, in the capacity of overseer, upon one of the out-farms, and had shown himself worthy of the high station of overseer upon the home or Great House Farm.

Mr. Gore was proud, ambitious, and persevering. He was artful, cruel, and obdurate. He was just the man for such a place, and it was just the place for such a man. It afforded scope for the full exercise of all his powers, and he seemed to be perfectly at home in it. He was one of those who could torture the slightest look, word, or gesture, on the part of the slave, into impudence, and would treat it accordingly. There must be no answering back to him; no explanation was allowed a slave, showing himself to have been wrongfully accused. Mr. Gore acted fully up to the maxim laid down by slaveholders,— "It is better that a dozen slaves suffer under the lash, than that the overseer should be convicted, in the presence of the slaves, of having been at fault." No matter how innocent a slave might be—it availed him nothing, when accused by Mr. Gore of any misdemeanor. To be accused was to be convicted, and to be convicted was to be punished; the one always following the other with immutable certainty. To escape punishment was to escape accusation; and few slaves had the fortune to do either, under the overseership of Mr. Gore. He was just proud enough to demand the most debasing homage of the slave, and quite servile enough to crouch, himself, at the feet of the master. He was ambitious enough to be contented with nothing short of the highest rank of overseers, and persevering enough to reach the height of his ambition. He was cruel enough to inflict the severest punishment, artful enough to descend to the lowest trickery, and obdurate enough to be insensible to the voice of a reproving conscience. He was, of all the overseers, the most dreaded by the slaves. His presence was painful; his eye flashed confusion; and seldom was his sharp, shrill voice heard, without producing horror and trembling in their ranks.

Mr. Gore was a grave man, and, though a young man, he indulged in no jokes, said no funny words, seldom smiled. His words were in perfect keeping with his looks, and his looks were in perfect keeping with his words. Overseers will sometimes indulge in a witty word, even with the slaves; not so with Mr. Gore. He spoke but to command, and commanded but to be obeyed; he dealt sparingly with his words, and bountifully with his whip, never using the former where the latter would answer as well. When he whipped, he seemed to do so from a sense of duty, and feared no consequences. He did nothing reluctantly, no matter how disagreeable; always at his post, never inconsistent. He never promised but to fulfil. He was, in a word, a man of the most inflexible firmness and stone-like coolness.

His savage barbarity was equalled only by the consummate coolness with which he committed the grossest and most savage deeds upon the slaves under his charge. Mr. Gore once undertook to whip one of Colonel Lloyd's slaves, by the name of Demby. He had given Demby but few stripes, when, to get rid of the scourging, he ran and plunged himself into a creek, and stood there at the depth of his shoulders, refusing to come out. Mr. Gore told him that he would give him three calls, and that, if he did not come out at the third call, he would shoot him. The first call was given. Demby made no response, but stood his ground. The second and third calls were given with the same result. Mr. Gore then, without consultation or deliberation with any one, not even giving Demby an additional call, raised his musket to his face, taking deadly aim at his standing victim, and in an instant poor Demby was no more. His mangled body sank out of sight, and blood and brains marked the water where he had stood.

A thrill of horror flashed through every soul upon the plantation, excepting Mr. Gore. He alone seemed cool and collected. He was asked by Colonel Lloyd and my old master, why he resorted to this extraordinary expedient. His reply was, (as well as I can remember,) that Demby had become unmanageable. He was setting a dangerous example to the other slaves,—one which, if suffered to pass without some such demonstration on his part, would finally lead to the total subversion of all rule and order upon the plantation. He argued that if one slave refused to be corrected, and escaped with his life, the other slaves would soon copy the example; the result of which would be, the freedom of the slaves, and the enslavement of the whites. Mr. Gore's defence was satisfactory. He was continued in his station as overseer upon the home plantation. His fame as an overseer went abroad. His horrid crime was not even submitted to judicial investigation. It was committed in the presence of slaves, and they of course could neither institute a suit, nor testify against him; and thus the guilty perpetrator of one of the bloodiest and most foul murders goes unwhipped of justice, and uncensured by the community in which he lives. Mr. Gore lived in St. Michael's, Talbot county, Maryland, when I left there; and if he is still alive, he very probably lives there now; and if so, he is now, as he was then, as highly esteemed and as much respected as though his guilty soul had not been stained with his brother's blood.

I speak advisedly when I say this,—that killing a slave, or any colored person, in Talbot county, Maryland, is not treated as a crime, either by the courts or the community. Mr. Thomas Lanman, of St. Michael's, killed two slaves, one of whom he killed with a hatchet, by knocking his brains out. He used to boast of the commission of the awful and bloody deed. I have heard him do so laughingly, saying, among other things, that he was the only benefactor of his country in the company, and that when others would do as much as he had done, we should be relieved of "the d———d niggers."

The wife of Mr. Giles Hicks, living but a short distance from where I used to live, murdered my wife's cousin, a young girl between fifteen and sixteen years of age, mangling her person in the most horrible manner, breaking her nose and breastbone with a stick, so that the poor girl expired in a few hours afterward. She was immediately buried, but had not been in her untimely grave but a few hours before she was taken up and examined by the coroner, who decided that she had come to her death by severe beating. The offence for which this girl was thus murdered was this:—She had been set that night to mind Mrs. Hicks's baby, and during the night she fell asleep, and the baby cried. She, having lost her rest for several nights previous, did not hear the crying. They were both in the room with Mrs. Hicks. Mrs. Hicks, finding the girl slow to move, jumped from her bed, seized an oak stick of wood by the fireplace, and with it broke the girl's nose and breastbone, and thus ended her life. I will not say that this most horrid murder produced no sensation in the community. It did produce sensation, but not enough to bring the murderess to punishment. There was a warrant issued for her arrest, but it was never served. Thus she escaped not only punishment, but even the pain of being arraigned before a court for her horrid crime.

Whilst I am detailing bloody deeds which took place during my stay on Colonel Lloyd's plantation, I will briefly narrate another, which occurred about the same time as the murder of Demby by Mr. Gore.

Colonel Lloyd's slaves were in the habit of spending a part of their nights and Sundays in fishing for oysters, and in this way made up the deficiency of their scanty allowance. An old man belonging to Colonel Lloyd, while thus engaged, happened to get beyond the limits of Colonel Lloyd's, and on the premises of Mr. Beal Bondly. At this trespass, Mr. Bondly took offence, and with his musket came down to the shore, and blew its deadly contents into the poor old man.

Mr. Bondly came over to see Colonel Lloyd the next day, whether to pay him for his property, or to justify himself in what he had done, I know not. At any rate, this whole fiendish transaction was soon hushed up. There was very little said about it at all, and nothing done. It was a common saying, even among little white boys, that it was worth a half-cent to kill a "nigger," and a half-cent to bury one.

CHAPTER V

As to my own treatment while I lived on Colonel Lloyd's plantation, it was very similar to that of the other slave children. I was not old enough to work in the field, and there being little else than field work to do, I had a great deal of leisure time. The most I had to do was to drive up the cows at evening, keep the fowls out of the garden, keep the front yard clean, and run off errands for my old master's daughter, Mrs. Lucretia Auld. The most of my leisure time I spent in helping Master Daniel Lloyd in finding his birds, after he had shot them. My connection with Master Daniel was of some advantage to me. He became quite attached to me, and was a sort of protector of me. He would not allow the older boys to impose upon me, and would divide his cakes with me.

I was seldom whipped by my old master, and suffered little from any thing else than hunger and cold. I suffered much from hunger, but much more from cold. In hottest summer and coldest winter, I was kept almost naked— no shoes, no stockings, no jacket, no trousers, nothing on but a coarse tow linen shirt, reaching only to my knees. I had no bed. I must have perished with cold, but that, the coldest nights, I used to steal a bag which was used for carrying corn to the mill. I would crawl into this bag, and there sleep on the cold, damp, clay floor, with my head in and feet out. My feet had been so cracked with the frost, that the pen with which I am writing might be laid in the gashes.

We were not regularly allowanced. Our food was coarse corn meal boiled. This was called *mush*. It was put into a large wooden tray or trough, and set down upon the ground. The children were then called, like so many pigs, and like so many pigs they would come and devour the mush; some with oystershells, others with pieces of shingle, some with naked hands, and none with spoons. He that ate fastest got most; he that was strongest secured the best place; and few left the trough satisfied.

I was probably between seven and eight years old when I left Colonel Lloyd's plantation. I left it with joy. I shall never forget the ecstasy with which I received the intelligence that my old master (Anthony) had determined to let me go to Baltimore, to live with Mr. Hugh Auld, brother to my old master's son-in-law, Captain Thomas Auld. I received this information about three days before my departure. They were three of the happiest days I ever enjoyed. I spent the most part of all these three days in the creek, washing off the plantation scurf, and preparing myself for my departure.

The pride of appearance which this would indicate was not my own. I spent the time in washing, not so much because I wished to, but because Mrs. Lucretia had told me I must get all the dead skin off my feet and knees before I could go to Baltimore; for the people in Baltimore were very cleanly, and would laugh at me if I looked dirty. Besides, she was going to give me a pair of trousers, which I should not put on unless I got all the dirt off me. The thought of owning a pair of trousers was great indeed! It was almost a sufficient motive, not only to make me take off what would be called by pig-drovers the mange, but the skin itself. I went at it in good earnest, working for the first time with the hope of reward.

The ties that ordinarily bind children to their homes were all suspended in my case. I found no severe trial in my departure. My home was charmless; it was not home to me; on parting from it, I could not feel that I was leaving any thing which I could have enjoyed by staying. My mother was dead, my grandmother lived far off, so that I seldom saw her. I had two sisters and one brother, that lived in the same house with me; but the early separation of us from our mother had well nigh blotted the fact of our relationship from our memories. I looked for home elsewhere, and was confident of finding none which I should relish less than the one which I was leaving. If, however, I found in my new home hardship, hunger, whipping, and nakedness, I had the consolation that I should not have escaped any one of them by staying. Having already had more than a taste of them in the house of my old master, and having endured them there, I very naturally inferred my ability to endure them elsewhere, and especially at Baltimore; for I had something of the feeling about Baltimore that is expressed in the proverb, that "being hanged in England is preferable to dying a natural death in Ireland." I had the strongest desire to see Baltimore. Cousin Tom, though not fluent in speech, had inspired me with that desire by his eloquent description of the place. I could never point out any thing at the Great House, no matter how beautiful or powerful, but that he had seen something at Baltimore far exceeding, both in beauty and strength, the object which I pointed out to him. Even the Great House itself, with all its pictures, was far inferior to many buildings in Baltimore. So strong was my desire, that I thought a gratification of it would fully compensate for whatever loss of comforts I should sustain by the exchange. I left without a regret, and with the highest hopes of future happiness.

We sailed out of Miles River for Baltimore on a Saturday morning. I remember only the day of the week, for at that time I had no knowledge of the days of the month, nor the months of the year. On setting sail, I walked aft, and gave to Colonel Lloyd's plantation what I hoped would be the last look. I then placed myself in the bows of the sloop, and there spent the remainder of the day in looking ahead, interesting myself in what was in the distance rather than in things near by or behind.

In the afternoon of that day, we reached Annapolis, the capital of the State. We stopped but a few moments, so that I had no time to go on shore. It was the first large town that I had ever seen, and though it would look small compared with some of our New England factory villages, I thought it a wonderful place for its size—more imposing even than the Great House Farm!

We arrived at Baltimore early on Sunday morning, landing at Smith's Wharf, not far from Bowley's Wharf. We had on board the sloop a large flock of sheep; and after aiding in driving them to the slaughterhouse of Mr. Curtis on Louden Slater's Hill, I was conducted by Rich, one of the hands belonging on board of the sloop, to my new home in Alliciana Street, near Mr. Gardner's ship-yard, on Fells Point.

Mr. and Mrs. Auld were both at home, and met me at the door with their little son Thomas, to take care of whom I had been given. And here I saw what I had never seen before; it was a white face beaming with the most kindly emotions; it was the face of my new mistress, Sophia Auld. I wish I could describe the rapture that flashed through my soul as I beheld it. It was a new and strange sight to me, brightening up my pathway with the light of happiness. Little Thomas was told, there was his Freddy,—and I was told to take care of little Thomas; and thus I entered upon the duties of my new home with the most cheering prospect ahead.

I look upon my departure from Colonel Lloyd's plantation as one of the most interesting events of my life. It is possible, and even quite probable, that but for the mere circumstance of being removed from that plantation to Baltimore, I should have to-day, instead of being here seated by my own table, in the enjoyment of freedom and the happiness of home, writing this Narrative, been confined in the galling chains of slavery. Going to live at Baltimore laid the foundation, and opened the gateway, to all my subsequent prosperity. I have ever regarded it as the first plain manifestation of that kind providence which has ever since attended me, and marked my life with so many favors. I regarded the selection of myself as being somewhat remarkable. There were a number of slave children that might have been sent from the plantation to Baltimore. There were those younger, those older, and those of the same age. I was chosen from among them all, and was the first, last, and only choice.

I may be deemed superstitious, and even egotistical, in regarding this event as a special interposition of divine Providence in my favor. But I should be false to the earliest sentiments of my soul, if I suppressed the opinion. I prefer to be true to myself, even at the hazard of incurring the ridicule of others, rather than to be false, and incur my own abhorrence. From my earliest recollection, I date the entertainment of a deep conviction that slavery would not always be able to hold me within its foul embrace; and in the darkest hours of my career in slavery, this living word of faith and spirit of hope departed not from me, but remained like ministering angels to cheer me through the gloom. This good spirit was from God, and to him I offer thanksgiving and praise.

CHAPTER VI

My new mistress proved to be all she appeared when I first met her at the door,—a woman of the kindest heart and finest feelings. She had never had a slave under her control previously to myself, and prior to her marriage she had been dependent upon her own industry for a living. She was by trade a weaver; and by constant application to her business, she had been in a good degree preserved from the blighting and dehumanizing effects of slavery. I was utterly astonished at her goodness. I scarcely knew how to behave towards her. She was entirely unlike any other white woman I had ever seen. I could not approach her as I was accustomed to approach other white ladies. My early instruction was all out of place. The crouching servility, usually so acceptable a quality in a slave, did not answer when manifested toward her. Her favor was not gained by it; she seemed to be disturbed by it. She did not deem it impudent or unmannerly for a slave to look her in the face. The meanest slave was put fully at ease in her presence, and none left without feeling better for having seen her. Her face was made of heavenly smiles, and her voice of tranquil music.

But, alas! this kind heart had but a short time to remain such. The fatal poison of irresponsible power was already in her hands, and soon commenced its infernal work. That cheerful eye, under the influence of slavery, soon became red with rage; that voice, made all of sweet accord, changed to one of harsh and horrid discord; and that angelic face gave place to that of a demon.

Very soon after I went to live with Mr. and Mrs. Auld, she very kindly commenced to teach me the A, B, C. After I had learned this, she assisted me in learning to spell words of three or four letters. Just at this point of my progress, Mr. Auld found out what was going on, and at once forbade Mrs. Auld to instruct me further, telling her, among other things, that it was unlawful, as well as unsafe, to teach a slave to read. To use his own words, further, he said, "If you give a nigger an inch, he will take an ell. A nigger should know nothing but to obey his master—to do as he is told to do. Learning would *spoil* the best nigger in the world. Now," said he, "if you teach that nigger (speaking of myself) how to read, there would be no keeping him. It would forever unfit him to be a slave. He would at once become unmanageable, and of no value to his master. As to himself, it could do him no good, but a great deal of harm. It would make him discontented and unhappy." These words sank deep into my heart, stirred up sentiments within that lay slumbering, and called into existence an entirely new train of thought. It was a new and special revelation, explaining dark and mysterious things, with which my youthful understanding had struggled, but struggled in vain. I now understood what had been to me a most perplexing difficulty— to wit, the white man's power to enslave the black man. It was a grand achievement, and I prized it highly. From that moment, I understood the pathway from slavery to freedom. It was just what I wanted, and I got it at a time when I the least expected it. Whilst I was saddened by the thought of losing the aid of my kind mistress, I was gladdened by the invaluable instruction which, by the merest accident, I had gained from my master. Though conscious of the difficulty of learning without a teacher, I set out with high hope, and a fixed purpose, at whatever cost of trouble, to learn how to read. The very decided manner with which he spoke, and strove to impress his wife with the evil consequences of giving me instruction, served to convince me that he was deeply sensible of the truths he was uttering. It gave me the best assurance that I might rely with the utmost confidence on the results which, he said, would flow from teaching me to read. What he most dreaded, that I most desired. What he most loved, that I most hated. That which to him was a great evil, to be carefully shunned, was to me a great good, to be diligently sought; and the argument which he so warmly urged, against my learning to read, only served to inspire me with a desire and determination to learn. In learning to read, I owe almost as much to the bitter opposition of my master, as to the kindly aid of my mistress. I acknowledge the benefit of both.

I had resided but a short time in Baltimore before I observed a marked difference, in the treatment of slaves, from that which I had witnessed in the country. A city slave is almost a freeman, compared with a slave on the plantation. He is much better fed and clothed, and enjoys privileges altogether unknown to the slave on the plantation. There is a vestige of decency, a sense of shame, that does much to curb and check those outbreaks of atrocious cruelty so commonly enacted upon the plantation. He is a desperate slaveholder, who will shock the humanity of his nonslaveholding neighbors with the cries of his lacerated slave. Few are willing to incur the odium attaching to the reputation of being a cruel master; and above all things, they would not be known as not giving a slave enough to eat. Every city slaveholder is anxious to have it known of him, that he feeds his slaves well; and it is due to them to say, that most of them do give their slaves enough to eat. There are, however, some painful exceptions to this rule. Directly opposite to us, on Philpot Street, lived Mr. Thomas Hamilton. He owned two slaves. Their names were Henrietta and Mary. Henrietta was about twenty-two years of age, Mary was about fourteen; and of all the mangled and emaciated creatures I ever looked upon, these two were the most so. His heart must be harder than stone, that could look upon these unmoved. The head, neck, and shoulders of Mary were literally cut to pieces. I have frequently felt her head, and found it nearly covered with festering sores, caused by the lash of her cruel mistress. I do not know that her master ever whipped her, but I have been an eye-witness to the cruelty of Mrs. Hamilton. I used to be in Mr. Hamilton's house nearly every day. Mrs. Hamilton used to sit in a large chair in the middle of the room, with a heavy cowskin always by her side, and scarce an hour passed during the day but was marked by the blood of one of these slaves. The girls seldom passed her without her saying, "Move faster, you *black gip!*"[6] at the same time giving them a blow with the cowskin over the head or shoulders, often drawing the blood. She would then say, "Take that, you *black gip!*"—continuing, "If you don't move faster, I'll move you!" Added to the cruel lashings to which these slaves were subjected, they were kept nearly half-starved. They seldom knew what it was to

6. Cheat, swindler.

eat a full meal. I have seen Mary contending with the pigs for the offal thrown into the street. So much was Mary kicked and cut to pieces, that she was oftener called *"pecked"* than by her name.

CHAPTER VII

I lived in Master Hugh's family about seven years. During this time, I succeeded in learning to read and write. In accomplishing this, I was compelled to resort to various stratagems. I had no regular teacher. My mistress, who had kindly commenced to instruct me, had, in compliance with the advice and direction of her husband, not only ceased to instruct, but had set her face against my being instructed by any one else. It is due, however, to my mistress to say of her, that she did not adopt this course of treatment immediately. She at first lacked the depravity indispensable to shutting me up in mental darkness. It was at least necessary for her to have some training in the exercise of irresponsible power, to make her equal to the task of treating me as though I were a brute.

My mistress was, as I have said, a kind and tender-hearted woman; and in the simplicity of her soul she commenced, when I first went to live with her, to treat me as she supposed one human being ought to treat another. In entering upon the duties of a slaveholder, she did not seem to perceive that I sustained to her the relation of a mere chattel, and that for her to treat me as a human being was not only wrong, but dangerously so. Slavery proved as injurious to her as it did to me. When I went there, she was a pious, warm, and tender-hearted woman. There was no sorrow or suffering for which she had not a tear. She had bread for the hungry, clothes for the naked, and comfort for every mourner that came within her reach. Slavery soon proved its ability to divest her of these heavenly qualities. Under its influence, the tender heart became stone, and the lamblike disposition gave way to one of tiger-like fierceness. The first step in her downward course was in her ceasing to instruct me. She now commenced to practise her husband's precepts. She finally became even more violent in her opposition than her husband himself. She was not satisfied with simply doing as well as he had commanded; she seemed anxious to do better. Nothing seemed to make her more angry than to see me with a newspaper. She seemed to think that here lay the danger. I have had her rush at me with a face made all up of fury, and snatch from me a newspaper, in a manner that fully revealed her apprehension. She was an apt woman; and a little experience soon demonstrated, to her satisfaction, that education and slavery were incompatible with each other.

From this time I was most narrowly watched. If I was in a separate room any considerable length of time, I was sure to be suspected of having a book, and was at once called to give an account of myself. All this, however, was too late. The first step had been taken. Mistress, in teaching me the alphabet, had given me the *inch*, and no precaution could prevent me from taking the *ell*.

The plan which I adopted, and the one by which I was most successful, was that of making friends of all the little white boys whom I met in the street. As many of these as I could, I converted into teachers. With their kindly aid, obtained at different times and in different places, I finally succeeded in learning to read. When I was sent of errands, I always took my book with me, and by going one part of my errand quickly, I found time to get a lesson before my return. I used also to carry bread with me, enough of which was always in the house, and to which I was always welcome; for I was much better off in this regard than many of the poor white children in our neighborhood. This bread I used to bestow upon the hungry little urchins, who, in return, would give me that more valuable bread of knowledge. I am strongly tempted to give the names of two or three of those little boys, as a testimonial of the gratitude and affection I bear them; but prudence forbids;—not that it would injure me, but it might embarrass them; for it is almost an unpardonable offence to teach slaves to read in this Christian country. It is enough to say of the dear little fellows, that they lived on Philpot Street, very near Durgin and Bailey's ship-yard. I used to talk this matter of slavery over with them. I would sometimes say to them, I wished I could be as free as they would be when they got to be men. "You will be free as soon as you are twenty-one, *but I am a slave for life!* Have not I as good a right to be free as you have?" These words used to trouble them; they would express for me the liveliest sympathy, and console me with the hope that something would occur by which I might be free.

I was now about twelve years old, and the thought of being *a slave for life* began to bear heavily upon my heart. Just about this time, I got hold of a book entitled "The Columbian Orator."[7] Every opportunity I got, I used to read this book. Among much of other interesting matter, I found in it a dialogue between a master and his slave. The slave was represented as having run away from his master three times. The dialogue represented the conversation which took place between them, when the slave was retaken the third time. In this dialogue, the whole argument in behalf of slavery was brought forward by the master, all of which was disposed of by the slave. The slave was made to say some very smart as well as impressive things in reply to his master—things which had the desired though unexpected effect; for the conversation resulted in the voluntary emancipation of the slave on the part of the master.

In the same book, I met with one of Sheridan's[8] mighty speeches on and in behalf of Catholic emancipation. These were choice documents to me. I read them over and over again with unabated interest. They gave tongue to interesting thoughts of my own soul, which had frequently flashed through my mind, and died away for want of utterance. The moral which I gained from the dialogue was the power of truth over the conscience of even a slaveholder. What I got from Sheridan was a bold denunciation of slavery, and a powerful vindication of human rights. The reading of these documents enabled me to utter my thoughts, and to meet the arguments brought forward to sustain slavery; but while they relieved me of one difficulty, they brought on another even more painful than the one of which I was relieved. The more I read, the more I was led to abhor and detest my enslavers. I could regard them in no other light than a band of successful robbers, who had left their homes, and gone to Africa, and stolen us from our homes, and in a strange land reduced us to slavery. I loathed them as being the meanest as well as the most wicked of men. As I read and contemplated the subject,

7. Caleb Bingham, *The Columbian Orator: Containing a Variety of Original and Selected Pieces: Together with Rules, Calculated to Improve Youth and Others in the Ornamental and Useful Art of Eloquence* (1807).
8. Thomas Sheridan (1719–1788), lecturer and writer on elocution.

behold! that very discontentment which Master Hugh had predicted would follow my learning to read had already come, to torment and sting my soul to unutterable anguish. As I writhed under it, I would at times feel that learning to read had been a curse rather than a blessing. It had given me a view of my wretched condition, without the remedy. It opened my eyes to the horrible pit, but to no ladder upon which to get out. In moments of agony, I envied my fellow-slaves for their stupidity. I have often wished myself a beast. I preferred the condition of the meanest reptile to my own. Any thing, no matter what, to get rid of thinking! It was this everlasting thinking of my condition that tormented me. There was no getting rid of it. It was pressed upon me by every object within sight or hearing, animate or inanimate. The silver trump of freedom had roused my soul to eternal wakefulness. Freedom now appeared, to disappear no more forever. It was heard in every sound, and seen in every thing. It was ever present to torment me with a sense of my wretched condition. I saw nothing without seeing it, I heard nothing without hearing it, and felt nothing without feeling it. It looked from every star, it smiled in every calm, breathed in every wind, and moved in every storm.

I often found myself regretting my own existence, and wishing myself dead; and but for the hope of being free, I have no doubt but that I should have killed myself, or done something for which I should have been killed. While in this state of mind, I was eager to hear any one speak of slavery. I was a ready listener. Every little while, I could hear something about the abolitionists. It was some time before I found what the word meant. It was always used in such connections as to make it an interesting word to me. If a slave ran away and succeeded in getting clear, or if a slave killed his master, set fire to a barn, or did any thing very wrong in the mind of a slaveholder, it was spoken of as the fruit of *abolition.* Hearing the word in this connection very often, I set about learning what it meant. The dictionary afforded me little or no help. I found it was "the act of abolishing;" but then I did not know what was to be abolished. Here I was perplexed. I did not dare to ask any one about its meaning, for I was satisfied that it was something they wanted me to know very little about. After a patient waiting, I got one of our city papers, containing an account of the number of petitions from the north, praying for the abolition of slavery in the District of Columbia, and of the slave trade between the States. From this time I understood the words *abolition* and *abolitionist,* and always drew near when that word was spoken, expecting to hear something of importance to myself and fellow-slaves. The light broke in upon me by degrees. I went one day down on the wharf of Mr. Waters; and seeing two Irishmen unloading a scow of stone, I went, unasked, and helped them. When we had finished, one of them came to me and asked me if I were a slave. I told him I was. He asked, "Are ye a slave for life?" I told him that I was. The good Irishman seemed to be deeply affected by the statement. He said to the other that it was a pity so fine a little fellow as myself should be a slave for life. He said it was a shame to hold me. They both advised me to run away to the north; that I should find friends there, and that I should be free. I pretended not to be interested in what they said, and treated them as if I did not understand them; for I feared they might be treacherous. White men have been known to encourage slaves to escape, and then, to get the reward, catch them and return them to their masters. I was afraid that these seemingly good men might use me so; but I nevertheless remembered their advice, and from that time I resolved to run away. I looked forward to a time at which it would be safe for me to escape. I was too young to think of doing so immediately; besides, I wished to learn how to write, as I might have occasion to write my own pass. I consoled myself with the hope that I should one day find a good chance. Meanwhile, I would learn to write.

The idea as to how I might learn to write was suggested to me by being in Durgin and Bailey's ship-yard, and frequently seeing the ship carpenters, after hewing, and getting a piece of timber ready for use, write on the timber the name of that part of the ship for which it was intended. When a piece of timber was intended for the larboard side, it would be marked thus—"L." When a piece was for the starboard side, it would be marked thus—"S." A piece for the larboard forward, would be marked thus—"L.F." When a piece was for starboard side forward, it would be marked thus—"S.F." For larboard aft, it would be marked thus—"L.A." For starboard aft, it would be marked thus—"S.A." I soon learned the names of these letters, and for what they were intended when placed upon a piece of timber in the ship-yard. I immediately commenced copying them, and in a short time was able to make the four letters named. After that, when I met with any boy who I knew could write, I would tell him I could write as well as he. The next word would be, "I don't believe you. Let me see you try it." I would then make the letters which I had been so fortunate as to learn, and ask him to beat that. In this way I got a good many lessons in writing, which it is quite possible I should never have gotten in any other way. During this time, my copy-book was the board fence, brick wall, and pavement; my pen and ink was a lump of chalk. With these, I learned mainly how to write. I then commenced and continued copying the Italics in Webster's Spelling Book, until I could make them all without looking on the book. By this time, my little Master Thomas had gone to school, and learned how to write, and had written over a number of copy-books. These had been brought home, and shown to some of our near neighbors, and then laid aside. My mistress used to go to class meeting at the Wilk Street meetinghouse every Monday afternoon, and leave me to take care of the house. When left thus, I used to spend the time in writing in the spaces left in Master Thomas's copy-book, copying what he had written. I continued to do this until I could write a hand very similar to that of Master Thomas. Thus, after a long, tedious effort for years, I finally succeeded in learning how to write.

CHAPTER VIII

In a very short time after I went to live at Baltimore, my old master's youngest son Richard died; and in about three years and six months after his death, my old master, Captain Anthony, died, leaving only his son, Andrew, and daughter, Lucretia, to share his estate. He died while on a visit to see his daughter at Hillsborough. Cut off thus unexpectedly, he left no will as to the disposal of his property. It was therefore necessary to have a valuation of the property, that it might be equally divided between Mrs. Lucretia and Master Andrew. I was immediately sent for, to be valued with the other property. Here again my feelings rose up in detestation of slavery. I had now a new conception of my degraded condition. Prior to this, I had become, if not insensible to my lot, at least partly so. I left Baltimore with a young heart overborne with sadness, and a soul full of apprehension. I took passage with Captain Rowe, in the schooner *Wild Cat,* and, after a sail of about twenty-four hours, I found myself near the place of my birth. I had now been absent from it almost, if not quite, five years. I, however, remembered the place very well. I was only about five years old when I left it, to go and live with my old master on Colonel Lloyd's plantation; so that I was now between ten and eleven years old.

We were all ranked together at the valuation. Men and women, old and young, married and single, were ranked with horses, sheep, and swine. There were horses and men, cattle and women, pigs and children, all holding the same rank in the scale of being, and all were subjected to the same narrow examination. Silvery-headed age and sprightly youth, maids and matrons, had to undergo the same indelicate inspection. At this moment, I saw more clearly than ever the brutalizing effects of slavery upon both slave and slaveholder.

After the valuation, then came the division. I have no language to express the high excitement and deep anxiety which were felt among us poor slaves during this time. Our fate for life was now to be decided. We had no more voice in that decision than the brutes among whom we were ranked. A single word from the white men was enough—against all our wishes, prayers, and entreaties—to sunder forever the dearest friends, dearest kindred, and strongest ties known to human beings. In addition to the pain of separation, there was the horrid dread of falling into the hands of Master Andrew. He was known to us all as being a most cruel wretch,—a common drunkard, who had, by his reckless mismanagement and profligate dissipation, already wasted a large portion of his father's property. We all felt that we might as well be sold at once to the Georgia traders, as to pass into his hands; for we knew that that would be our inevitable condition,—a condition held by us all in the utmost horror and dread.

I suffered more anxiety than most of my fellow-slaves. I had known what it was to be kindly treated; they had known nothing of the kind. They had seen little or nothing of the world. They were in very deed men and women of sorrow, and acquainted with grief.[9] Their backs had been made familiar with the bloody lash, so that they had become callous; mine was yet tender; for while at Baltimore I got few whippings, and few slaves could boast of a kinder master and mistress than myself; and the thought of passing out of their hands into those of Master Andrew—a man who, but a few days before, to give me a sample of his bloody disposition, took my little brother by the throat, threw him on the ground, and with the heel of his boot stamped upon his head till the blood gushed from his nose and ears—was well calculated to make me anxious as to my fate. After he had committed this savage outrage upon my brother, he turned to me, and said that was the way he meant to serve me one of these days,—meaning, I suppose, when I came into his possession.

Thanks to a kind Providence, I fell to the portion of Mrs. Lucretia, and was sent immediately back to Baltimore, to live again in the family of Master

---

9. In Isaiah 53.3, the Lord's servant is described as "a man of sorrows, and acquainted with grief."

Hugh. Their joy at my return equalled their sorrow at my departure. It was a glad day to me. I had escaped a [fate] worse than lion's jaws. I was absent from Baltimore, for the purpose of valuation and division, just about one month, and it seemed to have been six.

Very soon after my return to Baltimore, my mistress, Lucretia, died, leaving her husband and one child, Amanda; and in a very short time after her death, Master Andrew died. Now all the property of my old master, slaves included, was in the hands of strangers,—strangers who had had nothing to do with accumulating it. Not a slave was left free. All remained slaves, from the youngest to the oldest. If any one thing in my experience, more than another, served to deepen my conviction of the infernal character of slavery, and to fill me with unutterable loathing of slaveholders, it was their base ingratitude to my poor old grandmother. She had served my old master faithfully from youth to old age. She had been the source of all his wealth; she had peopled his plantation with slaves; she had become a great grandmother in his service. She had rocked him in infancy, attended him in childhood, served him through life, and at his death wiped from his icy brow the cold death-sweat, and closed his eyes forever. She was nevertheless left a slave—a slave for life—a slave in the hands of strangers; and in their hands she saw her children, her grandchildren, and her great-grandchildren, divided, like so many sheep, without being gratified with the small privilege of a single word, as to their or her own destiny. And, to cap the climax of their base ingratitude and fiendish barbarity, my grandmother, who was now very old, having outlived my old master and all his children, having seen the beginning and end of all of them, and her present owners finding she was of but little value, her frame already racked with the pains of old age, and complete helplessness fast stealing over her once active limbs, they took her to the woods, built her a little hut, put up a little mud-chimney, and then made her welcome to the privilege of supporting herself there in perfect loneliness; thus virtually turning her out to die! If my poor old grandmother now lives, she lives to suffer in utter loneliness; she lives to remember and mourn over the loss of children, the loss of grandchildren, and the loss of great-grandchildren. They are, in the language of the slave's poet, Whittier,—

> "Gone, gone, sold and gone
> To the rice swamp dank and lone,
> Where the slave-whip ceaseless swings,
> Where the noisome insect stings,
> Where the fever-demon strews
> Poison with the falling dews,
> Where the sickly sunbeams glare
> Through the hot and misty air:—
> Gone, gone, sold and gone
> To the rice swamp dank and lone,
> From Virginia hills and waters—
> Woe is me, my stolen daughters!"[1]

The hearth is desolate. The children, the unconscious children, who once sang and danced in her presence, are gone. She gropes her way, in the dark-

---

1. John Greenleaf Whittier, American poet (1807–1892), wrote a large group of antislavery poems. This one is *The Farewell of a Virginia Slave Mother to her Daughters Sold into Southern Bondage.*

ness of age, for a drink of water. Instead of the voices of her children, she hears by day the moans of the dove, and by night the screams of the hideous owl. All is gloom. The grave is at the door. And now, when weighed down by the pains and aches of old age, when the head inclines to the feet, when the beginning and ending of human existence meet, and helpless infancy and painful old age combine together—at this time, this most needful time, the time for the exercise of that tenderness and affection which children only can exercise towards a declining parent—my poor old grandmother, the devoted mother of twelve children, is left all alone, in yonder little hut, before a few dim embers. She stands—she sits—she staggers—she falls—she groans—she dies—and there are none of her children or grandchildren present, to wipe from her wrinkled brow the cold sweat of death, or to place beneath the sod her fallen remains. Will not a righteous God visit[2] for these things?

In about two years after the death of Mrs. Lucretia, Master Thomas married his second wife. Her name was Rowena Hamilton. She was the eldest daughter of Mr. William Hamilton. Master now lived in St. Michael's. Not long after his marriage, a misunderstanding took place between himself and Master Hugh; and as a means of punishing his brother, he took me from him to live with himself at St. Michael's. Here I underwent another most painful separation. It, however, was not so severe as the one I dreaded at the division of property; for, during this interval, a great change had taken place in Master Hugh and his once kind and affectionate wife. The influence of brandy upon him, and of slavery upon her, had effected a disastrous change in the characters of both; so that, as far as they were concerned, I thought I had little to lose by the change. But it was not to them that I was attached. It was to those little Baltimore boys that I felt the strongest attachment. I had received many good lessons from them, and was still receiving them, and the thought of leaving them was painful indeed. I was leaving, too, without the hope of ever being allowed to return. Master Thomas had said he would never let me return again. The barrier betwixt himself and brother he considered impassable.

I then had to regret that I did not at least make the attempt to carry out my resolution to run away; for the chances of success are tenfold greater from the city than from the country.

I sailed from Baltimore for St. Michael's in the sloop *Amanda*, Captain Edward Dodson. On my passage, I paid particular attention to the direction which the steamboats took to go to Philadelphia. I found, instead of going down, on reaching North Point they went up the bay, in a north-easterly direction. I deemed this knowledge of the utmost importance. My determination to run away was again revived. I resolved to wait only so long as the offering of a favorable opportunity. When that came, I was determined to be off.

CHAPTER IX

I have now reached a period of my life when I can give dates. I left Baltimore, and went to live with Master Thomas Auld, at St. Michael's, in March, 1832. It was now more than seven years since I lived with him in

---

2. I.e., visit vengeance. Compare Exodus 32.34: "Nevertheless, in the day when I visit their sin upon them."

the family of my old master, on Colonel Lloyd's plantation. We of course were now almost entire strangers to each other. He was to me a new master, and I to him a new slave. I was ignorant of his temper and disposition; he was equally so of mine. A very short time, however, brought us into full acquaintance with each other. I was made acquainted with his wife not less than with himself. They were well matched, being equally mean and cruel. I was now, for the first time during a space of more than seven years, made to feel the painful gnawings of hunger—a something which I had not experienced before since I left Colonel Lloyd's plantation. It went hard enough with me then, when I could look back to no period at which I had enjoyed a sufficiency. It was tenfold harder after living in Master Hugh's family, where I had always had enough to eat, and of that which was good. I have said Master Thomas was a mean man. He was so. Not to give a slave enough to eat, is regarded as the most aggravated development of meanness even among slaveholders. The rule is, no matter how coarse the food, only let there be enough of it. This is the theory; and in the part of Maryland from which I came, it is the general practice,—though there are many exceptions. Master Thomas gave us enough of neither coarse nor fine food. There were four of us slaves in the kitchen—my sister Eliza, my aunt Priscilla, Henny, and myself; and we were allowed less than a half of a bushel of corn-meal per week, and very little else, either in the shape of meat or vegetables. It was not enough for us to subsist upon. We were therefore reduced to the wretched necessity of living at the expense of our neighbors. This we did by begging and stealing, whichever came handy in the time of need, the one being considered as legitimate as the other. A great many times have we poor creatures been nearly perishing with hunger, when food in abundance lay mouldering in the safe and smoke-house, and our pious mistress was aware of the fact; and yet that mistress and her husband would kneel every morning, and pray that God would bless them in basket and store!

Bad as all slaveholders are, we seldom meet one destitute of every element of character commanding respect. My master was one of this rare sort. I do not know of one single noble act ever performed by him. The leading trait in his character was meanness; and if there were any other element in his nature, it was made subject to this. He was mean; and, like most other mean men, he lacked the ability to conceal his meanness. Captain Auld was not born a slaveholder. He had been a poor man, master only of a Bay craft. He came into possession of all his slaves by marriage; and of all men, adopted slaveholders are the worst. He was cruel, but cowardly. He commanded without firmness. In the enforcement of his rules, he was at times rigid, and at times lax. At times, he spoke to his slaves with the firmness of Napoleon and the fury of a demon; at other times, he might well be mistaken for an inquirer who had lost his way. He did nothing of himself. He might have passed for a lion, but for his ears.[3] In all things noble which he attempted, his own meanness shone most conspicuous. His airs, words, and actions, were the airs, words, and actions of born slaveholders, and, being assumed, were awkward enough. He was not even a good imitator. He possessed all the disposition to deceive, but wanted the power. Having no resources within himself,

3. A variation on Aesop's fable of the ass in the lion's skin, in which the fox says, "I should have been frightened too, if I had heard you bray."

he was compelled to be the copyist of many, and being such, he was forever the victim of inconsistency; and of consequence he was an object of contempt, and was held as such even by his slaves. The luxury of having slaves of his own to wait upon him was something new and unprepared for. He was a slaveholder without the ability to hold slaves. He found himself incapable of managing his slaves either by force, fear, or fraud. We seldom called him "master;" we generally called him "Captain Auld," and were hardly disposed to title him at all. I doubt not that our conduct had much to do with making him appear awkward, and of consequence fretful. Our want of reverence for him must have perplexed him greatly. He wished to have us call him master, but lacked the firmness necessary to command us to do so. His wife used to insist upon our calling him so, but to no purpose. In August, 1832, my master attended a Methodist camp-meeting held in the Bay-side, Talbot county, and there experienced religion. I indulged a faint hope that his conversion would lead him to emancipate his slaves, and that, if he did not do this, it would, at any rate, make him more kind and humane. I was disappointed in both these respects. It neither made him to be humane to his slaves, nor to emancipate them. If it had any effect on his character, it made him more cruel and hateful in all his ways; for I believe him to have been a much worse man after his conversion than before. Prior to his conversion, he relied upon his own depravity to shield and sustain him in his savage barbarity; but after his conversion, he found religious sanction and support for his slaveholding cruelty. He made the greatest pretensions to piety. His house was the house of prayer. He prayed morning, noon, and night. He very soon distinguished himself among his brethren, and was soon made a class-leader and exhorter. His activity in revivals was great, and he proved himself an instrument in the hands of the church in converting many souls. His house was the preachers' home. They used to take great pleasure in coming there to put up; for while he starved us, he stuffed them. We have had three or four preachers there at a time. The names of those who used to come most frequently while I lived there, were Mr. Storks, Mr. Ewery, Mr. Humphry, and Mr. Hickey. I have also seen Mr. George Cookman at our house. We slaves loved Mr. Cookman. We believed him to be a good man. We thought him instrumental in getting Mr. Samuel Harrison, a very rich slaveholder, to emancipate his slaves; and by some means got the impression that he was laboring to effect the emancipation of all the slaves. When he was at our house, we were sure to be called in to prayers. When the others were there, we were sometimes called in and sometimes not. Mr. Cookman took more notice of us than either of the other ministers. He could not come among us without betraying his sympathy for us, and, stupid as we were, we had the sagacity to see it.

While I lived with my master in St. Michael's, there was a white young man, a Mr. Wilson, who proposed to keep a Sabbath school for the instruction of such slaves as might be disposed to learn to read the New Testament. We met but three times, when Mr. West and Mr. Fairbanks, both class-leaders, with many others, came upon us with sticks and other missiles, drove us off, and forbade us to meet again. Thus ended our little Sabbath school in the pious town of St. Michael's.

I have said my master found religious sanction for his cruelty. As an example, I will state one of many facts going to prove the charge. I have seen him tie up a lame young woman, and whip her with a heavy cowskin upon her naked shoulders, causing the warm red blood to drip; and, in justification of the bloody deed, he would quote this passage of Scripture—"He that knoweth his master's will, and doeth it not, shall be beaten with many stripes."[4]

Master would keep this lacerated young woman tied up in this horrid situation four or five hours at a time. I have known him to tie her up early in the morning, and whip her before breakfast; leave her, go to his store, return to dinner, and whip her again, cutting her in the places already made raw with his cruel lash. The secret of master's cruelty toward "Henny" is found in the fact of her being almost helpless. When quite a child, she fell into the fire, and burned herself horribly. Her hands were so burnt that she never got the use of them. She could do very little but bear heavy burdens. She was to master a bill of expense; and as he was a mean man, she was a constant offence to him. He seemed desirous of getting the poor girl out of existence. He gave her away once to his sister; but, being a poor gift, she was not disposed to keep her. Finally, my benevolent master, to use his own words, "set her adrift to take care of herself." Here was a recently-converted man, holding on upon the mother, and at the same time turning out her helpless child, to starve and die! Master Thomas was one of the many pious slaveholders who hold slaves for the very charitable purpose of taking care of them.

My master and myself had quite a number of differences. He found me unsuitable to his purpose. My city life, he said, had had a very pernicious effect upon me. It had almost ruined me for every good purpose, and fitted me for every thing which was bad. One of my greatest faults was that of letting his horse run away, and go down to his father-in-law's farm, which was about five miles from St. Michael's. I would then have to go after it. My reason for this kind of carelessness, or carefulness, was, that I could always get something to eat when I went there. Master William Hamilton, my master's father-in-law, always gave his slaves enough to eat. I never left there hungry, no matter how great the need of my speedy return. Master Thomas at length said he would stand it no longer. I had lived with him nine months, during which time he had given me a number of severe whippings, all to no good purpose. He resolved to put me out, as he said, to be broken; and, for this purpose, he let me for one year to a man named Edward Covey. Mr. Covey was a poor man, a farm-renter. He rented the place upon which he lived, as also the hands with which he tilled it. Mr. Covey had acquired a very high reputation for breaking young slaves, and this reputation was of immense value to him. It enabled him to get his farm tilled with much less expense to himself than he could have had it done without such a reputation. Some slaveholders thought it not much loss to allow Mr. Covey to have their slaves one year, for the sake of the training to which they were subjected, without any other compensation. He could hire young help with great ease, in consequence of this reputation. Added to the natural good qualities of Mr. Covey, he was a professor of religion—a pious soul—a member and a class-leader in the Methodist church. All of this added weight to his reputation as a "nigger-breaker." I was aware of all the facts, having been made acquainted with them by a young man who had lived there. I nevertheless

4. Luke 12.47.

made the change gladly; for I was sure of getting enough to eat, which is not the smallest consideration to a hungry man.

CHAPTER X

I left Master Thomas's house, and went to live with Mr. Covey, on the 1st of January, 1833. I was now, for the first time in my life, a field hand. In my new employment, I found myself even more awkward than a country boy appeared to be in a large city. I had been at my new home but one week before Mr. Covey gave me a very severe whipping, cutting my back, causing the blood to run, and raising ridges on my flesh as large as my little finger. The details of this affair are as follows: Mr. Covey sent me, very early in the morning of one of our coldest days in the month of January, to the woods, to get a load of wood. He gave me a team of unbroken oxen. He told me which was the in-hand ox, and which the off-hand ox. He then tied the end of a large rope around the horns of the in-hand ox, and gave me the other end of it, and told me, if the oxen started to run, that I must hold on upon the rope. I had never driven oxen before, and of course I was very awkward. I, however, succeeded in getting to the edge of the woods with little difficulty; but I had got a very few rods into the woods, when the oxen took fright, and started full tilt, carrying the cart against trees, and over stumps, in the most frightful manner. I expected every moment that my brains would be dashed out against the trees. After running thus for a considerable distance, they finally upset the cart, dashing it with great force against a tree, and threw themselves into a dense thicket. How I escaped death, I do not know. There I was, entirely alone, in a thick wood, in a place new to me. My cart was upset and shattered, my oxen were entangled among the young trees, and there was none to help me. After a long spell of effort, I succeeded in getting my cart righted, my oxen disentangled, and again yoked to the cart. I now proceeded with my team to the place where I had, the day before, been chopping wood, and loaded my cart pretty heavily, thinking in this way to tame my oxen. I then proceeded on my way home. I had now consumed one half of the day. I got out of the woods safely, and now felt out of danger. I stopped my oxen to open the woods gate; and just as I did so, before I could get hold of my ox-rope, the oxen again started, rushed through the gate, catching it between the wheel and the body of the cart, tearing it to pieces, and coming within a few inches of crushing me against the gate-post. Thus twice, in one short day, I escaped death by the merest chance. On my return, I told Mr. Covey what had happened, and how it happened. He ordered me to return to the woods again immediately. I did so, and he followed on after me. Just as I got into the woods, he came up and told me to stop my cart, and that he would teach me how to trifle away my time, and break gates. He then went to a large gum-tree, and with his axe cut three large switches, and, after trimming them up neatly with his pocket-knife, he ordered me to take off my clothes. I made him no answer, but stood with my clothes on. He repeated his order. I still made him no answer, nor did I move to strip myself. Upon this he rushed at me with the fierceness of a tiger, tore off my clothes, and lashed me till he had worn out his switches, cutting me so savagely as to leave the marks visible for a long time after. This whipping was the first of a number just like it, and for similar offences.

I lived with Mr. Covey one year. During the first six months, of that year, scarce a week passed without his whipping me. I was seldom free from a sore back. My awkwardness was almost always his excuse for whipping me. We were worked fully up to the point of endurance. Long before day we were up, our horses fed, and by the first approach of day we were off to the field with our hoes and ploughing teams. Mr. Covey gave us enough to eat, but scarce time to eat it. We were often less than five minutes taking our meals. We were often in the field from the first approach of day till its last lingering ray had left us; and at saving-fodder time, midnight often caught us in the field binding blades.[5]

Covey would be out with us. The way he used to stand it was this. He would spend the most of his afternoons in bed. He would then come out fresh in the evening, ready to urge us on with his words, example, and frequently with the whip. Mr. Covey was one of the few slaveholders who could and did work with his hands. He was a hard-working man. He knew by himself just what a man or a boy could do. There was no deceiving him. His work went on in his absence almost as well as in his presence; and he had the faculty of making us feel that he was ever present with us. This he did by surprising us. He seldom approached the spot where we were at work openly, if he could do it secretly. He always aimed at taking us by surprise. Such was his cunning, that we used to call him, among ourselves, "the snake." When we were at work in the cornfield, he would sometimes crawl on his hands and knees to avoid detection, and all at once he would rise nearly in our midst, and scream out, "Ha, ha! Come, come! Dash on, dash on!" This being his mode of attack, it was never safe to stop a single minute. His comings were like a thief in the night. He appeared to us as being ever at hand. He was under every tree, behind every stump, in every bush, and at every window, on the plantation. He would sometimes mount his horse, as if bound to St. Michael's, a distance of seven miles, and in half an hour afterwards you would see him coiled up in the corner of the wood-fence, watching every motion of the slaves. He would, for this purpose, leave his horse tied up in the woods. Again, he would sometimes walk up to us, and give us orders as though he was upon the point of starting on a long journey, turn his back upon us, and make as though he was going to the house to get ready; and, before he would get half way thither, he would turn short and crawl into a fence-corner, or behind some tree, and there watch us till the going down of the sun.

Mr. Covey's *forte* consisted in his power to deceive. His life was devoted to planning and perpetrating the grossest deceptions. Every thing he possessed in the shape of learning or religion, he made conform to his disposition to deceive. He seemed to think himself equal to deceiving the Almighty. He would make a short prayer in the morning, and a long prayer at night; and, strange as it may seem, few men would at times appear more devotional than he. The exercises of his family devotions were always commenced with singing; and, as he was a very poor singer himself, the duty of raising the hymn generally came upon me. He would read his hymn, and nod at me to commence. I would at times do so; at others, I would not. My non-

---

5. Gathering cut grain into bundles or sheaves.

compliance would almost always produce much confusion. To show himself independent of me, he would start and stagger through with his hymn in the most discordant manner. In this state of mind, he prayed with more than ordinary spirit. Poor man! such was his disposition, and success at deceiving, I do verily believe that he sometimes deceived himself into the solemn belief, that he was a sincere worshipper of the most high God; and this, too, at a time when he may be said to have been guilty of compelling his woman slave to commit the sin of adultery. The facts in the case are these: Mr. Covey was a poor man; he was just commencing in life; he was only able to buy one slave; and, shocking as is the fact, he bought her, as he said, for a *breeder*. This woman was named Caroline. Mr. Covey bought her from Mr. Thomas Lowe, about six miles from St. Michael's. She was a large, able-bodied woman, about twenty years old. She had already given birth to one child, which proved her to be just what he wanted. After buying her, he hired a married man of Mr. Samuel Harrison, to live with him one year; and him he used to fasten up with her every night! The result was, that, at the end of the year, the miserable woman gave birth to twins. At this result Mr. Covey seemed to be highly pleased, both with the man and the wretched woman. Such was his joy, and that of his wife, that nothing they could do for Caroline during her confinement was too good, or too hard, to be done. The children were regarded as being quite an addition to his wealth.

If at any one time of my life more than another, I was made to drink the bitterest dregs of slavery, that time was during the first six months of my stay with Mr. Covey. We were worked in all weathers. It was never too hot or too cold; it could never rain, blow, hail, or snow, too hard for us to work in the field. Work, work, work, was scarcely more the order of the day than of the night. The longest days were too short for him, and the shortest nights too long for him. I was somewhat unmanageable when I first went there, but a few months of this discipline tamed me. Mr. Covey succeeded in breaking me. I was broken in body, soul, and spirit. My natural elasticity was crushed, my intellect languished, the disposition to read departed, the cheerful spark that lingered about my eye died; the dark night of slavery closed in upon me; and behold a man transformed into a brute!

Sunday was my only leisure time. I spent this in a sort of beast-like stupor, between sleep and wake, under some large tree. At times I would rise up, a flash of energetic freedom would dart through my soul, accompanied with a faint beam of hope, that flickered for a moment, and then vanished. I sank down again, mourning over my wretched condition. I was sometimes prompted to take my life, and that of Covey, but was prevented by a combination of hope and fear. My sufferings on this plantation seem now like a dream rather than a stern reality.

Our house stood within a few rods of the Chesapeake Bay, whose broad bosom was ever white with sails from every quarter of the habitable globe. Those beautiful vessels, robed in purest white, so delightful to the eye of freemen, were to me so many shrouded ghosts, to terrify and torment me with thoughts of my wretched condition. I have often, in the deep stillness of a summer's Sabbath, stood all alone upon the lofty banks of that noble bay, and traced, with saddened heart and tearful eye, the countless number of sails moving off to the mighty ocean. The sight of these always affected me powerfully. My thoughts would compel utterance; and there, with no audience but the Almighty, I would pour out my soul's complaint, in my rude way, with an apostrophe[6] to the moving multitude of ships:—

"You are loosed from your moorings, and are free; I am fast in my chains, and am a slave! You move merrily before the gentle gale, and I sadly before the bloody whip! You are freedom's swift-winged angels, that fly round the world; I am confined in bands of iron! O that I were free! O, that I were on one of your gallant decks, and under your protecting wing! Alas! betwixt me and you, the turbid waters roll. Go on, go on. O that I could also go! Could I but swim! If I could fly! O, why was I born a man, of whom to make a brute! The glad ship is gone; she hides in the dim distance. I am left in the hottest hell of unending slavery. O God, save me! God, deliver me! Let me be free! Is there any God? Why am I a slave? I will run away. I will not stand it. Get caught, or get clear, I'll try it. I had as well die with ague as the fever. I have only one life to lose. I had as well be killed running as die standing. Only think of it; one hundred miles straight north, and I am free! Try it? Yes! God helping me, I will. It cannot be that I shall live and die a slave. I will take to the water. This very bay shall bear me into freedom. The steam boats steered in a north-east course from North Point. I will do the same; and when I get to the head of the bay, I will turn my canoe adrift, and walk straight through Delaware into Pennsylvania. When I get there, I shall not be required to have a pass; I can travel without being disturbed. Let but the first opportunity offer, and, come what will, I am off. Meanwhile, I will try to bear up under the yoke. I am not the only slave in the world. Why should I fret? I can bear as much as any of them. Besides, I am but a boy, and all boys are bound to some one. It may be that my misery in slavery will only increase my happiness when I get free. There is a better day coming."

Thus I used to think, and thus I used to speak to myself; goaded almost to madness at one moment, and at the next reconciling myself to my wretched lot.

I have already intimated that my condition was much worse, during the first six months of my stay at Mr. Covey's, than in the last six. The circumstances leading to the change in Mr. Covey's course toward me form an epoch in my humble history. You have seen how a man was made a slave; you shall see how a slave was made a man. On one of the hottest days of the month of August, 1833, Bill Smith, William Hughes, a slave named Eli, and myself, were engaged in fanning wheat.[7] Hughes was clearing the fanned wheat from before the fan, Eli was turning, Smith was feeding, and I was carrying wheat to the fan. The work was simple, requiring strength rather than intellect; yet, to one entirely unused to such work, it came very hard. About three o'clock of that day, I broke down; my strength failed me; I was seized with a violent aching of the head, attended with extreme dizziness; I trembled in every limb. Finding what was coming, I nerved myself up, feeling it would never do to stop work. I stood as long as I could stagger to the hopper with grain. When I could stand no longer, I fell, and felt as if held down by an immense weight. The fan of course stopped; every one had his own work to do; and no one could do the work of the other, and have his own go on at the same time.

6. An exclamatory form of address.   7. Separating the grain from the chaff.

Mr. Covey was at the house, about one hundred yards from the treading-yard where we were fanning. On hearing the fan stop, he left immediately, and came to the spot where we were. He hastily inquired what the matter was. Bill answered that I was sick, and there was no one to bring wheat to the fan. I had by this time crawled away under the side of the post and rail-fence by which the yard was enclosed, hoping to find relief by getting out of the sun. He then asked where I was. He was told by one of the hands. He came to the spot, and, after looking at me awhile, asked me what was the matter. I told him as well as I could, for I scarce had strength to speak. He then gave me a savage kick in the side, and told me to get up. I tried to do so, but fell back in the attempt. He gave me another kick, and again told me to rise. I again tried, and succeeded in gaining my feet; but, stooping to get the tub with which I was feeding the fan, I again staggered and fell. While down in this situation, Mr. Covey took up the hickory slat with which Hughes had been striking off the half-bushel measure, and with it gave me a heavy blow upon the head, making a large wound, and the blood ran freely; and with this again told me to get up. I made no effort to comply, having now made up my mind to let him do his worst. In a short time after receiving this blow, my head grew better. Mr. Covey had now left me to my fate. At this moment I resolved, for the first time, to go to my master, enter a complaint, and ask his protection. In order to [do] this, I must that afternoon walk seven miles; and this, under the circumstances, was truly a severe undertaking. I was exceedingly feeble; made so as much by the kicks and blows which I received, as by the severe fit of sickness to which I had been subjected. I, however, watched my chance, while Covey was looking in an opposite direction, and started for St. Michael's. I succeeded in getting a considerable distance on my way to the woods, when Covey discovered me, and called after me to come back, threatening what he would do if I did not come. I disregarded both his calls and his threats, and made my way to the woods as fast as my feeble state would allow; and thinking I might be overhauled by him if I kept the road, I walked through the woods, keeping far enough from the road to avoid detection, and near enough to prevent losing my way. I had not gone far before my little strength again failed me. I could go no farther. I fell down, and lay for a considerable time. The blood was yet oozing from the wound on my head. For a time I thought I should bleed to death; and think now that I should have done so, but that the blood so matted my hair as to stop the wound. After lying there about three quarters of an hour, I nerved myself up again, and started on my way, through bogs and briers, barefooted and bareheaded, tearing my feet sometimes at nearly every step; and after a journey of about seven miles, occupying some five hours to perform it, I arrived at master's store. I then presented an appearance enough to affect any but a heart of iron. From the crown of my head to my feet, I was covered with blood. My hair was all clotted with dust and blood; my shirt was stiff with blood. My legs and feet were torn in sundry places with briers and thorns, and were also covered with blood. I suppose I looked like a man who had escaped a den of wild beasts, and barely escaped them. In this state I appeared before my master, humbly entreating him to interpose his authority for my protection. I told him all the circumstances as well as I could, and it seemed, as I spoke, at times to affect him. He would then walk the floor, and seek to justify Covey by saying he expected I deserved it. He asked me what I wanted. I told him, to let me get a new home; that as sure as I lived with Mr. Covey again, I should live with but to die with him; that Covey would surely kill me; he was in a fair way for it. Master Thomas ridiculed the idea that there was any danger of Mr. Covey's killing me, and said that he knew Mr. Covey; that he was a good man, and that he could not think of taking me from him; that, should he do so, he would lose the whole year's wages; that I belonged to Mr. Covey for one year, and that I must go back to him, come what might; and that I must not trouble him with any more stories, or that he would himself *get hold of me*. After threatening me thus, he gave me a very large dose of salts, telling me that I might remain in St. Michael's that night, (it being quite late) but that I must be off back to Mr. Covey's early in the morning; and that if I did not, he would *get hold of me,* which meant that he would whip me. I remained all night, and, according to his orders, I started off to Covey's in the morning, (Saturday morning), wearied in body and broken in spirit. I got no supper that night, or breakfast that morning. I reached Covey's about nine o'clock; and just as I was getting over the fence that divided Mrs. Kemp's fields from ours, out ran Covey with his cowskin, to give me another whipping. Before he could reach me, I succeeded in getting to the cornfield; and as the corn was very high, it afforded me the means of hiding. He seemed very angry, and searched for me a long time. My behavior was altogether unaccountable. He finally gave up the chase, thinking, I suppose, that I must come home for something to eat; he would give himself no further trouble in looking for me. I spent that day mostly in the woods, having the alternative before me,—to go home and be whipped to death, or stay in the woods and be starved to death. That night, I fell in with Sandy Jenkins, a slave with whom I was somewhat acquainted. Sandy had a free wife who lived about four miles from Mr. Covey's; and it being Saturday, he was on his way to see her. I told him my circumstances, and he very kindly invited me to go home with him. I went home with him, and talked this whole matter over, and got his advice as to what course it was best for me to pursue. I found Sandy an old adviser. He told me, with great solemnity, I must go back to Covey; but that before I went, I must go with him into another part of the woods, where there was a certain *root*, which, if I would take some of it with me, carrying it *always on my right side,* would render it impossible for Mr. Covey, or any other white man, to whip me. He said he had carried it for years; and since he had done so, he had never received a blow, and never expected to while he carried it. I at first rejected the idea, that the simple carrying of a root in my pocket would have any such effect as he had said, and was not disposed to take it; but Sandy impressed the necessity with much earnestness, telling me it could do no harm, if it did no good. To please him, I at length took the root, and, according to his direction, carried it upon my right side. This was Sunday morning. I immediately started for home; and upon entering the yard gate, out came Mr. Covey on his way to meeting. He spoke to me very kindly, bade me drive the pigs from a lot near by, and passed on towards the church. Now, this singular conduct of Mr. Covey really made me begin to think that there was something in the *root* which Sandy had given me; and had it been on any other day than Sunday, I could have attributed the conduct to no other cause than the influence of that root; and as it was, I was half inclined to think the *root* to be something more than I at first had taken it to be. All went well till Monday morning. On this morning, the virtue of the *root* was fully tested.

Long before daylight, I was called to go and rub, curry, and feed, the horses. I obeyed, and was glad to obey. But whilst thus engaged, whilst in the act of throwing down some blades from the loft, Mr. Covey entered the stable with a long rope; and just as I was half out of the loft, he caught hold of my legs, and was about tying me. As soon as I found what he was up to, I gave a sudden spring, and as I did so, he holding to my legs, I was brought sprawling on the stable floor. Mr. Covey seemed now to think he had me, and could do what he pleased; but at this moment—from whence came the spirit I don't know—I resolved to fight; and, suiting my action to the resolution, I seized Covey hard by the throat; and as I did so, I rose. He held on to me, and I to him. My resistance was so entirely unexpected, that Covey seemed taken all aback. He trembled like a leaf. This gave me assurance, and I held him uneasy, causing the blood to run where I touched him with the ends of my fingers. Mr. Covey soon called out to Hughes for help. Hughes came, and, while Covey held me, attempted to tie my right hand. While he was in the act of doing so, I watched my chance, and gave him a heavy kick close under the ribs. This kick fairly sickened Hughes, so that he left me in the hands of Mr. Covey. This kick had the effect of not only weakening Hughes, but Covey also. When he saw Hughes bending over with pain, his courage quailed. He asked me if I meant to persist in my resistance. I told him I did, come what might; that he had used me like a brute for six months, and that I was determined to be used so no longer. With that, he strove to drag me to a stick that was lying just out of the stable door. He meant to knock me down. But just as he was leaning over to get the stick, I seized him with both hands by his collar, and brought him by a sudden snatch to the ground. By this time, Bill came. Covey called upon him for assistance. Bill wanted to know what he could do. Covey said, "Take hold of him, take hold of him!" Bill said his master hired him out to work, and not to help to whip me; so he left Covey and myself to fight our own battle out. We were at it for nearly two hours. Covey at length let me go, puffing and blowing at a great rate, saying that if I had not resisted, he would not have whipped me half so much. The truth was, that he had not whipped me at all. I considered him as getting entirely the worst end of the bargain; for he had drawn no blood from me, but I had from him. The whole six months afterwards, that I spent with Mr. Covey, he never laid the weight of his finger upon me in anger. He would occasionally say, he didn't want to get hold of me again. "No," thought I, "you need not; for you will come off worse than you did before."

This battle with Mr. Covey was the turning-point in my career as a slave. It rekindled the few expiring embers of freedom, and revived within me a sense of my own manhood. It recalled the departed self-confidence, and inspired me again with a determination to be free. The gratification afforded by the triumph was a full compensation for whatever else might follow, even death itself. He only can understand the deep satisfaction which I experienced, who has himself repelled by force the bloody arm of slavery. I felt as I never felt before. It was a glorious resurrection, from the tomb of slavery, to the heaven of freedom. My long-crushed spirit rose, cowardice departed, bold defiance took its place; and I now resolved that, however long I might remain a slave in form, the day had passed forever when I could be a slave in fact. I did not hesitate to let it be known of me, that the white man who expected to succeed in whipping, must also succeed in killing me.

From this time I was never again what might be called fairly whipped, though I remained a slave four years afterwards. I had several fights, but was never whipped.

It was for a long time a matter of surprise to me why Mr. Covey did not immediately have me taken by the constable to the whipping-post, and there regularly whipped for the crime of raising my hand against a white man in defence of myself. And the only explanation I can now think of does not entirely satisfy me; but such as it is, I will give it. Mr. Covey enjoyed the most unbounded reputation for being a first-rate overseer and negro-breaker. It was of considerable importance to him. That reputation was at stake; and had he sent me—a boy about sixteen years old—to the public whipping-post, his reputation would have been lost; so, to save his reputation, he suffered me to go unpunished.

My term of actual service to Mr. Edward Covey ended on Christmas day, 1833. The days between Christmas and New Year's day are allowed as holidays; and, accordingly, we were not required to perform any labor, more than to feed and take care of the stock. This time we regarded as our own, by the grace of our masters; and we therefore used or abused it nearly as we pleased. Those of us who had families at a distance, were generally allowed to spend the whole six days in their society. This time, however, was spent in various ways. The staid, sober, thinking and industrious ones of our number would employ themselves in making corn-brooms, mats, horse-collars, and baskets; and another class of us would spend the time in hunting opossums, hares, and coons. But by far the larger part engaged in such sports and merriments as playing ball, wrestling, running foot-races, fiddling, dancing, and drinking whisky; and this latter mode of spending the time was by far the most agreeable to the feelings of our masters. A slave who would work during the holidays was considered by our masters as scarcely deserving them. He was regarded as one who rejected the favor of his master. It was deemed a disgrace not to get drunk at Christmas; and he was regarded as lazy indeed, who had not provided himself with the necessary means, during the year, to get whisky enough to last him through Christmas.

From what I know of the effect of these holidays upon the slave, I believe them to be among the most effective means in the hands of the slaveholder in keeping down the spirit of insurrection. Were the slaveholders at once to abandon this practice, I have not the slightest doubt it would lead to an immediate insurrection among the slaves. These holidays serve as conductors, or safety-valves, to carry off the rebellious spirit of enslaved humanity. But for these, the slave would be forced up to the wildest desperation; and woe betide the slaveholder, the day he ventures to remove or hinder the operation of those conductors! I warn him that, in such an event, a spirit will go forth in their midst, more to be dreaded than the most appalling earthquake.

The holidays are part and parcel of the gross fraud, wrong, and inhumanity of slavery. They are professedly a custom established by the benevolence of the slaveholders; but I undertake to say, it is the result of selfishness, and one of the grossest frauds committed upon the down-trodden slave. They do not give the slaves this time because they would not like to have their work during its continuance, but because they know it would be unsafe to deprive them of it. This will be seen by the fact, that the slaveholders like to have their slaves spend those days just in such a manner as to make them as glad of their ending as of their beginning. Their object seems to be, to disgust their slaves with freedom, by plunging them into the lowest depths of dissipation. For instance, the slaveholders not only like to see the slave drink of his own accord, but will adopt various plans to make him drunk. One plan is, to make bets on their slaves, as to who can drink the most whisky without getting drunk; and in this way they succeed in getting whole multitudes to drink to excess. Thus, when the slave asks for virtuous freedom, the cunning slaveholder, knowing his ignorance, cheats him with a dose of vicious dissipation, artfully labelled with the name of liberty. The most of us used to drink it down, and the result was just what might be supposed: many of us were led to think that there was little to choose between liberty and slavery. We felt, and very properly too, that we had almost as well be slaves to man as to rum. So, when the holidays ended, we staggered up from the filth of our wallowing, took a long breath, and marched to the field,—feeling, upon the whole, rather glad to go, from what our master had deceived us into a belief was freedom, back to the arms of slavery.

I have said that this mode of treatment is a part of the whole system of fraud and inhumanity of slavery. It is so. The mode here adopted to disgust the slave with freedom, by allowing him to see only the abuse of it, is carried out in other things. For instance, a slave loves molasses; he steals some. His master, in many cases, goes off to town, and buys a large quantity; he returns, takes his whip, and commands the slave to eat the molasses, until the poor fellow is made sick at the very mention of it. The same mode is sometimes adopted to make the slaves refrain from asking for more food than their regular allowance. A slave runs through his allowance, and applies for more. His master is enraged at him; but, not willing to send him off without food, gives him more than is necessary, and compels him to eat it within a given time. Then, if he complains that he cannot eat it, he is said to be satisfied neither full nor fasting, and is whipped for being hard to please! I have an abundance of such illustrations of the same principle, drawn from my own observation, but think the cases I have cited sufficient. The practice is a very common one.

On the first of January, 1834, I left Mr. Covey, and went to live with Mr. William Freeland, who lived about three miles from St. Michael's. I soon found Mr. Freeland a very different man from Mr. Covey. Though not rich, he was what would be called an educated southern gentleman. Mr. Covey, as I have shown, was a well-trained negro-breaker and slave-driver. The former (slaveholder though he was) seemed to possess some regard for honor, some reverence for justice, and some respect for humanity. The latter seemed totally insensible to all such sentiments. Mr. Freeland had many of the faults peculiar to slaveholders, such as being very passionate and fretful; but I must do him the justice to say, that he was exceedingly free from those degrading vices to which Mr. Covey was constantly addicted. The one was open and frank, and we always knew where to find him. The other was a most artful deceiver, and could be understood only by such as were skilful enough to detect his cunningly-devised frauds. Another advantage I gained in my new master was, he made no pretensions to, or profession of, religion; and this, in my opinion, was truly a great advantage. I assert most unhesitatingly, that the religion of the south is a mere covering for the most horrid crimes,—a justifier of the most appalling barbarity,—a sanctifier of the most hateful frauds,—and a dark shelter under which the darkest, foulest, gross-est, and most infernal deeds of slaveholders find the strongest protection. Were I to be again reduced to the chains of slavery, next to that enslavement, I should regard being the slave of a religious master the greatest calamity that could befall me. For of all slaveholders with whom I have ever met, religious slaveholders are the worst. I have ever found them the meanest and basest, the most cruel and cowardly, of all others. It was my unhappy lot not only to belong to a religious slaveholder, but to live in a community of such religionists. Very near Mr. Freeland lived the Rev. Daniel Weeden, and in the same neighborhood lived the Rev. Rigby Hopkins. These were members and ministers in the Reformed Methodist Church. Mr. Weeden owned, among others, a woman slave, whose name I have forgotten. This woman's back, for weeks, was kept literally raw, made so by the lash of this merciless, *religious* wretch. He used to hire hands. His maxim was, Behave well or behave ill, it is the duty of a master occasionally to whip a slave, to remind him of his master's authority. Such was his theory, and such his practice.

Mr. Hopkins was even worse than Mr. Weeden. His chief boast was his ability to manage slaves. The peculiar feature of his government was that of whipping slaves in advance of deserving it. He always managed to have one or more of his slaves to whip every Monday morning. He did this to alarm their fears, and strike terror into those who escaped. His plan was to whip for the smallest offences, to prevent the commission of large ones. Mr. Hop-kins could always find some excuse for whipping a slave. It would astonish one, unaccustomed to a slaveholding life, to see with what wonderful ease a slaveholder can find things, of which to make occasion to whip a slave. A mere look, word, or motion,—a mistake, accident, or want of power,—are all matters for which a slave may be whipped at any time. Does a slave look dissatisfied? It is said, he has the devil in him, and it must be whipped out. Does he speak loudly when spoken to by his master? Then he is getting high-minded, and should be taken down a button-hole lower. Does he forget to pull off his hat at the approach of a white person? Then he is wanting in reverence, and should be whipped for it. Does he ever venture to vindicate his conduct, when censured for it? Then he is guilty of impudence,—one of the greatest crimes of which a slave can be guilty. Does he ever venture to suggest a different mode of doing things from that pointed out by his master? He is indeed presumptuous, and getting above himself; and nothing less than a flogging will do for him. Does he, while ploughing, break a plough,—or, while hoeing, break a hoe? It is owing to his carelessness, and for it a slave must always be whipped. Mr. Hopkins could always find something of this sort to justify the use of the lash, and he seldom failed to embrace such opportunities. There was not a man in the whole county, with whom the slaves who had the getting their own home, would not prefer to live, rather than with this Rev. Mr. Hopkins. And yet there was not a man any where round, who made higher professions of religion, or was more active in reviv-als,—more attentive to the class, love-feast, prayer and preaching meetings, or more devotional in his family,—that prayed earlier, later, louder, and longer,—than this same reverend slave-driver, Rigby Hopkins.

But to return to Mr. Freeland, and to my experience while in his employ-ment. He, like Mr. Covey, gave us enough to eat; but, unlike Mr. Covey, he also gave us sufficient time to take our meals. He worked us hard, but always between sunrise and sunset. He required a good deal of work to be done, but gave us good tools with which to work. His farm was large, but he employed hands enough to work it, and with ease, compared with many of his neighbors. My treatment, while in his employment, was heavenly, compared with what I experienced at the hands of Mr. Edward Covey.

Mr. Freeland was himself the owner of but two slaves. Their names were Henry Harris and John Harris. The rest of his hands he hired. These consisted of myself, Sandy Jenkins,[8] and Handy Caldwell. Henry and John were quite intelligent, and in a very little while after I went there, I succeeded in creating in them a strong desire to learn how to read. This desire soon sprang up in the others also. They very soon mustered up some old spelling-books, and nothing would do but that I must keep a Sabbath school. I agreed to do so, and accordingly devoted my Sundays to teaching these my loved fellow-slaves how to read. Neither of them knew his letters when I went there. Some of the slaves of the neighboring farms found what was going on, and also availed themselves of this little opportunity to learn to read. It was understood, among all who came, that there must be as little display about it as possible. It was necessary to keep our religious masters at St. Michael's unacquainted with the fact, that, instead of spending the Sabbath in wrestling, boxing, and drinking whiskey, we were trying to learn how to read the will of God; for they had much rather see us engaged in those degrading sports, than to see us behaving like intellectual, moral, and accountable beings. My blood boils as I think of the bloody manner in which Messrs. Wright Fairbanks and Garrison West, both class-leaders, in connection with many others, rushed in upon us with sticks and stones, and broke up our virtuous little Sabbath school, at St. Michael's—all calling themselves Christians! humble followers of the Lord Jesus Christ! But I am again digressing.

I held my Sabbath school at the house of a free colored man, whose name I deem it imprudent to mention; for should it be known, it might embarrass him greatly, though the crime of holding the school was committed ten years ago. I had at one time over forty scholars, and those of the right sort, ardently desiring to learn. They were of all ages, though mostly men and women. I look back to those Sundays with an amount of pleasure not to be expressed. They were great days to my soul. The work of instructing my dear fellow-slaves was the sweetest engagement with which I was ever blessed. We loved each other, and to leave them at the close of the Sabbath was a severe cross indeed. When I think that those precious souls are to-day shut up in the prison-house of slavery, my feelings overcome me, and I am almost ready to ask, "Does a righteous God govern the universe? and for what does he hold the thunders in his right hand, if not to smite the oppressor, and deliver the spoiled out of the hand of the spoiler?" These dear souls came not to Sabbath school because it was popular to do so, nor did I teach them because it was reputable to be thus engaged. Every moment they spent in that school, they were liable to be taken up, and given thirty-nine lashes. They came because they wished to learn. Their minds had been starved by their cruel masters. They had been shut up in mental darkness. I taught them, because it was

8. This is the same man who gave me the roots to prevent my being whipped by Mr. Covey. He was "a clever soul." We used frequently to talk about the fight with Covey, and as often as we did so, he would claim my success as the result of the roots which he gave me. This superstition is very common among the more ignorant slaves. A slave seldom dies but that his death is attributed to trickery [Douglass's note].

the delight of my soul to be doing something that looked like bettering the condition of my race. I kept up my school nearly the whole year I lived with Mr. Freeland; and, beside my Sabbath school, I devoted three evenings in the week, during the winter, to teaching the slaves at home. And I have the happiness to know, that several of those who came to Sabbath school learned how to read; and that one, at least, is now free through my agency.

The year passed off smoothly. It seemed only about half as long as the year which preceded it. I went through it without receiving a single blow. I will give Mr. Freeland the credit of being the best master I ever had, *till I became my own master.* For the ease with which I passed the year, I was, however, somewhat indebted to the society of my fellow-slaves. They were noble souls; they not only possessed loving hearts, but brave ones. We were linked and interlinked with each other. I loved them with a love stronger than any thing I have experienced since. It is sometimes said that we slaves do not love and confide in each other. In answer to this assertion, I can say, I never loved any or confided in any people more than my fellow-slaves, and especially those with whom I lived at Mr. Freeland's. I believe we would have died for each other. We never undertook to do any thing, of any importance, without a mutual consultation. We never moved separately. We were one; and as much so by our tempers and dispositions, as by the mutual hardships to which we were necessarily subjected by our condition as slaves.

At the close of the year 1834, Mr. Freeland again hired me of my master, for the year 1835. But, by this time, I began to want to live *upon free land* as well as *with Freeland;* and I was no longer content, therefore, to live with him or any other slaveholder. I began, with the commencement of the year, to prepare myself for a final struggle, which should decide my fate one way or the other. My tendency was upward. I was fast approaching manhood, and year after year had passed, and I was still a slave. These thoughts roused me—I must do something. I therefore resolved that 1835 should not pass without witnessing an attempt, on my part, to secure my liberty. But I was not willing to cherish this determination alone. My fellow-slaves were dear to me. I was anxious to have them participate with me in this, my life-giving determination. I therefore, though with great prudence, commenced early to ascertain their views and feelings in regard to their condition, and to imbue their minds with thoughts of freedom. I bent myself to devising ways and means for our escape, and meanwhile strove, on all fitting occasions, to impress them with the gross fraud and inhumanity of slavery. I went first to Henry, next to John, then to the others. I found, in them all, warm hearts and noble spirits. They were ready to hear, and ready to act when a feasible plan should be proposed. This was what I wanted. I talked to them of our want of manhood, if we submitted to our enslavement without at least one noble effort to be free. We met often, and consulted frequently, and told our hopes and fears, recounted the difficulties, real and imagined, which we should be called on to meet. At times we were almost disposed to give up, and try to content ourselves with our wretched lot; at others, we were firm and unbending in our determination to go. Whenever we suggested any plan, there was shrinking—the odds were fearful. Our path was beset with the greatest obstacles; and if we succeeded in gaining the end of it, our right to be free was yet questionable—we were yet liable to be returned to bondage. We could see no spot, this side of the ocean, where we could be free. We knew nothing about Canada. Our knowledge of the north did not extend farther than New York; and to go there, and be forever harassed with the frightful liability of being returned to slavery—with the certainty of being treated tenfold worse than before—the thought was truly a horrible one, and one which it was not easy to overcome. The case sometimes stood thus: At every gate through which we were to pass, we saw a watchman—at every ferry a guard—on every bridge a sentinel—and in every wood a patrol. We were hemmed in upon every side. Here were the difficulties, real or imagined—the good to be sought, and the evil to be shunned. On the one hand, there stood slavery, a stern reality, glaring frightfully upon us,—its robes already crimsoned with the blood of millions, and even now feasting itself greedily upon our own flesh. On the other hand, away back in the dim distance, under the flickering light of the north star, behind some craggy hill or snow-covered mountain, stood a doubtful freedom—half frozen—beckoning us to come and share its hospitality. This in itself was sometimes enough to stagger us; but when we permitted ourselves to survey the road, we were frequently appalled. Upon either side we saw grim death, assuming the most horrid shapes. Now it was starvation, causing us to eat our own flesh;—now we were contending with the waves, and were drowned;—now we were overtaken, and torn to pieces by the fangs of the terrible bloodhound. We were stung by scorpions, chased by wild beasts, bitten by snakes, and finally, after having nearly reached the desired spot,—after swimming rivers, encountering wild beasts, sleeping in the woods, suffering hunger and nakedness,—we were overtaken by our pursuers, and, in our resistance, we were shot dead upon the spot! I say, this picture sometimes appalled us, and made us

> "rather bear those ills we had,
> Than fly to others, that we knew not of."[9]

In coming to a fixed determination to run away, we did more than Patrick Henry,[1] when he resolved upon liberty or death. With us it was a doubtful liberty at most, and almost certain death if we failed. For my part, I should prefer death to hopeless bondage.

Sandy, one of our number, gave up the notion, but still encouraged us. Our company then consisted of Henry Harris, John Harris, Henry Bailey, Charles Roberts, and myself. Henry Bailey was my uncle, and belonged to my master. Charles married my aunt: he belonged to my master's father-in-law, Mr. William Hamilton.

The plan we finally concluded upon was, to get a large canoe belonging to Mr. Hamilton, and upon the Saturday night previous to Easter holidays, paddle directly up the Chesapeake Bay. On our arrival at the head of the bay, a distance of seventy or eighty miles from where we lived, it was our purpose to turn our canoe adrift, and follow the guidance of the north star till we got beyond the limits of Maryland. Our reason for taking the water route was, that we were less liable to be suspected as runaways; we hoped to be regarded as fishermen; whereas, if we should take the land route, we should be subjected to interruptions of almost every kind. Any one hav-

9. Shakespeare's *Hamlet* 3.1.81–82: "rather bear those ills we have, / Than fly to others, that we know not of."   1. American statesman and orator (1736–1799) whose most famous utterance was "Give me liberty or give me death."

ing a white face, and being so disposed, could stop us, and subject us to examination.

The week before our intended start, I wrote several protections, one for each of us. As well as I can remember, they were in the following words, to wit:—

"This is to certify that I, the undersigned, have given the bearer, my servant, full liberty to go to Baltimore, and spend the Easter holidays. Written with mine own hand, &c., 1835.

"WILLIAM HAMILTON,
"Near St. Michael's, in Talbot county, Maryland."

We were not going to Baltimore; but, in going up the bay, we went toward Baltimore, and these protections were only intended to protect us while on the bay.

As the time drew near for our departure, our anxiety became more and more intense. It was truly a matter of life and death with us. The strength of our determination was about to be fully tested. At this time, I was very active in explaining every difficulty, removing every doubt, dispelling every fear, and inspiring all with the firmness indispensable to success in our undertaking; assuring them that half was gained the instant we made the move; we had talked long enough; we were now ready to move; if not now, we never should be; and if we did not intend to move now, we had as well fold our arms, sit down, and acknowledge ourselves fit only to be slaves. This, none of us were prepared to acknowledge. Every man stood firm; and at our last meeting, we pledged ourselves afresh, in the most solemn manner, that, at the time appointed, we would certainly start in pursuit of freedom. This was in the middle of the week, at the end of which we were to be off. We went, as usual, to our several fields of labor, but with bosoms highly agitated with thoughts of our truly hazardous undertaking. We tried to conceal our feelings as much as possible; and I think we succeeded very well.

After a painful waiting, the Saturday morning, whose night was to witness our departure, came. I hailed it with joy, bring what of sadness it might. Friday night was a sleepless one for me. I was, by common consent, at the head of the whole affair. The responsibility of success or failure lay heavily upon me. The glory of the one, and the confusion of the other, were alike mine. The first two hours of that morning were such as I never experienced before, and hope never to again. Early in the morning, we went, as usual, to the field. We were spreading manure; and all at once, while thus engaged, I was overwhelmed with an indescribable feeling, in the fulness of which I turned to Sandy, who was near by, and said, "We are betrayed!" "Well," said he, "that thought has this moment struck me." We said no more. I was never more certain of any thing.

The horn was blown as usual, and we went up from the field to the house for breakfast. I went for the form, more than for want of any thing to eat that morning. Just as I got to the house, in looking out at the lane gate, I saw four white men, with two colored men. The white men were on horseback, and the colored ones were walking behind, as if tied. I watched them a few moments till they got up to our lane gate. Here they halted, and tied the colored men to the gate-post. I was not yet certain as to what the matter was. In a few moments, in rode Mr. Hamilton, with a speed betokening great excitement. He came to the door, and inquired if Master William was in. He was told he was at the barn. Mr. Hamilton, without dismounting, rode up to the barn with extraordinary speed. In a few moments, he and Mr. Freeland returned to the house. By this time, the three constables rode up, and in great haste dismounted, tied their horses, and met Master William and Mr. Hamilton returning from the barn; and after talking awhile, they all walked up to the kitchen door. There was no one in the kitchen but myself and John. Henry and Sandy were up at the barn. Mr. Freeland put his head in at the door, and called me by name, saying, there were some gentlemen at the door who wished to see me. I stepped to the door, and inquired what they wanted. They at once seized me, and, without giving me any satisfaction, tied me—lashing my hands closely together. I insisted upon knowing what the matter was. They at length said, that they had learned I had been in a "scrape," and that I was to be examined before my master; and if their information proved false, I should not be hurt.

In a few moments, they succeeded in tying John. They then turned to Henry, who had by this time returned, and commanded him to cross his hands. "I won't!" said Henry, in a firm tone, indicating his readiness to meet the consequences of his refusal. "Won't you?" said Tom Graham, the constable. "No, I won't!" said Henry, in a still stronger tone. With this, two of the constables pulled out their shining pistols, and swore, by their Creator, that they would make him cross his hands or kill him. Each cocked his pistol, and, with fingers on the trigger, walked up to Henry, saying, at the same time, if he did not cross his hands, they would blow his damned heart out. "Shoot me, shoot me!" said Henry; "you can't kill me but once. Shoot, shoot,—and be damned! *I won't be tied!*" This he said in a tone of loud defiance; and at the same time, with a motion as quick as lightning, he with one single stroke dashed the pistols from the hand of each constable. As he did this, all hands fell upon him, and, after beating him some time, they finally overpowered him, and got him tied.

During the scuffle, I managed, I know not how, to get my pass out, and, without being discovered, put it into the fire. We were all now tied; and just as we were to leave for Easton jail, Betsy Freeland, mother of William Freeland, came to the door with her hands full of biscuits, and divided them between Henry and John. She then delivered herself of a speech, to the following effect:—addressing herself to me, she said, *"You devil! You yellow devil!* it was you that put it into the heads of Henry and John to run away. But for you, you long-legged mulatto devil! Henry nor John would never have thought of such a thing." I made no reply, and was immediately hurried off towards St. Michael's. Just a moment previous to the scuffle with Henry, Mr. Hamilton suggested the propriety of making a search for the protections which he had understood Frederick had written for himself and the rest. But, just at the moment he was about carrying his proposal into effect, his aid was needed in helping to tie Henry; and the excitement attending the scuffle caused them either to forget, or to deem it unsafe, under the circumstances, to search. So we were not yet convicted of the intention to run away.

When we got about half way to St. Michael's, while the constables having us in charge were looking ahead, Henry inquired of me what he should do with his pass. I told him to eat it with his biscuit, and own nothing; and we passed the word around, *"Own nothing"*; and *"Own nothing!"* said we all. Our confidence in each other was unshaken. We were resolved to succeed or fail together, after the calamity had befallen us as much as before. We were now prepared for any thing. We were to be dragged that morning fifteen miles behind horses, and then to be placed in the Easton jail. When we reached St. Michael's, we underwent a sort of examination. We all denied that we ever intended to run away. We did this more to bring out the evidence against us, than from any hope of getting clear of being sold; for, as I have said, we were ready for that. The fact was, we cared but little where we went, so we went together. Our greatest concern was about separation. We dreaded that more than any thing this side of death. We found the evidence against us to be the testimony of one person; our master would not tell who it was; but we came to a unanimous decision among ourselves as to who their informant was. We were sent off to the jail at Easton. When we got there, we were delivered up to the sheriff, Mr. Joseph Graham, and by him placed in jail. Henry, John, and myself, were placed in one room together—Charles, and Henry Bailey, in another. Their object in separating us was to hinder concert.

We had been in jail scarcely twenty minutes, when a swarm of slave traders, and agents for slave traders, flocked into jail to look at us, and to ascertain if we were for sale. Such a set of beings I never saw before! I felt myself surrounded by so many fiends from perdition. A band of pirates never looked more like their father, the devil. They laughed and grinned over us, saying, "Ah, my boys! we have got you, haven't we?" And after taunting us in various ways, they one by one went into an examination of us, with intent to ascertain our value. They would impudently ask us if we would not like to have them for our masters. We would make them no answer, and leave them to find out as best they could. Then they would curse and swear at us, telling us that they could take the devil out of us in a very little while, if we were only in their hands.

While in jail, we found ourselves in much more comfortable quarters than we expected when we went there. We did not get much to eat, nor that which was very good; but we had a good clean room, from the windows of which we could see what was going on in the street, which was very much better than though we had been placed in one of the dark, damp cells. Upon the whole, we got along very well, so far as the jail and its keeper were concerned. Immediately after the holidays were over, contrary to all our expectations, Mr. Hamilton and Mr. Freeland came up to Easton, and took Charles, the two Henrys, and John, out of jail, and carried them home, leaving me alone. I regarded this separation as a final one. It caused me more pain than any thing else in the whole transaction. I was ready for any thing rather than separation. I supposed that they had consulted together, and had decided that, as I was the whole cause of the intention of the others to run away, it was hard to make the innocent suffer with the guilty; and that they had, therefore, concluded to take the others home, and sell me, as a warning to the others that remained. It is due to the noble Henry to say, he seemed almost as reluctant at leaving the prison as at leaving home to come to the prison. But we knew we should, in all probability, be separated, if we were sold; and since he was in their hands, he concluded to go peaceably home.

I was now left to my fate. I was all alone, and within the walls of a stone prison. But a few days before, and I was full of hope. I expected to have been safe in a land of freedom; but now I was covered with gloom, sunk down to the utmost despair. I thought the possibility of freedom was gone. I was kept in this way about one week, at the end of which, Captain Auld, my master, to my surprise and utter astonishment, came up, and took me out, with the intention of sending me, with a gentleman of his acquaintance, into Alabama. But, from some cause or other, he did not send me to Alabama, but concluded to send me back to Baltimore, to live again with his brother Hugh, and to learn a trade.

Thus, after an absence of three years and one month, I was once more permitted to return to my old home at Baltimore. My master sent me away, because there existed against me a very great prejudice in the community, and he feared I might be killed.

In a few weeks after I went to Baltimore, Master Hugh hired me to Mr. William Gardner, an extensive ship-builder, on Fell's Point. I was put there to learn how to calk. It, however, proved a very unfavorable place for the accomplishment of this object. Mr. Gardner was engaged that spring in building two large man-of-war brigs, professedly for the Mexican government. The vessels were to be launched in the July of that year, and in failure thereof, Mr. Gardner was to lose a considerable sum; so that when I entered, all was hurry. There was no time to learn any thing. Every man had to do that which he knew how to do. In entering the shipyard, my orders from Mr. Gardner were, to do whatever the carpenters commanded me to do. This was placing me at the beck and call of about seventy-five men. I was to regard all these as masters. Their word was to be my law. My situation was a most trying one. At times I needed a dozen pair of hands. I was called a dozen ways in the space of a single minute. Three or four voices would strike my ear at the same moment. It was—"Fred., come help me to cant this timber here."—"Fred., come carry this timber yonder."—"Fred., bring that roller here."—"Fred., go get a fresh can of water."—"Fred., come help saw off the end of this timber."—"Fred., go quick, and get the crowbar."—"Fred., hold on the end of this fall."—"Fred., go to the blacksmith's shop, and get a new punch."—"Hurra,[2] Fred.! run and bring me a cold chisel."—"I say, Fred., bear a hand, and get up a fire as quick as lightning under that steam-box."—"Halloo, nigger! come, turn this grindstone."—"Come, come! move, move! and bowse[3] this timber forward."—"I say, darky, blast your eyes, why don't you heat up some pitch?"—"Halloo! halloo! halloo!" (Three voices at the same time.) "Come here!—Go there!—Hold on where you are! Damn you, if you move, I'll knock your brains out!"

This was my school for eight months, and I might have remained there longer, but for a most horrid fight I had with four of the white apprentices, in which my left eye was nearly knocked out, and I was horribly mangled in other respects. The facts in the case were these: Until a very little while after I went there, white and black ship-carpenters worked side by side, and no one seemed to see any impropriety in it. All hands seemed to be very well satisfied. Many of the black carpenters were freemen. Things seemed to be going on very well. All at once, the white carpenters knocked off, and said they would not work with free colored workmen. Their reason for this, as alleged, was, that if free colored carpenters were encouraged, they would soon take the trade into their own hands, and poor white men would be

---

2. Hurry.   3. Lift or haul (usually with the help of block and tackle).

thrown out of employment. They therefore felt called upon at once to put a stop to it. And, taking advantage of Mr. Gardner's necessities, they broke off, swearing they would work no longer, unless he would discharge his black carpenters. Now, though this did not extend to me in form, it did reach me in fact. My fellow-apprentices very soon began to feel it degrading to them to work with me. They began to put on airs, and talk about the "niggers" taking the country, saying we all ought to be killed; and, being encouraged by the journeymen, they commenced making my condition as hard as they could, by hectoring me around, and sometimes striking me. I, of course, kept the vow I made after the fight with Mr. Covey, and struck back again, regardless of consequences; and while I kept them from combining, I succeeded very well; for I could whip the whole of them, taking them separately. They, however, at length combined, and came upon me, armed with sticks, stones, and heavy handspikes. One came in front with a half brick. There was one at each side of me, and one behind me. While I was attending to those in front, and on either side, the one behind ran up with the handspike, and struck me a heavy blow upon the head. It stunned me. I fell, and with this they all ran upon me, and fell to beating me with their fists. I let them lay on for a while, gathering strength. In an instant, I gave a sudden surge, and rose to my hands and knees. Just as I did that, one of their number gave me, with his heavy boot, a powerful kick in the left eye. My eyeball seemed to have burst. When they saw my eye closed, and badly swollen, they left me. With this I seized the handspike, and for a time pursued them. But here the carpenters interfered, and I thought I might as well give it up. It was impossible to stand my hand against so many. All this took place in sight of not less than fifty white ship-carpenters, and not one interposed a friendly word; but some cried, "Kill the damned nigger! Kill him! kill him! He struck a white person." I found my only chance for life was in flight. I succeeded in getting away without an additional blow, and barely so; for to strike a white man is death by Lynch law,—and that was the law in Mr. Gardner's ship-yard; nor is there much of any other out of Mr. Gardner's ship-yard.

I went directly home, and told the story of my wrongs to Master Hugh; and I am happy to say of him, irreligious as he was, his conduct was heavenly, compared with that of his brother Thomas under similar circumstances. He listened attentively to my narration of the circumstances leading to the savage outrage, and gave many proofs of his strong indignation of it. The heart of my once overkind mistress was again melted into pity. My puffed-out eye and blood-covered face moved her to tears. She took a chair by me, washed the blood from my face, and, with a mother's tenderness, bound up my head, covering the wounded eye with a lean piece of fresh beef. It was almost compensation for my suffering to witness, once more, a manifestation of kindness from this, my once affectionate old mistress. Master Hugh was very much enraged. He gave expression to his feelings by pouring out curses upon the heads of those who did the deed. As soon as I got a little the better of my bruises, he took me with him to Esquire Watson's, on Bond Street, to see what could be done about the matter. Mr. Watson inquired who saw the assault committed. Master Hugh told him it was done in Mr. Gardner's ship-yard, at midday, where there were a large company of men at work. "As to that," he said, "the deed was done, and there was no question as to who did it." His answer was, he could do nothing in the case, unless some white man would come forward and testify. He could issue no warrant on my word. If

I had been killed in the presence of a thousand colored people, their testimony combined would have been insufficient to have arrested one of the murderers. Master Hugh, for once, was compelled to say this state of things was too bad. Of course, it was impossible to get any white man to volunteer his testimony in my behalf, and against the white young men. Even those who may have sympathized with me were not prepared to do this. It required a degree of courage unknown to them to do so; for just at that time, the slightest manifestation of humanity toward a colored person was denounced as abolitionism, and that name subjected its bearer to frightful liabilities. The watchwords of the bloody-minded in that region, and in those days, were, "Damn the abolitionists!" and "Damn the niggers!" There was nothing done, and probably nothing would have been done if I had been killed. Such was, and such remains, the state of things in the Christian city of Baltimore.

Master Hugh, finding he could get no redress, refused to let me go back again to Mr. Gardner. He kept me himself, and his wife dressed my wound till I was again restored to health. He then took me into the ship-yard of which he was foreman, in the employment of Mr. Walter Price. There I was immediately set to calking, and very soon learned the art of using my mallet and irons. In the course of one year from the time I left Mr. Gardner's, I was able to command the highest wages given to the most experienced calkers. I was now of some importance to my master. I was bringing him from six to seven dollars per week. I sometimes brought him nine dollars per week: my wages were a dollar and a half a day. After learning how to calk, I sought my own employment, made my own contracts, and collected the money which I earned. My pathway became much more smooth than before; my condition was now much more comfortable. When I could get no calking to do, I did nothing. During these leisure times, those old notions about freedom would steal over me again. When in Mr. Gardner's employment, I was kept in such a perpetual whirl of excitement, I could think of nothing, scarcely, but my life; and in thinking of my life, I almost forgot my liberty. I have observed this in my experience of slavery,—that whenever my condition was improved, instead of its increasing my contentment, it only increased my desire to be free, and set me to thinking of plans to gain my freedom. I have found that, to make a contented slave, it is necessary to make a thoughtless one. It is necessary to darken his moral and mental vision, and, as far as possible, to annihilate the power of reason. He must be made to feel that slavery is right; and he can be brought to that only when he ceases to be a man.

I was now getting, as I have said, one dollar and fifty cents per day. I contracted for it; I earned it; it was paid to me; it was rightfully my own; yet, upon each returning Saturday night, I was compelled to deliver every cent of that money to Master Hugh. And why? Not because he earned it,—not because he had any hand in earning it,—not because I owed it to him,—nor because he possessed the slightest shadow of a right to it; but solely because he had the power to compel me to give it up. The right of the grim-visaged pirate upon the high seas is exactly the same.

CHAPTER XI

I now come to that part of my life during which I planned, and finally succeeded in making, my escape from slavery. But before narrating any of the peculiar circumstances, I deem it proper to make known my intention not to state all the facts connected with the transaction. My reasons for pursuing this course may be understood from the following: First, were I to give a minute statement of all the facts, it is not only possible, but quite probable, that others would thereby be involved in the most embarrassing difficulties. Secondly, such a statement would most undoubtedly induce greater vigilance on the part of slaveholders than has existed heretofore among them; which would, of course, be the means of guarding a door whereby some dear brother bondman might escape his galling chains. I deeply regret the necessity that impels me to suppress any thing of importance connected with my experience in slavery. It would afford me great pleasure indeed, as well as materially add to the interest of my narrative, were I at liberty to gratify a curiosity, which I know exists in the minds of many, by an accurate statement of all the facts pertaining to my most fortunate escape. But I must deprive myself of this pleasure, and the curious of the gratification which such a statement would afford. I would allow myself to suffer under the greatest imputations which evil-minded men might suggest, rather than exculpate myself, and thereby run the hazard of closing the slightest avenue by which a brother slave might clear himself of the chains and fetters of slavery.

I have never approved of the very public manner in which some of our western friends have conducted what they call the *underground railroad,*[4] but which, I think, by their open declarations, has been made most emphatically the *upperground railroad.* I honor those good men and women for their noble daring, and applaud them for willingly subjecting themselves to bloody persecution, by openly avowing their participation in the escape of slaves. I, however, can see very little good resulting from such a course, either to themselves or the slaves escaping; while, upon the other hand, I see and feel assured that those open declarations are a positive evil to the slaves remaining, who are seeking to escape. They do nothing towards enlightening the slave, whilst they do much towards enlightening the master. They stimulate him to greater watchfulness, and enhance his power to capture his slave. We owe something to the slaves south of the line[5] as well as to those north of it; and in aiding the latter on their way to freedom, we should be careful to do nothing which would be likely to hinder the former from escaping from slavery. I would keep the merciless slaveholder profoundly ignorant of the means of flight adopted by the slave. I would leave him to imagine himself surrounded by myriads of invisible tormentors, ever ready to snatch from his infernal grasp his trembling prey. Let him be left to feel his way in the dark; let darkness commensurate with his crime hover over him; and let him feel that at every step he takes, in pursuit of the flying bondman, he is running the frightful risk of having his hot brains dashed out by an invisible agency. Let us render the tyrant no aid; let us not hold the light by which he can trace the footprints of our flying brother. But enough of this. I will now proceed to the statement of those facts, connected with my escape, for which I am alone responsible, and for which no one can be made to suffer but myself.

In the early part of the year 1838, I became quite restless. I could see no

4. A system set up by opponents of slavery to help fugitive slaves from the South escape to free states and to Canada.   5. The Mason-Dixon line, the boundary between Pennsylvania and Maryland and between slave and free states.

reason why I should, at the end of each week, pour the reward of my toil into the purse of my master. When I carried to him my weekly wages, he would, after counting the money, look me in the face with a robber-like fierceness, and ask, "Is this all?" He was satisfied with nothing less than the last cent. He would, however, when I made him six dollars, sometimes give me six cents, to encourage me. It had the opposite effect. I regarded it as a sort of admission of my right to the whole. The fact that he gave me any part of my wages was proof, to my mind, that he believed me entitled to the whole of them. I always felt worse for having received any thing; for I feared that the giving me a few cents would ease his conscience, and make him feel himself to be a pretty honorable sort of robber. My discontent grew upon me. I was ever on the look-out for means of escape; and, finding no direct means, I determined to try to hire my time, with a view of getting money with which to make my escape. In the spring of 1838, when Master Thomas came to Baltimore to purchase his spring goods, I got an opportunity, and applied to him to allow me to hire my time. He unhesitatingly refused my request, and told me this was another stratagem by which to escape. He told me I could go nowhere but that he could get me; and that, in the event of my running away, he should spare no pains in his efforts to catch me. He exhorted me to content myself, and be obedient. He told me, if I would be happy, I must lay out no plans for the future. He said, if I behaved myself properly, he would take care of me. Indeed, he advised me to complete thoughtlessness of the future, and taught me to depend solely upon him for happiness. He seemed to see fully the pressing necessity of setting aside my intellectual nature, in order to [insure] contentment in slavery. But in spite of him, and even in spite of myself, I continued to think, and to think about the injustice of my enslavement, and the means of escape.

About two months after this, I applied to Master Hugh for the privilege of hiring my time. He was not acquainted with the fact that I had applied to Master Thomas, and had been refused. He too, at first, seemed disposed to refuse; but, after some reflection, he granted me the privilege, and proposed the following terms: I was to be allowed all my time, make all contracts with those for whom I worked, and find my own employment; and, in return for this liberty, I was to pay him three dollars at the end of each week; find myself in calking tools, and in board and clothing. My board was two dollars and a half per week. This, with the wear and tear of clothing and calking tools, made my regular expenses about six dollars per week. This amount I was compelled to make up, or relinquish the privilege of hiring my time. Rain or shine, work or no work, at the end of each week the money must be forthcoming, or I must give up my privilege. This arrangement, it will be perceived, was decidedly in my master's favor. It relieved him of all need of looking after me. His money was sure. He received all the benefits of slave-holding without its evils; while I endured all the evils of a slave, and suffered all the care and anxiety of a freeman. I found it a hard bargain. But, hard as it was, I thought it better than the old mode of getting along. It was a step towards freedom to be allowed to bear the responsibilities of a freeman, and I was determined to hold on upon it. I bent myself to the work of making money. I was ready to work at night as well as day, and by the most untiring perseverance and industry, I made enough to meet my expenses, and lay up a little money every week. I went on thus from May till August. Master Hugh then refused to allow me to hire my time longer. The ground for his refusal was a failure on my part, one Saturday night, to pay him for my week's time. This failure was occasioned by my attending a camp meeting about ten miles from Baltimore. During the week, I had entered into an engagement with a number of young friends to start from Baltimore to the camp ground early Saturday evening; and being detained by my employer, I was unable to get down to Master Hugh's without disappointing the company. I knew that Master Hugh was in no special need of the money that night. I therefore decided to go to camp meeting, and upon my return pay him the three dollars. I staid at the camp meeting one day longer than I intended when I left. But as soon as I returned, I called upon him to pay him what he considered his due. I found him very angry; he could scarce restrain his wrath. He said he had a great mind to give me a severe whipping. He wished to know how I dared go out of the city without asking his permission. I told him I hired my time, and while I paid him the price which he asked for it, I did not know that I was bound to ask him when and where I should go. This reply troubled him; and, after reflecting a few moments, he turned to me, and said I should hire my time no longer; that the next thing he should know of, I would be running away. Upon the same plea, he told me to bring my tools and clothing home forthwith. I did so; but instead of seeking work, as I had been accustomed to do previously to hiring my time, I spent the whole week without the performance of a single stroke of work. I did this in retaliation. Saturday night, he called upon me as usual for my week's wages. I told him I had no wages; I had done no work that week. Here we were upon the point of coming to blows. He raved, and swore his determination to get hold of me. I did not allow myself a single word; but was resolved, if he laid the weight of his hand upon me, it should be blow for blow. He did not strike me, but told me that he would find me in constant employment in future. I thought the matter over during the next day, Sunday, and finally resolved upon the third day of September, as the day upon which I would make a second attempt to secure my freedom. I now had three weeks during which to prepare for my journey. Early on Monday morning, before Master Hugh had time to make any engagement for me, I went out and got employment of Mr. Butler, at his ship-yard near the draw-bridge, upon what is called the City Block, thus making it unnecessary for him to seek employment for me. At the end of the week, I brought him between eight and nine dollars. He seemed very well pleased, and asked me why I did not do the same the week before. He little knew what my plans were. My object in working steadily was to remove any suspicion he might entertain of my intent to run away; and in this I succeeded admirably. I suppose he thought I was never better satisfied with my condition than at the very time during which I was planning my escape. The second week passed, and again I carried him my full wages; and so well pleased was he, that he gave me twenty-five cents, (quite a large sum for a slaveholder to give a slave,) and bade me to make a good use of it. I told him I would.

Things went on without very smoothly indeed, but within there was trouble. It is impossible for me to describe my feelings as the time of my contemplated start drew near. I had a number of warm-hearted friends in Baltimore,—friends that I loved almost as I did my life,—and the thought of being separated from them forever was painful beyond expression. It is my opinion that thousands would escape from slavery, who now remain, but for the strong cords of affection that bind them to their friends. The thought of leaving my friends was decidedly the most painful thought with which I had to contend. The love of them was my tender point, and shook my decision more than all things else. Besides the pain of separation, the dread and apprehension of a failure exceeded what I had experienced at my first attempt. The appalling defeat I then sustained returned to torment me. I felt assured that, if I failed in this attempt, my case would be a hopeless one— it would seal my fate as a slave forever. I could not hope to get off with any thing less than the severest punishment, and being placed beyond the means of escape. It required no very vivid imagination to depict the most frightful scenes through which I should have to pass, in case I failed. The wretchedness of slavery, and the blessedness of freedom, were perpetually before me. It was life and death with me. But I remained firm, and, according to my resolution, on the third day of September, 1838, I left my chains, and succeeded in reaching New York without the slightest interruption of any kind. How I did so,—what means I adopted,—what direction I travelled, and by what mode of conveyance,—I must leave unexplained, for the reasons before mentioned.

I have been frequently asked how I felt when I found myself in a free State. I have never been able to answer the question with any satisfaction to myself. It was a moment of the highest excitement I ever experienced. I suppose I felt as one may imagine the unarmed mariner to feel when he is rescued by a friendly man-of-war from the pursuit of a pirate. In writing to a dear friend, immediately after my arrival at New York, I said I felt like one who had escaped a den of hungry lions. This state of mind, however, very soon subsided; and I was again seized with a feeling of great insecurity and loneliness. I was yet liable to be taken back, and subjected to all the tortures of slavery. This in itself was enough to damp the ardor of my enthusiasm. But the loneliness overcame me. There I was in the midst of thousands, and yet a perfect stranger; without home and without friends, in the midst of thousands of my own brethren—children of a common Father, and yet I dared not to unfold to any one of them my sad condition. I was afraid to speak to any one for fear of speaking to the wrong one, and thereby falling into the hands of money-loving kidnappers, whose business it was to lie in wait for the panting fugitive, as the ferocious beasts of the forest lie in wait for their prey. The motto which I adopted when I started from slavery was this—"Trust no man!" I saw in every white man an enemy, and in almost every colored man cause for distrust. It was a most painful situation; and, to understand it, one must needs experience it, or imagine himself in similar circumstances. Let him be a fugitive slave in a strange land—a land given up to be the hunting-ground for slaveholders—whose inhabitants are legalized kidnappers—where he is every moment subjected to the terrible liability of being seized upon by his fellow-men, as the hideous crocodile seizes upon his prey!—I say, let him place himself in my situation—without home or friends—without money or credit—wanting shelter, and no one to give it— wanting bread, and no money to buy it,—and at the same time let him feel that he is pursued by merciless men-hunters, and in total darkness as to what to do, where to go, or where to stay,—perfectly helpless both as to the means of defence and means of escape,—in the midst of plenty, yet suffering the terrible gnawings of hunger,—in the midst of houses, yet having no home,—among fellow-men, yet feeling as if in the midst of wild beasts, whose greediness to swallow up the trembling and half-famished fugitive is only equalled by that with which the monsters of the deep swallow up the helpless fish upon which they subsist,—I say, let him be placed in this most trying situation,—the situation in which I was placed,—then, and not till then, will he fully appreciate the hardships of, and know how to sympathize with, the toil-worn and whip-scarred fugitive slave.

Thank Heaven, I remained but a short time in this distressed situation. I was relieved from it by the humane hand of Mr. DAVID RUGGLES,[6] whose vigilance, kindness, and perseverance, I shall never forget. I am glad of an opportunity to express, as far as words can, the love and gratitude I bear him. Mr. Ruggles is now afflicted with blindness, and is himself in need of the same kind offices which he was once so forward in the performance of toward others. I had been in New York but a few days, when Mr. Ruggles sought me out, and very kindly took me to his boarding-house at the corner of Church and Lespenard Streets. Mr. Ruggles was then very deeply engaged in the memorable *Darg* case, as well as attending to a number of other fugitive slaves, devising ways and means for their successful escape; and, though watched and hemmed in on almost every side, he seemed to be more than a match for his enemies. Very soon after I went to Mr. Ruggles, he wished to know of me where I wanted to go; as he deemed it unsafe for me to remain in New York. I told him I was a calker, and should like to go where I could get work. I thought of going to Canada; but he decided against it, and in favor of my going to New Bedford, thinking I should be able to get work there at my trade. At this time, Anna,[7] my intended wife, came on; for I wrote to her immediately after my arrival at New York, (notwithstanding my homeless, houseless, and helpless condition,) informing her of my successful flight, and wishing her to come on forthwith. In a few days after her arrival, Mr. Ruggles called in the Rev. J. W. C. Pennington, who, in the presence of Mr. Ruggles, Mrs. Michaels, and two or three others, performed the marriage ceremony, and gave us a certificate, of which the following is an exact copy:—

> "THIS may certify, that I joined together in holy matrimony Frederick Johnson[8] and Anna Murray, as man and wife, in the presence of Mr. David Ruggles and Mrs. Michaels.
>
> "JAMES W. C. PENNINGTON.
> "*New York, Sept.* 15, 1838."

Upon receiving this certificate, and a five-dollar bill from Mr. Ruggles, I shouldered one part of our baggage, and Anna took up the other, and we set out forthwith to take passage on board of the steamboat John W. Richmond for Newport, on our way to New Bedford. Mr. Ruggles gave me a letter to a Mr. Shaw in Newport, and told me, in case my money did not serve me to New Bedford, to stop in Newport and obtain further assistance; but upon

---

6. A black abolitionist (1810–1849), at this time living in New York, who helped many slaves to escape.
7. She was free [Douglass's note].   8. I had changed my name from Frederick *Bailey* to that of *Johnson* [Douglass's note].

our arrival at Newport, we were so anxious to get to a place of safety, that, notwithstanding we lacked the necessary money to pay our fare, we decided to take seats in the stage, and promise to pay when we got to New Bedford. We were encouraged to do this by two excellent gentlemen, residents of New Bedford, whose names I afterward ascertained to be Joseph Ricketson and William C. Taber. They seemed at once to understand our circumstances, and gave us such assurance of their friendliness as put us fully at ease in their presence. It was good indeed to meet with such friends, at such a time. Upon reaching New Bedford, we were directed to the house of Mr. Nathan Johnson, by whom we were kindly received, and hospitably provided for. Both Mr. and Mrs. Johnson took a deep and lively interest in our welfare. They proved themselves quite worthy of the name of abolitionists. When the stage-driver found us unable to pay our fare, he held on upon our baggage as security for the debt. I had but to mention the fact to Mr. Johnson, and he forthwith advanced the money.

We now began to feel a degree of safety, and to prepare ourselves for the duties and responsibilities of a life of freedom. On the morning after our arrival at New Bedford, while at the breakfast-table, the question arose as to what name I should be called by. The name given me by my mother was, "Frederick Augustus Washington Bailey." I, however, had dispensed with the two middle names long before I left Maryland so that I was generally known by the name of "Frederick Bailey." I started from Baltimore bearing the name of "Stanley." When I got to New York, I again changed my name to "Frederick Johnson," and thought that would be the last change. But when I got to New Bedford, I found it necessary again to change my name. The reason of this necessity was, that there were so many Johnsons in New Bedford, it was already quite difficult to distinguish between them. I gave Mr. Johnson the privilege of choosing me a name, but told him he must not take from me the name of "Frederick." I must hold on to that, to preserve a sense of my identity. Mr. Johnson had just been reading the "Lady of the Lake,"[9] and at once suggested that my name be "Douglass." From that time until now I have been called "Frederick Douglass;" and as I am more widely known by that name than by either of the others, I shall continue to use it as my own.

I was quite disappointed at the general appearance of things in New Bedford. The impression which I had received respecting the character and condition of the people of the north, I found to be singularly erroneous. I had very strangely supposed, while in slavery, that few of the comforts, and scarcely any of the luxuries, of life were enjoyed at the north, compared with what were enjoyed by the slaveholders of the south. I probably came to this conclusion from the fact that northern people owned no slaves. I supposed that they were about upon a level with the non-slaveholding population of the south. I knew *they* were exceedingly poor, and I had been accustomed to regard their poverty as the necessary consequence of their being non-slaveholders. I had somehow imbibed the opinion that, in the absence of slaves, there could be no wealth, and very little refinement. And upon coming to the north, I expected to meet with a rough, hard-handed, and uncultivated population, living in the most Spartan-like simplicity, knowing nothing of the ease, luxury, pomp, and grandeur of southern slaveholders. Such being

9. A narrative poem by Sir Walter Scott (1810) about the fortunes of the Douglas clan in Scotland.

my conjectures, any one acquainted with the appearance of New Bedford may very readily infer how palpably I must have seen my mistake.

In the afternoon of the day when I reached New Bedford, I visited the wharves, to take a view of the shipping. Here I found myself surrounded with the strongest proofs of wealth. Lying at the wharves, and riding in the stream, I saw many ships of the finest model, in the best order, and of the largest size. Upon the right and left, I was walled in by granite warehouses of the widest dimensions, stowed to their utmost capacity with the necessaries and comforts of life. Added to this, almost every body seemed to be at work, but noiselessly so, compared with what I had been accustomed to in Baltimore. There were no loud songs heard from those engaged in loading and unloading ships. I heard no deep oaths or horrid curses on the laborer. I saw no whipping of men; but all seemed to go smoothly on. Every man appeared to understand his work, and went at it with a sober, yet cheerful earnestness, which betokened the deep interest which he felt in what he was doing, as well as a sense of his own dignity as a man. To me this looked exceedingly strange. From the wharves I strolled around and over the town, gazing with wonder and admiration at the splendid churches, beautiful dwellings, and finely-cultivated gardens; evincing an amount of wealth, comfort, taste, and refinement, such as I had never seen in any part of slaveholding Maryland.

Every thing looked clean, new, and beautiful. I saw few or no dilapidated houses, with poverty-stricken inmates; no half-naked children and barefooted women, such as I had been accustomed to see in Hillsborough, Easton, St. Michael's, and Baltimore. The people looked more able, stronger, healthier, and happier, than those of Maryland. I was for once made glad by a view of extreme wealth, without being saddened by seeing extreme poverty. But the most astonishing as well as the most interesting thing to me was the condition of the colored people, a great many of whom, like myself, had escaped thither as a refuge from the hunters of men. I found many, who had not been seven years out of their chains, living in finer houses, and evidently enjoying more of the comforts of life, than the average of slave-holders in Maryland. I will venture to assert that my friend Mr. Nathan Johnson (of whom I can say with a grateful heart, "I was hungry, and he gave me meat; I was thirsty, and he gave me drink; I was a stranger, and he took me in")[1] lived in a neater house; dined at a better table; took, paid for, and read, more newspapers; better understood the moral, religious, and political character of the nation,—than nine tenths of the slaveholders in Talbot county Maryland. Yet Mr. Johnson was a working man. His hands were hardened by toil, and not his alone, but those also of Mrs. Johnson. I found the colored people much more spirited than I had supposed they would be. I found among them a determination to protect each other from the blood-thirsty kidnapper, at all hazards. Soon after my arrival, I was told of a circumstance which illustrated their spirit. A colored man and a fugitive slave were on unfriendly terms. The former was heard to threaten the latter with informing his master of his whereabouts. Straightway a meeting was called among the colored people, under the stereotyped notice, "Business of importance!" The betrayer was invited to attend. The people came at the appointed hour, and organized

1. Matthew 25.35: "For I was an hungered, and ye gave me meat: I was thirsty, and ye gave me drink: I was a stranger, and ye took me in."

the meeting by appointing a very religious old gentleman as president, who, I believe, made a prayer, after which he addressed the meeting as follows: *"Friends, we have got him here, and I would recommend that you young men just take him outside the door, and kill him!"* With this, a number of them bolted at him; but they were intercepted by some more timid than themselves, and the betrayer escaped their vengeance, and has not been seen in New Bedford since. I believe there have been no more such threats, and should there be hereafter, I doubt not that death would be the consequence.

I found employment, the third day after my arrival, in stowing a sloop with a load of oil. It was new, dirty, and hard work for me; but I went at it with a glad heart and a willing hand. I was now my own master. It was a happy moment, the rapture of which can be understood only by those who have been slaves. It was the first work, the reward of which was to be entirely my own. There was no Master Hugh standing ready, the moment I earned the money, to rob me of it. I worked that day with a pleasure I had never before experienced. I was at work for myself and newly-married wife. It was to me the starting-point of a new existence. When I got through with that job, I went in pursuit of a job of calking; but such was the strength of prejudice against color, among the white calkers, that they refused to work with me, and of course I could get no employment.[2] Finding my trade of no immediate benefit, I threw off my calking habiliments, and prepared myself to do any kind of work I could get to do. Mr. Johnson kindly let me have his wood-horse and saw, and I very soon found myself a plenty of work. There was no work too hard—none too dirty. I was ready to saw wood, shovel coal, carry the hod, sweep the chimney, or roll oil casks,—all of which I did for nearly three years in New Bedford, before I became known to the anti-slavery world.

In about four months after I went to New Bedford there came a young man to me, and inquired if I did not wish to take the "Liberator."[3] I told him I did; but, just having made my escape from slavery, I remarked that I was unable to pay for it then. I, however, finally became a subscriber to it. The paper came, and I read it from week to week with such feelings as it would be quite idle for me to attempt to describe. The paper became my meat and my drink. My soul was set all on fire. Its sympathy for my brethren in bonds— its scathing denunciations of slaveholders—its faithful exposures of slavery— and its powerful attacks upon the upholders of the institution—sent a thrill of joy through my soul, such as I had never felt before!

I had not long been a reader of the "Liberator," before I got a pretty correct idea of the principles, measures and spirit of the anti-slavery reform. I took right hold of the cause. I could do but little; but what I could, I did with a joyful heart, and never felt happier than when in an anti-slavery meeting. I seldom had much to say at the meetings, because what I wanted to say was said so much better by others. But, while attending an anti-slavery convention at Nantucket, on the 11th of August, 1841, I felt strongly moved to speak, and was at the same time much urged to do so by Mr. William C. Coffin, a gentleman who had heard me speak in the colored people's meeting at New Bedford. It was a severe cross, and I took it up reluctantly. The truth was, I felt myself a slave, and the idea of speaking to white people weighed

2. I am told that colored persons can now get employment at calking in New Bedford—a result of anti-slavery effort [Douglass's note].   3. William Lloyd Garrison's antislavery newspaper, which began publication in 1831.

me down. I spoke but a few moments, when I felt a degree of freedom, and said what I desired with considerable ease. From that time until now, I have been engaged in pleading the cause of my brethren—with what success, and with what devotion, I leave those acquainted with my labors to decide.

APPENDIX

I find, since reading over the foregoing Narrative, that I have, in several instances, spoken in such a tone and manner, respecting religion, as may possibly lead those unacquainted with my religious views to suppose me an opponent of all religion. To remove the liability of such misapprehension, I deem it proper to append the following brief explanation. What I have said respecting and against religion, I mean strictly to apply to the *slaveholding religion* of this land, and with no possible reference to Christianity proper; for, between the Christianity of this land, and the Christianity of Christ, I recognize the widest possible difference—so wide, that to receive the one as good, pure, and holy, is of necessity to reject the other as bad, corrupt, and wicked. To be the friend of the one, is of necessity to be the enemy of the other. I love the pure, peaceable, and impartial Christianity of Christ: I therefore hate the corrupt, slaveholding, women-whipping, cradle-plundering, partial and hypocritical Christianity of this land. Indeed, I can see no reason, but the most deceitful one, for calling the religion of this land Christianity. I look upon it as the climax of all misnomers, the boldest of all frauds, and the grossest of all libels. Never was there a clearer case of "stealing the livery of the court of heaven to serve the devil in." I am filled with unutterable loathing when I contemplate the religious pomp and show, together with the horrible inconsistencies, which every where surround me. We have men-stealers for ministers, women-whippers for missionaries, and cradle-plunderers for church members. The man who wields the blood-clotted cowskin during the week fills the pulpit on Sunday, and claims to be a minister of the meek and lowly Jesus. The man who robs me of my earnings at the end of each week meets me as a class-leader on Sunday morning, to show me the way of life, and the path of salvation. He who sells my sister, for purposes of prostitution, stands forth as the pious advocate of purity. He who proclaims it a religious duty to read the Bible denies me the right of learning to read the name of the God who made me. He who is the religious advocate of marriage robs whole millions of its sacred influence, and leaves them to the ravages of wholesale pollution. The warm defender of the sacredness of the family relation is the same that scatters whole families,—sundering husbands and wives, parents and children, sisters and brothers,—leaving the hut vacant, and the hearth desolate. We see the thief preaching against theft, and the adulterer against adultery. We have men sold to build churches, women sold to support the gospel, and babes sold to purchase Bibles for the *poor heathen! all for the glory of God and the good of souls!* The slave auctioneer's bell and the church-going bell chime in with each other, and the bitter cries of the heart-broken slave are drowned in the religious shouts of his pious master. Revivals of religion and revivals in the slave-trade go hand in hand together. The slave prison and the church stand near each other. The clanking of fetters and the rattling of chains in the prison, and the pious psalm and solemn prayer in the church, may be heard at the same time. The dealers in the bodies and souls of men erect their stand in the presence of the pulpit, and they mutually help each other. The dealer gives his blood-stained gold to support the pulpit, and the pulpit, in return, covers his infernal business with the garb of Christianity. Here we have religion and robbery the allies of each other—devils dressed in angels' robes, and hell presenting the semblance of paradise.

> "Just God! and these are they,
>   Who minister at thine altar, God of right!
> Men who their hands, with prayer and blessing, lay
>   On Israel's ark of light.
>
> "What! preach, and kidnap men?
>   Give thanks, and rob thy own afflicted poor?
> Talk of thy glorious liberty, and then
>   Bolt hard the captive's door?
>
> "What! servants of thy own
>   Merciful Son, who came to seek and save
> The homeless and the outcast, fettering down
>   The tasked and plundered slave!
>
> "Pilate and Herod friends!
>   Chief priests and rulers, as of old, combine!
> Just God and holy! is that church which lends
>   Strength to the spoiler thine?"

The Christianity of America is a Christianity, of whose votaries it may be as truly said, as it was of the ancient scribes and Pharisees, "They bind heavy burdens, and grievous to be borne, and lay them on men's shoulders, but they themselves will not move them with one of their fingers. All their works they do for to be seen of men.—— They love the uppermost rooms at feasts, and the chief seats in the synagogues, ... and to be called of men, Rabbi, Rabbi.—— But woe unto you, scribes and Pharisees, hypocrites! for ye neither go in yourselves, neither suffer ye them that are entering to go in. Ye devour widows' houses, and for a pretence make long prayers; therefore ye shall receive the greater damnation. Ye compass sea and land to make one proselyte, and when he is made, ye make him twofold more the child of hell than yourselves.—— Woe unto you, scribes and Pharisees, hypocrites! for ye pay tithe of mint, and anise, and cumin, and have omitted the weightier matters of the law, judgment, mercy, and faith; these ought ye to have done, and not to leave the other undone. Ye blind guides! which strain at a gnat, and swallow a camel. Woe unto you, scribes and Pharisees, hypocrites! for ye make clean the outside of the cup and of the platter; but within, they are full of extortion and excess.—— Woe unto you, scribes and Pharisees, hypocrites! for ye are like unto whited sepulchres, which indeed appear beautiful outward, but are within full of dead men's bones, and of all uncleanness. Even so ye also outwardly appear righteous unto men, but within ye are full of hypocrisy and iniquity."[4]

Dark and terrible as is this picture, I hold it to be strictly true of the overwhelming mass of professed Christians in America. They strain at a gnat,

---

4. Matthew 23.

and swallow a camel. Could any thing be more true of our churches? They would be shocked at the proposition of fellowshipping a *sheep*-stealer; and at the same time they hug to their communion a *man*-stealer, and brand me with being an infidel, if I find fault with them for it. They attend with Pharisaical strictness to the outward forms of religion, and at the same time neglect the weightier matters of the law, judgment, mercy, and faith. They are always ready to sacrifice, but seldom to show mercy. They are they who are represented as professing to love God whom they have not seen, whilst they hate their brother whom they have seen. They love the heathen on the other side of the globe. They can pray for him, pay money to have the Bible put into his hand, and missionaries to instruct him; while they despise and totally neglect the heathen at their own doors.

Such is, very briefly, my view of the religion of this land; and to avoid any misunderstanding, growing out of the use of general terms, I mean, by the religion of this land, that which is revealed in the words, deeds, and actions, of those bodies, north and south, calling themselves Christian churches, and yet in union with slaveholders. It is against religion, as presented by these bodies, that I have felt it my duty to testify.

I conclude these remarks by copying the following portrait of the religion of the south, (which is, by communion and fellowship, the religion of the north) which I soberly affirm is "true to the life," and without caricature or the slightest exaggeration. It is said to have been drawn, several years before the present anti-slavery agitation began, by a northern Methodist preacher, who, while residing at the south, had an opportunity to see slaveholding morals, manners, and piety, with his own eyes. "Shall I not visit for these things? saith the Lord. Shall not my soul be avenged on such a nation as this?"[5]

"A Parody.

"Come, saints and sinners, hear me tell
How pious priests whip Jack and Nell,
And women buy and children sell,
And preach all sinners down to hell,
    And sing of heavenly union.

"They'll bleat and baa, dona[6] like goats,
Gorge down black sheep, and strain at motes,
Array their backs in fine black coats,
Then seize their negroes by their throats,
    And choke, for heavenly union.

"They'll church you if you sip a dram,
And damn you if you steal a lamb;
Yet rob old Tony, Doll, and Sam,
Of human rights, and bread and ham;
    Kidnapper's heavenly union.

"They'll loudly talk of Christ's reward,
And bind his image with a cord,

---

5. Jeremiah 5.9.   6. Believed to be a printer's error in the original edition for "go on" or "go n-a-a-ah."

And scold, and swing the lash abhorred,
And sell their brother in the Lord
   To handcuffed heavenly union.

"They'll read and sing a sacred song,
And make a prayer both loud and long,
And teach the right and do the wrong,
Hailing the brother, sister throng,
   With words of heavenly union.

"We wonder how such saints can sing,
Or praise the Lord upon the wing,
Who roar, and scold, and whip, and sting,
And to their slaves and mammon cling,
   In guilty conscience union.

"They'll raise tobacco, corn, and rye,
And drive, and thieve, and cheat, and lie,
And lay up treasures in the sky,
By making switch and cowskin fly,
   In hope of heavenly union.

"They'll crack old Tony on the skull,
And preach and roar like Bashan bull,
Or braying ass, of mischief full,
Then seize old Jacob by the wool,
   And pull for heavenly union.

"A roaring, ranting, sleek man-thief,
Who lived on mutton, veal, and beef,
Yet never would afford relief
To needy, sable sons of grief,
   Was big with heavenly union.

" 'Love not the world,' the preacher said,
And winked his eye, and shook his head;
He seized on Tom, and Dick, and Ned,
Cut short their meat, and clothes, and bread,
   Yet still loved heavenly union.

"Another preacher whining spoke
Of One whose heart for sinners broke:
He tied old Nanny to an oak,
And drew the blood at every stroke,
   And prayed for heavenly union.

"Two others oped their iron jaws,
And waved their children-stealing paws;
There sat their children in gewgaws;
By stinting negroes' backs and maws,
   They kept up heavenly union.

"All good from Jack another takes,
And entertains their flirts and rakes,
Who dress as sleek as glossy snakes,
And cram their mouths with sweetened cakes;
   And this goes down for union."

Sincerely and earnestly hoping that this little book may do something toward throwing light on the American slave system, and hastening the glad day of deliverance to the millions of my brethren in bonds—faithfully relying upon the power of truth, love, and justice, for success in my humble efforts— and solemnly pledging my self anew to the sacred cause,—I subscribe myself,

FREDERICK DOUGLASS.

Lynn, Mass., April 28, 1845.

WALT WHITMAN
1819–1892

Walt Whitman in his poetry makes himself the center of the universe, but he is richly aware of the nature and the importance of his social context. He brings to his emphatic self-presentation a detailed, partly ironic, partly celebratory sense of what it means to be an American; his poetry suggests something of what life in the United States must have felt like in the middle of the nineteenth century.

Born on Long Island, Whitman in his childhood moved with his family to Brooklyn. He was christened Walter, but shortened his first name to distinguish himself from his father. As a young man, he worked as schoolteacher, builder, bookstore owner, journalist, and poet, before moving to Washington to work as a government clerk. There he also served as a volunteer nurse, helping to care for the Civil War wounded. In 1873 he settled in Camden, New Jersey, where he remained for the rest of his life.

Whitman began writing in his youth, producing a good deal of bad poetry and a novel, a fictionalized temperance tract. He first published *Leaves of Grass* in 1855, after having become an admirer of Emerson and a Jeffersonian Democrat; he continued enlarging and revising the book for the rest of his life. In 1865, he published *Drum Taps,* poems derived from his Civil War experiences; in 1871, *Democratic Vistas,* a collection of political and philosophical essays.

Whitman's shifting diction—familiar, even slangy, to formal and rhetorical—makes possible a large range of tones in *Song of Myself.* In a single section (21), for example, these two sequences occur in close conjunction:

> I chant the chant of dilation or pride,
> We have had ducking and deprecating about enough,
> I show that size is only development.

> Smile O voluptuous cool-breathed earth!
> Earth of the slumbering and liquid trees!
> Earth of departed sunset—earth of the mountains misty-topt!
> Earth of the vitreous pour of the full moon just tinged with blue!

The first three-line passage, after its formal opening, falls into a pattern like that of colloquial speech. "About enough" belongs to an informal vocabulary; the final line, turning on the word *only,* makes the kind of joke one might make in conversation. ("Size doesn't matter, really, it only comes from growing.") The speaker's claim that he does not endorse conventional judgments, by which bigger is better, and his slightly mocking tone declare his independence and his willingness not to take himself with undue seriousness. Only a few lines later, when he turns to the "voluptuous cool-breathed earth," he sounds like a different person, entirely serious, almost grandiose, about his personal perceptions. Now his rhapsodic tone unites him with the Romantic poets, though his vocabulary still insists on his individuality. The conjunction of "voluptuous" with "cool-breathed," the use of "vitreous" (glasslike) to modify "pour" used as a noun, the idea of "liquid trees": such choices demand the reader's close attention to figure out exactly what the poem is saying, and they emphasize a fresh way of seeing, a precise attention to the look of things. But they also sound like poetry, in a sense familiar to readers of earlier nineteenth-century works—unlike the lines quoted just before, which resemble colloquial prose.

The range of tones here exemplified helps to communicate an important theme of Whitman's poem: the tension and exchange between desire for individuality and for community. *Narrative of the Life of Frederick Douglass* directly and without apparent conflict expresses a sense of community as part of a sense of personal identity. *Song of Myself,* on the other hand, alternates between assertions of specialness and of identification with others.

> I am of old and young, of the foolish as much as the wise, . . .
> One of the Nation of many nations, the smallest the same and the largest the
>   same,
> A Southerner soon as a Northerner, a planter nonchalant and hospitable down
>   by the Oconee I live, . . .
> At home on Kanadian snow-shoes or up in the bush, or with fishermen off
>   Newfoundland,
> At home in the fleet of ice-boats, sailing with the rest and tacking.

Declaring his union not, like Wordsworth, with the natural universe, but with the society of his compatriots, Whitman identifies himself with the enormous variety he perceives and celebrates in his country. But his poem opens "I celebrate myself, and sing myself, / And what I assume you shall assume," insisting on his uniqueness and dominance. Toward the end, these two lines occur: "I too am not a bit tamed, I too am untranslatable, / I sound my barbaric yawp over the roofs of the world." One hears the note of defiant specialness: another characteristic aspect of *Song of Myself.* The poem's power derives partly from its capacity to embody both feelings, the feeling of uniqueness and the sense of shared humanity, feelings that most people experience, sometimes in confusing conjunction. Like his Romantic predecessors, Whitman values emotion, every kind of emotion, for its own sake. He suggests the irrelevance of the notion of contradiction to any understanding of inner life. In the realm of emotion, everything coexists. *Song of Myself* attempts to include all of it.

The poetic daring of *Song of Myself* expresses itself not only in choice of subject matter but in poetic technique. Whitman's lines are unrhymed and avoid the blank verse that had been the norm, instead establishing a new sort of rhythm—one that proved of crucial importance to twentieth-century American poets, who adapted it to their own purposes. Not metrical in any familiar sense, the verse establishes its own hypnotic rhythms, evoking an individual speaking voice, an individual idiom. It even risks the prosaic in its insistence that poetry implies, above all, personal perception and personal voice: "everything" can be included in technique as well as in material.

Out of the Cradle Endlessly Rocking, another of Whitman's best-known pre–Civil War poems, develops a child's imaginative relation with nature in a way that Wordsworth might have approved. A man hears a bird song that evokes for him a past experience—just as, at the beginning of *Remembrance of Things Past,* Proust's narrator finds his childhood returning to his memory at the taste of a madeleine. Reduced to tears by the song and the memory, the speaker, "chanter of pains and joys, uniter of here and hereafter," records and explores his youthful revelation of lyric power, achieved by identification with the bird mourning the loss of its mate.

> Now in a moment I know what I am for, I awake,
> And already a thousand singers, a thousand songs, clearer, louder, and more
>   sorrowful than yours,
> A thousand warbling echoes have started to life within me, never to die.

The poem concludes with the adult speaker meditating on the nature of his creative force in terms recalling Keats's in *Ode to a Nightingale*. Whitman, too, muses about the attraction of death, feels the demonic and the beautiful united in the song that inspires him. His own songs merge in his imagination with the "strong and delicious word" spoken by the sea, another aspect of nature, and one traditionally associated with death (as well as with birth). In poetry marked, like *Song of Myself,* by his powerfully individual rhythm and meter, Whitman reminds us once more of a great Romantic theme: the mystery of creativity.

G. W. Allen, *The Solitary Singer: A Critical Biography of Walt Whitman* (1959), provides both biography and criticism. An important recent study is D. S. Reynolds, *Walt Whitman's America: A Cultural Biography* (1995). J. E. Miller Jr., *A Critical Guide to Leaves of Grass* (1957), is helpful. Also valuable are R. Chase, *Walt Whitman Reconsidered* (1955); B. Erkkila, *Whitman the Political Poet* (1989); J. E. Miller, *Leaves of Grass: America's Lyric-Epic of Self and Democracy* (1992); S. Ceniza, *Walt Whitman and 19th-Century Women Reformers* (1998); J. Loving, *Walt Whitman: The Song of Himself* (1999); and R. Asselineau and others, *The Evolution of Walt Whitman* (1999). A general guide is G. W. Allen, *The New Walt Whitman Handbook* (1986).

[POEMS]

From Song of Myself[1]

1

I celebrate myself, and sing myself,
And what I assume you shall assume,
For every atom belonging to me as good belongs to you.

I loafe and invite my soul,
I lean and loafe at my ease observing a spear of summer grass.   5

My tongue, every atom of my blood, formed from this soil, this air,
Born here of parents born here from parents the same, and their parents
    the same,
I, now thirty-seven years old in perfect health begin,
Hoping to cease not till death.

Creeds and schools in abeyance,   10
Retiring back a while sufficed at what they are, but never forgotten,
I harbor for good or bad, I permit to speak at every hazard,
Nature without check with original energy.

*   *   *

4

Trippers and askers surround me,
People I meet, the effect upon me of my early life or the ward and city I
    live in, or the nation,
The latest dates, discoveries, inventions, societies, authors old and new,
My dinner, dress, associates, looks, compliments, dues,
The real or fancied indifference of some man or woman I love,   5

---

1. First published in 1855. This text is from the 1891–92 edition of *Leaves of Grass,* the so-called Deathbed Edition.

The sickness of one of my folks or of myself, or ill-doing or loss or lack
    of money, or depressions or exaltations,
Battles, the horrors of fratricidal war, the fever of doubtful news, the
    fitful events;
These come to me days and nights and go from me again,
But they are not the Me myself.

Apart from the pulling and hauling stands what I am,   10
Stands amused, complacent, compassionating, idle, unitary,
Looks down, is erect, or bends an arm on an impalpable certain rest,
Looking with side-curved head curious what will come next,
Both in and out of the game and watching and wondering at it.

Backward I see in my own days where I sweated through fog with
    linguists and contenders,   15
I have no mockings or arguments, I witness and wait.

         *   *   *

7

Has any one supposed it lucky to be born?
I hasten to inform him or her it is just as lucky to die, and I know it.

I pass death with the dying and birth with the new-washed babe, and am
    not contained between my hat and boots,
And peruse manifold objects, no two alike and every one good,
The earth good and the stars good, and their adjuncts all good.   5

I am not an earth nor an adjunct of an earth,
I am the mate and companion of people, all just as immortal and
    fathomless as myself,
(They do not know how immortal, but I know.)

Every kind for itself and its own, for me mine male and female,
For me those that have been boys and that love women,   10
For me the man that is proud and feels how it stings to be slighted,
For me the sweet-heart and the old maid, for me mothers and the
    mothers of mothers,
For me lips that have smiled, eyes that have shed tears,
For me children and the begetters of children.

Undrape! you are not guilty to me, nor stale nor discarded,   15
I see through the broadcloth and gingham whether or no,
And am around, tenacious, acquisitive, tireless, and cannot be shaken
    away.

         *   *   *

16

I am of old and young, of the foolish as much as the wise,
Regardless of others, ever regardful of others,
Maternal as well as paternal, a child as well as a man,
Stuffed with the stuff that is coarse and stuffed with the stuff that is fine,
One of the Nation of many nations, the smallest the same and the
    largest the same,   5

A Southerner soon as a Northerner, a planter nonchalant and hospitable
    down by the Oconee[2] I live,
A Yankee bound my own was ready for trade, my joints the limberest joints
    on earth and the sternest joints on earth,
A Kentuckian walking the vale of the Elkhorn in my deer-skin leggings,
    a Louisianian or Georgian,
A boatman over lakes or bays or along coasts, a Hoosier, Badger,
    Buckeye;
At home on Kanadian snow-shoes or up in the bush, or with fishermen off
    Newfoundland,   10
At home in the fleet of ice-boats, sailing with the rest and tacking,
At home on the hills of Vermont or in the woods of Maine, or the
    Texan ranch,
Comrade of Californians, comrade of free North-Westerners, (loving their
    big proportions,)
Comrade of raftsmen and coalmen, comrade of all who shake hands
    and welcome to drink and meat,
A learner with the simplest, a teacher of the thoughtfullest,   15
A novice beginning yet experient of myriads of seasons,
Of every hue and caste am I, of every rank and religion,
A farmer, mechanic, artist, gentleman, sailor, quaker,
Prisoner, fancy-man, rowdy, lawyer, physician, priest.

I resist any thing better than my own diversity,   20
Breathe the air but leave plenty after me,
And am not stuck up, and am in my place.

(The moth and the fish-eggs are in their place,
The bright suns I see and the dark suns I cannot see are in their place,
The palpable is in its place and the impalpable is in its place.)   25

                ❊   ❊   ❊

21

I am the poet of the Body and I am the poet of the Soul,
The pleasures of heaven are with me and the pains of hell are with me,
The first I graft and increase upon myself, the latter I translate into a
    new tongue.

I am the poet of the woman the same as the man,
And I say it is as great to be a woman as to be a man,   5
And I say there is nothing greater than the mother of men.

I chant the chant of dilation or pride,
We have had ducking and deprecating about enough,
I show that size is only development.

Have you outstript the rest? are you the President?   10
It is a trifle, they will more than arrive there every one, and still pass on.

I am he that walks with the tender and growing night,
I call to the earth and sea half-held by the night.

2. River in Georgia.

Press close bare-bosomed night—press close magnetic nourishing night!
Night of south winds—night of the large few stars!   15
Still nodding night—mad naked summer night.

Smile O voluptuous cool-breathed earth!
Earth of the slumbering and liquid trees!
Earth of departed sunset—earth of the mountains misty-topt!
Earth of the vitreous pour of the full moon just tinged with blue!   20
Earth of shine and dark mottling the tide of the river!
Earth of the limpid gray of clouds brighter and clearer for my sake!
Far-swooping elbowed earth—rich apple-blossomed earth!
Smile, for your lover comes.

Prodigal, you have given me love—therefore I to you give love!   25
O unspeakable passionate love.

*   *   *

24

Walt Whitman, a kosmos, of Manhattan the son,
Turbulent, fleshy, sensual, eating, drinking and breeding,
No sentimentalist, no stander above men and women or apart from them,
No more modest than immodest.

Unscrew the locks from the doors!   5
Unscrew the doors themselves from their jambs!

Whoever degrades another degrades me,
And whatever is done or said returns at last to me.

Through me the afflatus surging and surging, through me the current and
      index.

I speak the pass-word primeval, I give the sign of democracy,   10
By God! I will accept nothing which all cannot have their counterpart
      of on the same terms.

*   *   *

32

I think I could turn and live with animals, they are so placid and self-
      contained,
I stand and look at them long and long.

They do not sweat and whine about their condition,
They do not lie awake in the dark and weep for their sins,
They do not make me sick discussing their duty to God,   5
Not one is dissatisfied, not one is demented with the mania of owning
      things,
Not one kneels to another, nor to his kind that lived thousands of years
      ago,
Not one is respectable or unhappy over the whole earth.

So they show their relations to me and I accept them,
They bring me tokens of myself, they evince them plainly in their
      possession.   10

I wonder where they get those tokens,
Did I pass that way huge times ago and negligently drop them?

Myself moving forward then and now and forever,
Gathering and showing more always and with velocity,
Infinite and omnigenous,[3] and the like of these among them,   15
Not too exclusive toward the reachers of my remembrancers,
Picking out here one that I love, and now go with him on brotherly terms.

A gigantic beauty of a stallion, fresh and responsive to my caresses,
Head high in the forehead, wide between the ears,
Limbs glossy and supple, tail dusting the ground,   20
Eyes full of sparkling wickedness, ears finely cut, flexibly moving.

His nostrils dilate as my heels embrace him,
His well-built limbs tremble with pleasure as we race around and return.

I but use you a minute, then I resign you, stallion,
Why do I need your paces when I myself out-gallop them?   25
Even as I stand or sit passing faster than you.

*   *   *

46

I know I have the best of time and space, and was never measured and
    never will be measured.

I tramp a perpetual journey, (come listen all!)
My signs are a rain-proof coat, good shoes, and a staff cut from the woods,
No friend of mine takes his ease in my chair,
I have no chair, no church, no philosophy,   5
I lead no man to a dinner-table, library, exchange,
But each man and each woman of you I lead upon a knoll,
My left hand hooking you round the waist,
My right hand pointing to landscapes of continents and the public road.

Not I, not any one else can travel that road for you,   10
You must travel it for yourself.

It is not far, it is within reach,
Perhaps you have been on it since you were born and did not know,
Perhaps it is everywhere on water and on land.

Shoulder your duds dear son, and I will mine, and let us hasten forth,   15
Wonderful cities and free nations we shall fetch as we go.

*   *   *

51

The past and present wilt—I have filled them, emptied them,
And proceed to fill my next fold of the future.

Listener up there! what have you to confide to me?
Look in my face while I snuff the sidle of evening,[4]
(Talk honestly, no one else hears you, and I stay only a minute longer.)   5

---

3. Belonging to all races.   4. I.e., smell the fragrance of the slowly descending evening.

Do I contradict myself?
Very well then I contradict myself,
(I am large, I contain multitudes.)

I concentrate toward them that are nigh, I wait on the door-slab.

Who has done his day's work? who will soonest be through with his
    supper?   10
Who wishes to walk with me?

Will you speak before I am gone? will you prove already too late?

52

The spotted hawk swoops by and accuses me, he complains of my gab and
    my loitering.

I too am not a bit tamed, I too am untranslatable,
I sound my barbaric yawp over the roofs of the world.

The last scud of day holds back for me,
It flings my likeness after the rest and true as any on the shadowed
    wilds,   5
It coaxes me to the vapor and the dusk.

I depart as air, I shake my white locks at the runaway sun,
I effuse my flesh in eddies, and drift it in lacy jags.

I bequeath myself to the dirt to grow from the grass I love,
If you want me again look for me under your boot-soles.   10

You will hardly know who I am or what I mean,
But I shall be good health to you nevertheless,
And filter and fibre your blood.

Failing to fetch me at first keep encouraged,
Missing me one place search another,   15
I stop somewhere waiting for you.

Out of the Cradle Endlessly Rocking

Out of the cradle endlessly rocking,
Out of the mocking-bird's throat, the musical shuttle,
Out of the Ninth-month[1] midnight,
Over the sterile sands and the fields beyond, where the child leaving
    his bed wandered alone, bareheaded, barefoot,
Down from the showered halo,   5
Up from the mystic play of shadows twining and twisting as if they
    were alive,
Out from the patches of briers and blackberries,
From the memories of the bird that chanted to me,

1. September, in Quaker usage.

From your memories sad brother, from the fitful risings and fallings I
    heard,
From under that yellow half-moon late-risen and swollen as if with
    tears,   10
From those beginning notes of yearning and love there in the mist,
From the thousand responses of my heart never to cease,
From the myriad thence-aroused words,
From the word stronger and more delicious than any,
From such as now they start the scene revisiting,   15
As a flock, twittering, rising, or overhead passing,
Borne hither, ere all eludes me, hurriedly,
A man, yet by these tears a little boy again,
Throwing myself on the sand, confronting the waves,
I, chanter of pains and joys, uniter of here and hereafter,   20
Taking all hints to use them, but swiftly leaping beyond them,
A reminiscence sing.

Once Paumanok,[2]
When the lilac-scent was in the air and Fifth-month[3] grass was growing,
Up this seashore in some briers,   25
Two feathered guests from Alabama, two together,
And their nest, and four light-green eggs spotted with brown,
And every day the he-bird to and fro near at hand,
And every day the she-bird crouched on her nest, silent, with bright eyes,
And every day I, a curious boy, never too close, never disturbing them, 30
Cautiously peering, absorbing, translating.

Shine! shine! shine!
Pour down your warmth, great sun!
While we bask, we two together.

Two together!   35
Winds blow south, or winds blow north,
Day come white, or night come black,
Home, or rivers and mountains from home,
Singing all time, minding no time,
While we two keep together.   40

Till of a sudden,
Maybe killed, unknown to her mate,
One forenoon the she-bird crouched not on the nest,
Nor returned that afternoon, nor the next,
Nor ever appeared again.   45

And thenceforward all summer in the sound of the sea,
And at night under the full of the moon in calmer weather,
Over the hoarse surging of the sea,
Or flitting from brier to brier by day,
I saw, I heard at intervals the remaining one, the he-bird,   50
The solitary guest from Alabama.

Blow! blow! blow!
Blow up sea-winds along Paumanok's shore;
I wait and I wait till you blow my mate to me.

---

2. Pronounced *paw-mah'-nok.* The Native American name for Long Island, where Whitman grew up.
3. May.

Yes, when the stars glistened,   55
All night long on the prong of a moss-scalloped stake,
Down almost amid the slapping waves,
Sat the lone singer wonderful causing tears.

He called on his mate,
He poured forth the meanings which I of all men know.   60

Yes my brother I know,
The rest might not, but I have treasured every note,
For more than once dimly down to the beach gliding,
Silent, avoiding the moonbeams, blending myself with the shadows,
Recalling now the obscure shapes, the echoes, the sounds and sights
    after their sorts,   65
The white arms out in the breakers tirelessly tossing,
I, with bare feet, a child, the wind wafting my hair,
Listened long and long.

Listened to keep, to sing, now translating the notes,
Following you my brother.   70

Soothe! soothe! soothe!
Close on its wave soothes the wave behind,
And again another behind embracing and lapping, every one close,
But my love soothes not me, not me.

Low hangs the moon, it rose late,   75
It is lagging—O I think it is heavy with love, with love.

O madly the sea pushes upon the land,
With love, with love.

O night! do I not see my love fluttering out among the breakers?
What is that little black thing I see there in the white?   80

Loud! loud! loud!
Loud I call to you, my love!
High and clear I shoot my voice over the waves,
Surely you must know who is here, is here,
You must know who I am, my love.   85

Low-hanging moon!
What is that dusky spot in your brown yellow?
O it is the shape, the shape of my mate!
O moon do not keep her from me any longer.

Land! land! O land!   90
Whichever way I turn, O I think you could give me my mate back again
    if you only would,
For I am almost sure I see her dimly whichever way I look.

O rising stars!
Perhaps the one I want so much will rise, will rise with some of you.

O throat! O trembling throat!   95
Sound clearer through the atmosphere!
Pierce the woods, the earth,
Somewhere listening to catch you must be the one I want.

Shake out carols!
Solitary here, the night's carols!   100
Carols of lonesome love! death's carols!
Carols under that lagging, yellow, waning moon!
O under that moon where she droops almost down into the sea!
O reckless despairing carols.

But soft! sink low!   105
Soft! let me just murmur,
And do you wait a moment you husky-noised sea,
For somewhere I believe I heard my mate responding to me,
So faint, I must be still, be still to listen,
But not altogether still, for then she might not come immediately to me. 110

Hither my love!
Here I am! here!
With this just-sustained note I announce myself to you,
This gentle call is for you my love, for you.

Do not be decoyed elsewhere,   115
That is the whistle of the wind, it is not my voice,
That is the fluttering, the fluttering of the spray,
Those are the shadows of leaves.

O darkness! O in vain!
O I am very sick and sorrowful.   120

O brown halo in the sky near the moon, drooping upon the sea!
O troubled reflection in the sea!

O throat! O throbbing heart!
And I singing uselessly, uselessly all the night.

O past! O happy life! O songs of joy!   125
In the air, in the woods, over fields,
Loved! loved! loved! loved! loved!
But my mate no more, no more with me!
We two together no more.

The aria sinking,   130
All else continuing, the stars shining,
The winds blowing, the notes of the bird continuous echoing,
With angry moans the fierce old mother incessantly moaning,
On the sands of Paumanok's shore gray and rustling,
The yellow half-moon enlarged, sagging down, drooping, the face of
　　the sea almost touching,   135
The boy ecstatic, with his bare feet the waves, with his hair the atmo-
　　sphere dallying,
The love in the heart long pent, now loose, now at last tumultuously
　　bursting,
The aria's meaning, the ears, the soul, swiftly depositing,
The strange tears down the cheeks coursing,
The colloquy there, the trio, each uttering,   140
The undertone, the savage old mother incessantly crying,
To the boy's soul's questions sullenly timing, some drowned secret hissing,
To the outsetting bard.

Demon or bird! (said the boy's soul,)
Is it indeed toward your mate you sing? or is it really to me? 145
For I, that was a child, my tongue's use sleeping, now I have heard you,
Now in a moment I know what I am for, I awake,
And already a thousand singers, a thousand songs, clearer, louder and
   more sorrowful than yours,
A thousand warbling echoes have started to life within me, never to die.

O you singer solitary, singing by yourself, projecting me, 150
O solitary me listening, never more shall I cease perpetuating you,
Never more shall I escape, never more the reverberations,
Never more the cries of unsatisfied love be absent from me,
Never again leave me to be the peaceful child I was before what there
   in the night,
By the sea under the yellow and sagging moon, 155
The messenger there aroused, the fire, the sweet hell within,
The unknown want, the destiny of me.

O give me the clue! (it lurks in the night here somewhere,)
O if I am to have so much, let me have more!

A word then, (for I will conquer it,) 160
The word final, superior to all,
Subtle, sent up—what is it?—I listen;
Are you whispering it, and have been all the time, you sea-waves?
Is that it from your liquid rims and wet sands?

Whereto answering, the sea, 165
Delaying not, hurrying not,
Whispered me through the night, and very plainly before daybreak,
Lisped to me the low and delicious word death,
And again death, death, death, death,
Hissing melodious, neither like the bird nor like my aroused child's
   heart, 170
But edging near as privately for me rustling at my feet,
Creeping thence steadily up to my ears and laving me softly all over.
Death, death, death, death, death.

Which I do not forget,
But fuse the song of my dusky demon and brother, 175
That he sang to me in the moonlight on Paumanok's gray beach,
With the thousand responsive songs at random,
My own songs awaked from that hour,
And with them the key, the word up from the waves,
The word of the sweetest song and all songs, 180
That strong and delicious word which, creeping to my feet,
(Or like some old crone rocking the cradle, swathed in sweet garments,
   bending aside,)
The sea whispered me.

HERMAN MELVILLE
1819–1891

Herman Melville's *Billy Budd, Sailor* has always absorbed and puzzled its readers. Its story appears to deal with the eternal struggle of good and evil as manifested in mortal affairs, but critics disagree about who or what the author considered "good." It has something to say about the nature of justice and of the individual's relation to society—but what? Commentators have asserted that the book affirms Melville's final serene acceptance of life as it is but also that it documents his ironic defiance. We don't know whether Melville had completed the work before he died, or what he intended its title to be. The challenging experience of becoming implicated in the novel's dilemmas, of confronting its perplexing characters, of trying to follow its moral logic, may lead to no firm conclusions, but it can hardly fail to generate imaginative excitement.

Melville's father died when the boy was thirteen, leaving the family in near poverty. This fact helps to account for young Melville's varied moneymaking enterprises. He taught school, kept a store, and clerked in a bank; at the age of twenty, he for the first time shipped out as a sailor. Subsequent ventures at sea included several whaling expeditions. On one of these, he jumped ship in the South Pacific, living for a month on an island in the Marquesas; on another whaling trip, he participated in a mutiny. In 1847, Melville married Elizabeth Shaw. The couple settled in Pittsfield, Massachusetts, where Melville spent his time writing. He attempted in vain to get an appointment to a foreign consulate as a means of support; his lecture tours, also intended to make money, were unsuccessful. Finally, with his wife and four children, he moved to New York City, where in 1867 he obtained a position at the Custom House, which he held for the next eighteen years.

Melville's first novels, including *Typee* (1846) and *Omoo* (1847), seafaring adventure stories based on his own experience, won popular success. His masterpiece, *Moby-Dick* (1851), however, puzzled readers by its allegorical obscurity, its apparent shapelessness, and its highly elaborate language. Melville thought it his best work and felt disappointed and somewhat embittered by its critical failure. Although he continued writing and publishing short stories, novels, and poems, none of his later works achieved popularity.

Billy Budd, Sailor existed only in a heavily revised and at some points barely comprehensible manuscript at the time of the novelist's death. It was printed for the first time, in an imperfect version (*Billy Budd, Foretopman*), in a 1924 edition of Melville's works. In 1948, Frederick Barron Freeman re-edited the novel as *Billy Budd*; his text was supplemented in 1956 by emendations from the manuscript by Elizabeth Treeman. In 1962, *Billy Budd, Sailor,* source of the text printed here, was produced by Harrison Hayford and Merton M. Sealts Jr., who returned to the original manuscript, distinguished Elizabeth Melville's handwriting in it from her husband's, and generated a version substantially different from its predecessors. Although the nature of Melville's intention must remain finally impossible to ascertain, this careful effort to recapture what the novelist actually wrote at least has clear authority for every editorial choice.

The issues raised by the French Revolution, so vivid a part of literary consciousness at the beginning of the nineteenth century, once more provide a novelistic theme at the century's end—but with a new perspective. The events reported in *Billy Budd, Sailor* are said to occur in 1797. The narrator speaks of "those invading waters of novel opinion social, political, and otherwise, which carried away as in a torrent no few minds in those days." His metaphor suggests disapproval of the "novel opinion" that so greatly excited the early Romantics. Captain Vere, an important character whose name associates him with truth ("verity"), utterly resists the "invading waters." The only direct evidence, within the novel, of the actual effects of revolution is the reported mutinies, of which the narrator also appears to disapprove. Such evidence suggests a negative view of the French Revolution in its moral and political effects.

On the other hand, the narrator provides evidence of abundant cause for mutiny, particularly in the brutal practice of impressment, by which men were removed forcibly from nonnaval ships (or from their hometown streets, or their farms) and pressed into navy service, with no legal or practical recourse. When Billy Budd says good-bye to his ship, *Rights-of-Man*, he intends no irony, but others hear irony, as well they may: the concept of human rights is violated in every instance of impressment. Captain Vere's absolute devotion to legality and rule, his lack of openness to new possibility, arguably amount to extreme rigidity, even, possibly, to insanity. The narrator's wariness about "invading waters" may, like Billy's good-bye, be heard as ironic.

The conflicting claims of this series of statements, all supportable, need not be resolved; the important point is that by the end of the nineteenth century, everything that seemed true and exciting at the beginning had been called into question—not refuted, only made dubious. One can readily multiply examples from *Billy Budd, Sailor*. Billy, powerfully associated with images of innocence, resembles a child; a baby, even; a friendly dog; a big horse; Adam before the Fall. A hundred years earlier, Blake had suggested the perceptive power of the innocent, the child who points out that the emperor wears no clothes (or that chimney sweepers must rely on dreams and a black child on his mother's wishful stories to compensate for social injustice). Billy's innocence, on the other hand, has ambiguous implications. What does it mean to be an unfallen man in a fallen world? Billy can neither acquire from experience nor learn from others the knowledge that might make him capable of self-protective suspicion. His utter helplessness indicts his society but also raises troubling questions about the desirability of innocence.

Of course, one might argue that we in the twenty-first-century, "cynical" in the same sense as the old Dansker in the novel, are suspicious of such figures as Billy and Captain Vere in ways that our forebears would not be. Perhaps so; yet virtually all the questions suggested in the last two paragraphs appear more or less directly in the novelistic text. The narrator reflects about troubling aspects of Billy's innocence; the surgeon raises the possibility that Captain Vere is "unhinged." At many points, the narrative's symbolic language calls insistent attention to itself. It too, however, typically leaves one poised between interpretive alternatives. Here, for instance, is the description of Billy's hanging. "At the same moment it chanced that the vapory fleece hanging low in the East was shot through with a soft glory as of the fleece of the Lamb of God seen in mystical vision, and simultaneously therewith, watched by the wedged mass of upturned faces, Billy ascended; and, ascending, took the full rose of dawn." Are we to take seriously the implicit identification of Billy with Christ? Billy has willingly taken guilt upon himself, has forgiven his condemner, dies in his innocence, and "ascends." On the other hand, he ascends not to heaven but to the yard-arm, not in resurrection but in death. Is this a form of transcendence? Or is it irony again, at the expense of those who comfort themselves for social injustice by religious sentimentality?

Possibilities for interpretation depend, the novel tells us, on who formulates the story and who receives it. The book's subtitle, "An Inside Narrative," proves as ambiguous as everything else about it. This account, it suggests, will tell what really happened, as opposed to the newspaper report quoted late in the narrative that makes Billy into a suspicious foreigner who nefariously stabs the noble English Claggart. The storyteller returns intermittently to his insistence that he deals with facts; hence he draws back from the climactic scene between Billy and Captain Vere. Because no one else was present, the narrator can only speculate; in this instance, we will never know what really happened. The dialogue between the purser and the surgeon about the physical peculiarities of the hanging exemplifies the universal difficulty of interpretation. The storyteller is only one more interpreter, with his own biases. Educating us in mistrust by the nature of his story, he leaves us no certainties. The last word on Billy is presented in the sailor's ballad at the end, in which Billy's execution becomes a matter of pathos, not of moral speculation. Perhaps this story does not after all involve the conflict of good and evil; maybe it only provides a record of social contingency. This final possibility explains events as adequately—and as inadequately—as any other hypothesis.

In its questioning of the Romantic verities, revolution and innocence, as in its possibly ironic use of nature ("a soft glory as of the fleece of the Lamb of God"), Melville's novel reminds us how much can happen in a century. It may also remind us how insistently the nineteenth century foretells the twentieth. We are accustomed to feeling that we never get enough dependable information to make accurate judgments in matters of morality; we often distrust, if we think about it, the reliability of the "news" we are lavishly offered. *Billy Budd, Sailor* evokes a world that feels in many troubling respects like our own.

N. Arvin's *Herman Melville* (1950) is an excellent biographical study. Also valuable is L. Robertson-Lorant, *Melville: A Biography* (1996). Important critical works include L. Thompson, *Melville's Quarrel with God* (1952); W. Berthoff, *The Example of Melville* (1962); H. Parker, *Reading Billy Budd* (1990); C. S. Durer, *Herman Melville, Romantic and Prophet: A Study of His Romantic Sensibility and His Relationship to European Romantics* (1996), which provides valuable historical perspective; and B. Zimmerman, *Herman Melville: Stargazer* (1998). Useful collections of critical essays include R. A. Lee, ed., *Herman Melville: Reassessments* (1984), and R. Milder, ed., *Critical Essays on Melville's Billy Budd, Sailor* (1989). General guides are J. Bryant, ed., *A Companion to Melville Studies* (1986), and K. E. Kier, ed., *A Melville Encyclopedia: The Novels* (1990).

PRONOUNCING GLOSSARY

The following list uses common English syllables and stress accents to provide rough equivalents of selected words whose pronunciation may be unfamiliar to the general reader.

Aldebaran: *al-deb'-ar-an*

Anacharsis: *an-u-kahr'-sis*

Ananias: *a-nu-nai'-us*

Athée: *ah-tay'*

Bucephalus: *boo-sef'-u-lus*

Chiron: *kai'-ron*

Erebus: *ay-ray'-bus*

Hesperides: *hes-payr'-i-deez*

Montaigne: *mohn-ten'-yu*

Murat: *myoo-rah'*

Tecumseh: *tay-kum'-se*

Trafalgar: *trah-fahl'-gar*

Billy Budd, Sailor[1]

(An Inside Narrative)

1

In the time before steamships, or then more frequently than now, a stroller along the docks of any considerable seaport would occasionally have his attention arrested by a group of bronzed mariners, man-of-war's men or merchant sailors in holiday attire, ashore on liberty. In certain instances they would flank, or like a bodyguard quite surround, some superior figure of their own class, moving along with them like Aldebaran[2] among the lesser lights

---

1. Edited by Harrison Hayford and Merton M. Sealts Jr.   2. A star of the first magnitude in the constellation of Taurus, the Bull, frequently used in navigation.

of his constellation. That signal object was the 'Handsome Sailor' of the less prosaic time alike of the military and merchant navies. With no perceptible trace of the vainglorious about him, rather with the offhand unaffectedness of natural regality, he seemed to accept the spontaneous homage of his shipmates.

A somewhat remarkable instance recurs to me. In Liverpool, now half a century ago, I saw under the shadow of the great dingy street-wall of Prince's Dock (an obstruction long since removed) a common sailor so intensely black that he must needs have been a native African of the unadulterate blood of Ham[3]—a symmetric figure much above the average height. The two ends of a gay silk handkerchief thrown loose about the neck danced upon the displayed ebony of his chest, in his ears were big hoops of gold, and a Highland bonnet with a tartan band set off his shapely head. It was a hot noon in July; and his face, lustrous with perspiration, beamed with barbaric good humor. In jovial sallies right and left, his white teeth flashing into view, he rollicked along, the center of a company of his shipmates. These were made up of such an assortment of tribes and complexions as would have well fitted them to be marched up by Anacharsis Cloots[4] before the bar of the first French Assembly as Representatives of the Human Race. At each spontaneous tribute rendered by the wayfarers to this black pagod[5] of a fellow—the tribute of a pause and stare, and less frequently an exclamation—the motley retinue showed that they took that sort of pride in the evoker of it which the Assyrian priests doubtless showed for their grand sculptured Bull when the faithful prostrated themselves.

To return. If in some cases a bit of a nautical Murat[6] in setting forth his person ashore, the Handsome Sailor of the period in question evinced nothing of the dandified Billy-be-Dam, an amusing character all but extinct now, but occasionally to be encountered, and in a form yet more amusing than the original, at the tiller of the boats on the tempestuous Erie Canal or, more likely, vaporing in the groggeries[7] along the towpath. Invariably a proficient in his perilous calling, he was also more or less of a mighty boxer or wrestler. It was strength and beauty. Tales of his prowess were recited. Ashore he was the champion; afloat the spokesman; on every suitable occasion always foremost. Close-reefing topsails in a gale, there he was, astride the weather yardarm-end, foot in the Flemish horse[8] as stirrup, both hands tugging at the earing as at a bridle, in very much the attitude of young Alexander curbing the fiery Bucephalus.[9] A superb figure, tossed up as by the horns of Taurus against the thunderous sky, cheerily hallooing to the strenuous file along the spar.

The moral nature was seldom out of keeping with the physical make. Indeed, except as toned by the former, the comeliness and power, always attractive in masculine conjunction, hardly could have drawn the sort of

3. It was thought that Noah cursed his second son, Ham, for mocking him; that black skin resulted from the curse; and that all black people descended from Ham. In fact, according to Genesis 9.20–27 and 10.6–14, Noah cursed not Ham but Ham's son Canaan, while Ham's son Cush was black.   4. Jean-Baptiste du Val-de-Grâce, baron de Cloots, or Clootz (1755–1794), assembled a crowd of assorted nationalities and introduced them at the French National Assembly during the Revolution; he was popularly called "Anacharsis."   5. Meaning not only a pagoda but "an image of a deity, an idol" (Oxford English Dictionary). 6. Joachim Murat (1767–1815), marshal of France and king of Naples, Napoleon's brother-in-law, famous as a dandy.   7. Taverns. Vaporing: boasting or blustering.   8. A hazardous activity: sailors go out on a yardarm (a spar supporting a sail) by means of foot ropes, one of which is called the Flemish horse. 9. Alexander the Great's warhorse.

honest homage the Handsome Sailor in some examples received from his less gifted associates.

Such a cynosure, at least in aspect, and something such too in nature, though with important variations made apparent as the story proceeds, was welkin-eyed[1] Billy Budd—or Baby Budd, as more familiarly, under circumstances hereafter to be given, he at last came to be called—aged twenty-one, a foretopman[2] of the British fleet toward the close of the last decade of the eighteenth century. It was not very long prior to the time of the narration that follows that he had entered the King's service, having been impressed on the Narrow Seas from a homeward-bound English merchantman into a seventy-four[3] outward bound, H.M.S. *Bellipotent;* which ship, as was not unusual in those hurried days, having been obliged to put to sea short of her proper complement of men. Plump upon Billy at first sight in the gangway the boarding officer, Lieutenant Ratcliffe, pounced, even before the merchantman's crew was formally mustered on the quarter-deck for his deliberate inspection. And him only he elected. For whether it was because the other men when ranged before him showed to ill advantage after Billy, or whether he had some scruples in view of the merchantman's being rather short-handed, however it might be, the officer contented himself with his first spontaneous choice. To the surprise of the ship's company, though much to the lieutenant's satisfaction, Billy made no demur. But, indeed, any demur would have been as idle as the protest of a goldfinch popped into a cage.

Noting this uncomplaining acquiescence, all but cheerful, one might say, the shipmaster turned a surprised glance of silent reproach at the sailor. The shipmaster was one of those worthy mortals found in every vocation, even the humbler ones—the sort of person whom everybody agrees in calling 'a respectable man.' And—nor so strange to report as it may appear to be—though a ploughman of the troubled waters, lifelong contending with the intractable elements, there was nothing this honest soul at heart loved better than simple peace and quiet. For the rest, he was fifty or thereabouts, a little inclined to corpulence, a prepossessing face, unwhiskered, and of an agreeable color—a rather full face, humanely intelligent in expression. On a fair day with a fair wind and all going well, a certain musical chime in his voice seemed to be the veritable unobstructed outcome of the innermost man. He had much prudence, much conscientiousness, and there were occasions when these virtues were the cause of overmuch disquietude in him. On a passage, so long as his craft was in any proximity to land, no sleep for Captain Graveling. He took to heart those serious responsibilities not so heavily borne by some shipmasters.

Now while Billy Budd was down in the forecastle getting his kit together, the *Bellipotent's* lieutenant, burly and bluff, nowise disconcerted by Captain Graveling's omitting to proffer the customary hospitalities on an occasion so unwelcome to him, an omission simply caused by preoccupation of thought, unceremoniously invited himself into the cabin, and also to a flask from the spirit locker, a receptacle which his experienced eye instantly discovered. In fact he was one of those sea dogs in whom all the hardship and peril of naval

1. Blue-eyed (*welkin:* sky).   2. Junior to a maintopman like Jack Chase, to whom the book is dedicated. 3. A third-rate ship of the line, equivalent to a light cruiser today. The designation refers to the number of guns the ship carried. *Narrow Seas:* the English Channel and the waters between England and Ireland.

life in the great prolonged wars of his time never impaired the natural instinct for sensuous enjoyment. His duty he always faithfully did; but duty is sometimes a dry obligation, and he was for irrigating its aridity, whensoever possible, with a fertilizing decoction of strong waters. For the cabin's proprietor there was nothing left but to play the part of the enforced host with whatever grace and alacrity were practicable. As necessary adjuncts to the flask, he silently placed tumbler and water jug before the irrepressible guest. But excusing himself from partaking just then, he dismally watched the unembarrassed officer deliberately diluting his grog[4] a little, then tossing it off in three swallows, pushing the empty tumbler away, yet not so far as to be beyond easy reach, at the same time settling himself in his seat and smacking his lips with high satisfaction, looking straight at the host.

These proceedings over, the master broke the silence; and there lurked a rueful reproach in the tone of his voice: 'Lieutenant, you are going to take my best man from me, the jewel of 'em.'

'Yes, I know,' rejoined the other, immediately drawing back the tumbler preliminary to a replenishing. 'Yes, I know. Sorry.'

'Beg pardon, but you don't understand, Lieutenant. See here, now. Before I shipped that young fellow, my forecastle was a rat-pit of quarrels. It was black times, I tell you, aboard the *Rights* here. I was worried to that degree my pipe had no comfort for me. But Billy came; and it was like a Catholic priest striking peace in an Irish shindy.[5] Not that he preached to them or said or did anything in particular; but a virtue went out of him, sugaring the sour ones. They took to him like hornets to treacle; all but the buffer[6] of the gang, the big shaggy chap with the fire-red whiskers. He indeed, out of envy, perhaps, of the newcomer, and thinking such a "sweet and pleasant fellow," as he mockingly designated him to the others, could hardly have the spirit of a gamecock, must needs bestir himself in trying to get up an ugly row with him. Billy forebore with him and reasoned with him in a pleasant way—he is something like myself, Lieutenant, to whom aught like a quarrel is hateful—but nothing served. So, in the second dogwatch[7] one day, the Red Whiskers in presence of the others, under pretense of showing Billy just whence a sirloin steak was cut—for the fellow had once been a butcher—insultingly gave him a dig under the ribs. Quick as lightning Billy let fly his arm. I dare say he never meant to do quite so much as he did, but anyhow he gave the burly fool a terrible drubbing. It took about half a minute, I should think. And lord bless you, the lubber was astonished at the celerity. And will you believe it, Lieutenant, the Red Whiskers now really loves Billy—loves him, or is the biggest hypocrite that ever I heard of. But they all love him. Some of 'em do his washing, darn his old trousers for him; the carpenter is at odd times making a pretty little chest of drawers for him. Anybody will do anything for Billy Budd; and it's the happy family here. But now, Lieutenant, if that young fellow goes—I know how it will be aboard the *Rights*. Not again very soon shall I, coming up from dinner, lean over the capstan smoking a quiet pipe—no, not very soon again, I think. Ay, Lieutenant, you are going to take away the jewel of 'em; you are going to take away my peacemaker!' And with that the good soul had really some ado in checking a rising sob.

4. A mixture of rum and water.   5. Free-for-all fight.   6. Big fellow.   7. From 6:00 to 8:00 P.M.

'Well,' said the lieutenant, who had listened with amused interest to all this and now was waxing merry with his tipple: 'well, blessed are the peace-makers, especially the fighting peacemakers. And such are the seventy-four beauties some of which you see poking their noses out of the portholes of yonder warship lying to for me,' pointing through the cabin window at the *Bellipotent.* 'But courage! Don't look so downhearted, man. Why, I pledge you in advance the royal approbation. Rest assured that His Majesty will be delighted to know that in a time when his hardtack is not sought for by sailors with such avidity as should be, a time also when some shipmasters privily resent the borrowing from them a tar[8] or two for the service; His Majesty, I say, will be delighted to learn that *one* shipmaster at least cheerfully surrenders to the King the flower of his flock, a sailor who with equal loyalty makes no dissent.—But where's my beauty? Ah,' looking through the cabin's open door, 'here he comes; and, by Jove, lugging along his chest—Apollo with his portmanteau!—My man,' stepping out to him, 'you can't take that big box aboard a warship. The boxes there are mostly shot boxes. Put your duds in a bag, lad. Boot and saddle for the cavalryman, bag and hammock for the man-of-war's man.'

The transfer from chest to bag was made. And, after seeing his man into the cutter and then following him down, the lieutenant pushed off from the *Rights-of-Man.* That was the merchant ship's name, though by her master and crew abbreviated in sailor fashion into the *Rights.* The hardheaded Dundee owner was a staunch admirer of Thomas Paine,[9] whose book in rejoinder to Burke's arraignment of the French Revolution had then been published for some time and had gone everywhere. In christening his vessel after the title of Paine's volume the man of Dundee was something like his contemporary ship-owner, Stephen Girard[1] of Philadelphia, whose sympathies, alike with his native land and its liberal philosophers, he evinced by naming his ships after Voltaire, Diderot, and so forth.

But now, when the boat swept under the merchantman's stern, and officer and oarsmen were noting—some bitterly and others with a grin—the name emblazoned there; just then it was that the new recruit jumped up from the bow where the coxswain had directed him to sit, and waving hat to his silent shipmates sorrowfully looking over at him from the taffrail, bade the lads a genial good-bye. Then, making a salutation as to the ship herself, 'And good-bye to you too, old *Rights-of-Man.*'

'Down, sir!' roared the lieutenant, instantly assuming all the rigor of his rank, though with difficulty repressing a smile.

To be sure, Billy's action was a terrible breach of naval decorum. But in that decorum he had never been instructed; in consideration of which the lieutenant would hardly have been so energetic in reproof but for the concluding farewell to the ship. This he rather took as meant to convey a covert sally on the new recruit's part, a sly slur at impressment in general, and that of himself in especial. And yet, more likely, if satire it was in effect, it was hardly so by intention, for Billy, though happily endowed with the gaiety of high health, youth, and a free heart, was yet by no means of a satirical turn.

---

8. Sailor.   9. American Revolutionary patriot (1737–1809), born in England, published *The Rights of Man* in 1791 as a response to Edmund Burke's *Reflections on the Revolution in France* (1790). Dundee is a seaport in Scotland.   1. Merchant, banker, and philanthropist (1750–1831), a native of France who emigrated at the age of twenty-seven.

The will to it and the sinister dexterity were alike wanting. To deal in double meanings and insinuations of any sort was quite foreign to his nature.

As to his enforced enlistment, that he seemed to take pretty much as he was wont to take any vicissitude of weather. Like the animals, though no philosopher, he was, without knowing it, practically a fatalist. And it may be that he rather liked this adventurous turn in his affairs, which promised an opening into novel scenes and martial excitements.

Aboard the *Bellipotent* our merchant sailor was forthwith rated as an able seaman and assigned to the starboard watch of the foretop. He was soon at home in the service, not at all disliked for his unpretentious good looks and a sort of genial happy-go-lucky air. No merrier man in his mess: in marked contrast to certain other individuals included like himself among the impressed portion of the ship's company; for these when not actively employed were sometimes, and more particularly in the last dogwatch when the drawing near of twilight induced revery, apt to fall into a saddish mood which in some partook of sullenness. But they were not so young as our foretopman, and no few of them must have known a hearth of some sort, others may have had wives and children left, too probably, in uncertain circumstances, and hardly any but must have had acknowledged kith and kin, while for Billy, as will shortly be seen, his entire family was practically invested in himself.

2

Though our new-made foretopman was well received in the top and on the gun decks, hardly here was he that cynosure he had previously been among those minor ship's companies of the merchant marine, with which companies only had he hitherto consorted.

He was young; and despite his all but fully developed frame, in aspect looked even younger than he really was, owing to a lingering adolescent expression in the as yet smooth face all but feminine in purity of natural complexion but where, thanks to his seagoing, the lily was quite suppressed and the rose had some ado visibly to flush through the tan.

To one essentially such a novice in the complexities of factitious life, the abrupt transition from his former and simpler sphere to the ampler and more knowing world of a great warship; this might well have abashed him had there been any conceit or vanity in his composition. Among her miscellaneous multitude, the *Bellipotent* mustered several individuals who however inferior in grade were of no common natural stamp, sailors more signally susceptive of that air which continuous martial discipline and repeated presence in battle can in some degree impart even to the average man. As the Handsome Sailor, Billy Budd's position aboard the seventy-four was something analogous to that of a rustic beauty transplanted from the provinces and brought into competition with the highborn dames of the court. But this change of circumstances he scarce noted. As little did he observe that something about him provoked an ambiguous smile in one or two harder faces among the bluejackets. Nor less unaware was he of the peculiar favorable effect his person and demeanor had upon the more intelligent gentlemen of the quarter-deck. Nor could this well have been otherwise. Cast in a mold peculiar to the finest physical examples of those Englishmen in whom the

Saxon strain would seem not at all to partake of any Norman or other admixture, he showed in face that humane look of reposeful good nature which the Greek sculptor in some instances gave to his heroic strong man, Hercules. But this again was subtly modified by another and pervasive quality. The ear, small and shapely, the arch of the foot, the curve in mouth and nostril, even the indurated hand dyed to the orange-tawny of the toucan's bill, a hand telling alike of the halyards and tar bucket; but, above all, something in the mobile expression, and every chance attitude and movement, something suggestive of a mother eminently favored by Love and the Graces; all this strangely indicated a lineage in direct contradiction to his lot. The mysteriousness here became less mysterious through a matter of fact elicited when Billy at the capstan was being formally mustered into the service. Asked by the officer, a small, brisk little gentleman as it chanced, among other questions, his place of birth, he replied, 'Please, sir, I don't know.'

'Don't know where you were born? Who was your father?'

'God knows, sir.'

Struck by the straightforward simplicity of these replies, the officer next asked, 'Do you know anything about your beginning?'

'No, sir. But I have heard that I was found in a pretty silk-lined basket hanging one morning from the knocker of a good man's door in Bristol.'

'Found, say you? Well,' throwing back his head and looking up and down the new recruit; 'well, it turns out to have been a pretty good find. Hope they'll find some more like you, my man; the fleet sadly needs them.'

Yes, Billy Budd was a foundling, a presumable by-blow, and, evidently, no ignoble one. Noble descent was as evident in him as in a blood horse.

For the rest, with little or no sharpness of faculty or any trace of the wisdom of the serpent, nor yet quite a dove, he possessed that kind and degree of intelligence going along with the unconventional rectitude of a sound human creature, one to whom not yet has been proffered the questionable apple of knowledge. He was illiterate; he could not read, but he could sing, and like the illiterate nightingale was sometimes the composer of his own song.

Of self-consciousness he seemed to have little or none, or about as much as we may reasonably impute to a dog of Saint Bernard's breed.

Habitually living with the elements and knowing little more of the land than as a beach, or, rather, that portion of the terraqueous globe providentially set apart for dance-houses, doxies, and tapsters, in short what sailors call a 'fiddler's green,'[2] his simple nature remained unsophisticated by those moral obliquities which are not in every case incompatible with that manufacturable thing known as respectability. But are sailors, frequenters of fiddler's greens, without vices? No; but less often than with landsmen do their vices, so called, partake of crookedness of heart, seeming less to proceed from viciousness than exuberance of vitality after long constraint: frank manifestations in accordance with natural law. By his original constitution aided by the co-operating influences of his lot, Billy in many respects was little more than a sort of upright barbarian, much such perhaps as Adam presumably might have been ere the urbane Serpent wriggled himself into his company.

2. A sailor's utopia.

And here be it submitted that apparently going to corroborate the doctrine of man's Fall, a doctrine now popularly ignored, it is observable that where certain virtues pristine and unadulterate peculiarly characterize anybody in the external uniform of civilization, they will upon scrutiny seem not to be derived from custom or convention, but rather to be out of keeping with these, as if indeed exceptionally transmitted from a period prior to Cain's city[3] and citified man. The character marked by such qualities has to an unvitiated taste an untampered-with flavor like that of berries, while the man thoroughly civilized, even in a fair specimen of the breed, has to the same moral palate a questionable smack as of a compounded wine. To any stray inheritor of these primitive qualities found, like Caspar Hauser,[4] wandering dazed in any Christian capital of our time, the good-natured poet's famous invocation, near two thousand years ago, of the good rustic out of his latitude in the Rome of the Caesars, still appropriately holds:

> Honest and poor, faithful in word and thought,
> What hath thee, Fabian, to the city brought?[5]

Though our Handsome Sailor had as much of masculine beauty as one can expect anywhere to see; nevertheless, like the beautiful woman in one of Hawthorne's minor tales,[6] there was just one thing amiss in him. No visible blemish indeed, as with the lady; no, but an occasional liability to a vocal defect. Though in the hour of elemental uproar or peril he was everything that a sailor should be, yet under sudden provocation of strong heart-feeling his voice, otherwise singularly musical, as if expressive of the harmony within, was apt to develop an organic hesitancy, in fact more or less of a stutter or even worse. In this particular Billy was a striking instance that the arch interferer, the envious marplot of Eden, still has more or less to do with every human consignment to this planet of Earth. In every case, one way or another he is sure to slip in his little card, as much as to remind us—I too have a hand here.

The avowal of such an imperfection in the Handsome Sailor should be evidence not alone that he is not presented as a conventional hero, but also that the story in which he is the main figure is no romance.

3

At the time of Billy Budd's arbitrary enlistment into the *Bellipotent* that ship was on her way to join the Mediterranean fleet. No long time elapsed before the junction was effected. As one of that fleet the seventy-four participated in its movements, though at times on account of her superior sailing qualities, in the absence of frigates, dispatched on separate duty as a scout and at times on less temporary service. But with all this the story has little concernment, restricted as it is to the inner life of one particular ship and the career of an individual sailor.

It was the summer of 1797. In the April of that year had occurred the commotion at Spithead followed in May by a second and yet more serious

---

3. I.e., in the time of the Garden of Eden. Cain "builded a city" in Genesis 4.16–17.   4. A German foundling (1812?–1833) who claimed to have been brought up in a primitive wilderness.   5. Martial's *Epigrams* 1.4.1–2, from Cowley's translation in the Bohn edition.   6. *The Birthmark*, in which the *blemish* is on the lady's cheek.

outbreak in the fleet at the Nore. The latter is known, and without exaggeration in the epithet, as 'the Great Mutiny.' It was indeed a demonstration more menacing to England than the contemporary manifestoes and conquering and proselyting armies of the French Directory.[7] To the British Empire the Nore Mutiny was what a strike in the fire brigade would be to London threatened by general arson. In a crisis when the kingdom might well have anticipated the famous signal that some years later published along the naval line of battle what it was that upon occasion England expected of Englishmen;[8] *that* was the time when at the mastheads of the three-deckers and seventy-fours moored in her own roadstead—a fleet the right arm of a Power then all but the sole free conservative one of the Old World—the bluejackets, to be numbered by thousands, ran up with huzzas the British colors with the union and cross[9] wiped out; by that cancellation transmuting the flag of founded law and freedom defined, into the enemy's red meteor of unbridled and unbounded revolt. Reasonable discontent growing out of practical grievances in the fleet had been ignited into irrational combustion as by live cinders blown across the Channel from France in flames.

The event converted into irony for a time those spirited strains of Dibdin[1]—as a song-writer no mean auxiliary to the English government at that European conjuncture—strains celebrating, among other things, the patriotic devotion of the British tar: 'And as for my life,'tis the King's!'

Such an episode in the Island's grand naval story her naval historians naturally abridge, one of them (William James)[2] candidly acknowledging that fain would he pass it over did not 'impartiality forbid fastidiousness.' And yet his mention is less a narration than a reference, having to do hardly at all with details. Nor are these readily to be found in the libraries. Like some other events in every age befalling states everywhere, including America, the Great Mutiny was of such character that national pride along with views of policy would fain shade it off into the historical background. Such events cannot be ignored, but there is a considerate way of historically treating them. If a well-constituted individual refrains from blazoning aught amiss or calamitous in his family, a nation in the like circumstance may without reproach be equally discreet.

Though after parleyings between government and the ringleaders, and concessions by the former as to some glaring abuses, the first uprising—that at Spithead—with difficulty was put down, or matters for the time pacified; yet at the Nore the unforeseen renewal of insurrection on a yet larger scale, and emphasized in the conferences that ensued by demands deemed by the authorities not only inadmissible but aggressively insolent, indicated—if the Red Flag did not sufficiently do so—what was the spirit animating the men. Final suppression, however, there was; but only made possible perhaps by the unswerving loyalty of the marine corps and a voluntary resumption of loyalty among influential sections of the crews.

To some extent the Nore Mutiny may be regarded as analogous to the distempering irruption of contagious fever in a frame constitutionally sound, and which anon throws it off.

7. The five directors who governed France from 1795 to 1799, during the Revolution.   8. "England expects every man to do his duty!": Lord Nelson, before the battle at Trafalgar, October 21, 1805.   9. The British Union Jack, or national flag, carries the crosses of Saint Andrew, Saint George, and Saint Patrick, patron saints of Scotland, England, and Ireland.   1. Charles Dibdin (1745–1814), English dramatist, chiefly remembered for his sea chanteys. The ballad quoted is "Poor Jack."   2. *The Naval History of Great Britain* (1860). Melville mistakenly wrote "G. P. R. James."

At all events, of these thousands of mutineers were some of the tars who not so very long afterwards—whether wholly prompted thereto by patriotism, or pugnacious instinct, or by both—helped to win a coronet for Nelson at the Nile, and the naval crown of crowns for him at Trafalgar.[3] To the mutineers, those battles and especially Trafalgar were a plenary absolution and a grand one. For all that goes to make up scenic naval display and heroic magnificance in arms, those battles, especially Trafalgar, stand unmatched in human annals.

4

In this matter of writing, resolve as one may to keep to the main road, some bypaths have an enticement not readily to be withstood. I am going to err into such a bypath. If the reader will keep me company I shall be glad. At the least, we can promise ourselves that pleasure which is wickedly said to be in sinning, for a literary sin the divergence will be.

Very likely it is no new remark that the inventions of our time have at last brought about a change in sea warfare in degree corresponding to the revolution in all warfare effected by the original introduction from China into Europe of gunpowder. The first European firearm, a clumsy contrivance, was, as is well known, scouted[4] by no few of the knights as a base implement, good enough peradventure for weavers too craven to stand up crossing steel with steel in frank fight. But as ashore knightly valor, though shorn of its blazonry, did not cease with the knights, neither on the sea—though nowadays in encounters there a certain kind of displayed gallantry be fallen out of date as hardly applicable under changed circumstances—did the nobler qualities of such naval magnates as Don John of Austria, Doria, Van Tromp, Jean Bart, the long line of British admirals, and the American Decaturs of 1812 become obsolete with their wooden walls.[5]

Nevertheless, to anybody who can hold the Present at its worth without being inappreciative of the Past, it may be forgiven, if to such an one the solitary old hulk at Portsmouth, Nelson's *Victory*, seems to float there, not alone as the decaying monument of a fame incorruptible, but also as a poetic reproach, softened by its picturesqueness, to the *Monitors*[6] and yet mightier hulls of the European ironclads. And this not altogether because such craft are unsightly, unavoidably lacking the symmetry and grand lines of the old battleships, but equally for other reasons.

There are some, perhaps, who while not altogether inaccessible to that poetic reproach just alluded to, may yet on behalf of the new order be disposed to parry it; and this to the extent of iconoclasm, if need be. For example, prompted by the sight of the star inserted in the *Victory's* quarter-deck designating the spot where the Great Sailor fell, these martial utilitarians may suggest considerations implying that Nelson's ornate publication of his person in battle was not only unnecessary, but not military, nay, savored of

3. Nelson was made a baronet for his victory over the French at Aboukir in 1798; his 1805 victory at Trafalgar is considered one of the greatest in naval history.   4. Scoffed at.   5. A reference to the wooden ships made obsolete by ironclads. Don Juan of Austria (1547–1578) commanded a fleet against the Turks at Lepanto in 1571, the last major sea battle in which oared ships predominated. Andrea Doria (1468–1560) liberated Genoa from the French. Maarten Van Tromp (1596–1653), Dutch admiral, fought successfully against the English. Jean Bart (1651?–1702), a French captain, battled the Dutch. Stephen Decatur (1779–1820) won victories over the Barbary Coast pirates at Tripoli and over the British in the War of 1812.   6. The *Monitor* was an ironclad launched in 1862 to fight the Confederate *Virginia* (formerly the frigate *Merrimack*) in a battle effectively ending the era of wooden ships.

foolhardiness and vanity. They may add, too, that at Trafalgar it was in effect nothing less than a challenge to death; and death came; and that but for his bravado the victorious admiral might possibly have survived the battle, and so, instead of having his sagacious dying injunctions overruled by his immediate successor in command, he himself when the contest was decided might have brought his shattered fleet to anchor, a proceeding which might have averted the deplorable loss of life by shipwreck in the elemental tempest that followed the martial one.

Well, should we set aside the more than disputable point whether for various reasons it was possible to anchor the fleet, then plausibly enough the Benthamites[7] of war may urge the above. But the *might-have-been* is but boggy ground to build on. And, certainly, in foresight as to the larger issue of an encounter, and anxious preparations for it—buoying the deadly way and mapping it out, as at Copenhagen[8]—few commanders have been so painstakingly circumspect as this same reckless declarer of his person in fight.

Personal prudence, even when dictated by quite other than selfish considerations, surely is no special virtue in a military man; while an excessive love of glory, impassioning a less burning impulse, the honest sense of duty, is the first. If the name *Wellington* is not so much of a trumpet to the blood as the simpler name *Nelson,* the reason for this may perhaps be inferred from the above. Alfred in his funeral ode on the victory of Waterloo ventures not to call him the greatest soldier of all time, though in the same ode he invokes Nelson as 'the greatest sailor since our world began.'[9]

At Trafalgar Nelson on the brink of opening the fight sat down and wrote his last brief will and testament. If under the presentiment of the most magnificent of all victories to be crowned by his own glorious death, a sort of priestly motive led him to dress his person in the jewelled vouchers of his own shining deeds; if thus to have adorned himself for the altar and the sacrifice were indeed vainglory, then affectation and fustian is each more heroic line in the great epics and dramas, since in such lines the poet but embodies in verse those exaltations of sentiment that a nature like Nelson, the opportunity being given, vitalizes into acts.

5

Yes, the outbreak at the Nore was put down. But not every grievance was redressed. If the contractors, for example, were no longer permitted to ply some practices peculiar to their tribe everywhere, such as providing shoddy cloth, rations not sound, or false in the measure; not the less impressment, for one thing, went on. By custom sanctioned for centuries, and judicially maintained by a Lord Chancellor as late as Mansfield,[1] that mode of manning the fleet, a mode now fallen into a sort of abeyance but never formally renounced, it was not practicable to give up in those years. Its abrogation would have crippled the indispensable fleet, one wholly under canvas, no steam power, its innumerable sails and thousands of cannon, everything in

---

7. Utilitarian thinkers and followers of Jeremy Bentham (1748–1832), who believed in the greatest good for the greatest number.   8. Where Nelson's careful planning defeated the Danish on April 2, 1801.
9. The quotation comes from Tennyson's *Ode on the Death of the Duke of Wellington* (1852) 6.7.
1. William Murray, Baron Mansfield (1705–1793), lord chief justice of Great Britain from 1756 to 1788.

short, worked by muscle alone; a fleet the more insatiate in demand for men, because then multiplying its ships of all grades against contingencies present and to come of the convulsed Continent.

Discontent foreran the Two Mutinies, and more or less it lurkingly survived them. Hence it was not unreasonable to apprehend some return of trouble sporadic or general. One instance of such apprehensions: In the same year with this story, Nelson, then Rear Admiral Sir Horatio, being with the fleet off the Spanish coast, was directed by the admiral in command to shift his pennant from the *Captain* to the *Theseus*; and for this reason: that the latter ship having newly arrived on the station from home, where it had taken part in the Great Mutiny, danger was apprehended from the temper of the men; and it was thought that an officer like Nelson was the one, not indeed to terrorize the crew into base subjection, but to win them, by force of his mere presence and heroic personality, back to an allegiance if not as enthusiastic as his own yet as true.

So it was that for a time, on more than one quarter-deck, anxiety did exist. At sea, precautionary vigilance was strained against relapse. At short notice an engagement might come on. When it did, the lieutenants assigned to batteries felt it incumbent on them, in some instances, to stand with drawn swords behind the men working the guns.

6

But on board the seventy-four in which Billy now swung his hammock, very little in the manner of the men and nothing obvious in the demeanor of the officers would have suggested to an ordinary observer that the Great Mutiny was a recent event. In their general bearing and conduct the commissioned officers of a warship naturally take their tone from the commander, that is if he have that ascendancy of character that ought to be his.

Captain the Honorable Edward Fairfax Vere, to give his full title, was a bachelor of forty or thereabouts, a sailor of distinction even in a time prolific of renowned seamen. Though allied to the higher nobility, his advancement had not been altogether owing to influences connected with that circumstance. He had seen much service, been in various engagements, always acquitting himself as an officer mindful of the welfare of his men, but never tolerating an infraction of discipline; thoroughly versed in the science of his profession, and intrepid to the verge of temerity, though never injudiciously so. For his gallantry in the West Indian waters as flag lieutenant under Rodney in that admiral's crowning victory over De Grasse,[2] he was made a post captain.

Ashore, in the garb of a civilian, scarce anyone would have taken him for a sailor, more especially that he never garnished unprofessional talk with nautical terms, and grave in his bearing, evinced little appreciation of mere humor. It was not out of keeping with these traits that on a passage when nothing demanded his paramount action, he was the most undemonstrative of men. Any landsman observing this gentleman not conspicuous by his stature and wearing no pronounced insignia, emerging from his cabin to the open deck, and noting the silent deference of the officers retiring to leeward,

---

2. The British admiral George Brydges, Baron Rodney (1719–1792), defeated the French admiral de Grasse off Dominica, in the Leeward Islands, in 1782.

might have taken him for the King's guest, a civilian aboard the King's ship, some highly honorable discreet envoy on his way to an important post. But in fact this unobtrusiveness of demeanor may have proceeded from a certain unaffected modesty of manhood sometimes accompanying a resolute nature, a modesty evinced at all times not calling for pronounced action, which shown in any rank of life suggests a virtue aristocratic in kind. As with some others engaged in various departments of the world's more heroic activities, Captain Vere though practical enough upon occasion would at times betray a certain dreaminess of mood. Standing alone on the weather side of the quarter-deck, one hand holding by the rigging, he would absently gaze off at the blank sea. At the presentation to him then of some minor matter interrupting the current of his thoughts, he would show more or less irascibility; but instantly he would control it.

In the navy he was popularly known by the appellation 'Starry Vere.' How such a designation happened to fall upon one who whatever his sterling qualities was without any brilliant ones, was in this wise: A favorite kinsman, Lord Denton, a freehearted fellow, had been the first to meet and congratulate him upon his return to England from his West Indian cruise; and but the day previous turning over a copy of Andrew Marvell's[3] poems had lighted, not for the first time, however, upon the lines entitled 'Appleton House,' the name of one of the seats of their common ancestor, a hero in the German wars of the seventeenth century, in which poem occur the lines:

> This 'tis to have been from the first
> In a domestic heaven nursed,
> Under the discipline severe
> Of Fairfax and the starry Vere.

And so, upon embracing his cousin fresh from Rodney's great victory wherein he had played so gallant a part, brimming over with just family pride in the sailor of their house, he exuberantly exclaimed, 'Give ye joy, Ed; give ye joy, my starry Vere!' This got currency, and the novel prefix serving in familiar parlance readily to distinguish the *Bellipotent*'s captain from another Vere his senior, a distant relative, an officer of like rank in the navy, it remained permanently attached to the surname.

7

In view of the part that the commander of the *Bellipotent* plays in scenes shortly to follow, it may be well to fill out that sketch of him outlined in the previous chapter.

Aside from his qualities as a sea officer Captain Vere was an exceptional character. Unlike no few of England's renowned sailors, long and arduous service with signal devotion to it had not resulted in absorbing and *salting* the entire man. He had a marked leaning toward everything intellectual. He loved books, never going to sea without a newly replenished library, compact but of the best. The isolated leisure, in some cases so wearisome, falling at intervals to commanders even during a war cruise, never was tedious to Captain Vere. With nothing of that literary taste which less heeds the thing conveyed than the vehicle, his bias was toward those books to which every

3. English lyric poet (1621–1678).

serious mind of superior order occupying any active post of authority in the world naturally inclines: books treating of actual men and events no matter of what era—history, biography, and unconventional writers like Montaigne,[4] who, free from cant and convention, honestly and in the spirit of common sense philosophize upon realities. In this line of reading he found confirmation of his own more reserved thoughts—confirmation which he had vainly sought in social converse, so that as touching most fundamental topics, there had got to be established in him some positive convictions which he forefelt would abide in him essentially unmodified so long as his intelligent part remained unimpaired. In view of the troubled period in which his lot was cast, this was well for him. His settled convictions were as a dike against those invading waters of novel opinion social, political, and otherwise, which carried away as in a torrent no few minds in those days, minds by nature not inferior to his own. While other members of that aristocracy to which by birth he belonged were incensed at the innovators mainly because their theories were inimical to the privileged classes, Captain Vere disinterestedly opposed them not alone because they seemed to him insusceptible of embodiment in lasting institutions, but at war with the peace of the world and the true welfare of mankind.

With minds less stored than his and less earnest, some officers of his rank, with whom at times he would necessarily consort, found him lacking in the companionable quality, a dry and bookish gentleman, as they deemed. Upon any chance withdrawal from their company one would be apt to say to another something like this: 'Vere is a noble fellow, Starry Vere. 'Spite the gazettes,[5] Sir Horatio' (meaning him who became Lord Nelson) 'is at bottom scarce a better seaman or fighter. But between you and me now, don't you think there is a queer streak of the pedantic running through him? Yes, like the King's yarn in a coil of navy rope?'[6]

Some apparent ground there was for this sort of confidential criticism; since not only did the captain's discourse never fall into the jocosely familiar, but in illustrating of any point touching the stirring personages and events of the time he would be as apt to cite some historic character or incident of antiquity as he would be to cite from the moderns. He seemed unmindful of the circumstance that to his bluff company such remote allusions, however pertinent they might really be, were altogether alien to men whose reading was mainly confined to the journals. But considerateness in such matters is not easy to natures constituted like Captain Vere's. Their honesty prescribes to them directness, sometimes far-reaching like that of a migratory fowl that in its flight never heeds when it crosses a frontier.

8

The lieutenants and other commissioned gentlemen forming Captain Vere's staff it is not necessary here to particularize, nor needs it to make any mention of any of the warrant officers. But among the petty officers[7] was one who, having much to do with the story, may as well be forthwith intro-

---

4. Michel Eyquem de Montaigne (1533–1592), French essayist.   5. Official gazettes that printed accounts of naval careers and honors.   6. A thread was worked into hempen cable to mark it as belonging to the Royal Navy.   7. Enlisted men corresponding in rank to noncommissioned officers in the army. *Warrant officers*: ranked above petty and just below commissioned officers.

duced. His portrait I essay, but shall never hit it. This was John Claggart, the master-at-arms. But that sea title may to landsmen seem somewhat equivocal. Originally, doubtless, that petty officer's function was the instruction of the men in the use of arms, sword or cutlass. But very long ago, owing to the advance in gunnery making hand-to-hand encounters less frequent and giving to niter and sulphur the pre-eminence over steel, that function ceased; the master-at-arms of a great warship becoming a sort of chief of police charged among other matters with the duty of preserving order on the populous lower gun decks.

Claggart was a man about five-and-thirty, somewhat spare and tall, yet of no ill figure upon the whole. His hand was too small and shapely to have been accustomed to hard toil. The face was a notable one, the features all except the chin cleanly cut as those on a Greek medallion; yet the chin, beardless as Tecumseh's,[8] had something of strange protuberant broadness in its make that recalled the prints of the Reverend Dr Titus Oates,[9] the historic deponent with the clerical drawl in the time of Charles II and the fraud of the alleged Popish Plot. It served Claggart in his office that his eye could cast a tutoring glance. His brow was of the sort phrenologically associated with more than average intellect; silken jet curls partly clustering over it, making a foil to the pallor below, a pallor tinged with a faint shade of amber akin to the hue of time-tinted marbles of old. This complexion, singularly contrasting with the red or deeply bronzed visages of the sailors, and in part the result of his official seclusion from the sunlight, though it was not exactly displeasing, nevertheless seemed to hint of something defective or abnormal in the constitution and blood. But his general aspect and manner were so suggestive of an education and career incongruous with his naval function that when not actively engaged in it he looked like a man of high quality, social and moral, who for reasons of his own was keeping incog.[1] Nothing was known of his former life. It might be that he was an Englishman; and yet there lurked a bit of accent in his speech suggesting that possibly he was not such by birth, but through naturalization in early childhood. Among certain grizzled sea gossips of the gun decks and forecastle went a rumor perdue[2] that the master-at-arms was a *chevalier*[3] who had volunteered into the King's navy by way of compounding for some mysterious swindle whereof he had been arraigned at the King's Bench.[4] The fact that nobody could substantiate this report was, of course, nothing against its secret currency. Such a rumor once started on the gun decks in reference to almost anyone below the rank of a commissioned officer would, during the period assigned to this narrative, have seemed not altogether wanting in credibility to the tarry old wiseacres of a man-of-war crew. And indeed a man of Claggart's accomplishments, without prior nautical experience entering the navy at mature life, as he did, and necessarily allotted at the start to the lowest grade in it; a man too who never made allusion to his previous life ashore; these were circumstances which in the dearth of exact knowledge as to his true antecedents opened to the invidious a vague field for unfavorable surmise.

But the sailors' dogwatch gossip concerning him derived a vague plausi-

8. Shawnee chief (1768?–1813) who attempted to unite the American Indians against the United States.
9. In 1678 Oates (1649–1705) invented a plot accusing Jesuits of planning to assassinate Charles II, burn London, and slaughter English Protestants.   1. Incognito, unrecognized.   2. Surreptitious.   3. A man of high rank.   4. Formerly the supreme court of common law in Great Britain.

bility from the fact that now for some period the British navy could so little afford to be squeamish in the matter of keeping up the muster rolls, that not only were press gangs notoriously abroad both afloat and ashore, but there was little or no secret about another matter, namely, that the London police were at liberty to capture any able-bodied suspect, any questionable fellow at large, and summarily ship him to the dockyard or fleet. Furthermore, even among voluntary enlistments there were instances where the motive thereto partook neither of patriotic impulse nor yet of a random desire to experience a bit of sea life and martial adventure. Insolvent debtors of minor grade, together with the promiscuous lame ducks of morality, found in the navy a convenient and secure refuge, secure because, once enlisted aboard a King's ship, they were as much in sanctuary as the transgressor of the Middle Ages harboring himself under the shadow of the altar. Such sanctioned irregularities, which for obvious reasons the government would hardly think to parade at the time and which consequently, and as affecting the least influential class of mankind, have all but dropped into oblivion, lend color[5] to something for the truth whereof I do not vouch, and hence have some scruple in stating; something I remember having seen in print though the book I cannot recall; but the same thing was personally communicated to me now more than forty years ago by an old pensioner in a cocked hat with whom I had a most interesting talk on the terrace at Greenwich, a Baltimore Negro, a Trafalgar man.[6] It was to this effect: In the case of a warship short of hands whose speedy sailing was imperative, the deficient quota, in lack of any other way of making it good, would be eked out by drafts culled direct from the jails. For reasons previously suggested it would not perhaps be easy at the present day directly to prove or disprove the allegation. But allowed as a verity, how significant would it be of England's straits at the time confronted by those wars which like a flight of harpies rose shrieking from the din and dust of the fallen Bastille.[7] That era appears measurably clear to us who look back at it, and but read of it. But to the grandfathers of us graybeards, the more thoughtful of them, the genius of it presented an aspect like that of Camoëns' Spirit of the Cape,[8] an eclipsing menace mysterious and prodigious. Not America was exempt from apprehension. At the height of Napoleon's unexampled conquests, there were Americans who had fought at Bunker Hill who looked forward to the possibility that the Atlantic might prove no barrier against the ultimate schemes of this French portentous upstart from the revolutionary chaos who seemed in act of fulfilling judgment prefigured in the Apocalypse.

But the less credence was to be given to the gun-deck talk touching Claggart, seeing that no man holding his office in a man-of-war can ever hope to be popular with the crew. Besides, in derogatory comments upon anyone against whom they have a grudge, or for any reason or no reason mislike, sailors are much like landsmen: they are apt to exaggerate or romance it.

About as much was really known to the Bellipotent's tars of the master-at-arms' career before entering the service as an astronomer knows about a comet's travels prior to its first observable appearance in the sky. The verdict

5. Appearance of truth.   6. A veteran of the Battle of Trafalgar. Greenwich: a hospital near London, a home for retired personnel.   7. The fall of the Bastille (July 14, 1789) signaled the beginning of the French Revolution.   8. The Portuguese poet Luiz Vaz de Camoëns (1524–1580) describes in his epic poem, the Lusiads, a monster named Adamastor who attempts to destroy Vasco da Gama and his crew.

of the sea quidnuncs[9] has been cited only by way of showing what sort of moral impression the man made upon rude uncultivated natures whose conceptions of human wickedness were necessarily of the narrowest, limited to ideas of vulgar rascality—a thief among the swinging hammocks during a night watch, or the man-brokers and land-sharks of the seaports.

It was no gossip, however, but fact that though, as before hinted, Claggart upon his entrance into the navy was, as a novice, assigned to the least honorable section of a man-of-war's crew, embracing the drudgery, he did not long remain there. The superior capacity he immediately evinced, his constitutional sobriety, an ingratiating deference to superiors, together with a peculiar ferreting genius manifested on a singular occasion; all this, capped by a certain austere patriotism, abruptly advanced him to the position of master-at-arms.

Of this maritime chief of police the ship's corporals, so called, were the immediate subordinates, and compliant ones; and this, as is to be noted in some business departments ashore, almost to a degree inconsistent with entire moral volition. His place put various converging wires of underground influence under the chief's control, capable when astutely worked through his understrappers of operating to the mysterious discomfort, if nothing worse, of any of the sea commonalty.

9

Life in the foretop well agreed with Billy Budd. There, when not actually engaged on the yards yet higher aloft, the topmen, who as such had been picked out for youth and activity, constituted an aerial club lounging at ease against the smaller stun'sails[1] rolled up into cushions, spinning yarns like the lazy gods, and frequently amused with what was going on in the busy world of the decks below. No wonder then that a young fellow of Billy's disposition was well content in such society. Giving no cause of offense to anybody, he was always alert at a call. So in the merchant service it had been with him. But now such a punctiliousness in duty was shown that his topmates would sometimes good-naturedly laugh at him for it. This heightened alacrity had its cause, namely, the impression made upon him by the first formal gangway-punishment he had ever witnessed, which befell the day following his impressment. It had been incurred by a little fellow, young, a novice afterguardsman absent from his assigned post when the ship was being put about; a dereliction resulting in a rather serious hitch to that maneuver, one demanding instantaneous promptitude in letting go and making fast. When Billy saw the culprit's naked back under the scourge, gridironed with red welts and worse, when he marked the dire expression in the liberated man's face as with his woolen shirt flung over him by the executioner he rushed forward from the spot to bury himself in the crowd, Billy was horrified. He resolved that never through remissness would he make himself liable to such a visitation or do or omit aught that might merit even verbal reproof. What then was his surprise and concern when ultimately he found himself getting into petty trouble occasionally about such matters as the stowage of his bag or something amiss in his hammock, matters under

9. What now (Latin, literal trans.); a busybody.   1. Studding sails (small auxiliaries to the mainsails).

the police oversight of the ship's corporals of the lower decks, and which brought down on him a vague threat from one of them.

So heedful in all things as he was, how could this be? He could not understand it, and it more than vexed him. When he spoke to his young topmates about it they were either lightly incredulous or found something comical in his unconcealed anxiety. 'Is it your bag, Billy?' said one. 'Well, sew yourself up in it, bully boy, and then you'll be sure to know if anybody meddles with it.'

Now there was a veteran aboard who because his years began to disqualify him for more active work had been recently assigned duty as mainmastman in his watch, looking to the gear belayed[2] at the rail roundabout that great spar near the deck. At off-times the foretopman had picked up some acquaintance with him, and now in his trouble it occurred to him that he might be the sort of person to go to for wise counsel. He was an old Dansker[3] long anglicized in the service, of few words, many wrinkles, and some honorable scars. His wizened face, time-tinted and weather-stained to the complexion of an antique parchment, was here and there peppered blue by the chance explosion of a gun cartridge in action.

He was an *Agamemnon* man, some two years prior to the time of this story having served under Nelson when still captain in that ship immortal in naval memory, which dismantled and in part broken up to her bare ribs is seen a grand skeleton in Haden's etching.[4] As one of a boarding party from the *Agamemnon* he had received a cut slantwise along one temple and cheek leaving a long pale scar like a streak of dawn's light falling athwart the dark visage. It was on account of that scar and the affair in which it was known that he had received it, as well as from his blue-peppered complexion, that the Dansker went among the *Bellipotent*'s crew by the name of 'Board-Her-in-the-Smoke.'

Now the first time that his small weasel eyes happened to light on Billy Budd, a certain grim internal merriment set all his ancient wrinkles into antic play. Was it that his eccentric unsentimental old sapience, primitive in its kind, saw or thought it saw something which in contrast with the warship's environment looked oddly incongruous in the Handsome Sailor? But after slyly studying him at intervals, the old Merlin's[5] equivocal merriment was modified; for now when the twain would meet, it would start in his face a quizzing[6] sort of look, but it would be but momentary and sometimes replaced by an expression of speculative query as to what might eventually befall a nature like that, dropped into a world not without some mantraps and against whose subtleties simple courage lacking experience and address,[7] and without any touch of defensive ugliness, is of little avail; and where such innocence as man is capable of does yet in a moral emergency not always sharpen the faculties or enlighten the will.

However it was, the Dansker in his ascetic way rather took to Billy. Nor was this only because of a certain philosophic interest in such a character. There was another cause. While the old man's eccentricities, sometimes bordering on the ursine, repelled the juniors, Billy, undeterred thereby, revering him as a salt hero, would make advances, never passing the old

2. Stowed.   3. Dane.   4. *Breaking up of the Agamemnon*, the masterpiece of Sir Francis Seymour Haden (1818–1910).   5. King Arthur's court magician.   6. Mocking.   7. Skill and tact in handling situations.

Agamemnon man without a salutation marked by that respect which is seldom lost on the aged, however crabbed at times or whatever their station in life.

There was a vein of dry humor, or what not, in the mastman; and, whether in freak of patriarchal irony touching Billy's youth and athletic frame, or for some other and more recondite reason, from the first in addressing him he always substituted *Baby* for Billy, the Dansker in fact being the originator of the name by which the foretopman eventually became known aboard ship.

Well then, in his mysterious little difficulty going in quest of the wrinkled one, Billy found him off duty in a dogwatch ruminating by himself, seated on a shot box of the upper gun deck, now and then surveying with a somewhat cynical regard certain of the more swaggering promenaders there. Billy recounted his trouble, again wondering how it all happened. The salt seer attentively listened, accompanying the foretopman's recital with queer twitchings of his wrinkles and problematical little sparkles of his small ferret eyes. Making an end of his story, the foretopman asked, 'And now, Dansker, do tell me what you think of it.'

The old man, shoving up the front of his tarpaulin and deliberately rubbing the long slant scar at the point where it entered the thin hair, laconically said, 'Baby Budd, *Jemmy Legs*'[8] (meaning the master-at-arms) 'is down on you.'

'*Jemmy Legs!*' ejaculated Billy, his welkin eyes expanding.

'What for? Why, he calls me "the sweet and pleasant young fellow," they tell me.'

'Does he so?' grinned the grizzled one; then said, 'Ay, Baby lad, a sweet voice has Jemmy Legs.'

'No, not always. But to me he has. I seldom pass him but there comes a pleasant word.'

'And that's because he's down upon you, Baby Budd.'

Such reiteration, along with the manner of it, incomprehensible to a novice, disturbed Billy almost as much as the mystery for which he had sought explanation. Something less unpleasingly oracular he tried to extract; but the old sea Chiron,[9] thinking perhaps that for the nonce he had sufficiently instructed his young Achilles, pursed his lips, gathered all his wrinkles together, and would commit himself to nothing further.

Years, and those experiences which befall certain shrewder men subordinated lifelong to the will of superiors, all this had developed in the Dansker the pithy guarded cynicism that was his leading characteristic.

10

The next day an incident served to confirm Billy Budd in his incredulity as to the Dansker's strange summing up of the case submitted. The ship at noon, going large before the wind, was rolling on her course, and he below at dinner and engaged in some sportful talk with the members of his mess, chanced in a sudden lurch to spill the entire contents of his soup pan upon the new-scrubbed deck. Claggart, the master-at-arms, official rattan[1] in

---

8. A disparaging nickname for the master-at-arms, still used in the American navy.   9. A Centaur, half man and half horse, skilled in healing and the wisest of his species; he taught the Greek heroes Achilles, Hercules, and Aesculapius.   1. Swagger stick, light whip.

hand, happened to be passing along the battery in a bay of which the mess was lodged, and the greasy liquid streamed just across his path. Stepping over it, he was proceeding on his way without comment, since the matter was nothing to take notice of under the circumstances, when he happened to observe who it was that had done the spilling. His countenance changed. Pausing, he was about to ejaculate something hasty at the sailor, but checked himself, and pointing down to the streaming soup, playfully tapped him from behind with his rattan, saying in a low musical voice peculiar to him at times, 'Handsomely done, my lad! And handsome is as handsome did it, too!' And with that passed on. Not noted by Billy as not coming within his view was the involuntary smile, or rather grimace, that accompanied Claggart's equivocal words. Aridly it drew down the thin corners of his shapely mouth. But everybody taking his remark as meant for humorous, and at which therefore as coming from a superior they were bound to laugh 'with counterfeited glee,'[2] acted accordingly; and Billy, tickled, it may be, by the allusion to his being the Handsome Sailor, merrily joined in; then addressing his messmates exclaimed, 'There now, who says that Jemmy Legs is down on me!'

'And who said he was, Beauty?' demanded one Donald with some surprise. Whereat the foretopman looked a little foolish, recalling that it was only one person, Board-Her-in-the-Smoke, who had suggested what to him was the smoky idea that his master-at-arms was in any peculiar way hostile to him. Meantime that functionary, resuming his path, must have momentarily worn some expression less guarded than that of the bitter smile, usurping the face from the heart—some distorting expression perhaps, for a drummer-boy heedlessly frolicking along from the opposite direction and chancing to come into light collision with his person was strangely disconcerted by his aspect. Nor was the impression lessened when the official, impetuously giving him a sharp cut with the rattan, vehemently exclaimed, 'Look where you go!'

11

What was the matter with the master-at-arms? And, be the matter what it might, how could it have direct relation to Billy Budd, with whom prior to the affair of the spilled soup he had never come into any special contact official or otherwise? What indeed could the trouble have to do with one so little inclined to give offense as the merchantship's 'peacemaker,' even him who in Claggart's own phrase was 'the sweet and pleasant young fellow'? Yes, why should Jemmy Legs, to borrow the Dansker's expression, be 'down' on the Handsome Sailor? But, at heart and not for nothing, as the late chance encounter may indicate to the discerning, down on him, secretly down on him, he assuredly was.

Now to invent something touching the more private career of Claggart, something involving Billy Budd, of which something the latter should be wholly ignorant, some romantic incident implying that Claggart's knowledge of the young bluejacket began at some period anterior to catching sight of him on board the seventy-four—all this, not so difficult to do, might avail in a way more or less interesting to account for whatever of enigma may appear to lurk in the case. But in fact there was nothing of the sort. And yet the

2. Oliver Goldsmith (1730–1774), *The Deserted Village*, line 201, alluding to the response of students to a severe schoolmaster.

cause necessarily to be assumed as the sole one assignable is in its very realism as much charged with that prime element of Radcliffian romance, the mysterious, as any that the ingenuity of the author of *The Mysteries of Udolpho*[3] would devise. For what can more partake of the mysterious than an antipathy spontaneous and profound such as is evoked in certain exceptional mortals by the mere aspect of some other mortal, however harmless he may be, if not called forth by this very harmlessness itself?

Now there can exist no irritating juxtaposition of dissimilar personalities comparable to that which is possible aboard a great warship fully manned and at sea. There, every day among all ranks, almost every man comes into more or less of contact with almost every other man. Wholly there to avoid even the sight of an aggravating object one must needs give it Jonah's toss[4] or jump overboard himself. Imagine how all this might eventually operate on some peculiar human creature the direct reverse of a saint!

But for the adequate comprehending of Claggart by a normal nature these hints are insufficient. To pass from a normal nature to him one must cross 'the deadly space between.' And this is best done by indirection.

Long ago an honest scholar, my senior, said to me in reference to one who like himself is now no more, a man so unimpeachably respectable that against him nothing was ever openly said though among the few something was whispered, 'Yes, X—— is a nut not to be cracked by the tap of a lady's fan. You are aware that I am the adherent of no organized religion, much less of any philosophy built into a system. Well, for all that, I think that to try and get into X——, enter his labyrinth and get out again, without a clue derived from some source other than what is known as "knowledge of the world"—that were hardly possible, at least for me.'

'Why,' said I, 'X——, however singular a study to some, is yet human, and knowledge of the world assuredly implies the knowledge of human nature, and in most of its varieties.'

'Yes, but a superficial knowledge of it, serving ordinary purposes. But for anything deeper, I am not certain whether to know the world and to know human nature be not two distinct branches of knowledge, which while they may co-exist in the same heart, yet either may exist with little or nothing of the other. Nay, in an average man of the world, his constant rubbing with it blunts that finer spiritual insight indispensable to the understanding of the essential in certain exceptional characters, whether evil ones or good. In a matter of some importance I have seen a girl wind an old lawyer about her little finger. Nor was it the dotage of senile love. Nothing of the sort. But he knew law better than he knew the girl's heart. Coke and Blackstone[5] hardly shed so much light into obscure spiritual places as the Hebrew prophets. And who were they? Mostly recluses.'

At the time, my inexperience was such that I did not quite see the drift of all this. It may be that I see it now. And, indeed, if that lexicon which is based on Holy Writ were any longer popular, one might with less difficulty define and denominate certain phenomenal men. As it is, one must turn to some authority not liable to the charge of being tinctured with the biblical element.

3. An immensely popular Gothic novel by Ann Radcliffe (1764–1823). 4. Jonah 1.15: "So they took up Jonah, and cast him forth into the sea." A nautical expression when an unlucky object or person is put overboard. 5. Sir Edward Coke (1552–1634) and Sir William Blackstone (1723–1780), noted British jurists and writers on the law.

In a list of definitions included in the authentic translation of Plato, a list attributed to him, occurs this: 'Natural Depravity: a depravity according to nature,' a definition which, though savoring of Calvinism,[6] by no means involves Calvin's dogma as to total mankind. Evidently its intent makes it applicable but to individuals. Not many are the examples of this depravity which the gallows and jail supply. At any rate, for notable instances, since these have no vulgar alloy of the brute in them, but invariably are dominated by intellectuality, one must go elsewhere. Civilization, especially if of the austerer sort, is auspicious to it. It folds itself in the mantle of respectability. It has certain negative virtues serving as silent auxiliaries. It never allows wine to get within its guard. It is not going too far to say that it is without vices or small sins. There is a phenomenal pride in it that excludes them. It is never mercenary or avaricious. In short, the depravity here meant partakes nothing of the sordid or sensual. It is serious, but free from acerbity. Though no flatterer of mankind it never speaks ill of it.

But the thing which in eminent instances signalizes so exceptional a nature is this: Though the man's even temper and discreet bearing would seem to intimate a mind peculiarly subject to the law of reason, not the less in heart he would seem to riot in complete exemption from that law, having apparently little to do with reason further than to employ it as an ambidexter[7] implement for effecting the irrational. That is to say: Toward the accomplishment of an aim which in wantonness of atrocity would seem to partake of the insane, he will direct a cool judgment sagacious and sound. These men are madmen, and of the most dangerous sort, for their lunacy is not continuous, but occasional, evoked by some special object; it is protectively secretive, which is as much as to say it is self-contained, so that when, moreover, most active it is to the average mind not distinguishable from sanity, and for the reason above suggested: that whatever its aims may be—and the aim is never declared—the method and the outward proceeding are always perfectly rational.

Now something such an one was Claggart, in whom was the mania of an evil nature, not engendered by vicious training or corrupting books or licentious living, but born with him and innate, in short 'a depravity according to nature.'

Dark sayings are these, some will say. But why? Is it because they somewhat savor of Holy Writ in its phrase 'mystery of iniquity'?[8] If they do, such savor was far enough from being intended, for little will it commend these pages to many a reader of today.

The point of the present story turning on the hidden nature of the master-at-arms has necessitated this chapter. With an added hint or two in connection with the incident at the mess, the resumed narrative must be left to vindicate, as it may, its own credibility.

12

That Claggart's figure was not amiss, and his face, save the chin, well molded, has already been said. Of these favorable points he seemed not insensible, for he was not only neat but careful in his dress. But the form of Billy Budd was heroic; and if his face was without the intellectual look of

---

6. The religious system founded by John Calvin (1509–1564), which emphasizes predestination.
7. Two-handed.   8. 2 Thessalonians 2.7.

the pallid Claggart's, not the less was it lit, like his, from within, though from a different source. The bonfire in his heart made luminous the rose-tan in his cheek.

In view of the marked contrast between the persons of the twain, it is more than probable that when the master-at-arms in the scene last given applied to the sailor the proverb 'Handsome is as handsome does,' he there let escape an ironic inkling, not caught by the young sailors who heard it, as to what it was that had first moved him against Billy, namely, his significant personal beauty.

Now envy and antipathy, passions irreconcilable in reason, nevertheless in fact may spring conjoined like Chang and Eng[9] in one birth. Is Envy then such a monster? Well, though many an arraigned mortal has in hopes of mitigated penalty pleaded guilty to horrible actions, did ever anybody seriously confess to envy? Something there is in it universally felt to be more shameful than even felonious crime. And not only does everybody disown it, but the better sort are inclined to incredulity when it is in earnest imputed to an intelligent man. But since its lodgment is in the heart not the brain, no degree of intellect supplies a guarantee against it. But Claggart's was no vulgar form of the passion. Nor, as directed toward Billy Budd, did it partake of that streak of apprehensive jealousy that marred Saul's visage perturbedly brooding on the comely young David.[1] Claggart's envy struck deeper. If askance he eyed the good looks, cheery health, and frank enjoyment of young life in Billy Budd, it was because these went along with a nature that, as Claggart magnetically felt, had in its simplicity never willed malice or experienced the reactionary bite of that serpent. To him, the spirit lodged within Billy, and looking out from his welkin eyes as from windows, that ineffability it was which made the dimple in his dyed cheek, suppled his joints, and dancing in his yellow curls made him pre-eminently the Handsome Sailor. One person excepted, the master-at-arms was perhaps the only man in the ship intellectually capable of adequately appreciating the moral phenomenon presented in Billy Budd. And the insight but intensified his passion, which assuming various secret forms within him, at times assumed that of cynic disdain, disdain of innocence—to be nothing more than innocent! Yet in an aesthetic way he saw the charm of it, the courageous free-and-easy temper of it, and fain would have shared it, but he despaired of it.

With no power to annul the elemental evil in him, though readily enough he could hide it; apprehending the good, but powerless to be it; a nature like Claggart's, surcharged with energy as such natures almost invariably are, what recourse is left to it but to recoil upon itself and, like the scorpion for which the Creator alone is responsible, act out to the end the part allotted it.

13

Passion, and passion in its profoundest, is not a thing demanding a palatial stage whereon to play its part. Down among the groundlings,[2] among the beggars and rakers of the garbage, profound passion is enacted. And the

9. Famous Siamese twins (1811–1874) who toured the United States.   1. David's comeliness and Saul's jealousy are described in 1 Samuel 16.18, 18.8ff.   2. The part of the audience that stood on the ground in an Elizabethan theater; the poorest spectators.

circumstances that provoke it, however trivial or mean, are no measure of its power. In the present instance the stage is a scrubbed gun deck, and one of the external provocations a man-of-war's man's spilled soup.

Now when the master-at-arms noticed whence came that greasy fluid streaming before his feet, he must have taken it—to some extent wilfully, perhaps—not for the mere accident it assuredly was, but for the sly escape of a spontaneous feeling on Billy's part more or less answering to the antipathy on his own. In effect a foolish demonstration, he must have thought, and very harmless, like the futile kick of a heifer, which yet were the heifer a shod stallion would not be so harmless. Even so was it that into the gall of Claggart's envy he infused the vitriol of his contempt. But the incident confirmed to him certain telltale reports purveyed to his ear by 'Squeak,' one of his more cunning corporals, a grizzled little man, so nicknamed by the sailors on account of his squeaky voice and sharp visage ferreting about the dark corners of the lower decks after interlopers, satirically suggesting to them the idea of a rat in a cellar.

From his chief's employing him as an implicit tool in laying little traps for the worriment of the foretopman—for it was from the master-at-arms that the petty persecutions heretofore adverted to had proceeded—the corporal, having naturally enough concluded that his master could have no love for the sailor, made it his business, faithful understrapper that he was, to foment the ill blood by perverting to his chief certain innocent frolics of the good-natured foretopman, besides inventing for his mouth sundry contumelious epithets he claimed to have overheard him let fall. The master-at-arms never suspected the veracity of these reports, more especially as to the epithets, for he well knew how secretly unpopular may become a master-at-arms, at least a master-at-arms of those days, zealous in his function, and how the bluejackets shoot at him in private their raillery and wit; the nickname by which he goes among them (Jemmy Legs) implying under the form of merriment their cherished disrespect and dislike. But in view of the greediness of hate for pabulum[3] it hardly needed a purveyor to feed Claggart's passion.

An uncommon prudence is habitual with the subtler depravity, for it has everything to hide. And in case of an injury but suspected, its secretiveness voluntarily cuts it off from enlightenment or disillusion; and, not unreluctantly, action is taken upon surmise as upon certainty. And the retaliation is apt to be in monstrous disproportion to the supposed offense; for when in anybody was revenge in its exactions aught else but an inordinate usurer? But how with Claggart's conscience? For though consciences are unlike as foreheads, every intelligence, not excluding the scriptural devils who 'believe and tremble,'[4] has one. But Claggart's conscience being but the lawyer to his will, made ogres of trifles, probably arguing that the motive imputed to Billy in spilling the soup just when he did, together with the epithets alleged, these, if nothing more, made a strong case against him; nay, justified animosity into a sort of retributive righteousness. The Pharisee is the Guy Fawkes[5] prowling in the hid chambers underlying some natures like Claggart's. And they can really form no conception of an unreciprocated malice.

3. Sustenance.   4. James 2.19: "The devils also believe, and tremble."   5. Instigator of the Gunpowder Plot, the plan to blow up the Houses of Parliament and King James I on November 5, 1605. *Pharisee*: follower of a Jewish sect known for its strict observance of the Torah; hence anyone extremely rigid and dogmatic.

Probably the master-at-arms' clandestine persecution of Billy was started to try the temper of the man; but it had not developed any quality in him that enmity could make official use of or even pervert into plausible self-justification; so that the occurrence at the mess, petty if it were, was a welcome one to that peculiar conscience assigned to be the private mentor of Claggart; and, for the rest, not improbably it put him upon new experiments.

14

Not many days after the last incident narrated, something befell Billy Budd that more graveled him than aught that had previously occurred.

It was a warm night for the latitude; and the foretopman, whose watch at the time was properly below, was dozing on the uppermost deck whither he had ascended from his hot hammock, one of hundreds suspended so closely wedged together over a lower gun deck that there was little or no swing to them. He lay as in the shadow of a hillside, stretched under the lee of the booms, a piled ridge of spare spars amidships between foremast and mainmast among which the ship's largest boat, the launch, was stowed. Alongside of three other slumberers from below, he lay near that end of the booms which approaches the foremast; his station aloft on duty as a foretopman being just over the deckstation of the forecastlemen, entitling him according to usage to make himself more or less at home in that neighborhood.

Presently he was stirred into semiconsciousness by somebody, who must have previously sounded the sleep of the others, touching his shoulder, and then, as the foretopman raised his head, breathing into his ear in a quick whisper, 'Slip into the lee forechains, Billy; there is something in the wind. Don't speak. Quick, I will meet you there,' and disappearing.

Now Billy, like sundry other essentially good-natured ones, had some of the weaknesses inseparable from essential good nature; and among these was a reluctance, almost an incapacity of plumply[6] saying *no* to an abrupt proposition not obviously absurd on the face of it, nor obviously unfriendly, nor iniquitous. And being of warm blood, he had not the phlegm[7] tacitly to negative any proposition by unresponsive inaction. Like his sense of fear, his apprehension as to aught outside of the honest and natural was seldom very quick. Besides, upon the present occasion, the drowse from his sleep still hung upon him.

However it was, he mechanically rose and, sleepily wondering what could be in the wind, betook himself to the designated place, a narrow platform, one of six, outside of the high bulwarks and screened by the great deadeyes and multiple columned lanyards of the shrouds and backstays; and, in a great warship of that time, of dimensions commensurate to the hull's magnitude; a tarry balcony in short, overhanging the sea, and so secluded that one mariner of the *Bellipotent,* a Nonconformist[8] old tar of a serious turn, made it even in daytime his private oratory.[9]

In this retired nook the stranger soon joined Billy Budd. There was no moon as yet; a haze obscured the starlight. He could not distinctly see the stranger's face. Yet from something in the outline and carriage, Billy took him, and correctly, for one of the afterguard.

---

6. Bluntly.   7. Sluggishness, apathy.   8. A Protestant dissenter from the Church of England.   9. A small chapel, especially for private prayer.

'Hist! Billy,' said the man, in the same quick cautionary whisper as before. 'You were impressed, weren't you? Well, so was I'; and he paused, as to mark the effect. But Billy, not knowing exactly what to make of this, said nothing. Then the other: 'We are not the only impressed ones, Billy. There's a gang of us.—Couldn't you—help—at a pinch?'

'What do you mean?' demanded Billy, here thoroughly shaking off his drowse.

'Hist, hist!' the hurried whisper now growing husky. 'See here,' and the man held up two small objects faintly twinkling in the night-light; 'see, they are yours, Billy, if you'll only—'

But Billy broke in, and in his resentful eagerness to deliver himself his vocal infirmity somewhat intruded. 'D—d—damme, I don't know what you are d—d—driving at, or what you mean, but you had better g—g—go where you belong!' For the moment the fellow, as confounded, did not stir; and Billy, springing to his feet, said, 'If you d—don't start, I'll t—t—toss you back over the r—rail!' There was no mistaking this, and the mysterious emissary decamped, disappearing in the direction of the mainmast in the shadow of the booms.

'Hallo, what's the matter?' here came growling from a forecastleman awakened from his deck-doze by Billy's raised voice. And as the foretopman reappeared and was recognized by him: 'Ah, Beauty, is it you? Well, something must have been the matter, for you st—st—stuttered.'

'Oh,' rejoined Billy, now mastering the impediment, 'I found an afterguardsman in our part of the ship here, and I bid him be off where he belongs.'

'And is that all you did about it, Foretopman?' gruffly demanded another, an irascible old fellow of brick-colored visage and hair who was known to his associate forecastlemen as 'Red Pepper.' 'Such sneaks I should like to marry to the gunner's daughter!'—by that expression meaning that he would like to subject them to disciplinary castigation over a gun.

However, Billy's rendering of the matter satisfactorily accounted to these inquirers for the brief commotion, since of all the sections of a ship's company the forecastlemen, veterans for the most part and bigoted in their sea prejudices, are the most jealous in resenting territorial encroachments, especially on the part of any of the afterguard, of whom they have but a sorry opinion—chiefly landsmen, never going aloft except to reef or furl the mainsail, and in no wise competent to handle a marlinspike or turn in a deadeye, say.

15

This incident sorely puzzled Billy Budd. It was an entirely new experience, the first time in his life that he had ever been personally approached in underhand intriguing fashion. Prior to this encounter he had known nothing of the afterguardsman, the two men being stationed wide apart, one forward and aloft during his watch, the other on deck and aft.

What could it mean? And could they really be guineas,[1] those two glittering objects the interloper had held up to his (Billy's) eyes? Where could the

1. English gold coins, not minted after 1813, worth 21 shillings (approximately $84).

fellow get guineas? Why, even spare buttons are not so plentiful at sea. The more he turned the matter over, the more he was nonplussed, and made uneasy and discomfited. In his disgustful recoil from an overture which, though he but ill comprehended, he instinctively knew must involve evil of some sort, Billy Budd was like a young horse fresh from the pasture suddenly inhaling a vile whiff from some chemical factory, and by repeated snortings trying to get it out of his nostrils and lungs. This frame of mind barred all desire of holding further parley with the fellow, even were it but for the purpose of gaining some enlightenment as to his design in approaching him. And yet he was not without natural curiosity to see how such a visitor in the dark would look in broad day.

He espied him the following afternoon in his first dogwatch below, one of the smokers on that forward part of the upper gun deck allotted to the pipe. He recognized him by his general cut and build more than by his round freckled face and glassy eyes of pale blue, veiled with lashes all but white. And yet Billy was a bit uncertain whether indeed it were he—yonder chap about his own age chatting and laughing in freehearted way, leaning against a gun; a genial young fellow enough to look at, and something of a rattlebrain, to all appearance. Rather chubby too for a sailor, even an afterguardsman. In short, the last man in the world, one would think, to be overburdened with thoughts, especially those perilous thoughts that must needs belong to a conspirator in any serious project, or even to the underling of such a conspirator.

Although Billy was not aware of it, the fellow, with a sidelong watchful glance, had perceived Billy first, and then noting that Billy was looking at him, thereupon nodded a familiar sort of friendly recognition as to an old acquaintance, without interrupting the talk he was engaged in with the group of smokers. A day or two afterwards, chancing in the evening promenade on a gun deck to pass Billy, he offered a flying word of good-fellowship, as it were, which by its unexpectedness, and equivocalness under the circumstances, so embarrassed Billy that he knew not how to respond to it, and let it go unnoticed.

Billy was now left more at a loss than before. The ineffectual speculations into which he was led were so disturbingly alien to him that he did his best to smother them. It never entered his mind that here was a matter which, from its extreme questionableness, it was his duty as a loyal bluejacket to report in the proper quarter. And, probably, had such a step been suggested to him, he would have been deterred from taking it by the thought, one of novice magnanimity, that it would savor overmuch of the dirty work of a telltale. He kept the thing to himself. Yet upon one occasion he could not forebear a little disburdening himself to the old Dansker, tempted thereto perhaps by the influence of a balmy night when the ship lay becalmed; the twain, silent for the most part, sitting together on deck, their heads propped against the bulwarks. But it was only a partial and anonymous account that Billy gave, the unfounded scruples above referred to preventing full disclosure to anybody. Upon hearing Billy's version, the sage Dansker seemed to divine more than he was told; and after a little meditation, during which his wrinkles were pursed as into a point, quite effacing for the time that quizzing expression his face sometimes wore: 'Didn't I say so, Baby Budd?'

'Say what?' demanded Billy.

'Why, *Jemmy Legs* is *down* on you.'

'And what,' rejoined Billy in amazement, 'has *Jemmy Legs* to do with that cracked afterguardsman?'

'Ho, it was an afterguardsman, then. A cat's-paw,[2] a cat's-paw!' And with that exclamation, whether it had reference to a light puff of air just then coming over the calm sea, or a subtler relation to the afterguardsman, there is no telling, the old Merlin gave a twisting wrench with his black teeth at his plug of tobacco, vouchsafing no reply to Billy's impetuous question, though now repeated, for it was his wont to relapse into grim silence when interrogated in skeptical sort as to any of his sententious oracles, not always very clear ones, rather partaking of that obscurity which invests most Delphic[3] deliverances from any quarter.

Long experience had very likely brought this old man to that bitter prudence which never interferes in aught and never gives advice.

16

Yes, despite the Dansker's pithy insistence as to the master-at-arms being at the bottom of these strange experiences of Billy on board the *Bellipotent*, the young sailor was ready to ascribe them to almost anybody but the man who, to use Billy's own expression, 'always had a pleasant word for him.' This is to be wondered at. Yet not so much to be wondered at. In certain matters, some sailors even in mature life remain unsophisticated enough. But a young seafarer of the disposition of our athletic foretopman is much of a child-man. And yet a child's utter innocence is but its blank ignorance, and the innocence more or less wanes as intelligence waxes. But in Billy Budd intelligence, such as it was, had advanced while yet his simple-mindedness remained for the most part unaffected. Experience is a teacher indeed; yet did Billy's years make his experience small. Besides, he had none of that intuitive knowledge of the bad which in natures not good or incompletely so foreruns experience, and therefore may pertain, as in some instances it too clearly does pertain, even to youth.

And what could Billy know of man except of man as a mere sailor? And the old-fashioned sailor, the veritable man before the mast, the sailor from boyhood up, he, though indeed of the same species as a landsman, is in some respects singularly distinct from him. The sailor is frankness, the landsman is finesse. Life is not a game with the sailor, demanding the long head—no intricate game of chess where few moves are made in straightforwardness and ends are attained by indirection, an oblique, tedious, barren game hardly worth that poor candle burnt out in playing it.

Yes, as a class, sailors are in character a juvenile race. Even their deviations are marked by juvenility, this more especially holding true with the sailors of Billy's time. Then too, certain things which apply to all sailors do more pointedly operate here and there upon the junior one. Every sailor, too, is accustomed to obey orders without debating them; his life afloat is externally ruled for him; he is not brought into that promiscuous[4] commerce with mankind where unobstructed free agency on equal terms—equal superficially, at

---

2. Either a light wind perceived by its impressions on the sea or a seaman employed to entice volunteers.
3. Literally, issuing from the ancient Greek oracle of Apollo at Delphi, which made ambiguous prophecies; hence, obscure in meaning, ambiguous.   4. Indiscriminate.

least—soon teaches one that unless upon occasion he exercise a distrust keen in proportion to the fairness of the appearance, some foul turn may be served him. A ruled undemonstrative distrustfulness is so habitual, not with businessmen so much as with men who know their kind in less shallow relations than business, namely, certain men of the world, that they come at last to employ it all but unconsciously; and some of them would very likely feel real surprise at being charged with it as one of their general characteristics.

17

But after the little matter at the mess Billy Budd no more found himself in strange trouble at times about his hammock or his clothes bag or what not. As to that smile that occasionally sunned him, and the pleasant passing word, these were, if not more frequent, yet if anything more pronounced than before.

But for all that, there were certain other demonstrations now. When Claggart's unobserved glance happened to light on belted Billy rolling along the upper gun deck in the leisure of the second dogwatch, exchanging passing broadsides of fun with other young promenaders in the crowd, that glance would follow the cheerful sea Hyperion[5] with a settled meditative and melancholy expression, his eyes strangely suffused with incipient feverish tears. Then would Claggart look like the man of sorrows.[6] Yes, and sometimes the melancholy expression would have in it a touch of soft yearning, as if Claggart could even have loved Billy but for fate and ban. But this was an evanescence, and quickly repented of, as it were, by an immitigable look, pinching and shriveling the visage into the momentary semblance of a wrinkled walnut. But sometimes catching sight in advance of the foretopman coming in his direction, he would, upon their nearing, step aside a little to let him pass, dwelling upon Billy for the moment with the glittering dental satire of a Guise.[7] But upon any abrupt unforeseen encounter a red light would flash forth from his eye like a spark from an anvil in a dusk smithy. That quick, fierce light was a strange one, darted from orbs which in repose were of a color nearest approaching a deeper violet, the softest of shades.

Though some of these caprices of the pit[8] could not but be observed by their object, yet were they beyond the construing of such a nature. And the thews of Billy were hardly compatible with that sort of sensitive spiritual organization which in some cases instinctively conveys to ignorant innocence an admonition of the proximity of the malign. He thought the master-at-arms acted in a manner rather queer at times. That was all. But the occasional frank air and pleasant word went for what they purported to be, the young sailor never having heard as yet of the 'too fair-spoken man.'

Had the foretopman been conscious of having done or said anything to provoke the ill will of the official, it would have been different with him, and his sight might have been purged if not sharpened. As it was, innocence was his blinder.

---

5. In Greek mythology, the Titan god who came to be identified with Apollo, god of youth and beauty.
6. In Isaiah 53.3, the Lord's servant is described as "despised and rejected of men; a man of sorrows, and acquainted with grief."   7. Henri de Guise (1550–1588), a famed conspirator who could smile throughout his villainy.   8. Of hell.

So was it with him in yet another matter. Two minor officers, the armorer and captain of the hold, with whom he had never exchanged a word, his position in the ship not bringing him into contact with them, these men now for the first began to cast upon Billy, when they chanced to encounter him, that peculiar glance which evidences that the man from whom it comes has been some way tampered with, and to the prejudice of him upon whom the glance lights. Never did it occur to Billy as a thing to be noted or a thing suspicious, though he well knew the fact, that the armorer and captain of the hold, with the ship's yeoman, apothecary, and others of that grade, were by naval usage messmates of the master-at-arms, men with ears convenient to his confidential tongue.

But the general popularity that came from our Handsome Sailor's manly forwardness upon occasion and irresistible good nature, indicating no mental superiority tending to excite an invidious feeling, this good will on the part of most of his shipmates made him the less to concern himself about such mute aspects toward him as those whereto allusion has just been made, aspects he could not so fathom as to infer their whole import.

As to the afterguardsman, though Billy for reasons already given necessarily saw little of him, yet when the two did happen to meet, invariably came the fellow's offhand cheerful recognition, sometimes accompanied by a passing pleasant word or two. Whatever that equivocal young person's original design may really have been, or the design of which he might have been the deputy, certain it was from his manner upon these occasions that he had wholly dropped it.

It was as if his precocity of crookedness (and every vulgar villain is precocious) had for once deceived him, and the man he had sought to entrap as a simpleton had through his very simplicity ignominiously baffled him.

But shrewd ones may opine that it was hardly possible for Billy to refrain from going up to the afterguardsman and bluntly demanding to know his purpose in the initial interview so abruptly closed in the forechains. Shrewd ones may also think it but natural in Billy to set about sounding some of the other impressed men of the ship in order to discover what basis, if any, there was for the emissary's obscure suggestions as to plotting disaffection aboard. Yes, shrewd ones may so think. But something more, or rather something else than mere shrewdness is perhaps needful for the due understanding of such a character as Billy Budd's.

As to Claggart, the monomania in the man—if that indeed it were—as involuntarily disclosed by starts in the manifestations detailed, yet in general covered over by his self-contained and rational demeanor; this, like a subterranean fire, was eating its way deeper and deeper in him. Something decisive must come of it.

18

After the mysterious interview in the forechains, the one so abruptly ended there by Billy, nothing especially germane to the story occurred until the events now about to be narrated.

Elsewhere it has been said that in the lack of frigates (of course better sailers than line-of-battle ships) in the English squadron up the Straits at that period, the *Bellipotent* 74 was occasionally employed not only as an available substitute for a scout, but at times on detached service of more important kind. This was not alone because of her sailing qualities, not common in a ship of her rate,[9] but quite as much, probably, that the character of her commander, it was thought, specially adapted him for any duty where under unforeseen difficulties a prompt initiative might have to be taken in some matter demanding knowledge and ability in addition to those qualities implied in good seamanship. It was on an expedition of the latter sort, a somewhat distant one, and when the *Bellipotent* was almost at her furthest remove from the fleet, that in the latter part of an afternoon watch she unexpectedly came in sight of a ship of the enemy. It proved to be a frigate. The latter, perceiving through the glass that the weight of men and metal would be heavily against her, invoking her light heels crowded sail to get away. After a chase urged almost against hope and lasting until about the middle of the first dogwatch, she signally succeeded in effecting her escape.

Not long after the pursuit had been given up, and ere the excitement incident thereto had altogether waned away, the master-at-arms, ascending from his cavernous sphere, made his appearance cap in hand by the mainmast respectfully waiting the notice of Captain Vere, then solitary walking the weather side of the quarter-deck, doubtless somewhat chafed at the failure of the pursuit. The spot where Claggart stood was the place allotted to men of lesser grades seeking some more particular interview either with the officer of the deck or the captain himself. But from the latter it was not often that a sailor or petty officer of those days would seek a hearing; only some exceptional cause would, according to established custom, have warranted that.

Presently, just as the commander, absorbed in his reflections, was on the point of turning aft in his promenade, he became sensible of Claggart's presence, and saw the doffed cap held in deferential expectancy. Here be it said that Captain Vere's personal knowledge of his petty officer had only begun at the time of the ship's last sailing from home, Claggart then for the first, in transfer from a ship detained for repairs, supplying on board the *Bellipotent* the place of a previous master-at-arms disabled and ashore.

No sooner did the commander observe who it was that now deferentially stood awaiting his notice than a peculiar expression came over him. It was not unlike that which uncontrollably will flit across the countenance of one at unawares encountering a person who, though known to him indeed, has hardly been long enough known for thorough knowledge, but something in whose aspect nevertheless now for the first provokes a vaguely repellent distaste. But coming to a stand and resuming much of his wonted official manner, save that a sort of impatience lurked in the intonation of the opening word, he said, 'Well? What is it, Master-at-arms?'

With the air of a subordinate grieved at the necessity of being a messenger of ill tidings, and while conscientiously determined to be frank yet equally resolved upon shunning overstatement, Claggart at this invitation, or rather summons to disburden, spoke up. What he said, conveyed in the language of no uneducated man, was to the effect following, if not altogether in these words, namely, that during the chase and preparations for the possible encounter he had seen enough to convince him that at least one sailor aboard

9. Classification.

was a dangerous character in a ship mustering some who not only had taken a guilty part in the late serious troubles, but others also who, like the man in question, had entered His Majesty's service under another form than enlistment.

At this point Captain Vere with some impatience interrupted him: 'Be direct, man; say *impressed men.*'

Claggart made a gesture of subservience, and proceeded. Quite lately he (Claggart) had begun to suspect that on the gun decks some sort of movement prompted by the sailor in question was covertly going on, but he had not thought himself warranted in reporting the suspicion so long as it remained indistinct. But from what he had that afternoon observed in the man referred to, the suspicion of something clandestine going on had advanced to a point less removed from certainty. He deeply felt, he added, the serious responsibility assumed in making a report involving such possible consequences to the individual mainly concerned, besides tending to augment those natural anxieties which every naval commander must feel in view of extraordinary outbreaks so recent as those which, he sorrowfully said it, it needed not to name.

Now at the first broaching of the matter Captain Vere, taken by surprise, could not wholly dissemble his disquietude. But as Claggart went on, the former's aspect changed into restiveness under something in the testifier's manner in giving his testimony. However, he refrained from interrupting him. And Claggart, continuing, concluded with this: 'God forbid, your honor, that the *Bellipotent*'s should be the experience of the—'

'Never mind that!' here peremptorily broke in the superior, his face altering with anger, instinctively divining the ship that the other was about to name, one in which the Nore Mutiny had assumed a singularly tragical character that for a time jeopardized the life of its commander. Under the circumstances he was indignant at the purposed allusion. When the commissioned officers themselves were on all occasions very heedful how they referred to the recent events in the fleet, for a petty officer unnecessarily to allude to them in the presence of his captain, this struck him as a most immodest presumption. Besides, to his quick sense of self-respect it even looked under the circumstances something like an attempt to alarm him. Nor at first was he without some surprise that one who so far as he had hitherto come under his notice had shown considerable tact in his function should in this particular evince such lack of it.

But these thoughts and kindred dubious ones flitting across his mind were suddenly replaced by an intuitional surmise which, though as yet obscure in form, served practically to affect his reception of the ill tidings. Certain it is that, long versed in everything pertaining to the complicated gun-deck life, which like every other form of life has its secret mines and dubious side, the side popularly disclaimed, Captain Vere did not permit himself to be unduly disturbed by the general tenor of his subordinate's report.

Furthermore, if in view of recent events prompt action should be taken at the first palpable sign of recurring insubordination, for all that, not judicious would it be, he thought, to keep the idea of lingering disaffection alive by undue forwardness in crediting an informer, even if his own subordinate and charged among other things with police surveillance of the crew. This feeling would not perhaps have so prevailed with him were it not that upon a prior occasion the patriotic zeal officially evinced by Claggart had somewhat irritated him as appearing rather supersensible and strained. Furthermore something even in the official's self-possessed and somewhat ostentatious manner in making his specifications strangely reminded him of a bandsman,[1] a perjurous witness in a capital case before a courtmartial ashore of which when a lieutenant he (Captain Vere) had been a member.

Now the peremptory check given to Claggart in the matter of the arrested allusion was quickly followed up by this: 'You say that there is at least one dangerous man aboard. Name him.'

'William Budd, a foretopman, your honor.'

'William Budd!' repeated Captain Vere with unfeigned astonishment. 'And mean you the man that Lieutenant Ratcliffe took from the merchantman not very long ago, the young fellow who seems to be so popular with the men—Billy the Handsome Sailor, as they call him?'

'The same, your honor; but for all his youth and good looks, a deep one. Not for nothing does he insinuate himself into the good will of his shipmates, since at the least they will at a pinch say—all hands will—a good word for him, and at all hazards. Did Lieutenant Ratcliffe happen to tell your honor of that adroit fling of Budd's, jumping up in the cutter's bow under the merchantman's stern when he was being taken off? It is even masked by that sort of good-humored air that at heart he resents his impressment. You have but noted his fair cheek. A mantrap may be under the ruddy-tipped daisies.'

Now the Handsome Sailor as a signal figure among the crew had naturally enough attracted the captain's attention from the first. Though in general not very demonstrative to his officers, he had congratulated Lieutenant Ratcliffe upon his good fortune in lighting on such a fine specimen of the *genus homo,* who in the nude might have posed for a statue of a young Adam before the Fall. As to Billy's adieu to the ship *Rights-of-Man,* which the boarding lieutenant had indeed reported to him, but, in a deferential way, more as a good story than aught else, Captain Vere, though mistakenly understanding it as a satiric sally, had but thought so much the better of the impressed man for it; as a military sailor, admiring the spirit that could take an arbitrary enlistment so merrily and sensibly. The foretopman's conduct, too, so far as it had fallen under the captain's notice, had confirmed the first happy augury, while the new recruit's qualities as a 'sailor-man' seemed to be such that he had thought of recommending him to the executive officer for promotion to a place that would more frequently bring him under his own observation, namely, the captaincy of the mizzentop, replacing there in the starboard watch a man not so young whom partly for that reason he deemed less fitted for the post. Be it parenthesized here that since the mizzentopmen have not to handle such breadths of heavy canvas as the lower sails on the mainmast and foremast, a young man if of the right stuff not only seems best adapted to duty there, but in fact is generally selected for the captaincy of that top, and the company under him are light hands and often but striplings. In sum, Captain Vere had from the beginning deemed Billy Budd to be what in the naval parlance of the time was called a 'King's bargain': that is to say, for His Britannic Majesty's navy a capital investment at small outlay or none at all.

After a brief pause, during which the reminiscences above mentioned

---

1. Crewman charged with the task of stitching bands of canvas into sails to strengthen them.

passed vividly through his mind and he weighed the import of Claggart's last suggestion conveyed in the phrase 'mantrap under the daisies,' and the more he weighed it the less reliance he felt in the informer's good faith, suddenly he turned upon him and in a low voice demanded: 'Do you come to me, Master-at-arms, with so foggy a tale? As to Budd, cite me an act or spoken word of his confirmatory of what you in general charge against him. Stay,' drawing nearer to him; 'heed what you speak. Just now, and in a case like this, there is a yardarm-end for the false witness.'

'Ah, your honor!' sighed Claggart, mildly shaking his shapely head as in sad deprecation of such unmerited severity of tone. Then, bridling—erecting himself as in virtuous self-assertion—he circumstantially alleged certain words and acts which collectively, if credited, led to presumptions morally inculpating Budd. And for some of these averments, he added, substantiating proof was not far.

With gray eyes impatient and distrustful essaying to fathom to the bottom Claggart's calm violet ones, Captain Vere again heard him out; then for the moment stood ruminating. The mood he evinced, Claggart—himself for the time liberated from the other's scrutiny—steadily regarded with a look difficult to render: a look curious of the operation of his tactics, a look such as might have been that of the spokesman of the envious children of Jacob deceptively imposing upon the troubled patriarch the blood-dyed coat of young Joseph.[2]

Though something exceptional in the moral quality of Captain Vere made him, in earnest encounter with a fellow man, a veritable touchstone of that man's essential nature, yet now as to Claggart and what was really going on in him his feeling partook less of intuitional conviction than of strong suspicion clogged by strange dubieties. The perplexity he evinced proceeded less from aught touching the man informed against—as Claggart doubtless opined—than from considerations how best to act in regard to the informer. At first, indeed, he was naturally for summoning that substantiation of his allegations which Claggart said was at hand. But such a proceeding would result in the matter at once getting abroad, which in the present stage of it, he thought, might undesirably affect the ship's company. If Claggart was a false witness—that closed the affair. And therefore, before trying the accusation, he would first practically test the accuser; and he thought this could be done in a quiet, undemonstrative way.

The measure he determined upon involved a shifting of the scene, a transfer to a place less exposed to observation than the broad quarter-deck. For although the few gunroom officers there at the time had, in due observance of naval etiquette, withdrawn to leeward the moment Captain Vere had begun his promenade on the deck's weather side; and though during the colloquy with Claggart they of course ventured not to diminish the distance; and though throughout the interview Captain Vere's voice was far from him, and Claggart's silvery and low; and the wind in the cordage and the wash of the sea helped the more to put them beyond earshot; nevertheless, the interview's continuance already had attracted observation from some topmen aloft and other sailors in the waist or further forward.

<hr />

2. Genesis 37.1–32: "And they took Joseph's coat, and killed a kid of the goats, and dipped the coat in the blood; and they sent the coat of many colours, and they brought it to their father; and said, This have we found: know now whether it be thy son's coat or no."

Having determined upon his measures, Captain Vere forthwith took action. Abruptly turning to Claggart, he asked, 'Master-at-arms, is it now Budd's watch aloft?'

'No, your honor.'

Whereupon, 'Mr Wilkes!' summoning the nearest midshipman. 'Tell Albert to come to me.' Albert was the captain's hammock-boy, a sort of sea valet in whose discretion and fidelity his master had much confidence. The lad appeared.

'You know Budd, the foretopman?'

'I do, sir.'

'Go find him. It is his watch off. Manage to tell him out of earshot that he is wanted aft. Contrive it that he speaks to nobody. Keep him in talk yourself. And not till you get well aft here, not till then let him know that the place where he is wanted is my cabin. You understand. Go.—Master-at-arms, show yourself on the decks below, and when you think it time for Albert to be coming with his man, stand by quietly to follow the sailor in.'

19

Now when the foretopman found himself in the cabin, closeted there, as it were, with the captain and Claggart, he was surprised enough. But it was a surprise unaccompanied by apprehension or distrust. To an immature nature essentially honest and humane, forewarning intimations of subtler danger from one's kind come tardily if at all. The only thing that took shape in the young sailor's mind was this: Yes, the captain, I have always thought, looks kindly upon me. Wonder if he's going to make me his coxswain. I should like that. And may be now he is going to ask the master-at-arms about me.

'Shut the door there, sentry,' said the commander; 'stand without, and let nobody come in.—Now, Master-at-arms, tell this man to his face what you told of him to me,' and stood prepared to scrutinize the mutually confronting visages.

With the measured step and calm collected air of an asylum physician approaching in the public hall some patient beginning to show indications of a coming paroxysm, Claggart deliberately advanced within short range of Billy and, mesmerically looking him in the eye, briefly recapitulated the accusation.

Not at first did Billy take it in. When he did, the rose-tan of his cheek looked struck as by white leprosy. He stood like one impaled and gagged. Meanwhile the accuser's eyes, removing not as yet from the blue dilated ones, underwent a phenomenal change, their wonted rich violet color blurring into a muddy purple. Those lights of human intelligence, losing human expression, were gelidly protruding like the alien eyes of certain uncatalogued creatures of the deep. The first mesmeristic glance was one of serpent fascination; the last was as the paralyzing lurch of the torpedo fish.

'Speak, man!' said Captain Vere to the transfixed one, struck by his aspect even more than by Claggart's. 'Speak! Defend yourself!' Which appeal caused but a strange dumb gesturing and gurgling in Billy; amazement at such an accusation so suddenly sprung on inexperienced nonage; this, and, it may be, horror of the accuser's eyes, serving to bring out his lurking defect and in this instance for the time intensifying it into a convulsed tongue-tie; while the intent head and entire form straining forward in an agony of ineffectual eagerness to obey the injunction to speak and defend himself, gave an expression to the face like that of a condemned vestal priestess in the moment of being buried alive, and in the first struggle against suffocation.[3]

Though at the time Captain Vere was quite ignorant of Billy's liability to vocal impediment, he now immediately divined it, since vividly Billy's aspect recalled to him that of a bright young schoolmate of his whom he had once seen struck by much the same startling impotence in the act of eagerly rising in the class to be foremost in response to a testing question put to it by the master. Going close up to the young sailor, and laying a soothing hand on his shoulder, he said, 'There is no hurry, my boy. Take your time, take your time.' Contrary to the effect intended, these words so fatherly in tone, doubtless touching Billy's heart to the quick, prompted yet more violent efforts at utterance—efforts soon ending for the time in confirming the paralysis, and bringing to his face an expression which was as a crucifixion to behold. The next instant, quick as the flame from a discharged cannon at night, his right arm shot out, and Claggart dropped to the deck. Whether intentionally or but owing to the young athlete's superior height, the blow had taken effect full upon the forehead, so shapely and intellectual-looking a feature in the master-at-arms; so that the body fell over lengthwise, like a heavy plank tilted from erectness. A gasp or two, and he lay motionless.

'Fated boy,' breathed Captain Vere in tone so low as to be almost a whisper, 'what have you done! But here, help me.'

The twain raised the felled one from the loins up into a sitting position. The spare form flexibly acquiesced, but inertly. It was like handling a dead snake. They lowered it back. Regaining erectness, Captain Vere with one hand covering his face stood to all appearance as impassive as the object at his feet. Was he absorbed in taking in all the bearings of the event and what was best not only now at once to be done, but also in the sequel? Slowly he uncovered his face; and the effect was as if the moon emerging from eclipse should reappear with quite another aspect than that which had gone into hiding. The father in him, manifested towards Billy thus far in the scene, was replaced by the military disciplinarian. In his official tone he bade the foretopman retire to a stateroom aft (pointing it out), and there remain till thence summoned. This order Billy in silence mechanically obeyed. Then going to the cabin door where it opened on the quarter-deck, Captain Vere said to the sentry without, 'Tell somebody to send Albert here.' When the lad appeared, his master so contrived it that he should not catch sight of the prone one. 'Albert,' he said to him, 'tell the surgeon I wish to see him. You need not come back till called.'

When the surgeon entered—a self-poised character of that grave sense and experience that hardly anything could take him aback—Captain Vere advanced to meet him, thus unconsciously intercepting his view of Claggart, and interrupting the other's wonted ceremonious salutation, said, 'Nay. Tell me how it is with yonder man,' directing his attention to the prostrate one.

The surgeon looked, and for all his self-command somewhat started at the abrupt revelation. On Claggart's always pallid complexion, thick black blood

---

3. Vestal virgins in Rome were buried alive if they violated their vows.

was now oozing from nostril and ear. To the gazer's professional eye it was unmistakably no living man that he saw.

'Is it so, then?' said Captain Vere, intently watching him. 'I thought it. But verify it.' Whereupon the customary tests confirmed the surgeon's first glance, who now, looking up in unfeigned concern, cast a look of intense inquisitiveness upon his superior. But Captain Vere, with one hand to his brow, was standing motionless. Suddenly, catching the surgeon's arm convulsively, he exclaimed, pointing down to the body, 'It is the divine judgment on Ananias![4] Look!'

Disturbed by the excited manner he had never before observed in the *Bellipotent*'s captain, and as yet wholly ignorant of the affair, the prudent surgeon nevertheless held his peace, only again looking an earnest interrogatory as to what it was that had resulted in such a tragedy.

But Captain Vere was now again motionless, standing absorbed in thought. Again starting, he vehemently exclaimed, 'Struck dead by an angel of God! Yet the angel must hang!'

At these passionate interjections, mere incoherences to the listener as yet unapprised of the antecedents, the surgeon was profoundly discomposed. But now, as recollecting himself, Captain Vere in less passionate tone briefly related the circumstances leading up to the event. 'But come, we must dispatch,' he added. 'Help me to remove him' (meaning the body) 'to yonder compartment,' designating one opposite that where the foretopman remained immured. Anew disturbed by a request that, as implying a desire for secrecy, seemed unaccountably strange to him, there was nothing for the subordinate to do but comply.

'Go now,' said Captain Vere with something of his wonted manner. 'Go now. I presently shall call a drumhead court.[5] Tell the lieutenants what has happened, and tell Mr Mordant' (meaning the captain of marines), 'and charge them to keep the matter to themselves.'

20

Full of disquietude and misgiving, the surgeon left the cabin. Was Captain Vere suddenly affected in his mind, or was it but a transient excitement, brought about by so strange and extraordinary a tragedy? As to the drumhead court, it struck the surgeon as impolitic, if nothing more. The thing to do, he thought, was to place Billy Budd in confinement, and in a way dictated by usage, and postpone further action in so extraordinary a case to such time as they should rejoin the squadron, and then refer it to the admiral. He recalled the unwonted agitation of Captain Vere and his excited exclamations, so at variance with his normal manner. Was he unhinged?

But assuming that he is, it is not so susceptible of proof. What then can the surgeon do? No more trying situation is conceivable than that of an officer subordinate under a captain whom he suspects to be not mad, indeed, but yet not quite unaffected in his intellects. To argue his order to him would be insolence. To resist him would be mutiny.

In obedience to Captain Vere, he communicated what had happened to

---

4. Acts 5.3–5: "Peter said, Ananias . . . thou hast not lied unto men, but unto God. And Ananias hearing these words fell down, and gave up the ghost." **5.** A court-martial, originally held around an upturned drum, to try offences committed during military operations.

the lieutenants and captain of marines, saying nothing as to the captain's state. They fully shared his own surprise and concern. Like him too, they seemed to think that such a matter should be referred to the admiral.

21

Who in the rainbow can draw the line where the violet tint ends and the orange tint begins? Distinctly we see the difference of the colors, but where exactly does the one first blendingly enter into the other? So with sanity and insanity. In pronounced cases there is no question about them. But in some supposed cases, in various degrees supposedly less pronounced, to draw the exact line of demarcation few will undertake, though for a fee becoming considerate some professional experts will. There is nothing nameable but that some men will, or undertake to, do it for pay.

Whether Captain Vere, as the surgeon professionally and privately surmised, was really the sudden victim of any degree of aberration, every one must determine for himself by such light as this narrative may afford.

That the unhappy event which has been narrated could not have happened at a worse juncture was but too true. For it was close on the heel of the suppressed insurrections, an aftertime very critical to naval authority, demanding from every English sea commander two qualities not readily interfusable—prudence and rigor. Moreover, there was something crucial in the case.

In the jugglery of circumstances preceding and attending the event on board the *Bellipotent,* and in the light of that martial code whereby it was formally to be judged, innocence and guilt personified in Claggart and Budd in effect changed places. In a legal view the apparent victim of the tragedy was he who had sought to victimize a man blameless; and the indisputable deed of the latter, navally regarded, constituted the most heinous of military crimes. Yet more. The essential right and wrong involved in the matter, the clearer that might be, so much the worse for the responsibility of a loyal sea commander, inasmuch as he was not authorized to determine the matter on that primitive basis.

Small wonder then that the *Bellipotent*'s captain, though in general a man of rapid decision, felt that circumspectness not less than promptitude was necessary. Until he could decide upon his course, and in each detail; and not only so, but until the concluding measure was upon the point of being enacted, he deemed it advisable, in view of all the circumstances, to guard as much as possible against publicity. Here he may or may not have erred. Certain it is, however, that subsequently in the confidential talk of more than one or two gun rooms and cabins he was not a little criticized by some officers, a fact imputed by his friends and vehemently by his cousin Jack Denton to professional jealousy of Starry Vere. Some imaginative ground for invidious comment there was. The maintenance of secrecy in the matter, the confining all knowledge of it for a time to the place where the homicide occurred, the quarter-deck cabin; in these particulars lurked some resemblance to the policy adopted in those tragedies of the palace which have occurred more than once in the capital founded by Peter the Barbarian.[6]

6. St. Petersburg, founded by Peter the Great (1672–1725) in 1703.

The case indeed was such that fain would the *Bellipotent's* captain have deferred taking any action whatever respecting it further than to keep the foretopman a close prisoner till the ship rejoined the squadron and then submitting the matter to the judgment of his admiral.

But a true military officer is in one particular like a true monk. Not with more of self-abnegation will the latter keep his vows of monastic obedience than the former his vows of allegiance to martial duty.

Feeling that unless quick action was taken on it, the deed of the foretop-man, so soon as it should be known on the gun decks, would tend to awaken any slumbering embers of the Nore among the crew, a sense of the urgency of the case overruled in Captain Vere every other consideration. But though a conscientious disciplinarian, he was no lover of authority for mere author-ity's sake. Very far was he from embracing opportunities for monopolizing to himself the perils of moral responsibility, none at least that could properly be referred to an official superior or shared with him by his official equals or even subordinates. So thinking, he was glad it would not be at variance with usage to turn the matter over to a summary court of his own officers, reserving to himself, as the one on whom the ultimate accountability would rest, the right of maintaining a supervision of it, or formally or informally interposing at need. Accordingly a drum-head court was summarily con-vened, he electing the individuals composing it: the first lieutenant, the cap-tain of marines, and the sailing master.

In associating an officer of marines with the sea lieutenant and the sailing master in a case having to do with a sailor, the commander perhaps deviated from general custom. He was prompted thereto by the circumstance that he took that soldier to be a judicious person, thoughtful, and not altogether incapable of grappling with a difficult case unprecedented in his prior expe-rience. Yet even as to him he was not without some latent misgiving, for withal he was an extremely good-natured man, an enjoyer of his dinner, a sound sleeper, and inclined to obesity—a man who though he would always maintain his manhood in battle might not prove altogether reliable in a moral dilemma involving aught of the tragic. As to the first lieutenant and the sailing master, Captain Vere could not but be aware that though honest natures, of approved gallantry upon occasion, their intelligence was mostly confined to the matter of active seamanship and the fighting demands of their profession.

The court was held in the same cabin where the unfortunate affair had taken place. This cabin, the commander's, embraced the entire area under the poop deck. Aft, and on either side, was a small stateroom, the one now temporarily a jail and the other a dead-house, and a yet smaller compartment, leaving a space between expanding forward into a goodly oblong of length coinciding with the ship's beam. A skylight of moderate dimension was over-head, and at each end of the oblong space were two sashed porthole windows easily convertible back into embrasures for short carronades.[7]

All being quickly in readiness, Billy Budd was arraigned, Captain Vere necessarily appearing as the sole witness in the case, and as such temporarily sinking his rank, though singularly maintaining it in a matter apparently trivial, namely, that he testified from the ship's weather side, with that object

---

7. Large pieces of artillery.

having caused the court to sit on the lee side. Concisely he narrated all that had led up to the catastrophe, omitting nothing in Claggart's accusation and deposing as to the manner in which the prisoner had received it. At this testimony the three officers glanced with no little surprise at Billy Budd, the last man they would have suspected either of the mutinous design alleged by Claggart or the undeniable deed he himself had done. The first lieutenant, taking judicial primacy and turning toward the prisoner, said, 'Captain Vere has spoken. Is it or is it not as Captain Vere says?'

In response came syllables not so much impeded in the utterance as might have been anticipated. They were these: 'Captain Vere tells the truth. It is just as Captain Vere says, but it is not as the master-at-arms said. I have eaten the King's bread and I am true to the King.'

'I believe you, my man,' said the witness, his voice indicating a suppressed emotion not otherwise betrayed.

'God will bless you for that, your honor!' not without stammering said Billy, and all but broke down. But immediately he was recalled to self-control by another question, to which with the same emotional difficulty of utterance he said, 'No, there was no malice between us. I never bore malice against the master-at-arms. I am sorry that he is dead. I did not mean to kill him. Could I have used my tongue I would not have struck him. But he foully lied to my face and in presence of my captain, and I had to say something, and I could only say it with a blow, God help me!'

In the impulsive aboveboard manner of the frank one the court saw confirmed all that was implied in words that just previously had perplexed them, coming as they did from the testifier to the tragedy and promptly following Billy's impassioned disclaimer of mutinous intent—Captain Vere's words, 'I believe you, my man.'

Next it was asked of him whether he knew of or suspected aught savoring of incipient trouble (meaning mutiny, though the explicit term was avoided) going on in any section of the ship's company.

The reply lingered. This was naturally imputed by the court to the same vocal embarrassment which had retarded or obstructed previous answers. But in main it was otherwise here, the question immediately recalling to Billy's mind the interview with the afterguardsman in the forechains. But an innate repugnance to playing a part at all approaching that of an informer against one's own shipmates—the same erring sense of uninstructed honor which had stood in the way of his reporting the matter at the time, though as a loyal man-of-war's man it was incumbent on him, and failure so to do, if charged against him and proven, would have subjected him to the heaviest of penalties; this, with the blind feeling now his that nothing really was being hatched, prevailed with him. When the answer came it was a negative.

'One question more,' said the officer of marines, now first speaking and with a troubled earnestness. 'You tell us that what the master-at-arms said against you was a lie. Now why should he have so lied, so maliciously lied, since you declare there was no malice between you?'

At that question, unintentionally touching on a spiritual sphere wholly obscure to Billy's thoughts, he was nonplussed, evincing a confusion indeed that some observers, such as can readily be imagined, would have construed into involuntary evidence of hidden guilt. Nevertheless, he strove some way to answer, but all at once relinquished the vain endeavor, at the same time turning an appealing glance towards Captain Vere as deeming him his best helper and friend. Captain Vere, who had been seated for a time, rose to his feet, addressing the interrogator. 'The question you put to him comes naturally enough. But how can he rightly answer it?—or anybody else, unless indeed it be he who lies within there,' designating the compartment where lay the corpse. 'But the prone one there will not rise to our summons. In effect, though, as it seems to me, the point you make is hardly material. Quite aside from any conceivable motive actuating the master-at-arms, and irrespective of the provocation to the blow, a martial court must needs in the present case confine its attention to the blow's consequence, which consequence justly is to be deemed not otherwise than as the striker's deed.'

This utterance, the full significance of which it was not at all likely that Billy took in, nevertheless caused him to turn a wistful interrogative look toward the speaker, a look in its dumb expressiveness not unlike that which a dog of generous breed might turn upon his master, seeking in his face some elucidation of a previous gesture ambiguous to the canine intelligence. Nor was the same utterance without marked effect upon the three officers, more especially the soldier. Couched in it seemed to them a meaning unanticipated, involving a prejudgment on the speaker's part. It served to augment a mental disturbance previously evident enough.

The soldier once more spoke, in a tone of suggestive dubiety addressing at once his associates and Captain Vere: 'Nobody is present—none of the ship's company, I mean—who might shed lateral light, if any is to be had, upon what remains mysterious in this matter.'

'That is thoughtfully put,' said Captain Vere; 'I see your drift. Ay, there is a mystery; but, to use a scriptural phrase, it is a "mystery of iniquity," a matter for psychologic theologians to discuss. But what has a military court to do with it? Not to add that for us any possible investigation of it is cut off by the lasting tongue-tie of—him—in yonder,' again designating the mortuary stateroom. 'The prisoner's deed—with that alone we have to do.'

To this, and particularly the closing reiteration, the marine soldier, knowing not how aptly to reply, sadly abstained from saying aught. The first lieutenant, who at the outset had not unnaturally assumed primacy in the court, now overrulingly instructed by a glance from Captain Vere, a glance more effective than words, resumed that primacy. Turning to the prisoner, 'Budd,' he said, and scarce in equable tones, 'Budd, if you have aught further to say for yourself, say it now.'

Upon this the young sailor turned another quick glance toward Captain Vere; then, as taking a hint from that aspect, a hint confirming his own instinct that silence was now best, replied to the lieutenant, 'I have said all, sir.'

The marine—the same who had been the sentinel without the cabin door at the time that the foretopman, followed by the master-at-arms, entered it—he, standing by the sailor throughout these judicial proceedings was now directed to take him back to the after compartment originally assigned to the prisoner and his custodian. As the twain disappeared from view, the three officers, as partially liberated from some inward constraint associated with Billy's mere presence, simultaneously stirred in their seats. They exchanged looks of troubled indecision, yet feeling that decide they must and without long delay. For Captain Vere, he for the time stood—unconsciously with his back toward them, apparently in one of his absent fits—gazing out from a sashed porthole to windward upon the monotonous blank of the twilight sea. But the court's silence continuing, broken only at moments by brief consultations, in low earnest tones, this served to arouse him and energize him. Turning, he to-and-fro paced the cabin athwart; in the returning ascent to windward climbing the slant deck in the ship's lee roll, without knowing it symbolizing thus in his action a mind resolute to surmount difficulties even if against primitive instincts strong as the wind and the sea. Presently he came to a stand before the three. After scanning their faces he stood less as mustering his thoughts for expression than as one inly deliberating how best to put them to well-meaning men not intellectually mature, men with whom it was necessary to demonstrate certain principles that were axioms to himself. Similar impatience as to talking is perhaps one reason that deters some minds from addressing any popular assemblies.

When speak he did, something, both in the substance of what he said and his manner of saying it, showed the influence of unshared studies modifying and tempering the practical training of an active career. This, along with his phraseology, now and then was suggestive of the grounds whereon rested that imputation of a certain pedantry socially alleged against him by certain naval men of wholly practical cast, captains who nevertheless would frankly concede that His Majesty's navy mustered no more efficient officer of their grade than Starry Vere.

What he said was to this effect: 'Hitherto I have been but the witness, little more; and I should hardly think now to take another tone, that of your coadjutor for the time, did I not perceive in you—at the crisis too—a troubled hesitancy, proceeding, I doubt not, from the clash of military duty with moral scruple—scruple vitalized by compassion. For the compassion, how can I otherwise than share it? But, mindful of paramount obligations, I strive against scruples that may tend to enervate decision. Not, gentlemen, that I hide from myself that the case is an exceptional one. Speculatively regarded, it well might be referred to a jury of casuists. But for us here, acting not as casuists or moralists, it is a case practical, and under martial law practically to be dealt with.

'But your scruples: do they move as in a dusk? Challenge them. Make them advance and declare themselves. Come now; do they import something like this: If, mindless of palliating circumstances, we are bound to regard the death of the master-at-arms as the prisoner's deed, then does that deed constitute a capital crime whereof the penalty is a mortal one. But in natural justice is nothing but the prisoner's overt act to be considered? How can we adjudge to summary and shameful death a fellow creature innocent before God, and whom we feel to be so?—Does that state it aright? You sign sad assent. Well, I too feel that, the full force of that. It is Nature. But do these buttons that we wear attest that our allegiance is to Nature? No, to the King. Though the ocean, which is inviolate Nature primeval, though this be the element where we move and have our being as sailors, yet as the King's officers lies our duty in a sphere correspondingly natural? So little is that true, that in receiving our commissions we in the most important regards ceased to be natural free agents. When war is declared are we the commissioned fighters previously consulted? We fight at command. If our judgments approve the war, that is but coincidence. So in other particulars. So now.

For suppose condemnation to follow these present proceedings. Would it be so much we ourselves that would condemn as it would be martial law operating through us? For that law and the rigor of it, we are not responsibile. Our vowed responsibility is in this: That however pitilessly that law may operate in any instances, we nevertheless adhere to it and administer it.

'But the exceptional in the matter moves the hearts within you. Even so too is mine moved. But let not warm hearts betray heads that should be cool. Ashore in a criminal case, will an upright judge allow himself off the bench to be waylaid by some tender kinswoman of the accused seeking to touch him with her tearful plea? Well, the heart here, sometimes the feminine in man, is as that piteous woman, and hard though it be, she must here be ruled out.'

He paused, earnestly studying them for a moment; then resumed.

'But something in your aspect seems to urge that it is not solely the heart that moves in you, but also the conscience, the private conscience. But tell me whether or not, occupying the position we do, private conscience should not yield to that imperial one formulated in the code under which alone we officially proceed?'

Here the three men moved in their seats, less convinced than agitated by the course of an argument troubling but the more the spontaneous conflict within.

Perceiving which, the speaker paused for a moment; then abruptly changing his tone, went on.

'To steady us a bit, let us recur to the facts.—In wartime at sea a man-of-war's man strikes his superior in grade, and the blow kills. Apart from its effect the blow itself is, according to the Articles of War, a capital crime. Furthermore—'

'Ay, sir,' emotionally broke in the officer of marines, 'in one sense it was. But surely Budd proposed neither mutiny nor homicide.'

'Surely not, my good man. And before a court less arbitrary and more merciful than a martial one, that plea would largely extenuate. At the Last Assizes[8] it shall acquit. But how here? We proceed under the law of the Mutiny Act.[9] In feature no child can resemble his father more than that Act resembles in spirit the thing from which it derives—War. In His Majesty's service—in this ship, indeed—there are Englishmen forced to fight for the King against their will. Against their conscience, for aught we know. Though as their fellow creatures some of us may appreciate their position, yet as navy officers what reck we of it? Still less recks the enemy. Our impressed men he would fain cut down in the same swath with our volunteers. As regards the enemy's naval conscripts, some of whom may even share our own abhorrence of the regicidal French Directory, it is the same on our side. War looks but to the frontage, the appearance. And the Mutiny Act, War's child, takes after the father. Budd's intent or non-intent is nothing to the purpose.

'But while, put to it by those anxieties in you which I cannot but respect, I only repeat myself—while thus strangely we prolong proceedings that should be summary—the enemy may be sighted and an engagement result. We must do; and one of two things must we do—condemn or let go.'

8. The highest courts of appeal in Great Britain. Melville refers here to the Last Judgment.   9. First passed in 1689; the act and its successors applied only to the army. The navy followed the King's Regulations and Admiralty Instructions of 1772.

'Can we not convict and yet mitigate the penalty?' asked the sailing master, here speaking, and falteringly, for the first.

'Gentlemen, were that clearly lawful for us under the circumstances, consider the consequences of such clemency. The people' (meaning the ship's company) 'have native sense; most of them are familiar with our naval usage and tradition; and how would they take it? Even could you explain to them—which our official position forbids—they, long molded by arbitrary discipline, have not that kind of intelligent responsiveness that might qualify them to comprehend and discriminate. No, to the people the foretopman's deed, however it be worded in the announcement, will be plain homicide committed in a flagrant act of mutiny. What penalty for that should follow, they know. But it does not follow. *Why?* they will ruminate. You know what sailors are. Will they not revert to the recent outbreak at the Nore? Ay. They know the well-founded alarm—the panic it struck throughout England. Your clement sentence they would account pusillanimous. They would think that we flinch, that we are afraid of them—afraid of practicing a lawful rigor singularly demanded at this juncture, lest it should provoke new troubles. What shame to us such a conjecture on their part, and how deadly to discipline. You see then, whither, prompted by duty and the law, I steadfastly drive. But I beseech you, my friends, do not take me amiss. I feel as you do for this unfortunate boy. But did he know our hearts, I take him to be of that generous nature that he would feel even for us on whom in this military necessity so heavy a compulsion is laid.'

With that, crossing the deck he resumed his place by the sashed porthole, tacitly leaving the three to come to a decision. On the cabin's opposite side the troubled court sat silent. Loyal lieges, plain and practical, though at bottom they dissented from some points Captain Vere had put to them, they were without the faculty, hardly had the inclination, to gainsay one whom they felt to be an earnest man, one too not less their superior in mind than in naval rank. But it is not improbable that even such of his words as were not without influence over them, less came home to them than his closing appeal to their instinct as sea officers: in the forethought he threw out as to the practical consequences to discipline, considering the unconfirmed tone of the fleet at the time, should a man-of-war's man's violent killing at sea of a superior in grade be allowed to pass for aught else than a capital crime demanding prompt infliction of the penalty.

Not unlikely they were brought to something more or less akin to that harassed frame of mind which in the year 1842 actuated the commander of the U.S. brig-of-war *Somers* to resolve, under the so-called Articles of War, Articles modeled upon the English Mutiny Act, to resolve upon the execution at sea of a midshipman and two sailors as mutineers designing the seizure of the brig.[1] Which resolution was carried out though in a time of peace and within not many days' sail of home. An act vindicated by a naval court of inquiry subsequently convened ashore. History, and here cited without comment. True, the circumstances on board the *Somers* were different from those on board the *Bellipotent*. But the urgency felt, well-warranted or otherwise, was much the same.

---

1. Melville's cousin, Guert Gansevoort, was first lieutenant of the *Somers* at the time of a mutiny. The incident may have been in the back of Melville's mind when he wrote *Billy Budd*.

Says a writer whom few know,[2] 'Forty years after a battle it is easy for a noncombatant to reason about how it ought to have been fought. It is another thing personally and under fire to have to direct the fighting while involved in the obscuring smoke of it. Much so with respect to other emergencies involving considerations both practical and moral, and when it is imperative promptly to act. The greater the fog the more it imperils the steamer, and speed is put on though at the hazard of running somebody down. Little ween the snug card players in the cabin of the responsibilities of the sleepless man on the bridge.'

In brief, Billy Budd was formally convicted and sentenced to be hung at the yardarm in the early morning watch, it being now night. Otherwise, as is customary in such cases, the sentence would forthwith have been carried out. In wartime on the field or in the fleet, a mortal punishment decreed by a drumhead court—on the field sometimes decreed by but a nod from the general—follows without delay on the heel of conviction, without appeal.

22

It was Captain Vere himself who of his own motion communicated the finding of the court to the prisoner, for that purpose going to the compartment where he was in custody and bidding the marine there to withdraw for the time.

Beyond the communication of the sentence, what took place at this interview was never known. But in view of the character of the twain briefly closeted in that stateroom, each radically sharing in the rarer qualities of our nature—so rare indeed as to be all but incredible to average minds however much cultivated—some conjectures may be ventured.

It would have been in consonance with the spirit of Captain Vere should he on this occasion have concealed nothing from the condemned one—should he indeed have frankly disclosed to him the part he himself had played in bringing about the decision, at the same time revealing his actuating motives. On Billy's side it is not improbable that such a confession would have been received in much the same spirit that prompted it. Not without a sort of joy, indeed, he might have appreciated the brave[3] opinion of him implied in his captain's making such a confidant of him. Nor, as to the sentence itself, could he have been insensible that it was imparted to him as to one not afraid to die. Even more may have been. Captain Vere in end may have developed the passion sometimes latent under an exterior stoical or indifferent. He was old enough to have been Billy's father. The austere devotee of military duty, letting himself melt back into what remains primeval in our formalized humanity, may in end have caught Billy to his heart, even as Abraham may have caught young Isaac on the brink of resolutely offering him up in obedience to the exacting behest.[4] But there is no telling the sacrament, seldom if in any case revealed to the gadding world, wherever under circumstances at all akin to those here attempted to be set forth two of great Nature's nobler order embrace. There is privacy at the time, invio-

2. Melville himself.   3. Fine, superior.   4. Genesis 22.1–18: "God did tempt Abraham, and said . . . Take now thy son, thine only son Isaac, whom thou lovest . . . and offer him . . . for a burnt offering. . . . And Abraham . . . bound Isaac his son, and laid him on the altar upon the wood. And Abraham stretched forth his hand, and took the knife to slay his son. And the angel of the Lord . . . said, Lay not thine hand upon the lad, neither do thou anything unto him: for now I know that thou fearest God. . . . And the angel of the Lord . . . said, . . . I will bless thee . . . because thou hast obeyed my voice."

lable to the survivor; and holy oblivion, the sequel to each diviner magnanimity, providentially covers all at last.

The first to encounter Captain Vere in act of leaving the compartment was the senior lieutenant. The face he beheld, for the moment one expressive of the agony of the strong, was to that officer, though a man of fifty, a startling revelation. That the condemned one suffered less than he who mainly had effected the condemnation was apparently indicated by the former's exclamation in the scene soon perforce to be touched upon.

23

Of a series of incidents within a brief term rapidly following each other, the adequate narration may take up a term less brief, especially if explanation or comment here and there seem requisite to the better understanding of such incidents. Between the entrance into the cabin of him who never left it alive, and him who when he did leave it left it as one condemned to die; between this and the closeted interview just given, less than an hour and a half had elapsed. It was an interval long enough, however, to awaken speculations among no few of the ship's company as to what it was that could be detaining in the cabin the master-at-arms and the sailor; for a rumor that both of them had been seen to enter it and neither of them had been seen to emerge, this rumor had got abroad upon the gun decks and in the tops, the people of a great warship being in one respect like villagers, taking microscopic note of every outward movement or non-movement going on. When therefore, in weather not at all tempestuous, all hands were called in the second dogwatch, a summons under such circumstances not usual in those hours, the crew were not wholly unprepared for some announcement extraordinary, one having connection too with the continued absence of the two men from their wonted haunts.

There was a moderate sea at the time; and the moon, newly risen and near to being at its full, silvered the white spar deck wherever not blotted by the clear-cut shadows horizontally thrown of fixtures and moving men. On either side the quarter-deck the marine guard under arms was drawn up; and Captain Vere, standing in his place surrounded by all the wardroom officers, addressed his men. In so doing, his manner showed neither more nor less than that properly pertaining to his supreme position aboard his own ship. In clear terms and concise he told them what had taken place in the cabin: that the master-at-arms was dead, that he who had killed him had been already tried by a summary court and condemned to death, and that the execution would take place in the early morning watch. The word *mutiny* was not named in what he said. He refrained too from making the occasion an opportunity for any preachment as to the maintenance of discipline, thinking perhaps that under existing circumstances in the navy the consequence of violating discipline shoud be made to speak for itself.

Their captain's announcement was listened to by the throng of standing sailors in a dumbness like that of a seated congregation of believers in hell listening to the clergyman's announcement of his Calvinistic text.

At the close, however, a confused murmur went up. It began to wax. All but instantly, then, at a sign, it was pierced and suppressed by shrill whistles of the boatswain and his mates. The word was given to about ship.

To be prepared for burial Claggart's body was delivered to certain petty officers of his mess. And here, not to clog the sequel with lateral matters, it may be added that at a suitable hour, the master-at-arms was committed to the sea with every funeral honor properly belonging to his naval grade.

In this proceeding as in every public one growing out of the tragedy strict adherence to usage was observed. Nor in any point could it have been at all deviated from, either with respect to Claggart or Billy Budd, without begetting undersirable speculations in the ship's company, sailors, and more particularly men-of-war's men, being of all men the greatest sticklers for usage. For similar cause, all communication between Captain Vere and the condemned one ended with the closeted interview already given, the latter being now surrendered to the ordinary routine preliminary to the end. His transfer under guard from the captain's quarters was effected without unusual precautions—at least no visible ones. If possible, not to let the men so much as surmise that their officers anticipate aught amiss from them is the tacit rule in a military ship. And the more that some sort of trouble should really be apprehended, the more do the officers keep that apprehension to themselves, though not the less unostentatious vigilance may be augmented. In the present instance, the sentry placed over the prisoner had strict orders to let no one have communication with him but the chaplain. And certain unobtrusive measures were taken absolutely to insure this point.

24

In a seventy-four of the old order the deck known as the upper gun deck was the one covered over by the spar deck, which last, though not without its armament, was for the most part exposed to the weather. In general it was at all hours free from hammocks; those of the crew swinging on the lower gun deck and berth deck, the latter being not only a dormitory but also the place for the stowing of the sailors' bags, and on both sides lined with the large chests or movable pantries of the many messes of the men.

On the starboard side of the *Bellipotent's* upper gun deck, behold Billy Budd under sentry lying prone in irons in one of the bays formed by the regular spacing of the guns comprising the batteries on either side. All these pieces were of the heavier caliber of that period. Mounted on lumbering wooden carriages, they were hampered with cumbersome harness of breeching and strong side-tackles for running them out. Guns and carriages, together with the long rammers and shorter linstocks lodged in loops overhead—all these, as customary, were painted black; and the heavy hempen breechings, tarred to the same tint, wore the like livery of the undertakers. In contrast with the funereal hue of these surroundings, the prone sailor's exterior apparel, white jumper and white duck trousers, each more or less soiled, dimly glimmered in the obscure light of the bay like a patch of discolored snow in early April lingering at some upland cave's black mouth. In effect he is already in his shroud, or the garments that shall serve him in lieu of one. Over him but scarce illuminating him, two battle lanterns swing from two massive beams of the deck above. Fed with the oil supplied by the war contractors (whose gains, honest or otherwise, are in every land an anticipated portion of the harvest of death), with flickering splashes of dirty yellow light they pollute the pale moonshine all but ineffectually struggling in obstructed flecks through the open ports from which the tampioned[5] cannon

---

5. Plugged with a tampion, which fits into the muzzle of a gun not in use.

protrude. Other lanterns at intervals serve but to bring out somewhat the obscurer bays which, like small confessionals or side-chapels in a cathedral, branch from the long dim-vistaed broad aisle between the two batteries of that covered tier.

Such was the deck where now lay the Handsome Sailor. Through the rose-tan of his complexion no pallor could have shown. It would have taken days of sequestration from the winds and the sun to have brought about the effacement of that. But the skeleton in the cheekbone at the point of its angle was just beginning delicately to be defined under the warm-tinted skin. In fervid hearts self-contained, some brief experiences devour our human tissue as secret fire in a ship's hold consumes cotton in the bale.

But now lying between the two guns, as nipped in the vice of fate, Billy's agony, mainly proceeding from a generous young heart's virgin experience of the diabolical incarnate and effective in some men—the tension of that agony was over now. It survived not the something healing in the closeted interview with Captain Vere. Without movement, he lay as in a trance, that adolescent expression previously noted as his taking on something akin to the look of a slumbering child in the cradle when the warm hearthglow of the still chamber at night plays on the dimples that at whiles mysteriously form in the cheek, silently coming and going there. For now and then in the gyved[6] one's trance a serene happy light born of some wandering reminiscence or dream would diffuse itself over his face, and then wane away only anew to return.

The chaplain, coming to see him and finding him thus, and perceiving no sign that he was conscious of his presence, attentively regarded him for a space, then slipping aside, withdrew for the time, peradventure feeling that even he, the minister of Christ though receiving his stipend from Mars,[7] had no consolation to proffer which could result in a peace transcending that which he beheld. But in the small hours he came again. And the prisoner, now awake to his surroundings, noticed his approach, and civilly, all but cheerfully, welcomed him. But it was to little purpose that in the interview following, the good man sought to bring Billy Budd to some godly understanding that he must die, and at dawn. True, Billy himself freely referred to his death as a thing close at hand; but it was something in the way that children will refer to death in general, who yet among their other sports will play a funeral with hearse and mourners.

Not that like children Billy was incapable of conceiving what death really is. No, but he was wholly without irrational fear of it, a fear more prevalent in highly civilized communities than those so-called barbarous ones which in all respects stand nearer to unadulterate Nature. And, as elsewhere said, a barbarian Billy radically was—as much so, for all the costume, as his countrymen the British captives, living trophies, made to march in the Roman triumph of Germanicus.[8] Quite as much so as those later barbarians, young men probably, and picked specimens among the earlier British converts to Christianity, at least nominally such, taken to Rome (as today converts from lesser isles of the sea may be taken to London), of whom the Pope at that time, admiring the strangeness of their personal beauty so unlike the Italian stamp, their clear ruddy complexion and curled flaxen locks,

---

6. Shackled, chained.　　7. The god of war. I.e., paid by the navy.　　8. Germanicus Caesar (15 B.C.–A.D. 19), granted a triumph in Rome in A.D. 17.

exclaimed, 'Angles' (meaning *English,* the modern derivative), 'Angles, do you call them? And is it because they look so like angels?'[9] Had it been later in time, one would think that the Pope had in mind Fra Angelico's seraphs, some of whom, plucking apples in gardens of the Hesperides,[1] have the faint rosebud complexion of the more beautiful English girls.

If in vain the good chaplain sought to impress the young barbarian with ideas of death akin to those conveyed in the skull, dial, and crossbones on old tombstones, equally futile to all appearance were his efforts to bring home to him the thought of salvation and a Savior. Billy listened, but less out of awe or reverence, perhaps, than from a certain natural politeness, doubtless at bottom regarding all that in much the same way that most mariners of his class take any discourse abstract or out of the common tone of the workaday world. And this sailor way of taking clerical discourse is not wholly unlike the way in which the primer of Christianity, full of transcendent miracles, was received long ago on tropic isles by any superior *savage,* so called—a Tahitian, say, of Captain Cook's time or shortly after that time.[2] Out of a natural courtesy he received, but did not appropriate. It was like a gift placed in the palm of an outreached hand upon which the fingers do not close.

But the *Bellipotent's* chaplain was a discreet man possessing the good sense of a good heart. So he insisted not in his vocation here. At the instance of Captain Vere, a lieutenant had apprised him of pretty much everything as to Billy; and since he felt that innocence was even a better thing than religion wherewith to go to Judgment, he reluctantly withdrew; but in his emotion not without first performing an act strange enough in an Englishman, and under the circumstances yet more so in any regular priest. Stooping over, he kissed on the fair cheek his fellow man, a felon in martial law, one whom though on the confines of death he felt he could never convert to a dogma; nor for all that did he fear for his future.

Marvel not that having been made acquainted with the young sailor's essential innocence the worthy man lifted not a finger to avert the doom of such a martyr to martial discipline. So to do would not only have been as idle as invoking the desert, but would also have been an audacious transgression of the bounds of his function, one as exactly prescribed to him by military law as that of the boatswain or any other naval officer. Bluntly put, a chaplain is the minister of the Prince of Peace serving in the host of the God of War—Mars. As such, he is as incongruous as a musket would be on the altar at Christmas. Why, then, is he there? Because he indirectly subserves the purpose attested by the cannon; because too he lends the sanction of the religion of the meek to that which practically is the abrogation of everything but brute Force.

25

The night so luminous on the spar deck, but otherwise on the cavernous ones below, levels so like the tiered galleries in a coal mine—the luminous night passed away. But like the prophet in the chariot disappearing in heaven

9. Bede's *Ecclesiastical History of the English People* tells this anecdote about Pope Gregory the Great (540?–604).   1. Daughters of Atlas who guarded a tree bearing golden apples on an enchanted island in the western sea. Fra Angelico (1387–1455), the Florentine painter Giovanni da Fiesole.   2. James Cook (1728–1779) was in Tahiti in 1769 and from 1772 to 1775.

and dropping his mantle to Elisha,[3] the withdrawing night transferred its pale robe to the breaking day. A meek, shy light appeared in the East, where stretched a diaphanous fleece of white furrowed vapor. That light slowly waxed. Suddenly *eight bells* was struck aft, responded to by one louder metallic stroke from forward. It was four o'clock in the morning. Instantly the silver whistles were heard summoning all hands to witness punishment. Up through the great hatchways rimmed with racks of heavy shot the watch below came pouring, overspreading with the watch already on deck the space between the mainmast and foremast including that occupied by the capacious launch and the black booms tiered on either side of it, boat and booms making a summit of observation for the powder-boys and younger tars. A different group comprising one watch of topmen leaned over the rail of that sea balcony, no small one in a seventy-four, looking down on the crowd below. Man or boy, none spake but in whisper, and few spake at all. Captain Vere—as before, the central figure among the assembled commissioned officers—stood nigh the break of the poop deck facing forward. Just below him on the quarter-deck the marines in full equipment were drawn up much as at the scene of the promulgated sentence.

At sea in the old time, the execution by halter of a military sailor was generally from the foreyard. In the present instance, for special reasons[4] the mainyard was assigned. Under an arm of that yard the prisoner was presently brought up, the chaplain attending him. It was noted at the time, and remarked upon afterwards, that in this final scene the good man evinced little or nothing of the perfunctory. Brief speech indeed he had with the condemned one, but the genuine Gospel was less on his tongue than in his aspect and manner towards him. The final preparations personal to the latter being speedily brought to an end by two boatswain's mates, the consummation impended. Billy stood facing aft. At the penultimate moment, his words, his only ones, words wholly unobstructed in the utterance, were these: 'God bless Captain Vere!' Syllables so unanticipated coming from one with the ignominious hemp about his neck—a conventional felon's benediction[5] directed aft towards the quarters of honor; syllables too delivered in the clear melody of a singing bird on the point of launching from the twig—had a phenomenal effect, not unenhanced by the rare personal beauty of the young sailor, spiritualized now through late experiences so poignantly profound.

Without volition, as it were, as if indeed the ship's populace were but the vehicles of some vocal current electric, with one voice from alow and aloft came a resonant sympathetic echo: 'God bless Captain Vere!' And yet at that instant Billy alone must have been in their hearts, even as in their eyes.

At the pronounced words and the spontaneous echo that voluminously rebounded them, Captain Vere, either through stoic self-control or a sort of momentary paralysis induced by emotional shock, stood erectly rigid as a musket in the ship-armorer's rack.

The hull, deliberately recovering from the periodic roll to leeward, was just regaining an even keel when the last signal, a preconcerted dumb one, was given. At the same moment it chanced that the vapory fleece hanging low in

---

3. 2 Kings 2.11–13: "There appeared a chariot of fire, and horses of fire, and parted them both asunder; and Elijah went up by a whirlwind into heaven. And Elisha . . . took up . . . the mantle of Elijah that fell from him." **4.** The *special reasons* remain obscure. The text editors suggest that the captain's motives were precautionary; the phrase, an insertion, previously read, "for strategic reasons." **5.** It is a traditional ritual for the condemned man to forgive the official compelled by duty to order his death.

the East was shot through with a soft glory as of the fleece of the Lamb of God seen in mystical vision, and simultaneously therewith, watched by the wedged mass of upturned faces, Billy ascended; and, ascending, took the full rose of the dawn.

In the pinioned figure arrived at the yard-end, to the wonder of all no motion was apparent, none save that created by the slow roll of the hull in moderate weather, so majestic in a great ship ponderously cannoned.

26

When some days afterwards, in reference to the singularity just mentioned, the purser, a rather ruddy, rotund person more accurate as an accountant than profound as a philosopher, said at mess to the surgeon, "What testimony to the force lodged in will power," the latter, saturnine, spare, and tall, one in whom a discreet causticity went along with a manner less genial than polite, replied. 'Your pardon, Mr Purser. In a hanging scientifically conducted—and under special orders I myself directed how Budd's was to be effected—any movement following the completed suspension and originating in the body suspended, such movement indicates mechanical spasm in the muscular system. Hence the absence of that is no more attributable to will power, as you call it, than to horsepower—begging your pardon.'

'But this muscular spasm you speak of, is not that in a degree more or less invariable in these cases?'

'Assuredly so, Mr Purser.'

'How then, my good sir, do you account for its absence in this instance?'

'Mr Purser, it is clear that your sense of the singularity in this matter equals not mine. You account for it by what you call will power—a term not yet included in the lexicon of science. For me, I do not, with my present knowledge, pretend to account for it at all. Even should we assume the hypothesis that at the first touch of the halyards the action of Budd's heart, intensified by extraordinary emotion at its climax, abruptly stopped—much like a watch when in carelessly winding it up you strain at the finish, thus snapping the chain—even under that hypothesis how account for the phenomenon that followed?'

'You admit, then, that the absence of spasmodic movement was phenomenal.'

'It was phenomenal, Mr Purser, in the sense that it was an appearance the cause of which is not immediately to be assigned.'

'But tell me, my dear sir,' pertinaciously continued the other, 'was the man's death effected by the halter, or was it a species of euthanasia?'[6]

'Euthanasia, Mr Purser, is something like your *will power*: I doubt its authenticity as a scientific term—begging your pardon again. It is at once imaginative and metaphysical—in short, Greek.—But,' abruptly changing his tone, 'there is a case in the sick bay that I do not care to leave to my assistants. Beg your pardon, but excuse me.' And rising from the mess he formally withdrew.

6. A quiet and easy death.

27

The silence at the moment of execution and for a moment or two continuing thereafter, a silence but emphasized by the regular wash of the sea against the hull or the flutter of a sail caused by the helmsman's eyes being tempted astray, this emphasized silence was gradually disturbed by a sound not easily to be verbally rendered. Whoever has heard the freshet-wave of a torrent suddenly swelled by pouring showers in tropical mountains, showers not shared by the plain; whoever has heard the first muffled murmur of its sloping advance through precipitous woods may form some conception of the sound now heard. The seeming remoteness of its source was because of its murmurous indistinctness, since it came from close by, even from the men massed on the ship's open deck. Being inarticulate, it was dubious in significance further than it seemed to indicate some capricious revulsion of thought or feeling such as mobs ashore are liable to, in the present instance possibly implying a sullen revocation on the men's part of their involuntary echoing of Billy's benediction. But ere the murmur had time to wax into clamor it was met by a strategic command, the more telling that it came with abrupt unexpectedness: 'Pipe down the starboard watch, Boatswain, and see that they go.'

Shrill as the shriek of the sea hawk, the silver whistles of the boatswain and his mates pierced that ominous low sound, dissipating it; and yielding to the mechanism of discipline the throng was thinned by one-half. For the remainder, most of them were set to temporary employments connected with trimming the yards and so forth, business readily to be got up to serve occasion by any officer of the deck.

Now each proceeding that follows a mortal sentence pronounced at sea by a drumhead court is characterized by promptitude not perceptibly merging into hurry, though bordering that. The hammock, the one which had been Billy's bed when alive, having already been ballasted with shot and otherwise prepared to serve for his canvas coffin, the last offices of the sea undertakers, the sailmakers' mates, were now speedily completed. When everything was in readiness a second call for all hands, made necessary by the strategic movement before mentioned, was sounded, now to witness burial.

The details of this closing formality it needs not to give. But when the tilted plank let slide its freight into the sea, a second strange human murmur was heard, blended now with another inarticulate sound proceeding from certain larger seafowl who, their attention having been attracted by the peculiar commotion in the water resulting from the heavy sloped dive of the shotted hammock into the sea, flew screaming to the spot. So near the hull did they come, that the stridor or bony creak of their gaunt double-jointed pinions was audible. As the ship under light airs passed on, leaving the burial spot astern, they still kept circling it low down with the moving shadow of their outstretched wings and the croaked requiem of their cries.

Upon sailors as superstitious as those of the age preceding ours, men-of-war's men too who had just beheld the prodigy of repose in the form suspended in air, and now foundering in the deeps; to such mariners the action of the seafowl, though dictated by mere animal greed for prey, was big with no prosaic significance. An uncertain movement began among them, in which some encroachment was made. It was tolerated but for a moment.

For suddenly the drum beat to quarters,[7] which familiar sound happening at least twice every day, had upon the present occasion a signal peremptoriness in it. True martial discipline long continued superinduces in average man a sort of impulse whose operation at the official word of command much resembles in its promptitude the effect of an instinct.

The drumbeat dissolved the multitude, distributing most of them along the batteries of the two covered gun decks. There, as wonted, the guns' crew stood by their respective cannon erect and silent. In due course the first officer, sword under arm and standing in his place on the quarter-deck, formally received the successive reports of the sworded lieutenants commanding the sections of batteries below; the last of which reports being made, the summed report he delivered with the customary salute to the commander. All this occupied time, which in the present case was the object in beating to quarters at an hour prior to the customary one. That such variance from usage was authorized by an officer like Captain Vere, a martinet as some deemed him, was evidence of the necessity for unusual action implied in what he deemed to be temporarily the mood of his men. 'With mankind,' he would say, 'forms, measured forms, are everything; and this is the import couched in the story of Orpheus with his lyre spellbinding the wild denizens of the wood.'[8] And this he once applied to the disruption of forms going on across the Channel and the consequences thereof.

At this unwonted muster at quarters, all proceeded as at the regular hour. The band on the quarter-deck played a sacred air, after which the chaplain went through the customary morning service. That done, the drum beat the retreat; and toned by music and religious rites subserving the discipline and purposes of war, the men in their wonted orderly manner dispersed to the places allotted them when not at the guns.

And now it was full day. The fleece of low-hanging vapor had vanished, licked up by the sun that late had so glorified it. And the circumambient air in the clearness of its serenity was like smooth white marble in the polished block not yet removed from the marble-dealer's yard.

28

The symmetry of form attainable in pure fiction cannot so readily be achieved in a narration essentially having less to do with fable than with fact. Truth uncompromisingly told will always have its ragged edges; hence the conclusion of such a narration is apt to be less finished than an architectural finial.

How it fared with the Handsome Sailor during the year of the Great Mutiny has been faithfully given. But though properly the story ends with his life, something in way of sequel will not be amiss. Three brief chapters will suffice.

In the general rechristening under the Directory of the craft originally forming the navy of the French monarchy, the *St. Louis* line-of-battle ship was named the *Athée* (the *Atheist*). Such a name, like some other substituted ones in the Revolutionary fleet, while proclaiming the infidel audacity of the

---

7. The signal for the sailors to return to their assigned stations.   8. When Orpheus, in Greek mythology, played his lyre and sang, wild animals were charmed, trees and stones followed him, fish left the water in which they swam, and birds flew about his head.

ruling power, was yet, though not so intended to be, the aptest name, if one consider it, ever given to a warship; far more so indeed than the *Devastation,* the *Erebus* (the *Hell*), and similar names bestowed upon fighting ships.

On the return passage to the English fleet from the detached cruise during which occurred the events already recorded, the *Bellipotent* fell in with the *Athée.* An engagement ensued, during which Captain Vere, in the act of putting his ship alongside the enemy with a view of throwing his boarders across her bulwarks, was hit by a musket ball from a porthole of the enemy's main cabin. More than disabled, he dropped to the deck and was carried below to the same cockpit where some of his men already lay. The senior lieutenant took command. Under him the enemy was finally captured, and though much crippled was by rare good fortune successfully taken into Gibraltar, an English port not very distant from the scene of the fight. There, Captain Vere with the rest of the wounded was put ashore. He lingered for some days, but the end came. Unhappily he was cut off too early for the Nile and Trafalgar. The spirit that 'spite its philosophic austerity may yet have indulged in the most secret of all passions, ambition, never attained to the fulness of fame.

Not long before death, while lying under the influence of that magical drug[9] which, soothing the physical frame, mysteriously operates on the subtler element in man, he was heard to murmur words inexplicable to his attendant: 'Billy Budd, Billy Budd.' That these were not the accents of remorse would seem clear from what the attendant said to the *Bellipotent*'s senior officer of marines, who, as the most reluctant to condemn of the members of the drumhead court, too well knew, though here he kept the knowledge to himself, who Billy Budd was.

29

Some few weeks after the execution, among other matters under the head of 'News from the Mediterranean,' there appeared in a naval chronicle of the time, an authorized weekly publication, an account of the affair. It was doubtless for the most part written in good faith, though the medium, partly rumor, through which the facts must have reached the writer served to deflect and in part falsify them. The account was as follows:

'On the tenth of the last month a deplorable occurrence took place on board H.M.S. *Bellipotent.* John Claggart, the ship's master-at-arms, discovering that some sort of plot was incipient among an inferior section of the ship's company, and that the ringleader was one William Budd; he, Claggart, in the act of arraigning the man before the captain, was vindictively stabbed to the heart by the suddenly drawn sheath knife of Budd.

'The deed and the implement employed sufficiently suggest that though mustered into the service under an English name the assassin was no Englishman, but one of those aliens adopting English cognomens whom the present extraordinary necessities of the service have caused to be admitted into it in considerable number.

'The enormity of the crime and the extreme depravity of the criminal appear the greater in view of the character of the victim, a middle-aged man

9. Opium.

respectable and discreet, belonging to that minor official grade, the petty officers, upon whom, as none know better than the commissioned gentlemen, the efficiency of His Majesty's navy so largely depends. His function was a responsible one, at once onerous and thankless; and his fidelity in it the greater because of his strong patriotic impulse. In this instance as in so many other instances in these days, the character of this unfortunate man signally refutes, if refutation were needed, that peevish saying attributed to the late Dr Johnson, that patriotism is the last refuge of a scoundrel.[1]

'The criminal paid the penalty of his crime. The promptitude of the punishment has proved salutary. Nothing amiss is now apprehended aboard H.M.S. *Bellipotent.*'

The above, appearing in a publication now long ago superannuated and forgotten, is all that hitherto has stood in human record to attest what manner of men respectively were John Claggart and Billy Budd.

30

Everything is for a term venerated in navies. Any tangible object associated with some striking incident of the service is converted into a monument. The spar from which the foretopman was suspended was for some few years kept trace of by the bluejackets. Their knowledges followed it from ship to dockyard and again from dockyard to ship, still pursuing it even when at last reduced to a mere dockyard boom. To them a chip of it was as a piece of the Cross. Ignorant though they were of the secret facts of the tragedy, and not thinking but that the penalty was somehow unavoidably inflicted from the naval point of view, for all that, they instinctively felt that Billy was a sort of man as incapable of mutiny as of wilful murder. They recalled the fresh young image of the Handsome Sailor, that face never deformed by a sneer or subtler vile freak of the heart within. This impression of him was doubtless deepened by the fact that he was gone, and in a measure mysteriously gone. On the gun decks of the *Bellipotent* the general estimate of his nature and its unconscious simplicity eventually found rude utterance from another foretopman, one of his own watch, gifted, as some sailors are, with an artless *poetic* temperament. The tarry hand made some lines which, after circulating among the shipboard crews for a while, finally got rudely printed at Portsmouth as a ballad. The title given to it was the sailor's.

Billy in the Darbies[2]

Good of the chaplain to enter Lone Bay
And down on his marrowbones here and pray
For the likes just o' me, Billy Budd.—But, look:
Through the port comes the moonshine astray!
It tips the guard's cutlass and silvers this nook;   5
But 'twill die in the dawning of Billy's last day.
A jewel-block[3] they'll make of me tomorrow,

---

1. The saying is quoted in James Boswell's *Life of Samuel Johnson Ll. D.* (1791).   2. Handcuffs or fetters.
3. Carries a studding-sail to the very end of the yard where it is hoisted.

Pendant pearl from the yardarm-end
Like the eardrop I gave to Bristol Molly—
O, 'tis me, not the sentence they'll suspend.   10
Ay, ay, all is up; and I must up too,
Early in the morning, aloft from alow.
On an empty stomach now never it would do.
They'll give me a nibble—bit o' biscuit ere I go.
Sure, a messmate will reach me the last parting cup;   15
But, turning heads away from the hoist and the belay,
Heaven knows who will have the running of me up!
No pipe to those halyards.—But aren't it all sham?
A blur's in my eyes; it is dreaming that I am.
A hatchet to my hawser? All adrift to go?   20
The drum roll to grog, and Billy never know?
But Donald he has promised to stand by the plank;
So I'll shake a friendly hand ere I sink.
But—no! It is dead then I'll be, come to think.
I remember Taff the Welshman when he sank.   25
And his cheek it was like the budding pink.
But me they'll lash in hammock, drop me deep.
Fathoms down, fathoms down, how I'll dream fast asleep.
I feel it stealing now. Sentry, are you there?
Just ease these darbies at the wrist,   30
And roll me over fair!
I am sleepy, and the oozy weeds about me twist.

EMILY DICKINSON
1830–1886

Emily Dickinson forces her readers to acknowledge the startling aspects of ordinary life. "Ordinary life" includes the mysterious actuality of death, but it also includes birds and woods and oceans, arguments between people, the weight of depression. In small facts and large, Dickinson perceives enormous meaning.

The poet's life, like her verse, was somewhat mysterious. Born to a prosperous and prominent Amherst, Massachusetts, family (her father, a lawyer, was also treasurer of Amherst College), Dickinson attended Amherst Academy and later, for a year, the Mount Holyoke Female Seminary. Thereafter, however, she remained almost entirely in her father's house, leading the life of a recluse. She had close family attachments and a few close friendships, pursued mainly through correspondence. The most important of these relationships, from a literary point of view, was with the Boston writer and critic Thomas Wentworth Higginson, who eventually published her poems. She had begun writing verse in the late 1850s; in 1862, after seeing an essay of Higginson's in the *Atlantic Monthly*, Dickinson wrote him to ask his opinion of her poems, about three hundred of them in existence by this time. The correspondence thus begun continued to the end of Dickinson's life; Higginson also visited her in Amherst.

At Dickinson's death, 1,775 poems survived; only seven had been published, anonymously. With the help of another friend, Mabel Todd Loomis, Higginson selected poems for a volume, published in 1890, which proved extremely popular. Further selections continued to appear, but not until 1955 did Dickinson's entire body of work reach print.

By 1843, the English poet Elizabeth Barrett Browning had written in verse an exhortation to social reform (*The Cry of the Children*); in 1857, she published a long poem, *Aurora Leigh,* commenting on the oppressed situation of women. Christina Rossetti, born the same year as Dickinson and like her unmarried, in poems like *Goblin Market* (1862) found indirect ways to meditate on female predicaments. Dickinson, on the other hand, seems only peripherally aware of social facts. She alludes to church services, locomotives, female costume; very occasionally (for example, in "My Life had stood—a Loaded Gun—") she refers to the way a woman's life is defined in relation to a man's. More centrally, she finds brilliant and provocative formulations of the emotional import of universal phenomena. We may feel already that death amounts to an incomprehensible and indigestible fact, but we are unlikely to have imagined conversations within a tomb or a personified version of death as carriage driver. By using such images, Dickinson disarmingly suggests a kind of playful innocence. Only gradually does one realize that the naive, childlike perception, devoid of obviously ominous suggestion, conceals a complex, disturbing sense of human self-deception and reluctance to face the truth of experience.

Truth is an important word in Dickinson's poetry. "Tell all the Truth but tell it slant," she advises, pointing out that "The Truth must dazzle gradually / Or every man be blind—." She tells of a man who preaches about " 'Truth' until it proclaimed him a Liar—": truth remains an absolute, both challenging and judging us all. In one of her most haunting poems, she claims the identity of Beauty and Truth (an identity tellingly asserted earlier in Keats's *Ode on a Grecian Urn*) through the fiction of two dead people discussing their profound commitments:

> I died for Beauty—but was scarce
> Adjusted in the Tomb
> When One who died for Truth, was lain
> In an adjoining Room—

Her neighbor asks her why she "failed"; when she explains, he says that beauty and truth "are One":

> And so, as Kinsmen, met a Night—
> We talked between the Rooms—
> Until the Moss had reached our lips—
> And covered up—our names—

Until the last two lines, about the moss, the poem appears to evoke a rather cozy vision of death: neighbors amiably conversing from one room to another, as though at a slumber party ("met a Night"), two "Kinsmen" dedicated to noble abstractions and comforted by the companionship of their dedication. Only the word *failed* (meaning "died") disturbs the comfortable atmosphere, by suggesting a view of death as defeat.

The Keats poem that ends by asserting the identity of truth and beauty implies the permanence of both, as embodied in the work of art, the Grecian urn that stimulates the poet's reflections. Dickinson's poem concludes with troubling suggestions of impermanence. Talk of beauty and truth may reassure the talkers, but death necessarily implies forgetfulness: the dead forget and are forgotten, their very identities ("names") lost, their capacity for communication eliminated. Death *is* defeat; the high Romanticism of Keats's ode, on which this poem implicitly comments, blurs that fact. Despite Dickinson's fanciful images and allegories, her poems insist on their own kind of uncompromising realism. They speak of the universal human effort to imagine experience in reassuring terms, but they do not suggest that reality offers much in the way of reassurance: only brief experiences of natural beauty; and even those challenge human constructions. "I started Early—Took my dog—" a poem about visiting the sea begins; but it ends with the sea encountering "the Solid Town— / No One He seemed to know—" and withdrawing.

Dickinson's eccentric punctuation, with dashes as the chief mark of emphasis and interruption, emphasizes the movements of consciousness in her lyrics. In their early publication, the poems were typically given conventional punctuation; only in 1955 did the body of work appear as Dickinson wrote it. The highly personal mode of punctuation emphasizes the fact that this verse contains also a personal and demanding vision.

Emily Dickinson: An Interpretive Biography (1955), by T. H. Johnson, Dickinson's editor, is indispensable. Useful critical sources include C. Blake, ed., *The Recognition of Emily Dickinson* (1964), a collection of criticism since 1890; Albert Gelpi, *Emily Dickinson: The Mind of the Poet* (1966); P. Bennett, *Emily Dickinson: Woman Poet* (1990); S. Juhasz, ed., *Feminist Critics Read Emily Dickinson* (1983), a collection with a specifically feminist orientation; and J. Dobson, *Dickinson and the Strategies of Reticence* (1989). Other critical studies are K. Stocks, *Emily Dickinson and the Modern Consciousness* (1988); M. N. Smith, *Rowing in Eden: Rereading Emily Dickinson* (1992); J. Farr, *The Passion of Emily Dickinson* (1992); and E. Phillips, *Emily Dickinson: Personae and Performance* (1996). E. A. Petrino, *Emily Dickinson and Her Contemporaries: Women's Verse in America, 1820–1885* (1998), places the verse in an illuminating context.

[POEMS]

216

Safe in their Alabaster Chambers—
Untouched by Morning
And untouched by Noon—
Sleep the meek members of the Resurrection—
Rafter of satin,   5
And Roof of stone.

Light laughs the breeze
In her Castle above them—
Babbles the Bee in a stolid Ear,
Pipe the Sweet Birds in ignorant cadence—   10
Ah, what sagacity perished here!

258

There's a certain Slant of light,
Winter Afternoons—
That oppresses, like the Heft
Of Cathedral Tunes—

Heavenly Hurt, it gives us—   5
We can find no scar,
But internal difference,
Where the Meanings, are—

None may teach it—Any—
'Tis the Seal Despair—
An imperial affliction   10
Sent us of the Air—

When it comes, the Landscape listens—
Shadows—hold their breath—
When it goes, 'tis like the Distance   15
On the look of Death—

303

The Soul selects her own Society—
Then—shuts the Door—
To her divine Majority—
Present no more—

Unmoved—she notes the Chariots—pausing   5
At her low Gate—
Unmoved—an Emperor be kneeling
Upon her Mat—

I've known her—from an ample nation—
Choose One—   10
Then—close the Valves of her attention—
Like Stone—

328

A Bird came down the Walk—
He did not know I saw—
He bit an Angleworm in halves
And ate the fellow, raw,

And then he drank a Dew   5
From a convenient Grass—
And then hopped sidewise to the Wall
To let a Beetle pass—

He glanced with rapid eyes
That hurried all around—   10
They looked like frightened Beads, I thought—
He stirred his Velvet Head

Like one in danger, Cautious,
I offered him a Crumb
And he unrolled his feathers   15
And rowed him softer home—

Than Oars divide the Ocean,
Too silver for a seam—
Or Butterflies, off Banks of Noon
Leap, plashless as they swim.   20

341

After great pain, a formal feeling comes—
The Nerves sit ceremonious, like Tombs—
The stiff Heart questions was it He, that bore,
And Yesterday, or Centuries before?

The Feet, mechanical, go round—   5
Of Ground, or Air, or Ought[1]—
A Wooden way
Regardless grown,
A Quartz contentment, like a stone—

This is the Hour of Lead—   10
Remembered, if outlived,
As Freezing persons, recollect the Snow—
First—Chill—then Stupor—then the letting go—

435

Much Madness is divinest Sense—
To a discerning Eye—
Much Sense—the starkest Madness—
'Tis the Majority
In this, as All, prevail—   5
Assent—and you are sane—
Demur—you're straightway dangerous—
And handled with a Chain—

449

I died for Beauty—but was scarce
Adjusted in the Tomb
When One who died for Truth, was lain
In an adjoining Room—

He questioned softly "Why I failed"?   5
"For Beauty", I replied—
"And I—for Truth—Themself are One—
We Brethren, are", He said—

And so, as Kinsmen, met a Night—
We talked between the Rooms—   10
Until the Moss had reached our lips—
And covered up—our names—

1. Zero.

465

I heard a Fly buzz—when I died—
The Stillness in the Room
Was like the Stillness in the Air—
Between the Heaves of Storm—

The Eyes around—had wrung them dry—   5
And Breaths were gathering firm
For that last Onset—when the King
Be witnessed—in the Room—

I willed my Keepsakes—Signed away
What portion of me be   10
Assignable—and then it was
There interposed a Fly—

With Blue—uncertain stumbling Buzz—
Between the light—and me—
And then the Windows failed—and then   15
I could not see to see—

519

'Twas warm—at first—like Us—
Until there crept upon
A Chill—like frost upon a Glass—
Till all the scene—be gone.

The Forehead copied Stone—   5
The Fingers grew too cold
To ache—and like a Skater's Brook—
The busy eyes—congealed—

It straightened—that was all—
It crowded Cold to Cold   10
It multiplied indifference—
As[1] Pride were all it could—

And even when with Cords—
'Twas lowered, like a Weight—
It made no Signal, nor demurred,   15
But dropped like Adamant.

1. As if.

585

I like to see it lap the Miles—
And lick the Valleys up—
And stop to feed itself at Tanks—
And then—prodigious step

Around a Pile of Mountains—   5
And supercilious peer
In Shanties—by the sides of Roads—
And then a Quarry pare

To fit its Ribs
And crawl between   10
Complaining all the while
In horrid—hooting stanza—
Then chase itself down Hill—

And neigh like Boanerges[1]—
Then—punctual as a Star   15
Stop—docile and omnipotent
At its own stable door—

632

The Brain—is wider than the Sky—
For—put them side by side—
The one the other will contain
With ease—and You—beside—

The Brain is deeper than the sea—   5
For—hold them—Blue to Blue—
The one the other will absorb—
As Sponges—Buckets—do—

The Brain is just the weight of God—
For—Heft them—Pound for Pound—   10
And they will differ—if they do—
As Syllable from Sound—

657

I dwell in Possibility—
A fairer House than Prose—
More numerous of Windows—
Superior—for Doors—

---

1. "Sons of thunder," name given by Jesus to the brothers and disciples James and John, presumably because they were thunderous preachers.

Of Chambers as the Cedars—   5
Impregnable of Eye—
And for an Everlasting Roof
The Gambrels[1] of the Sky—

Of Visitors—the fairest—
For Occupation—This—   10
The spreading wide my narrow Hands
To gather Paradise—

712

Because I could not stop for Death—
He kindly stopped for me—
The Carriage held but just Ourselves—
And Immortality.

We slowly drove—He knew no haste   5
And I had put away
My labor and my leisure too,
For His Civility—

We passed the School, where Children strove
At Recess—in the Ring—   10
We passed the Fields of Gazing Grain—
We passed the Setting Sun—

Or rather—He passed Us—
The Dews drew quivering and chill—
For only Gossamer, my Gown—   15
My Tippet—only Tulle[1]—

We paused before a House that seemed
A Swelling of the Ground—
The Roof was scarcely visible—
The Cornice—in the Ground—   20

Since then—'tis Centuries—and yet
Feels shorter than the Day
I first surmised the Horses' Heads
Were toward Eternity—

754

My Life had stood—a Loaded Gun—
In Corners—till a Day
The Owner passed—identified—
And carried Me away—

---

1. Slopes, as in the large, arched roofs often seen on barns.   1. Fine, silken netting. *Tippet:* a scarf.

And now We roam in Sovereign Woods—   5
And now We hunt the Doe—
And every time I speak for Him—
The Mountains straight reply—

And do I smile, such cordial light
Upon the Valley glow—   10
It is as a Vesuvian face[1]
Had let its pleasure through—

And when at Night—Our good Day done—
I guard My Master's Head—
'Tis better than the Eider-Duck's   15
Deep Pillow—to have shared—

To foe of His—I'm deadly foe—
None stir the second time—
On whom I lay a Yellow Eye—
Or an emphatic Thumb—   20

Though I than He—may longer live
He longer must—than I—
For I have but the power to kill,
Without—the power to die—

1084

At Half past Three, a single Bird
Unto a silent Sky
Propounded but a single term
Of cautious melody.

At Half past Four, Experiment   5
Had subjugated test
And lo, Her silver Principle
Supplanted all the rest.

At Half past Seven, Element
Nor Implement, be seen—   10
And Place was where the Presence was
Circumference between.

1129

Tell all the Truth but tell it slant—
Success in Circuit lies
Too bright for our infirm Delight
The Truth's superb surprise

1. A face glowing with light like that from an erupting volcano.

As Lightning to the Children eased   5
With explanation kind
The Truth must dazzle gradually
Or every man be blind—

1207

He preached upon "Breadth" till it argued him narrow—
The Broad are too broad to define
And of "Truth" until it proclaimed him a Liar—
The Truth never flaunted a Sign—

Simplicity fled from his counterfeit presence   5
As Gold the Pyrites[1] would shun—
What confusion would cover the innocent Jesus
To meet so enabled[2] a Man!

1564

Pass to thy Rendezvous of Light,
Pangless except for us—
Who slowly ford the Mystery
Which thou hast leaped across!

1593

There came a Wind like a Bugle—
It quivered through the Grass
And a Green Chill upon the Heat
So ominous did pass
We barred the Windows and the Doors   5
As from an Emerald Ghost—
The Doom's electric Moccasin[1]
That very instant passed—
On a strange Mob of panting Trees
And Fences fled away   10
And Rivers where the Houses ran
Those looked that lived—that Day—
The Bell within the steeple wild
The flying tidings told—
How much can come   15
And much can go,
And yet abide the World!

---

1. Iron bisulfide, sometimes called fool's gold.   2. Competent.   1. I.e., water moccasin, a poisonous snake.

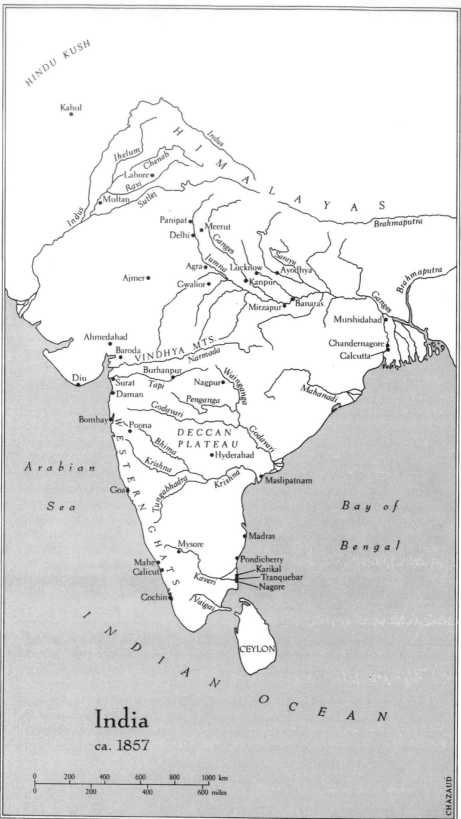

India
ca. 1857

Urdu Lyric Poetry in North India

The *ghazal* is the quintessential lyric genre in Urdu, a language that evolved out of the interaction of dialects of Hindi (a north Indian language) with Persian, the principal language of literature and administration for the Muslim dynasties who ruled various parts of India from the twelfth century onward. The Urdu *ghazal* reached its perfection during the age of the Mughals, Muslim rulers who commanded an extensive Indian empire between the sixteenth and eighteenth centuries. At first, the poets of the hybrid Indo-Muslim culture wrote mainly in the court language, Persian. However, impelled by the desire to express Indian sensibilities and experiences in an Indian idiom, they turned more and more to Urdu; and by the eighteenth century, the *ghazal*, an import from Persian poetry (see p. 1064), had emerged as a mature and productive form in Urdu. A poetry of introspection and reflection, the Urdu *ghazal* was at the same time a public, performative genre, cultivated in "poets' gatherings" (*mushā'irah*), at which poets met to recite their poems and compose verses extemporaneously before enthusiastic audiences. It remains an essential element of South Asian culture at all levels. *Mushā'irahs* are as important in intellectual circles in India, Pakistan, and Bangladesh today as they were in Mughal India, and songs in the popular Hindi cinema are modeled on the *ghazal*.

The typical *ghazal* is a poem of reflections on love in all its aspects. Originally a part of the Arabic praise-poem genre known as *qasīdah*, the *ghazal* became, in its independent form, the favored vehicle for Persian and Indian mystical poets writing about the soul's yearning for God, as well as for secular poets whose theme was human love. Ideally, however, secular and sacred concerns merge in the *ghazal*'s philosophical tenor, and its deliberately ambiguous vocabulary and imagery. Important among these built-in ambiguities is the use of masculine grammatical forms for the beloved person, which some scholars relate to an original context of homosexual love. The Urdu poets, however, use it to suggest both an idealized Beloved, usually a woman, and also God Himself. Thus the *ghazal* is not a poem about a specific love affair, or even about a particular mood of love, but a lyrical contemplation of love as a metaphor for the relations that exist among human beings, God, and the world. Vast as these themes are, it is the individual poet's unique imagination that unifies and reveals these relations and is thus central to the conception of the *ghazal*.

The aesthetic effect of the Urdu *ghazal* derives from thematic and formal conventions. Images from Persian and Arabic poetry—the garden, the fellowship of men drinking wine, the lover in the desert, the nightingale, and the rose, each capable of evoking a web of associations, all contribute to the *ghazal*'s pervasive mood of sadness and unfulfilled love. At the same time, the genre is recognizable by a set of stringent and complex formal conventions. The *ghazal* is composed of anywhere between three and seven couplets (*she'r*), each focusing on a separate thought, image, or mood but connected by a common meter and a rhyme scheme in the pattern *aa, ba, ca, da,* and so on. Another rhyming element is the *qāfiyah*, a syllable or sequence of sounds that appears in both lines of the first couplet and the second line of the following ones; it may be followed by a refrain (*radīf*), a word or phrase repeated without change as a refrain at the end of the couplet. The final couplet usually contains the *takhallus*, the poet's pen name or signature. The concentration of images, the highly condensed form of expression, and the juxtaposition of brief sentences and phrases in each couplet require the reader or listener to respond to the couplet as a self-contained unit. However, while each of the couplets in a *ghazal* may be enjoyed by itself, the appreciation of the *ghazal* as a whole involves the cumulative effect of several couplets linked by verbal and emotional associations as well as by the litany-like repeated elements.

TIME LINE

TEXTS	CONTEXTS
	1816 A group of Bengali and English men found the Hindu College in Calcutta "for the education of native youths in European literature and science"
	1817 James Mill writes a *History of India,* justifying British rule in India
ca. 1820–1865 Mirza Asadulla Khan Ghalib, preeminent poet in the Urdu language, writes ***ghazal* lyric poems** expressing the aesthetic of Islamic culture in India	
	1828 Bengali reformer Ram Mohun Roy founds the Brahmo Samaj, an organization dedicated to Hindu religious and social reform
	1835 British politician Thomas Macaulay publishes his *Minute on Education on India,* arguing for English education for Indians
ca. 1837–1841 Henry David Thoreau reads and is influenced by the ***Bhagavad-Gītā***	
ca. 1855 Walt Whitman's *Passage to India* is published in *Leaves of Grass*	
1861 Michael Madhusudan Datta, Indian Christian convert in Calcutta, publishes *Meghanadvadh,* a Bengali version of the *Rāmāyaṇa* epic in blank verse, modeled after Homer and Milton	
1882 Bankim Chandra Chatterjee writes the novel *Ananda Math,* an allegory of resistance to colonial rule	
	1885 A group of Indian and English intellectuals found the Indian National Congress, an organization devoted to Indian representation in the British colonial government of India
1894 Rudyard Kipling publishes *The Jungle Book*	

Boldface titles indicate works in the anthology.

GHALIB
1797–1869

Although several poets of the Mughal era, such as Mir, Sauda, and Momin, are greatly admired for particular effects, Mirza Asadullah Khan, known by his pen name Ghalib ("Conqueror"), is celebrated as the pre-eminent exponent of the Urdu *ghazal*. Born in the north Indian city of Agra into an aristocratic Muslim family of Turkish origin, the poet was educated in Agra and in Delhi. In 1812 he settled permanently in Delhi, devoting his time to writing poetry, mainly in Persian. By Ghalib's time, although Delhi continued to be the seat of the Mughals, the Mughal king was subservient to to the British East India Company, which ruled India on behalf of the British Crown.

Financial support was a major problem for Ghalib throughout his life. After the death of his uncle, who was also his guardian, the poet spent many years negotiating with the British colonial government for his share of the uncle's military pension. It was not until 1847 that he secured a major patron. In that year Bahadur Shah, the last Mughal "emperor," accepted Ghalib at his court. Three years later, the king commissioned from the poet a Persian prose history of the Mughals, tracing their lineage back to the Central Asian conqueror Timur. In 1855, a year after the death of his rival, the court poet Zauq (also a pen name, a tradition in Persian and Urdu poetry), Ghalib was appointed as Bahadur Shah's tutor in versification.

Ghalib's good fortune was short lived. When Indian princes and soldiers (*sepoys*) rose in revolt against the British regime in 1857, Delhi was beseiged and looted. The British suppressed the revolt, and Bahadur Shah was deposed and exiled to Burma. Earlier events, such as the Persian king Nadir Shah's sack of Delhi in 1739, had forced poets and artists to flee from the capital city and had led to the rise of Lucknow, the capital of the north Indian state of Oudh, as a major center for Urdu literature. The chaos that surrounded the revolt of 1857 resulted in a new exodus of poets and artists from Delhi to lesser provincial towns. Ghalib, however, remained in Delhi till his death in 1869. In addition to Persian poetry the poet left a number of works in Urdu: a collection (*dīvān*) of *ghazals*; two volumes of letters; and *Dastamboh* (Bouquet of Flowers), the diary he wrote during the revolt of 1857. While the lyric *ghazals* are unquestionably Ghalib's masterpieces, his letters and diary are exemplars of elegant Urdu prose style. If the former reflect an intense poetic and moral sensibility, the latter reveal Ghalib as a man of keen intelligence who possessed an observant eye and a sense of humor, and was deeply engaged with literary and political issues.

Ghalib's couplets have become an integral part of the consciousness of Urdu speakers, who will quote them freely in the course of everyday conversation to illustrate a point or to express a mood. Among the Urdu poets, Ghalib achieves to perfection the *ghazal* poet's goal of balancing subjectivity with a universalizing philosophical vision. Like other forms of classical Indian and Persian poetry, the *ghazal* is a highly conventional genre. In his poems Ghalib molds the very conventions of the *ghazal* into a personal, even private, poetic language that perfectly expresses his sensibility. In the couplet "Because of you the goblet had a thousand faces; Because of me it was mirrored in a single eye" (Ghazal XIX), the stock images of the wine goblet and mirror fuse to place the relationship between subject and object in an entirely new light. In "The dove is a clutch of ashes, nightingale a clench of color" (Ghazal XXI), the blurring of sense-experience images the intensity of feeling. Other couplets reveal the reflective, personal aspect of the *ghazal*: "Fire doesn't do it; lust for fire does it. / The heart hurts for the spirit's fading" (Ghazal XXI). The range of style and interpretation represented in the translations given here testifies to the combination of complex, brilliant images and ambiguities of language that renders Ghalib's couplets at once direct and elusive, precise and enigmatic, in much the same manner as the poems of the German poet Rilke.

Ghalib's poems are startlingly intense. Here, more than in the verse of any other Urdu poet, the *ghazal*'s characteristic melancholy deepens into a profound loneliness, an overwhelming sense of loss. Some have seen in these traits a reflection of the uncertain age in which Ghalib lived, when Indian rulers were being ousted by British colonial agencies, and English was beginning to take the place of Persian and Urdu language and literature among the Indian elites. The poet survived the revolt of 1857, a cataclysmic event that effectively ended Indian political power on the subcontinent. His letters and diary reveal a life constantly troubled by financial instability as well as by the decay of civilization as he knew it. Yet the voice that speaks to us most compellingly in Ghalib's *ghazals* is the private, personal one, testifying to the poet's visceral response to the enduring pain of the human condition, a darkness far more unsettling than "this time's great shadow."

A NOTE ON THE METERS OF GHALIB'S *GHAZALS*

The *ghazal* poets use a number of Persian quantitative meters. Stress patterns may vary from line to line, but the lines must be of equal length. Here is the first couplet of Ghazal XIX, in a meter with thirteen syllables per line:

har kadam dūrī-e-manzil   numāyān mujh se
= – = ==– = =   – = =   =   =

With every step, my goal seems farther away from me.

meri raftār se bhāge hai   biyābān mujh se
= – = = = = = =   – = =   =   =

As fast as I run, the desert runs away from me.

The – and = represent short and long syllables, respectively; *ān* in numāyā*n* and biyābā*n* is the rhyme (*qāfiyah*); the fixed phrase *mujh se*, which is repeated at the end of each of the couplets that follows, is the end refrain or end rhyme (*radīf*).

Aijaz Ahmad, *Ghazals of Ghalib* (1971), presents a selection of Ghalib's *ghazals*, each one translated by different poets and preceded by a literal translation with explanatory notes. Ralph Russell and Khurshidul Islam, *Ghalib: Life and Letters* (1969), provide an excellent account of Ghalib's life and a translation of his letters. For further discussion of the Urdu *ghazal* and selections from the major poets, see Ralph Russell and Khurshidul Islam, *Three Mughal Poets* (1968), and Ahmed Ali, *The Golden Tradition: An Anthology of Urdu Poetry* (1973). Anita Desai's novel *In Custody* (1984) successfully evokes the fascination of *ghazal* poetry for modern South Asians.

PRONOUNCING GLOSSARY

The following list uses common English syllables and stress accents to provide rough equivalents of selected words whose pronunciation may be unfamiliar to the general reader.

Bahadur Shah: *buh-hah'-door shah*

dīvān: *dee-vahn'*

Ghalib: *ghah'-lib*

ghazal: *g-huh-zuhl'*

Mirza Asadulla Khan: *meer-zah' uh-suhd-ool'-lah khahn*

mushāi'rah: *moo-shai'-rah*

qāfiyah: *quah'-fee-yah*

qasīdah: *quh-seeh'-dah*

radīf: *ruh-deehf*

she'r: *shayr*

takhallus: *tuhk-huhl'-loos*

Urdu: *oor'-dooh*

[Ghazals]

V[1]

Waterbead ecstasy: dying in a stream;
Too strong a pain brings its own balm.

So weak now we weep sighs only;
Learn surely how water turns to air.

Spring cloud thinning after rain: 5
Dying into its own weeping.

Would you riddle the miracle of the wind's shaping?
Watch how a mirror greens in spring.[2]

Rose, Ghalib, the rose changes give us our joy in seeing.
All colors and kinds, what is should and be open always.[3]   10

VIII[4]

Here in the splendid court the great verses flow:
may such treasure tumble open for us always.

Night has arrived; again the stars tumble forth,
a stream rich as wealth from a temple.

Ignorant as I am, foreign to the Beauty's mystery,   5
yet I could rejoice that the fair[5] face begins to commune with me.

Why in this night do I find grief? Why the storm of remembered affliction?
Will the stars always avert their gaze? Choose others?

Exiled, how can I rejoice, forced here from home,
and even my letters torn open?   10

X[6]

Why didn't I shrink in the blaze of that face?
I flare up, apprehending the gaze that returned that vision unblinded.[7]

Out in the world they call me a disciple of fire
because the words of my grief fall like a shower of sparks.[8]

Many have fallen in love with the slim neck of the decanter;   5
seeing you walk, the wave of the wine trembles with envy.

1. Translated by Thomas Fitzsimmons.   2. The face of the mirror turns green with mildew, thus rivaling
its metallic back, which is normally kept green with a kind of polish. In *ghazal* poetry the mirror is a mystical
image of perfect truth and clarity.   3. Ahmad's literal rendering of this couplet reads: "The appearance
of the rose has vouchsafed us the desire to witness (and enjoy), Ghalib! / Whatever the color and condition
of things, the eyes should always be open."   4. Translated by William Stafford.   5. Angelic.
6. Translated by Adrienne Rich.   7. The verse alludes to the Muslim myth of Moses in which God
revealed Himself to Moses on Mount Sinai in a dazzling flash, rendering him unconscious; the mountain
was burned to ashes.   8. Possibly a reference to the Parsis or Zoroastrians of India, who worship fire.

We and the poems we make get bought and sold together;
but we knew all along for whom they were intended.

The lightning-stroke of the vision was meant for us, not for Sinai;
the wine should be poured for him who possesses the goblet.   10

XII[9]

I'm neither the loosening of song nor the close-drawn tent of music;
I'm the sound, simply, of my own breaking.[1]

You were meant to sit in the shade of your rippling hair;
I was made to look further, into a blacker tangle.[2]

All my self-possession is self-delusion;   5
what violent effort, to maintain this nonchalance!

Now that you've come, let me touch you in greeting
as the forehead of the beggar touches the ground.

No wonder you came looking for me, you
who care for the grieving, and I the sound of grief.[3]   10

XIII[4]

No more those meetings, partings, tears!
No more those days, nights, months, and years!

Who has time for love, its lore?
Delight in beauty?—now no more.

All that was from the thought of someone,   5
a grace that's taken, now long gone.

Tears now hurt more; they flow deep.
Heartsick these days, it's blood we weep.[5]

Oh, Ghalib!—weak limbs, no hope, disgust:
no balance now, even in this dust.   10

XIV[6]

Wings are like dust, weightless; the wind may steal them;
otherwise they would have neither power nor endurance.[7]

9. Translated by Adrienne Rich.   1. *Gul-e-naghmā*, literally, "blossoming of song." *Tent:* or *pardah*,
which can suggest web, curtain, tapestry, screen, veil, and note of music.   2. The beloved's dark curls
are a stock image.   3. Ahmad's literal rendering of this couplet reads: "Now that you ask for me, it is no
wonder; / I am helpless / poor / afflicted / Miserable, and you who look after the afflicted."   4. Translated
by William Stafford.   5. Ahmad's literal rendering of this couplet reads: "Weeping tears of blood is not
so easy; / No more is strength in the heart, stability in our condition!"   6. Translated by W. S. Merwin.
7. Dust (*khāk*) is the leitmotif of this *ghazal*, appearing in the refrain phrase *khāk nahīñ*, which conveys a
different meaning in each couplet.

What beauty now is bringing nearer the face of heaven
So that the path bears not dust but flower visions?

At the mere thought of the flower's face, some are drunk.　　　5
There is nothing else in the cellar, in the wineskins.[8]

I have been shamed by my love's power to destroy.
In this house the wish to build lives alone.

Now Ghalib, these verses are idle amusements.
Clearly nothing is gained by such a performance.　　　10

XIX[9]

With every step I took, my goal seemed farther away.
I ran my fastest, but the desert ran faster.

That lonely night fire inhabited my heart
And my shadow drifted from me in a thin cloud of smoke.

Because my feet were blistered in the desert　　　5
Of my madness, my wake shone like a chain of pearls.[1]

Because of you the goblet had a thousand faces;
Because of me it was mirrored in a single eye.

Fire runs from my burning eyes, Asad![2]
I light up the soil and the dead leaves in the garden.　　　10

XXI[3]

Dew on a flower[4]—tears, or something:
hidden spots mark the heart of a cruel woman.

The dove is a clutch of ashes, nightingale a clench of color:[5]
a cry in a scarred, burnt heart, to that, is nothing.

Fire doesn't do it; lust for fire does it.　　　5
The heart hurts for the spirit's fading.

To cry like Love's prisoner is forced by Love's prison:[6]
hand under a stone, pinned there, faithful.

Sun that bathes our world! Hold us all here!
This time's great shadow estranges us all.　　　10

---

8. Here *khāk nahīñ* means "There is nothing." 　9. Translated by Mark Strand. 　1. Possibly an allusion
to the Arabian legend of Majnoon, who wandered in the desert, mad with passion for his beloved Laila.
2. Ghalib's first name, which he used as a pen name until he adopted "Ghalib." 　3. Translated by William Stafford. 　4. The *lālā*, tulip, or Indian red poppy. 　5. Or *qafas-e-rang*, literally, "prison of color."
6. Ahmad's literal rendering of this line reads: "To claim to be love's prisoner is itself a consequence of
constraint (compulsion)."

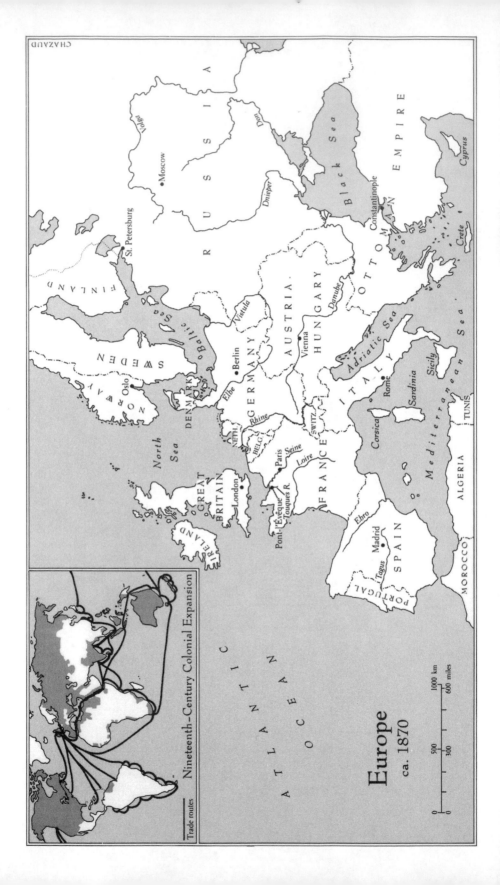

Europe
ca. 1870

Nineteenth-Century Colonial Expansion

Trade routes

Realism, Naturalism, and Symbolism in Europe

The nineteenth century is (apart from the twentieth) the century of greatest change in the history of Western civilization. The upheavals following the French Revolution broke up the old order of Europe. The Holy Roman Empire and the Papal States were dissolved. Nationalism, nourished by the political and social aspirations of the middle classes, grew by leaps and bounds. Colonial empires were created and vast sections of the globe opened up forcibly to Western trade. "Liberty" became the dominant political slogan of the century, although the various calls for liberty focused on Western society and not on the colonies. In different countries and different decades *liberty* meant different things: here liberation from the rule of the foreigner, there the emancipation of the serf; here the removal of economic restrictions on trade and manufacturing, there the introduction of a constitution, free speech, parliamentary institutions, and agitation for the rights of women. Almost everywhere in Europe, the middle classes established their effective rule, though revolutions in 1830 and 1848 were crushed across Europe and monarchs remained in more or less nominal power. Two large European countries, Germany and Italy, achieved their centuries-old dreams of political unification. The predominance of France, still marked at the beginning of the century, was broken, and England—or rather Great Britain—ruled the seas throughout the century. The smaller European nations, especially in the Balkans, began to emancipate themselves from foreign rule.

These major political changes were caused by, and in their turn caused, great social and economic changes. The Industrial Revolution, which had begun in England in the eighteenth century, spread over the Continent and transformed living conditions radically. The enormous increase in the speed and availability of transportation owing to the development of railroads and steamships and the rapid urbanization following from the establishment of industries changed the whole pattern of human life in most countries and made possible, within a century, an unprecedented increase in population (as much as threefold in most European countries), which was also fostered by the advances of medicine and hygiene. The development of transportation and communication systems brought areas of the world into closer contact and prepared the way for global economic and political systems. The existence of widespread wealth and prosperity is undeniable, although it coexisted with wretched living conditions and other hardships of the early factory workers, many of them women. As the social and political power of the aristocracy declined, the barriers between the social classes diminished appreciably almost everywhere. Middle-class values dominated, and the industrial laborer began to be felt as a political force.

These social and economic changes were closely bound up with shifts in prevailing outlooks and philosophies. Technological innovation is impossible without the discoveries of science. The scientific outlook, hitherto dominant only in a comparatively limited area, spread widely and permeated almost all fields of human thought and endeavor. It raised enormous hopes for the future betterment of our condition on Earth, especially when Darwin's evolutionary theories fortified the earlier, vaguer faith in unlimited progress. "Liberty," "science," "progress," and "evolution" are the concepts that define the mental atmosphere of the nineteenth century in Europe.

But tendencies hostile to these were by no means absent. Feudal or Catholic conservatism succeeded, especially in Austria-Hungary, in Russia, and in much of southern Europe, in preserving old regimes, and the philosophies of a conservative and religious society were reformulated in modern terms. At the same time, in England the very assumptions of the new industrial middle-class society were powerfully attacked by writers such as Carlyle and Ruskin who recommended a return to medieval forms of social cooperation and handicraft. The industrial civilization of the nineteenth century was also opposed by the fierce individualism of many artists and thinkers who were unhappy in the ugly, commercial, and "Philistine" society of the age. The writings of Nietzsche, toward the end of the century, and the whole movement of art for art's sake, which asserted the independence of the artist from society, are the most obvious symptoms of this revolt. The free-enterprise system and the liberalism of the ruling middle classes also early clashed with the rising proletariat; diverse forms of socialism developed, preaching a new collectivism with the stress on equality. Socialism could have Christian or romantic motivations, or it could become "scientific" and revolutionary, as Marx's brand of socialism (a certain stage of which he called "communism") claimed to be.

While up through the eighteenth century religion was, at least in name, a major force in European civilization, in the nineteenth century there was a marked decrease in its influence on both intellectual leaders and ordinary people. Local, intense revivals of religious consciousness, such as the Oxford movement in England, did occur, and the traditional religious institutions were preserved everywhere, but the impact of science on religion was such that many tenets of the old faiths crumbled or were severely weakened. The discoveries of astronomy, geology, evolutionary biology, and archaeology as well as biblical criticism forced, almost everywhere, a restatement of the old creeds. Religion, especially in the Protestant countries, was frequently confined to an inner feeling of religiosity or to a system of morality that preserved the ancient Christian virtues. In Germany during the early nineteenth century, Hegel and his predecessors and followers tried to interpret the world in spiritual terms, outside the bounds of traditional religion. There were many attempts even late in the century to restate this view, but the methods and discoveries of science seemed to invalidate it, and various formulas that took science as their base in building new lay religions of hope in humanity gained popularity. French positivism, English utilitarianism, the evolutionism of Herbert Spencer are some of the best-known examples. Meanwhile, for the first time in history, at least in Europe, profoundly pessimistic and atheistic philosophies arose, of which Schopenhauer's was the most subtle, while extreme materialism was the most widespread. Thus the whole gamut of views of the universe was represented during the century in new and impressive formulations.

The plastic arts did not show a similar vitality. For a long time, in most countries, painting and architecture floundered in a sterile eclecticism—in a bewildering variety of historical masquerades in which the neo-Gothic style was replaced by the neo-Renaissance and that by the neo-Baroque and other decorative revivals of past forms. Only in France did painting (with the Impressionists) find a new style that was genuinely original. In music the highly Romantic art of Richard Wagner attracted the most attention. Wagner's concept of the *Gesamtkunstwerk*—the "total work" combining music, drama, poetry, and spectacle—influenced Symbolist writers and encouraged the tendency to break down distinctions between genres. Otherwise, the individual national schools either continued in their tradition, like Italian opera (Verdi), or founded an idiom of their own, often based on a revival of folklore, as in Russia (Tchaikovsky), Poland (Chopin), Bohemia (Dvořák), and Norway (Grieg).

But literature was the most representative and the most widely influential art of nineteenth-century Europe. It found new forms and methods and expressed the social and intellectual situation of the time most fully and memorably. It was this literature, moreover, that served as a model for many non-Western writers seeking to modernize their own literary traditions on the basis of European masterworks. Nowadays, the cultural assumptions of such literary emulation are criticized by some, and many writers seek to rediscover an earlier, precolonial tradition. The literature of nineteenth-century Europe continues nonetheless to be read and admired in its own right.

REALISM AND NATURALISM

After the great wave of the international Romantic movement had spent its force in the fourth decade of the nineteenth century, European literature moved in the direction of what is usually called *realism*. Realism was not a coherent general movement that established itself unchallenged for a long period of time, as classicism had succeeded in doing during the eighteenth century. Exceptions and reservations there were, but still in retrospect the nineteenth century appears as the period of the great realistic writers: Flaubert in France, Dostoevsky and Tolstoy in Russia, Charles Dickens in England, Henry James in America, Ibsen in Norway.

What is meant by *realism*? The term, in literary use (there is a much older philosophical use), apparently dates back to the Germans at the turn of the century—to Friedrich Schiller and August and Friedrich Schlegel. It cropped up in France as early as 1826 but became a commonly accepted literary and artistic slogan only in the 1850s. When Gustave Courbet's paintings were rejected by the Paris World's Fair of 1855, the artist exhibited them separately as "realist" art and wrote a preface to the exhibit catalog that became an unofficial manifesto for realist art. In the following year, a review called *Réalisme* began publication, and in 1857 a novelist and critic, Champfleury (the pseudonym of Jules-François-Félix Husson), published a volume of critical articles with the title *Le Réalisme*. Since then the word has been bandied about, discussed, analyzed, and abused as all slogans are. It is frequently confused with naturalism, an ancient philosophical term for materialism, epicureanism, or any secularism. As a specifically literary term, it crystallized only in France. In French, as in English, naturalist means, of course, simply student of nature, and the analogy between the writer and the naturalist, specifically the botanist and zoologist, was ready at hand. Émile Zola, in the preface to a new edition of his early novel *Thérèse Raquin* (1866), proclaimed the naturalist creed most boldly. His book, he claims, is "an analytical labor on two living bodies like that of a surgeon on corpses." He proudly counts himself among the group of "naturalist writers."

The program of the groups of writers and critics who used these terms can be easily summarized. The realists wanted a truthful representation in literature of reality—that is, of contemporary life and manners. They thought of their method as inductive, observational, and hence "objective." The personality of the author was to be suppressed or was at least to recede into the background, since reality was to be seen "as it is." The naturalistic program, as formulated by Zola, was substantially the same, except that Zola put greater stress on the analogies to science, considering the procedure of the novelist as identical with that of the experimenting scientist. He also more definitely and exclusively embraced the philosophy of scientific materialism, with its deterministic implications and its stress on heredity and environment, while the older realists were not always so clear in drawing the philosophical consequences. These French theories were anticipated, paralleled, or imitated all over the world of Western literature. In Germany, the movement called Young Germany, with which Heine was associated, had propounded a substantially anti-Romantic realistic program as early as the 1830s, but versions of the French theories definitely triumphed there only in the 1880s. In Russia, as early as the 1840s, the most prominent critic of the time, Vissarion Belinsky, praised the "natural" school of Russian fiction, which described contemporary Russia with fidelity. Italy also, from the late 1870s on, produced an analogous movement, which called itself *verismo*. The English-speaking countries were the last to adopt the critical programs and slogans of the Continent: George Moore and George Gissing brought the French theories to England in the late 1880s, and in the United States William Dean Howells began his campaign for realism in 1886, when he became editor of *Harper's Magazine*. Realistic and naturalistic theories of literature have since been widely accepted, either as the basis of writing or as a standard against which later generations rebel. The once officially promoted doctrine in Russia is called "Socialist Realism," a combination of factual observation and implied socialist message; the novel in the United States is usually considered naturalistic and judged by the standards of nature and truth. Yet twentieth-century novelists in Europe and America have also pushed realism to an extreme in the "literature of fact," in documentary novels, and in often-bewildering series of undifferentiated "objective" perceptions reported by the narrator.

The slogans "realism" and "naturalism" were thus new to the nineteenth century and served as effective formulas directed against the Romantic creed. Truth, contemporaneity, and objectivity were the obvious counterparts of Romantic imagination, of Romantic historicism and its glorification of the past, and of Romantic subjectivity, the exaltation of the ego and the individual. But, of course, the emphasis on truth and objectivity was not really new: these qualities had been demanded by many older, classical theories of imitation, and in the eighteenth century there were great writers such as Denis Diderot who wanted a literal "imitation of life" even on the stage.

The practice of realism, it could be argued, is very old indeed. There are realistic scenes in the *Iliad* and *Odyssey*, and there is plenty of realism in ancient comedy and satire, in medieval stories (fabliaux) like some of Chaucer's and Boccaccio's, in many Elizabethan plays, in the Spanish rogue novels, in the English eighteenth-century novel beginning with Daniel Defoe, and so on almost ad infinitum. But while it would be easy to find in early literature anticipations of almost every single element of modern realism, still the systematic description of contemporary society, with a serious purpose, often even with a tragic tone as well, and with sympathy for heroes drawn from the middle and lower classes, was a real innovation of the nineteenth century.

It is usually rash to explain a literary movement in social and political terms. But the new realistic art surely had something to do with the triumph of the middle classes in France after the July revolution in 1830, and in England after the passage of the Reform Bill in 1832, and with the increasing influence of the middle classes in almost every country. Russia is somewhat of an exception as no large middle class could develop there during the nineteenth century. An absolute feudal regime continued in power and the special character of most of Russian literature must be the result of this distinction, but even in Russia there emerged an "intelligentsia" (the term comes from Russia) that was open to Western ideas and was highly critical of the czarist regime and its official ideology.

But while much nineteenth-century literature reflects the triumph of the middle classes, it would be an error to think of the great realistic writers as spokespeople or mouthpieces of the society they described. Honoré de Balzac was politically a Catholic monarchist who applauded the Bourbon restoration after the fall of Napoleon, but he had an extraordinary imaginative insight into the processes leading to the victory of the middle classes. Flaubert despised the middle-class society of the Third Empire with an intense hatred and the pride of a self-conscious artist. Dickens became increasingly critical of the middle classes and the assumptions of industrial civilization. Dostoevsky, though he took part in a conspiracy against the Russian government early in his life and spent ten years in exile in Siberia, became the propounder of an extremely conservative nationalistic and religious creed that was definitely directed against the revolutionary forces in Russia. Tolstoy, himself a count and a landowner, was violent in his criticism of the czarist regime, especially later in his life, but he cannot be described as friendly to the middle classes, to the aims of the democratic movements in Western Europe, or to the science of the time. Ibsen's political attitude was that of a proud individualist who condemns the "compact majority" and its tyranny. Possibly all art is critical of its society, but in the nineteenth century this criticism became much more explicit, as social and political issues became much more urgent or, at least, were regarded as more urgent by those writing about or within them. To a far greater degree than in earlier centuries, writers felt their isolation from society, viewed the structure and problems of the prevailing order as debatable and reformable, and in spite of all demands for objectivity became, in many cases, social propagandists and reformers in their own right.

The program of realism, while defensible enough as a reaction against Romanticism, raises critical questions that were not answered theoretically by its defenders. What is meant by *truth of representation*? Photographic copying? This seems the implication of many famous pronouncements: "A novel is a mirror walking along the road," said Stendhal (the pseudonym of Marie-Henri Beyle) as early as 1830. But such statements can hardly be taken literally. All art must select and represent; it cannot be and has never been a simple transcript of reality. What such analogies are intended to convey is rather a claim for an all-inclusiveness of subject matter, a protest against the exclusion of themes that before were considered low, sordid, or trivial (like the puddles along the road the mirror walks). Chekhov formulated this protest with the usual parallel between the scientist and the writer: "To a chemist nothing on earth is unclean. A writer must be as objective as a chemist; he must abandon the subjective line: he must know that dung heaps play a very respectable part in a landscape, and that evil passions are as inherent in life as good ones." Thus the truth of realistic art includes the sordid, the low, the disgusting, and the evil; and the implication is that the subject is treated objectively, without interference and falsification by the artist's personality and his own desires.

But in practice, while realistic art succeeded in expanding the themes of art, it could not fulfill the demand for total objectivity. Works of art are written by human beings and inevitably express their personalities and their points of view. As Joseph Conrad admitted, "even the most artful of writers will give himself (and his morality) away in about every third sentence." Objectivity, in the sense that Zola had in mind when he proposed a scientific method in the writing of novels and conceived of the novelist as a sociologist collecting human documents, is impossible in practice. When it has been attempted, it has led only to bad art, to dullness and the display of inert materials, to the confusion between the art of the novel and reporting, documentation. The demand for objectivity can be understood only as a demand for a specific method of narration, in which the author does not interfere explicitly, in his or her own name, and as a rejection of personal themes of introspection and reverie.

The realistic program, while it has made innumerable new subjects available to art, also implies a narrowing of its themes and methods—a condemnation of the fantastic, the historical, the remote, the idealized, the unsullied, the idyllic. Realism professes to present us with a slice of life. But one should recognize that it is an artistic method and convention like any other. Romantic art could, without offending its readers, use coincidences, improbabilities, and even impossibilities that were not, theoretically at least, tolerated in realistic art. Ibsen, for instance, avoided many older conventions of the stage: asides, soliloquies, eavesdropping, sudden unmotivated appearances of new characters, and so on; but his dramas have their own marked conventions, which seem today almost as "unnatural" as those of the Romantics. Realistic theories of literature cannot be upheld in their literal sense; objective and impersonal truth is unobtainable, at least in art, since all art is a making, a creating of a world of symbols that differs radically from the world that we call reality. The value of realism lies in its negation of the conventions of Romanticism, its expansion of the themes of art, and its new demonstration (never forgotten by artists) that literature has to deal also with its time and society and has, at its best, an insight into reality (not only social reality) that is not necessarily identical with that of science. Many of the great writers make us realize the world of their time, evoke an imaginative picture of it that seems truer and will last longer than that of historians and sociologists. But this achievement is owing to their imagination and their art, or craft, two requisites that realistic theory tended to forget or minimize.

When we observe the actual practice of the great realistic writers of the nineteenth century, we notice a sharp contradiction between theory and practice, and an independent evolution of the art of the novel that is obscured for us if we pay too much attention to the theories and slogans of the time, even those that the authors themselves propounded. Flaubert, the high priest of a cult of art for art's sake, the most consistent advocate of absolute objectivity, was actually, at least in a good half of his work, a writer of Romantic fantasies of blood and gold, flesh and jewels. There is some truth in his saying that Madame Bovary is himself, for in the drab story of a provincial adulteress he castigated his own Romanticism and Romantic dreams.

So too with Dostoevsky. Although some of his settings resemble those of the crime novel, he is actually a writer of high tragedy, of a drama of ideas in which ordinary reality is transformed into a symbol of the spiritual world. His technique is closely associated with Balzac's (it is significant that his first publication was a translation of Balzac's *Eugénie Grandet*) and thus with many devices of the sensational melodramatic novel of French Romanticism. Tolstoy's art is more concretely real than that of any of the other great masters mentioned, yet he is, at the same time, the most personal and even literally autobiographical author in the history of the novel—a writer, besides, who knows nothing of detachment toward social and religious problems but frankly preaches his own very personal religion. And if we turn to Ibsen, we find essentially the same situation. Ibsen began as a writer of historical and fantastic dramas and slowly returned to a style that is fundamentally symbolist. All his later plays are organized by symbols, from the duck of *The Wild Duck* (1884) to the white horses in *Rosmersholm* (1886), the burned manuscript in *Hedda Gabler* (1890), and the tower in *The Master Builder* (1892). Even Zola, the propounder of the most scientific theory, was in practice a novelist who used the most extreme devices of melodrama and Symbolism. In *Germinal* (1885), his novel of mining, the mine is the central symbol, alive as an animal, heaving, breathing. It would be an odd reader who could find literal truth in the final catastrophe of the cave-in or even in such naturalistic scenes as a dance where the beer oozes from the nostrils of the drinkers.

One could assert, in short, that all the great realists were at bottom Romanticists, but it is probably wiser to conclude that they were simply artists who created worlds of imagination and knew (at least instinctively) that in art one can say something about reality only through symbols. The attempts at documentary art, at mere reporting and transcribing, are today forgotten.

SYMBOLISM

The later nineteenth century cannot, however, be considered simply an age of realism and naturalism. Poetry addressed in its own way the same questions of truth and reality. By the middle of the century, it was embarked on an exploration of language that would influence all forms of twentieth-century literature. Where prose fiction and drama faced outward, aiming to mirror the real world, poetry turned its attention to the mirror itself: the words that reflect and represent reality. Preserving the Romantic notion of the poet as seer or visionary, emphasizing a heightened self-consciousness and an inquiry into poetic language, the innovators of nineteenth-century poetry explored both creativity and human identity. They examined the perceiving subject's awareness of perceptions and illustrated this awareness in allusive poetry that played with multiple and shifting perspectives and frequently led to a blurring of boundaries between real and imaginary. Traditional verse forms exploded, and the new forms heralded not only modern free verse, prose poems, and spatial poetry but also the innovative language of novelists such as James Joyce, William Faulkner, Alain Robbe-Grillet, and Marguerite Duras.

The evolution was gradual until the middle of the century. Some poets continued to practice a substantially Romantic art: Tennyson, for instance, and Victor Hugo. In England, the Pre-Raphaelite movement—painters and writers such as J. E. Millais (1829–1896), W. H. Hunt (1827–1910), and D. G. Rossetti (1828–1882)—drew their inspiration from the sensuous detail of Italian medieval art in opposition to the honored Renaissance painter Raphael (1483–1520); they upheld a Romantic, escapist, and antirealist program. In France, a large and diverse group of Parnassian poets stemming from Leconte de Lisle (1818–1894) retained Romantic themes while focusing on a precise and delicate use of detail. The most important writer of this period is Charles Baudelaire (1821–1867), whose poetry and writings on art deeply influenced the course of European poetry. Baudelaire's major collection of poems, *The Flowers of Evil*, was published in the same year that Flaubert was brought to trial for *Madame Bovary* (1857). He inspired a poetic movement that would later be called Symbolism, and he remains today the French poet most widely read outside France.

Symbolism as *symbolic representation* is a philosophical concept, and the use of symbols is not restricted to the nineteenth and twentieth centuries. Using one thing to suggest another, or an image to suggest an idea, is as old as art and language. The Neolithic paintings in the caves at Lascaux, France, are symbolic pictures of the hunt. Medieval Christian literature used a shared set of symbols to signify religious concepts through earthly images: the rose symbolized love, the dove the Holy Spirit, and the serpent Satan. As a literary movement, however, Symbolism is a nineteenth-century French phenomenon with affinities to the visionary writings of eighteenth-century German Romanticism, to the Parnassian cult of artistic form and art for art's sake, and to the poetic theories of Edgar Allan Poe. Confusingly enough, the official Symbolist "movement"—whose manifesto appeared only in 1886—derives from, but does not include, the great midcentury poets Baudelaire, Verlaine, Rimbaud, and Mallarmé. These highly individual writers were never part of any movement. Yet there are elements in common, and the ancestors of Symbolism are often discussed in the same breath as their followers. Symbolist poetry tries to manipulate language in an almost magical way to evoke hidden meanings behind the appearances of this world. A symbol in this sense is an image or cluster of images created to suggest another plane of reality that cannot be expressed in more direct and rational terms. Each poem transforms reality in its own manner, leading the reader to its own version of truth. The aim is to touch a primitive level of being where, for example, in Baudelaire's poem *Correspondences,* the five senses fuse: colors have taste, sights have physical texture, sounds have odors, and so on. (This fusion is called *synesthesia.*) Symbolist poetry may lead to abstract or visionary conclusions, but it is firmly based in images as realistic as a rotting carcass, logs falling on the pavement, and a mangy cat trying to find a comfortable spot in rainy weather (Baudelaire's *A Carcass, Song of Autumn I,* and *Spleen LXXVIII*). It is not, therefore, an escape from natural reality so much as a transformation of it, the creation of a new world reassembled in the mind from pieces of the old.

After Symbolic allusion, the second great theme of Symbolist poetry is language: language as a means of communication and language as the necessary but flawed tool of poetic creation. Like Flaubert seeking *le mot juste* (the exact word), Symbolist poets are haunted by the difficulty of writing: Baudelaire described his exhausted brain as a graveyard, and Stéphane Mallarmé felt paralyzed by "the empty paper whose whiteness defends it." The difficulty for the Symbolists is that their ideal poetic language must be distilled out of ordinary language through a totally controlled arrangement of all possible levels of form. Sound patterns, image clusters, and intertwined systems of logical and psychological associations act to create a complex architecture of inner reference. It is the relationship of words that counts, not just their dictionary definitions; the artist is, in a sense, a technician. The extraordinary self-consciousness of the Symbolist poet soon became an accepted element of the poem itself. Some poems focused on difficulties of communication (a characteristic Romantic theme); others, like Baudelaire's *Windows*, asserted joy in using language to imagine other existences and to sense, in return, their own reality. The Symbolists' acute awareness of the possibilities and limitations of language influenced both philosophers of language and literary theorists in the twentieth century.

Symbolist writers frequently compared their poetry to music, whose characteristics they tried to reproduce; Paul Verlaine (1844–1896) is especially known for the musicality of his verse. Both poetry and music they felt to be pure arts, in which line and harmony (including calculated dissonance) meant more than separate notes or the definitions of individual words. They saw analogies, too, between their art and painting, where distinctive new methods of depicting reality were being developed in the same period. Symbolist poetry and Impressionist art both represented moves away from the conventional realistic representation of reality; and in the poetic as in the art world, they both outraged the average citizen by their apparent betrayal of common sense.

Baudelaire's most important successors were very different figures: an English teacher, Stéphane Mallarmé (1842–1898); a sometime clerk and French teacher, Paul Verlaine; and the adolescent prodigy Arthur Rimbaud (1854–1891). In a short and violent literary career between the ages of fifteen and twenty, Rimbaud attempted to become a seer or *voyant* through hallucinatory writing expressing the "disorder of all the senses." His rebellion against home and authority, his experiments with drugs and alcohol, his love affair with Verlaine, and his search for a transfigured condition beyond ordinary experience all provide themes for this poetic quest. Ultimately, the poet became disenchanted with the efficacy of his magical or "alchemical" art, and he abruptly stopped writing. He left for Africa, where he spent the last eighteen years of his life trying to make a living. A good deal of Rimbaud's legend comes from this extraordinary example of a great poet who simply did not find what he sought in literature and, therefore, ceased to write. Rimbaud's work and the integrity of his spiritual commitment had enormous influence on later writers, especially the surrealists.

Paul Verlaine, conversely, had an immediate influence on the new generation of French poets for whom his revolutionary verse forms held a fascination almost equaled by the scandalous figure of the poet himself. Verlaine's *Art of Poetry* recommended music, nuance, and ambiguity instead of the conventionally prized intellect, clarity, and force; and his own poetry emphasized emotion and mood rather than philosophy or moral persuasion. He introduced short, impressionistic sketches that establish a mood, usually melancholy alienation, and strengthened that mood by creating a related music of word sounds and rhythm. Unlike previous classical poetry with its regular alexandrines (twelve-syllable lines), Verlaine's poems used shorter, irregular, continuous, and almost conversational lines that echo the rhythms of speech. Although his example directly inspired the free verse of later Symbolist and modern poetry, he himself cherished the musicality achieved by patterns of rhythm and rhyme.

Stéphane Mallarmé was a quiet and somewhat scholarly poet who spent his life in a search for absolute poetry *in language*. Mallarmé loved words and distrusted the sloppiness of everyday speech. He envisaged a special poetic language that would be built out of the precisely planned interaction of ordinary words, in poems that would "give a purer sense to the words of the crowd." Mallarmé's long poem *Dice Thrown*, with its startling arrangement of different type sizes and words scattered to create patterns on the page, heralded concrete poetry and other modern attempts to use the silence of blank space as part of poetry. Toward the end of his life, he considered everything he produced to be a fragment of an ultimate Work that he feared he would never be able to write: a massively interrelated composition of pure poetry whose function would be to assert the dignity of human imagination in the face of universal nothingness. Mallarmé uses Symbolist tactics in that he prefers allusion and suggestion to direct speech, or—a specifically Mallarméan theme—potentiality and absence to a fixed and limited reality. Material objects like a bracelet, a fan, a harp, or a lace curtain, are described so as to evoke other elements in another realm of being. A carved angel's wing gilded by the sun evokes a harp; the harp exists only in the imagination, however, and its implied music is doubly unreal because the source is merely suggested, not represented. This music is even more ambiguous than Keats's "melodies . . . unheard," for it is a musical *silence*.

It is paradoxical that none of these poets—Baudelaire, Mallarmé, Rimbaud, or Verlaine—was a member of the Symbolist movement. Symbolist doctrine as such dates to a manifesto issued in 1886 by a minor poet, Jean Moréas (Yánnis Papadiamantópoulous, 1856–1910). In many ways the movement is a systematization and popularization of ideas gleaned from Baudelaire, Rimbaud, Mallarmé, and Verlaine; especially influential were Verlaine's essays in 1884 describing Rimbaud, Mallarmé, and Tristan Corbière (1845–1875) as outcast or "accursed poets." A number of young poets (often called "Decadents") were attracted to Symbolist ideas and proclaimed Verlaine their master; their publication and literary reviews flourished around the turn of the century. Symbolism as a movement, however, had less impact than the major poets from whom it sprang; and it was the example of these earlier poets that especially influenced writers such as W. B. Yeats, T. S. Eliot, Marcel Proust, Rainer Maria Rilke, Wallace Stevens, and others around the world for whom Symbolist poetry became the model for contemporary poetry and poetics.

A NOTE ON FRENCH POETRY

English poetry receives its rhythm from the accent or stress in words, and the most common English line is iambic pentameter ("Whatever is begotten, born, and dies"). In contrast, the rhythm of French poetry is based on *quantity*—on the number and pattern of syllables in a line. The most common French line is the twelve-syllable, or alexandrine, verse, usually divided into balanced segments of six or four syllables. Baudelaire's *Correspondances* (given in French on page 1385) is a sonnet written in alexandrines that displays many of the conventions of French poetry.

Syllables are divided to reflect the sound of the line when read aloud; thus every syllable should begin with a consonant whenever possible. ("Na / tu / re . . . con / fu / ses / pa / roles.") In traditional French poetry, the unaccented or mute *e* counts as a syllable and is pronounced when it occurs before a sounded consonant (but not otherwise): thus "Com / me / les / prai / ries" (line 10) sound the mute *e* but "La / Na / tu / re est / un / tem / ple où" (line 1) does not. The subtle use of the mute *e* provides rich sonorous effects that are evident only in reading aloud.

French rhymes are categorized as rich, sufficient, or weak and also as masculine or feminine. Weak rhymes have only one accented vowel in common: prairies / infinies (the *ee* sound). Sufficient rhymes have two elements in common: en*fants* / triom*phants*. A rich rhyme has three or more elements in common: pi*liers* / famil*iers* (*i*, *l*, and the diphthong *ier*). A variety of rhymes is desirable. Feminine rhymes end in the sound of a mute *e*: pa*roles* / sym*boles* or *rose* / *chose*. All other rhymes are masculine. After the sixteenth century most poets alternated masculine and feminine rhymes. In *Correspondances*, Baudelaire uses the Petrarchan sonnet form (two quatrains, two tercets) with a rhyme scheme alternating masculine and feminine rhymes as follows: *mffm fmmf mfm fmm*. The intricacy of these and other poetic effects makes clear why later poets revered Baudelaire as a master of classical form as well as a visionary.

FURTHER READING

E. Auerbach, *Mimesis: The Representation of Reality in Western Literature* (1953), is a wide-ranging book (from Homer to Proust), with chapters on nineteenth-century realism. G. J. Becker, ed., *Documents of Modern Literary Realism* (1973), surveys the development of modern realism and offers documents and essays from 1835 to 1955. H. Levin, *The Gates of Horn: A Study of Five French Realists* (1963), contains much on realism in general, including Stendhal, Balzac, Flaubert, Zola, and Proust. Linda Nochlin, *Realism* (1971), discusses realism in the visual arts. Marcel Raymond, *From Baudelaire to Surrealism* (1933), is a fundamental study of the evolution of the new poetry. Naomi Schor, *Breaking the Chain: Women, Theory, and French Realist Fiction* (1985), discusses the realist fiction of Flaubert, Zola, Balzac, and others in terms of feminist and psychoanalytic theory. Also helpful is R. Wellek, "The Concept of Realism in Literary Scholarship," in *Concepts of Criticism* (1963). Nicholas Boyle and Martin Swales, eds., *Realism in European Literature: Essays in Honour of J. P. Stern* (1986), is a varied and useful collection that includes a discussion of realism related to modernism and language consciousness. Elise Boulding, *The Underside of History: A View of Women through Time* (1992), arranged by periods and sociological categories, contains much pertinent information about the role of women that is omitted from traditional histories. John Rignall, *Realist Fiction and the Strolling Spectator* (1992), indebted to Nietzsche and Walter Benjamin, analyzes realism's distanced point of view in eight nineteenth-century and three twentieth-century novelists. Laurence M. Porter, *The Crisis of French Symbolism* (1990), situates the poetry of Baudelaire, Mallarmé, Verlaine, and Rimbaud between neoclassicism and the Symbolist school. An influential and still valuable presentation is found in *The Symbolist Movement in Literature* (1980, orig. 1899), by the English Symbolist Arthur Symons. P. Mansell Jones, *The Background of Modern French Poetry* (1951, repr. 1968), describes the influence of Poe, Baudelaire, Mallarmé, and Whitman on modern free verse. Georges Poulet, *Exploding Poetry* (1984), trans. Françoise Meltzer, interprets the poetry of Baudelaire and Rimbaud.

PRONOUNCING GLOSSARY

The following list uses common English syllables and stress accents to provide rough equivalents of selected words whose pronunciation may be unfamiliar to the general reader.

Balzac: *bahl-zak'*

Baudelaire: *boh-d'lair'*

Champfleury: *shom-fler-ee'*

Chekhov: *chek'-hoff*

Chopin: *sho-panh*

Corbière: *core-bee-air'*

Courbet: *coor-bay'*

Dostoevsky: *dos-toy-eff'-skee*

Dvořák: *dvor'-zhak*

fabliaux: *fah-blee-oh'*

Gesamtkunstwerk: *ge-zamt-koonst'-varck*

Grieg: *greeg*

Mallarmé: *mal-ahr-may'*

Nietzsche: *neech'-uh*

Réalisme: *ray-al-eezm'*

Rimbaud: *ram-boh'*

Schlegel: *shlay'-gel*

Stendhal: *ston-dall'*

Tchaikovsky: *chai-kof'-skee*

Verlaine: *vehr-len'*

Wagner: *vahg'-ner*

Zola: *zoh-lah'*

TIME LINE

TEXTS	CONTEXTS
1856 Gustave Flaubert, *Madame Bovary*	
1857 Charles Baudelaire, *The Flowers of Evil*	
	1859 Charles Darwin, *Origin of Species*
	1861 Serfs emancipated in Russia
	1861–1865 Civil War in the United States
1864 Fyodor Dostoevsky, *Notes from Underground*	
1866 Dostoevsky, *Crime and Punishment*	
1866 Émile Zola's preface to his novel *Thérèse Raquin* argues for a "naturalist" style analogous to methods in experimental science	
1869 Leo Tolstoy, *War and Peace*	**1869** Suez Canal completed
	1870 Ernest Renan's *Life of Jesus* offers a historical approach to the New Testament
1871 George Eliot (Mary Ann Evans), *Middlemarch*	
	1874 Claude Monet's painting *Impression: Rising Sun* launches Impressionism as a style
	1876 Invention of the telephone
	1884–1885 Berlin Conference agrees on procedures for European acquisition of African territory; by 1914, all Africa except Ethiopia and Liberia succumbs to European rule
1886 Arthur Rimbaud's *Illuminations* • Tolstoy, *The Death of Ivan Ilyich*	**1886** Friedrich Nietzsche's *Beyond Good and Evil* proclaims a "life force," a "will to power," and a "superman" who embodies these qualities

Boldface titles indicate works in the anthology.

TIME LINE

TEXTS	CONTEXTS
	1887 Eiffel Tower built for the 1889 Paris World's Fair • Gottlieb Daimler's internal combustion engine for the automobile
1890 Henrik Ibsen, *Hedda Gabler* • **Poems** of Emily Dickinson (1830–1886) published posthumously	
	1894 X-rays discovered
	1894–1906 In the Dreyfus Affair, anti-Semitic sentiment polarizes France
	1898 Radium discovered by Marie and Pierre Curie • Spanish-American War breaks out
1904 Anton Chekhov, *The Cherry Orchard* performed	

GUSTAVE FLAUBERT
1821–1880

Gustave Flaubert is rightly considered the exemplary realist novelist and *Madame Bovary* his masterpiece. He displays the objectivity, the detachment from his characters demanded by the theory, and is a great virtuoso of the arts of composition and of style while giving a clear picture of the society of his time. It is likewise a picture in which we can see much of ourselves.

Flaubert was born in Rouen, Normandy, on December 12, 1821, to the chief surgeon of the Hôtel Dieu. He was extremely precocious: by the age of sixteen he was writing stories in the romantic taste, which were published only after his death. In 1840 he went to Paris to study law (he had received his baccalaureate from the local *lycée*), but he failed in his examinations and in 1843 suffered a sudden nervous breakdown that kept him at home. In 1846 he moved to Croisset, just outside Rouen on the Seine, where he made his home for the rest of his life, devoting himself to writing. The same year, in Paris, Flaubert met Louise Colet, a minor writer and socialite, who became his mistress. In 1849–51 he visited the Levant, traveling extensively in Greece, Syria, and Egypt. After his return he settled down to the writing of *Madame Bovary*, which took him five full years and which, despite accusations of immorality, was a great popular success. The remainder of his life was uneventful. He made occasional trips to Paris, and one trip, in 1860, to Tunisia to see the ruins of Carthage in preparation for the writing of his novel *Salammbô* (1862). Three more novels followed: *The Sentimental Education* (1869), *The Temptation of St. Anthony* (1874), and the unfinished *Bouvard and Pecuchet* (1881), as well as *Three Tales* (1877), consisting of *A Simple Heart, The Legend of St. Julian the Hospitaler,* and *Herodias.* Flaubert died in Croisset on May 8, 1880.

Madame Bovary (1856) is deservedly considered the showpiece of French realism. It would be impossible to find a novel, certainly before Flaubert, in which relatively humble persons in a humble setting are treated with such seriousness, restraint, verisimilitude, and imaginative clarity. At first sight, *Madame Bovary* is a solidly documented and clearly visualized account of life in a village of the French province of Normandy sometime in the 1840s. We meet a whole spectrum of social types found in such a time and place: the doctor (actually a "health officer" with a lower degree), a pharmacist, a storekeeper, a notary and his clerk, a tax collector, a woman innkeeper and her stable boy, the priest and his sacristan, a neighboring landowner, and a farmer. We are told the story of a young peasant woman brought up in a convent, who marries a dull man and commits adultery first with a ruthless philanderer and then with a spineless younger man. Overwhelmed by debts concealed from her unsuspecting husband, faced by sudden demands for repayment, disillusioned in love, rebuffed by everybody who might help her, she commits suicide by poisoning herself with arsenic. Nothing seems simpler or more ordinary, and the manner of telling seems completely objective, detached, impersonal. A case is presented that is observed with almost scientific curiosity. The descriptions are obviously accurate, sometimes based on expert knowledge; the clubfoot operation and the effects of arsenic poisoning agree with medical evidence. The setting—the topography of the two villages, the interior of the houses, the inn, the pharmacy, the city of Rouen, the cathedral there, the river landscape, and the particular things and sounds—imprints itself vividly on our memory. Every detail serves its purpose of characterization—from the absurd cap of the schoolboy Charles to the mirror and the crucifix in the deathbed scene; from the sound of Binet's lathe turning out napkin rings to the tap of the stable boy's wooden leg. "The technique of *Madame Bovary* has become the model of all novels" (Albert Thibaudet).

But surely the book could not have kept its grip on modern readers if it were only a superbly accurate description of provincial life in France, as the added subtitle,

Mœurs de province (provincial manners) suggests. The book transcends its time and place if one thinks of Emma Bovary as the type of the unfulfilled dreamer, as the failed and foiled romanticist, as a female Don Quixote, corrupted by sentimental reading, caught in a trap of circumstance, pitiful and to be pitied in her horrible self-inflicted death.

This central theme has, however, remained ambiguous. What attracted and shocked readers was the uncertainty about the author's attitude toward Emma, particularly at the time of publication when readers were accustomed to being told clearly by addresses and comments what they were to think of the actions and morals of the characters of a novel. *Madame Bovary*, at publication, caused a scandal. The *Paris Review*, in which it was published serially, and the author were hauled into court for immorality and blasphemy; and the prosecutor described the book as an incitement to adultery and atheism. In his rebuttal, the defense counsel argued that the novel is rather a highly moral work in which adultery is punished, even excessively. Flaubert was acquitted, but neither the prosecutor nor the defending attorney interpreted the book correctly. It is neither a salacious novel nor a didactic tract. Some parts of the book are frankly satirical (and thus far from purely objective): the gross village priest who cannot even understand the distress of Emma is flanked by the fussy, shallow, pseudoscientific, enlightened, "progressive" pharmacist Homais. Though they argue and quarrel, they are finally reduced to a common level when they eat and snore at the wake next to Emma's corpse. The rightly famous scene of the country fair satirizes and parodies the pompous rhetoric of the officials extolling the glories of agriculture, counterpointing it to the equally platitudinous love talk of Rodolphe and the lowing of the cattle in an amalgam that reduces men and women to a common level of animality. Even Emma is not spared: her sentimental religiosity, her taste for luxury, her financial improvidence are diagnosed as disguised eroticism. She would not have minded if Rodolphe had drawn a pistol against her husband. In her desperate search for escape she asks Léon to steal for her. In the last attempt to get money she is ready to sell herself. She is indifferent to her child, deceitful even in small matters. Her longing for sensual satisfaction becomes, in the scenes with Léon in the hotel at Rouen, frantic and corrupt. The author weighted the scales against her: she married an excessively stupid and insensitive man; she met two callous lovers; she is tricked by a merciless usurer; she is utterly alone at last. When Charles meeting Rodolphe after her death and after he had discovered her infidelities tells him, ineptly, awkwardly, "It was the fault of destiny," the author expressly approves of this statement. The novel conveys a sense of inexorable determinism, of the vanity of dreaming, of the impossibility of escape from one's nature and station. It conveys a sense of despair, of alienation in an incomprehensible universe—but also a hatred for all the stupidity, mediocrity and baseness of people there and everywhere. (Flaubert called them bourgeois, but included the proletarian masses in his contempt.) Emma is pitied because she has, at least, a spark of discontent, the yearning to escape the cage of her existence. But baseness triumphs and the book ends with a sudden change to the present tense: "Homais has just received the Cross of the Legion of Honor."

This sense of the inexorable, the fatal, the inescapable is secured also by the precision and firmness of Flaubert's style and the carefully planned architectonics of his composition. If we mean by style the systematic exploitation of the syntactical and lexical possibilities of a language we must class Flaubert with the great stylists. His keen sense of the exact descriptive epithet, the one right word (*le mot juste*)— even when he uses the most trivial cliché or the most recondite scientific term— coheres with the skillful modulations and rhythms of the sentences; the organization of the paragraphs; and the divisions of the sections, which are grouped around a series of pictorial scenes: the schoolroom, the rustic wedding, the ball, the visit to the priest, the country fair, the ride in the woods, the clubfoot operation, the opera, the cathedral, the cab ride, the deathbed, to mention only the most memorable.

Madame Bovary is constantly cited as an example for the handling of narrative perspective. The story begins in the schoolroom ostensibly told by a schoolfellow (the word *we* is used in the first pages); it shifts then to the narration of an omniscient author and, off and on, narrows to the point of view of Emma. Much is seen only through her eyes, but one cannot say that the author identifies with her or enters her mind sympathetically. He keeps his distance and on occasion conveys his own opinion. He is not averse even to moral judgments: he speaks of Emma's hard-hearted and tightfisted peasant nature (p. 1127), he refers to her depravity (p. 1256), and Rodolphe is several times condemned for his brutality and cynicism (pp. 1165, 1203, 1209). In the description of extreme unction (p. 1285) the author pronounces solemnly his forgiveness (which he suggests would be also God's) for her coveting all worldly goods, her greediness "for the warm breeze and scents of love," and even her sensuality and lust. But mostly Flaubert depicts the scenes by simple description or reproduction of speech or imagined silent reflections. Things and people become at times symbolic even in an obtrusive way: the wedding bouquet, the plate of boiled beef, and the apparition of the blind beggar who turns up conveniently at the hour of Emma's death. Much is said about her that she could not have observed herself. The famous saying "Madame Bovary c'est moi" ("I am Madame Bovary") cannot be traced back to an earlier date than 1909, when it is reported on distant hearsay in René Descharmes, *Flaubert before 1857*. There are dozens of passages in the letters during the composition of *Madame Bovary* that express Flaubert's distaste for the "vulgarity of his subject," "the fetid smell of the milieu," and his opinion of Emma Bovary as "a woman of false poetry and false sentiments." Usually he defends his choice of theme as a "prodigious *tour de force*," as "an act of crude willpower," as "a deliberate made-up thing," though we suspect him sometimes of exaggerating his efforts to impress his correspondent in Paris, a facile and prolific novelist and poet, Louise Colet.

Still, the saying "Madame Bovary c'est moi" has been widely quoted and accepted because it contains a kernel of truth. In Emma, Flaubert combats his own vices of daydreaming, romanticism, exoticism, of which he thought he could cure himself by writing this antiromantic book. But the identification with Emma distracts us from noticing Flaubert's deep-seated sympathies with the slow-witted, abused, but honest and loving Charles, who rightly opens and closes the book, and for the other good people: Emma's father, the farmer Rouault, kind and distressed by all he could not foresee; Justin, the pharmacist's apprentice adoring Emma from afar, praying on her grave; the clubfoot stable boy tortured and exploited for a dream of medical reputation; poor neglected Berthe sent to the cotton mill; the old peasant woman at the fair who for fifty-four years of service got a medal worth twenty-five francs; and even the blind beggar with his horrible skin disease. Moreover, there is the admirable Dr. Larivière, who appears fleetingly like an apparition from a saner, loftier world of good sense and professional devotion. Thus it seems unjust of the critic Martin Turnell to say that the novel is "an onslaught on the whole basis of human feeling and on all spiritual and moral values."

In Flaubert's mind, the novel was also an assertion of the redeeming power of art. His long struggle with its composition, which took him more than five years of grinding drudgery: five days in which he had written a single page, five or six pages in a week, twenty-five pages in six weeks, thirteen pages in seven weeks, a whole night spent in hunting for the right adjective; the ruthless pruning to which he subjected his enormous manuscript, eliminating many fine touches, similes, metaphors, and descriptions of elusive mental states (as a study of the manuscripts has shown) were to him a victory of art over reality, a passionate search for Beauty, which he knew to be an illusion. But one wonders whether the conflict of Flaubert's scientific detachment and cruel observation with the intense adoration of beauty, the thirst for calculated purity and structure, for "style" as perfection, can be resolved. He tried to achieve this synthesis in *Madame Bovary*. Watching this struggle between heterogeneous elements, and even opposites, explains some of the fascination of the book.

Editor's Note   An explanation of the plot and the stage business is needed to understand properly the performance in *Madame Bovary* of the opera *Lucia di Lammermoor,* which occurs on pages 1222–26 of this text. There are substantial differences between the French version, which Flaubert apparently followed, and the original Italian libretto, which will be more familiar to modern music lovers. The basic story is one of family hatred: Edgar, the owner of the castle of Ravenswood in the Scottish Highlands, has been expelled by Lord Henry Ashton who had killed his father. He is in hiding as an outlaw. He loves and is loved clandestinely by Lucy, Lord Henry's sister. The opera opens with a hunting scene on the grounds of Ravenswood castle where Henry, his forester called Gilbert (Normanno in the Italian), and other followers comb the grounds for traces of a mysterious stranger whom they suspect to be the outcast Edgar. They are joined by Lord Arthur, who is a suitor for Lucy's hand and is favored by her brother, as he can save him from financial ruin. Arthur declares his love for Lucy (no such scene is in the Italian). Lucy in the next scene prepares to meet Edgar in a secluded spot; she gives a purse to Gilbert, whom she believes to be her friend though Gilbert is actually scheming with Lord Henry against her. (The scene is not in the Italian original.) Then Lucy is left alone and sings a cavatina beginning: "Que n'avons-nous des ailes" ("If only we had wings"). Edgar appears then, played by Lagardy, a fictional tenor. He tells of his hatred for Lucy's brother because of the death of his father. He had sworn vengeance but is ready to forget it in his love for her. Edgar has to leave on a mission to France, but in parting the lovers pledge their troth and exchange rings. The stretto contains the words "Une fleur pour ma tombe" ("A flower for my tomb"), "donne une larme à l'exilé" ("give a tear for the exiled one"), phrases alluded to in Flaubert's account.

Charles is so obtuse that he thinks Edgar is torturing Lucy, and Emma has to tell him that he is her lover. Charles protests that he heard him vowing vengeance on her family. He had heard him saying: "J'ai juré vengeance et guerre" ("I have sworn vengeance and war"). Charles has also heard Lord Arthur say, "J'aime Lucie et m'en crois aimé" ("I love Lucie and I believe she loves me") and has seen Lord Arthur going off with her father arm in arm. But Charles obviously takes her brother Henry for her father.

The second act begins with Gilbert telling his master Henry that he slipped Lucy's ring from the sleeping Edgar, had made a copy, and will produce it to convince Lucy of Edgar's faithlessness. Charles mistakes the false ring, which is shown to Lucy, for a love gift sent by Edgar. The business with the rings replaces an analogous deception with forged letters in the Italian libretto. Lucy appears dressed for the wedding with Lord Arthur, unhappily resisting and imploring, reminding Emma of her own wedding day and the contrast with her false joy soon turned to bitterness. Brandishing a sword, Edgar suddenly returns voicing his indignation. There follows a sextet (Lucy, Henry, Edgar, Raimondo the minister, Arthur, Gilbert) that suggests to Emma her desire to flee and to be carried off as Edgar wants to carry off Lucy. But the marriage contract has been signed and Edgar curses her. The third act does not interest Emma any more as Léon has appeared in the interval. She does not care for the scene between Lord Henry and his retainer (called here "servant") Gilbert, who introduces a disguised stranger, Edgar, of course. The duet between Henry Lord Ashton and Edgar reaffirms their mutual hatred. The mad scene follows. Lucy flees the marriage chamber; she has stabbed her husband and gone mad. She dreams of Edgar and dies. The great aria that was considered the climax of coloratura singing was lost on Emma, who is absorbed in Léon.

One must assume that Flaubert had the French libretto in front of him or remembered its wordings and stage business accurately. (He had seen the opera first in Rouen in 1840 and again in Constantinople in November 1850.) A modern reader who knows the Italian libretto from recordings may be puzzled by the discrepancies and ascribe to Flaubert's imagination or confused memory what is actually an accurate description of the French version.

William Berg and Laurey K. Martin, *Gustave Flaubert* (1997), is a general introduction to Flaubert's life and work. Victor Brombert, *The Novels of Flaubert* (1966), has an excellent chapter on *Madame Bovary*; Raymond D. Giraud, ed., *Flaubert: A Collection of Critical Essays* (1964), and Harold Bloom, ed., *Emma Bovary* (1994), provide a range of short studies. Paul de Man, ed., *Gustave Flaubert: Madame Bovary. Backgrounds and Sources: Essays in Criticism* (1965), will help the reader, as will Alison Fairlie, *Flaubert: Madame Bovary* (1962), a good discussion of problems, structures, people, and values addressed to students. The chapter on *Madame Bovary* in Anthony Thorlby, *Gustave Flaubert and the Art of Realism* (1957), is still to be recommended, as is Margaret Lowe, *Toward the Real Flaubert: A Study of Madame Bovary* (1984).

PRONUNCIATION GLOSSARY

The following list uses common English syllables and stress accents to provide rough equivalents of selected words whose pronunciation may be unfamiliar to the general reader.

Berthe: *behrt*

Binet: *bee-nay'*

Bovary: *boh-vahr-ee'*

Canivet: *cah-nee-vay'*

Flaubert: *floh-bair'*

Guillaumin: *gee-oh-manh'*

Homais: *oh-me'*

huissier: *wee-syay'*

Larivière: *lah-ree-vyehr'*

La Vaubyessard: *lah-vohb-yes-ahr'*

Léon Dupuis: *lay-ohn' dyew-pwee'*

Les Bertaux: *lay behr-toh'*

Lestiboudois: *les-tee-boo-dwah'*

Lheureux: *leu-reu'*

Rodolphe Boulanger de la Huchette:
     ro-dawlf' boo-lawn-zhay'
     deu la ew-shet'

Rouault: *roo-oh'*

Rouen: *roo-awnh'*

Tostes: *toht*

Vinçart: *vanh-sahr'*

Yonville: *yohnh-veel'*

Yvetot: *eev-toh'*

Madame Bovary[1]

Part One

I

We were in study-hall when the headmaster entered, followed by a new boy not yet in school uniform and by the handyman carrying a large desk. Their arrival disturbed the slumbers of some of us, but we all stood up in our places as though rising from our work.

The headmaster motioned us to be seated; then, turning to the teacher:

"Monsieur Roger," he said in an undertone, "here's a pupil I'd like you to keep your eye on. I'm putting him in the last year of the lower school. If he does good work and behaves himself we'll move him up to where he ought to be at his age."

The newcomer, who was hanging back in the corner so that the door half hid him from view, was a country lad of about fifteen, taller than any of us.

---

1. Translated by Francis Steegmuller.

He had his hair cut in bangs like a cantor in a village church, and he had a gentle, timid look. He wasn't broad in the shoulders, but his green jacket with its black buttons seemed tight under the arms; and through the vents of his cuffs we could see red wrists that were clearly unaccustomed to being covered. His yellowish breeches were hiked up by his suspenders, and from them emerged a pair of blue-stockinged legs. He wore heavy shoes, hobnailed and badly shined.

We began to recite our lessons. He listened avidly, as though to a sermon— he didn't dare even cross his legs or lean on his elbows; and at two o'clock, when the bell rang for the next class, the teacher had to tell him to line up with the rest of us.

We always flung our caps on the floor when entering a classroom, to free our hands; we hurled them under the seats from the doorway itself, in such a way that they struck the wall and raised a cloud of dust: that was "how it was done."

But whether he had failed to notice this ritual or hadn't dared join in observance of it, his cap was still in his lap when we'd finished reciting our prayer. It was a headgear of composite order, containing elements of an ordinary hat, a hussar's busby, a lancer's cap, a sealskin cap and a nightcap: one of those wretched things whose mute hideousness suggests unplumbed depths, like an idiot's face. Ovoid and stiffened with whalebone, it began with three convex strips; then followed alternating lozenges of velvet and rabbit's fur, separated by a red band; then came a kind of bag, terminating in a cardboard-lined polygon intricately decorated with braid. From this hung a long, excessively thin cord ending in a kind of tassel of gold netting. The cap was new; its peak was shiny.

"Stand up," said the teacher.

He rose. His cap dropped to the floor. Everyone began to laugh.

He bent over for it. A boy beside him sent it down again with his elbow. Once again he picked it up.

"How about getting rid of your helmet?" suggested the teacher, who was something of a wit.

Another loud laugh from the students confused the poor fellow. He didn't know whether to keep the cap in his hand, drop it on the floor, or put it on his head. He sat down again and placed it in his lap.

"Stand up," repeated the professor, "and tell me your name."

The new boy mumbled a name that was unintelligible.

"Say it again!"

The same jumble of syllables came out, drowned in the jeers of the class.

"Louder!" cried the teacher. "Louder!"

With desperate resolve the new boy opened a mouth that seemed enormous, and as though calling someone he cried at the top of his lungs the word "Charbovari!"

This touched off a roar that rose *crescendo,* punctuated with shrill screams. There was a shrieking, a banging of desks as everyone yelled, "Charbovari! Charbovari!" Then the din broke up into isolated cries that slowly diminished, occasionally starting up again along a line of desks where a stifled laugh would burst out here and there like a half-spent firecracker.

But a shower of penalties gradually restored order; and the teacher, finally grasping the name Charles Bovary after it had been several times spelled out and repeated and he had read it aloud himself, at once commanded the poor devil to sit in the dunce's seat, at the foot of the platform. He began to move toward it, then hesitated.

"What are you looking for?" the teacher demanded.

"My c—" the new boy said timidly, casting an uneasy glance around him.

"Everybody will stay and write five hundred lines!"

Like Neptune's *"Quos ego,"*[2] those words, furiously uttered, cut short the threat of a new storm. "Quiet!" the indignant teacher continued, mopping his forehead with a handkerchief he took from his toque. "As for you," he said to the new boy, "you'll copy out for me twenty times all the tenses of *ridiculus sum.*"[3]

Then, more gently: "You'll find your cap. No one has stolen it."

All was calm again. Heads bent over copybooks, and for the next two hours the new boy's conduct was exemplary, even though an occasional spitball, sent from the nib of a pen, struck him wetly in the face. He wiped himself each time with his hand, and otherwise sat there motionless, his eyes lowered.

That evening, in study period, he took his sleeveguards from his desk, arranged his meager equipment, and carefully ruled his paper. We saw him working conscientiously, looking up every word in the dictionary, taking great pains. It was doubtless thanks to this display of effort that he was not demoted to a lower form. For while he had a fair knowledge of grammatical rules, his translations lacked elegance. He had begun his Latin with his village priest: his thrifty parents had sent him away to school as late as possible.

His father, Monsieur Charles-Denis-Bartholomé Bovary, had been an army surgeon's aide, forced to leave the service about 1812 as a result of involvement in a conscription scandal. He had then turned his personal charms to advantage, picking up a dowry of 60,000 francs brought to him by a knit-goods dealer's daughter who had fallen in love with his appearance. He was a handsome man, much given to bragging and clanking his spurs. His side whiskers merged with his mustache, his fingers were always loaded with rings, his clothes were flashy: he had the look of a bully and the easy cajoling ways of a traveling salesman. Once married, he lived off his wife's money for two or three years. He ate well, rose late, smoked big porcelain pipes, stayed out every night to see a show, spent much of his time in cafés. His father-in-law died and left very little; this made him indignant, and he "went into textiles" and lost some money. Then he retired to the country, with the intention of "making things pay." But he knew as little about crops as he did about calico; and since he rode his horses instead of working them in the fields, drank his cider bottled instead of selling it by the barrel, ate his best poultry, and greased his hunting boots with the fat from his pigs, he soon realized that he had better give up all idea of profit-making.

So for two hundred francs[4] a year he rented, in a village on the border of Normandy and Picardy, a dwelling that was half farm, half gentleman's res-

---

2. An unfinished threat (Latin: "you whom I . . .") delivered by the sea god Neptune to winds that had caused ocean storms without his permission (*Aeneid* 1.135).   3. I am a fool (Latin).   4. It is very difficult to transpose monetary values from 1840 into present-day figures, since relationships between the actual value of the franc, the cost of living, and the relative cost of specific items (e.g., rent and real estate) have undergone fundamental changes. A rough calculation of inflation and exchange rates between the franc and the dollar in 1840 and 1998 gives approximately $45; that would show Madame Bovary destroyed, at the end of the book, by an $18,000 debt.

idence; and there, surly, eaten by discontent, cursing heaven, envying everyone, he shut himself up at the age of forty-five, disgusted with mankind, he
said, and resolved to live in peace.

His wife had been mad about him at the beginning; in her love she had
tendered him a thousand servilities that had alienated him all the more. Once
sprightly, all outgoing and affectionate, with age she had grown touchy, nagging and nervous, like stale wine turning to vinegar. At first she had suffered
uncomplainingly, watching him chase after every trollop in the village and
having him come back to her at night from any one of twenty disgusting
places surfeited and stinking of drink. Then her pride rebelled. She withdrew
into her shell; and swallowing her rage she bore up stoically until her death.
She was always busy, always doing things. She was constantly running to
lawyers, to the judge, remembering when notes fell due and obtaining renew-
als; and at home she was forever ironing, sewing, washing, keeping an eye
on the hired men, figuring their wages. Monsieur, meanwhile, never lifted a
finger. He sat smoking in the chimney corner and spitting into the ashes,
continually falling into a grumpy doze and waking to utter uncomplimentary
remarks.

When she had a child it had to be placed out with a wet nurse. And then
later, when the little boy was back with its parents, he was pampered like a
prince. His mother stuffed him with jams and jellies; his father let him run
barefoot, and fancied himself a disciple of Rousseau to the point of saying
he'd be quite willing to have the boy go naked like a young animal. To counter
his wife's maternal tendencies he tried to form his son according to a certain
virile ideal of childhood and to harden his constitution by subjecting him to
strict discipline, Spartan-style. He sent him to bed without a fire, taught him
to take great swigs of rum and to ridicule religious processions. But the child
was pacific by nature, and such training had little effect. His mother kept
him tied to her apron-strings: she made him paper cutouts, told him stories,
and conversed with him in endless bitter-sweet monologues full of coaxing
chatter. In the isolation of her life she transferred to her baby all her own
poor frustrated ambitions. She dreamed of glamorous careers: she saw him
tall, handsome, witty, successful—a bridge builder or a judge. She taught
him to read, and even, on an old piano she had, to sing two or three sentimental little songs. But from Monsieur Bovary, who cared little for culture,
all this brought merely the comment that it was "useless." Could they ever
afford to give him an education, to buy him a practice or a business? Besides,
"with enough nerve a man could always get ahead in the world." Madame
Bovary pursed her lips, and the boy ran wild in the village.

He followed the hired men and chased crows, pelting them with clods of
earth until they flew off. He ate the wild blackberries that grew along the
ditches, looked after the turkeys with a long stick, pitched hay, roamed the
woods, played hopscotch in the shelter of the church porch when it rained,
and on important feast-days begged the sexton to let him toll the bells so
that he could hang with his full weight from the heavy rope and feel it sweep
him off his feet as it swung in its arc.

He throve like an oak. His hands grew strong and his complexion ruddy.

When he was twelve, his mother had her way: he began his studies. The
priest was asked to tutor him. But the lessons were so short and irregular
that they served little purpose. They took place at odd hurried moments—

in the sacristy between a baptism and a funeral; or else the priest would send for him after the Angelus, when his parish business was over for the day. They would go up to his bedroom and begin, midges and moths fluttering around the candle. There in the warmth the child would fall asleep; and the old man, too, would soon be dozing and snoring, his hands folded over his stomach and his mouth open. Other times, as Monsieur le curé was returning from a sickbed with the holy oils, he would catch sight of Charles scampering in the fields, and would call him over and lecture him for a few minutes, taking advantage of the occasion to make him conjugate a verb right there, under a tree. Rain would interrupt them, or some passer-by whom they knew. However, he was always satisfied with him, and even said that "the young fellow had a good memory."

Things weren't allowed to stop there. Madame was persistent. Shamed into consent—or, rather, his resistance worn down—Monsieur gave in without further struggle. They waited a year, until the boy had made his First Communion, then six months more; and finally Charles was sent to the lycée in Rouen. His father delivered him himself, toward the end of October, during the fortnight of the Saint-Romain fair.

It would be very difficult today for any of us to say what he was like. There was nothing striking about him: he played during recess, worked in study-hall, paid attention in class, slept soundly in the dormitory, ate heartily in the refectory. His local guardian was a wholesale hardware dealer in the rue Ganterie, who called for him one Sunday a month after early closing, sent him for a walk along the riverfront to look at the boats, then brought him back to school by seven, in time for supper. Every Thursday night Charles wrote a long letter to his mother, using red ink and three seals; then he looked over his history notes, or leafed through an old volume of *Anacharsis*[5] that lay around the study-hall. When his class went for outings he talked with the school servant who accompanied them, a countryman like himself.

By working hard he managed to stay about in the middle of the class; once he even got an honorable mention in natural history. But before he finished upper school his parents took him out of the lycée entirely and sent him to study medicine, confident that he could get his baccalaureate degree anyway by making up the intervening years on his own.

His mother choose a room for him, four flights up overlooking the stream called the Eau-de-Robec,[6] in the house of a dyer she knew. She arranged for his board, got him a table and two chairs, and sent home for an old cherry bed; and to keep her darling warm she bought him a small cast-iron stove and a load of wood. Then after a week she went back to her village, urging him a thousand times over to behave himself now that he was on his own.

The curriculum that he read on the bulletin board staggered him. Courses in anatomy, pathology, pharmacy, chemistry, botany, clinical practice, therapeutics, to say nothing of hygiene and materia medica—names of unfamiliar etymology that were like so many doors leading to solemn shadowy sanctuaries.

5. *Voyage du jeune Anacharsis en Grèce* (The Voyage of Young Anacharsis in Greece; 1788) was a popular account of ancient Greece as seen by a barbarian, by Jean-Jacques Barthélemy (1716–1795).   6. Small river, now covered up, that flows through the poorest neighborhood of Rouen, used as a sewer by the factories that border it, thus suggesting Flaubert's description as "une ignoble petite Venise" (squalid little Venise).

He understood absolutely nothing of any of it. He listened in vain: he could not grasp it. Even so, he worked. He filled his notebooks, attended every lecture, never missed hospital rounds. In the performance of his daily task he was like a mill-horse that treads blindfolded in a circle, utterly ignorant of what he is grinding.

To save him money, his mother sent him a roast of veal each week by the stagecoach, and off this he lunched when he came in from the hospital, warming his feet by beating them against the wall. Then he had to hurry off to lectures, to the amphitheatre, to another hospital, crossing the entire city again when he returned. At night, after eating the meager dinner his landlord provided, he climbed back up to his room, back to work. Steam rose from his damp clothes as he sat beside the red-hot stove.

On fine summer evenings, at the hour when the warm streets are empty and servant girls play at shuttlecock in front of the houses, he would open his window and lean out. The stream, which makes this part of Rouen a kind of squalid little Venice, flowed just below, stained yellow, purple or blue between its bridges and railings. Workmen from the dye plants, crouching on the bank, washed their arms in the water. Above him, on poles projecting from attics, skeins of cotton were drying in the open. And beyond the roof-tops stretched the sky, vast and pure, with the red sun setting. How good it must be in the country! How cool in the beech grove! And he opened his nostrils wide, longing for a whiff of the fresh and fragrant air, but none was ever wafted to where he was.

He grew thinner and taller, and his face took on a kind of plaintive expression that almost made it interesting.

The fecklessness that was part of his nature soon led him to break all his good resolutions. One day he skipped rounds; the next, a lecture; idleness, he found, was to his taste, and gradually he stayed away entirely.

He began to go to cafés. Soon he was crazy about dominoes. To spend his evenings shut up in a dirty public room, clinking black-dotted pieces of sheep's bone on a marble table, seemed to him a marvelous assertion of his freedom that raised him in his own esteem. It was like an initiation into the world, admission to a realm of forbidden delights; and every time he entered the café the feel of the doorknob in his hand gave him a pleasure that was almost sensual. Now many things pent up within him burst their bonds; he learned verses by heart and sang them at student gatherings, developed an enthusiasm for Béranger,[7] learned to make punch, and knew, at long last, the joys of love.

Thanks to that kind of preparation he failed completely the examination that would have entitled him to practice medicine as an *officier de santé*.[8] And his parents were waiting for him at home that very night to celebrate his success!

He set out on foot; at the outskirts of the village he stopped, sent someone for his mother, and told her all. She forgave him, laying his downfall to the unfairness of the examiners, and steadied him by promising to make all expla-

---

7. Pierre-Jean de Béranger (1780–1857), an extremely popular writer of songs that often exalt the glories of the empire of Napoleon I.   8. Health officer (French). Instituted during the French Revolution, a kind of second-class medical degree, well below the doctorate. The student was allowed to attend a medical school without having passed the equivalent of the *baccalauréat* and could practice only in the administrative region in which the diploma had been conferred (Bovary is thus tied down to the vicinity of Rouen) and was not allowed to perform major operations, except in the presence of a full-fledged doctor. This diploma was suppressed in 1892.

nations. (It was five years before Monsieur Bovary learned the truth: by that time it was an old story and he could accept it, especially since he couldn't conceive of his own offspring as being stupid.)

Charles set to work again and crammed ceaselessly, memorizing everything on which he could possibly be questioned. He passed with a fairly good grade. What a wonderful day for his mother! Everyone was asked to dinner.

Where should he practice? At Tostes. In that town there was only one elderly doctor, whose death Madame Bovary had long been waiting for; and the old man hadn't yet breathed his last when Charles moved in across the road as his successor.

But it wasn't enough to have raised her son, sent him into medicine, and discovered Tostes for him to practice in: he had to have a wife. She found him one: a *huissier's*[9] widow in Dieppe, forty-five years old, with twelve hundred francs a year.

Ugly though she was, and thin as a lath, with a face as spotted as a meadow in springtime, Madame Dubuc unquestionably had plenty of suitors to choose from. To gain her ends Madame Bovary had to get rid of all the rivals, and her outwitting of one of them, a butcher whose candidacy was favored by the local clergy, was nothing short of masterly.

Charles had envisaged marriage as the beginning of a better time, thinking that he would have greater freedom and be able to do as he liked with himself and his money. But it was his wife who ruled: in front of company he had to say certain things and not others, he had to eat fish on Friday, dress the way she wanted, obey her when she ordered him to dun nonpaying patients. She opened his mail, watched his every move, and listened through the thinness of the wall when there were women in his office.

She had to have her cup of chocolate every morning: there was no end to the attentions she required. She complained incessantly of her nerves, of pains in her chest, of depressions and faintnesses. The sound of anyone moving about near her made her ill; when people left her she couldn't bear her loneliness; when they came to see her it was, of course, "to watch her die." When Charles came home in the evening she would bring her long thin arms out from under her bedclothes, twine them around his neck, draw him down beside her on the edge of the bed, and launch into the tale of her woes: he was forgetting her, he was in love with someone else! How right people had been, to warn her that he'd make her unhappy! And she always ended by asking him to give her a new tonic and a little more love.

II

One night about eleven o'clock they were awakened by a noise: a horse had stopped just at their door. The maid opened the attic window and parleyed for some time with a man who stood in the street below. He had been sent to fetch the doctor; he had a letter. Nastasie came downstairs, shivering, turned the key in the lock and pushed back the bolts one by one. The man left his horse, followed the maid, and entered the bedroom at her heels. Out of his gray-tasseled woolen cap he drew a letter wrapped in a piece of cloth, and with a careful gesture handed it to Charles, who raised himself on his

9. Bailiff's.

pillow to read it. Nastasie stood close to the bed, holding the light. Madame had modestly turned her back and lay facing the wall.

This letter, sealed with a small blue wax seal, begged Monsieur Bovary to come immediately to a farm called Les Bertaux, to set a broken leg. Now, from Tostes to Les Bertaux is at least fifteen miles, going by way of Longueville and Saint-Victor. It was a pitch-black night. Madame Bovary was fearful lest her husband meet with an accident. So it was decided that the stable hand who had brought the letter should start out ahead, and that Charles should follow three hours later: by that time there would be a moon. A boy would be sent out to meet him, to show him the way to the farm and open the field gates.

About four o'clock in the morning Charles set out for Les Bertaux, wrapped in a heavy coat. He was still drowsy from his warm sleep, and the peaceful trot of his mare lulled him like the rocking of a cradle. Whenever she stopped of her own accord in front of one of those spike-edged holes that farmers dig along the roadside to protect their crops, he would wake up with a start, quickly remember the broken leg, and try to recall all the fractures he had ever seen. The rain had stopped; day was breaking, and on the leafless branches of the apple trees birds were perched motionless, ruffling up their little feathers in the cold morning wind. The countryside stretched flat as far as eye could see; and the tufts of trees clustered around the farmhouses were widely spaced dark purple stains on the vast gray surface that merged at the horizon into the dull tone of the sky. From time to time Charles would open his eyes; and then, his senses dimmed by a return of sleep, he would fall again into a drowsiness in which recent sensations became confused with older memories to give him double visions of himself: as husband and as student—lying in bed as he had been only an hour or so before, and walking through a surgical ward as in the past. In his mind the hot smell of poultices mingled with the fresh smell of the dew; he heard at once the rattle of the curtain rings on hospital beds, and the sound of his wife's breathing as she lay asleep. At Vassonville he saw a little boy sitting in the grass beside a ditch.

"Are you the doctor?" the child asked.

And when Charles answered, he took his wooden shoes in his hands and began to run in front of him.

As they continued on their way, the *officier de santé* gathered from what his guide told him that Monsieur Rouault must be a very well-to-do farmer indeed. He had broken his leg the previous evening, on his way back from celebrating Twelfth Night at the home of a neighbor. His wife had been dead for two years. He had with him only his "demoiselle"—his daughter—who kept house for him.

Now the road was more deeply rutted: they were approaching Les Bertaux. The boy slipped through an opening in a hedge, disappeared, then reappeared ahead, opening a farmyard gate from within. The horse was slipping on the wet grass; Charles had to bend low to escape overhanging branches. Kenneled watchdogs were barking, pulling at their chains. As he passed through the gate of Les Bertaux, his horse took fright and shied wildly.

It was a prosperous-looking farm. Through the open upper-halves of the stable doors great plough-horses could be seen placidly feeding from new racks. Next to the outbuildings stood a big manure pile, and in among the chickens and turkeys pecking at its steaming surface were five or six peacocks—favorite show pieces of *cauchois* farmyards.[1] The sheepfold was long, the barn lofty, its walls as smooth as your hand. In the shed were two large carts and four ploughs complete with whips, horse collars and full trappings, the blue wool pads gray under the fine dust that sifted down from the lofts. The farmyard sloped upwards, planted with symmetrically spaced trees, and from near the pond came the merry sound of a flock of geese.

A young woman wearing a blue merino dress with three flounces came to the door of the house to greet Monsieur Bovary, and she ushered him into the kitchen, where a big open fire was blazing. Around its edges the farm hands' breakfast was bubbling in small pots of assorted sizes. Damp clothes were drying inside the vast chimney-opening. The fire shovel, the tongs, and the nose of the bellows, all of colossal proportions, shone like polished steel; and along the walls hung a lavish array of kitchen utensils, glimmering in the bright light of the fire and in the first rays of the sun that were now beginning to come in through the windowpanes.

Charles went upstairs to see the patient. He found him in bed, sweating under blankets, his nightcap lying where he had flung it. He was a stocky little man of fifty, fair-skinned, blue-eyed, bald in front and wearing earrings. On a chair beside him was a big decanter of brandy: he had been pouring himself drinks to keep up his courage. But as soon as he saw the doctor he dropped his bluster, and instead of cursing as he had been doing for the past twelve hours he began to groan weakly.

The fracture was a simple one, without complications of any kind. Charles couldn't have wished for anything easier. Then he recalled his teachers' bed-side manner in accident cases, and proceeded to cheer up his patient with all kinds of facetious remarks—a truly surgical attention, like the oiling of a scalpel. For splints, they sent someone to bring a bundle of laths from the carriage shed. Charles selected one, cut it into lengths and smoothed it down with a piece of broken window glass, while the maidservant tore sheets for bandages and Mademoiselle Emma tried to sew some pads. She was a long time finding her workbox, and her father showed his impatience. She made no reply; but as she sewed she kept pricking her fingers and raising them to her mouth to suck.

Charles was surprised by the whiteness of her fingernails. They were almond shaped, tapering, as polished and shining as Dieppe ivories. Her hands, however, were not pretty—not pale enough, perhaps, a little rough at the knuckles; and they were too long, without softness of line. The finest thing about her was her eyes. They were brown, but seemed black under the long eyelashes; and she had an open gaze that met yours with fearless candor.

When the binding was done, the doctor was invited by Monsieur Rouault himself to "have something" before he left.

Charles went down to the parlor on the ground floor. At the foot of a great canopied bed, its calico hangings printed with a design of people in Turkish dress, there stood a little table on which places had been laid for two, a silver mug beside each plate. From a tall oaken cupboard facing the window came an odor of orris root and damp sheets. In corners stood rows of grain sacks—the overflow from the granary, which was just adjoining, approached by three stone steps. The room's only decoration, hanging from a nail in the center

1. From the Caux area, a large chalky plateau region in Normandy (northern France).

of the flaking green-painted wall, was a black pencil drawing of a head of Minerva framed in gold and inscribed at the bottom in Gothic letters "To my dear Papa."

They spoke about the patient first, and then about the weather, about the bitter cold, about the wolves that roamed the fields at night. Mademoiselle Rouault didn't enjoy country life, especially now, with almost the full responsibility of the farm on her shoulders. The room was chilly, and she shivered as she ate. Charles noticed that her lips were full, and that she had the habit of biting them in moments of silence.

Her neck rose out of the low fold of a white collar. The two black sweeps of her hair, pulled down from a fine center part that followed the curve of her skull, were so sleek that each seemed to be one piece. Covering all but the very tips of her ears, it was gathered at the back into a large chignon, and toward the temples it waved a bit—a detail that the country doctor now observed for the first time in his life. Her skin was rosy over her cheekbones. A pair of shell-rimmed eyeglasses, like a man's, was tucked between two buttons of her bodice.

When Charles came back downstairs after going up to take leave of Monsieur Rouault, he found her standing with her forehead pressed against the windowpane, looking out at the garden, where the beanpoles had been thrown down by the wind. She turned around.

"Are you looking for something?" she asked.

"For my riding crop," he said.

And he began to rummage on the bed, behind doors, under chairs. It had fallen on the floor between the grain bags and the wall. Mademoiselle Emma caught sight of it and reached for it, bending down across the sacks. Charles hurried over politely, and as he, too, stretched out his arm he felt his body in slight contact with the girl's back, bent there beneath him. She stood up, blushing crimson, and glanced at him over her shoulder as she handed him his crop.

Instead of returning to Les Bertaux three days later, as he had promised, he went back the very next day, then twice a week regularly, not to mention unscheduled calls he made from time to time, as though by chance.

Everything went well; the bone knit according to the rules; and after forty-six days, when Monsieur Rouault was seen trying to get around his farmyard by himself, everyone began to think of Monsieur Bovary as a man of great competence. Monsieur Rouault said he wouldn't have been better mended by the biggest doctors of Yvetot or even Rouen.

As for Charles, he didn't ask himself why he enjoyed going to Les Bertaux. Had he thought of it, he would doubtless have attributed his zeal to the seriousness of the case, or perhaps to the fee he hoped to earn. Still, was that really why his visits to the farm formed so charming a contrast to the drabness of the rest of his life? On such days he would rise early, set off at a gallop, urge his horse; and when he was almost there he would dismount to dust his shoes on the grass, and put on his black gloves. He enjoyed the moment of arrival, the feel of the gate as it yielded against his shoulder; he enjoyed the rooster crowing on the wall, the farm boys coming to greet him. He enjoyed the barn and the stables; he enjoyed Monsieur Rouault, who would clap him in the palm of the hand and call him his "savior"; he enjoyed hearing Mademoiselle Emma's little sabots on the newly washed flagstones of the kitchen floor. With their high heels they made her a little taller; and when she walked in them ahead of him their wooden soles kept coming up with a quick, sharp, tapping sound against the leather of her shoes.

She always accompanied him to the foot of the steps outside the door. If his horse hadn't been brought around she would wait there with him. At such moments they had already said good-bye, and stood there silent; the breeze eddied around her, swirling the stray wisps of hair at her neck, or sending her apron strings flying like streamers around her waist. Once she was standing there on a day of thaw, when the bark of the trees in the farmyard was oozing sap and the snow was melting on the roofs. She went inside for her parasol, and opened it. The parasol was of rosy iridescent silk, and the sun pouring through it painted the white skin of her face with flickering patches of light. Beneath it she smiled at the springlike warmth; and drops of water could be heard falling one by one on the taut moiré.

During the first period of Charles's visits to Les Bertaux, Madame Bovary never failed to ask about the patient's progress; and in her double-entry ledger she had given Monsieur Rouault a fine new page to himself. But when she heard that he had a daughter she began to make inquiries; and she learned that Mademoiselle Rouault had had her schooling in a convent, with the Ursuline nuns—had received, as the saying went, a "fine education," in the course of which she had been taught dancing, geography, drawing, needlework and a little piano. Think of that!

"So that's why he brightens up when he goes there! That's why he wears his new waistcoat, even in the rain! Ah! So she's at the bottom of it!"

Instinctively she hated her. At first she relieved her feelings by making insinuations. Charles didn't get them. Then she let fall parenthetical remarks which he left unanswered out of fear of a storm; and finally she was driven to point-blank reproaches which he didn't know how to answer. Why was it that he kept going back to Les Bertaux, now that Monsieur Rouault was completely mended and hadn't even paid his bill? Ah! Because there was *a certain person* there. Somebody who knew how to talk. Somebody who did embroidery. Somebody clever. That's what he enjoyed: he had to have city girls! And she went on:

"Rouault's daughter, a city girl! Don't make me laugh! The grandfather was a shepherd, and there's a cousin who barely escaped sentence for assault and battery. Scarcely good reasons for giving herself airs, for wearing silk dresses to church like a countess! Besides—her father, poor fellow: if it hadn't been for last year's colza crop he'd have been hard put to it to pay his debts."

For the sake of peace, Charles stopped going to Les Bertaux. Heloise had made him swear—his hand on his prayer book—that he would never go back there again: she had accomplished it after much sobbing and kissing, in the midst of a great amorous explosion. He yielded; but the strength of his desire kept protesting against the servility of his behavior, and with a naïve sort of hypocrisy he told himself that this very prohibition against seeing her implicitly allowed him to love her. And then the widow he was married to was skinny; she was long in the tooth; all year round she wore a little black shawl with a corner hanging down between her shoulder blades; her rigid form was always sheathed in dresses that were like scabbards; they were always too short; they showed her ankles, her big shoes, and her shoelaces crisscrossing their way up her gray stockings.

Charles's mother came to see them from time to time; but after a few days she invariably took on her daughter-in-law's sharpness against her son, and like a pair of knives they kept scarifying him with their comments and criticisms. He oughtn't to eat so much! Why always offer a drink to everyone who called? So pigheaded not to wear flannel underwear!

Early in the spring it happened that a notary in Ingouville, custodian of the Widow Dubuc's capital, sailed away one fine day, taking with him all his clients' money. To be sure, Heloise still owned her house in the rue Saint-François in Dieppe, as well as a six-thousand-franc interest in a certain ship; nevertheless, of the great fortune she'd always talked so much about, nothing except a few bits of furniture and some clothes had ever been seen in the household. Now, inevitably, everything came under investigation. The house in Dieppe, it turned out, was mortgaged up to its eaves; what she had placed with the notary, God only knew; and her share in the boat didn't amount to more than three thousand. So she'd been lying—lying all along, the dear, good lady! In his rage the older Monsieur Bovary dashed a chair to pieces on the floor and accused his wife of ruining their son's life by yoking him to such an ancient nag, whose harness was worth even less than her carcass. They came to Tostes. The four of them had it out. There were scenes. The weeping Heloise threw herself into her husband's arms and appealed to him to defend her against his parents. Charles began to take her part. The others flew into a rage and left.

But—"the fatal blow had been struck." A week later she was hanging out washing in her yard when suddenly she began to spit blood; and the next day, while Charles was looking the other way, drawing the window curtain, she gave a cry, then a sigh, and fainted. She was dead! Who would have believed it?

When everything was over at the cemetery, Charles returned to the house. There was no one downstairs, and he went up to the bedroom. One of her dresses was still hanging in the alcove. He stayed there until dark, leaning against the writing desk, his mind full of sad thoughts. Poor thing! She had loved him, after all.

III

One morning Monsieur Rouault came to pay Charles for setting his leg—seventy-five francs in two-franc pieces, with a turkey thrown in for good measure. He had heard of his bereavement, and offered him what consolation he could.

"I know what it is," he said, patting him on the shoulder. "I've been through just what you're going through. When I lost my wife I went out into the fields to be by myself. I lay down under a tree and cried. I talked to God, told him all kinds of crazy things. I wished I were dead, like the maggoty moles I saw hanging on the branches. And when I thought of how other men were holding their wives in their arms at that very moment, I began to pound my stick on the ground. I was almost out of my mind. I couldn't eat: the very thought of going to a café made me sick—you'd never believe it. Well, you know, what with one day gradually nosing out another, and spring coming on top of winter and then fall after the summer—it passed bit by bit, drop by drop. It just went away; it disappeared; I mean it grew less and less—there's always part of it you never get rid of entirely; you always feel something here." And he put his hand on his chest. "But it happens to us all, and you mustn't let yourself go, you mustn't want to die just because other people are dead. You must brace up, Monsieur Bovary: things will get better. Come and see us. My daughter talks about you every once in a while; she says you've probably forgotten her. Spring will soon be here: you and I'll go out after a rabbit—it will take your mind off things."

Charles took his advice. He went back to Les Bertaux; he found it unchanged since yesterday—since five months before, that is. The pear trees were already in flower; and the sight of Monsieur Rouault coming and going normally around the place made everything livelier.

The farmer seemed to think that the doctor's grief-stricken condition called for a special show of consideration, and he urged him to keep his hat on, addressed him in a low voice as though he were ill, and even pretended to be angry that no one had thought to cook him something special and light, like custard or stewed pears. He told him funny stories. Charles found himself laughing, but then the thought of his wife returned to sober him. By the end of the meal he had forgotten her again.

He thought of her less and less as he grew used to living alone. The novelty and pleasure of being independent soon made solitude more bearable. Now he could change his meal hours at will, come and go without explanation, stretch out across the bed if he was particularly tired. So he pampered and coddled himself and accepted all the comforting everyone offered. Besides, he wife's death had helped him quite a bit professionally: for a month or so everyone had kept saying, "Poor young man! What a tragedy!" His reputation grew; more and more patients came. Now he went to Les Bertaux whenever he pleased. He was aware of a feeling of hope—nothing very specific, a vague happiness: he thought himself better-looking when he stood at the mirror to brush his whiskers.

One day he arrived about three o'clock. Everyone was in the fields. He went into the kitchen, and at first didn't see Emma. The shutters were closed; the sun, streaming in between the slats, patterned the floor with long thin stripes that broke off at the corners of the furniture and quivered on the ceiling. On the table, flies were climbing up the sides of glasses that had recently been used, and buzzing as they struggled to keep from drowning in the cider at the bottom. The light coming down the chimney turned the soot on the fireback to velvet and gave a bluish cast to the cold ashes. Between the window and the hearth Emma sat sewing; her shoulders were bare, beaded with little drops of sweat.

Country-style, she offered him something to drink. He refused, she insisted, and finally suggested with a laugh that he take a liqueur with her. She brought a bottle of curaçao from the cupboard, reached to a high shelf for two liqueur glasses, filled one to the brim and poured a few drops in the other. She touched her glass to his and raised it to her mouth. Because it was almost empty she had to bend backwards to be able to drink; and with her head tilted back, her neck and her lips outstretched, she began to laugh at tasting nothing; and then the tip of her tongue came out from between her small teeth and began daintily to lick the bottom of the glass.

She sat down again and resumed her work—she was darning a white cotton stocking. She sewed with her head bowed, and she did not speak: nor did Charles. A draft was coming in under the door and blowing a little dust across the stone floor; he watched it drift, and was aware of a pulsating sound inside his head—that, and the clucking of a laying hen outside in the yard. From time to time Emma cooled her cheeks with the palms of her hands, and then cooled her hands against the iron knobs of the tall andirons.

She complained that the heat had been giving her dizzy spells, and asked whether sea bathing would help; then she began to talk about her convent school and Charles about his lycée: words came to them both. They went upstairs to her room. She showed him her old music exercise books, and the little volumes and the oak-leaf wreaths—the latter now lying abandoned in the bottom of a cupboard—that she had won as prizes. Then she spoke of her mother, and the cemetery, and took him out to the garden to see the bed where she picked flowers the first Friday of every month to put on her grave. But their gardener had no understanding of such things: farm help was so trying! She would love, if only for the winter, to live in the city—though she had to say that it was really in summer, with the days so long, that the country was most boring of all. Depending on what she talked about, her voice was clear, or shrill, or would grow suddenly languorous and trail off almost into a murmur, as though she were speaking to herself. One moment she would be gay and wide-eyed; the next, she would half shut her eyelids and seem to be drowned in boredom, her thoughts miles away.

That evening, on his homeward ride, Charles went over one by one the things she had said, trying to remember her exact words and sense their implications, in an effort to picture what her life had been like before their meeting. But in his thoughts he could never see her any differently from the way she had been when he had seen her the first time, or as she had been just now, when he left her. Then he wondered what would become of her, whether she would marry, and whom. Alas! Monsieur Rouault was very rich, and she . . . so beautiful! But Emma's face appeared constantly before his eyes, and in his ears there was a monotonous throbbing, like the humming of a top: "But why don't *you* get married! Why don't *you* get married!"

That night he didn't sleep, his throat was tight, he was thirsty; he got up to drink from his water jug and opened the window; the sky was covered with stars, a hot wind was blowing, dogs were barking in the distance. He stared out in the direction of Les Bertaux.

After all, he thought, nothing would be lost by trying; and he resolved to ask his question when the occasion presented itself; but each time it did, the fear of not finding the proper words paralyzed his lips.

Actually, Rouault wouldn't have been a bit displeased to have someone take his daughter off his hands. She was of no use to him on the farm. He didn't really hold it against her, being of the opinion that she was too clever to have anything to do with farming—that accursed occupation that had never yet made a man a millionaire. Far from having grown rich at it, the poor fellow was losing money every year: he more than held his own in the market place, where he relished all the tricks of the trade, but no one was less suited than he to the actual growing of crops and the managing of a farm. He never lifted a finger if he could help it, and never spared any expense in matters of daily living: he insisted on good food, a good fire, and a good bed. He liked his cider hard, his leg of mutton rare, his coffee well laced with brandy. He took his meals in the kitchen, alone, facing the fire, at a little table that was brought in to him already set, like on the stage.

So when he noticed that Charles tended to be flushed in his daughter's presence—meaning that one of these days he would ask for her hand—he pondered every aspect of the question well in advance. Charles was a bit namby-pamby, not his dream of a son-in-law; but he was said to be reliable, thrifty, very well educated; and he probably wouldn't haggle too much over the dowry. Moreover, Rouault was soon going to have to sell twenty-two of his acres: he owed considerable to the mason and considerable to the harness maker, and the cider press needed a new shaft. "If he asks me for her," he said to himself, "I won't refuse."

Toward the beginning of October, Charles spent three days at Les Bertaux. The last day had slipped by like the others, with the big step put off from one minute to the next. Rouault was escorting him on the first lap of his homeward journey; they were walking along a sunken road; they were just about to part—the moment had come. Charles gave himself to the corner of the hedge; and finally, when they had passed it: "Monsieur Rouault," he murmured, "there's something I'd like to say to you."

They stopped. Charles fell silent.

"Well, tell me what's on your mind! I know it already anyway!" Rouault said with a gentle laugh.

"Monsieur Rouault . . . Monsieur Rouault . . ." Charles stammered.

"Personally I wouldn't like anything better," continued the farmer. "I imagine the child agrees with me, but we'd better ask her. I'll leave you here now, and go back to the house. If it's 'Yes'—now listen to what I'm saying—you won't have to come in: there are too many people around, and besides she'd be too upset. But to take you off the anxious seat I'll slam a shutter against the wall: you can look back and see, if you lean over the hedge."

And he went off.

Charles tied his horse to a tree. He hastily stationed himself on the path and waited. Half an hour went by; then he counted nineteen minutes by his watch. Suddenly there was a noise against the wall: the shutter had swung back; the catch was still quivering.

The next morning he was at the farm by nine. Emma blushed when he entered, laughing a little in an attempt to be casual. Rouault embraced his future son-in-law. They postponed all talk of financial arrangements: there was plenty of time, since the wedding couldn't decently take place before the end of Charles's mourning—that is, toward the spring of the next year.

It was a winter of waiting. Mademoiselle Rouault busied herself with her trousseau. Part of it was ordered in Rouen, and she made her slips and nightcaps herself, copying fashion drawings that she borrowed. Whenever Charles visited the farm they spoke about preparations for the wedding, discussing which room the dinner should be served in, wondering how many courses to have and what the entrees should be.

Emma herself would have liked to be married at midnight, by torchlight; but Rouault wouldn't listen to the idea. So there was the usual kind of wedding, with forty-three guests, and everybody was sixteen hours at table, and the festivities began all over again the next day and even carried over a little into the days following.

IV

The invited guests arrived early in a variety of vehicles—one-horse shays, two-wheeled charabancs, old gigs without tops, vans with leather curtains; and the young men from the nearest villages came in farm carts, standing one behind the other along the sides and grasping the rails to keep from being thrown, for the horses trotted briskly and the roads were rough. They came from as far as twenty-five miles away, from Goderville, from Normanville, from Cany. All the relations of both families had been asked, old quarrels had been patched up, letters sent to acquaintances long lost sight of.

From time to time the crack of a whip would be heard behind the hedge, then after a moment the gate would open and a cart would roll in; it would come at a gallop as far as the doorstep, then stop with a lurch, and out would pour its passengers, rubbing their knees and stretching their arms. The ladies wore country-style headdresses and city-style gowns, with gold watch chains, tippets (the ends crossed and tucked into their belts), or small colored fichus[2] attached at the back with pins and leaving the neck bare. The boys, attired exactly like their papas, looked ill at ease in their new clothes (and indeed many of them were wearing leather shoes that day for the first time in their lives); and next to them would be some speechless, gangling girl of fourteen or sixteen, probably their cousin or their older sister, flushed and awkward in her white First Communion dress let down for the occasion, her hair sticky with scented pomade, terribly worried lest she dirty her gloves. Since there weren't enough stable hands to unharness all the carriages, the men rolled up their sleeves and went to it themselves. According to their social status, they wore tail coats, frock coats, long jackets or short jackets. The tail coats were worthy garments, each of them a prized family possession taken out of the closet only on great occasions; the frock coats had great flaring skirts that billowed in the wind, cylindrical collars, and pockets as capacious as bags; the long jackets were double-breasted, of coarse wool, and usually worn with a cap of some kind, its peak trimmed with brass; and the short jackets were very short indeed, with two back buttons set close together like a pair of eyes, and stiff tails that looked as though a carpenter had hacked them with his axe out of a single block of wood. A few guests (these, of course, would sit at the foot of the table) wore dress smocks—that is, smocks with turned-down collars, fine pleating at the back, and stitched belts low on the hips.

And the shirts! They bulged like breastplates. Every man was freshly shorn; ears stood out from heads; faces were of a holiday smoothness. Some of the guests from farthest away, who had got up before dawn and had to shave in the dark, had slanting gashes under their noses, or patches of skin the size of a three-franc piece peeled from their jaws. During the journey their wounds had been inflamed by the wind, and as a result red blotches adorned many a big beaming white face.

Since the mayor's office was scarcely more than a mile from the farm, the wedding party went there on foot and came back the same way after the church ceremony. The procession was compact at first, like a bright sash festooning the countryside as it followed the narrow path winding between

2. Triangular scarves. *Tippets:* shoulder capes with hanging ends.

the green grain fields; but soon it lengthened out and broke up into different groups, which lingered to gossip along the way. The fiddler went first, the scroll of his violin gay with ribbons; then came the bridal pair; then their families; then their friends in no particular order; and last of all the children, having a good time pulling the bell-shaped flowers from the oat stalks or playing among themselves out of sight of their elders. Emma's gown was too long, and trailed a little; from time to time she stopped to pull it up; and at such moments she would carefully pick off the coarse grasses and thistle spikes with her gloved fingers, as Charles waited empty-handed beside her. Rouault, in a new silk hat, the cuffs of his black tail coat coming down over his hands as far as his fingertips, had given his arm to the older Madame Bovary. The older Monsieur Bovary, who looked on all these people with contempt, and had come wearing simply a single-breasted overcoat of military cut, was acting the barroom gallant with a blond young peasant girl. She bobbed and blushed, tongue-tied and confused. The other members of the wedding party discussed matters of business, or played tricks behind each other's backs, their spirits already soaring in anticipation of the fun. If they listened, they could hear the steady scraping of the fiddle in the fields. When the fiddler realized that he had left everyone far behind, he stopped for breath, carefully rubbed his bow with rosin to make his strings squeak all the better, and then set off again on his course, raising and lowering the neck of his violin to keep time. The sound of the instrument frightened away all the birds for a long distance ahead.

The table was set up in the carriage shed. On it were four roasts of beef, six fricassees of chicken, a veal casserole, three legs of mutton, and in the center a charming little suckling pig flanked by four *andouilles à l'oseille*—pork sausages flavored with sorrel. At the corners stood decanters of brandy. The sweet cider foamed up around its corks, and before anyone was seated, every glass had been filled to the brim with wine. Great dishes of yellow custard, their smooth surfaces decorated with the newlyweds' initials in candy-dot arabesques, were set trembling whenever the table was given the slightest knock. The pies and cakes had been ordered from a caterer in Yvetot. Since he was just starting up in the district, he had gone to considerable pains; and when dessert time came he himself brought to the table a wedding cake that drew exclamations from all. Its base was a square of blue cardboard representing a temple with porticos and colonnades and adorned on all sides with stucco statuettes standing in niches spangled with gold-paper stars. The second tier was a medieval castle in *gâteau de Savoie,* surrounded by miniature fortifications of angelica, almonds, raisins, and orange sections. And finally, on the topmost layer—which was a green meadow, with rocks, jelly lakes, and boats of hazelnut shells—a little Cupid was swinging in a chocolate swing. The tips of the two uprights, the highest points of the whole, were two real rosebuds.

The banquet went on till nightfall. Those who grew tired of sitting took a stroll in the yard or played a kind of shuffleboard in the barn; then they returned to table. A few, toward the end, fell asleep and snored. But everything came to life again with the coffee: there were songs, displays of strength. The men lifted weights, played the game of passing their heads under their arms while holding one thumb on the table, tried to raise carts to their shoulders. Dirty jokes were in order; the ladies were kissed. In the evening, when it came time to go, the horses, stuffed with oats to the bursting point, could scarcely be forced between the shafts; they kicked and reared, broke their harness, brought curses or laughs from their masters. And all night long, under the light of the moon on the country roads, runaway carts were bouncing along ditches at a gallop, leaping over gravel piles and crashing into banks, with women leaning out trying desperately to seize the reins.

Those who stayed at Les Bertaux spent the night drinking in the kitchen. The children fell asleep on the floor.

The bride had begged her father that she be spared the usual pranks. However, a fishmonger cousin (who had actually brought a pair of soles as a wedding present) was just beginning to spurt water from his mouth through the keyhole when Rouault came along and stopped him, explaining that the importance of his son-in-law's position didn't permit such unseemliness. The cousin complied very grudgingly. In his heart he accused Rouault of being a snob, and he joined a group of four or five other guests, who had happened several times in succession to be given inferior cuts of meat at table and so considered that they, too, had been badly treated. The whole group sat there whispering derogatory things about their host, and in veiled language expressed hopes for his downfall.

The older Madame Bovary hadn't opened her mouth all day. No one had consulted her about her daughter-in-law's bridal dress, or the arrangements for the party: she went up to bed early. Her husband didn't accompany her; instead, he sent to Saint-Victor for cigars and sat up till dawn smoking and drinking kirsch and hot water. This variety of grog was new to his fellow guests, and made him feel that their respect for him rose all the higher.

Charles was far from being a wag. He had been dull throughout the festivities, responding but feebly to the witticisms, puns, *doubles-entendres,* teasings and dubious jokes that everyone had felt obliged to toss at him from the moment they had sat down to the soup.

The next day, however, he seemed a different man. It was he who gave the impression of having lost his virginity overnight: the bride made not the slightest sign that could be taken to betray anything at all. Even the shrewdest were nonplused, and stared at her with the most intense curiosity whenever she came near. But Charles hid nothing. He addressed her as *"ma femme,"* using the intimate *"tu,"*[3] kept asking everyone where she was and looking for her everywhere, and often took her out into the yard, where he could be glimpsed through the trees with his arm around her waist, leaning over her as they walked, his head rumpling the yoke of her bodice.

Two days after the wedding the bridal pair left: because of his patients Charles could stay away no longer. Rouault had them driven to Tostes in his cart, going with them himself as far as Vassonville. There he kissed his daughter a last time, got out, and retraced his way. When he had walked about a hundred yards he stopped; and the sight of the cart disappearing in the distance, its wheels spinning in the dust, made him utter a deep sigh. He remembered his own wedding, his own earlier days, his wife's first pregnancy. He, too, had been very happy, the day he had taken her from her father's house to his own. She had ridden pillion behind him as their horse trotted over the snow, for it had been close to Christmas and the fields were

---

3. The intimate form of "you" (French). *Ma femme:* my wife (French).

white; she had clutched him with one arm, her basket hooked over the other; the wind was whipping the long lace streamers of her *coiffure cauchoise*[4] so that at times they blew across his mouth; and by turning his head he could see her rosy little face close behind his shoulder, smiling silently at him under the gold buckle of her bonnet. From time to time she would warm her fingers by sliding them inside his coat. How long ago it all was! Their boy would be thirty if he were alive today! Then he looked back again, and there was nothing to be seen on the road. He felt dismal, like a stripped and empty house; and as tender memories and black thoughts mingled in his brain, dulled by the vapors of the feast, he considered for a moment turning his steps toward the church. But he was afraid that the sight of it might make him even sadder, so he went straight home.

Monsieur and Madame Charles reached Tostes about six o'clock. The neighbors came to their windows to see their doctor's new wife.

The elderly maidservant appeared, greeted them, apologized for not having dinner ready, and suggested that Madame, in the meantime, might like to make a tour of inspection of her house.

V

The brick house-front was exactly flush with the street, or rather the road. Behind the door hung a coat with a short cape, a bridle, and a black leather cap; and on the floor in the corner lay a pair of gaiters still caked with mud. To the right was the parlor, which served as both dining and sitting room. A canary yellow wallpaper, set off at the top by a border of pale flowers, rippled everywhere on its loose canvas lining; white calico curtains edged with red braid hung crosswise down the length of the windows; and on the narrow mantelpiece a clock ornamented with a head of Hippocrates stood proudly between two silver-plated candlesticks under oval glass domes. Across the hall was Charles's small consulting room, about eighteen feet wide, with a table, three straight chairs and an office armchair. There was a fir bookcase with six shelves, occupied almost exclusively by a set of the *Dictionary of the Medical Sciences,* its pages uncut but its binding battered by a long succession of owners. Cooking smells seeped through the wall during office hours, and the patients' coughs and confidences were quite audible in the kitchen. In the rear, opening directly into the yard (which contained the stables), was a big ramshackle room with an oven, now serving as woodshed, wine bin and storeroom; it was filled with old junk, empty barrels, broken tools, and a quantity of other objects all dusty and nondescript.

The long narrow garden ran back between two clay walls covered with espaliered apricot trees to the thorn hedge that marked it off from the fields. In the middle was a slate sundial on a stone pedestal. Four beds of scrawny rose bushes were arranged symmetrically around a square plot given over to vegetables. At the far end, under some spruces, a plaster priest stood reading his breviary.

Emma went up to the bedrooms. The first was empty; in the second, the conjugal chamber, a mahogany bed stood in an alcove hung with red draperies. A box made of seashells adorned the chest of drawers; and on the desk

4. Cauchois headdress.

near the window, standing in a decanter and tied with white satin ribbon, was a bouquet of orange blossoms—a bride's bouquet: the *other* bride's bouquet! She stared at it. Charles noticed, picked it up, and took it to the attic; and as her boxes and bags were brought up and placed around her, she sat in an armchair and thought of her own bridal bouquet, which was packed in one of those very boxes, wondering what would be done with it if she were to die.

She spent the first few days planning changes in the house. She took the domes off the candlesticks, had the parlor repapered, the stairs painted, and seats made to go around the sundial in the garden. She even made inquiries as to the best way of installing a fountain and a fish pond. And her husband, knowing that she liked to go for drives, bought a secondhand two-wheeled buggy. With new lamps and quilted leather mudguards it looked almost like a tilbury.

He was happy now, without a care in the world. A meal alone with her, a stroll along the highway in the evening, the way she touched her hand to her hair, the sight of her straw hat hanging from a window hasp, and many other things in which it had never occurred to him to look for pleasure—such now formed the steady current of his happiness. In bed in the morning, his head beside hers on the pillow, he would watch the sunlight on the downy gold of her cheeks, half covered by the scalloped tabs of her nightcap. Seen from so close, her eyes appeared larger than life, especially when she opened and shut her eyelids several times on awakening: black when looked at in shadow, dark blue in bright light, they seemed to contain layer upon layer of color, thicker and cloudier beneath, lighter and more transparent toward the lustrous surface. As his own eyes plunged into those depths, he saw himself reflected there in miniature down to his shoulders—his foulard on his head, his nightshirt open. After he had dressed she would go to the window and watch him leave for his rounds; she would lean out between two pots of geraniums, her elbows on the sill, her dressing gown loose around her. In the street, Charles would strap on his spurs at the mounting block; and she would continue to talk to him from above, blowing down to him some bit of flower or leaf she had bitten off in her teeth. It would flutter down hesitantly, weaving semicircles in the air like a bird, and before reaching the ground it would catch in the tangled mane of the old white mare standing motionless at the door. From the saddle Charles would send her a kiss; she would respond with a wave; then she would close the window, and he was off. And on the endless dusty ribbon of the highway, on sunken roads vaulted over by branches, on paths between stands of grain that rose to his knees—the sun on his shoulders and the morning air in his nostrils, his heart full of the night's bliss, his spirit at peace and his flesh content—he would ride on his way ruminating his happiness, like someone who keeps savoring, hours later, the fragrance of the truffles he has eaten for dinner.

Up until now, had there ever been a happy time in his life? His years at the lycée, where he had lived shut in behind high walls, lonely among richer, cleverer schoolmates who laughed at his country accent and made fun of his clothes and whose mothers brought them cookies in their muffs on visiting days? Or later, when he was studying medicine and hadn't enough in his purse to go dancing with some little working girl who might have become his mistress? After that he had lived fourteen months with the widow, whose feet in bed had been like icicles. But now he possessed, and for always, this pretty wife whom he so loved. The universe, for him, went not beyond the silken circuit of her petticoat; and he would reproach himself for not showing her his love, and yearn to be back with her. He would gallop home, rush upstairs, his heart pounding. Emma would be at her dressing table; he would creep up silently behind her and kiss her; she would cry out in surprise.

He couldn't keep from constantly touching her comb, her rings, everything she wore; sometimes he gave her great full-lipped kisses on the cheek, or a whole series of tiny kisses up her bare arm, from her fingertips to her shoulder; and half amused, half annoyed, she would push him away as one does an importunate child.

Before her marriage she had thought that she had love within her grasp; but since the happiness which she had expected this love to bring her hadn't come, she supposed she must have been mistaken. And Emma tried to imagine just what was meant, in life, by the words "bliss," "passion," and "rapture"—words that had seemed so beautiful to her in books.

VI

She had read *Paul and Virginia*,[5] and had dreamed of the bamboo cabin, of the Negro Domingo and the dog Fidèle; and especially she dreamed that she, too, had a sweet little brother for a devoted friend, and that he climbed trees as tall as church steeples to pluck her their crimson fruit, and came running barefoot over the sand to bring her a bird's nest.

When she was thirteen, her father took her to the city to enter her as a boarder in the convent. They stayed at a hotel near Saint-Gervais, where their supper plates were decorated with scenes from the life of Mademoiselle de La Vallière.[6] The explanatory captions, slashed here and there by knife scratches, were all in praise of piety, the sensibilities of the heart, and the splendors of the court.

Far from being unhappy in the convent, at first, she enjoyed the company of the nuns: it was fun when they took her to the chapel, down a long corridor from the refectory. She rarely played during recess, and she was very quick at catechism: it was always Mademoiselle Rouault who answered Monsieur le vicaire's hardest questions. As she continued to live uninterruptedly in the insipid atmosphere of the classrooms, among the white-faced women with their brass crucifixes dangling from their rosaries, she gently succumbed to the mystical languor induced by the perfumes of the altar, the coolness of the holy-water fonts, the gleaming of the candles. Instead of following the Mass she kept her prayer book open at the holy pictures with their sky-blue borders; and she loved the Good Shepherd, the Sacred Heart pierced by sharp arrows, and poor Jesus stumbling and falling under his cross. To mortify herself she tried to go a whole day without eating. She looked for some vow that she might accomplish.

5. A 1784 story of the sentimental tragic love of two young people on the tropical island of Île de France (today, Mauritius). It was the most popular work of Bernardin de Saint-Pierre (1737–1814).   6. One of Louis XIV's mistresses, whose mythologized character is familiar to all readers of Alexandre Dumas's *Le Vicomte de Bragelonne* (a sequel to *The Three Musketeers*).

When she went to confession she invented small sins in order to linger on her knees there in the darkness, her hands joined, her face at the grille, the priest whispering just above her. The metaphors constantly used in sermons—"betrothed," "spouse," "heavenly lover," "mystical marriage"— excited her in a thrilling new way.

Every evening before prayers a piece of religious writing was read aloud in study hall. During the week it would be some digest of Biblical history or the Abbé Frayssinous's lectures; on Sunday it was always a passage from the *Génie du Christianisme*,[7] offered as entertainment. How intently she listened, the first times, to the ringing lamentations of that romantic melancholy, echoed and reechoed by all the voices of earth and heaven! Had her childhood been spent in cramped quarters behind some city shop, she might have been open to the lyric appeal of nature—which usually reaches us only by way of literary interpretations. But she knew too much about country life: she was well acquainted with lowing herds, with dairy maids and ploughs. From such familiar, peaceful aspects, she turned to the picturesque. She loved the sea for its storms alone, cared for vegetation only when it grew here and there among ruins. She had to extract a kind of personal advantage from things; and she rejected as useless everything that promised no immediate gratification—for her temperament was more sentimental than artistic, and what she was looking for was emotions, not scenery.

At the convent there was an old spinster who came for a week every month to look after the linen. As a member of an ancient noble family ruined by the Revolution she was a protégée of the archdiocese; and she ate at the nuns' table in the refectory and always stayed for a chat with them before returning upstairs to her work. The girls often slipped out of study-hall to pay her a visit. She had a repertoire of eighteenth-century love songs, and sang them in a low voice as she sewed. She told stories, kept the girls abreast of the news, did errands for them in the city, and to the older ones would surreptitiously lend one of the novels she always carried in her apron pocket—novels of which the good spinster herself was accustomed to devour long chapters in the intervals of her task. They were invariably about love affairs, lovers, mistresses, harassed ladies swooning in remote pavilions. Couriers were killed at every relay, horses ridden to death on every page; there were gloomy forests, broken hearts, vows, sobs, tears and kisses, skiffs in the moonlight, nightingales in thickets; the noblemen were all brave as lions, gentle as lambs, incredibly virtuous, always beautifully dressed, and wept copiously on every occasion. For six months, when she was fifteen, Emma begrimed her hands with this dust from old lending libraries. Later, reading Walter Scott, she became infatuated with everything historical and dreamed about oaken chests and guardrooms and troubadours. She would have liked to live in some old manor, like those long-waisted chatelaines who spent their days leaning out of fretted Gothic casements, elbow on parapet and chin in hand, watching a white-plumed knight come galloping out of the distance on a black horse. At that time she worshiped Mary Queen of

7. An enormously influential book (1802), by François-René de Chateaubriand, celebrating the truths and beauties of Roman Catholicism, just before Napoleon's concordat with Rome. Denis de Frayssinous (1765– 1841) was a popular preacher who wrote *Défense du Christianisme* (1825). Under Louis XVIII (restored to the throne after the fall of Napoleon I) he became a bishop and minister of ecclesiastical affairs.

Scots, and venerated women illustrious or ill-starred. In her mind Joan of Arc, Héloise, Agnès Sorel, La Belle Ferronière and Clémence Isaure[8] stood out like comets on the shadowy immensity of history; and here and there (though less clearly outlined than the others against the dim background, and quite unrelated among themselves) were visible also St. Louis and his oak, the dying Bayard, certain atrocities of Louis XI, bits of the Massacre of St. Bartholomew,[9] the plumed crest of Henri IV, and, always, the memory of the hotel plates glorifying Louis XIV.

The sentimental songs she sang in music class were all about little angels with golden wings, madonnas, lagoons, gondoliers—mawkish compositions that allowed her to glimpse, through the silliness of the words and the indiscretions of the music, the alluring, phantasmagoric realm of genuine feeling. Some of her schoolmates brought to the convent the keepsake albums they had received as New Year's gifts. They had to hide them—it was very exciting; they could be read only at night, in the dormitory. Careful not to harm the lovely satin bindings, Emma stared bedazzled at the names of the unknown authors—counts or viscounts, most of them—who had written their signatures under their contributions.

She quivered as she blew back the tissue paper from each engraving: it would curl up into the air, then sink gently down against the page. Behind a balcony railing a young man in a short cloak clasped in his arms a girl in a white dress, a chatelaine bag fastened to her belt; or there were portraits of unidentified aristocratic English beauties with blond curls, staring out at you with their wide light-colored eyes from under great straw hats. Some were shown lolling in carriages, gliding through parks; their greyhound ran ahead, and two little grooms in white knee breeches drove the trotting horses. Others, dreaming on sofas, an opened letter lying beside them, gazed at the moon through a window that was half open, half draped with a black curtain. Coy maidens with tears on their cheeks kissed turtledoves through the bars of Gothic bird cages; or, smiling, their cheeks practically touching their own shoulders, they pulled the petals from daisies with pointed fingers that curved up at the ends like Eastern slippers. Then there were sultans with long pipes swooning under arbors in the arms of dancing girls; there were Giaours,[1] Turkish sabres, fezzes. And invariably there were blotchy, pale landscapes of fantastic countries: pines and palms growing together, tigers on the right, a lion on the left, Tartar minarets on the horizon. Roman ruins in the foreground, a few kneeling camels—all of it set in a very neat and orderly virgin forest, with a great perpendicular sunbeam quivering in the water; and standing out on the water's surface—scratched in white on the steel-gray background—a few widely spaced floating swans.

The bracket lamp above Emma's head shone down on those pictures of

8. A half-fictional lady from Toulouse (14th century), popularized in a novel by Florian as an incarnation of the mystical poetry of the troubadours. Héloise, famous for her love affair with the philosopher Abelard (1101–1164). Agnès Sorel (1422–1450), a mistress of Charles VII, rumored to have been poisoned by the future Louis XI. La Belle Ferronière (d. 1540), one of François I's mistresses, wife of the lawyer Le Ferron, who is said to have contracted syphilis for the mere satisfaction of passing it on to the king.   **9.** Massacre of the Protestants ordered by Catherine de Medici on the night of August 23, 1572. St. Louis (1215–1270), king of France as Louis IX, led the seventh and eighth crusades and was canonized in 1297. According to tradition, he dispensed justice under an oak tree at Vincennes (near Paris). *Bayard:* Seigneur de Pierre du Terrail (1473–1542), one of the most famous French captains, distinguished himself by feats of bravery during the wars of François I. When dying, he chided the connétable de Bourbon for his treason in a famous speech. Louis XI (b. 1421; ruled 1461–83), ruthlessly suppressed the rebellious noblemen.   **1.** Romantic heroes of the outcast desperado type.

every corner of the world as she turned them over one by one in the silence of the dormitory, the only sound, coming from the distance, that of some belated cab on the boulevards.

When her mother died, she wept profusely for several days. She had a memorial picture made for herself from the dead woman's hair; and in a letter filled with sorrowful reflections on life that she sent to Les Bertaux, she begged to be buried, when her time came, in the same grave. Her father thought she must be ill, and went to see her. Emma was privately pleased to feel that she had so very quickly attained this ideal of ethereal languor, inaccessible to mediocre spirits. So she let herself meander along Lamartinian² paths, listening to the throbbing of harps on lakes, to all the songs of dying swans, to the falling of every leaf, to the flight of pure virgins ascending to heaven, and to the voice of the Eternal speaking in the valleys. Gradually these things began to bore her, but she refused to admit it and continued as before, first out of habit, then out of vanity; until one day she discovered with surprise that the whole mood had evaporated, leaving her heart as free of melancholy as her brow was free of wrinkles.

The good nuns, who had been taking her vocation quite for granted, were greatly surprised to find that Mademoiselle Rouault was apparently slipping out of their control. And indeed they had so deluged her with prayers, retreats, novenas and sermons, preached so constantly the respect due the saints and the martyrs, and given her so much good advice about modest behavior and the saving of her soul, that she reacted like a horse too tightly reined: she balked, and the bit fell from her teeth. In her enthusiasms she had always looked for something tangible: she had loved the church for its flowers, music for its romantic words, literature for its power to stir the passions; and she rebelled before the mysteries of faith just as she grew ever more restive under discipline, which was antipathetic to her nature. When her father took her out of school no one was sorry to see her go. The Mother Superior, indeed, remarked that she had lately been displaying a certain lack of reverence toward the community.

Back at home, Emma at first enjoyed giving orders to the servants, then grew sick of country life and longed to be back in the convent. By the time Charles first appeared at Les Bertaux she thought that she was cured of illusions—that she had nothing more to learn, and no great emotions to look forward to.

But in her eagerness for a change, or perhaps overstimulated by this man's presence, she easily persuaded herself that love, that marvelous thing which had hitherto been like a great rosy-plumaged bird soaring in the splendors of poetic skies, was at last within her grasp. And now she could not bring herself to believe that the uneventful life she was leading was the happiness of which she had dreamed.

VII

She reflected occasionally that these were, nevertheless, the most beautiful days of her life—the honeymoon days, as people called them. To be sure, their sweetness would be best enjoyed far off, in one of those lands

---

2. Alphonse de Lamartine (1790–1869), French Romantic poet, whose *Méditations poétiques* (1820) resounds with amorous and religious melancholy.

with exciting names where the first weeks of marriage can be savored so much more deliciously and languidly! The post chaise with its blue silk curtains would have climbed slowly up the mountain roads, and the postilion's song would have reechoed among the cliffs, mingling with the tinkling of goat bells and the dull roar of waterfalls. They would have breathed the fragrance of lemon trees at sunset by the shore of some bay; and at night, alone on the terrace of a villa, their fingers intertwined, they would have gazed at the stars and planned their lives. It seemed to her that certain portions of the earth must produce happiness—as though it were a plant native only to those soils and doomed to languish elsewhere. Why couldn't she be leaning over the balcony of some Swiss chalet? Or nursing her melancholy in a cottage in Scotland, with a husband clad in a long black velvet coat and wearing soft leather shoes, a high-crowned hat and fancy cuffs?

She might have been glad to confide all these things to someone. But how speak about so elusive a malaise, one that keeps changing its shape like the clouds and its direction like the winds? She could find no words; and hence neither occasion nor courage came to hand.

Still, if Charles had made the slightest effort, if he had had the slightest inkling, if his glance had a single time divined her thought, it seemed to her that her heart would have been relieved of its fullness as quickly and easily as a tree drops its ripe fruit at the touch of a hand. But even as they were brought closer together by the details of daily life, she was separated from him by a growing sense of inward detachment.

Charles's conversation was flat as a sidewalk, a place of passage for the ideas of everyman; they wore drab everyday clothes, and they inspired neither laughter nor dreams. When he had lived in Rouen, he said, he had never had any interest in going to the theatre to see the Parisian company that was acting there. He couldn't swim or fence or fire a pistol; one day he couldn't tell her the meaning of a riding term she had come upon in a novel.

Wasn't it a man's role, though, to know everything? Shouldn't he be expert at all kinds of things, able to initiate you into the intensities of passion, the refinements of life, all the mysteries? *This* man could teach you nothing; he knew nothing, he wished for nothing. He took it for granted that she was content; and she resented his settled calm, his serene dullness, the very happiness she herself brought him.

She drew occasionally; and Charles enjoyed nothing more than standing beside her watching her bent over her sketchbook, half shutting his eyes the better to see her work, or rolling her bread-crumb erasers between his thumb and finger. As for the piano, the faster her fingers flew the more he marveled. She played with dash, swooping up and down the keyboard without a break. The strings of the old instrument jangled as she pounded, and when the window was open it could be heard to the end of the village. The *huissier*'s clerk often stopped to listen as he passed on the road—bareheaded, shuffling along in slippers, holding in his hand the notice he was about to post.

Moreover, Emma knew how to run her house. She let Charles's patients know how much they owed him, writing them nicely phrased letters that didn't sound like bills. When a neighbor came to Sunday dinner she always managed to think up some attractive dish. She would arrange greengages in a pyramid on a bed of vine leaves; she served her jellies not in their jars but neatly turned out on a plate; she spoke of buying finger bowls for dessert. All this redounded greatly to Bovary's credit.

He came to esteem himself the higher for having such a wife. He had two of her pencil sketches framed in wide frames, and hung them proudly in the parlor, at the end of long green cords. Citizens returning from Mass saw him standing on his doorstep, wearing a splendid pair of carpet slippers.

He came home from his rounds late—ten o'clock, sometimes midnight. He was hungry at that hour, and since the servant had gone to bed it was Emma who served him. He would take off his coat to be more comfortable at table, tell her every person he had seen, every village he had been to, every prescription he had written; and he would complacently eat what was left of the stew, pare his cheese, munch an apple, pour himself the last drop of wine. Then he would go up to bed, fall asleep the minute he was stretched on his back, and begin to snore.

He had so long been used to wearing cotton nightcaps that he couldn't get his foulard to stay on his head, and in the morning his hair was all over his face and white with down—the strings of his pillowcase often came undone during the night. He always wore heavy boots, with deep creases slanting from instep to ankle and the rest of the uppers so stiff that they seemed to be made of wood. He said that they were "plenty good enough for the country."

His mother approved his thriftiness. As in the past, she came to visit him whenever there was a particularly violent crisis in her own home; and yet she seemed to be prejudiced against her new daughter-in-law. She considered her "too grand in her tastes for the kind of people they were": the younger Bovarys ran through wood, sugar and candles at the rate of some great establishment; and the amount of charcoal they used would have done the cooking for twenty-five. She rearranged Emma's linen in the closets and taught her to check on the butcher when he delivered the meat. Emma listened to these lectures; Madame Bovary did not stint herself; and all day there would be a tremulous-lipped exchange of "ma fille" and "ma mère,"[3] each of the ladies uttering the sugary words in a voice that quivered with rage.

In Madame Dubuc's day the older woman had known herself to be the favorite; but now Charles's love for Emma seemed to her a desertion, an invasion of her own right; and she looked on sadly at Charles's happiness, like a ruined man staring through a window at revelers in a house that was once his own. Using the device of "Do you remember?" she reminded him of everything she had suffered and sacrificed for his sake; and contrasting all this with Emma's careless ways she pointed out how wrong he was to adore his wife to the exclusion of herself.

Charles didn't know what to answer. He respected his mother, and his love for his wife was boundless; he considered the former's opinions infallible, and yet Emma seemed to him perfect. After the older Madame Bovary's departure he made a fainthearted attempt to repeat one or two of the milder things he had heard her say, using her own phraseology; but with a word or two Emma convinced him he was wrong, and sent him back to his patients.

3. My mother (French). *Ma fille:* my daughter (French).

Throughout all this, following formulas she believed efficacious, she kept trying to experience love. Under the moonlight in the garden she would recite to Charles all the amorous verses she knew by heart, and sing him soulful sighing songs; but it all left her as unruffled as before, and Charles, too, seemed as little lovesick, as little stirred, as ever.

Having thus failed to produce the slightest spark of love in herself, and since she was incapable of understanding what she didn't experience, or of recognizing anything that wasn't expressed in conventional terms, she reached the conclusion that Charles's desire for her was nothing very extraordinary. His transports had become regularized; he embraced her only at certain times. This had now become a habit like any other—like a dessert that could be counted on to end a monotonous meal.

A gamekeeper whom Monsieur had cured of pneumonia made Madame a present of a little Italian greyhound bitch, and she took her with her whenever she went for a stroll: she did this every now and then, for the sake of a moment's solitude, a momentary relief from the everlasting sight of the back garden and the dusty road.

She would walk to the avenue of beeches at Banneville, near the abandoned pavilion at the corner of the wall along the fields. Rushes grow in the ditch there, tall and sharp edged among the grass.

Once arrived she would look around her, to see whether anything had changed since the last time she had come. The foxgloves and the wallflowers were where they had been; clumps of nettles were still growing around the stones; patches of lichen still clung along the three windows, whose perennially closed shutters were rotting away from their rusty iron bars. Her thoughts would be vague at first, straying like her dog, who would be running in circles, barking at yellow butterflies, chasing field mice, nibbling poppies at the edge of a wheatfield. Then her ideas would gradually focus; and sitting on the grass, jabbing it with little pokes of her parasol, Emma would ask herself again and again: "Why—*why*—did I ever marry?"

She wondered whether some different set of circumstances might not have resulted in her meeting some different man; and she tried to picture those imaginary circumstances, the life they would have brought her, the unknown other husband. However she imagined him, he wasn't a bit like Charles. He might have been handsome, witty, distinguished, magnetic—the kind of man her convent schoolmates had doubtless married. What kind of lives were they leading now? Cities, busy streets, buzzing theatres, brilliant balls—such surroundings afforded them unlimited opportunities for deep emotions and exciting sensations. But *her* life was as cold as an attic facing north; and boredom, like a silent spider, was weaving its web in the shadows, in every corner of her heart. She remembered Prize Days, when she had gone up onto the stage to receive her little wreaths. She had been charming, with her braids, her white dress, her prunella-cloth slippers. Gentlemen had leaned over, when she was back in her seat, and paid her compliments; the courtyard had been full of carriages; guests called good-bye to her as they rolled away; the music teacher with his violin case bowed to her as he passed. How far away it all was! How far!

She would call Djali,[4] take her between her knees, stroke her long delicate

---

4. The name of the little she-goat in Hugo's *Notre Dame de Paris*.

head. "Kiss your mistress," she would say, "you happy, carefree thing." The slender Djali would yawn slowly, as a dog does; and the melancholy look in her eyes would touch Emma, and she would liken her to herself, talking to her aloud as though comforting someone in distress.

Sometimes squalls blew up, winds that suddenly swept in from the sea over the plateau of the *pays de Caux*[5] and filled the countryside with fresh, salt-smelling air. The whistling wind would flatten the reeds and rustle the trembling beech leaves, while the tops of the trees swayed and murmured. Emma would pull her shawl close about her shoulders and get up.

Under the double row of trees a green light filtered down through the leaves onto the velvety moss that crunched softly beneath her feet. The sun was setting; the sky showed red between the branches; and the identical trunks of the straight line of trees were like a row of brown columns against a golden backdrop; a terror would seize her, she would call Djali and walk quickly back to Tostes along the highway. There she would sink into an armchair, and sit silent all evening.

Then, late in September, something exceptional happened: she was invited to La Vaubyessard, home of the marquis d'Andervilliers.

The marquis had been a member of the cabinet under the Restoration; and now, hoping to reenter political life, he was paving the way for his candidature to the Chamber of Deputies. He made generous distributions of firewood among the poor in the winter, and in sessions of the departmental council he was always eloquent in demanding better roads for his district. During the hot weather he had had a mouth abscess, which Charles had relieved—miraculously, it seemed—by a timely nick of the scalpel. His steward, sent to Tostes to pay the bill for the operation, reported that evening that he had seen some superb cherries in the doctor's little garden. The cherry trees at La Vaubyessard weren't doing well; Monsieur le marquis asked Charles for a few grafts, made a point of going to thank him personally, saw Emma, and noticed that she had a pretty figure and didn't curtsy like a peasant. So at the château it was decided that the doctor and his young wife could be invited without any transgression of the limits of condescension, and at the same time could be counted on to behave with decorum among their betters.

One Wednesday at three in the afternoon, therefore, Monsieur and Madame Bovary set out in their buggy for La Vaubyessard, a large trunk tied on behind and a hatbox in front. Charles had another box between his legs.

They arrived at nightfall, just as lanterns were being lit in the grounds to illuminate the driveway.

VIII

The château, a modern building in the Italian style, with two projecting wings and three entrances along the front, stretched across the far end of a vast expanse of turf where cows grazed in the open spaces between groups of tall trees. Tufts of shrubbery—rhododendrons, syringas and snowballs—made a variegated border along the curving line of the graveled drive. A stream flowed under a bridge; through the evening haze the thatched farm

---

5. See n. 1, p. 1096.

buildings could be seen scattered over a meadow shut in by two gently rising wooded ridges; and at the rear, in among thick plantings of trees, were the two parallel lines of the coach houses and the stables—remains of the original, ancient château that had been torn down.

Charles's buggy drew up before the middle door; servants appeared, then the marquis, who gave the doctor's wife his arm and led her into the entrance hall.

This had a marble floor and a high ceiling; footsteps and voices echoed as in a church. From the far side rose a straight staircase; and to the left a gallery giving on the garden led to the billiard room: the sound of clicking ivory balls could be heard ahead. As she passed through on her way to the drawing room Emma noticed the men around the table: dignified-looking, with cravats reaching up to their chins and decorations on their chests, they smiled silently as they made their shots. On the dark wall-paneling hung great gilded frames, inscribed at the base with names in black letters. "Jean-Antoine d'Andervilliers d' Yverbonville, comte de la Vaubyessard and baron de la Fresnaye, killed at the battle of Coutras,[6] October 20, 1587." Or: "Jean-Antoine-Henry-Guy d'Andervilliers de la Vaubyessard, admiral of the fleet and knight of the order of St. Michael, wounded in the battle of La Hogue, May 29, 1692, died at La Vaubyessard January 23, 1693." The rest were barely visible, for the lamplight was directed down on the green felt of the tables, and much of the room was in shadow. This darkened the row of pictures: only the crackle of their varnish caught an occasional broken gleam, and here and there some detail of painting lighter than the rest stood out from one of the dim, gold-framed rectangles: a pale forehead, two staring eyes, powdered wigs cascading onto red-coated shoulders, a garter buckle high up on a fleshy calf.

The marquis opened the drawing-room door, and one of the ladies rose. It was the marquise, and she came over to Emma, greeted her, drew her down beside her on a settee and talked to her as easily as though they were old acquaintances. She was a woman of forty or so, with fine shoulders, a hooked nose and a drawling voice; on her auburn hair she was wearing a simple bit of lace, the points falling down behind. Close beside her sat a blond young woman in a high-backed chair; and around the fireplace gentlemen with flowers in their buttonholes were chatting with the ladies.

Dinner was served at seven. The men, more numerous than the ladies, were put at a table in the entrance hall; the ladies sat down in the dining room, with the marquis and the marquise.

Here the air was warm and fragrant; the scent of flowers and fine linen mingled with the odor of cooked meats and truffles. Candle flames cast long gleams on rounded silver dish-covers; the clouded facets of the cut glass shone palely; there was a row of bouquets all down the table; and on the wide bordered plates the napkins stood like bishops' mitres, each with an oval-shaped roll between its folds. Red lobster claws protruded from platters; oversized fruit was piled up on moss in openwork baskets; quail were served in their plumage; steam rose from open dishes; and the platters of carved meat were brought round by the maître d'hotel himself, grave as a judge in silk stockings, knee breeches, white neckcloth and jabot. He reached them

6. In the Gironde; the battle was won by Henri de Navarre against the duc de Joyeuse.

down between the guests, and with a flick of his spoon transferred to each plate the piece desired. Atop the high copper-banded porcelain stove the statue of a woman swathed to the chin in drapery stared down motionless at the company.

Madame Bovary was surprised to notice that several of the ladies had failed to put their gloves in their wineglasses.[7]

At the head of the table, alone among ladies, was an old man. His napkin was tied around his neck like a child's, and he sat hunched over his heaped plate, gravy dribbling from his mouth. The underlids of his eyes hung down and showed red inside, and he wore his hair in a little pigtail wound with black ribbon. This was the marquis's father-in-law, the old duc de Laverdière, favorite of the duc d'Artois in the days of the marquis de Conflans's hunting parties at Le Vaudreuil: he was said to have been Marie-Antoinette's lover between Monsieur de Coigny and Monsieur de Lauzun. He had led a wild, dissipated life, filled with duels, wagers and abductions; he had gone through his money and been the terror of his family. Now, muttering unintelligibly, he pointed his finger at one dish after another, and a servant standing behind his chair shouted their names in his ear. Emma's eyes kept coming back to this pendulous-lipped old man as though he were someone extraordinary, someone august. He had lived at court! He had slept with a queen!

Iced champagne was served, and the feel of the cold wine in her mouth gave Emma a shiver that ran over her from head to toe. She had never seen pomegranates or eaten pineapple. Even the powdered sugar seemed to her whiter and finer than elsewhere.

Then the ladies went up to their rooms to dress for the ball.

Emma devoted herself to her toilette with the meticulous care of an actress the night of her debut. She did her hair as the hairdresser advised, and slipped into her gauzy *barège*[8] gown, which had been laid out for her on the bed.

Charles's trousers were too tight at the waist. And then, "The shoe straps will interfere with my dancing," he said.

"You? Dance?" Emma cried.

"Of course!"

"But you're crazy! Everybody would laugh. You mustn't. It's not suitable for a doctor, anyway," she added.

Charles said no more. He walked up and down waiting for Emma to be ready.

He saw her from behind in a mirror, between two sconces. Her dark eyes seemed darker than ever. Her hair, drawn down smoothly on both sides and slightly fluffed out over the ears, shone with a blue luster; in her chignon a rose quivered on its flexible stem, with artificial dewdrops at the leaf-tips. Her gown was pale saffron, trimmed with three bunches of pompon roses and green sprays.

Charles came up to kiss her on the shoulder. "Don't!" she cried. "You're rumpling me."

The strains of a violin floated up the stairs; a horn joined in. As Emma went down she had to restrain herself from running.

---

7. The ladies in the provinces, unlike their Paris counterparts, did not drink wine at public dinner parties and signified their intention by putting their gloves in their wineglasses. The fact that they fail to do so suggests to Emma the high degree of sophistication of the company.   8. A filmy fabric.

The quadrilles[9] had begun. More and more guests were arriving; there was something of a crush. Emma stayed near the door on a settee.

When the music stopped, the dance floor was left to the men, who stood there talking in groups, and to the liveried servants, who crossed it with their heavy trays. Along the line of seated women there was a flutter of painted fans; smiles were half hidden behind bouquets; gold-stoppered scent bottles twisted and turned in white-gloved hands, the tight silk binding the wrists and showing the form of the nails. There was a froth of lace around décolletages, a flashing of diamonds at throats; bracelets dangling medals and coins tinkled on bare arms. Hair was sleek and shining in front, twisted and knotted behind; and every coiffure had its wreath or bunch or sprig—of forget-me-nots, jasmine, pomegranate blossoms, wheat-sprays, cornflowers. The dowagers, sitting calm and formidable, wore red headdresses like turbans.

Emma's heart pounded a bit as her partner led her out by the fingertips and she waited in line for the starting signal on the violin. But her nervousness soon wore off, and swaying and nodding in time with the orchestra, she glided forward. She responded with a smile to the violinist's flourishes as he continued to play solo when the other instruments stopped; at such moments the chink of gold pieces came clearly from the gaming tables in the next room; then everything was in full swing again: the cornet blared, once again feet tramped in rhythm, skirts ballooned and brushed together, hands joined and separated; eyes lowered one moment looked intently into yours the next.

Scattered among the dancers or talking in doorways were a number of men—a dozen or so, aged from twenty-five to forty—who were clearly distinguishable from the rest by a certain look of overbreeding common to them all despite differences of age, dress, or feature.

Their coats were better cut and seemed to be of finer cloth; their hair, brought forward in ringlets over the temples, seemed to glisten with more expensive pomades. Their complexion bespoke wealth: they had the pale, very white skin that goes so well with the diaphanous tints of porcelain, the luster of satin, the patina of old wood, and is kept flawless by simple, exquisite fare. These men moved their heads unconstrainedly above low cravats; their long side whiskers drooped onto turned-down collars; they wiped their lips with handkerchiefs that were deliciously scented and monogrammed with huge initials. Those who were beginning to age preserved a youthful look, while the faces of the young had a touch of ripeness. There was an air of indifference about them, a calm produced by the gratification of every passion; and though their manners were suave, one could sense beneath them that special brutality which comes from the habit of breaking down half-hearted resistances that keep one fit and tickle ones vanity—the handling of blooded horses, the pursuit of loose women.

A few steps from Emma a blue-coated gentleman was deep in Italy with a pale young woman in pearls. They were gushing about the massiveness of the piers in St. Peter's, about Tivoli, Vesuvius, Castellamare and the Cascine,[1] the roses in Genoa, the Colosseum by moonlight. And the conversation heard with her other ear was full of words she didn't understand: it was coming from a circle that had formed around a very young man who only the week before had "beaten Miss Arabella and Romulus" and seemed

---

9. A square dance with four couples, fashionable in the 19th century. 1. A park near Florence. Castellamare is a port south of Naples.

to have won two thousand louis d'or by jumping a certain ditch in England. One of the speakers was complaining that his racers were putting on weight, another that misprints had made the name of his horse unrecognizable in the newspapers.

The air in the ballroom had grown heavy; the lamps were beginning to dim; a number of the men disappeared in the direction of the billiard room. A servant climbed on a chair and broke two panes in a window; at the sound of the smash Madame Bovary turned her head and saw peasants peering in from the garden, their faces pressed against the glass. She thought of Les Bertaux: she saw the farm, the muddy pond, her father in a smock under the apple trees; and she saw herself as she had been there, skimming cream with her finger from the milk jars in the dairy. But amid the splendors of this night her past life, hitherto so vividly present, was vanishing utterly; indeed she was beginning almost to doubt that she had lived it. She was here: and around the brilliant ball was a shadow that veiled all else. She was eating a maraschino ice, at that precise moment, from a gilded silver scallop-shell that she was holding in her left hand; the spoon was between her teeth, her eyes were half shut.

A lady near her dropped her fan just as a gentleman was passing. "Would you be good enough to pick up my fan, Monsieur?" she asked him. "It's there behind the sofa."

The gentleman bowed, and as he stretched out his arm Emma saw the lady toss something into his hat, something white, folded in the shape of a triangle. The gentleman recovered the fan and handed it to the lady respectfully; she thanked him with a nod and began to sniff at her bouquet.

For supper there was an array of Spanish wines and Rhine wines, bisque soup and cream of almond soup. Trafalgar pudding, and platters of all kinds of cold meat in trembling aspic; and after it the carriages began gradually to leave. Drawing back a corner of a muslin curtain, Emma could see their lamps slipping away into the darkness. The settees emptied; some of the card players stayed on; the musicians cooled the tips of their fingers on their tongues; Charles was half asleep, propped up against a door.

At three in the morning the closing cotillion began. Emma had never waltzed. Everyone else was waltzing, including Mademoiselle d'Andervilliers and the marquise; by this time only the hosts and the house guests remained, about a dozen in all. One of the waltzers, whom everyone called simply "Vicomte," and whose very low-cut waistcoat seemed to be molded on his torso, came up to Madame Bovary and for the second time asked her to be his partner. He would lead her, he urged; she'd do very well.

They started out slowly, then quickened their step. They whirled: or, rather, everything—lamps, furniture, walls, floor—whirled around them, like a disc on a spindle. As they passed close to a door the hem of Emma's gown caught on her partner's trousers, and for a moment their legs were all but intertwined; he looked down at her, she up at him; a paralyzing numbness came over her, and she stopped. Then they resumed; and spinning more quickly the vicomte swept her off until they were alone at the very end of the gallery; there, out of breath, she almost fell, and for an instant leaned her head against his chest. Then, still circling, but more slowly, he returned her to her seat. She sank back with her head against the wall, and put her hand over her eyes.

When she opened them, a lady was sitting on a low stool in the middle of the salon, three waltzers on their knees before her. The lady chose the vicomte, and the violin struck up again.

Everyone watched them as they went round and round. She held her body rigid, her head inclined; he maintained the same posture as before, very erect, elbow curved, chin forward. This time he had a partner worthy of him! They danced on and on, long after all the others had dropped out exhausted.

Hosts and guests chatted a few minutes longer; and then, bidding each other good night, or rather good morning, they all went up to bed.

Charles dragged himself up the stairs by the handrail; his legs, he said, were "ready to drop off." He had spent five solid hours on his feet by the card tables watching people play whist, unable to make head or tail of it. So he gave a great sigh of relief when he pulled his shoes off at last.

Emma slipped a shawl over her shoulders, opened the window and leaned out.

The night was very dark. A few drops of rain were falling. She breathed the moist wind, so cooling to her eyeballs. The music was still throbbing in her ears, and she forced herself to stay awake in order to prolong the illusion of this luxurious life she would so soon have to be leaving.

The sky began to lighten. Her glance lingered on the windows of the various rooms as she tried to imagine which of them were occupied by the people she had seen the night before. She longed to know all about their lives, to penetrate into them, to be part of them.

But she was shivering with cold. She undressed and crept into bed beside the sleeping Charles.

Everyone came downstairs for breakfast. The meal lasted ten minutes; to the doctor's surprise, no liqueurs were served. Mademoiselle d'Andervilliers gathered up the remains of the brioches in a basket to feed the swans in the lake; and everyone went for a stroll in the greenhouse, where strange hairy plants were displayed on pyramidal stands, and hanging jars that looked like nests crawling with snakes dripped long, dangling, intertwined green tendrils. From the orangery at the end of the greenhouse a roofed passage led to the outbuildings. To please the young woman the marquis took her to see the stables. Above the basket-shaped racks were porcelain name plates with the horses' names in black letters. Each horse moved restlessly in his stall at the approach of the visitors and the coaxing, clicking sounds they made with their tongues. The boards of the harness-room floor shone like the parquet floor of a drawing room. The carriage harness hung in the middle, on two revolving posts; and the bits, whips, stirrups and curbs were on a line of hooks along the wall.

Charles, meanwhile, had gone to ask a groom to harness his buggy. It was brought around to the front door, and when all the bundles were stowed away, the Bovarys said their thank-yous to the marquis and the marquise and set out for home.

Emma sat silent, watching the turning wheels. Charles drove perched on the edge of the seat, arms wide apart; and the little horse went along at an ambling trot between the overwide shafts. The slack reins slapped against his rump and grew wet with lather; and the case tied on behind thumped heavily and regularly against the body of the buggy.

They were climbing one of the rises near Thibourville when just ahead of them, coming from the opposite direction, there appeared a group of riders, who passed by laughing and smoking cigars. Emma thought she recognized the vicomte; she turned and stared; but all she saw was the bobbing heads of trotting or galloping riders silhouetted against the sky.

Half a mile further along they had to stop: the breeching broke, and Charles mended it with rope. As he was checking his harness he saw something on the ground between the horse's feet, and he picked up a cigar case trimmed with green silk and bearing a crest in the center like a carriage door.

"A couple of cigars in it, too," he said. "I'll smoke them after dinner."

"You've taken up smoking?" Emma demanded.

"Once in a while, when I get the chance."

He put his find in his pocket and gave the pony a flick of the whip.

When they reached home dinner was far from ready. Madame lost her temper. Nastasie talked back.

"It's too much!" Emma cried. "I've had enough of your insolence!" And she gave her notice on the spot.

For dinner there was onion soup and veal with sorrel. Charles, sitting opposite Emma, rubbed his hands with satisfaction: "How good to be home!"

They could hear Nastasie weeping. Charles had an affection for the poor thing. She had kept him company on many an idle evening during his widowerhood. She had been his first patient, his first acquaintance in the village.

"Are you really letting her go?" he finally asked.

"Yes—what's to stop me?"

Then they warmed themselves in the kitchen while their room was made ready. Charles proceeded to smoke. He curled and pursed his lips around the cigar, spat every other minute, shrank back from every puff.

"You're going to make yourself sick," she said scornfully.

He put down his cigar and rushed to the pump for a drink of cold water. Emma snatched the cigar case and quickly flung it to the back of the closet.

The next day was endless. She walked in her garden, up and down the same paths over and over again, stopping to look at the flower beds, the fruit trees, the plaster priest, staring with a kind of amazement at all these things from her past life, things once so familiar. How remote the ball already was! What was it that made tonight seem so very far removed from the day before yesterday? Her visit to La Vaubyessard had opened a breach in her life, like one of those great crevasses that a storm can tear across the face of a mountain in the course of a single night. But there was nothing to do about it. She put her beautiful ball costume reverently away in a drawer—even to her satin slippers, whose soles were yellow from the slippery wax of the dance floor. Her heart was like them: contact with luxury had left an indelible mark on it.

The memory of the ball would not leave her. Every Wednesday she told herself as she woke: "Ah! One week ago . . . two weeks ago . . . three weeks ago, I was there!" Little by little the faces grew confused in her mind; she forgot the tune of the quadrille, the liveries and the splendid rooms became blurred. Some of the details departed—but the yearning remained.

IX

Often when Charles was out she went to the closet and took the green silk cigar case from among the piles of linen where she kept it.

She would look at it, open it, even sniff its lining, fragrant with verbena and tobacco. Whose was it? The vicomte's. A present from his mistress, perhaps. It had been embroidered on some rosewood frame, a charming little piece of furniture kept hidden from prying eyes, over which a pensive girl had bent for hours and hours, her soft curls brushing its surface. Love had breathed through the mesh of the canvas; every stroke of the needle had recorded a hope or a memory; and all these intertwined silken threads bespoke one constant, silent passion. And then one morning the vicomte had taken it away with him. What words had they exchanged as he stood leaning his elbow on one of those elaborate mantelpieces decked with vases of flowers and rococo clocks? She was in Tostes. Whereas he now, was in Paris— in Paris! What was it like, Paris? The very name had such a vastness about it! She repeated it to herself under her breath with a thrill of pleasure; it sounded in her ears like the great bell of a cathedral; it blazed before her eyes everywhere, glamorous even on the labels of her jars of pomade.

At night when the fishmongers passed below her window in their carts, singing *La Marjolaine,* she would awaken; and listening to the sound of the iron-rimmed wheels on the pavement, and then the quick change in the sound as they reached the unpaved road at the end of the village, she would tell herself: "They'll be there tomorrow!"

And she followed them in thought, up and down hills, through villages, along the highway by the light of the stars. Then, somewhere along the way, her dream always petered out.

She bought a map of Paris, and with her fingertip she went for walks. She followed the boulevards, stopping at every corner, between the lines indicating the streets, in front of the white squares that were the houses. Then, closing her tired eyes, she would have a shadowy vision of gas lamps flickering in the wind and carriage steps clattering open in front of theatres.

She subscribed to a women's magazine called *La Corbeille,* and to *Le Sylphe des salons.* She devoured every word of every account of a first night, a horse race, a soirée; she was fascinated by the debut of every new singer, the opening of every new shop. She knew the latest fashions, the addresses of the best tailors, the proper days to go to the Bois[2] and the opera. She pored over the interior decorating details in the novels of Eugène Sue; she read Balzac and George Sand,[3] seeking in their pages vicarious satisfactions for her own desires. She brought her book with her even to meals, and turned the leaves while Charles ate and talked to her. Her readings always brought the vicomte back to her mind: she continually found similarities between him and the fictitious characters. But the circle whose center he was gradually widened; and the halo she had given him spread beyond his image, gilding other dreams.

Paris, city vaster than the ocean, glittered before Emma's eyes in a rosy light. But the teeming life of the tumultuous place was divided into compartments, separated into distinct scenes. Emma was aware of only two or three, which shut out the sight of the others and stood for all of mankind. In drawing rooms with mirrored walls and gleaming floors, around oval tables covered with gold-fringed velvet, moved the world of the ambassadors. It was full of trailing gowns, deep secrets, and unbearable tensions concealed

2. Horse races at the Bois de Boulogne.   3. Pseudonym of Aurore Dudevant (1804–1876), prolific woman novelist. Sue (1804–1857), a popular novelist, was extremely successful at that period, both as a writer and as a fashionable dandy.

beneath smiles. Then came the circle of the duchesses: here everyone was pale and lay in bed till four; the women—poor darlings!—wore English lace on their petticoat hems; and the men, their true worth unsuspected under their frivolous exteriors, rode horses to death for the fun of it, spent their summers at Baden-Baden,[4] and eventually, when they were about forty, married heiresses. After midnight, the gay, motley world of writers and actresses congregated at candlelit suppers in the private rooms of restaurants. They were profligate as kings, full of idealistic ambitions and fantastic frenzies. They lived on a higher plane than other people, somewhere sublime between heaven and earth, up among the storm clouds. As for the rest of the world, it was in some indeterminate pale beyond the pale; it could scarcely be said to exist. Indeed the closer to her things were, the further away from them her thoughts turned. Everything immediately surrounding her—boring countryside, inane petty bourgeois, the mediocrity of daily life—seemed to her the exception rather than the rule. She had been caught in it all by some accident: out beyond, there stretched as far as eye could see the immense territory of rapture and passions. In her longing she made no difference between the pleasures of luxury and the joys of the heart, between elegant living and sensitive feeling. Didn't love, like Indian plants, require rich soils, special temperatures? Sighs in the moonlight, long embraces, hands bathed in lovers' tears—all the fevers of the flesh and the languors of love—were inseparable from the balconies of great idle-houred castles, from a silk-curtained, thick-carpeted, beflowered boudoir with its bed on a dais, from the sparkle of precious stones and the swank of liveries.

The hired boy at the relay post across the road, who came in every morning to rub down the mare, walked through the hall in his heavy wooden shoes; his smock was in holes, his feet were innocent of stockings. Such was the groom in knee breeches she had to content herself with! When his work was done he left for the day: Charles stabled his horse himself when he returned from his rounds—took off the saddle and attached the halter; and the maid brought a truss of straw and tossed it as best she could into the manger.

To replace Nastasie (who finally departed from Tostes in a torrent of tears) Emma hired a sweet-faced orphan girl of fourteen. She forbade her to wear a cotton nightcap during the day, taught her to address her superiors in the third person, to hand a glass of water on a tray, to knock on doors before entering, and to iron, to starch, to help her dress—tried to turn her into a lady's maid. The girl obeyed without a murmur because she was afraid of losing her place; and since Madame usually left the key in the sideboard, Félicité took a little sugar upstairs with her every night, and ate it by herself in bed after saying her prayers.

Afternoons she sometimes crossed the road for a chat with the postilions while Madame was up in her room.

There Emma wore a shawl-collared dressing gown, open very low over a pleated dicky with three gold buttons. Her belt was a cord with large tassels, and her little garnet-colored slippers had rosettes of wide ribbons at the instep. Though she had no one to write to, she had bought herself a blotter, a writing case, a pen and envelopes; she would dust off her whatnot, look at

---

4. A fashionable German spa with hot mineral-water springs.

herself in the mirror, take up a book, and then begin to daydream and let it fall to her lap.

She longed to travel; she longed to go back and live in the convent. She wanted to die. And she wanted to live in Paris.

Charles jogged back and forth across the countryside under snow and rain. He ate omelettes at farmhouse tables, thrust his arm into damp beds, had his face spattered with jets of warm blood at bleedings; he listened to death rattles, examined the contents of basins, handled a lot of soiled undercloth-ing. But every night he came home to a blazing fire, a well-set table, a com-fortable chair, and a dainty, prettily dressed wife smelling so sweet that he never quite knew where the scent came from, and half wondered whether it wasn't her skin that was perfuming her slip.

She delighted him by countless little niceties: a new way of making sconces out of paper to catch the wax under candles, a flounce that she changed on her dress, or the fancy name of some very plain dish that the maid hadn't got right but that Charles enjoyed eating every bit of. In Rouen she saw ladies with charms dangling from their watch fobs; she bought some charms. She took a fancy to a pair of large blue glass vases for her mantelpiece, and a little later to an ivory workbox with a silver-gilt thimble. The less Charles understood these refinements, the more alluring he found them. They added something to the pleasure of his senses and the charm of his home. They were like a trickle of golden dust along the petty pathway of his life.

His health was good, his appearance hearty; his reputation was secure. The country people liked him because he gave himself no airs. He always fondled the children and never went to a café; moreover, his morals inspired confidence. He was especially successful in treating catarrhs and chest ail-ments. Actually, Charles had such a dread of killing his patients that he seldom prescribed anything but sedatives—once in a while an emetic or a foot bath or leeches. Not that surgery held any terrors for him: when he bled a patient he bled him hard, like a horse; and he was famous for his iron grip as a tooth puller.

Eventually, "to keep himself up to date," he took out a subscription to the *La Ruche médicale,* a new publication whose prospectus had been sent him. He read a little in it after his dinner, but the heat of the room plus digestion resulted in his falling asleep at the end of five minutes; and he sat there under the lamp with his chin in his hands and his hair falling forward like a mane. Emma looked at him and shrugged her shoulders. Why didn't she at least have for a husband one of those silent, dedicated men who spend their nights immersed in books and who by the time they're sixty and rheumatic have acquired a row of decorations to wear on their ill-fitting black coats? She would have liked the name Bovary—her name—to be famous, on display in all the bookshops, constantly mentioned in the newspapers, known all over France. But Charles had no ambition! A doctor from Yvetot with whom he had recently held a consultation had humiliated him right at the sickbed, in front of the assembled relatives. When Charles told her the story that evening, Emma burst out furiously against the other doctor. Charles was so moved that he shed a tear and kissed her on the forehead. But it was shame that had exasperated her: she wanted to strike him. She went into the hall, opened the window and took a breath of fresh air to calm herself.

"It's pathetic!" she whispered to herself, despair in her heart. "What a booby!"

And indeed he got on her nerves more and more. As he grew older he grew coarser: at the end of a meal he whittled the cork of the wine bottle with his dessert knife and cleaned his teeth with his tongue; he made a gulping noise every time he took a mouthful of soup; and as he put on weight his eyes, small to begin with, seemed to be pushed toward his temples by the puffing of his cheeks.

Emma sometimes tucked the red edge of his sweater up under his vest, or straightened his tie, or threw away a pair of faded old gloves he was about to put on; and it was never, as he believed, for his sake that she did it, but for her own, out of exasperated vanity. And sometimes she told him about things she had read—a passage in a novel or a new play, some high-life anecdote recounted in a gossip column, for Charles was a presence, at least, an ear that was always open, a sure source of approval. She confided many a secret to her dog, after all! She could almost have opened her heart to the logs in the fireplace and the pendulum of the clock.

Deep down, all the while, she was waiting for something to happen. Like a sailor in distress, she kept casting desperate glances over the solitary waste of her life, seeking some white sail in the distant mists of the horizon. She had no idea by what wind it would reach her, toward what shore it would bear her, or what kind of craft it would be—tiny boat or towering vessel, laden with heartbreaks or filled to the gunwales with rapture. But every morning when she awoke she hoped that today would be the day; she listened for every sound, gave sudden starts, was surprised when nothing happened; and then, sadder with each succeeding sunset, she longed for tomorrow.

Spring came again. She found it hard to breathe, the first warm days, when the pear trees were bursting into bloom.

From early in July she began to count on her fingers how many weeks there were till October, thinking that the marquis d'Andervilliers might give another ball at La Vaubyessard. But September passed without letters or visitors.

After the pain of this disappointment had gone, her heart stood empty once more; and then the series of identical days began all over again.

So from now on they were going to continue one after the other like this, always the same, innumerable, bringing nothing! Other people's lives, drab though they might be, held at least the possibility of an event. One unexpected happening often set in motion a whole chain of change: the entire setting of one's life could be transformed. But to her nothing happened. It was God's will. The future was a pitch-black tunnel ending in a locked door.

She gave up her music: why should she play? Who was there to listen? There wasn't a chance of her ever giving a concert in a short-sleeved velvet gown, skimming butterfly fingers over the ivory keys of a grand piano, feeling the public's ecstatic murmur flow around her like a breeze—so why go through the tedium of practicing? She left her drawing books and her embroidery in a closet. What was the use of anything? What was the use? She loathed sewing.

"I've read everything there is to read," she told herself.

And so she sat—holding the fire tongs in the fire till they glowed red, or watching the falling of the rain.

How depressed she was on Sundays, when the churchbell tolled for vespers! With a dull awareness she listened to the cracked sound as it rang out again and again. Sometimes a cat walking slowly along one of the roofs outside her window arched its back against the pale rays of the sun. The wind blew trails of dust on the highway. Far off somewhere a dog was howling. And the bell would keep on giving its regular, monotonous peals that died away over the countryside.

People came out of church. Women with their wooden shoes polished, peasant men in new smocks, little children skipping bareheaded in front of them—all moved toward home. And until dark five or six men, always the same ones, stayed playing their shuffleboard game before the main entrance of the inn.

The winter was a cold one. Every morning the windowpanes were frosted over, and the whitish light that came through—as though filtered through ground glass—sometimes didn't vary all day. By four o'clock it was time to light the lamps.

On sunny days she went out into the garden. The dew had garnished the cabbages with silvery lace, and joined head to head with long shining filaments. There was no sound of birds, everything seemed to be sleeping—the espaliered trees under their straw, the vine like a great sick snake under the wall coping, where she could see many-legged wood lice crawling as she came near. In among the spruces near the hedge the priest in a tricorn reading his breviary had lost his right foot, and the scaling of the plaster in the frost had left a white scurf on his face.

Then she would return upstairs, close her door, poke the coals; and languid in the heat of the fire she would feel boredom descend again, heavier than before. She would have liked to go down for a chat with the maid, but self-respect held her back.

Every day at the same time the schoolmaster in his black silk skullcap opened the shutters of his house; every day at the same time the village policeman passed, his sword buckled around his smock. Morning and evening the post horses crossed the road in threes to drink at the pond. Now and again the bell of a café door would tinkle as it opened; and when there was a wind she could hear the little copper basins that formed the barber's shop-sign creaking on their two rods. His window display consisted of an old fashion plate on one of the panes, and a wax bust of a woman with yellow hair. The barber, too, was accustomed to bewail the waste of his talents, his ruined career; and dreaming of a shop in a large city—in Rouen, perhaps, on the river front, or near the theatre—he paced back and forth all day between the mayor's office and the church, gloomily waiting for customers. When Madame Bovary raised her eyes she always saw him there with his cap over one ear, and his short work jacket, like a sentry on duty.

In the afternoon, sometimes, a man's face appeared outside the parlor windows, a swarthy face with black side whiskers and a slow, wide, gentle smile that showed very white teeth. Then would come the strain of a waltz; and in a miniature drawing room on top of the hurdy-gurdy a set of tiny dancers would begin to revolve. Women in pink turbans, Tyrolians in jackets, monkeys in black tailcoats, gentlemen in knee breeches—they all spun around among the armchairs, sofas and tables, and were reflected in bits of mirror glass joined together at the edges by strips of gold paper. As he turned his crank the man would glance to his right, to his left, and toward the windows. Now and then he would let out a spurt of brown saliva against the curb and raise his knee to lift the instrument and ease the heavy shoulder strap; and the music, now doleful and dragging, now merry and quick, came out of the box through a pink taffeta curtain under a fancy brasswork grill. The tunes it played were tunes that were being heard in other places—in theatres, in drawing rooms, under the lighted chandeliers of ballrooms: echoes from the world that reached Emma this way. Sarabands ran on endlessly in her head; and her thoughts, like dancing girls on some flowery carpet, leapt with the notes from dream to dream, from sorrow to sorrow. Then, when the man had caught in his cap the coin she threw him, he would pull down an old blue wool cover, hoist his organ onto his back, and move heavily off. She always watched him till he disappeared.

But it was above all at mealtime that she could bear it no longer—in that small ground-floor room with its smoking stove, its squeaking door, its sweating walls and its damp floor tiles. All the bitterness of life seemed to be served up to her on her plate; and the steam rising from the boiled meat brought gusts of revulsion from the depths of her soul. Charles was a slow eater; she would nibble a few hazelnuts, or lean on her elbow and draw lines on the oilcloth with the point of her table knife.

Now she let everything in the house go, and the older Madame Bovary was amazed by the change she found when she came to spend part of Lent in Tostes. Emma, once so careful and dainty, now went whole days without putting on a dress; she wore gray cotton stockings, lit the house with cheap tallow candles. She kept saying that they had to be careful, since they weren't rich; and she always went on to add that she was very contented, very happy, that she liked Tostes very much; and she made other surprising statements that shut up her mother-in-law. However, she seemed no more inclined than ever to follow her advice. Once, indeed, when Madame Bovary took it into her head to suggest that employers should keep an eye on their servants' religious life, Emma replied with such a terrible look and such a freezing smile that the dear woman henceforth kept her fingers out of things.

Emma was becoming capricious, hard to please. She would order special dishes for herself and then not touch them; one day she would drink nothing but fresh milk; the next, cups of tea by the dozen. Often she refused absolutely to go out; then she would feel stifled, open the windows, change to a light dress. She would give the maid a tongue-lashing and then turn around and give her presents, or time off to visit the neighbors, just as occasionally she would give a beggar all the silver she had in her purse, though she was anything but tenderhearted or sympathetic to other people's troubles. (In this she was like most sons and daughters of country folk: their souls always keep some of the horniness of their fathers' hands.)

Toward the end of February, Monsieur Rouault celebrated the anniversary of his recovery by bringing his son-in-law a magnificent turkey, and he stayed on at Tostes for three days. Charles was out most of the time with his patients, and it was Emma who kept her father company. He smoked in her bedroom, spit on the andirons, talked about crops, calves, cows, chickens and the village council; when he finally left and she had shut the door behind him, her feeling of relief surprised even herself. But then she no longer hid her scorn for anything or anyone; and she was beginning now and then to express peculiar opinions, condemning what everyone else approved and approving things that were perverse or immoral—a way of talking that made her husband stare at her wide-eyed.

Would this wretchedness last forever? Was there no way out? And yet she was every bit as good as all the other women, who lived in contentment! She had seen duchesses at La Vaubyessard who were dumpier and more common than she, and she cursed God for his injustice. She leaned her head against the wall and wept. She thought, with envy of riotous living, of nights spent at masked balls, of shameless revels and all the mysterious raptures they must bring in their train.

She grew pale and developed palpitations. Charles gave her valerian drops and camphor baths. Everything he tried seemed to exacerbate her the more.

Some days she chattered endlessly, almost feverishly; and such a period of overexcitement would suddenly be followed by a torpor in which she neither spoke nor moved. At such times she would revive herself with eau de Cologne, pouring a bottle of it over her arms.

Since she continually complained about Tostes, Charles supposed that the cause of her illness must have something to do with the town's situation; and struck by this idea he thought seriously of settling somewhere else.

As soon as she knew this she began to drink vinegar to lose weight, acquired a little dry cough, and lost her appetite completely.

It was a wrench for Charles to leave Tostes, after living there four years and just when he was beginning to be really established. Still, if it had to be—He took her to Rouen, to see one of his old teachers. The diagnosis was that she was suffering from a nervous illness: a change of air was indicated.

After looking here and there, Charles learned that in the district of Neufchâtel there was a good-sized market town named Yonville-l'Abbaye, whose doctor, a Polish refugee, had decamped just the week before. So he wrote to the local pharmacist and inquired about the population, the distance to the nearest doctor, how much his predecessor had earned a year, etc.; and when the answers were satisfactory he decided to move by spring if Emma's health didn't improve.

One day when she was going through a drawer in preparation for moving, something pricked her finger. It was the wire around her bridal bouquet. The orange-blossom buds were yellow with dust, and the silver-edged satin ribbons were frayed. She tossed it into the fire. It blazed up quicker than dry straw. Then it lay like a red bush on the ashes, slowly consuming itself. She watched it burn. The pasteboard berries burst open, the brass wire curled, the braid melted; and the shriveled paper petals hovered along the fireback like black butterflies and finally flew away up the chimney.

When they left Tostes in March, Madame Bovary was pregnant.

Part Two

I

Yonville-l'Abbaye (even the ruins of the ancient Capuchin friary from which it derives its name are no longer there) is a market town twenty miles from Rouen, between the highways to Abbeville and Beauvais in the valley of the Rieule. This is a small tributary of the Andelle: it turns the wheels of three mills before joining the larger stream, and contains some trout that boys like to fish for on Sundays.

Branching off from the highway at La Boissière, the road to Yonville continues level until it climbs the hill at Les Leux; and from there it commands a view of the valley. This is divided by the Rieule into two contrasting bits of countryside: everything to the left is grazing land, everything to the right is ploughed field. The pastures extend along the base of a chain of low hills and merge at the far end with the meadows of Bray; while eastward the plain rises gently and grows steadily wider, flaunting its golden grainfields as far as eye can see. The stream, flowing along the edge of the grass, is a white line dividing the color of the meadows from that of the ploughed earth: the country thus resembles a great spread-out cloak, its green velvet collar edged with silver braid.

On the horizon, beyond Yonville loom the oaks of the Arguel forest and the escarpments of the bluffs of Saint-Jean, the latter streaked from top to bottom with long, irregular lines of red: these are marks left by rain, and their brickish color, standing out so sharply against the gray rock of the hill, comes from the iron content of the many springs in the country just beyond.

This is where Normandy, Picardy and the Ile-de-France come together, a mongrel region where the speech of the natives is as colorless as the landscape is lacking in character. Here they make the worst Neufchâtel cheeses in the entire district; and here farming calls for considerable investment: great quantities of manure are needed to fertilize the friable, sandy, stony soil.

Up until 1835 no road was kept open to Yonville, but about that time the cross-cut was made that links the Abbeville and Amiens highways and is sometimes used by carters traveling from Rouen to Flanders. Nevertheless, despite its "new avenues for trade," Yonville-l'Abbaye has stood still. Instead of adopting improved methods of farming, the natives stick to their pastures, worn-out though they are; and the lazy town, spurning the farmland, has continued its spontaneous growth in the direction of the river. The sight of it from a distance, stretched out along the bank, brings to mind a cowherd taking a noonday nap beside the stream.

At the foot of the hill the road crosses the Rieule on a bridge, and then, becoming an avenue planted with young aspens, leads in a straight line to the first outlying houses. These are surrounded by hedges, and their yards are full of scattered outbuildings—cider presses, carriage houses and distilling sheds standing here and there under thick trees with ladders and poles leaning against their trunks and scythes hooked over their branches. The thatched roofs hide the top third or so of the low windows like fur caps pulled down over eyes, and each windowpane, thick and convex, has a bull's-eye in its center like the bottom of a bottle. Some of the plastered house walls with their diagonal black timbers are the background for scraggly espaliered pear trees; and the house doors have little swinging gates to keep out the baby chicks, who come to the sill to peck at brown-bread crumbs soaked in cider. Gradually the yards become narrower, houses are closer together, the hedges disappear; occasionally a fern broom put out to dry is seen hanging from a window; there is a blacksmith shop, a cart-maker's with two or three new carts outside half blocking the roadway. Then comes a white house behind an iron fence, its circular lawn adorned by a cupid holding finger to lips. Two cast-iron urns stand at either end of the entrance terrace; brass plates gleam brightly at the door: this is the notary's house, the finest in town.

The church is across the street, twenty yards further on, at the corner of the main square. The little graveyard surrounding it, enclosed by an elbow-high wall, is so full of graves that the old tombstones, lying flat on the ground, form a continuous pavement divided into rectangular blocks by the grass that pushes up between. The church was remodeled during the last years of the reign of Charles X.[5] The wooden vaulting is beginning to rot at the top: black cavities are appearing here and there in the blue paint. Above the door, in the place usually occupied by an organ, is a gallery for the men, reached by a spiral staircase that echoes loudly under the tread of wooden shoes.

Daylight, coming through the windows of plain glass, falls obliquely on the pews; and here and there on the wall from which they jut out at right angles is tacked a bit of straw matting, with the name of the pew holder in large letters below. Beyond, where the nave narrows, stands the confessional, and opposite it a statuette of the Virgin: she is dressed in a satin gown and a tulle veil spangled with silver stars, and her cheeks are daubed red like some idol from the Sandwich Islands.[6] A painting by a copyist, inscribed "Holy Family: Presented by the Minister of the Interior," hangs over the main altar; and there, flanked by four candlesticks, it closes the vista. The cheap fir choir stalls have never been painted.

The market—that is, a tile roof supported by about twenty pillars—takes up approximately half the main square of Yonville. The town hall, designed, as everyone will tell you, "by a Paris architect," is a kind of Greek temple forming one corner of the square, next door to the pharmacy. Its lower story has three Ionic columns; above is a row of arched windows; and the culminating pediment is filled with a figure of the Gallic cock, one of its claws resting on the Constitution[7] and the other holding the scales of justice.

But what catches the eye the most is across the square from the Lion d'Or hotel: Monsieur Homais' pharmacy! Especially at night, when his lamp is lit, and the red and green glass jars decorating his window cast the glow of their two colors far out across the roadway! Peering through it, as through the glare of Bengal lights,[8] one can catch a glimpse, at that hour, of the dim figure of the pharmacist himself, bent over his desk. The entire façade of his establishment is plastered from top to bottom with inscriptions—in running script, in round hand, in block capitals: "Vichy, Seltzer and Barèges Waters; Depurative Fruit Essences; Raspail's Remedy; Arabian Racahout; Darcet's Pastilles; Regnauk's Ointment; Bandages, Baths, Laxative Chocolates, etc." And the shop sign, as wide as the shop itself, proclaims in gold letters: "Homais Pharmacy." At the rear of the shop, behind the great scales fastened to the counter, the word "Laboratory" is inscribed above a glass door; and this door itself, halfway up, bears once again the name "Homais," in gold letters on a black ground.

That is as much as there is to see in Yonville. The street (the only street), long as a rifle shot and lined with a few shops, abruptly ceases to be a street at a turn of the road. If you leave it on the right and follow the base of the bluffs of Saint-Jean, you soon reach the cemetery.

5. The last Bourbon king (1757–1836), son of Louis XV. He was expelled by the July Revolution (1830).
6. Old name for Hawaii, after John Montagu, fourth earl of Sandwich (1718–1792), who served as first lord of admiralty when the islands were discovered.   7. The *Charte constitutiouelle de la France,* basis of the French constitution after the revolution, bestowed in 1814 by Louis XVIII and revised in 1830, after the downfall of Charles X.   8. Blue flares used in signaling.

This was enlarged the year of the cholera—one wall was torn down and three adjoining acres were added; but all this new portion is almost uninhabited, and new graves continue as in the past to be dug in the crowded area near the gate. The caretaker, who is also gravedigger and sexton at the church (thus profiting doubly from the parish corpses), has taken advantage of the empty land to plant potatoes. Nevertheless, his little field grows smaller every year, and when there is an epidemic he doesn't know whether to rejoice in the deaths or lament the space taken by the new graves.

"You are feeding on the dead, Lestiboudois!" Monsieur le curé told him, one day.

The somber words gave him pause, and for a time he desisted; but today he continues to plant his tubers, coolly telling everyone that they come up by themselves.

Since the events which we are about to relate, absolutely nothing has changed in Yonville. To this day the tin tricolor still turns atop the church tower; the two calico streamers outside the dry-goods shop still blow in the wind; the spongy foetuses in the pharmacy window continue to disintegrate in their cloudy alcohol; and over the main entrance of the hotel the old golden lion, much discolored by the rains, stares down like a curly-headed poodle on passers-by.

The evening the Bovarys were expected at Yonville, Madame Lefrançois, the widow who owned this hotel, was so frantically busy with her saucepans that large beads of sweat stood out on her face. Tomorrow was market-day, and she had to get everything ready in advance—cut the meat, clean the chickens, make soup, roast and grind the coffee. In addition, she had tonight's dinner to get for her regular boarders and for the new doctor and his wife and their maid. Bursts of laughter came from the billiard room; in the small dining room three millers were calling for brandy; logs were blazing, charcoal was crackling, and on the long table in the kitchen, in among the quarters of raw mutton, stood high piles of plates that shook with the chopping of the spinach on the chopping-block. From the yard came the squawking of the chickens that the kitchen maid was chasing with murderous intent.

Warming his back at the fire was a man in green leather slippers, wearing a velvet skullcap with a gold tassel. His face, slightly pitted by smallpox, expressed nothing, but self-satisfaction, and he seemed as contented with life as the goldfinch in a wicker cage hanging above his head. This was the pharmacist.

"Artémise!" cried the mistress of the inn. "Chop some kindling, fill the decanters, bring some brandy—hurry up! Lord! If I only knew what dessert to offer these people you're waiting for! Listen to their moving-men starting up that racket in the billiard room again! They've left their van in the driveway, too: the Hirondelle will probably crash into it. Call 'Polyte and tell him to put it in the shed! Would you believe it, Monsieur Homais—since this morning they've played at least fifteen games and drunk eight pots of cider! But they're going to ruin my table," she said, staring over at them across the room, her skimming spoon in her hand.

"That wouldn't be much of a loss," replied Monsieur Homais. "You'd buy another one."

"Another billiard table!" cried the widow.

"But this one's falling apart, Madame Lefrançois! I tell you again; it's shortsighted of you not to invest in a new one! Very shortsighted! Players today want narrow pockets and heavy cues, you know. They don't play billiards the way they used to. Everything's changed. We must keep up with the times! Just look at Tellier . . ."

The hostess flushed with anger.

"Say what you like," the pharmacist went on, "his billiard table is nicer than yours. And if a patriotic tournament were to be got up, for Polish independence or Lyons flood relief . . ."[9]

"We're not afraid of fly-by-nights like Tellier," the hostess interrupted, shrugging her heavy shoulders. "Don't worry, Monsieur Homais. As long as the Lion d'Or exists we'll keep our customers. We're a well-established house. But the Café Français . . . One of these mornings you'll find it sealed up, with a nice big notice on the window blinds. A new billiard table?" she went on, talking as though to herself. "But this one's so handy to stack the washing on! And in the hunting season it's slept as many as six! . . . But what's keeping that slowpoke Hivert?"

"You'll wait till he arrives, to give your gentlemen their dinner?" the pharmacist asked.

"Wait? And what about Monsieur Binet? You'll see him come in on the stroke of six: he's the most punctual man in the world. He always has to sit at the same place in the little room: he'd die rather than eat his dinner anywhere else. And finicky! So particular about his cider! Not like Monsieur Léon! Monsieur Léon sometimes doesn't come in till seven, or even half-past, and half the time he doesn't even know what he's eating. What a nice young man! So polite! So soft-spoken!"

"Ah, Madame! There's a great difference, you know, between someone who's been properly brought up and a tax collector who got his only schooling in the army."

The clock struck six. Binet entered.

He was clad in a blue frock coat that hung straight down all around his skinny body; and the raised peak of his leather cap, its earflaps pulled up and fastened at the top, displayed a bald, squashed-looking forehead, deformed by long pressure of a helmet. He was wearing a coarse wool vest, a crinoline collar, gray trousers, and—as he did in every season—well-shined shoes that bulged in two parallel lines over the rising of his two big toes. Not a hair was out of place in the blond chin whisker outlining his jaw: it was like the edging of a flower bed around his long, dreary face with its small eyes and hooked nose. He was a clever card player, a good hunter, and wrote a fine hand. His hobby was making napkin rings on his own lathe: jealous as an artist and stingy as a bourgeois, he cluttered up his house with his handiwork.

He headed for the small room, but the three millers had to be got out before he would go in. While his table was being set he stood next to the stove without saying a word; then he closed the door and took off his cap as usual.

---

9. The allusion dates the action of the novel as taking place in 1840; during the winter of 1840, the Rhône overflowed with catastrophic results. At the same time, Louis Philippe was under steady attack for his failure to offer sufficient assistance to the victims of the repression that followed the insurrection of Warsaw (1831).

"He won't wear out his tongue with civilities," the pharmacist remarked, as soon as he was alone with the hostess.

"He never talks a bit more than that," she answered. "Last week I had two cloth salesmen here—two of the funniest fellows you ever listened to. They told me stories that made me laugh till I cried. Would you believe it? He sat there like a clam—didn't open his mouth."

"No imagination," pronounced the pharmacist. "Not a hint of a spark! No manners whatever!"

"And yet they say he has something to him," objected the hostess.

"Something to him?" cried Monsieur Homais. "That man? Something to him? Still, in his own line I suppose he may have," he conceded.

And he went on: "Ah! A business man with vast connections, a lawyer, a doctor, a pharmacist—I can understand it if they get so engrossed in their affairs that they become eccentric, even surly: history is full of such examples. But at least they have important affairs to be engrossed in! Take me, for instance: how often I've turned my desk upside down looking for my pen to write some labels, only to find I'd stuck it behind my ear!"

Meanwhile Madame Lefrançois had approached the door to see whether the Hirondelle wasn't in sight, and she started as a black-clad man that moment entered the kitchen. In the last faint light of dusk it was just possible to make out his florid face and athletic figure.

"What can I offer you, Monsieur le curé?" she asked, reaching down a brass candlestick from a row that stood all ready and complete with candles on the mantelpiece. "A drop of cassis? A glass of wine?"

The priest very politely declined. He had come to fetch his umbrella, he said: he had left it at the convent in Ernemont the other day, and had supposed the Hirondelle would have delivered it by now. He asked Madame Lefrançois to have it brought to him at the rectory during the evening, and then left for the church, where the bell was tolling the Angelus.

When the sound of his footsteps in the square had died away, the pharmacist declared that in his opinion the priest's behavior had been most improper. His refusal to take a glass of something was the most revolting kind of hypocrisy: all priests were secret tipplers, he said, and they were all doing their best to bring back the days of the tithe.

The hostess said some words in the curé's defense. "Besides," she went on, "he could take on four like you. Last year he helped our men get in the straw: he carried as many as six bundles at a time—that shows you how strong he is."

"Bravo!" cried the pharmacist. "Go ahead! Keep sending your daughters to confession to strapping fellows like that! But if I were the government I'd have every priest bled once a month. Yes, a fine generous phlebotomy every month, Madame, in the interests of morals and decency."

"That's enough, Monsieur Homais! You've no respect for religion!"

"On the contrary, I'm a very religious man, in my own way, far more so than all these people with their mummeries and their tricks. I worship God, I assure you! I believe in a Supreme Being, a Creator. Whoever he is—and what difference does it make?—he put us here on earth to fulfill our duties as citizens and parents. But I don't have to go into church and kiss silver platters and hand over my money to fatten up a lot of rascals that eat better than you and I! To him, one can do full honor in a forest, a field—or merely by gazing up at the ethereal vault, like the ancients. My God is the God of Socrates, of Franklin, of Voltaire, of Béranger! My credo is the credo of Rousseau![1] I adhere to the immortal principles of '89! I have no use for the kind of God who goes walking in his garden with a stick, sends his friends to live in the bellies of whales, gives up the ghost with a groan and then comes back to life three days later! Those things aren't only absurd in themselves, Madame—they're completely opposed to all physical laws. It goes to prove, by the way, that priests have always wallowed in squalid ignorance and have wanted nothing better than to drag the entire world down to their own level."

As he ended, he glanced about in search of an audience: for a moment, during his outburst, he had had the illusion that he was addressing the village council. But the mistress of the inn was no longer listening to him: her ears had caught a distant sound of wheels. There was the rattle of a coach, the pounding of loose horseshoes on the road; and the Hirondelle drew up before the door at last.

It was a yellow box-shaped affair mounted on two large wheels that came up as high as the top, blocking the passengers' view and spattering their shoulders. When the carriage was closed the tiny panes of its narrow windows rattled in their frames, and there were mud stains here and there on the ancient coating of dust that even heavy rainstorms never washed off completely. It was drawn by three horses, one ahead and two abreast. Its under side bumped against the ground on down grades.

A number of the local inhabitants made their appearance in the square, and all speaking at once they asked for news, for explanations of the delay, for their packages. Hivert didn't know whom to answer first. It was he who attended to things in the city for the Yonvillians. He shopped for them, brought back rolls of leather for the shoemaker, scrap iron for the blacksmith, a keg of herrings for Madame Lefrançois his employer, ladies' bonnets from the milliner, wigs from the hairdresser; and all along the road on the way back he distributed his packages, standing up on his seat and hurling them over the farmyard fences with a shout as his horses kept galloping ahead.

An accident had delayed him: Madame Bovary's greyhound had run away—disappeared across the fields. They had whistled for her a good fifteen minutes. Hivert had even turned his coach around and gone back over the road for more than a mile, expecting to come upon her any minute; but they'd had to go on without her. Emma had wept and made a scene, blaming it all on Charles. Monsieur Lheureux, the Yonville dry-goods dealer, who was also in the carriage, had tried to comfort her by citing numerous examples of lost dogs' recognizing their masters many years later. There was a famous one, he said, that had returned to Paris all the way from Constantinople. Another had traveled one hundred twenty-five miles in a straight line, swimming four rivers. And his own father had had a poodle who after being gone for twelve years had suddenly jumped up on his back one night in the street, as he was on his way to a friend's house for dinner.

1. Rousseau's declaration (1762) of faith in God, a religion of his heart, coupled with a criticism of revealed religion. It is included in book 4 of his pedagogic treatise *Émile* but was frequently reprinted as an independent pamphlet.

II

Emma stepped out first, followed by Félicité, Monsieur Lheureux, and a wet nurse; and Charles had to be shaken awake in his corner, where he had dozed off as soon as darkness had fallen.

Homais introduced himself: he paid his compliments to Madame and spoke politely to Monsieur, said he was delighted to have been of service to them, and cordially added that he had taken the liberty of inviting himself to share their dinner, his wife being for the moment out of town.

In the kitchen, Madame Bovary crossed to the fireplace. Reaching halfway down her skirt, she grasped it with the tips of two of her fingers, raised it to her ankles, and stretched out a black-shod foot toward the flame, over the leg of mutton that was turning on the spit. She was standing in the full light of the fire, and by its harsh glare one could see the weave of her dress, the pores of her white skin, even her eyelids when she briefly shut her eyes. Now and again she was flooded by a great flow of red, as a gust of wind blew into the fire from the half-open kitchen door.

From the other side of the fireplace a fair-haired young man was silently watching her.

This was Monsieur Léon Dupuis, the second of the Lion d'Or's regular diners, clerk to Maître Guillaumin the notary. Finding Yonville very dull, he dined as late as possible, in the hope that some traveler might turn up at the inn with whom he could have an evening's conversation. On days where there was no work to detain him at the office, he had no way of filling the interval, and ended up arriving on time and enduring a tête-à-tête with Binet straight through from soup to cheese. So it was with pleasure that he accepted the hostess' suggestion that he dine with the new arrivals, and they all went into the large dining room, where their four places had been set: Madame Lefrançois was making an occasion of it.

Homais asked permission to keep his cap on; he had a dread of head colds. Then, turning to his neighbor: "Madame is a bit tired, I presume? Our old Hirondelle does such a frightful lot of bumping and shaking!"

"It does," Emma answered. "But I always love traveling anyway. I enjoy a change of scene."

The clerk sighed. "It's so boring to be always stuck in the same place!"

"If you were like me," said Charles, "always having to be on horseback . . ."

"But there's nothing more charming than riding, I think," said the clerk, addressing Madame Bovary. "If you have the opportunity, of course."

"As a matter of fact," said the apothecary, "the practice of medicine isn't particularly arduous in this part of the world. The condition of our roads makes it possible to use a gig, and, generally speaking, payment is good— the farmers are well off. Aside from the usual cases of enteritis, bronchitis, liver complaint, etc., our roster of illnesses includes an occasional intermittent fever at harvest time, but on the whole very little that's serious except for a good deal of scrofula, probably the result of the deplorable hygienic conditions in our countryside. Ah! You'll have to fight many a prejudice, Monsieur Bovary; every day your scientific efforts will be thwarted by the peasant's stubborn adherence to his old ways. Plenty of our people still have recourse to novenas and relics and the priest, instead of doing the natural thing and coming to the doctor or the pharmacist. To tell the truth, however, the climate isn't at all bad: we even have a few nonagenarians. The thermometer—this I can tell you from personal observation—goes down in winter to four degrees, and in the hottest season touches twenty-five or thirty degrees Centigrade at the most—that is, twenty-four degrees Réaumur at a maximum, or, in other words, fifty-four degrees Fahrenheit, to use the English scale—not more! You see, we're sheltered from the north winds by the Argueil forest on the one side and from the west winds by the bluffs of Saint-Jean on the other. However, this warmth, which because of the dampness given off by the river and the number of cattle in the pastures, which themselves exhale, as you know, a great deal of ammonia, that is nitrogen, hydrogen, and oxygen (no, just nitrogen and hydrogen), and which, sucking up the humus from the soil, mixing all these different emanations together—making a package of them, so to speak—and combining also with the electricity in the atmosphere when there is any, could in the long run result in noxious miasmas, as in tropical countries; this warmth, I was saying, is actually moderated from the direction from which it comes, or rather the direction from which it could come, namely, from the south, by southeast winds, which being of course cool themselves as a result of crossing the Seine sometimes burst on us all of a sudden like arctic air from Russia!"

"Are there some nice walks in the neighborhood, at least?" Madame Bovary asked, speaking to the young man.

"Oh, hardly any," he answered. "There's one place, called the Pasture, on top of the bluffs at the edge of the woods. I go there Sundays sometimes with a book and watch the sunset."

"There's nothing I love as much as sunsets," she said. "But my favorite place for them is the seashore."

"Oh, I adore the sea," said Monsieur Léon.

"Don't you have the feeling," asked Madame Bovary, "that something happens to free your spirit in the presence of all that vastness? It raises up my soul to look at it, somehow. It makes me think of the infinite, and all kinds of wonderful things."

"Mountain scenery does the same," said Léon. "A cousin of mine traveled in Switzerland last year, and he told me that no one who hasn't been there can imagine the poetry and charm of the lakes and waterfalls and the majesty of the glaciers. You can look across the rivers there and see pine trees so high you can't believe your eyes. They build their chalets right on the edge of precipices. If you look down you can see whole valleys a thousand feet below you through openings in the clouds. Think what it must do to you to see things like that! I'd fall on my knees, I think. I'd want to pray. I can well understand the famous composer who used to play the piano in such places, to get inspiration."

"Are you a musician?" she asked.

"No, but I love music," he answered.

"Ah, don't listen to him, Madame Bovary," interrupted Homais, leaning across his plate. "He's just being modest. What about the other day, my friend? You were singing L'Ange gardien[2] in your room—it was delightful. I heard you from the laboratory; you rendered it like a real actor."

---

2. The guardian angel (French). A sentimental romance written by Mme. Pauline Duchambre, author of several such songs that appeared in the keepsakes.

Léon lived at the pharmacist's, in a small third-floor room looking out on the square. He blushed at his landlord's compliment. But the latter had already turned back to the doctor and was briefing him on the leading citizens of Yonville. He told stories about them and gave vital statistics. No one knew for sure how well off the notary was; and then there was the Tuvache family, all of them hard to get on with.

Emma went on: "What is your favorite kind of music?"

"Oh, German music. It's the most inspiring."

"Do you know Italian opera?"

"Not yet—but I'll hear some next year when I go to Paris to finish law school."

"As I was just telling your husband," the pharmacist said, "speaking of our poor runaway friend Yanoda, thanks to his extravagance you're going to enjoy one of the most comfortable houses in Yonville. What's especially convenient about it for a doctor is that it has a door opening on the lane, so that people can come and go without being seen. Besides, it has everything a housekeeper needs: laundry, kitchen and pantry, sitting room, fruit closet, etc. Yanoda didn't care how he spent his money! He built an arbor alongside the river at the foot of the garden, just to drink beer in during the summer! If Madame likes gardening, she'll be able to . . ."

"My wife never gardens," said Charles. "She's been advised to take exercise, but even so she'd much rather stay in her room and read."

"So would I," said Léon. "What's more delightful than an evening beside the fire with a nice bright lamp and a book, listening to the wind beating against the windows . . . ?"

"How true!" she said, her great dark eyes fixed widely on him.

"I'm absolutely removed from the world at such times," he said. "The hours go by without my knowing it. Sitting there I'm wandering in countries I can see every detail of—I'm playing a role in the story I'm reading. I actually feel I'm the characters—I live and breathe with them."

"I know!" she said. "I feel the same!"

"Have you ever had the experience," Léon went on, "of running across in a book some vague idea you've had, some image that you realize has been lurking all the time in the back of your mind and now seems to express absolutely your most subtle feelings?"

"Indeed I have," she answered.

"That's why I'm especially fond of poetry," he said. "I find it much more affecting than prose. It's much more apt to make me cry."

"Still, it's tiresome in the long run," Emma replied. "Nowadays I'm crazy about a different kind of thing—stories full of suspense, stories that frighten you. I hate to read about low-class heroes and their down-to-earth concerns, the sort of thing the real world's full of."

"You're quite right," the clerk approved. "Writing like that doesn't move you: it seems to me to miss the whole true aim of art. Noble characters and pure affections and happy scenes are very comforting things. They're a refuge from life's disillusionments. As for me, they're my *only* means of relief, living here as I do, cut off from the world. Yonville has so little to offer!"

"It's like Tostes, I suppose," Emma said. "That's why I always subscribed to a lending library."

"If Madame would do me the honor of using it," said the pharmacist, who had heard her last words, "I can offer her a library composed of the best authors—Voltaire, Rousseau, Delille,[3] Walter Scott, the *Echo des Feuilletons*. I subscribe to a number of periodicals, too. The *Fanal de Rouen*[4] comes every day: as a matter of fact I happen to be its local correspondent for Buchy, Forges, Neufchâtel, Yonville and all this vicinity."

They had been at table two hours and a half. Artémise was a wretched waitress: she dragged her cloth slippers over the tile floor, brought plates one by one, forgot everything, paid no attention to what was told her, and constantly left the door of the billiard room ajar so that the latch kept banging against the wall.

As he talked, Léon had unconsciously rested his foot on one of the rungs of Madame Bovary's chair. She was wearing a little blue silk scarf that held her pleated batiste collar stiff as a ruff; and as she moved her head the lower part of her face buried itself in the folds or gently rose out of them. Sitting thus side by side while Charles and the pharmacist chatted, they entered into one of those vague conversations in which every new subject that comes up proves to be one more aspect of a core of shared feelings. The names of plays running in Paris, the titles of novels, new dance tunes, the inaccessible great world, Tostes where she had just come from, Yonville where they both were now—all this they went into and talked about until dinner was over.

When coffee was brought in, Félicité went off to prepare the bedroom in the new house, and soon they all got up from the table. Madame Lefrançois was asleep beside her smoldering fire, and the stable-boy, lantern in hand, was waiting to light Monsieur and Madame Bovary home. There were wisps of straw in his red hair, and his left leg was lame. He took Monsieur le curé's umbrella in his other hand, and the company set out.

The town was asleep. The pillars of the market cast long shadows, and the pallor of the road in the moonlight gave the effect of a summer night.

But the doctor's house was only fifty yards from the inn, and almost at once it was time to say good night and they went their separate ways.

The moment she stepped inside the entrance hall Emma felt the chill from the plaster walls fall on her shoulders, like the touch of a damp cloth. The walls were new and the wooden stairs creaked. Upstairs in the bedroom a whitish light came through the uncurtained windows. She could glimpse the tops of trees, and, beyond them, meadows half drowned in the mist that rose up in the moonlight along the river. In the middle of the room was a heap of bureau drawers, bottles, metal and wooden curtain rods; mattresses lying on chairs, basins strewn over the floor—everything had been left there in disorder by the two moving-men.

It was the fourth time that she had gone to bed in a strange place. The first was the day she entered the convent, the second the day she arrived in Tostes, the third at La Vaubyessard, and now the fourth: each time it had been like the opening of a new phase of her life. She refused to believe that things could be the same in different places; and since what had gone before was so bad, what was to come must certainly be better.

---

3. Jacques Delille (1738–1813), who wrote idyllic descriptive poems; *Les Jardins* (1782) is best known.
4. The *Rouen Beacon* (a fictitious newspaper).

III

The next morning she was barely up when she saw the clerk in the square. She was in her dressing gown. He caught sight of her and bowed. She responded with a brief nod and closed the window.

Léon waited all day for six o'clock to come, but when he entered the inn he found only Monsieur Binet, already at table.

The dinner of the previous evening had been a notable event for him: never before had he spoken for two consecutive hours with a "lady." How did it happen that he had been able to tell her so many things, in words that previously he wouldn't have thought of? He was ordinarily timid, with a reticence that was part modesty, part dissimulation. In Yonville he was thought to have very gentlemanly manners. He listened respectfully to his elders, and seemed not to get excited about politics—a remarkable trait in a young man. Besides, he was talented. He painted in water colors, could read the key of G, and when he didn't play cards after dinner he often took up a book. Monsieur Homais esteemed him because he was educated; Madame Homais liked him because he was helpful: he often spent some time with her children in the garden. They were brats, the Homais children, always dirty, wretchedly brought up, sluggish like their mother. Besides the maid, they were looked after by the pharmacist's apprentice, Justin, a distant cousin of Monsieur Homais, who had been taken in out of charity and was exploited as a servant.

The apothecary proved the best of neighbors. He advised Madame Bovary about tradesmen, had his cider dealer make a special delivery, tasted the brew himself, and saw to it that the barrel was properly installed in the cellar. He told her how to buy butter most advantageously, and made an arrangement for her with Lestiboudois the sacristan, who in addition to his ecclesiastical and funerary functions tended the principal gardens in Yonville by the hour or by the year, depending on the owners' preference.

It wasn't mere kindness that prompted the pharmacist to such obsequious cordiality: there was a scheme behind it.

He had violated the law of 19th Ventôse, Year XI,[5] Article I, which forbids anyone not holding a diploma to practice medicine; and in consequence had been denounced by anonymous informants and summoned to Rouen to the private chambers of the royal prosecutor. The magistrate had received him standing, clad in his robe of office banded at the shoulders with ermine and wearing his high official toque. It was in the morning, before the opening of court. Homais could hear the heavy tread of policemen in the corridor, and in the distance what sounded like heavy locks snapping shut. His ears rang so that he thought he was going to have a stroke; he had a vision of underground dungeons, his family in tears, his pharmacy sold, all his glass jars scattered among strangers; and when the interview was over he had to go to a café and drink a rum and soda to steady his nerves.

Gradually the memory of this warning faded, and he continued as before to give innocuous consultations in his back room. But his relations with the mayor were not good; he had competitors who would rejoice in his ruin: he

---

5. The government of the French Republic established a new calendar. The new year began on September 22, 1792; thus the year is 1803. Ventôse: windy (French); the sixth month of the new calendar (from February 19 to March 20), making the date March 9.

had to watch his step. By being polite to Monsieur Bovary he could win his gratitude and insure his looking the other way should he notice anything. So every morning Homais brought him "the paper," and often left the pharmacy in the afternoon to call on him for a moment's conversation.

Charles was in a gloomy state: he had no patients. He sat silent for hours on end, took naps in his consulting room, or watched his wife as she sewed. To keep occupied he acted as handyman around the house, even attempting to paint the attic with what the painters had left behind. But he was worried about money. He had spent so much for repairs at Tostes, for dresses for Madame, for the move, that the entire dowry and three thousand écus besides had been swallowed up in two years. Besides, so many things had been broken or lost between Tostes and Yonville! The plaster priest was one of them: a particularly violent bump had thrown it out of the van, and it had been smashed into a thousand pieces on the cobblestones of Quincampoix.

He had another, happier concern—his wife's pregnancy. As her term drew near she became ever dearer to him. Another bond of the flesh was being forged between them, one which gave him an all-pervasive feeling that their union was now closer. The indolence of her gait, the gentle sway of her uncorseted body, her tired way of sitting in a chair, all filled him with uncontrollable happiness: he would go up to her and kiss her, stroke her face, call her "little mother," try to dance with her; and half laughing, half weeping, he would think of a thousand playful endearments to shower her with. The idea of having begotten a child enchanted him. Now he had everything he could ever hope for. He had been granted all that human life had to offer, and he was serenely ready to enjoy it.

Emma's first reaction to her condition was one of great surprise; and then she was eager to be delivered and know what it was like to be a mother. But since she couldn't spend the money she would have liked and buy embroidered baby bonnets and a boat-shaped cradle with pink silk curtains, she resentfully gave up her own ideas about the layette and ordered the whole thing from a seamstress in the village without indicating any preferences or discussing any details. Thus she had none of the pleasure she might have had in the preparations that whet the appetite of mother love; and this perhaps did something to blunt her affection from the beginning. But Charles spoke of the baby every time they sat down to a meal, and gradually she became accustomed to the idea.

She wanted a son. He would be strong and dark; she would call him Georges; and this idea of having a male child was like a promise of compensation for all her past frustrations. A man is free, at least—free to range the passions and the world, to surmount obstacles, to taste the rarest pleasures. Whereas a woman is continually thwarted. Inert, compliant, she has to struggle against her physical weakness and legal subjection. Her will, like the veil tied to her hat, quivers with every breeze: there is always a desire that entices, always a convention that restrains.

The baby was born one Sunday morning, about six o'clock, as the sun was rising.

"It's a girl!" cried Charles.

She turned her head away and fainted.

Almost immediately Madame Homais rushed in and kissed her, followed by Madame Lefrançois of the Lion d'Or. The pharmacist, a man of discretion, confined himself to a few provisional words of congratulations, spoken through the half-open door. He asked to see the child and pronounced it well formed.

During her convalescence she gave a great deal of thought to a name for her daughter. First she went over all she could think of that had Italian endings—Clara, Louisa, Amanda, Atala; she was tempted by Galsuinde, too, and even more by Isolde and Léocadie. Charles wanted the child named for its mother; Emma was opposed. They went through the almanac from end to end and asked everyone for suggestions.

"Monsieur Léon," said the pharmacist, "told me the other day he's surprised you haven't decided on Madeleine: it's so very fashionable just now."

But the older Madame Bovary protested loudly against a name so associated with sin. Monsieur Homais' predilection was for names that recalled great men, illustrious deeds or noble thoughts: such had been his guiding principle in baptising his own four children. Napoléon stood for fame, Franklin for liberty; Irma was perhaps a concession to romanticism; but Athalie[6] was a tribute to the most immortal masterpiece of the French stage. For— mind you!—his philosophical convictions didn't interfere with his artistic appreciation: in him, the thinker didn't stifle the man of feeling; he was a man of discrimination, quite capable of differentiating between imagination and fanaticism. In the tragedy in question, for example, he condemned the ideas but admired the style, abhorred the conception but praised all the details, found the characters impossible but their speeches marvelous. When he read the famous passages he was carried away, but the thought that the clergy made use of it all for their own purposes distressed him immensely; and so troubling was his confusion of feelings that he would have liked to place a wreath on Racine's brow with his own hands and then have a good long argument with him.

In the end, Emma remembered hearing the marquise at Vaubyessard address a young woman as Berthe, and that promptly became the chosen name. Since Monsieur Rouault was unable to come, Monsieur Homais was asked to be godfather. As presents he brought several items from his pharmaceutical stock, namely, six boxes of jujubes, a full jar of racahout, three packages of marshmallow paste, and six sticks of sugar candy that he found in a cupboard and threw in for good measure. The evening of the ceremony there was a large dinner party. The priest was present: words became rather heated, and with the liqueurs Monsieur Homais broke into Béranger's *Le Dieu des bonnes gens.*[7] Monsieur Léon sang a barcarolle, and the older Madame Bovary (who was godmother) a Napoleonic ballad. Finally the older Monsieur Bovary insisted that the baby be brought down, and proceeded to baptize it with a glass of champagne, pouring the wine over its head. This mockery of the first sacrament brought indignant words from the Abbé Bournisien; the older Monsieur Bovary replied with a quotation from *La Guerre des dieux;*[8] and the priest started to leave. The ladies implored him to stay; Homais intervened; and after considerable persuasion the abbé sat down

6. A tragedy by Jean Racine, written in 1691 for the pupils of Saint-Cyr. Racine had abandoned the regular stage after a spiritual crisis and wrote two sacred tragedies, *Esther* and *Athalie*, for the young girls of Saint-Cyr.   7. The god of good people; a deistic song by Béranger (see n. 7, p. 1093).   8. The war of the gods; a satirical poem by Evarite-Désiré Deforge (later vicomte de Parny; 1753–1814) published in 1799. It ridicules the Christian religion.

again in his chair and calmly took up his saucer and his half-finished demitasse.

The older Monsieur Bovary stayed on for a month at Yonville, dazzling the inhabitants with a magnificent silver-braided policeman's cap that he wore mornings when he smoked his pipe in the square. He was used to drinking large quantities of brandy, and often sent the maid to the Lion d'Or to buy a bottle, which was charged to his son's account; and to perfume his foulards he used up his daughter-in-law's entire supply of eau de Cologne.

Emma didn't in the least dislike his company. He had seen the world: he spoke of Berlin, of Vienna, of Strasbourg, of his years as an army officer, of the mistresses he had had, of the official banquets he had attended. Then he would become gallant; and sometimes, on the stairs or in the garden, he would even seize hold of her waist and cry, "Better watch out, Charles!" The older Madame Bovary was alarmed for her son's happiness, and began to urge her husband to take her home, lest in the long run he corrupt the young woman's mind. Possibly her fears went further: Monsieur Bovary was a man to whom nothing was sacred.

One day Emma suddenly felt that she had to see her little daughter, who had been put out to nurse with the cabinetmaker's wife; and without looking at the almanac to see whether the six weeks of the Virgin[9] had elapsed, she made her way toward the house occupied by Rollet, at the end of the village at the foot of the hills, between the main road and the meadows.

It was noon: the houses had their shutters closed, and under the harsh light of the blue sky the ridges of the glittering slate roofs seemed to be shooting sparks. A sultry wind was blowing. Emma felt weak as she walked; the stones of the footpath hurt her feet, and she wondered whether she shouldn't return home or stop in somewhere to rest.

At that moment Monsieur Léon emerged from a nearby door, a sheaf of papers under his arm. He advanced to greet her and stood in the shade in front of Lheureux's store, under the gray awning.

Madame Bovary said that she was on her way to see her child but was beginning to feel tired.

"If . . ." Léon began, and then dared go no further.

"Have you an appointment somewhere?" she asked him.

And when he replied that he hadn't she asked him to accompany her. By evening the news of this had spread throughout Yonville, and Madame Tuvache, the wife of the mayor, said in her maid's presence that Madame Bovary was risking her reputation.

To reach the wet-nurse's house they had to turn left at the end of the village street, as though going to the cemetery, and follow a narrow path that led them past cottages and yards between privet hedges. These were in bloom; and blooming, too, were veronicas and wild roses and nettles and the wild blackberries that thrust out their slender sprays from the thickets. Through holes in the hedges they could see, in the farmyards, a pig on a manure pile or cows in wooden collars rubbing their horns against tree trunks. The two of them walked on slowly side by side, she leaning on his arm and he shortening his step to match hers; in front of them hovered a swarm of flies, buzzing in the warm air.

9. Originally the six weeks that separate Christmas from Purification (February 2); in those days, the normal period of confinement for a woman after childbirth.

They recognized the house by an old walnut tree that shaded it. It was low, roofed with brown tiles, and from the attic window hung a string of onions. Brushwood propped up against a thorn hedge formed a fence around a bit of garden given over to lettuce, a few plants of lavender, and sweet peas trained on poles. A trickle of dirty water ran off into the grass, and all around were odds and ends of rags, knitted stockings, a red calico wrapper, a large coarsely woven sheet spread out on the hedge. At the sound of the gate the wet nurse appeared, carrying an infant at her breast. With her other hand she was pulling along a frail, unhappy-looking little boy, his face covered with scrofulous sores—the son of a Rouen knit-goods dealer whom his parents were too busy in their shop to bother with.

"Come in," she said. "Your little girl's asleep inside."

The ground-floor bedroom—the only bedroom in the house—had a wide uncurtained bed standing against its rear wall; the window wall (one pane was mended with a bit of wrapping paper) was taken up by the kneading trough. In the corner behind the door was a raised slab for washing, and under it stood a row of heavy boots with shiny hobnails and a bottle of oil with a feather in its mouth. A Mathieu Laensberg almanac[1] lay on the dusty mantelpiece among gun flints, candle ends and bits of tinder. And as a final bit of clutter there was a figure of Fame blowing her trumpets—a picture probably cut out of a perfume advertisement and now fastened to the wall with six shoe tacks.

Emma's baby was asleep in a wicker cradle on the floor, and she took it up in its little blanket and began to sing softly to it and rock it in her arms.

Léon walked around the room: it seemed to him a strange sight, this elegant lady in her nankeen gown here among all this squalor. Madame Bovary blushed; he turned away, fearing that his glance might have been indiscreet; and she put the baby back in its cradle—it had just thrown up over the collar of her dress. The wet nurse quickly wiped off the mess, assuring her it wouldn't show.

"It isn't the first time, you know," she said. "I do nothing but wipe up after her all day long. Would you mind leaving word with Camus the grocer to let me pick up a little soap when I need it? That would be the easiest for you—I wouldn't have to trouble you."

"I will, I will," said Emma. "Good-bye, Madame Rollet."

And she left the house, wiping her feet on the doorsill.

The wet nurse walked with her as far as the gate, talking about how hard it was to have to get up during the night.

"I'm so worn out sometimes I fall asleep in my chair. So couldn't you at least let me have just a pound of ground coffee? It would last me a month; I'd drink it with milk in the morning."

After undergoing a deluge of thanks, Madame Bovary moved on; and then when she had gone a little way down the path there was the sound of sabots and she turned around: it was the wet nurse again.

"What is it now?"

And the peasant woman drew her aside behind an elm and began to talk to her about her husband. He "had only his trade and the six francs a year the captain gave him, so . . ."

"Come to the point!" said Emma brusquely.

---

1. A farmer's almanac, begun in 1635 by Laensberg, frequently found in farms and country houses.

"Well, what I mean is," the wet nurse said, sighing after every word, "I'm afraid he wouldn't like it, seeing me sitting there drinking coffee by myself; you know how men are, they . . ."

"But you'll both have coffee!" Emma cried. "I just told you I'd give you some! Leave me alone!"

"Ah, Madame, you see he's had terrible cramps in his chest ever since he was wounded, and he says cider makes him feel worse, and . . ."

"Won't you please let me go?"

"So," she went on, making a curtsy, "if it isn't too much to ask"—she curtsied again—"if you would"—and she gave a beseeching glance—"just a little jug of brandy," she finally got out, "and I'll rub your little girl's feet with it—they're as tender as your tongue."

When she was finally rid of the wet nurse, Emma once again took Monsieur Léon's arm. She walked rapidly for a little while; then she slowed, and her glance fell on the shoulder of the young man she was with. His brown hair, smooth and neatly combed, touched the black velvet collar of his frock coat. She noticed that his fingernails were longer than those of most other inhabitants of Yonville. The clerk spent a great deal of time caring for them: he kept a special penknife in his desk for the purpose.

They returned to Yonville along the river. The summer weather had reduced its flow and left uncovered the river walls and water steps of the gardens along its bank. It ran silently, swift and cold-looking; long fine grasses bent with the current, like masses of loose green hair streaming in its limpid depths. Here and there on the tip of a reed or on a water-lily pad a spidery-legged insect was poised or crawling. Sunbeams pierced the little blue air bubbles that kept forming and breaking on the ripples; branchless old willows mirrored their gray bark in the water; in the distance the meadows seemed empty all around them. It was dinner time on the farms, and as they walked the young woman and her companion heard only the rhythm of their own steps on the earth of the path, the words they themselves were uttering, and the whisper of Emma's dress as it rustled around her.

The garden walls, their copings bristling with broken bits of bottles, were as warm as the glass of a greenhouse. Wallflowers had taken root between the bricks; and as she passed, the edge of Madame Bovary's open parasol crumbled some of their faded flowers into yellow dust; or an overhanging branch of honeysuckle or clematis would catch in the fringe and cling for a moment to the silk.

They talked about a company of Spanish dancers scheduled soon to appear at the theatre in Rouen.

"Are you going?" she asked.

"If I can," he answered.

Had they nothing more to say to each other? Their eyes, certainly, were full of more meaningful talk; and as they made themselves utter banalities they sensed the same languor invading them both: it was like a murmur of the soul, deep and continuous, more clearly audible than the sound of their words. Surprised by a sweetness that was new to them, it didn't occur to them to tell each other how they felt or to wonder why. Future joys are like tropic shores: out into the immensity that lies before them they waft their native softness, a fragrant breeze that drugs the traveler into drowsiness and makes him careless of what awaits him on the horizon beyond his view.

In one spot the ground was boggy from the trampling of cattle, and they had to walk on large green stones that had been laid in the mud. She kept stopping to see where to place her foot; and teetering on an unsteady stone, her arms lifted, her body bent, a hesitant look in her eye, she laughed, fearing lest she fall into the puddles.

When they reached her garden, Madame Bovary pushed open the little gate, ran up the steps and disappeared.

Léon returned to his office. His employer was out; he glanced at the piles of papers, sharpened a quill pen, and then—took up his hat and went out again.

He climbed to the Pasture, on the hilltop at the edge of the Argueil forest, and there he stretched out on the ground under the firs and looked up at the sky through his fingers.

"God!" he said to himself. "What a boring existence!"

He felt that he was much to be pitied for having to live in this village, with Homais for a friend and Maître Guillaumin for a master. The latter, completely taken up with business, wore gold-framed spectacles, red side whiskers and a white tie; fine feelings were a closed book to him, though the stiff British manner he affected had impressed the clerk at first. As for Madame Homais, she was the best wife in Normandy, placid as a sheep and devoted to her children, her father, her mother and her cousins; she wept at others' misfortunes, let everything in the house go, and hated corsets. But she was so slow-moving, so boring to listen to, so common-looking and limited in conversation, that it never occurred to him—though she was thirty and he twenty, and they slept in adjoining rooms and he spoke to her every day— that anyone could look on her as a woman, that she had any attributes of her sex except the dress she wore.

Who was there besides? Binet, a few shopkeepers, two or three tavern keepers, the priest, and lastly, Monsieur Tuvache, the mayor, and his two sons—a comfortably-off, surly, dull-witted trio who farmed their own land, ate huge meals with never a guest, faithful churchgoers for all that, and utterly insufferable in company.

But against the background of all these human faces, Emma's stood out— isolated from them and yet further removed than they, for he sensed that some abyss separated him from her.

At first he had gone to her house several times with the pharmacist. Charles had not seemed too eager to have him; and Léon felt helpless, torn as he was between fear of being indiscreet and desire for an intimacy that he considered all but impossible.

IV

With the coming of cold weather Emma moved out of her bedroom into the parlor, a long low-ceilinged room where a chunky branch of coral stood on the mantelpiece in front of the mirror. Sitting in her armchair beside the window, she could watch the villagers go by on the sidewalk.

Twice a day Léon went from his office to the Lion d'Or. Emma could hear him coming in the distance; she would lean forward as she listened, and the young man would slip past on the other side of the window curtain, always dressed the same, never turning his head. At twilight, when she had put down her embroidery and was sitting there with her chin in her left hand, she often started at the sudden appearance of this gliding shadow. She would jump up, order the maid to set the table.

Monsieur Homais often called during dinner. Tasseled cap in hand, he would tiptoe in so as to disturb no one, and he always gave the same greeting: "Good evening, everybody!" Then, sitting down at the table between them, he would ask the doctor for news of his patients, and Charles would ask him what the chances were of being paid. Then they would talk about what was "in the paper." By this time of day Homais knew it almost by heart, and he would repeat it *in toto,* complete with editorials and the news of each and every disaster that had occurred in France and abroad. When these topics ran dry he never failed to comment on the dishes he saw being served. Sometimes, half rising, he would even considerately point out to Madame the tenderest piece of meat; or, turning to the maid, he would advise her on the preparation of her stews and the use of seasoning from a health point of view: he was quite dazzling on the subject of aromas, osmazomes, juices and gelatines. Indeed, Homais had more recipes in his head than there were bottles in his pharmacy, and he excelled at making all kinds of jellies, vinegars and cordials. He was acquainted with all the latest fuel-saving stoves, and with the arts of preserving cheeses and treating spoiled wine.

At eight o'clock Justin always called for him: it was time to shut the pharmacy. Monsieur Homais would give him a quizzical glance, especially if Félicité were in the room, for he had noticed that his pupil was partial to the doctor's house. "My young man's beginning to get ideas," he would say. "Something tells me he's after your maid!"

And there was worse: despite all rebukes, the boy persisted in his habit of listening to conversations. On Sundays, for instance, Madame Homais would summon him to the parlor to take away the children, who had fallen asleep in armchairs, dragging down the loose calico slip covers, and there was no way of getting him to leave the room.

These soirées at the pharmacist's were not very well attended, for his slanderous tongue and his political opinions had alienated one respectable person after another. The clerk was invariably present. At the sound of the doorbell he would run down to greet Madame Bovary, take her shawl, and stow away under the desk in the pharmacy the overshoes she wore when it snowed.

First they would play a few rounds of *trente-et-un;* then Monsieur Homais would play *écarté*[2] with Emma, Léon standing behind her and giving advice. With his hands on the back of her chair, he would look down and see the teeth of her comb piercing her chignon. Each time she threw down a card the right side of her dress gave an upward twist, and he could follow the gradually paling shadow cast down her neck by the knot of her hair, until it was lost in a darker shadow. Then her dress would drop down on both sides of her chair, swelling out in full folds and spreading to the floor. Sometimes Léon would feel himself touching it with the sole of his shoe, and he would quickly move away, as though he had been treading on someone.

---

2. A card game similar to euchre, in which players win tricks by playing a higher card in the suit. *Trente-et-un:* Thirty-one (French), also called Red and Black; a French gambling game in which cards are dealt in two categories (red and black) until a total of thirty-one or more points is reached; players bet on the winning color.

When they finished their cards, the apothecary and the doctor played dominoes; and Emma would move to another chair, lean her elbows on the table and leaf through *L'Illustration,* or take up the fashion magazine she usually brought with her. Léon would sit beside her, and together they would look at the pictures and wait for each other before turning a page. Often she would ask him to read a poem aloud, and Léon would recite it in a languid voice that he carefully let die away at the love passages. But the noise of the dominoes annoyed him: Monsieur Homais was an expert, easily outplaying Charles. When the score reached three hundred the two of them would stretch out before the fireplace and quickly fall asleep. The fire smoldered, the teapot was empty; Léon continued to read, and Emma listened, absent-mindedly turning the lampshade, its gauzy surface painted with pierrots in carriages and tightrope dancers balancing with their poles. Léon would stop, indicating with a gesture his sleeping audience; and then they would talk in low voices, their conversation seeming the sweeter for not being overheard.

Thus a kind of intimacy grew up between them, a continual exchange of books and ballads. Monsieur Bovary was not jealous; he found it all quite natural.

For his birthday he received a splendid phrenological head, all marked over with numerals down to the thorax and painted blue. This was an offering from the clerk. He was attentive in many other ways, too, even doing errands for Charles in Rouen. When a new novel launched a craze for exotic plants, Léon bought some for Madame, holding them on his knees in the Hirondelle and pricking his fingers on their spikes.

Emma had a railed shelf installed in her window to hold her flowerpots. The clerk, too, had his hanging garden, and they could look out and see each other tending their blossoms.

There was one person in the village who spent even more time at his window than they: from morning till night on Sunday, and every afternoon in good weather, the lean profile of Monsieur Binet could be seen in a dormer bent over his lathe, its monotonous drone audible as far as the Lion d'Or.

One evening when he returned home Léon found in his room a velvet and wool coverlet, with foliage designs on a pale ground. He showed it to Madame Homais, Monsieur Homais, Justin, the children, and the cook, and spoke about it to his employer. Everybody wanted to see it: why should the doctor's wife give presents to the clerk? The whole thing seemed suspicious, and everyone was sure that they must be having an affair.

By speaking incessantly about Emma's charms and intelligence, Léon gave plenty of grounds for the belief. Binet turned on him one day with a snarl: "What's it to me? She doesn't let *me* hang around her!"

He was in agony trying to think of a way of "declaring himself" to her. He was constantly torn between the fear of offending her and shame at his own cowardice; he shed tears of despair and frustrated desire. Every so often he resolved to take energetic action: he wrote letters, only to tear them up; he gave himself time limits, only to extend them. More than once he started out intending to dare all; but in Emma's presence he quickly lost his courage, and if Charles happened to appear at such a moment and invited him to get into the buggy and go with him to see a patient living somewhere nearby, he would accept at once, bow to Madame and drive off. Her husband, after all, was part of herself, was he not?

As for Emma, she never tried to find out whether she was in love with him. Love, to her, was something that comes suddenly, like a blinding flash of lightning—a heaven-sent storm hurled into life, uprooting it, sweeping every will before it like a leaf, engulfing all feelings. It never occurred to her that if the drainpipes of a house are clogged, the rain may collect in pools on the roof; and she suspected no danger until suddenly she discovered a crack in the wall.

V

It was a snowy Sunday afternoon in February.

All of them—Monsieur and Madame Bovary, Homais and Monsieur Léon—had gone to see a new flax mill that was being built in the valley, a mile or so from Yonville. The apothecary had taken Napoléon and Athalie along to give them some exercise, and Justin accompanied them, carrying a supply of umbrellas over his shoulder.

Nothing, however, could have been less interesting than this point of interest. A long rectangular building pierced with innumerable little windows stood in the midst of a large tract of bare land, with a few already rusty gear wheels lying here and there among piles of sand and gravel. It was still unfinished, and the sky could be seen between the rafters. Attached to the ridgepole at the peak of one of the gables was a bouquet of straw and wheat, tied with red, white and blue ribbons that flapped in the wind.

Homais was holding forth. He expatiated to them all on how important the mill was going to be, estimated the strength of the floors and the thickness of the walls, and keenly regretted not owning a carpenter's rule, such as Monsieur Binet possessed for his personal use.

Emma, who had taken his arm, was leaning slightly against his shoulder and looking up at the far-off disc of the sun that was suffusing the mist with its pale brilliance; then she turned her head, and saw—Charles. His cap was pulled down over his eyes; and the quivering of his thick lips in the cold gave him a stupid look. Even his back, his placid back, was irritating to look at: all his dullness was written right there, on his coat.

As she was looking at him, deriving a kind of perverse enjoyment from her very irritation, Léon moved a step closer. White in the cold, his face was more languorous and appealing than ever; a bit of his bare skin showed through a gap in his shirt collar; she could see the tip of one of his ears below a lock of his hair; and his large blue eyes, lifted toward the clouds, seemed to Emma more limpid and lovely than mountain lakes mirroring the sky.

"Stop that!" the apothecary suddenly cried.

And he rushed over to his son, who had just jumped into a heap of lime to whiten his shoes. To his father's scoldings Napoléon replied with howls; Justin scraped off the shoes with a bit of plaster; but a knife was needed, and Charles offered his.

"Ah!" she cried to herself. "He carries a knife around with him, like a peasant!"

The cold was beginning to pinch, and they turned back toward Yonville.

That evening Madame Bovary did not attend her neighbor's soirée; and when Charles had gone and she felt herself alone, the comparison returned to her mind almost with the sharpness of an actual sensation, and with the increased perspective conferred on things by memory. Watching the brightly burning fire from her bed, she saw once again, as at the scene itself, Léon standing there, leaning with one hand on his slender, flexing cane and with the other holding Athalie, who was placidly sucking a piece of ice. She found him charming; she could not take her mind off him; she remembered how he had looked on other occasions, things he had said, the sound of his voice, everything about him; and she kept saying to herself, protruding her lips as though for a kiss: "Charming, charming! . . . Isn't he in love? Who could it be?" she asked herself. "Why—he's in love with me!"

All the evidence burst on her at once; her heart leapt up. The flames in the fireplace cast a merry, flickering light on the ceilings; she lay on her back and stretched out her arms.

Then began the eternal lament: "Oh, if only fate had willed it so! Why didn't it? What stood in the way?"

When Charles came in at midnight she pretended to wake up. He made some noise as he undressed, and she complained of migraine; then she casually asked what had happened during the evening.

"Monsieur Léon went up to his room early," said Charles.

She couldn't help smiling, and she fell asleep filled with new happiness.

At nightfall the next day she had a visit from Monsieur Lheureux, the proprietor of the local dry-goods store. He was a clever man, this tradesman.

Born a Gascon, but long settled in Normandy, he combined his southern volubility with the cunning of his adopted region. His fat, flabby, clean-shaven face looked as though it had been dyed with a faint tincture of lico-rice, and his white hair emphasized the piercing boldness of his small black eyes. What he had been in earlier life was a mystery to all: peddler, some said; and others, banker in Routot. What was certain was that he could do in his head intricate feats of calculation that startled Binet himself. Polite to the point of obsequiousness, he was continually in a semi-bent position, like someone making a bow or extending an invitation.

He left his hat with its black mourning band at the door, placed a green case on the table, and began by complaining, with many civilities, at not having been honored up till now with Madame's patronage. A poor shop like his could scarcely be expected to attract so elegant a lady: he emphasized the adjective. But she had only to give him an order and he would undertake to supply anything she wanted, whether accessories, lingerie, hosiery and other knit goods, or notions, for he went to the city four times a month regularly. He was in constant touch with the biggest firms. She could men-tion his name at the Trois Frères, at the Barbe d'Or or at the Grand Sauvage: everyone in those places knew all about him. Today he would just like to show Madame a few articles he happened to have with him, thanks to a lucky buy; out of his box he took half a dozen embroidered collars.

Madame Bovary looked them over.

"I don't need anything," she said.

Then Monsieur Lheureux daintily held out for her inspection three Alger-ian scarves, some packages of English needles, a pair of straw slippers, and finally four coconut-shell egg cups, carved in an openwork design by con-victs. Then, both hands on the table, leaning forward, his neck outstretched, he watched Emma open-mouthed, following her gaze as it wandered uncer-tainly over the merchandise. From time to time, as though to brush off a bit of dust, he gave a flick of a fingernail to the silk of the scarves, lying there unfolded to their full length; and they quivered and rustled under his touch, their gold sequins gleaming like little stars in the greenish light of the dusk.

"How much are they?"

"They're absurdly cheap," he said. "Besides, there's no hurry. Pay whenever you like—we're not Jews!"

She meditated a few moments, then finally told Monsieur Lheureux once more that she didn't want to buy.

"That's quite all right," he answered impassively. "You and I will do business some other time. I've always known how to get along with the ladies—except my wife."

Emma smiled.

"I just want you to know," he said, dropping his facetious tone and assuming an air of candor, "that I'm not worried about the money. In fact, I could let you have some if you needed it."

Emma made a gesture of surprise.

"Ah," he said quickly, in a low voice. "I wouldn't have to go far to find it, believe me!"

Then he turned the conversation to the subject of Monsieur Tellier, proprietor of the Café Français, whom Monsieur Bovary was treating.

"What's his trouble, anyway? He's got a cough that shakes the house. I'm afraid he may soon need a wooden overcoat more than a flannel undershirt! He was a wild one in his younger days! The kind that doesn't know even the meaning of self-control, Madame! He literally burned his insides out with brandy! Still, it's hard to see an old friend go."

And as he tied up his box he talked on about the doctor's patients.

"It must be the weather," he said, scowling at the windowpanes, "that's causing all this illness. I don't feel right myself: one of these days I'll have to come and talk to Monsieur about a pain I have in my back. Well—au revoir, Madame Bovary; at your service, any time."

And he shut the door softly behind him.

Emma had her dinner brought to her in her bedroom on a tray, and ate it beside the fire. She lingered over her food: everything tasted good.

"How sensible I was!" she told herself, as she thought of the scarves.

She heard footsteps on the stairs: it was Léon. She jumped up and snatched the topmost dish towel from a pile she had left for hemming on the chest of drawers. She looked very busy when he came in.

Conversation languished: Madame Bovary kept letting his remarks drop unanswered, and he seemed very ill at ease. He sat in a low chair beside the fire, toying with her ivory needlecase; she continued to sew, occasionally creasing the cloth together with her fingernail. She said nothing, and he, too, was quiet, captivated by her silence as he would have been by her words.

"Poor fellow!" she was thinking.

"What does she dislike about me?" he was wondering.

Finally Léon said that he would be going to Rouen some day soon on office business.

"Your subscription at the music library has run out," he said. "Shall I renew it?"

"No," she answered.

"Why not?"

"Because . . ."

And pursing her lips she slowly drew out a new length of gray thread.

Her sewing irritated Léon: the cloth seemed to be roughening the tips of her fingers. A compliment occurred to him, but he hadn't the courage to utter it.

"You're giving it up?"

"What?" she asked quickly. "Oh, my music? Heavens, yes! Haven't I got my house and my husband to look after—a thousand things—all kinds of duties that come first?"

She looked at the clock. Charles was late. She pretended to be worried. "He's such a good man," she said, two or three times.

The clerk was fond of Monsieur Bovary, but he was unpleasantly surprised to hear her speak so affectionately of him. Nevertheless he continued the praises she had begun, and assured her that he heard them from everyone, especially the pharmacist.

"Ah, Monsieur Homais is a fine man," said Emma.

"He certainly is," said the clerk.

He began to speak of Madame Homais, whose sloppy appearance usually made them laugh.

"What of it?" Emma interrupted. "A good wife and mother doesn't worry about her clothes."

And once again she fell silent.

It was the same the following days: her talk, her manner, everything changed. She immersed herself in household tasks, went regularly to church, and was stricter with the maid.

She took Berthe away from the wet nurse. Félicité brought her in when there was company, and Madame Bovary undressed her to show off her little legs and arms. She adored children, she said: they were her consolation, her joy, her delight; and she accompanied her caresses with gushings that would have reminded anyone except the Yonvillians of Esmeralda's mother in *Notre-Dame de Paris*.[3]

Nowadays when Charles came in, he found his slippers set out to warm by the fire. Now his vests were never without linings, his shirts never without buttons; it was a pleasure to see the piles of cotton nightcaps stacked so neatly in the closet. She no longer frowned at the idea of taking a walk in the garden; she agreed to all his suggestions without trying to understand his reasons. And when Léon saw him beside the fire in the evening, his face flushed from dinner, his hands folded over his stomach, his feet on the andirons, his eyes moist with happiness, the baby crawling on the carpet, and this slender woman leaning over the back of his armchair to kiss him on the forehead—"I must be mad," he told himself. "How can I ever hope to come near her?"

She seemed so virtuous and inaccessible that he lost all hope, even the faintest.

But by thus renouncing her, he transformed her into an extraordinary being. She was divested in his eyes of the earthly attributes that held no promise for him; and in his heart she rose higher and higher, withdrawing further from him in a magnificent, soaring apotheosis. His feeling for her

---

3. A historical novel (1831) by Victor Hugo, in which the mother of Agnes, a girl abducted by gypsies who takes the name Esmeralda, worships a shoe of her stolen child.

was so pure that it did not interfere with his daily life—it was one of those feelings that are cherished because of their very rarity: the distress caused by their loss would be greater than the happiness given by their possession.

Emma grew thinner: her face became paler, more emaciated. With her smooth black hair, her large eyes, her straight nose, her birdlike movements, her new habit of silence, she seemed all but out of contact with life, bearing on her brow the vague mark of a sublime fate. She was so melancholy and so subdued, so sweet and yet so withdrawn, that in her presence he felt transfixed by a glacial spell—just as in a church the fragrance of flowers and the cold given off by marble will sometimes set us shivering. Even other men were not immune to this seduction. The pharmacist put it this way:

"She's got class! She'd hold her own in Le Havre or Dieppe!"

The village housewives admired her for her thrift; Charles's patients for her politeness; the poor for her charity.

And all this time she was torn by wild desires, by rage, by hatred. The trim folds of her dress hid a heart in turmoil, and her reticent lips told nothing of the storm. She was in love with Léon, and she sought the solitude that allowed her to revel undisturbed in his image. The sight of his person spoiled the voluptuousness of her musings. She trembled at the sound of his footsteps; then, with him before her, the agitation subsided, and she was left with nothing but a vast bewilderment that turned gradually into sadness.

Léon did not know, when he left her house in despair, that she went immediately to the window and watched him disappear down the street. She worried over his every move, watched every expression that crossed his face; she concocted an elaborate story to have a pretext for visiting his room. The pharmacist's wife seemed to her blessed to sleep under the same roof; and her thoughts came continually to rest on that house, like the pigeons from the Lion d'Or that alighted there to soak their pink feet and white wings in the eaves-trough. But the more aware Emma became of her love the more she repressed it in an effort to conceal it and weaken it. She would have been glad had Léon guessed; and she kept imagining accidents and disasters that would open his eyes. It was indolence, probably, or fear, that held her back, and a feeling of shame. She had kept him at too great a distance, she decided: now it was too late; the occasion was lost. Besides, the pride and pleasure she derived from thinking of herself as "virtuous" and from wearing an air of resignation as she looked at herself in the mirror consoled her a little for the sacrifice she thought she was making.

Her carnal desires, her cravings for money, and the fits of depression engendered by her love gradually merged into a single torment; and instead of trying to put it out of her mind she cherished it, spurring herself on to suffer, never missing an opportunity to do so. A dish poorly served or a door left ajar grated on her nerves; she sighed thinking of the velvet gowns she didn't own, the happiness that eluded her, her unattainable dreams, her entire cramped existence.

What exasperated her was Charles's total unawareness of her ordeal. His conviction that he was making her happy she took as a stupid insult: such self-righteousness could only mean that he didn't appreciate her. For whose sake, after all, was she being virtuous? Wasn't he the obstacle to every kind of happiness, the cause of all her wretchedness, the sharp-pointed prong of this many-stranded belt that bound her on all sides?

So he became the sole object of her resentment. Her attempts to conquer this feeling served only to strengthen it, for their failure gave her additional cause for despair and deepened her estrangement from her husband. She had moments of revulsion against her own meekness. She reacted to the drabness of her home by indulging in daydreams of luxury, and to matrimonial caresses by adulterous desires. She wished that Charles would beat her: then she would feel more justified in hating him and betraying him out of revenge. Sometimes she was surprised by the horrible possibilities that she imagined; and yet she had to keep smiling, hear herself say time and again that she was happy, pretend to be so, let everyone believe it!

Still, there were times when she could scarcely stomach the hypocrisy. She would be seized with a longing to run off with Léon, escape to some far-off place where they could begin life anew; but at such moments she would shudder, feeling herself at the brink of a terrifying precipice.

"What's the use—he doesn't love me any more," she would decide. What was to become of her? What help could she hope for? What comfort? What relief?

Such a crisis always left her shattered, gasping, prostrate, sobbing to herself, tears streaming down her face.

"Why in the world don't you tell Monsieur?" the maid would ask her, finding her thus distraught.

"It's nerves," Emma would answer. "Don't mention it to him. It would only upset him."

"Ah, yes," Félicité said, one day. "You're just like the daughter of old Guérin, the fisherman at Le Pollet.[4] I knew her at Dieppe before I came to you. She used to be so sad, so terribly sad, that when she stood in her door she made you think of a funeral pall hanging there. It seems it was some kind of a fog in her head that ailed her. The doctors couldn't do anything for her, or the priest either. When it came over her worst, she'd go off by herself along the beach, and sometimes the customs officer would find her stretched out flat on her face on the pebbles and crying, when he made his rounds. It passed off after she was married, they say."

"With me," said Emma, "it was after I married that it began."

VI

One evening when the window was open and she had been sitting beside it watching Lestiboudois the sacristan trim the boxwood, she suddenly heard the tolling of the Angelus.

It was the beginning of April, primrose time, when soft breezes blow over newly spaded flower beds, and gardens, like women, seem to be primping themselves for the gaieties of summer. Through the slats of the arbor, and all around beyond, she could see the stream flowing through the meadows, winding its vagabond course amid the grass. The evening mist was rising among the bare poplars, blurring their outlines with a tinge of purple that was paler and more transparent than the sheerest gauze caught on their branches. In the distance cattle were moving: neither their steps nor their lowing could be heard, and the steadily sounding church bell sent its peaceful lament into the evening air.

As the ringing continued, the young woman's thoughts began to stray

4. Suburb of Dieppe, where the fishermen live.

among old memories of girlhood and the convent. She remembered the tall altar candlesticks that soared above the vases full of flowers and the columned tabernacle. She wished she could be again what she once had been, one in the long line of white-veiled girls, black specked here and there by the stiff cowls of the nuns bowed over their *prie-dieus*. Sundays at Mass when she raised her head she used to see the gentle features of the Virgin among the bluish clouds of rising incense. The memory filled her with emotion: she felt limp and passive, like a bit of bird's-down whirling in a storm; and automatically she turned her steps toward the church, ready for any devotion that would enable her to humble her heart and lose herself entirely.

In the square she met Lestiboudois on his way back: in order not to lose pay by cutting his workday short, he preferred to interrupt his gardening and then go back to it, with the result that he rang the Angelus when it suited him. Besides, early ringing served to remind the village boys that it was time for catechism.

Some of them were already there, playing marbles on the slabs in the cemetery. Others, astride the wall, were swinging their legs, their wooden shoes breaking off the tall nettles that grew between the wall itself and the nearest graves. This was the only spot that was green: all the rest was stones, always covered with a fine dust despite the sacristan's sweeping.

Other boys had taken off their sabots and were running about on the stones as though the cemetery were a smooth floor made specially for them. Their shouts could be heard above the dying sounds of the bell; the heavy rope that hung down from the top of the bell tower and trailed on the ground was swaying ever more slowly. Swallows flew past, twittering as they sliced the air with their swift flight, and disappeared into their yellow nests under the eave-tiles. At the far end of the church a lamp was burning—a wick in a hanging glass, whose light seemed from a distance like a whitish spot dancing on the oil. A long shaft of sunlight cutting across the nave deepened the darkness in the side aisles and corners.

"Where is the priest?" Madame Bovary asked a boy who was happily trying to wrench the turnstile loose from its socket.

"He'll be here," he answered.

Just then the door of the rectory creaked open and the abbé Bournisien appeared. The boys fled helter-skelter into the church.

"Won't they ever behave?" he muttered to himself. "No respect for anything." He picked up a tattered catechism that he had almost stepped on. Then he saw Madame Bovary. "Excuse me," he said. "I didn't place you for a minute."

He stuffed the catechism into his pocket and stood swinging the heavy sacristy key between two fingers.

The setting sun was full in his face; and the black cloth of his cassock, shiny at the elbows and frayed at the hem, seemed paler in its glow. Grease spots and snuff stains ran parallel to the row of little buttons on his broad chest; they were thickest below his neckband, which held back the heavy folds of his red skin; this was sprinkled with yellow splotches, half hidden by the bristles of his graying beard. He had just had his dinner, and was breathing heavily.

"How are you?" he went on.

"Poorly," said Emma. "Not well at all."

"Neither am I," the priest answered. "These first hot days take it out of you terribly, don't they? But what can we do? We're born to suffer, as St. Paul says. What does your husband think is the trouble?"

"My husband!" she said, with a scornful gesture.

The country priest looked surprised. "He must have prescribed something for you, hasn't he?"

"Ah!" said Emma. "It isn't earthly remedies that I need."

But the priest kept looking away, into the church, where the boys were kneeling side by side, each shoving his neighbor with his shoulder and all of them falling down like ninepins.

"Could you tell me . . ." she began.

"Just wait, Riboudet!" he shouted furiously. "I'll box your ears when I get hold of you!"

Then, turning to Emma: "That's the son of Boudet the carpenter; his parents don't bother with him, they let him do as he likes. He'd learn fast if he wanted to: he's very bright. Sometimes as a joke I call him Riboudet—you know, from the name of the hill near Maromme; sometimes I say 'mon Riboudet'—Mont Riboudet! Ha! Ha! The other day I told my little joke to the bishop. He laughed. He was good enough to laugh. And Monsieur Bovary—how is he?"

She seemed not to hear him, and he went on: "Always on the move, probably? He and I are certainly the two busiest people in the parish. He takes care of the bodies," he added, with a heavy laugh, "and I look after the souls."

She fastened her imploring eyes upon him. "Yes," she said. "You must be called on to relieve all kinds of suffering."

"Believe me, I am, Madame Bovary! This very morning I had to go to Bas-Diauville for a cow that had the colic: the peasants thought it was a spell. All their cows, for some reason . . . Excuse me, Madame! Longuemarre! Boudet! Drat you both! Will you cut it out?"

And he rushed into the church.

By now the boys were crowding around the high lectern, climbing up on the cantor's bench and opening the missal; and others, moving stealthily, were about to invade the confessional. But the priest was suddenly upon them, slapping them right and left; seizing them by the coat collar, he lifted them off the ground and then set them on their knees on the stone floor of the choir, pushing them down hard as though he were trying to plant them there.

"Well!" he said, returning to Emma. And then, as he opened his large calico handkerchief, holding a corner of it between his teeth: "As we were saying, farmers have plenty of troubles."

"Other people, too," she answered.

"Of course! Workingmen in the cities, for instance . . ."

"I wasn't thinking of them . . ."

"Ah, but I assure you I've known mothers of families, good women, true saints, who didn't even have a crust of bread."

"I was thinking of women who have bread, Monsieur le curé," Emma said, the corners of her mouth twisting as she spoke, "but who lack . . ."

"Firewood for the winter," the priest anticipated.

"Ah, never mind . . ."

"What do you mean, never mind? It seems to me that to be warm and well fed . . ."

"Oh, my God!" Emma whispered to herself. "My God!"

"Are you feeling ill?" he asked. He looked concerned, and advanced a step. "Something must have disagreed with you. You'd better go home, Madame Bovary, and drink a cup of tea; that will pick you up. Or a glass of water with a little brown sugar."

"What for?"

She looked as though she were emerging from a dream.

"You were holding your hand to your forehead. I thought you must be feeling faint." Then: "But weren't you asking me a question? What was it? I can't recall . . ."

"I? Oh, no, nothing . . . nothing," Emma said.

And her wandering glance came slowly to rest on the old man in his cassock. For a few moments they looked at each other without speaking.

"Well, Madame Bovary," he said, finally, "you'll excuse me, but duty calls. I have to look after my youngsters. First Communion will be here soon: it will be on us before we know it. Time's so short I always keep them an extra hour on Wednesdays after Ascension. Poor things! We can't begin too soon to steer their young souls in the Lord's path—indeed it's what he Himself tells us to do, through the mouth of His divine Son. Keep well, Madame; remember me kindly to your husband!"

And he entered the church, genuflecting just inside the door.

Emma watched him as he disappeared between the double line of pews, treading heavily, his head slightly bent to one side, his half-open hands held with palms outward.

Then she turned stiffly, like a statue on a pivot, and set out for home. Behind her she heard the booming voice of the priest and the lighter voices of the boys.

"Are you a Christian?"

"Yes, I am a Christian."

"What is a Christian?"

"A Christian is one who, after being baptized . . . baptized . . . baptized . . ."

She climbed her stairs holding tight to the rail, and once in her room she sank heavily into a chair.

The whitish light coming through the windowpanes was slowly fading and ebbing away. The various pieces of furniture seemed to be fixed more firmly in their places, lost in shadow as in an ocean of darkness. The fire was out, the clock kept up its tick-tock; and Emma vaguely marveled that all these things should be so quiet while she herself was in such turmoil. Then little Berthe was in front of her, tottering in her knitted shoes between the window and the sewing table, trying to reach her mother and catch hold of the ends of her apron strings.

"Let me alone!" Emma cried, pushing her away.

But a few moments later the little girl was back, this time coming closer. Leaning her arms on her mother's knees she looked up at her with her big blue eyes, and a thread of clear saliva dripped from her lip onto the silk of the apron.

"Let me alone!" Emma cried again, very much annoyed.

The expression on her face frightened the child, who began to scream.

"Won't you let me alone!" she cried, thrusting her off with her elbow.

Berthe fell just at the foot of the chest of drawers, cutting her cheek on one of its brasses. She began to bleed. Madame Bovary rushed to pick her up, broke the bell-rope, called loudly for the maid; and words of self-reproach were on her lips when Charles appeared. It was dinner time; he had just come in.

"Look what's happened, darling," she said, in an even voice. "The baby fell down and hurt herself playing."

Charles reassured her: it was nothing serious, he said, and he went for some adhesive plaster.

Madame Bovary didn't go downstairs for dinner that evening: she insisted on staying alone with her child. As she watched her lying there asleep, her anxiety, such as it was, gradually wore off; and she thought of herself as having been silly and good-hearted indeed to let herself be upset over so small a matter. Berthe had stopped sobbing; and now the cotton coverlet rose and fell imperceptibly with her regular breathing. A few large tears had gathered in the corners of her half-closed eyelids; through the lashes could be seen the pupils, pale and sunken-looking; the adhesive stuck on her cheek pulled the skin to one side.

"It's a strange thing," Emma thought, "what an ugly child she is."

At eleven o'clock, when Charles came back from the pharmacy, where he had gone after dinner to take back the plaster that was left, he found his wife on her feet beside the cradle.

"Really, believe me—it will be all right," he said, kissing her on the forehead. "Don't worry about it, darling: you'll make yourself ill."

He had stayed out a long time. He had not seemed unduly upset, but even so Monsieur Homais had done his best to cheer him up, "raise his morale." The conversation had then turned on the various dangers that beset children because of the absentmindedness of servants. Madame Homais could speak from experience, bearing as she did to this day on her chest the marks of a panful of burning coals that a cook had dropped inside her pinafore when she was small. No wonder the Homais' went out of their way to be careful with their children! In their house knives were never sharpened, floors never waxed. There were iron grills at the windows and heavy bars across the fireplaces. Though taught to be self-reliant, the Homais children couldn't move a step without someone in attendance; at the slightest sign of a cold their father stuffed them with cough syrups, and well past their fourth birthdays they were all mercilessly made to wear padded caps. This, it must be said, was a pet idea of Madame Homais': her husband was secretly worried about it, fearing lest the intellectual organs suffer as a result of such pressure; and he sometimes went so far as to say:

"Do you want to turn them into Caribs or Botocudos?"[5]

Charles, meanwhile, had tried several times to end the conversation. "I'd like to have a word with you," he whispered in the clerk's ear; and Léon walked downstairs ahead of him.

"Can he be suspecting something?" he wondered. His heart pounded, and he imagined a thousand contingencies.

Charles, after closing the door behind them, asked him to inquire in Rouen as to the price of a good daguerreotype: he was thinking of paying a delicate tribute to his wife by giving her a sentimental surprise—a portrait of himself in his black tail coat. But he wanted to know, first, "what he was letting

---

5. Two South American peoples.

himself in for." Such inquiries would be no trouble for Monsieur Léon, since he went to the city almost every week.

What was the purpose of these visits? Homais suspected that there was a story there, an intrigue of some kind. But he was mistaken: Léon was not carrying on any amourette. These days his spirits were lower than ever: Madame Lefrançois could tell it from the amount of food he left on his plate. To find out more about it she questioned the tax collector; but Binet rebuffed her, saying that he "wasn't in the pay of the police."

Nevertheless his table companion struck him as exceedingly odd. Léon often lay back in his chair, stretched out his arms and complained vaguely about life.

"That's because you have no hobbies," said the tax collector.

"What would you advise?"

"If I were you I'd buy myself a lathe!"

"But I wouldn't know how to use it," the clerk answered.

"That's so, you wouldn't," said Binet. And he stroked his chin with an air of mingled scorn and satisfaction.

Léon was tired of loving without having anything to show for it, and he was beginning to feel the depression that comes from leading a monotonous life without any guiding interest or buoyant hope. He was so sick of Yonville and the Yonvillians that the sight of certain people and certain buildings irritated him beyond endurance: the pharmacist, worthy soul that he was, he found utterly unbearable. Still, though he longed for a new position, the prospect of change frightened him.

But now timidity gave way to impatience, and Paris beckoned from afar, with the fanfare of its masked balls, the laughter of its grisettes. Since he would have to finish his law studies there sooner or later, why shouldn't he go now? What was preventing him? And he began to make imaginary plans, sketch out his new existence. He furnished a dream apartment. He would lead an artist's life—take guitar lessons, wear a dressing gown, a Basque beret, blue velvet slippers! And in his mind's eye he particularly admired his overmantel arrangement: a pair of crossed fencing foils, with a skull and the guitar hanging above.

The difficulty lay in obtaining his mother's consent; still, there could scarcely be a more reasonable request. Even his employer was urging him to think of another office, where he could widen his experience. Taking a middle course, therefore, Léon looked for a place as second clerk in Rouen, found nothing, and finally wrote his mother a long detailed letter in which he set forth his reasons for moving to Paris at once. She consented.

He didn't hurry. Every day for a month Hivert transported for him, from Yonville to Rouen and from Rouen to Yonville, trunks, valises and bundles; and after Léon had had his wardrobe restocked and his three armchairs reupholstered and had bought a whole new supply of foulard handkerchiefs—after he had made more preparations than for a trip around the world—he kept putting off his departure from week to week, until he received a second letter from his mother urging him to be on his way, since he wanted to pass his examination before the summer vacation.

When the moment came for farewells, Madame Homais wept and Justin sobbed. Homais hid his emotion as a strong man should, and insisted on carrying his friend's overcoat as far as the notary's. Maître Guillaumin was to drive Léon to Rouen in his carriage.

There was just time to say good-bye to Monsieur Bovary. When Léon reached the top of the stairs he was so breathless that he stood still for a moment. As he entered the room Madame Bovary rose quickly to her feet.

"Here I am again," said Léon.

"I knew you'd come!"

She bit her lip, and the blood rushed under her skin, reddening it from the roots of her hair to the edge of her collar. She remained standing, leaning against the wall paneling.

"Monsieur isn't here?" he said.

"He's out."

He repeated: "He's out."

There was a silence. They looked at each other; and their thoughts clung together in their common anguish like two throbbing hearts.

"I'd love to kiss Berthe," said Léon.

Emma went down a few steps and called Félicité.

He glanced quickly around him, taking in the walls, the tables, the fireplace, as though to record them forever down to their last detail and carry them away in his memory.

Then she was back, and the maid brought in Berthe, who was swinging a pinwheel upside down on a string.

Léon kissed her several times on the neck. "Good-bye, sweetheart! Good-bye!" And he handed her back to her mother.

"You may take her," Emma said to the maid.

They were left alone.

Madame Bovary had turned her back, her face pressed to a window-pane. Léon was holding his cap in his hand and kept brushing it against his thigh.

"It's going to rain," said Emma.

"I have a coat," he answered.

"Ah!"

She half turned to him, her face lowered. The light seemed to glide down her forehead to her arching brows as on a marble statue; and there was no way of knowing what she was gazing at on the horizon or what her deepest thoughts might be.

"Good-bye, then," he said, sighing deeply.

She raised her head with an abrupt movement.

"Yes, good-bye—you must be on your way."

They both stepped forward: he held out his hand; she hesitated.

"A handshake, then—English style," she said, with a forced laugh, putting her hand in his.

Léon felt her moist palm in his grasp, and into it seemed to flow the very essence of his being.

Then he released it; their eyes met again; and he was off.

As he crossed the roofed market he stopped behind a pillar to stare for a last time at the white house with its four green shutters. He thought he saw a shadowy form at the bedroom window; then the curtain, released from its hook as though of its own accord, swung slowly for a moment in long slanting folds and sprang fully out to hang straight and motionless as a plaster wall. Léon set off at a run.

Ahead he saw his employer's gig in the road, and beside it a man in an apron holding the horse. Homais and Maître Guillaumin were talking together, waiting for him.

The apothecary embraced him, tears in his eyes. "Here's your overcoat, my boy: wrap up warm! Look after yourself! Take it easy!"

"Come, Léon—jump in!" said the notary.

Homais leaned over the mudguard, and in a voice broken by sobs gulped the sad, familiar words of parting: *"Bon voyage!"*

"Bon soir!" replied Maître Guillaumin. "Anchors aweigh!"

They rolled off, and Homais went home.

Madame Bovary had opened her window that gave on to the garden, and was watching the clouds.

They were gathering in the west, in the direction of Rouen, twisting rapidly in black swirls; out from behind them shot great sun rays, like the golden arrows of a hanging trophy; and the rest of the sky was empty, white as porcelain. Then came a gust of wind; the poplars swayed; and suddenly the rain was pattering on the green leaves. But soon the sun came out again; chickens cackled; sparrows fluttered their wings in the wet bushes; and rivulets flowing along the gravel carried away the pink flowers of an acacia.

"Ah, by now he must be far away!" she thought.

Monsieur Homais dropped in as usual at half-past six, during dinner.

"Well," he said, sitting down, "so we've sent our young man on his way, have we?"

"I guess so," said the doctor. And then, turning in his chair: "What's new at your house?"

"Nothing much. Just that my wife wasn't quite herself this afternoon. You know how women are—anything upsets them, mine especially. We've no right to complain: their nervous system is much more impressionable than ours."

"Poor Léon!" said Charles. "How will he get along in Paris, do you think? Will he get used to it?"

Madame Bovary sighed.

"Never fear!" said the pharmacist, making a clicking noise with his tongue. "Think of the gay parties in restaurants, the masked balls! The champagne! Everything will go at a merry pace, I assure you!"

"I don't think he'll do anything wrong," Bovary objected.

"Nor do I," Monsieur Homais said quickly, "but he'll have to go along with the others if he doesn't want to be taken for a Jesuit. You have no idea of the life those bohemians lead in the Latin Quarter with their actresses! You know, students are very highly thought of in Paris. If they have even the slightest social grace they're admitted to the very best circles. They're even fallen in love with sometimes by ladies of the Faubourg Saint-Germain.[6] Some of them make very good marriages."

"But," said the doctor, "I'm afraid that in the city he may . . ."

6. The aristocratic quarter of Paris.

"You're right," interrupted the apothecary. "It's the reverse of the medal. In the city you've got to keep your hand in your watch pocket every minute. Suppose you're sitting in a park. Some fellow comes up to you—well dressed, perhaps even wearing a decoration—somebody you could take for a diplomat. He addresses you, you talk, he ingratiates himself—offers you a pinch of snuff or picks up your hat for you. Then you get friendlier; he takes you to a café, invites you to visit him in the country, introduces you to all kinds of people over your drinks—and three-quarters of the time it's only to get his hands on your purse or lead you into evil ways."

"That's true," said Charles, "but I was thinking chiefly of diseases—typhoid fever, for example: students from the country are susceptible to it."

Emma shuddered.

"Because of the change of diet," agreed the pharmacist, "and the way it upsets the entire system. And don't forget the Paris water! The dishes they serve in restaurants—all those spicy foods—they overheat the blood: don't let anybody tell you they're worth a good stew. I've always said there's nothing like home cooking: it's better for the health. That was why when I was studying pharmacy in Rouen I went to board in a boarding house: I ate where my teachers ate."

And he continued to expound his general opinions and personal preferences until Justin came to fetch him to make an eggnog for a customer.

"Not a moment's peace!" he cried. "It's grind, grind, grind! I can't leave the shop for a minute. I'm like a plough-horse—sweating blood every second. It's a heavy yoke, my friends!"

And when he was at the door: "By the way," he said, "have you heard the news?"

"What news?"

"It is very likely," Homais announced, raising his eyebrows and looking excessively solemn, "that the annual Agricultural Show of the department of the Seine-Inférieure will be held this year at—Yonville-l'Abbaye. There is, at least, a rumor to that effect. The paper referred to it this morning. An event of the very greatest importance for our district! But we'll talk about it later. I can see, thank you. Justin has the lantern."

VII

The next day was a funereal one for Emma. Everything appeared to her as though shrouded in vague, hovering blackness; and grief swirled into her soul, moaning softly like the winter wind in a deserted castle. She was prey to the brooding brought on by irrevocable partings, to the weariness that follows every consummation, to the pain caused by the breaking off of a confirmed habit or the brusque stopping of a prolonged vibration.

It was like the days following her return from La Vaubyessard, when the dance tunes had kept whirling in her head: she was sunk in the same mournful melancholy, the same torpid despair. Léon seemed taller, handsomer, more charming and less distinct: though he had gone, he had not left her; he was there, and the walls of her house seemed to retain his shadow. She kept staring at the rug he had walked on, the empty chairs he had sat in. The stream at the foot of her garden flowed on as usual, rippling past the slippery bank. They had often strolled there, listening to this same murmur of the water over the moss-covered stones. How they had enjoyed the sun!

And the shade, too, afternoons by themselves in the garden! He had read aloud to her, bareheaded on a rustic bench, the cool wind from the meadows ruffling the pages of his book and the nasturtiums on the arbor. . . . And now he was gone, the one bright spot in her life, her one possible hope of happiness! Why hadn't she grasped that good fortune when it had offered itself? And when it had first threatened to slip away—why hadn't she seized it with both hands, implored it on her knees? She cursed herself for not having surrendered to her love for Léon: she thirsted for his lips. She was seized with a longing to run after him, to fling herself into his arms, to cry, "Take me! I'm yours!" But the difficulties of such an enterprise discouraged her in advance; and her longings, increased by regret, became all the more violent.

Thereafter, the image she had of Léon became the center of her distress: it glowed more brightly than a travelers' fire left burning on the snow of a Russian steppe. She ran up to it, crouched beside it, stirred it carefully when it was on the verge of extinction, grasped at everything within reach that might bring it back to life. Distant memories and present-day events, experiences actual and imagined, her starved sensuality, her plans for happiness, blown down like dead branches in the wind, her barren "virtue," the collapse of her hopes, the litter of her domestic life—all these she gathered up and used as fuel for her misery.

Nevertheless the flames did die down—whether exhausted from lack of supplies or choked by excessive feeding. Little by little, love was quenched by absence; regret was smothered by routine; and the fiery glow that had reddened her pale sky grew gray and gradually vanished. In this growing inner twilight she even mistook her recoil from her husband for an aspiration toward her lover, the searing waves of hatred for a rekindling of love. But the storm kept raging, her passion burned itself to ashes, no help was forthcoming, no new sun rose on the horizon. Night closed in completely around her, and she was left alone in a horrible void of piercing cold.

Then the bad days of Tostes began all over again. She considered herself far more unhappy now than she had been then, for now she had experienced grief, and she knew that it would never end.

A woman who had assumed such a burden of sacrifice was certainly entitled to indulge herself a little. She bought herself a Gothic *prie-dieu,* and in a month spent fourteen francs on lemons to blanch her fingernails; she wrote to Rouen for a blue cashmere dress; and at Lheureux's she chose the finest of his scarves. She wound it around her waist over her dressing gown, and thus arrayed she closed the shutters and stretched out on her sofa with a book.

She kept changing her way of wearing her hair: she tried it *à la chinoise,*[7] in soft curls, in braids; she tried parting it on one side and turning it under, like a man's.

She decided to learn Italian: she bought dictionaries, a grammar, a supply of paper. She went in for serious reading—history and philosophy. Sometimes at night Charles would wake up with a start, thinking that someone had come to fetch him to a sickbed. "I'm coming," he would mutter, and it would be the sound of the match that Emma was striking to light her lamp. But her books were like her many pieces of needlepoint: barely begun, they

7. Chinese fashion (French).

were tossed into the cupboard; she started them, abandoned them, discarded them in favor of new ones.

She had spells in which she would have gone to extremes with very little urging. One day she insisted, Charles to the contrary, that she could drink half a water glass of brandy; and when Charles was foolish enough to dare her, she downed every drop of it.

For all her "flightiness"—that was the Yonville ladies' word for it—Emma did not have a happy look. The corners of her mouth were usually marked with those stiff, pinched lines so often found on the faces of old maids and failures. She was pale, white as a sheet all over; the skin of her nose was drawn down toward the nostrils, and she had a way of staring vacantly at whoever she was talking with. When she discovered two or three gray hairs at her temples she began to talk about growing old.

She often had dizzy spells. One day she even spat blood; and when Charles hovered over her and showed his concern she shrugged. "What of it?" she said.

Charles shut himself in his consulting room, and sitting in his office armchair under the phrenological head he put his elbows on the table and wept.

He wrote his mother asking her to come, and they had long conversations on the subject of Emma.

What course to follow? What could be done, since she refused all treatment?

"Do you know what your wife needs?" said the older Madame Bovary. "She needs to be put to work—hard, manual work. If she had to earn her living like so many other people, she wouldn't have those vapors—they come from all those ideas she stuffs her head with, and the idle life she leads."

"She keeps busy, though," Charles said.

"Busy at what? Reading novels and all kinds of bad books—anti-religious books that quote Voltaire and ridicule the priests. It's a dangerous business, son: anyone who lacks respect for religion comes to a bad end."

So it was decided to prevent Emma from reading novels. The project presented certain difficulties, but the old lady undertook to carry it out: on her way through Rouen she would personally call on the proprietor of the lending library and tell him that Emma was canceling her subscription. If he nevertheless persisted in spreading his poison, they would certainly have the right to report him to the police.

Farewells between mother-in-law and daughter-in-law were curt. During the three weeks they had been together they hadn't exchanged four words apart from the formal greetings and absolute essentials called for at mealtime and bedtime.

The older Madame Bovary left on a Wednesday—market day at Yonville.

From early morning, one side of the square was taken up with a row of carts—all tipped up on end, with their shafts in the air, stretching along the house fronts from the church to the hotel. On the other side were canvas booths for the sale of cotton goods, woolen blankets and stockings, horse halters, and rolls of blue ribbon whose ends fluttered in the wind. Heavy hardware was spread out on the ground between pyramids of eggs and cheese baskets bristling with sticky straw; and close by the harvesting machines were the flat poultry boxes, with clucking hens sticking their necks out between the slats. The crowd always filled the same corner, unwilling to move on:

sometimes it seemed on the point of pushing through the glass of the pharmacy window. On Wednesdays the shop was never empty, and everyone elbowed his way in, less to buy pharmaceutical products than to consult the pharmacist, so celebrated was Monsieur Homais' reputation in the villages round about. His hearty self-confidence bewitched the country folk: to them he was a greater doctor than all the doctors.

Emma was leaning out her window (she often did this: in the provinces windows take the place of boulevards and theaters) watching the crowd of yokels, when she caught sight of a gentleman in a green velvet frock coat. His dressy yellow gloves contrasted with his heavy gaiters, and he was approaching the doctor's house. Behind him was a peasant who followed along with lowered head and decidedly pensive expression.

"May I see Monsieur?" he asked Justin, who was chatting in the doorway with Félicité. And assuming that he was one of the house servants, he added: "Give him my name—Monsieur Rodolphe Boulanger de la Huchette."

The new arrival had added the "de" and the "La Huchette" to his name not out of vanity as a landowner but rather to indicate more clearly who he was. La Huchette was an estate near Yonville, and he had recently bought the château and its two dependent farms. The latter he worked himself— not too seriously. He kept a bachelor establishment and was rumored to have "a private income of at least fifteen thousand francs a year."

Charles came into the parlor, and Monsieur Boulanger introduced his man, who wanted to be bled because "he felt prickly all over." There was no arguing with him: he said it would "clear him out."

So Bovary told the maid to bring a bandage, and a basin that he asked Justin to hold. The peasant turned pale at once. "There's nothing to be afraid of," Charles told him.

"I'm all right," the man said. "Go ahead."

He held out his sturdy arm with an air of bravado. At the prick of the scalpel the blood spurted out and spattered against the mirror.

"Hold the basin closer!" Charles cried.

"Look at that!" said the peasant. "Just like a fountain! I've got real red blood: that's a good sign, isn't it?"

"Sometimes," remarked the *officier de santé*, "they don't feel anything at first, and then they keel over—especially the husky ones, like this one here."

At those words the peasant dropped the scalpel case, which he had been twisting in his fingers. The back of the chair creaked under the heavy impact of his shoulders, and his hat fell to the floor.

"Just what I thought," said Bovary, pressing the vein with his finger.

The basin began to shake in Justin's hands; his knees wobbled and he turned pale.

"Where's my wife?" Charles cried, and he called her loudly. She came rushing down the stairs.

"Vinegar!" he cried. "We've got a pair of them, damn it!"

In his excitement he had trouble applying the compress.

"It's nothing," said Monsieur Boulanger, quite calmly; and he lifted Justin in his arms and propped him up on the table with his back against the wall.

Madame Bovary set about loosening Justin's cravat. There was a knot in the strings that fastened his shirt, and when she had undone it she rubbed his boyish neck lightly for a few minutes; then she moistened her batiste handkerchief in vinegar and patted his forehead with it, blowing gently on it as she did so.

The teamster revived; but Justin remained in his faint, the pupils of his eyes sunk into the whites like blue flowers in milk.

"We'd better not let him see this," said Charles.

Madame Bovary took away the basin. As she bent down to put it under the table, her dress—a long-waisted, full-skirted yellow summer dress with four flounces—belled out around her on the tile floor of the parlor; and as she put out her arms to steady herself the material billowed and settled, revealing the lines of her body. Then she brought in a pitcher of water, and was dissolving sugar in it when the pharmacist arrived. The maid had gone after him in the midst of the fracas, and when he found his apprentice with his eyes open he breathed a sigh of relief. Then he stalked back and forth in front of him, staring him up and down.

"Idiot!" he said. "Idiot, with a capital *I*! A terrible thing, a little bloodletting, isn't it! A fine fearless fellow, too. Just look at him! And yet I've seen him go up a tree after nuts like a squirrel—up to the dizziest heights, *Messieurs et Madame!* Say something, can't you? Tell us how good you are! You'll certainly make a fine pharmacist! Don't you know that some day you may be called on to give important evidence in court? The judges may need your expert opinion. You'll have to keep calm at such times, and know what to say! You'll have to show them you're a man, or else be called a fool!"

Justin made no answer, and the apothecary went on:

"Who asked you to come here anyway? You're always bothering Monsieur and Madame! You know perfectly well I always need you Wednesdays! There are twenty people in the shop right now—I left everything out of consideration for you! Go on! Get back there! Keep an eye on things till I come!"

When Justin had put himself to rights and gone, they talked a little about fainting spells. Madame Bovary had never had one.

"That's unusual for a lady," said Monsieur Boulanger. "But there are men who are extraordinarily susceptible, you know. I've seen a second at a duel lose consciousness at the mere sound of the loading of the pistols."

"I don't mind the sight of other people's blood a bit," said the pharmacist. "But the very idea of shedding my own would be enough to turn my stomach if I thought about it too much."

Meanwhile Monsieur Boulanger sent away his man, urging him to stop worrying now that he'd got what he wanted.

"His whim has afforded me the privilege of making your acquaintance," he said; and as he spoke the words he looked at Emma.

Then he put three francs on the corner of the table, bowed casually, and left.

He was soon on the other side of the river (it was the way back to La Huchette); and Emma saw him crossing the meadow under the poplars, occasionally slowing his pace as though he were pondering something.

"She's very nice," he was saying to himself, "very nice, that wife of the doctor's! Lovely teeth, black eyes, a dainty foot—she's like a real Parisian. Where the devil does she come from? How did such a clodhopper ever get hold of her?"

Monsieur Rodolphe Boulanger was thirty-four. He was brutal and shrewd. He was something of a connoisseur: there had been many women in his life.

This one seemed pretty, so the thought of her and her husband stayed with him.

"I have an idea he's stupid. I'll bet she's tired of him. His fingernails are dirty and he hasn't shaved in three days. He trots off to see his patients and leaves her home to darn his socks. How bored she must be! Dying to live in town, to dance the polka every night! Poor little thing! She's gasping for love like a carp on a kitchen table gasping for water. A compliment or two and she'd adore me, I'm positive. She'd be sweet! But—how would I get rid of her later?"

And the thought of the troubles inevitable in such an affair brought to his mind by contrast his present mistress, an actress he kept in Rouen. He found he could not evoke her image without a feeling of satiety, and after a time he said to himself:

"Ah, Madame Bovary is much prettier—and what's more, much fresher. Virginie's certainly growing too fat. She's getting on my nerves with all her enthusiasms. And her mania for shrimps . . . !"

The countryside was deserted, and the only sounds were the regular swish of the tall grass against his gaiters and the chirping of crickets hidden in the distant oats. He thought of Emma in the parlor, dressed as he had seen her, and he undressed her.

"I'll have her!" he said aloud, bringing his stick down on a clod of earth in front of him.

And he immediately began to consider the question of strategy.

"Where could we meet? How could we arrange it? The brat would always be around, and the maid, and the neighbors, and the husband—there'd be a lot of headaches. Bah! It would all take too much time."

Then he began all over again:

"Those eyes really bore into you, though! And that pale complexion . . . God! How I love pale women. . . ."

By the time he had reached the top of the hill his mind was made up.

"The only thing to do now is keep my eyes open for opportunities. I'll call on them occasionally and send them presents—game and chickens. I'll have myself bled, if I have to. We'll get to be friends. I'll invite them to the house. . . . And . . . Oh, yes"—it came to him—"we'll soon be having the show. She'll be there. I'll see her. We'll get started. The approach direct: that's the best."

VIII

The great day arrived at last.

The morning of the Agricultural Show all the Yonvillians were standing on their doorsteps discussing the preparations. The pediment of the town hall had been looped with ivy; a marquee had been set up for the banquet in one of the meadows; and in the middle of the square, in front of the church, stood an antiquated fieldpiece that was to be fired as a signal announcing the arrival of the prefect and the proclamation of the prize winners. The Buchy national guard (Yonville had none) had come to join forces with the fire brigade, commanded by Binet. Today he wore a collar even higher than usual; and his bust, tightly encased in his tunic, was so stiff and inflexible that all his animal fluids seemed to be concentrated in his legs, which rose and fell with the music in rhythmic jerks. Since the tax collector and the colonel were rivals, each showed off his talents by drilling his men separately. First the red epaulettes would march up and down, and then the black breastplates. And then it would begin all over again: there was no end to it. Never had there been such a display of pomp! A number of citizens had washed their housefronts the day before; tricolor flags were hanging from half-open windows; all the cafés were full; and in the perfect weather the headdresses of the women seemed whiter than snow, their gold crosses glittered in the bright sun, and their multicolored neckcloths relieved the somber monotony of the men's frock coats and blue smocks. As the farm women dismounted from their horses they undid the big pins that had held their skirts tucked up away from splashing. The men's concern was for their hats: to protect them they had covered them with large pocket handkerchiefs, holding the corners between their teeth as they rode.

The crowd converged on the main street from both ends of the village, from the paths between the houses, from the lanes, and from the houses themselves; knockers could be heard falling against doors as housewives in cotton gloves emerged to watch the festivities. Particularly admired were the two large illumination frames laden with colored glass lamps that flanked the official grandstand; and against the four columns of the town hall stood four poles, each with a little banner bearing a legend in gold letters on a greenish ground. One said "Commerce," another "Agriculture," the third "Industry," and the fourth "Fine Arts."

But the jubilation brightening all faces seemed to cast a gloom over Madame Lefrançois, the hotel-keeper. She was standing on her kitchen steps muttering to herself:

"It's a crime—a crime, that canvas shack! Do they really think the prefect will enjoy eating his dinner in a tent, like a circus performer? They pretend the whole thing's for the good of this village—so why bring a third-class cook over from Neufchâtel? And who's it all for, anyway? A lot of cowherds and riffraff."

The apothecary came by. He was wearing a black tail coat, yellow nankeen trousers, reverse-calf shoes, and—most exceptionally—a hat: a stiff, low-crowned hat.

"Good morning!" he said. "Forgive me for being in such a hurry."

And as the buxom widow asked him where he was going:

"I imagine it must seem funny to you, doesn't it? Considering that most of the time I can't be pried loose from my laboratory any more than the old man's rat from his cheese."

"What cheese is that?" asked the landlady.

"Oh, nothing, nothing," said Homais. "I was merely referring to the fact, Madame Lefrançois, that I usually stay at home, like a recluse. But today things are different. I must absolutely . . ."

"You don't mean you're going *there?*" she said with a scornful look.

"Of course I'm going there," the apothecary replied, surprised. "Don't you know I'm on the advisory committee?"

Madame Lefrançois looked at him for a moment or two and then answered with a smile:

"That's all right, then. But what have you got to do with farming? Do you know anything about it?"

"Certainly I know something about it, being a pharmacist! A pharmacist is a chemist, Madame Lefrançois; and since the aim of chemistry is to discover the laws governing the reciprocal and molecular action of all natural bodies, it follows that agriculture falls within its domain! Take the composition of manures, the fermentation of liquids, the analysis of gasses, the effects of noxious effluvia—what's all that, I ask you, if it isn't chemistry in the strictest sense of the word?"

The landlady made no reply. Homais went on:

"Do you think that to be an agronomist you must till the soil or fatten chickens with your own hands? No: you have to study the composition of various substances—geological strata, atmospheric phenomena, the properties of the various soils, minerals, types of water, the density of different bodies, their capillary attraction. And a hundred other things. You have to be thoroughly versed in all the principles of hygiene—that's an absolute prerequisite if you're going to serve in a supervisory or consultant capacity in anything relating to the construction of farm buildings, the feeding of livestock, the preparation of meals for hired men. And then you've got to know botany, Madame Lefrançois: be able to tell one plant from another—you know what I mean? Which ones are benign and which ones are poisonous, which ones are unproductive and which ones are nutritive; whether it's a good thing to pull them out here and resow them there, propagate some and destroy others. In short, you've got to keep abreast of science by reading pamphlets and publications; you've got to be always on the alert, always on the lookout for possible improvements. . . ."

All this time the landlady never took her eyes off the door of the Café Français. The pharmacist continued:

"Would to God our farmers were chemists, or at least that they listened more carefully to what science has to say. I myself recently wrote a rather considerable little treatise—a monograph of over seventy-two pages, entitled: *Cider: Its Manufacture and Its Effects; Followed by Certain New Observations on This Subject.* I sent it to the Agronomical Society of Rouen, and it even brought me the honor of being admitted to membership in that body—Agricultural Section, Pomology Division. Now if this work of mine had been made available to the public . . ."

The apothecary broke off: Madame Lefrançois' attention was obviously elsewhere.

"Just look at them," she said. "How can they patronize such a filthy place?"

And with shrugs that stretched her sweater tight over her bosom, she pointed with both hands to her competitor's café, out of which came the sound of singing.

"Anyway, it won't be there much longer," she said. "Just a few days more, and then—*finis.*"

Homais drew back in amazement, and she came down her three steps and put her lips to his ear:

"What! Haven't you heard? They're padlocking it this week. It's Lheureux who's forcing the sale; all those notes Tellier signed were murder."

"What an unutterable catastrophe!" The apothecary always had the proper expression ready, whatever the occasion.

The landlady proceeded to tell him the story, which she had from Théodore, Maître Guillaumin's servant; and although she detested Tellier she had nothing but harsh words for Lheureux. He was a wheedler, a cringer.

"Look—there he is now, in the market," she said. "He's greeting Madame Bovary. She's wearing a green hat. In fact, she's on Monsieur Boulanger's arm."

"Madame Bovary!" cried Homais. "I must go and pay her my respects. She might like to have a seat in the enclosure, under the portico."

And ignoring Madame Lefrançois' attempts to detain him with further details, he hurried off, smiling and with springy step, bestowing innumerable salutations right and left, and taking up a good deal of room with his long black coat tails that streamed in the wind behind him.

Rodolphe had seen him coming and had quickened his pace; but Madame Bovary was out of breath, and he slowed and smiled at her. "I was trying to avoid that bore," he said savagely. "You know, the apothecary."

She nudged him with her elbow.

"What does that mean?" he wondered, glancing at her out of the corner of his eye as they moved on.

Her face, seen in profile, was so calm that it gave him no hint. It stood out against the light, framed in the oval of her bonnet, whose pale ribbons were like streaming reeds. Her eyes with their long curving lashes looked straight ahead: they were fully open, but seemed a little narrowed because of the blood that was pulsing gently under the fine skin of her cheekbones. The rosy flesh between her nostrils was all but transparent in the light. She was inclining her head to one side, and the pearly tips of her white teeth showed between her lips.

"Is she laughing at me?" Rodolphe wondered.

But Emma's nudge had been no more than a warning, for Monsieur Lheureux was walking along beside them, now and then addressing them as though to begin conversation.

"What a marvelous day! Everybody's out! The wind is from the east."

Neither Madame Bovary nor Rodolphe made any reply, though at their slightest movement he edged up to them saying, "Beg your pardon?" and touching his hat.

When they were in front of the blacksmith's, instead of following the road as far as the gate Rodolphe turned abruptly into a side path, drawing Madame Bovary with him.

"Good-bye, Monsieur Lheureux!" he called out. "We'll be seeing you!"

"You certainly got rid of him!" she said, laughing.

"Why should we put up with intruders?" he said. "Today I'm lucky enough to be with you, so . . ."

Emma blushed. He left his sentence unfinished, and talked instead about the fine weather and how pleasant it was to be walking on the grass. A few late daisies were blooming around them.

"They're pretty, aren't they?" he said. "If any of the village girls are in love they can come here for their oracles." And he added: "Maybe I should pick one. What do you think?"

"Are you in love?" she asked, coughing a little.

"Ah, ah! Who knows?" answered Rodolphe.

The meadow was beginning to fill up, and housewives laden with big umbrellas, picnic baskets and babies were bumping into everyone. It was constantly necessary to turn aside, out of the way of long lines of girls— servants from farms, wearing blue stockings, low-heeled shoes and silver rings and smelling of the dairy when they came close. They walked holding hands, forming chains the whole length of the meadow, from the row of aspens to the banquet tent. It was time for the judging, and one after another the farmers were filing into a kind of hippodrome marked off by a long rope hung on stakes.

Here stood the livestock, noses to the rope, rumps of all shapes and sizes forming a ragged line. Lethargic pigs were nuzzling the earth with their snouts; calves were lowing and sheep bleating; cows with their legs folded under them lay on the grass, slowly chewing their cud and blinking their heavy eyelids under the midges buzzing around them. Bare-armed teamsters were holding rearing stallions by the halter: these were neighing loudly in the direction of the mares, who stood there quietly, necks outstretched and manes drooping, as their foals rested in their shadow or came now and again to suck. Above the long undulating line of these massed bodies a white mane would occasionally surge up like a wave in the wind, or a pair of sharp horns would stick out, or men's heads would bob up as they ran. Quite apart, outside the arena, a hundred yards off, was a big black bull with a strap harness and an iron ring through its nose, motionless as a brazen image. A ragged little boy held it by a rope.

Meanwhile a group of gentlemen were solemnly advancing between the two rows, inspecting each animal and then conferring in an undertone. One, who seemed the most important, was writing details in a notebook as he walked. This was the chairman of the jury, Monsieur Derozerays de la Panville. As soon as he recognized Rodolphe he quickly stepped forward and addressed him with a cordial smile: "What's this, Monsieur Boulanger? You've deserted us?"

Rodolphe assured him that he was coming directly. But when the chairman had passed:

"I'll certainly *not* be going," he said to Emma. "I like your company better than his."

And though he kept making fun of the show, Rodolphe displayed his blue pass to the guard so that they could walk about unmolested, and he even stopped from time to time in front of some particularly fine exhibit. It was never anything that Madame Bovary cared about: he noticed this, and began to make jokes about the Yonville ladies and the way they dressed; then he apologized for the carelessness of his own costume. This was a mixture of the casual and the refined—the kind of thing that both fascinates and exasperates the common herd, hinting as it does at an eccentric way of life, indulgence in wild passions and "artistic" affections, and a contempt for social conventions. His batiste shirt (it had pleated cuffs) puffed out from the opening of his gray twill vest at each gust of wind; and his broad-striped trousers ended at nankeen shoes trimmed with patent leather so shiny that the grass was reflected in it. He tramped unconcernedly through horse dung, one thumb in his vest pocket, his straw hat tilted over one ear.

"Anyway," he said, "when you live in the country . . ."

"Any trouble you take is wasted," said Emma.

"Completely," replied Rodolphe. "Think of it: there isn't a single person here today capable of appreciating the cut of a coat."

And they talked about the mediocrity of provincial life, so suffocating, so fatal to all noble dreams.

"So," said Rodolphe, "I just get more and more engulfed in gloom as time goes on. . . ."

"You do!" she cried, in surprise. "I thought of you as being very jolly."

"Of course—that's the impression I give: I've learned to wear a mask of mockery when I'm with other people. But many's the time I've passed a cemetery in the moonlight and asked myself if I wouldn't be better off lying there with the rest. . . ."

"Oh! And what about your friends?" she asked. "Have you no thought for them?"

"My friends? What friends? Have I any? Who cares anything about me?"

And he accompanied those last words with a kind of desperate whistle.

But they had to draw apart to make way for a tall tower of chairs borne by a man coming up behind them. He was so excessively laden that the only parts of him visible were the tips of his wooden shoes and his two out-stretched hands. It was Lestiboudois, the gravedigger, who was renting out church seats to the crowd. He was highly inventive where his own interests were concerned, and had thought up this way of profiting from the show. It was a good idea: everyone was hailing him at once. The villagers were hot; they clamored for the straw-seated chairs that gave off a smell of incense, and they leaned back with a certain veneration against the heavy slats stained with candle wax.

Then once again Madame Bovary took Rodolphe's arm, and he went on as though talking to himself:

"Yes, so many things have passed me by! I've always been so alone! Ah! If I'd had a purpose in life, if I'd met anyone with true affection, if I'd found somebody who . . . Oh! Then I wouldn't have spared any effort; I'd have sur-mounted every obstacle, let nothing stand in my way . . . !"

"It seems to me, though," said Emma, "that you're scarcely to be pitied."

"Oh? You think that?" said Rodolphe.

"Yes," she answered, "because after all you're free"—she hesitated—"rich . . ."

"Don't make fun of me," he begged.

And she was swearing that she was doing nothing of the kind, when a cannon shot resounded and everyone began to hurry toward the village.

It was a false alarm: the prefect wasn't even in sight, and the members of the jury were in a quandary, not knowing whether to begin the proceedings or wait a while longer.

Finally at the far end of the square appeared a big hired landau drawn by two skinny horses who were being furiously whipped on by a white-hatted coachman. Binet had just time to shout, "Fall in!" and the colonel to echo him; there was a rush for the stacked rifles; and in the confusion some of the men forgot to button their collars. But the official coach-and-pair seemed to sense the difficulty, and the emaciated beasts, dawdling on their chain, drew up at a slow trot in front of the portico of the town hall just at the moment when the national guard and the fire brigade were deploying into line to the beating of the drums.

"Mark time!" cried Binet.

"Halt!" cried the colonel. "Left, turn!"

And after a present-arms during which the rattle of the metal bands as they slid down the stocks and barrels sounded like a copper cauldron rolling down a flight of stairs, all the rifles were lowered.

Then there emerged from the carriage a gentleman clad in a short, silver-embroidered coat, his forehead high and bald, the back of his head tufted, his complexion wan and his expression remarkably benign. His eyes, very large and heavy-lidded, half shut as he peered at the multitude; and at the same time he lifted his sharp nose and curved his sunken mouth into a smile. He recognized the mayor by his sash, and explained that the prefect had been unable to come. He himself was a prefectural councilor, and he added a few words of apology. Tuvache replied with compliments, the emissary declared himself unworthy of them; and the two officials stood there face to face, their foreheads almost touching, all about them the members of the jury, the village council, the local elite, the national guard and the crowd. Holding his little black three-cornered hat against his chest, the prefectural councilor reiterated his greetings; and Tuvache, bent like a bow, returned his smiles, stammered, clutched uncertainly for words, protested his devotion to the monarchy and his awareness of the honor that was being bestowed on Yonville.

Hippolyte, the stable-boy at the hotel, came to take the horses from the coachman; and limping on his clubfoot he led them through the gateway of the Lion d'Or, where a crowd of peasants gathered to stare at the carriage. There was a roll of the drums, the howitzer thundered, and the gentlemen filed up and took their seats on the platform in red plush armchairs loaned by Madame Tuvache.

All in this group looked alike. Their flabby, fair-skinned, slightly suntanned faces were the color of new cider, and their bushy side whiskers stuck out over high, stiff collars that were held in place by white cravats tied in wide bows. Every vest was of velvet, with a shawl collar; every watch had an oval carnelian seal at the end of a long ribbon; and every one of the gentlemen sat with his hands planted on his thighs, his legs carefully apart, the hard-finished broadcloth of his trousers shining more brightly than the leather of his heavy shoes.

The invited ladies were seated to the rear, under the portico between the columns, while the ordinary citizens faced the platform, either standing, or sitting on chairs. Lestiboudois had retransported to this new location all those that he had previously taken to the meadow; now he kept bringing still more from the church; and he was crowding the place so with his chair-rental business that it was almost impossible for anyone to reach the few steps leading to the platform.

"In my opinion," said Monsieur Lheureux, addressing the pharmacist, who was passing by on his way to take his seat, "they should have set up a pair of Venetian flagstaffs: trimmed with something rich and not too showy they'd have made a very pretty sight."

"Certainly," said Homais. "But what can you expect? The mayor took everything into his own hands. He hasn't much taste, poor Tuvache: in fact, he's completely devoid of what is known as the artistic sense."

Meanwhile Rodolphe, with Madame Bovary, had gone up to the second floor of the town hall, into the "council chamber": it was quite empty—a perfect place, he said, from which to have a comfortable view of the ceremonies. He took three of the stools that stood around the oval table under the king's bust and moved them over to one of the windows; and there they sat down close together.

There was a certain agitation on the platform—prolonged whisperings and consultations. Finally the prefectural councilor rose to his feet. It had become known that he was called Lieuvain, and his name was repeated from one to another in the crowd. He made sure that his sheets of paper were in proper order, peered at them closely, and began:

"Gentlemen: I should like, with your permission (before speaking to you about the object of today's meeting—and this sentiment, I am sure, will be shared by all of you), I should like, with your permission, to pay tribute to the national administration, to the government, to the monarch, gentlemen, to our sovereign, to the beloved king to whom no branch of public or private prosperity is indifferent, and who, with so firm and yet so wise a hand, guides the chariot of state amidst the constant perils of a stormy sea, maintaining at the same time public respect for peace as well as for war—for industry, for commerce, for agriculture, for the fine arts."

"I ought to move a little further back," said Rodolphe.

"Why?" said Emma.

But at that moment the councilor's voice rose to an extraordinary pitch. He was declaiming:

"Gone forever, gentlemen, are the days when civil discord drenched our streets with blood; when the landlord, the businessman, nay, the worker, sank at night into a peaceful slumber trembling lest they be brutally awakened by the sound of inflammatory tocsins; when the most subversive principles were audaciously undermining the foundations . . ."

"It's just that I might be caught sight of from below," said Rodolphe. "If I were, I'd have to spend the next two weeks apologizing; and what with my bad reputation . . ."

"Oh! You're slandering yourself," said Emma.

"No, no, my reputation's execrable, I assure you."

"But, gentlemen," continued the councilor, "if I dismiss those depressing evocations and turn my eyes to the present situation of our cherished fatherland, what do I see before me? Commerce and the arts are thriving everywhere; everywhere new channels of communication, like so many new arteries in the body politic, are multiplying contacts between its various parts; our great manufacturing centers have resumed their activity; religion, its foundations strengthened, appeals to every heart; shipping fills our ports; confidence returns; at long last, France breathes again!"

"Moreover, from the point of view of society it's probably deserved," Rodolphe said.

"What do you mean?" she asked.

"Do you really not know," he said, "that there exist souls that are ceaselessly in torment? That are driven now to dreams, now to action, driven from the purest passions to the most orgiastic pleasures? No wonder we fling ourselves into all kinds of fantasies and follies!"

She stared at him as if he were a traveler from mythical lands. "We poor women," she said, "don't have even that escape."

"A poor escape," he said, "since it doesn't bring happiness."

"But do we ever find happiness?" she asked.

"Yes, it comes along one day," he answered.

"And the point has not been lost on you," the councilor was saying. "Not on you, farmers and workers in the fields! Not on you, champions of progress and morality! The point has not been lost on you, I say, that the storms of political strife are truly more to be dreaded than the disorders of the elements!"

"Yes, it comes along one day," Rodolphe repeated. "All of a sudden, just when we've given up hope. Then new horizons open before us: it's like a voice crying, 'Look! It's here!' We feel the need to pour out our hearts to a given person, to surrender, to sacrifice everything. In such a meeting no words are necessary: each senses the other's thoughts. Each is the answer to the other's dreams." He kept staring at her. "There it is, the treasure so long sought for—there before us: it gleams, it sparkles. But still we doubt; we daren't believe; we stand there dazzled, as though we'd come from darkness into light."

As he ended, Rodolphe enhanced his words with pantomime. He passed his hand over his face, like someone dazed; then he let it fall on Emma's hand. She withdrew hers. The councilor read on:

"And who is there who would wonder at such a statement, gentlemen? Only one so blind, so sunk (I use the word advisedly), so sunk in the prejudices of another age as to persist in his misconceptions concerning the spirit of our farming population. Where, I ask you, is there to be found greater patriotism than in rural areas, greater devotion to the common weal, greater —in one word—intelligence? And by intelligence, gentlemen, I do not mean that superficial intelligence that is a futile ornament of idle minds, but rather that profound and moderate intelligence that applies itself above all to useful ends, contributing in this manner to the good of all, to public improvement and the upholding of the state—that intelligence that is the fruit of respect for law and the performance of duty!"

"Ah, there they go again!" said Rodolphe. "Duty, duty, always duty—I'm sick of that word. Listen to them! They're a bunch of doddering old morons and bigoted old church mice with foot warmers and rosaries, always squeaking, 'Duty! Duty!' at us. I have my own idea of duty. Our duty is to feel what is great and love what is beautiful—not to accept all the social conventions and the infamies they impose on us."

"Still . . . still . . ." objected Madame Bovary.

"No! Why preach against the passions? Aren't they the only beautiful thing in this world, the source of heroism, enthusiasm, poetry, music, the arts, everything?"

"But still," said Emma, "we have to be guided a little by society's opinions; we have to follow its standards of morality."

"Ah! But there are two moralities," he replied. "The petty one, the conventional one, the one invented by man, the one that keeps changing and screaming its head off—that one's noisy and vulgar, like that crowd of fools you see out there. But the other one, the eternal one . . . Ah! This one's all around us and above us, like the landscape that surrounds us and the blue sky that gives us light."

Monsieur Lieuvain had just wiped his mouth with his pocket handkerchief. He resumed:

"Why should I presume, gentlemen, to prove to you who are here today the usefulness of agriculture? Who is it that supplies our needs, who is it that provisions us, if not the farmer? The farmer, gentlemen, sowing with laborious hand the fertile furrows of our countryside, brings forth the wheat which, having been ground and reduced to powder by means of ingenious machinery, emerges in the form of flour, and from thence, transported to our cities, is presently delivered to the baker, who fashions from it a food for the poor man as well as for the rich. Is it not the farmer, once again, who fattens his plentiful flocks in the pastures to provide us with our clothing? For how would we be clothed, for how would we be nourished, without agriculture? Indeed, gentlemen—is there need to seek so far afield for examples? Who among you has not often given thought to the immense benefit we derive from that modest creature—adornment of our kitchen yards— which provides at one and the same time a downy pillow for our beds, its succulent meat for our tables, and eggs? But I should never end, had I to enumerate one after another the different products which properly cultivated soil lavishes on its children like a generous mother. Here, the grape; there, the cider apple; yonder, the colza;[8] elsewhere, a thousand kinds of cheese. And flax, gentlemen, do not forget flax!—an area in which within the past few years there has been considerable development, and one to which I particularly call your attention."

There was no need for him to "call their attention": every mouth in the crowd was open, as though to drink in his words. Tuvache, sitting beside him, listened wide-eyed; Monsieur Derozerays' lids now and again gently shut; and further along the pharmacist, holding his son Napoléon between his knees, cupped his hand to his ear lest he miss a single syllable. The other members of the jury kept slowly nodding their chins against their vests to express their approval. The fire brigade, at the foot of the platform, leaned on their bayonets; and Binet stood motionless, elbow bent, the tip of his sword in the air. He could hear, perhaps, but he certainly could not see, for the visor of his helmet had fallen forward onto his nose. His lieutenant, who was Monsieur Tuvache's younger son, had gone him one better: the helmet he was wearing was far too big for him and kept teetering on his head and showing a corner of the calico nightcap he had on under it. He was smiling from beneath his headgear as sweetly as a baby; and his small pale face, dripping with sweat, wore an expression of enjoyment, exhaustion and drowsiness.

The square was packed solidly with people as far as the houses. Spectators were leaning out of every window and standing on every doorstep; and Justin, in front of the pharmacy show window, seemed nailed to the spot in contemplation of the spectacle. Despite the crowd's silence, Monsieur Lieuvain's voice didn't carry too well in the open air. What came was fragmentary bits of sentences interrupted here and there by the scraping of chairs; then all at once from behind there would resound the prolonged lowing of an ox, and lambs bleated to one another on the street corners. For the cowherds and shepherds had driven their animals in that close, and from time to time a cow would bellow as her tongue tore off some bit of foliage hanging down over her muzzle.

Rodolphe had come close to Emma and was speaking rapidly in a low voice:

"Don't you think it's disgusting, the way they conspire to ruin everything? Is there a single sentiment that society doesn't condemn? The noblest instincts, the purest sympathies are persecuted and dragged in the mud; and if two poor souls do find one another, everything is organized to keep them apart. They'll try, just the same; they'll beat their wings, they'll call to each other. Oh! Never fear! Sooner or later, in six months or ten years, they'll

---

8. A plant yielding rapeseed, or canola oil, used in cooking.

come together and love one another, because they can't go against fate and because they were born for each other."

He was leaning forward with his arms crossed on his knees, and lifting his face to Emma's he looked at her fixedly from very near. In his eyes she could see tiny golden lines radiating out all around his black pupils, and she could even smell the perfume of the pomade that lent a gloss to his hair. Then a languor came over her; she remembered the vicomte who had waltzed with her at La Vaubyessard and whose beard had given off this same odor of vanilla and lemon; and automatically she half closed her eyes to breathe it more deeply. But as she did this, sitting up straight in her chair, she saw in the distance, on the farthest horizon, the old stagecoach, the Hirondelle, slowly descending the hill of Les Leux, trailing a long plume of dust behind it. It was in this yellow carriage that Léon had so often returned to her; and that was the road he had taken when he had left forever. For a moment she thought she saw him across the square, at his window; then everything became confused, and clouds passed before her eyes; it seemed to her that she was still whirling in the waltz, under the blaze of the chandeliers, in the vicomte's arms, and that Léon was not far off, that he was coming. . . . And yet all the while she was smelling the perfume of Rodolphe's hair beside her. The sweetness of this sensation permeated her earlier desires, and like grains of sand in the wind these whirled about in the subtle fragrance that was filling her soul. She opened her nostrils wide to breathe in the freshness of the ivy festooning the capitals outside the window. She took off her gloves and wiped her hands; then she fanned herself with her handkerchief, hearing above the beating of the pulse in her temples the murmur of the crowd and the councilor's voice as he intoned his periods.

"Persist!" he was saying. "Perservere! Follow neither the beaten tracks of routine nor the rash counsels of reckless empiricism. Apply yourselves above all to the improvement of the soil, to rich fertilizers, to the development of fine breeds—equine, bovine, ovine and porcine. May this exhibition be for you a peaceful arena where the winner, as he leaves, will stretch out his hand to the loser and fraternize with him, wishing him better luck another time! And you, venerable servants, humblest members of the household, whose painful labors have by no government up until today been given the slightest consideration: present yourselves now, and receive the reward of your silent heroism! And rest assured that the state henceforth has its eyes upon you, that it encourages you, that it protects you, that it will honor your just demands, and lighten, to the best of its ability, the burden of your painful sacrifices!"

Monsieur Lieuvain sat down.

Monsieur Derozerays stood up, and began another speech. His was perhaps not quite so flowery as the councilor's; but it had the advantage of being characterized by a more positive style—by a more specialized knowledge, that is, and more pertinent arguments. There was less praise of the government, and more mention of religion and agriculture. He showed the relation between the two and how they had always worked together for the good of civilization. Rodolphe was talking to Madame Bovary about dreams, forebodings, magnetism. Going back to the cradle of human society, the orator depicted the savage ages when men lived off acorns in the depths of the forest. Then they had cast off their animal skins, garbed themselves in cloth, dug the ground and planted the vine. Was this an advance? Didn't this discovery entail more disadvantages than benefits? That was the problem Monsieur Derozerays set himself. From magnetism Rodolphe gradually moved on to affinities; and as the chairman cited Cincinnatus and his plough, Diocletian planting his cabbages[9] and the Chinese emperors celebrating the New Year by sowing seed, the young man was explaining to the young woman that these irresistible attractions had their roots in some earlier existence.

"Take us, for example," he said. "Why should we have met? How did it happen? It can only be that something in our particular inclinations made us come closer and closer across the distance that separated us, the way two rivers flow together."

He took her hand, and this time she did not withdraw it.

"First prize for all-round farming!" cried the chairman.

"Just this morning, for example, when I came to your house . . ."

"To Monsieur Bizet, of Quincampoix."

"Did I have any idea that I'd be coming with you to the show?"

"Seventy francs!"

"A hundred times I was on the point of leaving, and yet I followed you and stayed with you . . ."

"For the best manures."

" . . . as I'd stay with you tonight, tomorrow, every day, all my life!"

"To Monsieur Caron, of Argueil, a gold medal!"

"Never have I been so utterly charmed by anyone . . ."

"To Monsieur Bain, of Givry-Saint-Martin!"

" . . . so that I'll carry the memory of you with me. . . ."

"For a merino ram . . ."

"Whereas you'll forget me: I'll vanish like a shadow."

"To Monsieur Belot, of Notre-Dame . . ."

"No, though! Tell me it isn't so! Tell me I'll have a place in your thoughts, in your life!"

"Hogs: a tie! To Messieurs Lehérissé and Cullembourg, sixty francs!"

Rodolphe squeezed her hand, and he felt it all warm and trembling in his, like a captive dove that longs to fly away; but then, whether in an effort to free it, or in response to his pressure, she moved her fingers.

"Oh! Thank God! You don't repulse me! How sweet, how kind! I'm yours: you know that now! Let me see you! Let me look at you!"

A gust of wind coming in the windows ruffled the cloth on the table; and down in the square all the tall headdresses of the peasant women rose up like fluttering white butterfly wings.

"Use of oil cakes!" continued the chairman.

He was going faster now.

"Flemish fertilizer . . . flax-raising . . . drainage, long-term leases . . . domestic service!"

Rodolphe had stopped speaking. They were staring at each other. As their desire rose to a peak their dry lips quivered; and, languidly, of their own accord, their fingers intertwined.

"Catherine-Nicaise-Elizabeth Leroux, of Sassetot-la-Guerrière, for fifty-

---

9. Diocletian (A.D. 245–313), Roman emperor from 284 to 305. He resigned in 305 and retired to Salonae (now Split) in Dalmatia, to cultivate his garden. Cincinnatus was a Roman consul (460 B.C.) who was supposedly called to his office while found plowing.

four years of service on the same farm, a silver medal, value twenty-five francs!"

"Where is Catherine Leroux?" repeated the councilor.

There was no sign of her, but there was the sound of whispering voices:
"Go ahead!"

"No!"

"To the left!"

"Don't be scared!"

"Stupid old thing!"

"Is she there or isn't she?" cried Tuvache.

"Yes! Here she is!"

"Then send her up!"

Everyone watched her as she climbed to the platform: a frightened-looking little old woman who seemed to have shriveled inside her shabby clothes. On her feet were heavy wooden clogs, and she wore a long blue apron. Her thin face, framed in a simple coif, was more wrinkled than a withered russet, and out of the sleeves of her red blouse hung her large, gnarled hands. Years of barn dust, washing soda and wool grease had left them so crusted and rough and hard that they looked dirty despite all the clear water they'd been rinsed in; and from long habit of service they hung half open, as though offering their own humble testimony to the hardships they had endured. A kind of monklike rigidity gave a certain dignity to her face, but her pale stare was softened by no hint of sadness or human kindness. Living among animals, she had taken on their muteness and placidity. This was the first time she had ever been in the midst of so great a crowd; and inwardly terrified by the flags and the drums, by the gentlemen in tail coats and by the decoration worn by the councilor, she stood still, uncertain whether to move ahead or to turn and run, comprehending neither the urgings of the crowd nor the smiles of the jury. Thus did half a century of servitude stand before these beaming bourgeois.

"Step forward, venerable Catherine-Nicaise-Elizabeth Leroux!" cried the councilor, who had taken the list of prize winners from the chairman.

Looking at the sheet of paper and at the old woman in turn, he kept urging her forward like a father: "Come right here, come ahead!"

"Are you deaf?" cried Tuvache, jumping up from his chair.

And he proceeded to shout into her ear: "Fifty-four years of service! A silver medal! Twenty-five francs! For you!"

She took the medal and stared at it. Then a beatific smile spread over her face, and as she left the platform those nearby could hear her mumble: "I'll give it to our priest and he'll say some Masses for me."

"Such fanaticism!" hissed the pharmacist, bending toward the notary.

The ceremonies were ended; the crowd dispersed; and now that the speeches had been read everyone resumed his rank and everything reverted to normal. Masters bullied their servants, the servants beat their cows and their sheep, and the cows and the sheep—indolent in their triumph—moved slowly back to their sheds, their horns decked with the green wreaths that were their trophies.

Meanwhile the national guard had gone up to the second floor of the town hall: brioches were impaled on their bayonets, and their drummer bore a basketful of bottles. Madame Bovary took Rodolphe's arm; he escorted her home; they said good-bye at her door; and then he went for a stroll in the meadow until it was time for the banquet.

The feast was long, noisy, clumsily served: the guests were so crowded that they could scarcely move their elbows; and the narrow planks that were used for benches threatened to snap under their weight. They ate enormously, each piling his plate high to get full value for his assessment. Sweat poured off every forehead; and over the table, between the hanging lamps, hovered a whitish vapor, like a river mist on an autumn morning. Rodolphe, his back against the cloth side of the tent, was thinking so much about Emma that he was aware of nothing going on around him. Out on the grass behind him servants were stacking dirty plates; his tablemates spoke to him and he didn't answer; someone kept filling his glass, and his mind was filled with stillness despite the growing noise. He was thinking of the things she had said and of the shape of her lips; her face shone out from the plaques on the shakos as from so many magic mirrors; the folds of her dress hung down the walls; and days of lovemaking stretched endlessly ahead in the vistas of the future.

He saw her again that evening, during the fireworks, but she was with her husband and Madame Homais and the pharmacist. The latter was very worried about stray rockets, and constantly left the others to give Binet a word of advice.

Through overprecaution, the fireworks, which had been delivered in care of Monsieur Tuvache, had been stored in his cellar, with the result that the damp powder could scarcely be got to light; and the culminating number, which was to have depicted a dragon swallowing its own tail, was a complete fiasco. Now and then some pathetic little Roman candle would go off and bring a roar from the gaping crowd—a roar amidst which could be heard the screams of women, fair game for ticklers in the darkness. Emma nestled silently against Charles's shoulder, raising her head to follow the bright trail of the rockets in the black sky. Rodolphe watched her in the glow of the colored lamps.

Gradually these went out, the stars gleamed; then came a few drops of rain, and she tied a scarf over her hair.

Just then the councilor's landau drove out of the hotel yard. The drunken coachman chose that moment to collapse; and high above the hood, between the two lamps, everyone could see the mass of his body swaying right and left with the pitching of the springs.

"There ought to be strong measures taken against drunkenness," said the apothecary. "If I had my way, there'd be a special bulletin board put up on the door of the town hall, and every week there'd be a list posted of all who had intoxicated themselves with alcoholic liquors during that period. Such a thing would be very valuable statistically, a public record that might . . . Excuse me!"

And once again he hurried off toward the captain.

The latter was homeward bound. He was looking forward to rejoining his lathe.

"It might not do any harm," said Homais, "to send one of your men, or go yourself, to . . ."

"Get away and leave me alone," replied the tax collector. "Everything's taken care of."

"You can all stop worrying," the apothecary announced when he was back with his friends. "Monsieur Binet guarantees that all necessary measures have been taken. Not a spark has fallen. The pumps are full. We can safely retire to our beds."

"I can certainly do with some sleep," said Madame Homais, with a vast yawn. "Never mind—we had a wonderfully beautiful day for the show."

Rodolphe echoed her words in a low voice, his eyes soft: "Yes, it was: wonderfully beautiful."

They exchanged good-byes and went their respective ways.

Two days later, in the *Fanal de Rouen,* there was a great article about the Agricultural Show. Homais had written it in a burst of inspiration the very next day.

"Why these festoons, these flowers, these garlands? Whither was it bound, this crowd rushing like the billows of a raging sea under a torrential tropic sun that poured its torrid rays upon our fertile meadows?"

Then he went on to speak of the condition of the peasants. The government was doing something, certainly, but not enough. "Be bold!" he cried, addressing the administration. "A thousand reforms are indispensable: let us accomplish them." Then, describing the arrival of the councilor, he didn't forget "the warlike air of our militia," or "our sprightliest village maidens," or the bald-headed old men, veritable patriarchs, "some of whom, survivors of our immortal phalanxes, felt their hearts throb once again to the manly sound of the drums." His own name came quite early in his listing of the members of the jury, and he even reminded his readers in a footnote that Monsieur Homais, the pharmacist, had sent a monograph concerning cider to the Agricultural Society. When he came to the distribution of the prizes, he depicted the joy of the winners in dithyrambic terms. Father embraced son, brother embraced brother, husband embraced wife. More than one worthy rustic proudly displayed his humble medal to the assemblage; and, returning home to his helpmeet, doubtless wept tears of joy as he hung it on the modest wall of his cot.

"About six o'clock the leading participants in the festivities forgathered at a banquet in the pasture belonging to Monsieur Liégeard. The utmost cordiality reigned throughout. A number of toasts were proposed. By Monsieur Lieuvain: 'To the king!' By Monsieur Tuvache: 'To the prefect!' By Monsieur Derozerays: 'To agriculture!' By Monsieur Homais: 'To those twin sisters, industry and the fine arts!' By Monsieur Leplichey: 'To progress!' After nightfall a brilliant display of fireworks all at once illumined the heavens. It was a veritable kaleidoscope, a true stageset for an opera, and for a moment our modest village imagined itself transported into the midst of an Arabian Nights dream.

"We may mention that no untoward incidents arose to disturb this family gathering."

And he added:

"Only the clergy was conspicuous by its absence. Doubtless a totally different idea of progress obtains in the sacristies. Suit yourselves, *messieurs de Loyola!*"[1]

---

1. Ignatius of Loyola (1491–1556), a Spaniard, founded the order of the Jesuits in 1534. The Jesuits were expelled from France in 1762.

IX

Six weeks went by without further visit from Rodolphe. Then one evening he came.

The day after the show he had admonished himself: "I mustn't go back right away. That would be a mistake." And at the end of the week he had left for a hunting trip.

After his hunting was over he thought he had waited too long. But then: "If she loved me from the first, she must be impatient to see me again," he reasoned. "And this means she must love me all the more by now. So—back to the attack!"

And when he saw Emma turn pale as he entered the parlor he knew he was right.

She was alone. Daylight was fading. The muslin sash curtains deepened the twilight; and the gilt barometer had just caught a ray of sun and was blazing in the mirror between the lacy edges of the coral.

Rodolphe remained standing, and Emma scarcely replied to his first conventionally polite phrases.

"I've been having all kinds of things happen," he said. "I was ill."

"Anything serious?" she cried.

"Well, not really," he said, sitting beside her on a stool. "It was just that I didn't want to come here again."

"Why?"

"Can't you guess?"

He stared at her—this time so intently that she blushed and lowered her head.

"Emma . . ." he said.

"Monsieur!" she exclaimed, drawing away a little.

"Ah, you can see for yourself," he said, in a resigned voice, "that I was right not to want to come here again. Your name—my heart's full of it—I spoke it without meaning to, and you stopped me. 'Madame Bovary'! Everyone calls you that, and it's not your name at all. It's somebody else's. Somebody else's," he said a second time; and he buried his face in his hands. "I think of you every minute! The thought of you drives me crazy! Forgive me—I won't stay with you. I'll go away—far away—so far that you'll never hear of me again. But today . . . I don't know what power it was that made me come. We can't fight against fate. There's no resisting when an angel smiles. Once something lovely and charming and adorable has wound itself around your heart. . . ."

It was the first time that Emma had had such things said to her; and her pride, like someone relaxing in a steam bath, stretched luxuriously in the warmth of his words.

"No," he continued. "I didn't come, these past few weeks. I haven't seen you. But everything close to you I've looked at and looked at. At night—night after night—I got up and came here and stared at your house—the roof shining in the moonlight, the trees in the garden swaying at your window, and a little lamp, just a gleam, shining through the windowpanes in the dark. Ah! You little knew that a poor wretch was standing there, so near you and yet so far. . . ."

She turned to him with a sob. "How kind you are . . . !"

"I'm not kind! I love you, that's all! You must know it. Tell me you do: one word! Just one word!"

And Rodolphe was sliding imperceptibly from the stool to his knees when there was a sound of sabots in the kitchen and he saw that the door of the room was ajar.

"You'd be doing me a favor," he said, resuming his position on the stool, "if you'd gratify a whim I have."

The whim was to be taken through her house: he wanted to see it. Madame Bovary saw nothing out of the way in the request, and they were both just rising to their feet when Charles appeared.

"*Bonjour, docteur,*" Rodolphe greeted him.

Flattered to be so addressed, the *officier de santé* was profusely obsequious, and Rodolphe profited from those few moments to regain some of his composure.

"Madame was talking to me about her health," he began, "and . . ."

Charles interrupted him. He was very worried indeed; his wife was having difficulty breathing again. Rodolphe asked whether horseback riding might not be good for her.

"Certainly it would! Just the thing! An excellent suggestion, darling! You ought to follow it."

She pointed out that she had no horse; Monsieur Rodolphe offered her one of his; she declined; he did not insist; and finally, to explain the purpose of his visit, he told Charles that his teamster, the man who had been bled, was still having dizzy spells.

"I'll stop by and see him," said Bovary.

"No, no, I'll send him to you. We'll come here; that will be easier for you."

"Very good; thank you."

As soon as they were alone:

"Why don't you accept Monsieur Boulanger's suggestions? He's being so gracious."

She pouted, made one excuse after another, and finally said that "it might look strange."

"A lot I care about that!" said Charles, turning on his heel. "Health comes first! You're wrong!"

"But how do you expect me to ride a horse if I have no habit?"

"You must order one," he replied.

It was the riding habit that decided her.

When it was ready, Charles wrote to Monsieur Boulanger that his wife was at his disposition, and that they thanked him in advance for his kindness.

The next day at noon Rodolphe presented himself at Charles's door with two riding horses. One of them had pink pompons decorating its ears and bore a lady's buckskin saddle.

Rodolphe had put on a pair of high soft boots, telling himself that she had probably never seen anything like them; and Emma was indeed charmed with his appearance when he came up to the landing in his velvet frock coat and white tricot riding breeches. She was ready and waiting for him.

Justin ran out of the pharmacy to take a look at her, and the apothecary himself left his work for a few moments. He gave Monsieur Boulanger several bits of advice:

"Accidents happen so quickly! Take care! Your horses may be more spirited than you know!"

She heard a sound above her head: it was Félicité drumming on the windowpanes to amuse little Berthe. The child blew her a kiss, and Emma made a sign with her riding crop in answer.

"Have a good ride!" cried Monsieur Homais. "Be careful! That's the main thing! Careful!"

And he waved his newspaper after them as he watched them ride away.

As soon as it felt soft ground, Emma's horse broke into a gallop. Rodolphe galloped at her side. Now and again they exchanged a word. With her head slightly lowered, her hand raised and her right arm outstretched, she let herself go to the rhythmic rocking motion.

At the foot of the hill Rodolphe gave his horse its head: both horses leapt forward as one, and then at the top they as suddenly stopped, and Emma's large blue veil settled and hung still.

It was early October. There was a mist over the countryside. Wisps of vapor lay along the horizon, following the contours of the hills, and elsewhere they were drifting and rising and evaporating. Now and then as the clouds shifted, a ray of sun would light up the roofs of Yonville in the distance, with its riverside gardens, its yards and its church steeple. Emma half closed her eyes trying to pick out her house, and never had the wretched village she lived in looked so very small. From the height on which they were standing the whole valley was like an immense pale lake, dissolving into thin air: clumps of trees stood out here and there like dark rocks, and the tall lines of poplars piercing the fog were like its leafy banks, swaying in the wind.

To one side, over the turf between the firs, the light was dim and the air mild. The reddish earth, the color of snuff, deadened the sound of the hoofs; and the horses kicked fir cones before them as they walked.

For a time Rodolphe and Emma continued to follow the edge of the wood. Now and then she turned her head away to avoid his eyes, and at such moments she saw only the regularly spaced trunks of the firs, almost dizzying in their unbroken succession. The horses were blowing, and the leather creaked in the saddles.

Then they turned into the forest, and at that moment the sun came out.

"God's watching over us," said Rodolphe.

"You think so?" she said.

"Let's go on!" he said.

He clicked his tongue, and both horses broke into a trot.

Tall ferns growing along the path kept catching in Emma's stirrup, and Rodolphe bent over as he rode and pulled them out. At other times he came close to her to push aside overhanging branches, and she felt his knee brush against her leg. Now the sky was blue, and the leaves were still. There were clearings full of heather in bloom, and the sheets of purple alternated with the multicolored tangle of the trees, gray, fawn and gold. Often a faint rustling and fluttering of wings would come from under the bushes; or there would be the cry, at once raucous and sweet, of crows flying off among the oaks.

They dismounted. Rodolphe tethered the horses. She walked ahead of him on the moss between the cart tracks.

But the long skirt of her habit impeded her, even though she held it up by the end; and Rodolphe, walking behind her, kept staring at her sheer white stocking that showed between the black broadcloth and the black shoe as though it were a bit of her naked flesh.

She stopped.

"I'm tired," she said.

"Just a little further," he said. "Come along, try."

Then a hundred yards further on she stopped again; and the veil that slanted down from her man's hat to below her waist covered her face with a translucent blue film, as though she were swimming under limpid water.

"Where are we going?"

He didn't answer. She was breathing quickly. Rodolphe looked this way and that, biting his mustache.

They came to a larger open space, one that had recently been cleared of saplings. They sat down on a log, and Rodolphe spoke to her of his love.

He was careful not to frighten her, at first, by saying anything overbold: he was calm, serious, melancholy.

She listened to him with lowered head, stirring the wood chips on the ground with the toe of her shoe.

But when he said, "Our lives are bound up together now, aren't they?" she answered, "No—you know they can't be."

She rose to leave. He grasped her wrist. She stood still and gave him a long look, her eyes moist and tender. Then she said hastily:

"Please—let's not talk about it any more. Where are the horses? Let's go back."

A movement of angry displeasure escaped him.

"Where are the horses?" she asked again. "Where are the horses?"

Then, smiling a strange smile, staring fixedly, his teeth clenched, he advanced toward her with arms outstretched. She drew back trembling.

"You're frightening me!" she stammered. "What are you doing? Take me back!"

His expression changed. "Since you insist," he said.

And abruptly he was once more considerate, tender, timid. She took his arm and they turned back.

"What was the matter?" he asked. "What came over you? I don't understand. You must have some mistaken idea. I have you in my heart like a Madonna on a pedestal—in an exalted place, secure, immaculate. But I need you if I'm to go on living! I need your eyes, your voice, your thoughts. I beseech you: be my friend, my sister, my angel!"

And he reached out his arm and put it around her waist. She made a half-hearted effort to free herself, but he kept it there, holding her as they walked.

Now they were so close to the horses that they heard them munching leaves.

"Just a little longer," begged Rodolphe. "Let's not go yet. Wait."

He drew her further on, to the edge of a little pond whose surface was green with duck weed and where faded water lilies lay still among the rushes. At the sound of their steps in the grass, frogs leaped to hiding.

"It's wrong of me," she said. "Wrong. I must be out of my mind to listen to you."

"Why? Emma! Emma!"

"Oh! Rodolphe!" The syllables came out slowly, and she pressed against his shoulder.

The broadcloth of her habit clung to the velvet of his coat. She leaned back her head, her white throat swelled in a sigh, and, her resistance gone, weeping, hiding her face, with a long shudder she gave herself to him.

Evening shadows were falling, and the level rays of the sun streamed through the branches and dazzled her eyes. Here and there, all about her, among the leaves and on the ground, were shimmering patches of light, as though hummingbirds winging by had scattered their feathers. All was silent; a soft sweetness seemed to be seeping from the trees; she felt her heart beating again, and her blood flowing in her flesh like a river of milk. Then from far off, beyond the woods in distant hills, she heard a vague, long, drawn-out cry—a sound that lingered; and she listened silently as it mingled like a strain of music with the last vibrations of her quivering nerves. Rodolphe, a cigar between his teeth, was mending a broken bridle with his penknife.

They returned to Yonville by the same route. In the mud they saw, side by side, the hoof prints left there by their own two horses; they saw the same bushes, the same stones in the grass. Nothing around them had changed: and yet to her something had happened that was more momentous than if mountains had moved. Rodolphe reached over, now and then, and raised her hand to his lips.

She was charming on horseback—erect and slender, her knee bent against the animal's mane, her face flushed a little by the air in the red glow of evening.

As she entered the village she made her horse prance on the stone pavement, and people stared at her from their windows.

Her husband, at dinner, found that she looked well; but she seemed not to hear him when he asked about her ride; and she leaned her elbow on the table beside her plate, between the two lighted candles.

"Emma!" he said.

"What?"

"Well, I called on Monsieur Alexandre this afternoon. He bought a filly a few years ago and she's still in fine shape, just a little broken in the knees; I'm sure I could get her for a hundred écus. . . ."

And he went on:

"I thought you might like to have her, so I reserved her. . . . I bought her. . . . Did I do right? Tell me."

She nodded her head in assent. Then, a quarter of an hour later:

"Are you going out tonight?" she asked.

"Yes, why?"

"Oh, nothing—nothing, dear."

And as soon as she was rid of Charles she went upstairs and shut herself in her room.

At first it was as though she were in a daze: she saw the trees, the paths, the ditches, Rodolphe; once again she felt his arms tighten around her as the leaves were all a-tremble and the reeds whistled in the wind.

Then she caught sight of herself in the mirror, and was amazed by the way she looked. Never had her eyes been so enormous, so dark, so deep: her whole being was transfigured by some subtle emanation.

"I have a lover! I have a lover!" she kept repeating to herself, reveling in the thought as though she were beginning a second puberty. At last she was going to know the joys of love, the fever of the happiness she had despaired of. She was entering a marvelous realm where all would be passion, ecstasy, rapture: she was in the midst of an endless blue expanse, scaling the glittering heights of passion; everyday life had receded, and lay far below, in the shadows between those peaks.

She remembered the heroines of novels she had read, and the lyrical legion of those adulterous women began to sing in her memory with sisterly voices that enchanted her. Now she saw herself as one of those *amoureuses* whom she had so envied: she was becoming, in reality, one of that gallery of fictional figures; the long dream of her youth was coming true. She was full of a delicious sense of vengeance. How she had suffered! But now her hour of triumph had come; and love, so long repressed, was gushing forth in joyful effervescence. She savored it without remorse, without anxiety, without distress.

The next day brought a new delight. They exchanged vows. She told him her sorrows. Rodolphe interrupted her with kisses; and she begged him, gazing at him with half-shut eyes, to say her name again and tell her once more that he loved her. They were in the forest, like the day before, this time in a hut used by sabot-makers. The walls were of straw, and the roof was so low that they could not stand erect. They sat side by side on a bed of dry leaves.

From that day on they wrote each other regularly every night. Emma took her letter out into the garden and slipped it into a crack in the terrace wall beside the river; Rodolphe came, took it, and left one for her—one that was always, she complained, too short.

One morning when Charles had gone out before sunrise she was seized with a longing to see Rodolphe at once. She could go quickly to La Huchette, stay there an hour, and be back in Yonville before anyone was up. The thought made her pant with desire, and soon she was halfway across the meadow, walking fast and not looking back.

Day was just breaking. From far off Emma recognized her lover's farm, with its two swallow-tailed weathervanes silhouetted in black against the pale twilight.

Beyond the farmyard was a building that could only be the château. She entered it as though the walls opened of themselves at her approach. A long straight staircase led to an upper hall. Emma turned the latch of a door, and there at the far end of a room she saw a man asleep. It was Rodolphe. She uttered a cry.

"It's you!" he cried. "You, here! How did you come? Ah! Your dress is wet!"

"I love you!" was her answer; and she flung her arms around his neck.

She had dared and won; and from then on, each time that Charles went out early she quickly dressed and stole down the river stairs.

If the cow plank had been raised she had to follow the garden walls that bordered the stream; the bank was slippery, and to keep from falling she would clutch at tufts of faded wallflowers. Then she would strike out across the plowed fields, sinking in, stumbling, her light shoes getting continually stuck in the soft soil. The scarf she had tied over her head fluttered in the wind as she crossed the meadows; she was afraid of the oxen, and would begin to run; and she would arrive breathless, rosy cheeked, everything about her smelling of sap and verdure and fresh air. Rodolphe would still be asleep. She was like a spring morning entering his room.

The yellow curtains masking the windows let through a soft, dull golden light. Emma would grope her way, squinting, dewdrops clinging to her hair like a halo of topazes around her face. And Rodolphe would laugh and draw her to him and strain her to his heart.

Afterwards she would explore the room, opening drawers, combing her hair with his comb, looking at herself in his shaving mirror. Often she took the stem of his pipe in her teeth—a large pipe that he kept on his night table, beside the lemons and lumps of sugar that were there with his water jug.

It always took them a good quarter of an hour to say good-bye. Emma invariably wept: she wished that she never had to leave him. Some irresistible force kept driving her time and again to his side, until one day when she arrived unexpectedly he frowned as though displeased.

"What's wrong?" she cried. "Are you ill? Tell me!"

After some urging, he declared gravely that her visits were becoming foolhardy and that she was risking her reputation.

X

As time went on she came to share Rodolphe's fears. Love had intoxicated her at first, and she had had no thought beyond it. But now that life was inconceivable without it she was terrified lest she be deprived of any portion of this love, or even that it be in any way interfered with. Each time she returned from one of her visits she cast uneasy glances about her, peering at every figure moving on the horizon, at every dormer in the village from which she might be seen. Her ears picked up the sound of every footstep, every voice, every plow; and she would stand still, paler and more trembling than the leaves of the swaying poplars overhead.

One morning on her way back she suddenly thought she saw a rifle pointing at her. It was slanting out over the edge of a small barrel half hidden in the grass beside a ditch. She felt faint with fright, but continued to walk ahead, and a man emerged from the barrel like a jack-in-the-box. He wore gaiters buckled up to his knees, and his cap was pulled down over his eyes; his lips were trembling with cold and his nose was red. It was Captain Binet, out after wild duck.

"You should have called!" he cried. "When you see a gun you must always give warning."

That reproach was actually the tax collector's attempt to cover up the fright that Emma had given *him*. There was a police ordinance prohibiting duck shooting except from boats, and for all his respect for the law, Monsieur Binet was in the process of committing a violation. He had been expecting the game warden to appear any minute. But fear had added spice to his enjoyment, and in the solitude of his barrel he had been congratulating himself on his luck and his deviltry.

At the sight of Emma he felt relieved of a great weight, and he opened conversation:

"Chilly, isn't it! Really nippy!"

Emma made no answer.

"You're certainly out bright and early," he went on.

"Yes," she stammered. "I've been to see my baby at the nurse's."

"Ah, I see! As for me, I've been right here where I am now ever since daybreak, but it's such dirty weather that unless you have the bird at the very end of your gun . . ."

"Good-bye, Monsieur Binet," she interrupted, turning away.

"Good-bye, Madame," he answered dryly.

And he went back into his barrel.

Emma regretted having taken such brusque leave of the tax collector. Whatever surmises he made would certainly be to her discredit. What she had said about the wet nurse was the worst possible story she could have invented: everyone in Yonville knew perfectly well that little Berthe had been back with her parents for a year. Besides, no one lived out in that direction; that particular path led only to La Huchette. Binet must certainly have guessed where she was coming from: he wouldn't keep his mouth shut, either; he would gossip, unquestionably. All day she racked her brains, trying to dream up all possible lies; and she brooded incessantly about that fool with his game bag.

After dinner Charles, seeing that she looked worried about something, had the idea of distracting her from whatever it was by taking her to call on the pharmacist; and the first person she saw in the pharmacy was, once again, the tax collector! He was standing at the counter in the glow of the red jar, saying, "Give me a half-ounce of vitriol."

"Justin," called the pharmacist, "bring the sulphuric acid."

Then, to Emma, who was about to go up to Madame Homais' quarters:

"No, don't bother to climb the stairs: she'll be coming down directly. Warm yourself at the stove while you wait. Excuse me . . . *Bonjour, docteur.*" (The pharmacist greatly enjoyed uttering the word *docteur,* as though by applying it to someone else he caused some of the glory it held for him to be reflected on himself.) "But be careful not to knock over the mortars," he called to Justin. "No, no! Go get some of the chairs from the little room! You know perfectly well we never move the parlor armchairs."

And Homais was just bustling out from behind the counter to put his armchair back where it belonged when Binet asked him for a half-ounce of sugar acid.

"Sugar acid?" said the pharmacist scornfully. "I don't know what that is. I never heard of it. You want oxalic acid, perhaps? Oxalic is what you mean, isn't it?"

Binet explained that he needed a corrosive: he wanted to make some metal polish to clean the rust off parts of his hunting gear. Emma stood rigid.

"Yes, the weather is certainly unpropitious," said the pharmacist, "what with all this dampness."

"Still," said the tax collector slyly, "there are people who don't mind it."

She was choking.

"Now give me . . ."

"He'll never go!" she thought.

" . . . a half-ounce of rosin and turpentine, four ounces of beeswax, and an ounce and a half of boneblack to clean the patent leather on my outfit."

As the apothecary began cutting the wax, Madame Homais appeared with Irma in her arms, Napoléon beside her and Athalie bringing up the rear. She sat down on the plush-covered bench by the window, while the boy took a stool and his elder sister kept close to the jujube jar, near her dear papa. The latter was pouring things into funnels, corking bottles, gluing labels and wrapping parcels. Everyone watched him in silence: the only sound was an occasional clink of weights in the scales, and a few low-voiced words of advice from the pharmacist to his apprentice.

"How is your little girl?" Madame Homais suddenly asked.

"Quiet!" cried her husband, who was jotting figures on a scratch-pad.

"Why didn't you bring her?" she went on, in an undertone.

"Sh! Sh!" said Emma, pointing to the apothecary.

But Binet, absorbed in checking the pharmacist's arithmetic, seemed to have heard nothing. Then at last he left. Emma gave a deep sigh of relief.

"How heavily you're breathing!" said Madame Homais.

"Don't you find it rather warm?" she answered.

The next day, therefore, Emma and Rodolphe discussed the best way of arranging their meetings. Emma was for bribing her maid with a present, but it would be better if they could find some other, safer place in Yonville. Rodolphe promised to look for one.

From then on, three or four times a week throughout the winter, he came to the garden in the dark of the night. Emma had removed the key from the gate, letting Charles think it was lost.

To announce himself, Rodolphe threw a handful of gravel against the shutters. She always started up; but sometimes she had to wait, for Charles loved to chat beside the fire, and went on and on. She would grow wild with impatience: if she could have accomplished it with a look, she would have flung him out a window. Finally she would begin to get ready for bed, and then she would take up a book and sit quietly reading, as though absorbed. Charles, in bed by this time, would call her.

"Come, Emma," he would say. "It's time."

"Yes, I'm coming," she would answer.

But the candles shone in his eyes, and he would turn to the wall and fall asleep. Then she slipped out, holding her breath, smiling, palpitating, half undressed.

Rodolphe would enfold her in the large full cape he wore and, with his arm around her waist, lead her without a word to the foot of the garden.

It was in the arbor that they spent their time together, on the same dilapidated rustic bench from which Léon used to stare at her so amorously on summer evenings. She scarcely thought of him now.

The stars glittered through the bare branches of the jasmine. Behind them they heard the flowing of the river, and now and again the crackle of dry reeds on the bank. Here and there in the darkness loomed patches of deeper shadow; and sometimes these would suddenly seem to shudder, rear up and then curve downward, like huge black waves threatening to engulf them. In the cold of the night they clasped each other the more tightly, the sighs that came from their lips seemed deeper, their half-seen eyes looked larger; and amidst the silence their soft-spoken words had a crystalline ring that echoed and reechoed in their hearts.

If the night was rainy they sought shelter in the consulting room, between the shed and the stable. She would light a kitchen lamp that she kept hidden behind the books. Rodolphe made himself at home here, as though the place belonged to him. The sight of the bookcase and the desk—indeed the whole room—aroused his hilarity: he couldn't keep from joking about Charles in a way that made Emma uncomfortable. She would have liked him to be more serious—or even more dramatic sometimes, like the night she thought she heard the sound of approaching footsteps in the lane.

"Someone's coming," she whispered.

He blew out the light.

"Have you got your pistols?"

"What for?"

"Why—to defend yourself," said Emma.

"You mean against your husband? That poor . . . ?"

And Rodolphe ended his sentence with a gesture that meant that he could annihilate Charles with a flick of his finger.

This display of fearlessness dazzled her, even though she sensed in it a crudity and bland vulgarity that shocked her.

Rodolphe thought a good deal about that episode of the pistols. If she had spoken in earnest, it was absurd of her, he thought, really an odious thing, for he had no cause to hate poor Charles. He was by no means "devoured by jealousy," as the saying went: and indeed, in this connection, Emma had made him a tremendous vow that he, for his part, thought in rather poor taste.

Besides, she was becoming frightfully sentimental. They had had to exchange miniatures and cut handfuls of each other's hair; and now she was asking for a ring—a real wedding band, as a sign of eternal union. She often talked to him about the "bells of evening," or the "voices of nature"; and then she would go on about her mother and his. Rodolphe's mother had been dead for twenty years, but Emma kept consoling him in the kind of affected language one uses to a bereaved child; and sometimes she would even look at the moon and say to him, "Somewhere up there I'm sure they're both looking down at us and approving of our love."

But she was so pretty! He couldn't remember ever having had so unspoiled a mistress. The purity of her love was something entirely new to him. It was a change from his usual loose habits, and it both flattered his pride and inflamed his senses. Emma's continual raptures, which his bourgeois common sense despised, seemed to him in his heart of hearts charming, since it was he who inspired them.

As time went on he stopped making any effort, secure in the knowledge that he was loved; and imperceptibly his manner changed. No longer did he speak to her, as before, in words so sweet that they made her weep; nor were there any more of those fervid embraces that frenzied her. Their great love, in which she lived completely immersed, seemed to be ebbing away, like the water of a river that was sinking into its own bed; and she saw the mud at the bottom. She refused to believe it; she redoubled her caresses; and Rodolphe hid his indifference less and less.

She didn't know whether she regretted having yielded to him or whether she didn't rather long to love him more dearly. Her humiliating feeling of weakness was turning into resentment: but this melted away in the heat of his embraces. It was not an attachment; it was a kind of permanent seduction. She was in his bondage. It almost frightened her.

Nevertheless, from the outside everything looked more serene than ever, Rodolphe having succeeded in conducting the affair as he pleased; and at the end of six months, when spring came, they were like a married couple peacefully tending to a domestic flame.

It was the time of the year when Monsieur Rouault always sent his turkey, in commemoration of his mended leg. As usual, the present was accompanied by a letter. Emma cut the string tying it to the basket, and read the following:

Dear Children:

I hope these lines find you well and that this one will be up to the others: it seems to me a little tenderer, if I may say so, and meatier. But next time I'll send you a cock for a change, unless you'd rather stick to gobblers, and please send me back the basket along with the last two. I had an accident with the cart shed, one night a heavy wind blew the roof off into the trees. Crops haven't been too good either. I can't tell when I'll come to see you. It's so hard for me to leave the place now that I'm alone.

Here there was a space between the lines, as though the old man had put down his pen to think a while.

As for me, I'm all right, except for a cold I caught the other day at the fair in Yvetot, where I went to hire a shepherd, having got rid of the one I had because he was too particular about his food. All these good-for-nothings give you more trouble than they're worth. This one was disrespectful besides.

I heard from a peddler who stopped in your town to have a tooth drawn that Bovary keeps busy. It doesn't surprise me, and he showed me his tooth; we took a cup of coffee together. I asked if he'd seen you, Emma, he said no, but he'd seen two horses in the stable from which I assume that business is prospering. I'm glad of it, dear children, may the good Lord send you every possible happiness.

It grieves me that I've never seen my beloved granddaughter Berthe Bovary. I've planted a tree of September plums for her under the window of your room and I won't let anybody touch it except to make some jam for her later that I'll keep in the cupboard for her when she comes.

Good-bye, dear children. I kiss you on both cheeks, all three of you.

I am, with all good wishes,
Your loving father,
Théodore Rouault

She sat for a few minutes with the sheet of coarse paper in her hand. The letter was thick with spelling mistakes, and Emma brooded on the affectionate thought that cackled through them like a hen half hidden in a thorn hedge. Her father had dried his writing with ash from the fireplace, for a bit of gray dust drifted out of the letter onto her dress, and she could almost see the old man bending down toward the hearth to take up the tongs. How long it was since she had sat there beside him, on the fireseat, burning the end of a stick in the flame of the crackling furze! She remembered summer evenings, full of sunshine. The foals would whinny when anyone came near, and gallop and gallop to their hearts' content. There had been a beehive under her window, and sometimes the bees, wheeling in the light, would strike against the panes like bouncing golden balls. How happy she had been in those days! How free! How full of hope! How rich in illusions! There were no illusions left now! She had had to part with some each time she had ventured on a new path, in each of her successive conditions—as virgin, as wife, as mistress; all along the course of her life she had been losing them, like a traveler leaving a bit of his fortune in every inn along the road.

But what was making her so unhappy? Where was the extraordinary disaster that had wrought havoc with her life? And she lifted her head and looked about her, as though trying to discover the cause of her suffering.

An April sunbeam was dancing on the china in the whatnot; the fire was burning; she felt the rug soft beneath her slippers; the day was cloudless, the air mild, and she could hear her child shouting with laughter.

The little girl was rolling on the lawn, in the cut grass that Lestiboudois was raking. She was lying on her stomach on a pile that he had got together; Félicité was holding her by the skirt; the gardener was working nearby, and whenever he came close she leaned over toward him, waving her arms in the air.

"Bring her in to me!" her mother cried. And she rushed over and kissed her. "How I love you, darling! How I love you!"

Then, noticing that the tips of the child's ears were a little dirty, she quickly rang for hot water; and she washed her, changed her underclothes, stockings, and shoes, asked a thousand questions about how she felt, as though she were just back from a trip, and finally, giving her more and more kisses, and weeping a little, she handed her back to the maid, who stood gaping at this overflow of affection.

That night Rodolphe found her more reserved than usual.

"It will pass," he thought. "It's some whim."

And on three successive evenings he didn't appear for their rendezvous. When he finally came she was cold, almost disdainful.

"Ah! You'll get nowhere playing that game . . . !" And he pretended not to notice her melancholy sighs or the handkerchief she kept bringing out.

Then Emma's repentance knew no bounds.

She even wondered why she detested Charles, and whether it mightn't be better to try to love him. But there was so little about him to which her resurgent feeling could attach itself that she was at a loss as to how to put her noble resolution into effect. And then one day the apothecary provided the desired opportunity.

XI

Homais had lately read an article extolling a new method of curing club-foot; and since he was on the side of progress he conceived the patriotic idea that Yonville, to keep abreast of the times, should have its own operation for talipes, as he learnedly called the deformity.

"After all," he said to Emma, "what's the risk? Look." And he enumerated on his fingers the advantages that would accrue from the attempt. "Almost sure success, relief and improved appearance for the patient, and for the surgeon a rapid rise to fame. Why shouldn't your husband fix up poor Hippolyte, at the Lion d'Or? The boy would unquestionably talk about his cure to every traveler at the inn, and then"—here Homais lowered his voice and cast a glance about him—"what is there to keep me from sending a little piece about it to the paper? Ah! An article gets around—people talk about it—a thing like that really snowballs. Who can tell? Who can tell?"

He was right: Bovary might very well succeed. Emma had never had any reason to think that he wasn't skillful in his work; and what satisfaction *she* would derive from persuading him to take a step that would increase his fame and fortune! Something more solid than love to lean on would be only too welcome.

Egged on by her and by the apothecary, Charles consented. He sent to

Rouen for Doctor Duval's treatise; and every night, his head in his hands, he buried himself in its pages.

He studied talipes in its various forms—equinus, varus and valgus: in other words, the varying malformations of the foot downwards, inwards, or outwards, sometimes scientifically called *strephocatopodia, strephendopodia* and *strephexopodia;* and he studied *strephypopodia* and *strephanopodia*— downward or upward torsion. And meanwhile Monsieur Homais tried to persuade the stable boy to agree to be operated on. He used every possible argument.

"You'll scarcely feel it—there'll be the very slightest pain if any. It's just a prick, like the tiniest bloodletting. Not nearly as bad as cutting out certain kinds of corns."

Hippolyte rolled his eyes stupidly as he thought it over.

"Besides," the pharmacist went on, "it's not for my sake that I'm urging you, but for yours—out of pure humanity. I'd like to see you rid of that ugly limp, my boy, and that swaying in the lumbar region that must interfere seriously with your work, whatever you say."

Then Homais painted a picture of how much more lively and nimble he would feel, and even intimated that he'd be much more successful with women. The stable boy grinned sheepishly at that. Then Homais played on his vanity:

"Are you a man or aren't you? Think what it would have been like if you'd had to serve in the army and go into combat! Ah, Hippolyte!"

And Homais moved off, declaring that such stubbornness, such blindness in refusing the benefits of science were beyond his understanding.

In the end the poor wretch yielded, unable to stand up against what was a veritable conspiracy. Binet, who never meddled in other people's affairs, Madame Lefrançois, Artémise, the neighbors, even the mayor, Monsieur Tuvache—everybody urged him, lectured him, shamed him; but what finally decided him was that it wouldn't cost him anything. Bovary even offered to supply the apparatus that would be used after the operation. Emma had thought up that bit of generosity, and Charles had agreed, inwardly marveling at what an angel his wife was.

Guided by the pharmacist's advice, he finally succeeded on the third try in having the cabinetmaker and the locksmith construct a sort of box weighing about eight pounds—a complicated mass of iron, wood, tin, leather, screws and nuts.

Meanwhile, in order to know which of Hippolyte's tendons had to be cut, he first had to find out what variety of clubfoot his was.

The foot made almost a straight line with the leg, and at the same time was twisted inward, so that it was an equinus with certain characteristics of a varus, or else a varus with strong equinus features. But with his equinus— which actually was as wide across as an equine hoof, with rough skin, stringy tendons, oversized toes, and black nails that were like the nails of a horseshoe—the taliped[2] ran about fleet as a deer from morning to night. He was constantly to be seen in the square, hopping about among the carts, thrusting his clubfoot ahead of him. Actually, the affected leg seemed to be stronger than the other. From its long years of service it had taken on moral qualities, as it were—qualities of patience and energy; and whenever Hip-

---

2. A person with clubfoot, or talipes.

polyte was given a particularly heavy task to do, it was that leg that he threw his weight on.

Since it was an equinus, the Achilles tendon would have to be cut, and then later, perhaps, the anterior tibial muscle, to take care of the varus. Charles didn't dare risk two operations at once, and indeed he was trembling already lest he interfere with some important part of the foot he knew nothing about.

Neither Ambroise Paré, applying an immediate ligature to an artery for the first time since Celsus had done it fifteen centuries before; nor Dupuytren cutting open an abscess through a thick layer of the brain; nor Gensoul, when he performed the first removal of an upper maxillary—none of them, certainly, felt such a beating of the heart, such a quivering of the hand, such a tenseness of the mind, as Monsieur Bovary when he approached Hippolyte with his tenotomy knife. On a table nearby, just as in a hospital, lay a pile of lint, waxed thread, and a quantity of bandages—a veritable pyramid of bandages, the apothecary's entire stock. It was Monsieur Homais who had been making these preparations ever since early morning, as much to dazzle the multitude as to inflate his self-importance. Charles pierced the skin: there was a sharp snap. The tendon was cut; the operation was over. Hippolyte couldn't stop marveling: he bent over Bovary's hands and covered them with kisses.

"Don't get excited," said the apothecary. "You'll have plenty of occasion to express your gratitude to your benefactor."

And he went out to announce the result to five or six sensation seekers who were waiting in the yard expecting Hippolyte to make his appearance walking normally. Then Charles strapped his patient into the apparatus and went home, where Emma was anxiously awaiting him at the door. She flung her arms around his neck; they sat down at table; he ate heartily, and even asked for a cup of coffee with his dessert—a bit of intemperance he ordinarily allowed himself only on Sunday when there was company.

Their evening together was charming: they spoke of their future, the improvement they expected in their fortunes, changes they would make in their house. He saw himself a man of renown and riches, adored by his wife; and she felt herself pleasantly revived by this new sensation—this noble, wholesome experience of returning at least some of poor Charles's love. For a moment the thought of Rodolphe crossed her mind; but then her eyes swung back to Charles, and she noticed with surprise that his teeth weren't bad at all.

They were in bed when Monsieur Homais suddenly entered their room: he had brushed aside the cook's attempts to announce him, and was holding a newly written sheet of paper. It was the publicity article he had prepared for the *Fanal de Rouen:* he had brought it for them to read.

"You read it to us," said Bovary.

He began:

" 'Despite the network of prejudices that still extends across part of the face of Europe, our country districts are beginning to see the light. Just this Tuesday our small community of Yonville was the scene of a surgical experiment that was also an act of pure philanthropy. Monsieur Bovary, one of our most distinguished practitioners . . .' "

"That's going too far! Too far!" cried Charles, choked with emotion.

"Not at all! Certainly not! '. . . performed an operation on a clubfoot. . . .'

I didn't use the scientific term—in a newspaper, you know . . . not everybody would understand; the masses have to be . . ."

"You're right," said Bovary. "Go ahead."

"Where was I?" said the pharmacist. "Oh, yes. 'Monsieur Bovary, one of our most distinguished practitioners, performed an operation on a clubfoot. The patient was one Hippolyte Tautain, stable boy for the past twenty-five years at the Lion d'Or hotel, owned by Madame Lefrançois, on the Place d'Armes. The novelty of the enterprise and the interest felt in the patient had attracted such a large throng of our local citizenry that there was a veritable crush outside the establishment. The operation went off like magic, and only a few drops of blood appeared on the skin, as though to announce that the rebellious tendon had finally surrendered to the surgeon's art. The patient, strange though it may seem (we report this fact *de visu*), experienced not the slightest pain. Up to the moment of the present writing, his condition is entirely satisfactory. Everything gives us reason to expect that his convalescence will be rapid. Who knows? At the next village festival we may well see our good friend Hippolyte tripping Bacchic measures amidst a chorus of joyous companions, thus demonstrating to all, by his high spirits and his capers, the completeness of his cure. All honor to our generous men of science! All honor to those tireless benefactors who go without sleep to work for the improvement or the relief of mankind! All honor to them! Now indeed we can proclaim that the blind shall see, the deaf shall hear and the lame shall walk! But what fanaticism promised in times past to the elect, science is now achieving for all men! We shall keep our readers informed concerning the subsequent stages of this remarkable cure.' "

But all that eloquence did not alter the course of events. Five days later Madame Lefrançois rushed into the doctor's house frightened out of her wits, crying: "Help! He's dying! It's driving me mad!"

Charles made a dash for the Lion d'Or; and the pharmacist, catching sight of him as he rushed bareheaded across the square, hurriedly left his pharmacy. He, too, arrived at the hotel breathless, flushed and worried. "What has happened," he inquired of the numerous people climbing the stairs, "to our interesting taliped?"

The taliped was writhing—writhing in frightful convulsions, so severe that the apparatus locked around his leg was beating against the wall, threatening to demolish it.

Taking every precaution not to disturb the position of the leg, Charles and Monsieur Homais removed the box—and a terrible sight met their eyes. The foot was completely formless, so immensely swollen that the skin seemed ready to burst; and the entire surface was covered with black and blue spots caused by the much-vaunted apparatus. Hippolyte had been complaining of pain for some time, but no one had paid any attention; now it was clear that he hadn't entirely imagined it, and he was allowed to keep his foot out of the box for several hours. But hardly had the swelling subsided a little than the two experts decided that the treatment should be resumed; and they screwed the apparatus on more tightly than before, to hasten results. Finally, three days later, when Hippolyte could bear it no longer, they removed the box again and were amazed by what they saw. A livid tumescence now extended up the leg, and a dark liquid was oozing from a number of blood blisters. Things were taking a serious turn. Hippolyte had no courage left; and

Madame Lefrançois moved him into the small room, just off the kitchen, so that he might at least have some distraction.

But the tax collector, who took his dinner there every evening, complained bitterly of such company, so Hippolyte was moved again, this time into the billiard room.

He lay there, groaning under his heavy blankets, pale, unshaven, hollow eyed, turning and twisting his sweaty head on the dirty, fly-covered pillow. Madame Bovary came to see him. She brought him linen for his poultices, comforted him, tried to cheer him. He had no lack of company, especially on market days, when the peasants crowded around him, playing billiards, dueling with the cues, smoking, drinking, singing, shouting.

"How're you getting along?" they would say, giving him a poke in the shoulder. "You don't look too good. But it's your own fault. You should have . . ." And they would give their advice, telling him about people who had all been cured by methods quite different from the one that had been used on him. Then they would add, by way of comfort: "You fuss too much! Why don't you get up, instead of having everybody wait on you? Well, never mind, old boy—you certainly stink!"

And indeed the gangrene was climbing higher and higher. Bovary was sick about it. He kept coming in every hour, every few minutes. Hippolyte would look at him with terror-filled eyes, and sob and stammer:

"When will I be cured? Help me! Help me! Oh, God, it's terrible!"

And each time the doctor could only go away again, advising him to eat lightly.

"Don't listen to him," Madame Lefrançois would say, when Bovary had left. "They've made you suffer enough already. You'll lose still more of your strength. Here, swallow this!"

And she would give him some tasty soup, or a slice from a leg of mutton, or a bit of bacon, and now and again a little glass of brandy that he hardly dared drink.

The abbé Bournisien, learning that he was getting worse, came to the hotel and asked to see him. He began by condoling with him on his suffering—declaring, however, that he should rejoice in it, since it was the Lord's will, and lose no time taking advantage of this occasion to become reconciled with heaven.

"You've been a little neglectful of your religious duties," he pointed out in a paternal tone. "I've seldom seen you at Mass. How many years is it since you've been to Communion? It's understandable that your work and other distractions should have made you careless about your eternal salvation. But now is the time to think about it. Don't give way to despair: I've known grievous sinners who implored God's mercy when they were about to appear before Him—I know you haven't reached that point yet—and who certainly made better deaths as a result. Be an example to us, as they were! What's to prevent you from saying a Hail Mary and an Our Father every night and morning just as a precaution? Do it! Do it for me, to oblige me! It doesn't amount to much. Will you promise?"

The poor devil promised. The priest came again the following days. He chatted with the hotel keeper, told stories, made jokes and puns that were over Hippolyte's head. Then, at the first possible opening, he would return to religious matters, his face taking on an appropriate expression as he did so.

His zeal seemed to have some effect, for soon the taliped expressed a wish to make a pilgrimage to Bon-Secours if he was cured—to which the abbé replied that he could see nothing against it: two precautions were better than one. What—as he put it—was the risk?

The apothecary railed against what he called the priest's "maneuvers": they were interfering, he claimed, with Hippolyte's convalescence; and he kept saying to Madame Lefrançois, "Leave him alone! Leave him alone! You're confusing him with all your mysticism!"

But the lady wouldn't listen to him. He was "to blame for everything." And on a nail in the wall at the head of the sickbed she defiantly hung a brimming holy-water font with a sprig of boxwood in it.

However, religion seemed to be of no greater help than surgery, and the gangrenous process continued to extend inexorably upward toward the groin. In vain did they change medications and poultices: each day the muscles rotted a little more, and finally Charles replied with an affirmative nod when Madame Lefrançois asked him whether as a last resort she couldn't call in Monsieur Canivet, a celebrated surgeon in Neufchâtel.

This fellow practitioner, a fifty-year-old M.D. of considerable standing and equal self-assurance, laughed with unconcealed scorn when he saw Hippolyte's leg, by now gangrenous to the knee. Then, after declaring flatly that he would have to amputate, he visited the pharmacist and inveighed against the jackasses capable of reducing an unfortunate man to such a plight. He grasped Monsieur Homais by one of his coat buttons and shook him, shouting:

"New-fangled ideas from Paris! It's like strabismus and chloroform and lithotrity—the government ought to forbid such tomfoolery! But everybody wants to be smart nowadays, and they stuff you full of remedies without caring about the consequences! We don't pretend to be so clever, here in the country. We're not such know-it-alls, such la-di-das! We're practitioners, healers! It doesn't occur to us to operate on somebody who's perfectly well! Straighten a clubfoot! Who ever heard of straightening a clubfoot? It's like wanting to iron out a hunchback!"

Those words were a whiplash to Homais, but he hid his discomfiture under an obsequious smile: it was important to humor Canivet, whose prescriptions were sometimes brought into the pharmacy by Yonvillians, and so he made no defense of Bovary and expressed no opinion; he cast principles to the winds, and sacrificed his dignity to the weightier interests of his business.

It was quite an event in the village, that mid-thigh amputation by Doctor Canivet! All the citizens rose early that morning; and the Grande-Rue, thronged though it was, had something sinister about it, as though it were execution day. At the grocer's, Hippolyte's case was discussed from every angle, none of the stores did any business; and Madame Tuvache, the mayor's wife, didn't budge from her window, so eager was she not to miss the surgeon's arrival.

He drove up in his gig, holding the reins himself. Over the years the right-hand spring had given way under the weight of his corpulence, so that the carriage sagged a little to one side as it rolled along. Beside him, on the higher half of the seat cushion, could be seen a huge red leather case, its three brass clasps gleaming magisterially.

The doctor drew up in the hotel yard with a flourish and called loudly for someone to unharness his mare; and then he went to the stable to see whether she was really being given oats as he had ordered. His first concern, whenever he arrived at a patient's, was always for his mare and his gig. "That Canivet—he's a character!" people said of him; and they thought the more of him for his unshakable self-assurance. The universe might have perished to the last man, and he wouldn't have altered his habits a jot.

Homais made his appearance.

"I'm counting on you," said the doctor. "Are we ready? Let's go!"

But the apothecary blushingly confessed that he was too sensitive to be present at such an operation.

"When you just stand there watching," he said, "your imagination begins to play tricks on you, you know. And I'm of such a nervous temperament anyway that . . ."

"Bah!" interrupted Canivet. "You look more like the apoplectic type to me. It doesn't surprise me, either: you pharmacists are always cooped up in your kitchens—it can't help undermining your constitutions in the long run. Look at me: I'm up every day at four, shave in cold water every season of the year; I'm never chilly, never wear flannel underwear, never catch cold—I'm sound as a bell. I eat well one day, badly the next, however it comes. I take it philosophically. That's why I'm not a bit squeamish, like you. And that's why it's all the same to me whether I carve up a Christian or any old chicken they put in front of me. It's all a question of habit."

Thereupon, with no consideration whatever for Hippolyte, who was sweating with pain and terror under his bedclothes in the billiard room, the two gentlemen proceeded there in the kitchen to engage in a conversation in which the apothecary likened the coolness of a surgeon to that of a general. The comparison pleased Canivet, who expatiated on the demands made by his profession. He looked on it as a kind of sacred charge, even though dishonored nowadays by the activities of the *officiers de santé*. Then, finally giving thought to his patient, he inspected the bandages Homais had brought—the same ones he had furnished the day of the earlier operation— and asked for someone to hold the leg for him while he worked. Lestiboudois was sent for, and Canivet rolled up his sleeves and went into the billiard room. The apothecary stayed outside with Artémise and the landlady, both of the latter whiter than their aprons and all three of them with their ears to the door.

Bovary, meanwhile, didn't dare show himself outside his house. He sat downstairs in the parlor beside the empty fireplace, his chin on his chest, his hands folded, his eyes set. What a misfortune! he was thinking. What a disappointment! Certainly he had taken all conceivable precautions. Fate had played a hand in it. Be that as it may, if Hippolyte were later to die it would be he who would have murdered him. And then—how was he to answer the questions his patients were sure to ask him? What reason could he give for his failure? Perhaps he *had* made some mistake? He sought for what it might be, and failed to find it. The greatest surgeons made mistakes, didn't they? That was something no one would ever believe. Everyone would laugh at him, talk about him. The news would spread to Forges, to Neufchâtel, to Rouen—everywhere! Who knew—other doctors might write letters and articles attacking him! There would be a controversy: he would have to send replies to the newspapers. Hippolyte himself might sue him. He saw himself dishonored, ruined, lost! And his imagination, engendering countless fears, was tossed about like an empty barrel carried out to sea and bobbing on the waves.

Emma, sitting opposite, was watching him. She was not participating in his humiliation. She was experiencing a humiliation of a different sort: the humiliation of having imagined that such a man might be worth something—as though she hadn't twenty times already had full proof of his mediocrity.

Charles began to stride up and down the room. The floor creaked under his heavy boots.

"Sit down!" she said. "You're getting on my nerves!"

He sat down.

How in the world had she managed (she who was so intelligent) to commit yet another blunder? What deplorable mania was it that had made her wreck her life by constant self-sacrifice? She recalled all her desires for luxury, all her spiritual privations, the sordid details of marriage and housekeeping, her dreams mired like wounded swallows, everything she had ever craved for, everything she had denied herself, all the things she might have had. And for whose sake had she given up so much?

The silence that hung over the village was suddenly rent by a scream. Bovary went deathly pale. For an instant her brows contracted in a nervous frown; then she resumed her brooding. It was for him that she had done it—for this creature here, this man who understood nothing, who felt nothing. He was sitting quite calmly, utterly oblivious of the fact that the ridicule henceforth inseparable from his name would disgrace her as well. And she had tried to love him! She had wept tears of repentance at having given herself to another!

"I wonder—could it perhaps have been a valgus?"[3] The question came abruptly from the musing Charles.

At the sudden impact of those words, crashing into her mind like a leaden bullet into a silver dish, Emma felt herself shudder; and she raised her head, straining to understand what he had meant by them. They looked at each other in silence, almost wonderstruck, each of them, to see that the other was there, so far apart had their thoughts carried them. Charles stared at her with the clouded gaze of a drunken man; motionless in his chair, he was listening to the screams that continued to come from the hotel. One followed after another; each was a long, drawn-out succession of tones, and they were interspersed with short, shrill shrieks; it was all like the howling of some animal being butchered far away. Emma bit her pale lips; and twisting and turning in her fingers a sliver she had broken off the coral, she stared fixedly at Charles with blazing eyes that were like twin fiery arrows. Everything, everything about him exasperated her now—his face, his clothes, what he didn't say, his entire person, his very existence. She repented her virtue of days past as though it had been a crime; and what virtue she had left now crumbled under the furious assault of her pride. Adultery was triumphant; and she reveled in the prospect of its sordid ironies. The thought of her lover made her reel with desire; heart and soul she flung herself into her longing, borne toward him on waves of new rapture; and Charles seemed to her as detached from her life, as irrevocably gone, as impossible and done for, as though he were a dying man, gasping his last before her eyes.

There was a sound of footsteps on the sidewalk. Charles looked through

---

3. A twisting of the first toe above or below the other toes.

the lowered blind: in the hot sun near the market Doctor Canivet was mopping his forehead with his handkerchief. Behind him was Homais, carrying a large red box, and they were both heading for the pharmacy.

Flooded with sudden tenderness and despondency, Charles turned to his wife. "Kiss me!" he cried. "Kiss me, darling!"

"Don't touch me!" she flared, scarlet with fury.

"What . . . what is it?" he stammered, bewildered. "What's wrong? You're not yourself! You know how I love you! I need you!"

"Stop!" she cried in a terrible voice.

And rushing from the room she slammed the door so violently that the barometer was flung from the wall and broke to pieces on the floor.

Charles sank into his chair, crushed, wondering what her trouble was, fearing some nervous illness, weeping, and vaguely aware that the air about him was heavy with something baleful and incomprehensible.

When Rodolphe came to the garden that night he found his mistress waiting for him on the lowest step of the river stairs. They fell into each other's arms: and all their accumulated resentments melted like snow in the heat of this embrace.

XII

Once again their love was at high tide.

Now Emma would often take it into her head to write him during the day. Through her window she would signal to Justin, and he would whip off his apron and fly to La Huchette. And when Rodolphe arrived in response to her summons, it was to hear that she was miserable, that her husband was odious, that her life was a torment.

"Can I do anything about it?" he snapped at her one day.

"Ah, if you only would . . ."

She was sitting at his feet staring at nothing, her head between his knees, her hair streaming.

"What could I do?" Rodolphe demanded.

She sighed. "We could go live somewhere else, away from here. . . ."

"You're really crazy!" he said, laughing. "You know it's impossible!"

She tried to pursue the subject, but he pretended not to understand, and spoke of other things.

He saw no reason why there should be all this to-do about so simple a thing as lovemaking.

But for her there was a reason: there was a motive force that gave an additional impetus to her passion. Every day her love for Rodolphe was fanned by her aversion for her husband. The more completely she surrendered to the one, the more intensely she loathed the other: never did Charles seem to her so repulsive, so thick-fingered, so heavy-witted, so common, as when she was alone with him after her meetings with Rodolphe. Acting, at such times, the role of wife, of virtuous woman, she thought feverishly of her lover—of his black hair curling over his tanned forehead, of his body so powerful and yet so elegant, of the cool judgment that went hand in hand with his fiery passion. It was for him that she filed her fingernails with the care of the most exquisite artist, that she kept massaging her skin with cold cream, scenting her handkerchiefs with patchouli. She decked herself with bracelets, rings and necklaces. Whenever he was expected she filled her two big blue glass vases with roses; both her room and herself were made ready for him, as though she were a courtesan awaiting a prince. Félicité was perpetually bleaching lingerie: all day long she was in the kitchen, and Justin often sat there with her, watching her work.

His elbows on the ironing board, he would stare hungrily at all the feminine garments strewn about him—the dimity petticoats, the fichus, the collars, the drawstring pantaloons enormously wide at the waist and narrowing below.

"What is this for?" the boy would ask, touching a crinoline lining or a set of fastenings.

"Don't tell me you've never seen anything!" Félicité would laugh. "As if your Madame Homais didn't wear these same things!"

"Oh, Madame Homais . . ." And he would wonder aloud: "Is she a lady, like Madame?"

But Félicité was getting tired of having him hang around her. She was six years his elder, and Théodore, Maître Guillaumin's servant, was beginning to court her.

"Leave me alone!" she would say, reaching for her starch pot. "Go pound your almonds. You're always fussing around the women. You're a nasty little boy: better wait till you get some hair on your face for that sort of thing."

"Don't be cross. I'll do her shoes for you."

And he would go over to the doorsill and reach for Emma's shoes, all caked with the mud she had brought in from her meetings. It would fall away powdery under his fingers, and he would watch the particles float gently upward in a shaft of sun.

"You act as though you're afraid of spoiling them!" the cook would jeer. She herself wasn't so careful when she cleaned them, for Madame always gave them to her as soon as they looked the least bit worn.

Emma had countless pairs in her wardrobe, and discarded them on the slightest pretext. Charles never said a word.

Nor did he protest at paying three hundred francs for a wooden leg that she felt should be given to Hippolyte. It was cork trimmed and had spring joints—a complicated mechanism hidden under a black trouser leg that ended in a patent-leather shoe. But Hippolyte didn't dare use such a beautiful leg every day, and he begged Madame Bovary to get him another that would be more suitable. Naturally Charles paid for the new one as well.

The stable boy gradually resumed his work. He went about the village as before; and whenever Charles heard the sharp tap of his stick on the cobblestones in the distance, he quickly changed his direction.

It was Monsieur Lheureux, the shopkeeper, who had taken charge of the order. It gave him an opportunity to see a good deal of Emma. He chatted with her about the latest novelties from Paris, about a thousand feminine trifles; he was more than obliging, and never pressed for payment. Emma let herself slide into this easy way of gratifying all her whims. When she decided she wanted to give Rodolphe a handsome riding crop she had seen in an umbrella shop in Rouen, she told Lheureux to get it for her, and he set it on her table a week later.

The next day, however, he appeared with his bill—two hundred and seventy francs, not to mention the centimes. Emma didn't know what to do: all the desk drawers were empty, they owed Lestiboudois two weeks' pay and the maid six months' wages, there were a number of other bills, and Bovary was waiting impatiently for a remittance from Monsieur Derozerays, who usually settled with him once a year, toward the end of June.

She was able to put Lheureux off for a time, but eventually he lost patience: he was hard pressed, he said, his capital was tied up, and if she couldn't give him something on account he'd be forced to take back all the items she had chosen.

"All right, take them!" she said.

"I didn't really mean that," he answered. "Except perhaps for the riding crop. I guess I'll have to ask Monsieur for it back."

"No! No!" she cried.

"Ah ha!" Lheureux thought. "I've got you!"

And feeling sure that he had ferreted out her secret, he left her. "We'll see," he murmured to himself, with his customary little whistle. "We'll see!"

She was wondering how to extricate herself when the cook came in and put a little cylindrical parcel on the mantel. "From Monsieur Derozerays," she said. Emma seized it and opened it. It contained fifteen napoleons—full payment. She heard Charles on the stairs, and she flung the gold pieces into one of her drawers and took the key.

Three days later Lheureux came again.

"I have a suggestion," he said. "If instead of paying the amount we agreed on you'd like to take . . ."

"Here!" she said, and she handed him fourteen napoleons.

The shopkeeper was taken aback. To hide his disappointment he over-flowed with apologies and offers of service, all of which Emma declined. When he had left she stood a few moments with her hand in her apron, fingering the two five-franc pieces he had given her in change. She resolved to economize, so that eventually she could pay Charles back. . . .

"Bah!" she said to herself. "He'll never give it a thought."

Besides the riding crop with the silver-gilt knob, Rodolphe had been given a signet ring with the motto *"Amor nel cor"*; also a scarf to use as a muffler, and a cigar case very like the vicomte's that Charles had picked up on the road and Emma still kept.

But he found her presents humiliating, and on several occasions refused them. She was insistent, however, and he gave in, grumbling to himself that she was high-handed and interfering.

Then she had such crazy notions.

"When the bell strikes midnight," she would command him, "think of me."

And if he confessed that he hadn't done so, there were strings of reproaches, always ending with the eternal:

"Do you love me?"

"Of course I love you!"

"Very much?"

"Of course."

"You've never loved anybody else, have you?"

That made him laugh: "Do you think you deflowered me?"

When Emma burst into tears he tried to comfort her, protesting his love and saying things to make her smile.

"It's because I love you," she would interrupt. "I love you so much that I can't do without you—you know that, don't you? Sometimes I want so much to see you that it tears me to pieces. 'Where is he?' I wonder. 'Maybe he's with other women. They're smiling at him, he's going up close to them. . . .' Tell me it isn't true! Tell me you don't like any of them! Some of them are prettier than I am, but none of them can love you the way I do. I'm your slave and your concubine! You're my king, my idol! You're good! You're beautiful! You're wise! You're strong!"

He had had such things said to him so many times that none of them had any freshness for him. Emma was like all his other mistresses; and as the charm of novelty gradually slipped from her like a piece of her clothing, he saw revealed in all its nakedness the eternal monotony of passion, which always assumes the same forms and always speaks the same language. He had no perception—this man of such vast experience—of the dissimilarity of feeling that might underlie similarities of expression. Since he had heard those same words uttered by loose women or prostitutes, he had little belief in their sincerity when he heard them now: the more flowery a person's speech, he thought, the more suspect the feelings, or lack of feelings, it concealed. Whereas the truth is that fullness of soul can sometimes overflow in utter vapidity of language, for none of us can ever express the exact measure of his needs or his thoughts or his sorrows; and human speech is like a cracked kettle on which we tap crude rhythms for bears to dance to, while we long to make music that will melt the stars.

But with the superior acumen of those who keep aloof in any relationship, Rodolphe discovered that the affair offered still further possibilities of sensual gratification. He abandoned every last shred of restraint and consideration. He made her into something compliant, something corrupt. Hers was an infatuation to the point of idiocy; the intensity of her admiration for him was matched by the intensity of her own voluptuous feelings; she was in a blissful torpor, a drunkenness in which her very soul lay drowned and shriveled, like the duke of Clarence in his butt of malmsey.[4]

This constant indulgence had its effect on her daily behavior. Her glance grew bolder, her language freer; she went so far as to be seen smoking a cigarette in public, in Rodolphe's company—"as though," people said, "to show her contempt for propriety." Even those who had given her the benefit of the doubt stopped doing so when they saw her step out of the Hirondelle one day wearing a tight-fitting vest, like a man's. The elder Madame Bovary, who had taken refuge with her son following a particularly unpleasant scene with her husband, was as scandalized as any of the Yonville matrons. There were many other things that she disliked, too: first of all, Charles hadn't followed her advice about the ban on novels; and then she disapproved of "the way the house was run." She took the liberty of saying how she felt, and there were quarrels—one, especially, about Félicité.

Going down the hall the previous night the elder Madame Bovary had

---

4. The duke of Clarence was the younger brother of King Edward IV of England and the elder brother of Richard, duke of Gloucester. He was condemned to death for treason and, according to rumor, drowned in a butt of malmsey (a sweet aromatic wine) in February 1478. See Shakespeare's *Richard III* 1.4.155.

surprised her with a man—a man of about forty, with dark chin whiskers, who had slipped out through the kitchen when he had heard her coming. When she reported this, Emma burst out laughing; the older woman lost her temper, declaring that unless one cared nothing for morals oneself, one was bound to keep an eye on the morals of one's servants.

"What kind of social circles do *you* frequent?" Emma retorted, with such an impertinent stare that her mother-in-law asked her whether in taking her servant's part it wasn't really herself that she was defending.

"Get out!" the young woman cried, springing from her chair.

"Emma! Mother!" cried Charles, trying to stop the argument. But in their rage they both rushed from the room.

"What manners!" Emma sneered when he came to her. And she stamped with fury: "What a peasant!"

He hurried to his mother and found her close to hysterics. "Such insolence! She's irresponsible! Maybe worse!"

And she declared she would leave the house at once unless her daughter-in-law came to her and apologized. So Charles sought out his wife again and begged her to give in. He implored her on his knees. "Oh, all right, I'll do it," she said finally.

She held out her hand to her mother-in-law with the dignity of a marquise: *"Excusez-moi, Madame."* And then in her own room she flung herself flat on the bed and wept like a child, her head buried in the pillow.

She and Rodolphe had agreed that in case of an emergency she would fasten a piece of white paper to the blind, so that if he happened to be in Yonville he could go immediately into the lane behind the house. Emma hung out the signal; after waiting three-quarters of an hour she suddenly saw Rodolphe at the corner of the market. She was tempted to open the window and call to him; as she hesitated he disappeared. She sank back hopelessly in her chair.

But after a short time she thought she heard someone on the sidewalk: it must be he. She went downstairs and across the yard. He was outside the gate. She flung herself into his arms.

"Be careful!" he warned.

"Ah, if you knew what I've been through," she breathed.

And she proceeded to tell him everything—hurriedly, disjointedly, exaggerating some facts and inventing others, and putting in so many parentheses that he lost the thread of her story.

"Come, angel, be brave! Cheer up! Be patient!"

"But I've been patient for four years! I've suffered for four years! A love like ours is something to boast of! I'm on the rack, with those people! I can't stand it any longer! Rescue me, for God's sake!"

She clung to him. Her tear-filled eyes were flashing like undersea fires; her breast rose and fell in quick gasps; never had he found her so desirable. He lost his head. "What must we do?" he said. "What do you want me to do?"

"Oh! Take me away!" she cried. "I implore you: take me away!"

And she crushed her lips to his, as though to catch the consent she hadn't dared hope for—the consent that was now breathed out in a kiss.

"But . . ." Rodolphe began.

"What is it?"

"What about your little girl?"

She pondered a few moments; then: "We'll take her with us—it's the only way."

"What a woman!" he thought as he watched her move off. She had quickly slipped back into the garden: someone was calling her.

The elder Madame Bovary was astonished, the next few days, by her daughter-in-law's transformation. Emma was docility itself, deferential to the point of asking her for a recipe for pickles.

Was it her way of covering her tracks more thoroughly? Or was it a kind of voluptuous stoicism—a deliberate, deeper savoring of the bitterness of everything she was about to abandon? Scarcely the latter, for she noticed nothing around her: she was living as though immersed in advance in her future happiness. With Rodolphe she talked of nothing else. She would lean on his shoulder, and murmur:

"Think of what it will be like when we're in the stagecoach! Can you imagine it? Is it possible? The moment I feel the carriage moving, I think I'll have the sensation we're going up in a balloon, sailing up into the clouds. I'm counting the days. Are you?"

Never had Madame Bovary been as beautiful as now. She had that indefinable beauty that comes from happiness, enthusiasm, success—a beauty that is nothing more or less than a harmony of temperament and circumstances. Her desires, her sorrows, her experience of sensuality, her evergreen illusions, had developed her step by step, like a flower nourished by manure and by the rain, by the wind and the sun; and she was finally blooming in the fullness of her nature. Her eyelids seemed strangely perfect when she half closed them in a long amorous glance; and each of her deep sighs dilated her fine nostrils and raised the fleshy corners of her lips, lightly shadowed by dark down. Some artist skilled in corruption seemed to have designed the knot of her hair: it lay on her neck coiled in a heavy mass, twisted carelessly and always a little differently, for every day it was loosened by embraces. Her voice now took on softer inflections; her body, too; something subtle and penetrating emanated from the very folds of her dress, from the very arch of her foot. Charles found her exquisite and utterly irresistible, as in the first days of their marriage.

When he returned home in the middle of the night he dared not wake her. The porcelain night-light cast a trembling circular glow on the ceiling; and the drawn curtains of the cradle made it look like a tiny white hut swelling out in the darkness beside the bed. Charles looked at both sleepers. He thought he could hear the light breathing of his child. She would be growing rapidly now; every season would bring a change. Already he saw her coming home from school at the end of the day, laughing, her blouse spotted with ink, her basket on her arm. Then they would have to send her away to boarding school: that would cost a good deal—how would they manage? He thought and thought about it. He had the idea of renting a little farm on the outskirts, one that he could supervise himself mornings, as he rode out to see his patients. He would put the profits aside, in the savings bank; later he would buy securities of some kind. Besides, his practice would grow: he was counting on it, for he wanted Berthe to have a good education; he wanted her to be accomplished, to take piano lessions. Ah! How pretty she would be later, at fifteen! She would look just like her mother; and like her, in the summer, she would wear a great straw hat: from a distance they'd be taken for sisters. He pictured her sewing at night beside them in the lamplight; she would embroider slippers for him, and look after the house; she would fill their lives with her sweetness and her gaiety. And then he would think about her marriage. They would find her some fine young man with a good position, who would make her happy. And her happiness would last for ever and ever.

Emma wasn't asleep at such times. She was only pretending to be; and as Charles gradually sank into slumber beside her she lay awake dreaming different dreams.

A team of four horses, galloping every day for a week, had been whirling her and Rodolphe toward a new land from which they would never return. On and on the carriage bore them, and they sat there, arms entwined, saying not a word. Often from a mountaintop they would espy some splendid city, with domes, bridges, ships, forests of lemon trees, and white marble cathedrals whose pointed steeples were crowned with storks' nests. Here the horses slowed, picking their way over the great paving-stones, and the ground was strewn with bouquets of flowers tossed at them by women laced in red bodices. The ringing of bells and the braying of mules mingled with the murmur of guitars and the sound of gushing fountains; pyramids of fruit piled at the foot of pale statues were cooled by the flying spray, and the statues themselves seemed to smile through the streaming water. And then one night they arrived in a fishing village, where brown nets were drying in the wind along the cliff and the line of cottages. Here they stopped: this would be their dwelling place. They would live in a low flat-roofed house in the shade of a palm tree, on a bay beside the sea. They would ride in gondolas, swing in hammocks; and their lives would be easy and ample like the silk clothes they wore, warm like the soft nights that enveloped them, starry like the skies they gazed upon. Nothing specific stood out against the vast background of the future that she thus evoked: the days were all of them splendid, and as alike as the waves of the sea; and the whole thing hovered on the horizon, infinite, harmonious, blue and sparkling in the sun. But then the baby would cough in the cradle, or Bovary would give a snore louder than the rest, and Emma wouldn't fall asleep till morning, when dawn was whitening the windowpanes and Justin was already opening the shutters of the pharmacy.

She had sent for Monsieur Lheureux and told him she would be needing a cloak: "A long cloak with a deep collar and a lining."

"You're going on a trip?" he asked.

"No! But . . . Anyway, I can count on you to get it, can't I? Soon?"

He bowed.

"I'll want a trunk, too. Not too heavy, roomy."

"I know the kind you mean. About three feet by a foot and a half, the sort they're making now."

"And an overnight bag."

"A little too much smoke not to mean fire," Lheureux said to himself.

"And here," said Madame Bovary, unfastening her watch from her belt. "Take this: you can pay for the things out of what you get for it."

But the shopkeeper protested. She was wrong to suggest such a thing, he said; they were well acquainted; he trusted her completely. She mustn't be childish. But she insisted that he take at least the chain, and Lheureux had put it in his pocket and was on his way out when she called him back.

"Hold the luggage for me," she said. "As for the cloak"—she pretended to ponder the question—"don't bring that to me, either. But give me the address of the shop and tell them to have it ready for me when I come."

They were to elope the following month. She would leave Yonville as though to go shopping in Rouen. Rodolphe was to arrange for their reservations and their passports, and would write to Paris to make sure that they would have the coach to themselves as far as Marseilles; and there they would buy a barouche and continue straight on toward Genoa. She would send her things to Lheureux's, whence they would be loaded directly onto the Hirondelle, thus arousing no one's suspicions. In all these plans there was never a mention of little Berthe. Rodolphe avoided speaking of her: perhaps Emma had forgotten her.

He said he needed two weeks more, to wind up some affairs; then, at the end of the first of them, he said he would need an additional two; then he said he was sick; then he went on a trip somewhere. The month of August passed. Finally they decided they would leave without fail on the fourth of September, a Monday.

The Saturday night before that Monday, Rodolphe arrived earlier than usual.

"Is everything ready?" she asked him.

"Yes."

They strolled around the flower beds and sat on the terrace wall.

"You seem sad," said Emma.

"No, why?"

But he kept looking at her strangely—with unusual softness and tenderness.

"Is it because you're going away?" she asked. "Leaving everything that's dear to you, everything that makes up your life? I understand that. . . . But I have nothing—nothing in the world. You're my everything. And I'll be yours. I'll be your family, your country; I'll look after you, I'll love you."

"How sweet you are!" he cried, clasping her in his arms.

"Am I really?" she laughed, melting with pleasure. "Do you love me? Swear that you do?"

"Do I love you! Do I! I adore you, darling!"

The moon, a deep red disc, was rising straight out of the earth beyond the meadows. They could see it climb swiftly between the poplar branches that partially screened it like a torn black curtain; and finally, dazzlingly white, it shone high above them in the empty sky illumined by its light. Now, moving more slowly, it poured onto a stretch of the river a great brightness that flashed like a million stars; and this silvery gleam seemed to be writhing in its depths like a headless serpent covered with luminous scales. It looked, too, like a monstrous many-branched candlestick dripping with molten diamonds. The night spread softly around them; patches of shadow hung in the leaves of the trees. Emma, her eyes half closed, drank in the cool breeze with deep sighs. Lost in their revery, they said not a word. Full and silent as the flowing river, languid as the perfume of the syringas, the sweetness they had known in earlier days once again surged up in their hearts, casting on their memories longer and more melancholy shadows than those of the motionless willows on the grass. Now and again some prowling night animal, hedgehog or weasel, disturbed the leaves; or they heard the sound of a ripe peach as it dropped to the ground.

"What a lovely night!" said Rodolphe.

"We'll have many more," Emma answered.

And as though speaking to herself:

"Yes, it will be good to be traveling. . . . But why should I feel sad? Is it fear of the unknown, or the effect of leaving everything I'm used to? No— it's from too much happiness. How weak of me! Forgive me!"

"There's still time," he cried. "Think carefully—you might be sorry!"

"Never!" she answered impetuously.

And moving close to him:

"What harm can come to me? There's not a desert, not a precipice, not an ocean, that I wouldn't cross with you. Living together will be like an embrace that's tighter and more perfect every day. There'll be nothing to bother us, no cares—nothing in our way. We'll be alone, entirely to ourselves, for ever and ever. Say something, darling! Answer me!"

At regular intervals he answered, "Yes . . . yes . . ." Her fingers were in his hair, and through the great tears that were welling from her eyes she kept repeating his name in a childish voice:

"Rodolphe! Rodolphe! Sweet little Rodolphe!"

Midnight struck.

"Midnight!" she said. "Now it's tomorrow! One more day!"

He stood up to go; and as though his movement were the signal for their flight, Emma suddenly brightened.

"You have the passports?"

"Yes."

"You haven't forgotten anything?"

"No."

"You're sure?"

"Absolutely."

"And you'll be waiting for me at the Hotel de Provence at noon?"

He nodded.

"Till tomorrow, then," said Emma, giving him a last caress.

And she watched him go.

He did not turn around. She ran after him, and leaning out over the water among the bushes:

"Till tomorrow!" she cried.

Already he was on the other side of the river, walking quickly across the meadow.

After several minutes Rodolphe stopped; and when he saw her in her white dress gradually vanishing into the shadows like a wraith, his heart began to pound so violently that he leaned against a tree to keep from falling.

"God, what a fool I am!" he muttered with an obscene curse. "But she certainly made a pretty mistress!"

Emma's beauty and all the joys of their love rushed back into his mind; and for a moment he softened. But then he turned against her.

"After all," he cried, gesticulating and talking aloud to himself to strengthen his resolution, "I can't spend the rest of my life abroad! I can't be saddled with a child! All that trouble! All that expense! No! No! Absolutely not! It would be too stupid!"

XIII

As soon as he reached home Rodolphe sat down at his desk, under the stag's-head trophy that hung on the wall. But when he took up his pen he couldn't think of what to write, and he leaned on his elbows and pondered. Emma seemed to have receded into a far-off past, as though the resolution he had just made had put a great distance between them.

In order to recapture some feeling of her he went to the wardrobe at the head of his bed and took out an old Rheims cookie box that was his storage place for letters from women. Out of it came a smell of damp dust and withered roses. The first thing his eye fell on was a handkerchief spotted with faint stains. It was one of Emma's: she had had a nosebleed one day when they were out together—he hadn't remembered it till now. Then he took up something that had been knocking against the sides of the box: it was the miniature she had given him; she looked much too fussily dressed, he thought, and her ogling expression was preposterous. He kept staring at the artist's handiwork in an attempt to evoke the model as he remembered her, and this gradually resulted in Emma's features becoming confused in his memory, as though the real face and the painted face had been rubbing against each other and wearing each other away. Finally he read some of her letters. They were as brief, as technical, as urgent as business letters, filled chiefly with details pertaining to their trip. He wanted to reread the longer ones, the earlier ones; they were further down in the box, and to get at them he had to disarrange everything else. He found himself mechanically going through the pile of letters and other things, turning up a heterogeneous assortment—bouquets, a garter, a black mask, pins, locks of hair. So many locks of hair! Brunette and blond: some of them, catching in the metal hinges of the box, had broken off as he opened it.

He rummaged among his souvenirs, lingering on the differences of handwriting and style in the letters—as marked as the differences of spelling. There were affectionate letters, jolly letters, facetious letters, melancholy letters; there were some that begged for love and others that begged for money. Now and then a word brought back a face, a gesture, the sound of a voice; certain letters brought back nothing at all.

All those women, thronging into his memory, got in each other's way; none of them stood out above the rest, leveled down as they all were by the measure of his love. He took up handfuls of the various letters and for some minutes amused himself by letting them stream from one hand to another. In the end he lost interest in the game and put the box back into the wardrobe. "What a lot of nonsense!" he said to himself.

This accurately summed up his opinion, for his companions in pleasure, like children playing in a schoolyard, had so trampled his heart that nothing green could grow there; indeed they were more casual than children—they hadn't even scribbled their names on the walls.

"Come now," he said to himself. "Get busy."

He began to write:

"You must be courageous, Emma: the last thing I want to do is ruin your life. . . ."

"That's absolutely true, after all," he assured himself. "I'm acting in her interest; I'm only being honest."

"Have you given really serious thought to your decision? Do you realize into what abyss I was about to hurl you, poor darling? You don't, I'm sure. You were going ahead blind and confident, full of faith in happiness, in the future. . . . Ah! Poor wretched, insane creatures that we are!"

Here Rodolphe paused, looking for some good excuse.

"I could tell her that I've lost all my money. . . . No—that wouldn't stop her anyway: I'd have to go through the whole thing again later. Is there any way of making such women come to their senses?"

He thought for a while, then added:

"I'll never forget you—believe me—and I'll always feel the deepest devotion to you. But some day sooner or later our passion would have cooled—inevitably—it's the way with everything human. We would have had moments of weariness. Who knows—I might even have had the dreadful anguish of witnessing your remorse—and of sharing in it, since it would have been I who caused it. The very thought of the grief in store for you is a torture to me, Emma! Forget me! Why was it ordained that we should meet? Why were you so beautiful? Is the fault mine? In God's name, no! No! Fate alone is to blame—nothing and no one but fate!"

"That's always an effective word," he remarked to himself.

"Ah! Had you been a shallow-hearted creature like so many others, I could very well have gone ahead and let things happen as they might—purely for what was in it for myself—in that case without danger to you. But that marvelous intensity of feelings you have—such a delight for those who know you, such a source of anguish for yourself!—kept you—adorable woman that you are—from realizing the falsity of the position the future held for us. At first I, too, gave it no thought—I was lying in the shade of that ideal happiness we dreamed of as under a poison tree, without thought for the consequences."

"Maybe she'll think I'm giving her up out of stinginess. . . . What's it to me if she does! Let her. . . . And let's get it over with!"

"The world is cruel, Emma. It would have pursued us everywhere. You'd have been subjected to indiscreet questions—calumny—scorn—even insult, perhaps. You—insulted! Oh, my darling! And I would have been the cause of it—I, who wanted to put you on a throne—I, who shall carry away the thought of you like a talisman! Yes—away—for I am punishing myself for the harm I have done you—I am going into exile! Where? How can I tell? My poor mad brain can give no answer. Adieu, Emma! Continue to be as good as you have always been! Never forget the unfortunate man who lost you! Teach your child my name: tell her to include me in her prayers."

The flames of the two candles were flickering. Rodolphe got up to close the window; and then, back at his desk:

"That's all, I guess," he said to himself. "Oh—just this little bit more, to keep her from coming after me":

"I shall be far away when you read these unhappy lines; I dare not linger—the temptation to see you again is all but irresistible! This is no moment for weakness! I shall come back; and perhaps one day we'll be able to speak of our love with detachment, as a thing of the past. Adieu!"

And he appended one more, last adieu, this time written as two words— "*A Dieu!*": it seemed to him in excellent taste.

"How shall I sign it?" he wondered. " 'Devotedly'? No . . . 'Your friend'? Yes—that's it."

"Your friend."

He read over his letter and thought it was good.

"Poor little thing!" he thought, suddenly sentimental. "She'll think me as unfeeling as a stone. There ought to be a few tears on it, but weeping's beyond me—what can I do?" He poured some water in a glass, wet a finger, and holding it high above the page shook off a large drop. It made a pale blot on the ink. Then, looking around for something to seal the letter with, his eye fell on the signet ring with the motto *"Amor nel cor."* "Scarcely appropriate under the circumstances, but what the . . ."

Whereupon he smoked three pipes and went to bed.

When he got up the next day (about two in the afternoon—he slept late) Rodolphe had some apricots picked and arranged in a basket. At the bottom, hidden under some vine leaves, he put the letter; and he ordered Girard, his plough-boy, to deliver it carefully to Madame Bovary. This was his usual way of corresponding with her, sending her fruit or game according to the season.

"If she asks you anything about me," he said, "tell her I've left for a trip. Be sure to give the basket to her personally. Get going, now, and do it right!"

Girard put on his new smock, tied his handkerchief over the apricots, and plodding along in his great hobnailed boots, he set out tranquilly for Yonville.

When he reached Madame Bovary's he found her helping Félicité stack linen on the kitchen table.

"Here," said the plough-boy. "My master sent you this."

A feeling of dread came over her, and as she fumbled in her pocket for some change she stared at the peasant with haggard eyes; he in turn looked at her in bewilderment, failing to understand why anyone should be so upset by such a present. Finally he left. Félicité stayed where she was. The suspense was too great for Emma: she ran into the other room as though for the purpose of carrying in the apricots, dumped them out of the basket, tore away the leaves, found the letter and opened it; and as though she were fleeing from a fire she ran panic-stricken up the stairs toward her room.

Charles had come in: she caught sight of him; he spoke to her; whatever he said, she didn't hear it; and she hurried on up the second flight of stairs, breathless, distracted, reeling, clutching the horrible piece of paper that rattled in her hand like a sheet of tin. At the third-floor landing she stopped outside the closed attic door.

She tried to calm herself: only then did she think of the letter. She must finish it—she didn't dare. Besides, where could she read it? How? She'd be seen.

"I'll be all right in here," she thought; and she pushed open the door and went in.

There the roof slates were throwing down a heat that was all but unbearable; it pressed on her so that she could scarcely breathe. She dragged herself over to the dormer, whose shutters were closed; she pulled back the bolt, and the dazzling sunlight poured in.

Out beyond the rooftops, the open countryside stretched as far as eye could see. Below her the village square was empty; the stone sidewalk glittered; the weathervanes on the houses stood motionless. From the lower floor of a house at the corner came a whirring noise with strident changes of tone: Binet was at his lathe.

Leaning against the window frame she read the letter through, now and then giving an angry sneer. But the more she tried to concentrate, the more confused her thoughts became. She saw Rodolphe, heard his voice, clasped him in her arms; and a series of irregular palpitations, thudding in her breast like great blows from a battering ram, came faster and faster. She cast her eyes about her, longing for the earth to open up. Why not end it all? What was holding her back? She was free to act. And she moved forward. "Do it! Do it!" she ordered herself, peering down at the pavement.

The rays of bright light reflected directly up to her from below were pulling the weight of her body toward the abyss. The surface of the village square seemed to be sliding dizzily up the wall of her house; the floor she was standing on seemed to be tipped up on end, like a pitching ship. Now she was at the very edge, almost hanging out, a great emptiness all around her. The blue of the sky was flooding her; her head felt hollow and filled with the rushing of the wind: all she had to do now was to surrender, yield to the onrush. And the lathe kept whirring, like an angry voice calling her.

But then she heard another voice: "Where are you?" It was Charles.

She listened.

"Where are you? Come down!"

The thought that she had just escaped death almost made her faint from terror; she closed her eyes; then she gave a start as she felt the touch of a hand on her sleeve. It was Félicité.

"Monsieur is waiting, Madame. The soup is on the table."

And she had to go down—had to sit through a meal!

She did her best to eat. Each mouthful choked her. She unfolded her napkin as though to inspect the darns, and began really seriously to devote her attention to it and count the stitches. Suddenly the thought of the letter came back to her. Had she lost it? Where would she lay hands on it? But in her exhaustion of mind she could invent no excuse for leaving the table. Besides, she didn't dare: she was terrified of Charles; he knew everything—she was sure he must! And oddly enough he chose that moment to say:

"I gather we shan't be seeing Monsieur Rodolphe for some time."

She started: "Who told you so?"

"Who told me?" he said, surprised by her abrupt tone. "Girard—I saw him a few minutes ago at the door of the Café Français. He's left for a trip, or he's about to leave."

A sob escaped her.

"What's so surprising about it? He's always going off on pleasure trips. Why shouldn't he? When you're a bachelor and well off . . . Besides, he knows how to give himself a good time, our friend. He's a real playboy. Monsieur Langlois once told me . . ."

He decorously broke off as the maid came in.

Félicité gathered up the apricots that lay scattered over the sideboard and put them back into the basket. Unaware that his wife had turned scarlet, Charles asked for them, took one, and bit into it.

"Oh, perfect!" he said. "Try one."

He held the basket out toward her, and she gently pushed it away.

"Smell them: such fragrance!" he said, moving it back and forth before her.

"I'm stifling in here!" she cried, leaping to her feet. But she forced herself to conquer her spasm. "It's nothing," she said. "Nothing. Just nerves. Sit down; eat your fruit."

Her great dread was lest he question her, insist on doing something for her, never leave her to herself.

Charles had obediently sat down and was spitting apricot pits into his hand and transferring them to his plate.

Suddenly a blue tilbury crossed the square at a smart trot. Emma gave a cry, fell abruptly backwards and lay on the floor.

Rodolphe had decided, after a good deal of thought, to leave for Rouen. Since the Yonville road was the only route from La Huchette to Buchy, he had to pass through the village; and Emma had recognized him in the glow of his carriage lights as they flashed in the gathering dusk like a streak of lightning.

The commotion at the Bovarys' brought the pharmacist running. The table had been knocked over and all the plates were on the floor; gravy, meat, knives, the salt cellar and the cruet stand littered the room; Charles was calling for help; Berthe was frightened and in tears; and Félicité with trembling hands was unlacing Madame, whose entire body was racked with convulsions.

"I'll run to my laboratory and get a little aromatic vinegar," said the apothecary.

And when he had returned and held the flacon under her nostrils and she opened her eyes:

"I knew it," he said. "This stuff would resuscitate a corpse."

"Speak to us!" cried Charles. "Say something! Can you hear me? It's Charles—Charles, who loves you. Do you recognize me? See—here's your little girl—kiss her, darling."

The child stretched out her arms toward her mother, trying to clasp them around her neck. But Emma turned her head away. "No, no," she said brokenly. "Leave me alone."

She fainted again, and they carried her to her bed.

She lay there on her back, mouth open, eyes closed, hands flat beside her, motionless, white as a wax statue. Two rivulets of tears trickled slowly from her eyes onto the pillow.

Charles stood at the foot of the bed. At his side the pharmacist was observing the thoughtful silence appropriate to life's solemn occasions. Then:

"I think she'll be all right," he said. "The paroxysm seems to be over."

"Yes, she's resting a little now," Charles answered, watching her sleep. "Poor thing! Poor thing! It's a real relapse."

Then Homais asked for details, and Charles told him how she had been stricken suddenly while eating apricots.

"Extraordinary!" said the pharmacist. "Still, the apricots may very well have caused the syncope. Some natures react so strongly to certain odors! It would be an interesting subject to study, in both its pathological and its physiological aspects. The priests are well aware of the importance of this phenomenon—they've always made use of aromatics in their ceremonies. They employ them deliberately, to deaden the understanding and induce ecstatic states—women lend themselves to it easily, they're so much more delicate than the rest of us. Cases are recorded of women fainting from the smell of burnt horn, fresh bread . . ."

"Take care not to wake her!" Bovary warned softly.

"And it's not only humans who are subject to such anomalies," continued the apothecary. "Animals are, too. You are certainly not ignorant of the intensely aphrodisiac effect produced by *nepeta cataria,* vulgarly called cat-nip, on the feline species; and to mention another example—one whose authenticity I myself can vouch for—Bridoux, one of my old schoolmates, now in business in the Rue Malpalu, has a dog which has convulsions if you show it a snuffbox. Bridoux sometimes makes him perform for his friends, at his suburban residence in Bois-Guillaume. Would you believe that a sim-ple sternutative could work such havoc in the organism of a quadruped? It's extremely curious, don't you find?"

"Yes," said Charles, who wasn't listening.

"This is but another illustration," said the pharmacist, smiling with an air of benign self-satisfaction, "of the innumerable irregularities of the nervous system. As far as Madame is concerned, I confess she has always seemed to me a genuine sensitive. For that reason, my good friend, I advise you not to use any of those so-called remedies which attack the temperament under the guise of attacking the symptoms. No—no futile medication. Just a regi-men. Sedatives, emollients, dulcifiers. And then, don't you think it would be a good thing to rouse her imagination—something striking?"

"How? What?"

"Ah, that's the problem. That is indeed the problem. *'That is the question,'* " he quoted in English, "as I read in the paper recently."

Just then Emma, waking from her sleep, cried: "The letter? Where is the letter?"

They thought her delirious, and from midnight on she was: there could be no doubt that it was brain fever.

For forty-three days Charles did not leave her side. He neglected all his patients; he never lay down; he was constantly feeling her pulse, applying mustard plasters and cold compresses. He sent Justin to Neufchâtel for ice; the ice melted on the way; he sent him back. He called in Doctor Canivet for consultation; he had Doctor Larivière, his old teacher, come from Rouen; he was desperate. What frightened him most was Emma's degree of prostra-tion: she didn't speak, she gave no sign of comprehending or even hearing anything that was said to her; and she seemed to be in no pain. It was as though her body and her soul together had sought rest after all their tribu-lations. Toward the middle of October she could sit up in bed, propped against pillows. Charles wept when he saw her eat her first slice of bread and jam. Her strength returned; she left her bed for a few hours each after-noon; and one day when she felt better than usual he got her to take his arm and try a walk in the garden. The gravel on the paths was almost hidden under dead leaves; she walked slowly, dragging her slippers; and leaning on Charles's shoulder she smiled continuously.

They made their way to the far end, near the terrace. She drew herself up slowly and held her hand above her eyes: she stared into the distance, the far distance; but on the horizon there were only great grass fires, smoking on the hills.

"You'll tire yourself, darling," said Bovary.

And guiding her gently, trying to induce her to enter the arbor:

"Sit on this bench: you'll be comfortable."

"Oh no! Not there! Not there!" she said in a faltering voice.

Immediately she felt dizzy; and beginning that night there was another onset of her illness. This time it was less clearly identifiable, more complex. Now her heart would pain her, now her chest, now her head, now her limbs. She had vomiting spells, which Charles feared were the first symptoms of cancer.

And as though that were not enough, the poor fellow had money worries!

XIV

To begin with, he didn't know how to make good to Monsieur Homais for all the medicaments that had come from the pharmacy: as a doctor he might have been excused from paying for them, but the obligation embarrassed him. Then, what with the cook acting as mistress, the household expenses were getting to be alarming; there was a deluge of bills; the tradespeople were grumbling; Monsieur Lheureux, especially, was harassing him. The dry-goods dealer, taking advantage of the circumstances to pad his bill, had chosen a moment at the very height of Emma's illness to deliver the cloak, the overnight bag, two trunks instead of one, and a number of other things as well. Charles protested that he had no use for them, but the shopkeeper arrogantly retorted that all those items had been ordered and that he wouldn't take them back. Besides, he said, it would be upsetting to Madame in her convalescence. Monsieur should think it over. In short, he was determined to stand on his rights and carry the matter to court rather than give in. A little later Charles ordered that everything be sent back to the shop; but Félicité forgot; and he had other things on his mind and didn't think of them. Monsieur Lheureux brought the matter up again, and by alternating threats and moans got Charles to sign a six-months' promissory note. No sooner had he signed than he had a bold idea: he would try to borrow a thousand francs from Monsieur Lheureux. So he awkwardly asked whether there was any chance of this, explaining that it would be for one year and at any rate of interest Lheureux might specify. Lheureux ran to his shop, brought back the money, and dictated another promissory note, whereby Bovary promised to pay to his order, the first of the following September, the sum of 1,070 francs. Together with the 180 already stipulated, that came to just 1,250. In this way, loaning at the rate of six percent, plus his commission and at least one-third mark-up on the goods, the whole thing would bring him in a clear 130 francs' profit in twelve months; and he hoped that it wouldn't stop there, that the notes wouldn't be met but renewed, and that his poor little capital, after benefiting from the doctor's care like a patient in a sanatorium, would eventually come back to him considerably plumper, fat enough to burst the bag.

Everything Lheureux touched was successful at this moment. His had been the winning bid for the cider-supply contract at the Neufchâtel public hospital; Maître Guillaumin was promising him some shares in the peatery at Grumesnil; and he was thinking of setting up a new coach service between Argueil and Rouen: such a thing would quickly spell the end of the old rattletrap at the Lion d'Or, and being faster and cheaper and carrying a bigger pay load would give him a monopoly of the Yonville trade.

Charles wondered more than once how he was going to be able to pay back so large a sum the following year; and racking his brains he imagined various expedients, such as applying to his father or selling off something. But his father would turn a deaf ear, and he himself owned nothing that could be sold. The difficulties he foresaw were so formidable that he quickly banished the disagreeable subject from his mind. He reproached himself for having let it distract him from Emma—as though his every thought were her property and he were filching something from her if he took his mind off her for a second.

It was a severe winter. Madame's convalescence was slow. On fine days they pushed her armchair to the window—the one overlooking the square, for she had taken an aversion to the garden, and the blind on that side was always down. She asked that her horse be sold: things that had once given her pleasure she now disliked. She seemed to have no thought for anything beyond her own health. She ate her tiny meals in bed, rang for the maid to ask about her tisanes or just to chat. All this while the snow on the roof of the market filled the room with its monotonous white reflection; then came a spell of rain. And every day Emma looked forward, with a kind of anxious expectation, to the same, unfailingly recurring, trivial events, little though they mattered to her. The greatest of these was the nightly arrival of the Hirondelle, when Madame Lefrançois shouted, other voices replied, and Hippolyte's stable lamp, as he looked for luggage under the hood, shone out like a star in the darkness. At noon Charles always returned from his rounds; after lunch he went out again; then she took a cup of bouillon; and toward five, at the close of day, children passed the house on their way home from school, dragging their wooden shoes along the sidewalk, and invariably, one after the other, hitting their rulers against the shutter hooks.

About this time Monsieur Bournisien usually stopped in. He would ask after her health, give her news, and exhort her to prayer in an affectionate, informal way that wasn't without its charm. Just the sight of his cassock she found comforting.

One day at the height of her sickness, when she thought she was dying, she had asked for Communion; and as her room was made ready for the sacrament—the chest of drawers cleared of its medicine bottles and transformed into an altar, the floor strewn with dahlia blossoms by Félicité—Emma felt something powerful pass over her that rid her of all pain, all perception, all feeling. Her flesh had been relieved of its burdens, even the burden of thought; another life was beginning; it seemed to her that her spirit, ascending to God, was about to find annihilation in this love, like burning incense dissolving in smoke. The sheets of her bed were sprinkled with holy water; the priest drew the white host from the sacred pyx; and she was all but swooning with celestial bliss as she advanced her lips to receive the body of the Saviour. The curtains of her alcove swelled out softly around her like clouds; and the beams of the two wax tapers burning on the chest of drawers seemed to her like dazzling emanations of divine light. Then she let her head fall back: through the vastnesses of space seemed to come the music of seraphic harps; and on a golden throne in an azure sky she thought she saw God the Father in all His glory, surrounded by the saints bearing branches of green palm; He was gesturing majestically, and obedient angels with flaming wings were descending to the earth to bear her to Him in their arms.

This splendid vision, the most beautiful of all possible dreams, stayed in her memory—not eclipsing all else as at the time it occurred, but no less intensely sweet; and she kept straining to recapture the original sensation. Her soul, aching with pride, was at last finding rest in Christian humility; and luxuriating in her own weakness she turned her eyes inward and watched the destruction of her will, which was to open wide the way for an onrush of grace. She was filled with wonderment at the discovery that there was a bliss greater than mere happiness—a love different from and transcending all others—a love without break and without end, a love that increased throughout eternity! Among the illusions born of her hope she glimpsed a realm of purity in which she aspired to dwell: it hovered above the earth, merging with the sky. She conceived the idea of becoming a saint. She bought rosaries and festooned herself with holy medals; she wished she had an emerald-studded reliquary within reach at her bed's head, to kiss every night.

The priest was enchanted by her change of heart, though he was of the opinion that her faith might by its very fervor come to border on heresy and even on extravagance. But not being versed in these matters once they went beyond a certain point, he wrote Monsieur Boulard, the bishop's bookseller, and asked him to send him "something particularly good for a lady who had a very fine mind." As casually as though he were shipping trinkets to savages, the bookseller made up a heterogeneous package of everything just then current in the religious book trade—little question-and-answer manuals, pamphlets couched in the contemptuous language made popular by Monsieur de Maistre,[5] so-called novels in pink bindings and sugary style concocted by romantic-minded seminarists or reformed blue-stockings. There were titles such as *Think It Over Carefully; The Man of the World at the Feet of Mary, by Monsieur de——, recipient of several decorations; The Errors of Voltaire, for the use of the young;* etc.

Madame Bovary wasn't yet sufficiently recovered in mind to apply herself seriously to anything; and besides, she plunged into all this literature far too precipitately. The regulations governing worship annoyed her; she disliked the arrogance of the polemical writings because of their relentless attacks on people she had never heard of; and the secular stories flavored with religion seemed to her written out of such ignorance of the world that she was unwittingly led away from the very truths she was longing to have confirmed. Nevertheless she persisted; and when the volume fell from her hands she was convinced that hers was the most exquisite Catholic melancholy that had ever entered an ethereal soul.

As for the memory of Rodolphe, she had buried it in the depths of her heart; and there it remained, as solemn and motionless as the mummy of a pharaoh in an underground chamber. Her great love that lay thus embalmed

---

5. A major theorist (1753–1821) of Catholic conservatism. His books, *Du Pape* (1819) and *Soirées de Saint-Petersbourg* (1821), defended the power of the pope and the sovereign king and argued that the reign of evil on Earth has to be curbed by authority.

gave off a fragrance that permeated everything, adding a touch of tenderness to the immaculate atmosphere in which she longed to live. When she knelt at her Gothic *prie-dieu* she addressed the Lord in the same ardent words she had formerly murmured to her lover in the ecstasies of adultery. It was her way of praying for faith; but heaven showered no joy upon her, and she would rise, her limbs aching, with a vague feeling that it was all a vast fraud. This quest she considered meritorious in itself; and in the pride of her piety Emma likened herself to those great ladies of yore whose fame she had dreamed of while gazing at a portrait of La Vallière: how majestically they had trailed the gorgeous trains of their long gowns, as they withdrew into seclusion to shed at the feet of Christ all the tears of their life-wounded hearts!

Now she became wildly charitable. She sewed clothes for the poor, sent firewood to women in childbed; and one day Charles came home to find three tramps sitting at the kitchen table eating soup. She sent for her daughter—during her illness Charles had left the child with the nurse—and she determined to teach her to read. Berthe wept and wept, but she never lost her temper with her. It was a deliberately adopted attitude of resignation, of indulgence toward all. She used a lofty term whenever she could:

"Is your stomach-ache all gone, my angel?" she would say to her daughter.

The elder Madame Bovary found nothing to reproach her for in all this, except perhaps her mania for knitting undershirts for orphans instead of mending her own dish towels. Harassed by the incessant quarrels in her own home, the old lady enjoyed the peaceful atmosphere of this house; and she prolonged her visit through Easter to escape the jibes of her husband, whose invariable habit it was to order pork sausage on Good Friday.

In addition to the company of her mother-in-law, whom she found a steadying influence because of her unswerving principles and solemn demeanor, Emma nearly every day had other visits—from Madame Langlois, Madame Caron, Madame Dubreuil, Madame Tuvache, and, regularly from two to five, from Madame Homais, who—good soul that she was—had always refused to believe any of the gossip that was spread about her neighbor. The Homais children visited her, too; Justin brought them. He came with them up into her bedroom and stood quietly near the door, never saying a word. Often while he was there Madame Bovary would start to dress, oblivious of him. She would begin by taking out her comb and tossing her head; and the first time he saw her mass of black hair fall in ringlets to her knees, it was for the boy like the sudden opening of a door upon something marvelous and new, something whose splendor frightened him.

Emma never noticed his silent eagerness or his timidity. She knew only that love had disappeared from her life: she had no suspicion that it was pulsating there so close to her, beneath that coarse shirt, in that adolescent heart so open to the emanations of her beauty. Moreover, her detachment from everything had become so complete, her language was so sweet and the look in her eye so haughty, her behavior was so mercurial, that there was no longer any way of telling where selfishness and corruption ended and charity and virtue began. One night, for instance, she lost her temper with her servant, who was asking permission to go out and stammering some pretended reason. Then:

"So you love him, do you?" Emma suddenly demanded.

And without waiting for the blushing Félicité to answer, she added, resignedly:

"All right—run along! Enjoy yourself!"

When the weather turned mild she had the garden completely dug up and relandscaped. Bovary objected a little, but he was glad to see her finally caring about things, and she gave more and more evidence of this as her strength returned. She forbade the house to Madame Rollet the nurse, who during her convalescence had formed the habit of coming too often to the kitchen with her own two babes and her little boarder, the latter more ravenous than a cannibal. She cut down on visits from the Homais', discouraged all her other callers, and even went less regularly to church, thus eliciting the apothecary's approval.

"I was afraid you'd been taken in by the mumbo-jumbo," he said amicably.

The abbé Bournisien still came every day, after catechism class. He preferred to sit outdoors in the fresh air—in the "grove," as he called the arbor. This was the hour of Charles's return. Both men would be hot; Félicité would bring them sweet cider, and they would raise their glasses and drink to Madame's complete recovery.

Binet was often there: just below, that is—beside the terrace wall, fishing for crayfish. Bovary would invite him to join them for a drink; he prided himself on being an expert uncorker of cider jugs.

"First," he would say—glancing at his companions complacently and then giving an equally smug look at the landscape—"first you must hold the bottle upright on the table, like this. Then you cut the strings. And then you pry up the cork, a little at a time, gently, gently—the way they open seltzer water in restaurants."

But during this demonstration the cork would often pop out and the cider would splash one or another of them in the face; and the curé never failed to laugh his thick laugh and make his joke:

"Its excellence is certainly *striking!*"

He was a good-hearted fellow—there was no denying it—and he even expressed no objection one day when the pharmacist advised Charles to give Madame a treat and take her to the opera in Rouen, to hear the famous tenor, Lagardy. Homais was surprised at his silence, and asked him how he felt about it; and the priest declared that he considered music less dangerous to morals than literature.

The pharmacist sprang to the defense of letters. The theater, he claimed, served to expose prejudice: it taught virtue under the guise of entertainment:

"*Castigat ridendo mores,*[6] Monsieur Bournisien! Take most of Voltaire's tragedies, for example: it's clever the way he's stuck them full of philosophical remarks—they're a complete education in morals and diplomacy for the people."

"I saw a play once, called the *Gamin de Paris,*[7] said Binet. "There's an old general in it that's absolutely first-class. A rich fellow seduces a working girl and the general slaps him down and at the end . . ."

"Of course," Homais went on, "there's bad literature just as there's bad pharmaceutics. But to make a blanket condemnation of the greatest of the

6. "It [comedy] reproves the manners, through laughter" (Latin); a slogan for comedy invented by the poet Jean de Santeuil (1630–1697) and given to the harlequin Dominique to put on the curtain of his theater.
7. A comedy by Bayard and Vanderbusch performed in 1836 in Paris.

fine arts seems to be a yokelism, a medievalism worthy of that abominable age when they imprisoned Galileo."[8]

"I know perfectly well," objected the priest, "that there are good writers who write good things. Still, the fact alone that people of different sexes are brought together in a glamorous auditorium that's the last word in worldly luxury—and then the heathenish disguises, the painted faces, the footlights, the effeminate voices—it all can't help encouraging a certain licentiousness and inducing evil thoughts and impure temptations. Such, at least, is the opinion of all the church fathers. After all," he added, suddenly assuming an unctuous tone and rolling himself a pinch of snuff, "if the church condemns play-going she has good reason for doing so: we must submit to her decrees."

"Why," demanded the apothecary, "does she excommunicate actors? They used to take part openly in ecclesiastical ceremonies, you know. Yes, they used to act right in the middle of the choir—put on farcical plays called mysteries. These often violated the laws of decency, I may say."

The priest's only answer was a groan, and the pharmacist persisted:

"It's the same in the Bible. There's more than one spicy bit in that book, you know—some pret-ty dar-ing things!"

And as Monsieur Bournisien made a gesture of annoyance:

"Ah! You'll agree that it's no book to give a young person! I'd be sorry if my daughter Athalie . . ."

"But *we* don't recommend the reading of the Bible!" cried the abbé impatiently. "It's the Protestants!"

"It makes no difference," said Homais. "I'm astonished that in this day and age—an age of enlightenment—anyone should persist in forbidding a form of intellectual diversion that's harmless, morally uplifting, and sometimes—isn't it true, Doctor?—even good for the health."

"I guess so." Charles made his answer in a vacant tone—perhaps because he shared Homais' opinion and didn't want to offend the priest, or perhaps because he had no opinion.

The conversation seemed to be at an end, when the pharmacist saw fit to make one last dig.

"I've known priests," he said, "who made a practice of going out in civilian clothes and watching leg shows."

"Come now," said the priest.

"Oh yes, I've known some!"

And once again separating his syllables by way of significant emphasis, Homais repeated:

"I—have—known—some!"

"Well, then, they did wrong," said Bournisien with truly Christian patience.

"I should think so! And that wasn't all they were up to, either!" exclaimed the apothecary.

"*Monsieur!*" The priest jumped to his feet and glared so fiercely that the pharmacist was intimidated.

"All I mean," he said, much more mildly, "is that tolerance is the surest means of bringing souls into the church."

8. Galileo Galilei (1564–1642), astronomer who was confined to his house in Arcetri (near Florence) after his book propounding the view that the Earth circled around the sun was condemned by the Inquisition (in 1633).

"Quite true, quite true," the curé conceded, sitting down again.

He left a moment or two later, however, and Homais said to the doctor:

"Quite a squabble! How did you like the way I got the better of him? Pretty good, eh? Anyway—follow my advice and take Madame to the opera, if only to give a priest a black eye for once in your life. If I could find a substitute I'd come with you. Don't lose any time getting tickets: Lagardy's giving only one performance—he's scheduled for an English tour at staggering fees. From what they say, he must be quite a lad. He's filthy with money. Everywhere he goes he takes along three mistresses and a cook. All those great artists burn their candles at both ends: they have to lead a wild kind of life—it stimulates their imagination. But they die in the poorhouse, because they haven't the sense to save money when they're young. Well, *bon appétit: à demain!*"

The idea of the opera took rapid root in Bovary's mind. He lost no time suggesting it to his wife. She shook her head, pleading fatigue, trouble and expense; but for once Charles didn't give in, so convinced was he that she would benefit from the excursion. He saw no reason for them not to go: his mother had sent him three hundred francs they had given up hope of getting, their debts of the moment were nothing tremendous, and Lheureux's notes weren't due for so long that there was no use thinking about them. Fancying that Emma was refusing out of consideration for him, Charles insisted the more strongly, and finally she gave in. The next day, at eight in the morning, they bundled themselves into the Hirondelle.

The apothecary, who had nothing in the world to keep him in Yonville, but who was firmly convinced that he couldn't absent himself even briefly, gave a sigh as he watched their departure.

"*Bon voyage!*" he called to them. "Some people have all the luck!"

And to Emma, who was wearing a blue silk dress with four rows of flounces:

"You're pretty as a picture! You'll be the belle of Rouen!"

The coach took them to the Hotel de la Croix-Rouge in the Place Beauvoisine. It was one of those inns such as you find on the edge of every provincial city, with large stables and small bedrooms, and chickens scratching for oats in the coach yard under muddy gigs belonging to traveling salesmen—comfortable, old-fashioned stopovers, with worm-eaten wooden balconies that creak in the wind on winter nights, constantly full of people, bustle and victuals, their blackened tabletops sticky with spilled coffee-and-brandies, their thick windowpanes yellowed by flies, their napkins spotted blue by cheap red wine. They always seem a little rustic, like farmhands in Sunday clothes; on the street side they have a café, and in back—on the country side—a vegetable garden. Charles went at once to buy tickets. He got the stage boxes mixed up with the top balconies, and the rest of the boxes with the orchestra; he asked for explanations, didn't understand them, was sent from the box office to the manager, came back to the hotel, went back to the box office again. All in all, between the theater and the outer boulevard he covered the entire length of the city several times over.

Madame bought herself a hat, gloves and a bouquet. Monsieur was nervous about missing the beginning; and without stopping for as much as a cup of bouillon they arrived at the theater before the doors were even open.

XV

There was a crowd waiting outside, lined up behind railings on both sides of the entrance. At the adjoining street corners huge posters in fancy lettering announced: *"Lucie de Lammermoor*[9] . . . Lagardy . . . Opéra . . . etc." It was a fine evening; everyone was hot: many a set of curls was drenched in sweat, and handkerchiefs were out, mopping red brows; now and again a soft breeze blowing from the river gently stirred the edges of the canvas awnings over café doors. But just a short distance away there was a coolness, provided by an icy draft smelling of tallow, leather and oil—the effluvia of the Rue des Charettes, with its great, gloomy, barrel-filled warehouses.

Fearing lest they appear ridiculous, Emma insisted that they stroll a bit along the river front before going in; and Bovary, by way of precaution, kept the tickets in his hand and his hand in his trousers pocket, pressed reassuringly against his stomach.

Her heart began to pound as they entered the foyer. A smile of satisfaction rose involuntarily to her lips at seeing the crowd hurry off to the right down the corridor, while she climbed the stairs leading to the first tier. She took pleasure, like a child, in pushing open the wide upholstered doors with one finger; she filled her lungs with the dusty smell of the corridors; and seated in her box she drew herself up with all the airs of a duchess.

The theater began to fill; opera glasses came out of cases; and subscribers exchanged greetings as they glimpsed one another across the house. The arts, for them, were a relaxation from the worries of buying and selling; that was why they had come; but it was quite impossible for them to forget business even here, and their conversation was about cotton, spirits and indigo. The old men looked blank and placid: with their gray-white hair and gray-white skin they were like silver medals that had been tarnished by lead fumes. The young beaux strutted in the orchestra: the openings of their waistcoats were bright with pink or apple-green cravats; and Madame Bovary looked admiringly down at them as they leaned with tightly yellow-gloved hands on their gold-knobbed walking sticks.

Meanwhile the candles were lighted on the music stands and the chandelier came down from the ceiling, the sparkle of its crystals filling the house with sudden gaiety; then the musicians filed in and there was a long cacophony of booming cellos, scraping violins, blaring horns, and piping flutes and flageolets. Then three heavy blows came from the stage; there was a roll of kettledrums and a series of chords from the brasses; and the curtain rose on an outdoor scene.

It was a crossroad in a forest, on the right a spring shaded by an oak. A group of country folk and nobles, all with tartans over their shoulders, sang a hunting chorus; then a captain strode in and inveighed against an evil spirit, raising both arms to heaven; another character joined him; they both walked off, and the huntsmen repeated their chorus.

She was back in the books she had read as a girl—deep in Walter Scott. She imagined she could hear the sound of Scottish pipes echoing through the mist across the heather. Her recollection of the novel made it easy for her to grasp the libretto; and she followed the plot line by line, elusive, half-

---

9. An opera by Gaetano Donizetti (1797–1848), first performed in Naples in 1835 (in Paris in 1837), based on Walter Scott's novel *The Bride of Lammermoor* (1819). See "Editor's Note," p. 1087.

forgotten memories drifting into her thoughts only to be dispelled by the onrush of the music. She let herself be lulled by the melodies, feeling herself vibrate to the very fiber of her being, as though the bows of the violins were playing on her nerve strings. She couldn't take in enough of the costumes, the sets, the characters, the painted trees that shook at the slightest footstep, the velvet bonnets, the cloaks, the swords—all those fanciful things that fluttered on waves of music as though in another world. Then a young woman came forward, tossing a purse to a squire in green. She was left along on the stage, and there came the sound of a flute, like the ripple of a spring or the warbling of a bird. Lucie, looking solemn, began her cavatina in G major: she uttered love laments, begged for wings. And at the moment Emma, too, longed that she might leave life behind and take wing in an embrace. Suddenly Edgar Lagardy came on stage.

He was pale to the point of splendor, with that marmoreal majesty sometimes found among the passionate races of the south. His stalwart figure was clad in a tight brown doublet; a small chased dagger swung at his left hip; and he rolled his eyes about him languorously and flashed his white teeth. People said that a Polish princess had heard him sing one night on the beach at Biarritz, where he was a boat boy, and had fallen in love with him; she had beggared herself for him, and he had left her for other women. This reputation as a ladies' man had done no disservice to his professional career. Shrewd ham actor that he was, he always saw to it that his publicity should include a poetic phrase or two about the charm of his personality and the sensibility of his soul. A fine voice, utter self-possession, more temperament than intelligence, more bombast than feeling—such were the principal attributes of this magnificent charlatan. There was a touch of the hairdresser about him, and a touch of the toreador.

He had the audience in transports from the first. He clasped Lucie in his arms, left her, returned to her, seemed in despair: he would shout with rage, then let his voice expire, plaintive and infinitely sweet; and the notes that poured from his bare throat were full of sobs and kisses. Emma strained forward to watch him, her fingernails scratching the plush of her box. Her heart drank its full of the melodious laments that hung suspended in the air against the sound of the double basses like the cries of shipwrecked sailors against the tumult of a storm. Here was the same ecstasy, the same anguish that had brought her to the brink of death. The soprano's voice seemed but the echo of her own soul, and this illusion that held her under its spell a part of her own life. But no one on earth had ever loved her with so great a love. That last moonlight night, when they had told each other, "Till tomorrow! Till tomorrow!" he had not wept as Edgar was weeping now. The house was bursting with applause. The whole stretto was repeated: the lover sang about the flowers on their graves, about vows and exile and fate and hope; and when their voices rose in the final farewell, Emma herself uttered a sharp cry that was drowned in the blast of the final chords.

"What's that lord doing, mistreating her like that?" Charles asked.

"No, no," she answered. "That's her lover."

"But he's swearing vengeance on her family, whereas the other one—the one that came on a while ago—said 'I love Lucie and I think she loves me!' Besides, he walked off arm in arm with her father. That is her father, isn't it, the ugly little one with the cock feather in his hat?"

Despite Emma's explanations, Charles got everything mixed up beginning with the duet in recitative in which Gilbert explains his abominable machinations to his master Ashton. The false engagement ring serving to trick Lucie he took to be a love token sent by Edgar. In fact he couldn't follow the story at all, he said, because of the music: it interfered so with the words.

"What difference does it make?" said Emma. "Be quiet!"

"But I like to know what's going on," he persisted, leaning over her shoulder. "You know I do."

"Be quiet! Be quiet!" she whispered impatiently.

Lucie came on, half borne up by her women; there was a wreath of orange blossoms in her hair, and she was paler than the white satin of her gown. Emma thought of her own wedding day: she saw herself walking toward the church along the little path amid the wheatfields. Why in heaven's name hadn't she resisted and entreated, like Lucie? But no—she had been light-hearted, unaware of the abyss she was rushing toward. Ah! If only in the freshness of her beauty, before defiling herself in marriage, before the disillusionments of adultery, she could have found some great and noble heart to be her life's foundation! Then virtue and affection, sensual joys and duty would all have been one; and she would never have fallen from her high felicity. But that kind of happiness was doubtless a lie, invented to make one despair of any love. Now she well knew the true paltriness of the passions that art painted so large. So she did her best to think of the opera in a different light: she resolved to regard this image of her own griefs as a vivid fantasy, an enjoyable spectacle and nothing more; and she was actually smiling to herself in scornful pity when from behind the velvet curtains at the back of the stage there appeared a man in a black cloak.

A single gesture sent his broad-brimmed Spanish hat to the ground; and the orchestra and the singers abruptly broke into the sextet. Edgar, flashing fury, dominated all the others with his high, clear voice. Ashton flung him his homicidal challenge in solemn tones; Lucie uttered her shrill lament; Arthur sang his asides in middle register; and the chaplain's baritone boomed like an organ while the women, echoing his words, repeated them in delicious chorus. All the characters now formed a single line across the stage; all were gesticulating at once; and rage, vengeance, jealousy, terror, pity and amazement poured simultaneously from their open mouths. The outraged lover brandished his naked sword; his lace collar rose and fell with the heaving of his chest; and he strode up and down, clanking the silver-gilt spurs on his soft, flaring boots. His love, she thought, must be inexhaustible, since he could pour it out in such great quantities on the crowd. Her resolution not to be taken in by the display of false sentiment was swept away by the impact of the singer's eloquence; the fiction that he was embodying drew her to his real life, and she tried to imagine what it was like—that glamorous, fabulous, marvelous life that she, too, might have lived had chance so willed it. They might have met! They might have loved! With him she might have traveled over all the kingdoms of Europe, from capital to capital, sharing his hardships and his triumphs, gathering up the flowers his admirers threw, embroidering his costumes with her own hands; and every night behind the gilded lattice of her box she might have sat open-mouthed, breathing in the outpourings of that divine creature who would be singing for her alone: he would have gazed at her from the stage as he played his role. A mad idea seized her: he was gazing at her now! She was sure of it! She longed to rush into his arms and seek refuge in his strength as in the very incarnation of love; she longed to cry: "Ravish me! Carry me off! Away from here! All my passion and all my dreams are yours—yours alone!"

The curtain fell.

The smell of gas mingled with human exhalations, and the air seemed the more stifling for being stirred up by fans. Emma tried to get out, but there was a crush in the corridors, and she sank back onto a chair, oppressed by palpitations. Charles, fearful lest she fall into a faint, hurried to the bar for a glass of orgeat.

He had a hard time getting back to the box: he held the glass in both hands because his elbows were being jarred at every other step, but even so he spilled three-quarters of it over the shoulders of a Rouen lady in short sleeves, who began to scream like a peacock, as though she were being murdered, when she felt the cold liquid trickling down her spine. While she took her handkerchief to the spots on her beautiful cerise taffeta gown, her mill-owner husband gave poor clumsy Charles a piece of his mind, angrily muttering the words "damages," "cost," and "replacement." Finally Charles made his way to his wife.

"I thought I'd never get out of there," he gasped. "Such a crowd! Such a crowd!"

And he added:

"Guess who I ran into: Monsieur Léon!"

"Léon?"

"Absolutely. He'll be coming along to pay you his respects."

As he uttered the words the former Yonville clerk entered the box.

He held out his hand with aristocratic casualness; and Madame Bovary automatically extended hers—yielding, no doubt, to the attraction of a stronger will. She hadn't touched it since that spring evening when the rain was falling on the new green leaves—the evening they had said farewell as they stood beside the window. But quickly reminding herself of the social requirements of the situation, she roused herself with an effort from her memories and began to stammer hurried phrases:

"Ah, good evening! You here? How amazing . . . !"

"Quiet!" cried a voice from the orchestra, for the third act was beginning.

"So you're living in Rouen?"

"Yes."

"Since when?"

"Sh! Sh!"

People were turning around at them indignantly, and they fell silent.

But from that moment on Emma no longer listened to the music. The chorus of guests, the scene between Ashton and his attendant, the great duet in D major—for her it all took place at a distance, as though the instruments had lost their sound and the characters had moved away. She recalled the card games at the pharmacist's and the walk to the wet nurse's, their readings under the arbor, the tête-à-têtes beside the fire—the whole poor story of their love, so quiet and so long, so discreet, so tender, and yet discarded from her memory. Why was he returning like this? What combination of events was bringing him back into her life? He sat behind her, leaning a shoulder against the wall of the box; and from time to time she quivered as she felt his warm breath on her hair.

"Are you enjoying this?" he asked, leaning over so close that the tip of his mustache brushed against her cheek.

"Heavens no," she said carelessly, "not particularly."

And he suggested that they leave the theater and go somewhere for an ice.

"Oh, not yet! Let's stay!" said Bovary. "Her hair's down: it looks as though it's going to be tragic."

But the mad scene interested Emma not at all: the soprano, she felt, was overdoing her role.

"She's shrieking too loud," she said, turning toward Charles, who was drinking it in.

"Yes . . . perhaps . . . a little," he replied, torn between the fullness of his enjoyment and the respect he had for his wife's opinions.

"It's so hot. . . ." sighed Léon.

"It is. . . . Unbearable."

"Are you uncomfortable?" asked Bovary.

"Yes, I'm stifling; let's go."

Monsieur Léon carefully laid her long lace shawl over her shoulders, and the three of them walked to the river front and sat down on the outdoor terrace of a café. First they spoke of her sickness, Emma interrupting Charles now and then lest, as she said, he bore Monsieur Léon; and Monsieur Léon told them he had just come to Rouen to spend two years in a large office to familiarize himself with the kind of business carried on in Normandy, which was different from anything he had learned about in Paris. Then he asked about Berthe, the Homais', and Madame Lefrançois; and since they had no more to say to each other in front of Charles the conversation soon died.

People coming from the theater strolled by on the sidewalk, humming or bawling at the top of their voices: *"O bel ange, ma Lucie!"* Léon began to show off his musical knowledge. He had heard Tamburini, Rubini, Persiani, Grisi;[1] and in comparison with them, Lagardy, for all the noise he made, was nothing.

"Still," interrupted Charles, who was eating his rum sherbet a tiny bit at a time, "they say he's wonderful in the last act. I was sorry to leave before the end: I was beginning to like it."

"Don't worry," said the clerk, "he'll be giving another performance soon."

But Charles said they were leaving the next day.

"Unless," he said, turning to his wife, "you'd like to stay on by yourself, sweetheart?"

And changing his tune to suit this unexpected opportunity, the young man sang the praises of Lagardy in the final scenes. He was superb, sublime! Charles insisted:

"You can come home Sunday. Yes, make up your mind to do it. You'd be wrong not to, if you think there's the slightest chance it might do you some good."

Meanwhile the tables around them were emptying; a waiter came and

---

1. Antonio Tamburini (1800–1876); Gian-Battista Rubini (1794–1854); Fanny Tacchinardi Persiani, who was the first Lucia (1812–1867); and Giulia Grisi (1811–1869) were all famous bel canto singers who appeared in Paris in the operas of Rossini and Donizetti.

stood discreetly nearby; Charles took the hint and drew out his purse; the clerk put a restraining hand on his arm, paid the bill, and noisily threw down a couple of silver coins for the waiter.

"I'm really embarrassed," murmured Bovary, "at the money that you . . ."

The younger man shrugged him off in a friendly way and took up his hat: "So it's agreed?" he said. "Tomorrow at six?"

Charles repeated that he couldn't stay away that much longer, but that there was nothing to prevent Emma . . .

"Oh," she murmured, smiling a peculiar smile, "I really don't know whether . . ."

"Well, think it over," said Charles. "Sleep on it and we'll decide in the morning."

Then, to Léon, who was walking with them:

"Now that you're back in our part of the world I hope you'll drop in now and then and let us give you dinner?"

The clerk said that he certainly would, especially since he'd soon be going to Yonville anyway on a business matter. They said good night at the corner of the Passage Saint-Herbland as the cathedral clock was striking half past eleven.

Part Three

I

Busy though he had been with his law studies, Monsieur Léon had nevertheless found time to frequent the Chaumière, and in that cabaret he had done very well for himself with the grisettes, who considered him "distinguished-looking." He was the best-behaved student imaginable; his hair was neither too long nor too short, he didn't spend his entire quarter's allowance the day he got it, and he kept on good terms with his professors. As for excesses, he had been too timorous as well as too squeamish to go in for them.

Often, when he sat reading in his room, or under the lindens of the Luxembourg[2] in the evening, he let his law book fall to the ground, and the memory of Emma came back to him. But gradually his feeling for her faded, and other sensual appetites supplanted it. Even so, it persisted in the background, for Léon never gave up all hope: it was as though a vague promise kept dangling before him in the future, like a golden fruit hanging from some exotic tree.

Then, seeing her again after three years, his passion revived. This time, he decided he must make up his mind to possess her. Much of his shyness had worn off as a result of the gay company he had kept, and he had returned to the provinces filled with contempt for the local ladies, so different from the trim-shod creatures of the boulevards. Before an elegant Parisienne in the salon of some famous, rich, bemedaled physician, the poor clerk would doubtless have trembled like a child; but here on the Rouen river front, in

---

2. The gardens of the Palace of Luxembourg (built between 1615 and 1620 for Marie de Médici); they are open to the public and much frequented by students, as they are near the Sorbonne.

the presence of this wife of an *officier de santé,* he felt at ease, sure in advance that she would be dazzled. Self-confidence depends on surroundings: the same person talks quite differently in the drawing room and in the garret, and a rich woman's virtue is protected by her banknotes quite as effectively as by any cuirass worn under a corset.

After taking leave of Monsieur and Madame Bovary the previous night, Léon had followed them at a distance in the street; and when he saw them turn into the Croix-Rouge, he retraced his steps and spent the rest of the night working out a plan of action.

The next afternoon about five, pale faced, with a tightness in his throat and with the blind resolution of the panic-stricken, he walked into the inn kitchen.

"Monsieur isn't here," a servant told him.

He took that to be a good omen, and went upstairs.

She received him calmly, and even apologized for having forgotten to mention where they were staying.

"Oh, I guessed!" said Léon.

"How?"

He pretended that he had been led to her by pure chance, a kind of instinct. That made her smile; and, ashamed of his blunder, he quickly told her that he had spent the morning looking for her all over the city, in one hotel after another.

"So you decided to stay?" he asked.

"Yes," she said, "and I was wrong. One can't afford to be self-indulgent if one has a thousand things to attend to."

"Oh, I can imagine . . ."

"No, you can't! You're not a woman."

But men had their troubles, too; and so the conversation got under way, with philosophical reflections. Emma expatiated on the vanity of earthly attachments and on the eternal isolation of every human heart. Either to impress her, or naturally taking on the color of her melancholy, the young man declared that he had found his studies prodigiously frustrating. The technicalities of law irritated him, he was tempted by other careers, and in her letters his mother never stopped pestering him. Indeed, as they talked on they both became more specific in their complaints, and less reserved in their confidences. Occasionally they shrank from giving full expression to their thought, and groped for phrases that would convey it obliquely. But she never disclosed having had another passion, and he said nothing about having forgotten her.

Perhaps he no longer remembered the suppers following fancy-dress balls, with the girls costumed as stevedores; and doubtless she didn't recall those early-morning meetings when she had run through the fields to her lover's château. The sounds of the city reached them only faintly, and the room seemed small, designed with them in mind, to make their solitude the closer. Emma, in a dimity dressing gown, leaned her chignon against the back of the old armchair; the yellow wallpaper was like a gold ground behind her; and her bare head was reflected in the mirror, with the white line of her center part and the tips of her ears peeping out from under the sweeps of her hair.

"But forgive me," she said. "I shouldn't bore you with all my complaints!"

"How can you say that!" he said reproachfully.

"Ah!" she said, lifting her lovely tear-bright eyes to the ceiling. "If you knew all the dreams I've dreamed!"

"It's the same with me! Oh, I had a terrible time! Very often I dropped everything and went out and wandered along the quays, trying to forget my thoughts in the noise of the crowd. But I could never drive out the obsession that haunted me. In the window of a print shop on the boulevard there's an Italian engraving showing one of the Muses. She's draped in a tunic and looking at the moon—her hair's streaming down, with forget-me-nots in it. Something made me go back there over and over again: I used to stand in front of that window for hours on end."

Then, in a trembling voice:

"She looked like you a little."

Madame Bovary averted her face lest he see the smile that she couldn't suppress.

"I kept writing you letters," he said, "and then tearing them up."

She made no answer. He went on:

"I used to imagine we'd meet by chance. I kept thinking I saw you on street corners, and I even ran after cabs sometimes, if I saw a shawl or a veil at the window that looked like yours. . . ."

She seemed determined to let him speak without interruption. Arms crossed and head lowered, she stared at the rosettes on her slippers, now and again moving her toes a little under the satin.

Finally she gave a sigh. "The worst thing of all, it seems to me, is to go on leading a futile life the way I do. If our unhappiness were of use to someone, we could find consolation in the thought of sacrifice!"

He launched into a eulogy of virtue, duty, silent renunciation: he, too, he said, had a fantastic need for selfless dedication that he was unable to satisfy.

"What I should love to do," she said, "would be to join an order of nursing Sisters."

"Alas!" he answered. "No such sacred missions are open to men. I can't think of any calling . . . except maybe becoming a doctor. . . ."

She gave a slight shrug and interrupted him, expressing regret that her illness had not been fatal. What a pity! By now she would be past all suffering. Léon at once chimed in with a longing for "the peace of the grave." One night he had even written out his will, asking to be buried in the beautiful velvet-striped coverlet she had given him.

That was how they would have liked to be: what they were doing was to dream up ideals and then refashion their past lives to match them. Speech is a rolling-machine that always stretches the feelings it expresses!

But:

"Why?" she asked him, at his made-up tale about the coverlet.

"Why?" He hesitated. "Because—I was terribly in love with you."

And congratulating himself on having got over the hurdle, Léon watched her face out of the corner of his eye.

It was like the sky when a gust of wind sweeps away the clouds. The mass of sad thoughts that had darkened her blue eyes seemed to lift: her whole face was radiant.

He waited. Finally she answered:

"I always thought so."

They went over, then, the tiny happenings of that far-off time, whose joys and sorrows had been evoked by a single word. He spoke of the clematis bower, of the dresses she had worn, of the furniture in her room—of everything in the house.

"And our poor cactuses—what's become of them?"

"The cold killed them last winter."

"I've thought about them so often, would you believe it? I've pictured them the way they used to look on summer mornings, with the sun on the blinds and your bare arms in among the flowers."

"Poor boy," she said, holding out her hand.

Léon lost no time pressing it to his lips. Then, after taking a deep breath:

"You were a strange, mysterious, captivating force in my life in those days. There was one time, for example, when I came to call on you . . . But you probably don't remember."

"Yes, I do. Go on."

"You were downstairs in the hall, ready to go out, standing on the bottom step. I even remember your hat—it had little blue flowers on it. And without your asking me at all I went with you. I couldn't help it. I felt more and more foolish every minute, though, and I kept on walking near you. I didn't dare really follow you, and yet I couldn't bear to go away. When you went into a shop I stayed in the street, watching you through the window take off your gloves and count the change on the counter. Then you rang Madame Tuvache's bell; you went in; and I stood there like an idiot in front of the big heavy door even after it had closed behind you."

As she listened to him, Madame Bovary marveled at how old she was: all those reemerging details made her life seem vaster, as though she had endless emotional experiences to look back on. Her voice low, her eyes half closed, she kept saying:

"Yes, I remember! I remember! I remember . . . !"

They heard eight o'clock strike from several belfries near the Place Beauvoisine, a section of Rouen full of boarding schools, churches and great deserted mansions. They were no longer speaking; but as they looked at one another they felt a throbbing in their heads: it was as though their very glances had set off a physical vibration. Now they had clasped hands; and in the sweetness of their ecstasy everything merged—the past, the future, their memories and their dreams. Night was darkening the walls of the room: still gleaming in the dimness were the garish colors of four prints showing four scenes from *La Tour de Nesle*,[3] with captions below in Spanish and French. Through the sash window they could see a patch of dark sky between peaked roofs.

She rose to light two candles on the chest of drawers, and then sat down again.

"Well . . . ?" said Léon.

"Well . . . ?" she echoed.

And as he wondered how to resume the interrupted conversation, she asked:

"Why has no one ever said such things to me before?"

---

3. The Nesle Tower (French); a melodrama by Alexandre Dumas the elder (1803–1870) and Gaillardet (1832) in which Marie de Bourgogne, famous for her crimes, is the main heroine.

The clerk assured her warmly that idealistic natures were rarely understood. But he had loved her the moment he saw her, and despair filled him whenever he thought of the happiness that might have been theirs. Had fortune been kind, had they met earlier, they would long since have been united indissolubly.

"I've thought about that, sometimes," she said.

"What a dream!" murmured Léon.

And then, gently fingering the blue border of her long white belt:

"What's to prevent us from beginning all over again, now?"

"No, no," she said. "I'm too old . . . you're too young . . . forget me! You'll find other women to love you . . . and to love."

"Not as I do you!" he cried.

"What a child you are! Come, let's be sensible. I want us to be."

And she explained why they couldn't be lovers, why they must continue to be friends—like brother and sister—as in the past.

Did she mean those things she was saying? Doubtless Emma herself couldn't tell, engrossed as she was by the charm of seduction and the need to defend herself. Looking fondly at the young man, she gently repulsed the timid caresses his trembling hands essayed.

"Ah! Forgive me!" he said, drawing back.

And Emma was seized by a vague terror in the face of this timidity, a greater danger for her than Rodolphe's boldness when he had advanced with outstretched arms. Never had any man seemed to her so handsome. There was an exquisite candor about him. His long, fine, curving eyelashes were lowered; the smooth skin of his cheek was flushing with desire for her—so she thought; and she felt an all but invincible longing to touch it with her lips. She leaned away toward the clock, as though to see the time.

"Heavens!" she said. "How late! How we've been chattering!"

He understood, and rose to go.

"I forgot all about the opera! And poor Bovary left me here on purpose to see it! It was all arranged that I was to go with Monsieur and Madame Lormeaux, of the Rue Grand-Pont!"

It was her last chance, too, for she was leaving the next day.

"Really?" said Léon.

"Yes."

"But I must see you again," he said. "I had something to tell you. . . ."

"What?"

"Something . . . something serious, important. No—really: you mustn't go, you mustn't. If you knew . . . Listen . . . You haven't understood me, then? You haven't guessed . . ."

"On the contrary, you have a very clear way of putting things," said Emma.

"Ah! Now you're laughing at me! Please don't! Have pity on me: let me see you again. Once—just once."

"Well . . ."

She paused; then, as though changing her mind:

"Not here, certainly!"

"Wherever you like."

"Will you . . ."

She seemed to ponder; and then, tersely:

"Tomorrow at eleven in the cathedral."

"I'll be there!" he cried. He seized her hands, but she pulled them away.

They were standing close together, he behind and she with lowered head, and he bent over and kissed her long and lingeringly on the nape of the neck.

"You're crazy, crazy!" she cried between short bursts of laughter as he kissed her again and again.

Then, leaning his head over her shoulder, he seemed to be imploring her eyes to say yes, but the gaze he received was icy and aloof.

Léon stepped back; in the doorway he paused, and tremblingly whispered: "Till tomorrow."

Her only reply was a nod, and like a bird she vanished into the adjoining room.

That night Emma wrote the clerk an endless letter canceling their appointment: everything was over between them, and for the sake of their own happiness they must never meet again. But when she finished the letter she didn't know what to do with it—she hadn't Léon's address.

"I'll give it to him myself," she thought, "when he comes."

Léon, the next morning—humming a tune on his balcony beside his open window—polished his pumps himself, going over them again and again. He donned a pair of white trousers, fine socks, and a green tail coat; he doused his handkerchief with all the perfumes he possessed, had his hair curled, then uncurled it again to make it look more elegantly natural.

"Still too early!" he thought: he was looking at the barber's cuckoo clock, and it pointed to nine.

He read an old fashion magazine, went out, smoked a cigar, walked a few blocks. Finally he decided it was time to go, and set off briskly toward the Parvis Notre-Dame.

It was a fine summer morning. Silver gleamed in jewelers' windows, and the sunlight slanting onto the cathedral flashed on the cut surface of the gray stone; a flock of birds was swirling in the blue sky around the trefoiled turrets; the square, echoing with cries, smelled of the flowers that edged its pavement—roses, jasmine, carnations, narcissus and tuberoses interspersed with well-watered plants of catnip and chickweed. The fountain gurgled in the center; and under great umbrellas, among piles of cantaloupes, bare headed flower women were twisting paper around bunches of violets.

The young man chose one. It was the first time he had bought flowers for a woman; and his chest swelled with pride as he inhaled their fragrance, as though this homage that he intended for another were being paid, instead, to him.

But he was afraid of being seen, and resolutely entered the church.

The verger was just then standing in the left doorway, under the figure of the dancing Salomé. He was in full regalia, with plumed hat, rapier and staff, more majestic than a cardinal, shining like a pyx.

He advanced toward Léon, and with the smiling, bland benignity of a priest questioning a child, he said:

"Monsieur is from out of town, perhaps? Monsieur would like to visit the church?"

"No," said Léon.

He walked down one of the side aisles and up the other, then stood outside and looked over the square; there was no sign of Emma, and he reentered the church and strolled as far as the choir.

The nave was mirrored in the holy-water fonts, with the lower portions of the ogives and some of the stained glass; the reflection of the painted windows broke off at the marble rim only to continue beyond, on the pavement, like a many-colored carpet. Brilliant daylight streamed into the church in three enormous shafts through the three open portals. Now and again a sacristan moved across the far end, dipping before the altar in the half-sidewise genuflection practiced by hurried worshipers. The crystal chandeliers hung motionless. A silver lamp was burning in the choir; and from the side chapels and shadowy corners of the church came an occasional sound like a sigh, and the noise of a metal gate clanging shut and echoing under the lofty vaults.

Léon walked meditatively, keeping near the walls. Never had life seemed so good. Any minute now she would appear, charming, all aquiver, turning around to see whether anyone was looking—with her flounced dress, her gold eyeglass, her dainty shoes, all kinds of feminine elegances he had never had a taste of, and all the ineffable allurement of virtue on the point of yielding. The church was like a gigantic boudoir, suffused by her image: the vaults curved dimly down to breathe in the avowal of her love; the windows were ablaze to cast their splendor on her face; and even the incense burners were lighted, to welcome her like an angel amid clouds of perfume.

But still she didn't come. He took a chair and his eyes rested on a blue stained-glass window showing boatmen carrying baskets. He stared at it fixedly, counting the scales on the fish and the buttonholes in the doublets, his thoughts meanwhile roving in search of Emma.

The verger, standing to one side, was raging inwardly at this person who was taking it upon himself to admire the cathedral on his own. He was behaving monstrously, he considered: he was stealing from him, really—almost committing sacrilege.

Then there was a rustle of silk on the stone pavement, the edge of a hat under a hooded cape. . . . It was she! Léon jumped up and ran to meet her.

She was pale. She walked quickly.

"Read this!" she said, holding out a sheet of paper. "Oh, no!"

And abruptly she drew back her hand and turned into the chapel of the Virgin, where she knelt down against a chair and began to pray.

The young man was irritated by this sanctimonious bit of whimsy; then he felt a certain charm at seeing her, in the midst of a love meeting, plunged into devotions like an Andalusian *marquesa*; but he soon grew impatient, for there seemed to be no end to it.

Emma was praying, or rather forcing herself to pray, in the hope that heaven might miraculously send her strength of will; and to draw down divine aid she filled her eyes with the splendors of the tabernacle, she breathed the fragrance of the sweet-rockets, white and lush in their tall vases, and she listened intently to the silence of the church, which only increased the tumult of her heart.

She rose, and they were about to leave when the verger came swiftly over:

"Madame is perhaps from out of town? Madame would like to visit the church?"

"Oh, no!" the clerk cried.

"Why not?" she retorted.

Her desperate attempt to steady her virtue made her clutch at the Virgin, at the sculptures, at the tombs, at anything that came to hand.

Insisting that they must "begin at the beginning," the verger led them outside the entrance door to the edge of the square, and there pointed with his staff to a large circle of black stones in the pavement, devoid of carving or inscription:

"That," he said majestically, "is the circumference of the great Amboise bell. It weighed forty thousand pounds. It was without equal in all Europe. The workman who cast it died of joy. . . ."

"Let's get away from here," said Léon.

The guide moved on; and back in the chapel of the Virgin he extended his arms in a showman's gesture that took in everything, and addressed them more proudly than a gentleman farmer displaying his fruit trees:

"This plain stone marks the resting place of Pierre de Brézé, lord of La Varenne and Brissac, grand marshal of Poitou and governor of Normandy, killed at the battle of Montlhéry, July 16, 1465."

Léon bit his lips in a fury of impatience.

"And on the right the nobleman in full armor on a rearing horse is his grandson Louis de Brézé, lord of Braval and Montchauvet, comte de Mau-levrier, baron de Mauny, royal chamberlain, knight of the order and likewise governor of Normandy, who died July 23, 1531, a Sunday, as it says on the inscription; and below, the man about to descend into the tomb represents the same person exactly. Human mortality has never been more perfectly represented."

Madame Bovary raised her eyeglass. Léon stood still and stared at her, no longer even trying to utter a word or make the slightest move, so discouraged was he by this combination of patter and indifference.

The guide droned on:

"Near him, there, that kneeling weeping woman is his wife, Diane de Poitiers, comtesse de Brézé, duchesse de Valentinois, born 1499, died 1566; and on the left, holding a child, the Holy Virgin. Now face this way: those are the tombs of the Amboises. They were both cardinals and archbishops of Rouen. That one was one of King Louis XII's ministers. He was a great benefactor of the cathedral. In his will he left 30,000 *écus d'or* for the poor."

And immediately, without interrupting his stream of talk, he pushed them into a chapel cluttered with railings, some of which he moved aside to reveal a blockish object that looked like a roughly carved statue.

"This," he said with a deep sigh, "once formed part of the decoration of the tomb of Richard Coeur-de-Lion,[4] king of England and duke of Nor-mandy. It was the Calvinists, Monsieur, who reduced it to the condition in which you see it now. Out of pure malice they buried it in the earth, under Monseigneur's episcopal throne. That door, there, by the way, is the one he uses—Monseigneur, I mean—to reach his residence. Now we'll move on to the gargoyle windows."

But Léon hastily took a silver piece from his pocket and grasped Emma's arm. The verger was taken aback, mystified by such premature munificence: the visitor still had so much to see! He called after him:

"Monsieur! The steeple! The steeple!"[5]

4. Richard the Lion-Hearted (b. 1157), who was king of England from 1189 to 1199; he died at the siege of the castle of Châlus.   5. Added to the cathedral of Rouen, which was built in the Gothic style in stages from the 13th century to the early 16th, it is a high cast-iron spire (485 feet), generally considered a tasteless disfigurement. Construction was begun in 1824 but not finished until 1876.

"No, thanks," said Léon.

"Monsieur is wrong! It's going to be four hundred forty feet high, only nine feet lower than the Great Pyramid of Egypt. It's entirely of cast iron, it . . ."

Léon fled, for it seemed to him that his love, after being reduced to stone-like immobility in the church for nearly two hours, was now going to vanish like smoke up that truncated pipe, that elongated cage, that fretwork chimney, or what you will, that perches so precariously and grotesquely atop the cathedral like the wild invention of a crazy metalworker.

"But where are we going?" she asked.

Making no answer, he continued swiftly on, and Madame Bovary was already dipping a finger in the holy water when behind them they heard a sound of heavy panting regularly punctuated by the tapping of a staff. Léon turned around.

"Monsieur!"

"What?"

It was the verger, holding about twenty thick paperbound volumes against his stomach. They were "books about the cathedral."

"Fool!" muttered Léon, hurrying out of the church.

An urchin was playing in the square:

"Go get me a cab!"

The youngster vanished like a shot up the Rue des Quatre-Vents, and for a few minutes they were left alone, face to face and a little constrained.

"Oh, Léon! Really—I don't know whether I should . . . !"

She simpered. Then, in a serious tone:

"It's very improper, you know."

"What's improper about it?" retorted the clerk. "Everybody does it in Paris!"

It was an irresistible and clinching argument.

But there was no sign of a cab. Léon was terrified lest she retreat into the church. Finally the cab appeared.

"Drive past the north door, at least!" cried the verger, from the entrance. "Take a look at the Resurrection, the Last Judgment, Paradise, King David, and the souls of the damned in the flames of hell!"

"Where does Monsieur wish to go?" asked the driver.

"Anywhere!" said Léon, pushing Emma into the carriage.

And the lumbering contraption rolled away.

It went down the Rue Grand-Pont, crossed the Place des Arts, the Quai Napoléon and the Pont Neuf, and stopped in front of the statue of Pierre Corneille.

"Keep going!" called a voice from within.

It started off again, and gathering speed on the downgrade beyond the Carrefour Lafayette it came galloping up to the railway station.

"No! Straight on!" cried the same voice.

Rattling out through the station gates, the cab soon turned into the Boulevard, where it proceeded at a gentle trot between the double row of tall elms. The coachman wiped his brow, stowed his leather hat between his legs, and veered the cab off beyond the side lanes to the grass strip along the river front.

It continued along the river on the cobbled towing path for a long time in the direction of Oyssel, leaving the islands behind.

But suddenly it rushed off through Quatre-Mares, Sotteville, the Grande-Chaussée, the Rue d'Elbeuf, and made its third stop—this time at the Jardin des Plantes.

"Drive on!" cried the voice, more furiously.

And abruptly starting off again it went through Saint-Sever, along the Quai des Curandiers and the Quai aux Meules, recrossed the bridge, crossed the Place du Champ-de-Mars and continued on behind the garden of the hospital, where old men in black jackets were strolling in the sun on a terrace green with ivy. It went up the Boulevard Bouvreuil, along the Boulevard Cauchoise, and traversed Mont-Riboudet as far as the hill at Deville.

There it turned back; and from then on it wandered at random, without apparent goal. It was seen at Saint-Pol, at Lescure, at Mont-Gargan, at Rouge-Mare and the Place du Gaillardbois; in the rue Maladrerie, the Rue Dinanderie, and in front of one church after another—Saint-Romain, Saint-Vivien, Saint-Maclou, Saint-Nicaise; in front of the customs house, at the Basse Vieille-Tour, at Trois-Pipes, and at the Cimetière Monumental. From his seat the coachman now and again cast a desperate glance at a café. He couldn't conceive what locomotive frenzy was making these people persist in refusing to stop. He tried a few times, only to hear immediate angry exclamation from behind. So he lashed the more furiously at his two sweating nags, and paid no attention whatever to bumps in the road; he hooked into things right and left; he was past caring—demoralized, and almost weeping from thirst, fatigue, and despair.

Along the river front amidst the trucks and the barrels, along the streets from the shelter of the guard posts, the bourgeois stared wide-eyed at this spectacle unheard of in the provinces—a carriage with drawn shades that kept appearing and reappearing, sealed tighter than a tomb and tossing like a ship.

At a certain moment in the early afternoon, when the sun was blazing down most fiercely on the old silver-plated lamps, a bare hand appeared from under the little yellow cloth curtains and threw out some torn scraps of paper. The wind caught them and scattered them, and they alighted at a distance, like white butterflies, on a field of flowering red clover.

Then, about six o'clock, the carriage stopped in a side street near the Place Beauvoisine. A woman alighted from it and walked off, her veil down, without a backward glance.

II

When she reached the hotel, Madame Bovary was surprised to see no sign of the stagecoach. Hivert had waited for her fifty-three minutes, and then driven off.

Nothing really obliged her to go, even though she had said that she would be back that evening. But Charles would be waiting for her: and in advance her heart was filled with that craven submissiveness with which many women both redeem their adultery and punish themselves for it.

She quickly packed her bag, paid her bill, and hired a gig in the yard. She told the driver to hurry, and kept urging him on and asking him the time and how many miles they had gone. They caught up with the Hirondelle on the outskirts of Quincampoix.

She shut her eyes almost before she was seated in her corner, and opened them at the outskirts of the village: ahead she saw Félicité standing watch outside the blacksmith's. Hivert pulled up the horses, and the cook, standing on tiptoe to address her through the window, said with an air of mystery:

"Madame, you must go straight to Monsieur Homais'. It's something urgent."

The village was silent as usual. Little pink mounds were steaming in the gutters: it was jelly-making time, and everyone in Yonville was putting up the year's supply the same day. The mound in front of the pharmacy was by far the largest and most impressive, and quite properly so: a laboratory must always be superior to home kitchens; a universal demand must always over-shadow mere individual tastes!

She went in. The big armchair was overturned, and—what was more shocking—the *Fanal de Rouen* itself had been left lying on the floor between the two pestles. She pushed open the hall door, and in the middle of the kitchen—amid earthenware jars full of stemmed currants, grated sugar, lump sugar, scales on the table and pans on the fire—she found all the Homais, big and little, swathed to the chin in aprons and wielding forks. Justin was standing there hanging his head, and the pharmacist was shouting:

"Who told you to go get it in the Capharnaum?"

"What is it?" Emma asked. "What's the matter?"

"What's the matter?" replied the apothecary. "We're making jelly. It's on the fire. It threatens to boil over. I call for another pan. And this good-for-nothing, out of sheer laziness, goes and takes—goes into my laboratory and takes off the hook—the key to the Capharnaum!"

Such was the apothecary's name for a small room under the eaves, filled with pharmaceutical utensils and supplies. He often spent long hours there alone, labeling, decanting, repackaging. He considered it not a mere store-room, but a veritable sanctuary, birthplace of all kinds of pills, boluses, tisanes, lotions and potions concocted by himself and destined to spread his renown throughout the countryside. Not another soul ever set foot in it: so fiercely did he respect the place that he even swept it out himself. If the pharmacy, open to all comers, was the arena where he paraded in all his glory, the Capharnaum was the hideaway where he rapturously pursued his favorite occupations in selfish seclusion. No wonder Justin's carelessness seemed to him a monstrous bit of irreverence. His face was redder than the currants as he continued his tirade:

"Yes, the key to the Capharnaum! The key that guards the acids and the caustic alkalis! And to calmly go and take one of the spare pans! A pan with a lid! One I may never use! Every detail is important in an art as precise as ours! Distinctions must be preserved! Pharmaceutical implements mustn't be used for near-domestic tasks! It's like carving a chicken with a scalpel, as though a judge were to . . ."

"Stop exciting yourself!" Madame Homais kept saying.

And Athalie pulled at his frock coat and cried: "Papa! Papa!"

"No! Leave me alone!" ordered the apothecary. "Leave me alone! God! I might as well be a grocer, I swear! Go ahead—go right ahead—*don't* respect anything! Smash! Crash! Let the leeches loose! Burn the marshmallow! Make pickles in the medicine jars! Slash up the bandages!"

"But you had something to . . ." said Emma.

"One moment, Madame!—Do you know the risk you were running? Didn't you notice anything in the corner, on the left, on the third shelf? Open your mouth! Say something!"

"I . . . don't . . . know . . ." stammered the boy.

"Ah! You don't know! Well, I know! You saw a bottle, a blue glass bottle sealed with yellow wax, with white powder in it, and that I myself marked *Dangerous!*? Do you know what's in that bottle? Arsenic! And you go meddling with that! You take a pan that's standing right beside it!"

"Right beside it!" cried Madame Homais, clasping her hands. "Arsenic! You might have poisoned us all!"

And the children began to scream, as though they were already prey to the most frightful gastric pains.

"Or you might have poisoned a patient!" the apothecary persisted. "Do you want me to be hauled into court as a common criminal? Do you want to see me dragged to the scaffold? Don't you know how very careful I am about handling anything, no matter how many million times I may have done it before? Sometimes I'm terrified at the thought of my responsibilities! The government positively hounds us! The legal restrictions are absurd—a veritable sword of Damocles hanging over our heads!"

Emma had given up any attempt to ask what was wanted of her, and the pharmacist breathlessly continued:

"That's your way of being grateful for all the kindness you've been shown! That's how you repay me for the father's care I've showered on you! Where would you be if it weren't for me? What would you be doing? Who gives you your food and your lodging, and training, and clothing—everything you need to become a respectable member of society someday? But to achieve that you've got to bend your back to the oar—get some calluses on your hands, as the saying goes. *Fabricando fit faber, age quod agis.*"[6]

His rage had sent him into Latin: he would have spouted Chinese or Greenlandic had he been able to, for he was in the throes of one of those crises in which the soul lays bare its every last corner, just as the ocean, in the travail of storm, splits open to display everything from the seaweed on its shores to the sand of its deepest bottom.

And he went on:

"I'm beginning to repent bitterly that I ever took you into my charge! I'd have done far better to leave you as I found you—let you wallow in the misery and filth you were born in! You'll never be fit to do anything except look after the cows! You haven't the makings of a scientist! You're scarcely capable of sticking on a label! And you live here at my expense, gorging yourself like a priest, like a pig in clover!"

Emma turned to Madame Homais:

"I was told to come . . ."

"I know," the lady said, wringing her hands, "but how can I possibly tell you . . . ? It's a calamity . . ."

She left her words unfinished. The apothecary was thundering on:

"Empty it out! Scour it! Take it back! Be quick about it!"

---

6. The artisan becomes proficient through practice; practice what you are supposed to do (Latin).

And as he shook Justin by the collar of his overall a book fell out of one of the pockets.

The boy bent down for it, but Homais was quicker, and he picked up the book and stared at it open-mouthed.

"*Conjugal . . . Love!*" he cried, placing a deliberate pause between the two words. "Ah! Very good! *Very good!* Charming, in fact! And with illustrations . . . Really! This goes beyond everything!"

Madame Homais stepped forward as though to look.

"No! Don't touch it!"

The children clamored to see the pictures.

"Leave the room!" he said imperiously.

They left.

First he strode up and down, holding the volume open, rolling his eyes, choking, puffing, apoplectic. Then he walked straight up to his apprentice and stood in front of him, arms folded.

"So you're going in for *all* the vices, are you, you little wretch? Watch out, you're on the downward path! Did it ever occur to you that this wicked book might fall into my children's hands? It might be just the spark that . . . It might sully the purity of Athalie! It might corrupt Napoléon! Physically, he's a man already! Are you sure, at least, that they haven't read it? Can you swear to me . . ."

"Really, Monsieur," said Emma. "Did you have something to tell me?"

"So I did, Madame. . . . Your father-in-law is dead!"

It was true: the elder Bovary had died two days before, very suddenly, from an apoplectic stroke, as he was leaving the table; and Charles, overanxious to spare Emma's sensibilities, had asked Monsieur Homais to acquaint her tactfully with the horrible news.

The pharmacist had devoted much thought to the wording of his announcement. He had rounded it and polished it and given it cadence. It was a masterpiece of discretion and transition, of subtlety and shading. But anger had swept away rhetoric.

Emma, seeing that it was useless to ask for details, left the pharmacy, for Monsieur Homais had resumed his vituperations. He was quieting down, however, and now was grumbling in a fatherly way as he fanned himself with his cap:

"It's not that I disapprove entirely of the book. The author was a doctor. It deals with certain scientific aspects that it does a man no harm to know about—aspects, if I may say so, that a man *has* to know about. But later, later! Wait till you're a man yourself, at least; wait till your character's formed."

The sound of the knocker told the expectant Charles that Emma had arrived, and he came toward her with open arms. There were tears in his voice:

"Ah! *Ma chère amie* . . ."

And he bent down gently to kiss her. But at the touch of his lips the memory of Léon gripped her, and she passed her hand over her face and shuddered.

Nevertheless she answered him. "Yes," she said. "I know . . . I know . . ."

He showed her the letter in which his mother told what had happened, without any sentimental hypocrisy. Her only regret was that her husband had not received the succor of the church: he had died not at home, but at Doudeville, in the street, just outside a café, after a patriotic banquet with some ex-army officers.

Emma handed back the letter. At dinner she pretended a little for the sake of good manners to have no appetite, but when Charles urged her, she proceeded to eat heartily, while he sat opposite her motionless, weighed down by grief.

Now and again he lifted his head and gave her a long, stricken look. "I wish I could have seen him again!" he sighed.

She made no answer. And finally, when she knew that she must say something:

"How old was your father?"

"Fifty-eight."

"Ah!"

And that was all.

A little later:

"My poor mother!" he said. "What's to become of her now?"

She conveyed with a gesture that she had no idea.

Seeing her so silent, Charles supposed that she, too, was affected, and he forced himself to say no more lest he exacerbate her sorrow, which he found touching. But for a moment he roused himself from his own.

"Did you have a good time yesterday?" he asked.

"Yes."

When the tablecloth was removed, Bovary did not get up, nor did Emma; and as she continued to look at him the monotony of the sight gradually banished all compassion from her heart. He seemed to her insignificant, weak, a nonentity—contemptible in every way. How could she rid herself of him? What an endless evening! She felt torpid, drugged, as though from opium fumes.

From the entry came the sharp tap of a stick on the wooden floor. It was Hippolyte, bringing Madame's bags. To set them down, he swung his wooden leg around in an awkward quarter-circle.

"Charles doesn't even think about him anymore," she remarked to herself as she watched the poor devil, his mop of red hair dripping sweat.

Bovary fumbled in his purse for a coin; and, apparently unaware of the humiliation implicit in the very presence of the man who was standing there, like a living reproach for his incurable ineptitude:

"Oh, you have a pretty bouquet!" he said, noticing Léon's violets on the mantelpiece.

"Yes," she said carelessly. "I bought it just before I left—from a beggar woman."

Charles took up the violets, held their coolness against his tear-reddened eyes, and gently sniffed them. She quickly took them from his hand, and went to put them in a glass of water.

The following day the older Madame Bovary arrived. She and her son did a good deal of weeping. Emma, pleading household duties, kept out of the way. The day after that, they had to consult about mourning, and the three of them sat down together, the ladies with their workboxes, under the arbor on the river bank.

Charles thought about his father, and was surprised to feel so much affection for one whom up till then he had thought he loved but little. The older Madame Bovary thought of her husband. The worst of her times with him seemed desirable now. Everything was submerged in grief, so intensely did she miss the life she was used to; and from time to time as she plied her needle a great tear rolled down her nose and hung there for a moment before dropping. Emma was thinking that scarcely forty-eight hours before they had been together, shut away from the world, in ecstasy, devouring each other with their eyes. She tried to recapture the tiniest details of that vanished day. But the presence of her mother-in-law and her husband interfered. She wished she could hear nothing, see nothing: she wanted merely to be left alone to evoke her love, which depite her best efforts was becoming blurred under the impact of external impressions.

She was ripping the lining of a dress, and scraps of the material lay scattered around her; the older Madame Bovary, never raising her eyes, kept squeaking away with her scissors; and Charles, in his cloth slippers and the old brown frock coat that he used as a dressing gown, kept his hand in his pockets and said no more than the others. Near them, Berthe, in a little white apron, was scraping the gravel of the path with her shovel.

Suddenly they saw Monsieur Lheureux, the dry-goods dealer, push open the gate.

He had come to offer his services "on this very sad occasion." Emma answered that she thought she could do without them. But the shopkeeper did not concede defeat.

"If you'll excuse me," he said, "I'd like to speak to you privately."

And in a low voice:

"It's about that little matter . . . you know what I'm referring to?"

Charles blushed to the roots of his hair.

"Oh, yes . . . of course."

And in his embarrassment he turned to his wife:

"Darling, would you take care of . . . ?"

She seemed to understand, for she rose; and Charles said to his mother:

"It's nothing—just some household detail, I imagine."

He didn't want her to learn about the promissory note: he dreaded her comments.

As soon as Emma was alone with Monsieur Lheureux he began to congratulate her rather bluntly on coming into money, and then spoke of indifferent matters—fruit trees, the harvest, and his own health, which was always the same, "so-so, could be worse." He worked like a galley slave, he informed her, and even so, despite what people said about him, he didn't make enough to buy butter for his bread.

Emma let him talk. She had been so prodigiously bored these last two days!

"And you're entirely well again?" he went on. "Your husband was in quite a state, I can tell you! He's a fine fellow, even if we did have a little trouble."

"What trouble?" she asked, for Charles had told her nothing about the dispute over the various items.

"But you know perfectly well!" said Lheureux. "About the little things you wanted—the trunks."

He had pushed his hat forward over his eyes, and with his hands behind his back, smiling, and whistling to himself under his breath, he was staring straight at her in a way she found intolerable. Did he suspect something? She waited in a panic of apprehension. But finally he said:

"We made it up, and I came today to propose another arrangement."

What he proposed was the renewal of the note signed by Bovary. Monsieur should of course do as he pleased: he shouldn't worry, especially now that he was going to have so many other things on his mind.

"He'd really do best to turn it over to somebody else—you, for example. With a power of attorney everything would be very simple, and then you and I could attend to our little affairs together."

She didn't understand. He let the matter drop, and turned the conversation back to dry goods: Madame really couldn't not order something from him. He'd send her a piece of black barège—twelve meters, enough to make a dress.

"The one you have there is all right for the house, but you need another for going out. I saw that the minute I came in. I've got an eye like a Yankee!"

He didn't send the material: he brought it. Then he came again to do the measuring, and again and again on other pretexts, each time putting himself out to be agreeable and helpful—making himself her liegeman, as Homais might have put it—and always slipping in a few words of advice about the power of attorney. He didn't mention the promissory note. It didn't occur to her to think of it: early in her convalescence Charles had, in fact, said something to her about it, but her mind had been so agitated that she had forgotten. Moreover she was careful never to bring up anything about money matters. This surprised her mother-in-law, who attributed her new attitude to the religious sentiments she had acquired during her illness.

But as soon as the older woman left, Emma lost no time in impressing Bovary with her practical good sense. It was up to them, she said, to make inquiries, check on mortgages, see if there were grounds for liquidating the property by auction or otherwise. She used technical terms at random, and impressive words like "order," "the future" and "foresight," and she continually exaggerated the complications attendant on inheritance. Then one day she showed him the draft of a general authorization to "manage and administer his affairs, negotiate all loans, sign and endorse all promissory notes, pay all sums," etc. She had profited from Lheureux's lessons.

Charles naïvely asked her where the document came from.

"From Maître Guillaumin."

And with the greatest coolness imaginable she added:

"I haven't too much confidence in him. You hear such dreadful things about notaries! Perhaps we ought to consult . . . We don't know anyone except . . . We don't know anyone, really."

"Unless Léon . . ." said Charles, who was thinking hard.

But it was difficult to make things clear by letter. So she offered to make the trip. He thanked her but said she mustn't. She insisted. Each outdid the other in consideration. Finally, imitating the pert disobedience of a child, she cried:

"I will, too, go! I will!"

"How good you are!" he said, kissing her on the forehead.

The next morning she set out in the Hirondelle for Rouen to consult Monsieur Léon, and she stayed there three days.

III

They were three full, exquisite, glorious days, a real honeymoon.

They stayed at the Hotel de Boulogne on the river front, living there behind drawn shutters and locked doors; their room was strewn with flowers, and iced fruit drinks were brought up to them all day long.

At dusk they hired a covered boat and went to dine on one of the islands.

From the shipyards came the thumping of caulking irons against hulls. Wisps of tar smoke curled up from among the trees, and on the river floated great oily patches, the color of Florentine bronze, undulating unevenly in the purple glow of the sun.

They drifted downstream amidst anchored craft whose long slanting cables grazed the top of their boat.

The sounds of the city gradually receded—the rattle of wagons, the tumult of voices, the barking of dogs on the decks of ships. As they touched the shore of their island she loosened the silk ribbon of her hat.

They sat in the low-ceilinged room of a restaurant with black fishnets hanging at its door, and ate fried smelts, cream and cherries. Then they stretched out on the grass in an out-of-the-way corner and lay in each other's arms under the poplars: they wished they might live forever, like two Robinson Crusoes, in this little spot that seemed to them in their bliss the most magnificent on earth. It wasn't the first time in their lives that they had seen trees, blue sky and lawn, or heard the flowing of water or the rustle of the breeze in the branches, but never before, certainly, had they looked on it all with such wonder: it was as though nature had not existed before, or had only begun to be beautiful with the slaking of their desires.

At nightfall they returned to the city. The boat followed the shoreline of the islands, and they crouched deep in its shadow, not saying a word. The square-tipped oars clicked in the iron oarlocks: it sounded, in the silence, like the beat of a metronome, and the rope trailing behind kept up its gentle splashing in the water.

One night the moon shone out, and of course they rhapsodized about how melancholy and poetical it was. She even sang a little:

> One night—dost thou remember?—
> We were sailing . . .[7]

Her sweet, small voice died away over the river: borne off on the breeze were the trills that Léon heard flit past him like the fluttering of wings.

She was sitting opposite him, leaning against the wall of the little cabin, the moonlight streaming in on her through an open shutter. In her black dress, its folds spreading out around her like a fan, she looked taller, slimmer. Her head was raised, her hands were clasped, her eyes turned heavenward. One moment she would be hidden by the shadow of some willows; the next, she would suddenly reemerge in the light of the moon like an apparition.

---

7. The beginning of Alphonse de Lamartine's *The Lake* (see p. 1111).

Léon, sitting on the bottom beside her, picked up a bright red ribbon. The boatman looked at it.

"Oh," he said, "that's probably from a party I took out the other day. They were a jolly lot, all right, the men *and* the girls: they brought along food and champagne and music—the whole works. There was one of them, especially—a big, good-looking fellow with a little mustache—he was a riot. They all kept after him. 'Come on, tell us a story, Adolphe'—or Dodolphe, or some name like that."

She shuddered.

"Don't you feel well?" asked Léon, moving closer to her.

"Oh, it's nothing. Just a chill."

"He was another one who never had to worry about where his women would come from," the old boatman added softly, as a compliment to his present passenger.

Then he spit on his hands and took up his oars.

But finally they had to part. Their farewells were sad. He was to write her in care of Madame Rollet; and she gave him such detailed instructions about using a double envelope that he marveled greatly at her shrewdness in love matters.

"So I have your word for it that everything's in order?" she said, as they kissed for the last time.

"Absolutely—But why the devil," he wondered, as he walked home alone through the streets, "is she so set on having that power of attorney?"

IV

Before long, Léon began to give himself superior airs around the office. He kept aloof from his colleagues and totally neglected his work. He waited for Emma's letters, and read them over and over. He wrote to her. He evoked her image with all the strength of his passion and his memories. Far from being lessened by absence, his longing to see her again increased, until finally one Saturday morning he took the road to Yonville.

When he looked down on the valley from the top of the hill and saw the church steeple with its tin flag turning in the wind, he was filled with an exquisite pleasure: smug satisfaction and selfish sentimentality were mingled in it—it was the feeling that a millionaire must experience on revisiting his boyhood village.

He prowled around her house. A light was burning in the kitchen. He watched for her shadow behind the curtains. Not a soul was to be seen.

Madame Lefrançois uttered loud cries at the sight of him, and said that he was "taller and thinner." Artémise, on the other hand, found that he had grown "heavier and darker."

He took his dinner in the small dining room, just as in the old days, but alone, without the tax collector: for Binet, sick of waiting for the Hirondelle, had permanently changed his mealtime to an hour earlier, and now dined on the stroke of five. Even so he never missed a chance to grumble that "the rusty old clock was slow."

Finally Léon got up his courage and knocked on the doctor's door. Madame was in her room: it was a quarter of an hour before she came down. Monsieur seemed delighted to see him again, but didn't stir from the house all evening or all the next day.

Only late Sunday evening did he see her alone, in the lane behind the garden—in the lane, just like Rodolphe. It was during a thunderstorm, and they talked under an umbrella, with lightning flashing around them.

The thought of parting was unbearable.

"I'd rather die!" said Emma.

She clung convulsively to his arm and wept:

"Adieu! Adieu! When will I see you again?"

They separated, then turned back for a last embrace; and it was at that moment that she promised him to find, soon, no matter how, some way in which they would be able to see each other alone and regularly, at least once a week. Emma had no doubt about succeeding. She looked forward to the future with confidence: the inheritance money would shortly be coming in.

On the strength of it she bought, for her bedroom, a pair of wide-striped yellow curtains that Monsieur Lheureux extolled as a bargain. She said she wished she could have a carpet; and Lheureux, assuring her that she wasn't "reaching for the moon," promised very obligingly to find her one. By now she didn't know how she could get along without him. She sent for him twenty times a day, and he always promptly left whatever he was doing and came, without a word of protest. Nor was it clear to anyone why Madame Rollet lunched at her house every day, and even visited with her privately.

It was about this time—the beginning of winter—that she became intensely musical.

One evening while Charles was listening she started the same piece over again four times, each time expressing annoyance with herself. Charles was unaware of anything wrong. "Bravo!" he cried. "Very good! Why stop? Keep going."

"No, I'm playing abominably. My fingers are rusty."

The next day he asked her to "play him something else."

"Very well, if you like."

Charles had to admit that she seemed a little out of practice. She fumbled, struck wrong notes, and finally broke off abruptly:

"That's enough of that! I should take some lessons, but . . ."

She bit her lips and added: "Twenty francs an hour—it's too expensive."

"Yes, it certainly is . . . a little . . ." said Charles, with a silly giggle. "But it seems to me you ought to be able to find somebody for less. There are plenty of musicians without big names who are better than the celebrities."

"Try and find some," said Emma.

When he came in the next day he gave her a sly look, and finally came out with: "You certainly have a way sometimes of thinking you know better than anybody else. I was at Barfeuchères today and Madame Liégeard told me that her three girls—the three at school at the Miséricorde—take lessons at two and a half francs an hour, and from a marvelous teacher!"

She shrugged, and from then on left her instrument unopened.

But whenever she walked by it she would sigh (if Bovary happened to be there): "Ah, my poor piano!"

And she always made a point of telling visitors that she had given up her music and now couldn't possibly go on with it again, for imperative reasons. Everybody pitied her. What a shame! She had so much talent! People even spoke to Bovary about it. They made him feel ashamed, especially the pharmacist.

"You're making a mistake! Natural faculties must never be let lie fallow!

Besides, my friend, look at it this way: by encouraging Madame to take lessons now, you'll save money later on your daughter's lessons. In my opinion, mothers should teach their children themselves. It's an idea of Rousseau's—maybe a little new, still, but bound to prevail eventually, I'm sure, like mother's breast-feeding and vaccination."

So Charles brought up the question of the piano again. Emma answered tartly that they'd better sell it. Poor old piano! It had so often been a source of pride for him, that to see it go would be like watching Emma commit partial suicide.

"If you really want to go ahead with it," he said, "I suppose a lesson now and then wouldn't ruin us."

"But lessons aren't worth taking," she said, "unless they're taken regularly."

That was how she obtained her husband's permission to go to the city once a week to meet her lover. By the end of the first month everyone found that her playing had improved considerably.

V

And so, every Thursday, she rose and dressed without a sound, lest she wake Charles, who would have remarked on her getting ready too early. Then she paced up and down, stood at the windows, looked out at the square. The first light of morning was stealing into the pillared market place; and on the pharmacist's house, its shutters still drawn, the pale tints of dawn were picking out the capital letters of the shop sign.

When the clock said quarter past seven she made her way to the Lion d'Or and was let in by the yawning Artémise. The servant paid her the attention of digging out the smoldering coals from under the ashes, and then left her to herself in the kitchen. From time to time she walked out into the yard. Hivert would be harnessing the horses. He went about it very deliberately, listening as he did so to Madame Lefrançois, who had stuck her head, nightcap and all, out of a window and was briefing him on his errands in a way that anyone else would have found bewildering. Emma tapped her foot on the cobbles.

Finally, when he had downed his bowl of soup, put on his overcoat, lighted his pipe and picked up his whip, he unhurriedly climbed onto the seat.

The Hirondelle set off at a gentle trot, and for the first mile or two kept stopping here and there to take on passengers who stood watching for it along the road, outside their gates. Those who had booked seats the day before kept the coach waiting: some, even, were still in their beds, and Hivert would call, shout, curse, and finally get down from his seat and pound on the doors. The wind whistled in through the cracked blinds.

Gradually the four benches filled up, the coach rattled along, row upon row of apple trees flashed by; and the road, lined on each side by a ditch of yellow water, stretched on and on, narrowing toward the horizon.

Emma knew every inch of it: she knew that after a certain meadow came a road sign, then an elm, a barn, or a road-mender's cabin; sometimes she even shut her eyes, trying to give herself a surprise. But she always knew just how much farther there was to go.

Finally the brick houses crowded closer together, the road rang under the wheels, and now the Hirondelle moved smoothly between gardens: through iron fences were glimpses of statues, artificial mounds crowned by arbors, clipped yews, a swing. Then, all at once, the city came into view.

Sloping downward like an amphitheatre, drowned in mist, it sprawled out shapelessly beyond its bridges. Then open fields swept upward again in a monotonous curve, merging at the top with the uncertain line of the pale sky. Thus seen from above, the whole landscape had the static quality of a painting: ships at anchor were crowded into one corner, the river traced its curve along the foot of the green hills, and on the water the oblong-shaped islands looked like great black fish stopped in their course. From the factory chimneys poured endless trails of brown smoke, their tips continually dissolving in the wind. The roar of foundries mingled with the clear peal of chimes that came from the churches looming in the fog. The leafless trees along the boulevards were like purple thickets in amongst the houses; and the roofs, all of them shiny with rain, gleamed with particular brilliance in the upper reaches of the town. Now and again a gust of wind blew the clouds toward the hill of Sainte-Catherine, like aerial waves breaking soundlessly against a cliff.

A kind of intoxication was wafted up to her from those closely packed lives, and her heart swelled as though the 120,000 souls palpitating below had sent up to her as a collective offering the breath of all the passions she supposed them to be feeling. In the face of the vastness her love grew larger, and was filled with a turmoil that echoed the vague ascending hum. All this love she, in turn, poured out—onto the squares, onto the tree-lined avenues, onto the streets; and to her the old Norman city was like some fabulous capital, a Babylon into which she was making her entry. She leaned far out the window and filled her lungs with air; the three horses galloped on, there was a grinding of stones in the mud beneath the wheels; the coach swayed; Hivert shouted warningly ahead to the wagons he was about to overtake, and businessmen leaving their suburban villas in Bois-Guillaume descended the hill at a respectable pace in their little family carriages.

There was a stop at the city gate: Emma took off her overshoes, changed her gloves, arranged her shawl, and twenty paces farther on she left the Hirondelle.

The city was coming to life. Clerks in caps were polishing shop windows, and women with baskets on their hips stood on street corners uttering loud, regular cries. She walked on, her eyes lowered, keeping close to the house walls and smiling happily under her lowered black veil.

For fear of being seen, she usually didn't take the shortest way. She would plunge into a maze of dark alleys, and emerge, hot and perspiring, close to the fountain at the lower end of the Rue Nationale. This is the part of town near the theater, full of bars and prostitutes. Often a van rumbled by, laden with shaky stage sets. Aproned waiters were sanding the pavement between the tubs of green bushes. There was a smell of absinthe, cigars and oysters.

Then she turned a corner. She recognized him from afar by the way his curly hair hung down below his hat.

He walked ahead on the sidewalk. She followed him to the hotel; he went upstairs, opened the door of the room, went in—What an embrace!

Then, after kisses, came a flood of words. They spoke of the troubles of the week, of their forebodings, their worries about letters; but now they could forget everything, and they looked into each other's eyes, laughing with delight and exchanging loving names.

The bed was a large mahogany one in the form of a boat. Red silk curtains hung from the ceiling and were looped back very low beside the flaring headboard, and there was nothing so lovely in the world as her dark hair and white skin against the deep crimson when she brought her bare arms together in a gesture of modesty, hiding her face in her hands.

The warm room, with its discreet carpet, its pretty knickknacks and its tranquil light, seemed designed for the intimacies of passion. The arrow-tipped curtain rods, the brass ornaments on the furniture and the big knobs on the andirons—all gleamed at once if the sun shone in. Between the candlesticks on the mantelpiece was a pair of those great pink shells that sound like the ocean when you hold them to your ear.

How they loved that sweet, cheerful room, for all its slightly faded splendor! Each piece of furniture was always waiting for them in its place, and sometimes the hairpins she had forgotten the Thursday before were still there, under the pedestal of the clock. They lunched beside the fire, on a little table inlaid with rosewood. Emma carved, murmuring all kinds of endearments as she put the pieces on his plate; and she gave a loud, wanton laugh when the champagne foamed over the fine edge of the glass onto the rings on her fingers. They were so completely lost in their possession of each other that they thought of themselves as being in their own home, destined to live there for the rest of their days, eternal young husband and eternal young wife. They said "our room," "our carpet," "our chairs"; she even said "our slippers," meaning a pair that Léon had given her to gratify a whim. They were of pink satin, trimmed with swansdown. When she sat in his lap her legs swung in the air, not reaching the floor, and the dainty slippers, open all around except at the tip, hung precariously from her bare toes.

He was savoring for the first time the ineffable subtleties of feminine refinement. Never had he encountered this grace of language, this quiet taste in dress, these relaxed, dovelike postures. He marveled at the sublimity of her soul and at the lace on her petticoat. Besides—wasn't she a "lady," and married besides? Everything, in short, that a mistress should be?

With her ever-changing moods, by turns brooding and gay, chattering and silent, fiery and casual, she aroused in him a thousand desires, awakening instincts or memories. She was the *amoureuse* of all the novels, the heroine of all the plays, the vague "she" of all the poetry books. Her shoulders were amber toned, like the bathing odalisques he had seen in pictures; she was long waisted like the feudal chatelaines; she resembled Musset's *"pâle femme de Barcelone,"*[8] too: but at all times she was less woman than angel!

Often, as he looked at her, it seemed to him that his soul, leaving him in quest of her, flowed like a wave around the outline of her head, and then was drawn down into the whiteness of her breast.

He would kneel on the floor before her, and with his elbows on her knees gaze at her smilingly, his face lifted.

She would bend toward him and murmur, as though choking with rapture:

"Don't move! Don't say a word! Just look at me! There's something so sweet in your eyes, something that does me so much good!"

She called him "child": "Do you love me, child?"

---

8. Pale woman of Barcelona (French). Alfred de Musset (1810–1857) frequently incarnates, for Flaubert, the type of stilted romantic sensibility he despises.

She never heard his answer, so fast did his lips always rise to meet her mouth.

On the clock there was a little bronze cupid, simpering and curving its arms under a gilded wreath. They often laughed at it, but when it came time to part, everything grew serious.

Motionless, face to face, they would say, over and over:

"Till Thursday! Till Thursday!"

Then she would abruptly take his face between her hands, quickly kiss him on the forehead, cry, "Adieu!" and run out into the hall.

She always went to a hairdresser in the Rue de la Comédie and had her hair brushed and put in order. Darkness would be falling; in the shops they would be lighting the gas.

She could hear the bell in the theater summoning the actors to the performance, and across the street she would see white-faced men and shabbily dressed women going in through the stage door.

It was hot in this little place with its too-low ceiling and its stove humming in the midst of wigs and pomades. The smell of the curling irons and the touch of the soft hands at work on her head soon made her drowsy, and she dozed off a little in her dressing gown. Often, as he arranged her hair, the coiffeur would ask her to buy tickets for a masked ball.

Then she was off. She retraced her way through the streets, reached the Croix-Rouge, retrieved the overshoes that she had hidden there that morning under a bench, and squeezed herself in among the impatient passengers. To spare the horses, the men got out at the foot of the hill, leaving Emma alone in the coach.

At each bend of the road more and more of the city lights came into view, making a layer of luminous mist that hung over the mass of the houses. Emma would kneel on the cushions and look back, letting her eyes wander over the brilliance. Sobs would burst from her, she would call Léon's name, and send him sweet words, and kisses that were lost in the wind.

On this hill road was a wretched beggar, who wandered with his stick in the midst of the traffic. His clothes were a mass of rags, and his face was hidden under a battered old felt hat that was turned down all around like a basin; when he took this off, it was to reveal two gaping, bloody sockets in place of eyelids. The flesh continually shredded off in red gobbets, and from it oozed a liquid matter, hardening into greenish scabs that reached down to his nose. His black nostrils sniffled convulsively. Whenever he began to talk, he leaned his head far back and gave an idiot laugh; and at such times his bluish eyeballs, rolling round and round, pushed up against the edges of the live wound.

As he walked beside the coaches he sang a little song:

A clear day's warmth will often move
A lass to stay in dreams of love . . .

And the rest of it was all about the birds, the sun, and the leaves on the trees.

Sometimes he would loom up all at once from behind Emma, bareheaded. She would draw back with a cry. Hivert always joked with him, urging him to hire a booth at the Saint-Romain fair, or laughingly asking after the health of his sweetheart.

Often while the coach was moving slowly up the hill his hat would suddenly come through the window, and he would be there, clinging with his other hand to the footboard, between the spattering wheels. His voice, at the outset a mere wail, would grow shrill. It would linger in the darkness like a plaintive cry of distress; and through the jingle of the horse bells, the rustle of the trees and the rumble of the empty coach, there was something eerie about it that gave Emma a shudder of horror. The sound spiraled down into the very depths of her soul, like a whirlwind in an abyss, and swept her off into the reaches of a boundless melancholy. But Hivert would become aware that his vehicle was weighed down on one side, and would strike out savagely at the blind man with his whip. The stinging lash would cut into his wounds, and he would drop off into the mud with a shriek.

One by one the Hirondelle's passengers would fall asleep, some with their mouths open, others with their chins on their chests, leaning on their neighbor's shoulder or with an arm in the strap, all the while rocking steadily with the motion of the coach; and the gleam of the lamp, swaying outside above the rumps of the shaft horses and shining in through the chocolate-colored calico curtains, cast blood-red shadows on all those motionless travelers. Emma, numb with sadness, would shiver under her coat; her feet would grow colder and colder, and she felt like death.

Charles would be at the house, waiting: the Hirondelle was always late on Thursdays. Then at last Madame would arrive! She would scarcely take time to kiss her little girl. Dinner wasn't ready—no matter! She forgave the cook: Félicité seemed to have everything her own way, these days.

Often her husband would notice her pallor, and ask whether she were ill.

"No," Emma would say.

"But you're acting so strangely tonight!"

"Oh, it's nothing! It's nothing!"

Some Thursdays she went up to her room almost the minute she came in. Justin would be there and would busy himself silently, cleverer at helping her than an experienced ladies' maid. He would arrange matches, candlesticks, a book, lay out her dressing jacket, open her bed.

"Very good," she would tell him. "Now run along."

For he would be standing there, his hands at his sides and his eyes staring, as though a sudden revery had tied him to the spot with a thousand strands.

The next day was always an ordeal, and the days that followed were even more unbearable, so impatient was she to recover her happiness. It was a fierce desire that was kept aflame by the vividness of her memories, and on the seventh day burst forth freely under Léon's caresses. His transports took the form of overflowing wonderment and gratitude. Emma enjoyed this passion in a way that was both deliberate and intense, keeping it alive by every amorous device at her command, and fearing all the while that someday it would come to an end.

Often she would say to him, sweetly and sadly:

"Ah! Sooner or later you'll leave me! You'll marry! You'll be like all the others."

"What others?"

"Why, men—all men."

And, languidly pushing him away, she would add: "You're faithless, every one of you!"

One day when they were having a philosophical discussion about earthly disillusionments, she went so far as to say (whether testing his jealousy, or yielding to an irresistible need to confide) that in the past, before him, she had loved someone else. "Not like you!" she quickly added; and she swore by her daughter that "nothing had happened."

The young man believed her, but nevertheless asked her what kind of man "he" had been.

"He was a sea captain," she told him.

Did she say that, perhaps, to forestall his making any inquiries, and at the same time to exalt herself by making the supposed victim of her charms sound like an imperious kind of man accustomed to having his way?

This impressed upon the clerk the mediocrity of his own status: he longed to have epaulettes, decorations and titles. Such things must be to her liking, he suspected, judging by her spendthrift ways.

There were a number of her wildest ideas, however, that Emma never said a word about, such as her craving to be driven to Rouen in a blue tilbury drawn by an English horse, with a groom in turned-down boots on the seat. It was Justin who had inspired her with this particular fancy, by begging her to take him into her service as footman; and though being deprived of it didn't prevent her from enjoying each weekly arrival in the city, it certainly added to the bitterness of each return to Yonville.

Often, when they spoke of Paris, she would murmur:

"Ah! How happy we'd be, living there!"

"Aren't we happy here?" the young man would softly ask, passing his hand over her hair.

"Of course we are! I'm being foolish. Kiss me!"

With her husband she was more charming than ever; she made him pistachio creams and played waltzes for him after dinner. He considered himself the luckiest of mortals, and Emma had no fear of discovery—until suddenly, one evening:

"It is Mademoiselle Lempereur you take lessons from, isn't it?"

"Yes."

"Well, I just saw her," said Charles, "at Madame Liégeard's. I talked to her about you: she doesn't know you."

It was like a thunderbolt. But she answered in a natural tone.

"Oh, she must have forgotten my name."

"Or else maybe there's more than one Mademoiselle Lempereur in Rouen who teaches piano."

"Maybe so."

Then, quickly:

"Besides, it just occurs to me: I have her receipts. Look!"

And she went to the secretary, rummaged in all the drawers, mixed up all the papers, and finally grew so rattled that Charles begged her not to go to so much trouble for a few wretched receipts.

"Oh, I'll find them," she said.

And indeed, the following Friday, while Charles was putting on one of his shoes in the dark dressing room where his clothes were kept, he felt a piece of paper between the sole and his sock, and pulled it out and read:

"Three months' lessons, plus supplies. Sixty-five francs. Paid. Félicité Lempereur, *Professeur de musique.*"

"How the devil did this get in my shoe?"

"It probably fell down from the old bill file on the shelf."

From that moment on, she piled lie upon lie, using them as veils to conceal her love.

Lying became a need, a mania, a positive joy—to such a point that if she said that she had walked down the right-hand side of a street the day before, it meant that she had gone down the left.

One morning just after she had gone, rather lightly clad as usual, there was a sudden snowfall; and Charles, looking out the window at the weather, saw Monsieur Bournisien setting out for Rouen in Monsieur Tuvache's buggy. So he ran down with a heavy shawl and asked the priest to give it to Madame as soon as he got to the Croix-Rouge. The moment he reached the inn, Bournisien asked where the wife of the Yonville doctor was. The hotel keeper replied that she spent very little time there. That evening, therefore, finding Madame Bovary in the Hirondelle, the curé told her of the *contretemps:* he seemed to attach little importance to it, however, for he launched into praise of a preacher, the sensation at the cathedral, adored by all the ladies.

Still, though he hadn't asked for explanations, others, in the future, might be less discreet. So she thought it practical to take a room each time at the Croix-Rouge, in order that her fellow villagers might see her there and have no suspicion.

One day, however, Monsieur Lheureux ran into her as she was leaving the Hotel de Boulogne on Léon's arm. She was frightened, thinking that he might talk. He was too smart for that.

But three days later he came into her room, closed the door, and said:

"I'd like some money."

She declared that she had none to give him. Lheureux began to moan, and reminded her of how many times he'd gone out of his way to oblige her.

And indeed, of the two notes signed by Charles, Emma had so far paid off only one. As for the second, the shopkeeper had agreed at her request to replace it with two others, which themselves had been renewed for a very long term. Then he drew out of his pocket a list of goods still unpaid for: the curtains, the carpet, upholstery material for armchairs, several dresses and various toilet articles, totaling about two thousand francs.

She hung her head.

"You may not have any cash," he said, "but you do have some property."

And he mentioned a wretched, tumbledown cottage situated at Barneville, near Aumale, which didn't bring in very much. It had once been part of a small farm that the elder Bovary had sold: Lheureux knew everything, down to the acreage and the neighbors' names.

"If I were you I'd get rid of it," he said. "You'd still have a balance after paying me."

She brought up the difficulty of finding a buyer; he was encouraging about the possibility of locating one. But: "What would I have to do to be able to sell?" she asked.

"Haven't you power of attorney?" he countered.

The words came to her like a breath of fresh air.

"Leave your bill with me," said Emma.

"Oh, it's not worth bothering about," replied Lheureux.

He came again the following week, very proud of having unearthed, after a lot of trouble, a certain Monsieur Langlois, who had been eying the property for a long time without ever mentioning the price he was willing to pay.

"The price doesn't matter!" she cried.

On the contrary, he said: they should take their time, sound Langlois out. The affair was worth the bother of a trip, and since she couldn't make it he offered to go himself and talk things over with Langlois on the spot. On his return he announced that the buyer offered 4,000 francs.

Emma beamed at the news.

"Frankly," he said, "it's a good price."

Half the amount was paid her at once, and when she said that now she'd settle his bill, he told her:

"Honestly, it hurts me to see you hand over every bit of all that money right away."

She stared at the banknotes and had a vision of the countless love-meetings those 2,000 francs represented. "What?" she stammered. "What do you mean?"

"Oh," he said, with a jovial laugh, "there's more than one way of making out a bill. Don't you think I know how it is with married couples?"

And he stared at her, running his fingernails up and down two long sheets of paper he had in his hand. After a long moment he opened his billfold and spread out on the table four more promissory notes, each for a thousand francs.

"Sign these," he said, "and keep all the money."

She gave a choked cry.

"But if I give you the balance," Monsieur Lheureux answered, "don't you see that I'm doing you a service?"

And taking up a pen he wrote at the bottom of the bill: "Received from Madame Bovary the sum of 4,000 francs."

"What's there to worry you? In six months you'll have the rest of the money due on your cottage, and I'll make the last note payable after that date."

She was getting a little mixed up in her arithmetic, and she felt a ringing in her ears as though gold pieces were bursting out of their bags and dropping to the floor all about her. Finally Lheureux explained that he had a friend named Vinçart, a Rouen banker, who would discount these four new notes, following which he himself would pay Madame the balance of what was really owed.

But instead of 2,000 francs, he brought her only 1,800; for his friend Vinçart (as was "only right") had deducted 200, representing commission and discount.

Then he casually asked for a receipt.

"You know . . . in business . . . sometimes . . . And put down the date, please, the date."

A host of things that she could do with the money stretched out before Emma in perspective. She had enough sense to put 3,000 francs aside, and with them she paid, as they came due, the first three notes; but the fourth, as luck would have it, arrived at the house on a Thursday; and Charles, stunned, patiently awaited his wife's return to have it explained to him.

Ah! If she hadn't told him anything about that note it was because she hadn't wanted to bother him with household worries; she sat in his lap, caressed him, cooed at him, and gave a long list of all the indispensables she had bought on credit.

"You'll have to admit," she said, "that considering how many things there were, the bill's not too high."

Charles, at his wits' end, soon had recourse to the inevitable Lheureux, who promised to straighten everything out if Monsieur would sign two more notes, one of them for 700 francs, payable in three months. Charles wrote a pathetic letter to his mother, asking for help. Instead of sending an answer, she came herself; and when Emma asked him if he'd got anything out of her:

"Yes," he answered. "But she insists on seeing the bill."

So early the next morning Emma rushed to Monsieur Lheureux and begged him to make out a different note, for not more than 1,000 francs, for if she were to show the one for 4,000 she would have to say that she had paid off two-thirds of it, and consequently reveal the sale of the cottage. That transaction had been handled very cleverly by the shopkeeper, and never did leak out until later.

Despite the low price of each article, the elder Madame Bovary naturally found such expenditure excessive.

"Couldn't you get along without a carpet? Why re-cover the armchairs? In my day every house had exactly one armchair, for elderly persons—at least, that's the way it was at my mother's, and she was a respectable woman, I assure you. Everybody can't be rich! No amount of money will last if you throw it out the window. It would make me blush to pamper myself the way you do—and I'm an old woman and need looking after. . . . Who's ever seen so much finery? What, silk for linings at two francs when you can find jaconet for half a franc and even less that does perfectly well?"

Emma, stretched out on the settee, answered with the greatest calm:

"That's enough, Madame, that's enough."

Her mother-in-law continued to sermonize, prophesying that they'd end in the poorhouse. Besides, it was all Bovary's fault, she said. At least, though, he'd promised her he'd cancel the power of attorney.

"What!"

"Yes, he's given me his word," said the lady.

Emma opened the window and called Charles in, and the poor fellow had to confess the promise his mother had extracted from him.

Emma disappeared, then quickly returned, majestically holding out to her a large sheet of paper.

"I thank you," said the old woman.

And she threw the power of attorney into the fire.

Emma burst out laughing and didn't stop: her laughter was loud and strident—it was an attack of hysterics.

"Ah, my God!" cried Charles. "You're overdoing things, too! You've no right to come here and make scenes."

His mother shrugged her shoulders and said that "it was all put on."

But Charles, rebellious for the first time in his life, took his wife's part, and the older Madame Bovary said she wanted to go. She departed the next day, and on the doorstep, as he was trying to make her change her mind, she answered:

"No! No! You love her more than you do me, and you're right; that's as it should be. There's nothing I can do about it. You'll see, though . . . Take care of yourself . . . I can promise you it will be a long time before I come back here to 'make scenes,' as you put it."

Nevertheless Charles was very hangdog with Emma, and she didn't hide her resentment at having been distrusted. He had to entreat her many times before she would consent to accept power of attorney again, and he even went with her to Maître Guillaumin to have a new one drawn up, identical with the first.

"I well understand your doing this," said the notary. "A man of science can't be expected to burden himself with the practical details of existence."

Charles felt soothed by those oily words: they flattered his weakness, making it look like preoccupation with lofty things.

What exultation there was the next Thursday in their room at the hotel, with Léon! She laughed, cried, sang, danced, sent for water ices, insisted on smoking cigarettes. He found her wild, but adorable, superb.

He had no idea what it was that was driving her more and more to fling herself into a reckless pursuit of pleasure. She grew irritable, greedy, voluptuous; and she walked boldly with him in the street—unafraid, she said, of compromising herself. There were times, though, when Emma trembled at the sudden thought of meeting Rodolphe, for she suspected that even though they had parted forever, he still retained some of his power over her.

One night she didn't return to Yonville at all. Charles lost his head, and little Berthe, unwilling to go to bed without *maman*, sobbed as though her heart would break. Justin had gone off down the road to look for her. Monsieur Homais actually stepped out of his pharmacy.

Finally, at eleven o'clock, unable to stand it any longer, Charles harnessed his buggy, jumped in, whipped the horse on, and reached the Croix-Rouge at two in the morning. No sign of her. It occurred to him that Léon might have seen her: but where did he live? Luckily, Charles remembered the address of his employer, and he hastened there.

The sky was beginning to lighten. He made out some escutcheons over a door, and knocked. Without opening, someone shouted the information he wanted, together with a good deal of abuse about people who disturb other people at night.

The house the clerk lived in boasted neither bell nor knocker nor doorman. Charles pounded with his fists on the shutters, but just then a policeman came along: this frightened him, and he slunk away.

"I'm crazy," he told himself. "The Lormeaux' probably kept her to dinner."

But the Lormeaux' no longer lived in Rouen.

"She must have stayed to look after Madame Dubreuil. Oh, no—Madame Dubreuil died ten months ago. So where can she be?"

He had an idea. In a café he asked for the directory and looked up Mademoiselle Lempereur: 74 Rue de la Renelle-des-Maroquiniers was her address.

Just as he turned into that street, Emma herself appeared at the other end. It would be wrong to say that he embraced her: he flung himself on her, crying:

"What kept you, yesterday?"

"I was ill."

"Ill? How? Where?"

She passed her hand over her forehead:

"At Mademoiselle Lempereur's."

"I knew it! I was on my way there."

"Well, there's no use going there now. She's just gone out. But after this don't get so excited. I won't feel free to do a thing if I know that the slightest delay upsets you like this."

It was a kind of permit that she was giving herself—a permit to feel completely unhampered in her escapades. And she proceeded to make free and frequent use of it. Whenever she felt like seeing Léon, she would go off, using any excuse that came to mind; and since he wouldn't be expecting her that day, she would call for him at his office.

It was all very joyous, the first few times. But before long he stopped hiding the truth from her: his employer was complaining loudly of these incursions.

"Bah!" she said. "Come along."

And he slipped out.

She demanded that he dress entirely in black and grow a little pointed beard, to make himself look like the portraits of Louis XIII.⁹ She asked to see his rooms, and found them very so-so; he reddened at that, but she didn't notice, and advised him to buy curtains like hers. When he objected to the expense:

"Ah! So you pinch your pennies!" she said, laughing.

Each time, Léon had to tell her everything he had done since their last rendezvous. She asked for a poem, a poem for herself, a love piece written in her honor: he could never find a rhyme for the second line, and ended up copying a sonnet from a keepsake.

He did that less out of vanity than out of a desire to please her. He never disputed any of her ideas; he fell in with all her tastes: he was becoming her mistress, far more than she was his. Her sweet words and her kisses swept away his soul. Her depravity was so deep and so dissembled as to be almost intangible: where could she have learned it?

VI

On his trips to see her he had often taken dinner at the pharmacist's, and he felt obliged out of politeness to invite him in return.

"With pleasure!" Homais answered. "A change will do me good: my life here is such a rut. We'll see a show and eat in a restaurant and really go out on the town."

"Out on the town!" Madame Homais' exclamation was affectionate: she was alarmed by the vague perils he was girding himself to meet.

"Why shouldn't I? Don't you think I ruin my health enough, exposing myself to all those drug fumes? That's women for you! They're jealous of Science, and yet they're up in arms at the mention of even the most legitimate distraction. Never mind, I'll be there. One of these days I'll turn up in Rouen, and we'll turn the town upside down."

In the past, the apothecary would have been careful to avoid such an expression; but now he was going in for a daredevil, Parisian kind of language that he considered very à la mode, and like his neighbor Madame Bovary he asked the clerk many searching questions about life in the big city. He even

9. French king (1601–1643), who ruled 1610–43; the father of Louis XIV.

talked slang in order to show off in front of the "bourgeois," using such terms as *turne, bazar, chicard, chicanard,* the English "Breda Street" for Rue de Bréda and *je me la casse* for *je m'en vais.*[1]

So one Thursday Emma was surprised to find, in the kitchen of the Lion d'Or, none other than Monsieur Homais in traveling garb—that is, wrapped in an old cape that no one had ever seen on him before, with a suitcase in one hand and in the other the foot warmer from his shop. He hadn't breathed a word about his trip to anyone, fearing lest the public be made nervous by his absence.

The idea of revisiting the scenes of his youth apparently excited him, for he didn't stop talking all the way. The wheels had barely stopped turning when he leapt from the coach in search of Léon; and despite the clerk's struggles he dragged him off to lunch at the Café de Normandie. Here Monsieur Homais made a majestic entrance: he kept his hat on, considering it highly provincial to uncover in a public place.

Emma waited for Léon three-quarters of an hour, then rushed to his office. She was at a loss as to what could have happened: in her mind she heaped him with reproaches for his indifference and herself for her weakness; all afternoon she stood with her forehead glued to the windowpanes of their room.

At two o'clock Léon and Homais were still facing each other across their table. The big dining room was emptying; the stovepipe, designed to resemble a palm tree, spread out in a circle of gilded fronds on the white ceiling; and near them, just inside the window, in full sun, a little fountain gurgled into a marble basin, where among watercress and asparagus three sluggish lobsters stretched their claws toward a heap of quail.

Homais was in heaven. He found the *luxe* even more intoxicating than the fine food and drink; still, the Pommard went to his head a little; and when the rum omelet made its appearance he advanced certain immoral theories concerning women. What particularly captivated him was the quality of *chic.* He adored an elegant *toilette* in a handsome *décor,* and as for physical qualities, he wasn't averse to a "plump little morsel."

Léon desperately watched the clock. The apothecary kept drinking, eating, talking.

"You must feel quite deprived, here in Rouen," he suddenly remarked. "But then, your lady-love doesn't live *too* far away."

And as Léon blushed:

"Come, be frank! You won't deny, will you, that in Yonville . . ."

The young man began to stammer.

". . . at the Bovarys', you did quite some courting of . . ."

"Of whom?"

"Of the maid!"

Homais wasn't joking. But Léon's vanity got the better of his discretion, and despite himself he protested indignantly. Besides, he said, he liked only brunettes.

"I approve your preference," said the pharmacist. "They have more temperament."

And putting his mouth close to his friend's ear, he enumerated the sure

---

1. I'm leaving (French). *Turne:* sweet. *Bazar:* fabulous. *Chicard:* "in." *Chicanard:* con artist. *Je me la casse:* I'm breaking (out) (French).

signs of temperament in a woman. He even launched into an ethnographical digression: German women were moody, French women licentious, Italian women passionate.

"What about Negro women?" demanded the clerk.

"Much favored by artists," said Homais. "Waiter—two demitasses!"

"Shall we go?" said Léon finally, his patience at an end.

"Yes," said Homais, in English.

But before leaving he insisted on seeing the manager, and offered him his congratulations.

Léon, in the hope of being left alone, now pleaded a business appointment.

"Ah! I'll go with you!" said Homais.

And as he accompanied him through the streets he talked about his wife, about his children, about their future, about his pharmacy, told him in what a rundown state he had found it and to what a peak of perfection he had brought it.

When they reached the Hotel de Boulogne, Léon brusquely took leave of him, ran upstairs and found his mistress close to hysterics.

The mention of the pharmacist's name put her into a rage. He pleaded his case persuasively: it wasn't his fault—surely she knew Monsieur Homais. Could she think for a moment that he preferred his company? But she turned away; he caught hold of her, and winding his arms around her waist he sank to his knees, languorous, passionate, imploring.

She stood there, solemn, almost terrible, transfixing him with her great blazing eyes. Then tears came to cloud them, she lowered her reddened eyelids, held out her hands, and Léon was just pressing them to his lips when a servant knocked and said that someone was asking for Monsieur.

"You'll come back?" she said.

"Yes."

"When?"

"Right away."

"How do you like my little trick?" said the pharmacist, when Léon appeared. "I wanted to help you get away from your company: you gave me the impression you didn't expect to enjoy it. Let's go to Bridoux's and have a glass of cordial."

Léon insisted that he had to return to his office. The apothecary made facetious remarks about legal papers and legal flummery.

"Forget about Cujas and Barthole[2] for a bit, for heaven's sake. Who's to stop you? Be a sport. Let's go to Bridoux's. You'll see his dog: it's very interesting."

And when the clerk stubbornly held out:

"I'll come, too. I'll read a newspaper while I wait, or look through a law book."

Overcome by Emma's anger, Monsieur Homais' chatter, and perhaps by the heavy lunch, Léon stood undecided, as though under the pharmacist's spell.

"Let's go to Bridoux's!" the latter kept repeating. "It's only a step from here—Rue Malpalu."

2. Or Bartole (1313–1357), an Italian jurist in Bologna. Jacques Cujas (1552–1590), a famous jurist who interpreted Roman law in contemporary terms.

Out of cowardice or stupidity, or perhaps yielding to that indefinable impulse that leads us to do the things we most deplore, he let himself be carried off to Bridoux's. They found him in his little yard, superintending three workmen who were pantingly turning the great wheel of a Seltzer-water machine. Homais offered them several bits of advice and embraced Bridoux; they had their cordial. Twenty times Léon started to leave, but the pharmacist caught him by the arm, saying:

"Just a minute! I'm coming. We'll go to the *Fanal de Rouen* and say hello to everybody. I'll introduce you to Thomassin."

He got rid of him, however, and flew to the hotel. Emma was gone.

She had just left in a fury. She hated him. His failure to keep their appointment seemed to her an insult, and she sought additional reasons for seeing no more of him. He was unheroic, weak, commonplace, spineless as a woman, and stingy and timorous to boot.

Gradually, growing calmer, she came to see that she had been unjust to him. But casting aspersions on those we love always does something to loosen our ties. We shouldn't maltreat our idols: the gilt comes off on our hands.

From then on, matters extraneous to their love occupied a greater place in their talk. The letters that Emma sent him were all about flowers, poetry, the moon and the stars: she resorted to these naïve expedients as her passion weakened, trying to keep it alive by artificial means. She continually promised herself that the next rendezvous would carry her to the peak of bliss; but when it was over she had to admit that she had felt nothing extraordinary. Each disappointment quickly gave way to new hope; each time, Emma returned to him more feverish, more avid. She could hardly wait to undress: she pulled so savagely at her corset string that it hissed around her hips like a gliding snake. Then she would tiptoe barefoot to see once again that the door was locked, and in a single movement let fall all her clothes; and, pale, silent, solemn, she would fling herself against his body with a long shudder.

There was something mad, though, something strange and sinister, about that cold, sweating forehead, about those stammering lips, those wildly staring eyes, the clasp of those arms—something that seemed to Léon to be creeping between them, subtly, as though to tear them apart.

He didn't dare question her; but realizing how experienced she was, he told himself that she must have known the utmost extremes of suffering and pleasure. What had once charmed him he now found a little frightening. Then, too, he rebelled against the way his personality was increasingly being submerged: he resented her perpetual triumph over him. He even did his best to stop loving her; then at the sound of her footsteps he would feel his will desert him, like a drunkard at the sight of strong liquor.

She made a point, it is true, of showering him with all kinds of attentions—everything from fine foods to coquetries of dress and languorous glances. She brought roses from Yonville in her bosom and tossed them at him; she worried over his health, gave him advice about how to conduct himself; and one day, to bind him the closer, hoping that heaven itself might take a hand in things, she slipped over his head a medal of the Blessed Virgin. Like a virtuous mother, she inquired about his associates:

"Don't see them," she would say. "Don't go out. Just think about us: love me!"

She wished she could keep an eye on him continually, and it occurred to her to have him followed on the street. There was a kind of tramp near the hotel who always accosted travelers and who would certainly be willing to . . . But her pride rebelled.

"What if he does betray me? Do I care?"

One day when they had said farewell earlier than usual, she caught sight of the walls of her convent as she was walking back alone down the boulevard, and she sank onto a bench in the shade of the elms. How peaceful those days had been! How she had longed for that ineffable emotion of love that she had tried to imagine from her books!

The first months of her marriage, her rides in the forest, the vicomte she had waltzed with, Lagardy singing—all passed again before her eyes. And Léon suddenly seemed as far removed as the others.

"I do love him, though!" she told herself.

No matter: she wasn't happy, and never had been. Why was life so unsatisfactory? Why did everything she leaned on crumble instantly to dust? But why, if somewhere there existed a strong and handsome being—a man of valor, sublime in passion and refinement, with a poet's heart and an angel's shape, a man like a lyre with strings of bronze, intoning elegiac epithalamiums to the heavens—why mightn't she have the luck to meet him? Ah, fine chance! Besides, nothing was worth looking for: everything was a lie! Every smile concealed a yawn of boredom; every joy, a curse; every pleasure, its own surfeit; and the sweetest kisses left on one's lips but a vain longing for fuller delight.

Through the air came a hoarse, prolonged metallic groan, and then the clock of the convent struck four. Only four! And it seemed to her that she had been there on that bench since eternity. But an infinity of passions can be compressed into a minute, like a crowd into a little space. Emma's passions were the sole concern of her life: for money she had no more thought than an archduchess.

One day, however, she was visited by an ill-kempt individual, red faced and bald, who said he had been sent by Monsieur Vinçart of Rouen. He pulled out the pins fastening the side pocket of his long green frock coat, stuck them in his sleeve, and politely handed her a document.

It was a note for 500 francs, signed by her, which Lheureux, despite all his promises, had endorsed over to Vinçart.

She sent her maid for Lheureux. He couldn't come.

The stranger had remained standing, dissimulating under his thick blond eyebrows the inquisitive glances that he cast left and right. "What answer am I to give Monsieur Vinçart?" he asked, with an innocent air.

"Well," said Emma, "tell him . . . that I haven't got . . . I'll have it next week. . . . He should wait . . . yes, I'll have it next week."

Whereupon the fellow went off without a word.

But the next day, at noon, she received a protest of nonpayment; and the sight of the official document, bearing the words "Maître Hareng, *huissier* at Buchy" several times in large letters, gave her such a fright that she hurried to the dry-goods merchant.

She found him in his shop tying up a parcel.

"At your service!" he said. "What can I do for you?"

He didn't interrupt his task: his clerk, a slightly hunchbacked girl of thirteen or so, who also did his cooking, was helping him.

Finally he clattered across the shop in his wooden shoes, climbed up ahead of Madame to the second floor, and showed her into a small office. Here on a large fir desk lay several ledgers, fastened down by a padlocked metal bar that stretched across them. A safe could be glimpsed against the wall, under some lengths of calico—a safe of such size that it certainly contained something besides cash and promissory notes. And indeed Monsieur Lheureux did some pawnbroking: it was here that he kept Madame Bovary's gold chain, along with some earrings that had belonged to poor Tellier. The latter had finally had to sell the Café Français, and had since bought a little grocery business in Quincampoix, where he was dying of his catarrh, his face yellower than the tallow candles he sold.

Lheureux sat down in his broad, rush-bottomed armchair.

"What's new?" he asked her.

"Look!"

And she showed him the document.

"Well, what can I do about it?"

She flew into a rage, reminding him that he had promised not to endorse her notes. He admitted it.

"But my hand was forced: my creditors had a knife at my throat."

"And what's going to happen now?" she asked.

"Oh, it's very simple: a court warrant, then execution; there's no way out."

Emma had to restrain herself from hitting him. She asked quietly whether there wasn't some way of appeasing Monsieur Vinçart.

"Ha! Appease Vinçart! You don't know him: he's fiercer than an Arab."

But Monsieur Lheureux *had* to do something about it!

"Now listen!" he said. "It seems to me I've been pretty nice to you so far."

And opening one of his ledgers:

"Look!"

He moved his finger up the page:

"Let's see . . . let's see . . . August 3,200 francs . . . June 17, 150 . . . March 23, 46. In April . . ."

He stopped, as though afraid of making a blunder.

"I won't even mention the notes your husband signed, one for seven hundred francs, another for three hundred. And as for your payments on account, and the interest, there's no end to it. It's a mess. I won't have anything more to do with it."

She wept; she even called him her "dear Monsieur Lheureux." But he kept laying the blame on "that scoundrelly Vinçart." Besides, he himself didn't have a centime: no one was paying him at the moment; his creditors were tearing the clothes from his back; a poor shopkeeper like himself couldn't advance money.

Emma stopped speaking; and Monsieur Lheureux, nibbling the quill of his pen, seemed disturbed by her silence.

"Of course," he said, "if I were to have something come in one of these days I might . . ."

"After all," she said, "as soon as the balance on Barneville . . ."

"What's that?"

And when he heard that Langlois hadn't yet paid he seemed very surprised. Then, in an oily voice:

"And our terms will be . . . ?"

"Oh, anything you say!"

Then he shut his eyes to help himself think, wrote down a few figures, and assuring her that he was making things hard for himself, taking a great risk, "bleeding himself white," he made out four notes for 250 francs each, payable a month apart.

"Let's hope that Vinçart's willing to listen to me! Anyway, you have my word: I don't say one thing and mean another; I'm open and aboveboard."

Afterwards he casually showed her a few items, not one of which, in his opinion, was worthy of Madame.

"When I think of dress goods like this selling at seven sous a meter and guaranteed dye-fast! Everybody believes it, too! And they don't get undeceived. I can assure you." The admission that he swindled others was meant as clinching proof of his frankness with herself.

Then he called her back and showed her several yards of point lace that he had come upon recently "in a vendue."

"Isn't it splendid?" he said. "It's being used a good deal now for antimacassars: it's the last word."

And quicker than a juggler he wrapped up the lace and handed it to Emma.

"At least," she said, "let me know how much it . . ."

"Oh, we'll talk about that later," he answered, turning abruptly away.

That very evening she made Bovary write his mother and ask her to send the balance of his inheritance at once. Her mother-in-law replied that there was nothing to send: the estate was settled, and in addition to Barneville they could count on a yearly income of 600 francs, which she would forward punctually.

So Madame sent bills to two or three patients, and before long she was sending them to many more, so successful did the expedient prove. She was always careful to add, in a postscript: "Don't speak of this to my husband— you know how proud he is. With regrets. Your humble servant." There were a few complaints, but she intercepted them.

To raise money she began to sell her old gloves, her old hats, all kinds of household odds and ends. She drove a hard bargain: her peasant blood stood her in good stead. And on her trips to the city she combed the curiosity shops for knickknacks, telling herself that Monsieur Lheureux, if no one else, would take them off her hands. She brought ostrich feathers, Chinese porcelains, old chests; she borrowed from Félicité, from Madame Lefrançois, from the landlady of the Croix-Rouge, from anyone and everyone. With part of the money she finally got from Barneville, she paid off two notes, the rest—1,500 francs—dribbled away. She signed new notes—always new notes.

Occasionally she tried to add up some figures, but the totals were so enormous that she couldn't believe them. Then she'd begin all over again, quickly become confused, and push it all aside and forget it.

The house was a gloomy place these days. Tradesmen called, and left with angry faces. Handkerchiefs lay strewn about on the stoves; and Madame Homais was shocked to see little Berthe with holes in her stockings. If Charles ventured some timid remark, Emma retorted savagely that *she* certainly wasn't to blame.

Why these fits of rage? He laid it all to her old nervous illness; and, penitent at having mistaken her infirmities for faults, he cursed his selfishness and longed to run up to her and take her in his arms.

"Oh, no!" he told himself. "I'd only annoy her."

And he did nothing.

After dinner he would walk alone in the garden. Then, with little Berthe in his lap and his medical journal open, he would try to teach the child to read. But she had never been given the slightest schooling, and after a few moments her eyes would grow round and sad, and the tears would come. He would comfort her: he filled the watering can to help her make rivulets in the paths, or broke privet branches that she could plant as trees in the flower beds. None of this harmed the garden, particularly—it was so choked with high grass anyway: they owed so many days' pay to Lestiboudois! Then the little girl would feel chilly and ask for her mother.

"Call Félicité," Charles would tell her. "You know *maman* doesn't like to be disturbed."

It was the onset of autumn, and already the leaves were falling—like two years before, when she had been so ill. When would there be an end to all this? And he would walk up and down, his hands behind his back.

Madame was in her room. No one else was admitted. She stayed there all day long in a torpor, not bothering to dress, now and again burning incense that she had bought at an Algerian shop in Rouen. She couldn't stand having Charles lying like a log at her side all night, and her repeated complaints finally drove him to sleep in the attic. She would read till morning—lurid novels full of orgies and bloodshed.

Sometimes, in sudden terror, she screamed; but when Charles ran in she dismissed him:

"Oh, get out."

At other times, seared by that hidden fire which her adultery kept feeding, consumed with longing, feverish with desire, she would open her window, inhale the cold air, let the heavy mass of her hair stream out in the wind: as she gazed at the stars she wished she were loved by a prince. Thoughts of Léon filled her. At such moments she would have given anything for a single one of their trysts—the trysts that sated her lust.

Those were her gala days. She was determined that they be glorious; and when he couldn't pay for everything himself she freely made up the difference. This happened almost every time. He tried to convince her that they would be just as well off elsewhere, in a more modest hotel, but she always objected.

One day she opened her bag, produced six little silver-gilt spoons—they had been her father's wedding present—and asked him to run out and pawn them for her. Léon obeyed, though he disliked the errand: he was afraid it might compromise him.

Thinking it over later, he came to the conclusion that his mistress was certainly beginning to act strangely: maybe the people who were urging him to break with her weren't so mistaken after all.

For indeed someone had sent his mother a long anonymous letter, warning her that he was "ruining himself with a married woman"; and the lady, having visions of the perennial bogey of respectable families—that ill-defined, baleful female, that siren, that fantastic monster forever lurking in the abysses of love—wrote to Maître Bocage, his employer. This gentleman's handling of the matter was flawless. He talked to the young man for three-quarters of an hour, trying to unseal his eyes and warn him of the precipice ahead. Sooner or later, such an affair would harm his career. He begged him to break it off—and if he couldn't make the sacrifice for his own sake, then he should at least do it for his—namely, for the sake of Maître Bocage.

In the end Léon had promised never to see Emma again; and he reproached himself for not having kept his word, especially considering all the trouble and reproaches she still probably held in store for him—not to mention the jokes his fellow clerks cracked every morning around the stove. Besides, he was about to be promoted to head clerk: this was the time to turn over a new leaf. So he gave up playing the flute and said good-bye to exalted sentiments and romantic dreams. There isn't a bourgeois alive who in the ferment of his youth, if only for a day or for a minute, hasn't thought himself capable of boundless passions and noble exploits. The sorriest little woman-chaser has dreamed of Oriental queens; in a corner of every notary's heart lie the moldy remains of a poet.

These days it only bored him when Emma suddenly burst out sobbing on his breast: like people who can stand only a certain amount of music, he was drowsy and apathetic amidst the shrillness of her love; his heart had grown deaf to its subtler overtones.

By now they knew each other too well: no longer did they experience, in their mutual possession, that wonder that multiplies the joy a hundredfold. She was as surfeited with him as he was tired of her. Adultery, Emma was discovering, could be as banal as marriage.

But what way out was there? She felt humiliated by the degradation of such pleasures; but to no avail: she continued to cling to them, out of habit or out of depravity; and every day she pursued them more desperately, destroying all possible happiness by her excessive demands. She blamed Léon for her disappointed hopes, as though he had betrayed her; and she even longed for a catastrophe that would bring about their separation, since she hadn't the courage to bring it about herself.

Still, she continued to write him loving letters, faithful to the idea that a woman must always write her lover.

But as her pen flew over the paper she was aware of the presence of another man, a phantom embodying her most ardent memories, the most beautiful things she had read and her strongest desires. In the end he became so real and accessible that she tingled with excitement, unable though she was to picture him clearly, so hidden was he, godlike, under his manifold attributes. He dwelt in that enchanted realm where silken ladders swing from balconies moon-bright and flower-scented. She felt him near her: he was coming—coming to ravish her entirely in a kiss. And the next moment she would drop back to earth, shattered; for these rapturous love-dreams drained her more than the greatest orgies.

She lived these days in a state of constant and total exhaustion. She was continually receiving writs—official documents that she barely looked at. She wished she were dead, or in a state of continual sleep.

The Thursday night of the mi-carême—the mid-Lenten festivities—she didn't return to Yonville, but went to a masked ball. She wore velvet knee breeches and red stockings and a peruke, and a cocked hat over one ear. She danced all night to the wild sound of trombones; she was the center of an admiring throng; and morning found her under the portico of the theatre with five or six maskers dressed as stevedores and sailors—friends of Léon's, who were wondering where they might have something to eat.

The nearby cafés were all full. On the river front they found a nondescript restaurant whose owner showed them up to a little room on the fifth floor.

The men whispered in a corner, doubtless consulting about the expense. A clerk, two medical students and a shop assistant: what company she was keeping! As for the women, Emma was quickly aware from their voices that most of them must be of the lowest class. That frightened her, and she drew back her chair and lowered her eyes.

The others began to eat. She did not. Her forehead was afire, her eyelids were smarting, her skin was icy cold. In her head she still felt the quaking of the dance floor under the rhythmic tread of a thousand feet. The smell of punch and cigar smoke made her dizzy. She fainted, and they carried her to the window.

Day was beginning to break, and in the pale sky toward Sainte-Catherine a large streak of red was widening. The leaden river shivered in the wind; the bridges were empty; the street lamps were going out.

Gradually she revived, and somehow she thought of Berthe, asleep out there beyond the horizon, in Félicité's room. But a wagon laden with long strips of iron went by, and the impact of its metallic clang shook the house walls.

Abruptly, she left the place. She took off her costume, told Léon she had to go home, and at last was alone in the Hotel de Boulogne. She loathed everything, including herself. She longed to fly away like a bird, to recapture her youth somewhere far away in the immaculate reaches of space.

She went out, followed the boulevard, crossed the Place Cauchoise and walked through the outskirts of the city to an open street overlooking gardens. She walked swiftly; the fresh air calmed her; and gradually the faces of the crowd, the maskers, the quadrilles, the blazing lights, the supper, and those women she had found herself with all disappeared like mist blown off by the wind. Then she returned to the Croix-Rouge and flung herself down on her bed in the little third-floor room with the prints of the Tour de Nesle. At four that afternoon Hivert woke her.

When she arrived home Félicité showed her a gray sheet of paper stuck behind the clock.

"By virtue of an instrument," she read, "duly setting forth the terms of a judgment to be enforced . . ."

What judgment? The previous day, she found, another paper had arrived; she hadn't seen it; and now she was dumbfounded to read these words:

"To Madame Bovary: You are hereby commanded by order of the king, the law and the courts . . ."

Then, skipping several lines, she saw:

"Within twenty-four hours." What was this? "Pay the total amount of 8,000 francs." And lower down: "There to be subjected to all due processes of law, and notably to execution of distraint upon furniture and effects."

What was to be done? In twenty-four hours: tomorrow! Lheureux, she thought, was probably trying to frighten her again. Suddenly she saw through all his schemes; the reason for his amiability burst upon her. What reassured her was the very enormity of the amount.

Nonetheless, as a result of buying and never paying, borrowing, signing notes and then renewing those same notes, which grew larger and larger each time they came due, she had gradually built up a capital for Monsieur Lheureux that he was impatient to lay his hands on to use in his speculations.

She called on him, assuming a nonchalant air.

"You know what's happened? It's a joke, I suppose?"

"No."

"What do you mean?"

He slowly turned his head away and folded his arms.

"Did you think, my dear lady," he said, "that I was going to go on to the end of time being your supplier and banker just for the love of God? I have to get back what I laid out: let's be fair!"

She was indignant about the size of the amount claimed.

"What can I do about it? The court upheld it. There's a judgment. You were notified. Besides, I have nothing to do with it—it's Vinçart."

"Couldn't you . . . ?"

"Absolutely nothing."

"But . . . still . . . let's talk it over."

And she stammered incoherently that she had known nothing about it, that the whole thing had come as a surprise. . . .

"Whose fault is that?" said Lheureux, with an ironic bow. "I work like a slave, and you go out enjoying yourself."

"Ah! No preaching!"

"It never did anybody any harm," he retorted.

She was craven: she pled with him, she even put her pretty slender white hand on his knee.

"None of that! Are you trying to seduce me, or what?"

"You're contemptible!" she cried.

"Oh! Oh! How you go on!" he said, laughing.

"I'll let everybody know what you're like. I'll tell my husband. . . ."

"Will you? I have something to *show* your husband!"

And out of his safe Lheureux took the receipt for 1,800 francs that she had given him for the note discounted by Vinçart.

"Do you think," he said, "that he won't see through your little swindle, the poor dear man?"

She crumpled, as though hit over the head with a club. He paced back and forth between the window and the desk, saying over and over:

"I'll show it to him! I'll show it to him!"

Then he came close to her and said softly:

"It's no fun, I know; but nobody's ever died of it, after all, and since it's the only way you have left of paying me back my money . . ."

"But where can I find some?" cried Emma, wringing her hands.

"Ah! Bah! A woman like you, with plenty of friends!"

And he transfixed her with a stare so knowing and so terrible that she shuddered to the depths of her being.

"I promise you!" she said. "I'll sign . . ."

"I have enough of your signatures!"

"I'll sell more . . ."

"Face it!" he said, shrugging his shoulders. "You've got nothing left."

And he called through a peephole that communicated with the shop:

"Annette! Don't forget the three cuttings of No. 14."

The servant entered; Emma took the hint, and asked how much money would be required to stop all proceedings.

"It's too late!"

"But if I brought you a few thousand francs—a quarter of the amount, a third, almost all?"

"No—there's no use!"

He pushed her gently toward the stairs.

"I implore you, Monsieur Lheureux—just a few days more!"

She was sobbing.

"Ah! Tears! Very good!"

"You'll drive me to do something desperate!"

"A lot I care!" he said, closing the door behind her.

VII

She was stoical, the next day, when Maître Hareng, the *huissier,* arrived with two witnesses to take inventory of the goods and chattels to be sold.

They began with Bovary's consulting room, and didn't include the phrenological head, which was considered a "professional instrument"; but in the kitchen they counted the plates and the pans, the chairs and the candlesticks, and in the bedroom all the knickknacks on the whatnot. They inspected her dresses, the linen, the *cabinet de toilette:* and her very being, down to its most hidden and intimate details, was laid open, like a dissected corpse, to the stares of those three men.

Maître Hareng, bottomed up in a close-fitting black tail coat, with a white cravat, his shoe straps very tight, kept repeating:

"*Vous permettez,*[3] *Madame? Vous permettez?*"

And frequently he exclaimed:

"Charming! Very pretty!"

Then he would resume his writing, dipping his pen in the inkhorn he held in his left hand.

When they had finished with the various rooms they went up to the attic.

She kept a desk there, where Rodolphe's letters were locked away. They made her open it.

"Ah! Personal papers!" said Maître Hareng, with a discreet smile. "*Mais permettez!* I have to make sure there's nothing else in the box."

And he held the envelopes upside down, very gently, as though expecting them to disgorge gold pieces. She was put into a fury by the sight of that great red hand, with its soft, sluglike fingers, touching those pages that had caused her so many heartthrobs.

They left at last. Félicité came back: she had sent her out to watch for Bovary and keep him away. They quickly installed the watchman in the attic, and he promised to stay there.

Charles, she thought during the evening, looked careworn. She scrutinized him with an agonized stare, reading accusations in the drawn lines of his face. Then, as her eyes roved over the mantelpiece, gay with Chinese fans, over the full curtains, the armchairs, all the things that had tempered the bitterness of her life, she was overcome with remorse, or rather with immense regret; and this, far from eclipsing her passion, only exasperated it. Charles placidly stirred the fire, lounging in his chair.

At one moment the watchman—bored, no doubt, in his hiding place—made a slight noise.

---

3. Permit me (French).

"Is somebody walking around up there?" said Charles.

"No!" she answered. "It's a dormer that's been left open, blowing in the wind."

The next day, Sunday, she left for Rouen, determined to call on every banker she had heard of. Most of them were away in the country or traveling. She persisted, however, and those whom she succeeded in seeing she asked for money, insisting that she must have it, swearing to repay. Some of them laughed in her face; they all refused.

At two o'clock she hurried to Léon's and knocked on his door. No one came to open. Finally he appeared.

"What brings you here?"

"Are you sorry to see me?"

"No . . . but . . ."

And he confessed that his landlord didn't like the tenants to entertain "women."

"I've got to talk to you," she said.

He reached for his key. She stopped him:

"Oh, no—let's go to our place."

And they went to their room in the Hotel de Boulogne.

There she drank a large glass of water. She was very pale.

"Léon," she said to him, "you have to do something for me."

And clutching both his hands tightly in hers, she shook them and said:

"Listen! I've got to have eight thousand francs!"

"But you're out of your mind!"

"Not yet!"

And in a rush she told him all about the execution. She was in desperate straits: Charles had been kept in total ignorance, her mother-in-law hated her, her father could do nothing. He—Léon—must save her. He must go out at once and find her the money that she absolutely had to have.

"How in the world do you expect me . . . ?"

"Don't just stand there, like a spineless fool!"

"You're making things out to be worse than they are," he said stupidly. "You could probably quiet your man with three thousand francs."

All the more reason for trying to do something: it wasn't conceivable that three thousand francs couldn't be found. Besides, Léon's signature could go on the notes instead of hers.

"Go ahead! Try! I've got to have it! Hurry! Oh, try! Try! Then I'll show you how I love you!"

He went out. In an hour he was back.

"I've seen three people," he told her, solemn-faced. "Nothing doing."

They sat face to face across the fire, still and silent. Emma kept shrugging her shoulders, tapping her foot. Then he heard her say, low-voiced:

"If I were in your place I'd know where to find the money!"

"You would? Where?"

"In your office!"

She stared at him.

There was a demonic desperation burning in her eyes, and she narrowed them in a look of lascivious provocation: the young man felt himself giving way before the mute will of this woman who was urging him to crime. He took fright; and to avoid hearing anything further he clapped his hand to his forehead.

"Morel should be back tonight!" he cried. "He won't refuse me, I hope!" (Morel was one of his friends, the son of a wealthy businessman.) "I'll bring it to you tomorrow," he promised.

Emma didn't appear to welcome this hope of relief as joyfully as he had thought. Did she suspect his lie? He blushed as he added:

"But if I'm not back by three, don't wait for me any longer, darling. Now I have to go out. Forgive me! Good-bye!"

He pressed her hand, but it lay inert in his: Emma was drained of all feeling.

Four o'clock struck; and she got up to go back to Yonville, automatic in her obedience to the force of habit.

The day was fine—one of those clear, sharp March days with the sun brilliant in a cloudless sky. Contented-looking Rouennais were strolling in their Sunday best. As she came to the Place du Parvis, vespers in the cathedral had just ended: crowds were pouring out through the three portals, like a river through the three arches of a bridge; and in their midst, immovable as a rock, stood the verger.

She remembered how tremulous she had been, how full of hope, the day she had entered that lofty nave: how it had stretched away before her, on and on—and yet not as infinite as her love! And she kept walking, weeping under her veil, dazed, tottering, almost in a faint.

"Watch out!" The cry came from within a porte-cochère that was swinging open; she stopped, and out came a black horse, prancing between the shafts of a tilbury. A gentleman in sables was holding the reins. Who was he? She knew him. . . . The carriage leapt forward and was gone.

The vicomte! It was the vicomte! She turned to stare: the street was empty. And the encounter left her so crushed, so immeasurably sad, that she leaned against a wall to keep from falling.

Then she thought that she might be mistaken. How could she tell? She had no way of knowing. Everything—everything within her, everything without—was abandoning her. She felt lost, rolling dizzily down into some dark abyss; and she was almost glad, when she reached the Croix-Rouge, to see good old Monsieur Homais. He was watching a case of pharmaceutical supplies being loaded onto the Hirondelle, and in his hand he carried a present for his wife—six *cheminots* wrapped in a foulard handkerchief.

Madame Homais was particularly fond of those heavy turban-shaped rolls, which the Rouennais eat in Lent with salted butter—a last relic of Gothic fare, going back perhaps to the times of the Crusades. The lusty Normans of those days gorged themselves on *cheminots*, picturing them as the heads of Saracens, to be devoured by the light of yellow torches along with flacons of spiced wine and giant slabs of meat. Like those ancients, the apothecary's wife crunched them heroically, despite her wretched teeth; and every time Monsieur Homais made a trip to the city he faithfully brought some back to her, buying them always at the best baker's, in the Rue Massacre.

"Delighted to see you!" he said, offering Emma a hand to help her into the Hirondelle.

Then he put the *cheminots* in the baggage net and sat there hatless, his arms folded, in a pose that was pensive and Napoleonic.

But when the blind beggar made his appearance as usual at the foot of the hill, he exclaimed in indignation:

"I cannot understand why the authorities continue to tolerate such dishonest occupations! All these unfortunates should be put away—and put to work! Progress moves at a snail's pace, no doubt about it: we're still wallowing in the midst of barbarism!"

The blind man held out his hat, and it swung to and fro at the window like a loose piece of upholstery.

"That," pronounced the pharmacist, "is a scrofulous disease."

And though he had often seen the poor devil before, he pretended now to be looking at him for the first time, and he murmured the words "cornea," "opaque cornea," "sclerotic," "facies." Then, in a paternal tone:

"Have you had that frightful affliction long, my friend? You'd do well to follow a diet, instead of getting drunk in cafés."

He urged him to take only good wine and good beer, and to eat good roast meat. The blind man kept singing his song: actually, he seemed fairly close to idiocy. Finally Monsieur Homais took out his purse:

"Here—here's a sou: change it for me and keep half of it for yourself. And don't forget my suggestions—you'll find they help."

Hivert presumed to express certain doubts about their efficacy. But the apothecary swore that he could cure the fellow himself, with an antiphlogistic[4] salve of his own invention, and he gave him his address:

"Monsieur Homais, near the market—ask anyone."

"Come now," said Hivert. "Show the gentleman you're grateful by doing your act."

The blind man squatted on his haunches and threw back his head, and rolling his greenish eyes and sticking out his tongue he rubbed his stomach with both hands, meanwhile uttering a kind of muffled howl, like a famished dog. Emma, shuddering with disgust, flung him a five-franc piece over her shoulder. It was all the money she had in the world: there was something grand, she thought, in thus throwing it away.

The coach was again in motion, when suddenly Monsieur Homais leaned out the window.

"Nothing farinaceous!" he shouted. "No dairy products! Wear woolens next to your skin! Fumigate the diseased areas with the smoke of juniper berries!"

The sight of all the familiar things they passed gradually took Emma's mind off her misery. She was oppressed, crushed with fatigue, and she reached home numb and spiritless, almost asleep.

"Let come what may!" she told herself.

Besides—who knew? Something extraordinary might happen any moment. Lheureux himself might die.

She was awakened the next morning at nine by the sound of voices in the square. People were crowding around the market to read a large notice posted on one of the pillars, and she saw Justin climb on a guard post and deface the notice. Just then the village policeman seized him by the collar. Monsieur Homais came out of his pharmacy, and Madame Lefrançois seemed to be holding forth in the midst of the crowd.

"Madame! Madame!" cried Félicité, rushing in. "It's an outrage!"

And the poor girl, much agitated, showed her a yellow paper she had just

---

4. Anti-inflammatory.

torn off the front door. Emma read in a glance that all the contents of her house were subject to sale.

They looked at each other in silence. There were no secrets between mistress and maid. Finally Félicité murmured:

"If I were you, Madame, I'd go see Maître Guillaumin."

"Do you think so?"

"You know all about the Guillaumins from their manservant," the question meant; "does the master mention me, sometimes?"

"Yes, go ahead: it's worth trying."

She put on her black dress and her bonnet with jade beads; and to keep from being seen (there was still quite a crowd in the square) she avoided the village and took the river path.

She was breathless when she reached the notary's gate. The sky was dark; it was snowing a little.

At the sound of her ring Théodore, in a red vest, emerged from the front door; and he opened the gate for her with an air of familiarity, as though she were someone he knew well, and showed her into the dining room.

A large porcelain stove was purring; the niche above it was filled with a cactus plant; and against the oak-grained wallpaper hung Steuben's "Esmeralda" and Schopin's "Potiphar,"[5] both in black wood frames. The table set for breakfast, the two silver dish warmers, the crystal doorknobs, the parquet floor and the furniture—all gleamed with a meticulous English spotlessness; in the corners of each of the windows were panes of colored glass.

"This," thought Emma, "is the kind of dining room I should have."

The notary came in. He was wearing a dressing gown with palm designs, which he clutched about him with his left hand; and with his right he doffed and then quickly replaced his brown velvet skullcap. This he wore rakishly tilted to the right, and out from under it emerged the ends of three strands of fair hair that were combed up from the back and drawn carefully over his bald cranium.

After offering her a chair he sat down to his breakfast, apologizing profusely for his discourtesy.

"Monsieur," she said, "I want to ask you . . ."

"What, Madame? I'm listening."

She told him of her predicament.

It was no news to Maître Guillaumin: he was secretly associated with the dry-goods merchant, who could always be counted on to supply him with capital for the mortgage loans he arranged for his clients.

Thus he knew—far better than she—the long story of the notes, small at first, carrying the names of various endorsers, made out for long terms and continually renewed; he knew how the shopkeeper had gradually accumulated the various protests of nonpayment, and how he had finally had his friend Vinçart institute the necessary legal proceedings in his name, wishing to avoid acquiring a reputation for bloodthirstiness among his fellow villagers.

She interspersed her story with recriminations against Lheureux, and to

5. The official of the court of Egypt who was Joseph's master; the wife of Potiphar tried to seduce him. The painting represents the seduction scene. Karl Steuben (1877–1856), a German history painter. Esmeralda is the gypsy girl in Hugo's *Notre Dame de Paris*. A painting titled *Esmeralda et Quasimodo* was exhibited in 1839. Schopin was the brother of the composer Chopin.

these the notary returned occasional, empty answers. He ate his chop and drank his tea; his chin kept rubbing against his sky-blue cravat, whose two diamond stickpins were linked by a fine gold chain; and he smiled a strange, sugary, ambiguous smile. Then he noticed that her feet were wet.

"Move closer to the stove! Put them up—higher—against the porcelain."

She was afraid of dirtying it, but his retort was gallant:

"Pretty things never do any harm."

Then she tried to appeal to his emotions: growing emotional herself, she told him about her cramped household budget, her harassments, her needs. He was very sympathetic—an elegant woman like herself!—and without interrupting his meal he gradually turned so that he faced her and his knee brushed against her shoe, whose sole was beginning to curl a little as it steamed in the heat of the stove.

But when she asked him for 3,000 francs he tightened his lips and said that he was very sorry not to have had charge of her capital in the past, for there were a hundred easy ways in which even a lady could invest her money profitably. The Grumesnil peatery, building lots in Le Havre—such speculations were excellent, almost risk-proof; and he let her consume herself with rage at the thought of the fantastic sums she could certainly have made.

"How come," he asked her, "that you never called on me?"

"I really don't know," she said.

"Why didn't you? Did I seem so very frightening to you? But I'm the one who has cause for complaint: we barely know each other! I feel very warmly toward you, though; you realize that now, I hope?"

He reached out his hand, took hers, pressed it to his lips in a greedy kiss, and then kept it on his knee; and he gently fondled her fingers, murmuring a thousand compliments.

His monotonous voice rustled on like a running brook; his eyes were gleaming through the glitter of his glasses; and his hands crept up inside Emma's sleeve and stroked her arm. She felt a panting breath on her cheek. This man was more than she could stand.

She leapt to her feet.

"Monsieur! I'm waiting!"

"What for?" cried the notary, suddenly extremely pale.

"The money."

"But . . ."

Then, yielding to an irresistible surge of desire:

"Yes! Yes!"

He dragged himself toward her on his knees, careless of his dressing gown.

"Please! Don't go! I love you!"

He seized her by the waist.

A flood of crimson rushed to Madame Bovary's face. She shrank back, and with a terrible look she cried:

"It's shameless of you to take advantage of my distress! I'm to be pitied, but I'm not for sale!"

And she walked out.

The notary sat there dumbfounded, his eyes fixed on his beautiful embroidered slippers. They were a gift from a mistress, and the sight of them gradually comforted him. Anyway, he told himself, such an affair would have involved too many risks.

"What a contemptible, lowdown cad!" she said to herself, as she fled tremulously under the aspens lining the road. Disappointment at having failed made her all the more indignant at the insult offered her honor: it seemed to her that Providence was hounding her relentlessly. She was filled with pride at the way she had acted: never before had she esteemed herself so highly; never had she felt such contempt for everyone else. She was at war with the world, and the thought transported her. She longed to lash out at all men, to spit in their faces, grind them all to dust; and she hurried straight on, pale, trembling, furious, scanning the empty horizon with weeping eyes, almost gloating in the hatred that was choking her.

When she caught sight of her house she felt suddenly paralyzed. She couldn't go on, and yet she had to: what escape was there?

Félicité was waiting for her at the door.

"Well?"

"No," said Emma.

And for a quarter of an hour they discussed who in Yonville might be willing to help her. But every time Félicité mentioned someone, Emma answered:

"Out of the question! They'd refuse!"

"And Monsieur will soon be home!"

"I know. . . . Go away and leave me alone."

She had tried everything. Now there was nothing more to be done; so when Charles appeared there would be only one thing to tell him:

"Don't stay here! The very rug you're walking on isn't ours. Not a piece of all this furniture belongs to you—not a pin, not a wisp of straw; and I'm the one who has ruined you!"

Then he would utter a great sob, and then weep floods of tears; and in the end, once the shock was over, he would forgive her.

"Yes," she muttered, through clenched teeth, *"he'll* forgive *me*—the man *I* wouldn't forgive for setting eyes on me if he offered me a million. . . . Never! Never!"

This thought of Bovary in a position to be condescending put her beside herself. But whether she confessed or not, he would inevitably—sooner or later, today or tomorrow—learn of the disaster; so she could only look forward to that horrible scene and to being subjected to the weight of his magnanimity. Suddenly she felt an urge to try Lheureux once more: but what was the use? Or to write to her father: but it was too late. And perhaps she was regretting, now, not having yielded to the notary, when she heard a horse's trot in the lane. It was Charles: he was opening the gate, his face more ashen than the plaster on the wall. Rushing downstairs, she slipped quickly out into the square; and the mayor's wife, who was chatting in front of the church with Lestiboudois, saw her enter the house of the tax collector.

Madame Tuvache ran to tell Madame Caron. The two ladies climbed up to the latter's attic; and there, hidden behind some laundry that was hanging up to dry, they stood so that they could easily see into Binet's.

He was alone in his garret, busily copying, in wood, one of those ivory ornaments that beggar description, a conglomeration of half-moons and of spheres carved one inside the other, the whole thing standing erect like an obelisk and perfectly useless. He was just beginning on the last section: the end was in sight! In the chiaroscuro of his workshop the golden sawdust flew from his lathe like a spray of sparks under the hooves of a galloping horse; the two wheels spun and whirred; Binet was smiling, chin down and nostrils wide: he looked absorbed, in one of those states of utter bliss such as men seem to find only in humble activities, which divert the mind with easy challenges and gratify it with the most utter and complete success.

"Ah! There she is!" said Madame Tuvache.

But the sound of the lathe made it impossible to know what she was saying.

Finally the two ladies thought they heard the word "francs," and Madame Tuvache whispered:

"She's asking him for a postponement of her taxes."

"Looks like it," said the other.

They saw her pacing up and down the room, looking at the shelves along the wall laden with napkin rings, candlesticks and finials, while Binet contentedly stroked his beard.

"Would she be coming to order something from him?" suggested Madame Tuvache.

"But he never sells anything!" the other reminded her.

The tax collector seemed to be listening, staring as though he didn't understand. She continued to talk, her manner gentle and supplicating. She came close to him; her breast was heaving; now they seemed not to be speaking.

"Is she making advances to him?" said Madame Tuvache.

Binet had gone red to the roots of his hair. She grasped his hands.

"Ah! Just look at that . . . !"

And she must have been suggesting something abominable, for the tax collector—and he was a man of courage: he had fought at Bautzen and Lützen, and taken part in the French campaign,[6] and even been proposed for the Legion of Honor—suddenly recoiled as though he had seen a snake.

"Madame!" he cried. "You must be dreaming!"

"Women like that should be horsewhipped," said Madame Tuvache.

"Where has she gone to?" said Madame Caron.

For even as he was speaking she had vanished. Then they saw her darting down the Grande Rue and turning to the right, as though to reach the cemetery, and they didn't know what to make of it.

"Madame Rollet!" she cried, when she reached the wet nurse's. "I can't breathe! Unlace me!"

She fell sobbing onto the bed. Madame Rollet covered her with a petticoat and stood beside her. Then, when she didn't speak, the peasant woman moved away, took up her wheel and began spinning flax.

"Don't do that!" she murmured: she thought it was Binet's lathe.

"What's the matter with her?" wondered the nurse. "Why did she come here?"

She had come because a kind of terror had sent her—a terror that made her flee her home. Lying on her back, motionless, her eyes vacant, she saw things only in a blur, though she focused her attention on them with idiotic persistence. She stared at the flaking plaster on the wall, at two half-burned sticks smoking end to end in the fireplace, at a large spider crawling overhead in a crack in the rafter. Gradually she collected her thoughts. She remem-

6. The battles in France before the Allies captured Paris and forced the abdication of Napoleon and his banishment to Elba in 1814. Bautzen, in Saxony, was the scene of an 1813 battle in which Napoleon defeated the Prussians and Russians. Lützen, in Saxony, was the scene of another victory by Napoleon.

bered . . . one day with Léon . . . Oh, how far away it was . . . ! The sun was shining on the river, and the air was full of the scent of clematis. . . . Then, swept along in her memories as in a raging torrent, she quickly recalled the previous day.

"What time is it?" she asked.

Madame Rollet went out, held up the fingers of her right hand against the brightest part of the sky, and came slowly back, saying:

"Almost three."

"Ah! Thank you! Thank you!"

For he would be coming. There could be no question about it: by now he had found the money. But probably he would go to her house, having no idea that she was here; and she ordered the nurse to run and fetch him.

"Hurry!"

"I'm on my way, dear lady! I'm on my way!"

She marveled, now, at not having thought of him in the first place: yesterday he had given his word; he wouldn't fail her; and already she saw herself at Lheureux's, laying the three banknotes on his desk. Then she'd have to invent some story that would satisfy Bovary. What would it be?

But the nurse was a long time returning. Still, since there was no clock in the cottage, Emma feared that she might be exaggerating the duration of her absence, and she walked slowly around and around the garden, and down the path by the hedge and quickly back, hoping that the nurse might have returned some other way. Finally, weary of waiting, a prey to suspicions that she resolutely put out of her mind, no longer sure whether she had been there a hundred years or a minute, she sat down in a corner and closed her eyes and put her hands to her ears. The gate squeaked: she leapt up. Before she could speak Madame Rollet said:

"He's not there!"

"What?"

"No, he's not! And Monsieur's crying. He keeps calling your name. Everybody's looking for you."

Emma made no answer. She was gasping and staring wildly about her; the peasant woman, frightened by the expression on her face, instinctively shrank back, thinking her crazed. All at once she clapped her hand to her forehead and gave a cry, for into her mind had come the memory of Rodolphe, like a great lightning-flash in a black night. He was so kind, so sensitive, so generous! And if he should hesitate to help her she'd know how to persuade him: one glance from her eyes would remind him of their lost love. So she set out for La Huchette, unaware that now she was eager to yield to the very thing that had made her so indignant only a short while ago, and totally unconscious that she was prostituting herself.

VIII

As she walked she wondered: "What am I going to say? What shall I tell him first?" Drawing nearer, she recognized the thickets, the trees, the furze on the hill, the château in the distance. She was reliving the sensations of her first love, and at the memory her poor anguished heart swelled tenderly. A warm wind was blowing in her face; melting snow dripped from the leaf buds onto the grass.

She entered, as she always had, by the little park gate, and then came to the main courtyard, planted around with a double row of thick-crowned lindens, their long branches rustling and swaying. All the dogs in the kennel barked, but though their outcry echoed and reechoed, no one came.

She climbed the wide, straight, wooden-banistered stairs that led up to the hall with its paving of dusty flagstones. A row of doors opened onto it, as in a monastery or an inn. His room was at the far end, the last on the left. When her fingers touched the latch her strength suddenly left her: she was afraid that he would not be there—she almost wished that he wouldn't be, and yet he was her only hope, her last chance of salvation. For a minute she collected her thoughts; then, steeling her courage to the present necessity, she entered.

He was smoking a pipe before the fire, his feet against the mantelpiece.

"Oh, it's you!" he said, rising quickly.

"Yes, here I am. . . . Rodolphe, I want . . . I need some advice. . . ."

Despite her best efforts she couldn't go on.

"You haven't changed—you're as charming as ever!"

"Oh, my charms!" she answered bitterly. "They can't amount to much, since you scorned them."

He launched into apology, justifying his conduct in terms that were vague but the best he could muster.

She let herself be taken in—not so much by what he said, as by the sound of his voice and the very sight of him; and she pretended to believe—or perhaps she actually did believe—the reason he gave for their break. It was a secret, he said, involving the honor—the life, even—of a third person.

She looked at him sadly. "Whatever it was," she said, "I suffered a great deal."

He answered philosophically:

"That's how life is!"

"Has it been kind to you, at least," asked Emma, "since we parted?"

"Oh, neither kind nor unkind, particularly."

"Perhaps it would have been better had we stayed together."

"Yes . . . perhaps!"

"Do you really think so?" she said, coming closer.

And she sighed:

"Oh, Rodolphe! If you knew! I loved you very much!"

She took his hand; and for a few moments their fingers were intertwined—like that first day, at the Agricultural Show! Pride made him struggle against giving in to his feelings. But she leaned heavily against him, and said:

"How did you ever think that I could live without you? Happiness is a habit that's hard to break! I was desperate! I thought I'd die! I'll tell you all about it. And you . . . you stayed away from me . . . !"

It was true: for the past three years he had carefully avoided her, out of the natural cowardice that characterizes the stronger sex; and now Emma went on, twisting and turning her head in coaxing little movements that were loving and catlike.

"You have other women—admit it. Oh, I sympathize with them: I don't blame them. You seduced them, the way you seduced me. You're a man! You have everything to make us love you. But you and I'll begin all over again, won't we? We'll love each other! Look—I'm laughing, I'm happy! Speak to me!"

And indeed she was ravishing to see, with a tear trembling in her eye like a raindrop in a blue flower-cup after a storm.

He drew her onto his lap, and with the back of his hand caressed her sleek hair: in the twilight a last sunbeam was gleaming on it like a golden arrow. She lowered her head, and soon he was kissing her on the eyelids, very gently, just brushing them with his lips.

"But you've been crying!" he said. "Why?"

She burst into sobs: Rodolphe thought it was from the violence of her love; when she didn't answer him he interpreted her silence as the ultimate refuge of her womanly modesty, and exclaimed:

"Ah! Forgive me! You're the only one I really care about! I've been stupid and heartless! I love you—I'll always love you. . . . What is it? Tell me!"

He was on his knees.

"Well, then . . . I'm ruined, Rodolphe! You've got to lend me three thousand francs!"

"But . . . but . . . ?" he said, slowly rising, a worried expression coming over his face.

"You know," she went on quickly, "my husband gave his money to a notary to invest, and the notary absconded. We've borrowed, patients haven't paid. . . . The estate isn't settled yet: we'll be getting something later. But today— just for three thousand francs—they're going to sell us out: now, this very instant. I counted on your friendship. I came to you."

"Ah," thought Rodolphe, suddenly pale. "So that's why she came!"

And after a moment he said, calmly:

"I haven't got it, dear lady."

He wasn't lying. If he had had it he would probably have given it to her, unpleasant though it usually is to make such generous gifts: of all the icy blasts that blow on love, a request for money is the most chilling and havoc wreaking.

For a long moment she stared at him. Then:

"You haven't got it!"

She said it again, several times:

"You haven't got it! I might have spared myself this final humiliation. You never loved me! You're no better than the rest!"

She was giving herself away; she no longer knew what she was saying.

Rodolphe broke in, assuring her that he was "hard up" himself.

"Ah, I pity you!" said Emma. "How I pity you!"

And as her eyes fell on a damascened rifle that glittered in a trophy on the wall:

"When you're as poor as all that you don't put silver on the stock of your gun! You don't buy things with tortoiseshell inlay!" she went on, pointing to the Boulle clock. "Or silver-gilt whistles for your whip!"—she touched them—"or charms for your watch chain! Oh, he has everything! Even a liqueur case in his bedroom! You pamper yourself, you live well, you have a château, farms, woods; you hunt, you make trips to Paris. . . . Why, even things like this," she cried, snatching up his cuff links from the mantelpiece, "the tiniest trifles, you can raise money on . . . ! Oh, I don't want them! Keep them."

And she hurled the two buttons so violently that their gold chain snapped as they struck the wall.

"But I—I'd have given you everything, I'd have sold everything, worked my fingers to the bone, begged in the streets, just for a smile from you, for a look, just to hear you say 'Thank you.' And you sit there calmly in your chair, as though you hadn't made me suffer enough already! If it hadn't been for you I could have been happy! What made you do it? Was it a bet? You loved me, though: you used to say so. . . . And you said so again just now. Ah, you'd have done better to throw me out! My hands are still hot from your kisses; and right there on the rug you swore on your knees that you'd love me forever. You made me believe it: for two years you led me on in a wonderful, marvelous dream. . . . Our plans for going away—you remember? Oh! That letter you wrote me! It tore my heart in two! And now when I come back to him—and find him rich and happy and free—to implore him for help that anybody would give me—come in distress, bringing him all my love—he refuses me, because it would cost him three thousand francs!"

"I haven't got it," answered Rodolphe, with that perfect calm that resigned anger employs as a shield.

She walked out. The walls were quaking, the ceiling was threatening to crush her; and she went back down the long avenue of trees, stumbling against piles of dead leaves that were scattering in the wind. At last she reached the ditch before the gate: she broke her nails on the latch, so frantically did she open it. Then, a hundred yards farther on, out of breath, ready to drop, she paused. She turned: and once again she saw the impassive château, with its park, its gardens, its three courtyards, its many-windowed façade.

She stood there in a daze. Only the pulsing of her veins told her that she was alive: she thought she heard it outside herself, like some deafening music filling the countryside. The earth beneath her feet was as yielding as water, and the furrows seemed to her like immense, dark, breaking waves. All the memories and thoughts in her mind poured out at once, like a thousand fireworks. She saw her father, Lheureux's office, their room in Rouen, another landscape. Madness began to take hold of her; she was frightened, but managed to control herself—without, however, emerging from her confusion, for the cause of her horrible state—the question of money—had faded from her mind. It was only her love that was making her suffer, and she felt her soul leave her at the thought—just as a wounded man, as he lies dying, feels his life flowing out with his blood through the gaping hole.

Night was falling; crows flew overhead.

It suddenly seemed to her that fiery particles were bursting in the air, like bullets exploding as they fell, and spinning and spinning and finally melting in the snow among the tree branches. In the center of each of them appeared Rodolphe's face. They multiplied; they came together; they penetrated her; everything vanished. She recognized the lights of houses, shining far off in the mist.

Suddenly her plight loomed before her, like an abyss. She panted as though her lungs would burst. Then, with a heroic resolve that made her almost happy, she ran down the hill and across the cow plank, ran down the river path and the lane, crossed the square, and came to the pharmacy.

It was empty. She was about to go in, when it occurred to her that the sound of the bell might bring someone; and slipping through the side gate, holding her breath, feeling her way along the walls, she came to the kitchen door. A lighted tallow candle was standing on the stove, and Justin, in shirt-sleeves, was just leaving the room carrying a dish.

"Ah, they're at dinner," she said to herself. "Better wait."

Justin returned to the kitchen. She tapped on the window. He came out.

"The key! The one for upstairs, where the . . ."

"What?"

And he stared at her, astounded by the pallor of her face, which stood out white against the blackness of the night. She seemed to him extraordinarily beautiful, majestic as an apparition from another world; without understanding what she wanted, he had a foreboding of something terrible.

But she went on quickly, in a low voice, a voice that was gentle and melting:

"I want it! Give it to me."

The wall was thin, and they could hear the clinking of forks on plates in the dining room.

She pretended she had to kill some rats that were keeping her awake nights.

"I must go ask Monsieur."

"No! Stay here!"

Then, with a casual air:

"There's no use bothering him: I'll tell him later. Come along, give me a light."

She passed into the hall off which opened the laboratory door. There against the wall hung a key marked "capharnaum."

"Justin!" called the apothecary impatiently.

"Let's go up!"

He followed her.

The key turned in the lock, and she went straight to the third shelf—so well did her memory serve her as guide—seized the blue jar, tore out the cork, plunged in her hand, withdrew it full of white powder, and ate greedily.

"Stop!" he cried, flinging himself on her.

"Be quiet! Someone might come. . . ."

He was frantic, wanted to call out.

"Don't say a word about it: all the blame would fall on your master!"

Then she went home, suddenly at peace—almost as serene as though she had done her duty.

When Charles reached home, overwhelmed by the news of the execution, Emma had just left. He called her name, wept, fainted away, but she didn't come back. Where could she be? He sent Félicité to the pharmacist's, to the mayor's, to the dry-goods shop, to the Lion d'Or—everywhere; and whenever his anguish about her momentarily subsided he saw his reputation ruined, all their money gone, Berthe's future wrecked! What was the cause of it all . . . ? Not a word! He waited until six that evening. Finally, unable to bear it any longer, and imagining that she must have gone to Rouen, he went out to the highway, followed it for a mile or so, met no one, waited a while, and returned.

She was back.

"What happened? . . . Why? . . . Tell me!"

She sat down at her desk and wrote a letter, sealed it slowly, and added the date and the hour. Then she said in a solemn tone:

"Read it tomorrow. Till then, please don't ask me a single question—not one!"

"But . . ."

"Oh, leave me alone!"

And she stretched out on her bed.

An acrid taste in her mouth woke her. She caught sight of Charles and reclosed her eyes.

She observed herself with interest, to see whether there was any pain. No—nothing yet. She heard the ticking of the clock, the sound of the fire, and Charles breathing, standing there beside her bed.

"Dying doesn't amount to much!" she thought. "I'll fall asleep, and everything will be over."

She swallowed a mouthful of water and turned to the wall.

There was still that dreadful taste of ink.

"I'm thirsty! I'm so thirsty!" she whispered.

"What's wrong with you, anyway?" said Charles, handing her a glass.

"Nothing! Open the window . . . I'm choking!"

She was seized by an attack of nausea so sudden that she scarcely had time to snatch her handkerchief from under the pillow.

"Get rid of it!" she said quickly. "Throw it out!"

He questioned her, but she made no answer. She lay very still, fearing that the slightest disturbance would make her vomit. Now she felt an icy coldness creeping up from her feet toward her heart.

"Ah! It's beginning!" she murmured.

"What did you say?"

She twisted her head from side to side in a gentle movement expressive of anguish, and kept opening her jaws as though she had something very heavy on her tongue. At eight o'clock the vomiting resumed.

Charles noticed that there was a gritty white deposit on the bottom of the basin, clinging to the porcelain.

"That's extraordinary! That's peculiar!" he kept saying.

"No!" she said loudly. "You're mistaken."

Very gently, almost caressingly, he passed his hand over her stomach. She gave a sharp scream. He drew back in fright.

She began to moan, softly at first. Her shoulders heaved in a great shudder, and she grew whiter than the sheet her clenched fingers were digging into. Her irregular pulse was almost imperceptible now.

Beads of sweat stood out on her face, which had turned blue and rigid, as though from the breath of some metallic vapor. Her teeth chattered, her dilated eyes stared about her vaguely, and her sole answer to questions was a shake of her head; two or three times she even smiled. Gradually her groans grew louder. A muffled scream escaped her; she pretended that she was feeling better and that she'd soon be getting up. But she was seized with convulsions.

"God!" she cried. "It's horrible!"

He flung himself on his knees beside her bed.

"Speak to me! What did you eat? Answer, for heaven's sake!"

And in his eyes she read a love such as she had never known.

"There . . . over there . . ." she said in a faltering voice.

He darted to the secretary, broke open the seal and read aloud: "No one is to blame . . ." He stopped, passed his hand over his eyes, read it again.

"What . . . ! Help! Help!"

He could only repeat the word: "Poisoned! Poisoned!" Félicité ran to Homais, who spoke loudly as he crossed the square; Madame Lefrançois heard him at the Lion d'Or, other citizens left their beds to tell their neighbors, and all night long the village was awake.

Distracted, stammering, close to collapse, Charles walked in circles around the room. He stumbled against the furniture, tore his hair: never had the pharmacist dreamed there could be so frightful a sight.

He went back to his own house and wrote letters to Monsieur Canivet and Doctor Larivière. He couldn't concentrate, had to begin them over fifteen times. Hippolyte left for Neufchâtel, and Justin spurred Bovary's horse so hard that he left it on the hill at Bois-Guillaume, foundered and all but done for.

Charles tried to consult his medical dictionary: he couldn't see; the lines danced before his eyes.

"Don't lose your head!" said the apothecary. "It's just a question of administering some powerful antidote. What poison is it?"

Charles showed him the letter. It was arsenic.

"Well then!" said Homais. "We must make an analysis."

For he knew that an analysis always had to be made in cases of poisoning.

Charles, who hadn't understood, answered with a groan:

"Do it! Do it! Save her . . . !"

And returning to her side, he sank down on the carpet and leaned his head on the edge of her bed, sobbing.

"Don't cry!" she said. "I shan't be tormenting you much longer."

"Why did you do it? What made you?"

"It was the only thing," she answered.

"Weren't you happy? Am I to blame? But I did everything I could . . . !"

"Yes . . . I know . . . You're good, you're different. . . ."

She slowly passed her hand through his hair. The sweetness of her touch was more than his grief could bear. He felt his entire being give way to despair at the thought of having to lose her just when she was showing him more love than ever in the past; and he could think of nothing to do—he knew nothing, dared nothing: the need for immediate action took away the last of his presence of mind.

Emma was thinking that now she was through with all the betrayals, the infamies, the countless fierce desires that had racked her. She hated no one, now; a twilight confusion was falling over her thoughts, and of all the world's sounds she heard only the intermittent lament of this poor man beside her, gentle and indistinct, like the last echo of an ever-fainter symphony.

"Bring me my little girl," she said, raising herself on her elbow.

"You're not feeling worse, are you?" Charles asked.

"No! No!"

Berthe was carried in by the maid. Her bare feet peeped out from beneath her long nightdress; she looked serious, still half dreaming. She stared in surprise to see the room in such disorder, and she blinked her eyes, dazzled by the candles that were standing here and there on the furniture. They probably reminded her of other mornings—New Year's day or mi-carême,[7] when she was wakened early in just this same way by candlelight and carried to her mother's bed to be given a shoeful of presents; for she asked:

"Where is it, *maman?*"

And when no one answered:

"I don't see my little shoe!"

Félicité held her over the bed, but she kept looking toward the fireplace.

"Did nurse take it away?" she asked.

At the word "nurse," which brought back her adulteries and her calamities, Madame Bovary averted her head, as though another, stronger, poison had risen to her mouth and filled her with revulsion.

"Oh, how big your eyes are, *maman!*" cried Berthe, whom the maid had put on the bed. "How pale you are! You're sweating . . . !"

Her mother looked at her.

"I'm afraid!" cried the little girl, shrinking back.

Emma took her hand to kiss it; she struggled.

"Enough! Take her away!" cried Charles, sobbing at the foot of the bed.

The symptoms momentarily stopped; she seemed calmer; and at each insignificant word she said, each time she breathed a little more easily, his hope gained ground. When Canivet finally arrived he threw himself in his arms, weeping.

"Ah! You've come! Thank you! You're kind! But she's doing better. Here: look at her!"

His colleague was not at all of this opinion. There was no use—as he himself put it—"beating around the bush," and he prescribed an emetic, to empty the stomach completely.

Soon she was vomiting blood. Her lips pressed together more tightly. Her limbs were contorted, her body was covered with brown blotches, her pulse quivered under the doctor's fingers like a taut thread, like a harp string about to snap.

Then she began to scream, horribly. She cursed the poison, railed against it, begged it to be quick; and with her stiffened arms she pushed away everything that Charles, in greater agony than herself, tried to make her drink. He was standing, his handkerchief to his mouth, moaning, weeping, choked by sobs and shaking all over; Félicité rushed about the room; Homais, motionless, kept sighing heavily; and Monsieur Canivet, for all his air of self-assurance, began to manifest some uneasiness:

"What the devil . . . ! But she's purged, and since the cause is removed . . ."

"The effect should subside," said Homais. "It's self-evident."

"Do something to save her!" cried Bovary.

Paying no attention to the pharmacist, who was venturing the hypothesis that "this paroxysm may mark the beginning of improvement," Canivet was about to give her theriaca when there came the crack of a whip, all the windows rattled, and a post chaise drawn at breakneck speed by three mud-covered horses flashed around the corner of the marketplace. It was Doctor Larivière.

The sudden appearance of a god wouldn't have caused greater excitement.

7. Mid-Lent.

Bovary raised both hands, Canivet broke off his preparations, and Homais doffed his cap well before the doctor entered.

He belonged to that great surgical school created by Bichat[8]—that generation, now vanished, of philosopher-practitioners, who cherished their art with fanatical love and applied it with enthusiasm and sagacity. Everyone in his hospital trembled when he was angry; and his students so revered him that the moment they set up for themselves they imitated him as much as they could. There was scarcely a town in the district where one of them couldn't be found, wearing a long merino overcoat and a full black tail coat, exactly like his. Doctor Larivière's unbuttoned cuffs partly covered his fleshy hands—extraordinary hands, always ungloved, as though to be the readier to grapple with suffering. Disdainful of decorations, titles and academies, hospitable, generous, a father to the poor, practicing Christian virtues although an unbeliever, he might have been thought of as a saint if he hadn't been feared as a devil because of the keenness of his mind. His scalpel-sharp glance cut deep into your soul, exposing any lie buried under excuses and reticences. His manner was majestic and genial, conscious as he was of his great gifts and his wealth and the forty years of hard work and blameless living he had behind him.

While he was still in the doorway he frowned, catching sight of Emma's cadaverous face as she lay on her back, her mouth open. Then, seeming to listen to Canivet, he passed his forefinger back and forth beneath his nostrils, repeating:

"Yes, yes."

But his shoulders lifted in a slow shrug. Bovary noticed it; their eyes met. The sight of a grieving face was no novelty to the doctor, yet he couldn't keep a tear from dropping onto his shirt front.

He asked Canivet to step into the next room. Charles followed him.

"She's very low, isn't she? How about poultices? What else? Can't you think of something? You've saved so many lives!"

Charles put his arms around him, sagged against his chest, and looked at him anxiously and beseechingly.

"Come, my poor boy, be brave! There's nothing to be done."

And Doctor Larivière turned away.

"You're leaving?"

"I'll be back."

He pretended he had something to say to the coachman, and went out with Canivet, who was no more eager than he to watch Emma die.

The pharmacist joined them in the square. He was temperamentally incapable of staying away from celebrities, and he begged Monsieur Larivière to do him the signal honor of being his guest at lunch.

Someone was quickly sent to the Lion d'Or for pigeons, the butcher was stripped of all his chops, Tuvache supplied cream and Lestiboudois eggs. The apothecary himself helped with the preparations, while Madame Homais pulled at her wrapper strings and said:

"I hope you'll forgive us, Monsieur. In this wretched village, if we don't have a full day's warning . . ."

"The stemmed glasses!!!" whispered Homais.

8. Marie-Françoise-Xavier Bichat (1771–1802), author of an *Anatomie générale* (1801).

"If we lived in the city we'd at least have stuffed pigs' feet to fall back on."

"Don't talk so much . . . ! Sit down, Doctor!"

After the first few mouthfuls he considered it appropriate to supply a few details concerning the catastrophe.

"First we had a sensation of siccity in the pharynx, then intolerable pain in the epigastrium, superpurgation, coma."

"How did she poison herself?"

"I have no idea, Doctor, and I can't even imagine where she managed to procure that arsenous oxide."

Justin, who was just then carrying in a pile of plates, was seized with a fit of trembling.

"What's the matter with you?" asked the pharmacist.

At the question the young man dropped everything with a great crash.

"Imbecile!" cried Homais. "Clumsy lout! Damned idiot!"

Then, quickly regaining his self-control:

"I wanted to try an analysis, Doctor, and, *primo,* I carefully inserted into a tube . . ."

"It would have been better," said the surgeon, "if you'd inserted your fingers into her throat."

Canivet said nothing, having just a few minutes before been given, in private, a severe rebuke concerning his emetic. Today he was as meek as he had been arrogant and verbose the day he had operated on Hippolyte: his face was fixed in a continual, approving smile.

Homais blossomed in his role of proud host, and the thought of Bovary's distress added something to his pleasure as he selfishly contrasted their lots. Moreover, the doctor's presence excited him. He displayed all his erudition, dragging in, pell-mell, mention of cantharides, the upas, the manchineel, the bite of the adder.

"I've even read about people being poisoned, Doctor—positively struck down—by blood sausages that had been subjected to excessive fumigation! At least, so it says in a very fine report, written by one of our leading pharmaceutical lights, one of our masters, the illustrious Cadet de Gassicourt!"[9]

Madame Homais reappeared, bearing one of those rickety contraptions that are heated with alcohol, for Homais insisted on brewing his coffee at table—having, needless to say, previously done his own roasting, his own grinding and his own blending.

"*Saccharum,* Doctor?" he said, passing the sugar.

Then he called in all his children, eager to have the surgeon's opinion on their constitutions.

Finally, when Monsieur Larivière was about to leave, Madame Homais asked him to advise her about her husband. His "blood was getting thicker" because of his habit of falling asleep every evening after dinner.

"Oh, he's not thick-*blooded!*"

And smiling a little at his joke, which passed unnoticed, the doctor opened the door. But the pharmacy was thronged, and he had a hard time getting rid of Monsieur Tuvache, who was afraid that his wife would get pneumonia because of her habit of spitting into the fire; then Monsieur Binet com-

---

9. The pharmacist of Emperor Napoleon I who had considerable trouble under the Restoration because of his liberal ideas.

plained of often feeling ravenous; Madame Caron had prickling sensations; Lheureux suffered from dizzy spells; Lestiboudois was rheumatic; and Madame Lefrançois had heartburn. Finally the three horses bore him away, and the general verdict was that he had been far from obliging.

Then the attention of the public was distracted by the appearance of Monsieur Bournisien, crossing the market with the holy oils.

Homais paid his debt to his principles by likening priests to ravens: both are attracted by the odor of the dead. Actually, he had a more personal reason for disliking the sight of a priest: a cassock made him think of a shroud, and his execration of the one owed something to his fear of the other.

Nevertheless, not flinching in the face of what he called his "mission," he returned to the Bovary house along with Canivet, whom Monsieur Larivière had urged to stay on to the end. But for his wife's protests, the pharmacist would have taken his two sons along, to inure them to life's great moments, to provide them with a lesson, an example, a momentous spectacle that they would remember later.

The bedroom, as they entered, was mournful and solemn. On the sewing table, now covered with a white napkin, were five or six small wads of cotton in a silver dish, and nearby a large crucifix between two lighted candelabra. Emma lay with her chin sunk on her breast, her eyelids unnaturally wide apart; and her poor hands picked at the sheets in the ghastly and poignant way of the dying, who seem impatient to cover themselves with their shrouds. Pale as a statue, his eyes red as coals, but no longer weeping, Charles stood facing her at the foot of the bed; the priest, on one knee, mumbled under his breath.

She slowly turned her face, and seemed overjoyed at suddenly seeing the purple stole—doubtless recognizing in this interval of extraordinary peace, the lost ecstasy of her first mystical flights and the first visions of eternal bliss.

The priest stood up and took the crucifix; she stretched out her head like someone thirsting; and pressing her lips to the body of the God-Man, she imprinted on it, with every ounce of her failing strength, the most passionate love-kiss she had ever given. Then he recited the *Misereatur* and the *Indulgentiam,* dipped his right thumb in the oil, and began the unctions. First he anointed her eyes, once so covetous of all earthly luxuries; then her nostrils, so gluttonous of caressing breezes and amorous scents; then her mouth, so prompt to lie, so defiant in pride, so loud in lust; then her hands, that had thrilled to voluptuous contacts; and finally the soles of her feet, once so swift when she had hastened to slake her desires, and now never to walk again.

The curé wiped his fingers, threw the oil-soaked bits of cotton into the fire, and returned to the dying woman, sitting beside her and telling her that now she must unite her sufferings with Christ's and throw herself on the divine mercy.

As he ended his exhortations he tried to have her grasp a blessed candle, symbol of the celestial glories soon to surround her. Emma was too weak, and couldn't close her fingers: but for Monsieur Bournisien the candle would have fallen to the floor.

Yet she was no longer so pale, and her face was serene, as though the sacrament had cured her.

The priest didn't fail to point this out: he even explained to Bovary that the Lord sometimes prolonged people's lives when He judged it expedient for their salvation; and Charles remembered another day, when, similarly close to death, she had received communion.

"Perhaps there's hope after all," he thought.

And indeed, she looked all about her, slowly, like someone waking from a dream; then, in a distinct voice, she asked for her mirror, and she remained bowed over it for some time, until great tears flowed from her eyes. Then she threw back her head with a sigh, and sank onto the pillow.

At once her breast began to heave rapidly. Her tongue hung at full length from her mouth; her rolling eyes grew dim like the globes of two lamps about to go out; and one might have thought her dead already but for the terrifying, ever-faster movement of her ribs, which were shaken by furious gasps, as though her soul were straining violently to break its fetters. Félicité knelt before the crucifix, and even the pharmacist flexed his knees a little. Monsieur Canivet stared vaguely out into the square. Bournisien had resumed his praying, his face bowed over the edge of the bed and his long black cassock trailing out behind him into the room. Charles was on the other side, on his knees, his arms stretched out toward Emma. He had taken her hands, and was pressing them, shuddering at every beat of her heart, as at the tremors of a falling ruin. As the death-rattle grew louder, the priest speeded his prayers: they mingled with Bovary's stifled sobs, and at moments everything seemed drowned by the monotonous flow of Latin syllables that sounded like the tolling of a bell.

Suddenly from out on the sidewalk came a noise of heavy wooden shoes and the scraping of a stick, and a voice rose up, a raucous voice singing:

> A clear day's warmth will often move
> A lass to stray in dreams of love.

Emma sat up like a galvanized corpse, her hair streaming, her eyes fixed and gaping.

> To gather up the stalks of wheat
> The swinging scythe keeps laying by,
> Nanette goes stooping in the heat
> Along the furrows where they lie.

"The blind man!" she cried.

Emma began to laugh—a horrible, frantic, desperate laugh—fancying that she saw the beggar's hideous face, a figure of terror looming up in the darkness of eternity.

> The wind blew very hard that day
> And snatched her petticoat away!

A spasm flung her down on the mattress. Everyone drew close. She had ceased to exist.

IX

Anyone's death always releases something like an aura of stupefaction, so difficult is it to grasp this irruption of nothingness and to believe that it has actually taken place. But when Charles realized how still she was, he threw himself on her, crying:

"Adieu! Adieu!"

Homais and Canivet led him from the room.

"Control yourself!"

"Let me stay!" he said, struggling. "I'll be reasonable; I won't do anything I shouldn't. But I want to be near her—she's my wife!"

And he wept.

"Weep, weep," said the pharmacist. "Let yourself go: you'll feel the better for it."

Helpless as a child, Charles let himself be taken downstairs to the parlor. Monsieur Homais soon went home.

In the square he was accosted by the blind beggar. Lured by the hope of the antiphlogistic salve, he had dragged himself all the way to Yonville, and now was asking every passer-by where the apothecary lived.

"Good Lord! As though I didn't have other things on my mind! Too bad! Come back later."

He hurried into the pharmacy.

He had to write two letters, prepare a sedative for Bovary, and invent a plausible lie that would cover up the suicide for an article in the *Fanal* and for the crowd that was awaiting him in order to learn the news. When all the Yonvillians had heard his story about the arsenic that Emma had mistaken for sugar while making a custard, Homais returned once more to Bovary.

He found him alone (Canivet had just left), sitting in the armchair beside the window, staring vacantly at the parlor floor.

"Now," said the pharmacist, "what you've got to do is decide on a time for the ceremony."

"Why? What ceremony?"

Then, in a frightened stammer:

"Oh no! I don't have to, do I? I want to keep her!"

To hide his embarrassment Homais took a carafe from the whatnot and began to water the geraniums.

"Ah, thank you!" said Charles. "You're so good!"

He broke off, choked by the flood of memories the pharmacist's action evoked.

To distract him, Homais thought it well to talk about horticulture: plants, he ventured, had to be kept moist. Charles nodded in agreement.

"Anyway, we'll soon be having fine spring weather."

"Ah!" said Bovary.

Not knowing what to say next, the apothecary twitched the sash curtain.

"Ah—there's Monsieur Tuvache going by."

Charles repeated mechanically:

"Monsieur Tuvache going by."

Homais didn't dare broach the subject of funeral arrangements again: it was the priest who eventually made Charles see reason.

He locked himself in his consulting room, took a pen, and after sobbing a while he wrote:

"I want her buried in her bridal dress, with white shoes and a wreath and her hair spread over her shoulders. Three coffins—one oak, one mahogany, one lead. No one has to say anything to me: I'll have the strength to go through with it. Cover her with a large piece of green velvet. I want this done. Do it."

The priest and the pharmacist were much taken aback by Bovary's romantic ideas. Homais expostulated:

"The velvet seems to be supererogatory. Not to mention the expense . . ."

"Is it any concern of yours?" cried Charles. "Leave me alone! You didn't love her! Go away!"

The priest took him by the arm and walked him around the garden, discoursing on the vanity of earthly things. God is all-great, all-good; we must submit to His decrees without complaint; more than that, we must be grateful.

Charles burst into a stream of blasphemy.

"I detest your God!"

"The spirit of rebellion is still in you," sighed the priest.

Bovary had strode away from him and was pacing up and down beside the wall of espaliered fruit trees, grinding his teeth and looking curses at heaven: but not even a leaf stirred in answer.

A fine rain was falling. Charles's shirt was open, and soon he began to shiver. He went back into the house and sat in the kitchen.

At six o'clock there was a clanking in the square. It was the Hirondelle arriving, and he stood with his head against the windowpanes, watching all the passengers get out, one after the other. Félicité put down a mattress for him in the parlor, and he threw himself on it and fell asleep.

Rationalist though he was, Monsieur Homais respected the dead. So, bearing no grudge against poor Charles, he returned that night to watch beside the body. He brought three books with him, and a writing pad for making notes.

He found Monsieur Bournisien already there. Two tall candles were burning at the head of the bed, which had been moved out of the alcove.

The apothecary, oppressed by the silence, soon made a few elegiac remarks concerning "this hapless young woman"; and the priest replied that now there was nothing left to do but pray for her.

"Still," said Homais, "it's one thing or the other: either she died in a state of grace (as the church puts it), and therefore had no need of our prayers; or else she died unrepentant (I believe that is the ecclesiastical term) and in that case . . ."

Bournisien interrupted him, replying testily that prayer was called for nonetheless.

"But," objected the pharmacist, "since God knows all our needs, what purpose can be served by prayer?"

"What?" said the priest. "Prayer? Aren't you a Christian, then?"

"I beg your pardon!" said Homais. "I admire Christianity. It freed the slaves, for one thing; it introduced into the world a moral code that . . ."

"That's not the point! All the texts . . ."

"Oh! Oh! The texts! Look in any history book: everybody knows they were falsified by the Jesuits."

Charles came in, walked up to the bed and slowly parted the curtains.

Emma's head was turned toward her right shoulder. The corner of her open mouth was like a black hole in the lower part of her face; her two thumbs were bent inward toward the palms of her hands; a kind of white dust powdered her lashes; and the outline of her eyes was beginning to disappear in a viscous pallor, as though spiders had been spinning cobwebs over her face. From her breasts to her knees the sheet sagged, rising again at her toes; and it seemed to Charles that some infinite mass, some enormous weight, was pressing on her.

The church clock struck two. The flowing river murmured deeply in the darkness at the foot of the terrace. Now and again Monsieur Bournisien blew his nose loudly, and Homais' pen was scratching on his paper.

"Go back to bed, my friend," he said. "Stop torturing yourself."

When Charles had gone, the pharmacist and the curé resumed their arguments.

"Read Voltaire!" said the one. "Read Holbach! Read the Encyclopedia!"[1]

"Read the *Letters of Some Portuguese Jews!*" said the other. "Read the *Proof of Christianity,*[2] by ex-magistrate Nicolas!"

They grew excited and flushed; both spoke at once, neither listening to the other; Bournisien was shocked by such audacity; Homais marveled at such stupidity; and they were on the point of exchanging insults when Charles suddenly reappeared. He couldn't keep away: it was as though a spell kept drawing him upstairs.

He stood at the foot of the bed to see her better, absorbed in contemplation so intense that he no longer felt any pain.

He recalled stories about catalepsy and the miracles of magnetism; and he told himself that by straining his will to the utmost he might resuscitate her. Once he even leaned over toward her and cried very softly "Emma! Emma!" The force of his breath blew the flickering candle flames against the wall.

At daybreak the older Madame Bovary arrived, and as Charles embraced her he had another fit of weeping. Like the pharmacist, she ventured a few remarks about the funeral expenses, but he flew into such a rage that she said no more, and he sent her straight to the city to buy what was needed.

Charles spent all afternoon alone. Berthe had been taken to Madame Homais'; Félicité stayed upstairs in the bedroom with Madame Lefrançois.

That evening, people called. He rose and shook hands with them, unable to speak; each then took a seat alongside the others, gradually forming a wide semicircle in front of the fireplace. Eyes lowered and legs crossed, they dangled their feet, sighing deeply from time to time. Everyone was bored beyond measure, but no one was willing to be the first to leave.

When Homais returned at nine o'clock (during the past two days he had seemed to spend all his time crossing the square) he brought with him a supply of camphor, benzoin and aromatic herbs. He also had a vase full of chlorine water, to "drive out the miasmas." At that moment the maid, Madame Lefrançois and the older Madame Bovary were clustered around Emma, putting the finishing touches to her toilette: they drew down the long, stiff veil, covering her even to her satin shoes.

Félicité sobbed:

"Ah! Poor mistress! Poor mistress!"

---

1. Paul-Henri Dietrich, baron d'Holbach (1723–1789), friend and disciple of Diderot and one of the most outspoken opponents of religion in the French Enlightenment. The *Encyclopedia,* a dictionary of the sciences, arts, and letters, edited by Diderot and d'Alembert (1751–72), is the intellectual monument of the French Enlightenment, a fountainhead of later secular and agnostic thought.   2. One of the many books defending Roman Catholicism by Jean-Jacques-Auguste Nicolas (1807–1888). *Letters of Some Portuguese Jews* (1769) refers to a book by Abbé Antoine Guéné directed against Voltaire.

"Look at her," said the hotel keeper, with a sigh. "How pretty she still is! You'd swear she'd be getting up any minute."

Then they bent over to put on her wreath.

They had to lift her head a little, and as they did so a black liquid poured out of her mouth like vomit.

"Heavens! Watch out for her dress!" cried Madame Lefrançois. "Help us, won't you?" she said to the pharmacist. "You wouldn't be afraid, would you?"

"I, afraid?" he answered, shrugging his shoulders. "Take it from me: I saw plenty of things like this at the hospital, when I was studying pharmacy. We used to make punch in the dissecting room while we worked. Death holds no terrors for a philosopher. In fact, as I often say, I intend to leave my body to the hospitals, so that it can eventually be of service to science."

When the curé arrived he asked how Monsieur was; and at the apothecary's reply he said:

"Of course: he still hasn't got over the shock."

Homais went on to congratulate him on not being exposed, like other men, to the risk of losing a beloved wife; and there followed a discussion on the celibacy of the clergy.

"After all," said the pharmacist, "it's against nature for a man to do without women. We've all heard of crimes . . ."

"But drat it all!" cried the priest. "How would you expect anyone who was married to be able to keep the secrets of the confessional, for example?"

Homais attacked confession. Bournisien defended it: he dilated on the acts of restitution it was constantly responsible for, told stories about thieves suddenly turning honest. Soldiers, approaching the tribunal of repentance, had felt the scales drop from their eyes. There was a minister at Fribourg . . .

His fellow watcher had fallen asleep. Bournisien found it somewhat hard to breathe, the air of the room was so heavy, and he opened a window. This woke the pharmacist.

"Here," the priest said. "Take a pinch of snuff. Do—it clears the head."

There was a continual barking somewhere in the distance.

"Do you hear a dog howling?" said the pharmacist.

"People say that they scent the dead," answered the priest. "It's like bees: they leave the hive when someone dies."

Homais didn't challenge those superstitions, for once again he had fallen asleep.

Monsieur Bournisien, more resistant, continued for some time to move his lips in a murmur, then his chin sank gradually lower, his thick black book slipped from his hand, and he began to snore.

They sat opposite one another, stomachs out, faces swollen, both of them scowling—united, after so much dissension, in the same human weakness; and they stirred no more than the corpse that was like another sleeper beside them.

Charles's coming didn't wake them. This was the last time. He had come to bid her farewell.

The aromatic herbs were still smoking, and at the window their swirls of bluish vapor mingled with the mist that was blowing in.

There were a few stars. The night was mild.

Great drops of wax were falling onto the bedsheets from the candles.

Charles watched them burn, tiring his eyes in the gleam of their yellow flames.

The watered satin of her dress was shimmering with the whiteness of moonbeams. Emma was invisible under it; and it seemed to him as though she were spreading out beyond herself, melting confusedly into the surroundings—the silence, the night, the passing wind, the damp fragrance that rose from the earth.

Then, suddenly, he saw her in the garden at Tostes, on the seat, against the thorn hedge—or in Rouen, in the street—or on the doorstep of their house, in the farmyard at Les Bertaux. Once again he heard the laughter of the merry lads dancing under the apple trees; the wedding chamber was full of the perfume of her hair, and her dress rustled in his arms with a sound of flying sparks. And now she was wearing that very dress!

He stood there a long time thus recalling all his past happiness—her poses, her gestures, the sound of her voice. Wave of despair followed upon wave, endlessly, like the waters of an overflowing tide.

A terrible curiosity came over him: slowly, with the tips of his fingers, his heart pounding, he lifted her veil. He gave a scream of horror that woke the sleepers. They took him downstairs to the parlor.

Then Félicité came up, to say that he was asking for a lock of her hair.

"Cut some!" answered the apothecary.

She didn't dare, and he stepped forward himself, scissors in hand. He trembled so violently that he nicked the skin on the temples in several places. Finally, steeling himself, Homais slashed blindly two or three times, leaving white marks in the beautiful black tresses.

The pharmacist and the curé resumed their respective occupations—not without dozing off now and again and reproaching each other for doing so each time they awoke. Then Monsieur Bournisien would sprinkle the room with holy water and Homais would pour a little chlorine water on the floor.

Félicité had thought to leave a bottle of brandy for them on the chest of drawers, along with a cheese and a big brioche. Finally, about four in the morning, the apothecary could hold out no longer.

"I confess," he sighed, "that I'd gladly partake of some nourishment."

The priest didn't have to be asked twice. He went out, said his Mass, came back; and they proceeded to eat and clink their glasses, chuckling a little without knowing why, prey to that indefinable gaiety that often succeeds periods of gloom. With the last drink of brandy the priest slapped the pharmacist on the back:

"We'll be good friends yet!" he said.

Downstairs in the hall they met the workmen arriving, and for two hours Charles had to suffer the torture of the sound of the hammer on the planks. Then they brought her down in her oaken coffin, which they fitted inside the two others. The outermost was too wide, and they had to stuff the space between with wool from a mattress. Finally, when the three lids had been planed, nailed on and soldered, the bier was exposed at the door. The house was thrown open, and the Yonvillians began to flock in.

Monsieur Rouault arrived. He fell in a faint in the square at the sight of the black cloth.

X

The pharmacist's letter hadn't reached him until thirty-six hours after the event; and to spare his feelings Monsieur Homais had worded it in such a way that it was impossible for him to know what to think.

On reading it he fell to the ground, as though stricken by apoplexy. Then he gathered that she was *not* dead. But she might be . . . He put on his smock and his hat, fastened a spur to his boot, and set off at a gallop; and during the entire length of his breathless ride he was frantic with anguish. At one point he had to stop and dismount: he couldn't see, he heard voices, he thought he was losing his mind.

At daybreak he caught sight of three black hens asleep in a tree, and he shuddered, terrified by the omen. He promised the Holy Virgin three chasubles for the church, and vowed to walk barefoot from the cemetery at Les Bertaux to the chapel at Vassonville.

He rode into Maromme, shouting ahead to the people at the inn, burst open the gate with his shoulder, dashed up to the oats bag, poured a bottle of sweet cider into the manger; then he remounted his nag, and it was off again, striking sparks from all four shoes.

He kept telling himself that she would certainly live: the doctors would find a remedy—there was no question. He reminded himself of all the miraculous recoveries people had told him of.

Then he had a vision of her dead. She was there, before him stretched on her back in the middle of the road. He pulled at the reins, and the hallucination vanished.

At Quincampoix he drank three coffees in a row to fortify himself.

It occurred to him that they might have put the wrong name on the letter. He rummaged for it in his pocket, felt it there, but didn't dare open it.

He even began to imagine that it might be a practical joke, an attempt to get even with him for something, or a wag's idea of a prank. Besides—if she was dead, he'd know it! But no—the countryside was as always: the sky was blue, the trees were swaying; a flock of sheep crossed the road. He caught sight of the village; people saw him racing by, hunched over his horse, beating it furiously, its saddle girths dripping blood.

Then, when he had regained consciousness, he fell weeping into Bovary's arms:

"My daughter! Emma! My baby! Tell me . . ."

Charles answered, sobbing:

"I don't know, I don't know! It's a curse . . ."

The apothecary drew them apart.

"There's no use going into the horrible details. I'll tell Monsieur all about it later. People are coming. Have some dignity, for heaven's sake! Take it like a philosopher!"

Poor Charles made an effort, and repeated several times:

"Yes! . . . Be brave!"

"All right, then, I'll be brave, God damn it to hell!" the old man cried. "I'll stay with her to the end."

The bell was tolling. Everything was ready. It was time to set out.

Sitting side by side in one of the choir stalls, they watched the three cantors continually crossing back and forth in front of them, intoning. The serpent[3] player blew with all his might. Monsieur Bournisien, in full regalia, sang in a shrill voice: he bowed to the tabernacle, raised his hands, stretched out his arms, Lestiboudois moved about the church with his verger's staff; near the lectern stood the coffin, between four rows of candles. Charles had to restrain himself from getting up and putting them out.

He did his best, however, to work himself up into a religious frame of mind, to seize on the hope of a future life in which he would see her again. He tried to imagine that she had gone on a trip—far off—a long time ago. But when he remembered that she was right there, in the coffin, and that everything was over, and that now she was going to be buried, he was filled with a rage that was fierce and black and desperate. At moments he thought he was beyond feeling; and he relished this ebbing of grief, cursing himself in the same breath for a scoundrel.

A sharp, regular noise, like the tapping of a metal-tipped walking stick, was heard on the stone floor. It came from the far end of the church and stopped abruptly in the side aisle. A man in a coarse brown jacket sank painfully to his knees. It was Hippolyte, the stable boy at the Lion d'Or. He had put on his new leg.

One of the cantors came through the nave, taking up the collection, and one after another the heavy coins clattered onto the silver plate.

"Get it over with! I can't stand much more of this!" cried Bovary, angrily throwing him a five-franc piece.

The cantor thanked him with a ceremonious bow.

The singing and the kneeling and the rising went on and on. He remembered that once, early in their marriage, they had attended Mass together, and that they had sat on the other side, at the right, against the wall. The bell began to toll again. There was a great scraping of chairs. The pallbearers slipped their three poles under the bier, and everyone left the church.

At that moment Justin appeared in the doorway of the pharmacy and abruptly retreated, white-faced and trembling.

People stood at their windows to watch the procession. Charles, at the head, held himself very straight. He put on a brave front and nodded to those who came out from the lanes and the doorways to join the crowd.

The six men, three on each side, walked with short steps, panting a little. The priests, the cantors and the two choirboys recited the *De profundis;* and their voices carried over the fields, rising and falling in waves. Sometimes they disappeared from view at a twist of the path; but the great silver cross was always visible, high up among the trees.

At the rear were the women, in their black cloaks with turned-down hoods; each of them carried a thick lighted candle; and Charles felt himself overcome amidst this endless succession of prayers and lights, these cloying odors of wax and cassocks. A cool breeze was blowing, the rye and the colza were sprouting green; dewdrops shimmered on the thorn hedges along the road. All kinds of joyous sounds filled the air—the rattle of a jolting cart in distant ruts, the repeated crowing of a cock, the thudding of a colt as it bolted off under the apple trees. The pure sky was dappled with rosy clouds; wisps of bluish smoke trailed down over the thatched cottages, their roofs abloom with iris. Charles recognized each farmyard as he passed. He remembered

---

3. A woodwind instrument no longer in use.

leaving them on mornings like this after making sick calls, on his way back home to where she was.

The black pall, embroidered with white tears, flapped up now and again, exposing the coffin beneath. The tired pallbearers were slowing down, and the bier moved forward in a series of jerks, like a boat pitching at every wave.

They reached the cemetery.

The pallbearers continued on to where the grave had been dug in the turf.

Everyone stood around it; and as the priest spoke, the reddish earth, heaped up on the edges, kept sliding down at the corners, noiselessly and continuously.

Then, when the four ropes were in position, the coffin was pushed onto them. He watched it go down. It went down and down.

Finally there was a thud, and the ropes creaked as they came back up. Then Bournisien took the shovel that Lestiboudois held out to him. With his left hand—all the while sprinkling holy water with his right—he vigorously pushed in a large spadeful of earth; and the stones striking the wood of the coffin made that awesome sound that seems to us like the very voice of eternity.

The priest passed his sprinkler to the person beside him. It was Homais. He shook it gravely, then handed it to Charles, who sank on his knees in the pile of earth and threw it into the grave in handfuls, crying, *"Adieu!"* He blew her kisses, and dragged himself toward the grave as though to be swallowed up in it with her.

They led him away, and he soon grew calmer—vaguely relieved, perhaps, like everyone else, that it was all over.

On the way back Monsieur Rouault calmly lit his pipe—a gesture that Homais silently condemned as improper. He noticed, too, that Monsieur Binet had stayed away, that Tuvache had "sneaked off" after the Mass, and that Théodore, the notary's servant, was wearing a blue coat—"as if he couldn't find a black coat, since it's the custom, for heaven's sake!" And he went from group to group communicating his sentiments. Everyone was deploring Emma's death, especially Lheureux, who hadn't failed to attend the funeral.

"Poor little lady! How terrible for her husband!"

"If it hadn't been for me, let me tell you," the apothecary assured him, "he would have tried to do away with himself!"

"Such a good woman! To think that just last Saturday I saw her in my shop!"

"I didn't have the leisure," said Homais, "to prepare a little speech. I'd have liked to say a few words at the grave."

Back home, Charles took off his funeral clothes and Monsieur Rouault got back into his blue smock. It was a new one: all the way from Les Bertaux he had kept wiping his eyes with the sleeve, and the dye had come off on his face, which was still dusty and tear-streaked.

The older Madame Bovary was with them. All three were silent. Finally the old man sighed:

"You remember, my friend, I came to Tostes once, when you had just lost your first wife. That time I tried to comfort you. I could think of something to say; but now . . ."

Then, his chest heaving in a long groan:

"Ah! Everything's over for me! I've seen my wife go . . . then my son . . . and now today my daughter!"

He insisted on leaving immediately for Les Bertaux, saying that he couldn't sleep in that house. He even refused to see his granddaughter.

"No! No! It would be too hard on me. . . . But give her a big kiss for me! Good-bye! . . . You're a good man! And—I'll never forget this!" he said, slapping his thigh. "Don't worry—you'll always get your turkey."

But when he reached the top of the hill he turned around as he had turned around once before, after parting from her on the road to Saint-Victor. The windows of the village were all ablaze in the slanting rays of the sun that was setting beyond the meadow. He shaded his eyes with his hand; and on the horizon he made out a walled enclosure where trees stood in dark clumps here and there among white stones; then he continued on his way at a gentle trot, for his nag was limping.

Weary though they were, Charles and his mother sat up very late that night talking. They spoke of days gone by and of the future: she would come and live in Yonville, she would keep house for him; never again would they be apart. She was astute and ingratiating with him, rejoicing inwardly at the thought of recapturing his affection, which had eluded her for so many years. Midnight struck. The village was silent as usual; and Charles lay awake, thinking ceaselessly of *her*.

Rodolphe, who had spent all day roaming the woods to keep his mind off things, was peacefully asleep in his château; and Léon was sleeping, too, in the distant city.

But there was someone else—someone who was not asleep at that late hour.

On the grave among the firs knelt a young boy, weeping and sobbing in the darkness, his heart overflowing with an immense grief that was tender as the moon and unfathomable as night. Suddenly the gate creaked. It was Lestiboudois, come to fetch his spade, which he had forgotten a while before. He recognized Justin clambering over the wall: at last he knew who was stealing his potatoes!

XI

The next day Charles sent for Berthe. She asked for *maman:* she was away on a trip, she was told, and would bring her back some toys. She mentioned her again several times, then gradually forgot her. Charles found the little girl's cheerfulness depressing. The pharmacist's consolations, too, were an ordeal.

Before long the question of money came up again. Monsieur Lheureux egged on his friend Vinçart as before, and Charles signed notes for enormous sums: he refused absolutely to consider selling the slightest bit of furniture that had belonged to her. His mother fumed; he flew into an even greater rage. He was a completely changed man. She packed up and left.

Then everyone began to snatch what he could. Mademoiselle Lempereur demanded her fees for six months' lessons. Emma had never taken a single one, despite the receipted bills that she had shown Bovary: the two ladies had concocted this device between them. The lending-library proprietor demanded three years' subscription fees. Madame Rollet demanded postage fees for twenty or so letters, and when Charles asked for an explanation she was tactful enough to answer:

"Oh, I don't know anything about them—some personal matters."

Each debt he paid, Charles thought was the last. Then more came—a continual stream.

He dunned patients for back bills, but they showed him the letters his wife had sent and he had to apologize.

Félicité now wore Madame's dresses. Not all, for he had kept a few and used to shut himself up in her dressing room and look at them. The maid was just about her size, and often when Charles caught sight of her from behind he thought it was Emma, and cried out:

"Oh! Don't go! Don't go!"

But at Pentecost she left Yonville without warning, eloping with Théodore and stealing everything that was left of the wardrobe.

It was about this time that "Madame *veuve* Dupuis" had the honor of announcing to him the "marriage of M. Léon Dupuis, her son, notary at Yvetot, and Mlle. Léocadie Leboeuf, of Bondeville." Charles's letter of congratulation contained the sentence: "How happy this would have made my poor wife!"

One day, wandering aimlessly about the house, he went up to the attic; and through the sole of his slipper he felt a wad of thin paper. He opened it. "You must be courageous, Emma," he read. "The last thing I want to do is ruin your life." It was Rodolphe's letter. It had fallen to the floor in among some boxes and had remained there, and now the draught from the dormer had blown it toward the door. Charles stood there motionless and open-mouthed—in the very spot where Emma, desperate and even paler than he was now, had longed to die. Finally he discovered a small "R" at the bottom of the second page. Who was it? He remembered Rodolphe's attentiveness, his sudden disappearance, and his air of constraint the two or three times they had met since. But the respectful tone of the letter deceived him.

"Perhaps they loved each other platonically," he told himself.

In any case, Charles wasn't one to go to the root of things: he closed his eyes to the evidence, and his hesitant jealousy was drowned in the immensity of his grief.

Everyone must have adored her, he thought. Every man who saw her must certainly have coveted her. This made her the lovelier in his mind; and he conceived a furious desire for her that never stopped; it fed the flames of his despair, and it grew stronger and stronger because now it could never be satisfied.

To please her, as though she were still alive, he adopted her tastes, her ideas: he bought himself patent leather shoes, took to wearing white cravats. He waxed his mustache, and signed—just as she had—more promissory notes. She was corrupting him from beyond the grave.

He was forced to sell the silver piece by piece, then he sold the parlor furniture. But though all the other rooms grew bare, the bedroom—her bedroom—remained as before. Charles went there every day after dinner. He pushed the round table up to the fire, pulled her armchair close to it. He sat opposite. A tallow candle burned in one of the gilded sconces. Berthe, at his side, colored pictures.

It pained him, poor fellow, to see her so shabbily dressed, with her shoes

unlaced and the armholes of her smock torn and gaping to below her waist—
for the cleaning woman completely neglected her. But she was so sweet and
gentle, and she bent her little head so gracefully, letting her fair hair fall
against her rosy cheek, that he was flooded with infinite pleasure—an enjoyment that was mixed with bitterness, like an inferior wine tasting of resin.
He mended her toys, made puppets for her out of cardboard, sewed up the
torn stomachs of her dolls. But the sight of the sewing box, or a bit of loose
ribbon, or even a pin caught in a crack in the table, would send him brooding;
and then he looked so gloomy that she, too, grew sad.

No one came to see them now, for Justin had run off to Rouen, where he
found work as a grocery clerk, and the apothecary's children saw less and
less of Berthe. Monsieur Homais was not eager to prolong the intimacy,
considering the difference in their social status.

The blind man, whom his salve had not cured, had resumed his beat on
the hill at Bois-Guillaume, where he told everyone about the pharmacist's
failure—to such a point that Homais, whenever he went to the city, hid
behind the Hirondelle's curtains to avoid meeting him face to face. He hated
him. He must get rid of him at all costs, he decided, for the sake of his own
reputation; and he launched an underhand campaign against him in which
he revealed his deep cunning and his criminal vanity. During the next six
months paragraphs like the following would appear in the *Fanal de Rouen*:

> Anyone who has ever wended his way toward the fertile fields of Picardy
> cannot help but have noticed, on the hill at Bois-Guillaume, an unfor-
> tunate afflicted with a horrible facial deformity. He pesters travelers,
> persecutes them, levies a veritable tax upon them. Are we back in the
> monstrous days of the Middle Ages, when vagabonds were permitted to
> display, in our public squares, the leprous ulcers and scrofulous sores
> they brought back from the Crusades?

Or:

> Despite the laws against vagrancy, the approaches to our large cities
> continue to be infested by bands of beggars. There are some who operate
> single-handed; and these, perhaps, are not the least dangerous of the
> lot. What are our Municipal Authorities waiting for?

Sometimes Homais invented ancedotes:

> Yesterday, on the hill at Bois-Guillaume, a skittish horse . . .

And there would follow the story of an accident caused by the blind man.
This went on until the beggar was locked up. But he was released. He took
up where he had left off. So did Homais. It was a fight to the finish. Homais
was victorious: his enemy was committed to an asylum for the rest of his
days.

This success emboldened him; and from then on whenever a dog was run
over in the district, or a barn set on fire, or a woman beaten, Homais hastened
to publicize the event, inspired always by love of progress and hatred of the
clergy. He instituted comparisons between public and religious schools, to
the detriment of the latter; he referred to Saint Bartholomew's Eve apropos
of every hundred-franc subsidy the government granted the church; he
denounced abuses, he flashed the rapier of satire. Such, at least, was the

way he put it. In short, Homais was "undermining the foundations": he was becoming a dangerous man.

He found the narrow limitations of journalism stifling, however, and soon he felt the need to produce a book, a "work." So he composed his *General Statistics Concerning the Canton of Yonville, Followed by Climatological Observations;* and statistics led him into philosophy. He dealt with burning issues: the social problem, raising the moral standards of the poor, pisciculture,[4] rubber, railroads, etc. In the end, he felt it a disgrace to be a bourgeois. He affected bohemian ways, he even smoked! He bought two rococo statuettes, very *chic*, to decorate his parlor.

Not that he gave up pharmacy. Far from it! He kept up with all the latest discoveries. He followed every stage in the great development of chocolates. He was the first to introduce into the department of the Seine-Inférieure those two great chocolate health foods, Cho-ca and Revalentia. He became an enthusiastic partisan of Pulvermacher electric health belts; he wore one himself, and at night when he took off his flannel undershirt Madame Homais never failed to be dazzled by the golden spiral that almost hid him from view, and her passion redoubled for this man she saw before her swaddled like a Scythian and splendid as a Magian priest.

He had brilliant ideas for Emma's tombstone. First he suggested a broken column with a drapery; then a pyramid, then a Temple of Vesta, a kind of rotunda, or perhaps a romantic pile of ruins. One element was constant in all his plans—a weeping willow, which he considered the obligatory symbol of grief.

Charles and he made a trip to Rouen together to look at tombstones at a burial specialist's, accompanied by an artist named Vaufrilard, a friend of Bridoux's, who never stopped making puns. Finally, after examining a hundred designs, getting an estimate, and making a second trip to Rouen, Charles decided in favor of a mausoleum whose two principal sides were to be adorned with "a spirit bearing an extinguished torch."

As for the inscription, Homais could think of nothing as eloquent as *Sta viator.* He couldn't get beyond it, rack his brains as he might: he kept repeating "*Sta viator*" to himself over and over again. Finally he had an inspiration— *amabilem conjugem calcas;*[5] and this was adopted.

The strange thing was that Bovary, even though he thought of Emma continually, was forgetting her; and he felt desperate realizing that her image was fading from his memory, struggle as he might to keep it alive. Each night, however, he dreamed of her. It was always the same dream: he approached her, but just when he was about to embrace her she fell into decay in his arms.

The first week, he went to church every evening. Monsieur Bournisien called on him two or three times, then left him alone. The fact is that the priest was becoming decidedly less tolerant—sinking into real fanaticism, as Homais put it. He thundered against the spirit of the modern age, and regularly once a fortnight included in his sermon an account of the last agony of Voltaire—who died eating his own excrement, as everyone knows.

Despite Bovary's frugality, he was quite unable to pay off his old debts.

---

4. Fish breeding.   5. You are treading on a beloved spouse (Latin). Based on the Latin inscription placed over the spot where the valorous Bavarian field marshal Baron Franz von Mercy died in the Second Battle of Nördlingen (1645): *Sta viator, heroem calcas* (Halt, traveler, you are treading on a hero).

Lheureux refused to renew a single note. Execution was imminent. He had recourse to his mother, who agreed to let him mortgage her house; but she seized the occasion to write him many harsh things about Emma, and in return for her sacrifice she demanded a shawl that had escaped Félicité's depredations. Charles refused to let her have it, and they quarreled.

She made the first overtures toward a reconciliation by offering to take the little girl to live with her: the child could help her in the house. Charles consented. But when the time came for her to leave he couldn't face it, and there was a new break between mother and son, this time irrevocable.

As his bonds with others weakened, his love for his child grew ever stronger. She worried him, however, for occasionally she coughed and had red patches on her cheekbones.

Across the square, in constant view, thriving and jovial, was the family of the pharmacist. He had every reason to be satisfied with his lot. Napoléon helped him in the laboratory, Athalie embroidered him a smoking cap, Irma cut paper circles to cover the jelly jars, and Franklin could recite the multiplication table without stumbling. Homais was the happiest of fathers, the luckiest of men.

Not quite, though! He was eaten with a secret ambition: he wanted the cross of the Legion of Honor. He had plenty of qualifications:

"*First:* during the cholera epidemic, was conspicuous for devotion above and beyond the call of professional duty. *Second:* have published at my own expense various works of public usefulness, such as . . ." (And he cited his treatise on *Cider: Its Manufacture and Its Effects:* also, some observations on the woolly aphis that he had sent to the Academy; his volume of statistics, and even his pharmacist's thesis.) "Not to mention that I am a member of several learned societies." (He belonged to only one.)

"And even suppose," he said with a caper, "that the only thing I had to my credit was my perfect record as a volunteer fireman!"

Homais proceeded to ingratiate himself with the powers that be; he secretly rendered great services to Monsieur le Préfet during an electoral campaign. In short he sold himself; he prostituted himself. He went so far as to address a petition to the sovereign in which he begged him to "do him justice": he called him "our good king" and compared him to Henri IV.

Every morning the apothecary rushed to the newspaper, hoping to find the news of his nomination, but it didn't come. Finally, in his impatience, he had a star-shaped grass plot designed for his garden, to represent the decoration, with two little tufts of greenery as the ribbon. He would walk around it, his arms folded, pondering on governmental stupidity and human ingratitude.

Out of respect, or to prolong the almost sensual pleasure he took in his investigations, Charles had not yet opened the secret compartment of the rosewood desk that Emma had always used. At last, one day, he sat down at it, turned the key and pressed the spring. All Léon's letters were there. No possible doubt, this time! He devoured every last one of them. Then he rummaged in every corner, every piece of furniture, every drawer, looked for hiding places in the walls: he was sobbing, screaming with rage, beside himself, stark mad. He came upon a box, kicked it open. Rodolphe's picture jumped out at him, and all the love letters spilled out with it.

Everyone was amazed at the depth of his depression. He no longer went out, had no visitors, refused even to call on his patients. Everyone said that he "locked himself up to get drunk."

Now and again someone more curious than the rest would peer over the garden hedge and would be startled at the sight of him, wild-eyed, long-bearded, clad in sordid rags, walking and weeping aloud.

Summer evenings he would take his daughter with him and go to the cemetery. They always came back after dark, when the only light in the square was in Binet's dormer.

Still, he was unable to savor his grief to the full, since he had no one with whom he could share it. From time to time he called on Madame Lefrançois, for the sole purpose of talking about "her." But the innkeeper listened to him with only one ear, having her troubles just as he had his: Monsieur Lheureux had finally established his transportation service, *Les Favorites du commerce*, and Hivert, who enjoyed a considerable reputation for his dependability as doer of errands, was demanding an increase in wages and threatening to go to work for her competitor.

One day, at the market in Argueuil, where he had gone to sell his horse—his last asset—he met Rodolphe.

Both men turned pale when they caught sight of each other, Rodolphe, who had merely sent his card with a message of condolence, began by stammering a few excuses; then he grew bolder, and even had the cheek (it was a very hot August day) to invite him to take a bottle of beer in a café.

Sitting opposite him, his elbows on the table, he chewed his cigar as he talked; and Charles was lost in revery as he looked into the face that she had loved. In it, he felt, he was seeing something of her. It was a revelation. He would have liked to be that man.

Rodolphe talked farming, livestock, fertilizers—making use of banalities to stop up all the gaps through which any compromising reference might creep in. Charles wasn't listening. Rodolphe became aware of this; and in the play of expression on Charles's face he could read the sequence of his thoughts. Gradually it grew crimson; Charles's nostrils fluttered, his lips quivered; at one point, filled with somber fury, he stared fixedly at Rodolphe, who in his fright stopped speaking. But almost at once the other man's features reassumed their habitual expression of mournful weariness.

"I don't hold it against you," he said.

Rodolphe sat speechless. And Charles, his head in his hands, repeated, in a dull voice, with all the resignation of a grief that can never be assuaged:

"No, I don't hold it against you, any more."

And he added a bit of rhetoric, the only such utterance that had ever escaped him:

"No one is to blame. It was decreed by fate."

Rodolphe, who had been the instrument of that fate, thought him very meek indeed for a man in his situation—comical, even, and a little contemptible.

The next day Charles sat down on the bench in the arbor. Rays of light came through the trellis, grape leaves traced their shadow on the gravel, the jasmine was fragrant under the blue sky, beetles buzzed about the flowering lilies. A vaporous flood of love-memories swelled in his sorrowing heart, and he was overcome with emotion, like an adolescent.

At seven o'clock little Berthe, who hadn't seen him all afternoon, came to call him to dinner.

She found him with his head leaning back against the wall, his eyes closed, his mouth open; and there was a long lock of black hair in his hands.

"Papa! Come along!" she said.

She thought that he was playing, and gave him a little push. He fell to the ground. He was dead.

Thirty-six hours later Monsieur Canivet arrived, summoned by the apothecary. He performed an autopsy, but found nothing.

When everything was sold, there remained twelve francs and fifteen centimes—enough to pay Mademoiselle Bovary's coach fare to her grandmother's. The old lady died the same year; and since Monsieur Rouault was now paralyzed, it was an aunt who took charge of her. She is poor, and sends her to work for her living in a cotton mill.

Since Bovary's death, three doctors have succeeded one another in Yonville, and not one of them has gained a foothold, so rapidly and so utterly has Homais routed them. The devil himself doesn't have a greater following than the pharmacist: the authorities treat him considerately, and public opinion is on his side.

He has just been awarded the cross of the Legion of Honor.

FYODOR DOSTOEVSKY
1821–1881

Fyodor Dostoevsky has been a central figure in the formation of the modern sensibility. His works are fundamental to the Western tradition of the novel and a strong influence on modern literature in China and Japan. Dostoevsky formulated in fictional terms, in dramatic and even sensational scenes, some of the central predicaments of our time: the choices between God and atheism, good and evil, freedom and tyranny; the recognition of the limits and even of the fall of humanity against the belief in progress, revolution, and utopia. Most important, he captured unforgettably the enormous contradictions of which our common human nature is capable and by which it is torn.

Fyodor Mikhailovich Dostoevsky was born in Moscow on October 30, 1821. His father was a staff doctor at the Hospital for the Poor. Later he acquired an estate and serfs. In 1839 he was killed by one of his peasants in a quarrel. Dostoevsky was sent to the Military Engineering Academy in St. Petersburg, from which he graduated in 1843. He became a civil servant, a draftsman in the St. Petersburg Engineering Corps, but soon resigned because he feared that he would be transferred to the provinces when his writing was discovered. His first novel, *Poor People* (1846), proved a great success with the critics; his second, *The Double* (1846), which followed immediately, was a failure.

Subsequently, Dostoevsky became involved in the Petrashevsky circle, a secret society of antigovernment and socialist tendencies. He was arrested on April 23, 1849, and condemned to be shot. On December 22 he was led to public execution, but he was reprieved at the last moment and sent to penal servitude in Siberia (near Omsk), where he worked for four years in a stockade, wearing fetters, completely cut off from communications with Russia. On his release in February 1854, he was assigned as a common soldier to Semipalatinsk, a small town near the Mongolian frontier. There he received several promotions (eventually becoming an ensign); his rank of nobility, forfeited by his sentence, was restored; and he married the widow of a customs official. In July 1859, Dostoevsky was permitted to return to Russia and, finally, in December 1859, to St. Petersburg—after ten years of his life had been spent in Siberia.

In the last year of his exile, Dostoevsky had resumed writing; and in 1861, shortly after his return, he founded a review, *Time* (*Vremya*). This was suppressed in 1863, though Dostoevsky had changed his political opinions and was now strongly nationalistic and conservative in outlook. He made his first trip to France and England in 1862 and traveled in Europe again in 1863 and 1865, to follow a young woman friend, Apollinaria Suslova, and to indulge in gambling. After his wife's death in 1864 and another unsuccessful journalistic venture, *The Epoch* (*Epokha,* 1864–65), Dostoevsky was for a time almost crushed by gambling debts, emotional entanglements, and frequent epileptic seizures. He barely managed to return from Germany in 1865. In the winter of 1866 he wrote *Crime and Punishment* and, before he had finished it, dictated a shorter novel, *The Gambler,* to meet a deadline. He married his secretary, Anna Grigoryevna Snitkina, early in 1867 and left Russia with her to avoid his creditors. For years they wandered through Germany, Italy, and Switzerland, frequently in abject poverty. Their first child died. In 1871, when the initial chapters of *The Possessed* proved a popular success, Dostoevsky returned to St. Petersburg. He was the editor of a weekly, *The Citizen* (*Grazhdanin*), for a short time and then published a periodical written by himself, *The Diary of a Writer* (1876–81), which won great acclaim. His last novel, *The Brothers Karamazov* (1880), was an immense success, and honors and some prosperity came to him at last. At a Pushkin anniversary celebrated in Moscow in 1880 he gave the main speech. But soon after his return to St. Petersburg he died, on January 28, 1881, not yet sixty years old.

Dostoevsky, like every great writer, can be approached in different ways and read on different levels. We can try to understand him as a religious philosopher, a political commentator, a psychologist, and a novelist; and if we know much about his fascinating and varied life, we might also interpret his works as biographical.

The biographical interpretation is the one that has been pushed furthest. The lurid crimes of Dostoevsky's characters (such as the rape of a young girl) have been ascribed to him, and all his novels have been studied as if they constituted a great personal confession. Dostoevsky certainly did draw from his experiences in his books, as every writer does: he several times described the feelings of a man facing a firing squad as he himself faced it on December 22, 1849, only to be reprieved at the last moment. His writings also reflect his years in Siberia: four years working in a loghouse, in chains, as he describes it in an oddly impersonal book, *Memoirs from the House of the Dead* (1862), and six more years as a common soldier on the borders of Mongolia, in a small, remote provincial town. Similarly, he used the experience of his disease (epilepsy), ascribing great spiritual significance to the ecstatic rapture preceding the actual seizure. He assigned his disease to both his most angelic "good" man, the "Idiot" Prince Myshkin, and his most diabolical, inhuman figure, the cold-blooded unsexed murderer of the old Karamazov, the flunky Smerdyakov. Dostoevsky also used something of his experiences in Germany, where in the 1860s he succumbed to a passion for gambling, which he overcame only much later, during his second marriage. The short novel *The Gambler* (1866) gives an especially vivid account of this life and its moods.

There are other autobiographical elements in Dostoevsky's works, but it seems a gross misunderstanding of his methods and the procedures of art in general to conclude from his writings (as Thomas Mann has done) that he was a "saint and criminal" in one. Dostoevsky, after all, was an extremely hard worker who wrote and rewrote some twenty volumes. He was a novelist who employed the methods of the French sensational novel; he was constantly on the lookout for the most striking occurrences—the most shocking crimes and the most horrible disasters and scandals—because only in such fictional situations could he exalt his characters to their highest pitch, bringing out the clash of ideas and temperaments, revealing the deepest layers of their souls. But these fictions cannot be taken as literal transcriptions of reality and actual experience.

Whole books have been written to explain Dostoevsky's religious philosophy and conception of human nature. The Russian philosopher Berdyayev concludes his excellent study by saying, "So great is the value of Dostoevsky that to have produced him is by itself sufficient justification for the existence of the Russian people in the world." But there is no need for such extravagance. Dostoevsky's philosophy of religion is rather a personal version of extreme mystical Christianity and assumes flesh and blood only in the context of the novels. Reduced to the bare bones of abstract propositions, it amounts to saying that humanity is fallen but is free to choose between evil and Christ. And choosing Christ means taking on oneself the burden of humanity in love and pity, since "everybody is guilty for all and before all." Hence in Dostoevsky there is tremendous stress on personal freedom of choice; and his affirmation of the worth of every individual is combined, paradoxically, with an equal insistence on the substantial identity of all human beings, their equality before God, the bond of love that unites them.

Dostoevsky also develops a philosophy of history, with practical political implications, based on this point of view. According to him, the West is in complete decay; only Russia has preserved Christianity in its original form. The West is either Catholic (and Catholicism is condemned by Dostoevsky as an attempt to force salvation by magic and authority) or bourgeois, and hence materialistic and fallen away from Christ, or socialist, and socialism is to Dostoevsky identical with atheism, as it dreams of a utopia in which human beings would not be free to choose even at the expense of suffering. Dostoevsky—who himself had belonged to a revolutionary group and come into contact with Russian revolutionaries abroad—had an extraordinary insight into the mentality of the Russian underground. In *The Possessed* (1871–72) he gives a lurid satiric picture of these would-be saviors of Russia and humankind. But although he was afraid of the revolution, Dostoevsky himself hoped and prophesied that Russia would save Europe from the dangers of communism, as Russia alone was the uncorrupted Christian land. Put in terms of political propositions (as Dostoevsky himself preaches them in his journal, *The Diary of a Writer*, 1876–81), what he propounds is a conservative Russian nationalism with messianic hopes for Russian Christianity.

When translated into abstractions, Dostoevsky's psychology is as unimpressive as his political theory. It is merely a derivative of theories propounded by German writers about the unconscious, the role of dreams, the ambivalence of human feelings. What makes it electric in the novels is his ability to dramatize it in scenes of sudden revelation, in characters who in today's terminology would be called split personalities, in people twisted by isolation, lust, humiliation, and resentment. The dreams of Raskolnikov may be interpreted according to Freudian psychology; but to the reader without any knowledge of science they are comprehensible in their place in the novel and function as warnings and anticipations.

Dostoevsky was first of all an artist—a novelist who succeeded in using his ideas (many old and venerable, many new and fantastic) and psychological insights for the writing of stories of absorbing interest. As an artist, Dostoevsky treated the novel like a drama, constructing it in large, vivid scenes that end with a scandal or a crime or some act of violence, filling it with unforgettable "stagelike" figures torn by great passions and swayed by great ideas. Then he set this world in an environment of St. Petersburg slums or of towns, monasteries, and country houses, all so vividly realized that we forget how the setting, the figures, and the ideas blend together into one cosmos of the imagination only remotely and obliquely related to any reality of nineteenth-century Russia. We take part in a great drama of pride and humility, good and evil, in a huge allegory of humanity's search for God and itself. We understand and share in this world because it is not merely Russia in the nineteenth century, where people could hardly have talked and behaved as Dostoevsky's people do, but a myth of humanity, universalized as all art is.

Notes from Underground (1864) precedes the four great novels: Crime and Punishment (1866), The Idiot (1868), The Possessed, and The Brothers Karamazov (1880). The Notes can be viewed as a prologue, an important introduction to the cycle of the four great novels, an anticipation of the mature Dostoevsky's method and thought. Though it cannot compare in dramatic power and scope with these, the story has its own peculiar and original artistry. It is made up of two parts, at first glance seemingly independent: the monologue of the Underground man and the confession that he makes about himself, called Apropos of Wet Snow. The monologue, though it includes no action, is dramatic—a long address to an imaginary hostile reader, whom the Underground man ridicules, defies, jeers at, but also flatters. The confession is an autobiographical reminiscence of the Underground man. It describes events that occurred long before the delivery of the monologue, but it functions as a confirmation in concrete terms of the self-portrait drawn in the monologue and as an explanation of the isolation of the hero.

The narrative of the confession is a comic variation on the old theme of the rescue of a fallen woman from vice, a seesaw series of humiliations permitting Dostoevsky to display all the cruelty of his probing psychology. The hero, out of spite and craving for human company, forces himself into the company of former schoolfellows and is shamefully humiliated by them. He reasserts his ego (as he cannot revenge himself on them) in the company of a humble prostitute by impressing her with florid and moving speeches, which he knows to be insincere, about her horrible future. Ironically, he converts her, but when she comes to him and surprises him in a degrading scene with his servant, he humiliates her again. When, even then, she understands and forgives and thus shows her moral superiority, he crowns his spite by deliberately misunderstanding her and forcing money on her. She is the moral victor, and the Underground man returns to his hideout to jeer at humanity. It is hard not to feel that we are shown a tortured and twisted soul almost too despicable to elicit our compassion.

Still it would be a complete misunderstanding of Dostoevsky's story to take the philosophy expounded jeeringly in the long monologue of the first part merely as the irrational railings of a sick personality. The Underground man, though abject and spiteful, represents not only a specific Russian type of the time—the intellectual divorced from the soil and his nation—but also modern humanity, even Everyman, and strangely enough, even the author, who through the mouth of this despicable character, as through a mask, expresses his boldest and most intimate convictions. In spite of all the exaggerated pathos, wild paradox, and jeering irony used by the speaker, his self-criticism and his criticism of society and history must be taken seriously and interpreted patiently if we are to extract the meaning accepted by Dostoevsky.

The Underground man is also the hyperconscious man who examines himself as if in a mirror and sees himself with pitiless candor. His very self-consciousness cripples his will and poisons his feelings. He cannot escape from his ego; he knows that he has acted badly toward the woman, but at the same time he cannot help acting as he does. He knows that he is alone, that there is no bridge from him to humanity, that the world is hostile to him, and that he is humiliated by everyone he meets. But though he resents the humiliation, he cannot help courting it, provoking it, and even enjoying it in his perverse manner. He understands (and knows from his own experience) that something within us all enjoys evil and destruction.

His self-criticism widens, then, into a criticism of the assumptions of modern civilization, of nineteenth-century optimism about human nature and progress, of utilitarianism, and of all kinds of utopias. It is possible to identify specific allusions to a contemporary novel by a radical socialist and revolutionary, Chernyshevsky, titled *What Is to Be Done?* (1863), but we do not need to know the exact target of Dostoevsky's satire to recognize what he attacks: the view that human nature is good, that we generally seek our enlightened self-interest, that science propounds immutable truths, and that a paradise on Earth will be just around the corner once society is reformed along scientific lines. In a series of vivid symbols these assumptions are represented, parodied, exposed. Science says that "twice two makes four" but the Underground man laughs that "twice two makes five is sometimes a very charming thing too." Science means to him (and to Dostoevsky) the victory of the doctrine of fatality, of iron necessity, of determinism, and thus finally of death. Humanity would become an "organ stop," a "piano key," if deterministic science were valid.

Equally disastrous are the implications of the social philosophy of liberalism and of socialism (which Dostoevsky considers its necessary consequence). In this view, we need only follow our enlightened self-interest, need only be rational, and we will become noble and good and the Earth will be a place of prosperity and peace. But the Underground man knows that this conception of human nature is entirely false. What if humankind does not follow, and never will follow, its own enlightened self-interest, is consciously and purposely irrational, even bloodthirsty and evil? History seems to the Underground man to speak a clear language: "civilization has made mankind if not more bloodthirsty, at least more vilely, more loathsomely bloodthirsty." Humanity wills the irrational and evil because it does not want to become an organ stop, a piano key, because it wants to be left with the freedom to choose between good and evil. This freedom of choice, even at the expense of chaos and destruction, is what makes us human.

Actually, we love something other than our own well-being and happiness, love even suffering and pain, because we are human and not animals inhabiting some great organized rational "ant heap." The ant heap, the hen house, the block of tenements, and finally the Crystal Palace (then the newest wonder of architecture, a great hall of iron and glass erected for the Universal Exhibition in London) are the images used by the Underground man to represent his hated utopia. The heroine of *What Is to Be Done?* had dreamed of a building made of cast iron and glass and placed in the middle of a beautiful garden where there would be eternal spring and summer, eternal joy. Dostoevsky had recognized there the utopian dream of Charles Fourier, the French socialist whom he had admired in his youth and whose ideals he had come to hate with a fierce revulsion. But we must realize that the Underground man, and Dostoevsky, despise this "ant heap," this perfectly organized society of automatons, in the name of something higher, in the name of freedom. Dostoevsky does not believe that humanity can achieve freedom and happiness at the same time; happiness can be bought only at the expense of freedom, and all utopian schemes seem to him devices to lure us into the yoke of slavery. This freedom is, of course, not political freedom but freedom of choice, indeterminism, even caprice and willfulness, in the paradoxical formulation of the Underground man.

There are hints at a positive solution in only the one chapter (Part I, Chapter X) that was mutilated by the censor. A letter by Dostoevsky to his brother about the "swine of a censor who let through the passages where I jeered at everything and blasphemed ostensibly" refers to the fact that he "suppressed everything where I drew the conclusion that faith in Christ is needed." In Part I, Chapter XI, of the text printed here (and Dostoevsky never restored the suppressed passages) the Underground man says merely, "I am lying because I know myself that it is not underground that is better, but something different, quite different, for which I am thirsting, but which I cannot find!" This "something . . . quite different" all the other writings of Dostoevsky show to be the voluntary following of the Christian savior even at the expense of suffering and pain.

In a paradoxical form, through the mouth of one of his vilest characters, Dostoevsky reveals in the story his view of humanity and history—of the evil in human nature and of the blood and tragedy in history—and his criticism of the optimistic, utilitarian, utopian, progressive view of humanity that was spreading to Russia from the West during the nineteenth century and that found its most devoted adherents in the Russian revolutionaries. Preoccupied with criticism, Dostoevsky does not here suggest any positive remedy. But if we understand the *Notes,* we can understand how Raskolnikov, the murderer out of intellect in *Crime and Punishment,* can find salvation at last and how Dmitri, the guilty-guiltless parricide of *The Brothers Karamazov,* can sing his hymn to joy in the Siberian mines. We can even understand the legend of the Grand Inquisitor told by Ivan Karamazov, in which we meet the same criticism of a utopia (this time that of Catholicism) and the same exaltation of human freedom even at the price of suffering.

Monroe C. Beardsley, "Dostoevsky's Metaphor of the 'Underground,' " *Journal of the History of Ideas* 3 (June 1942), is a subtle interpretation of the central metaphor of the *Notes.* Joseph Frank, "Nihilism and *Notes from Underground,*" *Sewanee Review* 69 (1961), interprets the *Notes* in the context of the history of the times. Robert L. Jackson, *The Underground Man in Russian Literature* (1981), traces the impact of the *Notes* on Russian literature. Konstantin Mochulsky, *Dostoevsky: Life and Work* (1967), is the best general work translated from Russian, the work of an emigré in Paris. A useful short overview is Victor Terras, *Reading Dostoevsky* (1998). René Wellek, ed., *Dostoevsky: A Collection of Critical Essays* (1962), contains an essay by the editor on the history of Dostoevsky criticism. Alba della Fazia Amoia, *Feodor Dostoevsky* (1993), is a general introduction to Dostoevsky's work, aimed at a student audience. Joseph Frank, *Dostoevsky* (1976–95), is an impressive, though still-unfinished, biographical study in four volumes. Frank's *Through the Russian Prism* (1990) includes review essays that examine various approaches to Dostoevsky. Louis Breger, *Dostoevsky: The Author as Psychoanalyst* (1989), takes a psychoanalytic approach in analyzing levels of meaning in Dostoevsky's work as a new sensibility that anticipates the modern novel; he includes a chapter on *Notes.* Liza Knapp, *The Annihilation of Inertia: Dostoevsky and Metaphysics* (1996), discusses the "tragedy of the underground." Malcolm V. Jones, *Dostoyevsky After Bakhtin: Readings in Dostoyevsky's Fantastic Realism* (1990), examines Dostoevsky's "higher realism" in various perspectives and includes a chapter on *Notes.* Nina Pelikan Straus, *Dostoevsky and the Woman Question: Rereadings at the End of a Century* (1994), examines the presence of women and Dostoevsky's construction of the feminine; other pertinent essays are found in Sona Stephan Hoisington, ed., *A Plot of Her Own: The Female Protagonist in Russian Literature* (1995).

PRONOUNCING GLOSSARY

The following list uses common English syllables and stress accents to provide rough equivalents of selected words whose pronunciation may be unfamiliar to the general reader.

Anton Antonych: *an'-ton an'-tonych*

Apollon: *ah-poll-on'*

Ferfichkin: *fair-fich'-kin*

Fyodor Dostoevsky: *fyo'-dor dos-toy-eff'-skee*

Karamazov: *kah-rah-mah'-zoff*

Kolya: *kol'-ya*

Podkharzhevsky: *pod-har-zheff'-skee*

Simonov: *see-mon'-off*

Trudolyubov: *troo-doll-yoo'-boff*

Zverkov: *zvyer-koff'*

Notes from Underground[1]

I

Underground[2]

1

I am a sick man. . . . [3] I am a spiteful man. I am a most unpleasant man. I think my liver is diseased. Then again, I don't know a thing about my illness; I'm not even sure what hurts. I'm not being treated and never have been, though I respect both medicine and doctors. Besides, I'm extremely superstitious—well at least enough to respect medicine. (I'm sufficiently educated not to be superstitious; but I am, anyway.) No, gentlemen, it's out of spite that I don't wish to be treated. Now then, that's something you probably won't understand. Well, I do. Of course, I won't really be able to explain to you precisely who will be hurt by my spite in this case; I know perfectly well that I can't possibly "get even" with doctors by refusing their treatment; I know better than anyone that all this is going to hurt me alone, and no one else. Even so, if I refuse to be treated, it's out of spite. My liver hurts? Good, let it hurt even more!

I've been living this way for some time—about twenty years. I'm forty now. I used to be in the civil service. But no more. I was a nasty official. I was rude and took pleasure in it. After all, since I didn't accept bribes, at least I had to reward myself in some way. (That's a poor joke, but I won't cross it out. I wrote it thinking that it would be very witty; but now, having realized that I merely wanted to show off disgracefully, I'll make a point of not crossing it out!) When petitioners used to approach my desk for information, I'd gnash my teeth and feel unending pleasure if I succeeded in causing someone distress. I almost always succeeded. For the most part they were all timid people: naturally, since they were petitioners. But among the dandies there was a certain officer whom I particularly couldn't bear. He simply refused to be humble, and he clanged his saber in a loathsome manner. I waged war with him over that saber for about a year and a half. At last I prevailed. He stopped clanging. All this, however, happened a long time ago, during my youth. But do you know, gentlemen, what the main component of my spite really was? Why, the whole point, the most disgusting thing, was the fact that I was shamefully aware at every moment, even at the moment of my greatest bitterness, that not only was I not a spiteful man, I was not even an embittered one, and that I was merely scaring sparrows to no effect and consoling myself by doing so. I was foaming at the mouth—but just bring me some trinket to play with, just serve me a nice cup of tea with sugar, and I'd probably have calmed down. My heart might even have been touched,

---

1. Translated by Michael Katz.　　2. Both the author of these notes and the *Notes* themselves are fictitious, of course. Nevertheless, people like the author of these notes not only may, but actually must exist in our society, considering the general circumstances under which our society was formed. I wanted to bring before the public with more prominence than usual one of the characters of the recent past. He's a representative of the current generation. In the excerpt entitled "Underground" this person introduces himself and his views, and, as it were, wants to explain the reasons why he appeared and why he had to appear in our midst. The following excerpt [*Apropos of Wet Snow*] contains the actual "notes" of this person about several events in his life [Author's note].　　3. The ellipses are the author's and do not indicate omissions from this text.

although I'd probably have gnashed my teeth out of shame and then suffered from insomnia for several months afterward. That's just my usual way.

I was lying about myself just now when I said that I was a nasty official. I lied out of spite. I was merely having some fun at the expense of both the petitioners and that officer, but I could never really become spiteful. At all times I was aware of a great many elements in me that were just the opposite of that. I felt how they swarmed inside me, these contradictory elements. I knew that they had been swarming inside me my whole life and were begging to be let out; but I wouldn't let them out, I wouldn't, I deliberately wouldn't let them out. They tormented me to the point of shame; they drove me to convulsions and—and finally I got fed up with them, oh how fed up! Perhaps it seems to you, gentlemen, that I'm repenting about something, that I'm asking your forgiveness for something? I'm sure that's how it seems to you. . . . But really, I can assure you, I don't care if that's how it seems. . . .

Not only couldn't I become spiteful, I couldn't become anything at all: neither spiteful nor good, neither a scoundrel nor an honest man, neither a hero nor an insect. Now I live out my days in my corner, taunting myself with the spiteful and entirely useless consolation that an intelligent man cannot seriously become anything and that only a fool can become something. Yes, sir, an intelligent man in the nineteenth century must be, is morally obliged to be, principally a characterless creature; a man possessing character, a man of action, is fundamentally a limited creature. That's my conviction at the age of forty. I'm forty now; and, after all, forty is an entire lifetime; why it's extreme old age. It's rude to live past forty, it's indecent, immoral! Who lives more than forty years? Answer sincerely, honestly. I'll tell you who: only fools and rascals. I'll tell those old men that right to their faces, all those venerable old men, all those silver-haired and sweet-smelling old men! I'll say it to the whole world right to its face! I have a right to say it because I myself will live to sixty. I'll make it to seventy! Even to eighty! . . . Wait! Let me catch my breath. . . .

You probably think, gentlemen, that I want to amuse you. You're wrong about that, too. I'm not at all the cheerful fellow I seem to be, or that I may seem to be; however, if you're irritated by all this talk (and I can already sense that you are irritated), and if you decide to ask me just who I really am, then I'll tell you: I'm a collegiate assessor. I worked in order to have something to eat (but only for that reason); and last year, when a distant relative of mine left me six thousand rubles in his will, I retired immediately and settled down in this corner. I used to live in this corner before, but now I've settled down in it. My room is nasty, squalid, on the outskirts of town. My servant is an old peasant woman, spiteful out of stupidity; besides, she has a foul smell. I'm told that the Petersburg climate is becoming bad for my health, and that it's very expensive to live in Petersburg with my meager resources. I know all that; I know it better than all those wise and experienced advisers and admonishers. But I shall remain in Petersburg; I shall not leave Petersburg! I shall not leave here because . . . Oh, what difference does it really make whether I leave Petersburg or not?

Now, then, what can a decent man talk about with the greatest pleasure? Answer: about himself.

Well, then, I too will talk about myself.

II

Now I would like to tell you, gentlemen, whether or not you want to hear it, why it is that I couldn't even become an insect. I'll tell you solemnly that I wished to become an insect many times. But not even that wish was granted. I swear to you, gentlemen, that being overly conscious is a disease, a genuine, full-fledged disease. Ordinary human consciousness would be more than sufficient for everyday human needs—that is, even half or a quarter of the amount of consciousness that's available to a cultured man in our unfortunate nineteenth century, especially to one who has the particular misfortune of living in St. Petersburg, the most abstract and premeditated city in the whole world.[4] (Cities can be either premeditated or unpremeditated.) It would have been entirely sufficient, for example, to have the consciousness with which all so-called spontaneous people and men of action are endowed. I'll bet that you think I'm writing all this to show off, to make fun of these men of action, that I'm clanging my saber just like that officer did to show off in bad taste. But, gentlemen, who could possibly be proud of his illnesses and want to show them off?

But what am I saying? Everyone does that; people do take pride in their illnesses, and I, perhaps, more than anyone else. Let's not argue; my objection is absurd. Nevertheless, I remain firmly convinced that not only is being overly conscious a disease, but so is being conscious at all. I insist on it. But let's leave that alone for a moment. Tell me this: why was it, as if on purpose, at the very moment, indeed, at the precise moment that I was most capable of becoming conscious of the subtleties of everything that was "beautiful and sublime,"[5] as we used to say at one time, that I didn't become conscious, and instead did such unseemly things, things that . . . well, in short, probably everyone does, but it seemed as if they occurred to me deliberately at the precise moment when I was most conscious that they shouldn't be done at all? The more conscious I was of what was good, of everything "beautiful and sublime," the more deeply I sank into the morass and the more capable I was of becoming entirely bogged down in it. But the main thing is that all this didn't seem to be occurring accidentally; rather, it was as if it all had to be so. It was as if this were my most normal condition, not an illness or an affliction at all, so that finally I even lost the desire to struggle against it. It ended when I almost came to believe (perhaps I really did believe) that this might really have been my normal condition. But at first, in the beginning, what agonies I suffered during that struggle! I didn't believe that others were experiencing the same thing; therefore, I kept it a secret about myself all my life. I was ashamed (perhaps I still am even now); I reached the point where I felt some secret, abnormal, despicable little pleasure in returning home to my little corner on some disgusting Petersburg night, acutely aware that once again I'd committed some revolting act that day, that what had been done could not be undone, and I used to gnaw and gnaw at myself inwardly, secretly, nagging away, consuming myself until finally the bitterness turned

---

4. Petersburg was conceived as an imposing city; plans called for regular streets, broad avenues, and spacious squares.   5. This phrase originated in Edmund Burke's (1729–1797) *Philosophical Inquiry into the Origin of Our Ideas of the Sublime and Beautiful* (1756) and was repeated in Immanuel Kant's (1724–1804) *Observations on the Feeling of the Beautiful and the Sublime* (1756). It became a cliché in the writings of Russian critics during the 1830s.

into some kind of shameful, accursed sweetness and at last into genuine, earnest pleasure! Yes, into pleasure, real pleasure! I absolutely mean that. . . . That's why I first began to speak out, because I want to know for certain whether other people share this same pleasure. Let me explain: the pleasure resulted precisely from the overly acute consciousness of one's own humiliation; from the feeling that one had reached the limit; that it was disgusting, but couldn't be otherwise; you had no other choice—you could never become a different person; and that even if there were still time and faith enough for you to change into something else, most likely you wouldn't even want to change, and if you did, you wouldn't have done anything, perhaps because there really was nothing for you to change into. But the main thing and the final point is that all of this was taking place according to normal and fundamental laws of overly acute consciousness and of the inertia which results directly from these laws; consequently, not only couldn't one change, one simply couldn't do anything at all. Hence it follows, for example, as a result of this overly acute consciousness, that one is absolutely right in being a scoundrel, as if this were some consolation to the scoundrel. But enough of this. . . . Oh, my, I've gone on rather a long time, but have I really explained anything? How can I explain this pleasure? But I will explain it! I shall see it through to the end! That's why I've taken up my pen. . . .

For example, I'm terribly proud. I'm as mistrustful and as sensitive as a hunchback or a dwarf; but, in truth, I've experienced some moments when, if someone had slapped my face, I might even have been grateful for it. I'm being serious. I probably would have been able to derive a peculiar sort of pleasure from it—the pleasure of despair, naturally, but the most intense pleasures occur in despair, especially when you're very acutely aware of the hopelessness of your own predicament. As for a slap in the face—why, here the consciousness of being beaten to a pulp would overwhelm you. The main thing is, no matter how I try, it still turns out that I'm always the first to be blamed for everything and, what's even worse, I'm always the innocent victim, so to speak, according to the laws of nature. Therefore, in the first place, I'm guilty inasmuch as I'm smarter than everyone around me. (I've always considered myself smarter than everyone around me, and sometimes, believe me, I've been ashamed of it. At the least, all my life I've looked away and never could look people straight in the eye.) Finally, I'm to blame because even if there were any magnanimity in me, it would only have caused more suffering as a result of my being aware of its utter uselessness. After all, I probably wouldn't have been able to make use of that magnanimity: neither to forgive, as the offender, perhaps, had slapped me in accordance with the laws of nature, and there's no way to forgive the laws of nature; nor to forget, because even if there were any laws of nature, it's offensive nonetheless. Finally, even if I wanted to be entirely unmagnanimous, and had wanted to take revenge on the offender, I couldn't be revenged on anyone for anything because, most likely, I would never have decided to do anything, even if I could have. Why not? I'd like to say a few words about that separately.

III

Let's consider people who know how to take revenge and how to stand up for themselves in general. How, for example, do they do it? Let's suppose that they're seized by an impulse to take revenge—then for a while nothing else remains in their entire being except for that impulse. Such an individual simply rushes toward his goal like an enraged bull with lowered horns; only a wall can stop him. (By the way, when actually faced with a wall such individuals, that is, spontaneous people and men of action, genuinely give up. For them a wall doesn't constitute the evasion that it does for those of us who think and consequently do nothing; it's not an excuse to turn aside from the path, a pretext in which a person like me usually doesn't believe, but one for which he's always extremely grateful. No, they give up in all sincerity. For them the wall possesses some kind of soothing, morally decisive and definitive meaning, perhaps even something mystical . . . But more about the wall later.) Well, then, I consider such a spontaneous individual to be a genuine, normal person, just as tender mother nature wished to see him when she lovingly gave birth to him on earth. I'm green with envy at such a man. He's stupid, I won't argue with you about that; but perhaps a normal man is supposed to be stupid—how do we know? Perhaps it's even very beautiful. And I'm all the more convinced of the suspicion, so to speak, that if, for example, one were to take the antithesis of a normal man—that is, a man of overly acute consciousness, who emerged, of course, not from the bosom of nature, but from a laboratory test tube (this is almost mysticism, gentlemen, but I suspect that it's the case), then this test tube man sometimes gives up so completely in the face of his antithesis that he himself, with his overly acute consciousness, honestly considers himself not as a person, but a mouse. It may be an acutely conscious mouse, but a mouse nonetheless, while the other one is a person and consequently, . . . and so on and so forth. But the main thing is that he, he himself, considers himself to be a mouse; nobody asks him to do so, and that's the important point. Now let's take a look at this mouse in action. Let's assume, for instance, that it feels offended (it almost always feels offended), and that it also wishes to be revenged. It may even contain more accumulated malice than *l'homme de la nature et de la vérité*.[6] The mean, nasty, little desire to pay the offender back with evil may indeed rankle in it even more despicably than in *l'homme de la nature et de la vérité*, because *l'homme de la nature et de la vérité*, with his innate stupidity, considers his revenge nothing more than justice, pure and simple; but the mouse, as a result of its overly acute consciousness, rejects the idea of justice. Finally, we come to the act itself, to the very act of revenge. In addition to its original nastiness, the mouse has already managed to pile up all sorts of other nastiness around itself in the form of hesitations and doubts; so many unresolved questions have emerged from that one single question, that some kind of fatal blow is concocted unwillingly, some kind of stinking mess consisting of doubts, anxieties and, finally, spittle showered upon it by the spontaneous men of action who stand by solemnly as judges and arbiters, roaring with laughter until their sides split. Of course, the only thing left to do is dismiss it with a wave of its paw and a smile of assumed contempt which it doesn't even believe in, and creep ignominiously back into its mousehole. There, in its disgusting, stinking underground, our offended, crushed, and ridiculed mouse immediately plunges into cold, malicious, and,

6. The man of nature and truth (French). The basic idea is borrowed from Jean-Jacques Rousseau's *Confessions* (1782–89), namely, that human beings in a state of nature are honest and direct and that they are corrupted only by civilization.

above all, everlasting spitefulness. For forty years on end it will recall its insult down to the last, most shameful detail; and each time it will add more shameful details of its own, spitefully teasing and irritating itself with its own fantasy. It will become ashamed of that fantasy, but it will still remember it, rehearse it again and again, fabricating all sorts of incredible stories about itself under the pretext that they too could have happened; it won't forgive a thing. Perhaps it will even begin to take revenge, but only in little bits and pieces, in trivial ways, from behind the stove, incognito, not believing in its right to be revenged, nor in the success of its own revenge, and knowing in advance that from all its attempts to take revenge, it will suffer a hundred times more than the object of its vengeance, who might not even feel a thing. On its deathbed it will recall everything all over again, with interest compounded over all those years and. . . . But it's precisely in that cold, abominable state of half-despair and half-belief, in that conscious burial of itself alive in the underground for forty years because of its pain, in that powerfully created, yet partly dubious hopelessness of its own predicament, in all that venom of unfulfilled desire turned inward, in all that fever of vacillation, of resolutions adopted once and for all and followed a moment later by repentance—herein precisely lies the essence of that strange enjoyment I was talking about earlier. It's so subtle, sometimes so difficult to analyze, that even slightly limited people, or those who simply have strong nerves, won't understand anything about it. "Perhaps," you'll add with a smirk, "even those who've never received a slap in the face won't understand," and by so doing you'll be hinting to me ever so politely that perhaps during my life I too have received such a slap in the face and that therefore I'm speaking as an expert. I'll bet that's what you're thinking. Well, rest assured, gentlemen, I've never received such a slap, although it's really all the same to me what you think about it. Perhaps I may even regret the fact that I've given so few slaps during my lifetime. But that's enough, not another word about this subject which you find so extremely interesting.

I'll proceed calmly about people with strong nerves who don't understand certain refinements of pleasure. For example, although under particular circumstances these gentlemen may bellow like bulls as loudly as possible, and although, let's suppose, this behavior bestows on them the greatest honor, yet, as I've already said, when confronted with impossibility, they submit immediately. Impossibility—does that mean a stone wall? What kind of stone wall? Why, of course, the laws of nature, the conclusions of natural science and mathematics. As soon as they prove to you, for example, that it's from a monkey you're descended,[7] there's no reason to make faces; just accept it as it is. As soon as they prove to you that in truth one drop of your own fat is dearer to you than the lives of one hundred thousand of your fellow creatures and that this will finally put an end to all the so-called virtues, obligations, and other such similar ravings and prejudices, just accept that too; there's nothing more to do, since two times two is a fact of mathematics. Just you try to object.

"For goodness sake," they'll shout at you, "it's impossible to protest: it's two times two makes four! Nature doesn't ask for your opinion; it doesn't

---

7. A reference to the theory of evolution by natural selection developed by Charles Darwin (1809–1882). A book on the subject was translated into Russian in 1864.

care about your desires or whether you like or dislike its laws. You're obliged to accept it as it is, and consequently, all its conclusions. A wall, you see, is a wall . . . etc. etc." Good Lord, what do I care about the laws of nature and arithmetic when for some reason I dislike all these laws and I dislike the fact that two times two makes four? Of course, I won't break through that wall with my head if I really don't have the strength to do so, nor will I reconcile myself to it just because I'm faced with such a stone wall and lack the strength.

As though such a stone wall actually offered some consolation and contained some real word of conciliation, for the sole reason that it means two times two makes four. Oh, absurdity of absurdities! How much better it is to understand it all, to be aware of everything, all the impossibilities and stone walls; not to be reconciled with any of those impossibilities or stone walls if it so disgusts you; to reach, by using the most inevitable logical combinations, the most revolting conclusions on the eternal theme that you are somehow or other to blame even for that stone wall, even though it's absolutely clear once again that you're in no way to blame, and, as a result of all this, while silently and impotently gnashing your teeth, you sink voluptuously into inertia, musing on the fact that, as it turns out, there's no one to be angry with; that an object cannot be found, and perhaps never will be; that there's been a substitution, some sleight of hand, a bit of cheating, and that it's all a mess—you can't tell who's who or what's what; but in spite of all these uncertainties and sleights-of-hand, it hurts you just the same, and the more you don't know, the more it hurts!

IV

"Ha, ha, ha! Why, you'll be finding enjoyment in a toothache next!" you cry out with a laugh.

"Well, what of it? There is some enjoyment even in a toothache," I reply. I've had a toothache for a whole month; I know what's what. In this instance, of course, people don't rage in silence; they moan. But these moans are insincere; they're malicious, and malice is the whole point. These moans express the sufferer's enjoyment; if he didn't enjoy it, he would never have begun to moan. This is a good example, gentlemen, and I'll develop it. In the first place, these moans express all the aimlessness of the pain which consciousness finds so humiliating, the whole system of natural laws about which you really don't give a damn, but as a result of which you're suffering nonetheless, while nature isn't. They express the consciousness that while there's no real enemy to be identified, the pain exists nonetheless; the awareness that, in spite of all possible Wagenheims,[8] you're still a complete slave to your teeth; that if someone so wishes, your teeth will stop aching, but that if he doesn't so wish, they'll go on aching for three more months; and finally, that if you still disagree and protest, all there's left to do for consolation is flagellate yourself or beat your fist against the wall as hard as you can, and absolutely nothing else. Well, then, it's these bloody insults, these jeers coming from nowhere, that finally generate enjoyment that can sometimes reach the highest degree of voluptuousness. I beseech you, gentlemen, to listen to

---

8. The *General Address Book of St. Petersburg* listed eight dentists named Wagenheim; contemporary readers would have recognized the name from signs throughout the city.

the moans of an educated man of the nineteenth century who's suffering from a toothache, especially on the second or third day of his distress, when he begins to moan in a very different way than he did on the first day, that is, not simply because his tooth aches; not the way some coarse peasant moans, but as a man affected by progress and European civilization, a man "who's renounced both the soil and the common people," as they say nowadays. His moans become somehow nasty, despicably spiteful, and they go on for days and nights. Yet he himself knows that his moans do him no good; he knows better than anyone else that he's merely irritating himself and others in vain; he knows that the audience for whom he's trying so hard, and his whole family, have now begun to listen to him with loathing; they don't believe him for a second, and they realize full well that he could moan in a different, much simpler way, without all the flourishes and affectation, and that he's only indulging himself out of spite and malice. Well, it's precisely in this awareness and shame that the voluptuousness resides. "It seems I'm disturbing you, tearing at your heart, preventing anyone in the house from getting any sleep. Well, then, you won't sleep; you too must be aware at all times that I have a toothache. I'm no longer the hero I wanted to pass for earlier, but simply a nasty little man, a rogue. So be it! I'm delighted that you've seen through me. Does it make you feel bad to hear my wretched little moans? Well, then, feel bad. Now let me add an even nastier flourish. . . ." You still don't understand, gentlemen? No, it's clear that one has to develop further and become even more conscious in order to understand all the nuances of this voluptuousness! Are you laughing? I'm delighted. Of course my jokes are in bad taste, gentlemen; they're uneven, contradictory, and lacking in self-assurance. But that's because I have no respect for myself. Can a man possessing consciousness ever really respect himself?

V

Well, and is it possible, is it really possible for a man to respect himself if he even presumes to find enjoyment in the feeling of his own humiliation? I'm not saying this out of any feigned repentance. In general I could never bear to say: "I'm sorry, Daddy, and I won't do it again," not because I was incapable of saying it, but, on the contrary, perhaps precisely because I was all too capable, and how! As if on purpose it would happen that I'd get myself into some sort of mess for which I was not to blame in any way whatsoever. That was the most repulsive part of it. What's more, I'd feel touched deep in my soul; I'd repent and shed tears, deceiving even myself of course, though not feigning in the least. It seemed that my heart was somehow playing dirty tricks on me. . . . Here one couldn't even blame the laws of nature, although it was these very laws that continually hurt me during my entire life. It's disgusting to recall all this, and it was disgusting even then. Of course, a moment or so later I would realize in anger that it was all lies, lies, revolting, made-up lies, that is, all that repentance, all that tenderness, all those vows to mend my ways. But you'll ask why I mauled and tortured myself in that way? The answer is because it was so very boring to sit idly by with my arms folded; so I'd get into trouble. That's the way it was. Observe yourselves better, gentlemen; then you'll understand that it's true. I used to think up adventures for myself, inventing a life so that at least I could live. How many times did it happen, well, let's say, for example, that I took offense, deliberately, for no reason at all? All the while I knew there was no reason for it; I put on airs nonetheless, and would take it so far that finally I really did feel offended. I've been drawn into such silly tricks all my life, so that finally I lost control over myself. Another time, even twice, I tried hard to fall in love. I even suffered, gentlemen, I can assure you. In the depths of my soul I really didn't believe that I was suffering; there was a stir of mockery, but suffer I did, and in a genuine, normal way at that; I was jealous, I was beside myself with anger. . . . And all as a result of boredom, gentlemen, sheer boredom; I was overcome by inertia. You see, the direct, legitimate, immediate result of consciousness is inertia, that is, the conscious sitting idly by with one's arms folded. I've referred to this before. I repeat, I repeat emphatically: all spontaneous men and men of action are so active precisely because they're stupid and limited. How can one explain this? Here's how: as a result of their limitations they mistake immediate and secondary causes for primary ones, and thus they're convinced more quickly and easily than other people that they've located an indisputable basis for action, and this puts them at ease; that's the main point. For, in order to begin to act, one must first be absolutely at ease, with no lingering doubts whatsoever. Well, how can I, for example, ever feel at ease? Where are the primary causes I can rely upon, where's the foundation? Where shall I find it? I exercise myself in thinking, and consequently, with me every primary cause drags in another, an even more primary one, and so on to infinity. This is precisely the essence of all consciousness and thought. And here again, it must be the laws of nature. What's the final result? Why, the very same thing. Remember: I was talking about revenge before. (You probably didn't follow.) I said: a man takes revenge because he finds justice in it. That means, he's found a primary cause, a foundation: namely, justice. Therefore, he's completely at ease, and, as a result, he takes revenge peacefully and successfully, convinced that he's performing an honest and just deed. But I don't see any justice here at all, nor do I find any virtue in it whatever; consequently, if I begin to take revenge, it's only out of spite. Of course, spite could overcome everything, all my doubts, and therefore could successfully serve instead of a primary cause precisely because it's not a cause at all. But what do I do if I don't even feel spite (that's where I began before)? After all, as a result of those damned laws of consciousness, my spite is subject to chemical disintegration. You look—and the object vanishes, the arguments evaporate, a guilty party can't be identified, the offense ceases to be one and becomes a matter of fate, something like a toothache for which no one's to blame, and, as a consequence, there remains only the same recourse: that is, to bash the wall even harder. So you throw up your hands because you haven't found a primary cause. Just try to let yourself be carried away blindly by your feelings, without reflection, without a primary cause, suppressing consciousness even for a moment; hate or love, anything, just in order not to sit idly by with your arms folded. The day after tomorrow at the very latest, you'll begin to despise yourself for having deceived yourself knowingly. The result: a soap bubble and inertia. Oh, gentlemen, perhaps I consider myself to be an intelligent man simply because for my whole life I haven't been able to begin or finish anything. All right, suppose I am a babbler, a harmless, annoying babbler, like the rest of us. But then what is to be done[9] if the direct and single vocation of every intelligent man consists in babbling, that is, in deliberately talking in endless circles?

VI

Oh, if only I did nothing simply as a result of laziness. Lord, how I'd respect myself then. I'd respect myself precisely because at least I'd be capable of being lazy; at least I'd possess one more or less positive trait of which I could be certain. Question: who am I? Answer: a sluggard. Why, it would have been very pleasant to hear that said about oneself. It would mean that I'd been positively identified; it would mean that there was something to be said about me. "A sluggard!" Why, that's a calling and a vocation, a whole career! Don't joke, it's true. Then, by rights I'd be a member of the very best club and would occupy myself exclusively by being able to respect myself continually. I knew a gentleman who prided himself all his life on being a connoisseur of Lafite.[1] He considered it his positive virtue and never doubted himself. He died not merely with a clean conscience, but with a triumphant one, and he was absolutely correct. I should have chosen a career for myself too: I would have been a sluggard and a glutton, not an ordinary one, but one who, for example, sympathized with everything beautiful and sublime. How do you like that? I've dreamt about it for a long time. The "beautiful and sublime" have been a real pain in the neck during my forty years, but then it's been *my* forty years, whereas then—oh, then it would have been otherwise! I would've found myself a suitable activity at once—namely, drinking to everything beautiful and sublime. I would have seized upon every opportunity first to shed a tear into my glass and then drink to everything beautiful and sublime. Then I would have turned everything into the beautiful and sublime; I would have sought out the beautiful and sublime in the nastiest, most indisputable trash. I would have become as tearful as a wet sponge. An artist, for example, has painted a portrait of Ge.[2] At once I drink to the artist who painted that portrait of Ge because I love everything beautiful and sublime. An author has written the words, "Just as you please,"[3] at once I drink to "Just as you please," because I love everything "beautiful and sublime." I'd demand respect for myself in doing this, I'd persecute anyone who didn't pay me any respect. I'd live peacefully and die triumphantly—why, it's charming, perfectly charming! And what a belly I'd have grown by then, what a triple chin I'd have acquired, what a red nose I'd have developed—so that just looking at me any passerby would have said, "Now that's a real plus! That's something really positive!" Say what you like, gentlemen, it's extremely pleasant to hear such comments in our negative age.

---

9. An oblique reference to the controversial novel by Nikolai Chernyshevsky (1828–1889) titled *What Is to Be Done?* (1863). *Notes from Underground* is in part Dostoevsky's polemical response to it.   1. A variety of red wine from Médoc in France.   2. N. N. Ge (1831–1894), Russian artist, whose painting *The Last Supper* was displayed in St. Petersburg during the spring of 1863 and provoked considerable controversy. 3. An attack on the writer M. E. Saltykov-Shchedrin, who published a sympathetic review of Ge's painting titled *Just As You Please*.

VII

But these are all golden dreams. Oh, tell me who was first to announce, first to proclaim that man does nasty things simply because he doesn't know his own true interest; and that if he were to be enlightened, if his eyes were to be opened to his true, normal interests, he would stop doing nasty things at once and would immediately become good and noble, because, being so enlightened and understanding his real advantage, he would realize that his own advantage really did lie in the good; and that it's well known that there's not a single man capable of acting knowingly against his own interest; consequently, he would, so to speak, begin to do good out of necessity. Oh, the child! Oh, the pure, innocent babe! Well, in the first place, when was it during all these millennia, that man has ever acted only in his own self interest? What does one do with the millions of facts bearing witness to the one fact that people knowingly, that is, possessing full knowledge of their own true interests, have relegated them to the background and have rushed down a different path, that of risk and chance, compelled by no one and nothing, but merely as if they didn't want to follow the beaten track, and so they stubbornly, willfully forged another way, a difficult and absurd one, searching for it almost in the darkness? Why, then, this means that stubbornness and willfulness were really more pleasing to them than any kind of advantage. . . . Advantage! What is advantage? Will you take it upon yourself to define with absolute precision what constitutes man's advantage? And what if it turns out that man's advantage sometimes not only may, but even must in certain circumstances, consist precisely in his desiring something harmful to himself instead of something advantageous? And if this is so, if this can ever occur, then the whole theory falls to pieces. What do you think, can such a thing happen? You're laughing; laugh, gentlemen, but answer me: have man's advantages ever been calculated with absolute certainty? Aren't there some which don't fit, can't be made to fit into any classification? Why, as far as I know, you gentlemen have derived your list of human advantages from averages of statistical data and from scientific-economic formulas. But your advantages are prosperity, wealth, freedom, peace, and so on and so forth; so that a man who, for example, expressly and knowingly acts in opposition to this whole list, would be, in your opinion, and in mine, too, of course, either an obscurantist or a complete madman, wouldn't he? But now here's what's astonishing: why is it that when all these statisticians, sages, and lovers of humanity enumerate man's advantages, they invariably leave one out? They don't even take it into consideration in the form in which it should be considered, although the entire calculation depends upon it. There would be no great harm in considering it, this advantage, and adding it to the list. But the whole point is that this particular advantage doesn't fit into any classification and can't be found on any list. I have a friend, for instance. . . . But gentlemen! Why, he's your friend, too! In fact, he's everyone's friend! When he's preparing to do something, this gentleman straight away explains to you eloquently and clearly just how he must act according to the laws of nature and truth. And that's not all: with excitement and passion he'll tell you all about genuine, normal human interests; with scorn he'll reproach the shortsighted fools who understand neither their own advantage nor the real meaning of virtue; and then—exactly a quarter of an hour later, without any sudden outside cause, but precisely because of something internal that's stronger than all his interests—he does a complete about-face; that is, he does something which clearly contradicts what he's been saying: it goes against the laws of reason and his own advantage, in a word, against everything. . . . I warn you that my friend is a collective personage; therefore it's rather difficult to blame only him. That's just it, gentlemen; in fact, isn't there something dearer to every man than his own best advantage, or (so as not to violate the rules of logic) isn't there one more advantageous advantage (exactly the one omitted, the one we mentioned before), which is more important and more advantageous than all others and, on behalf of which, a man will, if necessary, go against all laws, that is, against reason, honor, peace, and prosperity—in a word, against all those splendid and useful things, merely in order to attain this fundamental, most advantageous advantage which is dearer to him than everything else?

"Well, it's advantage all the same," you say, interrupting me. Be so kind as to allow me to explain further; besides, the point is not my pun, but the fact that this advantage is remarkable precisely because it destroys all our classifications and constantly demolishes all systems devised by lovers of humanity for the happiness of mankind. In a word, it interferes with everything. But, before I name this advantage, I want to compromise myself personally; therefore I boldly declare that all these splendid systems, all these theories to explain to mankind its real, normal interests so that, by necessarily striving to achieve them, it would immediately become good and noble—are, for the time being, in my opinion, nothing more than logical exercises! Yes, sir, logical exercises! Why, even to maintain a theory of mankind's regeneration through a system of its own advantages, why, in my opinion, that's almost the same as . . . well, claiming, for instance, following Buckle,[4] that man has become kinder as a result of civilization; consequently, he's becoming less bloodthirsty and less inclined to war. Why, logically it all even seems to follow. But man is so partial to systems and abstract conclusions that he's ready to distort the truth intentionally, ready to deny everything that he himself has ever seen and heard, merely in order to justify his own logic. That's why I take this example, because it's such a glaring one. Just look around: rivers of blood are being spilt, and in the most cheerful way, as if it were champagne. Take this entire nineteenth century of ours during which even Buckle lived. Take Napoleon—both the great and the present one.[5] Take North America—that eternal union.[6] Take, finally, that ridiculous Schleswig-Holstein[7]. . . . What is it that civilization makes kinder in us? Civilization merely promotes a wider variety of sensations in man and . . . absolutely nothing else. And through the development of this variety man may even reach the point where he takes pleasure in spilling blood. Why, that's even happened to him already. Haven't you noticed that the most refined bloodshedders are almost always the most civilized gentlemen to

---

4. In his *History of Civilization in England* (1857–61), Henry Thomas Buckle (1821–1862) argued that the development of civilization necessarily leads to the cessation of war. Russia had recently been involved in fierce fighting in the Crimea (1853–56).   5. The French emperors Napoleon I (1769–1821) and his nephew Napoleon III (1808–1873), both of whom engaged in numerous wars, though on vastly different scales.   6. The United States was in the middle of its Civil War (1861–65).   7. The German duchies of Schleswig and Holstein, held by Denmark since 1773, were reunited with Prussia after a brief war in 1864.

whom all these Attila the Huns and Stenka Razins[8] are scarcely fit to hold a candle; and if they're not as conspicuous as Attila and Stenka Razin, it's precisely because they're too common and have become too familiar to us. At least if man hasn't become more bloodthirsty as a result of civilization, surely he's become bloodthirsty in a nastier, more repulsive way than before. Previously man saw justice in bloodshed and exterminated whomever he wished with a clear conscience; whereas now, though we consider bloodshed to be abominable, we nevertheless engage in this abomination even more than before. Which is worse? Decide for yourselves. They say that Cleopatra (forgive an example from Roman history) loved to stick gold pins into the breasts of her slave girls and take pleasure in their screams and writhing. You'll say that this took place, relatively speaking, in barbaric times; that these are barbaric times too, because (also comparatively speaking), gold pins are used even now; that even now, although man has learned on occasion to see more clearly than in barbaric times, *he's still far from having learned* how to act in accordance with the dictates of reason and science. Nevertheless, you're still absolutely convinced that he will learn how to do so, as soon as he gets rid of some bad, old habits and as soon as common sense and science have completely re-educated human nature and have turned it in the proper direction. You're convinced that then man will voluntarily stop committing blunders, and that he will, so to speak, never willingly set his own will in opposition to his own normal interests. More than that: then, you say, science itself will teach man (though, in my opinion, that's already a luxury) that in fact he possesses neither a will nor any whim of his own, that he never did, and that he himself is nothing more than a kind of piano key or an organ stop;[9] that, moreover, there still exist laws of nature, so that everything he's done has been not in accordance with his own desire, but in and of itself, according to the laws of nature. Consequently, we need only discover these laws of nature, and man will no longer have to answer for his own actions and will find it extremely easy to live. All human actions, it goes without saying, will then be tabulated according to these laws, mathematically, like tables of logarithms up to 108,000, and will be entered on a schedule; or even better, certain edifying works will be published, like our contemporary encyclopedic dictionaries, in which everything will be accurately calculated and specified so that there'll be no more actions or adventures left on earth.

At that time, it's still you speaking, new economic relations will be established, all ready-made, also calculated with mathematical precision, so that all possible questions will disappear in a single instant, simply because all possible answers will have been provided. Then the crystal palace[1] will be built. And then . . . Well, in a word, those will be our halcyon days. Of course, there's no way to guarantee (now this is me talking) that it won't be, for instance, terribly boring then (because there won't be anything left to do,

8. Cossack leader (d. 1671) who organized a peasant rebellion in Russia. Attila (406?–453 A.D.), king of the Huns, who conducted devastating wars against the Roman emperors.   9. A reference to the last discourse of the French philosopher Denis Diderot (1713–1784) in the *Conversation of D'Alembert and Diderot* (1769).   1. An allusion to the crystal palace described in Vera Pavlovna's fourth dream in Chernyshevsky's *What Is to Be Done?* and to the actual building designed by Sir Joseph Paxton, erected for the Great Exhibition in London in 1851 and at that time admired as the newest wonder of architecture; Dostoevsky described it in *Winter Notes on Summer Impressions* (1863).

once everything has been calculated according to tables); on the other hand, everything will be extremely rational. Of course, what don't people think up out of boredom! Why, even gold pins get stuck into other people out of boredom, but that wouldn't matter. What's really bad (this is me talking again) is that for all I know, people might even be grateful for those gold pins. For man is stupid, phenomenally stupid. That is, although he's not really stupid at all, he's really so ungrateful that it's hard to find another being quite like him. Why, I, for example, wouldn't be surprised in the least, if, suddenly, for no reason at all, in the midst of this future, universal rationalism, some gentleman with an offensive, rather, a retrograde and derisive expression on his face were to stand up, put his hands on his hips, and declare to us all: "How about it, gentlemen, what if we knock over all this rationalism with one swift kick for the sole purpose of sending all these logarithms to hell, so that once again we can live according to our own stupid will!" But that wouldn't matter either; what's so annoying is that he would undoubtedly find some followers; such is the way man is made. And all because of the most foolish reason, which, it seems, is hardly worth mentioning: namely, that man, always and everywhere, whoever he is, has preferred to act as he wished, and not at all as reason and advantage have dictated; one might even desire something opposed to one's own advantage, and sometimes (this is now my idea) one *positively must do so*. One's very own free, unfettered desire, one's own whim, no matter how wild, one's own fantasy, even though sometimes roused to the point of madness—all this constitutes precisely that previously omitted, most advantageous advantage which isn't included under any classification and because of which all systems and theories are constantly smashed to smithereens. Where did these sages ever get the idea that man needs any normal, virtuous desire? How did they ever imagine that man needs any kind of rational, advantageous desire? Man needs only one thing—his own *independent* desire, whatever that independence might cost and wherever it might lead. And as far as desire goes, the devil only knows. . . .

VIII

"Ha, ha, ha! But in reality even this desire, if I may say so, doesn't exist!" you interrupt me with a laugh. "Why science has already managed to dissect man so now we know that desire and so-called free choice are nothing more than . . ."

Wait, gentlemen, I myself wanted to begin like that. I must confess that even I got frightened. I was just about to declare that the devil only knows what desire depends on and perhaps we should be grateful for that, but then I remembered about science and I . . . stopped short. But now you've gone and brought it up. Well, after all, what if someday they really do discover the formula for all our desires and whims, that is, the thing that governs them, precise laws that produce them, how exactly they're applied, where they lead in each and every case, and so on and so forth, that is, the genuine mathematical formula—why, then all at once man might stop desiring, yes, indeed, he probably would. Who would want to desire according to some table? And that's not all: he would immediately be transformed from a person into an organ stop or something of that sort; because what is man without desire, without will, and without wishes if not a stop in an organ pipe? What do you think? Let's consider the probabilities—can this really happen or not?

"Hmmm . . . ," you decide, "our desires are mistaken for the most part because of an erroneous view of our own advantage. Consequently, we sometimes desire pure rubbish because, in our own stupidity, we consider it the easiest way to achieve some previously assumed advantage. Well, and when all this has been analyzed, calculated on paper (that's entirely possible, since it's repugnant and senseless to assume in advance that man will never come to understand the laws of nature) then, of course, all so-called desires will no longer exist. For if someday desires are completely reconciled with reason, we'll follow reason instead of desire simply because it would be impossible, for example, while retaining one's reason, to *desire* rubbish, and thus knowingly oppose one's reason, and desire something harmful to oneself. . . . And, since all desires and reasons can really be tabulated, since someday the laws of our so-called free choice are sure to be discovered, then, all joking aside, it may be possible to establish something like a table, so that we could actually desire according to it. If, for example, someday they calculate and demonstrate to me that I made a rude gesture because I couldn't possibly refrain from it, that I had to make precisely that gesture, well, in that case, what sort of *free choice* would there be, especially if I'm a learned man and have completed a course of study somewhere? Why, then I'd be able to calculate in advance my entire life for the next thirty years; in a word, if such a table were to be drawn up, there'd be nothing left for us to do; we'd simply have to accept it. In general, we should be repeating endlessly to ourselves that at such a time and in such circumstances nature certainly won't ask our opinion; that we must accept it as is, and not as we fantasize it, and that if we really aspire to prepare a table, a schedule, and, well . . . well, even a laboratory test tube, there's nothing to be done—one must even accept the test tube! If not, it'll be accepted even without you. . . ."

Yes, but that's just where I hit a snag! Gentlemen, you'll excuse me for all this philosophizing; it's a result of my forty years in the underground! Allow me to fantasize. Don't you see: reason is a fine thing, gentlemen, there's no doubt about it, but it's only reason, and it satisfies only man's rational faculty, whereas desire is a manifestation of all life, that is, of all human life, which includes both reason, as well as all of life's itches and scratches. And although in this manifestation life often turns out to be fairly worthless, it's life all the same, and not merely the extraction of square roots. Why, take me, for instance; I quite naturally want to live in order to satisfy all my faculties of life, not merely my rational faculty, that is, some one-twentieth of all my faculties. What does reason know? Reason knows only what it's managed to learn. (Some things it may never learn; while this offers no comfort, why not admit it openly?) But human nature acts as a whole, with all that it contains, consciously and unconsciously; and although it may tell lies, it's still alive. I suspect, gentlemen, that you're looking at me with compassion; you repeat that an enlightened and cultured man, in a word, man as he will be in the future, cannot knowingly desire something disadvantageous to himself, and that this is pure mathematics. I agree with you: it really is mathematics. But I repeat for the one-hundredth time, there is one case, only one, when a man may intentionally, consciously desire even something harmful to himself, something stupid, even very stupid, namely: in order *to have the right* to desire something even very stupid and not be bound by an obligation to desire only what's smart. After all, this very stupid thing, one's own whim, gentlemen, may in fact be the most advantageous thing on earth for people like me, especially in certain cases. In particular, it may be more advantageous than any other advantage, even in a case where it causes obvious harm and contradicts the most sensible conclusions of reason about advantage—because in any case it preserves for us what's most important and precious, that is, our personality and our individuality. There are some people who maintain that in fact this is more precious to man than anything else; of course, desire can, if it so chooses, coincide with reason, especially if it doesn't abuse this option, and chooses to coincide in moderation; this is useful and sometimes even commendable. But very often, even most of the time, desire absolutely and stubbornly disagrees with reason and . . . and . . . and, do you know, sometimes this is also useful and even very commendable? Let's assume, gentlemen, that man isn't stupid. (And really, this can't possibly be said about him at all, if only because if he's stupid, then who on earth is smart?) But even if he's not stupid, he is, nevertheless, monstrously ungrateful. Phenomenally ungrateful. I even believe that the best definition of man is this: a creature who walks on two legs and is ungrateful. But that's still not all; that's still not his main defect. His main defect is his perpetual misbehavior, perpetual from the time of the Great Flood to the Schleswig-Holstein period of human destiny. Misbehavior, and consequently, imprudence; for it's long been known that imprudence results from nothing else but misbehavior. Just cast a glance at the history of mankind; well, what do you see? Is it majestic? Well, perhaps it's majestic; why, the Colossus of Rhodes,[2] for example—that alone is worth something! Not without reason did Mr Anaevsky[3] report that some people consider it to be the product of human hands, while others maintain that it was created by nature itself. Is it colorful? Well, perhaps it's also colorful; just consider the dress uniforms, both military and civilian, of all nations at all times—why, that alone is worth something, and if you include everyday uniforms, it'll make your eyes bulge; not one historian will be able to sort it all out. Is it monotonous? Well, perhaps it's monotonous, too: men fight and fight; now they're fighting; they fought first and they fought last—you'll agree that it's really much too monotonous. In short, anything can be said about world history, anything that might occur to the most disordered imagination. There's only one thing that can't possibly be said about it—that it's rational. You'll choke on the word. Yet here's just the sort of thing you'll encounter all the time: why, in life you're constantly running up against people who are so well-behaved and so rational, such wise men and lovers of humanity who set themselves the lifelong goal of behaving as morally and rationally as possible, so to speak, to be a beacon for their nearest and dearest, simply in order to prove that it's really possible to live one's life in a moral and rational way. And so what? It's a well-known fact that many of these lovers of humanity, sooner or later, by the end of their lives, have betrayed themselves: they've pulled off some caper, sometimes even quite an indecent one. Now I ask

2. A large bronze statue of the sun god, Helios, built between 292 and 280 B.C. in the harbor of Rhodes (an island in the Aegean Sea) and considered one of the Seven Wonders of the Ancient World.   3. A. E. Anaevsky was a critic whose articles were frequently ridiculed in literary polemics of the period.

you: what can one expect from man as a creature endowed with such strange qualities? Why, shower him with all sorts of earthly blessings, submerge him in happiness over his head so that only little bubbles appear on the surface of this happiness, as if on water, give him such economic prosperity that he'll have absolutely nothing left to do except sleep, eat gingerbread, and worry about the continuation of world history—even then, out of pure ingratitude, sheer perversity, he'll commit some repulsive act. He'll even risk losing his gingerbread, and will intentionally desire the most wicked rubbish, the most uneconomical absurdity, simply in order to inject his own pernicious fantastic element into all this positive rationality. He wants to hold onto those most fantastic dreams, his own indecent stupidity solely for the purpose of assuring himself (as if it were necessary) that men are still men and not piano keys, and that even if the laws of nature play upon them with their own hands, they're still threatened by being overplayed until they won't possibly desire anything more than a schedule. But that's not all: even if man really turned out to be a piano key, even if this could be demonstrated to him by natural science and pure mathematics, even then he still won't become reasonable; he'll intentionally do something to the contrary, simply out of ingratitude, merely to have his own way. If he lacks the means, he'll cause destruction and chaos, he'll devise all kinds of suffering and have his own way! He'll leash a curse upon the world; and, since man alone can do so (it's his privilege and the thing that most distinguishes him from other animals), perhaps only through this curse will he achieve his goal, that is, become really convinced that he's a man and not a piano key! If you say that one can also calculate all this according to a table, this chaos and darkness, these curses, so that the mere possibility of calculating it all in advance would stop everything and that reason alone would prevail—in that case man would go insane deliberately in order not to have reason, but to have his own way! I believe this, I vouch for it, because, after all, the whole of man's work seems to consist only in proving to himself constantly that he's a man and not an organ stop! Even if he has to lose his own skin, he'll prove it; even if he has to become a troglodyte, he'll prove it. And after that, how can one not sin, how can one not praise the fact that all this hasn't yet come to pass and that desire still depends on the devil knows what . . . ?

You'll shout at me (if you still choose to favor me with your shouts) that no one's really depriving me of my will; that they're merely attempting to arrange things so that my will, by its own free choice, will coincide with my normal interests, with the laws of nature, and with arithmetic.

But gentlemen, what sort of free choice will there be when it comes down to tables and arithmetic, when all that's left is two times two makes four? Two times two makes four even without my will. Is that what you call free choice?

IX

Gentlemen, I'm joking of course, and I myself know that it's not a very good joke; but, after all, you can't take everything as a joke. Perhaps I'm gnashing my teeth while I joke. I'm tormented by questions, gentlemen; answer them for me. Now, for example, you want to cure man of his old habits and improve his will according to the demands of science and common sense. But how do you know not only whether it's possible, but even if it's *necessary* to remake him in this way? Why do you conclude that human desire *must* undoubtedly be improved? In short, how do you know that such improvement will really be to man's advantage? And, to be perfectly frank, why are you so *absolutely* convinced that not to oppose man's real, normal advantage guaranteed by the conclusions of reason and arithmetic is really always to man's advantage and constitutes a law for all humanity? After all, this is still only an assumption of yours. Let's suppose that it's a law of logic, but perhaps not a law of humanity. Perhaps, gentlemen, you're wondering if I'm insane? Allow me to explain. I agree that man is primarily a creative animal, destined to strive consciously toward a goal and to engage in the art of engineering, that, is, externally and incessantly building new roads for himself *wherever they lead*. But sometimes he may want to swerve aside precisely because he's *compelled* to build these roads, and perhaps also because, no matter how stupid the spontaneous man of action may generally be, nevertheless it sometimes occurs to him that the road, as it turns out, almost always leads *somewhere or other*, and that the main thing isn't so much where it goes, but the fact that it does, and that the well-behaved child, disregarding the art of engineering, shouldn't yield to pernicious idleness which, as is well known, constitutes the mother of all vices. Man loves to create and build roads; that's indisputable. But why is he also so passionately fond of destruction and chaos? Now, then, tell me. But I myself want to say a few words about this separately. Perhaps the reason that he's so fond of destruction and chaos (after all, it's indisputable that he sometimes really loves it, and that's a fact) is that he himself has an instinctive fear of achieving his goal and completing the project under construction? How do you know if perhaps he loves his building only from afar, but not from close up; perhaps he only likes building it, but not living in it, leaving it afterward *aux animaux domestiques*,[4] such as ants or sheep, or so on and so forth. Now ants have altogether different tastes. They have one astonishing structure of a similar type, forever indestructible—the anthill.

The worthy ants began with the anthill, and most likely, they will end with the anthill, which does great credit to their perseverance and steadfastness. But man is a frivolous and unseemly creature and perhaps, like a chess player, he loves only the process of achieving his goal, and not the goal itself. And, who knows (one can't vouch for it), perhaps the only goal on earth toward which mankind is striving consists merely in this incessant process of achieving or to put it another way, in life itself, and not particularly in the goal which, of course, must always be none other than two times two makes four, that is, a formula; after all, two times two makes four is no longer life, gentlemen, but the beginning of death. At least man has always been somewhat afraid of this two times two makes four, and I'm afraid of it now, too. Let's suppose that the only thing man does is search for this two times two makes four; he sails across oceans, sacrifices his own life in the quest; but to seek it out and find it—really and truly, he's very frightened. After all, he feels that as soon as he finds it, there'll be nothing left to search for. Workers, after finishing work, at least receive their wages, go off to a tavern, and then wind up at a police station—now that's a full week's occupation. But where

4. To domestic animals (French).

will man go? At any rate a certain awkwardness can be observed each time he approaches the achievement of similar goals. He loves the process, but he's not so fond of the achievement, and that, of course is terribly amusing. In short, man is made in a comical way; obviously there's some sort of catch in all this. But two times two makes four is an insufferable thing, nevertheless. Two times two makes four—why, in my opinion, it's mere insolence. Two times two makes four stands there brazenly with its hands on its hips, blocking your path and spitting at you. I agree that two times two makes four is a splendid thing; but if we're going to lavish praise, then two times two makes five is sometimes also a very charming little thing.

And why are you so firmly, so triumphantly convinced that only the normal and positive—in short, only well-being is advantageous to man? Doesn't reason ever make mistakes about advantage? After all, perhaps man likes something other than well-being? Perhaps he loves suffering just as much? Perhaps suffering is just as advantageous to him as well-being? Man sometimes loves suffering terribly, to the point of passion, and that's a fact. There's no reason to study world history on this point; if indeed you're a man and have lived at all, just ask yourself. As far as my own personal opinion is concerned, to love only well-being is somehow even indecent. Whether good or bad, it's sometimes also very pleasant to demolish something. After all, I'm not standing up for suffering here, nor for well-being, either. I'm standing up for . . . my own whim and for its being guaranteed to me whenever necessary. For instance, suffering is not permitted in vaudevilles,[5] that I know. It's also inconceivable in the crystal palace; suffering is doubt and negation. What sort of crystal palace would it be if any doubt were allowed? Yet, I'm convinced that man will never renounce real suffering, that is, destruction and chaos. After all, suffering is the sole cause of consciousness. Although I stated earlier that in my opinion consciousness is man's greatest misfortune, still I know that man loves it and would not exchange it for any other sort of satisfaction. Consciousness, for example, is infinitely higher than two times two. Of course, after two times two, there's nothing left, not merely nothing to do, but nothing to learn. Then the only thing possible will be to plug up your five senses and plunge into contemplation. Well, even if you reach the same result with consciousness, that is, having nothing left to do, at least you'll be able to flog yourself from time to time, and that will liven things up a bit. Although it may be reactionary, it's still better than nothing.

X[6]

You believe in the crystal palace, eternally indestructible, that is, one at which you can never stick out your tongue furtively nor make a rude gesture, even with your fist hidden away. Well, perhaps I'm so afraid of this building precisely because it's made of crystal and it's eternally indestructible, and because it won't be possible to stick one's tongue out even furtively.

Don't you see: if it were a chicken coop instead of a palace, and if it should rain, then perhaps I could crawl into it so as not to get drenched; but I would still not mistake a chicken coop for a palace out of gratitude, just because it

---

5. A dramatic genre, popular on the Russian stage, consisting of scenes from contemporary life acted with a satirical twist, often in racy dialogue.   6. This chapter was badly mutilated by the censor, as Dostoevsky makes clear in the letter to his brother Mikhail, dated March 26, 1864 (see p. 1305).

sheltered me from the rain. You're laughing, you're even saying that in this case there's no difference between a chicken coop and a mansion. Yes, I reply, if the only reason for living is to keep from getting drenched.

But what if I've taken it into my head that this is not the only reason for living, and, that if one is to live at all, one might as well live in a mansion? Such is my wish, my desire. You'll expunge it from me only when you've changed my desires. Well, then, change them, tempt me with something else, give me some other ideal. In the meantime, I still won't mistake a chicken coop for a palace. But let's say that the crystal palace is a hoax, that according to the laws of nature it shouldn't exist, and that I've invented it only out of my own stupidity, as a result of certain antiquated, irrational habits of my generation. But what do I care if it doesn't exist? What difference does it make if it exists only in my own desires, or, to be more precise, if it exists as long as my desires exist? Perhaps you're laughing again? Laugh, if you wish; I'll resist all your laughter and I still won't say I'm satiated if I'm really hungry; I know all the same that I won't accept a compromise, an infinitely recurring zero, just because it exists according to the laws of nature and it *really* does exist. I won't accept as the crown of my desires a large building with tenements for poor tenants to be rented for a thousand years and, just in case, with the name of the dentist Wagenheim on the sign. Destroy my desires, eradicate my ideals, show me something better and I'll follow you. You may say, perhaps, that it's not worth getting involved; but, in that case, I'll say the same thing in reply. We're having a serious discussion; if you don't grant me your attention, I won't grovel for it. I still have my underground.

And, as long as I'm still alive and feel desire—may my arm wither away before it contributes even one little brick to that building! Never mind that I myself have just rejected the crystal palace for the sole reason that it won't be possible to tease it by sticking out one's tongue at it. I didn't say that because I'm so fond of sticking out my tongue. Perhaps the only reason I got angry is that among all your buildings there's still not a single one where you don't feel compelled to stick out your tongue. On the contrary, I'd let my tongue be cut off out of sheer gratitude, if only things could be so arranged that I'd no longer want to stick it out. What do I care if things can't be so arranged and if I must settle for some tenements? Why was I made with such desires? Can it be that I was made this way only in order to reach the conclusion that my entire way of being is merely a fraud? Can this be the whole purpose? I don't believe it.

By the way, do you know what? I'm convinced that we underground men should be kept in check. Although capable of sitting around quietly in the underground for some forty years, once he emerges into the light of day and bursts into speech, he talks on and on and on. . . .

XI

The final result, gentlemen, is that it's better to do nothing! Conscious inertia is better! And so, long live the underground! Even though I said that I envy the normal man to the point of exasperation, I still wouldn't want to be him under the circumstances in which I see him (although I still won't keep from envying him. No, no, in any case the underground is more advantageous!) At least there one can . . . Hey, but I'm lying once again! I'm lying because I know myself as surely as two times two, that it isn't really the underground that's better, but something different, altogether different, something that I long for, but I'll never be able to find! To hell with the underground! Why, here's what would be better: if I myself were to believe even a fraction of everything I've written. I swear to you, gentlemen, that I don't believe one word, not one little word of all that I've scribbled. That is, I do believe it, perhaps, but at the very same time, I don't know why, I feel and suspect that I'm lying like a trooper.

"Then why did you write all this?" you ask me.

"What if I'd shut you up in the underground for forty years with nothing to do and then came back forty years later to see what had become of you? Can a man really be left alone for forty years with nothing to do?"

"Isn't it disgraceful, isn't it humiliating!" you might say, shaking your head in contempt. "You long for life, but you try to solve life's problems by means of a logical tangle. How importunate, how insolent your outbursts, and how frightened you are at the same time! You talk rubbish, but you're constantly afraid of them and make apologies. You maintain that you fear nothing, but at the same time you try to ingratiate yourself with us. You assure us that you're gnashing your teeth, yet at the same time you try to be witty and amuse us. You know that your witticisms are not very clever, but apparently you're pleased by their literary merit. Perhaps you really have suffered, but you don't even respect your own suffering. There's some truth in you, too, but no chastity; out of the pettiest vanity you bring your truth out into the open, into the marketplace, and you shame it. . . . You really want to say something, but you conceal your final word out of fear because you lack the resolve to utter it; you have only cowardly impudence. You boast about your consciousness, but you merely vacillate, because even though your mind is working, your heart has been blackened by depravity, and without a pure heart, there can be no full, genuine consciousness. And how importunate you are; how you force yourself upon others; you behave in such an affected manner. Lies, lies, lies!"

Of course, it was I who just invented all these words for you. That, too, comes from the underground. For forty years in a row I've been listening to all your words through a crack. I've invented them myself, since that's all that's occurred to me. It's no wonder that I've learned it all by heart and that it's taken on such a literary form. . . .

But can you really be so gullible as to imagine that I'll print all this and give it to you to read? And here's another problem I have: why do I keep calling you "gentlemen"? Why do I address you as if you really were my readers? Confessions such as the one I plan to set forth here aren't published and given to other people to read. Anyway, I don't possess sufficient fortitude, nor do I consider it necessary to do so. But don't you see, a certain notion has come into my mind, and I wish to realize it at any cost. Here's the point.

Every man has within his own reminiscences certain things he doesn't reveal to anyone, except, perhaps, to his friends. There are also some that he won't reveal even to his friends, only to himself perhaps, and even then, in secret. Finally, there are some which a man is afraid to reveal even to himself; every decent man has accumulated a fair number of such things. In fact, it can even be said that the more decent the man, the more of these things he's accumulated. Anyway, only recently I myself decided to recall some of my earlier adventures; up to now I've always avoided them, even with a certain anxiety. But having decided not only to recall them, but even to write them down, now is when I wish to try an experiment: is it possible to be absolutely honest even with one's own self and not to fear the whole truth? Incidentally, I'll mention that Heine maintains that faithful autobiographies are almost impossible, and that a man is sure to lie about himself.[7] In Heine's opinion, Rousseau, for example, undoubtedly told untruths about himself in his confession and even lied intentionally, out of vanity. I'm convinced that Heine is correct; I understand perfectly well that sometimes it's possible out of vanity alone to impute all sorts of crimes to oneself, and I can even understand what sort of vanity that might be. But Heine was making judgments about a person who confessed to the public. I, however, am writing for myself alone and declare once and for all that if I write as if I were addressing readers, that's only for show, because it's easier for me to write that way. It's a form, simply a form; I shall never have any readers. I've already stated that. . . . I don't want to be restricted in any way by editing my notes. I won't attempt to introduce any order or system. I'll write down whatever comes to mind.

Well, now, for example, someone might seize upon my words and ask me, if you really aren't counting on any readers, why do you make such compacts with yourself, and on paper no less; that is, if you're not going to introduce any order or system, if you're going to write down whatever comes to mind, etc., etc.? Why do you go on explaining? Why do you keep apologizing?

"Well, imagine that," I reply.

This, by the way, contains an entire psychology. Perhaps it's just that I'm a coward. Or perhaps it's that I imagine an audience before me on purpose, so that I behave more decently when I'm writing things down. There may be a thousand reasons.

But here's something else: why is it that I want to write? If it's not for the public, then why can't I simply recall it all in my own mind and not commit it to paper?

Quite so; but somehow it appears more dignified on paper. There's something more impressive about it; I'll be a better judge of myself; the style will be improved. Besides, perhaps I'll actually experience some relief from the process of writing it all down. Today, for example, I'm particularly oppressed by one very old memory from my distant past. It came to me vividly several days ago and since then it's stayed with me, like an annoying musical motif that doesn't want to leave you alone. And yet you must get rid of it. I have hundreds of such memories; but at times a single one emerges from those hundreds and oppresses me. For some reason I believe that if I write it down I can get rid of it. Why not try?

Lastly, I'm bored, and I never do anything. Writing things down actually seems like work. They say that work makes a man become good and honest. Well, at least there's a chance.

It's snowing today, an almost wet, yellow, dull snow. It was snowing yesterday too, a few days ago as well. I think it was apropos of the wet snow

---

7. A reference to the work *On Germany* (1853–54) by the German poet Heinrich Heine (1797–1856), in which on the very first page Heine speaks of Rousseau as lying and inventing disgraceful incidents about himself for his *Confessions*.

that I recalled this episode and now it doesn't want to leave me alone. And so, let it be a tale apropos of wet snow.

II

Apropos of Wet Snow

> When from the darkness of delusion
> I saved your fallen soul
> With ardent words of conviction,
> And, full of profound torment,
> Wringing your hands, you cursed
> The vice that had ensnared you;
> When, punishing by recollection
> Your forgetful conscience,
> You told me the tale
> Of all that had happened before,
> And, suddenly, covering your face,
> Full of shame and horror,
> You tearfully resolved,
> Indignant, shaken . . .
> Etc., etc., etc.
>   From the poetry of N. A. Nekrasov[8]

I

At that time I was only twenty-four years old. Even then my life was gloomy, disordered, and solitary to the point of savagery. I didn't associate with anyone; I even avoided talking, and I retreated further and further into my corner. At work in the office I even tried not to look at anyone; I was aware not only that my colleagues considered me eccentric, but that they always seemed to regard me with a kind of loathing. Sometimes I wondered why it was that no one else thinks that others regard him with loathing. One of our office-workers had a repulsive pock-marked face which even appeared somewhat villainous. It seemed to me that with such a disreputable face I'd never have dared look at anyone. Another man had a uniform so worn that there was a foul smell emanating from him. Yet, neither of these two gentlemen was embarrassed—neither because of his clothes, nor his face, nor in any moral way. Neither one imagined that other people regarded him with loathing; and if either had so imagined, it wouldn't have mattered at all, as long as their supervisor chose not to view him that way. It's perfectly clear to me now, because of my unlimited vanity and the great demands I accordingly made on myself, that I frequently regarded myself with a furious dissatisfaction verging on loathing; as a result, I intentionally ascribed my own view to everyone else. For example, I despised my own face; I considered it hideous, and I even suspected that there was something repulsive in its expression. Therefore, every time I arrived at work, I took pains to behave as independently as possible, so that I couldn't be suspected of any malice, and I tried to assume as noble an expression as possible. "It may not be a handsome face," I thought, "but let it be noble, expressive, and above all,

---

8. A famous Russian poet and editor of radical sympathies (1821–1878). The poem quoted dates from 1845 and is without title. It ends with the lines "And enter my house bold and free / To become its full mistress!"

extremely *intelligent*." But I was agonizingly certain that my face couldn't possibly express all these virtues. Worst of all, I considered it positively stupid. I'd have been reconciled if it had looked intelligent. In fact, I'd even have agreed to have it appear repulsive, on the condition that at the same time people would find my face terribly intelligent.

Of course, I hated all my fellow office-workers from the first to the last and despised every one of them; yet, at the same time it was as if I were afraid of them. Sometimes it happened that I would even regard them as superior to me. At this time these changes would suddenly occur: first I would despise them, then I would regard them as superior to me. A cultured and decent man cannot be vain without making unlimited demands on himself and without hating himself, at times to the point of contempt. But, whether hating them or regarding them as superior, I almost always lowered my eyes when meeting anyone. I even conducted experiments: could I endure someone's gaze? I'd always be the first to lower my eyes. This infuriated me to the point of madness. I slavishly worshipped the conventional in everything external. I embraced the common practice and feared any eccentricity with all my soul. But how could I sustain it? I was morbidly refined, as befits any cultured man of our time. All others resembled one another as sheep in a flock. Perhaps I was the only one in the whole office who constantly thought of himself as a coward and a slave; and I thought so precisely because I was so cultured. But not only did I think so, it actually was so: I was a coward and a slave. I say this without any embarrassment. Every decent man of our time is and must be a coward and a slave. This is his normal condition. I'm deeply convinced of it. This is how he's made and what he's meant to be. And not only at the present time, as the result of some accidental circumstance, but in general at all times, a decent man must be a coward and a slave. This is a law of nature for all decent men on earth. If one of them should happen to be brave about something or other, we shouldn't be comforted or distracted: he'll still lose his nerve about something else. That's the single and eternal way out. Only asses and their mongrels are brave, and even then, only until they come up against a wall. It's not worthwhile paying them any attention because they really don't mean anything at all.

There was one more circumstance tormenting me at that time: no one was like me, and I wasn't like anyone else. "I'm alone," I mused, "and they are *everyone*"; and I sank deep into thought.

From all this it's clear that I was still just a boy.

The exact opposite would also occur. Sometimes I would find it repulsive to go to the office: it reached the point where I would often return home from work ill. Then suddenly, for no good reason at all, a flash of skepticism and indifference would set in (everything came to me in flashes); I would laugh at my own intolerance and fastidiousness, and reproach myself for my *romanticism*. Sometimes I didn't even want to talk to anyone; at other times it reached a point where I not only started talking, but I even thought about striking up a friendship with others. All my fastidiousness would suddenly disappear for no good reason at all. Who knows? Perhaps I never really had any, and it was all affected, borrowed from books. I still haven't answered this question, even up to now. And once I really did become friends with others; I began to visit their houses, play préférance,[9] drink vodka, talk about promotions. . . . But allow me to digress.

We Russians, generally speaking, have never had any of those stupid, transcendent German romantics, or even worse, French romantics, on whom nothing produces any effect whatever: the earth might tremble beneath them, all of France might perish on the barricades, but they remain the same, not even changing for decency's sake; they go on singing their transcendent songs, so to speak, to their dying day, because they're such fools. We here on Russian soil have no fools. It's a well-known fact; that's precisely what distinguishes us from foreigners. Consequently, transcendent natures cannot be found among us in their pure form. That's the result of our "positive" publicists and critics of that period, who hunted for the Kostanzhouglo and the Uncle Pyotr Ivanoviches,[1] foolishly mistaking them for our ideal and slandering our own romantics, considering them to be the same kind of transcendents as one finds in Germany or France. On the contrary, the characteristics of our romantics are absolutely and directly opposed to the transcendent Europeans; not one of those European standards can apply here. (Allow me to use the word "romantic"—it's an old-fashioned little word, well-respected and deserving, familiar to everyone.) The characteristics of our romantics are to understand everything, *to see everything, often to see it much more clearly than our most positive minds*; not to be reconciled with anyone or anything, but, at the same time, not to balk at anything; to circumvent everything, to yield on every point, to treat everyone diplomatically; never to lose sight of some useful, practical goal (an apartment at government expense, a nice pension, a decoration)—to keep an eye on that goal through all his excesses and his volumes of lyrical verse, and, at the same time, to preserve intact the "beautiful and sublime" to the end of their lives; and, incidentally, to preserve themselves as well, wrapped up in cotton like precious jewelry, if only, for example, for the sake of that same "beautiful and sublime." Our romantic has a very broad nature and is the biggest rogue of all, I can assure you of that . . . even by my own experience. Of course, all this is true if the romantic is smart. But what am I saying? A romantic is always smart; I merely wanted to observe that although we've had some romantic fools, they really don't count at all, simply because while still in their prime they would degenerate completely into Germans, and, in order to preserve their precious jewels more comfortably, they'd settle over there, either in Weimar or in the Black Forest. For instance, I genuinely despised my official position and refrained from throwing it over merely out of necessity, because I myself sat there working and received good money for doing it. And, as a result, please note, I still refrained from throwing it over. Our romantic would sooner lose his mind (which, by the way, very rarely occurs) than give it up, if he didn't have another job in mind; nor is he ever kicked out, unless he's hauled off to the insane asylum as the "King of Spain,"[2] and only if he's gone completely mad. Then again, it's really only the weaklings

---

9. A card game for three players.   1. A character in Ivan Goncharov's novel *A Common Story* (1847). He is a high bureaucrat, a factory owner who teaches lessons of sobriety and good sense to the romantic hero, Alexander Aduyev. Konstanzhouglo is the ideal efficient landowner in the second part of Nikolai Gogol's novel *Dead Souls* (1852).   2. An allusion to the hero of Gogol's short story *Diary of a Madman* (1835). Poprishchin, a low-ranking civil servant, sees his aspirations crushed by the enormous bureaucracy. He ends by going insane and imagining himself to be king of Spain.

and towheads who go mad in our country. An enormous number of romantics later rise to significant rank. What extraordinary versatility! And what a capacity for the most contradictory sensations! I used to be consoled by these thoughts back then, and still am even nowadays. That's why there are so many "broad natures" among us, people who never lose their ideals, no matter how low they fall; even though they never lift a finger for the sake of their ideals, even though they're outrageous villains and thieves, nevertheless they respect their original ideals to the point of tears and are extremely honest men at heart. Yes, only among us Russians can the most outrageous scoundrel be absolutely, even sublimely honest at heart, while at the same time never ceasing to be a scoundrel. I repeat, nearly always do our romantics turn out to be very efficient rascals (I use the word "rascal" affectionately); they suddenly manifest such a sense of reality and positive knowledge that their astonished superiors and the general public can only click their tongues at them in amazement.

Their versatility is really astounding; God only knows what it will turn into, how it will develop under subsequent conditions, and what it holds for us in the future. The material is not all that bad! I'm not saying this out of some ridiculous patriotism or jingoism. However, I'm sure that once again you think I'm joking. But who knows? Perhaps it's quite the contrary, that is, you're convinced that this is what I really think. In any case, gentlemen, I'll consider that both of these opinions constitute an honor and a particular pleasure. And do forgive me for this digression.

Naturally, I didn't sustain any friendships with my colleagues, and soon I severed all relations after quarreling with them; and, because of my youthful inexperience at the same time, I even stopped greeting them, as if I'd cut them off entirely. That, however, happened to me only once. On the whole, I was always alone.

At home I spent most of my time reading. I tried to stifle all that was constantly seething within me with external sensations. And of all external sensations available, only reading was possible for me. Of course, reading helped a great deal—it agitated, delighted, and tormented me. But at times it was terribly boring. I still longed to be active; and suddenly I sank into dark, subterranean, loathsome depravity—more precisely, petty vice. My nasty little passions were sharp and painful as a result of my constant, morbid irritability. I experienced hysterical fits accompanied by tears and convulsions. Besides reading, I had nowhere else to go—that is, there was nothing to respect in my surroundings, nothing to attract me. In addition, I was overwhelmed by depression; I possessed a hysterical craving for contradictions and contrasts; and, as a result, I plunged into depravity. I haven't said all this to justify myself. . . . But, no, I'm lying. I did want to justify myself. It's for myself, gentlemen, that I include this little observation. I don't want to lie. I've given my word.

I indulged in depravity all alone, at night, furtively, timidly, sordidly, with a feeling of shame that never left me even in my most loathsome moments and drove me at such times to the point of profanity. Even then I was carrying around the underground in my soul. I was terribly afraid of being seen, met, recognized. I visited all sorts of dismal places.

Once, passing by some wretched little tavern late at night, I saw through a lighted window some gentlemen fighting with billiard cues; one of them was thrown out the window. At some other time I would have been disgusted; but just then I was overcome by such a mood that I envied the gentleman who'd been tossed out; I envied him so much that I even walked into the tavern and entered the billiard room. "Perhaps," I thought, "I'll get into a fight, and they'll throw me out the window, too."

I wasn't drunk, but what could I do—after all, depression can drive a man to this kind of hysteria. But nothing came of it. It turned out that I was incapable of being tossed out the window; I left without getting into a fight.

As soon as I set foot inside, some officer put me in my place.

I was standing next to the billiard table inadvertently blocking his way as he wanted to get by; he took hold of me by the shoulders and without a word of warning or explanation, moved me from where I was standing to another place, and he went past as if he hadn't even noticed me. I could have forgiven even a beating, but I could never forgive his moving me out of the way and entirely failing to notice me.

The devil knows what I would have given for a genuine, ordinary quarrel, a decent one, a more *literary* one, so to speak. But I'd been treated as if I were a fly. The officer was about six feet tall, while I'm small and scrawny. The quarrel, however, was in my hands; all I had to do was protest, and of course they would've thrown me out the window. But I reconsidered and preferred . . . to withdraw resentfully.

I left the tavern confused and upset and went straight home; the next night I continued my petty vice more timidly, more furtively, more gloomily than before, as if I had tears in my eyes—but I continued nonetheless. Don't conclude, however, that I retreated from that officer as a result of any cowardice; I've never been a coward at heart, although I've constantly acted like one in deed, but—wait before you laugh—I can explain this. I can explain anything, you may rest assured.

Oh, if only this officer had been the kind who'd have agreed to fight a duel! But no, he was precisely one of those types (alas, long gone) who preferred to act with their billiard cues or, like Gogol's Lieutenant Pirogov,[3] by appealing to the authorities. They didn't fight duels; in any case, they'd have considered fighting a duel with someone like me, a lowly civilian, to be indecent. In general, they considered duels to be somehow inconceivable, free-thinking, French, while they themselves, especially if they happened to be six feet tall, offended other people rather frequently.

In this case I retreated not out of any cowardice, but because of my unlimited vanity. I wasn't afraid of his height, nor did I think I'd receive a painful beating and get thrown out the window. In fact, I'd have had sufficient physical courage; it was moral fortitude I lacked. I was afraid that everyone present—from the insolent billiard marker to the foul-smelling, pimply little clerks with greasy collars who used to hang about—wouldn't understand and would laugh when I started to protest and speak to them in literary Russian. Because, to this very day, it's still impossible for us to speak about a point of honor, that is, not about honor itself, but a point of honor (*point d'honneur*), except in literary language. One can't even refer to a "point of honor" in everyday language. I was fully convinced (a sense of reality, in spite of all my

---

3. One of two main characters in Gogol's short story *Nevsky Prospect* (1835). A shallow and self-satisfied officer, he mistakes the wife of a German artisan for a woman of easy virtue and receives a sound thrashing. He decides to lodge an official complaint but, after consuming a cream-filled pastry, thinks better of it.

romanticism!) that they would all simply split their sides laughing, and that the officer, instead of giving me a simple beating, that is, an inoffensive one, would certainly apply his knee to my back and drive me around the billiard table; only then perhaps would he have the mercy to throw me out the window. Naturally, this wretched story of mine couldn't possibly end with this alone. Afterward I used to meet this officer frequently on the street and I observed him very carefully. I don't know whether he ever recognized me. Probably not; I reached that conclusion from various observations. As for me, I stared at him with malice and hatred, and continued to do so for several years! My malice increased and became stronger over time. At first I began to make discreet inquiries about him. This was difficult for me to do, since I had so few acquaintances. But once, as I was following him at a distance as though tied to him, someone called to him on the street: that's how I learned his name. Another time I followed him back to his own apartment and for a ten-kopeck piece learned from the doorman where and how he lived, on what floor, with whom, etc.—in a word, all that could be learned from a doorman. One morning, although I never engaged in literary activities, it suddenly occurred to me to draft a description of this officer as a kind of exposé, a caricature, in the form of a tale. I wrote it with great pleasure. I exposed him; I even slandered him. At first I altered his name only slightly, so that it could be easily recognized; but then, upon careful reflection, I changed it. Then I sent the tale off to *Notes of the Fatherland*.[4] But such exposés were no longer in fashion, and they didn't publish my tale. I was very annoyed by that. At times I simply choked on my spite. Finally, I resolved to challenge my opponent to a duel. I composed a beautiful, charming letter to him, imploring him to apologize to me; in case he refused, I hinted rather strongly at a duel. The letter was composed in such a way that if that officer had possessed even the smallest understanding of the "beautiful and sublime," he would have come running, thrown his arms around me, and offered his friendship. That would have been splendid! We would have led such a wonderful life! Such a life! He would have shielded me with his rank; I would have ennobled him with my culture, and, well, with my ideas. Who knows what might have come of it! Imagine it, two years had already passed since he'd insulted me; my challenge was the most ridiculous anachronism, in spite of all the cleverness of my letter in explaining and disguising that fact. But, thank God (to this day I thank the Almighty with tears in my eyes), I didn't send that letter. A shiver runs up and down my spine when I think what might have happened if I had. Then suddenly . . . suddenly, I got my revenge in the simplest manner, a stroke of genius! A brilliant idea suddenly occurred to me. Sometimes on holidays I used to stroll along Nevsky Prospect at about four o'clock in the afternoon, usually on the sunny side. That is, I didn't really stroll; rather, I experienced innumerable torments, humiliations, and bilious attacks. But that's undoubtedly just what I needed. I darted in and out like a fish among the strollers, constantly stepping aside before generals, cavalry officers, hussars, and young ladies. At those moments I used to experience painful spasms in my heart and a burning sensation in my back merely at the thought of my dismal apparel as well as the wretchedness and vulgarity of my darting little figure. This was sheer torture, uninterrupted and unbear-

4. A radical literary and political journal published in St. Petersburg from 1839 to 1867.

able humiliation at the thought, which soon became an incessant and immediate sensation, that I was a fly in the eyes of society,[5] a disgusting, obscene fly—smarter than the rest, more cultured, even nobler—all that goes without saying, but a fly, nonetheless, who incessantly steps aside, insulted and injured by everyone. For what reason did I inflict this torment on myself? Why did I stroll along Nevsky Prospect? I don't know. But something simply *drew* me there at every opportunity.

Then I began to experience surges of that pleasure about which I've already spoken in the first chapter. After the incident with the officer I was drawn there even more strongly; I used to encounter him along Nevsky most often, and it was there that I could admire him. He would also go there, mostly on holidays. He, too, would give way before generals and individuals of superior rank; he, too, would spin like a top among them. But he would simply trample people like me, or even those slightly superior; he would walk directly toward them, as if there were empty space ahead of him; and under no circumstance would he ever step aside. I revelled in my malice as I observed him, and . . . bitterly stepped aside before him every time. I was tortured by the fact that even on the street I found it impossible to stand on an equal footing with him. "Why is it you're always first to step aside?" I badgered myself in insane hysteria, at times waking up at three in the morning. "Why always you and not he? After all, there's no law about it; it isn't written down anywhere. Let it be equal, as it usually is when people of breeding meet: he steps aside halfway and you halfway, and you pass by showing each other mutual respect." But that was never the case, and I continued to step aside, while he didn't even notice that I was yielding to him. Then a most astounding idea suddenly dawned on me. "What if," I thought, "what if I were to meet him and . . . not step aside? Deliberately not step aside, even if it meant bumping into him: how would that be?" This bold idea gradually took such a hold that it afforded me no peace. I dreamt about it incessantly, horribly, and even went to Nevsky more frequently so that I could imagine more clearly how I would do it. I was in ecstasy. The scheme was becoming more and more possible and even probable to me. "Of course, I wouldn't really collide with him," I thought, already feeling more generous toward him in my joy, "but I simply won't turn aside. I'll bump into him, not very painfully, but just so, shoulder to shoulder, as much as decency allows. I'll bump into him the same amount as he bumps into me." At last I made up my mind completely. But the preparations took a very long time. First, in order to look as presentable as possible during the execution of my scheme, I had to worry about my clothes. "In any case, what if, for example, it should occasion a public scandal? (And the public there was *superflu:*[5] a countess, Princess D., and the entire literary world.) It was essential to be well-dressed; that inspires respect and in a certain sense will place us immediately on an equal footing in the eyes of high society." With that goal in mind I requested my salary in advance, and I purchased a pair of black gloves and a decent hat at Churkin's store. Black gloves seemed to me more dignified, more *bon ton*[6] than the lemon-colored ones I'd considered at first. "That would be too glaring, as if the person wanted to be noticed"; so I didn't buy the lemon-colored ones. I'd already procured a fine shirt with white bone cufflinks; but my overcoat

5. Excessively refined (French).   6. In good taste (French).

constituted a major obstacle. In and of itself it was not too bad at all; it kept me warm; but it was quilted and had a raccoon collar, the epitome of bad taste. At all costs I had to replace the collar with a beaver one, just like on an officer's coat. For this purpose I began to frequent the Shopping Arcade; and, after several attempts, I turned up some cheap German beaver. Although these German beavers wear out very quickly and soon begin to look shabby, at first, when they're brand new, they look very fine indeed; after all, I only needed it for a single occasion. I asked the price: it was still expensive. After considerable reflection I resolved to sell my raccoon collar. I decided to request a loan for the remaining amount—a rather significant sum for me—from Anton Antonych Setochkin, my office chief, a modest man, but a serious and solid one, who never lent money to anyone, but to whom, upon entering the civil service, I'd once been specially recommended by an important person who'd secured the position for me. I suffered terribly. It seemed monstrous and shameful to ask Anton Antonych for money. I didn't sleep for two or three nights in a row; in general I wasn't getting much sleep those days, and I always had a fever. I would have either a vague sinking feeling in my heart, or else my heart would suddenly begin to thump, thump, thump! . . . At first Anton Antonych was surprised, then he frowned, thought it over, and finally gave me the loan, after securing from me a note authorizing him to deduct the sum from my salary two weeks later. In this way everything was finally ready; the splendid beaver reigned in place of the mangy raccoon, and I gradually began to get down to business. It was impossible to set about it all at once, in a foolhardy way; one had to proceed in this matter very carefully, step by step. But I confess that after many attempts I was ready to despair: we didn't bump into each other, no matter what! No matter how I prepared, no matter how determined I was—it seems that we're just about to bump, when I look up—and once again I've stepped aside while he's gone by without even noticing me. I even used to pray as I approached him that God would grant me determination. One time I'd fully resolved to do it, but the result was that I merely stumbled and fell at his feet because, at the very last moment, only a few inches away from him, I lost my nerve. He stepped over me very calmly, and I bounced to one side like a rubber ball. That night I lay ill with a fever once again and was delirious. Then, everything suddenly ended in the best possible way. The night before I decided once and for all not to go through with my pernicious scheme and to give it all up without success; with that in mind I went to Nevsky Prospect for one last time simply in order to see how I'd abandon the whole thing. Suddenly, three paces away from my enemy, I made up my mind unexpectedly; I closed my eyes and— we bumped into each other forcefully, shoulder to shoulder! I didn't yield an inch and walked by him on a completely equal footing! He didn't even turn around to look at me and pretended that he hadn't even noticed; but he was merely pretending, I'm convinced of that. To this very day I'm convinced of that! Naturally, I got the worst of it; he was stronger, but that wasn't the point. The point was that I'd achieved my goal, I'd maintained my dignity, I hadn't yielded one step, and I'd publicly placed myself on an equal social footing with him. I returned home feeling completely avenged for everything. I was ecstatic. I rejoiced and sang Italian arias. Of course, I won't describe what happened to me three days later; if you've read the first part entitled "Underground," you can guess for yourself. The officer was later transferred somewhere else; I haven't seen him for some fourteen years. I wonder what he's doing nowadays, that dear friend of mine! Whom is he trampling underfoot?

II

But when this phase of my nice, little dissipation ended I felt terribly nauseated. Remorse set in; I tried to drive it away because it was too disgusting. Little by little, however, I got used to that, too. I got used to it all; that is, it wasn't that I got used to it, rather, I somehow voluntarily consented to endure it. But I had a way out that reconciled everything—to escape into "all that was beautiful and sublime," in my dreams, of course. I was a terrible dreamer; I dreamt for three months in a row, tucked away in my little corner. And well you may believe that in those moments I was not at all like the gentlemen who, in his faint-hearted anxiety, had sewn a German beaver onto the collar of his old overcoat. I suddenly became a hero. If my six-foot-tall lieutenant had come to see me then, I'd never have admitted him. I couldn't even conceive of him at that time. It's hard to describe now what my dreams consisted of then, and how I could've been so satisfied with them, but I was. Besides, even now I can take pride in them at certain times. My dreams were particularly sweet and vivid after my little debauchery; they were filled with remorse and tears, curses and ecstasy. There were moments of such positive intoxication, such happiness, that I felt not even the slightest trace of mockery within me, really and truly. It was all faith, hope and love. That's just it: at the time I believed blindly that by some kind of miracle, some external circumstance, everything would suddenly open up and expand; a vista of appropriate activity would suddenly appear—beneficent, beautiful, and most of all, *ready-made* (what precisely, I never knew, but, most of all, it had to be ready-made), and that I would suddenly step forth into God's world, almost riding on a white horse and wearing a laurel wreath. I couldn't conceive of a secondary role; and that's precisely why in reality I very quietly took on the lowest one. Either a hero or dirt—there was no middle ground. That was my ruin because in the dirt I consoled myself knowing that at other times I was a hero, and that the hero covered himself with dirt; that is to say, an ordinary man would be ashamed to wallow in filth, but a hero is too noble to become defiled; consequently, he can wallow. It's remarkable that these surges of everything "beautiful and sublime" occurred even during my petty depravity, and precisely when I'd sunk to the lowest depths. They occurred in separate spurts, as if to remind me of themselves; however, they failed to banish my depravity by their appearance. On the contrary, they seemed to add spice to it by means of contrast; they came in just the right amount to serve as a tasty sauce. This sauce consisted of contradictions, suffering, and agonizing internal analysis; all of these torments and trifles lent a certain piquancy, even some meaning to my depravity—in a word, they completely fulfilled the function of a tasty sauce. Nor was all this even lacking in a measure of profundity. Besides, I would never have consented to the simple, tasteless, spontaneous little debauchery of an ordinary clerk and have endured all that filth! How could it have attracted me then and lured me into the street late at night? No, sir, I had a noble loophole for everything. . . .

But how much love, oh Lord, how much love I experienced at times in those dreams of mine, in those "escapes into everything beautiful and sublime." Even though it was fantastic love, even though it was never directed at anything human, there was still so much love that afterward, in reality, I no longer felt any impulse to direct it: that would have been an unnecessary luxury. However, everything always ended in a most satisfactory way by a lazy and intoxicating transition into art, that is, into beautiful forms of being, ready-made, largely borrowed from poets and novelists, and adapted to serve every possible need. For instance, I would triumph over everyone; naturally, everyone else grovelled in the dust and was voluntarily impelled to acknowledge my superiority, while I would forgive them all for everything. Or else, being a famous poet and chamberlain, I would fall in love; I'd receive an enormous fortune and would immediately sacrifice it all for the benefit of humanity, at the same time confessing before all peoples my own infamies, which, needless to say, were not simple infamies, but contained a great amount of "the beautiful and sublime," something in the style of Manfred.[7] Everyone would weep and kiss me (otherwise what idiots they would have been), while I went about barefoot and hungry preaching new ideas and defeating all the reactionaries of Austerlitz.[8] Then a march would be played, a general amnesty declared, and the Pope would agree to leave Rome and go to Brazil;[9] a ball would be hosted for all of Italy at the Villa Borghese on the shores of Lake Como,[1] since Lake Como would have been moved to Rome for this very occasion; then there would be a scene in the bushes, etc., etc.—as if you didn't know. You'll say that it's tasteless and repugnant to drag all this out into the open after all the raptures and tears to which I've confessed. But why is it so repugnant? Do you really think I'm ashamed of all this or that it's any more stupid than anything in your own lives, gentlemen? Besides, you can rest assured that some of it was not at all badly composed. . . . Not everything occurred on the shores of Lake Como. But you're right; in fact, it is tasteless and repugnant. And the most repugnant thing of all is that now I've begun to justify myself before you. And even more repugnant is that now I've made that observation. But enough, otherwise there'll be no end to it: each thing will be more repugnant than the last. . . .

I was never able to dream for more than three months in a row, and I began to feel an irresistible urge to plunge into society. To me plunging into society meant paying a visit to my office chief, Anton Antonych Setochkin. He's the only lasting acquaintance I've made during my lifetime; I too now marvel at this circumstance. But even then I would visit him only when my dreams had reached such a degree of happiness that it was absolutely essential for me to embrace people and all humanity at once; for that reason I needed to have at least one person on hand who actually existed. However, one could only call upon Anton Antonych on Tuesdays (his receiving day); consequently, I always had to adjust the urge to embrace all humanity so

---

7. The romantic hero of Byron's poetic tragedy *Manfred* (1817), a lonely, defiant figure whose past conceals some mysterious crime.   8. The site of Napoleon's great victory in December 1805 over the combined armies of the Russian czar Alexander I and the Austrian emperor Francis II.   9. Napoleon announced his annexation of the Papal States to France in 1809 and was promptly excommunicated by Pope Pius VII. The pope was imprisoned and forced to sign a new concordat, but in 1814 he returned to Rome in triumph. 1. Located in the foothills of the Italian Alps in Lombardy. Villa Borghese was the elegant summer palace built by Scipione Cardinal Borghese outside the Porta del Popolo in Rome.

that it occurred on Tuesday. This Anton Antonych lived near Five Corners,[2] on the fourth floor, in four small, low-ceilinged rooms, each smaller than the last, all very frugal and yellowish in appearance. He lived with his two daughters and an aunt who used to serve tea. The daughters, one thirteen, the other fourteen, had little snub noses. I was very embarrassed by them because they used to whisper all the time and giggle to each other. The host usually sat in his study on a leather couch in front of a table together with some gray-haired guest, a civil servant either from our office or another one. I never saw more than two or three guests there, and they were always the same ones. They talked about excise taxes, debates in the Senate, salaries, promotions, His Excellency and how to please him, and so on and so forth. I had the patience to sit there like a fool next to these people for four hours or so; I listened without daring to say a word to them or even knowing what to talk about. I sat there in a stupor; several times I broke into a sweat; I felt numbed by paralysis; but it was good and useful. Upon returning home I would postpone for some time my desire to embrace all humanity.

I had one other sort of acquaintance, however, named Simonov, a former schoolmate of mine. In fact, I had a number of schoolmates in Petersburg, but I didn't associate with them, and I'd even stopped greeting them along the street. I might even have transferred into a different department at the office so as not to be with them and to cut myself off from my hated childhood once and for all. Curses on that school and those horrible years of penal servitude. In short, I broke with my schoolmates as soon as I was released. There remained only two or three people whom I would greet upon encountering them. One was Simonov, who hadn't distinguished himself in school in any way; he was even-tempered and quiet, but I detected in him a certain independence of character, even honesty. I don't even think that he was all that limited. At one time he and I experienced some rather bright moments, but they didn't last very long and somehow were suddenly clouded over. Evidently he was burdened by these recollections, and seemed in constant fear that I would lapse into that former mode. I suspect that he found me repulsive, but not being absolutely sure, I used to visit him nonetheless.

So once, on a Thursday, unable to endure my solitude, and knowing that on that day Anton Antonych's door was locked, I remembered Simonov. As I climbed the stairs to his apartment on the fourth floor, I was thinking how burdensome this man found my presence and that my going to see him was rather useless. But since it always turned out, as if on purpose, that such reflections would impel me to put myself even further into an ambiguous situation, I went right in. It had been almost a year since I'd last seen Simonov.

III

I found two more of my former schoolmates there with him. Apparently they were discussing some important matter. None of them paid any attention to me when I entered, which was strange since I hadn't seen them for several years. Evidently they considered me some sort of ordinary house fly.

---

2. A well-known landmark in St. Petersburg.

They hadn't even treated me like that when we were in school together, although they'd all hated me. Of course, I understood that they must despise me now for my failure in the service and for the fact that I'd sunk so low, was badly dressed, and so on, which, in their eyes, constituted proof of my ineptitude and insignificance. But I still hadn't expected such a degree of contempt. Simonov was even surprised by my visits. All this disconcerted me; I sat down in some distress and began to listen to what they were saying.

The discussion was serious, even heated, and concerned a farewell dinner which these gentlemen wanted to organize jointly as early as the following day for their friend Zverkov, an army officer who was heading for a distant province. Monsieur Zverkov had also been my schoolmate all along. I'd begun to hate him especially in the upper grades. In the lower grades he was merely an attractive, lively lad whom everyone liked. However, I'd hated him in the lower grades, too, precisely because he was such an attractive, lively lad. He was perpetually a poor student and had gotten worse as time went on; he managed to graduate, however, because he had influential connections. During his last year at school he'd come into an inheritance of some two hundred serfs, and, since almost all the rest of us were poor, he'd even begun to brag. He was an extremely uncouth fellow, but a nice lad nonetheless, even when he was bragging. In spite of our superficial, fantastic, and high-flown notions of honor and pride, all of us, except for a very few, would fawn upon Zverkov, the more so the more he bragged. They didn't fawn for any advantage; they fawned simply because he was a man endowed by nature with gifts. Moreover, we'd somehow come to regard Zverkov as a cunning fellow and an expert on good manners. This latter point particularly infuriated me. I hated the shrill, self-confident tone of his voice, his adoration for his own witticisms, which were terribly stupid in spite of his bold tongue; I hated his handsome, stupid face (for which, however, I'd gladly have exchanged my own intelligent one), and the impudent bearing typical of officers during the 1840s. I hated the way he talked about his future successes with women. (He'd decided not to get involved with them yet, since he still hadn't received his officer's epaulettes; he awaited those epaulettes impatiently.) And he talked about all the duels he'd have to fight. I remember how once, although I was usually very taciturn, I suddenly clashed with Zverkov when, during our free time, he was discussing future exploits with his friends; getting a bit carried away with the game like a little puppy playing in the sun, he suddenly declared that not a single girl in his village would escape his attention—that it was his *droit de seigneur*,[3] and that if the peasants even dared protest, he'd have them all flogged, those bearded rascals; and he'd double their quit-rent.[4] Our louts applauded, but I attacked him—not out of any pity for the poor girls or their fathers, but simply because everyone else was applauding such a little insect. I got the better of him that time, but Zverkov, although stupid, was also cheerful and impudent. Therefore he laughed it off to such an extent that, in fact, I really didn't get the better of him. The laugh remained on his side. Later he got the better of me several times, but without malice, just so, in jest, in passing, in fun. I was filled with spite and hatred, but I didn't

---

3. Lord's privilege (French); the feudal lord's right to spend the first night with the bride of a newly married serf.   4. The annual sum paid in cash or produce by serfs to landowners for the right to farm their land in feudal Russia, as opposed to the *corvée*, a certain amount of labor owed.

respond. After graduation he took a few steps toward me; I didn't object strongly because I found it flattering; but soon we came to a natural parting of the ways. Afterward I heard about his barrack-room successes as a lieutenant and about his *binges*. Then there were other rumors—about his *successes* in the service. He no longer bowed to me on the street; I suspected that he was afraid to compromise himself by acknowledging such an insignificant person as myself. I also saw him in the theater once, in the third tier, already sporting an officer's gold braids. He was fawning and grovelling before the daughters of some aged general. In those three years he'd let himself go, although he was still as handsome and agile as before; he sagged somehow and had begun to put on weight; it was clear that by the age of thirty he'd be totally flabby. So it was for this Zverkov, who was finally ready to depart, that our schoolmates were organizing a farewell dinner. They'd kept up during these three years, although I'm sure that inwardly they didn't consider themselves on an equal footing with him.

One of Simonov's two guests was Ferfichkin, a Russified German, a short man with a face like a monkey, a fool who made fun of everybody, my bitterest enemy from the lower grades—a despicable, impudent show-off who affected the most ticklish sense of ambition, although, of course, he was a coward at heart. He was one of Zverkov's admirers and played up to him for his own reasons, frequently borrowing money from him. Simonov's other guest, Trudolyubov, was insignificant, a military man, tall, with a cold demeanor, rather honest, who worshipped success of any kind and was capable of talking only about promotions. He was a distant relative of Zverkov's, and that, silly to say, lent him some importance among us. He'd always regarded me as a nonentity; he treated me not altogether politely, but tolerably.

"Well, if each of us contributes seven rubles," said Trudolyubov, "with three of us that makes twenty-one altogether—we can have a good dinner. Of course, Zverkov won't have to pay."

"Naturally," Simonov agreed, "since we're inviting him."

"Do you really think," Ferfichkin broke in arrogantly and excitedly, just like an insolent lackey bragging about his master-the-general's medals, "do you really think Zverkov will let us pay for everything? He'll accept out of decency, but then he'll order *half a dozen bottles* on his own."

"What will the four of us do with half a dozen bottles?" asked Trudolyubov, only taking note of the number.

"So then, three of us plus Zverkov makes four, twenty-one rubles, in the Hôtel de Paris, tomorrow at five o'clock," concluded Simonov definitively, since he'd been chosen to make the arrangements.

"Why only twenty-one?" I asked in trepidation, even, apparently, somewhat offended. "If you count me in, you'll have twenty-eight rubles instead of twenty-one."

It seemed to me that to include myself so suddenly and unexpectedly would appear as quite a splendid gesture and that they'd all be smitten at once and regard me with respect.

"Do you really want to come, too?" Simonov inquired with displeasure, managing somehow to avoid looking at me. He knew me inside out.

It was infuriating that he knew me inside out.

"And why not? After all, I was his schoolmate, too, and I must admit that I even feel a bit offended that you've left me out," I continued, just about to boil over again.

"And how were we supposed to find you?" Ferfichkin interjected rudely.

"You never got along very well with Zverkov," added Trudolyubov frowning. But I'd already latched on and wouldn't let go.

"I think no one has a right to judge that," I objected in a trembling voice, as if God knows what had happened. "Perhaps that's precisely why I want to take part now, since we didn't get along so well before."

"Well, who can figure you out . . . such lofty sentiments . . . ," Trudolyubov said with an ironic smile.

"We'll put your name down," Simonov decided, turning to me. "Tomorrow at five o'clock at the Hôtel de Paris. Don't make any mistakes."

"What about the money?" Ferfichkin started to say in an undertone to Simonov while nodding at me, but he broke off because Simonov looked embarrassed.

"That'll do," Trudolyubov said getting up. "If he really wants to come so much, let him."

"But this is our own circle of friends," Ferfichkin grumbled, also picking up his hat. "It's not an official gathering. Perhaps we really don't want you at all. . . ."

They left. Ferfichkin didn't even say goodbye to me as he went out; Trudolyubov barely nodded without looking at me. Simonov, with whom I was left alone, was irritated and perplexed, and he regarded me in a strange way. He neither sat down nor invited me to.

"Hmmm . . . yes . . . , so, tomorrow. Will you contribute your share of the money now? I'm asking just to know for sure," he muttered in embarrassment.

I flared up; but in doing so, I remembered that I'd owed Simonov fifteen rubles for a very long time, which debt, moreover, I'd forgotten, but had also never repaid.

"You must agree, Simonov, that I couldn't have known when I came here . . . oh, what a nuisance, but I've forgotten. . . ."

He broke off and began to pace around the room in even greater irritation. As he paced, he began to walk on his heels and stomp more loudly.

"I'm not detaining you, am I?" I asked after a few moments of silence.

"Oh, no!" he replied with a start. "That is, in fact, yes. You see, I still have to stop by at . . . It's not very far from here . . . ," he added in an apologetic way with some embarrassment.

"Oh, good heavens! Why didn't you say so?" I exclaimed, seizing my cap; moreover I did so with a surprisingly familiar air, coming from God knows where.

"But it's really not far . . . only a few steps away . . . ," Simonov repeated, accompanying me into the hallway with a bustling air which didn't suit him well at all. "So, then, tomorrow at five o'clock sharp!" he shouted to me on the stairs. He was very pleased that I was leaving. However, I was furious.

"What possessed me, what on earth possessed me to interfere?" I gnashed my teeth as I walked along the street. "And for such a scoundrel, a pig like Zverkov! Naturally, I shouldn't go. Of course, to hell with them. Am I bound to go, or what? Tomorrow I'll inform Simonov by post. . . ."

But the real reason I was so furious was that I was sure I'd go. I'd go on purpose. The more tactless, the more indecent it was for me to go, the more certain I'd be to do it.

There was even a definite impediment to my going: I didn't have any money. All I had was nine rubles. But of those, I had to hand over seven the next day to my servant Apollon for his monthly wages; he lived in and received seven rubles for his meals.

Considering Apollon's character it was impossible not to pay him. But more about that rascal, that plague of mine, later.

In any case, I knew that I wouldn't pay him his wages and that I'd definitely go.

That night I had the most hideous dreams. No wonder: all evening I was burdened with recollections of my years of penal servitude at school and I couldn't get rid of them. I'd been sent off to that school by distant relatives on whom I was dependent and about whom I've heard nothing since. They dispatched me, a lonely boy, crushed by their reproaches, already introspective, taciturn, and regarding everything around him savagely. My schoolmates received me with spiteful and pitiless jibes because I wasn't like any of them. But I couldn't tolerate their jibes; I couldn't possibly get along with them as easily as they got along with each other. I hated them all at once and took refuge from everyone in fearful, wounded and excessive pride. Their crudeness irritated me. Cynically they mocked my face and my awkward build; yet, what stupid faces they all had! Facial expressions at our school somehow degenerated and became particularly stupid. Many attractive lads had come to us, but in a few years they too were repulsive to look at. When I was only sixteen I wondered about them gloomily; even then I was astounded by the pettiness of their thoughts and the stupidity of their studies, games and conversations. They failed to understand essential things and took no interest in important, weighty subjects, so that I couldn't help considering them beneath me. It wasn't my wounded vanity that drove me to it; and, for God's sake, don't repeat any of those nauseating and hackneyed clichés, such as, "I was merely a dreamer, whereas they already understood life." They didn't understand a thing, not one thing about life, and I swear, that's what annoyed me most about them. On the contrary, they accepted the most obvious, glaring reality in a fantastically stupid way, and even then they'd begun to worship nothing but success. Everything that was just, but oppressed and humiliated, they ridiculed hard-heartedly and shamelessly. They mistook rank for intelligence; at the age of sixteen they were already talking about occupying comfortable little niches. Of course, much of this was due to their stupidity and the poor examples that had constantly surrounded them in their childhood and youth. They were monstrously depraved. Naturally, even this was more superficial, more affected cynicism; of course, their youth and a certain freshness shone through their depravity; but even this freshness was unattractive and manifested itself in a kind of rakishness. I hated them terribly, although, perhaps, I was even worse than they were. They returned the feeling and didn't conceal their loathing for me. But I no longer wanted their affection; on the contrary, I constantly longed for their humiliation. In order to avoid their jibes, I began to study as hard as I could on purpose and made my way to the top of the class. That impressed them. In addition, they all began to realize that I'd read certain books which they could never read and that I understood certain things (not included in our special course) about which they'd never even heard. They regarded this with savagery and sarcasm, but they submitted morally, all the more since even the teachers paid me some attention on this account. Their jibes ceased, but their hostility remained, and relations between us became cold and strained. In the end I myself couldn't stand it: as the years went by, my need for people, for friends, increased. I made several attempts to get closer to some of them; but these attempts always turned out to be unnatural and ended of their own accord. Once I even had a friend of sorts. But I was already a despot at heart; I wanted to exercise unlimited power over his soul; I wanted to instill in him contempt for his surroundings; and I demanded from him a disdainful and definitive break with those surroundings. I frightened him with my passionate friendship, and I reduced him to tears and convulsions. He was a naive and giving soul, but as soon as he'd surrendered himself to me totally, I began to despise him and reject him immediately—as if I only needed to achieve a victory over him, merely to subjugate him. But I was unable to conquer them all; my one friend was not at all like them, but rather a rare exception. The first thing I did upon leaving school was abandon the special job in the civil service for which I'd been trained, in order to sever all ties, break with my past, cover it over with dust. . . . The devil only knows why, after all that, I'd dragged myself over to see this Simonov! . . .

Early the next morning I roused myself from bed, jumped up in anxiety, just as if everything was about to start happening all at once. But I believed that some radical change in my life was imminent and was sure to occur that very day. Perhaps because I wasn't used to it, but all my life, at any external event, albeit a trivial one, it always seemed that some sort of radical change would occur. I went off to work as usual, but returned home two hours earlier in order to prepare. The most important thing, I thought, was not to arrive there first, or else they'd all think I was too eager. But there were thousands of most important things, and they all reduced me to the point of impotence. I polished my boots once again with my own hands. Apollon wouldn't polish them twice in one day for anything in the world; he considered it indecent. So I polished them myself, after stealing the brushes from the hallway so that he wouldn't notice and then despise me for it afterward. Next I carefully examined my clothes and found that everything was old, shabby, and worn out. I'd become too slovenly. My uniform was in better shape, but I couldn't go to dinner in a uniform. Worst of all, there was an enormous yellow stain on the knee of my trousers. I had an inkling that the spot alone would rob me of nine-tenths of my dignity. I also knew that it was unseemly for me to think that. "But this isn't the time for thinking. Reality is now looming," I thought, and my heart sank. I also knew perfectly well at that time, that I was monstrously exaggerating all these facts. But what could be done? I was no longer able to control myself, and was shaking with fever. In despair I imagined how haughtily and coldly that "scoundrel" Zverkov would greet me; with what dull and totally relentless contempt that dullard Trudolyubov would regard me; how nastily and impudently that insect Ferfichkin would giggle at me in order to win Zverkov's approval; how well Simonov would understand all this and how he'd despise me for my wretched vanity and cowardice; and worst of all, how petty all this would be, not *literary*, but commonplace. Of course, it would have been better not to go at all. But that was no longer possible; once I began to feel drawn to something, I plunged right in, head first. I'd have reproached myself for the rest of my life: "So, you retreated, you retreated before reality, you retreated!" On the contrary, I desperately wanted to prove to all this "rabble" that I really wasn't the coward I imagined myself to be. But that's not all: in the strongest paroxysm of cowardly fever I dreamt of gaining the upper hand, of conquering them, of carrying them away, compelling them to love me—if only "for the nobility of my thought and my indisputable wit." They would abandon Zverkov; he'd sit by in silence and embarassment, and I'd crush him. Afterward, perhaps, I'd be reconciled with Zverkov and drink to our *friendship*, but what was most spiteful and insulting for me was that I knew even then, I knew completely and for sure, that I didn't need any of this at all; that in fact I really didn't want to crush them, conquer them, or attract them, and that if I could have ever achieved all that, I'd be the first to say that it wasn't worth a damn. Oh, how I prayed to God that this day would pass quickly! With inexpressible anxiety I approached the window, opened the transom,[5] and peered out into the murky mist of the thickly falling wet snow. . . .

At last my worthless old wall clock sputtered out five o'clock. I grabbed my hat, and, trying not to look at Apollon—who'd been waiting since early morning to receive his wages, but didn't want to be the first one to mention it out of pride—I slipped out the door past him and intentionally hired a smart cab with my last half-ruble in order to arrive at the Hôtel de Paris in style.

IV

I knew since the day before that I'd be the first one to arrive. But it was no longer a question of who was first.

Not only was no one else there, but I even had difficulty finding our room. The table hadn't even been set. What did it all mean? After many inquiries I finally learned from the waiters that dinner had been ordered for closer to six o'clock, instead of five. This was also confirmed in the buffet. It was too embarrassing to ask any more questions. It was still only twenty-five minutes past five. If they'd changed the time, they should have let me know; that's what the city mail was for. They shouldn't have subjected me to such "shame" in my own eyes and . . . and, at least not in front of the waiters. I sat down. A waiter began to set the table. I felt even more ashamed in his presence. Toward six o'clock candles were brought into the room in addition to the lighted lamps already there, yet it hadn't occurred to the waiters to bring them in as soon as I'd arrived. In the next room two gloomy customers, angry-looking and silent, were dining at separate tables. In one of the distant rooms there was a great deal of noise, even shouting. One could hear the laughter of a whole crowd of people, including nasty little squeals in French—there were ladies present at that dinner. In short, it was disgusting. Rarely had I passed a more unpleasant hour, so that when they all arrived together precisely at six o'clock, I was initially overjoyed to see them, as if they were my liberators, and I almost forgot that I was supposed to appear offended.

Zverkov, obviously the leader, entered ahead of the rest. Both he and they

5. A small hinged pane in the window of a Russian house, used for ventilation especially during the winter when the main part of the window is sealed.

were laughing; but, upon seeing me, Zverkov drew himself up, approached me unhurriedly, bowed slightly from the waist almost coquettishly, and extended his hand politely, but not too, with a kind of careful civility, almost as if he were a general both offering his hand, but also guarding against something. I'd imagined, on the contrary, that as soon as he entered he'd burst into his former, shrill laughter with occasional squeals, and that he'd immediately launch into his stale jokes and witticisms. I'd been preparing for them since the previous evening; but in no way did I expect such condescension, such courtesy characteristic of a general. Could it be that he now considered himself so immeasurably superior to me in all respects? If he'd merely wanted to offend me by this superior attitude, it wouldn't have been so bad, I thought; I'd manage to pay him back somehow. But what if, without any desire to offend, the notion had crept into his dumb sheep's brain that he really was immeasurably superior to me and that he could only treat me in a patronizing way? From this possibility alone I began to gasp for air.

"Have you been waiting long?" Trudolyubov asked.

"I arrived at five o'clock sharp, just as I was told yesterday," I answered loudly and with irritation presaging an imminent explosion.

"Didn't you let him know that we changed the time?" Trudolyubov asked, turning to Simonov.

"No, I didn't. I forgot," he replied, but without any regret; then, not even apologizing to me, he went off to order the hors d'oeuvres.

"So you've been here for a whole hour, you poor fellow!" Zverkov cried sarcastically, because according to his notions, this must really have been terribly amusing. That scoundrel Ferfichkin chimed in after him with nasty, ringing laughter that sounded like a dog's yapping. My situation seemed very amusing and awkward to him, too.

"It's not the least bit funny!" I shouted at Ferfichkin, getting more and more irritated. "The others are to blame, not me. They neglected to inform me. It's, it's, it's . . . simply preposterous."

"It's not only preposterous, it's more than that," muttered Trudolyubov, naively interceding on my behalf. "You're being too kind. It's pure rudeness. Of course, it wasn't intentional. And how could Simonov have . . . hmm!"

"If a trick like that had been played on me," said Ferfichkin, "I'd . . ." "Oh, you'd have ordered yourself something to eat," interrupted Zverkov, "or simply asked to have dinner served without waiting for the rest of us."

"You'll agree that I could've done that without asking anyone's permission," I snapped. "If I did wait, it was only because . . ."

"Let's be seated, gentlemen," cried Simonov upon entering. "Everything's ready. I can vouch for the champagne; it's excellently chilled. . . . Moreover, I didn't know where your apartment was, so how could I find you?" he said turning to me suddenly, but once again not looking directly at me. Obviously he was holding something against me. I suspect he got to thinking after what had happened yesterday.

Everyone sat down; I did, too. The table was round. Trudolyubov sat on my left, Simonov, on my right. Zverkov sat across; Ferfichkin, next to him, between Trudolyubov and him.

"Tell-l-l me now, are you . . . in a government department?" Zverkov continued to attend to me. Seeing that I was embarrassed, he imagined in earnest that he had to be nice to me, encouraging me to speak. "Does he want me to throw a bottle at his head, or what?" I thought in a rage. Unaccustomed as I was to all this, I was unnaturally quick to take offense.

"In such and such an office," I replied abruptly, looking at my plate.

"And . . . is it p-p-profitable? Tell-l-l me, what ma-a-de you decide to leave your previous position?"

"What ma-a-a-de me leave my previous position was simply that I wanted to," I dragged my words out three times longer than he did, hardly able to control myself. Ferfichkin snorted. Simonov looked at me ironically; Trudolyubov stopped eating and began to stare at me with curiosity.

Zverkov was jarred, but didn't want to show it.

"Well-l, and how is the support?"

"What support?"

"I mean, the s-salary?"

"Why are you cross-examining me?"

However, I told him right away what my salary was. I blushed terribly.

"That's not very much," Zverkov observed pompously.

"No, sir, it's not enough to dine in café-restaurants!" added Ferfichkin insolently.

"In my opinion, it's really very little," Trudolyubov observed in earnest.

"And how thin you've grown, how you've changed . . . since . . . ," Zverkov added, with a touch of venom now, and with a kind of impudent sympathy, examining me and my apparel.

"Stop embarrassing him," Ferfichkin cried with a giggle.

"My dear sir, I'll have you know that I'm not embarrassed," I broke in at last. "Listen! I'm dining in this 'café-restaurant' at my own expense, my own, not anyone else's; note that, Monsieur Ferfichkin."

"Wha-at? And who isn't dining at his own expense? You seem to be . . ." Ferfichkin seized hold of my words, turned as red as a lobster, and looked me straight in the eye with fury.

"Just so-o," I replied, feeling that I'd gone a bit too far, "and I suggest that it would be much better if we engaged in more intelligent conversation."

"It seems that you're determined to display your intelligence."

"Don't worry, that would be quite unnecessary here."

"What's all this cackling, my dear sir? Huh? Have you taken leave of your senses in that *duh*-partment of yours?"

"Enough, gentlemen, enough," cried Zverkov authoritatively.

"How stupid this is!" muttered Simonov.

"Really, it is stupid. We're gathered here in a congenial group to have a farewell dinner for our good friend, while you're still settling old scores," Trudolyubov said, rudely addressing only me. "You forced yourself upon us yesterday; don't disturb the general harmony now. . . ."

"Enough, enough," cried Zverkov. "Stop it, gentlemen, this'll never do. Let me tell you instead how I very nearly got married a few days ago . . ."

There followed some scandalous, libelous anecdote about how this gentleman very nearly got married a few days ago. There wasn't one word about marriage, however; instead, generals, colonels, and even gentlemen of the bed chamber figured prominently in the story, while Zverkov played the leading role among them all. Approving laughter followed; Ferfichkin even squealed.

Everyone had abandoned me by now, and I sat there completely crushed and humiliated.

"Good Lord, what kind of company is this for me?" I wondered. "And what a fool I've made of myself in front of them all! But I let Ferfichkin go too far. These numbskulls think they're doing me an honor by allowing me to sit with them at their table, when they don't understand that it's I who's done them the honor, and not the reverse. 'How thin I've grown! What clothes!' Oh, these damned trousers! Zverkov's already noticed the yellow spot on my knee. . . . What's the use? Right now, this very moment, I should stand up, take my hat, and simply leave without saying a single word. . . . Out of contempt! And tomorrow—I'll even be ready for a duel. Scoundrels! It's not the seven rubles I care about. But they may think that . . . To hell with it! I don't care about the seven rubles. I'm leaving at once! . . ."

Of course, I stayed.

In my misery I drank Lafite and sherry by the glassful. Being unaccustomed to it, I got drunk very quickly; the more intoxicated I became, the greater my annoyance. Suddenly I felt like offending them all in the most impudent manner—and then I'd leave. To seize the moment and show them all who I really was—let them say: even though he's ridiculous, he's clever . . . and . . . and . . . in short, to hell with them!

I surveyed them all arrogantly with my dazed eyes. But they seemed to have forgotten all about me. *They* were noisy, boisterous and merry. Zverkov kept on talking. I began to listen. He was talking about some magnificent lady whom he'd finally driven to make a declaration of love. (Of course, he was lying like a trooper.) He said that he'd been assisted in this matter particularly by a certain princeling, the hussar Kolya, who possessed some three thousand serfs.

"And yet, this same Kolya who has three thousand serfs hasn't even come to see you off," I said, breaking into the conversation suddenly. For a moment silence fell.

"You're drunk already," Trudolyubov said, finally deigning to notice me, and glancing contemptuously in my direction. Zverkov examined me in silence as if I were an insect. I lowered my eyes. Simonov quickly began to pour champagne.

Trudolyubov raised his glass, followed by everyone but me.

"To your health and to a good journey!" he cried to Zverkov. "To old times, gentlemen, and to our future, hurrah!"

Everyone drank up and pressed around to exchange kisses with Zverkov. I didn't budge; my full glass stood before me untouched.

"Aren't you going to drink?" Trudolyubov roared at me, having lost his patience and turning to me menacingly.

"I wish to make my own speech, all by myself . . . and then I'll drink, Mr. Trudolyubov."

"Nasty shrew!" Simonov muttered.

I sat up in my chair, feverishly seized hold of my glass, and prepared for something extraordinary, although I didn't know quite what I'd say.

"*Silence!*" cried Ferfichkin. "And now for some real intelligence!" Zverkov waited very gravely, aware of what was coming.

"Mr. Lieutenant Zverkov," I began, "you must know that I detest phrases, phrasemongers, and corsetted waists. . . . That's the first point; the second will follow."

Everyone stirred uncomfortably.

"The second point: I hate obscene stories and the men who tell them.[6] I especially hate the men who tell them!"

"The third point: I love truth, sincerity and honesty," I continued almost automatically, because I was beginning to become numb with horror, not knowing how I could be speaking this way. . . . "I love thought, Monsieur Zverkov. I love genuine comradery, on an equal footing, but not . . . hmmm . . . I love . . . But, after all, why not? I too will drink to your health, Monsieur Zverkov. Seduce those Circassian[7] maidens, shoot the enemies of the fatherland, and . . . and . . . To your health, Monsieur Zverkov!"

Zverkov rose from his chair, bowed, and said: "I'm most grateful."

He was terribly offended and had even turned pale.

"To hell with him," Trudolyubov roared, banging his fist down on the table.

"No, sir, people should be whacked in the face for saying such things!" squealed Ferfichkin.

"We ought to throw him out!" muttered Simonov.

"Not a word, gentlemen, not a move!" Zverkov cried triumphantly, putting a stop to this universal indignation. "I'm grateful to you all, but I can show him myself how much I value his words."

"Mr. Ferfichkin, tomorrow you'll give me satisfaction for the words you've just uttered!" I said loudly, turning to Ferfichkin with dignity.

"Do you mean a duel? Very well," he replied, but I must have looked so ridiculous as I issued my challenge, it must have seemed so out of keeping with my entire appearance, that everyone, including Ferfichkin, collapsed into laughter.

"Yes, of course, throw him out! Why, he's quite drunk already," Trudolyubov declared in disgust.

"I shall never forgive myself for letting him join us," Simonov muttered again.

"Now's the time to throw a bottle at the lot of them," I thought. So I grabbed a bottle and . . . poured myself another full glass.

" . . . No, it's better to sit it out to the very end!" I went on thinking. "You'd be glad, gentlemen, if I left. But nothing doing! I'll stay here deliberately and keep on drinking to the very end, as a sign that I accord you no importance whatsoever. I'll sit here and drink because this is a tavern, and I've paid good money to get in. I'll sit here and drink because I consider you to be so many pawns, nonexistent pawns. I'll sit here and drink . . . and sing too, if I want to, yes, sir, I'll sing because I have the right to . . . sing . . . hmm."

But I didn't sing. I just tried not to look at any of them; I assumed the most carefree poses and waited impatiently until they would be the first to speak to me. But, alas, they did not. How much, how very much I longed to be reconciled with them at that moment! The clock struck eight, then nine. They moved from the table to the sofa. Zverkov sprawled on the couch, placing one foot on the round table. They brought the wine over, too. He really had ordered three bottles at his own expense. Naturally, he didn't invite me to join them. Everyone surrounded him on the sofa. They listened to him almost with reverence. It was obvious they liked him. "What for? What for?" I wondered to myself. From time to time they were moved to drunken ecstasy

---

6. A phrase borrowed from the inveterate liar Nozdryov, one of the provincial landowners in the first volume of Gogol's *Dead Souls* (1842).   7. A Muslim people inhabiting a region in the northern Caucasus.

and exchanged kisses. They talked about the Caucasus, the nature of true passion, card games, profitable positions in the service; they talked about the income of a certain hussar Podkharzhevsky, whom none of them knew personally, and they rejoiced that his income was so large; they talked about the unusual beauty and charm of Princess D., whom none of them had ever seen; finally, they arrived at the question of Shakespeare's immortality.

I smiled contemptuously and paced up and down the other side of the room, directly behind the sofa, along the wall from the table to the stove and back again. I wanted to show them with all my might that I could get along without them; meanwhile, I deliberately stomped my boots, thumping my heels. But all this was in vain. *They* paid me no attention. I had the forbearance to pace like that, right in front of them, from eight o'clock until eleven, in the very same place, from the table to the stove and from the stove back to the table. "I'm pacing just as I please, and no one can stop me." A waiter who came into the room paused several times to look at me; my head was spinning from all those turns; there were moments when it seemed that I was delirious. During those three hours I broke out in a sweat three times and then dried out. At times I was pierced to the heart with a most profound, venomous thought: ten years would pass, twenty, forty; and still, even after forty years, I'd remember with loathing and humiliation these filthiest, most absurd, and horrendous moments of my entire life. It was impossible to humiliate myself more shamelessly or more willingly, and I fully understood that, fully; nevertheless, I continued to pace from the table to the stove and back again. "Oh, if you only knew what thoughts and feelings I'm capable of, and how cultured I really am!" I thought at moments, mentally addressing the sofa where my enemies were seated. But my enemies behaved as if I weren't even in the room. Once, and only once, they turned to me, precisely when Zverkov started in about Shakespeare, and I suddenly burst into contemptuous laughter. I snorted so affectedly and repulsively that they broke off their conversation immediately and stared at me in silence for about two minutes, in earnest, without laughing, as I paced up and down, from the table to the stove, while I *paid not the slightest bit of attention to them.* But nothing came of it; they didn't speak to me. A few moments later they abandoned me again. The clock struck eleven.

"Gentlemen," exclaimed Zverkov, getting up from the sofa, "Now let's all go *to that place.*"[8]

"Of course, of course!" the others replied.

I turned abruptly to Zverkov. I was so exhausted, so broken, that I'd have slit my own throat to be done with all this! I was feverish; my hair, which had been soaked through with sweat, had dried and now stuck to my forehead and temples.

"Zverkov, I ask your forgiveness," I said harshly and decisively. "Ferfichkin, yours too, and everyone's, everyone's. I've insulted you all!" "Aha! So a duel isn't really your sort of thing!" hissed Ferfichkin venomously.

His remark was like a painful stab to my heart.

"No, I'm not afraid of a duel, Ferfichkin! I'm ready to fight with you tomorrow, even after we're reconciled. I even insist upon it, and you can't refuse me. I want to prove that I'm not afraid of a duel. You'll shoot first, and I'll fire into the air."

---

8. I.e., a brothel.

"He's amusing himself," Simonov observed.

"He's simply taken leave of his senses!" Trudolyubov added.

"Allow us to pass; why are you blocking our way? . . . Well, what is it you want?" Zverkov asked contemptuously. They were all flushed, their eyes glazed. They'd drunk a great deal.

"I ask for your friendship, Zverkov, I've insulted you, but . . ."

"Insulted me? You? In-sul-ted me? My dear sir, I want you to know that never, under any circumstances, could you possibly insult *me!*"

"And that's enough from you. Out of the way!" Trudolyubov added. "Let's go."

"Olympia is mine, gentlemen, that's agreed!" cried Zverkov.

"We won't argue, we won't," they replied, laughing.

I stood there as if spat on. The party left the room noisily, and Trudolyubov struck up a stupid song. Simonov remained behind for a brief moment to tip the waiters. All of a sudden I went up to him.

"Simonov! Give me six rubles," I said decisively and desperately.

He looked at me in extreme amazement with his dulled eyes. He was drunk, too.

"Are you really going *to that place* with us?"

"Yes!"

"I have no money!" he snapped; then he laughed contemptuously and headed out of the room.

I grabbed hold of his overcoat. It was a nightmare.

"Simonov! I know that you have some money. Why do you refuse me? Am I really such a scoundrel? Beware of refusing me: if you only knew, if you only knew why I'm asking. Everything depends on it, my entire future, all my plans. . . ."

Simonov took out the money and almost threw it at me.

"Take it, if you have no shame!" he said mercilessly, then ran out to catch up with the others.

I remained behind for a minute. The disorder, the leftovers, a broken glass on the floor, spilled wine, cigarette butts, drunkenness and delirium in my head, agonizing torment in my heart; and finally, a waiter who'd seen and heard everything and who was now looking at me with curiosity.

"To that place!" I cried. "Either they'll all fall on their knees, embracing me, begging for my friendship, or . . . or else, I'll give Zverkov a slap in the face."

V

"So here it is, here it is at last, a confrontation with reality," I muttered, rushing headlong down the stairs. "This is no longer the Pope leaving Rome and going to Brazil; this is no ball on the shores of Lake Como!"

"You're a scoundrel," the thought flashed through my mind, "if you laugh at that now."

"So what!" I cried in reply. "Everything is lost now, anyway!"

There was no sign of them, but it didn't matter. I knew where they were going.

At the entrance stood a solitary, late-night cabby in a coarse peasant coat powdered with wet, seemingly warm snow that was still falling. It was steamy and stuffy outside. The little shaggy piebald nag was also dusted with snow and was coughing; I remember that very well. I headed for the rough-hewn sledge; but as soon as I raised one foot to get in, the recollection of how Simonov had just given me six rubles hit me with such force that I tumbled into the sledge like a sack.

"No! There's a lot I have to do to make up for that!" I cried. "But make up for it I will or else I'll perish on the spot this very night. Let's go!" We set off. There was an entire whirlwind spinning around inside my head.

"They won't fall on their knees to beg for my friendship. That's a mirage, an indecent mirage, disgusting, romantic, and fantastic; it's just like the ball on the shores of Lake Como. Consequently, I *must* give Zverkov a slap in the face! I am obligated to do it. And so, it's all decided; I'm rushing there to give him a slap in the face."

"Hurry up!"

The cabby tugged at the reins.

"As soon as I go in, I'll slap him. Should I say a few words first before I slap him in the face? No! I'll simply go in and slap him. They'll all be sitting there in the drawing room; he'll be on the sofa with Olympia. That damned Olympia! She once ridiculed my face and refused me. I'll drag Olympia around by the hair and Zverkov by the ears. No, better grab one ear and lead him around the room like that. Perhaps they'll begin to beat me, and then they'll throw me out. That's even likely. So what? I'll still have slapped him first; the initiative will be mine. According to the laws of honor, that's all that matters. He'll be branded, and nothing can wipe away that slap except a duel.[9] He'll have to fight. So just let them beat me now! Let them, the ingrates! Trudolyubov will hit me hardest, he's so strong. Ferfichkin will sneak up alongside and will undoubtedly grab my hair, I'm sure he will. But let them, let them. That's why I've come. At last these blockheads will be forced to grasp the tragedy in all this! As they drag me to the door, I'll tell them that they really aren't even worth the tip of my little finger!"

"Hurry up, driver, hurry up!" I shouted to the cabby.

He was rather startled and cracked his whip. I'd shouted very savagely.

"We'll fight at daybreak, and that's settled. I'm through with the department. Ferfichkin recently said duh-partment, instead of department. But where will I get pistols? What nonsense! I'll take my salary in advance and buy them. And powder? Bullets? That's what the second will attend to. And how will I manage to do all this by daybreak? And where will I find a second? I have no acquaintances. . . ."

"Nonsense!" I shouted, whipping myself up into even more of a frenzy, "Nonsense!"

"The first person I meet on the street will have to act as my second, just as he would pull a drowning man from the water. The most extraordinary possibilities have to be allowed for. Even if tomorrow I were to ask the director himself to act as my second, he too would have to agree merely out of a sense of chivalry, and he would keep it a secret! Anton Antonych . . ."

The fact of the matter was that at that very moment I was more clearly and vividly aware than anyone else on earth of the disgusting absurdity of my intentions and the whole opposite side of the coin, but . . .

"Hurry up, driver, hurry, you rascal, hurry up!"

---

9. Duels as a means of resolving points of honor were officially discouraged but still fairly common.

"Hey, sir!" that son of the earth replied.

A sudden chill came over me.

"Wouldn't it be better . . . wouldn't it be better . . . to go straight home right now? Oh, my God! Why, why did I invite myself to that dinner yesterday? But no, it's impossible. And my pacing for three hours from the table to the stove? No, they, and no one else will have to pay me back for that pacing! They must wipe out that disgrace!"

"Hurry up!"

"What if they turn me over to the police? They wouldn't dare! They'd be afraid of a scandal. And what if Zverkov refuses the duel out of contempt? That's even likely; but I'll show them. . . . I'll rush to the posting station when he's supposed to leave tomorrow; I'll grab hold of his leg, tear off his overcoat just as he's about to climb into the carriage. I'll fasten my teeth on his arm and bite him. 'Look, everyone, see what a desperate man can be driven to!' Let him hit me on the head while others hit me from behind. I'll shout to the whole crowd, 'Behold, here's a young puppy who's going off to charm Circassian maidens with my spit on his face!' "

"Naturally, it'll all be over after that. The department will banish me from the face of the earth. They'll arrest me, try me, drive me out of the service, send me to prison; ship me off to Siberia for resettlement. Never mind! Fifteen years later when they let me out of jail, a beggar in rags, I'll drag myself off to see him. I'll find him in some provincial town. He'll be married and happy. He'll have a grown daughter. . . . I'll say, 'Look, you monster, look at my sunken cheeks and my rags. I've lost everything—career, happiness, art, science, a *beloved woman*—all because of you. Here are the pistols. I came here to load my pistol, and . . . and I forgive you.' Then I'll fire into the air, and he'll never hear another word from me again. . . ."

I was actually about to cry, even though I knew for a fact at that very moment that all this was straight out of Silvio and Lermontov's *Masquerade*.[1] Suddenly I felt terribly ashamed, so ashamed that I stopped the horse, climbed out of the sledge, and stood there amidst the snow in the middle of the street. The driver looked at me in amazement and sighed.

What was I to do? I couldn't go there—that was absurd; and I couldn't drop the whole thing, because then it would seem like . . . Oh, Lord! How could I drop it? After such insults!

"No!" I cried, throwing myself back into the sledge. "It's predestined; it's fate! Drive on, hurry up, *to that place!*"

In my impatience, I struck the driver on the neck with my fist.

"What's the matter with you? Why are you hitting me?" cried the poor little peasant, whipping his nag so that she began to kick up her hind legs.

Wet snow was falling in big flakes; I unbuttoned my coat, not caring about the snow. I forgot about everything else because now, having finally resolved on the slap, *I felt with horror that it was imminent* and that *nothing on earth could possibly stop it.* Lonely street lamps shone gloomily in the snowy mist like torches at a funeral. Snow got in under my overcoat, my jacket, and my necktie, and melted there. I didn't button up; after all, everything was lost, anyway. At last we arrived. I jumped out, almost beside myself, ran up the

---

1. A drama by Mikhail Lermontov (1835) about romantic conventions of love and honor. Silvio is the protagonist of Alexander Pushkin's short story *The Shot* (1830), about a man dedicated to revenge. Both works conclude with bizarre twists.

stairs, and began to pound at the door with my hands and feet. My legs, especially my knees, felt terribly weak. The door opened rather quickly; it was as if they knew I was coming. (In fact, Simonov had warned them that there might be someone else, since at this place one had to give notice and in general take precautions. It was one of those "fashionable shops" of the period that have now been eliminated by the police. During the day it really was a shop; but in the evening men with recommendations were able to visit as guests.) I walked rapidly through the darkened shop into a familiar drawing-room where there was only one small lit candle, and I stopped in dismay: there was no one there.

"Where are they?" I asked.

Naturally, by now they'd all dispersed. . . .

Before me stood a person with a stupid smile, the madam herself, who knew me slightly. In a moment a door opened, and another person came in.

Without paying much attention to anything, I walked around the room, and, apparently, was talking to myself. It was as if I'd been delivered from death, and I felt it joyously in my whole being. I'd have given him the slap, certainly, I'd certainly have given him the slap. But now they weren't here and . . . everything had vanished, everything had changed! . . . I looked around. I still couldn't take it all in. I glanced up mechanically at the girl who'd come in: before me there flashed a fresh, young, slightly pale face with straight dark brows and a serious, seemingly astonished look. I liked that immediately; I would have hated her if she'd been smiling. I began to look at her more carefully, as though with some effort: I'd still not managed to collect my thoughts. There was something simple and kind in her face, but somehow it was strangely serious. I was sure that she was at a disadvantage as a result, and that none of those fools had even noticed her. She couldn't be called a beauty, however, even though she was tall, strong, and well built. She was dressed very simply. Something despicable took hold of me; I went up to her. . . .

I happened to glance into a mirror. My overwrought face appeared extremely repulsive: it was pale, spiteful and mean; and my hair was dishevelled. "It doesn't matter. I'm glad," I thought. "In fact, I'm even delighted that I'll seem so repulsive to her; that pleases me. . . ."

VI

Somewhere behind a partition a clock was wheezing as if under some strong pressure, as though someone were strangling it. After this unnaturally prolonged wheezing there followed a thin, nasty, somehow unexpectedly hurried chime, as if someone had suddenly leapt forward. It struck two. I recovered, although I really hadn't been asleep, only lying there half-conscious.

It was almost totally dark in the narrow, cramped, low-ceilinged room, which was crammed with an enormous wardrobe and cluttered with cartons, rags, and all sorts of old clothes. The candle burning on the table at one end of the room flickered faintly from time to time, and almost went out completely. In a few moments total darkness would set in.

It didn't take long for me to come to my senses; all at once, without any effort, everything returned to me, as though it had been lying in ambush ready to pounce on me again. Even in my unconscious state some point had constantly remained in my memory, never to be forgotten, around which my sleepy visions had gloomily revolved. But it was a strange thing: everything that had happened to me that day now seemed, upon awakening, to have occurred in the distant past, as if I'd long since left it all behind.

My mind was in a daze. It was as though something were hanging over me, provoking, agitating, and disturbing me. Misery and bile were welling inside me, seeking an outlet. Suddenly I noticed beside me two wide-open eyes, examining me curiously and persistently. The gaze was coldly detached, sullen, as if belonging to a total stranger. I found it oppressive.

A dismal thought was conceived in my brain and spread throughout my whole body like a nasty sensation, such as one feels upon entering a damp, mouldy underground cellar. It was somehow unnatural that only now these two eyes had decided to examine me. I also recalled that during the course of the last two hours I hadn't said one word to this creature, and that I had considered it quite unnecessary; that had even given me pleasure for some reason. Now I'd suddenly realized starkly how absurd, how revolting as a spider, was the idea of debauchery, which, without love, crudely and shamelessly begins precisely at the point where genuine love is consummated. We looked at each other in this way for some time, but she didn't lower her gaze before mine, nor did she alter her stare, so that finally, for some reason, I felt very uneasy.

"What's your name?" I asked abruptly, to put an end to it quickly.

"Liza," she replied, almost in a whisper, but somehow in a very unfriendly way; and she turned her eyes away.

I remained silent.

"The weather today . . . snow . . . foul!" I observed, almost to myself, drearily placing one arm behind my head and staring at the ceiling.

She didn't answer. The whole thing was obscene.

"Are you from around here?" I asked her a moment later, almost angrily, turning my head slightly toward her.

"No."

"Where are you from?"

"Riga," she answered unwillingly.

"German?"

"No, Russian."

"Have you been here long?"

"Where?"

"In this house."

"Two weeks." She spoke more and more curtly. The candle had gone out completely; I could no longer see her face.

"Are your mother and father still living?"

"Yes . . . no . . . they are."

"Where are they?"

"There . . . in Riga."

"Who are they?"

"Just . . ."

"Just what? What do they do?"

"Tradespeople."

"Have you always lived with them?"

"Yes."

"How old are you?"

"Twenty."

"Why did you leave them?"

"Just because . . ."

That "just because" meant: leave me alone, it makes me sick. We fell silent.

Only God knows why, but I didn't leave. I too started to feel sick and more depressed. Images of the previous day began to come to mind all on their own, without my willing it, in a disordered way. I suddenly recalled a scene that I'd witnessed on the street that morning as I was anxiously hurrying to work. "Today some people were carrying a coffin and nearly dropped it," I suddenly said aloud, having no desire whatever to begin a conversation, but just so, almost accidentally.

"A coffin?"

"Yes, in the Haymarket; they were carrying it up from an underground cellar."

"From a cellar?"

"Not a cellar, but from a basement . . . well, you know . . . from downstairs . . . from a house of ill repute . . . There was such filth all around. . . . Eggshells, garbage . . . it smelled foul . . . it was disgusting."

Silence.

"A nasty day to be buried!" I began again to break the silence.

"Why nasty?"

"Snow, slush . . ." (I yawned.)

"It doesn't matter," she said suddenly after a brief silence.

"No, it's foul. . . ." (I yawned again.) "The grave diggers must have been cursing because they were getting wet out there in the snow. And there must have been water in the grave."

"Why water in the grave?" she asked with some curiosity, but she spoke even more rudely and curtly than before. Something suddenly began to goad me on.

"Naturally, water on the bottom, six inches or so. You can't ever dig a dry grave at Volkovo cemetery."

"Why not?"

"What do you mean, why not? The place is waterlogged. It's all swamp. So they bury them right in the water. I've seen it myself . . . many times. . . ."

(I'd never seen it, and I'd never been to Volkovo cemetery, but I'd heard about it from other people.)

"Doesn't it matter to you if you die?"

"Why should I die?" she replied, as though defending herself.

"Well, someday you'll die; you'll die just like that woman did this morning. She was a . . . she was also a young girl . . . she died of consumption."

"The wench should have died in the hospital. . . ." (She knows all about it, I thought, and she even said "wench" instead of "girl.")

"She owed money to her madam," I retorted, more and more goaded on by the argument. "She worked right up to the end, even though she had consumption. The cabbies standing around were chatting with the soldiers, telling them all about it. Her former acquaintances, most likely. They were all laughing. They were planning to drink to her memory at the tavern." (I invented a great deal of this.)

Silence, deep silence. She didn't even stir.

"Do you think it would be better to die in a hospital?"

"Isn't it just the same? . . . Besides, why should I die?" she added irritably.

"If not now, then later?"

"Well, then later . . ."

"That's what you think! Now you're young and pretty and fresh—that's your value. But after a year of this life, you won't be like that any more; you'll fade."

"In a year?"

"In any case, after a year your price will be lower," I continued, gloating. "You'll move out of here into a worse place, into some other house. And a year later, into a third, each worse and worse, and seven years from now you'll end up in a cellar on the Haymarket. Even that won't be so bad. The real trouble will come when you get some disease, let's say a weakness in the chest . . . or you catch cold or something. In this kind of life it's no laughing matter to get sick. It takes hold of you and may never let go. And so, you die."

"Well, then, I'll die," she answered now quite angrily and stirred quickly.

"That'll be a pity."

"For what?"

"A pity to lose a life."

Silence.

"Did you have a sweetheart? Huh?"

"What's it to you?"

"Oh, I'm not interrogating you. What do I care? Why are you angry? Of course, you may have had your own troubles. What's it to me? Just the same, I'm sorry."

"For whom?"

"I'm sorry for you."

"No need . . . ," she whispered barely audibly and stirred once again.

That provoked me at once. What! I was being so gentle with her, while she . . .

"Well, and what do you think? Are you on the right path then?"

"I don't think anything."

"That's just the trouble—you don't think. Wake up, while there's still time. And there is time. You're still young and pretty; you could fall in love, get married, be happy.[2] . . ."

"Not all married women are happy," she snapped in her former, rude manner.

"Not all, of course, but it's still better than this. A lot better. You can even live without happiness as long as there's love. Even in sorrow life can be good; it's good to be alive, no matter how you live. But what's there besides . . . stench? Phew!"

I turned away in disgust; I was no longer coldly philosophizing. I began to feel what I was saying and grew excited. I'd been longing to expound these cherished *little ideas* that I'd been nurturing in my corner. Something had suddenly caught fire in me, some kind of goal had "manifested itself" before me.

"Pay no attention to the fact that I'm here. I'm no model for you. I may

---

2. A popular theme treated by Gogol, Chernyshevsky, and Nekrasov, among others. Typically, an innocent and idealistic young man attempts to rehabilitate a prostitute or "fallen" woman.

be even worse than you are. Moreover, I was drunk when I came here." I hastened nonetheless to justify myself. "Besides, a man is no example to a woman. It's a different thing altogether; even though I degrade and defile myself, I'm still no one's slave; if I want to leave, I just get up and go. I shake it all off and I'm a different man. But you must realize right from the start that you're a slave. Yes, a slave! You give away everything, all your freedom. Later, if you want to break this chain, you won't be able to; it'll bind you ever more tightly. That's the kind of evil chain it is. I know. I won't say anything else; you might not even understand me. But tell me this, aren't you already in debt to your madam? There, you see!" I added, even though she hadn't answered, but had merely remained silent; but she was listening with all her might. "There's your chain! You'll never buy yourself out. That's the way it's done. It's just like selling your soul to the devil. . . .

"And besides . . . I may be just as unfortunate, how do you know, and I may be wallowing in mud on purpose, also out of misery. After all, people drink out of misery. Well, I came here out of misery. Now, tell me, what's so good about this place? Here you and I were . . . intimate . . . just a little while ago, and all that time we didn't say one word to each other; afterward you began to examine me like a wild creature, and I did the same. Is that the way people love? Is that how one person is supposed to encounter another? It's a disgrace, that's what it is!"

"Yes!" she agreed with me sharply and hastily. The haste of her answer surprised even me. It meant that perhaps the very same idea was flitting through her head while she'd been examining me earlier. It meant that she too was capable of some thought. . . . "Devil take it; this is odd, this *kinship*," I thought, almost rubbing my hands together. "Surely I can handle such a young soul."

It was the sport that attracted me most of all.

She turned her face closer to mine, and in the darkness it seemed that she propped her head up on her arm. Perhaps she was examining me. I felt sorry that I couldn't see her eyes. I heard her breathing deeply.

"Why did you come here?" I began with some authority.

"Just so . . ."

"But think how nice it would be living in your father's house! There you'd be warm and free; you'd have a nest of your own."

"And what if it's worse than that?"

"I must establish the right tone," flashed through my mind. "I won't get far with sentimentality."

However, that merely flashed through my mind. I swear that she really did interest me. Besides, I was somewhat exhausted and provoked. After all, artifice goes along so easily with feeling.

"Who can say?" I hastened to reply. "All sorts of things can happen. Why, I was sure that someone had wronged you and was more to blame than you are. After all, I know nothing of your life story, but a girl like you doesn't wind up in this sort of place on her own accord. . . ."

"What kind of a girl am I?" she whispered hardly audibly; but I heard it.

"What the hell! Now I'm flattering her. That's disgusting! But, perhaps it's a good thing. . . ." She remained silent.

"You see, Liza, I'll tell you about myself. If I'd had a family when I was growing up, I wouldn't be the person I am now. I think about this often.

After all, no matter how bad it is in your own family—it's still your own father and mother, and not enemies or strangers. Even if they show you their love only once a year, you still know that you're at home. I grew up without a family; that must be why I turned out the way I did—so unfeeling."

I waited again.

"She might not understand," I thought. "Besides, it's absurd—all this moralizing."

"If I were a father and had a daughter, I think that I'd have loved her more than my sons, really," I began indirectly, talking about something else in order to distract her. I confess that I was blushing.

"Why's that?"

Ah, so she's listening!

"Just because. I don't know why, Liza. You see, I knew a father who was a stern, strict man, but he would kneel before his daughter and kiss her hands and feet; he couldn't get enough of her, really. She'd go dancing at a party, and he'd stand in one spot for five hours, never taking his eyes off her. He was crazy about her; I can understand that. At night she'd be tired and fall asleep, but he'd wake up, go in to kiss her, and make the sign of the cross over her while she slept. He used to wear a dirty old jacket and was stingy with everyone else, but would spend his last kopeck on her, buying her expensive presents; it afforded him great joy if she liked his presents. A father always loves his daughters more than their mother does. Some girls have a very nice time living at home. I think that I wouldn't even have let my daughter get married."

"Why not?" she asked with a barely perceptible smile.

"I'd be jealous, so help me God. Why, how could she kiss someone else? How could she love a stranger more than her own father? It's even painful to think about it. Of course, it's all nonsense; naturally, everyone finally comes to his senses. But I think that before I'd let her marry, I'd have tortured myself with worry. I'd have found fault with all her suitors. Nevertheless, I'd have ended up by allowing her to marry whomever she loved. After all, the one she loves always seems the worst of all to the father. That's how it is. That causes a lot of trouble in many families."

"Some are glad to sell their daughters, rather than let them marry honorably," she said suddenly.

Aha, so that's it!

"That happens, Liza, in those wretched families where there's neither God nor love," I retorted heatedly. "And where there's no love, there's also no good sense. There are such families, it's true, but I'm not talking about them. Obviously, from the way you talk, you didn't see much kindness in your own family. You must be very unfortunate. Hmm . . . But all this results primarily from poverty."

"And is it any better among the gentry? Honest folk live decently even in poverty."

"Hmmm . . . Yes. Perhaps. There's something else, Liza. Man only likes to count his troubles; he doesn't calculate his happiness. If he figured as he should, he'd see that everyone gets his share. So, let's say that all goes well in a particular family; it enjoys God's blessing, the husband turns out to be a good man, he loves you, cherishes you, and never leaves you. Life is good in that family. Sometimes, even though there's a measure of sorrow, life's still good. Where isn't there sorrow? If you choose to get married, *you'll find out for yourself*. Consider even the first years of a marriage to the one you love: what happiness, what pure bliss there can be sometimes! Almost without exception. At first even quarrels with your husband turn out well. For some women, the more they love their husbands, the more they pick fights with them. It's true; I once knew a woman like that. 'That's how it is,' she'd say. 'I love you very much and I'm tormenting you out of love, so that you'll feel it.' Did you know that one can torment a person intentionally out of love? It's mostly women who do that. Then she thinks to herself, 'I'll love him so much afterward, I'll be so affectionate, it's no sin to torment him a little now.' At home everyone would rejoice over you, and it would be so pleasant, cheerful, serene, and honorable. . . . Some other women are very jealous. If her husband goes away, I knew one like that, she can't stand it; she jumps up at night and goes off on the sly to see. Is he there? Is he in that house? Is he with that one? Now that's bad. Even she herself knows that it's bad; her heart sinks and she suffers because she really loves him. It's all out of love. And how nice it is to make up after a quarrel, to admit one's guilt or forgive him! How nice it is for both of them, how good they both feel at once, just as if they'd met again, married again, and begun their love all over again. No one, no one at all has to know what goes on between a husband and wife, if they love each other. However their quarrel ends, they should never call in either one of their mothers to act as judge or to hear complaints about the other one. They must act as their own judges. Love is God's mystery and should be hidden from other people's eyes, no matter what happens. This makes it holier, much better. They respect each other more, and a great deal is based on this respect. And, if there's been love, if they got married out of love, why should love disappear? Can't it be sustained? It rarely happens that it can't be sustained. If the husband turns out to be a kind and honest man, how can the love disappear? The first phase of married love will pass, that's true, but it's followed by an even better kind of love. Souls are joined together and all their concerns are managed in common; there'll be no secrets from one another. When children arrive, each and every stage, even a very difficult one, will seem happy, as long as there's both love and courage. Even work is cheerful; even when you deny yourself bread for your children's sake, you're still happy. After all, they'll love you for it afterward; you're really saving for your own future. Your children will grow up, and you'll feel that you're a model for them, a support. Even after you die, they'll carry your thoughts and feelings all during their life. They'll take on your image and likeness, since they received it from you. Consequently, it's a great obligation. How can a mother and father keep from growing closer? They say it's difficult to raise children. Who says that? It's heavenly joy! Do you love little children, Liza? I love them dearly. You know—a rosy little boy, suckling at your breast; what husband's heart could turn against his wife seeing her sitting there holding his child? The chubby, rosy little baby sprawls and snuggles; his little hands and feet are plump; his little nails are clean and tiny, so tiny it's even funny to see them; his little eyes look as if he already understood everything. As he suckles, he tugs at your breast playfully with his little hand. When the father approaches, the child lets go of the breast, bends way back, looks at his father, and laughs—as if God only knows how funny it is—and then takes to suckling again. Afterward, when he starts cutting teeth, he'll sometimes bite his mother's breast; looking at her sideways his little eyes seem to say, 'See, I bit you!' Isn't this pure bliss—the three of them, husband, wife, and child, all together? You can forgive a great deal for such moments. No, Liza, I think you must first learn how to live by yourself, and only afterward blame others."

"It's by means of images," I thought to myself, "just such images that I can get to you," although I was speaking with considerable feeling, I swear it; and all at once I blushed. "And what if she suddenly bursts out laughing—where will I hide then?" That thought drove me into a rage. By the end of my speech I'd really become excited, and now my pride was suffering somehow. The silence lasted for a while. I even considered shaking her.

"Somehow you . . ." she began suddenly and then stopped.

But I understood everything already: something was trembling in her voice now, not shrill, rude or unyielding as before, but something soft and timid, so timid that I suddenly was rather ashamed to watch her and felt guilty.

"What?" I asked with tender curiosity.

"Well, you . . ."

"What?"

"You somehow . . . it sounds just like a book," she said, and once again something which was noticeably sarcastic was suddenly heard in her voice.

Her remark wounded me dreadfully. That's not what I'd expected.

Yet, I didn't understand that she was intentionally disguising her feelings with sarcasm; that was usually the last resort of people who are timid and chaste of heart, whose souls have been coarsely and impudently invaded; and who, until the last moment, refuse to yield out of pride and are afraid to express their own feelings to you. I should've guessed it from the timidity with which on several occasions she tried to be sarcastic, until she finally managed to express it. But I hadn't guessed, and a malicious impulse took hold of me.

"Just you wait," I thought.

VII

"That's enough, Liza. What do books have to do with it, when this disgusts me as an outsider? And not only as an outsider. All this has awakened in my heart . . . Can it be, can it really be that you don't find it repulsive here? No, clearly habit means a great deal. The devil only knows what habit can do to a person. But do you seriously think that you'll never grow old, that you'll always be pretty, and that they'll keep you on here forever and ever? I'm not even talking about the filth. . . . Besides, I want to say this about your present life: even though you're still young, good-looking, nice, with soul and feelings, do you know, that when I came to a little while ago, I was immediately disgusted to be here with you! Why, a man has to be drunk to wind up here. But if you were in a different place, living as nice people do, I might not only chase after you, I might actually fall in love with you. I'd rejoice at a look from you, let alone a word; I'd wait for you at the gate and kneel down before you; I'd think of you as my betrothed and even consider that an honor. I wouldn't dare have any impure thoughts about you. But here, I know that I need only whistle, and you, whether you want to or not, will come to me, and that I don't have to do your bidding, whereas you have to do mine. The lowliest peasant may hire himself out as a laborer, but he doesn't make a complete slave of himself; he knows that it's only for a limited term. But what's your term? Just think about it. What are you giving up here? What are you enslaving? Why, you're enslaving your soul, something you don't really own, together with your body! You're giving away your love to be defiled by any drunkard! Love! After all, that's all there is! It's a precious jewel, a maiden's treasure, that's what it is! Why, to earn that love a man might be ready to offer up his own soul, to face death. But what's your love worth now? You've been bought, all of you; and why should anyone strive for your love, when you offer everything even without it? Why, there's no greater insult for a girl, don't you understand? Now, I've heard that they console you foolish girls, they allow you to see your own lovers here. But that's merely child's play, deception, making fun of you, while you believe it. And do you really think he loves you, that lover of yours? I don't believe it. How can he, if he knows that you can be called away from him at any moment? He'd have to be depraved after all that. Does he possess even one drop of respect for you? What do you have in common with him? He's laughing at you and stealing from you at the same time—so much for his love. It's not too bad, as long as he doesn't beat you. But perhaps he does. Go on, ask him, if you have such a lover, whether he'll ever marry you. Why, he'll burst out laughing right in your face, if he doesn't spit at you or smack you. He himself may be worth no more than a few lousy kopecks. And for what, do you think, did you ruin your whole life here? For the coffee they give you to drink, or for the plentiful supply of food? Why do you think they feed you so well? Another girl, an honest one, would choke on every bite, because she'd know why she was being fed so well. You're in debt here, you'll be in debt, and will remain so until the end, until such time comes as the customers begin to spurn you. And that time will come very soon; don't count on your youth. Why, here youth flies by like a stagecoach. They'll kick you out. And they'll not merely kick you out, but for a long time before that they'll pester you, reproach you, and abuse you—as if you hadn't ruined your health for the madam, hadn't given up your youth and your soul for her in vain, but rather, as if you'd ruined her, ravaged her, and robbed her. And don't expect any support. Your friends will also attack you to curry her favor, because they're all in bondage here and have long since lost both conscience and pity. They've become despicable, and there's nothing on earth more despicable, more repulsive, or more insulting than their abuse. You'll lose everything here, everything, without exception—your health, youth, beauty, and hope—and at the age of twenty-two you'll look as if you were thirty-five, and even that won't be too awful if you're not ill. Thank God for that. Why, you probably think that you're not even working, that it's all play! But there's no harder work or more onerous task than this one in the whole world and there never has been. I'd think that one's heart alone would be worn out by crying. Yet you dare not utter one word, not one syllable; when they drive you out, you leave as if you were the guilty one. You'll move to another place, then to a third, then somewhere else, and finally you'll wind up in the Haymarket. And there they'll start beating you for no good reason at all; it's a local custom; the clients there don't know how to be nice without beating you. You don't think it's so disgusting there? Maybe you should go and have a look sometime, and see it with your own eyes. Once, at New Year's, I saw a woman in a doorway.

Her own kind had pushed her outside as a joke, to freeze her for a little while because she was wailing too much; they shut the door behind her. At nine o'clock in the morning she was already dead drunk, dishevelled, half-naked, and all beaten up. Her face was powdered, but her eyes were bruised; blood was streaming from her nose and mouth; a certain cabby had just fixed her up. She was sitting on a stone step, holding a piece of salted fish in her hand; she was howling, wailing something about her 'fate,' and slapping the fish against the stone step. Cabbies and drunken soldiers had gathered around the steps and were taunting her. Don't you think you'll wind up the same way? I wouldn't want to believe it myself, but how do you know, perhaps eight or ten years ago this same girl, the one with the salted fish, arrived here from somewhere or other, all fresh like a little cherub, innocent, and pure; she knew no evil and blushed at every word. Perhaps she was just like you—proud, easily offended, unlike all the rest; she looked like a queen and knew that total happiness awaited the man who would love her and whom she would also love. Do you see how it all ended? What if at the very moment she was slapping the fish against that filthy step, dead drunk and dishevelled, what if, even at that very moment she'd recalled her earlier, chaste years in her father's house when she was still going to school, and when her neighbor's son used to wait for her along the path and assure her that he'd love her all his life and devote himself entirely to her, and when they vowed to love one another forever and get married as soon as they grew up! No, Liza, you'd be lucky, very lucky, if you died quickly from consumption somewhere in a corner, in a cellar, like that other girl. In a hospital, you say? All right—they'll take you off, but what if the madam still requires your services? Consumption is quite a disease—it's not like dying from a fever. A person continues to hope right up until the last minute and declares that he's in good health. He consoles himself. Now that's useful for your madam. Don't worry, that's the way it is. You've sold your soul; besides, you owe her money—that means you don't dare say a thing. And while you're dying, they'll all abandon you, turn away from you—because there's nothing left to get from you. They'll even reproach you for taking up space for no good reason and for taking so long to die. You won't even be able to ask for something to drink, without their hurling abuse at you: 'When will you croak, you old bitch? You keep on moaning and don't let us get any sleep—and you drive our customers away.' That's for sure; I've overheard such words myself. And as you're breathing your last, they'll shove you into the filthiest corner of the cellar—into darkness and dampness; lying there alone, what will you think about then? After you die, some stranger will lay you out hurriedly, grumbling all the while, impatiently—no one will bless you, no one will sigh over you; they'll merely want to get rid of you as quickly as possible. They'll buy you a wooden trough and carry you out as they did that poor woman I saw today; then they'll go off to a tavern and drink to your memory. There'll be slush, filth, and wet snow in your grave—why bother for the likes of you? 'Let her down, Vanyukha; after all, it's her fate to go down with her legs up, that's the sort of girl she was. Pull up on that rope, you rascal!' 'It's okay like that.' 'How's it okay? See, it's lying on its side. Was she a human being or not? Oh, never mind, cover it up.' They won't want to spend much time arguing over you. They'll cover your coffin quickly with wet, blue clay and then go off to the tavern. . . . That'll be the end of your memory on earth; for other women, children will visit their graves, fathers, husbands—but for you—no tears, no sighs; no remembrances. No one, absolutely no one in the whole world, will ever come to visit you; your name will disappear from the face of the earth, just as if you'd never been born and had never existed. Mud and filth, no matter how you pound on the lid of your coffin at night when other corpses arise: 'Let me out, kind people, let me live on earth for a little while! I lived, but I didn't really see life; my life went down the drain; they drank it away in a tavern at the Haymarket; let me out, kind people, let me live in the world once again!' "

I was so carried away by my own pathos that I began to feel a lump forming in my throat, and . . . I suddenly stopped, rose up in fright, and, leaning over apprehensively, I began to listen carefully as my own heart pounded. There was cause for dismay.

For a while I felt that I'd turned her soul inside out and had broken her heart; the more I became convinced of this, the more I strived to reach my goal as quickly and forcefully as possible. It was the sport, the sport that attracted me; but it wasn't only the sport. . . .

I knew that I was speaking clumsily, artificially, even bookishly; in short, I didn't know how to speak except "like a book." But that didn't bother me, for I knew, I had a premonition, that I would be understood and that this bookishness itself might even help things along. But now, having achieved this effect, I suddenly lost all my nerve. No, never, never before had I witnessed such despair! She was lying there, her face pressed deep into a pillow she was clutching with her hands. Her heart was bursting. Her young body was shuddering as if she were having convulsions. Suppressed sobs shook her breast, tore her apart, and suddenly burst forth in cries and moans. Then she pressed her face even deeper into the pillow: she didn't want anyone, not one living soul, to hear her anguish and her tears. She bit the pillow; she bit her hand until it bled (I noticed that afterward); or else, thrusting her fingers into her dishevelled hair, she became rigid with the strain, holding her breath and clenching her teeth. I was about to say something, to ask her to calm down; but I felt that I didn't dare. Suddenly, all in a kind of chill, almost in a panic, I groped hurriedly to get out of there as quickly as possible. It was dark: no matter how I tried, I couldn't end it quickly. Suddenly I felt a box of matches and a candlestick with a whole unused candle. As soon as the room was lit up, Liza started suddenly, sat up, and looked at me almost senselessly, with a distorted face and a half-crazy smile. I sat down next to her and took her hands; she came to and threw herself at me, wanting to embrace me, yet not daring to. Then she quietly lowered her head before me.

"Liza, my friend, I shouldn't have . . . you must forgive me," I began, but she squeezed my hands so tightly in her fingers that I realized I was saying the wrong thing and stopped.

"Here's my address, Liza. Come to see me."

"I will," she whispered resolutely, still not lifting her head.

"I'm going now, good-bye . . . until we meet again."

I stood up; she did, too, and suddenly blushed all over, shuddered, seized a shawl lying on a chair, threw it over her shoulders, and wrapped herself up to her chin. After doing this, she smiled again somewhat painfully, blushed, and looked at me strangely. I felt awful. I hastened to leave, to get away.

"Wait," she said suddenly as we were standing in the hallway near the door, and she stopped me by putting her hand on my overcoat. She quickly put the candle down and ran off; obviously she'd remembered something or wanted to show me something. As she left she was blushing all over, her eyes were gleaming, and a smile had appeared on her lips—what on earth did it all mean? I waited against my own will; she returned a moment later with a glance that seemed to beg forgiveness for something. All in all it was no longer the same face or the same glance as before—sullen, distrustful, obstinate. Now her glance was imploring, soft, and, at the same time, trusting, affectionate, and timid. That's how children look at people whom they love very much, or when they're asking for something. Her eyes were light hazel, lovely, full of life, as capable of expressing love as brooding hatred.

Without any explanation, as if I were some kind of higher being who was supposed to know everything, she held a piece of paper out toward me. At that moment her whole face was shining with a most naive, almost childlike triumph. I unfolded the paper. It was a letter to her from some medical student containing a high-flown, flowery, but very respectful declaration of love. I don't remember the exact words now, but I can well recall the genuine emotion that can't be feigned shining through that high style. When I'd finished reading the letter, I met her ardent, curious, and childishly impatient gaze. She'd fixed her eyes on my face and was waiting eagerly to see what I'd say. In a few words, hurriedly, but with some joy and pride, she explained that she'd once been at a dance somewhere, in a private house, at the home of some "very, very good people, *family people,* where they *knew nothing,* nothing at all," because she'd arrived at this place only recently and was just . . . well, she hadn't quite decided whether she'd stay here and she'd certainly leave as soon as she'd paid off her debt. . . . Well, and this student was there; he danced with her all evening and talked to her. It turned out he was from Riga; he'd known her as a child, they'd played together, but that had been a long time ago; he was acquainted with her parents—but he knew nothing, absolutely nothing *about this place* and he didn't even suspect it! And so, the very next day, after the dance (only some three days ago), he'd sent her this letter through the friend with whom she'd gone to the party . . . and . . . well, that's the whole story."

She lowered her sparkling eyes somewhat bashfully after she finished speaking.

The poor little thing, she'd saved this student's letter as a treasure and had run to fetch this one treasure of hers, not wanting me to leave without knowing that she too was the object of sincere, honest love, and that someone exists who had spoken to her respectfully. Probably that letter was fated to lie in her box without results. But that didn't matter; I'm sure that she'll guard it as a treasure her whole life, as her pride and vindication; and now, at a moment like this, she remembered it and brought it out to exult naively before me, to raise herself in my eyes, so that I could see it for myself and could also think well of her. I didn't say a thing; I shook her hand and left. I really wanted to get away. . . . I walked all the way home in spite of the fact that wet snow was still falling in large flakes. I was exhausted, oppressed, and perplexed. But the truth was already glimmering behind that perplexity. The ugly truth!

VIII

It was some time, however, before I agreed to acknowledge that truth. I awoke the next morning after a few hours of deep, leaden sleep. Instantly recalling the events of the previous day, even I was astonished at my *sentimentality* with Liza last night, at all of yesterday's "horror and pity." "Why, it's an attack of old woman's nervous hysteria, phew!" I decided. "And why on earth did I force my address on her? What if she comes? Then again, let her come, it doesn't make any difference. . . ." But *obviously* that was not the main, most important matter: I had to make haste and rescue at all costs my reputation in the eyes of Zverkov and Simonov. That was my main task. I even forgot all about Liza in the concerns of that morning.

First of all I had to repay last night's debt to Simonov immediately. I resolved on desperate means: I would borrow the sum of fifteen rubles from Anton Antonych. As luck would have it, he was in a splendid mood that morning and gave me the money at once, at my first request. I was so delighted that I signed a promissory note with a somewhat dashing air, and told him *casually* that on the previous evening "I'd been living it up with some friends at the Hôtel de Paris. We were holding a farewell dinner for a comrade, one might even say, a childhood friend, and, you know—he's a great carouser, very spoiled—well, naturally; he comes from a good family, has considerable wealth and a brilliant career; he's witty and charming, and has affairs with certain ladies, you understand. We drank up an extra 'half-dozen bottles' and . . ." There was nothing to it; I said all this very easily, casually, and complacently.

Upon arriving home I wrote to Simonov at once.

To this very day I recall with admiration the truly gentlemanly, good-natured, candid tone of my letter. Cleverly and nobly, and, above all, without unnecessary words, I blamed myself for everything. I justified myself, "if only I could be allowed to justify myself," by saying that, being so totally unaccustomed to wine, I'd gotten drunk with the first glass, which (supposedly) I'd consumed even before their arrival, as I waited for them in the Hôtel de Paris between the hours of five and six o'clock. In particular, I begged for Simonov's pardon; I asked him to convey my apology to all the others, especially to Zverkov, whom, "I recall, as if in a dream," it seems, I'd insulted. I added that I'd have called upon each of them, but was suffering from a bad headache, and, worst of all, I was ashamed. I was particularly satisfied by the "certain lightness," almost casualness (though, still very proper), unexpectedly reflected in my style; better than all possible arguments, it conveyed to them at once that I regarded "all of last night's unpleasantness" in a rather detached way, and that I was not at all, not in the least struck down on the spot as you, gentlemen, probably suspect. On the contrary, I regard this all serenely, as any self-respecting gentleman would. The true story, as they say, is no reproach to an honest young man.

"Why, there's even a hint of aristocratic playfulness in it," I thought admiringly as I reread my note. "And it's all because I'm such a cultured and educated man! Others in my place wouldn't know how to extricate themselves, but I've gotten out of it, and I'm having a good time once again, all because I'm an 'educated and cultured man of our time.' It may even be true that the whole thing occurred as a result of that wine yesterday. Hmmm . . .

well, no, it wasn't really the wine. And I didn't have anything to drink between five and six o'clock when I was waiting for them. I lied to Simonov; it was a bold-faced lie—yet I'm not ashamed of it even now. . . ."

But, to hell with it, anyway! The main thing is, I got out of it.

I put six rubles in the letter, sealed it up, and asked Apollon to take it to Simonov. When he heard that there was money in it, Apollon became more respectful and agreed to deliver it. Toward evening I went out for a stroll. My head was still aching and spinning from the events of the day before. But as evening approached and twilight deepened, my impressions changed and became more confused, as did my thoughts. Something hadn't yet died within me, deep within my heart and conscience; it didn't want to die, and it expressed itself as burning anguish. I jostled my way along the more populous, commercial streets, along Meshchanskaya, Sadovaya, near the Yusupov Garden. I particularly liked to stroll along these streets at twilight, just as they became most crowded with all sorts of pedestrians, merchants, and tradesmen, with faces preoccupied to the point of hostility, on their way home from a hard day's work. It was precisely the cheap bustle that I liked, the crass prosaic quality. But this time all that street bustle irritated me even more. I couldn't get a hold of myself or puzzle out what was wrong. Something was rising, rising up in my soul continually, painfully, and didn't want to settle down. I returned home completely distraught. It was just as if some crime were weighing on my soul.

I was constantly tormented by the thought that Liza might come to see me. It was strange, but from all of yesterday's recollections, the one of her tormented me most, somehow separately from all the others. I'd managed to forget the rest by evening, to shrug everything off, and I still remained completely satisfied with my letter to Simonov. But in regard to Liza, I was not at all satisfied. It was as though I were tormented by her alone. "What if she comes?" I thought continually. "Well, so what? It doesn't matter. Let her come. Hmm. The only unpleasant thing is that she'll see, for instance, how I live. Yesterday I appeared before her such a . . . hero . . . but now, hmm! Besides, it's revolting that I've sunk so low. The squalor of my apartment. And I dared go to dinner last night wearing such clothes! And that oilcloth sofa of mine with its stuffing hanging out! And my dressing gown that doesn't quite cover me! What rags! . . . She'll see it all—and she'll see Apollon. That swine will surely insult her. He'll pick on her, just to be rude to me. Of course, I'll be frightened, as usual. I'll begin to fawn before her, wrap myself up in my dressing gown. I'll start to smile and tell lies. Ugh, the indecency! And that's not even the worst part! There's something even more important, nastier, meaner! Yes, meaner! Once again, I'll put on that dishonest, deceitful mask! . . ."

When I reached this thought, I simply flared up.

"Why deceitful? How deceitful? Yesterday I spoke sincerely. I recall that there was genuine feeling in me, too. I was trying no less than to arouse noble feelings in her . . . and if she wept, that's a good thing; it will have a beneficial effect. . . ."

But I still couldn't calm down.

All that evening, even after I returned home, even after nine o'clock, when by my calculations Liza could no longer have come, her image continued to haunt me, and, what's most important, she always appeared in one and the

same form. Of all that had occurred yesterday, it was one moment in particular which stood out most vividly: that was when I lit up the room with a
match and saw her pale, distorted face with its tormented gaze. What a
pitiful, unnatural, distorted smile she'd had at that moment! But little did I
know then that even fifteen years later I'd still picture Liza to myself with
that same pitiful, distorted, and unnecessary smile which she'd had at that
moment.

The next day I was once again prepared to dismiss all this business as
nonsense, as the result of overstimulated nerves; but most of all, as exaggeration. I was well aware of this weakness of mine and sometimes was even
afraid of it; "I exaggerate everything, that's my problem," I kept repeating to
myself hour after hour. And yet, "yet, Liza may still come, all the same"; that
was the refrain which concluded my reflections. I was so distressed that I
sometimes became furious. "She'll come! She'll definitely come! If not today,
then tomorrow, she'll seek me out! That's just like the damned romanticism
of all these *pure hearts*! Oh, the squalor, the stupidity, the narrowness of
these 'filthy, sentimental souls!' How could all this not be understood, how
on earth could it not be understood? . . ." But at this point I would stop
myself, even in the midst of great confusion.

"And how few, how very few words were needed," I thought in passing,
"how little idyllic sentiment (what's more, the sentiment was artificial, bookish, composed) was necessary to turn a whole human soul according to my
wishes at once. That's innocence for you! That's virgin soil!"

At times the thought occurred that I might go to her myself "to tell her
everything," and to beg her not to come to me. But at this thought such
venom arose in me that it seemed I'd have crushed that "damned" Liza if
she'd suddenly turned up next to me. I'd have insulted her, spat at her, struck
her, and chased her away!

One day passed, however, then a second, and a third; she still hadn't come,
and I began to calm down. I felt particularly reassured and relaxed after nine
o'clock in the evening, and even began to daydream sweetly at times. For
instance, I'd save Liza, precisely because she'd come to me, and I'd talk to
her. . . . I'd develop her mind, educate her. At last I'd notice that she loved
me, loved me passionately. I'd pretend I didn't understand. (For that matter,
I didn't know why I'd pretend; most likely just for the effect.) At last, all
embarrassed, beautiful, trembling, and sobbing, she'd throw herself at my
feet and declare that I was her saviour and she loved me more than anything
in the world. I'd be surprised, but . . . "Liza," I'd say, "Do you really think
that I haven't noticed your love? I've seen everything. I guessed, but dared
not be first to make a claim on your heart because I had such influence over
you, and because I was afraid you might deliberately force yourself to respond
to my love out of gratitude, that you might forcibly evoke within yourself a
feeling that didn't really exist. No, I didn't want that because it would be . . .
despotism. . . . It would be indelicate (well, in short, here I launched on some
European, George Sandian,[3] inexplicably lofty subtleties . . .). But now,
now—you're mine, you're my creation, you're pure and lovely, you're my
beautiful wife."

---

3. George Sand was the pseudonym of the French woman novelist Aurore Dudevant (1804–1876), famous
also as a promoter of feminism.

> And enter my house bold and free
> To become its full mistress![4]

"Then we'd begin to live happily together, travel abroad, etc., etc." In short, it began to seem crude even to me, and I ended it all by sticking my tongue out at myself.

"Besides, they won't let her out of there, the 'bitch,' " I thought. "After all, it seems unlikely that they'd release them for strolls, especially in the evening (for some reason I was convinced that she had to report there every evening, precisely at seven o'clock). Moreover, she said that she'd yet to become completely enslaved there, and that she still had certain rights; that means, hmm. Devil take it, she'll come, she's bound to come!"

It was a good thing I was distracted at the time by Apollon's rudeness. He made me lose all patience. He was the bane of my existence, a punishment inflicted on me by Providence. We'd been squabbling constantly for several years now and I hated him. My God, how I hated him! I think that I never hated anyone in my whole life as much as I hated him, especially at those times. He was an elderly, dignified man who worked part-time as a tailor. But for some unknown reason he despised me, even beyond all measure, and looked down upon me intolerably. However, he looked down on everyone. You need only glance at that flaxen, slicked-down hair, at that single lock brushed over his forehead and greased with vegetable oil, at his strong mouth, always drawn up in the shape of the letter V,[5] and you felt that you were standing before a creature who never doubted himself. He was a pedant of the highest order, the greatest one I'd ever met on earth; in addition he possessed a sense of self-esteem appropriate perhaps only to Alexander the Great, King of Macedonia. He was in love with every one of his buttons, every one of his fingernails—absolutely in love, and he looked it! He treated me quite despotically, spoke to me exceedingly little, and, if he happened to look at me, cast a steady, majestically self-assured, and constantly mocking glance that sometimes infuriated me. He carried out his tasks as if he were doing me the greatest of favors. Moreover, he did almost nothing at all for me; nor did he assume that he was obliged to do anything. There could be no doubt that he considered me the greatest fool on earth, and, that if he "kept me on," it was only because he could receive his wages from me every month. He agreed to "do nothing" for seven rubles a month. I'll be forgiven many of my sins because of him. Sometimes my hatred reached such a point that his gait alone would throw me into convulsions. But the most repulsive thing about him was his lisping. His tongue was a bit larger than normal or something of the sort; as a result, he constantly lisped and hissed. Apparently, he was terribly proud of it, imagining that it endowed him with enormous dignity. He spoke slowly, in measured tones, with his hands behind his back and his eyes fixed on the ground. It particularly infuriated me when he used to read the Psalter to himself behind his partition. I endured many battles on account of it. He was terribly fond of reading during the evening in a slow, even singsong voice, as if chanting over the dead. It's curious, but that's how he ended up: now he hires himself out to recite the Psalter over the dead; in addition, he exterminates rats and makes shoe polish. But at

---

4. The last lines of the poem by Nekrasov used as the epigraph of Part II of this story (see p. 1329).
5. The last letter of the old Russian alphabet, triangular in shape.

that time I couldn't get rid of him; it was as if he were chemically linked to my own existence. Besides, he'd never have agreed to leave for anything. It was impossible for me to live in a furnished room: my own apartment was my private residence, my shell, my case, where I hid from all humanity. Apollon, the devil only knows why, seemed to belong to this apartment, and for seven long years I couldn't get rid of him.

It was impossible, for example, to delay paying him his wages for even two or three days. He'd make such a fuss that I wouldn't know where to hide. But in those days I was so embittered by everyone that I decided, heaven knows why or for what reason, to *punish* Apollon by not paying him his wages for two whole weeks. I'd been planning to do this for some time now, about two years, simply in order to teach him that he had no right to put on such airs around me, and that if I chose to, I could always withhold his wages. I resolved to say nothing to him about it and even remain silent on purpose, to conquer his pride and force him to be the first one to mention it. Then I would pull all seven rubles out of a drawer and show him that I actually had the money and had intentionally set it aside, but that "I didn't want to, didn't want to, simply didn't want to pay him his wages, and that I didn't want to simply because *that's what I wanted*," because such was "my will as his master," because he was disrespectful and because he was rude. But, if he were to ask respectfully, then I might relent and pay him; if not, he might have to wait another two weeks, or three, or even a whole month. . . .

But, no matter how angry I was, he still won. I couldn't even hold out for four days. He began as he always did, because there had already been several such cases (and, let me add, I knew all this beforehand; I knew his vile tactics by heart), to wit: he would begin by fixing an extremely severe gaze on me. He would keep it up for several minutes in a row, especially when meeting me or accompanying me outside of the house. If, for example, I held out and pretended not to notice these stares, then he, maintaining his silence as before, would proceed to further tortures. Suddenly, for no reason at all, he'd enter my room quietly and slowly, while I was pacing or reading; he'd stop at the door, place one hand behind his back, thrust one foot forward, and fix his gaze on me, no longer merely severe, but now utterly contemptuous. If I were suddenly to ask him what he wanted, he wouldn't answer at all. He'd continue to stare at me reproachfully for several more seconds; then, compressing his lips in a particular way and assuming a very meaningful air, he'd turn slowly on the spot and slowly withdraw to his own room. Two hours later he'd emerge again and suddenly appear before me in the same way. It's happened sometimes that in my fury I hadn't even asked what he wanted, but simply raised my head sharply and imperiously, and begun to stare reproachfully back at him. We would stare at each other thus for some two minutes or more; at last he'd turn slowly and self-importantly, and withdraw for another few hours.

If all this failed to bring me back to my senses and I continued to rebel, he'd suddenly begin to sigh while staring at me. He'd sigh heavily and deeply, as if trying to measure with each sigh the depth of my moral decline. Naturally, it would end with his complete victory: I'd rage and shout, but I was always forced to do just as he wished on the main point of dispute.

This time his usual maneuvers of "severe stares" had scarcely begun when I lost my temper at once and lashed out at him in a rage. I was irritated enough even without that.

"Wait!" I shouted in a frenzy, as he was slowly and silently turning with one hand behind his back, about to withdraw to his own room. "Wait! Come back, come back, I tell you!" I must have bellowed so unnaturally that he turned around and even began to scrutinize me with a certain amazement. He continued, however, not to utter one word, and that was what infuriated me most of all.

"How dare you come in here without asking permission and stare at me? Answer me!"

But after regarding me serenely for half a minute, he started to turn around again.

"Wait!" I roared, rushing up to him. "Don't move! There! Now answer me: why do you come in here to stare?"

"If you've got any orders for me now, it's my job to do 'em," he replied after another pause, lisping softly and deliberately, raising his eyebrows, and calmly shifting his head from one side to the other—what's more, he did all this with horrifying composure.

"That's not it! That's not what I'm asking you about, you executioner!" I shouted, shaking with rage. "I'll tell you myself, you executioner, why you came in here. You know that I haven't paid you your wages, but you're so proud that you don't want to bow down and ask me for them. That's why you came in here to punish me and torment me with your stupid stares, and you don't even sus-s-pect, you torturer, how stupid it all is, how stupid, stupid, stupid, stupid!"

He would have turned around silently once again, but I grabbed hold of him.

"Listen," I shouted to him. "Here's the money, you see! Here it is! (I pulled it out of a drawer.) All seven rubles. But you won't get it, you won't until you come to me respectfully, with your head bowed, to ask my forgiveness. Do you hear?"

"That can't be!" he replied with some kind of unnatural self-confidence.

"It will be!" I shrieked. "I give you my word of honor, it will be!"

"I have nothing to ask your forgiveness for," he said as if he hadn't even noticed my shrieks, "because it was you who called me an 'executioner,' and I can always go lodge a complaint against you at the police station."

"Go! Lodge a complaint!" I roared. "Go at once, this minute, this very second! You're still an executioner! Executioner! Executioner!" But he only looked at me, then turned and, no longer heeding my shouts, calmly withdrew to his own room without looking back.

"If it hadn't been for Liza, none of this would have happened!" I thought to myself. Then, after waiting a minute, pompously and solemnly, but with my heart pounding heavily and forcefully, I went in to see him behind the screen.

"Apollon!" I said softly and deliberately, though gasping for breath, "go at once, without delay to fetch the police supervisor!"

He'd already seated himself at his table, put on his eyeglasses, and picked up something to sew. But, upon hearing my order, he suddenly snorted with laughter.

"At once! Go this very moment! Go, go, or you can't imagine what will happen to you!"

"You're really not in your right mind," he replied, not even lifting his head, lisping just as slowly, and continuing to thread his needle. "Who's ever heard of a man being sent to fetch a policeman against himself? And as for trying to frighten me, you're only wasting your time, because nothing will happen to me."

"Go," I screeched, seizing him by the shoulder. I felt that I might strike him at any moment.

I never even heard the door from the hallway suddenly open at that very moment, quietly and slowly, and that someone walked in, stopped, and began to examine us in bewilderment. I glanced up, almost died from shame, and ran back into my own room. There, clutching my hair with both hands, I leaned my head against the wall and froze in that position.

Two minutes later I heard Apollon's deliberate footsteps.

"There's *some woman* asking for you," he said, staring at me with particular severity; then he stood aside and let her in—it was Liza. He didn't want to leave, and he scrutinized us mockingly.

"Get out, get out!" I commanded him all flustered. At that moment my clock strained, wheezed, and struck seven.

IX

And enter my house bold and free,
To become its full mistress!
From the same poem.[6]

I stood before her, crushed, humiliated, abominably ashamed; I think I was smiling as I tried with all my might to wrap myself up in my tattered, quilted dressing gown—exactly as I'd imagined this scene the other day during a fit of depression. Apollon, after standing over us for a few minutes, left, but that didn't make things any easier for me. Worst of all was that she suddenly became embarrassed too, more than I'd ever expected. At the sight of me, of course.

"Sit down," I said mechanically and moved a chair up to the table for her, while I sat on the sofa. She immediately and obediently sat down, staring at me wide-eyed, and, obviously, expecting something from me at once. This naive expectation infuriated me, but I restrained myself.

She should have tried not to notice anything, as if everything were just as it should be, but she . . . And I vaguely felt that she'd have to pay dearly *for everything*.

"You've found me in an awkward situation, Liza," I began, stammering and realizing that this was precisely the wrong way to begin.

"No, no, don't imagine anything!" I cried, seeing that she'd suddenly blushed. "I'm not ashamed of my poverty. . . . On the contrary, I regard it with pride. I'm poor, but noble. . . . One can be poor and noble," I muttered. "But . . . would you like some tea?"

"No . . . ," she started to say.

"Wait!"

I jumped up and ran to Apollon. I had to get away somehow.

"Apollon," I whispered in feverish haste, tossing down the seven rubles which had been in my fist the whole time, "here are your wages. There, you see, I've given them to you. But now you must rescue me: bring us some tea

6. I.e., from the poem quoted on pp. 1329 and 1369.

and a dozen rusks from the tavern at once. If you don't go, you'll make me a very miserable man. You have no idea who this woman is. . . . This means—everything! You may think she's . . . But you've no idea at all who this woman really is!"

Apollon, who'd already sat down to work and had put his glasses on again, at first glanced sideways in silence at the money without abandoning his needle; then, paying no attention to me and making no reply, he continued to fuss with the needle he was still trying to thread. I waited there for about three minutes standing before him with my arms folded *à la Napoleon*.[7] My temples were soaked in sweat. I was pale, I felt that myself. But, thank God, he must have taken pity just looking at me. After finishing with the thread, he stood up slowly from his place, slowly pushed back his chair, slowly took off his glasses, slowly counted the money and finally, after inquiring over his shoulder whether he should get a whole pot, slowly walked out of the room. As I was returning to Liza, it occurred to me: shouldn't I run away just as I was, in my shabby dressing gown, no matter where, and let come what may?

I sat down again. She looked at me uneasily. We sat in silence for several minutes.

"I'll kill him." I shouted suddenly, striking the table so hard with my fist that ink splashed out of the inkwell.

"Oh, what are you saying?" she exclaimed, startled.

"I'll kill him, I'll kill him!" I shrieked, striking the table in an absolute frenzy, but understanding full well at the same time how stupid it was to be in such a frenzy.

"You don't understand, Liza, what this executioner is doing to me. He's my executioner. . . . He's just gone out for some rusks; he . . ."

And suddenly I burst into tears. It was a nervous attack. I felt so ashamed amidst my sobs, but I couldn't help it. She got frightened.

"What's the matter? What's wrong with you?" she cried, fussing around me.

"Water, give me some water, over there!" I muttered in a faint voice, realizing full well, however, that I could've done both without the water and without the faint voice. But I was *putting on an act*, as it's called, in order to maintain decorum, although my nervous attack was genuine.

She gave me some water while looking at me like a lost soul. At that very moment Apollon brought in the tea. It suddenly seemed that this ordinary and prosaic tea was horribly inappropriate and trivial after everything that had happened, and I blushed. Liza stared at Apollon with considerable alarm. He left without looking at us.

"Liza, do you despise me?" I asked, looking her straight in the eye, trembling with impatience to find out what she thought.

She was embarrassed and didn't know what to say.

"Have some tea," I said angrily. I was angry at myself, but she was the one who'd have to pay, naturally. A terrible anger against her suddenly welled up in my heart; I think I could've killed her. To take revenge I swore inwardly not to say one more word to her during the rest of her visit. "She's the cause of it all," I thought.

Our silence continued for about five minutes. The tea stood on the table;

7. In the style of Napoleon.

we didn't touch it. It reached the point of my not wanting to drink on purpose, to make it even more difficult for her; it would be awkward for her to begin alone. Several times she glanced at me in sad perplexity. I stubbornly remained silent. I was the main sufferer, of course, because I was fully aware of the despicable meanness of my own spiteful stupidity; yet, at the same time, I couldn't restrain myself.

"I want to . . . get away from . . . that place . . . once and for all," she began just to break the silence somehow; but, poor girl, that was just the thing she shouldn't have said at that moment, stupid enough as it was to such a person as me, stupid as I was. My own heart even ached with pity for her tactlessness and unnecessary straightforwardness. But something hideous immediately suppressed all my pity; it provoked me even further. Let the whole world go to hell. Another five minutes passed.

"Have I disturbed you?" she began timidly, barely audibly, and started to get up.

But as soon as I saw this first glimpse of injured dignity, I began to shake with rage and immediately exploded.

"Why did you come here? Tell me why, please," I began, gasping and neglecting the logical order of my words. I wanted to say it all at once, without pausing for breath; I didn't even worry about how to begin.

"Why did you come here? Answer me! Answer!" I cried, hardly aware of what I was saying. "I'll tell you, my dear woman, why you came here. You came here because I spoke some *words of pity* to you that time. Now you've softened, and want to hear more 'words of pity.' Well, you should know that I was laughing at you then. And I'm laughing at you now. Why are you trembling? Yes, I was laughing at you! I'd been insulted, just prior to that, at dinner, by those men who arrived just before me that evening. I came intending to thrash one of them, the officer; but I didn't succeed; I couldn't find him; I had to avenge my insult on someone, to get my own back; you turned up and I took my anger out at you, and I laughed at you. I'd been humiliated, and I wanted to humiliate someone else; I'd been treated like a rag, and I wanted to exert some power. . . . That's what it was; you thought that I'd come there on purpose to save you, right? Is that what you thought? Is that it?"

I knew that she might get confused and might not grasp all the details, but I also knew that she'd understand the essence of it very well. That's just what happened. She turned white as a sheet; she wanted to say something. Her lips were painfully twisted, but she collapsed onto a chair just as if she'd been struck down with an ax. Subsequently she listened to me with her mouth gaping, her eyes wide open, shaking with awful fear. It was the cynicism, the cynicism of my words that crushed her. . . .

"To save you!" I continued, jumping up from my chair and rushing up and down the room in front of her, "to save you from what? Why, I may be even worse than you are. When I recited that sermon to you, why didn't you throw it back in my face? You should have said to me, 'Why did you come here? To preach morality or what?' Power, it was the power I needed then, I craved the sport, I wanted to reduce you to tears, humiliation, hysteria—that's what I needed then! But I couldn't have endured it myself, because I'm such a wretch. I got scared. The devil only knows why I foolishly gave you my address. Afterward, even before I got home, I cursed you like nothing on earth on account of that address. I hated you already because I'd lied to you then, because it was all playing with words, dreaming in my own mind. But, do you know what I really want now? For you to get lost, that's what! I need some peace. Why, I'd sell the whole world for a kopeck if people would only stop bothering me. Should the world go to hell, or should I go without my tea? I say, let the world go to hell as long as I can always have my tea. Did you know that or not? And I know perfectly well that I'm a scoundrel, a bastard, an egotist, and a sluggard. I've been shaking from fear for the last three days wondering whether you'd ever come. Do you know what disturbed me most of all these last three days? The fact that I'd appeared to you then as such a hero, and that now you'd suddenly see me in this torn dressing gown, dilapidated and revolting. I said before that I wasn't ashamed of my poverty; well, you should know that I am ashamed, I'm ashamed of it more than anything, more afraid of it than anything, more than if I were a thief, because I'm so vain; it's as if the skin's been stripped away from my body so that even wafts of air cause pain. By now surely even you've guessed that I'll never forgive you for having come upon me in this dressing gown as I was attacking Apollon like a vicious dog. Your saviour, your former hero, behaving like a mangy, shaggy mongrel, attacking his own lackey, while that lackey stood there laughing at me! Nor will I ever forgive you for those tears which, like an embarrassed old woman, I couldn't hold back before you. And I'll never forgive *you* for all that I'm confessing now. Yes—you, you alone must pay for everything because you turned up like this, because I'm a scoundrel, because I'm the nastiest, most ridiculous, pettiest, stupidest, most envious worm of all those living on earth who're no better than me in any way, but who, the devil knows why, never get embarrassed, while all my life I have to endure insults from every louse—that's my fate. What do I care that you don't understand any of this? What do I care, what do I care about you and whether or not you perish there? Why, don't you realize how much I'll hate you now after having said all this with your being here listening to me? After all, a man can only talk like this once in his whole life, and then only in hysteria! . . . What more do you want? Why, after all this, are you still hanging around here tormenting me? Why don't you leave?"

But at this point a very strange thing suddenly occurred.

I'd become so accustomed to inventing and imagining everything according to books, and picturing everything on earth to myself just as I'd conceived of it in my dreams, that at first I couldn't even comprehend the meaning of this strange occurrence. But here's what happened: Liza, insulted and crushed by me, understood much more than I'd imagined. She understood out of all this what a woman always understands first of all, if she sincerely loves—namely, that I myself was unhappy.

The frightened and insulted expression on her face was replaced at first by grieved amazement. When I began to call myself a scoundrel and a bastard, and my tears had begun to flow (I'd pronounced this whole tirade in tears), her whole face was convulsed by a spasm. She wanted to get up and stop me; when I'd finished, she paid no attention to my shouting, "Why are you here? Why don't you leave?" She only noticed that it must have been very painful for me to utter all this. Besides, she was so defenseless, the poor girl. She considered herself immeasurably beneath me. How could she get angry or take offense? Suddenly she jumped up from the chair with a kind of uncontrollable impulse, and yearning toward me, but being too timid and not daring to stir from her place, she extended her arms in my direction. . . . At this moment my heart leapt inside me, too. Then suddenly she threw herself at me, put her arms around my neck, and burst into tears. I, too, couldn't restrain myself and sobbed as I'd never done before.

"They won't let me . . . I can't be . . . good!"[8] I barely managed to say; then I went over to the sofa, fell upon it face down, and sobbed in genuine hysterics for a quarter of an hour. She knelt down, embraced me, and remained motionless in that position.

But the trouble was that my hysterics had to end sometime. And so (after all, I'm writing the whole loathsome truth), lying there on the sofa and pressing my face firmly into that nasty leather cushion of mine, I began to sense gradually, distantly, involuntarily, but irresistibly, that it would be awkward for me to raise my head and look Liza straight in the eye. What was I ashamed of? I don't know, but I was ashamed. It also occurred to my overwrought brain that now our roles were completely reversed; now she was the heroine, and I was the same sort of humiliated and oppressed creature she'd been in front of me that evening—only four days ago. . . . And all this came to me during those few minutes as I lay face down on the sofa!

My God! Was it possible that I envied her?

I don't know; to this very day I still can't decide. But then, of course, I was even less able to understand it. After all, I couldn't live without exercising power and tyrannizing over another person. . . . But . . . but, then, you really can't explain a thing by reason; consequently, it's useless to try.

However, I regained control of myself and raised my head; I had to sooner or later. . . . And so, I'm convinced to this day that it was precisely because I felt too ashamed to look at her, that another feeling was suddenly kindled and burst into flame in my heart—the feeling of domination and possession. My eyes gleamed with passion; I pressed her hands tightly. How I hated her and felt drawn to her simultaneously! One feeling intensified the other. It was almost like revenge! . . . At first there was a look of something resembling bewilderment, or even fear, on her face, but only for a brief moment. She embraced me warmly and rapturously.

X

A quarter of an hour later I was rushing back and forth across the room in furious impatience, constantly approaching the screen to peer at Liza through the crack. She was sitting on the floor, her head leaning against the bed, and she must have been crying. But she didn't leave, and that's what irritated me. By this time she knew absolutely everything. I'd insulted her once and for all, but . . . there's nothing more to be said. She guessed that my outburst of passion was merely revenge, a new humiliation for her, and that to my former, almost aimless, hatred there was added now a *personal*, *envious* hatred of her. . . . However, I don't think that she understood all this explicitly; on the other hand, she fully understood that I was a despicable man, and, most important, that I was incapable of loving her.

8. This epithet *dobryi* ("good") must be read in combination with that in the second sentence of the work, where the hero describes himself as *zloi*—not only "spiteful" but also "evil."

I know that I'll be told this is incredible—that it's impossible to be as spiteful and stupid as I am; you may even add that it was impossible not to return, or at least to appreciate, this love. But why is this so incredible? In the first place, I could no longer love because, I repeat, for me love meant tyrannizing and demonstrating my moral superiority. All my life I could never even conceive of any other kind of love, and I've now reached the point that I sometimes think that love consists precisely in a voluntary gift by the beloved person of the right to tyrannize over him. Even in my underground dreams I couldn't conceive of love in any way other than a struggle. It always began with hatred and ended with moral subjugation; afterward, I could never imagine what to do with the subjugated object. And what's so incredible about that, since I'd previously managed to corrupt myself morally; I'd already become unaccustomed to "real life," and only a short while ago had taken it into my head to reproach her and shame her for having come to hear "words of pity" from me. But I never could've guessed that she'd come not to hear words of pity at all, but to love me, because it's in that kind of love that a woman finds her resurrection, all her salvation from whatever kind of ruin, and her rebirth, as it can't appear in any other form. However, I didn't hate her so much as I rushed around the room and peered through the crack behind the screen. I merely found it unbearably painful that she was still there. I wanted her to disappear. I longed for "peace and quiet"; I wanted to remain alone in my underground. "Real life" oppressed me—so unfamiliar was it—that I even found it hard to breathe.

But several minutes passed, and she still didn't stir, as if she were oblivious. I was shameless enough to tap gently on the screen to remind her. . . . She started suddenly, jumped up, and hurried to find her shawl, hat, and coat, as if she wanted to escape from me. . . . Two minutes later she slowly emerged from behind the screen and looked at me sadly. I smiled spitefully; it was forced, however, for *appearance's sake only*; and I turned away from her look.

"Good-bye," she said, going toward the door.

Suddenly I ran up to her, grabbed her hand, opened it, put something in . . . and closed it again. Then I turned away at once and bolted to the other corner, so that at least I wouldn't be able to see. . . .

I was just about to lie—to write that I'd done all this accidentally, without knowing what I was doing, in complete confusion, out of foolishness. But I don't want to lie; therefore I'll say straight out, that I opened her hand and placed something in it . . . out of spite. It occurred to me to do this while I was rushing back and forth across the room and she was sitting there behind the screen. But here's what I can say for sure: although I did this cruel thing deliberately, it was not from my heart, but from my stupid head. This cruelty of mine was so artificial, cerebral, intentionally invented, *bookish*, that I couldn't stand it myself even for one minute—at first I bolted to the corner so as not to see, and then, out of shame and in despair, I rushed out after Liza. I opened the door into the hallway and listened. "Liza! Liza!" I called down the stairs, but timidly, in a soft voice.

There was no answer; I thought I could hear her footsteps at the bottom of the stairs.

"Liza!" I cried more loudly.

No answer. But at that moment I heard down below the sound of the tight outer glass door opening heavily with a creak and then closing again tightly. The sound rose up the stairs.

She'd gone. I returned to my room deep in thought. I felt horribly oppressed.

I stood by the table near the chair where she'd been sitting and stared senselessly into space. A minute or so passed, then I suddenly started: right before me on the chair I saw . . . in a word, I saw the crumpled blue five-ruble note, the very one I'd thrust into her hand a few moments before. It was the same one; it couldn't be any other; I had none other in my apartment. So she'd managed to toss it down on the table when I'd bolted to the other corner.

So what? I might have expected her to do that. Might have expected it? No. I was such an egotist, in fact, I so lacked respect for other people, that I couldn't even conceive that she'd ever do that. I couldn't stand it. A moment later, like a madman, I hurried to get dressed. I threw on whatever I happened to find, and rushed headlong after her. She couldn't have gone more than two hundred paces when I ran out on the street.

It was quiet; it was snowing heavily, and the snow was falling almost perpendicularly, blanketing the sidewalk and the deserted street. There were no passers-by; no sound could be heard. The street lights were flickering dismally and vainly. I ran about two hundred paces to the crossroads and stopped.

"Where did she go? And why am I running after her? Why? To fall down before her, sob with remorse, kiss her feet, and beg her forgiveness! That's just what I wanted. My heart was being torn apart; never, never will I recall that moment with indifference. But—why?" I wondered. "Won't I grow to hate her, perhaps as soon as tomorrow, precisely because I'm kissing her feet today? Will I ever be able to make her happy? Haven't I found out once again today, for the hundredth time, what I'm really worth? Won't I torment her?"

I stood in the snow, peering into the murky mist, and thought about all this.

"And wouldn't it be better, wouldn't it," I fantasized once I was home again, stifling the stabbing pain in my heart with such fantasies, "wouldn't it be better if she were to carry away the insult with her forever? Such an insult—after all, is purification; it's the most caustic and painful form of consciousness. Tomorrow I would have defiled her soul and wearied her heart. But now that insult will never die within her; no matter how abominable the filth that awaits her, that insult will elevate and purify her . . . by hatred . . . hmm . . . perhaps by forgiveness as well. But will that make it any easier for her?"

And now, in fact, I'll pose an idle question of my own. Which is better: cheap happiness or sublime suffering? Well, come on, which is better?

These were my thoughts as I sat home that evening, barely alive with the anguish in my soul. I'd never before endured so much suffering and remorse; but could there exist even the slightest doubt that when I went rushing out of my apartment, I'd turn back again after going only halfway? I never met Liza afterward, and I never heard anything more about her. I'll also add that for a long time I remained satisfied with my theory about the use of insults and hatred, in spite of the fact that I myself almost fell ill from anguish at the time.

Even now, after so many years, all this comes back to me as *very unpleasant*. A great deal that comes back to me now is very unpleasant, but . . . perhaps I should end these *Notes* here? I think that I made a mistake in beginning to write them. At least, I was ashamed all the time I was writing this *tale*: consequently, it's not really literature, but corrective punishment. After all, to tell you long stories about how, for example, I ruined my life through moral decay in my corner, by the lack of appropriate surroundings, by isolation from any living beings, and by futile malice in the underground— so help me God, that's not very interesting. A novel needs a hero, whereas here all the traits of an anti-hero have been assembled *deliberately*; but the most important thing is that all this produces an extremely unpleasant impression because we've all become estranged from life, we're all cripples, every one of us, more or less. We've become so estranged that at times we feel some kind of revulsion for genuine "real life," and therefore we can't bear to be reminded of it. Why, we've reached a point where we almost regard "real life" as hard work, as a job, and we've all agreed in private that it's really better in books. And why do we sometimes fuss, indulge in whims, and make demands? We don't know ourselves. It'd be even worse if all our whimsical desires were fulfilled. Go on, try it. Give us, for example, a little more independence; untie the hands of any one of us, broaden our sphere of activity, relax the controls, and . . . I can assure you, we'll immediately ask to have the controls reinstated. I know that you may get angry at me for saying this, you may shout and stamp your feet: "Speak for yourself," you'll say, "and for your own miseries in the underground, but don't you dare say '*all of us.*'" If you'll allow me, gentlemen; after all, I'm not trying to justify myself by saying *all of us*. What concerns me in particular, is that in my life I've only taken to an extreme that which you haven't even dared to take halfway; what's more, you've mistaken your cowardice for good sense; and, in so deceiving yourself, you've consoled yourself. So, in fact, I may even be "more alive" than you are. Just take a closer look! Why, we don't even know where this "real life" lives nowadays, what it really is, and what it's called. Leave us alone without books and we'll get confused and lose our way at once—we won't know what to join, what to hold on to, what to love or what to hate, what to respect or what to despise. We're even oppressed by being men— men with real bodies and blood of *our very own*. We're ashamed of it; we consider it a disgrace and we strive to become some kind of impossible "general-human-beings." We're stillborn; for some time now we haven't been conceived by living fathers; we like it more and more. We're developing a taste for it. Soon we'll conceive of a way to be born from ideas. But enough; I don't want to write any more "from Underground. . . ."

However, the "notes" of this paradoxalist don't end here. He couldn't resist and kept on writing. But it also seems to us that we might as well stop here.

CHARLES BAUDELAIRE
1821–1867

Few writers have had such impact on succeeding generations as Charles Baudelaire, called both the "first modern poet" and the "father of modern criticism." Nor is his reputation confined to the West, for Baudelaire is the most widely read French poet around the globe. Yet for a long time Baudelaire's literary image was dominated by his reputation as a scandalous writer whose blatant eroticism and open fascination with evil outraged all right-thinking people. Both he and Flaubert were brought to trial in 1857 for "offenses against public and religious morals"—Flaubert for *Madame Bovary* and Baudelaire for his just-published book of poetry *Les Fleurs du Mal* (The Flowers of Evil). Some of this reputation is justified; the poet did intend to shock, and he displayed in painfully vivid scenes his own spiritual and sensual torment. Haunted by a religiously framed vision of human nature as fallen and corrupt, he lucidly analyzed his own weaknesses as well as the hypocrisy and sins he found in society. Lust, hatred, laziness, a disabling self-awareness that ironized all emotions, a horror of death and decay, and finally an apathy that swallowed up all other vices— all contrasted bitterly with the poet's dreams of a lost Eden, an ideal harmony of being. Perfection existed only in the distance: in scenes of erotic love, faraway voyages, or artistic beauty created often out of ugliness and crude reality. Baudelaire's ability to present realistic detail inside larger symbolic horizons, his constant use of imagery and suggestion, his consummate craftsmanship and the intense musicality of his verse made him a precursor of Symbolism and, in the words of T. S. Eliot, "the greatest exemplar in *modern* poetry in any language."

Baudelaire was born in Paris on April 9, 1821. His father died when the poet was six, and his widowed mother married Captain (later General) Jacques Aupick the following year. In 1832 the family moved to Lyons, and young Charles was placed in boarding school; in 1836 Aupick and his family were reassigned to Paris. Throughout his life Baudelaire remained greatly attached to his mother and detested his disciplinarian stepfather. He was a rebellious and difficult youth whom his parents sent on a long voyage to the Indies in 1841 to remove him from bad influences; but he cut short the trip at Reunion Island and insisted on returning home after ten months. Baudelaire's unconventional behavior and extravagant lifestyle continued to worry his family, especially after he turned twenty-one and received his father's inheritance. In 1844, they obtained a court order to supervise his finances, and from then on the poet subsisted on allowances paid by a notary.

In contrast to the Romantics with their love of nature and pastoral scenes, Baudelaire was a city poet fascinated by the variety and excitement of modern urban life. Living in Paris, he collaborated with other writers; published poems, translations, and criticism in different journals; and in 1842 began a lifelong liaison with Jeanne Duval, the "black Venus" of many poems. When he read Edgar Allan Poe for the first time, he was struck by the similarity of their ideas: by Poe's dedication to beauty, his fascination with bizarre images and death, and above all his emphasis on craftsmanship and perfectly controlled art. The French poet recognized in Poe "not only subjects I had dreamed of, but SENTENCES that I had thought and he had written twenty years earlier." Baudelaire's translations of Poe, collected in five volumes published from 1856 to 1865, were immensely popular and introduced the American writer to a broad European audience.

Public scandal greeted the appearance in 1857 of Baudelaire's major work, *The Flowers of Evil*. French authorities, already annoyed at Flaubert's acquittal, seized the book immediately. Less than two months later, the poet and his publisher were condemned to pay a fine and to delete six poems. A second edition with more poems appeared in 1861, and new lyrics were added to later printings. By now the poet was also well known as a critic. He championed the modern art of his time, interpreting and upholding the spirit of modernity in the art criticism of his 1845, 1846, and 1859 *Salons*; in remarkable studies of the painters Eugène Delacroix and Constantin Guys; and in a spirited defense of the German composer Richard Wagner. His literary criticism, although it included studies of *Madame Bovary*, Victor Hugo, and Théophile Gautier, was in general limited to brief journal reviews. Baudelaire started publishing prose poetry at the beginning of the 1860s, experimenting with a form that was almost unknown in France and in which he hoped to achieve "the miracle of a poetic prose, musical without rhythm or rhyme, able . . . to adapt itself to the soul's lyric movements, to the undulations of reverie, to the sudden starts of consciousness." A slim book of twenty prose poems appeared in 1862; the complete *Little Poems in Prose* (also called *Paris Spleen*) would contain fifty poems in all. Baudelaire's health was precarious during these years. In 1862, he had what was apparently a minor stroke, which he called a "warning" and described with characteristically vivid imagery: "I felt pass over me a draft of wind from imbecility's wing." Four years later, in Belgium, he was stricken with aphasia and hemiplegia; unable to speak, he was brought back to Paris where he died on August 31, 1867.

His audience was never far from Baudelaire's mind. He wished to shock, to startle, to make the reader rethink cherished ideas and values. In the prefatory poem to *The Flowers of Evil, To the Reader*, Baudelaire ends a catalog of human vices by insisting that both he and the reader are caught in a common guilt: "You—hypocrite Reader—my double—my brother!" The poet's insistent theme of *ennui* (pathological boredom or apathy) occurs here at the beginning of the book: it is the melancholy inertia that keeps human beings from acting either for good or for evil, placing them outside the realm of choice, much as Dante relegated to Limbo those who were unwilling to take a moral stand. (In Catholic theology, such spiritual inertia is termed *acedia*.) This *spleen*, as it is also called (from the part of the body governing a splenetic or bilious humor), appears throughout *The Flowers of Evil* as an insidious, debilitating force. In *To the Reader* Baudelaire argues that the devil's most terrifying weapon against humankind is not the litany of sins so colorfully described, but rather his ability to diminish the possibility of action: to evaporate—like a chemist in a laboratory—the precious metal of human will.

The Voyage, placed by Baudelaire at the end of the collection, describes the opposite of inertia: an active search for goals always out of reach. Written in a consciously Byronic tone and intended, according to the poet, to upset current faith in human progress, *The Voyage* describes "progress" as a series of temporary advances that end in disappointment and disgust. These smaller achievements—discovering new lands, inventing new luxuries, gaining fame and fortune, seeking ecstasy in sadism and sensuality—are all bound to deceive because they are merely symbols of a larger unending voyage: the quest for the infinite. Since human beings contain an "inner [spiritual] infinite" they cannot be satisfied with any limits and must constantly travel toward the unknown and the new. The "country" of earthly experience is not adequate for travelers impelled by an inner fire; their voyage ends, therefore, with a final plunge—for answers—into the unfathomable obscurity of death. The last line, "In the depths of the Unknown, we'll discover the New!" became a famous rallying cry for generations who sought new insights by exploring such unmapped frontiers.

Baudelaire alternates between acid melancholy and glimpses of happiness. Not all voyages are unhappy; one of his rare contented and even tender poems is the lyrical *Invitation to the Voyage*, a lover's invitation to an exotic land of peace, beauty, and sensuous harmony. The voyage is imaginary, of course, implying two forms of escape from reality: an escape out of real time into a primeval accord of the senses, and an escape into another artistic vision—the glowing interiors painted by such Dutch masters as Jan Vermeer. A similar but more cynical voyage of escape occurs in *Her Hair*. Here the poet, abandoning himself to passion, buries his face in the dark tide of his mistress's hair as if to submerge himself in the dark ocean of dream. This escape is available only on a temporary basis, however; the woman remains his "oasis" only so long as he adorns her hair with jewels. In both poems, and probably in Baudelaire's poetry in general, we must admit that women do not exist as separate personalities even if there are specific historical figures behind the poems. They are foils for poetic inspiration, conventional images of beauty, coldness, vision, or vice given one or another form. The woman in *A Carcass* exists only as an appropriate listener in a poem that mocks Petrarchan ideals of feminine beauty. Even if male subjectivity governs the descriptions, men are absent, in a different way; they exist only generically, as brothers (or doubles) of the poet himself. What emerges is that Baudelaire is even more clamped in his own solitude, registering repeatedly a personal experience from which he builds an amazingly complex imaginative universe.

Baudelaire was convinced that "every good poet has always been a realist," and he himself was a master of realistic details used for effects that go beyond conventional or photographic realism. The rhythmic thump of firewood being delivered is repeated throughout *Song of Autumn I,* where it coordinates ascending images of death. Imagery in *A Carcass* is more brutal. Even if the contrast between the language of courtly love ("star of my eyes") and crude and obscene descriptions no longer shocks in quite the same way, there remains the striking feat of imagination in which Baudelaire superimposes a swarming, vibrating new life onto the blurred outlines of a decaying animal carcass. The poem's ostensible theme is familiar—*carpe diem,* "seize the day" or "think of the future and love me now," since only a poet can preserve beauty—but one has only to compare Yeats's poem *When You Are Old* to recognize the harshness of this address to the beloved. The mixture of tones is more subtle in the *Spleen* poems, celebrated for their evocation of gray misery. Here Baudelaire inserts mundane items like bats, spiders, old-fashioned clothes, uncorked perfume bottles, and noisy rainspouts. Such down-to-earth details give substance to concurrent mythical or allegorical scenes. A chill revelation of mortality emerges from the sequence of thoroughly practical references to water in *Spleen LXXVIII,* beginning with the rain and fog in the city and including a cat twisting and turning uncomfortably on clammy tiles, the whine of a rainspout, the wheeze of wet wood and a damp clock pendulum, and finally a deck of cards left by an old woman who died of dropsy. If the sequence is interesting as a tour de force of linked images, it also serves cumulatively to evoke an atmosphere of lethargy and decay climaxing in a tiny, altogether unrealistic final scene in which two face cards talk sinisterly of their past loves.

Similar themes are to be found in the prose poems (*Little Poems in Prose* or *Paris Spleen*), although with a more openly autobiographical tone and a more homely setting. This prose must also find its own way to be musical "without rhyme." Stanzas become paragraphs; rhythm is created through variations in sentence length, syntax, and sound patterns, and the juxtaposition of scenes and tones. Rhythm is undeniably present, however changed: it is audible in the triple cadence ending *Windows* (helping him "to live, to feel that I am, and what I am") or in the contrasting dialogue leading up to the soul's explosion at the end of *Anywhere out of the World.*

The realism that is often buried in the lyrics of *The Flowers of Evil* appears on the surface in the prose poems. Baudelaire reviews an irritating day in *One o'Clock in the Morning,* recasts the topics of *The Voyage* as an imaginary dialogue in *Anywhere out of the World,* and ponders his solitude and the nature of creative genius in *Crowds* and *Windows.* In *Windows,* after having deduced the life story of an old woman seen across the roofs, he ends by saying that her story is only a "legend"—or, at least, that he does not care whether it is true so long as it provides a point of departure for his own imagination. Correspondingly, the poet relishes crowds because, moving among so many people, he is able to imagine himself in their place: "to be himself or someone else, as he chooses." In each case the artist is visibly alone, experiencing either the melancholy of *spleen* or the joy of an artistic imagination that creates and populates its own world. In verse or in prose, the alternation between dream and reality continues.

Baudelaire is a complex and ironic poet, an inheritor of that Romantic irony that wishes to embrace all the opposites of human existence: good and evil, love and hate, self and other, dream and reality. His is a universe of relationships, of echoes and correspondences. His best-known poem, in fact, is the sonnet *Correspondences*. This poem describes a vision of the mystic unity of all nature, which is demonstrated by the reciprocity of our five senses (*synesthesia*). Nature, says the poet, is a system of perpetual analogies in which one thing always corresponds to another—physical objects to each other (colonnades in a temple, for example, to trees in the forest), spiritual reality to physical reality, and the five senses (taste, smell, touch, sight, and hearing) among themselves—to produce such combinations as "bitter green," a "soft look," or "a harsh sound." Human beings are not usually aware of the "universal analogy"—the forest of the first stanza watches us without our knowing it—but it is the role of the poet to act as seer and guide, urging us toward a state of awareness in which both mind and senses fuse in another dimension. *Correspondences* is no vaguely intuitive poem, however. Even though it describes a state of ecstatic awareness, it works through the stages of a logical argument. The thesis is set out in the first stanza, explained in the second, and illustrated with cumulative examples in the third and fourth. Baudelaire's yearning for mystic harmony does not make him neglect either a base in reality or a rigorous application of intellect. His fusion of idealist vision, realistic detail, and artistic discipline made him the most influential poet of the nineteenth century and the first poet of the modern age.

The selections printed here, from a range of Baudelaire's most influential lyric and prose poems, are translated by different modern poets. While remaining faithful to the original text, each translation necessarily stresses different aspects (for example, images, meter and rhyme, word order, tone, a particular set of associations when more than one is possible) to create a genuine English poem. The footnotes occasionally point out elements that are especially significant in the French text.

Lois Boe Hyslop, *Charles Baudelaire Revisited* (1992), is a useful introductory survey. F. W. Leakey, *Baudelaire, Les Fleurs du Mal* (1992), is a short guide to the poet's major work. Enid Starkie, *Baudelaire* (1953), is the fullest biography in English. Henri Peyre, ed., *Baudelaire: A Collection of Critical Essays* (1962), contains eleven essays on *The Flowers of Evil*, with selections by major writers. Harold Bloom, ed., *Charles Baudelaire* (1987), presents ten contemporary critics on Baudelaire's themes, literary and artistic criticism, selected texts, and relation to Poe. Nicolae Babuts, *Baudelaire: At the Limits and Beyond* (1997), describes the coherence of Baudelaire's texts by means of eight chapters examining different focal points. Patricia Clements, *Baudelaire and the English Tradition* (1985), is a penetrating analysis of Baudelaire's influence on English literature from Swinburne to T. S. Eliot; it includes comparisons and contrasts with late Symbolist tradition. Edward Kaplan, *Baudelaire's Prose Poems* (1990), studies the prose poems as a many-sided but coherent ensemble of "fables of modern life." Baudelaire's criticism of literature and art are discussed in Rosemary Lloyd, *Baudelaire's Literary Criticism* (1981) and David Carrier, *High Art: Charles Baudelaire and the Origins of Modernist Painting* (1996). Lloyd's *Selected Letters of Charles Baudelaire: The Conquest of Solitude* (1986) contains personal and literary letters. Laurence M. Porter, *The Crisis of French Symbolism* (1990), has an interesting chapter on Baudelaire's relation to his imagined audience.

PRONOUNCING GLOSSARY

The following list uses common English syllables and stress accents to provide rough equivalents of selected words whose pronunciation may be unfamiliar to the general reader.

Baudelaire: *boh-d'lair'*

ennui: *on-wee'*

Pylades: *pill'-ah-deez*

Venustre: *ven-yew'-struh*

FROM THE FLOWERS OF EVIL

To the Reader[1]

Infatuation, sadism, lust, avarice
possess our souls and drain the body's force;
we spoonfeed our adorable remorse,
like whores or beggars nourishing their lice.

Our sins are mulish, our confessions lies;   5
we play to the grandstand with our promises,
we pray for tears to wash our filthiness,
importantly pissing hogwash through our styes.

The devil, watching by our sickbeds, hissed
old smut and folk-songs to our soul, until   10
the soft and precious metal of our will
boiled off in vapor for this scientist.

Each day his flattery[2] makes us eat a toad,
and each step forward is a step to hell,
unmoved, though previous corpses and their smell   15
asphyxiate our progress on this road.

Like the poor lush who cannot satisfy,
we try to force our sex with counterfeits,
die drooling on the deliquescent tits,
mouthing the rotten orange we suck dry.   20

Gangs of demons are boozing in our brain—
ranked, swarming, like a million warrior-ants,[3]
they drown and choke the cistern of our wants;
each time we breathe, we tear our lungs with pain.

If poison, arson, sex, narcotics, knives   25
have not yet ruined us and stitched their quick,
loud patterns on the canvas of our lives,
it is because our souls are still too sick.[4]

Among the vermin, jackals, panthers, lice,
gorillas and tarantulas that suck   30
and snatch and scratch and defecate and fuck
in the disorderly circus of our vice,

there's one more ugly and abortive birth.
It makes no gestures, never beats its breast,
yet it would murder for a moment's rest,[5]   35
and willingly annihilate the earth.

---

1. Translated by Robert Lowell. The translation pays primary attention to the insistent rhythm of the original poetic language and keeps the *abba* rhyme scheme.　　2. The devil is literally described as a puppet master controlling our strings.　　3. Literally, intestinal worms.　　4. Literally, not bold enough. 5. Literally, swallow the world in a yawn.

It's BOREDOM. Tears have glued its eyes together.
You know it well, my Reader. This obscene
beast chain-smokes yawning for the guillotine—
you—hypocrite Reader—my double—my brother!   40

Correspondences[1]

Nature is a temple whose living colonnades
Breathe forth a mystic speech in fitful sighs;
Man wanders among symbols in those glades
Where all things watch him with familiar eyes.

Like dwindling echoes gathered far away   5
Into a deep and thronging unison
Huge as the night or as the light of day,
All scents and sounds and colors meet as one.

Perfumes there are as sweet as the oboe's sound,
Green as the prairies, fresh as a child's caress,[2]   10
—And there are others, rich, corrupt, profound[3]

And of an infinite pervasiveness,
Like myrrh, or musk, or amber,[4] that excite
The ecstasies of sense, the soul's delight.

Correspondances

La Nature est un temple où de vivants piliers
Laissent parfois sortir de confuses paroles;
L'homme y passe à travers des forêts de symboles
Qui l'observent avec des regards familiers.

Comme de longs échos qui de loin se confondent   5
Dans une ténébreuse et profonde unité,
Vaste comme la nuit et comme la clarté,
Les parfums, les couleurs et les sons se répondent.

Il est des parfums frais comme des chairs d'enfants,
Doux comme les hautbois, verts comme les prairies,   10
—Et d'autres, corrompus, riches et triomphants,

Ayant l'expansion des choses infinies,
Comme l'ambre, le musc, le benjoin et l'encens,
Qui chantent les transports de l'esprit et des sens.

1. Translated by Richard Wilbur. The translation keeps the intricate melody of the sonnet's original rhyme
scheme.   2. Literally, flesh.   3. Literally, triumphant.   4. Or ambergris, a substance secreted by
whales. Ambergris and musk (a secretion of the male musk deer) are used in making perfume.

Her Hair[1]

O fleece, that down the neck waves to the nape!
O curls! O perfume nonchalant and rare!
O ecstacy! To fill this alcove[2] shape
With memories that in these tresses sleep,
I would shake them like pennons in the air!   5

Languorous Asia, burning Africa,
And a far world, defunct almost, absent,
Within your aromatic forest stay!
As other souls on music drift away,
Mine, o my love! still floats upon your scent.   10

I shall go there where, full of sap, both tree
And man swoon in the heat of southern climes;
Strong tresses, be the swell that carries me!
I dream upon your sea of ebony
Of dazzling sails, of oarsmen, masts and flames: 15

A sun-drenched and reverberating port,
Where I imbibe color and sound and scent;
Where vessels, gliding through the gold and moire,
Open their vast arms as they leave the shore
To clasp the pure and shimmering firmament.   20

I'll plunge my head, enamored of its pleasure,
In this black ocean where the other hides;
My subtle spirit then will know a measure
Of fertile idleness and fragrant leisure,
Lulled by the infinite rhythm of its tides!   25

Pavilion, of blue-shadowed tresses spun,
You give me back the azure from afar;
And where the twisted locks are fringed with down
Lurk mingled odors I grow drunk upon
Of oil of coconut, of musk and tar.   30

A long time! always! my hand in your hair
Will sow the stars of sapphire, pearl, ruby,
That you be never deaf to my desire,
My oasis and gourd whence I aspire
To drink deep of the wine of memory![3]   35

A Carcass[1]

Remember, my love, the item you saw
That beautiful morning in June:

---

1. Translated by Doreen Bell. The translation emulates the French original's challenging *abaab* rhyme pattern.   2. Bedroom.   3. The last two lines are a question: "Are you not . . . ?"   1. Translated by James McGowan with special attention to imagery. The alternation of long and short lines in English emulates the French meter's rhythmic swing between twelve-syllable and eight-syllable lines in an *abab* rhyme scheme.

By a bend in the path a carcass reclined
  On a bed sown with pebbles and stones;

Her legs were spread out like a lecherous whore,   5
  Sweating out poisonous fumes,
Who opened in slick invitational style
  Her stinking and festering womb.

The sun on this rottenness focused its rays
  To cook the cadaver till done,   10
And render to Nature a hundredfold gift
  Of all she'd united in one.

And the sky cast an eye on this marvelous meat
  As over the flowers in bloom.
The stench was so wretched that there on the grass   15
  You nearly collapsed in a swoon.

The flies buzzed and droned on these bowels of filth
  Where an army of maggots arose,
Which flowed like a liquid and thickening stream
  On the animate rags of her clothes.[2]   20

And it rose and it fell, and pulsed like a wave,
  Rushing and bubbling with health.
One could say that this carcass, blown with vague breath,
  Lived in increasing itself.

And this whole teeming world made a musical sound   25
  Like babbling brooks and the breeze,
Or the grain that a man with a winnowing-fan
  Turns with a rhythmical ease.

The shapes wore away as if only a dream
  Like a sketch that is left on the page   30
Which the artist forgot and can only complete
  On the canvas, with memory's aid.

From back in the rocks, a pitiful bitch
  Eyed us with angry distaste,
Awaiting the moment to snatch from the bones   35
  The morsel she'd dropped in her haste.

—And you, in your turn, will be rotten as this:
  Horrible, filthy, undone,
Oh sun of my nature and star of my eyes,
  My passion, my angel[3] in one!   40

Yes, such will you be, oh regent of grace,
  After the rites have been read,

---

2. By extension. The torn flesh is described as "living rags."   3. Series of conventional Petrarchan images
that idealize the beloved.

Under the weeds, under blossoming grass
   As you molder with bones of the dead.

Ah then, oh my beauty, explain to the worms   45
   Who cherish your body so fine,
That I am the keeper for corpses of love
   Of the form, and the essence divine![4]

Invitation to the Voyage[1]

   My child, my sister, dream
   How sweet all things would seem
Were we in that kind land to live together,
   And there love slow and long,
   There love and die among   5
Those scenes that image you, that sumptuous weather.
   Drowned suns that glimmer there
   Through cloud-disheveled air
Move me with such a mystery as appears
   Within those other skies   10
   Of your treacherous eyes
When I behold them shining through their tears.

There, there is nothing else but grace and measure,
Richness, quietness, and pleasure.

   Furniture that wears   15
   The lustre of the years
Softly would glow within our glowing chamber,
   Flowers of rarest bloom
   Proffering their perfume
Mixed with the vague fragrances of amber;   20
   Gold ceilings would there be,
   Mirrors deep as the sea,
The walls all in an Eastern splendor hung—
   Nothing but should address
   The soul's loneliness,   25
Speaking her sweet and secret native tongue.

There, there is nothing else but grace and measure,
Richness, quietness, and pleasure.

   See, sheltered from the swells
   There in the still canals   30
Those drowsy ships that dream of sailing forth;
   It is to satisfy
   Your least desire, they ply

---

4. "Any form created by man is immortal. For form is independent of matter . . ." (from Baudelaire's journal *My Heart Laid Bare* 80).   **1.** Translated by Richard Wilbur. The translation maintains both the rhyme scheme and the rocking motion of the original meter, which follows an unusual pattern of two five-syllable lines followed by one seven-syllable line, and a seven-syllable couplet as refrain.

Hither through all the waters of the earth.
    The sun at close of day   35
    Clothes the fields of hay,
Then the canals, at last the town entire
    In hyacinth and gold:
    Slowly the land is rolled
Sleepward under a sea of gentle fire.   40

There, there is nothing else but grace and measure,
Richness, quietness, and pleasure.

Song of Autumn I[2]

Soon we shall plunge into the chilly fogs;
Farewell, swift light! our summers are too short!
I hear already the mournful fall of logs
Re-echoing from the pavement of the court.

All of winter will gather in my soul: 5
Hate, anger, horror, chills, the hard forced work;
And, like the sun in his hell by the north pole,
My heart will be only a red and frozen block.

I shudder, hearing every log that falls;
No scaffold could be built with hollower sounds.   10
My spirit is like a tower whose crumbling walls
The tireless battering-ram brings to the ground.

It seems to me, lulled by monotonous shocks,
As if they were hastily nailing a coffin today.
For whom?—Yesterday was summer. Now autumn knocks.   15
That mysterious sound is like someone's going away.

Spleen LXXVIII[1]

Old Pluvius,[2] month of rains, in peevish mood
Pours from his urn chill winter's sodden gloom
On corpses fading in the near graveyard,
On foggy suburbs pours life's tedium.

My cat seeks out a litter on the stones,   5
Her mangy body turning without rest.
An ancient poet's soul in monotones
Whines in the rain-spouts like a chilblained ghost.

---

2. Translated by C. F. MacIntyre to follow the original rhyme pattern.   1. Translated by Kenneth O. Hanson, with emphasis on the imagery. The French original uses identical *abab* rhymes in the two quatrains and shifts to *ccd, eed* in the tercets.   2. The rainy time (Latin, literal trans.); a period extending from January 20 to February 18 as the fifth month of the French Revolutionary calendar.

A great bell mourns, a wet log wrapped in smoke
Sings in falsetto to the wheezing clock,   10
While from a rankly perfumed deck of cards
(A dropsical old crone's fatal bequest)
The Queen of Spades, the dapper Jack of Hearts
Speak darkly of dead loves, how they were lost.

Spleen LXXIX[1]

I have more memories than if I had lived a thousand years.

Even a bureau crammed with souvenirs,
Old bills, love letters, photographs, receipts,
Court depositions, locks of hair in plaits,
Hides fewer secrets than my brain could yield.   5
It's like a tomb, a corpse-filled Potter's Field,[2]
A pyramid where the dead lie down by scores.
I am a graveyard that the moon abhors:
Like guilty qualms, the worms burrow and nest
Thickly in bodies that I loved the best.   10
I'm a stale boudoir where old-fashioned clothes
Lie scattered among wilted fern and rose,
Where only the Boucher girls[3] in pale pastels
Can breathe the uncorked scents and faded smells.

Nothing can equal those days for endlessness   15
When in the winter's blizzardy caress
Indifference expanding to Ennui[4]
Takes on the feel of Immortality.
O living matter, henceforth you're no more
Than a cold stone encompassed by vague fear   20
And by the desert, and the mist and sun;
An ancient Sphinx ignored by everyone,
Left off the map, whose bitter irony
Is to sing as the sun sets in that dry sea.[5]

Spleen LXXXI[1]

When the low heavy sky weighs like a lid
Upon the spirit aching for the light
And all the wide horizon's line is hid
By a black day sadder than any night;

When the changed earth is but a dungeon dank   5
Where batlike Hope goes blindly fluttering

---

1. Translated by Anthony Hecht. The translation follows the original rhymed couplets, except for one technical impossibility: Baudelaire's repetition (in a poem about monotony) of an identical rhyme for eight lines (lines 11–18, the sound of long *a*).   **2.** A general term describing the common cemetery for those buried at public expense.   **3.** François Boucher (1703–1770), court painter for Louis XV of France, drew many pictures of young women clothed and nude.   **4.** Melancholy, paralyzing boredom.   **5.** Baudelaire combines two references to ancient Egypt, the Sphinx and the legendary statue of Memnon at Thebes, which was supposed to sing at sunset.   **1.** Translated by Sir John Squire in accord with the original rhyme scheme.

And, striking wall and roof and mouldered plank,
Bruises his tender head and timid wing;

When like grim prison bars stretch down the thin,
Straight, rigid pillars of the endless rain,   10
And the dumb throngs of infamous spiders spin
Their meshes in the caverns of the brain,

Suddenly, bells leap forth into the air,
Hurling a hideous uproar to the sky
As 'twere a band of homeless spirits who fare   15
Through the strange heavens, wailing stubbornly.

And hearses, without drum or instrument,
File slowly through my soul; crushed, sorrowful,
Weeps Hope, and Grief, fierce and omnipotent,
Plants his black banner on my drooping skull.   20

The Voyage[1]

To Maxime du Camp[2]

I

The child, in love with prints and maps,
Holds the whole world in his vast appetite.
How large the earth is under the lamplight!
But in the eyes of memory, how the world is cramped!

We set out one morning, brain afire,   5
Hearts fat with rancor and bitter desires,
Moving along to the rhythm of wind and waves,
Lull the inner infinite on the finite of seas:

Some are glad, glad to leave a degraded home;
Others, happy to shake off the horror of their hearts,   10
Still others, astrologers drowned in the eyes of woman—
Oh the perfumes of Circe,[3] the power and the pig!—

To escape conversion to the Beast, get drunk
On space and light and the flames of skies;
The tongue of the sun and the ice that bites   15
Slowly erase the mark of the Kiss.

But the true voyagers are those who leave
Only to be going; hearts nimble as balloons,

1. Translated by Charles Henri Ford. The French poem is written in the traditional twelve-syllable (alexandrine) line with an *abab* rhyme scheme.   2. A wry dedication to the progress-oriented author of *Modern Songs* (1855), which began "I was born a traveler."   3. In Homer's *Odyssey*, an island sorceress who changed visitors into beasts. Odysseus's men were transformed into pigs.

They never diverge from luck's black sun,
And with or without reason, cry, Let's be gone!   20

Desire to them is nothing but clouds,
They dream, as a draftee dreams of the cannon,
Of vast sensualities, changing, unknown,
Whose name the spirit has never pronounced!

II

We imitate—horrible!—the top and ball   25
In their waltz and bounce; even in sleep
We're turned and tormented by Curiosity,
Who, like a mad Angel, lashes the stars.

Peculiar fortune that changes its goal,
And being nowhere, is anywhere at all!   30
And Man, who is never untwisted from hope,
Scrambling like a madman to get some rest!

The soul's a three-master seeking Icaria;[4]
A voice on deck calls: "Wake up there!"
A voice from the mast-head, vehement, wild: 35
"Love . . . fame . . . happiness!" We're on the rocks!

Every island that the lookout hails
Becomes the Eldorado[5] foretold by Fortune;
Then Imagination embarks on its orgy
But runs aground in the brightness of morning.   40

Poor little lover of visionary fields!
Should he be put in irons, dumped in the sea,
This drunken sailor, discoverer of Americas,
Mirage that makes the gulf more bitter?

So the old vagabond, shuffling in mud,   45
Dreams, nose hoisted, of a shining paradise,
His charmed eye lighting on Capua's[6] coast
At every candle aglow in a hovel.

III

Astounding voyagers! what noble stories
We read in your eyes, deeper than seas;   50
Show us those caskets, filled with rich memories,
Marvelous jewels, hewn from stars and aether.

---

4. Greek island in the Aegean Sea, named after the mythological Icarus, who, escaping from prison on wings made by his father, Daedalus, plunged into nearby waters and drowned when they gave way. His name was associated with utopian flights, as in Etienne Cabet's novel about a utopian community, *Voyage to Icaria* (1840). *Three-master:* a ship.   **5.** Fabled country of gold and abundance.   **6.** City on the Volturno River in southern Italy, famous for its luxury and sensuality.

Yes, we would travel, without sail or steam!
Gladden a little our jail's desolation,
Sail over our minds, stretched like a canvas,   55
All your memories, framed with gold horizons.

Tell us, what have you seen?

IV

                              "We have seen stars
And tides; we have seen sands, too,
And, despite shocks and unforeseen disasters,
We were often bored, just as we are here.   60

The glory of sun on a violet sea,
The glory of cities in the setting sun,
Kindled our hearts with torment and longing
To plunge into the sky's magnetic reflections.

Neither the rich cities nor sublime landscapes,   65
Ever possessed that mysterious attraction
Of Change and Chance having fun with the clouds.
And always Desire kept us anxious!

—Enjoyment adds force to Appetite!
Desire, old tree nurtured by pleasure,   70
Although your dear bark thicken and harden,
Your branches throb to hold the sun closer!

Great tree, will you outgrow the cypress?
Still we have gathered carefully
Some sketches for your hungry album,   75
Brothers, for whom all things from far away

Are precious! We've bowed down to idols;
To thrones encrusted with luminous rocks;
To figured palaces whose magic pomp
Would ruin your bankers with a ruinous dream;   80

To costumes that intoxicate the eye,
To women whose teeth and nails are dyed,
To clever jugglers, fondled by the snake."[7]

V

And then, and what more?

7. Snake charmers. The images in this stanza evoke India.

VI

"O childish minds!

Not to forget the principal thing,   85
We saw everywhere, without looking for it,
From top to toe of the deadly scale,
The tedious drama of undying sin:

Woman, low slave, vain and stupid,
Without laughter self-loving, and without disgust,   90
Man, greedy despot, lewd, hard and covetous,
Slave of the slave, rivulet in the sewer;

The hangman exulting, the martyr sobbing;
Festivals that season and perfume the blood;[8]
The poison of power unnerving the tyrant,   95
The masses in love with the brutalizing whip;

Many religions, very like our own,
All climbing to heaven; and Holiness,
Like a delicate wallower in a feather bed,
Seeking sensation from hair shirts and nails.   100

Jabbering humanity, drunk with its genius,
As crazy now as it was in the past,
Crying to God in its raging agony:
'O master, fellow creature, I curse thee forever!'

And then the least stupid, brave lovers of Lunacy,   105
Fleeing the gross herd that Destiny pens in,
Finding release in the vast dreams of opium!
—Such is the story, the whole world over."

VII

Bitter knowledge that traveling brings!
The globe, monotonous and small, today,   110
Yesterday, tomorrow, always, throws us our image:
An oasis of horror in a desert of boredom!

Should we go? Or stay? If you can stay, stay;
But go if you must. Some run, some hide
To outwit Time, the enemy so vigilant and   115
Baleful. And many, alas, must run forever

Like the wandering Jew[9] and the twelve apostles,
Who could not escape his relentless net[1]

---

8. Literally, Festivals seasoned and perfumed by blood.   9. According to medieval legend, a Jew who
mocked Christ on his way to the Cross and was condemned to wander unceasingly until Judgment Day.
1. These three stanzas describe Time (ultimately Death) as a Roman gladiator, the *retiarius,* who used a
net to trap his opponent.

By ship or by wheel; while others knew how
To destroy him without leaving home.   120

When finally he places his foot on our spine,
May we be able to hope and cry, Forward!
As in days gone by when we left for China,
Eyes fixed on the distance, hair in the wind,

With heart as light as a young libertine's   125
We'll embark on the sea of deepening shadows.
Do you hear those mournful, enchanting voices[2]
That sing: "Come this way, if you would taste

The perfumed Lotus. Here you may pick
Miraculous fruits for which the heart hungers.   130
Come and drink deep of this strange,
Soft afternoon that never ends?"

Knowing his voice, we visualize the phantom—
It is our Pylades there, his arms outstretched.
While she whose knees we used to kiss cries out,   135
"For strength of heart, swim back to your Electra!"[3]

VIII

O Death, old captain, it is time! weigh anchor!
This country confounds us; hoist sail and away!
If the sky and sea are black as ink,
Our hearts, as you know them, burst with blinding rays. 140

Pour us your poison, that last consoling draft!
For we long, so the fire burns in the brain,
To sound the abyss, Hell or Heaven, what matter?
In the depths of the Unknown, we'll discover the New!

FROM PARIS SPLEEN[1]

One o'Clock in the Morning

At last! I am alone! Nothing can be heard but the rumbling of a few belated and weary cabs. For a few hours at least silence will be ours, if not sleep. At last! The tyranny of the human face has disappeared, and now there will be no one but myself to make me suffer.

At last! I am allowed to relax in a bath of darkness! First a double turn of the key in the lock. This turn of the key will, it seems to me, increase my solitude and strengthen the barricades that, for the moment, separate me from the world.

2. The voices of the dead, luring the sailor to the Lotus-land of ease and forgetfulness.   3. In Greek mythology, Orestes and Pylades were close friends ready to sacrifice their lives for each other. Electra was Orestes' faithful sister, who saved him from the Furies.   1. Translated by Louis Varèse.

Horrible life! Horrible city! Let us glance back over the events of the day: saw several writers, one of them asking me if you could go to Russia by land (he thought Russia was an island, I suppose); disagreed liberally with the editor of a review who to all my objections kept saying: "Here we are on the side of respectability," implying that all the other periodicals were run by rascals; bowed to twenty or more persons of whom fifteen were unknown to me; distributed hand shakes in about the same proportion without having first taken the precaution of buying gloves; to kill time during a shower, dropped in on a dancer who asked me to design her a costume of *Venustre*;[2] went to pay court to a theatrical director who in dismissing me said: "Perhaps you would do well to see Z. . . . ; he is the dullest, stupidest and most celebrated of our authors; with him you might get somewhere. Consult him and then we'll see": boasted (why?) of several ugly things I never did, and cravenly denied some other misdeeds that I had accomplished with the greatest delight; offense of fanfaronnade,[3] crime against human dignity; refused a slight favor to a friend and gave a written recommendation to a perfect rogue; Lord! let's hope that's all!

Dissatisfied with everything, dissatisfied with myself, I long to redeem myself and to restore my pride in the silence and solitude of the night. Souls of those whom I have loved, souls of those whom I have sung, strengthen me, sustain me, keep me from the vanities of the world and its contaminating fumes; and You, dear God! grant me grace to produce a few beautiful verses to prove to myself that I am not the lowest of men, that I am not inferior to those whom I despise.

Crowds

It is not given to every man to take a bath of multitude; enjoying a crowd is an art; and only he can relish a debauch of vitality at the expense of the human species, on whom, in his cradle, a fairy has bestowed the love of masks and masquerading, the hate of home, and the passion for roaming.

Multitude, solitude: identical terms, and interchangeable by the active and fertile poet. The man who is unable to people his solitude is equally unable to be alone in a bustling crowd.

The poet enjoys the incomparable privilege of being able to be himself or someone else, as he chooses. Like those wandering souls who go looking for a body, he enters as he likes into each man's personality. For him alone everything is vacant; and if certain places seem closed to him, it is only because in his eyes they are not worth visiting.

The solitary and thoughtful stroller finds a singular intoxication in this universal communion. The man who loves to lose himself in a crowd enjoys feverish delights that the egoist locked up in himself as in a box, and the slothful man like a mollusk in his shell, will be eternally deprived of. He adopts as his own all the occupations, all the joys and all the sorrows that chance offers.

What men call love is a very small, restricted, feeble thing compared with

2. Venus. Baudelaire ironically reproduces the dancer's mispronunciation.   3. Boasting.

this ineffable orgy, this divine prostitution of the soul giving itself entire, all its poetry and all its charity, to the unexpected as it comes along, to the stranger as he passes.

It is a good thing sometimes to teach the fortunate of this world, if only to humble for an instant their foolish pride, that there are higher joys than theirs, finer and more uncircumscribed. The founders of colonies, shepherds of peoples, missionary priests exiled to the ends of the earth, doubtlessly know something of this mysterious drunkenness; and in the midst of the vast family created by their genius, they must often laugh at those who pity them because of their troubled fortunes and chaste lives.

Windows

Looking from outside into an open window one never sees as much as when one looks through a closed window. There is nothing more profound, more mysterious, more pregnant, more insidious, more dazzling than a window lighted by a single candle. What one can see out in the sunlight is always less interesting than what goes on behind a windowpane. In that black or luminous square life lives, life dreams, life suffers.

Across the ocean of roofs I can see a middle-aged woman, her face already lined, who is forever bending over something and who never goes out. Out of her face, her dress, and her gestures, out of practically nothing at all, I have made up this woman's story, or rather legend, and sometimes I tell it to myself and weep.

If it had been an old man I could have made up his just as well.

And I go to bed proud to have lived and to have suffered in some one besides myself.

Perhaps you will say "Are you sure that your story is the real one?" But what does it matter what reality is outside myself, so long as it has helped me to live, to feel that I am, and what I am?

Anywhere out of the World[1]

Life is a hospital where every patient is obsessed by the desire of changing beds. One would like to suffer opposite the stove, another is sure he would get well beside the window.

It always seems to me that I should be happy anywhere but where I am, and this question of moving is one that I am eternally discussing with my soul.

"Tell me, my soul, poor chilly soul, how would you like to live in Lisbon? It must be warm there, and you would be as blissful as a lizard in the sun. It is a city by the sea; they say that it is built of marble, and that its inhabitants have such a horror of the vegetable kingdom that they tear up all the trees.

---

1. The title (given in English by Baudelaire) is based on a line from Thomas Hood's poem *Bridge of Sighs*: "Anywhere, anywhere—out of the world." Baudelaire probably found the reference in Poe's *Poetic Principle*.

You see it is a country after my own heart; a country entirely made of mineral and light, and with liquid to reflect them."

My soul does not reply.

"Since you are so fond of being motionless and watching the pageantry of movement, would you like to live in the beatific land of Holland? Perhaps you could enjoy yourself in that country which you have so long admired in paintings on museum walls. What do you say to Rotterdam,[2] you who love forests of masts, and ships that are moored on the doorsteps of houses?"

My soul remains silent.

"Perhaps you would like Batavia[3] better? There, moreover, we should find the wit of Europe wedded to the beauty of the tropics."

Not a word. Can my soul be dead?

"Have you sunk into so deep a stupor that you are happy only in your unhappiness? If that is the case, let us fly to countries that are the counterfeits of Death. I know just the place for us, poor soul. We will pack up our trunks for Torneo.[4] We will go still farther, to the farthest end of the Baltic Sea; still farther from life if possible; we will settle at the Pole. There the sun only obliquely grazes the earth, and the slow alternations of daylight and night abolish variety and increase that other half of nothingness, monotony. There we can take deep baths of darkness, while sometimes for our entertainment, the Aurora Borealis will shoot up its rose-red sheafs like the reflections of the fireworks of hell!"

At last my soul explores! "Anywhere! Just so it is out of the world!"

2. Large Dutch seaport.   3. Former name of Djakarta, capital of the Dutch East Indies and now the
capital city of Indonesia.   4. A city in Finland.

STÉPHANE MALLARMÉ
1842–1898

Of all the Symbolist writers, Mallarmé (*mal-ahr-may*) is the most compulsive visionary. He uses ordinary words and concrete images, but only as raw material for a wholly imaginary creation. Like Rimbaud, he seeks a way out of sordid reality through the liberating power of the imagination, but unlike the younger poet, he did not turn his back on literature even though his lofty poetic ideals made it increasingly difficult for him to put words on paper. Mallarmé works to purify language; he avoids the direct approach because obliquely he can say more. Thus he suggests, rather than names; keeps several levels of meaning alive at the same time; complicates his syntax and sometimes even misleads us to prolong the pleasure of final discovery. Although Mallarmé's poems are immediately accessible on the level of visual imagery, they also offer the pleasure of a chess game for those who like to pursue intricate structures of thought. He constitutes another example of the poet adventuring on the frontiers of thought; by the second half of the twentieth century, Mallarmé's multileveled patterns of allusion and abstract theories of poetic language had found followers among not only poets but also philosophers of language.

Étienne (called Stéphane) Mallarmé was born in Paris on March 18, 1842, into a settled bourgeois family. His father was deputy clerk in the Registry, and ancestors on both sides of the family had been minor government bureaucrats as far back as the French Revolution. Mallarmé's mother died when he was five, and his sister in 1857: the pain of their loss recurs in images of his later poetry. After graduating from boarding school in 1860, he worked for two years in his grandfather's office before deciding to become a teacher of English. In 1863 he received a teaching position in the southeastern provincial town of Tournon and moved there with his new wife, a young German woman named Maria Gerhard. Their daughter, Geneviève, was born in 1864. A son, Anatole, was born in 1871 and died in 1879.

Mallarmé began publishing poems and articles in 1862, although his output was always meager and he did not produce a collection in book form until 1887. Much of his work was published separately in various journals. His first important group of poems was published in 1866 in the new literary magazine *Contemporary Parnassus*, and his translations of Edgar Allan Poe appeared in 1872. Mallarmé was eager to move to Paris, the capital of the arts, but as a young teacher in the state educational system he was dependent on governmental assignments. Sent in 1886 to Besançon and in 1867 to Avignon, he was finally able to move to Paris in 1871, and there he taught at the Lycée Fontanes. Mallarmé was not a particularly good language teacher, had little aptitude for drills and discipline, and was often a figure of fun for his students. On the other hand, he was an important and charismatic figure for the young writers, artists, and musicians who heard him talk about the nature of poetry at the "Tuesdays," gatherings held every Tuesday evening from 1880 until shortly before his death. Mallarmé's influence was widespread. In 1876 Edouard Manet illustrated Mallarmé's *L'Après-midi d'un faune* (The Afternoon of a Faun), and in 1894 Claude Debussy composed his musical *Prélude*, which was inspired by the same text. Verlaine included Mallarmé in his account of the new poets, *The Accursed Poets*, and after Verlaine's death Mallarmé was elected "Prince of Poets" by his colleagues in 1896. Upon his retirement from teaching in 1894, Mallarmé lectured on poetry and experimented with different kinds of poetic form, including the typographical arrangements of *Dice Thrown* (1897) that foreshadowed modern concrete poetry. For years, he had worked on the notion of a universal "Book," a complicated text that would be performed and not merely read. Yet he himself finally felt that his vision had outstripped technical possibilities; and when he died on September 9, 1898, the work remained incomplete.

The creative process itself is the central topic of Mallarmé's poetry, whether in the earlier autobiographical poems or in later impersonal scenes from which the narrator is excluded. Mallarmé's particular symbolism builds on allusion and suggestion to evoke a virtual reality, a richer dimension he prefers to ordinary limited realism. The poet is understandably haunted by the difficulty of writing. He describes himself as a grave digger digging his thoughts out of the "cold and niggard soil" of his brain or as paralyzed by the blank whiteness of the paper on which he must write. Escaping into art, he wishes in one poem to imitate the spare perfection of painted Chinese porcelain. Even such a banal object as a fan, fluttering open and then lying closed against a bracelet, can evoke the desired realm of absolute beauty. Oddly enough, a common characteristic of Mallarmé's evocations of beauty, and one that distinguishes them from scenes in Baudelaire, Rimbaud, and Verlaine, is his emphasis on absence. An early poem, *Saint*, illustrates the way the poet plays with a sense of loss or absence while using concrete details to create a series of vivid—though intangible—images.

The saint of the poem (according to a previous title, Saint Cecilia, the patron saint of music), is seen at—perhaps represented on—the window of a cabinet where musical instruments are kept. The cabinet's cedar-wood viol, which no longer gleams with gold as it did when formerly played with accompanying flute and mandolin, and the old book lying open at the Magnificat, together establish the idea of a real, historical music that is now stilled or absent. The poem's single sentence is divided into two contrasting scenes; in the last two stanzas, the saint plays an imaginary harp that suggests an ideal or soundless music. She, the "Musician of silences," has her finger poised on the shape of a golden harp implied by the outstretched wing of a sculptured angel, a "plumage instrumental" that receives from the evening sun all the gilding that was lost to the real instrument of the first stanza. By the end of the poem, the ideal music suggested by the saint's gesture is more present to the reader than the "real" music at the beginning.

The ideal music of this and other poems is created by refining and manipulating ordinary language: purifying "the language of the horde," as Mallarmé says in *The Tomb of Edgar Poe*. This "tomb" or epitaph poem was written for a Baltimore memorial ceremony at which a monument to Poe was erected. Mallarmé describes the American poet as a Saint George confronting the dragon of mediocrity and slander (that is, critics who accused him of writing only drunken fantasies). Another allegory of the alienated poet, *The virginal, vibrant, and beautiful dawn*, is built around the image of a swan who—refusing to sing about life, warmth, and mundane reality—is finally frozen into the dazzling glacier of his ideal dreams. The sonnet emphasizes images of whiteness, arrested movement, sterility, and chill; the French text intensifies this bleakness by reiterating a shrill *ee* sound throughout all fourteen lines and piling up negative linguistic forms. Mallarmé's artist is a technician, coordinating different relationships among words to invent his "purer" poetic language

Mallarmé's best-known poem, the source of Claude Debussy's orchestral *Prélude* in 1894 and Nijinsky's ballet in 1912, is *The Afternoon of a Faun*. Here the familiar themes of artistic creation, dream, and loss—the doomed attempt to capture perfect form in mere words—underly the warm and sensuous picture of a woodland satyr recounting his erotic pursuit of two nymphs. Was it a dream, he wonders, that he caught the two water nymphs—one passionate, one naive—only to lose them on the brink of possession? The poem is framed by the faun's desire first to "perpetuate" these nymphs in memory and finally to follow them back into dream. It is famous for its vivid and sensual descriptions, for its intricate imagery, and for the extraordinary musicality of its classical verse (the French alexandrine, or twelve-syllable line). Turning to his pipes and to drunken dreams to celebrate a perfect union he could not hold, the faun illustrates once more Mallarmé's theme of poetic creation, describing an ideal beauty that is absent and a sensuously intuited love that remains perpetually not just out of reach but in fact a figment of the imagination.

Frederic St. Aubyn, *Stéphane Mallarmé* (1989), provides a brief biography and thematically arranged discussions of Mallarmé's work. Harold Bloom, ed., *Stéphane Mallarmé* (1987), collects thirteen challenging essays on Mallarmé's work and its implications for poetic practice. Hans-Jost Frey, *Studies in Poetic Discourse* (1996), trans. William Whobrey, offers perceptive essays on Mallarmé, Baudelaire, Rimbaud, and Hölderlin.

[Poems]

The Afternoon of a Faun[1]

Eclogue[2]

THE FAUN

These nymphs that I would perpetuate:
                  so clear
And light, their carnation,[3] that it floats in the air
Heavy with leafy slumbers.

---

1. All poems translated by Henry Weinfield. In Greek mythology, a faun was a woodland satyr with goatlike hooves and horns.   2. A pastoral poem, usually in dialogue form, originating in Greek poetry. Here, italics indicate the divisions of the faun's internal dialogue.   3. A rosy flesh pink.

Did I love a dream?
My doubt, night's ancient hoard, pursues its theme
In branching labyrinths, which, being still
The veritable woods themselves, alas, reveal
My triumph as the ideal fault of roses.
Consider . . .

        if the women of your glosses
Are phantoms of your fabulous[4] desires!
Faun, the illusion flees from the cold, blue eyes
Of the chaster nymph like a fountain gushing tears;
But the other, all in sighs, you say, compares
To a hot wind through the fleece that blows at noon?
No! through the motionless and weary swoon
Of stifling heat that suffocates the morning,
Save from my flute, no waters murmuring
In harmony flow out into the groves;
And the only wind on the horizon no ripple moves,
Exhaled from my twin pipes and swift to drain
The melody in arid drifts of rain,
Is the visible, serene and fictive air
Of inspiration rising as if in prayer.

RELATE, Sicilian shores,[5] whose tranquil fens
My vanity disturbs as do the suns,
Silent beneath the brilliant flowers of flame:
"That cutting hollow reeds my art would tame,
I saw far off, against the glaucous gold
Of foliage twined to where the springs run cold,
An animal whiteness languorously swaying;
To the slow prelude that the pipes were playing,
This flight of swans—no! naiads[6]—rose in a shower
Of spray . . ."

        Day burns inert in the tawny hour
And excess of hymen is escaped away—
Without a sign, from one who pined for the primal A:[7]
And so, beneath a flood of antique light,
As innocent as are the lilies white,
To my first ardors I awake alone.

Besides sweet nothings by their lips made known,
Kisses that only mark their perfidy,
My chest reveals an unsolved mystery . . .
The toothmarks of some strange, majestic creature:
Enough! Arcana such as these disclose their nature
Only through vast twin reeds played to the skies,
That, turning to music all that clouds the eyes,

5

10

15

20

25

30

35

40

---

4. Fabled; i.e., both marvelous and narrated.   **5.** An invocation to the surrounding countryside, which recalls the openings of classical poems like the *Iliad* and the *Aeneid*.   6. Water nymphs.   7. The musical note A. In the French text it is *la* (from the *do-re-mi* scale), which is also the feminine article "the." *Hymen*: marriage or sexual union.

Dream, in a long solo, that we amused   45
The beauty all around us by confused
Equations[8] with our credulous melody;
And dream that the song can make love soar so high
That, purged of all ordinary fantasies
Of back or breast—incessant shapes that rise   50
In blindness—it distills sonorities
From every empty and monotonous line.[9]

Then, instrument of flights; Syrinx[1] malign,
At lakes where you attend me, bloom once more!
Long shall my discourse from the echoing shore   55
Depict those goddesses: by masquerades,[2]
I'll strip the veils that sanctify their shades;
And when I've sucked the brightness out of grapes,
To quell the flood of sorrow that escapes,
I'll lift the empty cluster to the sky,   60
Avidly drunk till evening has drawn nigh,
And blow in laughter through the luminous skins.

Let us inflate our MEMORIES, O nymphs.
"Piercing the reeds, my darting eyes transfix,
Plunged in the cooling waves, immortal necks,   65
And cries of fury echo through the air;
Splendid cascades of tresses disappear
In shimmering jewels. Pursuing them, I find
There, at my feet, two sleepers intertwined,
Bruised in the languor of duality,   70
Their arms about each other heedlessly.
I bear them, still entangled, to a height
Where frivolous shadow never mocks the light
And dying roses yield the sun their scent,
That with the day our passions might be spent."   75
I adore you, wrath of virgins—fierce delight
Of the sacred burden's writhing naked flight
From the fiery lightning of my lips that flash
With the secret terror of the thirsting flesh:
From the cruel one's feet to the heart of the shy,   80
Whom innocence abandons suddenly,
Watered in frenzied or less woeful tears.
"Gay with the conquest of those traitorous fears,
I sinned when I divided the dishevelled
Tuft of kisses that the gods had ravelled.   85
For hardly had I hidden an ardent moan
Deep in the joyous recesses of one
(Holding by a finger, that her swanlike pallor
From her sister's passion might be tinged with color,
The little one, unblushingly demure,   90

---

8. Playing his reed pipes, the faun creates a musical line that is equated with the nymphs' silhouette as he remembers it behind closed eyes.   9. Lines 51 and 52 are one line in the French text.   1. In Greek mythology, a nymph who fled from the god Pan and was changed into a reed, from which flutes, or panpipes, are made.   2. Literally, idolatrous pictures (of the nymphs).

When from my arms, loosened[3] by death obscure,
This prey, ungrateful to the end, breaks free,
Spurning the sobs that still transported me."

Others will lead me on to happiness,
Their tresses knotted round my horns, I guess.   95
You know, my passion, that, crimson with ripe seeds,
Pomegranates burst in a murmur of bees,
And that our blood, seized by each passing form,
Flows toward desire's everlasting swarm.
In the time when the forest turns ashen and gold   100
And the summer's demise in the leaves is extolled,
Etna![4] when Venus visits her retreat,
Treading your lava with innocent feet,
Though a sad sleep thunders and the flame burns cold,
I hold the queen!
                          Sure punishment[5] . . .

                                    No, but the soul,   105
Weighed down by the body, wordless, struck dumb,
To noon's proud silence must at last succumb:
And so, let me sleep, oblivious of sin,
Stretched out on the thirsty sand, drinking in
The bountiful rays of the wine-growing star!   110

Couple, farewell; I'll see the shade that now you are.

The Tomb[1] of Edgar Poe

As to Himself at last eternity changes him
The Poet reawakens with a naked sword
His century appalled at never having heard
That in this voice triumphant death had sung its hymn.

They, like a writhing hydra, hearing seraphim[2]   5
Bestow a purer sense on the language of the horde,
Loudly proclaimed that the magic potion[3] had been poured
From the dregs of some dishonored mixture of foul slime.

From the war between earth and heaven, what grief!
If understanding cannot sculpt a bas-relief   10
To ornament the dazzling tomb of Poe:

---

3. I.e., his arms were momentarily weakened.   **4.** A volcano in Sicily.   **5.** The faun imagines swift punishment when in his heightened desire he fantasizes seizing Venus, the goddess of love.   **1.** A *tomb* is also a funeral poem. The poem was written for a memorial ceremony honoring Edgar Allan Poe (1809–1849) in Baltimore, Maryland, and was first published in the 1877 memorial volume.   **2.** The Angel: the above said Poet [Mallarmé's note]. Mallarmé explained this in English to the memorial organizers. *Hydra:* a mythical many-headed serpent; here compared with those who slandered Poe when he was alive.   **3.** In plain prose: Charged him with always being drunk [Mallarmé's note]. Critics accused Poe of finding inspiration in drunken fantasies.

Calm block here fallen from obscure disaster,[4]
Let this granite at least mark the boundaries evermore
To the dark flights of Blasphemy[5] hurled to the future.

Saint[1]

At the window frame concealing
The viol old and destitute
Whose gilded sandalwood, now peeling,
Once shone with mandolin or flute,

Is the Saint, pale, unfolding   5
The old, worn missal,[2] a divine
Magnificat[3] in rivers flowing
Once at vespers and compline:[4]

At the glass of this monstrance,[5] vessel
Touched by a harp that took its shape   10
From the evening flight of an Angel
For the delicate fingertip

Which, without the old, worn missal
Or sandalwood, she balances
On the plumage instrumental,   15
Musician of silences.

[The virginal, vibrant, and beautiful dawn]

II

The virginal, vibrant, and beautiful dawn,
Will a beat of its drunken wing[1] not suffice
To rend this hard lake haunted beneath the ice
By the transparent glacier of flights never flown?

A swan of former times remembers it's the one   5
Magnificent but hopelessly struggling to resist
For never having sung of a land in which to exist
When the boredom of the sterile winter has shone.

Though its quivering neck will shake free of the agonies
Inflicted on the bird by the space it denies,   10
The horror of the earth will remain where it lies.

---

4. The memorial marker (*Calm block*) is seen as a meteorite fallen from a dark or negative star (*disaster*); a play on words: *aster* is Greek for "star."   **5.** Blasphemy: against poets, such as the charge of Poe being drunk [Mallarmé's note]. *Boundaries*: literally, the milestone along French roads, intended here to limit the batlike flights of slander.   **1.** The original title was "Saint Cecilia Playing on the Wing of an Angel." **2.** Literally, an old book, probably containing the music for the old instruments. Cecilia is the patron saint of music.   **3.** A hymn of praise to God.   **4.** Evening church services. *Once*: formerly.   **5.** An altar receptacle to hold the Host, with a small glass window in front.   **1.** A wild, impulsive gesture; also, an astonishing extended rhyme with *is freed* in French: *d'aile ivre / délivre*.

Phantom whose pure brightness assigns it this domain,
It stiffens in the cold dream of disdain
That clothes the useless exile of the Swan.[2]

2. The word *swan* rhymes with *sign* in French (*cygne* / *signe*), and the capitalized Swan may be read as a symbol of the writer's futile quest for the absolute Sign.

PAUL VERLAINE
1844–1896

The musicality of his verse, his impressionistic yet intimate scenes, and the complex melancholy of his poetic voice serve to distinguish Paul Verlaine among the three great Symbolist poets after Baudelaire. If the abstract Mallarmé and the flamboyant Rimbaud are better known to modern readers, it is Verlaine whose asymmetrical lines and fleeting images influenced the next generation of poets and helped shape twentieth-century free verse. Verlaine's love for the nuance that captures several dimensions of experience and his rejection of fixed categories as a kind of lesser vision are evoked in the mysterious figure of Pierrot, the mournful clown who stands slightly apart from society and recognizes his own alienation. It was an alienation Verlaine knew; he scandalized society by his irregular life and affair with Arthur Rimbaud, and by the time of his death he was both "Prince of Poets" and a symbol of decadence.

Paul-Marie Verlaine was born at Metz, France, in a well-to-do army family that indulged their only son. When Verlaine was seven, his father resigned his commission and the family moved to Paris, where the boy was educated, frequented the circles of the classically oriented Parnassian poets, and attended law school for a year before deciding to devote himself to poetry. Earning a living in a series of clerical positions, he published his first collection, *Saturnian Poems* (under the sign of Saturn, supposedly signaling a morbid imagination) in 1866; three years later, *Fêtes galantes* (Gallant Feasts; elegant pastoral festivities) appeared. Verlaine at this time was already having problems with alcoholism and showing signs of the sudden rages that punctuated his later life; several times, he went so far as to attack his mother. In 1870, under pressure from his family and perhaps hoping to settle down, he married Mathilde Mauté, a devout Catholic and sister of a friend. Anticipations of peace and happiness dominate the poems of *The Good Song*, written shortly before his marriage and published the same year. The next year, however, he met Arthur Rimbaud, and relations with his wife deteriorated sharply; Mathilde left Verlaine in 1872 when he would not break with Rimbaud, and the couple was divorced in 1874. The two poets spent much of the following year in London, but their tempestuous relationship ended in Belgium in July 1873 when Verlaine shot Rimbaud after a quarrel and was imprisoned for two years. Poems from this period were published in 1874 as *Songs Without Words*, a paradoxical title that recalls the poet's advice in his *Art of Poetry:* "You must have music first of all." (In fact, Verlaine's poetry has often been set to music.) While in prison, he turned for solace to his childhood Catholicism and wrote poems (later published in *Wisdom*, 1880) that evoke his pain, remorse, and renewed hope of salvation. Emerging from prison in 1875, Verlaine attempted to renew his relationship with Rimbaud but was rebuffed. The famous affair had ended, and with Rimbaud in Africa, Verlaine's only further connection was to edit the *Illuminations* in 1886 and a posthumous collection in 1895.

Verlaine's religious conversion in 1873 did not herald a life of peace and contemplation. After teaching French for a while in England, he returned to Paris and attempted unsuccessfully to regain his job with the city. He also tried farming with a former student, Lucien Létinois. After Létinois's death from typhoid fever, Verlaine moved in with his mother but was again imprisoned for violence. He moved to Paris in 1885, where he lived in poverty and ill health. His continued alcoholism was taking its toll, and he spent much of his life in hospitals until his death in 1896. During the last ten years, however, his literary reputation was on the rise. The next generation of poets in France and England looked to him as a master, admiring both his poetry and his anticonformist ways. Critical studies were written about him; he wrote prolifically, lectured in England, and was hailed as their leader by a new group of self-styled "Decadent" poets in France. In August 1894, Verlaine was elected "Prince of Poets" by his colleagues.

His later poetry is quite different from his early, ambivalent style: it stresses religious themes and a voice of absolute conviction. Some continuity is visible: previous images of the poet's vulnerability before life (*Autumn Song*) become the more reassuring image of a worshiper's humility before God; the sensuality and dissonances of earlier poems are later used as examples of evil in the poet's battle against sin. On several occasions, Verlaine even parodies his former style. For many readers, however, the volumes of poetry and prose after *Yesteryear and Yesterday* (*Jadis et Naguère*; 1884) are less compelling precisely because they turn to more assertive, explicit, and often conventional forms of expression. Gone is the taste for nuance and ambiguity, the irony and self-conscious pathos, the half-tones and the lilt of asymmetrical rhythms that seem peculiarly Verlaine and without which—as he says in *The Art of Poetry*—everything else is merely literary convention, or "literature."

The five poems printed here come from five different collections published from 1866 to 1884. *Autumn Song,* one of seven "Mournful Landscapes" in the *Saturnian Poems,* captures a moment of experience while displaying Verlaine's intense musicality in its short rhymed lines and gently rocking melody. (In the French, the indented lines have three syllables, the others four.) Dead leaves proclaim the end of the year, and the speaker—already disheartened by the melodious cry of the autumn wind—weeps quietly over the passage of time in his own life. In this acute evocation of a state of mind, the melancholy speaker is equated with a dead leaf blown helplessly on the wind (compare Shelley's *Ode to the West Wind*).

Another imaginary landscape, this time a painted one, appears in *Moonlight,* a poem from *Fêtes galantes* that evokes the dreamlike scenes in which the eighteenth-century French artist Antoine Watteau (1684–1721) portrayed aristocratic men and women playing at being romantic shepherds and shepherdesses. *Moonlight* is truly a poem of nuances and masks, of paradoxical images and elusive identity. The moon's half-light illuminates uncertain characters who dance dejectedly inside their fanciful costumes, sing in a sad minor key about love and good luck, and cannot believe in their own happiness; in this painted world, their song itself is part of the moonlight, and the whole scene an image of the addressee's (perhaps Verlaine's) soul. Moonlight reappears in *The white moonglow* (from *The Good Song*), one of the poems Verlaine gave his fiancée before their marriage. This "exquisite hour" celebrates a moment of intimacy between the two lovers walking at night; it is a swift, delicate sketch in which the human figures never actually appear. Instead, there are overheard voices, fragmentary or reflected images, and refracted moonlight.

Verlaine is not all moonlight and fading voices, however. In *Wooden Horses,* he depicts a busy merry-go-round in an amusement park peopled by pickpockets and by workers eager to make love on their day off. This time the music is harshly rhythmic, an insistent tempo that is echoed and reinforced by the poem's repetitions: the wooden horses gallop on and on, their riders drunk with dizziness in what begins to seem like a mindless pursuit of passion. Evening comes with velvet elegance in the last stanza, but here it is only a background for amorous couples pairing off to the beat of the drums. All four poems evoke a particular moment of experience, a fleeting subjective impression that is built out of a few telling details and associated rhythm patterns. Such, in fact, is the recommendation of Verlaine's *Art of Poetry,* published in *Yesteryear and Yesterday.* This poem, which became the unofficial manifesto of the new Symbolist school, not only reflects Verlaine's own preferences in 1874 but also outlines a program of antitraditional poetic strategies. No more four-square rhythm; no more fixed images with clear outlines and colors; no wit, eloquence, or rhyme for its own sake; in short, none of the traditional poetic techniques intended to create beautiful and lasting images in explicit, rational verse. Instead, Verlaine proclaimed the joys of the *vers impair,* the "uneven" line whose odd number of syllables creates a floating effect. (*The Art of Poetry* uses a nine-syllable line.) Words are slightly inexact, perhaps containing suggestive overtones. Composite images express a state of mind; nuances invite a blurring of boundaries and release the imagination; and above all, music and emotion are the poet's guide until words become "soluble" and poetry a natural experience. Verlaine's opposition of "poetry" and "literature," and the example of his own poems, became a model for the young Symbolist poets—among them Jules Laforgue, much admired by the early T. S. Eliot—and helped shape European lyric tradition for many years.

Joanna Richardson, *Verlaine* (1971), is a useful biography. Stefan Zweig, *Paul Verlaine* (1913), trans. O. F. Theis (1980), discusses the poet and his work.

PRONOUNCING GLOSSARY

The following list uses common English syllables and stress accents to provide rough equivalents of selected names whose pronunciation may be unfamiliar to the general reader.

Bois de la Cambre: *bwah d'lah cawm'-br*   Verlaine: *vehr-len'*

[POEMS]

Autumn Song[1]

With long sobs
the violin-throbs
  of autumn wound
my heart with languorous
and monotonous   5
  sound.

Choking and pale
when I mind the tale
  the hours keep,
my memory strays   10
down other days
  and I weep;

and I let me go
where ill winds blow,
  now here, now there,   15
harried and sped,
even as a dead
  leaf, anywhere.

---

1. All poems translated by C. F. MacIntyre. The poem is one of the "Mournful Landscapes" in *Saturnian Poems* (1866).

Moonlight[1]

Your soul is like a painter's landscape[2] where
charming masks in shepherd mummeries
are playing lutes[3] and dancing with an air
of being sad in their fantastic guise.

Even while they sing, all in a minor key,   5
of love triumphant and life's careless boon,
they seem in doubt of their felicity,
their song melts in the calm light of the moon,

the lovely melancholy light that sets
the little birds to dreaming in the tree   10
and among the statues makes the jets
of slender fountains sob with ecstasy.

[The white moonglow][1]

The white moonglow
shines on the trees;
from each bough
a voice flees
as the leaves move . . .   5

Oh, my love.

The pond reflects,
a mirror deep,
the black silhouette
of the willow tree   10
where the wind weeps . . .

Oh, reverie.

Now a tender
and vast appeasement
seems to descend   15
from the firmament
with the irised star[2] . . .

Ah, exquisite hour.

1. From *Fêtes galantes* (1869).   2. A reference to Antoine Watteau's (1684–1721) dreamlike paintings in which elegant men and women, costumed as shepherds and shepherdesses, play at being pastoral lovers. 3. Arab musical instrument associated with serenades that was fashionable in the 18th century. 1. From *The Good Song* (1870).   2. The multiple reflections of the moonlight.

Wooden Horses[1]

By Saint-Gille
let's away,
my light-footed bay.
        V. Hugo[2]

Turn, good wooden horses, round
a hundred turns, a thousand turns.
Forever turn till the axles burn,
turn, turn, to the oboes' sound.

The big soldier and the fattest maid   5
ride your backs as if in their chamber,
because their masters have also made
an outing today in the Bois de la Cambre.[3]

Turn, turn, horses of their hearts,
while all around your whirling there   10
are the clever sharpers[4] at their art;
turn to the cornet's bragging blare.

It's as much fun as getting dead
drunk, to ride in this silly ring!
Good for the belly, bad for the head,   15
a plenty good and a plenty bad thing.

Turn, turn, no need today
of any spurs to make you bound,
galloping around and round,
turn, turn, without hope of hay.   20

And hurry, horses of their love,
already night is falling here
and the pigeon flies to join the dove,
far from madame, far from the fair.

Turn! Turn! Slow evening comes,   25
in velvet, buttoned up with stars.
Away the lovers go, in pairs.
Turn to the beat of the joyous drums.

The Art of Poetry[1]

You must have music first of all,
and for that a rhythm uneven[2] is best,

---

1. From *Songs Without Words* (1874).   2. French poet (1802–1885). Saint-Gilles is a suburb of Brussels, Belgium, with a public fairground.   3. An elegant park south of Brussels.   4. Literally, pickpockets.   1. From *Yesteryear and Yesterday* (1884), written in 1874.   2. The *vers impair* (line with an uneven number of syllables), which gives traditional French readers a sense of "nothing at rest." This poem uses a nine-syllable line and—as here—often illustrates its points.

vague in the air and soluble,
with nothing heavy and nothing at rest.

You must not scorn to do some wrong   5
in choosing the words to fill your lines:
nothing more dear than the tipsy song
where the Undefined and Exact combine.

It is the veiled and lovely eye,
the full noon quivering with light;   10
it is, in the cool of an autumn sky,
the blue confusion of stars at night!

Never the Color, always the Shade,
always the nuance is supreme!
Only by shade is the trothal made   15
between flute and horn, of dream with dream!

Epigram's an assassin! Keep
away from him, fierce Wit, and vicious
laughter that makes the Azure[3] weep,
and from all that garlic of vulgar dishes!   20

Take Eloquence and wring his neck!
You would do well, by force and care,
wisely to hold Rhyme in check,
or she's off—if you don't watch—God knows where!

Oh, who will tell the wrongs of Rhyme?   25
What crazy negro or deaf child
made this trinket for a dime,
sounding hollow and false when filed?

Let there be music, again and forever!
Let your verse be a quick-wing'd thing and light—   30
such as one feels when a new love's fervor
to other skies wings the soul in flight.

Happy-go-lucky, let your lines
disheveled run where the dawn winds lure,
smelling of wild mint, smelling of thyme . . .   35
and all the rest is literature.

---

3. The sky's unbroken azure was, for many Symbolists, an image of absolute poetry as opposed to vulgarity.

ARTHUR RIMBAUD
1854–1891

In a dazzlingly brief literary career, which he abandoned at the age of twenty, Arthur Rimbaud (*ram-boh'*) put his indelible stamp on the visionary and experimental aspects of modern poetry. Taking literally the ancient (and Romantic) notion of the poet as prophet, he determined to make himself a seer, or *voyant*, by whatever violent means were necessary. His writing reveals the mixture of idealism, hope, and faith in his own genius that led him to believe in the possibility of a self-produced apocalypse. It also recounts a futile search for love that permeates his poetic quest; a stormy relationship with the older poet Paul Verlaine; and finally, the bitterness and sense of defeat that drove him to abandon his former life and become a fortune-hunter in Africa. Rimbaud was an especially strong model for the Surrealists and for others in twentieth-century literature who saw in him an example of complete dedication to a poetic ideal that surpassed mere written words: he exemplified a revolutionary reimagining of human experience that would open vistas, explode harmful patterns of thought, and thus bring about a better future. Despite—or perhaps because of— Rimbaud's admission of defeat, he became a mythic figure whose brilliant poems and prose were markers on the way of a career that, in the words of one admirer, passed like a lightning bolt through French literature.

Jean-Nicholas-Arthur Rimbaud was born on October 20, 1854, in Charleville, a town in northeastern France. Rimbaud's father abandoned the family when Arthur was seven, and his embittered mother raised her children in a repressive and disciplinarian atmosphere. In 1870, Rimbaud made the first of his flights from home and spent ten days in jail as a vagrant. Yet he proved to be an unusually gifted student and was encouraged in his literary tastes and endeavors by a sympathetic teacher who introduced him to current poetry. It was this teacher, Georges Izambard, to whom Rimbaud wrote of his poetic ambitions and his desire to make himself a seer by the systematic "derangement of all the senses." In 1871, the poet Paul Verlaine (to whom Rimbaud had sent some of his work) invited Rimbaud to Paris. It was the beginning of a stormy two-year relationship in Paris, London, and Brussels that ended in 1873 when Verlaine shot Rimbaud through the wrist and was sentenced to two years' imprisonment. In that year, at the age of nineteen, Rimbaud decided to give up writing and seek his fortune in commerce. He found his way to many parts of Europe, to Cyprus, to Java, and to Aden, where he worked for an exporting firm, later moving to Harar in Abyssinia. As an independent trader he went on expeditions in Abyssinia and engaged in gun running; despite rumor, it does not appear that he trafficked in slaves. Falling ill with a cancerous tumor on one knee and unable to find adequate treatment, Rimbaud returned to France with a gangrenous leg in May 1891. His leg was amputated at a Marseilles hospital, and he died six months later on November 10, 1891.

In a short and violent literary career—he wrote all his poetry between the ages of fifteen and twenty—Rimbaud combines an aggressive, cynical realism and attempts to transform both self and surroundings into a magically perfect whole. The visionary image sequences of his first major poem (a symbolic voyage titled *The Drunken Boat*), the agonized and mocking autobiographical prose of *A Season in Hell*, and finally the transfigured scenes from real life called *Illuminations* together represent stages in this endeavor to discover—or create—a state of natural innocence and harmony. For a while, Rimbaud believed that he could manipulate language to create the vision of an ideal world. "I have strung ropes from steeple to steeple; garlands from window to window; golden chains from star to star, and I dance."

The Drunken Boat, written when the poet was still sixteen and had never seen the sea, uses the traditional literary theme of the voyage to express his rebellion against guides and restraints. Speaking as a boat let loose on the high seas, the narrator describes a gradually intensifying series of encounters with a total reality—at once beautiful and terrifying—that goes beyond his individual power to sustain. Yet the concluding section is not a resolution of the original need for flight: Rimbaud's boat cannot accept the world of proud commercial shipping or of prison ships, and dreams of the childhood world of a solitary paper boat set adrift in a small pool. The poem ends in a clearer restatement of its original alienation and in an attitude that many have interpreted as prefiguring Rimbaud's eventual departure from Europe and his rejection of poetry.

Rimbaud's attempt to become a *voyant,* to transform his everyday reality by means of the re-creating power of poetry, is both summarized and mocked in the bitter autobiographical prose poem *A Season in Hell.* In an atmosphere of perpetual crisis, alternating between agonized idealism and cynical disbelief, he reviews his quest for perfect truth and love and vividly describes his effort to reach the unknown by pure hallucination. "I saw very plainly a mosque in place of a factory, a school of drummers composed of angels . . . a drawing room at the bottom of the lake . . . I became a fabulous opera." At the end of *A Season in Hell* he tells us that he has rejected these earlier illusions and embraced earth and rugged reality. Yet he never wrote poetry to celebrate his newly rediscovered realism (and may well have completed the *Illuminations* after that point), so that he remains best known for the passion and beauty of his apocalyptic vision.

The *Illuminations* offer a series of transformations that leave only traces of their varied points of departure: bridges in London, plowed fields, a park statue, dawn. They parade illusions and free association, and they cut short logical sequences to develop an almost musical organization of themes and images. Almost all are prose poems, intricately organized in complex rhythmic and visual patterns. Some echo autobiographical themes, but the scenes and allusions are transformed. *Bridges* recalls the London where Rimbaud lived for a time, but it is an impressionistic memory that transforms the real scene. *Barbarian* may echo a previous sea voyage and drug use, but the poem transcends the question of any single source in reality. Set outside normal time and space, "Long after the days and the seasons, and the creatures and the countries," it enacts a withdrawal that moves gradually from echoes of the real world to an elemental core of tenderness and beauty, completely inside the world of imagination.

Clearly the reader cannot approach *Barbarian* as if it were by Lamartine—or even by Baudelaire. Rimbaud's vision has leaped beyond the picturing of actual scenes and beyond the rational core that so often supports even a visionary poem. Instead, he cuts short all explanations and simply presents the vision for itself. *Barbarian* is not, however, merely an impressionistic, unstructured collection of words. It is carefully organized according to an almost musical development of themes and pattern of oppositions: red and white (raw meat and arctic flowers, embers and frost, fire and diamonds, flames and drift ice), heat and cold, subterranean volcanoes and starry sky. On a more fundamental level, it is a world that swings between the real and the ideal, from echoes of a former reality to an ideal world where there are ultimately no complete images, only "forms, sweats, eyes" that will be part of a new creation heralded by a feminine voice reaching into the very heart of this fiery, icy vortex. *Barbarian* ends on a note of openness and ambiguity, as the cyclical opposition of reality and imagination seem about to recommence with "The banner." The poem may foreshadow the future Symbolist doctrines: it disassembles scenes from recognizable reality to assemble a new transcendent vision, and it employs to this end a subtly nonrational language that emulates the patterns of music. Yet Rimbaud is even more closely associated with twentieth-century poetry and with those writers—including the Surrealists—who found in the explosion of poetic form a complete and often violent engagement of the self.

Frederic St. Aubyn, *Arthur Rimbaud* (1988), is a useful biography that also treats Rimbaud's work. Wallace Fowlie, *Rimbaud* (1966), discusses the *Illuminations* and the myth of childhood in Rimbaud. Harold Bloom, ed., *Arthur Rimbaud* (1988), collects eleven essays on various aspects of Rimbaud's work. Georges Poulet, *Exploding Poetry* (1984), trans. Françoise Meltzer, examines poetic worldviews in Baudelaire and Rimbaud.

[POEMS]

The Drunken Boat[1]

As I descended black, impassive Rivers,
I sensed that haulers[2] were no longer guiding me:
Screaming Redskins took them for their targets,
Nailed nude to colored stakes: barbaric trees.

I was indifferent to all my crews;   5
I carried English cottons, Flemish wheat.
When the disturbing din of haulers ceased,
The Rivers let me ramble where I willed.

Through the furious ripping of the sea's mad tides,
Last winter, deafer than an infant's mind,   10
I ran! And drifting, green Peninsulas
Did not know roar more gleefully unkind.

A tempest blessed my vigils on the sea.
Lighter than a cork I danced on the waves,
Those endless rollers, as they say, of graves:[3]   15
Ten nights beyond a lantern's[4] silly eye!

Sweeter than sourest apple-flesh to children,
Green water seeped into my pine-wood hull
And washed away blue wine[5] stains, vomitings,
Scattering rudder, anchor, man's lost rule.   20

And then I, trembling, plunged into the Poem
Of the Sea,[6] infused with stars, milk-white,
Devouring azure greens; where remnants, pale
And gnawed, of pensive corpses fell from light;

Where, staining suddenly the blueness, delirium.   25
The slow rhythms of the pulsing glow of day,
Stronger than alcohol and vaster than our lyres,
The bitter reds of love ferment the way!

1. Translated by Stephen Stepanchev.   2. The image is of a commercial barge being towed along a canal.
3. Victor Hugo's *Oceano nox* (Night on the ocean; Latin) describes the sea as a graveyard in which sailors' corpses roll eternally.   4. Port beacons.   5. A cheap, ordinary, bitter wine.   6. A play on words. *Poem* suggests "creation" (Greek *poiein*, "making"); *Sea*, the source or "mother" of life, sounds the same as "mother" in French (*mer / mère*).

I know skies splitting into light, whirled spouts
Of water, surfs, and currents: I know the night,   30
The dawn exalted like a flock of doves, pure wing,
And I have seen what men imagine they have seen.

I saw the low sun stained with mystic horrors,
Lighting long, curdled clouds of violet,
Like actors in a very ancient play,   35
Waves rolling distant thrills like lattice[7] light!

I dreamed of green night, stirred by dazzling snows,
Of kisses rising to the sea's eyes, slowly,
The sap-like coursing of surprising currents,
And singing phosphors,[8] flaring blue and gold!   40

I followed, for whole months, a surge like herds
Of insane cattle in assault on the reefs,
Unhopeful that three Marys,[9] come on luminous feet,
Could force a muzzle on the panting seas!

Yes, I struck incredible Floridas[1]   45
That mingled flowers and the eyes of panthers
In skins of men! And rainbows bridled green
Herds beneath the horizon of the seas.

I saw the ferment of enormous marshes, weirs
Where a whole Leviathan[2] lies rotting in the weeds!   50
Collapse of waters within calms at sea,
And distances in cataract toward chasms!

Glaciers, silver suns, pearl waves, and skies like coals,
Hideous wrecks at the bottom of brown gulfs
Where giant serpents eaten by red bugs   55
Drop from twisted trees and shed a black perfume!

I should have liked to show the young those dolphins
In blue waves, those golden fish, those fish that sing.
—Foam like flowers rocked my sleepy drifting,
And, now and then, fine winds supplied me wings.   60

When, feeling like a martyr, I tired of poles and zones,
The sea, whose sobbing made my tossing sweet,
Raised me its dark flowers, deep and yellow whirled,
And, like a woman, I fell on my knees . . .[3]

Peninsula, I tossed upon my shores   65
The quarrels and droppings of clamorous, blond-eyed birds.

---

7. Like the ripple of venetian blinds.   8. *Noctiluca*, tiny marine animals.   9. A legend that the three biblical Marys crossed the sea during a storm to land in Camargue, a region in southern France famous for its horses and bulls.   1. A name (plural) given to any exotic country.   2. Vast biblical sea monster (Job 41.1–10).   3. The poet's ellipses; nothing has been omitted.

I sailed until, across my rotting cords,
Drowned men, spinning backwards, fell asleep! . . .

Now I, a lost boat in the hair of coves,[4]
Hurled by tempest into a birdless air,   70
I, whose drunken carcass neither Monitors
Nor Hansa ships[5] would fish back for men's care;

Free, smoking, rigged with violet fogs,
I, who pierced the red sky like a wall
That carries exquisite mixtures for good poets,   75
Lichens of sun and azure mucus veils;

Who, spotted with electric crescents, ran
Like a mad plank, escorted by seashores,
When cudgel blows of hot Julys struck down
The sea-blue skies upon wild water spouts;   80

I, who trembled, feeling the moan at fifty leagues
Of rutting Behemoths[6] and thick Maelstroms, I,
Eternal weaver of blue immobilities,
I long for Europe with its ancient quays!

I saw sidereal archipelagoes! and isles   85
Whose delirious skies are open to the voyager:
—Is it in depthless nights you sleep your exile,
A million golden birds, O future Vigor?—

But, truly, I have wept too much! The dawns disturb.
All moons are painful, and all suns break bitterly: 90
Love has swollen me with drunken torpors.
Oh, that my keel might break and spend me in the sea!

Of European waters I desire
Only the black, cold puddle in a scented twilight
Where a child of sorrows squats and sets the sails   95
Of a boat as frail as a butterfly in May.

I can no longer, bathed in languors, O waves,
Cross the wake of cotton-bearers on long trips,
Nor ramble in a pride of flags and flares,
Nor swim beneath the horrible eyes of prison ships.[7]   100

4. Seaweed.   5. Vessels belonging to the German Hanseatic League of commercial maritime cities. *Monitors*: armored coast guard ships, after the iron-clad Union warship *Monitor* of the American Civil War. 6. Biblical animal resembling a hippopotamus (Job 40.15–24).   7. Portholes of ships tied at anchor and used as prisons.

From A Season in Hell[1]

Night of Hell

I have swallowed a first-rate draught of poison.—Thrice blessed be the counsel that came to me!—My entrails are on fire. The violence of the venom wrings my limbs, deforms me, fells me. I am dying of thirst, I am suffocating, I cannot cry out. This is hell, the everlasting punishment! Mark how the fire surges up again! I am burning properly. There you are, demon!

I had caught a glimpse of conversion to righteousness and happiness, salvation. May I describe the vision; the atmosphere of hell does not permit hymns! It consisted of millions of charming creatures, a sweet sacred concert, power and peace, noble ambitions, and goodness knows what else.

Noble ambitions![2]

And yet this is life!—What if damnation is eternal! A man who chooses to mutilate himself is rightly damned, isn't he? I believe that I am in hell, consequently I am there.[3] This is the effect of the catechism. I am the slave of my baptism.[4] Parents, you have caused my affliction and you have caused your own. Poor innocent!—Hell cannot assail pagans.—This is life, nevertheless! Later, the delights of damnation will be deeper. A crime, quickly, that I may sink to nothingness, in accordance with human law.

Be silent, do be silent! . . . There is shame, reproof, in this place: Satan who says that the fire is disgraceful, that my wrath is frightfully foolish.— Enough! . . . The errors that are whispered to me, enchantments, false perfumes, childish melodies.[5]—And to say that I possess truth, that I understand justice: I have a sound and steady judgment, I am prepared for perfection . . . Pride.—The skin of my head is drying up. Pity! Lord, I am terrified. I am thirsty, so thirsty! Ah! childhood, the grass, the rain, the lake upon the stones, *the moonlight when the bell tower was striking twelve*[6] . . . the devil is in the bell tower, at that hour. Mary! Blessed Virgin! . . . —The horror of my stupidity.

Over there, are they not honest-souls, who wish me well? . . . Come . . . I have a pillow over my mouth, they don't hear me, they are phantoms. Besides, no one ever thinks of others. Let no one approach. I reek of burning, that's certain.

The hallucinations are countless. It's exactly what I've always had: no more faith in history, neglect of principles. I shall be silent about this: poets and visionaries would be jealous. I am a thousand times the richest, let us be avaricious like the sea.

Now then! the clock of life has just stopped. I am no longer in the world.— Theology is serious, hell is certainly *below*—and heaven above.—Ecstasy, nightmare, sleep in a nest of flames.

What pranks during my vigilance in the country . . . Satan, Ferdinand,[7]

---

1. Translated by Enid Rhodes Peschel. *Night of Hell* is the second section (after the preface) of the autobiographical *A Season in Hell*. The first section, *Bad Blood*, describes his solitary childhood and sense of being a member of an "inferior race." It also contrasts an authoritarian and hypocritical European society with African paganism, which is seen as a freer and more natural existence.   2. Mockery of his childhood idealism and attraction to traditional Catholicism.   3. A parody of French philosopher René Descartes's (1596–1650) phrase "I think, therefore I am," which had become a symbol of well-ordered thought. 4. Because baptism creates the possibility of both heaven and hell.   5. The poetic visions and harmonies that Rimbaud explored with Paul Verlaine.   6. A collection of romanticized childhood memories. 7. Peasant name for the devil.

races with the wild seeds . . . Jesus walks on the purplish briers, without bending them . . . Jesus used to walk on the troubled waters.[8] The lantern revealed him to us, a figure standing, pale and with brown tresses, beside a wave of emerald. . . .

I am going to unveil all the mysteries: mysteries religious or natural, death, birth, futurity, antiquity, cosmogony, nothingness, I am a master of phantasmagories.

Listen! . . .

I have all the talents!—There is nobody here and there is somebody: I would not wish to scatter my treasure.—Do you wish for Negro chants, dances of houris?[9] Do you wish me to vanish, to dive in search of the *ring?*[1] Do you? I shall produce gold, cures.

Rely, then, upon me: faith comforts, guides, heals. All of you, come,— even the little children,[2]—that I may console you, that one may pour out his heart for you,—the marvelous heart!—Poor men, laborers! I do not ask for prayers; with your confidence alone, I shall be happy.

—And let's think of me. This makes me miss the world very little. I have the good fortune not to suffer any longer. My life was nothing but sweet follies, regrettably.

Bah! let's make all the grimaces imaginable.

Decidedly, we are out of the world. No more sound. My sense of touch has disappeared. Ah! my castle, my Saxony,[3] my forest of willows. The evenings, the mornings, the nights, the days . . . Am I weary!

I ought to have my hell for wrath, my hell for pride,—and the hell of the caress; a concert of hells.

I am dying of weariness. This is the tomb, I am going to the worms, horror of horrors! Satan, jester, you wish to undo me, with your spells. I protest. I protest! one jab of the pitchfork, one lick of fire.

Ah! to rise again to life! To cast eyes upon our deformities. And that poison, that kiss a thousand times accursed! My weakness, the cruelty of the world! Dear God, your mercy, hide me, I regard myself too poorly!—I am hidden and I am not.

It is the fire that rises again with the soul condemned to it.

FROM THE ILLUMINATIONS[1]

The Bridges[2]

Crystalline gray skies. A strange pattern of bridges, these straight, those arched, others descending obliquely at angles to the first, and these configurations repeating themselves in the other illuminated circuits of the canal,[3] but all so long and light that the shores, laden with domes, sink and diminish.

---

8. Jesus' disciples saw him walking on the sea at night (John 6.16–21).   9. Beautiful virgins in the Koranic paradise.   1. At the end of Wagner's opera *Götterdämmerung*, Hagen plunges into the river Rhine to recapture the golden ring of world power.   2. Parody of Jesus' words "Suffer little children, and forbid them not, to come unto me" (Matthew 19.14).   3. Germanic duchy, part of Rimbaud's visionary memories.   1. Translated by Enid Rhodes Peschel.   2. An impressionistic memory of London. 3. The river Thames as it winds through the city.

Some of these bridges are still encumbered with hovels.[4] Others support masts, signals, frail parapets. Minor chords interweave, and flow smoothly; ropes rise from the steep banks. One detects a red jacket, perhaps other costumes and musical instruments. Are these popular tunes, fragments of manorial concerts, remnants of public anthems? The water is gray and blue, ample as an arm of the sea.

A white ray, falling from the summit of the sky, reduces to nothingness this theatrical performance.

Barbarian

Long after the days and the seasons, and the creatures and the countries,
The banner of bleeding meat[1] on the silk of the seas and of the arctic flowers; (they do not exist.)
Delivered from the old fanfares of heroism—that still attack our heart and our head—far from the former assassins.
—Oh! the banner of bleeding meat on the silk of the seas and of the arctic flowers; (they do not exist.)
Delights!
Blazing coals, raining in squalls of hoarfrost—Delights!—fires in the rain of the wind of diamonds, rain hurled down by the earthly heart eternally carbonized for us—O world!—
(Far from the old retreats and the old flames, that are known, that are felt,)
Blazing coals and froths. Music, veering of whirlpools and collisions of drift ice with the stars.
O Delights, oh world, oh music! And there, the forms, the sweats, the heads of hair and the eyes, floating. And the white tears, boiling—oh delights!—and the feminine voice borne down to the bottom of the volcanoes and the arctic grottoes.
The banner . . .

4. Houses were once built on London Bridge.   1. Perhaps a description of the Danish flag (a white cross on a red field), which Rimbaud would have seen on a visit to Iceland, then a Danish possession.

LEO TOLSTOY
1828–1910

Count Leo Tolstoy excited the interest of Europe mainly as a public figure: a count owning large estates who decided to give up his wealth and live like a simple Russian peasant—to dress in a blouse, to eat peasant food, and even to plow the fields and make shoes with his own hands. By the time of his death he had become the leader of a religious cult, the propounder of a new religion. It was, in substance, a highly simplified primitive Christianity that he reduced to a few moral commands (such as "Do not resist evil") and from which he drew, with radical consistency, a complete condemnation of modern civilization: the state, courts and law, war, patriotism, marriage, modern art and literature, science and medicine. In debating this Christian anarchism people have tended to forget that Tolstoy established his command of the public ear as a novelist, or they have exaggerated the contrast between the early worldly novelist and the later prophet who repudiated all his early, great novelistic work: *War and Peace*, the enormous epic of the 1812 invasion of Russia, and *Anna Karenina*, the story of an adulterous love, superbly realized in accurately imagined detail.

Tolstoy was born at Yasnaya Polyana, his mother's estate near Tula (about 130 miles south of Moscow), on August 28, 1828. His father was a retired lieutenant colonel; one of his ancestors, the first count, had served Peter the Great as an ambassador. His mother's father was a Russian general-in-chief. Tolstoy lost both parents early in his life and was brought up by aunts. He went to the University of Kazan between 1844 and 1847, drifted along aimlessly for a few years more, and in 1851 became a cadet in the Caucasus. As an artillery officer he saw action in the wars with the mountain tribes and again, in 1854–55, during the Crimean War against the French and English. Tolstoy had written fictional reminiscences of his childhood while he was in the Caucasus; and during the Crimean War he wrote war stories, which established his literary reputation. For some years he lived on his estate, where he founded and himself taught at an extremely "progressive" school for peasant children. He made two trips to western Europe, in 1857 and in 1860–61. In 1862 he married a physician's daughter, Sonya Bers, with whom he had thirteen children.

In the first years of his married life, between 1863 and 1869, he wrote his enormous novel *War and Peace*. The book made him famous in Russia but was not translated into English until long afterward. Superficially, *War and Peace* is an historical novel about the Napoleonic invasion of Russia in 1812, a huge swarming epic of a nation's resistance to the foreigner. Tolstoy himself interprets history in general as a struggle of anonymous collective forces that are moved by unknown irrational impulses, waves of communal feeling. Heroes, great men and women, are actually not heroes but merely insignificant puppets; the best general is the one who does nothing to prevent the unknown course of Providence. But *War and Peace* is not only an impressive and vivid panorama of historical events but also the profound story—centered in two main characters, Pierre Bezukhov and Prince Andrey Bolkonsky—of a search for meaning in life. Andrey finds meaning in love and forgiveness of his enemies. Pierre, at the end of a long groping struggle, an education by suffering, finds it in an acceptance of ordinary existence, its duties and pleasures, the family, the continuity of the race.

Tolstoy's next long novel, *Anna Karenina* (1875–77), resumes this second thread of *War and Peace*. It is a novel of contemporary manners, a narrative of adultery and suicide. But this vivid story, told with incomparable concrete imagination, is counterpointed and framed by a second story, that of Levin, another seeker after the meaning of life, a figure who represents the author as Pierre did in the earlier book; the work ends with a promise of salvation, with the ideal of a life in which we should "remember God." Thus *Anna Karenina* also anticipates the approaching crisis in Tolstoy's life. When it came, with the sudden revulsion he describes in *A Confession* (1879), he condemned his earlier books and spent the next years in writing pamphlets and tracts expounding his religion.

Only slowly did Tolstoy return to the writing of fiction, now regarded entirely as a means of presenting his creed. The earlier novels seemed to him unclear in their message, overdetailed in their method. Hence Tolstoy tried to simplify his art; he wrote plays with a thesis, stories that are like fables or parables, and one long, rather inferior novel, *The Resurrection* (1899), his most savage satire on Russian and modern institutions.

In 1901 Tolstoy was excommunicated. A disagreement with his wife about the nature of the good life and about financial matters sharpened into a conflict over his last will, which finally led to a complete break: he left home in the company of a doctor friend. He caught cold on the train journey south and died in the house of the stationmaster of Astapovo, on November 20, 1910.

If we look back on Tolstoy's work as a whole, we must recognize its continuity. From the very beginning he was a Rousseauist. As early as 1851, when he was in the Caucasus, his diary announced his intention of founding a new, simplified religion. Even as a young man on his estate he had lived quite simply, like a peasant, except for occasional sprees and debauches. He had been horrified by war from the very beginning, though he admired the heroism of the individual soldier and had remnants of patriotic feeling. All his books concern the same theme, the good life, and they all say that the good life lies outside civilization, near the soil, in simplicity and humility, in love of one's neighbor. Power, the lust for power, luxury are always evil.

Tolstoy's roots as a novelist are part of another, older realistic tradition. He read and knew the English writers of the eighteenth century—and also William Makepeace Thackeray and Anthony Trollope—though he did not care for the recent French writers (he was strong in his disapproval of Gustave Flaubert) except for Guy de Maupassant, who struck him as truthful and useful in his struggle against hypocrisy. Tolstoy's long novels are loosely plotted, though they have large overall designs. They work by little scenes vividly visualized, by an accumulation of exact detail. Each character is drawn by means of repeated emphasis on certain physical traits, like Pierre's shortsightedness and his hairy, clumsy hands, or Princess Marya's luminous eyes, the red patches on her face, and her shuffling gait. This concretely realized surface, however, everywhere recedes into depths: to the depiction of disease, delirium, and death and to glimpses into eternity. In *War and Peace* the blue sky is the recurrent symbol for the metaphysical spirit within us. Tolstoy is so robust, has his feet so firmly on the ground, presents what he sees with such clarity and objectivity, that one can be easily deluded into considering his dominating quality to be physical, sensual, antithetical to Dostoevsky's spirituality. The contrasts between the two greatest Russian novelists are indeed obvious. While Tolstoy's method can be called epic, Dostoevsky's is dramatic; while Tolstoy's view of humanity is Rousseauistic, Dostoevsky stresses the Fall; while Tolstoy rejects history and status, Dostoevsky appeals to the past and desires a hierarchical society, and so on. But these profound differences should not obscure one basic similarity: the deep spirituality of both writers, their rejection of the basic materialism and the conception of truth propounded by modern science and theorists of realism.

The Death of Ivan Ilyich (1886) belongs to the period after Tolstoy's religious conversion when he slowly returned to fiction writing. It represents a happy medium between his early and late manner. Its story and moral are simple and obvious, as always with Tolstoy (in contrast to Dostoevsky). And it expresses what almost all of his works are intended to convey—that humanity is leading the wrong kind of life, that we should return to essentials, to "nature." In *The Death of Ivan Ilyich* Tolstoy combines a savage satire on the futility and hypocrisy of conventional life with a powerful symbolic presentation of isolation in the struggle with death and of hope for a final resurrection. Ivan Ilyich is a Russian judge, an official, but he is also the average man of the prosperous middle classes of his time and ours, and he is also Everyman confronted with disease and dying and death. He is an ordinary person, neither virtuous nor particularly vicious, a "go-getter" in his profession, a "family man," as marriages go, who has children but has drifted apart from his wife. Through his disease, which comes about by a trivial accident in the trivial business of fixing a curtain, Ivan Ilyich is slowly awakened to self-consciousness and a realization of the falsity of his life and ambitions. The isolation that disease imposes on him, the wall of hypocrisy erected around him by his family and his doctors, his suffering and pain, drive him slowly to the recognition of *It*: to a knowledge, not merely theoretical but proved on his pulses, of his own mortality. At first he would like simply to return to his former pleasant and normal life—even in the last days of his illness, knowing he must die, he screams in his agony, "I won't!"—but at the end, struggling in the black sack into which he is being pushed, he sees the light at the bottom. " 'Death is finished,' he said to himself. 'It is no more!' "

The people around him are egotists and hypocrites: his wife, who can remember only how she suffered during his agony; his daughter, who thinks only of the delay in her marriage; his colleagues, who speculate only about the room his death will make for promotions in the court; the doctors, who think only of the name of the disease and not of the patient; all except his shy and frightened son, Vasya, and the servant Gerasim. Because he is young, near to "nature," and free from hypocrisy, Gerasim is able to make his master more comfortable and even to mention death, while all the others conceal the truth from him. The doctors, especially, are shown as mere specialists, inhuman and selfish. The first doctor is like a judge—like Ivan himself when he sat in court—summing up and cutting off further questions of the patient. The satire at points appears ineffectively harsh in its violence, but it will not seem exceptional to those who know the older Tolstoy's general attitude toward courts, medicine, marriage, and even modern literature. The cult of art is jeered at, in small touches, only incidentally; it belongs, according to Tolstoy, to the falsities of modern civilization, alongside marriage (which merely hides bestial sensuality) and science (which merely hides rapacity and ignorance).

The story is deliberately deprived of any element of suspense, not only by the announcement contained in the title but by the technique of the cutback. We first hear of Ivan Ilyich's death and see the reaction of the widow and friends, and only then listen to the story of his life. The detail, as always in Tolstoy, is superbly concrete and realistic: he does not shy away from the smell of disease, the physical necessity of using a chamber pot, or the sound of screaming. He can employ the creaking of a hassock as a recurrent motif to point out the comedy of hypocrisy played by the widow and her visitor. He can seriously and tragically use the humble image of a black sack or the illusion of the movement of a train.

But all this naturalistic detail serves the one purpose of making us come to realize, as Ivan Ilyich realizes, that not only Caius is mortal but you and I also, and that the life of "civilized" people is a great lie simply because it disguises and ignores its dark background, the metaphysical abyss, the reality of Death. While the presentation of The Death of Ivan Ilyich approaches, at moments, the tone of a legend or fable ("Ivan Ilyich's life had been most simple and most ordinary and therefore most terrible"), Tolstoy in this story manages to stay within the concrete situation of his society and to combine the aesthetic method of realism with the universalizing power of symbolic art.

R. F. Christian, Tolstoy: A Critical Introduction (1969), is clear, instructive, and informative. E. B. Greenwood, Tolstoy: The Comprehensive Vision (1975), is helpful in placing The Death of Ivan Ilyich in the perspective of Tolstoy's work as a whole. Some good analysis is found in H. Gifford, ed., Leo Tolstoy: A Critical Anthology (1971). Ralph E. Matlaw, Tolstoy: A Collection of Critical Essays (1967), and Philip Rahv, Image and Idea (1949), both present essays on The Death of Ivan Ilyich. Theodore Redpath, Tolstoy (1960), provides a brief introduction with good criticism of ideas. Ernest J. Simmons, Leo Tolstoy (1946), and A. N. Wilson, Tolstoy (1988), are both excellent biographies. Rimvydas Silbajoris, Tolstoy's Aesthetics and His Art (1991), includes accounts of reactions to the author at home and abroad as well as many substantial quotations.

PRONOUNCING GLOSSARY

The following list uses common English syllables and stress accents to provide rough equivalents of selected words whose pronunciation may be unfamiliar to the general reader.

Fëdor Petrovich: *fyo'-dor pet-ro'-vich*

Fëdor Vasilievich: *fyo'-dor vas-eel'-ye-vich*

Gerasim: *jair-ah'-seem*

Golovin: *go-lo-veen'*

Ivan Ilyich: *ee-van' il'-yich*

Ivanovich: *ee-van'-oh-vich*

Karenina: *kah-ren'-yina*

The Death of Ivan Ilyich[1]

I

During an interval in the Melvinski trial in the large building of the Law Courts the members and public prosecutor met in Ivan Egorovich Shebek's private room, where the conversation turned on the celebrated Krasovski case. Fëdor Vasilievich warmly maintained that it was not subject to their jurisdiction, Ivan Egorovich maintained the contrary, while Peter Ivanovich, not having entered into the discussion at the start, took no part in it but looked through the *Gazette* which had just been handed in.

"Gentlemen," he said, "Ivan Ilyich has died!"

"You don't say!"

"Here read it yourself," replied Peter Ivanovich, handing Fëdor Vasilievich the paper still damp from the press. Surrounded by a black border were the words: "Praskovya Fëdorovna Golovina, with profound sorrow, informs relatives and friends of the demise of her beloved husband Ivan Ilyich Golovin, Member of the Court of Justice, which occurred on February the 4th of this year 1882. The funeral will take place on Friday at one o'clock in the afternoon."

Ivan Ilyich had been a colleague of the gentlemen present and was liked by them all. He had been ill for some weeks with an illness said to be incurable. His post had been kept open for him, but there had been conjectures that in case of his death Alexeev might receive his appointment, and that either Vinnikov or Shtabel would succeed Alexeev. So on receiving the news of Ivan Ilyich's death the first thought of each of the gentlemen in that private room was of the changes and promotions it might occasion among themselves or their acquaintances.

"I shall be sure to get Shtabel's place or Vinnikov's," thought Fëdor Vasilievich. "I was promised that long ago, and the promotion means an extra eight hundred rubles a year for me besides the allowance."

"Now I must apply for my brother-in-law's transfer from Kaluga," thought Peter Ivanovich. "My wife will be very glad, and then she won't be able to say that I never do anything for her relations."

"I thought he would never leave his bed again," said Peter Ivanovich aloud. "It's very sad."

"But what really was the matter with him?"

"The doctors couldn't say—at least they could, but each of them said something different. When last I saw him I thought he was getting better."

1. Translated by Louise Maude and Aylmer Maude.

"And I haven't been to see him since the holidays. I always meant to go."

"Had he any property?"

"I think his wife had a little—but something quite trifling."

"We shall have to go to see her, but they live so terribly far away."

"Far away from you, you mean. Everything's far away from your place."

"You see, he never can forgive my living on the other side of the river," said Peter Ivanovich, smiling at Shebek. Then, still talking of the distances between different parts of the city, they returned to the Court.

Besides considerations as to the possible transfers and promotions likely to result from Ivan Ilyich's death, the mere fact of the death of a near acquaintance aroused, as usual, in all who heard of it the complacent feeling that, "it is he who is dead and not I."

Each one thought or felt, "Well, he's dead but I'm alive!" But the more intimate of Ivan Ilyich's acquaintances, his so-called friends, could not help thinking also that they would now have to fulfil the very tiresome demands of propriety by attending the funeral service and paying a visit of condolence to the widow.

Fëdor Vasilievich and Peter Ivanovich had been his nearest acquaintances. Peter Ivanovich had studied law with Ivan Ilyich and had considered himself to be under obligations to him.

Having told his wife at dinner-time of Ivan Ilyich's death, and of his conjecture that it might be possible to get her brother transferred to their circuit, Peter Ivanovich sacrificed his usual nap, put on his evening clothes, and drove to Ivan Ilyich's house.

At the entrance stood a carriage and two cabs. Leaning against the wall in the hall downstairs near the cloak-stand was a coffin-lid covered with cloth of gold, ornamented with gold cord and tassels, that had been polished up with metal powder. Two ladies in black were taking off their fur cloaks. Peter Ivanovich recognized one of them as Ivan Ilyich's sister, but the other was a stranger to him. His colleague Schwartz was just coming downstairs, but on seeing Peter Ivanovich enter he stopped and winked at him, as if to say: "Ivan Ilyich has made a mess of things—not like you and me."

Schwartz's face with his Piccadilly whiskers, and his slim figure in evening dress, had as usual an air of elegant solemnity which contrasted with the playfulness of his character and had a special piquancy here, or so it seemed to Peter Ivanovich.

Peter Ivanovich allowed the ladies to precede him and slowly followed them upstairs. Schwartz did not come down but remained where he was, and Peter Ivanovich understood that he wanted to arrange where they should play bridge that evening. The ladies went upstairs to the widow's room, and Schwartz with seriously compressed lips but a playful look in his eyes, indicated by a twist of his eyebrows the room to the right where the body lay.

Peter Ivanovich, like everyone else on such occasions, entered feeling uncertain what he would have to do. All he knew was that at such times it is always safe to cross oneself. But he was not quite sure whether one should make obeisances while doing so. He therefore adopted a middle course. On entering the room he began crossing himself and made a slight movement resembling a bow. At the same time, as far as the motion of his head and arm allowed, he surveyed the room. Two young men—apparently nephews, one of whom was a high-school pupil—were leaving the room, crossing themselves as they did so. An old woman was standing motionless, and a lady with strangely arched eyebrows was saying something to her in a whisper. A vigorous, resolute Church Reader, in a frock-coat, was reading something in a loud voice with an expression that precluded any contradiction. The butler's assistant, Gerasim, stepping lightly in front of Peter Ivanovich, was strewing something on the floor. Noticing this, Peter Ivanovich was immediately aware of a faint odour of a decomposing body.

The last time he had called on Ivan Ilyich, Peter Ivanovich had seen Gerasim in the study. Ivan Ilyich had been particularly fond of him and he was performing the duty of a sick nurse.

Peter Ivanovich continued to make the sign of the cross slightly inclining his head in an intermediate direction between the coffin, the Reader, and the icons on the table in a corner of the room. Afterwards, when it seemed to him that this movement of his arm in crossing himself had gone on too long, he stopped and began to look at the corpse.

The dead man lay, as dead men always lie, in a specially heavy way, his rigid limbs sunk in the soft cushions of the coffin, with the head forever bowed on the pillow. His yellow waxen brow with bald patches over his sunken temples was thrust up in the way peculiar to the dead, the protruding nose seeming to press on the upper lip. He was much changed and had grown even thinner since Peter Ivanovich had last seen him, but, as is always the case with the dead, his face was handsomer and above all more dignified than when he was alive. The expression on the face said that what was necessary had been accomplished, and accomplished rightly. Besides this there was in that expression a reproach and a warning to the living. This warning seemed to Peter Ivanovich out of place, or at least not applicable to him. He felt a certain discomfort and so he hurriedly crossed himself once more and turned and went out of the door—too hurriedly and too regardless of propriety, as he himself was aware.

Schwartz was waiting for him in the adjoining room with legs spread wide apart and both hands toying with his top-hat behind his back. The mere sight of that playful, well-groomed, and elegant figure refreshed Peter Ivanovich. He felt that Schwartz was above all these happenings and could not surrender to any depressing influences. His very look said that this incident of a church service for Ivan Ilyich could not be a sufficient reason for infringing the order of the session—in other words, that it would certainly not prevent his unwrapping a new pack of cards and shuffling them that evening while a footman placed four fresh candles on the table: in fact, that there was no reason for supposing that this incident would hinder their spending the evening agreeably. Indeed he said this in a whisper as Peter Ivanovich passed him, proposing that they should meet for a game at Fëdor Vasilievich's. But apparently Peter Ivanovich was not destined to play bridge that evening. Praskovya Fëdorovna (a short, fat woman who despite all efforts to the contrary had continued to broaden steadily from her shoulders downwards and who had the same extraordinary arched eyebrows as the lady who had been standing by the coffin), dressed all in black, her head covered with lace, came out of her own room with some other ladies, conducted them to the room where the dead body lay, and said: "The service will begin immediately. Please go in."

Schwartz, making an indefinite bow, stood still, evidently neither accepting nor declining this invitation. Praskovya Fëdorovna recognizing Peter

Ivanovich, sighed, went close up to him, took his hand, and said: "I know you were a true friend to Ivan Ilyich . . ." and looked at him awaiting some suitable response. And Peter Ivanovich knew that, just as it had been the right thing to cross himself in that room, so what he had to do here was to press her hand, sigh, and say, "Believe me . . ." So he did all this and as he did it felt that the desired result had been achieved: that both he and she were touched.

"Come with me. I want to speak to you before it begins," said the widow. "Give me your arm."

Peter Ivanovich gave her his arm and they went to the inner rooms, passing Schwartz who winked at Peter Ivanovich compassionately.

"That does for our bridge! Don't object if we find another player. Perhaps you can cut in when you do escape," said his playful look.

Peter Ivanovich sighed still more deeply and despondently, and Praskovya Fëdorovna pressed his arm gratefully. When they reached the drawing-room, upholstered in pink cretonne and lighted by a dim lamp, they sat down at the table—she on a sofa and Peter Ivanovich on a low hassock, the springs of which yielded spasmodically under his weight. Praskovya Fëdorovna had been on the point of warning him to take another seat, but felt that such a warning was out of keeping with her present condition and so changed her mind. As he sat down on the hassock Peter Ivanovich recalled how Ivan Ilyich had arranged this room and had consulted him regarding this pink cretonne with green leaves. The whole room was full of furniture and knick-knacks, and on her way to the sofa the lace of the widow's black shawl caught on the carved edge of the table. Peter Ivanovich rose to detach it, and the springs of the hassock, relieved of his weight, rose also and gave him a push. The widow began detaching her shawl herself, and Peter Ivanovich again sat down, suppressing the rebellious springs of the hassock under him. But the widow had not quite freed herself and Peter Ivanovich got up again, and again the hassock rebelled and even creaked. When this was all over she took out a clean cambric handkerchief and began to weep. The episode with the shawl and the struggle with the hassock had cooled Peter Ivanovich's emotions and he sat there with a sullen look on his face. This awkward situation was interrupted by Sokolov, Ivan Ilyich's butler, who came to report that the plot in the cemetery that Praskovya Fëdorovna had chosen would cost two hundred rubles. She stopped weeping and, looking at Peter Ivanovich with the air of a victim, remarked in French that it was very hard for her. Peter Ivanovich made a silent gesture signifying his full conviction that it must indeed be so.

"Please smoke," she said in a magnanimous yet crushed voice, and turned to discuss with Sokolov the price of the plot for the grave.

Peter Ivanovich while lighting his cigarette heard her inquiring very circumstantially into the prices of different plots in the cemetery and finally decide which she would take. When that was done she gave instructions about engaging the choir. Sokolov then left the room.

"I look after everything myself," she told Peter Ivanovich, shifting the albums that lay on the table; and noticing that the table was endangered by his cigarette-ash, she immediately passed him an ashtray, saying as she did so: "I consider it an affectation to say that my grief prevents my attending to practical affairs. On the contrary, if anything can—I won't say console me, but—distract me, it is seeing to everything concerning him." She again took out her handkerchief as if preparing to cry, but suddenly, as if mastering her feeling, she shook herself and began to speak calmly. "But there is something I want to talk to you about."

Peter Ivanovich bowed, keeping control of the springs of the hassock, which immediately began quivering under him.

"He suffered terribly the last few days."

"Did he?" said Peter Ivanovich.

"Oh, terribly! He screamed unceasingly, not for minutes but for hours. For the last three days he screamed incessantly. It was unendurable. I cannot understand how I bore it; you could hear him three rooms off. Oh, what I have suffered!"

"Is it possible that he was conscious all that time?" asked Peter Ivanovich.

"Yes," she whispered. "To the last moment. He took leave of us a quarter of an hour before he died, and asked us to take Vasya away."

The thought of the sufferings of this man he had known so intimately, first as a merry little boy, then as a school-mate, and later as a grown-up colleague, suddenly struck Peter Ivanovich with horror, despite an unpleasant consciousness of his own and this woman's dissimulation. He again saw that brow, and that nose pressing down on the lip, and felt afraid for himself.

"Three days of frightful suffering and then death! Why, that might suddenly, at any time, happen to me," he thought, and for a moment felt terrified. But—he did not himself know how—the customary reflection at once occurred to him that this had happened to Ivan Ilyich and not to him, and that it should not and could not happen to him, and that to think that it could would be yielding to depression which he ought not to do, as Schwartz's expression plainly showed. After which reflection Peter Ivanovich felt reassured, and began to ask with interest about the details of Ivan Ilyich's death, as though death was an accident natural to Ivan Ilyich but certainly not to himself.

After many details of the really dreadful physical sufferings Ivan Ilyich had endured (which details he learnt only from the effect those sufferings had produced on Praskovya Fëdorovna's nerves) the widow apparently found it necessary to get to business.

"Oh, Peter Ivanovich, how hard it is! How terribly, terribly hard!" and she again began to weep.

Peter Ivanovich sighed and waited for her to finish blowing her nose. When she had done so he said, "Believe me . . ." and she again began talking and brought out what was evidently her chief concern with him—namely, to question him as to how she could obtain a grant of money from the government on the occasion of her husband's death. She made it appear that she was asking Peter Ivanovich's advice about her pension, but he soon saw that she already knew about that to the minutest detail, more even than he did himself. She knew how much could be got out of the government in consequence of her husband's death, but wanted to find out whether she could possibly extract something more. Peter Ivanovich tried to think of some means of doing so, but after reflecting for a while and, out of propriety, condemning the government for its niggardliness, he said he thought that nothing more could be got. Then she sighed and evidently began to devise means of getting rid of her visitor. Noticing this, he put out his cigarette, rose, pressed her hand, and went out into the anteroom.

In the dining-room where the clock stood that Ivan Ilyich had liked so much and had bought at an antique shop, Peter Ivanovich met a priest and a few acquaintances who had come to attend the service, and he recognized Ivan Ilyich's daughter, a handsome young woman. She was in black and her slim figure appeared slimmer than ever. She had a gloomy, determined, almost angry expression, and bowed to Peter Ivanovich as though he were in some way to blame. Behind her, with the same offended look, stood a wealthy young man, an examining magistrate, whom Peter Ivanovich also knew and who was her fiancé, as he had heard. He bowed mournfully to them and was about to pass into the death-chamber, when from under the stairs appeared the figure of Ivan Ilyich's schoolboy son, who was extremely like this father. He seemed a little Ivan Ilyich, such as Peter Ivanovich remembered when they studied law together. His tear-stained eyes had in them the look that is seen in the eyes of boys of thirteen or fourteen who are not pure-minded.

When he saw Peter Ivanovich he scowled morosely and shamefacedly. Peter Ivanovich nodded to him and entered the death-chamber. The service began: candles, groans, incense, tears, and sobs. Peter Ivanovich stood looking gloomily down at his feet. He did not look once at the dead man, did not yield to any depressing influence, and was one of the first to leave the room. There was no one in the anteroom, but Gerasim darted out of the dead man's room, rummaged with his strong hands among the fur coats to find Peter Ivanovich's and helped him on with it.

"Well, friend Gerasim," said Peter Ivanovich, so as to say something. "It's a sad affair, isn't it?"

"It's God's will. We shall all come to it some day," said Gerasim, displaying his teeth—the even, white teeth of a healthy peasant—and, like a man in the thick of urgent work, he briskly opened the front door, called the coachman, helped Peter Ivanovich into the sledge, and sprang back to the porch as if in readiness for what he had to do next.

Peter Ivanovich found the fresh air particularly pleasant after the smell of incense, the dead body, and carbolic acid.

"Where to, sir?" asked the coachman.

"It's not too late even now. . . . I'll call round on Fëdor Vasilievich."

He accordingly drove there and found them just finishing the first rubber, so that it was quite convenient for him to cut in.

II

Ivan Ilyich's life had been most simple and most ordinary and therefore most terrible.

He had been a member of the Court of Justice, and died at the age of forty-five. His father had been an official who after serving in various ministries and departments in Petersburg had made the sort of career which brings men to positions from which by reason of their long service they cannot be dismissed, though they are obviously unfit to hold any responsible position, and for whom therefore posts are specially created, which though fictitious, carry salaries of from six to ten thousand rubles that are not fictitious, and in receipt of which they live on to a great age.

Such was the Privy Councillor and superfluous member of various superfluous institutions, Ilya Efimovich Golovin.

He had three sons, of whom Ivan Ilyich was the second. The eldest son was following in his father's footsteps only in another department, and was already approaching that stage in the service at which a similar sinecure would be reached. The third son was a failure. He had ruined his prospects in a number of positions and was now serving in the railway department. His father and brothers, and still more their wives, not merely disliked meeting him, but avoided remembering his existence unless compelled to do so. His sister had married Baron Greff, a Petersburg official of her father's type. Ivan Ilyich was *le phénix de la famille*[2] as people said. He was neither as cold and formal as his elder brother nor as wild as the younger, but was a happy mean between them—an intelligent, polished, lively and agreeable man. He had studied with his younger brother at the School of Law, but the latter had failed to complete the course and was expelled when he was in the fifth class. Ivan Ilyich finished the course well. Even when he was at the School of Law he was just what he remained for the rest of his life: a capable, cheerful, good-natured, and sociable man, though strict in the fulfilment of what he considered to be his duty: and he considered his duty to be what was so considered by those in authority. Neither as a boy nor as a man was he a toady, but from early youth was by nature attracted to people of high station as a fly is drawn to the light, assimilating their ways and views of life and establishing friendly relations with them. All the enthusiasms of childhood and youth passed without leaving much trace on him; he succumbed to sensuality, to vanity, and latterly among the highest classes to liberalism, but always within limits which his instinct unfailingly indicated to him as correct.

At school he had done things which had formerly seemed to him very horrid and made him feel disgusted with himself when he did them; but when later on he saw that such actions were done by people of good position and that they did not regard them as wrong, he was able not exactly to regard them as right, but to forget about them entirely or not be at all troubled at remembering them.

Having graduated from the School of Law and qualified for the tenth rank of the civil service, and having received money from his father for his equipment, Ivan Ilyich ordered himself clothes at Scharmer's, the fashionable tailor, hung a medallion inscribed *respice finem*[3] on his watch-chain, took leave of his professor and the prince who was patron of the school, had a farewell dinner with his comrades at Donon's first-class restaurant, and with his new and fashionable portmanteau, linen, clothes, shaving and other toilet appliances, and a travelling rug, all purchased at the best shops, he set off for one of the provinces where, through his father's influence, he had been attached to the governor as an official for special service.

In the province Ivan Ilyich soon arranged as easy and agreeable a position for himself as he had at the School of Law. He performed his official tasks, made his career, and at the same time amused himself pleasantly and decorously. Occasionally he paid official visits to country districts, where he behaved with dignity both to his superiors and inferiors, and performed the duties entrusted to him, which related chiefly to the sectarians,[4] with an exactness and incorruptible honesty of which he could not but feel proud.

---

2. The phoenix of the family (French). The word *phoenix* is used here to mean "rare bird," "prodigy." 3. Regard the end (a Latin motto). 4. The Old Believers, a large group of Russians (about 25 million in 1900), members of a sect that originated in a break with the Orthodox Church in the 17th century; they were subject to many legal restrictions.

In official matters, despite his youth and taste for frivolous gaiety, he was exceedingly reserved, punctilious, and even severe; but in society he was often amusing and witty, and always good-natured, correct in his manner, and *bon enfant,* as the governor and his wife—with whom he was like one of the family—used to say of him.

In the province he had an affair with a lady who made advances to the elegant young lawyer, and there was also a milliner; and there were carousals with aides-de-camp who visited the district, and after-supper visits to a certain outlying street of doubtful reputation; and there was too some obsequiousness to his chief and even to his chief's wife, but all this was done with such a tone of good breeding that no hard names could be applied to it. It all came under the heading of the French saying: *"Il faut que jeunesse se passe."*[5] It was all done with clean hands, in clean linen, with French phrases, and above all among people of the best society and consequently with the approval of people of rank.

So Ivan Ilyich served for five years and then came a change in his official life. The new and reformed judicial institutions were introduced, and new men were needed. Ivan Ilyich became such a new man. He was offered the post of Examining Magistrate, and he accepted it though the post was in another province and obliged him to give up the connexions he had formed and to make new ones. His friends met to give him a send-off; they had a group-photograph taken and presented him with a silver cigarette-case, and he set off to his new post.

As examining magistrate Ivan Ilyich was just as *comme il faut* and decorous a man, inspiring general respect and capable of separating his official duties from his private life, as he had been when acting as an official on special service. His duties now as examining magistrate were far more interesting and attractive than before. In his former position it had been pleasant to wear an undress uniform made by Scharmer, and to pass through the crowd of petitioners and officials who were timorously awaiting an audience with the governor, and who envied him as with free and easy gait he went straight into his chief's private room to have a cup of tea and a cigarette with him. But not many people had then been directly dependent on him—only police officials and the sectarians when he went on special missions—and he liked to treat them politely, almost as comrades, as if he were letting them feel that he who had the power to crush them was treating them in this simple, friendly way. There were then but few such people. But now, as an examining magistrate, Ivan Ilyich felt that everyone without exception, even the most important and self-satisfied, was in his power, and that he need only write a few words on a sheet of paper with a certain heading, and this or that important, self-satisfied person would be brought before him in the role of an accused person or a witness, and if he did not choose to allow him to sit down, would have to stand before him and answer his questions. Ivan Ilyich never abused his power; he tried on the contrary to soften its expression, but the consciousness of it and of the possibility of softening its effect, supplied the chief interest and attraction of his office. In his work itself, especially in his examinations, he very soon acquired a method of eliminating all considerations irrelevant to the legal aspect of the case, and reducing even the most

---

5. Youth must have its fling [Translators' note].

complicated case to a form in which it would be presented on paper only in its externals, completely excluding his personal opinion of the matter, while above all observing every prescribed formality. The work was new and Ivan Ilyich was one of the first men to apply the new Code of 1864.[6]

On taking up the post of examining magistrate in a new town, he made new acquaintances and connexions, placed himself on a new footing, and assumed a somewhat different tone. He took up an attitude of rather dignified aloofness towards the provincial authorities, but picked out the best circle of legal gentlemen and wealthy gentry living in the town and assumed a tone of slight dissatisfaction with the government, of moderate liberalism, and of enlightened citizenship. At the same time, without at all altering the elegance of his toilet, he ceased shaving his chin and allowed his beard to grow as it pleased.

Ivan Ilyich settled down very pleasantly in this new town. The society there, which inclined towards opposition to the governor, was friendly, his salary was larger, and he began to play *vint* [a form of bridge], which he found added not a little to the pleasure of life, for he had a capacity for cards, played good-humouredly, and calculated rapidly and astutely, so that he usually won.

After living there for two years he met his future wife, Praskovya Fëdorovna Mikhel, who was the most attractive, clever, and brilliant girl of the set in which he moved, and among other amusements and relaxations from his labours as examining magistrate, Ivan Ilyich established light and playful relations with her.

While he had been an official on special service he had been accustomed to dance, but now as an examining magistrate it was exceptional for him to do so. If he danced now, he did it as if to show that though he served under the reformed order of things, and had reached the fifth official rank, yet when it came to dancing he could do it better than most people. So at the end of an evening he sometimes danced with Praskovya Fëdorovna, and it was chiefly during these dances that he captivated her. She fell in love with him. Ivan Ilyich had at first no definite intention of marrying, but when the girl fell in love with him he said to himself: "Really, why shouldn't I marry?"

Praskovya Fëdorovna came of a good family, was not bad looking, and had some little property. Ivan Ilyich might have aspired to a more brilliant match, but even this was good. He had his salary, and she, he hoped, would have an equal income. She was well connected, and was a sweet, pretty, and thoroughly correct young woman. To say that Ivan Ilyich married because he fell in love with Praskovya Fëdorovna and found that she sympathized with his views of life would be as incorrect as to say that he married because his social circle approved of the match. He was swayed by both these considerations: the marriage gave him personal satisfaction, and at the same time it was considered the right thing by the most highly placed of his associates.

So Ivan Ilyich got married.

The preparations for marriage and the beginning of married life, with its conjugal caresses, the new furniture, new crockery, and new linen, were very

6. The emancipation of the serfs in 1861 was followed by a thorough all-round reform of judicial proceedings [Translators' note].

pleasant until his wife became pregnant—so that Ivan Ilyich had begun to think that marriage would not impair the easy, agreeable, gay, and always decorous character of his life, approved of by society and regarded by himself as natural, but would even improve it. But from the first months of his wife's pregnancy, something new, unpleasant, depressing, and unseemly, and from which there was no way of escape, unexpectedly showed itself.

His wife, without any reason—*de gaieté de coeur*[7] as Ivan Ilyich expressed it to himself—began to disturb the pleasure and propriety of their life. She began to be jealous without any cause, expected him to devote his whole attention to her, found fault with everything, and made coarse and ill-mannered scenes.

At first Ivan Ilyich hoped to escape from the unpleasantness of this state of affairs by the same easy and decorous relation to life that had served him heretofore: he tried to ignore his wife's disagreeable moods, continued to live in his usual easy and pleasant way, invited friends to his house for a game of cards, and also tried going out to his club or spending his evenings with friends. But one day his wife began upbraiding him so vigorously, using such coarse words, and continued to abuse him every time he did not fulfil her demands, so resolutely and with such evident determination not to give way till he submitted—that is, till he stayed at home and was bored just as she was—that he became alarmed. He now realized that matrimony—at any rate with Praskovya Fëdorovna—was not always conducive to the pleasures and amenities of life, but on the contrary often infringed both comfort and propriety, and that he must therefore entrench himself against such infringement. And Ivan Ilyich began to seek for means of doing so. His official duties were the one thing that imposed upon Praskovya Fëdorovna, and by means of his official work and the duties attached to it he began struggling with his wife to secure his own independence.

With the birth of their child, the attempts to feed it and the various failures in doing so, and with the real and imaginary illnesses of mother and child, in which Ivan Ilyich's sympathy was demanded but about which he understood nothing, the need of securing for himself an existence outside his family life became still more imperative.

As his wife grew more irritable and exacting and Ivan Ilyich transferred the centre of gravity of his life more and more to his official work, so did he grow to like his work better and became more ambitious than before.

Very soon, within a year of his wedding, Ivan Ilyich had realized that marriage, though it may add some comforts to life, is in fact a very intricate and difficult affair towards which in order to perform one's duty, that is, to lead a decorous life approved of by society, one must adopt a definite attitude just as towards one's official duties.

And Ivan Ilyich evolved such an attitude towards married life. He only required of it those conveniences—dinner at home, housewife, and bed—which it could give him, and above all that propriety of external forms required by public opinion. For the rest he looked for light-hearted pleasure and propriety, and was very thankful when he found them, but if he met with antagonism and querulousness he at once retired into his separate fenced-off world of official duties, where he found satisfaction.

---

7. From sheer impulsiveness (French).

Ivan Ilyich was esteemed a good official, and after three years was made Assistant Public Prosecutor. His new duties, their importance, the possibility of indicting and imprisoning anyone he chose, the publicity his speeches received, and the success he had in all these things, made his work still more attractive.

More children came. His wife became more and more querulous and ill-tempered, but the attitude Ivan Ilyich had adopted towards his home life rendered him almost impervious to her grumbling.

After seven years' service in that town he was transferred to another province as Public Prosecutor. They moved, but were short of money and his wife did not like the place they moved to. Though the salary was higher the cost of living was greater, besides which two of their children died and family life became still more unpleasant for him.

Praskovya Fëdorovna blamed her husband for every inconvenience they encountered in their new home. Most of the conversations between husband and wife, especially as to the children's education, led to topics which recalled former disputes, and those disputes were apt to flare up again at any moment. There remained only those rare periods of amorousness which still came to them at times but did not last long. These were islets at which they anchored for a while and then again set out upon that ocean of veiled hostility which showed itself in their aloofness from one another. This aloofness might have grieved Ivan Ilyich had he considered that it ought not to exist, but he now regarded the position as normal, and even made it the goal at which he aimed in family life. His aim was to free himself more and more from those unpleasantnesses and to give them a semblance of harmlessness and propriety. He attained this by spending less and less time with his family, and when obliged to be at home he tried to safeguard his position by the presence of outsiders. The chief thing however was that he had his official duties. The whole interest of his life now centered in the official world and that interest absorbed him. The consciousness of his power, being able to ruin anybody he wished to ruin, the importance, even the external dignity of his entry into court, or meetings with his subordinates, his success with superiors and inferiors, and above all his masterly handling of cases, of which he was conscious—all this gave him pleasure and filled his life, together with chats with his colleagues, dinners, and bridge. So that on the whole Ivan Ilyich's life continued to flow as he considered it should do—pleasantly and properly.

So things continued for another seven years. His eldest daughter was already sixteen, another child had died, and only one son was left, a schoolboy and a subject of dissensions. Ivan Ilyich wanted to put him in the School of Law, but to spite him Praskovya Fëdorovna entered him at the High School. The daughter had been educated at home and had turned out well: the boy did not learn badly either.

III

So Ivan Ilyich lived for seventeen years after his marriage. He was already a Public Prosecutor of long standing, and had declined several proposed transfers while awaiting a more desirable post, when an unanticipated and unpleasant occurrence quite upset the peaceful course of his life. He was expecting to be offered the post of presiding judge in a University town, but Hoppe somehow came to the front and obtained the appointment instead. Ivan Ilyich became irritable, reproached Hoppe, and quarrelled both with him and with his immediate superiors—who became colder to him and again passed him over when other appointments were made.

This was in 1880, the hardest year of Ivan Ilyich's life. It was then that it became evident on the one hand that his salary was insufficient for them to live on, and on the other that he had been forgotten, and not only this, but that what was for him the greatest and most cruel injustice appeared to others a quite ordinary occurrence. Even his father did not consider it his duty to help him. Ivan Ilyich felt himself abandoned by everyone, and that they regarded his position with a salary of 3,500 rubles as quite normal and even fortunate. He alone knew that with the consciousness of the injustices done him, with his wife's incessant nagging, and with the debts he had contracted by living beyond his means his position was far from normal.

In order to save money that summer he obtained leave of absence and went with his wife to live in the country at her brother's place.

In the country, without his work, he experienced *ennui* for the first time in his life, and not only *ennui* but intolerable depression, and he decided that it was impossible to go on living like that, and that it was necessary to take energetic measures.

Having passed a sleepless night pacing up and down the veranda, he decided to go to Petersburg and bestir himself, in order to punish those who had failed to appreciate him and to get transferred to another ministry.

Next day, despite many protests from his wife and her brother, he started for Petersburg with the sole object of obtaining a post with a salary of five thousand rubles a year. He was no longer bent on any particular department, or tendency, or kind of activity. All he now wanted was an appointment to another post with a salary of five thousand rubles, either in the administration, in the banks, with the railways, in one of the Empress Marya's Institutions,[8] or even in the customs—but it had to carry with it a salary of five thousand rubles and be in a ministry other than that in which they had failed to appreciate him.

And this quest of Ivan Ilyich's was crowned with remarkable and unexpected success. At Kursk an acquaintance of his, F. I. Ilyin, got into the first class carriage, sat down beside Ivan Ilyich, and told him of a telegram just received by the governor of Kursk announcing that a change was about to take place in the ministry: Peter Ivanovich was to be superseded by Ivan Seménovich.

The proposed change, apart from its significance for Russia, had a special significance for Ivan Ilyich, because by bringing forward a new man, Peter Petrovich, and consequently his friend Zachar Ivanovich, it was highly favourable for Ivan Ilyich, since Zachar Ivanovich was a friend and colleague of his.

In Moscow his news was confirmed, and on reaching Petersburg Ivan Ilyich found Zachar Ivanovich and received a definite promise of an appointment in his former department of Justice.

8. Reference to the charitable organization founded by the empress Marya, wife of Paul I, late in the 18th century.

A week later he telegraphed to his wife: "Zachar in Miller's place. I shall receive appointment on presentation of report."

Thanks to this change of personnel, Ivan Ilyich had unexpectedly obtained an appointment in his former ministry which placed him two stages above his former colleagues besides giving him five thousand rubles salary and three thousand five hundred rubles for expenses connected with his removal. All his ill humour towards his former enemies and the whole department vanished, and Ivan Ilyich was completely happy.

He returned to the country more cheerful and contented than he had been for a long time. Praskovya Fëdorovna also cheered up and a truce was arranged between them. Ivan Ilyich told of how he had been fêted by everybody in Petersburg, how all those who had been his enemies were put to shame and now fawned on him, how envious they were of his appointment, and how much everybody in Petersburg had liked him.

Praskovya Fëdorovna listened to all this and appeared to believe it. She did not contradict anything, but only made plans for their life in the town to which they were going. Ivan Ilyich saw with delight that these plans were his plans, that he and his wife agreed, and that, after a stumble, his life was regaining its due and natural character of pleasant lightheartedness and decorum.

Ivan Ilyich had come back for a short time only, for he had to take up his new duties on the 10th of September. Moreover, he needed time to settle into the new place, to move all his belongings from the province, and to buy and order many additional things: in a word, to make such arrangements as he had resolved on, which were almost exactly what Praskovya Fëdorovna too had decided on.

Now that everything had happened so fortunately, and that he and his wife were at one in their aims and moreover saw so little of one another they got on together better than they had done since the first years of marriage. Ivan Ilyich had thought of taking his family away with him at once, but the insistence of his wife's brother and her sister-in-law, who had suddenly become particularly amiable and friendly to him and his family, induced him to depart alone.

So he departed, and the cheerful state of mind induced by his success and by the harmony between his wife and himself, the one intensifying the other, did not leave him. He found a delightful house, just the thing both he and his wife had dreamt of. Spacious, lofty reception rooms in the old style, a convenient and dignified study, rooms for his wife and daughter, a study for his son—it might have been specially built for them. Ivan Ilyich himself superintended the arrangements, chose the wallpapers, supplemented the furniture (preferably with antiques which he considered particularly *comme il faut*), and supervised the upholstering. Everything progressed and progressed and approached the ideal he had set himself: even when things were only half completed they exceeded his expectations. He saw what a refined and elegant character, free from vulgarity, it would all have when it was ready. On falling asleep he pictured to himself how the reception-room would look. Looking at the yet unfinished drawing-room he could see the fireplace, the screen, the what-not, the little chairs dotted here and there, the dishes and plates on the walls, and the bronzes, as they would be when everything was in place. He was pleased by the thought of how his wife and daughter, who shared his taste in this matter, would be impressed by it. They were certainly not expecting as much. He had been particularly successful in finding, and buying cheaply, antiques which gave a particularly aristocratic character to the whole place. But in his letters he intentionally understated everything in order to be able to surprise them. All this so absorbed him that his new duties—though he liked his official work—interested him less than he had expected. Sometimes he even had moments of absent-mindedness during the Court Sessions, and would consider whether he should have straight or curved cornices for his curtains. He was so interested in it all that he often did things himself, rearranging the furniture, or rehanging the curtains. Once when mounting a step-ladder to show the upholsterer, who did not understand, how he wanted the hangings draped, he made a false step and slipped, but being a strong and agile man he clung on and only knocked his side against the knob of the window frame. The bruised place was painful but the pain soon passed, and he felt particularly bright and well just then. He wrote: "I feel fifteen years younger." He thought he would have everything ready by September, but it dragged on till mid-October. But the result was charming not only in his eyes but to everyone who saw it.

In reality it was just what is usually seen in the houses of people of moderate means who want to appear rich, and therefore succeed only in resembling others like themselves: there were damasks, dark wood, plants, rugs, and dull and polished bronzes—all the things people of a certain class have in order to resemble other people of that class. His house was so like the others that it would never have been noticed, but to him it all seemed to be quite exceptional. He was very happy when he met his family at the station and brought them to the newly furnished house all lit up, where a footman in a white tie opened the door into the hall decorated with plants, and when they went on into the drawing room and the study uttering exclamations of delight. He conducted them everywhere, drank in their praises eagerly, and beamed with pleasure. At tea that evening, when Praskovya Fëdorovna among other things asked him about his fall, he laughed, and showed them how he had gone flying and had frightened the upholsterer.

"It's a good thing I'm a bit of an athlete. Another man might have been killed, but I merely knocked myself, just here; it hurts when it's touched, but it's passing off already—it's only a bruise."

So they began living in their new home—in which, as always happens, when they got thoroughly settled in they found they were just one room short—and with the increased income, which as always was just a little (some five hundred rubles) too little, but it was all very nice.

Things went particularly well at first, before everything was finally arranged and while something had still to be done: this thing bought, that thing ordered, another thing moved, and something else adjusted. Though there were some disputes between husband and wife, they were both so well satisfied and had so much to do that it all passed off without any serious quarrels. When nothing was left to arrange it became rather dull and something seemed to be lacking, but they were then making acquaintances, forming habits, and life was growing fuller.

Ivan Ilyich spent his mornings at the law court and came home to dinner, and at first he was generally in a good humour, though he occasionally became irritable just on account of his house. (Every spot on the tablecloth or the upholstery, and every broken window-blind string, irritated him. He had devoted so much trouble to arranging it all that every disturbance of it distressed him.) But on the whole his life ran its course as he believed life should do: easily, pleasantly, and decorously.

He got up at nine, drank his coffee, read the paper, and then put on his undress uniform and went to the law courts. There the harness in which he worked had already been stretched to fit him and he donned it without a hitch: petitioners, inquiries at the chancery, the chancery itself, and the sittings public and administrative. In all this the thing was to exclude everything fresh and vital, which always disturbs the regular course of official business, and to admit only official relations with people, and then only on official grounds. A man would come, for instance, wanting some information. Ivan Ilyich, as one in whose sphere the matter did not lie, would have nothing to do with him: but if the man had some business with him in his official capacity, something that could be expressed on officially stamped paper, he would do everything, positively everything he could within the limits of such relations, and in doing so would maintain the semblance of friendly human relations, that is, would observe the courtesies of life. As soon as the official relations ended, so did everything else. Ivan Ilyich possessed this capacity to separate his real life from the official side of affairs and not mix the two, in the highest degree, and by long practice and natural aptitude had brought it to such a pitch that sometimes, in the manner of a virtuoso, he would even allow himself to let the human and official relations mingle. He let himself do this just because he felt that he could at any time he chose resume the strictly official attitude again and drop the human relation. And he did it all easily, pleasantly, correctly, and even artistically. In the intervals between the sessions he smoked, drank tea, chatted a little about politics, a little about general topics, a little about cards, but most of all about official appointments. Tired, but with the feelings of a virtuoso—one of the first violins who has played his part in an orchestra with precision—he would return home to find that his wife and daughter had been out paying calls, or had a visitor, and that his son had been to school, had done his homework with his tutor, and was duly learning what is taught at High Schools. Everything was as it should be. After dinner, if they had no visitors, Ivan Ilyich sometimes read a book that was being much discussed at the time, and in the evening settled down to work, that is, read official papers, compared the depositions of witnesses, and noted paragraphs of the Code applying to them. This was neither dull nor amusing. It was dull when he might have been playing bridge, but if no bridge was available it was at any rate better than doing nothing or sitting with his wife. Ivan Ilyich's chief pleasure was giving little dinners to which he invited men and women of good social position, and just as his drawing-room resembled all other drawing-rooms so did his enjoyable little parties resemble all other such parties.

Once they even gave a dance. Ivan Ilyich enjoyed it and everything went off well, except that it led to a violent quarrel with his wife about the cakes and sweets. Praskovya Fëdorovna had made her own plans, but Ivan Ilyich insisted on getting everything from an expensive confectioner and ordered too many cakes, and the quarrel occurred because some of those cakes were left over and the confectioner's bill came to forty-five rubles. It was a great and disagreeable quarrel. Praskovya Fëdorovna called him "a fool and an imbecile," and he clutched at his head and made angry allusions to divorce.

But the dance itself had been enjoyable. The best people were there, and Ivan Ilyich had danced with Princess Trufonova, a sister of the distinguished founder of the Society "Bear my Burden."

The pleasures connected with his work were pleasures of ambition; his social pleasures were those of vanity; but Ivan Ilyich's greatest pleasure was playing bridge. He acknowledged that whatever disagreeable incident happened in his life, the pleasure that beamed like a ray of light above everything else was to sit down to bridge with good players, not noisy partners, and of course to four-handed bridge (with five players it was annoying to have to stand out, though one pretended not to mind), to play a clever and serious game (when the cards allowed it) and then to have supper and drink a glass of wine. After a game of bridge, especially if he had won a little (to win a large sum was unpleasant), Ivan Ilyich went to bed in specially good humour.

So they lived. They formed a circle of acquaintances among the best people and were visited by people of importance and by young folk. In their views as to their acquaintances, husband, wife, and daughter were entirely agreed, and tacitly and unanimously kept at arm's length and shook off the various shabby friends and relations who, with much show of affection, gushed into the drawing-room with its Japanese plates on the walls. Soon these shabby friends ceased to obtrude themselves and only the best people remained in the Golovins' set.

Young men made up to Lisa, and Petrishchev, an examining magistrate and Dmitri Ivanovich Petrischchev's son and sole heir, began to be so attentive to her that Ivan Ilyich had already spoken to Praskovya Fëdorovna about it, and considered whether they should not arrange a party for them, or get up some private theatricals.

So they lived, and all went well, without change, and life flowed pleasantly.

IV

They were all in good health. It could not be called ill health if Ivan Ilyich sometimes said that he had a queer taste in his mouth and felt some discomfort in his left side.

But this discomfort increased and, though not exactly painful, grew into a sense of pressure in his side accompanied by ill humour. And his irritability became worse and worse and began to mar the agreeable, easy, and correct life that had established itself in the Golovin family. Quarrels between husband and wife became more and more frequent, and soon the ease and amenity disappeared and even the decorum was barely maintained. Scenes again became frequent, and very few of those islets remained on which husband and wife could meet without an explosion. Praskovya Fëdorovna now had good reason to say that her husband's temper was trying. With characteristic exaggeration she said he had always had a dreadful temper, and that it had needed all her good nature to put up with it for twenty years. It was true that now the quarrels were started by him. His bursts of temper always came just before dinner, often just as he began to eat his soup. Sometimes he noticed that a plate or dish was chipped, or the food was not right, or his son put his elbow on the table, or his daughter's hair was not done as he liked it, and for all this he blamed Praskovya Fëdorovna. At first she retorted and said disagreeable things to him, but once or twice he fell into such a rage at the beginning of dinner that she realized it was due to some physical derangement brought on by taking food, and so she restrained herself and did not answer, but only hurried to get the dinner over. She regarded this self-restraint as highly praiseworthy. Having come to the conclusion that her husband had a dreadful temper and made her life miserable, she began to feel sorry for herself, and the more she pitied herself the more she hated her husband. She began to wish he would die; yet she did not want him to die because then his salary would cease. And this irritated her against him still more. She considered herself dreadfully unhappy just because not even his death could save her, and though she concealed her exasperation, that hidden exasperation of hers increased his irritation also.

After one scene in which Ivan Ilyich had been particularly unfair and after which he had said in explanation that he certainly was irritable but that it was due to his not being well, she said that if he was ill it should be attended to, and insisted on his going to see a celebrated doctor.

He went. Everything took place as he had expected and as it always does. There was the usual waiting and the important air assumed by the doctor, with which he was so familiar (resembling that which he himself assumed in court), and the sounding and listening, and the questions which called for answers that were foregone conclusions and were evidently unnecessary, and the look of importance which implied that "if only you put yourself in our hands we will arrange everything—we know indubitably how it has to be done, always in the same way for everybody alike." It was all just as it was in the law courts. The doctor put on just the same air towards him as he himself put on towards an accused person.

The doctor said that so-and-so indicated that there was so-and-so inside the patient, but if the investigation of so-and-so did not confirm this, then he must assume that and that. If he assumed that and that, then . . . and so on. To Ivan Ilyich only one question was important: was his case serious or not? But the doctor ignored that inappropriate question. From his point of view it was not the one under consideration, the real question was to decide between a floating kidney, chronic catarrh, or appendicitis. It was not a question of Ivan Ilyich's life or death, but one between a floating kidney and appendicitis. And that question the doctor solved brilliantly, as it seemed to Ivan Ilyich, in favour of the appendix, with the reservation that should an examination of the urine give fresh indications the matter would be reconsidered. All this was just what Ivan Ilyich had himself brilliantly accomplished a thousand times in dealing with men on trial. The doctor summed up just as brilliantly, looking over his spectacles triumphantly and even gaily at the accused. From the doctor's summing up Ivan Ilyich concluded that things were bad, but that for the doctor, and perhaps for everybody else, it was a matter of indifference, though for him it was bad. And this conclusion struck him painfully, arousing in him a great feeling of pity for himself and of bitterness towards the doctor's indifference to a matter of such importance.

He said nothing of this, but rose, placed the doctor's fee on the table, and remarked with a sigh: "We sick people probably often put inappropriate questions. But tell me, in general, is this complaint dangerous or not? . . ."

The doctor looked at him sternly over his spectacles with one eye, as if to say: "Prisoner, if you will not keep to the questions put to you, I shall be obliged to have you removed from the court."

"I have already told you what I consider necessary and proper. The analysis may show something more." And the doctor bowed.

Ivan Ilyich went out slowly, seated himself disconsolately in his sledge, and drove home. All the way home he was going over what the doctor had said, trying to translate those complicated, obscure, scientific phrases into plain language and find in them an answer to the question: "Is my condition bad? Is it very bad? Or is there as yet nothing much wrong?" And it seemed to him that the meaning of what the doctor had said was it was very bad. Everything in the streets seemed depressing. The cabmen, the houses, the passers-by, and the shops, were dismal. His ache, this dull gnawing ache that never ceased for a moment, seemed to have acquired a new and more serious significance from the doctor's dubious remarks. Ivan Ilyich now watched it with a new and oppressive feeling.

He reached home and began to tell his wife about it. She listened, but in the middle of his account his daughter came in with her hat on, ready to go out with her mother. She sat down reluctantly to listen to this tedious story, but could not stand it long, and her mother too did not hear him to the end.

"Well, I am very glad," she said. "Mind now to take your medicine regularly. Give me the prescription and I'll send Gerasim to the chemist's." And she went to get ready to go out.

While she was in the room Ivan Ilyich had hardly taken time to breathe, but he sighed deeply when she left it.

"Well," he thought, "perhaps it isn't so bad after all."

He began taking his medicine and following the doctor's directions, which had been altered after the examination of the urine. But then it happened that there was a contradiction between the indications drawn from the examination of the urine and the symptoms that showed themselves. It turned out that what was happening differed from what the doctor had told him, and that he had either forgotten, or blundered, or hidden something from him. He could not, however, be blamed for that, and Ivan Ilyich still obeyed his orders implicitly and at first derived some comfort from doing so.

From the time of his visit to the doctor, Ivan Ilyich's chief occupation was the exact fulfilment of the doctor's instructions regarding hygiene and the taking of medicine, and the observation of his pain and his excretions. His chief interests came to be people's ailments and people's health. When sickness, deaths, or recoveries were mentioned in his presence, especially when the illness resembled his own, he listened with agitation which he tried to hide, asked questions, and applied what he heard to his own case.

The pain did not grow less, but Ivan Ilyich made efforts to force himself to think that he was better. And he could do this so long as nothing agitated him. But as soon as he had any unpleasantness with his wife, any lack of success in his official work, or held bad cards at bridge, he was at once acutely sensible of his disease. He had formerly borne such mischances, hoping soon to adjust what was wrong, to master it and attain success, or make a grand slam. But now every mischance upset him and plunged him into despair. He would say to himself. "There now, just as I was beginning to get better and the medicine had begun to take effect, comes this accursed misfortune, or unpleasantness . . ." And he was furious with the mishap, or with the people who were causing the unpleasantness and killing him, for he felt that this fury was killing him but could not restrain it. One would have thought that it should have been clear to him that this exasperation with circumstances and people aggravated his illness, and that he ought therefore to ignore unpleasant occurrences. But he drew the very opposite conclusion: he said that he needed peace, and he watched for everything that might disturb it and became irritable at the slightest infringement of it. His condition was rendered worse by the fact that he read medical books and consulted doctors. The progress of his disease was so gradual that he could deceive himself when comparing one day with another—the difference was so slight. But when he consulted the doctors it seemed to him that he was getting worse, and even very rapidly. Yet despite this he was continually consulting them.

That month he went to see another celebrity, who told him almost the same as the first had done but put his questions rather differently, and the interview with this celebrity only increased Ivan Ilyich's doubts and fears. A friend of a friend of his, a very good doctor, diagnosed his illness again quite differently from the others, and though he predicted recovery, his questions and suppositions bewildered Ivan Ilyich still more and increased his doubts. A homeopathist diagnosed the disease in yet another way, and prescribed medicine which Ivan Ilyich took secretly for a week. But after a week, not feeling any improvement and having lost confidence both in the former doctor's treatment and in this one's, he became still more despondent. One day a lady acquaintance mentioned a cure effected by a wonder-working icon. Ivan Ilyich caught himself listening attentively and beginning to believe that it had occurred. This incident alarmed him. "Has my mind really weakened to such an extent?" he asked himself. "Nonsense! It's all rubbish. I mustn't give way to nervous fears but having chosen a doctor must keep strictly to his treatment. That is what I will do. Now it's all settled. I won't think about it, but will follow the treatment seriously till summer, and then we shall see. From now there must be no more of this wavering!" This was easy to say but impossible to carry out. The pain in his side oppressed him and seemed to grow worse and more incessant, while the taste in his mouth grew stranger and stranger. It seemed to him that his breath had a disgusting smell, and he was conscious of a loss of appetite and strength. There was no deceiving himself: something terrible, new, and more important than anything before in his life, was taking place within him of which he alone was aware. Those about him did not understand or would not understand it, but thought everything in the world was going on as usual. That tormented Ivan Ilyich more than anything. He saw that his household, especially his wife and daughter who were in a perfect whirl of visiting, did not understand anything of it and were annoyed that he was so depressed and so exacting, as if he were to blame for it. Though they tried to disguise it he saw that he was an obstacle in their path, and that his wife had adopted a definite line in regard to his illness and kept to it regardless of anything he said or did. Her attitude was this: "You know," she would say to her friends, "Ivan Ilyich can't do as other people do, and keep to the treatment prescribed for him. One day he'll take his drops and keep strictly to his diet and go to bed in good time, but the next day unless I watch him he'll suddenly forget his medicine, eat sturgeon—which is forbidden—and sit up playing cards till one o'clock in the morning."

"Oh, come, when was that?" Ivan Ilyich would ask in vexation. "Only once at Peter Ivanovich's."

"And yesterday with Shebek."

"Well, even if I hadn't stayed up, this pain would have kept me awake."

"Be that as it may you'll never get well like that, but will always make us wretched."

Praskovya Fedorovna's attitude to Ivan Ilyich's illness, as she expressed it both to others and to him, was that it was his own fault and was another of the annoyances he caused her. Ivan Ilyich felt that this opinion escaped her involuntarily—but that did not make it easier for him.

At the law courts too, Ivan Ilyich noticed, or thought he noticed, a strange attitude towards himself. It sometimes seemed to him that people were watching him inquisitively as a man whose place might soon be vacant. Then again, his friends would suddenly begin to chaff him in a friendly way about his low spirits, as if the awful, horrible, and unheard-of thing that was going on within him, incessantly gnawing at him and irresistibly drawing him away, was a very agreeable subject for jests. Schwartz in particular irritated him by his jocularity, vivacity, and *savoir-faire,* which reminded him of what he himself had been ten years ago.

Friends came to make up a set and they sat down to cards. They dealt, bending the new cards to soften them, and he sorted the diamonds in his hand and found he had seven. His partner said "No trumps" and supported him with two diamonds. What more could be wished for? It ought to be jolly and lively. They would make a grand slam. But suddenly Ivan Ilyich was conscious of that gnawing pain, that taste in his mouth, and it seemed ridiculous that in such circumstances he should be pleased to make a grand slam.

He looked at his partner Mikhail Mikhaylovich, who rapped the table with his strong hand and instead of snatching up the tricks pushed the cards courteously and indulgently towards Ivan Ilyich that he might have the pleasure of gathering them up without the trouble of stretching out his hand for them. "Does he think I am too weak to stretch out my arm?" thought Ivan Ilyich, and forgetting what he was doing he over-trumped his partner, missing the grand slam by three tricks. And what was most awful of all was that he saw how upset Mikhail Mikhaylovich was about it but did not himself care. And it was dreadful to realize why he did not care.

They all saw that he was suffering, and said: "We can stop if you are tired. Take a rest." Lie down? No, he was not at all tired, and he finished the rubber. All were gloomy and silent. Ivan Ilyich felt that he had diffused this gloom over them and could not dispel it. They had supper and went away, and Ivan Ilyich was left alone with the consciousness that his life was poisoned and was poisoning the lives of others, and that this poison did not weaken but penetrated more and more deeply into his whole being.

With this consciousness, and with physical pain besides the terror, he must go to bed, often to lie awake the greater part of the night. Next morning he had to get up again, dress, go to the law courts, speak, and write; or if he did not go out, spend at home those twenty-four hours a day each of which was a torture. And he had to live thus all alone on the brink of an abyss, with no one who understood or pitied him.

V

So one month passed and then another. Just before the New Year his brother-in-law came to town and stayed at their house. Ivan Ilyich was at the law courts and Praskovya Fëdorovna had gone shopping. When Ivan Ilyich came home and entered his study he found his brother-in-law there—a healthy, florid man—unpacking his portmanteau himself. He raised his head on hearing Ivan Ilyich's footsteps and looked up at him for a moment without a word. That stare told Ivan everything. His brother-in-law opened his mouth to utter an exclamation of surprise but checked himself, and that action confirmed it all.

"I have changed, eh?"

"Yes, there is a change."

And after that, try as he would to get his brother-in-law to return to the subject of his looks, the latter would say nothing about it. Praskovya Fëdorovna came home and her brother went out to her. Ivan Ilyich locked the door and began to examine himself in the glass, first full face, then in profile. He took up a portrait of himself taken with his wife, and compared it with what he saw in the glass. The change in him was immense. Then he bared his arms to the elbow, looked at them, drew the sleeves down again, sat down on an ottoman, and grew blacker than night.

"No, no, this won't do!" he said to himself, and jumped up, went to the table, took up some law papers and began to read them, but could not continue. He unlocked the door and went into the reception-room. The door leading to the drawing-room was shut. He approached it on tiptoe and listened.

"No, you are exaggerating!" Praskovya Fëdorovna was saying.

"Exaggerating! Don't you see it? Why, he's a dead man! Look at his eyes—there's no light in them. But what is it that is wrong with him?"

"No one knows. Nikolaevich [that was another doctor] said something, but I don't know what. And Leshchetitsky [this was the celebrated specialist] said quite the contrary . . ."

Ivan Ilyich walked away, went to his own room, lay down and began musing: "The kidney, a floating kidney." He recalled all the doctors had told him of how it detached itself and swayed about. And by an effort of imagination he tried to catch that kidney and arrest it and support it. So little was needed for this, it seemed to him. "No, I'll go to see Peter Ivanovich again." [That was the friend whose friend was a doctor.] He rang, ordered the carriage, and got ready to go.

"Where are you going, *Jean?*" asked his wife, with a specially sad and exceptionally kind look.

This exceptionally kind look irritated him. He looked morosely at her.

"I must go to see Peter Ivanovich."

He went to see Peter Ivanovich, and together they went to see his friend, the doctor. He was in, and Ivan Ilyich had a long talk with him.

Reviewing the anatomical and physiological details of what in the doctor's opinion was going on inside him, he understood it all.

There was something, a small thing, in the vermiform appendix. It might all come right. Only stimulate the energy of one organ and check the activity of another, then absorption would take place and everything would come right. He got home rather late for dinner, ate his dinner, and conversed cheerfully, but could not for a long time bring himself to go back to work in his room. At last, however, he went to his study and did what was necessary, but the consciousness that he had put something aside—an important, intimate matter which he would revert to when his work was done—never left him. When he had finished his work he remembered that this intimate matter was the thought of his vermiform appendix. But he did not give himself up to it, and went to the drawing-room for tea. There were callers there, including the examining magistrate who was a desirable match for his daughter, and they were conversing, playing the piano, and singing. Ivan Ilyich, as Praskovya Fëdorovna remarked, spent that evening more cheerfully than usual, but he never for a moment forgot that he had postponed the important matter of the appendix. At eleven o'clock he said good-night and went to his bedroom. Since his illness he had slept alone in a small room next to his study. He undressed and took up a novel by Zola,[9] but instead of reading it he fell into thought, and in his imagination that desired improvement in the vermiform appendix occurred. There was the absorption and evacuation and the reestablishment of normal activity. "Yes, that's it!" he said to himself. "One need only assist nature, that's all." He remembered his medicine, rose, took it, and lay down on his back watching for the beneficent action of the medicine and for it to lessen the pain. "I need only take it regularly and avoid all injurious influences. I am already feeling better, much better." He began touching his side: it was not painful to the touch. "There, I really don't feel it. It's much better already." He put out the light and turned on his side. . . . "The appendix is getting better, absorption is occurring." Suddenly he felt the old, familiar, dull, gnawing pain, stubborn and serious. There was the same familiar loathsome taste in his mouth. His heart sank and he felt dazed. "My God! My God!" he muttered. "Again, again! And it will never cease." And suddenly the matter presented itself in a quite different aspect. "Vermiform appendix! Kidney!" he said to himself. "It's not a question of appendix or kidney, but of life and . . . death. Yes, life was there and now it is going, going and I cannot stop it. Yes. Why deceive myself? Isn't it obvious to everyone but me that I'm dying, and that it's only a question of weeks, days . . . it may happen this moment. There was light and now there is darkness. I was here and now I'm going there! Where?" A chill came over him, his breathing ceased, and he felt only the throbbing of his heart.

"When I am not, what will there be? There will be nothing. Then where shall I be when I am no more? Can this be dying? No, I don't want to!" He jumped up and tried to light the candle, felt for it with trembling hands, dropped candle and candlestick on the floor, and fell back on his pillow.

"What's the use? It makes no difference," he said to himself, staring with wide-open eyes into the darkness. "Death. Yes, death. And none of them know or wish to know it, and they have no pity for me. Now they are playing." (He heard through the door the distant sound of a song and its accompaniment.) "It's all the same to them, but they will die too! Fools! I first, and they later, but it will be the same for them. And now they are merry . . . the beasts!"

Anger choked him and he was agonizingly, unbearably miserable. "It is impossible that all men have been doomed to suffer this awful horror!" He raised himself.

"Something must be wrong. I must calm myself—must think it all over

9. Émile Zola (1840–1902), French novelist, author of the *Rougon-Macquart* novels (*Nana, Germinal,* and so on). Tolstoy condemned Zola for his naturalistic theories and considered his novels crude and gross.

from the beginning." And he again began thinking. "Yes, the beginning of my illness: I knocked my side, but I was still quite well that day and the next. It hurt a little, then rather more. I saw the doctors, then followed despondency and anguish, more doctors, and I drew nearer to the abyss. My strength grew less and I kept coming nearer and nearer, and now I have wasted away and there is no light in my eyes. I think of the appendix—but this is death! I think of mending the appendix, and all the while here is death! Can it really be death!" Again terror seized him and he gasped for breath. He leant down and began feeling for the matches, pressing with his elbow on the stand beside the bed. It was in his way and hurt him, he grew furious with it, pressed on it still harder, and upset it. Breathless and in despair he fell on his back, expecting death to come immediately.

Meanwhile the visitors were leaving. Praskovya Fëdorovna was seeing them off. She heard something fall and came in.

"What has happened?"

"Nothing. I knocked it over accidentally."

She went out and returned with a candle. He lay there panting heavily, like a man who has run a thousand yards, and stared upwards at her with a fixed look.

"What is it, *Jean?*"

"No . . . o . . . thing. I upset it." ("Why speak of it? She won't understand," he thought.)

And in truth she did not understand. She picked up the stand, lit his candle, and hurried away to see another visitor off. When she came back he still lay on his back, looking upwards.

"What is it? Do you feel worse?"

"Yes."

She shook her head and sat down.

"Do you know, *Jean,* I think we must ask Leshchetitsky to come and see you here."

This meant calling in the famous specialist, regardless of expense. He smiled malignantly and said "No." She remained a little longer and then went up to him and kissed his forehead.

While she was kissing him he hated her from the bottom of his soul and with difficulty refrained from pushing her away.

"Good-night. Please God you'll sleep."

"Yes."

VI

Ivan Ilyich saw that he was dying, and he was in continual despair.

In the depth of his heart he knew he was dying, but not only was he not accustomed to the thought, he simply did not and could not grasp it.

The syllogism he had learned from Kiesewetter's *Logic:*[1] "Caius is a man, men are mortal, therefore Caius is mortal," had always seemed to him correct as applied to Caius, but certainly not as applied to himself. That Caius—man in the abstract—was mortal, was perfectly correct, but he was not Caius, not an abstract man, but a creature quite, quite separate from all others. He

---

1. Karl Kiesewetter (1766–1819) was a German popularizer of Kant's philosophy. His *Outline of Logic According to Kantian Principles* (1796) was widely used in Russian adaptations as a schoolbook.

had been little Vanya, with a mamma and a papa, with Mitya and Volodya, with the toys, a coachman and a nurse, afterwards with Katenka and with all the joys, griefs, and delights of childhood, boyhood, and youth. What did Caius know of the smell of that striped leather ball Vanya had been so fond of? Had Caius kissed his mother's hand like that, and did the silk of her dress rustle so for Caius? Had he rioted like that at school when the pastry was bad? Had Caius been in love like that? Could Caius preside at a session as he did? "Caius really was mortal, and it was right for him to die; but for me, little Vanya, Ivan Ilyich, with all my thoughts and emotions, it's altogether a different matter. It cannot be that I ought to die. That would be too terrible."

Such was his feeling.

"If I had to die like Caius I should have known it was so. An inner voice would have told me so, but there was nothing of the sort in me and I and all my friends felt that our case was quite different from that of Caius. And now here it is!" he said to himself. "It can't be. It's impossible! But here it is. How is this? How is one to understand it?"

He could not understand it, and tried to drive this false, incorrect, morbid thought away and to replace it by other proper and healthy thoughts. But that thought, and not the thought only but the reality itself, seemed to come and confront him.

And to replace that thought he called up a succession of others, hoping to find in them some support. He tried to get back into the former current of thoughts that had once screened the thought of death from him. But strange to say, all that had formerly shut off, hidden, and destroyed, his consciousness of death, no longer had that effect. Ivan Ilyich now spent most of his time in attempting to re-establish that old current. He would say to himself: "I will take up my duties again—after all I used to live by them." And banishing all doubts he would go to the law courts, enter into conversation with his colleagues, and sit carelessly as was his wont, scanning the crowd with a thoughtful look and leaning both his emaciated arms on the arms of his oak chair; bending over as usual to a colleague and drawing his papers nearer he would interchange whispers with him, and then suddenly raising his eyes and sitting erect would pronounce certain words and open the proceedings. But suddenly in the midst of those proceedings the pain in his side, regardless of the stage the proceedings had reached, would begin its own gnawing work. Ivan Ilyich would turn his attention to it and try to drive the thought of it away, but without success. *It* would come and stand before him and look at him, and he would be petrified and the light would die out of his eyes, and he would again begin asking himself whether *It* alone was true. And his colleagues and subordinates would see with surprise and distress that he, the brilliant and subtle judge, was becoming confused and making mistakes. He would shake himself, try to pull himself together, manage somehow to bring the sitting to a close, and return home with the sorrowful consciousness that his judicial labours could not as formerly hide from him what he wanted them to hide, and could not deliver him from *It*. And what was worst of all was that *It* drew his attention to itself not in order to make him take some action but only that he should look at *It*, look it straight in the face: look at it without doing anything, suffer inexpressibly.

And to save himself from this condition Ivan Ilyich looked for consolations—new screens—and new screens were found and for a while seemed to save him, but then they immediately fell to pieces or rather became transparent, as *It* penetrated them and nothing could veil *It*.

In these latter days he would go into the drawing-room he had arranged—that drawing-room where he had fallen and for the sake of which (how bitterly ridiculous it seemed) he had sacrificed his life—for he knew that his illness originated with that knock. He would enter and see that something had scratched the polished table. He would look for the cause of this and find that it was the bronze ornamentation of an album, that had got bent. He would take up the expensive album which he had lovingly arranged, and feel vexed with his daughter and her friends for their untidiness—for the album was torn here and there and some of the photographs turned upside down. He would put it carefully in order and bend the ornamentation back into position. Then it would occur to him to place all those things in another corner of the room, near the plants. He would call the footman, but his daughter or wife would contradict him, and he would dispute and grow angry. But that was all right, for then he did not think about *It*. *It* was invisible.

But then, when he was moving something himself, his wife would say: "Let the servants do it. You will hurt yourself again." And suddenly *It* would flash through the screen and he would see it. It was just a flash, and he hoped it would disappear, but he would involuntarily pay attention to his side. "It sits there as before, gnawing just the same!" And he could no longer forget *It*, but could distinctly see it looking at him from behind the flowers. "What is it all for?"

"It really is so! I lost my life over that curtain as I might have done when storming a fort. Is that possible? How terrible and how stupid. It can't be true! It can't, but it is."

He would go to his study, lie down, and again be alone with *It*: face to face with *It*. And nothing could be done with *It* except to look at it and shudder.

VII

How it happened it is impossible to say because it came about step by step, unnoticed, but in the third month of Ivan Ilyich's illness, his wife, his daughter, his son, his acquaintances, the doctors, the servants, and above all he himself, were aware that the whole interest he had for other people was whether he would soon vacate his place, and at last release the living from the discomfort caused by his presence and be himself released from his sufferings.

He slept less and less. He was given opium and hypodermic injections of morphine, but this did not relieve him. The dull depression he experienced in a somnolent condition at first gave him a little relief, but only as something new; afterwards it became as distressing as the pain itself or even more so.

Special foods were prepared for him by the doctors' orders, but all those foods became increasingly distasteful and disgusting to him.

For his excretions also special arrangements had to be made, and this was a torment to him every time—a torment from the uncleanliness, the unseemliness, and the smell, and from knowing that another person had to take part in it.

But just through this most unpleasant matter, Ivan Ilyich obtained comfort. Gerasim, the butler's young assistant, always came in to carry the things out. Gerasim was a clean, fresh peasant lad, grown stout on town food and always cheerful and bright. At first the sight of him, in his clean Russian peasant costume, engaged on that disgusting task embarrassed Ivan Ilyich.

Once when he got up from the commode too weak to draw up his trousers, he dropped into a soft armchair and looked with horror at his bare, enfeebled thighs with the muscles so sharply marked on them.

Gerasim with a firm light tread, his heavy boots emitting a pleasant smell of tar and fresh winter air, came in wearing a clean Hessian apron, the sleeves of his print shirt tucked up over his strong bare young arms; and refraining from looking at his sick master out of consideration for his feelings, and restraining the joy of life that beamed from his face, he went up to the commode.

"Gerasim!" said Ivan Ilyich in a weak voice.

Gerasim started, evidently afraid he might have committed some blunder, and with a rapid movement turned his fresh, kind, simple young face which just showed the first downy sign of a beard.

"Yes, sir?"

"That must be very unpleasant for you. You must forgive me. I am helpless."

"Oh, why, sir," and Gerasim's eyes beamed and he showed his glistening white teeth, "what's a little trouble? It's a case of illness with you, sir."

And his deft strong hands did their accustomed task, and he went out of the room stepping lightly. Five minutes later he as lightly returned.

Ivan Ilyich was still sitting in the same position in the armchair.

"Gerasim," he said when the latter had replaced the freshly-washed utensil. "Please come here and help me." Gerasim went up to him. "Lift me up. It is hard for me to get up, and I have sent Dmitri away."

Gerasim went up to him, grasped his master with his strong arms deftly but gently, in the same way that he stepped—lifted him, supported him with one hand, and with the other drew up his trousers and would have set him down again, but Ivan Ilyich asked to be led to the sofa. Gerasim, without an effort and without apparent pressure, led him, almost lifting him, to the sofa and placed him on it.

"Thank you. How easily and well you do it all!"

Gerasim smiled again and turned to leave the room. But Ivan Ilyich felt his presence such a comfort that he did not want to let him go.

"One thing more, please move up that chair. No, the other one—under my feet. It is easier for me when my feet are raised."

Gerasim brought the chair, set it down gently in place, and raised Ivan Ilyich's legs on to it. It seemed to Ivan Ilyich that he felt better while Gerasim was holding up his legs.

"It's better when my legs are higher," he said. "Place that cushion under them."

Gerasim did so. He again lifted the legs and placed them, and again Ivan Ilyich felt better while Gerasim held his legs. When he set them down Ivan Ilyich fancied he felt worse.

"Gerasim," he said. "Are you busy now?"

"Not at all, sir," said Gerasim, who had learnt from the townsfolk how to speak to gentlefolk.

"What have you still to do?"

"What have I to do? I've done everything except chopping the logs for to-morrow."

"Then hold my legs up a bit higher, can you?"

"Of course I can. Why not?" And Gerasim raised his master's legs higher and Ivan Ilyich thought that in that position he did not feel any pain at all.

"And how about the logs?"

"Don't trouble about that, sir. There's plenty of time."

Ivan Ilyich told Gerasim to sit down and hold his legs, and began to talk to him. And strange to say it seemed to him that he felt better while Gerasim held his legs up.

After that Ivan Ilyich would sometimes call Gerasim and get him to hold his legs on his shoulders, and he liked talking to him. Gerasim did it all easily, willingly, simply, and with a good nature that touched Ivan Ilyich. Health, strength, and vitality in other people were offensive to him, but Gerasim's strength and vitality did not mortify but soothed him.

What tormented Ivan Ilyich most was the deception, the lie, which for some reason they all accepted, that he was not dying but was simply ill, and that he only need keep quiet and undergo a treatment and then something very good would result. He however knew that do what they would nothing would come of it, only still more agonizing suffering and death. This deception tortured him—their not wishing to admit what they all knew and what he knew, but wanting to lie to him concerning his terrible condition, and wishing and forcing him to participate in that lie. Those lies—lies enacted over him on the eve of his death and destined to degrade this awful, solemn act to the level of their visitings, their curtains, their sturgeon for dinner— were a terrible agony for Ivan Ilyich. And strangely enough, many times when they were going through their antics over him he had been within a hair-breadth of calling out to them: "Stop lying! You know and I know that I am dying. Then at least stop lying about it!" But he had never had the spirit to do it. The awful, terrible act of his dying was, he could see, reduced by those about him to the level of a casual, unpleasant, and almost indecorous inci-dent (as if someone entered a drawing-room diffusing an unpleasant odour) and this was done by that very decorum which he had served all his life long. He saw that no one felt for him, because no one even wished to grasp his position. Only Gerasim recognized and pitied him. And so Ivan Ilyich felt at ease only with him. He felt comforted when Gerasim supported his legs (sometimes all night long) and refused to go to bed, saying: "Don't you worry, Ivan Ilyich. I'll get sleep enough later on," or when he suddenly became familiar and exclaimed: "If you weren't sick it would be another matter, but as it is, why should I grudge a little trouble?" Gerasim alone did not lie; everything showed that he alone understood the facts of the case and did not consider it necessary to disguise them, but simply felt sorry for his ema-ciated and enfeebled master. Once when Ivan Ilyich was sending him away he even said straight out: "We shall all of us die, so why should I grudge a little trouble?"—expressing the fact that he did not think his work burden-some, because he was doing it for a dying man and hoped someone would do the same for him when his time came.

Apart from this lying, or because of it, what most tormented Ivan Ilyich was that no one pitied him as he wished to be pitied. At certain moments after prolonged suffering he wished most of all (though he would have been ashamed to confess it) for someone to pity him as a sick child is pitied. He longed to be petted and comforted. He knew he was an important functionary, that he had a beard turning grey, and that therefore what he longed for was impossible, but still he longed for it. And in Gerasim's attitude towards him there was something akin to what he wished for, and so that attitude comforted him. Ivan Ilyich wanted to weep, wanted to be petted and cried over, and then his colleague Shebek would come, and instead of weeping and being petted, Ivan Ilyich would assume a serious, severe, and profound air, and by force of habit would express his opinion on a decision of the Court of Appeal and would stubbornly insist on that view. This falsity around him and within him did more than anything else to poison his last days.

VIII

It was morning. He knew it was morning because Gerasim had gone, and Peter the footman had come and put out the candles, drawn back one of the curtains, and begun quietly to tidy up. Whether it was morning or evening, Friday or Sunday, made no difference, it was all just the same: the gnawing, unmitigated, agonizing pain, never ceasing for an instant, the consciousness of life inexorably waning but not yet extinguished, the approach of that ever dreaded and hateful Death which was the only reality, and always the same falsity. What were days, weeks, hours, in such a case?

"Will you have some tea, sir?"

"He wants things to be regular, and wishes the gentlefolk to drink tea in the morning," thought Ivan Ilyich, and only said "No."

"Wouldn't you like to move onto the sofa, sir?"

"He wants to tidy up the room, and I'm in the way. I am uncleanliness and disorder," he thought, and said only:

"No, leave me alone."

The man went on bustling about. Ivan Ilyich stretched out his hand. Peter came up, ready to help.

"What is it, sir?"

"My watch."

Peter took the watch which was close at hand and gave it to his master.

"Half-past eight. Are they up?"

"No sir, except Vladimir Ivanich" (the son) "who has gone to school. Praskovya Fëdorovna ordered me to wake her if you asked for her. Shall I do so?"

"No, there's no need to." "Perhaps I'd better have some tea," he thought, and added aloud: "Yes, bring me some tea."

Peter went to the door, but Ivan Ilyich dreaded being left alone. "How can I keep him here? Oh yes, my medicine." "Peter, give me my medicine." "Why not? Perhaps it may still do me some good." He took a spoonful and swallowed it. "No, it won't help. It's all tomfoolery, all deception," he decided as soon as he became aware of the familiar, sickly, hopeless taste. "No, I can't believe in it any longer. But the pain, why this pain? If it would only cease just for a moment!" And he moaned. Peter turned towards him. "It's all right. Go and fetch me some tea."

Peter went out. Left alone Ivan Ilyich groaned not so much with pain, terrible though that was, as from mental anguish. Always and forever the same, always these endless days and nights. If only it would come quicker!

If only *what* would come quicker? Death, darkness? . . . No, no! Anything rather than death!

When Peter returned with the tea on a tray, Ivan Ilyich stared at him for a time in perplexity, not realizing who and what he was. Peter was disconcerted by that look and his embarrassment brought Ivan Ilyich to himself.

"Oh, tea! All right, put it down. Only help me to wash and put on a clean shirt."

And Ivan Ilyich began to wash. With pauses for rest, he washed his hands and then his face, cleaned his teeth, brushed his hair, and looked in the glass. He was terrified by what he saw, especially by the limp way in which his hair clung to his pallid forehead.

While his shirt was being changed he knew that he would be still more frightened at the sight of his body, so he avoided looking at it. Finally he was ready. He drew on a dressing-gown, wrapped himself in a plaid, and sat down in the armchair to take his tea. For a moment he felt refreshed, but as soon as he began to drink the tea he was again aware of the same taste, and the pain also returned. He finished it with an effort, and then lay down stretching out his legs, and dismissed Peter.

Always the same. Now a spark of hope flashes up, then a sea of despair rages, and always pain; always pain, always despair, and always the same. When alone he had a dreadful and distressing desire to call someone, but he knew beforehand that with others present it would be still worse. "Another dose of morphine—to lose consciousness. I will tell him, the doctor, that he must think of something else. It's impossible, impossible, to go on like this."

An hour and another pass like that. But now there is a ring at the door bell. Perhaps it's the doctor? It is. He comes in fresh, hearty, plump, and cheerful, with that look on his face that seems to say: "There now, you're in a panic about something, but we'll arrange it all for you directly!" The doctor knows this expression is out of place here, but he has put it on once for all and can't take it off—like a man who has put on a frock-coat in the morning to pay a round of calls.

The doctor rubs his hands vigorously and reassuringly.

"Brr! How cold it is! There's such a sharp frost; just let me warm myself!" he says, as if it were only a matter of waiting till he was warm, and then he would put everything right.

"Well now, how are you?"

Ivan Ilyich feels that the doctor would like to say: "Well, how are our affairs?" but that even he feels that this would not do, and says instead: "What sort of a night have you had?"

Ivan Ilyich looks at him as much as to say: "Are you really never ashamed of lying?" But the doctor does not wish to understand this question, and Ivan Ilyich says: "Just as terrible as ever. The pain never leaves me and never subsides. If only something . . ."

"Yes, you sick people are always like that. . . . There, now I think I'm warm enough. Even Praskovya Fëdorovna, who is so particular, could find no fault with my temperature. Well, now I can say good-morning," and the doctor presses his patient's hand.

Then, dropping his former playfulness, he begins with a most serious face to examine the patient, feeling his pulse and taking his temperature, and then begins the sounding and auscultation.

Ivan Ilyich knows quite well and definitely that all this is nonsense and pure deception, but when the doctor, getting down on his knee, leans over him, putting his ear first higher then lower, and performs various gymnastic movements over him with a significant expression on his face, Ivan Ilyich submits to it all as he used to submit to the speeches of the lawyers, though he knew very well that they were all lying and why they were lying.

The doctor, kneeling on the sofa, is still sounding him when Praskovya Fëdorovna's silk dress rustles at the door and she is heard scolding Peter for not having let her know of the doctor's arrival.

She comes in, kisses her husband, and at once proceeds to prove that she has been up a long time already, and only owing to a misunderstanding failed to be there when the doctor arrived.

Ivan Ilyich looks at her, scans her all over, sets against her the whiteness and plumpness and cleanness of her hands and neck, the gloss of her hair, and the sparkle of her vivacious eyes. He hates her with his whole soul. And the thrill of hatred he feels for her makes him suffer from her touch.

Her attitude towards him and his disease is still the same. Just as the doctor had adopted a certain relation to his patient which he could not abandon, so had she formed one towards him—that he was not doing something he ought to do and was himself to blame, and that she reproached him lovingly for this—and she could not now change that attitude.

"You see he doesn't listen to me and doesn't take his medicine at the proper time. And above all he lies in a position that is no doubt bad for him—with his legs up."

She described how he made Gerasim hold his legs up.

The doctor smiled with a contemptuous affability that said: "What's to be done? These sick people do have foolish fancies of that kind, but we must forgive them."

When the examination was over the doctor looked at his watch, and then Praskovya Fëdorovna announced to Ivan Ilyich that it was of course as he pleased, but she had sent to-day for a celebrated specialist who would examine him and have a consultation with Michael Danilovich (their regular doctor).

"Please don't raise any objections. I am doing this for my own sake," she said ironically, letting it be felt that she was doing it all for his sake and only said this to leave him no right to refuse. He remained silent, knitting his brows. He felt that he was so surrounded and involved in a mesh of falsity that it was hard to unravel anything.

Everything she did for him was entirely for her own sake, and she told him she was doing for herself what she actually was doing for herself, as if that was so incredible that he must understand the opposite.

At half-past eleven the celebrated specialist arrived. Again the sounding began and the significant conversations in his presence and in other rooms, about the kidneys and the appendix, and the questions and answers, with such an air of importance that again, instead of the real question of life and death which now alone confronted him, the question arose of the kidney and the appendix which were not behaving as they ought to and would now be attacked by Michael Danilovich and the specialist and forced to amend their ways.

The celebrated specialist took leave of him with a serious though not hopeless look, and in reply to the timid question in Ivan Ilyich, with eyes glistening with fear and hope, put to him as to whether there was a chance of recovery, said that he could not vouch for it but there was a possibility. The look of hope with which Ivan Ilyich watched the doctor out was so pathetic that Praskovya Fëdorovna, seeing it, even wept as she left the room to hand the doctor his fee.

The gleam of hope kindled by the doctor's encouragement did not last long. The same room, the same pictures, curtains, wallpaper, medicine bottles, were all there, and the same aching suffering body, and Ivan Ilyich began to moan. They gave him a subcutaneous injection and he sank into oblivion.

It was twilight when he came to. They brought him his dinner and he swallowed some beef tea with difficulty, and then everything was the same again and night was coming on.

After dinner, at seven o'clock, Praskovya Fëdorovna came into the room in evening dress, her full bosom pushed up by her corset, and with traces of powder on her face. She had reminded him in the morning that they were going to the theatre. Sarah Bernhardt[2] was visiting the town and they had a box, which he had insisted on their taking. Now he had forgotten about it and her toilet offended him, but he concealed his vexation when he remembered that he had himself insisted on their securing a box and going because it would be an instructive and aesthetic pleasure for the children.

Praskovya Fëdorovna came in, self-satisfied but yet with a rather guilty air. She sat down and asked how he was, but, as he saw, only for the sake of asking and not in order to learn about it, knowing that there was nothing to learn—and then went on to what she really wanted to say: that she would not on any account have gone but that the box had been taken and Helen and their daughter were going, as well as Petrishchev (the examining magistrate, their daughter's fiancé) and that it was out of the question to let them go alone; but that she would have much preferred to sit with him for a while; and he must be sure to follow the doctor's orders while she was away.

"Oh, and Fëdor Petrovich" (the fiancé) "would like to come in. May he? And Lisa?"

"All right."

Their daughter came in in full evening dress, her fresh young flesh exposed (making a show of that very flesh which in his own case caused so much suffering), strong, healthy, evidently in love, and impatient with illness, suffering, and death, because they interfered with her happiness.

Fëdor Petrovich came in too, in evening dress, his hair curled à la Capoul, a tight stiff collar round his long sinewy neck, an enormous white shirt-front and narrow black trousers tightly stretched over his strong thighs. He had one white glove tightly drawn on, and was holding his opera hat in his hand.

Following him the schoolboy crept in unnoticed, in a new uniform, poor little fellow, and wearing gloves. Terribly dark shadows showed under his eyes, the meaning of which Ivan Ilyich knew well.

His son had always seemed pathetic to him, and now it was dreadful to see the boy's frightened look of pity. It seemed to Ivan Ilyich that Vasya was the only one besides Gerasim who understood and pitied him.

2. Stage name of Rosine Bernard (1844–1923), famed for romantic and tragic roles.

They all sat down and again asked how he was. A silence followed. Lisa asked her mother about the opera-glasses, and there was an altercation between mother and daughter as to who had taken them and where they had been put. This occasioned some unpleasantness.

Fëdor Petrovich inquired of Ivan Ilyich whether he had ever seen Sarah Bernhardt. Ivan Ilyich did not at first catch the question, but then replied: "No, have you seen her before?"

"Yes, in *Adrienne Lecouvreur.*"[3]

Praskovya Fëdorovna mentioned some rôles in which Sarah Bernhardt was particularly good. Her daughter disagreed. Conversation sprang up as to the elegance and realism of her acting—the sort of conversation that is always repeated and is always the same.

In the midst of the conversation Fëdor Petrovich glanced at Ivan Ilyich and became silent. The others also looked at him and grew silent. Ivan Ilyich was staring with glittering eyes straight before him, evidently indignant with them. This had to be rectified, but it was impossible to do so. The silence had to be broken, but for a time no one dared to break it and they all became afraid that the conventional deception would suddenly become obvious and the truth become plain to all. Lisa was the first to pluck up courage and break that silence, but by trying to hide what everybody was feeling, she betrayed it.

"Well, if we are going it's time to start," she said, looking at her watch, a present from her father, and with a faint and significant smile at Fëdor Petrovich relating to something known only to them. She got up with a rustle of her dress.

They all rose, said good-night, and went away.

When they had gone it seemed to Ivan Ilyich that he felt better; the falsity had gone with them. But the pain remained—that same pain and that same fear that made everything monotonously alike, nothing harder and nothing easier. Everything was worse.

Again minute followed minute and hour followed hour. Everything remained the same and there was no cessation. And the inevitable end of it all became more and more terrible.

"Yes, send Gerasim here," he replied to a question Peter asked.

IX

His wife returned late at night. She came in on tiptoe, but he heard her, opened his eyes, and made haste to close them again. She wished to send Gerasim away and to sit with him herself, but he opened his eyes and said: "No, go away."

"Are you in great pain?"

"Always the same."

"Take some opium."

He agreed and took some. She went away.

Till about three in the morning he was in a state of stupefied misery. It seemed to him that he and his pain were being thrust into a narrow, deep

---

3. A play (1849) by the French dramatist Eugène Scribe (1791–1861), in which the heroine was a famous actress of the 18th century. Tolstoy considered Scribe, who wrote over four hundred plays, a shoddy, commercial playwright.

black sack, but though they were pushed further and further in they could not be pushed to the bottom. And this, terrible enough in itself, was accompanied by suffering. He was frightened yet wanted to fall through the sack, he struggled but yet co-operated. And suddenly he broke through, fell, and regained consciousness. Gerasim was sitting at the foot of the bed dozing quietly and patiently, while he himself lay with his emaciated stockinged legs resting on Gerasim's shoulders; the same shaded candle was there and the same unceasing pain.

"Go away, Gerasim," he whispered.

"It's all right, sir. I'll stay a while."

"No. Go away."

He removed his legs from Gerasim's shoulders, turned sideways onto his arm, and felt sorry for himself. He only waited till Gerasim had gone into the next room and then restrained himself no longer but wept like a child. He wept on account of his helplessness, his terrible loneliness, the cruelty of man, the cruelty of God, and the absence of God.

"Why hast Thou done all this? Why hast Thou brought me here? Why, dost Thou torment me so terribly?"

He did not expect an answer and yet wept because there was no answer and could be none. The pain again grew more acute, but he did not stir and did not call. He said to himself: "Go on! Strike me! But what is it for? What have I done to Thee? What is it for?"

Then he grew quiet and not only ceased weeping but even held his breath and became all attention. It was as though he were listening not to an audible voice but to a voice of his soul, to the current of thoughts arising within him.

"What is it you want?" was the first clear conception capable of expression in words, that he heard.

"What do you want? What do you want?" he repeated to himself.

"What do I want? To live and not to suffer," he answered.

And again he listened with such concentrated attention that even his pain did not distract him.

"To live? How?" asked his inner voice.

"Why, to live as I used to—well and pleasantly."

"As you lived before, well and pleasantly?" the voice repeated.

And in imagination he began to recall the moments of his pleasant life. But strange to say none of those best moments of his pleasant life now seemed at all what they had then seemed—none of them except the first recollections of childhood. There, in childhood, there had been something really pleasant with which it would be possible to live if it could return. But the child who had experienced that happiness existed no longer, it was like a reminiscence of somebody else.

As soon as the period began which had produced the present Ivan Ilyich, all that had then seemed joys now melted before his sight and turned into something trivial and often nasty.

And the further he departed from childhood and the nearer he came to the present the more worthless and doubtful were the joys. This began with the School of Law. A little that was really good was still found there—there was light-heartedness, friendship, and hope. But in the upper classes there had already been fewer of such good moments. Then during the first years of his official career, when he was in the service of the Governor, some pleasant moments again occurred: they were the memories of love for a woman. Then all became confused and there was still less of what was good; later on again there was still less that was good, and the further he went the less there was. His marriage, a mere accident, then the disenchantment that followed it, his wife's bad breath and the sensuality and hypocrisy: then that deadly official life and those preoccupations about money, a year of it, and two, and ten, and twenty, and always the same thing. And the longer it lasted the more deadly it became. "It is as if I had been going downhill while I imagined I was going up. And that is really what it was. I was going up in public opinion, but to the same extent life was ebbing away from me. And now it is all done and there is only death."

"Then what does it mean? Why? It can't be that life is so senseless and horrible. But if it really has been so horrible and senseless, why must I die and die in agony? There is something wrong!"

"Maybe I did not live as I ought to have done," it suddenly occurred to him. "But how could that be, when I did everything properly?" he replied, and immediately dismissed from his mind this, the sole solution of all the riddles of life and death, as something quite impossible.

"Then what do you want now? To live? Live how? Live as you lived in the law courts when the usher proclaimed 'The judge is coming!' The judge is coming, the judge!" he repeated to himself. "Here he is, the judge. But I am not guilty!" he exclaimed angrily. "What is it for?" And he ceased crying, but turning his face to the wall continued to ponder on the same question: Why, and for what purpose, is there all this horror? But however much he pondered he found no answer. And whenever the thought occurred to him, as it often did, that it all resulted from his not having lived as he ought to have done, he at once recalled the correctness of his whole life, and dismissed so strange an idea.

X

Another fortnight passed. Ivan Ilyich now no longer left his sofa. He would not lie in bed but lay on the sofa, facing the wall nearly all the time. He suffered ever the same unceasing agonies and in his loneliness pondered always on the same insoluble question: "What is this? Can it be that it is Death?" And the inner voice answered: "Yes, it is Death."

"Why these sufferings?" And the voice answered, "For no reason—they just are so." Beyond and besides this there was nothing.

From the very beginning of his illness, ever since he had first been to see the doctor, Ivan Ilyich's life had been divided between two contrary and alternating moods: now it was despair and the expectation of this uncomprehended and terrible death, and now hope and an intently interested observation of the functioning of his organs. Now before his eyes there was only a kidney or an intestine that temporarily evaded its duty, and now only that incomprehensible and dreadful death from which it was impossible to escape.

These two states of mind had alternated from the very beginning of his illness, but the further it progressed the more doubtful and fantastic became the conception of the kidney, and the more real the sense of impending death.

He had but to call to mind what he had been three months before and what he was now, to call to mind with what regularity he had been going downhill, for every possibility of hope to be shattered.

Latterly during that loneliness in which he found himself as he lay facing the back of the sofa, a loneliness in the midst of a populous town and surrounded by numerous acquaintances and relations but that yet could not have been more complete anywhere—either at the bottom of the sea or under the earth—during that terrible loneliness Ivan Ilyich had lived only in memories of the past. Pictures of his past rose before him one after another. They always began with what was nearest in time and then went back to what was most remote—to his childhood—and rested there. If he thought of the stewed prunes that had been offered him that day, his mind went back to the raw shrivelled French plums of his childhood, their peculiar flavour and the flow of saliva when he sucked their stones, and along with the memory of that taste came a whole series of memories of those days: his nurse, his brother, and their toys. "No, I mustn't think of that. . . . It is too painful," Ivan Ilyich said to himself, and brought himself back to the present—to the button on the back of the sofa and the creases in its morocco. "Morocco is expensive, but it does not wear well: there had been a quarrel about it. It was a different kind of quarrel and a different kind of morocco that time when we tore father's portfolio and were punished, and mamma brought us some tarts. . . ." And again his thoughts dwelt on his childhood, and again it was painful and he tried to banish them and fix his mind on something else.

Then again together with that chain of memories another series passed through his mind—of how his illness had progressed and grown worse. There also the further back he looked the more life there had been. There had been more of what was good in life and more of life itself. The two merged together. "Just as the pain went on getting worse and worse, so my life grew worse and worse," he thought. "There is one bright spot there at the back, at the beginning of life, and afterwards all becomes blacker and blacker and proceeds more and more rapidly—in inverse ratio to the square of the distance from death," thought Ivan Ilyich. And the example of a stone falling downwards with increasing velocity entered his mind. Life, a series of increasing sufferings, flies further and further towards its end—the most terrible suffering. "I am flying. . . ." He shuddered, shifted himself, and tried to resist, but was already aware that resistance was impossible, and again with eyes weary of gazing but unable to cease seeing what was before them, he stared at the back of the sofa and waited—awaiting that dreadful fall and shock and destruction.

"Resistance is impossible!" he said to himself. "If I could only understand what it is all for! But that too is impossible. An explanation would be possible if it could be said that I have not lived as I ought to. But it is impossible to say that," and he remembered all the legality, correctitude, and propriety of his life. "That at any rate can certainly not be admitted," he thought, and his lips smiled ironically as if someone could see that smile and be taken in by it. "There is no explanation! Agony, death. . . . What for?"

XI

Another two weeks went by in this way and during that fortnight an event occurred that Ivan Ilyich and his wife had desired. Petrishchev formally proposed. It happened in the evening. The next day Praskovya Fëdorovna came into her husband's room considering how best to inform him of it, but that very night there had been a fresh change for the worse in his condition. She found him still lying on the sofa but in a different position. He lay on his back, groaning and staring fixedly straight in front of him.

She began to remind him of his medicines, but he turned his eyes towards her with such a look that she did not finish what she was saying; so great an animosity, to her in particular, did that look express.

"For Christ's sake let me die in peace!" he said.

She would have gone away, but just then their daughter came in and went up to say good morning. He looked at her as he had done at his wife, and in reply to her inquiry about his health said dryly that he would soon free them all of himself. They were both silent and after sitting with him for a while went away.

"Is it our fault?" Lisa said to her mother. "It's as if we were to blame! I am sorry for papa, but why should we be tortured?"

The doctor came at his usual time. Ivan Ilyich answered "Yes" and "No," never taking his angry eyes from him, and at last said: "You know you can do nothing for me, so leave me alone."

"We can ease your sufferings."

"You can't even do that. Let me be."

The doctor went into the drawing-room and told Praskovya Fëdorovna that the case was very serious and that the only resource left was opium to allay her husband's sufferings, which must be terrible.

It was true, as the doctor said, that Ivan Ilyich's physical sufferings were terrible, but worse than the physical sufferings were his mental sufferings which were his chief torture.

His mental sufferings were due to the fact that that night, as he looked at Gerasim's sleepy, good-natured face with its prominent cheek-bones, the question suddenly occurred to him: "What if my whole life has really been wrong?"

It occurred to him that what had appeared perfectly impossible before, namely that he had not spent his life as he should have done, might after all be true. It occurred to him that his scarcely perceptible attempts to struggle against what was considered good by the most highly placed people, those scarcely noticeable impulses which he had immediately suppressed, might have been the real thing, and all the rest false. And his professional duties and the whole arrangement of his life and of his family, and all his social and official interests, might all have been false. He tried to defend all those things to himself and suddenly felt the weakness of what he was defending. There was nothing to defend.

"But if that is so," he said to himself, "and I am leaving this life with the consciousness that I have lost all that was given me and it is impossible to rectify it—what then?"

He lay on his back and began to pass his life in review in quite a new way. In the morning when he saw first his footman, then his wife, then his daughter, and then the doctor, their every word and movement confirmed to him the awful truth that had been revealed to him during the night. In them he saw himself—all that for which he had lived—and saw clearly that it was not real at all, but a terrible and huge deception which had hidden both life and death. This consciousness intensified his physical suffering tenfold. He groaned and tossed about, and pulled at his clothing which choked and sti-fled him. And he hated them on that account.

He was given a large dose of opium and became unconscious, but at noon his sufferings began again. He drove everybody away and tossed from side to side.

His wife came to him and said:

"*Jean,* my dear, do this for me. It can't do any harm and often helps. Healthy people often do it."

He opened his eyes wide.

"What? Take communion? Why? It's unnecessary! However . . ."

She began to cry.

"Yes, do, my dear. I'll send for our priest. He is such a nice man."

"All right. Very well," he muttered.

When the priest came and heard his confession, Ivan Ilyich was softened and seemed to feel a relief from his doubts and consequently from his suf-ferings, and for a moment there came a ray of hope. He again began to think of the vermiform appendix and the possibility of correcting it. He received the sacrament with tears in his eyes.

When they laid him down again afterwards he felt a moment's ease, and the hope that he might live awoke in him again. He began to think of the operation that had been suggested to him. "To live! I want to live!" he said to himself.

His wife came in to congratulate him after his communion, and when uttering the usual conventional words she added:

"You feel better, don't you?"

Without looking at her he said "Yes."

Her dress, her figure, the expression of her face, the tone of her voice, all revealed the same thing. "This is wrong, it is not as it should be. All you have lived for and still live for is falsehood and deception, hiding life and death from you." And as soon as he admitted that thought, his hatred and his agonizing physical suffering again sprang up, and with that suffering a con-sciousness of the unavoidable, approaching end. And to this was added a new sensation of grinding shooting pain and a feeling of suffocation.

The expression of his face when he uttered that "yes" was dreadful. Having uttered it, he looked her straight in the eyes, turned on his face with a rapidity extraordinary in his weak state and shouted:

"Go away! Go away and leave me alone!"

XII

From that moment the screaming began that continued for three days, and was so terrible that one could not hear it through two closed doors without horror. At the moment he answered his wife he realized that he was lost, that there was no return, that the end had come, the very end, and his doubts were still unsolved and remained doubts.

"Oh! Oh! Oh!" he cried in various intonations. He had begun by screaming "I won't!" and continued screaming on the letter "o."

For three whole days, during which time did not exist for him, he struggled in that black sack into which he was being thrust by an invisible, resistless force. He struggled as a man condemned to death struggles in the hands of the executioner, knowing that he cannot save himself. And every moment he felt that despite all his efforts he was drawing nearer and nearer to what terrified him. He felt that his agony was due to his being thrust into that black hole and still more to his not being able to get right into it. He was hindered from getting into it by his conviction that his life had been a good one. That very justification of his life held him fast and prevented his moving forward, and it caused him most torment of all.

Suddenly some force struck him in the chest and side, making it still harder to breathe, and he fell through the hole and there at the bottom was a light. What had happened to him was like the sensation one sometimes experiences in a railway carriage when one thinks one is going backwards while one is really going forwards and suddenly becomes aware of the real direction.

"Yes, it was all not the right thing," he said to himself, "but that's no matter. It can be done. But what *is* the right thing?" he asked himself, and suddenly grew quiet.

This occurred at the end of the third day, two hours before his death. Just then his schoolboy son had crept softly in and gone up to the bedside. The dying man was still screaming desperately and waving his arms. His hand fell on the boy's head, and the boy caught it, pressed it to his lips, and began to cry.

At that very moment Ivan Ilyich fell through and caught sight of the light, and it was revealed to him that though his life had not been what it should have been, this could still be rectified. He asked himself, "What *is* the right thing?" and grew still, listening. Then he felt that someone was kissing his hand. He opened his eyes, looked at his son, and felt sorry for him. His wife came up to him and he glanced at her. She was gazing at him open-mouthed, with undried tears on her nose and cheek and a despairing look on her face. He felt sorry for her too.

"Yes, I am making them wretched," he thought. "They are sorry, but it will be better for them when I die." He wished to say this but had not the strength to utter it. "Besides, why speak? I must act," he thought. With a look at his wife he indicated his son and said: "Take him away . . . sorry for him . . . sorry for you too. . . ." He tried to add, "forgive me," but said "forgo" and waved his hand, knowing that He whose understanding mattered would understand.

And suddenly it grew clear to him that what had been oppressing him and would not leave him was all dropping away at once from two sides, from ten sides, and from all sides. He was sorry for them, he must act so as not to hurt them: release them and free himself from these sufferings. "How good and how simple!" he thought. "And the pain?" he asked himself. "What has become of it? Where are you, pain?"

He turned his attention to it.

"Yes, here it is. Well, what of it? Let the pain be."

"And death . . . where is it?"

He sought his former accustomed fear of death and did not find it. "Where is it? What death?" There was no fear because there was no death.

In place of death there was light.

"So that's what it is!" he suddenly exclaimed aloud. "What joy!"

To him all this happened in a single instant, and the meaning of that instant did not change. For those present his agony continued for another two hours. Something rattled in his throat, his emaciated body twitched, then the gasping and rattle became less and less frequent.

"It is finished!" said someone near him.

He heard these words and repeated them in his soul.

"Death is finished," he said to himself. "It is no more!"

He drew in a breath, stopped in the midst of a sigh, stretched out, and died.

HENRIK IBSEN
1828–1906

Henrik Ibsen was the foremost playwright of his time—treating social themes and ideas and often satirizing the nineteenth-century bourgeoisie—and not only in Norway, his native land. His plays may be viewed historically as the culmination point of the bourgeois drama that has flourished fitfully, in France and Germany particularly, since the eighteenth century, when Diderot advocated and wrote plays about the middle classes, their "conditions" and problems. But they may also be seen as the fountainhead of much twentieth-century drama; in the West the plays of George Bernard Shaw and John Galsworthy, who discuss social problems, and of Maurice Maeterlinck and Anton Chekhov, who learned from the later "symbolist" Ibsen. Ibsen's drama of domestic and political crisis was also immensely popular in China and influenced a generation of modern playwrights.

Ibsen was born at Skien, in Norway, on March 20, 1828. His family had sunk into poverty and finally complete bankruptcy. In 1844, at the age of sixteen, he was sent to Grimstad, another small coastal town, as an apothecary's apprentice. There he lived in almost complete isolation and cut himself off from his family, except for his sister Hedvig. In 1850 he managed to get to Oslo (then Christiania) and to enroll at the university. But he never passed his examinations and in the following year left for Bergen, where he had acquired the position of playwright and assistant stage manager at the newly founded Norwegian Theater. Ibsen supplied the small theater with several historical and romantic plays. In 1857 he was appointed artistic director at the Mollergate Theater in Christiania, and a year later he married Susannah Thoresen. *Love's Comedy* (1862) was his first major success on the stage. Ibsen was then deeply affected by Scandinavianism, the movement for solidarity of the northern nations, and when in 1864 Norway refused to do anything to support Denmark in its war with Prussia and Austria over Schleswig-Holstein, he was so disgusted with his country that he left it for what he thought would be permanent exile. He lived in Rome, in Dresden, in Munich, and in smaller summer resorts, and during this time wrote all his later plays.

After a long period of incubation and experimentation with romantic and historical themes, Ibsen wrote a series of "problem" plays, beginning with *The Pillars of Society* (1877), which in their time created a furor by their fearless criticism of the nineteenth-century social scene: the subjection of women, hypocrisy, hereditary disease, seamy politics, and corrupt journalism. He wrote these plays using naturalistic modes of presentation: ordinary colloquial speech, a simple setting in a drawing room or study, a natural way of introducing or dismissing characters. Ibsen had learned from the "well-made" Parisian play (typified by those of Eugène Scribe) how to confine his action to one climactic situation and how gradually to uncover the past by retrogressive exposition. But he went far beyond it in technical skill and intellectual honesty.

The success of Ibsen's problem plays was international. But we must not forget that he was a Norwegian, the first writer of his small nation (its population at that time was less than two million) to win a reputation outside of Norway. Ibsen more than anyone else widened the scope of world literature beyond the confines of the "great" modern nations, which had entered its community roughly in this order: Italy, Spain, France, England, Germany, Russia. Since the time of Ibsen, other small nations have begun to play their part in the concert of world literature. Paradoxically, however, Ibsen rejected his own land. He had dreamed of becoming a great national poet. Instead, the plays he wrote during his voluntary exile depicted Norwegian society as consisting largely of a stuffy, provincial middle class, redeemed by a few upright, even fiery, individuals of initiative and courage. Only in 1891, when he was sixty-three, did Ibsen return to Christiania for good. He was then famous and widely honored, but lived a very retired life. In 1900 he suffered a stroke that made him a complete invalid for the last years of his life. He died on May 23, 1906.

Ibsen could hardly have survived his time if he had been merely a painter of society, a dialectician of social issues, and a magnificent technician of the theater. True, many of his discussions are now dated. We smile at some of what happens in *A Doll's House* (1879) and *Ghosts* (1881). His stagecraft is not unusual. But Ibsen stays with us because he has more to offer—because he was an artist who managed to create, at his best, works of poetry that, under their mask of sardonic humor, express his dream of humanity reborn by intelligence and self-sacrifice.

Hedda Gabler (1890) surprised and puzzled the large audience all over Europe that Ibsen had won in the 1880s. The play shows nothing of Ibsen's reforming zeal: no general theme emerges that could be used in spreading progressive ideas such as the emancipation of women dramatized in *A Doll's House* (1879), nor is the play an example of Ibsen's peculiar technique of retrospective revelation exhibited in *Rosmersholm* (1886). At first glance it seems mainly a study of a complex, exceptional, and even unique woman. Henry James, reviewing the first English performance, saw it as the picture of "a state of nerves as well as of soul, a state of temper, of health, of chagrin, of despair." Undoubtedly, Hedda is the central figure of the play, but she is no conventional heroine. She behaves atrociously to everyone with whom she comes in contact, and her moral sense is thoroughly defective: she is perverse, egotistical, sadistic, callous, even evil and demonic, truly a *femme fatale*. Still, this impression, while not mistaken, ignores another side of her personality and her situation. The play is, after all, a tragedy (though there are comic touches), and we are to feel pity and terror. Hedda is not simply evil and perverse. We must imagine her as distinguished, well bred, proud, beautiful, and even grand in her defiance of her surroundings and in the final gesture of her suicide. Not for nothing have great actresses excelled in this role. We must pity her as a tortured, tormented creature caught in a web of circumstance, as a victim, in spite of her desperate struggles to dominate and control the fate of those around her.

We are carefully prepared to understand her heritage. She is General Gabler's daughter. Ibsen tells us himself (in a letter to Count Moritz Prozor, dated December 4, 1890) that "I intended to indicate thereby that as a personality she is to be regarded rather as her father's daughter than as her husband's wife." She has inherited an aristocratic view of life. Her father's portrait hangs in her apartment. His pistols tell of the code of honor and the ready escape they offer in a self-inflicted death. Hedda lives in Ibsen's Norway, a stuffy, provincial, middle-class society, and is acutely, even morbidly afraid of scandal. She has, to her own regret, rejected the advances of Eilert, theatrically threatening him with her father's pistol. She envies Thea for the boldness with which she deserted her husband to follow Eilert. She admires Eilert for his escapades, which she romanticizes with the recurrent metaphor of his returning with "vine-leaves in his hair." But she cannot break out of the narrow confines of her society. She is not an emancipated woman.

When she is almost thirty, in reduced circumstances, she accepts a suitable husband, George Tesman. The marriage of convenience turns out to be a ghastly error for which she cannot forgive herself: Tesman is an amiable bore absorbed in his research into the "domestic industries of Brabant in the Middle Ages." His expectations of a professorship in his home town turn out to be uncertain. He has gone into debt, even to his guileless old aunt, in renting an expensive house, and, supreme humiliation for her, Hedda is pregnant by him. The dream of luxury, of becoming a hostess, of keeping thoroughbred horses, is shattered the very first day after their return from the prolonged honeymoon, which for Tesman was also a trip to rummage around in archives. Hedda is deeply stirred by the return of Eilert, her first suitor. She seems vaguely to think of a new relationship, at least, by spoiling his friendship with Thea. She plays with the attentions of Judge Brack. But everything quickly comes to nought: she is trapped in her marriage, unable and unwilling to become unfaithful to her husband; she is deeply disappointed by Eilert's ugly death, saying, "Oh, why does everything I touch become mean and ludicrous? It's like a curse!" She fears the scandal that will follow when her role in Eilert's suicide is discovered and she is called before the police; she can avoid it only by coming under the power of Judge Brack, who is prepared to blackmail her with his knowledge of the circumstances. Her plot to destroy Thea and Eilert's brainchild is frustrated by Thea's having preserved notes and drafts, which Thea eagerly starts to reconstruct with the help of Tesman. Still, while Hedda is in a terrible impasse, her suicide remains a shock, an abrupt, even absurd deed, eliciting the final line from the commonsensical Judge Brack: "But, good God! People don't do such things!" But we must assume that Hedda had pondered suicide long before: the pistol she gave to Eilert implies an unspoken suicide pact. He bungled it; she does it the right way, dying in beauty, shot in the temple and not in the abdomen.

The play is not, however, simply a character study, though Hedda is an extraordinarily complex, contradictory, subtle woman whose portrait, at least on the stage, could not be easily paralleled before Ibsen. It is also an extremely effective, swiftly moving play of action, deftly plotted in its clashes and climaxes. At the end of Act I Hedda seems to have won. The Tesmans, husband and aunt, are put in their place. Thea is lured into making confidences. The scene in Act II in which Hedda appeals to Eilert's pride in his independence and induces him to join in Judge Brack's party is a superb display of Hedda's power and skill. Act II ends with Eilert going off and the two women left alone in their tense though suppressed antagonism. Act III ends with Hedda alone, burning the precious manuscript about the "forces that will shape our civilization and the direction in which that civilization may develop," an obvious contrast to Tesman's research into an irrelevant past. (Ibsen himself always believed in progress, in a utopia he called "the Third Realm.")

The action is compressed into about thirty-six hours and located in a house where only the moving of furniture (the piano into the back room) or the change of light or costumes indicates the passing of time. Tesman is something of a fool. He is totally unaware of Hedda's inner turmoil, he obtusely misunderstands allusions to her pregnancy, he comically encourages the advances of Judge Brack, he complacently settles down to the task of assembling the fragments of Eilert's manuscript, recognizing that "putting other people's papers into order is rather my specialty." Though he seems amiably domestic in his love for his aunts, proud of having won Hedda, ambitious to provide an elegant home for her, his behavior is by no means above reproach. He envies and fears Eilert, gloats over his bad reputation, surreptitiously brings home the lost manuscript, conceals its recovery from Thea; when Hedda tells of its being burned, he is at first shocked, reacting comically with the legal phrase about "appropriating lost property," but is then easily persuaded to accept it when Hedda tells him that she did it for his sake and is completely won over when she reveals her pregnancy.

After Eilert's death he feels, however, some guilt and tries to make up by helping in the reconstruction of the manuscript, now that his rival no longer threatens his career. Tesman is given strong speech mannerisms: the frequent use of "what?"—which Hedda, commenting at the end on the progress of the work on the manuscript, imitates sarcastically—and the use of "fancy that." His last inappropriate words, "She's shot herself! Shot herself in the head! Fancy that!" lend a grotesque touch to the tragic end. Aunt Juliana belongs with him: she is a fussy, kindly person, proud of her nephew, awed by his new wife, eager to help with the expected baby, but also easily consoled after the death of her sister: "There's always some poor invalid who needs care and attention."

The other pair, Eilert Loevborg and Thea Elvsted, are sharply contrasted. Thea had the courage to leave her husband; she is devoted to Eilert and seems to have cured him of his addiction to drink but fears that he cannot resist a new temptation. Eilert tells Hedda unkindly that Thea is "silly," and there is some truth to that, inasmuch as she is so easily taken in by Hedda. Her quick settling down to work on the manuscript after Eilert's death suggests some obtuseness, though we must, presumably, excuse it as a theatrical foreshortening.

Judge Brack is a "man of the world," a sensualist who hardly conceals his desire to make Hedda his mistress, by blackmail if necessary, and is dismayed when she escapes his clutches: in his facile philosophy "people usually learn to accept the inevitable."

Eilert, we must assume, is some kind of genius. His book, we have to take on trust, is an important work. We are told that he had squandered an inheritance, had engaged in orgies, and had regaled Hedda with tales of his exploits before she chased him with her pistol. When he comes back to town, ostensibly reformed, dressed conventionally, he immediately starts courting Hedda again. Stung by her contempt for his abstinence, he rushes off to Brack's party, which degenerates into a disgraceful brawl in a brothel. His relapse and the loss of the manuscript destroy his self-esteem and hope for any future. He accepts Hedda's pistol but dies an ignominious, ugly death. We see Eilert mainly reflected in Hedda's imagination as a figure of pagan freedom who, she thinks, has done something noble, beautiful, and courageous in "rising from the feast of life so early." She dies in beauty as she wanted Eilert to die.

This aesthetic suicide must seem to us a supremely futile gesture of revolt. Ibsen always admired the great rebels, the fighters for freedom, but *Hedda Gabler* will appear almost a parodic version of his persistent theme: the individual against society, defying it and escaping it in death.

Yvonne Shafter, *Henrik Ibsen: Life, Work, and Criticism* (1985), is a general work; see also Robert Ferguson, *Henrik Ibsen: A New Biography* (1996). J. W. McFarlane, ed., *Discussions of Henrik Ibsen* (1962), contains Henry James's "On the Occasion of 'Hedda Gabler.'" Rolf Fjelde, ed., *Ibsen: A Collection of Critical Essays* (1965), has a good essay on *Hedda Gabler*; James McFarlane, ed., *The Cambridge Companion to Ibsen* (1994), and Harold Bloom, ed., *Henrik Ibsen* (1999), assemble essays on a variety of topics. *Ibsen's Heroines* (1985), by Ibsen's friend Lou Andreas-Salomé, has an interesting chapter on Hedda Gabler as an empty soul reaching for greatness. Joan Templeton, *Ibsen's Women* (1997), is an excellent study that includes a chapter on *Hedda Gabler* and a discussion of Ibsen's modernism. Frederick J. Marker and Lise-Lone Marker, *Ibsen's Lively Art: A Performance Study of the Major Plays* (1989), use descriptions of the various performances of *Hedda Gabler* to examine differing interpretations of the main characters.

PRONOUNCING GLOSSARY

The following list uses common English syllables and stress accents to provide rough equivalents of selected words whose pronunciation may be unfamiliar to the general reader.

Eilert Loevborg: *ai'-lert leuhv'-borg*	Rosmersholm: *ross'-merss-holm*
fjord: *fyoord*	Thea Elvsted: *tay'-ah aelf'-sted*

Hedda Gabler[1]

CHARACTERS

GEORGE TESMAN, *research graduate in*
    cultural history
HEDDA, *his wife*
MISS JULIANA TESMAN, *his aunt*

MRS. ELVSTED
JUDGE BRACK
EILERT LOEVBORG
BERTHA, *a maid*

The action takes place in TESMAN'S *villa in the fashionable quarter of town.*

Act I

SCENE—A *large drawing room, handsomely and tastefully furnished; decorated in dark colors. In the rear wall is a broad open doorway, with curtains drawn back to either side. It leads to a smaller room, decorated in the same style as the drawing room. In the right-hand wall of the drawing room, a folding door leads out to the hall. The opposite wall, on the left, contains french windows, also with curtains drawn back on either side. Through the glass we can see part of a verandah, and trees in autumn colors. Downstage stands an oval table, covered by a cloth and surrounded by chairs. Downstage right, against the wall, is a broad stove tiled with dark porcelain; in front of it stand a high-backed armchair, a cushioned footrest, and two footstools. Upstage right, in an alcove, is a corner sofa, with a small, round table. Downstage left, a little away from the wall, is another sofa. Upstage of the french windows, a piano. On either side of the open doorway in the rear wall stand what-nots holding ornaments of terra cotta and majolica. Against the rear wall of the smaller room can be seen a sofa, a table, and a couple of chairs. Above this sofa hangs the portrait of a handsome old man in general's uniform. Above the table a lamp hangs from the ceiling, with a shade of opalescent, milky glass. All round the drawing room bunches of flowers stand in vases and glasses. More bunches lie on the tables. The floors of both rooms are covered with thick carpets. Morning light. The sun shines in through the french windows.*

    MISS JULIANA TESMAN, *wearing a hat and carrying a parasol, enters from the hall, followed by* BERTHA, *who is carrying a bunch of flowers wrapped in paper.* MISS TESMAN *is about sixty-five, of pleasant and kindly appearance. She is neatly but simply dressed in grey outdoor clothes.* BERTHA, *the maid, is rather simple and rustic-looking. She is getting on in years.*

MISS TESMAN [*Stops just inside the door, listens, and says in a hushed voice.*]   No, bless my soul! They're not up yet.
BERTHA [*Also in hushed tones.*]   What did I tell you, miss? The boat didn't get in till midnight. And when they did turn up—Jesus, miss, you should have seen all the things Madam made me unpack before she'd go to bed!
MISS TESMAN   Ah, well. Let them have a good lie in. But let's have some nice fresh air waiting for them when they do come down. [*Goes to the french windows and throws them wide open.*]

1. Translated by Michael Meyer.

BERTHA [*Bewildered at the table, the bunch of flowers in her hand.*] I'm blessed if there's a square inch left to put anything. I'll have to let it lie here, miss. [*Puts it on the piano.*]

MISS TESMAN Well, Bertha dear, so now you have a new mistress. Heaven knows it nearly broke my heart to have to part with you.

BERTHA [*Snivels.*] What about me, Miss Juju? How do you suppose I felt? After all the happy years I've spent with you and Miss Rena?

MISS TESMAN We must accept it bravely, Bertha. It was the only way. George needs you to take care of him. He could never manage without you. You've looked after him ever since he was a tiny boy.

BERTHA Oh, but Miss Juju, I can't help thinking about Miss Rena, lying there all helpless, poor dear. And that new girl! She'll never learn the proper way to handle an invalid.

MISS TESMAN Oh, I'll manage to train her. I'll do most of the work myself, you know. You needn't worry about my poor sister, Bertha dear.

BERTHA But Miss Juju, there's another thing. I'm frightened Madam may not find me suitable.

MISS TESMAN Oh, nonsense, Bertha. There may be one or two little things to begin with——

BERTHA She's a real lady. Wants everything just so.

MISS TESMAN But of course she does! General Gabler's daughter! Think of what she was accustomed to when the General was alive. You remember how we used to see her out riding with her father? In that long black skirt? With the feather in her hat?

BERTHA Oh, yes, miss. As if I could forget! But, Lord! I never dreamed I'd live to see a match between her and Master Georgie.

MISS TESMAN Neither did I. By the way, Bertha, from now on you must stop calling him Master Georgie. You must say: Dr. Tesman.

BERTHA Yes, Madam said something about that too. Last night—the moment they'd set foot inside the door. Is it true, then, miss?

MISS TESMAN Indeed it is. Just imagine, Bertha, some foreigners have made him a doctor. It happened while they were away. I had no idea till he told me when they got off the boat.

BERTHA Well, I suppose there's no limit to what he won't become. He's that clever. I never thought he'd go in for hospital work, though.

MISS TESMAN No, he's not that kind of doctor. [*Nods impressively.*] In any case, you may soon have to address him by an even grander title.

BERTHA You don't say! What might that be, miss?

MISS TESMAN [*Smiles.*] Ah! If you only knew! [*Moved.*] Dear God, if only poor dear Joachim could rise out of his grave and see what his little son has grown into! [*Looks round.*] But Bertha, why have you done this? Taken the chintz covers off all the furniture!

BERTHA Madam said I was to. Can't stand chintz covers on chairs, she said.

MISS TESMAN But surely they're not going to use this room as a parlor?

BERTHA So I gathered, miss. From what Madam said. He didn't say anything. The Doctor.

[GEORGE TESMAN *comes into the rear room, from the right, humming, with an open, empty travelling bag in his hand. He is about thirty-three, of medium height and youthful appearance, rather plump, with an open, round, contented face, and fair hair and beard. He wears spectacles, and is dressed in comfortable, indoor clothes.*]

MISS TESMAN   Good morning! Good morning, George!

TESMAN [*In open doorway.*]   Auntie Juju! Dear Auntie Juju! [*Comes forward and shakes her hand.*] You've come all the way out here! And so early! What?

MISS TESMAN   Well, I had to make sure you'd settled in comfortably.

TESMAN   But you can't have had a proper night's sleep.

MISS TESMAN   Oh, never mind that.

TESMAN   We were so sorry we couldn't give you a lift. But you saw how it was—Hedda had so much luggage—and she insisted on having it all with her.

MISS TESMAN   Yes, I've never seen so much luggage.

BERTHA [*To* TESMAN.]   Shall I go and ask Madam if there's anything I can lend her a hand with?

TESMAN   Er—thank you, Bertha; no, you needn't bother. She says if she wants you for anything she'll ring.

BERTHA [*Over to right.*]   Oh. Very good.

TESMAN   Oh, Bertha—take this bag, will you?

BERTHA [*Takes it.*]   I'll put it in the attic. [*Goes out into the hall.*]

TESMAN   Just fancy, Auntie Juju, I filled that whole bag with notes for my book. You know, it's really incredible what I've managed to find rooting through those archives. By Jove! Wonderful old things no one even knew existed——

MISS TESMAN   I'm sure you didn't waste a single moment of your honeymoon, George dear.

TESMAN   No, I think I can truthfully claim that. But, Auntie Juju, do take your hat off. Here. Let me untie it for you. What?

MISS TESMAN [*As he does so.*]   Oh dear, oh dear! It's just as if you were still living at home with us.

TESMAN [*Turns the hat in his hand and looks at it.*]   I say! What a splendid new hat!

MISS TESMAN   I bought it for Hedda's sake.

TESMAN   For Hedda's sake? What?

MISS TESMAN   So that Hedda needn't be ashamed of me, in case we ever go for a walk together.

TESMAN [*Pats her cheek.*]   You still think of everything, don't you, Auntie Juju? [*Puts the hat down on a chair by the table.*] Come on, let's sit down here on the sofa. And have a little chat while we wait for Hedda.

[*They sit. She puts her parasol in the corner of the sofa.*]

MISS TESMAN [*Clasps both his hands and looks at him.*]   Oh, George, it's so wonderful to have you back, and be able to see you with my own eyes again! Poor dear Joachim's own son!

TESMAN   What about me! It's wonderful for me to see you again, Auntie Juju. You've been a mother to me. And a father, too.

MISS TESMAN   You'll always keep a soft spot in your heart for your old aunties, won't you, George dear?

TESMAN   I suppose Auntie Rena's no better? What?

MISS TESMAN   Alas, no. I'm afraid she'll never get better, poor dear. She's lying there just as she has for all these years. Please God I may be allowed to keep her for a little longer. If I lost her I don't know what I'd do. Especially now I haven't you to look after.

TESMAN [*Pats her on the back.*]   There, there, there!

MISS TESMAN [*With a sudden change of mood.*]   Oh, but George, fancy you being a married man! And to think it's you who've won Hedda Gabler! The beautiful Hedda Gabler! Fancy! She was always so surrounded by admirers.

TESMAN [*Hums a little and smiles contentedly.*]   Yes, I suppose there are quite a few people in this town who wouldn't mind being in my shoes. What?

MISS TESMAN   And what a honeymoon! Five months! Nearly six.

TESMAN   Well, I've done a lot of work, you know. All those archives to go through. And I've had to read lots of books.

MISS TESMAN   Yes, dear, of course. [*Lowers her voice confidentially.*] But tell me, George—haven't you any—any extra little piece of news to give me?

TESMAN   You mean, arising out of the honeymoon?

MISS TESMAN   Yes.

TESMAN   No, I don't think there's anything I didn't tell you in my letters. My doctorate, of course—but I told you about that last night, didn't I?

MISS TESMAN   Yes, yes, I didn't mean that kind of thing. I was just wondering—are you—are you expecting——?

TESMAN   Expecting what?

MISS TESMAN   Oh, come on, George, I'm your old aunt!

TESMAN   Well actually—yes, I am expecting something.

MISS TESMAN   I knew it!

TESMAN   You'll be happy to hear that before very long I expect to become a professor.

MISS TESMAN   Professor?

TESMAN   I think I may say that the matter has been decided. But, Auntie Juju, you know about this.

MISS TESMAN [*Gives a little laugh.*]   Yes, of course. I'd forgotten. [*Changes her tone.*] But we were talking about your honeymoon. It must have cost a dreadful amount of money, George?

TESMAN   Oh well, you know, that big research grant I got helped a good deal.

MISS TESMAN   But how on earth did you manage to make it do for two?

TESMAN   Well, to tell the truth it was a bit tricky. What?

MISS TESMAN   Especially when one's traveling with a lady. A little bird tells me that makes things very much more expensive.

TESMAN   Well, yes, of course it does make things a little more expensive. But Hedda has to do things in style, Auntie Juju. I mean, she has to. Anything less grand wouldn't have suited her.

MISS TESMAN   No, no, I suppose not. A honeymoon abroad seems to be the vogue nowadays. But tell me, have you had time to look round the house?

TESMAN   You bet. I've been up since the crack of dawn.

MISS TESMAN   Well, what do you think of it?

TESMAN   Splendid. Absolutely splendid. I'm only wondering what we're going to do with those two empty rooms between that little one and Hedda's bedroom.

MISS TESMAN [*Laughs slyly.*] Ah, George dear, I'm sure you'll manage to find some use for them—in time.

TESMAN Yes, of course, Auntie Juju, how stupid of me. You're thinking of my books. What?

MISS TESMAN Yes, yes, dear boy. I was thinking of your books.

TESMAN You know, I'm so happy for Hedda's sake that we've managed to get this house. Before we became engaged she often used to say this was the only house in town she felt she could really bear to live in. It used to belong to Mrs. Falk—you know, the Prime Minister's widow.

MISS TESMAN Fancy that! And what a stroke of luck it happened to come into the market. Just as you'd left on your honeymoon.

TESMAN Yes, Auntie Juju, we've certainly had all the luck with us. What?

MISS TESMAN But, George dear, the expense! It's going to make a dreadful hole in your pocket, all this.

TESMAN [*A little downcast.*] Yes, I—I suppose it will, won't it?

MISS TESMAN Oh, George, really!

TESMAN How much do you think it'll cost? Roughly, I mean? What?

MISS TESMAN I can't possibly say till I see the bills.

TESMAN Well, luckily Judge Brack's managed to get it on very favorable terms. He wrote and told Hedda so.

MISS TESMAN Don't you worry, George dear. Anyway I've stood security for all the furniture and carpets.

TESMAN Security? But dear, sweet Auntie Juju, how could you possibly stand security?

MISS TESMAN I've arranged a mortgage on our annuity.

TESMAN [*Jumps up.*] What? On your annuity? And—Auntie Rena's?

MISS TESMAN Yes. Well, I couldn't think of any other way.

TESMAN [*Stands in front of her.*] Auntie Juju, have you gone completely out of your mind? That annuity's all you and Auntie Rena have.

MISS TESMAN All right, there's no need to get so excited about it. It's a pure formality, you know. Judge Brack told me so. He was so kind as to arrange it all for me. A pure formality; those were his very words.

TESMAN I dare say. All the same——

MISS TESMAN Anyway, you'll have a salary of your own now. And, good heavens, even if we did have to fork out a little—tighten our belts for a week or two—why, we'd be happy to do so for your sake.

TESMAN Oh, Auntie Juju! Will you never stop sacrificing yourself for me?

MISS TESMAN [*Gets up and puts her hands on his shoulders.*] What else have I to live for but to smooth your road a little, my dear boy? You've never had any mother or father to turn to. And now at last we've achieved our goal. I won't deny we've had our little difficulties now and then. But now, thank the good Lord, George dear, all your worries are past.

TESMAN Yes, it's wonderful really how everything's gone just right for me.

MISS TESMAN Yes! And the enemies who tried to bar your way have been struck down. They have been made to bite the dust. The man who was your most dangerous rival has had the mightiest fall. And now he's lying there in the pit he dug for himself, poor misguided creature.

TESMAN   Have you heard any news of Eilert? Since I went away?

MISS TESMAN   Only that he's said to have published a new book.

TESMAN   What! Eilert Loevborg? You mean—just recently? What?

MISS TESMAN   So they say. I don't imagine it can be of any value, do you? When your new book comes out, that'll be another story. What's it going to be about?

TESMAN   The domestic industries of Brabant[2] in the Middle Ages.

MISS TESMAN   Oh, George! The things you know about!

TESMAN   Mind you, it may be some time before I actually get down to writing it. I've made these very extensive notes, and I've got to file and index them first.

MISS TESMAN   Ah, yes! Making notes; filing and indexing; you've always been wonderful at that. Poor dear Joachim was just the same.

TESMAN   I'm looking forward so much to getting down to that. Especially now I've a home of my own to work in.

MISS TESMAN   And above all, now that you have the girl you set your heart on, George dear.

TESMAN [*Embraces her.*]   Oh, yes, Auntie Juju, yes! Hedda's the loveliest thing of all! [*Looks towards the doorway.*] I think I hear her coming. What?

> [HEDDA *enters the rear room from the left, and comes into the drawing room. She is a woman of twenty-nine. Distinguished, aristocratic face and figure. Her complexion is pale and opalescent. Her eyes are steel-grey, with an expression of cold, calm serenity. Her hair is of a handsome auburn color, but is not especially abundant. She is dressed in an elegant, somewhat loose-fitting morning gown.*]

MISS TESMAN [*Goes to greet her.*]   Good morning, Hedda dear! Good morning!

HEDDA [*Holds out her hand.*]   Good morning, dear Miss Tesman. What an early hour to call. So kind of you.

MISS TESMAN [*Seems somewhat embarrassed.*]   And has the young bride slept well in her new home?

HEDDA   Oh—thank you, yes. Passably well.

TESMAN [*Laughs.*]   Passably. I say, Hedda, that's good! When I jumped out of bed, you were sleeping like a top.

HEDDA   Yes. Fortunately. One has to accustom oneself to anything new, Miss Tesman. It takes time. [*Looks left.*] Oh, that maid's left the french windows open. This room's flooded with sun.

MISS TESMAN [*Goes towards the windows.*]   Oh—let me close them.

HEDDA   No, no, don't do that. Tesman dear, draw the curtains. This light's blinding me.

TESMAN [*At the windows.*]   Yes, yes, dear. There, Hedda, now you've got shade and fresh air.

HEDDA   This room needs fresh air. All these flowers—But my dear Miss Tesman, won't you take a seat?

MISS TESMAN   No, really not, thank you. I just wanted to make sure you have everything you need. I must see about getting back home. My poor dear sister will be waiting for me.

---

2. In the Middle Ages, a duchy located in parts of what are now Belgium and the Netherlands.

TESMAN   Be sure to give her my love, won't you? Tell her I'll run over and see her later today.

MISS TESMAN   Oh yes, I'll tell her that. Oh, George—— [*Fumbles in the pocket of her skirt.*] I almost forgot. I've brought something for you.

TESMAN   What's that, Auntie Juju? What?

MISS TESMAN [*Pulls out a flat package wrapped in newspaper and gives it to him.*]   Open and see, dear boy.

TESMAN [*Opens the package.*]   Good heavens! Auntie Juju, you've kept them! Hedda, this is really very touching. What?

HEDDA [*By the what-nots, on the right.*]   What is it, Tesman?

TESMAN   My old shoes! My slippers, Hedda!

HEDDA   Oh, them. I remember you kept talking about them on our honeymoon.

TESMAN   Yes, I missed them dreadfully. [*Goes over to her.*] Here, Hedda, take a look.

HEDDA [*Goes away towards the stove.*]   Thanks, I won't bother.

TESMAN [*Follows her.*]   Fancy, Hedda, Auntie Rena's embroidered them for me. Despite her being so ill. Oh, you can't imagine what memories they have for me.

HEDDA [*By the table.*]   Not for me.

MISS TESMAN   No, Hedda's right there, George.

TESMAN   Yes, but I thought since she's one of the family now——

HEDDA [*Interrupts.*]   Tesman, we really can't go on keeping this maid.

MISS TESMAN   Not keep Bertha?

TESMAN   What makes you say that, dear? What?

HEDDA [*Points.*]   Look at that! She's left her old hat lying on the chair.

TESMAN [*Appalled, drops his slippers on the floor.*]   But, Hedda——!

HEDDA   Suppose someone came in and saw it?

TESMAN   But Hedda—that's Auntie Juju's hat.

HEDDA   Oh?

MISS TESMAN [*Picks up the hat.*]   Indeed it's mine. And it doesn't happen to be old, Hedda dear.

HEDDA   I didn't look at it very closely, Miss Tesman.

MISS TESMAN [*Tying on the hat.*]   As a matter of fact, it's the first time I've worn it. As the good Lord is my witness.

TESMAN   It's very pretty, too. Really smart.

MISS TESMAN   Oh, I'm afraid it's nothing much really. [*Looks round.*] My parasol? Ah, here it is. [*Takes it.*] This is mine, too. [*Murmurs.*] Not Bertha's.

TESMAN   A new hat and a new parasol! I say, Hedda, fancy that!

HEDDA   Very pretty and charming.

TESMAN   Yes, isn't it? What? But Auntie Juju, take a good look at Hedda before you go. Isn't she pretty and charming?

MISS TESMAN   Dear boy, there's nothing new in that. Hedda's been a beauty ever since the day she was born. [*Nods and goes right.*]

TESMAN [*Follows her.*]   Yes, but have you noticed how strong and healthy she's looking? And how she's filled out since we went away?

MISS TESMAN [*Stops and turns.*]   Filled out?

HEDDA [*Walks across the room.*]   Oh, can't we forget it?

TESMAN   Yes, Auntie Juju—you can't see it so clearly with that dress on. But I've good reason to know——

HEDDA [*By the french windows, impatiently.*]   You haven't good reason to know anything.

TESMAN   It must have been the mountain air up there in the Tyrol—

HEDDA [*Curtly, interrupts him.*]   I'm exactly the same as when I went away.

TESMAN   You keep on saying so. But you're not. I'm right, aren't I, Auntie Juju?

MISS TESMAN [*Has folded her hands and is gazing at her.*]   She's beautiful—beautiful. Hedda is beautiful. [*Goes over to* HEDDA, *takes her head between her hands, draws it down and kisses her hair.*] God bless and keep you, Hedda Tesman. For George's sake.

HEDDA [*Frees herself politely.*]   Oh—let me go, please.

MISS TESMAN [*Quietly, emotionally.*]   I shall come see you both every day.

TESMAN   Yes, Auntie Juju, please do. What?

MISS TESMAN   Good-bye! Good-bye!

[*She goes out into the hall.* TESMAN *follows her. The door remains open.* TESMAN *is heard sending his love to* AUNT RENA *and thanking* MISS TESMAN *for his slippers. Meanwhile* HEDDA *walks up and down the room raising her arms and clenching her fists as though in desperation. Then she throws aside the curtains from the french windows and stands there, looking out. A few moments later,* TESMAN *returns and closes the door behind him.*]

TESMAN [*Picks up his slippers from the floor.*]   What are you looking at, Hedda?

HEDDA [*Calm and controlled again.*]   Only the leaves. They're so golden. And withered.

TESMAN [*Wraps up the slippers and lays them on the table.*]   Well, we're in September now.

HEDDA [*Restless again.*]   Yes. We're already into September.

TESMAN   Auntie Juju was behaving rather oddly, I thought, didn't you? Almost as though she was in church or something. I wonder what came over her. Any idea?

HEDDA   I hardly know her. Does she often act like that?

TESMAN   Not to the extent she did today.

HEDDA [*Goes away from the french windows.*]   Do you think she was hurt by what I said about the hat?

TESMAN   Oh, I don't think so. A little at first, perhaps——

HEDDA   But what a thing to do, throw her hat down in someone's drawing room. People don't do such things.

TESMAN   I'm sure Auntie Juju doesn't do it very often.

HEDDA   Oh well, I'll make it up with her.

TESMAN   Oh Hedda, would you?

HEDDA   When you see them this afternoon invite her to come out here this evening.

TESMAN   You bet I will! I say, there's another thing which would please her enormously.

HEDDA   Oh?

TESMAN   If you could bring yourself to call her Auntie Juju. For my sake, Hedda? What?

HEDDA   Oh no, really Tesman, you mustn't ask me to do that. I've told you so once before. I'll try to call her Aunt Juliana. That's as far as I'll go.

TESMAN [*After a moment.*]   I say, Hedda, is anything wrong? What?

HEDDA   I'm just looking at my old piano. It doesn't really go with all this.

TESMAN   As soon as I start getting my salary we'll see about changing it.

HEDDA   No, no, don't let's change it. I don't want to part with it. We can move it into that little room and get another one to put in here.

TESMAN [A little downcast.]   Yes, we—might do that.

HEDDA [Picks up the bunch of flowers from the piano.]   These flowers weren't here when we arrived last night.

TESMAN   I expect Auntie Juju brought them.

HEDDA   Here's a card. [Takes it out and reads.] "Will come back later today." Guess who it's from?

TESMAN   No idea. Who? What?

HEDDA   It says: "Mrs. Elvsted."

TESMAN   No, really? Mrs. Elvsted! She used to be Miss Rysing, didn't she?

HEDDA   Yes. She was the one with that irritating hair she was always showing off. I hear she used to be an old flame of yours.

TESMAN [Laughs.]   That didn't last long. Anyway, that was before I got to know you, Hedda. By Jove, fancy her being in town!

HEDDA [Thinks for a moment, then says suddenly.]   Tell me, Tesman, doesn't he live somewhere up in those parts? You know—Eilert Loevborg?

TESMAN   Yes, that's right. So he does.
     [BERTHA enters from the hall.]

BERTHA   She's here again, madam. The lady who came and left the flowers. [Points.] The ones you're holding.

HEDDA   Oh, is she? Well, show her in.
     [BERTHA opens the door for MRS. ELVSTED and goes out. MRS. ELVSTED is a delicately built woman with gentle, attractive features. Her eyes are light blue, large, and somewhat prominent, with a frightened, questioning expression. Her hair is extremely fair, almost flaxen, and is exceptionally wavy and abundant. She is two or three years younger than HEDDA. She is wearing a dark visiting dress, in good taste but not quite in the latest fashion.]

HEDDA [Goes cordially to greet her.]   Dear Mrs. Elvsted, good morning. How delightful to see you again after all this time.

MRS. ELVSTED [Nervously, trying to control herself.]   Yes, it's many years since we met.

TESMAN   And since we met. What?

HEDDA   Thank you for your lovely flowers.

MRS. ELVSTED   Oh, please—I wanted to come yesterday afternoon. But they told me you were away—

TESMAN   You've only just arrived in town, then? What?

MRS. ELVSTED   I got here yesterday, around midday. Oh, I became almost desperate when I heard you weren't here.

HEDDA   Desperate? Why?

TESMAN   My dear Mrs. Rysing—Elvsted—

HEDDA   There's nothing wrong, I hope?

MRS. ELVSTED   Yes, there is. And I don't know anyone else here whom I can turn to.

HEDDA [Puts the flowers down on the table.]   Come and sit with me on the sofa—

MRS. ELVSTED   Oh, I feel too restless to sit down.

HEDDA   You must. Come along, now.

[*She pulls* MRS. ELVSTED *down on to the sofa and sits beside her.*]

TESMAN   Well? Tell us, Mrs.—er——

HEDDA   Has something happened at home?

MRS. ELVSTED   Yes—that is, yes and no. Oh, I do hope you won't misunderstand me——

HEDDA   Then you'd better tell us the whole story, Mrs. Elvsted.

TESMAN   That's why you've come. What?

MRS. ELVSTED   Yes—yes, it is. Well, then—in case you don't already know—Eilert Loevborg is in town.

HEDDA   Loevborg here?

TESMAN   Eilert back in town? By Jove, Hedda, did you hear that?

HEDDA   Yes, of course I heard.

MRS. ELVSTED   He's been here a week. A whole week! In this city. Alone. With all those dreadful people——

HEDDA   But my dear Mrs. Elvsted, what concern is he of yours?

MRS. ELVSTED   [*Gives her a frightened look and says quickly.*]   He's been tutoring the children.

HEDDA   Your children?

MRS. ELVSTED   My husband's. I have none.

HEDDA   Oh, you mean your stepchildren.

MRS. ELVSTED   Yes.

TESMAN   [*Gropingly.*]   But was he sufficiently—I don't know how to put it—sufficiently regular in his habits to be suited to such a post? What?

MRS. ELVSTED   For the past two to three years he has been living irreproachably.

TESMAN   You don't say! By Jove, Hedda, hear that?

HEDDA   I hear.

MRS. ELVSTED   Quite irreproachably, I assure you. In every respect. All the same—in this big city—with money in his pockets—I'm so dreadfully frightened something may happen to him.

TESMAN   But why didn't he stay up there with you and your husband?

MRS. ELVSTED   Once his book had come out, he became restless.

TESMAN   Oh, yes—Auntie Juju said he's brought out a new book.

MRS. ELVSTED   Yes, a big new book about the history of civilization. A kind of general survey. It came out a fortnight ago. Everyone's been buying it and reading it—it's created a tremendous stir——

TESMAN   Has it really? It must be something he's dug up, then.

MRS. ELVSTED   You mean from the old days?

TESMAN   Yes.

MRS. ELVSTED   No, he's written it all since he came to live with us.

TESMAN   Well, that's splendid news, Hedda. Fancy that!

MRS. ELVSTED   Oh, yes! If only he can go on like this!

HEDDA   Have you met him since you came here?

MRS. ELVSTED   No, not yet, I had such dreadful difficulty finding his address. But this morning I managed to track him down at last.

HEDDA   [*Looks searchingly at her.*]   I must say I find it a little strange that your husband—hm——

MRS. ELVSTED   [*Starts nervously.*]   My husband! What do you mean?

HEDDA   That he should send you all the way here on an errand of this kind. I'm surprised he didn't come himself to keep an eye on his friend.

MRS. ELVSTED   Oh, no, no—my husband hasn't the time. Besides, I—er—wanted to do some shopping here.

HEDDA [*With a slight smile.*]   Ah. Well, that's different.

MRS. ELVSTED [*Gets up quickly, restlessly.*]   Please, Mr. Tesman, I beg you—be kind to Eilert Loevborg if he comes here. I'm sure he will. I mean, you used to be such good friends in the old days. And you're both studying the same subject, as far as I can understand. You're in the same field, aren't you?

TESMAN   Well, we used to be, anyway.

MRS. ELVSTED   Yes—so I beg you earnestly, do please, please, keep an eye on him. Oh, Mr. Tesman, do promise me you will.

TESMAN   I shall be only too happy to do so, Mrs. Rysing.

HEDDA   Elvsted.

TESMAN   I'll do everything for Eilert that lies in my power. You can rely on that.

MRS. ELVSTED   Oh, how good and kind you are! [*Presses his hands.*] Thank you, thank you, thank you. [*Frightened.*] My husband's so fond of him, you see.

HEDDA [*Gets up.*]   You'd better send him a note, Tesman. He may not come to you of his own accord.

TESMAN   Yes, that'd probably be the best plan, Hedda. What?

HEDDA   The sooner the better. Why not do it now?

MRS. ELVSTED [*Pleadingly.*]   Oh yes, if only you would!

TESMAN   I'll do it this very moment. Do you have his address, Mrs.—er—Elvsted?

MRS. ELVSTED   Yes. [*Takes a small piece of paper from her pocket and gives it to him.*]

TESMAN   Good, good. Right, well, I'll go inside and—— [*Looks round.*] Where are my slippers? Oh yes, here. [*Picks up the package and is about to go.*]

HEDDA   Try to sound friendly. Make it a nice long letter.

TESMAN   Right, I will.

MRS. ELVSTED   Please don't say anything about my having seen you.

TESMAN   Good heavens no, of course not. What? [*Goes out through the rear room to the right.*]

HEDDA [*Goes over to* MRS. ELVSTED, *smiles, and says softly.*]   Well! Now we've killed two birds with one stone.

MRS. ELVSTED   What do you mean?

HEDDA   Didn't you realize I wanted to get him out of the room?

MRS. ELVSTED   So that he could write the letter?

HEDDA   And so that I could talk to you alone.

MRS. ELVSTED [*Confused.*]   About this?

HEDDA   Yes, about this.

MRS. ELVSTED [*In alarm.*]   But there's nothing more to tell, Mrs. Tesman. Really there isn't.

HEDDA   Oh, yes there is. There's a lot more. I can see that. Come along, let's sit down and have a little chat.

[*She pushes* MRS. ELVSTED *down into the armchair by the stove and seats herself on one of the footstools.*]

MRS. ELVSTED [*Looks anxiously at her watch.*] Really, Mrs. Tesman, I think I ought to be going now.

HEDDA There's no hurry. Well? How are things at home?

MRS. ELVSTED I'd rather not speak about that.

HEDDA But my dear, you can tell me. Good heavens, we were at school together.

MRS. ELVSTED Yes, but you were a year senior to me. Oh, I used to be terribly frightened of you in those days.

HEDDA Frightened of me?

MRS. ELVSTED Yes, terribly frightened. Whenever you met me on the staircase you used to pull my hair.

HEDDA No, did I?

MRS. ELVSTED Yes. And once you said you'd burn it all off.

HEDDA Oh, that was only in fun.

MRS. ELVSTED Yes, but I was so silly in those days. And then afterwards—I mean, we've drifted so far apart. Our backgrounds were so different.

HEDDA Well, now we must try to drift together again. Now listen. When we were at school we used to call each other by our Christian names——

MRS. ELVSTED No, I'm sure you're mistaken.

HEDDA I'm sure I'm not. I remember it quite clearly. Let's tell each other our secrets, as we used to in the old days. [*Moves closer on her footstool.*] There, now. [*Kisses her on the cheek.*] You must call me Hedda.

MRS. ELVSTED [*Squeezes her hands and pats them.*] Oh, you're so kind. I'm not used to people being so nice to me.

HEDDA Now, now, now. And I shall call you Tora, the way I used to.

MRS. ELVSTED My name is Thea.

HEDDA Yes, of course. Of course. I meant Thea. [*Looks at her sympathetically.*] So you're not used to kindness, Thea? In your own home?

MRS. ELVSTED Oh, if only I had a home! But I haven't. I've never had one.

HEDDA [*Looks at her for a moment.*] I thought that was it.

MRS. ELVSTED [*Stares blankly and helplessly.*] Yes—yes—yes.

HEDDA I can't remember exactly now, but didn't you first go to Mr. Elvsted as a housekeeper?

MRS. ELVSTED Governess, actually. But his wife—at the time, I mean—she was an invalid, and had to spend most of her time in bed. So I had to look after the house too.

HEDDA But in the end, you became mistress of the house.

MRS. ELVSTED [*Sadly.*] Yes, I did.

HEDDA Let me see. Roughly how long ago was that?

MRS. ELVSTED When I got married, you mean?

HEDDA Yes.

MRS. ELVSTED About five years.

HEDDA Yes; it must be about that.

MRS. ELVSTED Oh, those five years! Especially that last two or three. Oh, Mrs. Tesman, if you only knew——

HEDDA [*Slaps her hand gently.*] Mrs. Tesman? Oh, Thea!

MRS. ELVSTED I'm sorry, I'll try to remember. Yes—if you had any idea—

HEDDA [*Casually.*] Eilert Loevborg's been up there too, for about three years, hasn't he?

MRS. ELVSTED [*Looks at her uncertainly.*] Eilert Loevborg? Yes, he has.

HEDDA Did you know him before? When you were here?

MRS. ELVSTED   No, not really. That is—I knew him by name, of course.

HEDDA   But up there, he used to visit you?

MRS. ELVSTED   Yes, he used to come and see us every day. To give the children lessons. I found I couldn't do that as well as manage the house.

HEDDA   I'm sure you couldn't. And your husband——? I suppose being a magistrate he has to be away from home a good deal?

MRS. ELVSTED   Yes. You see, Mrs.——you see, Hedda, he has to cover the whole district.

HEDDA [Leans against the arm of MRS. ELVSTED's chair.]   Poor, pretty little Thea! Now you must tell me the whole story. From beginning to end.

MRS. ELVSTED   Well—what do you want to know?

HEDDA   What kind of a man is your husband, Thea? I mean, as a person. Is he kind to you?

MRS. ELVSTED [Evasively.]   I'm sure he does his best to be.

HEDDA   I only wonder if he isn't too old for you. There's more than twenty years between you, isn't there?

MRS. ELVSTED [Irritably.]   Yes, there's that too. Oh, there are so many things. We're different in every way. We've nothing in common. Nothing whatever.

HEDDA   But he loves you, surely? In his own way?

MRS. ELVSTED   Oh, I don't know. I think he just finds me useful. And then I don't cost much to keep. I'm cheap.

HEDDA   Now you're being stupid.

MRS. ELVSTED [Shakes her head.]   It can't be any different. With him. He doesn't love anyone except himself. And perhaps the children—a little.

HEDDA   He must be fond of Eilert Loevborg, Thea.

MRS. ELVSTED [Looks at her.]   Eilert Loevborg? What makes you think that?

HEDDA   Well, if he sends you all the way down here to look for him—— [Smiles almost imperceptibly.] Besides, you said so yourself to Tesman.

MRS. ELVSTED [With a nervous twitch.]   Did I? Oh yes, I suppose I did. [Impulsively, but keeping her voice low.] Well, I might as well tell you the whole story. It's bound to come out sooner or later.

HEDDA   But my dear Thea——?

MRS. ELVSTED   My husband had no idea I was coming here.

HEDDA   What? Your husband didn't know?

MRS. ELVSTED   No, of course not. As a matter of fact, he wasn't even there. He was away at the assizes. Oh, I couldn't stand it any longer, Hedda! I just couldn't. I'd be so dreadfully lonely up there now.

HEDDA   Go on.

MRS. ELVSTED   So I packed a few things. Secretly. And went.

HEDDA   Without telling anyone?

MRS. ELVSTED   Yes. I caught the train and came straight here.

HEDDA   But my dear Thea! How brave of you!

MRS. ELVSTED [Gets up and walks across the room.]   Well, what else could I do?

HEDDA   But what do you suppose your husband will say when you get back?

MRS. ELVSTED [By the table, looks at her.]   Back there? To him?

HEDDA   Yes. Surely——?

MRS. ELVSTED   I shall never go back to him.

HEDDA [*Gets up and goes closer.*]   You mean you've left your home for good?

MRS. ELVSTED   Yes. I didn't see what else I could do.

HEDDA   But to do it so openly!

MRS. ELVSTED   Oh, it's no use trying to keep a thing like that secret.

HEDDA   But what do you suppose people will say?

MRS. ELVSTED   They can say what they like. [*Sits sadly, wearily on the sofa.*] I had to do it.

HEDDA [*After a short silence.*]   What do you intend to do now? How are you going to live?

MRS. ELVSTED   I don't know. I only know that I must live wherever Eilert Loevborg is. If I am to go on living.

HEDDA [*Moves a chair from the table, sits on it near* MRS. ELVSTED *and strokes her hands.*]   Tell me, Thea, how did this—friendship between you and Eilert Loevborg begin?

MRS. ELVSTED   Oh, it came about gradually. I developed a kind of—power over him.

HEDDA   Oh?

MRS. ELVSTED   He gave up his old habits. Not because I asked him to. I'd never have dared to do that. I suppose he just noticed I didn't like that kind of thing. So he gave it up.

HEDDA [*Hides a smile.*]   So you've made a new man of him. Clever little Thea!

MRS. ELVSTED   Yes—anyway, he says I have. And he's made a—sort of—real person of me. Taught me to think—and to understand all kinds of things.

HEDDA   Did he give you lessons too?

MRS. ELVSTED   Not exactly lessons. But he talked to me. About—oh, you've no idea—so many things! And then he let me work with him. Oh, it was wonderful. I was so happy to be allowed to help him.

HEDDA   Did he allow you to help him?

MRS. ELVSTED   Yes. Whenever he wrote anything we always—did it together.

HEDDA   Like good pals?

MRS. ELVSTED [*Eagerly.*]   Pals! Yes—why, Hedda, that's exactly the word he used! Oh, I ought to feel so happy. But I can't. I don't know if it will last.

HEDDA   You don't seem very sure of him.

MRS. ELVSTED [*Sadly.*]   Something stands between Eilert Loevberg and me. The shadow of another woman.

HEDDA   Who can that be?

MRS. ELVSTED   I don't know. Someone he used to be friendly with in—in the old days. Someone he's never been able to forget.

HEDDA   What has he told you about her?

MRS. ELVSTED   Oh, he only mentioned her once, casually.

HEDDA   Well! What did he say?

MRS. ELVSTED   He said when he left her she tried to shoot him with a pistol.

HEDDA [*Cold, controlled.*] What nonsense. People don't do such things. The kind of people we know.

MRS. ELVSTED No, I think it must have been that red-haired singer he used to——

HEDDA Ah yes, very probably.

MRS. ELVSTED I remember they used to say she always carried a loaded pistol.

HEDDA Well then, it must be her.

MRS. ELVSTED But Hedda, I hear she's come back, and is living here. Oh, I'm so desperate——!

HEDDA [*Glances toward the rear room.*] Ssh! Tesman's coming. [*Gets up and whispers.*] Thea, we mustn't breathe a word about this to anyone.

MRS. ELVSTED [*Jumps up.*] Oh, no, no! Please don't!

[GEORGE TESMAN *appears from the right in the rear room with a letter in his hand, and comes into the drawing room.*]

TESMAN Well, here's my little epistle all signed and sealed.

HEDDA Good. I think Mrs. Elvsted wants to go now. Wait a moment—I'll see you as far as the garden gate.

TESMAN Er—Hedda, do you think Bertha could deal with this?

HEDDA [*Takes the letter.*] I'll give her instructions.

[BERTHA *enters from the hall.*]

BERTHA Judge Brack is here and asks if he may pay his respects to Madam and the Doctor.

HEDDA Yes, ask him to be so good as to come in. And—wait a moment—drop this letter in the post box.

BERTHA [*Takes the letter.*] Very good, madam.

[*She opens the door for* JUDGE BRACK, *and goes out.* JUDGE BRACK *is forty-five; rather short, but well-built, and elastic in his movements. He has a roundish face with an aristocratic profile. His hair, cut short, is still almost black, and is carefully barbered. Eyes lively and humorous. Thick eyebrows. His moustache is also thick, and is trimmed square at the ends. He is wearing outdoor clothes which are elegant but a little too youthful for him. He has a monocle in one eye; now and then he lets it drop.*]

BRACK [*Hat in hand, bows.*] May one presume to call so early?

HEDDA One may presume.

TESMAN [*Shakes his hand.*] You're welcome here any time. Judge Brack— Mrs. Rysing.

[HEDDA *sighs.*]

BRACK [*Bows.*] Ah—charmed——

HEDDA [*Looks at him and laughs.*] What fun to be able to see you by daylight for once, Judge.

BRACK Do I look—different?

HEDDA Yes. A little younger, I think.

BRACK Obliged.

TESMAN Well, what do you think of Hedda? What? Doesn't she look well? Hasn't she filled out——?

HEDDA Oh, do stop it. You ought to be thanking Judge Brack for all the inconvenience he's put himself to——

BRACK Nonsense, it was a pleasure——

HEDDA   You're a loyal friend. But my other friend is pining to get away. Au revoir, Judge. I won't be a minute.

> [*Mutual salutations.* MRS. ELVSTED *and* HEDDA *go out through the hall.*]

BRACK   Well, is your wife satisfied with everything?

TESMAN   Yes, we can't thank you enough. That is—we may have to shift one or two things around, she tells me. And we're short of one or two little items we'll have to purchase.

BRACK   Oh? Really?

TESMAN   But you musn't worry your head about that. Hedda says she'll get what's needed. I say, why don't we sit down? What?

BRACK   Thanks, just for a moment. [*Sits at the table.*] There's something I'd like to talk to you about, my dear Tesman.

TESMAN   Oh? Ah yes, of course. [*Sits.*] After the feast comes the reckoning. What?

BRACK   Oh, never mind about the financial side—there's no hurry about that. Though I could wish we'd arranged things a little less palatially.

TESMAN   Good heavens, that'd never have done. Think of Hedda, my dear chap. You know her. I couldn't possibly ask her to live like a suburban housewife.

BRACK   No, no—that's just the problem.

TESMAN   Anyway, it can't be long now before my nomination[3] comes through.

BRACK   Well, you know, these things often take time.

TESMAN   Have you heard any more news? What?

BRACK   Nothing definite. [*Changing the subject.*] Oh, by the way, I have one piece of news for you.

TESMAN   What?

BRACK   Your old friend Eilert Loevborg is back in town.

TESMAN   I know that already.

BRACK   Oh? How did you hear that?

TESMAN   She told me. That lady who went out with Hedda.

BRACK   I see. What was her name? I didn't catch it.

TESMAN   Mrs. Elvsted.

BRACK   Oh, the magistrate's wife. Yes, Loevborg's been living up near them, hasn't he?

TESMAN   I'm delighted to hear he's become a decent human being again.

BRACK   Yes, so they say.

TESMAN   I gather he's published a new book, too. What?

BRACK   Indeed he has.

TESMAN   I hear it's created rather a stir.

BRACK   Quite an unusual stir.

TESMAN   I say, isn't that splendid news! He's such a gifted chap—and I was afraid he'd gone to the dogs for good.

BRACK   Most people thought he had.

TESMAN   But I can't think what he'll do now. How on earth will he manage to make ends meet? What?

---

3. For the professorship. Professors at European universities were less numerous and more socially prominent than their contemporary American counterparts.

[*As he speaks his last words,* HEDDA *enters from the hall.*]

HEDDA [*To* BRACK, *laughs slightly scornfully.*]   Tesman is always worrying about making ends meet.

TESMAN   We were talking about poor Eilert Loevborg, Hedda dear.

HEDDA [*Gives him a quick look.*]   Oh, were you? [*Sits in the armchair by the stove and asks casually.*] Is he in trouble?

TESMAN   Well, he must have run through his inheritance long ago by now. And he can't write a new book every year. What? So I'm wondering what's going to become of him.

BRACK   I may be able to enlighten you there.

TESMAN   Oh?

BRACK   You mustn't forget he has relatives who wield a good deal of influence.

TESMAN   Relatives? Oh, they've quite washed their hands of him, I'm afraid.

BRACK   They used to regard him as the hope of the family.

TESMAN   Used to, yes. But he's put an end to that.

HEDDA   Who knows? [*With a little smile.*] I hear the Elvsteds have made a new man of him.

BRACK   And then this book he's just published——

TESMAN   Well, let's hope they find something for him. I've just written him a note. Oh, by the way, Hedda, I asked him to come over and see us this evening.

BRACK   But my dear chap, you're coming to me this evening. My bachelor party.[4] You promised me last night when I met you at the boat.

HEDDA   Had you forgotten, Tesman?

TESMAN   Good heavens, yes, I'd quite forgotten.

BRACK   Anyway, you can be quite sure he won't turn up here.

TESMAN   Why do you think that? What?

BRACK [*A little unwillingly, gets up and rests his hands on the back of his chair.*]   My dear Tesman—and you, too, Mrs. Tesman—there's something I feel you ought to know.

TESMAN   Concerning Eilert?

BRACK   Concerning him and you.

TESMAN   Well, my dear Judge, tell us, please!

BRACK   You must be prepared for your nomination not to come through quite as quickly as you hope and expect.

TESMAN [*Jumps up uneasily.*]   Is anything wrong? What?

BRACK   There's a possibility that the appointment may be decided by competition——

TESMAN   Competition! By Jove, Hedda, fancy that!

HEDDA [*Leans further back in her chair.*]   Ah! How interesting!

TESMAN   But who else——? I say, you don't mean——?

BRACK   Exactly. By competition with Eilert Loevborg.

TESMAN [*Clasps his hands in alarm.*]   No, no, but this is inconceivable! It's absolutely impossible! What?

BRACK   Hm. We may find it'll happen, all the same.

TESMAN   No, but—Judge Brack, they couldn't be so inconsiderate toward me! [*Waves his arms.*] I mean, by Jove, I—I'm a married man! It was on

---

4. A party for men only, whether single or married.

the strength of this that Hedda and I *got* married! We ran up some pretty hefty debts. And borrowed money from Auntie Juju! I mean, good heavens, they practically promised me the appointment. What?

BRACK   Well, well, I'm sure you'll get it. But you'll have to go through a competition.

HEDDA [*Motionless in her armchair.*]   How exciting, Tesman. It'll be a kind of duel, by Jove.

TESMAN   My dear Hedda, how can you take it so lightly?

HEDDA [*As before.*]   I'm not. I can't wait to see who's going to win.

BRACK   In any case, Mrs. Tesman, it's best you should know how things stand. I mean before you commit yourself to these little items I hear you're threatening to purchase.

HEDDA   I can't allow this to alter my plans.

BRACK   Indeed? Well, that's your business. Good-bye. [*To* TESMAN.] I'll come and collect you on the way home from my afternoon walk.

TESMAN   Oh, yes, yes. I'm sorry, I'm all upside down just now.

HEDDA [*Lying in her chair, holds out her hand.*]   Good-bye, Judge. See you this afternoon.

BRACK   Thank you. Good-bye, good-bye.

TESMAN [*Sees him to the door.*]   Good-bye, my dear Judge. You will excuse me, won't you?

[JUDGE BRACK *goes out through the hall.*]

TESMAN [*Pacing up and down.*]   Oh, Hedda! One oughtn't to go plunging off on wild adventures. What?

HEDDA [*Looks at him and smiles.*]   Like you're doing?

TESMAN   Yes. I mean, there's no denying it, it was a pretty big adventure to go off and get married and set up house merely on expectation.

HEDDA   Perhaps you're right.

TESMAN   Well, anyway, we have our home, Hedda. By Jove, yes. The home we dreamed of. And set our hearts on. What?

HEDDA [*Gets up slowly, wearily.*]   You agreed that we should enter society. And keep open house. That was the bargain.

TESMAN   Yes. Good heavens, I was looking forward to it all so much. To seeing you play hostess to a select circle! By Jove! What? Ah, well, for the time being we shall have to make do with each other's company, Hedda. Perhaps have Auntie Juju in now and then. Oh dear, this wasn't at all what you had in mind——

HEDDA   I won't be able to have a liveried footman.[5] For a start.

TESMAN   Oh no, we couldn't possibly afford a footman.

HEDDA   And that thoroughbred horse you promised me——

TESMAN [*Fearfully.*]   Thoroughbred horse!

HEDDA   I mustn't even think of that now.

TESMAN   Heaven forbid!

HEDDA [*Walks across the room.*]   Ah, well. I still have one thing left to amuse myself with.

TESMAN [*Joyfully.*]   Thank goodness for that. What's that, Hedda? What?

HEDDA [*In the open doorway, looks at him with concealed scorn.*]   My pistols, George darling.

TESMAN [*Alarmed.*]   Pistols!

---

5. A uniformed servant.

HEDDA [*Her eyes cold.*]   General Gabler's pistols.
[*She goes into the rear room and disappears.*]
TESMAN [*Runs to the doorway and calls after her.*]   For heaven's sake,
Hedda dear, don't touch those things. They're dangerous. Hedda—
please—for my sake! What?

Act II

SCENE—*The same as in Act I except that the piano has been removed and an
elegant little writing table, with a bookcase, stands in its place. By the sofa on
the left a smaller table has been placed. Most of the flowers have been removed.*
MRS. ELVSTED'S *bouquet stands on the larger table, downstage. It is afternoon.*
HEDDA, *dressed to receive callers, is alone in the room. She is standing by the
open french windows, loading a revolver. The pair to it is lying in an open pistol
case on the writing table.*

HEDDA [*Looks down into the garden and calls.*]   Good afternoon, Judge.
BRACK [*In the distance, below.*]   Afternoon, Mrs. Tesman.
HEDDA [*Raises the pistol and takes aim.*]   I'm going to shoot you, Judge
Brack.
BRACK [*Shouts from below.*]   No, no, no! Don't aim that thing at me!
HEDDA   This'll teach you to enter houses by the back door. [*Fires.*]
BRACK [*Below.*]   Have you gone completely out of your mind?
HEDDA   Oh dear! Did I hit you?
BRACK [*Still outside.*]   Stop playing these silly tricks.
HEDDA   All right, Judge. Come along in.
[JUDGE BRACK, *dressed for a bachelor party, enters through the
french windows. He has a light overcoat on his arm.*]
BRACK   For God's sake! Haven't you stopped fooling around with those
things yet? What are you trying to hit?
HEDDA   Oh, I was just shooting at the sky.
BRACK [*Takes the pistol gently from her hand.*]   By your leave, ma'am.
[*Looks at it.*] Ah, yes—I know this old friend well. [*Looks around.*]
Where's the case? Oh, yes. [*Puts the pistol in the case and closes it.*] That's
enough of that little game for today.
HEDDA   Well, what on earth *am* I to do?
BRACK   You haven't had any visitors?
HEDDA [*Closes the french windows.*]   Not one. I suppose the best people
are all still in the country.
BRACK   Your husband isn't home yet?
HEDDA [*Locks the pistol case away in a drawer of the writing table.*]   No.
The moment he'd finished eating he ran off to his aunties. He wasn't
expecting you so early.
BRACK   Ah, why didn't I think of that? How stupid of me.
HEDDA [*Turns her head and looks at him.*]   Why stupid?
BRACK   I'd have come a little sooner.
HEDDA [*Walks across the room.*]   There'd have been no one to receive you.
I've been in my room since lunch, dressing.
BRACK   You haven't a tiny crack in the door through which we might have
negotiated?

HEDDA   You forgot to arrange one.

BRACK   Another stupidity.

HEDDA   Well, we'll have to sit down here. And wait. Tesman won't be back for some time.

BRACK   Sad. Well, I'll be patient.

[HEDDA *sits on the corner of the sofa.* BRACK *puts his coat over the back of the nearest chair and seats himself, keeping his hat in his hand. Short pause. They look at each other.*]

HEDDA   Well?

BRACK [*In the same tone of voice.*]   Well?

HEDDA   I asked first.

BRACK [*Leans forward slightly.*]   Yes, well, now we can enjoy a nice, cosy little chat—Mrs. Hedda.

HEDDA [*Leans further back in her chair.*]   It seems such ages since we had a talk. I don't count last night or this morning.

BRACK   You mean: *à deux?*[6]

HEDDA   Mm—yes. That's roughly what I meant.

BRACK   I've been longing so much for you to come home.

HEDDA   So have I.

BRACK   You? Really, Mrs. Hedda? And I thought you were having such a wonderful honeymoon.

HEDDA   Oh, yes. Wonderful!

BRACK   But your husband wrote such ecstatic letters.

HEDDA   He! Oh, yes! He thinks life has nothing better to offer than rooting around in libraries and copying old pieces of parchment, or whatever it is he does.

BRACK [*A little maliciously.*]   Well, that *is* his life. Most of it, anyway.

HEDDA   Yes, I know. Well, it's all right for him. But for me! Oh no, my dear Judge. I've been bored to death.

BRACK [*Sympathetically.*]   Do you mean that? Seriously?

HEDDA   Yes. Can you imagine? Six whole months without ever meeting a single person who was one of us, and to whom I could talk about the kind of things we talk about.

BRACK   Yes, I can understand. I'd miss that, too.

HEDDA   That wasn't the worst, though.

BRACK   What was?

HEDDA   Having to spend every minute of one's life with—with the same person.

BRACK [*Nods.*]   Yes. What a thought! Morning; noon; and——

HEDDA [*Coldly.*]   As I said: every minute of one's life.

BRACK   I stand corrected. But dear Tesman is such a clever fellow, I should have thought one ought to be able——

HEDDA   Tesman is only interested in one thing, my dear Judge. His special subject.

BRACK   True.

HEDDA   And people who are only interested in one thing don't make the most amusing company. Not for long, anyway.

BRACK   Not even when they happen to be the person one loves?

HEDDA   Oh, don't use that sickly, stupid word.

6. Just the two of us.

BRACK [*Starts.*]   But, Mrs. Hedda——!

HEDDA [*Half laughing, half annoyed.*]   You just try it, Judge. Listening to the history of civilization morning, noon and——

BRACK [*Corrects her.*]   Every minute of one's life.

HEDDA   All right. Oh, and those domestic industries of Brabant in the Middle Ages! That really is beyond the limit.

BRACK [*Looks at her searchingly.*]   But, tell me—if you feel like this why on earth did you—? Ha——

HEDDA   Why on earth did I marry George Tesman?

BRACK   If you like to put it that way.

HEDDA   Do you think it so very strange?

BRACK   Yes—and no, Mrs. Hedda.

HEDDA   I'd danced myself tired, Judge. I felt my time was up—— [*Gives a slight shudder.*] No, I mustn't say that. Or even think it.

BRACK   You've no rational cause to think it.

HEDDA   Oh—cause, cause—— [*Looks searchingly at him.*] After all, George Tesman—well, I mean, he's a very respectable man.

BRACK   Very respectable, sound as a rock. No denying that.

HEDDA   And there's nothing exactly ridiculous about him. Is there?

BRACK   Ridiculous? No-o-o, I wouldn't say that.

HEDDA   Mm. He's very clever at collecting material and all that, isn't he? I mean, he may go quite far in time.

BRACK [*Looks at her a little uncertainly.*]   I thought you believed, like everyone else, that he would become a very prominent man.

HEDDA [*Looks tired.*]   Yes, I did. And when he came and begged me on his bended knees to be allowed to love and to cherish me, I didn't see why I shouldn't let him.

BRACK   No, well—if one looks at it like that——

HEDDA   It was more than my other admirers were prepared to do, Judge dear.

BRACK [*Laughs.*]   Well, I can't answer for the others. As far as I myself am concerned, you know I've always had a considerable respect for the institution of marriage. As an institution.

HEDDA [*Lightly.*]   Oh, I've never entertained any hopes of you.

BRACK   All I want is to have a circle of friends whom I can trust, whom I can help with advice or—or by any other means, and into whose houses I may come and go as a—trusted friend.

HEDDA   Of the husband?

BRACK [*Bows.*]   Preferably, to be frank, of the wife. And of the husband too, of course. Yes, you know, this kind of—triangle is a delightful arrangement for all parties concerned.

HEDDA   Yes, I often longed for a third person while I was away. Oh, those hours we spent alone in railway compartments——

BRACK   Fortunately your honeymoon is now over.

HEDDA [*Shakes her head.*]   There's a long way still to go. I've only reached a stop on the line.

BRACK   Why not jump out and stretch your legs a little, Mrs. Hedda?

HEDDA   I'm not the jumping sort.

BRACK   Aren't you?

HEDDA   No. There's always someone around who——

BRACK [*Laughs.*]   Who looks at one's legs?

HEDDA   Yes. Exactly.

BRACK   Well, but surely——

HEDDA [*With a gesture of rejection.*]   I don't like it. I'd rather stay where I am. Sitting in the compartment. À *deux.*

BRACK   But suppose a third person were to step into the compartment?

HEDDA   That would be different.

BRACK   A trusted friend—someone who understood——

HEDDA   And was lively and amusing——

BRACK   And interested in—more subjects than one——

HEDDA [*Sighs audibly.*]   Yes, that'd be a relief.

BRACK [*Hears the front door open and shut.*]   The triangle is completed.

HEDDA [*Half under breath.*]   And the train goes on.

[GEORGE TESMAN, *in grey walking dress with a soft felt hat, enters from the hall. He has a number of paper-covered books under his arm and in his pockets.*]

TESMAN [*Goes over to the table by the corner sofa.*]   Phew! It's too hot to be lugging all this around. [*Puts the books down.*] I'm positively sweating, Hedda. Why, hullo, hullo! You here already, Judge? What? Bertha didn't tell me.

BRACK [*Gets up.*]   I came in through the garden.

HEDDA   What are all those books you've got there?

TESMAN [*Stands glancing through them.*]   Oh, some new publications dealing with my special subject. I had to buy them.

HEDDA   Your special subject?

BRACK   His special subject, Mrs. Tesman.

[BRACK *and* HEDDA *exchange a smile.*]

HEDDA   Haven't you collected enough material on your special subject?

TESMAN   My dear Hedda, one can never have too much. One must keep abreast of what other people are writing.

HEDDA   Yes. Of course.

TESMAN [*Rooting among the books.*]   Look—I bought a copy of Eilert Loevborg's new book, too. [*Holds it out to her.*] Perhaps you'd like to have a look at it, Hedda? What?

HEDDA   No, thank you. Er—yes, perhaps I will, later.

TESMAN   I glanced through it on my way home.

BRACK   What's your opinion—as a specialist on the subject?

TESMAN   I'm amazed how sound and balanced it is. He never used to write like that. [*Gathers his books together.*] Well, I must get down to these at once. I can hardly wait to cut the pages.[7] Oh, I've got to change, too. [*To* BRACK.] We don't have to be off just yet, do we? What?

BRACK   Heavens, no. We've plenty of time yet.

TESMAN   Good, I needn't hurry, then. [*Goes with his books, but stops and turns in the doorway.*] Oh, by the way, Hedda, Auntie Juju won't be coming to see you this evening.

HEDDA   Won't she? Oh—the hat, I suppose.

TESMAN   Good heavens, no. How could you think such a thing of Auntie Juju? Fancy——! No, Auntie Rena's very ill.

HEDDA   She always is.

---

7. Books used to be sold with the pages folded but uncut as they came from the printing press; the owner had to cut the pages to read the book.

TESMAN   Yes, but today she's been taken really bad.

HEDDA   Oh, then it's quite understandable that the other one should want to stay with her. Well, I shall have to swallow my disappointment.

TESMAN   You can't imagine how happy Auntie Juju was in spite of everything. At your looking so well after the honeymoon!

HEDDA [*Half beneath her breath, as she rises.*]   Oh, these everlasting aunts!

TESMAN   What?

HEDDA [*Goes over to the french windows.*]   Nothing.

TESMAN   Oh. All right. [*Goes into the rear room and out of sight.*]

BRACK   What was that about the hat?

HEDDA   Oh, something that happened with Miss Tesman this morning. She'd put her hat down on a chair. [*Looks at him and smiles.*] And I pretended to think it was the servant's.

BRACK [*Shakes his head.*]   But my dear Mrs. Hedda, how could you do such a thing? To that poor old lady?

HEDDA [*Nervously, walking across the room.*]   Sometimes a mood like that hits me. And I can't stop myself. [*Throws herself down in the armchair by the stove.*] Oh, I don't know how to explain it.

BRACK [*Behind her chair.*]   You're not really happy. That's the answer.

HEDDA [*Stares ahead of her.*]   Why on earth should I be happy? Can you give me a reason?

BRACK   Yes. For one thing you've got the home you always wanted.

HEDDA [*Looks at him.*]   You really believe that story?

BRACK   You mean it isn't true?

HEDDA   Oh, yes, it's partly true.

BRACK   Well?

HEDDA   It's true I got Tesman to see me home from parties last summer—

BRACK   It was a pity my home lay in another direction.

HEDDA   Yes. Your interests lay in another direction, too.

BRACK [*Laughs.*]   That's naughty of you, Mrs. Hedda. But to return to you and Tesman——

HEDDA   Well, we walked past this house one evening. And poor Tesman was fidgeting in his boots trying to find something to talk about. I felt sorry for the great scholar——

BRACK [*Smiles incredulously.*]   Did you? Hm.

HEDDA   Yes, honestly I did. Well, to help him out of his misery, I happened to say quite frivolously how much I'd love to live in this house.

BRACK   Was that all?

HEDDA   That evening, yes.

BRACK   But—afterwards?

HEDDA   Yes. My little frivolity had its consequences, my dear Judge.

BRACK   Our little frivolities do. Much too often, unfortunately.

HEDDA   Thank you. Well, it was our mutual admiration for the late Prime Minister's house that brought George Tesman and me together on common ground. So we got engaged, and we got married, and we went on our honeymoon, and—Ah well, Judge, I've—made my bed and I must lie in it, I was about to say.

BRACK   How utterly fantastic! And you didn't really care in the least about the house?

HEDDA   God knows I didn't.

BRACK   Yes, but now that we've furnished it so beautifully for you?

HEDDA   Ugh—all the rooms smell of lavender and dried roses. But perhaps Auntie Juju brought that in.

BRACK [*Laughs.*]   More likely the Prime Minister's widow, rest her soul.

HEDDA   Yes, it's got the odor of death about it. It reminds me of the flowers one has worn at a ball—the morning after. [*Clasps her hands behind her neck, leans back in the chair and looks up at him.*] Oh, my dear Judge, you've no idea how hideously bored I'm going to be out here.

BRACK   Couldn't you find some kind of occupation, Mrs. Hedda? Like your husband?

HEDDA   Occupation? That'd interest me?

BRACK   Well—preferably.

HEDDA   God knows what. I've often thought—— [*Breaks off.*] No, that wouldn't work either.

BRACK   Who knows? Tell me about it.

HEDDA   I was thinking—if I could persuade Tesman to go into politics, for example.

BRACK [*Laughs.*]   Tesman! No, honestly, I don't think he's quite cut out to be a politician.

HEDDA   Perhaps not. But if I could persuade him to have a go at it?

BRACK   What satisfaction would that give you? If he turned out to be no good? Why do you want to make him do that?

HEDDA   Because I'm bored. [*After a moment.*] You feel there's absolutely no possibility of Tesman becoming Prime Minister, then?

BRACK   Well, you know, Mrs. Hedda, for one thing he'd have to be pretty well off before he could become that.

HEDDA [*Gets up impatiently.*]   There you are! [*Walks across the room.*] It's this wretched poverty that makes life so hateful. And ludicrous. Well, it is!

BRACK   I don't think that's the real cause.

HEDDA   What is, then?

BRACK   Nothing really exciting has ever happened to you.

HEDDA   Nothing serious, you mean?

BRACK   Call it that if you like. But now perhaps it may.

HEDDA [*Tosses her head.*]   Oh, you're thinking of this competition for that wretched professorship? That's Tesman's affair. I'm not going to waste my time worrying about that.

BRACK   Very well, let's forget about that then. But suppose you were to find yourself faced with what people call—to use the conventional phrase—the most solemn of human responsibilities? [*Smiles.*]   A new responsibility, little Mrs. Hedda.

HEDDA [*Angrily.*]   Be quiet! Nothing like that's going to happen.

BRACK [*Warily.*]   We'll talk about it again in a year's time. If not earlier.

HEDDA [*Curtly.*]   I've no leanings in that direction, Judge. I don't want any—responsibilities.

BRACK   But surely you must feel some inclination to make use of that— natural talent which every woman—

HEDDA [*Over by the french windows.*]   Oh, be quiet, I say! I often think there's only one thing for which I have any natural talent.

BRACK [*Goes closer.*]   And what is that, if I may be so bold as to ask?

HEDDA [*Stands looking out.*]   For boring myself to death. Now you know. [*Turns, looks toward the rear room and laughs.*] Talking of boring, here comes the Professor.

BRACK [*Quietly, warningly.*]   Now, now, now, Mrs. Hedda!

[GEORGE TESMAN, *in evening dress, with gloves and hat in his hand, enters through the rear room from the right.*]

TESMAN   Hedda, hasn't any message come from Eilert? What?

HEDDA   No.

TESMAN   Ah, then we'll have him here presently. You wait and see.

BRACK   You really think he'll come?

TESMAN   Yes, I'm almost sure he will. What you were saying about him this morning is just gossip.

BRACK   Oh?

TESMAN   Yes. Auntie Juju said she didn't believe he'd ever dare to stand in my way again. Fancy that!

BRACK   Then everything in the garden's lovely.

TESMAN [*Puts his hat, with his gloves in it, on a chair, right.*]   Yes, but you really must let me wait for him as long as possible.

BRACK   We've plenty of time. No one'll be turning up at my place before seven or half past.

TESMAN   Ah, then we can keep Hedda company a little longer. And see if he turns up. What?

HEDDA [*Picks up* BRACK's *coat and hat and carries them over to the corner sofa.*]   And if the worst comes to the worst, Mr. Loevborg can sit here and talk to me.

BRACK [*Offering to take his things from her.*]   No, please. What do you mean by "if the worst comes to the worst"?

HEDDA   If he doesn't want to go with you and Tesman.

TESMAN [*Looks doubtfully at her.*]   I say, Hedda, do you think it'll be all right for him to stay here with you? What? Remember Auntie Juju isn't coming.

HEDDA   Yes, but Mrs. Elvsted is. The three of us can have a cup of tea together.

TESMAN   Ah, that'll be all right then.

BRACK [*Smiles.*]   It's probably the safest solution as far as he's concerned.

HEDDA   Why?

BRACK   My dear Mrs. Tesman, you always say of my little bachelor parties that they should be attended only by men of the strongest principles.

HEDDA   But Mr. Loevborg is a man of principle now. You know what they say about a reformed sinner——

[BERTHA *enters from the hall.*]

BERTHA   Madam, there's a gentleman here who wants to see you——

HEDDA   Ask him to come in.

TESMAN [*Quietly.*]   I'm sure it's him. By Jove. Fancy that!

[EILERT LOEVBORG *enters from the hall. He is slim and lean, of the same age as* TESMAN, *but looks older and somewhat haggard. His hair and beard are of a blackish-brown; his face is long and pale, but with a couple of reddish patches on his cheekbones. He is dressed in an elegant and fairly new black suit, and carries black gloves and a top hat in his hand. He stops just inside the door and bows abruptly. He seems somewhat embarrassed.*]

TESMAN [*Goes over and shakes his hand.*] My dear Eilert! How grand to see you again after all these years!

EILERT LOEVBORG [*Speaks softly.*] It was good of you to write, George. [*Goes nearer to* HEDDA.] May I shake hands with you, too, Mrs. Tesman?

HEDDA [*Accepts his hand.*] Delighted to see you, Mr. Loevborg. [*With a gesture.*] I don't know if you two gentlemen——

LOEVBORG [*Bows slightly.*] Judge Brack, I believe.

BRACK [*Also with a slight bow.*] Correct. We—met some years ago

TESMAN [*Puts his hands on* LOEVBORG'S *shoulders.*] Now you're to treat this house just as though it were your own home, Eilert. Isn't that right, Hedda? I hear you've decided to settle here again? What?

LOEVBORG Yes, I have.

TESMAN Quite understandable. Oh, by the bye—I've just bought your new book. Though to tell the truth I haven't found time to read it yet.

LOEVBORG You needn't bother.

TESMAN Oh? Why?

LOEVBORG There's nothing much in it.

TESMAN By Jove, fancy hearing that from you!

BRACK But everyone's praising it.

LOEVBORG That was exactly what I wanted to happen. So I only wrote what I knew everyone would agree with.

BRACK Very sensible.

TESMAN Yes, but my dear Eilert——

LOEVBORG I want to try to re-establish myself. To begin again—from the beginning.

TESMAN [*A little embarrassed.*] Yes, I—er—suppose you do. What?

LOEVBORG [*Smiles, puts down his hat and takes a package wrapped in paper from his coat pocket.*] But when this gets published—George Tesman—read it. This is my real book. The one in which I have spoken with my own voice.

TESMAN Oh, really? What's it about?

LOEVBORG It's the sequel.

TESMAN Sequel? To what?

LOEVBORG To the other book.

TESMAN The one that's just come out?

LOEVBORG Yes.

TESMAN But my dear Eilert, that covers the subject right up to the present day.

LOEVBORG It does. But this is about the future.

TESMAN The future! But, I say, we don't know anything about that.

LOEVBORG No. But there are one or two things that need to be said about it. [*Opens the package.*] Here, have a look.

TESMAN Surely that's not your handwriting?

LOEVBORG I dictated it. [*Turns the pages.*] It's in two parts. The first deals with the forces that will shape our civilization. [*Turns further on towards the end.*] And the second indicates the direction in which that civilization may develop.

TESMAN Amazing! I'd never think of writing about anything like that.

HEDDA [*By the french windows, drumming on the pane.*] No. You wouldn't.

LOEVBORG [*Puts the pages back into their cover and lays the package on the table.*]   I brought it because I thought I might possibly read you a few pages this evening.

TESMAN   I say, what a kind idea! Oh, but this evening——? [*Glances at* BRACK.] I'm not quite sure whether——

LOEVBORG   Well, some other time, then. There's no hurry.

BRACK   The truth is, Mr. Loevborg, I'm giving a little dinner this evening. In Tesman's honor, you know.

LOEVBORG [*Looks round for his hat.*]   Oh—then I mustn't——

BRACK   No, wait a minute. Won't you do me the honor of joining us?

LOEVBORG [*Curtly, with decision.*]   No, I can't. Thank you so much.

BRACK   Oh, nonsense. Do—please. There'll only be a few of us. And I can promise you we shall have some good sport, as Mrs. Hed—as Mrs. Tesman puts it.

LOEVBORG   I've no doubt. Nevertheless——

BRACK   You could bring your manuscript along and read it to Tesman at my place. I could lend you a room.

TESMAN   By Jove, Eilert, that's an idea. What?

HEDDA [*Interposes.*]   But Tesman, Mr. Loevborg doesn't want to go. I'm sure Mr. Loevborg would much rather sit here and have supper with me.

LOEVBORG [*Looks at her.*]   With you, Mrs. Tesman?

HEDDA   And Mrs. Elvsted.

LOEVBORG   Oh. [*Casually.*]   I ran into her this afternoon.

HEDDA   Did you? Well, she's coming here this evening. So you really must stay, Mr. Loevborg. Otherwise she'll have no one to see her home.

LOEVBORG   That's true. Well—thank you, Mrs. Tesman, I'll stay then.

HEDDA   I'll just tell the servant.

[*She goes to the door which leads into the hall, and rings.* BERTHA *enters.* HEDDA *talks softly to her and points towards the rear room.* BERTHA *nods and goes out.*]

TESMAN [*To* LOEVBORG, *as* HEDDA *does this.*]   I say, Eilert. This new subject of yours—the—er—future—is that the one you're going to lecture about?

LOEVBORG   Yes.

TESMAN   They told me down at the bookshop that you're going to hold a series of lectures here during the autumn.

LOEVBORG   Yes, I am, I—hope you don't mind, Tesman.

TESMAN   Good heavens, no! But——?

LOEVBORG   I can quite understand it might queer your pitch a little.

TESMAN [*Dejectedly.*]   Oh well, I can't expect you to put them off for my sake.

LOEVBORG   I'll wait till your appointment's been announced.

TESMAN   You'll wait! But—but—aren't you going to compete with me for the post? What?

LOEVBORG   No. I only want to defeat you in the eyes of the world.

TESMAN   Good heavens! Then Auntie Juju was right after all! Oh, I knew it, I knew it! Hear that, Hedda? Fancy! Eilert *doesn't* want to stand in our way.

HEDDA [*Curtly.*]   Our? Leave me out of it, please.

[*She goes towards the rear room, where* BERTHA *is setting a tray with decanters and glasses on the table.* HEDDA *nods approval, and comes back into the drawing room.* BERTHA *goes out.*]

TESMAN [*While this is happening.*] Judge Brack, what do you think about all this? What?

BRACK Oh, I think honor and victory can be very splendid things——

TESMAN Of course they can. Still——

HEDDA [*Looks at* TESMAN *with a cold smile.*] You look as if you'd been hit by a thunderbolt.

TESMAN Yes, I feel rather like it.

BRACK There was a black cloud looming up, Mrs. Tesman. But it seems to have passed over.

HEDDA [*Points toward the rear room.*] Well, gentlemen, won't you go in and take a glass of cold punch?

BRACK [*Glances at his watch.*] A stirrup cup?[8] Yes, why not?

TESMAN An admirable suggestion, Hedda. Admirable! Oh, I feel so relieved!

HEDDA Won't you have one, too, Mr. Loevborg?

LOEVBORG No, thank you. I'd rather not.

BRACK Great heavens, man, cold punch isn't poison. Take my word for it.

LOEVBORG Not for everyone, perhaps.

HEDDA I'll keep Mr. Loevborg company while you drink.

TESMAN Yes, Hedda dear, would you?

[*He and* BRACK *go into the rear room, sit down, drink punch, smoke cigarettes and talk cheerfully during the following scene.* EILERT LOEVBORG *remains standing by the stove.* HEDDA *goes to the writing table.*]

HEDDA [*Raising her voice slightly.*] I've some photographs I'd like to show you, if you'd care to see them. Tesman and I visited the Tyrol on our way home.

[*She comes back with an album, places it on the table by the sofa and sits in the upstage corner of the sofa.* EILERT LOEVBORG *comes toward her, stops and looks at her. Then he takes a chair and sits down on her left, with his back toward the rear room.*]

HEDDA [*Opens the album.*] You see these mountains, Mr. Loevborg? That's the Ortler group. Tesman has written the name underneath. You see: "The Ortler Group near Meran."[9]

LOEVBORG [*Has not taken his eyes from her; says softly, slowly.*] Hedda— Gabler!

HEDDA [*Gives him a quick glance.*] Ssh!

LOEVBORG [*Repeats softly.*] Hedda Gabler!

HEDDA [*Looks at the album.*] Yes, that used to be my name. When we first knew each other.

LOEVBORG And from now on—for the rest of my life—I must teach myself never to say: Hedda Gabler.

HEDDA [*Still turning the pages.*] Yes, you must. You'd better start getting into practice. The sooner the better.

---

8. A drink before parting. (Originally, it was taken by riders on horseback just before setting forth.)
9. Or Merano, a city in the Austrian Tyrol, since 1918 in Italy. The scenic features mentioned here and later are tourist attractions. The Ortler Group and the Dolomites are ranges of the Alps. The Ampezzo Valley lies beyond the Dolomites to the east. The Brenner Pass is a major route through the Alps to Austria.

LOEVBORG [*Bitterly.*]   Hedda Gabler married? And to George Tesman?

HEDDA   Yes. Well—that's life.

LOEVBORG   Oh, Hedda, Hedda! How could you throw yourself away like that?

HEDDA [*Looks sharply at him.*]   Stop it.

LOEVBORG   What do you mean?

[TESMAN *comes in and goes toward the sofa.*]

HEDDA [*Hears him coming and says casually.*]   And this, Mr. Loevborg, is the view from the Ampezzo valley. Look at those mountains. [*Glances affectionately up at* TESMAN.] What did you say those curious mountains were called, dear?

TESMAN   Let me have a look. Oh, those are the Dolomites.

HEDDA   Of course. Those are the Dolomites, Mr. Loevborg.

TESMAN   Hedda, I just wanted to ask you, can't we bring some punch in here? A glass for you, anyway. What?

HEDDA   Thank you, yes. And a biscuit[1] or two, perhaps.

TESMAN   You wouldn't like a cigarette?

HEDDA   No.

TESMAN   Right.

[*He goes into the rear room and over to the right.* BRACK *is sitting there, glancing occasionally at* HEDDA *and* LOEVBORG.]

LOEVBORG [*Softly, as before.*]   Answer me, Hedda. How could you do it?

HEDDA [*Apparently absorbed in the album.*]   If you go on calling me Hedda I won't talk to you any more.

LOEVBORG   Mayn't I even when we're alone?

HEDDA   No. You can think it. But you mustn't say it.

LOEVBORG   Oh, I see. Because you love George Tesman.

HEDDA [*Glances at him and smiles.*]   Love? Don't be funny.

LOEVBORG   You don't love him?

HEDDA   I don't intend to be unfaithful to him. That's not what I want.

LOEVBORG   Hedda—just tell me one thing——

HEDDA   Ssh!

[TESMAN *enters from the rear room, carrying a tray.*]

TESMAN   Here we are! Here come the goodies! [*Puts the tray down on the table.*]

HEDDA   Why didn't you ask the servant to bring it in?

TESMAN [*Fills the glasses.*]   I like waiting on you, Hedda.

HEDDA   But you've filled both glasses. Mr. Loevborg doesn't want to drink.

TESMAN   Yes, but Mrs. Elvsted'll be here soon.

HEDDA   Oh yes, that's true. Mrs. Elvsted——

TESMAN   Had you forgotten her? What?

HEDDA   We're so absorbed with these photographs. [*Shows him one.*] You remember this little village?

TESMAN   Oh, that one down by the Brenner Pass. We spent a night there——

HEDDA   Yes, and met all those amusing people.

TESMAN   Oh yes, it was there, wasn't it? By Jove, if only we could have had you with us, Eilert! Ah, well. [*Goes back into the other room and sits down with* BRACK.]

---

1. Cookie.

LOEVBORG   Tell me one thing, Hedda.

HEDDA   Yes?

LOEVBORG   Didn't you love me either? Not—just a little?

HEDDA   Well now, I wonder? No, I think we were just good pals—Really good pals who could tell each other anything. [Smiles.] You certainly poured your heart out to me.

LOEVBORG   You begged me to.

HEDDA   Looking back on it, there was something beautiful and fascinating—and brave—about the way we told each other everything. That secret friendship no one else knew about.

LOEVBORG   Yes, Hedda, yes! Do you remember? How I used to come up to your father's house in the afternoon—and the General sat by the window and read his newspapers—with his back toward us——

HEDDA   And we sat on the sofa in the corner——

LOEVBORG   Always reading the same illustrated magazine——

HEDDA   We hadn't any photograph album.

LOEVBORG   Yes, Hedda. I regarded you as a kind of confessor. Told you things about myself which no one else knew about—then. Those days and nights of drinking and—Oh, Hedda, what power did you have to make me confess such things?

HEDDA   Power? You think I had some power over you?

LOEVBORG   Yes—I don't know how else to explain it. And all those— oblique questions you asked me——

HEDDA   You knew what they meant.

LOEVBORG   But that you could sit there and ask me such questions! So unashamedly——

HEDDA   I thought you said they were oblique.

LOEVBORG   Yes, but you asked them so unashamedly. That you could question me about—about that kind of thing!

HEDDA   You answered willingly enough.

LOEVBORG   Yes—that's what I can't understand—looking back on it. But tell me, Hedda—what you felt for me—wasn't that—love? When you asked me those questions and made me confess my sins to you, wasn't it because you wanted to wash me clean?

HEDDA   No, not exactly.

LOEVBORG   Why did you do it, then?

HEDDA   Do you find it so incredible that a young girl, given the chance to do so without anyone knowing, should want to be allowed a glimpse into a forbidden world of whose existence she is supposed to be ignorant?

LOEVBORG   So that was it?

HEDDA   One reason. One reason—I think.

LOEVBORG   You didn't love me, then. You just wanted—knowledge. But if that was so, why did you break it off?

HEDDA   That was your fault.

LOEVBORG   It was you who put an end to it.

HEDDA   Yes, when I realized that our friendship was threatening to develop into something—something else. Shame on you, Eilert Loevborg! How could you abuse the trust of your dearest friend?

LOEVBORG [Clenches his fists.]   Oh, why didn't you do it? Why didn't you shoot me dead? As you threatened to?

HEDDA   I was afraid. Of the scandal.

LOEVBORG   Yes, Hedda. You're a coward at heart.

HEDDA   A dreadful coward. [*Changes her tone.*] Luckily for you. Well, now you've found consolation with the Elvsteds.

LOEVBORG   I know what Thea's been telling you.

HEDDA   I dare say you told her about us.

LOEVBORG   Not a word. She's too silly to understand that kind of thing.

HEDDA   Silly?

LOEVBORG   She's silly about that kind of thing.

HEDDA   And I am a coward. [*Leans closer to him, without looking him in the eyes, and says quietly.*] But let me tell you something. Something you don't know.

LOEVBORG [*Tensely.*]   Yes?

HEDDA   My failure to shoot you wasn't my worst act of cowardice that evening.

LOEVBORG [*Looks at her for a moment, realizes her meaning and whispers passionately.*]   Oh, Hedda! Hedda Gabler! Now I see what was behind those questions. Yes! It wasn't knowledge you wanted! It was life!

HEDDA [*Flashes a look at him and says quietly.*]   Take care! Don't you delude yourself!

[*It has begun to grow dark.* BERTHA, *from outside, opens the door leading into the hall.*]

HEDDA [*Closes the album with a snap and cries, smiling.*]   Ah, at last! Come in, Thea dear!

[MRS. ELVSTED *enters from the hall, in evening dress. The door is closed behind her.*]

HEDDA [*On the sofa, stretches out her arms toward her.*]   Thea darling, I thought you were never coming!

[MRS. ELVSTED *makes a slight bow to the gentlemen in the rear room as she passes the open doorway, and they to her. Then she goes to the table and holds out her hand to* HEDDA. EILERT LOEVBORG *has risen from his chair. He and* MRS. ELVSTED *nod silently to each other.*]

MRS. ELVSTED   Perhaps I ought to go in and say a few words to your husband?

HEDDA   Oh, there's no need. They're happy by themselves. They'll be going soon.

MRS. ELVSTED   Going?

HEDDA   Yes, they're off on a spree this evening.

MRS. ELVSTED [*Quickly, to* LOEVBORG.]   You're not going with them?

LOEVBORG   No.

HEDDA   Mr. Loevborg is staying here with us.

MRS. ELVSTED [*Takes a chair and is about to sit down beside him.*]   Oh, how nice it is to be here!

HEDDA   No, Thea darling, not there. Come over here and sit beside me. I want to be in the middle.

MRS. ELVSTED   Yes, just as you wish.

[*She goes right of the table and sits on the sofa, on* HEDDA's *right.* LOEVBORG *sits down again in his chair.*]

LOEVBORG [*After a short pause, to* HEDDA.]   Isn't she lovely to look at?

HEDDA [*Strokes her hair gently.*]   Only to look at?

LOEVBORG   Yes. We're just good pals. We trust each other implicitly. We can talk to each other quite unashamedly.

HEDDA No need to be oblique?

MRS. ELVSTED [*Nestles close to* HEDDA *and says quietly.*] Oh, Hedda I'm so happy. Imagine—he says I've inspired him!

HEDDA [*Looks at her with a smile.*] Dear Thea! Does he really?

LOEVBORG She has the courage of her convictions, Mrs. Tesman.

MRS. ELVSTED I? Courage?

LOEVBORG Absolute courage. Where friendship is concerned.

HEDDA Yes. Courage. Yes. If only one had that——

LOEVBORG Yes?

HEDDA One might be able to live. In spite of everything. [*Changes her tone suddenly.*] Well, Thea darling, now you're going to drink a nice glass of cold punch.

MRS. ELVSTED No, thank you. I never drink anything like that.

HEDDA Oh. You, Mr. Loevborg?

LOEVBORG Thank you, I don't either.

MRS. ELVSTED No, he doesn't, either.

HEDDA [*Looks into his eyes.*] But if I want you to?

LOEVBORG That doesn't make any difference.

HEDDA [*Laughs.*] Have I no power over you at all? Poor me!

LOEVBORG Not where this is concerned.

HEDDA Seriously, I think you should. For your own sake.

MRS. ELVSTED Hedda!

LOEVBORG Why?

HEDDA Or perhaps I should say for other people's sake.

LOEVBORG What do you mean?

HEDDA People might think you didn't feel absolutely and unashamedly sure of yourself. In your heart of hearts.

MRS. ELVSTED [*Quietly.*] Oh, Hedda, no!

LOEVBORG People can think what they like. For the present.

MRS. ELVSTED [*Happily.*] Yes, that's true.

HEDDA I saw it so clearly in Judge Brack a few minutes ago.

LOEVBORG Oh. What did you see?

HEDDA He smiled so scornfully when he saw you were afraid to go in there and drink with them.

LOEVBORG Afraid! I wanted to stay here and talk to you.

MRS. ELVSTED That was only natural, Hedda.

HEDDA But the Judge wasn't to know that. I saw him wink at Tesman when you showed you didn't dare to join their wretched little party.

LOEVBORG Didn't dare! Are you saying I didn't dare?

HEDDA I'm not saying so. But that was what Judge Brack thought.

LOEVBORG Well, let him.

HEDDA You're not going, then?

LOEVBORG I'm staying here with you and Thea.

MRS. ELVSTED Yes, Hedda, of course he is.

HEDDA [*Smiles, and nods approvingly to* LOEVBORG.] Firm as a rock! A man of principle! That's how a man should be! [*Turns to* MRS. ELVSTED *and strokes her cheek.*] Didn't I tell you so this morning when you came here in such a panic——

LOEVBORG [*Starts.*] Panic?

MRS. ELVSTED [*Frightened.*] Hedda! But—Hedda!

HEDDA Well, now you can see for yourself. There's no earthly need for you to get scared to death just because—— [*Stops.*] Well! Let's all three cheer up and enjoy ourselves.

LOEVBORG   Mrs. Tesman, would you mind explaining to me what this is all about?

MRS. ELVSTED   Oh, my God, my God, Hedda, what are you saying? What are you doing?

HEDDA   Keep calm. That horrid Judge has his eye on you.

LOEVBORG   Scared to death, were you? For my sake?

MRS. ELVSTED [*Quietly, trembling.*]   Oh, Hedda! You've made me so unhappy!

LOEVBORG [*Looks coldly at her for a moment. His face is distorted.*]   So that was how much you trusted me.

MRS. ELVSTED   Eilert dear, please listen to me——

LOEVBORG [*Takes one of the glasses of punch, raises it and says quietly, hoarsely.*]   Skoal, Thea! [*Empties the glass, puts it down and picks up one of the others.*]

MRS. ELVSTED [*Quietly.*]   Hedda, Hedda! Why did you want this to happen?

HEDDA   I—want it? Are you mad?

LOEVBORG   Skoal to you too, Mrs. Tesman. Thanks for telling me the truth. Here's to the truth! [*Empties his glass and refills it.*]

HEDDA [*Puts her hand on his arm.*]   Steady. That's enough for now. Don't forget the party.

MRS. ELVSTED   No, no, no!

HEDDA   Ssh! They're looking at you.

LOEVBORG [*Puts down his glass.*]   Thea, tell me the truth——

MRS. ELVSTED   Yes!

LOEVBORG   Did your husband know you were following me?

MRS. ELVSTED   Oh, Hedda!

LOEVBORG   Did you and he have an agreement that you should come here and keep an eye on me? Perhaps he gave you the idea? After all, he's a magistrate.[2] I suppose he needed me back in his office. Or did he miss my companionship at the card table?

MRS. ELVSTED [*Quietly, sobbing.*]   Eilert, Eilert!

LOEVBORG [*Seizes a glass and is about to fill it.*]   Let's drink to him, too.

HEDDA   No more now. Remember you're going to read your book to Tesman.

LOEVBORG [*Calm again, puts down his glass.*]   That was silly of me, Thea. To take it like that, I mean. Don't be angry with me, my dear. You'll see— yes, and they'll see, too—that though I fell, I—I have raised myself up again. With your help, Thea.

MRS. ELVSTED [*Happily.*]   Oh, thank God!

[BRACK *has meanwhile glanced at his watch. He and* TESMAN *get up and come into the drawing room.*]

BRACK [*Takes his hat and overcoat.*]   Well, Mrs. Tesman. It's time for us to go.

HEDDA   Yes, I suppose it must be.

LOEVBORG [*Gets up.*]   Time for me too, Judge.

---

2. Also translated "sheriff." A civil official with duties associated with the courts.

MRS. ELVSTED [*Quietly, pleadingly.*]   Eilert, please don't!

HEDDA [*Pinches her arm.*]   They can hear you.

MRS. ELVSTED [*Gives a little cry.*]   Oh!

LOEVBORG [*To* BRACK.]   You were kind enough to ask me to join you.

BRACK   Are you coming?

LOEVBORG   If I may.

BRACK   Delighted.

LOEVBORG [*Puts the paper package in his pocket and says to* TESMAN.]   I'd like to show you one or two things before I send it off to the printer.

TESMAN   I say, that'll be fun. Fancy——! Oh, but Hedda, how'll Mrs. Elvsted get home? What?

HEDDA   Oh, we'll manage somehow.

LOEVBORG [*Glances over toward the ladies.*]   Mrs. Elvsted? I shall come back and collect her, naturally. [*Goes closer.*] About ten o'clock, Mrs. Tesman? Will that suit you?

HEDDA   Yes. That'll suit me admirably.

TESMAN   Good, that's settled. But you mustn't expect me back so early, Hedda.

HEDDA   Stay as long as you c—as long as you like, dear.

MRS. ELVSTED [*Trying to hide her anxiety.*]   Well then, Mr. Loevborg, I'll wait here till you come.

LOEVBORG [*His hat in his hand.*]   Pray do, Mrs. Elvsted.

BRACK   Well, gentlemen, now the party begins. I trust that, in the words of a certain fair lady, we shall enjoy good sport.

HEDDA   What a pity the fair lady can't be there, invisible.

BRACK   Why invisible?

HEDDA   So as to be able to hear some of your uncensored witticisms, your honor.

BRACK [*Laughs.*]   Oh, I shouldn't advise the fair lady to do that.

TESMAN [*Laughs too.*]   I say, Hedda, that's good. By Jove! Fancy that!

BRACK   Well, good night, ladies, good night!

LOEVBORG [*Bows farewell.*]   About ten o'clock, then.

> [BRACK, LOEVBORG *and* TESMAN *go out through the hall. As they do so* BERTHA *enters from the rear room with a lighted lamp. She puts it on the drawing-room table, then goes out the way she came.*]

MRS. ELVSTED [*Has got up and is walking uneasily to and fro.*]   Oh Hedda, Hedda! How is all this going to end?

HEDDA   At ten o'clock, then. He'll be here. I can see him. With a crown of vine-leaves in his hair.[3] Burning and unashamed!

MRS. ELVSTED   Oh, I do hope so!

HEDDA   Can't you see? Then he'll be himself again! He'll be a free man for the rest of his days!

MRS. ELVSTED   Please God you're right.

HEDDA   That's how he'll come! [*Gets up and goes closer.*] You can doubt him as much as you like. I believe in him! Now we'll see which of us——

MRS. ELVSTED   You're after something, Hedda.

HEDDA   Yes, I am. For once in my life I want to have the power to shape a man's destiny.

---

3. Like Bacchus, the Greek god of wine, and his followers.

MRS. ELVSTED   Haven't you that power already?

HEDDA   No, I haven't. I've never had it.

MRS. ELVSTED   What about your husband?

HEDDA   Him! Oh, if you could only understand how poor I am. And you're allowed to be so rich, so rich! [*Clasps her passionately.*] I think I'll burn your hair off after all!

MRS. ELVSTED   Let me go! Let me go! You frighten me, Hedda!

BERTHA [*In the open doorway.*]   I've laid tea in the dining room, madam.

HEDDA   Good, we're coming.

MRS. ELVSTED   No, no, no! I'd rather go home alone! Now—at once!

HEDDA   Rubbish! First you're going to have some tea, you little idiot. And then—at ten o'clock—Eilert Loevborg will come. With a crown of vine-leaves in his hair!

[*She drags* MRS. ELVSTED *almost forcibly toward the open doorway.*]

Act III

SCENE—*The same. The curtains are drawn across the open doorway, and also across the french windows. The lamp, half turned down, with a shade over it, is burning on the table. In the stove, the door of which is open, a fire has been burning, but it is now almost out.*

MRS. ELVSTED, *wrapped in a large shawl and with her feet resting on a footstool, is sitting near the stove, huddled in the armchair.* HEDDA *is lying asleep on this sofa, fully dressed, with a blanket over her.*

MRS. ELVSTED [*After a pause, suddenly sits up in her chair and listens tensely. Then she sinks wearily back again and sighs.*]   Not back yet! Oh, God! Oh, God! Not back yet!

[BERTHA *tiptoes cautiously in from the hall. She has a letter in her hand.*]

MRS. ELVSTED [*Turns and whispers.*]   What is it? Has someone come?

BERTHA [*Quietly.*]   Yes, a servant's just called with this letter.

MRS. ELVSTED [*Quickly, holding out her hand.*]   A letter! Give it to me!

BERTHA   But it's for the Doctor, madam.

MRS. ELVSTED   Oh. I see.

BERTHA   Miss Tesman's maid brought it. I'll leave it here on the table.

MRS. ELVSTED   Yes, do.

BERTHA [*Puts down the letter.*]   I'd better put the lamp out. It's starting to smoke.

MRS. ELVSTED   Yes, put it out. It'll soon be daylight.

BERTHA [*Puts out the lamp.*]   It's daylight already, madam.

MRS. ELVSTED   Yes. Broad day. And not home yet.

BERTHA   Oh dear, I was afraid this would happen.

MRS. ELVSTED   Were you?

BERTHA   Yes. When I heard that a certain gentleman had returned to town, and saw him go off with them. I've heard all about him.

MRS. ELVSTED   Don't talk so loud. You'll wake your mistress.

BERTHA [*Looks at the sofa and sighs.*]   Yes. Let her go on sleeping, poor dear. Shall I put some more wood on the fire?

MRS. ELVSTED   Thank you, don't bother on my account.

BERTHA   Very good. [*Goes quietly out through the hall.*]

HEDDA [*Wakes as the door closes and looks up.*]   What's that?

MRS. ELVSTED   It was only the maid.

HEDDA [*Looks round.*]   What am I doing here? Oh, now I remember. [*Sits up on the sofa, stretches herself and rubs her eyes.*] What time is it, Thea?

MRS. ELVSTED   It's gone seven.

HEDDA   When did Tesman get back?

MRS. ELVSTED   He's not back yet.

HEDDA   Not home yet?

MRS. ELVSTED [*Gets up.*]   No one's come.

HEDDA   And we sat up waiting for them till four o'clock.

MRS. ELVSTED   God! How I waited for him!

HEDDA [*Yawns and says with her hand in front of her mouth.*]   Oh, dear. We might have saved ourselves the trouble.

MRS. ELVSTED   Did you manage to sleep?

HEDDA   Oh, yes. Quite well, I think. Didn't you get any?

MRS. ELVSTED   Not a wink. I couldn't, Hedda. I just couldn't.

HEDDA [*Gets up and comes over to her.*]   Now, now, now. There's nothing to worry about. I know what's happened.

MRS. ELVSTED   What? Please tell me.

HEDDA   Well, obviously the party went on very late——

MRS. ELVSTED   Oh dear, I suppose it must have. But——

HEDDA   And Tesman didn't want to come home and wake us all up in the middle of the night. [*Laughs.*] Probably wasn't too keen to show his face either, after a spree like that.

MRS. ELVSTED   But where could he have gone?

HEDDA   I should think he's probably slept at his aunts'. They keep his old room for him.

MRS. ELVSTED   No, he can't be with them. A letter came for him just now from Miss Tesman. It's over there.

HEDDA   Oh? [*Looks at the envelope.*]   Yes, it's Auntie Juju's handwriting. Well, he must still be at Judge Brack's, then. And Eilert Loevborg is sitting there, reading to him. With a crown of vine-leaves in his hair.

MRS. ELVSTED   Hedda, you're only saying that. You don't believe it.

HEDDA   Thea, you really are a little fool.

MRS. ELVSTED   Perhaps I am.

HEDDA   You look tired to death.

MRS. ELVSTED   Yes. I am tired to death.

HEDDA   Go to my room and lie down for a little. Do as I say, now; don't argue.

MRS. ELVSTED   No, no. I couldn't possibly sleep.

HEDDA   Of course you can.

MRS. ELVSTED   But your husband'll be home soon. And I must know at once——

HEDDA   I'll tell you when he comes.

MRS. ELVSTED   Promise me, Hedda?

HEDDA   Yes, don't worry. Go and get some sleep.

MRS. ELVSTED   Thank you. All right, I'll try.

[*She goes out through the rear room.* HEDDA *goes to the french windows and draws the curtains. Broad daylight floods into the room.*

She goes to the writing table, takes a small hand mirror from it and arranges her hair. Then she goes to the door leading into the hall and presses the bell. After a few moments, BERTHA *enters.*]

BERTHA Did you want anything, madam?

HEDDA Yes, put some more wood on the fire. I'm freezing.

BERTHA Bless you, I'll soon have this room warmed up. [*She rakes the embers together and puts a fresh piece of wood on them. Suddenly she stops and listens.*] There's someone at the front door, madam.

HEDDA Well, go and open it. I'll see to the fire.

BERTHA It'll burn up in a moment.

[*She goes out through the hall.* HEDDA *kneels on the footstool and puts more wood in the stove. After a few seconds,* GEORGE TESMAN *enters from the hall. He looks tired, and rather worried. He tiptoes toward the open doorway and is about to slip through the curtains.*]

HEDDA [*At the stove, without looking up.*] Good morning.

TESMAN [*Turns.*] Hedda! [*Comes nearer.*] Good heavens, are you up already? What?

HEDDA Yes, I got up very early this morning.

TESMAN I was sure you'd still be sleeping. Fancy that!

HEDDA Don't talk so loud. Mrs. Elvsted's asleep in my room.

TESMAN Mrs. Elvsted? Has she stayed the night here?

HEDDA Yes. No one came to escort her home.

TESMAN Oh. No, I suppose not.

HEDDA [*Closes the door of the stove and gets up.*] Well. Was it fun?

TESMAN Have you been anxious about me? What?

HEDDA Not in the least. I asked if you'd had fun.

TESMAN Oh yes, rather! Well, I thought, for once in a while—The first part was the best; when Eilert read his book to me. We arrived over an hour too early—what about that, eh? By Jove! Brack had a lot of things to see to, so Eilert read to me.

HEDDA [*Sits at the right-hand side of the table.*] Well? Tell me about it.

TESMAN [*Sits on a footstool by the stove.*] Honestly, Hedda, you've no idea what a book that's going to be. It's really one of the most remarkable things that's ever been written. By Jove!

HEDDA Oh, never mind about the book——

TESMAN I'm going to make a confession to you, Hedda. When he'd finished reading a sort of beastly feeling came over me.

HEDDA Beastly feeling?

TESMAN I found myself envying Eilert for being able to write like that. Imagine that, Hedda!

HEDDA Yes. I can imagine.

TESMAN What a tragedy that with all those gifts he should be so incorrigible.

HEDDA You mean he's less afraid of life than most men?

TESMAN Good heavens, no. He just doesn't know the meaning of the word moderation.

HEDDA What happened afterwards?

TESMAN Well, looking back on it I suppose you might almost call it an orgy, Hedda.

HEDDA Had he vine-leaves in his hair?

TESMAN   Vine-leaves? No, I didn't see any of them. He made a long, ram-
bling oration in honor of the woman who'd inspired him to write this
book. Yes, those were the words he used.

HEDDA   Did he name her?

TESMAN   No. But I suppose it must be Mrs. Elvsted. You wait and see!

HEDDA   Where did you leave him?

TESMAN   On the way home. We left in a bunch—the last of us, that is—
and Brack came with us to get a little fresh air. Well, then, you see, we
agreed we ought to see Eilert home. He'd had a drop too much.

HEDDA   You don't say?

TESMAN   But now comes the funny part, Hedda. Or I should really say the
tragic part. Oh, I'm almost ashamed to tell you. For Eilert's sake, I
mean—

HEDDA   Why, what happened?

TESMAN   Well, you see, as we were walking toward town I happened to
drop behind for a minute. Only for a minute—er—you understand——

HEDDA   Yes, yes——

TESMAN   Well then, when I ran on to catch them up, what do you think
I found by the roadside. What?

HEDDA   How on earth should I know?

TESMAN   You mustn't tell anyone, Hedda. What? Promise me that—for
Eilert's sake. [*Takes a package wrapped in paper from his coat pocket.*]
Just fancy! I found this.

HEDDA   Isn't this the one he brought here yesterday?

TESMAN   Yes! The whole of that precious, irreplaceable manuscript! And
he went and lost it! Didn't even notice! What about that? By Jove! Tragic.

HEDDA   But why didn't you give it back to him?

TESMAN   I didn't dare to, in the state he was in.

HEDDA   Didn't you tell any of the others?

TESMAN   Good heavens, no. I didn't want to do that. For Eilert's sake, you
understand.

HEDDA   Then no one else knows you have his manuscript?

TESMAN   No. And no one must be allowed to know.

HEDDA   Didn't it come up in the conversation later?

TESMAN   I didn't get a chance to talk to him any more. As soon as we got
into the outskirts of town, he and one or two of the others gave us the
slip. Disappeared, by Jove!

HEDDA   Oh? I suppose they took him home.

TESMAN   Yes, I imagine that was the idea. Brack left us, too.

HEDDA   And what have you been up to since then?

TESMAN   Well, I and one or two of the others—awfully jolly chaps, they
were—went back to where one of them lived, and had a cup of morning
coffee. Morning after coffee—what? Ah, well. I'll just lie down for a bit
and give Eilert time to sleep it off, poor chap, then I'll run over and give
this back to him.

HEDDA   [*Holds out her hand for the package.*]   No, don't do that. Not just
yet. Let me read it first.

TESMAN   Oh no, really, Hedda dear, honestly, I daren't do that.

HEDDA   Daren't?

TESMAN   No—imagine how desperate he'll be when he wakes up and finds his manuscript's missing. He hasn't any copy, you see. He told me so himself.

HEDDA   Can't a thing like that be rewritten?

TESMAN   Oh no, not possibly, I shouldn't think. I mean, the inspiration, you know——

HEDDA   Oh, yes. I'd forgotten that. [*Casually.*] By the way, there's a letter for you.

TESMAN   Is there? Fancy that!

HEDDA [*Holds it out to him.*]   It came early this morning.

TESMAN   I say, it's from Auntie Juju! What on earth can it be? [*Puts the package on the other footstool, opens the letter, reads it and jumps up.*] Oh, Hedda! She says poor Auntie Rena's dying.

HEDDA   Well, we've been expecting that.

TESMAN   She says if I want to see her I must go quickly. I'll run over at once.

HEDDA [*Hides a smile.*]   Run?

TESMAN   Hedda dear, I suppose you wouldn't like to come with me? What about that, eh?

HEDDA [*Gets up and says wearily and with repulsion.*]   No, no, don't ask me to do anything like that. I can't bear illness or death. I loathe anything ugly.

TESMAN   Yes, yes. Of course. [*In a dither.*] My hat? My overcoat? Oh yes, in the hall. I do hope I won't get there too late, Hedda? What?

HEDDA   You'll be all right if you run.

[BERTHA *enters from the hall.*]

BERTHA   Judge Brack's outside and wants to know if he can come in.

TESMAN   At this hour? No, I can't possibly receive him now.

HEDDA   I can. [*To* BERTHA.] Ask his honor to come in.

[BERTHA *goes.*]

HEDDA [*Whispers quickly.*]   The manuscript, Tesman. [*She snatches it from the footstool.*]

TESMAN   Yes, give it to me.

HEDDA   No, I'll look after it for now.

[*She goes over to the writing table and puts it in the bookcase.* TES-MAN *stands dithering, unable to get his gloves on.* JUDGE BRACK *enters from the hall.*]

HEDDA [*Nods to him.*]   Well, you're an early bird.

BRACK   Yes, aren't I? [*To* TESMAN.] Are you up and about, too?

TESMAN   Yes, I've got to go and see my aunts. Poor Auntie Rena's dying.

BRACK   Oh dear, is she? Then you mustn't let me detain you. At so tragic a——

TESMAN   Yes, I really must run. Good-bye! Good-bye! [*Runs out through the hall.*]

HEDDA [*Goes nearer.*]   You seem to have had excellent sport last night— Judge.

BRACK   Indeed yes, Mrs. Hedda. I haven't even had time to take my clothes off.

HEDDA   *You* haven't either?

BRACK   As you see. What's Tesman told you about last night's escapades?

HEDDA   Oh, only some boring story about having gone and drunk coffee somewhere.

BRACK   Yes, I've heard about that coffee party. Eilert Loevborg wasn't with them, I gather?

HEDDA   No, they took him home first.

BRACK   Did Tesman go with him?

HEDDA   No, one or two of the others, he said.

BRACK [*Smiles.*]   George Tesman is a credulous man, Mrs. Hedda.

HEDDA   God knows. But—has something happened?

BRACK   Well, yes, I'm afraid it has.

HEDDA   I see. Sit down and tell me.
[*She sits on the left of the table,* BRACK *at the long side of it, near her.*]

HEDDA   Well?

BRACK   I had a special reason for keeping track of my guests last night. Or perhaps I should say some of my guests.

HEDDA   Including Eilert Loevborg?

BRACK   I must confess—yes.

HEDDA   You're beginning to make me curious.

BRACK   Do you know where he and some of my other guests spent the latter half of last night, Mrs. Hedda?

HEDDA   Tell me. If it won't shock me.

BRACK   Oh, I don't think it'll shock you. They found themselves participating in an exceedingly animated *soirée.*[4]

HEDDA   Of a sporting character?

BRACK   Of a highly sporting character.

HEDDA   Tell me more.

BRACK   Loevborg had received an invitation in advance—as had the others. I knew all about that. But he had refused. As you know, he's become a new man.

HEDDA   Up at the Elvsteds', yes. But he went?

BRACK   Well, you see, Mrs. Hedda, last night at my house, unhappily, the spirit moved him.

HEDDA   Yes, I hear he became inspired.

BRACK   Somewhat violently inspired. And as a result, I suppose, his thoughts strayed. We men, alas, don't always stick to our principles as firmly as we should.

HEDDA   I'm sure you're an exception, Judge Brack. But go on about Loevborg.

BRACK   Well, to cut a long story short, he ended up in the establishment of a certain Mademoiselle Danielle.

HEDDA   Mademoiselle Danielle?

BRACK   She was holding the *soirée.* For a selected circle of friends and admirers.

HEDDA   Has she got red hair?

BRACK   She has.

HEDDA   A singer of some kind?

BRACK   Yes—among other accomplishments. She's also a celebrated huntress—of men, Mrs. Hedda. I'm sure you've heard about her. Eilert Loevborg used to be one of her most ardent patrons. In his salad days.[5]

HEDDA   And how did all this end?

---

4. Evening party.   5. Indiscreet youth.

BRACK   Not entirely amicably, from all accounts. Mademoiselle Danielle began by receiving him with the utmost tenderness and ended by resorting to her fists.

HEDDA   Against Loevborg?

BRACK   Yes. He accused her, or her friends, of having robbed him. He claimed his pocketbook had been stolen. Among other things. In short, he seems to have made a bloodthirsty scene.

HEDDA   And what did this lead to?

BRACK   It led to a general free-for-all, in which both sexes participated. Fortunately, in the end the police arrived.

HEDDA   The police too?

BRACK   Yes. I'm afraid it may turn out to be rather an expensive joke for Master Eilert. Crazy fool!

HEDDA   Oh?

BRACK   Apparently he put up a very violent resistance. Hit one of the constables on the ear and tore his uniform. He had to accompany them to the police station.

HEDDA   Where did you learn all this?

BRACK   From the police.

HEDDA [To herself.]   So that's what happened. He didn't have a crown of vine-leaves in his hair.

BRACK   Vine-leaves, Mrs. Hedda?

HEDDA [In her normal voice again.]   But, tell me, Judge, why do you take such a close interest in Eilert Loevborg?

BRACK   For one thing it'll hardly be a matter of complete indifference to me if it's revealed in court that he came there straight from my house.

HEDDA   Will it come to court?

BRACK   Of course. Well, I don't regard that as particularly serious. Still, I thought it my duty, as a friend of the family, to give you and your husband a full account of his nocturnal adventures.

HEDDA   Why?

BRACK   Because I've a shrewd suspicion that he's hoping to use you as a kind of screen.

HEDDA   What makes you think that?

BRACK   Oh, for heaven's sake, Mrs. Hedda, we're not blind. You wait and see. This Mrs. Elvsted won't be going back to her husband just yet.

HEDDA   Well, if there were anything between those two there are plenty of other places where they could meet.

BRACK   Not in anyone's home. From now on every respectable house will once again be closed to Eilert Loevborg.

HEDDA   And mine should be too, you mean?

BRACK   Yes. I confess I should find it more than irksome if this gentleman were to be granted unrestricted access to this house. If he were superfluously to intrude into——

HEDDA   The triangle?

BRACK   Precisely. For me it would be like losing a home.

HEDDA [Looks at him and smiles.]   I see. You want to be the cock of the walk.

BRACK [Nods slowly and lowers his voice.]   Yes, that is my aim. And I shall fight for it with—every weapon at my disposal.

HEDDA [*As her smile fades.*]   You're a dangerous man, aren't you? When you really want something.

BRACK   You think so?

HEDDA   Yes. I'm beginning to think so. I'm deeply thankful you haven't any kind of hold over me.

BRACK [*Laughs equivocally.*]   Well, well, Mrs. Hedda—perhaps you're right. If I had, who knows what I might not think up?

HEDDA   Come, Judge Brack. That sounds almost like a threat.

BRACK [*Gets up.*]   Heaven forbid! In the creation of a triangle—and its continuance—the question of compulsion should never arise.

HEDDA   Exactly what I was thinking.

BRACK   Well, I've said what I came to say. I must be getting back. Goodbye, Mrs. Hedda. [*Goes toward the french windows.*]

HEDDA [*Gets up.*]   Are you going out through the garden?

BRACK   Yes, it's shorter.

HEDDA   Yes. And it's the back door, isn't it?

BRACK   I've nothing against back doors. They can be quite intriguing—sometimes.

HEDDA   When people fire pistols out of them, for example?

BRACK [*In the doorway, laughs.*]   Oh, people don't shoot tame cocks.

HEDDA [*Laughs too.*]   I suppose not. When they've only got one.

[*They nod good-bye, laughing. He goes. She closes the french windows behind him, and stands for a moment, looking out pensively. Then she walks across the room and glances through the curtains in the open doorway. Goes to the writing table, takes* LOEVBORG's *package from the bookcase and is about to leaf through the pages when* BERTHA *is heard remonstrating loudly in the hall.* HEDDA *turns and listens. She hastily puts the package back in the drawer, locks it and puts the key on the inkstand.* EILERT LOEVBORG, *with his overcoat on and his hat in his hand, throws the door open. He looks somewhat confused and excited.*]

LOEVBORG [*Shouts as he enters.*]   I must come in, I tell you! Let me pass! [*He closes the door, turns, sees* HEDDA, *controls himself immediately and bows.*]

HEDDA [*At the writing table.*]   Well, Mr. Loevborg, this is rather a late hour to be collecting Thea.

LOEVBORG   And an early hour to call on you. Please forgive me.

HEDDA   How do you know she's still here?

LOEVBORG   They told me at her lodgings that she has been out all night.

HEDDA [*Goes to the table.*]   Did you notice anything about their behavior when they told you?

LOEVBORG [*Looks at her, puzzled.*]   Notice anything?

HEDDA   Did they sound as if they thought it—strange?

LOEVBORG [*Suddenly understands.*]   Oh, I see what you mean. I'm dragging her down with me. No, as a matter of fact I didn't notice anything. I suppose Tesman isn't up yet?

HEDDA   No, I don't think so.

LOEVBORG   When did he get home?

HEDDA   Very late.

LOEVBORG   Did he tell you anything?

HEDDA   Yes. I gather you had a merry party at Judge Brack's last night.

LOEVBORG   He didn't tell you anything else?

HEDDA   I don't think so. I was so terribly sleepy——

[MRS. ELVSTED *comes through the curtains in the open doorway.*]

MRS. ELVSTED [*Runs toward him.*]   Oh, Eilert! At last!

LOEVBORG   Yes—at last. And too late.

MRS. ELVSTED   What is too late?

LOEVBORG   Everything—now. I'm finished, Thea.

MRS. ELVSTED   Oh, no, no! Don't say that!

LOEVBORG   You'll say it yourself, when you've heard what I——

MRS. ELVSTED   I don't want to hear anything!

HEDDA   Perhaps you'd rather speak to her alone? I'd better go.

LOEVBORG   No, stay.

MRS. ELVSTED   But I don't want to hear anything, I tell you!

LOEVBORG   It's not about last night.

MRS. ELVSTED   Then what——?

LOEVBORG   I want to tell you that from now on we must stop seeing each other.

MRS. ELVSTED   Stop seeing each other!

HEDDA [*Involuntarily.*]   I knew it!

LOEVBORG   I have no further use for you, Thea.

MRS. ELVSTED   You can stand there and say that! No further use for me! Surely I can go on helping you? We'll go on working together, won't we?

LOEVBORG   I don't intend to do any more work from now on.

MRS. ELVSTED [*Desperately.*]   Then what use have I for my life?

LOEVBORG   You must try to live as if you had never known me.

MRS. ELVSTED   But I can't!

LOEVBORG   Try to, Thea. Go back home——

MRS. ELVSTED   Never! I want to be wherever you are! I won't let myself be driven away like this! I want to stay here—and be with you when the book comes out.

HEDDA [*Whispers.*]   Ah, yes! The book!

LOEVBORG [*Looks at her.*]   Our book; Thea's and mine. It belongs to both of us.

MRS. ELVSTED   Oh, yes! I feel that, too! And I've a right to be with you when it comes into the world. I want to see people respect and honor you again. And the joy! The joy! I want to share it with you!

LOEVBORG   Thea—our book will never come into the world.

HEDDA   Ah!

MRS. ELVSTED   Not——?

LOEVBORG   It cannot. Ever.

MRS. ELVSTED   Eilert—what have you done with the manuscript? Where is it?

LOEVBORG   Oh, Thea, please don't ask me that!

MRS. ELVSTED   Yes, yes—I must know. I've a right to know. Now!

LOEVBORG   The manuscript. I've torn it up.

MRS. ELVSTED [*Screams.*]   No, no!

HEDDA [*Involuntarily.*]   But that's not——!

LOEVBORG [*Looks at her.*]   Not true, you think?

HEDDA [*Controls herself.*]   Why—yes, of course it is, if you say so. It just sounded so incredible——

LOEVBORG   It's true, nevertheless.

MRS. ELVSTED   Oh, my God, my God, Hedda—he's destroyed his own book!

LOEVBORG   I have destroyed my life. Why not my life's work, too?

MRS. ELVSTED   And you—did this last night?

LOEVBORG   Yes, Thea. I tore it into a thousand pieces. And scattered them out across the fjord.[6] It's good, clean, salt water. Let it carry them away; let them drift in the current and the wind. And in a little while, they will sink. Deeper and deeper. As I shall, Thea.

MRS. ELVSTED   Do you know, Eilert—this book—all my life I shall feel as though you'd killed a little child?

LOEVBORG   You're right. It is like killing a child.

MRS. ELVSTED   But how could you? It was my child, too!

HEDDA [Almost inaudibly.]   Oh—the child—!

MRS. ELVSTED [Breathes heavily.]   It's all over, then. Well—I'll go now, Hedda.

HEDDA   You're not leaving town?

MRS. ELVSTED   I don't know what I'm going to do. I can't see anything except—darkness.

[She goes out through the hall.]

HEDDA [Waits a moment.]   Aren't you going to escort her home, Mr. Loevborg?

LOEVBORG   I? Through the streets? Do you want me to let people see her with me?

HEDDA   Of course I don't know what else may have happened last night. But is it so utterly beyond redress?

LOEVBORG   It isn't just last night. It'll go on happening. I know it. But the curse of it is, I don't want to live that kind of life. I don't want to start all that again. She's broken my courage. I can't spit in the eyes of the world any longer.

HEDDA [As though to herself.]   That pretty little fool's been trying to shape a man's destiny. [Looks at him.] But how could you be so heartless toward her?

LOEVBORG   Don't call me heartless!

HEDDA   To go and destroy the one thing that's made her life worth living? You don't call that heartless?

LOEVBORG   Do you want to know the truth, Hedda?

HEDDA   The truth?

LOEVBORG   Promise me first—give me your word—that you'll never let Thea know about this.

HEDDA   I give you my word.

LOEVBORG   Good. Well; what I told her just now was a lie.

HEDDA   About the manuscript?

LOEVBORG   Yes. I didn't tear it up. Or throw it in the fjord.

HEDDA   You didn't? But where is it, then?

LOEVBORG   I destroyed it, all the same. I destroyed it, Hedda!

HEDDA   I don't understand.

LOEVBORG   Thea said that what I had done was like killing a child.

HEDDA   Yes. That's what she said.

6. Inlet of the sea.

LOEVBORG   But to kill a child isn't the worst thing a father can do to it.
HEDDA   What could be worse than that?
LOEVBORG   Hedda—suppose a man came home one morning, after a night of debauchery, and said to the mother of his child: "Look here. I've been wandering round all night. I've been to—such-and-such a place and such-and-such a place. And I had our child with me. I took him to—these places. And I've lost him. Just—lost him. God knows where he is or whose hands he's fallen into."
HEDDA   I see. But when all's said and done, this was only a book——
LOEVBORG   Thea's heart and soul were in that book. It was her whole life.
HEDDA   Yes. I understand.
LOEVBORG   Well, then you must also understand that she and I cannot possibly ever see each other again.
HEDDA   Where will you go?
LOEVBORG   Nowhere. I just want to put an end to it all. As soon as possible.
HEDDA [*Takes a step toward him.*]   Eilert Loevborg, listen to me. Do it—beautifully!
LOEVBORG   Beautifully? [*Smiles.*] With a crown of vine-leaves in my hair? The way you used to dream of me—in the old days?
HEDDA   No. I don't believe in that crown any longer. But—do it beautifully, all the same. Just this once. Good-bye. You must go now. And don't come back.
LOEVBORG   Adieu, madam. Give my love to George Tesman. [*Turns to go.*]
HEDDA   Wait. I want to give you a souvenir to take with you.
    [*She goes over to the writing table, opens the drawer and the pistol-case, and comes back to* LOEVBORG *with one of the pistols.*]
LOEVBORG [*Looks at her.*]   This? Is this the souvenir?
HEDDA [*Nods slowly.*]   You recognize it? You looked down its barrel once.
LOEVBORG   You should have used it then.
HEDDA   Here! Use it now!
LOEVBORG [*Puts the pistol in his breast pocket.*]   Thank you.
HEDDA   Do it beautifully, Eilert Loevborg. Only promise me that!
LOEVBORG   Good-bye, Hedda Gabler.
    [*He goes out through the hall.* HEDDA *stands by the door for a moment, listening. Then she goes over to the writing table, takes out the package containing the manuscript, glances inside it, pulls some of the pages half out and looks at them. Then she takes it to the armchair by the stove and sits down with the package in her lap. After a moment, she opens the door of the stove; then she opens the packet.*]
HEDDA [*Throws one of the pages into the stove and whispers to herself.*]   I'm burning your child, Thea! You with your beautiful wavy hair! [*She throws a few more pages into the stove.*] The child Eilert Loevborg gave you. [*Throws the rest of the manuscript in.*] I'm burning it! I'm burning your child!

Act IV

SCENE—*The same. It is evening. The drawing room is in darkness. The small room is illuminated by the hanging lamp over the table. The curtains are drawn across the french windows.* HEDDA, *dressed in black, is walking up and down in the darkened room. Then she goes into the small room and crosses to the left. A few chords are heard from the piano. She comes back into the drawing room.*

BERTHA *comes through the small room from the right with a lighted lamp, which she places on the table in front of the corner sofa in the drawing room. Her eyes are red with crying, and she has black ribbons on her cap. She goes quietly out, right.* HEDDA *goes over to the french windows, draws the curtains slightly to one side and looks out into the darkness.*

A few moments later, MISS TESMAN *enters from the hall. She is dressed in mourning, with a black hat and veil.* HEDDA *goes to meet her and holds out her hand.*

MISS TESMAN   Well, Hedda, here I am in the weeds of sorrow. My poor sister has ended her struggles at last.

HEDDA   I've already heard. Tesman sent me a card.

MISS TESMAN   Yes, he promised me he would. But I thought, no, I must go and break the news of death to Hedda myself—here, in the house of life.

HEDDA   It's very kind of you.

MISS TESMAN   Ah, Rena shouldn't have chosen a time like this to pass away. This is no moment for Hedda's house to be a place of mourning.

HEDDA [*Changing the subject.*]   She died peacefully, Miss Tesman?

MISS TESMAN   Oh, it was quite beautiful! The end came so calmly. And she was so happy at being able to see George once again. And say good-bye to him. Hasn't he come home yet?

HEDDA   No. He wrote that I mustn't expect him too soon. But please sit down.

MISS TESMAN   No, thank you, Hedda dear—bless you. I'd like to. But I've so little time. I must dress her and lay her out as well as I can. She shall go to her grave looking really beautiful.

HEDDA   Can't I help with anything?

MISS TESMAN   Why, you mustn't think of such a thing! Hedda Tesman mustn't let her hands be soiled by contact with death. Or her thoughts. Not at this time.

HEDDA   One can't always control one's thoughts.

MISS TESMAN [*Continues.*]   Ah, well, that's life. Now we must start to sew poor Rena's shroud. There'll be sewing to be done in this house too before long, I shouldn't wonder. But not for a shroud, praise God.

[GEORGE TESMAN *enters from the hall.*]

HEDDA   You've come at last! Thank heavens!

TESMAN   Are you here, Auntie Juju? With Hedda? Fancy that!

MISS TESMAN   I was just on the point of leaving, dear boy. Well, have you done everything you promised me?

TESMAN   No, I'm afraid I forgot half of it. I'll have to run over again tomorrow. My head's in a complete whirl today. I can't collect my thoughts.

MISS TESMAN   But George dear, you mustn't take it like this.

TESMAN   Oh? Well—er—how should I?

MISS TESMAN   You must be happy in your grief. Happy for what's happened. As I am.

TESMAN   Oh, yes, yes. You're thinking of Aunt Rena.

HEDDA   It'll be lonely for you now, Miss Tesman.

MISS TESMAN   For the first few days, yes. But it won't last long, I hope. Poor dear Rena's little room isn't going to stay empty.

TESMAN   Oh? Whom are you going to move in there? What?

MISS TESMAN   Oh, there's always some poor invalid who needs care and attention.

HEDDA   Do you really want another cross like that to bear?

MISS TESMAN   Cross! God forgive you, child. It's been no cross for me.

HEDDA   But now—if a complete stranger comes to live with you——

MISS TESMAN   Oh, one soon makes friends with invalids. And I need so much to have someone to live for. Like you, my dear. Well, I expect there'll soon be work in this house too for an old aunt, praise God!

HEDDA   Oh—please!

TESMAN   By Jove, yes! What a splendid time the three of us could have together if——

HEDDA   If?

TESMAN   [Uneasily.]   Oh, never mind. It'll all work out. Let's hope so—what?

MISS TESMAN   Yes, yes. Well, I'm sure you two would like to be alone. [Smiles.] Perhaps Hedda may have something to tell you, George. Goodbye. I must go home to Rena. [Turns to the door.] Dear God, how strange! Now Rena is with me and with poor dear Joachim.

TESMAN   Fancy that. Yes, Auntie Juju! What?

[MISS TESMAN goes out through the hall.]

HEDDA   [Follows TESMAN coldly and searchingly with her eyes.]   I really believe this death distresses you more than it does her.

TESMAN   Oh, it isn't just Auntie Rena. It's Eilert I'm so worried about.

HEDDA   [Quickly.]   Is there any news of him?

TESMAN   I ran over to see him this afternoon. I wanted to tell him his manuscript was in safe hands.

HEDDA   Oh? You didn't find him?

TESMAN   No. He wasn't at home. But later I met Mrs. Elvsted and she told me he'd been here early this morning.

HEDDA   Yes, just after you'd left.

TESMAN   It seems he said he'd torn the manuscript up. What?

HEDDA   Yes, he claimed to have done so.

TESMAN   You told him we had it, of course?

HEDDA   No. [Quickly.] Did you tell Mrs. Elvsted?

TESMAN   No, I didn't like to. But you ought to have told him. Think if he should go home and do something desperate! Give me the manuscript, Hedda. I'll run over to him with it right away. Where did you put it?

HEDDA   [Cold and motionless, leaning against the armchair.]   I haven't got it any longer.

TESMAN   Haven't got it? What on earth do you mean?

HEDDA   I've burned it.

TESMAN   [Starts, terrified.]   Burned it! Burned Eilert's manuscript!

HEDDA   Don't shout. The servant will hear you.

TESMAN   Burned it! But in heaven's name——! Oh, no, no, no! This is impossible!

HEDDA   Well, it's true.

TESMAN   But Hedda, do you realize what you've done? That's appropriating lost property! It's against the law! By Jove! You ask Judge Brack and see if I'm not right.

HEDDA   You'd be well advised not to talk about it to Judge Brack or anyone else.

TESMAN   But how could you go and do such a dreadful thing? What on earth put the idea into your head? What came over you? Answer me! What?

HEDDA [*Represses an almost imperceptible smile.*]   I did it for your sake, George.

TESMAN   For my sake?

HEDDA   When you came home this morning and described how he'd read his book to you——

TESMAN   Yes, yes?

HEDDA   You admitted you were jealous of him.

TESMAN   But, good heavens, I didn't mean it literally!

HEDDA   No matter. I couldn't bear the thought that anyone else should push you into the background.

TESMAN [*Torn between doubt and joy.*]   Hedda—is this true? But—but—but I never realized you loved me like that! Fancy——

HEDDA   Well, I suppose you'd better know. I'm going to have—— [*Breaks off and says violently.*] No, no—you'd better ask your Auntie Juju. She'll tell you.

TESMAN   Hedda! I think I understand what you mean. [*Clasps his hands.*] Good heavens, can it really be true! What?

HEDDA   Don't shout. The servant will hear you.

TESMAN [*Laughing with joy.*]   The servant! I say, that's good! The servant! Why, that's Bertha! I'll run out and tell her at once!

HEDDA [*Clenches her hands in despair.*]   Oh, it's destroying me, all this—it's destroying me!

TESMAN   I say, Hedda, what's up? What?

HEDDA [*Cold, controlled.*]   Oh, it's all so—absurd—George.

TESMAN   Absurd? That I'm so happy? But surely——? Ah, well—perhaps I won't say anything to Bertha.

HEDDA   No, do. She might as well know too.

TESMAN   No, no, I won't tell her yet. But Auntie Juju—I must let her know! And you—you called me George! For the first time! Fancy that! Oh, it'll make Auntie Juju so happy, all this! So very happy!

HEDDA   Will she be happy when she hears I've burned Eilert Loevborg's manuscript—for your sake?

TESMAN   No, I'd forgotten about that. Of course no one must be allowed to know about the manuscript. But that you're burning with love for me, Hedda, I must certainly let Auntie Juju know that. I say, I wonder if young wives often feel like that toward their husbands? What?

HEDDA   You might ask Auntie Juju about that too.

TESMAN I will, as soon as I get the chance. [*Looks uneasy and thoughtful again.*] But I say, you know, that manuscript. Dreadful business. Poor Eilert!

[MRS. ELVSTED, *dressed as on her first visit, with hat and overcoat, enters from the hall.*]

MRS. ELVSTED [*Greets them hastily and tremulously.*] Oh, Hedda dear, do please forgive me for coming here again.

HEDDA Why, Thea, what's happened?

TESMAN Is it anything to do with Eilert Loevborg? What?

MRS. ELVSTED Yes—I'm so dreadfully afraid he may have met with an accident.

HEDDA [*Grips her arm.*] You think so?

TESMAN But, good heavens, Mrs. Elvsted, what makes you think that?

MRS. ELVSTED I heard them talking about him at the boarding-house, as I went in. Oh, there are the most terrible rumors being spread about him in town today.

TESMAN Fancy. Yes, I heard about them too. But I can testify that he went straight home to bed. Fancy that!

HEDDA Well—what did they say in the boarding-house?

MRS. ELVSTED Oh, I couldn't find out anything. Either they didn't know, or else—— They stopped talking when they saw me. And I didn't dare to ask.

TESMAN [*Fidgets uneasily.*] We must hope—we must hope you misheard them, Mrs. Elvsted.

MRS. ELVSTED No, no, I'm sure it was he they were talking about. I heard them say something about a hospital——

TESMAN Hospital!

HEDDA Oh no, surely that's impossible!

MRS. ELVSTED Oh, I became so afraid. So I went up to his rooms and asked to see him.

HEDDA Do you think that was wise, Thea?

MRS. ELVSTED Well, what else could I do? I couldn't bear the uncertainty any longer.

TESMAN But you didn't manage to find him either? What?

MRS. ELVSTED No. And they had no idea where he was. They said he hadn't been home since yesterday afternoon.

TESMAN Since yesterday? Fancy that!

MRS. ELVSTED I'm sure he must have met with an accident.

TESMAN Hedda, I wonder if I ought to go into town and make one or two enquiries?

HEDDA No, no, don't you get mixed up in this.

[JUDGE BRACK *enters from the hall, hat in hand.* BERTHA, *who has opened the door for him, closes it. He looks serious and greets them silently.*]

TESMAN Hullo, my dear Judge. Fancy seeing you!

BRACK I had to come and talk to you.

TESMAN I can see Auntie Juju's told you the news.

BRACK Yes, I've heard about that too.

TESMAN Tragic, isn't it?

BRACK Well, my dear chap, that depends on how you look at it.

TESMAN [*Looks uncertainly at him.*]   Has something else happened?

BRACK   Yes.

HEDDA   Another tragedy?

BRACK   That also depends on how you look at it, Mrs. Tesman.

MRS. ELVSTED   Oh, it's something to do with Eilert Loevborg!

BRACK [*Looks at her for a moment.*]   How did you guess? Perhaps you've heard already——

MRS. ELVSTED [*Confused.*]   No, no, not at all—I——

TESMAN   For heaven's sake, tell us!

BRACK [*Shrugs his shoulders.*]   Well, I'm afraid they've taken him to the hospital. He's dying.

MRS. ELVSTED [*Screams.*]   Oh God, God!

TESMAN   The hospital! Dying!

HEDDA [*Involuntarily.*]   So quickly!

MRS. ELVSTED [*Weeping.*]   Oh, Hedda! And we parted enemies!

HEDDA [*Whispers.*]   Thea—Thea!

MRS. ELVSTED [*Ignoring her.*]   I must see him! I must see him before he dies!

BRACK   It's no use, Mrs. Elvsted. No one's allowed to see him now.

MRS. ELVSTED   But what's happened to him? You must tell me!

TESMAN   He hasn't tried to do anything to himself? What?

HEDDA   Yes, he has. I'm sure of it.

TESMAN   Hedda, how can you——?

BRACK [*Who has not taken his eyes from her.*]   I'm afraid you've guessed correctly, Mrs. Tesman.

MRS. ELVSTED   How dreadful!

TESMAN   Attempted suicide! Fancy that!

HEDDA   Shot himself!

BRACK   Right again, Mrs. Tesman.

MRS. ELVSTED [*Tries to compose herself.*]   When did this happen, Judge Brack?

BRACK   This afternoon. Between three and four.

TESMAN   But, good heavens—where? What?

BRACK [*A little hesitantly.*]   Where? Why, my dear chap, in his rooms of course.

MRS. ELVSTED   No, that's impossible. I was there soon after six.

BRACK   Well, it must have been somewhere else, then. I don't know exactly. I only know that they found him. He'd shot himself—through the breast.

MRS. ELVSTED   Oh, how horrible! That he should end like that!

HEDDA [*To* BRACK.]   Through the breast, you said?

BRACK   That is what I said.

HEDDA   Not through the head?

BRACK   Through the breast, Mrs. Tesman.

HEDDA   The breast. Yes; yes. That's good, too.

BRACK   Why, Mrs. Tesman?

HEDDA   Oh—no, I didn't mean anything.

TESMAN   And the wound's dangerous you say? What?

BRACK   Mortal. He's probably already dead.

MRS. ELVSTED   Yes, yes—I feel it! It's all over. All over. Oh Hedda——!

TESMAN But, tell me, how did you manage to learn all this?

BRACK [*Curtly.*] From the police. I spoke to one of them.

HEDDA [*Loudly, clearly.*] At last! Oh, thank God!

TESMAN [*Appalled.*] For God's sake, Hedda, what are you saying?

HEDDA I am saying there's beauty in what he has done.

BRACK Mm—Mrs. Tesman——

TESMAN Beauty! Oh, but I say!

MRS. ELVSTED Hedda, how can you talk of beauty in connection with a thing like this?

HEDDA Eilert Loevborg has settled his account with life. He's had the courage to do what—what he had to do.

MRS. ELVSTED No, that's not why it happened. He did it because he was mad.

TESMAN He did it because he was desperate.

HEDDA You're wrong! I know!

MRS. ELVSTED He must have been mad. The same as when he tore up the manuscript.

BRACK [*Starts.*] Manuscript? Did he tear it up?

MRS. ELVSTED Yes. Last night.

TESMAN [*Whispers.*] Oh, Hedda, we shall never be able to escape from this.

BRACK Hm. Strange.

TESMAN [*Wanders round the room.*] To think of Eilert dying like that. And not leaving behind him the thing that would have made his name endure.

MRS. ELVSTED If only it could be pieced together again!

TESMAN Yes, fancy! If only it could! I'd give anything——

MRS. ELVSTED Perhaps it can, Mr. Tesman.

TESMAN What do you mean?

MRS. ELVSTED [*Searches in the pocket of her dress.*] Look! I kept the notes he dictated it from.

HEDDA [*Takes a step nearer.*] Ah!

TESMAN You kept them, Mrs. Elvsted! What?

MRS. ELVSTED Yes, here they are. I brought them with me when I left home. They've been in my pocket ever since.

TESMAN Let me have a look.

MRS. ELVSTED [*Hands him a wad of small sheets of paper.*] They're in a terrible muddle. All mixed up.

TESMAN I say, just fancy if we can sort them out! Perhaps if we work on them together——?

MRS. ELVSTED Oh, yes! Let's try, anyway!

TESMAN We'll manage it. We must! I shall dedicate my life to this.

HEDDA *You*, George? Your life?

TESMAN Yes—well, all the time I can spare. My book'll have to wait. Hedda, you do understand? What? I owe it to Eilert's memory.

HEDDA Perhaps.

TESMAN Well, my dear Mrs. Elvsted, you and I'll have to pool our brains. No use crying over spilt milk, what? We must try to approach this matter calmly.

MRS. ELVSTED Yes, yes, Mr. Tesman. I'll do my best.

TESMAN Well, come over here and let's start looking at these notes right away. Where shall we sit? Here? No, the other room. You'll excuse us, won't you, Judge? Come along with me, Mrs. Elvsted.

MRS. ELVSTED   Oh, God! If only we can manage to do it!

[TESMAN and MRS. ELVSTED *go into the rear room. He takes off his hat and overcoat. They sit at the table beneath the hanging lamp and absorb themselves in the notes.* HEDDA *walks across to the stove and sits in the armchair. After a moment,* BRACK *goes over to her.*]

HEDDA [*Half aloud.*]   Oh, Judge! This act of Eilert Loevborg's—doesn't it give one a sense of release!

BRACK   Release, Mrs. Hedda? Well, it's a release for him, of course——

HEDDA   Oh, I don't mean him—I mean me! The release of knowing that someone can do something really brave! Something beautiful!

BRACK [*Smiles.*]   Hm—my dear Mrs. Hedda——

HEDDA   Oh, I know what you're going to say. You're a bourgeois at heart too, just like—ah, well!

BRACK [*Looks at her.*]   Eilert Loevborg has meant more to you than you're willing to admit to yourself. Or am I wrong?

HEDDA   I'm not answering questions like that from you. I only know that Eilert Loevborg has had the courage to live according to his own principles. And now, at last, he's done something big! Something beautiful! To have the courage and the will to rise from the feast of life so early!

BRACK   It distresses me deeply, Mrs. Hedda, but I'm afraid I must rob you of that charming illusion.

HEDDA   Illusion?

BRACK   You wouldn't have been allowed to keep it for long, anyway.

HEDDA   What do you mean?

BRACK   He didn't shoot himself on purpose.

HEDDA   Not on purpose?

BRACK   No. It didn't happen quite the way I told you.

HEDDA   Have you been hiding something? What is it?

BRACK   In order to spare poor Mrs. Elvsted's feelings, I permitted myself one or two small—equivocations.

HEDDA   What?

BRACK   To begin with, he is already dead.

HEDDA   He died at the hospital?

BRACK   Yes. Without regaining consciousness.

HEDDA   What else haven't you told us?

BRACK   The incident didn't take place at his lodgings.

HEDDA   Well, that's utterly unimportant.

BRACK   Not utterly. The fact is, you see, that Eilert Loevborg was found shot in Mademoiselle Danielle's boudoir.

HEDDA [*Almost jumps up, but instead sinks back in her chair.*]   That's impossible. He can't have been there today.

BRACK   He was there this afternoon. He went to ask for something he claimed they'd taken from him. Talked some crazy nonsense about a child which had got lost——

HEDDA   Oh! So that was the reason!

BRACK   I thought at first he might have been referring to his manuscript. But I hear he destroyed that himself. So he must have meant his pocket-book—I suppose.

HEDDA   Yes, I suppose so. So they found him there?

BRACK Yes; there. With a discharged pistol in his breast pocket. The shot had wounded him mortally.

HEDDA Yes. In the breast.

BRACK No. In the—hm—stomach. The—lower part——

HEDDA [*Looks at him with an expression of repulsion.*] That too! Oh, why does everything I touch become mean and ludicrous? It's like a curse!

BRACK There's something else, Mrs. Hedda. It's rather disagreeable, too.

HEDDA What?

BRACK The pistol he had on him——

HEDDA Yes? What about it?

BRACK He must have stolen it.

HEDDA [*Jumps up.*] Stolen it! That isn't true! He didn't!

BRACK It's the only explanation. He must have stolen it. Ssh!

[TESMAN *and* MRS. ELVSTED *have got up from the table in the rear room and come into the drawing room.*]

TESMAN [*His hands full of papers.*] Hedda, I can't see properly under that lamp. Think!

HEDDA I am thinking.

TESMAN Do you think we could possibly use your writing table for a little? What?

HEDDA Yes, of course. [*Quickly.*] No, wait! Let me tidy it up first.

TESMAN Oh, don't you trouble about that. There's plenty of room.

HEDDA No, no, let me tidy it up first, I say. I'll take this in and put them on the piano. Here.

[*She pulls an object, covered with sheets of music, out from under the bookcase, puts some more sheets on top and carries it all into the rear room and away to the left.* TESMAN *puts his papers on the writing table and moves the lamp over from the corner table. He and* MRS. ELVSTED *sit down and begin working again.* HEDDA *comes back.*]

HEDDA [*Behind* MRS. ELVSTED's *chair, ruffles her hair gently.*] Well, my pretty Thea! And how is work progressing on Eilert Loevborg's memorial?

MRS. ELVSTED [*Looks up at her, dejectedly.*] Oh, it's going to be terribly difficult to get these into any order.

TESMAN We've got to do it. We must! After all, putting other people's papers into order is rather my specialty, what?

[HEDDA *goes over to the stove and sits on one of the footstools.* BRACK *stands over her, leaning against the armchair.*]

HEDDA [*Whispers.*] What was that you were saying about the pistol?

BRACK [*Softly.*] I said he must have stolen it.

HEDDA Why do you think that?

BRACK Because any other explanation is unthinkable, Mrs. Hedda, or ought to be.

HEDDA I see.

BRACK [*Looks at her for a moment.*] Eilert Loevborg was here this morning. Wasn't he?

HEDDA Yes.

BRACK Were you alone with him?

EDDA For a few moments.

BRACK You didn't leave the room while he was here?

HEDDA No.

BRACK Think again. Are you sure you didn't go out for a moment?

HEDDA   Oh—yes, I might have gone into the hall. Just for a few seconds.

BRACK   And where was your pistol-case during this time?

HEDDA   I'd locked it in that——

BRACK   Er—Mrs. Hedda?

HEDDA   It was lying over there on my writing table.

BRACK   Have you looked to see if both the pistols are still there?

HEDDA   No.

BRACK   You needn't bother. I saw the pistol Loevborg had when they found him. I recognized it at once. From yesterday. And other occasions.

HEDDA   Have you got it?

BRACK   No. The police have it.

HEDDA   What will the police do with this pistol?

BRACK   Try to trace the owner.

HEDDA   Do you think they'll succeed?

BRACK [*Leans down and whispers.*]   No, Hedda Gabler. Not as long as I hold my tongue.

HEDDA [*Looks nervously at him.*]   And if you don't?

BRACK [*Shrugs his shoulders.*]   You could always say he'd stolen it.

HEDDA   I'd rather die!

BRACK [*Smiles.*]   People say that. They never do it.

HEDDA [*Not replying.*]   And suppose the pistol wasn't stolen? And they trace the owner? What then?

BRACK   There'll be a scandal, Hedda.

HEDDA   A scandal!

BRACK   Yes, a scandal. The thing you're so frightened of. You'll have to appear in court. Together with Mademoiselle Danielle. She'll have to explain how it all happened. Was it an accident, or was it—homicide? Was he about to take the pistol from his pocket to threaten her? And did it go off? Or did she snatch the pistol from his hand, shoot him and then put it back in his pocket? She might quite easily have done it. She's a resourceful lady, is Mademoiselle Danielle.

HEDDA   But I had nothing to do with this repulsive business.

BRACK   No. But you'll have to answer one question. Why did you give Eilert Loevborg this pistol? And what conclusions will people draw when it is proved you did give it to him?

HEDDA [*Bows her head.*]   That's true. I hadn't thought of that.

BRACK   Well, luckily there's no danger as long as I hold my tongue.

HEDDA [*Looks up at him.*]   In other words, I'm in your power, Judge. From now on, you've got your hold over me.

BRACK [*Whispers, more slowly.*]   Hedda, my dearest—believe me—I will not abuse my position.

HEDDA   Nevertheless, I'm in your power. Dependent on your will, and your demands. Not free. Still not free! [*Rises passionately.*] No. I couldn't bear that. No.

BRACK [*Looks half-derisively at her.*]   Most people resign themselves to the inevitable, sooner or later.

HEDDA [*Returns his gaze.*]   Possibly they do.

   [*She goes across to the writing table.*]

HEDDA [*Represses an involuntary smile and says in* TESMAN's *voice.*]   Well, George. Think you'll be able to manage? What?

TESMAN   Heaven knows, dear. This is going to take months and months.

HEDDA [*In the same tone as before.*]   Fancy that, by Jove! [*Runs her hands gently through* MRS. ELVSTED's *hair.*] Doesn't it feel strange, Thea? Here you are working away with Tesman just the way you used to work with Eilert Loevborg.

MRS. ELVSTED   Oh—if only I can inspire your husband too!

HEDDA   Oh, it'll come. In time.

TESMAN   Yes—do you know, Hedda, I really think I'm beginning to feel a bit—well—that way. But you go back and talk to Judge Brack.

HEDDA   Can't I be of use to you two in any way?

TESMAN   No, none at all. [*Turns his head.*] You'll have to keep Hedda company from now on, Judge, and see she doesn't get bored. If you don't mind.

BRACK [*Glances at* HEDDA.]   It'll be a pleasure.

HEDDA   Thank you. But I'm tired this evening. I think I'll lie down on the sofa in there for a little while.

TESMAN   Yes, dear—do. What?

[HEDDA *goes into the rear room and draws the curtain behind her. Short pause. Suddenly she begins to play a frenzied dance melody on the piano.*]

MRS. ELVSTED [*Starts up from her chair.*]   Oh, what's that?

TESMAN [*Runs to the doorway.*]   Hedda dear, please! Don't play dance music tonight! Think of Auntie Rena. And Eilert.

HEDDA [*Puts her head out through the curtains.*]   And Auntie Juju. And all the rest of them. From now on I'll be quiet. [*Closes the curtains behind her.*]

TESMAN [*At the writing table.*]   It distresses her to watch us doing this. I say, Mrs. Elvsted, I've an idea. Why don't you move in with Auntie Juju? I'll run over each evening, and we can sit and work there. What?

MRS. ELVSTED   Yes, that might be the best plan.

HEDDA [*From the rear room.*]   I can hear what you're saying, Tesman. But how shall I spend the evenings out here?

TESMAN [*Looking through his papers.*]   Oh, I'm sure Judge Brack'll be kind enough to come over and keep you company. You won't mind my not being here, Judge?

BRACK [*In the armchair, calls gaily.*]   I'll be delighted, Mrs. Tesman. I'll be here every evening. We'll have great fun together, you and I.

HEDDA [*Loud and clear.*]   Yes, that'll suit you, won't it, Judge? The only cock on the dunghill——!

[*A shot is heard from the rear room.* TESMAN, MRS. ELVSTED *and* JUDGE BRACK *start from their chairs.*]

TESMAN   Oh, she's playing with those pistols again.

[*He pulls the curtains aside and runs in.* MRS. ELVSTED *follows him.* HEDDA *is lying dead on the sofa. Confusion and shouting.* BERTHA *enters in alarm from the right.*]

TESMAN [*Screams to* BRACK.]   She's shot herself! Shot herself in the head! By Jove! Fancy that!

BRACK [*Half paralyzed in the armchair.*]   But, good God! People don't do such things!

ANTON CHEKHOV
1860–1904

In plays and stories Anton Chekhov depicts Russia around the turn of the twentieth century with great pity, gentleness, and kindness of heart. More important, with a deep humanity that has outlasted all the problems of his time, he dramatizes universal and almost timeless feelings rather than ideas that date and pass. He differs sharply from the two giants of Russian literature, Dostoevsky and Tolstoy. For one thing, his work is of smaller scope. With the exception of an immature, forgotten novel and a travel book, he wrote only short stories and plays. He belongs, furthermore, to a very different moral and spiritual atmosphere. Chekhov had studied medicine and practiced it for a time. He shared the scientific outlook of his age and had too skeptical a mind to believe in Christianity or in any metaphysical system. He confessed that an intelligent believer was a puzzle to him. His attitude toward his materials and characters is detached, "objective," and his letters to friends insist that a good writer must present both physical details and a character's state of mind without overt interpretation or judgment. He is thus much more in the stream of Western realism than either Tolstoy or Dostoevsky, and the delicate, precise realism of his short stories has served as a model for later writers in Europe, China, and the United States. But extended reading of Chekhov does convey an impression of his view of life. There is implied in his stories a philosophy of kindness and humanity, a love of beauty, a sense of the unexplainable mystery of life, a sense, especially, of the individual's utter loneliness in this universe and among other people. Chekhov's pessimism has nothing of the defiance of the universe or the horror at it that we meet in other writers with similar attitudes; it is somehow merely sad, often pathetic, and yet also comforting and comfortable.

The Russia depicted in Chekhov's stories and plays is of a later period than that presented by Tolstoy and Dostoevsky. It seems to be nearing its end; there is a sense of decadence and frustration that heralds the approach of catastrophe. The aristocracy still keeps up a beautiful front but is losing its fight without much resistance, resignedly. Officialdom is stupid and venal. The Church is backward and narrow minded. The intelligentsia are hopelessly ineffectual, futile, lost in the provinces or absorbed in their egos. The peasants live subject to the lowest degradations of poverty and drink, apparently rather aggravated than improved since the much-heralded emancipation of the serfs in 1861. There seems no hope for society except in a gradual spread of enlightenment, good sense, and hygiene, for Chekhov is skeptical of the revolution and revolutionaries as well as of Tolstoy's followers.

Anton Pavlovich Chekhov was born on January 17, 1860, at Taganrog, a small town on the Sea of Azov. His father was a grocer and haberdasher; his grandfather, a serf who had bought his freedom. Chekhov's father went bankrupt in 1876, and the family moved to Moscow, leaving Anton to finish school in his home town. After his graduation in 1879, he followed his family to Moscow, where he studied medicine. To earn additional money for his family and himself, he started to write humorous sketches and stories for magazines. In 1884 he became a doctor and published his first collection of stories, *Tales of Melpomene*. Over the next several years, two collections of light comic tales brought him success and the opportunity to publish serious literature regularly in Moscow's largest daily newspaper, the *New Times*. In 1884, he also had his first hemorrhage. All the rest of his life he struggled against tuberculosis. His first play, *Ivanov*, was performed in 1887; and by 1889 he had written nine volumes of short stories. The next year, he undertook an arduous journey through Siberia to the island of Sakhalin (north of Japan) and back by boat through the Suez Canal. He saw there the Russian penal settlements and wrote a moving account of his trip in *Sakhalin Island* (1892). In 1898 his play *The Sea Gull* was a great success at the Moscow Art Theater. The next year he moved to Yalta, in the

Crimea, and in 1901 married the actress Olga Knipper. He died on July 2, 1904, at Badenweiler in the Black Forest.

Chekhov's stories explore small but significant events in ordinary lives, emphasizing the twists and turns of interpersonal relations rather than (for example) the inexorably advancing plot recommended by Edgar Allan Poe. Whether it is a cabdriver's frustrated attempt to tell his fares about his son's recent death (*Misery*), a widow's final happiness in caring for another woman's child (*The Darling*), a retired clerk's delight in his gooseberry bushes (*Gooseberries*), or the aftermath of a businessman's brief affair at a resort (*The Lady with the Dog*), the author focuses on his characters' inner lives. They meditate on their own actions; observe the beauties of nature; wax philosophical about society or human nature; and most of all, react to the presence of other people. Typically, however, these characters find it hard to communicate with each other and frequently cannot do so at all; isolated in their own private worlds, they rarely make contact with the world of another. Successful or not, these relationships are all-important: they motivate events, illuminate actions, and shape the conclusion, which generally rounds off a stage in the character's life rather than resolving all issues. Chekhov's endings are famously ambiguous, and his conclusions remain— like events in real life—preludes to various possible sequels.

The Lady with the Dog is one of Chekhov's best-known stories. Published in 1899, it tells the story of a love affair sprung up between a man and woman vacationing in Yalta. Both are married, but not to each other, and each expects the affair to be a brief episode; one of many affairs for the banker Dmitri Gurov, and a single experience of romantic love for the dissatisfied Anna Sergeyevna von Diederitz. Anna Sergeyevna, the lady of the title, appears first as a nameless figure known only through local gossip. She is a tourist, walking her dog at a Crimean resort known for brief liaisons. Married young to an unimaginative minor official in a small town, she is bored, has probably read romantic novels, and is willing to risk anything rather than having her entire life pass without an intense experience. Dmitri Gurov, a prosperous Moscow bank official who likes the company of women, decides on a whim to seduce her and soon succeeds.

The physical seduction is strikingly minimized (quite unlike modern fiction); it happens offstage and is merely indicated through subsequent conversation revealing the couple's different reactions. Chekhov shows Gurov thinking about his various former lovers, and Anna Sergeyevna in self-conscious despair at having passed from the role of "lady with the dog" to that of a "fallen woman." He eats watermelon slices while she weeps (in a later scene, he drinks tea). Despite Anna Sergeyevna's remorse, with which Gurov fails to sympathize and in fact is utterly bored, neither is able to forget the other, and the affair resumes a few months after both have returned home. Anna continues to suffer over her position, and Gurov retreats from emotional entanglement into his role as man-about-town; she cannot bear living a double life, but he enjoys the contrast of public and private roles.

The story does not focus solely on the success or failure of a difficult love affair, nonetheless. As the relationship evolves, the protagonists emerge from the near-stereotypes of the beginning to individual personalities possessing a great deal of depth, ambiguity, and—perhaps—openness to change. Gurov's development from a self-satisfied to a self-conscious lover is particularly emphasized; it is his thoughts that we follow as he perceives Anna Sergeyevna first as an object of seduction, later as a woman tragically in love with him, and finally as his true partner. The gulf between the two remains unchanged until he looks in the mirror and realizes his own mortality; suddenly, a feeling of shared vulnerability enables him to reach out to Anna Sergeyevna. Whether or not it enables them to find a satisfactory solution to their dilemma is another question. If the conclusion of the story leaves the lovers' future undecided, it also demonstrates that any sequel we may imagine (and readers usually try to) must take into account both historical possibility and also our idea of what the characters have become.

The plays of Chekhov seem to go furthest in the direction of naturalism, the depiction of a "slice of life," on stage. Compared with Ibsen's plays they seem plotless; they could be described as a succession of little scenes, composed like a mosaic or like the dots or strokes in an Impressionist painting. The characters rarely engage in the usual dialogue; they speak often in little soliloquies, hardly justified by the situation; and they often do not listen to the words of their ostensible partners. They seem alone even in a crowd. Human communication seems difficult and even impossible. There is no clear message, no zeal for social reform; life seems to flow quietly, even sluggishly, until interrupted by some desperate outbreak or even a pistol shot.

Chekhov's last play, *The Cherry Orchard* (written in 1903, first performed at the Moscow Art Theater on January 17, 1904) differs, however, from this pattern in several respects. It has a strongly articulated central theme—the loss of the orchard—and it has a composition that roughly follows the traditional scheme of a well-made play. Arrival and departure from the very same room, the nursery, frame the two other acts: the outdoor idyll of Act II and the dance in Act III. Act III is the turning point of the action: Lopahin appears and announces, somewhat shamefacedly, that he has bought the estate. The orchard was lost from the very beginning—there is no real struggle to prevent its sale—but still the news of Lopahin's purchase is a surprise as he had no intention of buying it but did so only when during the auction sale a rival seemed to have a chance of acquiring it. A leading action runs its course, and many— one may even argue too many—subplots crisscross each other: the shy and awkward love affair of the student Trofimov and the daughter Anya; the love triangle among the three dependents, Yepihodov (the unlucky clerk), Dunyasha (the chambermaid), and Yasha (the conceited and insolent footman). Varya, the practical stepdaughter, has her troubles with Lopahin, and Simeonov-Pishchik is beset by the same financial problems as the owners of the orchard and is rescued by the discovery of some white clay on his estate. The German governess Charlotta drifts around alluding to her obscure origins and past. There are undeveloped references to events preceding the action on stage—the lover in Paris, the drowned boy Grisha—but there is no revelation of the past as in Ibsen, no mystery, no intrigue.

While the events on the stage follow each other naturally, though hardly always in a logical, causal order, a symbolic device is used conspicuously: in Act II after a pause, "suddenly a distant sound is heard, coming from the sky as it were, the sound of a snapping string, mournfully dying away." It occurs again at the very end of the play followed by "the strokes of the ax against a tree far away in the orchard." An attempt is made to explain this sound at its first occurrence as a bucket's fall in a faraway pit or as the cries of a heron or an owl, but the effect is weird and even supernatural; it establishes an ominous mood. Even the orchard carries more than its obvious meaning: it is white, drowned in blossoms when the party arrives in the spring; it is bare and desolate in the autumn when the axes are heard cutting it down. "The old bark on the trees gleams faintly, and the cherry trees seem to be dreaming of things that happened a hundred, two hundred years ago and to be tormented by painful visions," declaims Trofimov, defining his feeling for the orchard as a symbol of repression and serfdom. For Lubov Ranevskaya it is an image of her lost innocence and of the happier past, while Lopahin sees it only as an investment. It seems to draw together the meaning of the play.

But what is this meaning? Can we even decide whether it is a tragedy or a comedy? It has been commonly seen as the tragedy of the downfall of the Russian aristocracy (or more correctly, the landed gentry) victimized by the newly rich, upstart peasantry. One could see the play as depicting the defeat of a group of feckless people at the hand of a ruthless "developer" who destroys nature and natural beauty for profit. Or one could see it as prophesying, through the mouth of the student Trofimov, the approaching end of feudal Russia and the coming happier future. Soviet interpretations and performances leaned that way.

Surely none of these interpretations can withstand inspection in the light of the actual play. They all run counter to Chekhov's professed intentions. He called the play a comedy. In a letter of September 15, 1903, he declared expressly that the play "has not turned out as drama but as comedy, in places even a farce" and a few days later (September 21, 1903) he wrote that "the whole play is gay and frivolous." Chekhov did not like the staging of the play at the Moscow Art Theater and complained of its tearful tone and its slow pace. He objected that "they obstinately call my play a drama in playbill and newspaper advertisements" while he had called it a comedy (April 10, 1904).

No doubt, there are many comical and even farcical characters and scenes in the play. Charlotta with her nut-eating dog, her card tricks, her ventriloquism, her disappearing acts, is a clownish figure. Gayev, the landowner, though "suave and elegant," is a boor, obsessed by his passion for billiards, constantly popping candy into his mouth, telling the waiters in a restaurant about the "decadents" in Paris. Yepihodov, the clerk, carries a revolver and, threatening suicide, asks Charlotta foolishly whether she has read Buckle (the English historian) and complains of his ill luck: a spider on his chest, a cockroach in his drink. Simeonov-Pishchik empties a whole bottle of pills; eats half a bucket of pickles; quotes Nietzsche supposedly recommending the forging of banknotes; and fat as he is, puffs and prances at the dance ordering the "cavaliers à genoux." Even the serious characters are put into ludicrous predicaments: Trofimov falls down the stairs; Lopahin, coming to announce the purchase of the estate, is almost hit with a stick by Varya (and *was* hit in the original version). Lopahin, teasing his intended Varya, "moos like a cow." The ball, the hunting for the galoshes, and the champagne drinking by Yasha in the last act have all a touch of absurdity. The grand speeches, Gayev's addresses to the bookcase and to nature or Trofimov's about "mankind going forward" and "All Russia is our orchard," are undercut by the contrast between words and character: Gayev is callous and shallow; the "perpetual student," Trofimov never did a stitch of work. He is properly ridiculed and insulted by Lubov for his scant beard and his silly professions of being "above love." One can sympathize with Chekhov's irritation at the pervading gloom imposed by the Moscow production.

Still, we cannot, in spite of the author, completely dismiss the genuine pathos of the central situation and of the central figure, Lubov Ranevskaya. Whatever one may say about her recklessness in financial matters and her guilt in relation to her lover in France, we must feel her deep attachment to the house and the orchard, to the past and her lost innocence, clearly and unhumorously expressed in the first act on her arrival, again and again at the impending sale of the estate, and finally at the parting from her house: "Oh, my orchard—my dear, sweet, beautiful orchard! . . . My life, my youth, my happiness—Good-bye!" That Gayev, before the final parting, seems to have overcome the sense of loss and even looks forward to his job in the bank and that Lubov acknowledges that her "nerves are better" and that "she sleeps well" testifies to the indestructible spirit of brother and sister, but cannot minimize the sense of loss, the pathos of parting, the nostalgia for happier times. Nor is the conception of Lopahin simple. Chekhov emphasized, in a letter to Konstantin Stanislavsky, who was to play the part, that "Lopahin is a decent person in the full sense of the word, and his bearing must be that of a completely dignified and intelligent man." He is not, he says, a profiteering peasant (*kulachok*, October 30, 1903). He admires Lubov and thinks of her with gratitude. He senses the beauty of the poppies in his fields. Even the scene of the abortive encounter with Varya at the end has its quiet pathos in spite of all its awkwardness and the comic touches such as the reference to the broken thermometer. Firs, the eighty-seven-year-old valet, may be grotesque in his deafness and his nostalgia for the good old days of serfdom, but the very last scene when we see him abandoned in the locked-up house surely ends the play on a note of desolation and even despair.

Chekhov, we must conclude, achieved a highly original and even paradoxical blend of comedy and tragedy, or rather of farce and pathos. Both play and short story present a social picture firmly set in a specific historical time—the dissolution of the landed gentry, the rise of the peasant, the encroachment of the city, newly affluent bourgeoisie and its double standard for women—but they do not propound an obvious social thesis. Chekhov, in his tolerance and tenderness, in his distrust of ideologies and heroics, extends his sympathy to all his characters (with the exception of the crudely ambitious valet Yasha). The glow of his humanity, untrammeled by time and place, keeps *The Cherry Orchard* and *The Lady with the Dog* alive in quite different social and political conditions, as they have the universalizing power of great art.

Donald Rayfield, *The Cherry Orchard: Catastrophe and Comedy* (1994), presents an extended discussion of the play; his *Understanding Chekhov: A Critical Study of Chekhov's Prose and Drama* (1999) is a valuable study of Chekhov's life and work. Good chapters are also found in Beverly Hahn, *Chekhov: A Study of the Major Stories and Plays* (1977); Harvey Pitcher, *The Chekhov Play: A New Interpretation* (1973); and Richard Pearce, *Chekhov: A Study of the Four Major Plays* (1983). Francis Fergusson compares Ibsen and Chekhov in *"Ghosts* and *The Cherry Orchard,"* in *The Idea of the Theatre* (1949). There is helpful critical analysis in R. L. Jackson, ed., *Chekhov: A Collection of Critical Essays* (1967) and *Reading Chekhov's Text* (1993); in Harold Bloom, ed., *Anton Chekhov* (1999); and in René Wellek and N. D. Wellek, eds., *Chekhov: New Perspectives* (1984), which includes a sketch of Chekhov criticism in England and America. Lawrence Senelick, *The Chekhov Theatre: A Century of Plays in Performance* (1997), presents a different perspective. Ralph E. Matlaw, ed., *Anton Chekhov's Short Stories* (1979), includes eight valuable essays on aspects of the short stories and selections from Chekhov's letters. Virginia Llewellyn Smith, *Anton Chekhov and the Lady with the Dog* (1973), argues for autobiographical elements in Gurov's portrayal. J. Douglas Clayton, ed., *Chekhov Then and Now: The Reception of Chekhov in World Culture* (1996), includes a comparison of *The Lady with the Dog* and Joyce Carol Oates's retelling from the woman's point of view. Nicholas Worrall, *File on Chekhov* (1986), offers an introductory survey with useful cited passages and suggestions for further study. Donald Rayfield, *Anton Chekhov: A Life* (1998), is a revisionary biography that evokes a more complex personality based on newly discovered evidence; another useful biography is Philip Callow, *Chekhov, the Hiddend Ground: A Biography* (1998).

PRONOUNCING GLOSSARY

The following list uses common English syllables and stress accents to provide rough equivalents of selected words whose pronunciation may be unfamiliar to the general reader.

Anna Sergeyevna von Diederitz: *an-na sehr-gyeff'-nah fon deed'-rits*

Anton Chekhov: *ahn'-tonn cheh'-off*

Charlotta Ivanovna: *shar-lot'-ta ee-van'-ov-na*

Dmitri Gurov: *d'mee'-tree (or d'mit'-ree) goo'-roff*

Firs: *feers*

Leonid Andreyevich Gayev: *lay-on'-it ahn-dray'-ev-ich gah'-yeff*

Lubov Andreyevna Ranevskaya: *loo-boff' ahn-dray'-ev-na rahn-yeff'-ska-ya*

Pyotr Sergeyevich Trofimov: *pyo-tr sair-gyay'-evich traw-fee'-moff*

Semyon Yepihodov: *sem-yon' ye-pee-ho'doff*

Simeon Pishchik: *see-may-ohn' pish-chik*

Yermolay Alexeyevich Lopahin: *yair-moh-lai' ah-lex-ay'-evich loh-pah-heen'*

The Lady with the Dog[1]

I

People were telling one another that a newcomer had been seen on the promenade—a lady with a dog. Dmitri Dmitrich Gurov had been a fortnight in Yalta,[2] and was accustomed to its ways, and he, too, had begun to take an interest in fresh arrivals. From his seat in Vernet's outdoor café, he caught sight of a young woman in a toque, passing along the promenade; she was fair and not very tall; after her trotted a white Pomeranian.

Later he encountered her in the municipal park and in the square several times a day. She was always alone, wearing the same toque, and the Pomeranian always trotted at her side. Nobody knew who she was, and people referred to her simply as "the lady with the dog."

"If she's here without her husband, and without any friends," thought Gurov, "it wouldn't be a bad idea to make her acquaintance."

He was not yet forty but had a twelve-year-old daughter and two sons in high school. He had been talked into marrying in his second year at college, and his wife now looked nearly twice as old as he did. She was a tall woman with dark eyebrows, erect, dignified, imposing, and, as she said of herself, a "thinker." She was a great reader, omitted the "hard sign"[3] at the end of words in her letters, and called her husband "Dimitry" instead of Dmitry; and though he secretly considered her shallow, narrow-minded, and dowdy, he stood in awe of her, and disliked being at home. He had first begun deceiving her long ago and he was now constantly unfaithful to her, and this was no doubt why he spoke slightingly of women, to whom he referred as *the lower race.*

He considered that the ample lessons he had received from bitter experience entitled him to call them whatever he liked, but without this "lower race" he could not have existed a single day. He was bored and ill-at-ease in the company of men, with whom he was always cold and reserved, but felt quite at home among women, and knew exactly what to say to them, and how to behave; he could even be silent in their company without feeling the slightest awkwardness. There was an elusive charm in his appearance and disposition which attracted women and caught their sympathies. He knew this and was himself attracted to them by some invisible force.

Repeated and bitter experience had taught him that every fresh intimacy, while at first introducing such pleasant variety into everyday life, and offering itself as a charming, light adventure, inevitably developed, among decent people (especially in Moscow, where they are so irresolute and slow to move), into a problem of excessive complication leading to an intolerably irksome situation. But every time he encountered an attractive woman he forgot all about this experience, the desire for life surged up in him, and everything suddenly seemed simple and amusing.

One evening, then, while he was dining at the restaurant in the park, the lady in the toque came strolling up and took a seat at a neighboring table. Her expression, gait, dress, coiffure, all told him that she was from the upper

---

1. Translated by Ivy Litvinov.   2. A fashionable seaside resort in the Crimea.   3. Certain progressive intellectuals, anticipating the reform of the Russian alphabet, omitted the hard sign after consonants in writing; here, however, it is an affectation.

classes, that she was married, that she was in Yalta for the first time, alone and bored. . . . The accounts of the laxity of morals among visitors to Yalta are greatly exaggerated, and he paid no heed to them, knowing that for the most part they were invented by people who would gladly have transgressed themselves, had they known how to set about it. But when the lady sat down at a neighboring table a few yards away from him, these stories of easy conquests, of excursions to the mountains, came back to him, and the seductive idea of a brisk transitory liaison, an affair with a woman whose very name he did not know, suddenly took possession of his mind.

He snapped his fingers at the Pomeranian and, when it trotted up to him, shook his forefinger at it. The Pomeranian growled. Gurov shook his finger again.

The lady glanced at him and instantly lowered her eyes.

"He doesn't bite," she said, and blushed.

"May I give him a bone?" he asked, and on her nod of consent added in friendly tones: "Have you been long in Yalta?"

"About five days."

"And I am dragging out my second week here."

Neither spoke for a few minutes.

"The days pass quickly, and yet one is so bored here," she said, not looking at him.

"It's the thing to say it's boring here. People never complain of boredom in godforsaken holes like Belyev or Zhizdra, but when they get here it's: 'Oh, the dullness! Oh, the dust!' You'd think they'd come from Granada[4] to say the least."

She laughed. Then they both went on eating in silence, like complete strangers. But after dinner they left the restaurant together, and embarked upon the light, jesting talk of people free and contented, for whom it is all the same where they go, or what they talk about. They strolled along, remarking on the strange light over the sea. The water was a warm, tender purple, the moonlight lay on its surface in a golden strip. They said how close it was, after the hot day. Gurov told her he was from Moscow, that he was really a philologist, but worked in a bank; that he had at one time trained himself to sing in a private opera company, but had given up the idea; that he owned two houses in Moscow. . . . And from her he learned that she had grown up in Petersburg,[5] but had gotten married in the town of S., where she had been living two years, that she would stay another month in Yalta, and that perhaps her husband, who also needed a rest, would join her. She was quite unable to explain whether her husband was a member of the province council, or on the board of the *zemstvo*,[6] and was greatly amused at herself for this. Further, Gurov learned that her name was Anna Sergeyevna.

Back in his own room he thought about her, and felt sure he would meet her the next day. It was inevitable. As he went to bed he reminded himself that only a very short time ago she had been a schoolgirl, like his own daughter, learning her lessons, he remembered how much there was of shyness and constraint in her laughter, in her way of conversing with a stranger—it was probably the first time in her life that she found herself alone, and in a

4. A famous medieval city in Spain, once capital of the Moorish kingdom of Granada and now a tourist center known for its art and architecture. Belyev and Zhizdra are small provincial towns.   5. St. Petersburg, the former capital of Russia: an important port and cultural center.   6. District administration.

situation in which men could follow her and watch her, and speak to her, all the time with a secret aim she could not fail to divine. He recalled her slender, delicate neck, her fine gray eyes.

"And yet there's something pathetic about her," he thought to himself as he fell asleep.

II

A week had passed since the beginning of their acquaintance. It was a holiday. Indoors it was stuffy, but the dust rose in clouds out of doors, and people's hats blew off. It was a parching day and Gurov kept going to the outdoor café for fruit drinks and ices to offer Anna Sergeyevna. The heat was overpowering.

In the evening, when the wind had dropped, they walked to the pier to see the steamer come in. There were a great many people strolling about the landing-place; some, bunches of flowers in their hands, were meeting friends. Two peculiarities of the smart Yalta crowd stood out distinctly—the elderly ladies all tried to dress very youthfully, and there seemed to be an inordinate number of generals about.

Owing to the roughness of the sea the steamer arrived late, after the sun had gone down, and it had to maneuver for some time before it could get alongside the pier. Anna Sergeyevna scanned the steamer and passengers through her lorgnette,[7] as if looking for someone she knew, and when she turned to Gurov her eyes were glistening. She talked a great deal, firing off abrupt questions and forgetting immediately what it was she had wanted to know. Then she lost her lorgnette in the crush.

The smart crowd began dispersing, features could no longer be made out, the wind had quite dropped, and Gurov and Anna Sergeyevna stood there as if waiting for someone else to come off the steamer. Anna Sergeyevna had fallen silent, every now and then smelling her flowers, but not looking at Gurov.

"It's turned out a fine evening," he said. "What shall we do? We might go for a drive."

She made no reply.

He looked steadily at her and suddenly took her in his arms and kissed her lips, and the fragrance and dampness of the flowers closed round him, but the next moment he looked behind him in alarm—had anyone seen them?

"Let's go to your room," he murmured.

And they walked off together, very quickly.

Her room was stuffy and smelt of some scent she had bought in the Japanese shop.[8] Gurov looked at her, thinking to himself: "How full of strange encounters life is!" He could remember carefree, good-natured women who were exhilarated by love-making and grateful to him for the happiness he gave them, however short-lived; and there had been others—his wife among them—whose caresses were insincere, affected, hysterical, mixed up with a great deal of quite unnecessary talk, and whose expression seemed to say that all this was not just love-making or passion, but something much more

---

7. Small eyeglasses on a short handle.   8. Probably a tourist shop with imported goods.

significant; then there had been two or three beautiful, cold women, over whose features flitted a predatory expression, betraying a determination to wring from life more than it could give, women no longer in their first youth, capricious, irrational, despotic, brainless, and when Gurov had cooled to these, their beauty aroused in him nothing but repulsion, and the lace trimming on their underclothes reminded him of fish-scales.

But here the timidity and awkwardness of youth and inexperience were still apparent; and there was a feeling of embarrassment in the atmosphere, as if someone had just knocked at the door. Anna Sergeyevna, "the lady with the dog," seemed to regard the affair as something very special, very serious, as if she had become a fallen woman, an attitude he found odd and disconcerting. Her features lengthened and drooped, and her long hair hung mournfully on either side of her face. She assumed a pose of dismal meditation, like a repentant sinner in some classical painting.[9]

"It isn't right," she said. "You will never respect me anymore."

On the table was a watermelon. Gurov cut himself a slice from it and began slowly eating it. At least half an hour passed in silence.

Anna Sergeyevna was very touching, revealing the purity of a decent, naïve woman who had seen very little of life. The solitary candle burning on the table scarcely lit up her face, but it was obvious that her heart was heavy.

"Why should I stop respecting you?" asked Gurov. "You don't know what you're saying."

"May God forgive me!" she exclaimed, and her eyes filled with tears. "It's terrible."

"No need to seek to justify yourself."

"How can I justify myself? I'm a wicked, fallen woman, I despise myself and have not the least thought of self-justification. It isn't my husband I have deceived, it's myself. And not only now, I have been deceiving myself for ever so long. My husband is no doubt an honest, worthy man, but he's a flunky. I don't know what it is he does at his office, but I know he's a flunky. I was only twenty when I married him, and I was devoured by curiosity, I wanted something higher. I told myself that there must be a different kind of life I wanted to live, to live. . . . I was burning with curiosity . . . you'll never understand that, but I swear to God I could no longer control myself, nothing could hold me back, I told my husband I was ill, and I came here. . . . And I started going about like one possessed, like a madwoman . . . and now I have become an ordinary, worthless woman, and everyone has the right to despise me."

Gurov listened to her, bored to death. The naïve accents, the remorse, all was so unexpected, so out of place. But for the tears in her eyes, she might have been jesting or play-acting.

"I don't understand," he said gently. "What is it you want?"

She hid her face against his breast and pressed closer to him.

"Do believe me, I implore you to believe me," she said. "I love all that is honest and pure in life, vice is revolting to me, I don't know what I'm doing. The common people say they are snared by the Devil. And now I can say that I have been snared by the Devil, too."

---

9. A famous painting of Mary Magdalen (see Luke 7.36–50) by the French classical artist Georges de la Tour (1593–1652) shows her seated at a table meditating, her face and long hair illuminated by a candle.

"Come, come," he murmured.

He gazed into her fixed, terrified eyes, kissed her, and soothed her with gentle affectionate words, and gradually she calmed down and regained her cheefulness. Soon they were laughing together again.

When, a little later, they went out, there was not a soul on the promenade, the town and its cypresses looked dead, but the sea was still roaring as it dashed against the beach. A solitary fishing-boat tossed on the waves, its lamp blinking sleepily.

They found a carriage and drove to Oreanda.[1]

"I discovered your name in the hall, just now," said Gurov, "written up on the board. Von Diederitz. Is your husband a German?"

"No. His grandfather was, I think, but he belongs to the Orthodox Church himself."

When they got out of the carriage at Oreanda they sat down on a bench not far from the church, and looked down at the sea, without talking. Yalta could be dimly discerned through the morning mist, and white clouds rested motionless on the summits of the mountains. Not a leaf stirred, the grasshoppers chirruped, and the monotonous hollow roar of the sea came up to them, speaking of peace, of the eternal sleep lying in wait for us all. The sea had roared like this long before there was any Yalta or Oreanda, it was roaring now, and it would go on roaring, just as indifferently and hollowly, when we had passed away. And it may be that in this continuity, this utter indifference of life and death, lies the secret of our ultimate salvation, of the stream of life on our planet, and of its never-ceasing movement towards perfection.

Side by side with a young woman, who looked so exquisite in the early light, soothed and enchanted by the sight of all this magical beauty—sea, mountains, clouds and the vast expanse of the sky—Gurov told himself that, when you came to think of it, everything in the world is beautiful really, everything but our own thoughts and actions, when we lose sight of the higher aims of life, and of our dignity as human beings.

Someone approached them—a watchman, probably—looked at them and went away. And there was something mysterious and beautiful even in this. The steamer from Feodosia[2] could be seen coming towards the pier, lit up by the dawn, its lamps out.

"There's dew on the grass," said Anna Sergeyevna, breaking the silence.

"Yes. Time to go home."

They went back to the town.

After this they met every day at noon on the promenade, lunching and dining together, going for walks, and admiring the sea. She complained of sleeplessness, of palpitations, asked the same questions over and over again, alternately surrendering to jealousy and the fear that he did not really respect her. And often, when there was nobody in sight in the square or the park, he would draw her to him and kiss her passionately. The utter idleness, these kisses in broad daylight, accompanied by furtive glances and the fear of discovery, the heat, the smell of the sea, and the idle, smart, well-fed people continually crossing their field of vision, seemed to have given him a new lease of life. He told Anna Sergeyevna she was beautiful and seductive, made

---

1. A hotel and beach compound near Yalta; the whole area is known as the Ukrainian Riviera.   2. A coastal town seventy miles northeast of Yalta.

love to her with impetuous passion, and never left her side, while she was always pensive, always trying to force from him the admission that he did not respect her, that he did not love her a bit, and considered her just an ordinary woman. Almost every night they drove out of town, to Oreanda, the waterfall, or some other beauty-spot. And these excursions were invariably a success, each contributing fresh impressions of majestic beauty.

All this time they kept expecting her husband to arrive. But a letter came in which he told his wife that he was having trouble with his eyes, and implored her to come home as soon as possible. Anna Sergeyevna made hasty preparations for leaving.

"It's a good thing I'm going," she said to Gurov. "It's the intervention of fate."

She left Yalta in a carriage, and he went with her as far as the railway station. The drive took nearly a whole day. When she got into the express train, after the second bell had been rung, she said:

"Let me have one more look at you. . . . One last look. That's right."

She did not weep, but was mournful, and seemed ill, the muscles of her cheeks twitching.

"I shall think of you . . . I shall think of you all the time," she said. "God bless you! Think kindly of me. We are parting forever, it must be so, because we ought never to have met. Good-bye—God bless you."

The train steamed rapidly out of the station, its lights soon disappearing, and a minute later even the sound it made was silenced, as if everything were conspiring to bring this sweet oblivion, this madness, to an end as quickly as possible. And Gurov, standing alone on the platform and gazing into the dark distance, listened to the shrilling of the grasshoppers and the humming of the telegraph wires, with a feeling that he had only just awakened. And he told himself that this had been just one more of the many adventures in his life, and that it, too, was over, leaving nothing but a memory. . . . He was moved and sad, and felt a slight remorse. After all, this young woman whom he would never again see had not been really happy with him. He had been friendly and affectionate with her, but in his whole behaviour, in the tones of his voice, in his very caresses, there had been a shade of irony, the insulting indulgence of the fortunate male, who was, moreover, almost twice her age. She had insisted in calling him good, remarkable, high-minded. Evidently he had appeared to her different from his real self, in a word he had involuntarily deceived her. . . .

There was an autumnal feeling in the air, and the evening was chilly.

"It's time for me to be going north, too," thought Gurov, as he walked away from the platform. "High time!"

III

When he got back to Moscow it was beginning to look like winter; the stoves were heated every day, and it was still dark when the children got up to go to school and drank their tea, so that the nurse had to light the lamp for a short time. Frost had set in. When the first snow falls, and one goes for one's first sleigh-ride, it is pleasant to see the white ground, the white roofs; one breathes freely and lightly, and remembers the days of one's youth. The ancient lime-trees and birches, white with hoarfrost, have a good-natured look, they are closer to the heart than cypresses and palms, and beneath their branches one is no longer haunted by the memory of mountains and the sea.

Gurov had always lived in Moscow, and he returned to Moscow on a fine frosty day, and when he put on his fur-lined overcoat and thick gloves, and sauntered down Petrovka Street, and when, on Saturday evening, he heard the church bells ringing, his recent journey and the places he had visited lost their charm for him. He became gradually immersed in Moscow life, reading with avidity three newspapers a day, while declaring he never read Moscow newspapers on principle. Once more he was caught up in a whirl of restaurants, clubs, banquets, and celebrations, once more he glowed with the flattering consciousness that well-known lawyers and actors came to his house, that he played cards in the Medical Club opposite a professor. He could once again eat a whole serving of Moscow Fish Stew served in a pan.

He had believed that in a month's time Anna Sergeyevna would be nothing but a vague memory, and that hereafter, with her wistful smile, she would only occasionally appear to him in dreams, like others before her. But the month was now well over and winter was in full swing, and all was as clear in his memory as if he had parted with Anna Sergeyevna only the day before. And his recollections grew ever more insistent. When the voices of his children at their lessons reached him in his study through the evening stillness, when he heard a song, or the sounds of a music-box in a restaurant, when the wind howled in the chimney, it all came back to him: early morning on the pier, the misty mountains, the steamer from Feodosia, the kisses. He would pace up and down his room for a long time, smiling at his memories, and then memory turned into dreaming, and what had happened mingled in his imagination with what was going to happen. Anna Sergeyevna did not come to him in his dreams, she accompanied him everywhere, like his shadow, following him everywhere he went. When he closed his eyes, she seemed to stand before him in the flesh, still lovelier, younger, tenderer than she had really been, and looking back, he saw himself, too, as better than he had been in Yalta. In the evenings she looked out at him from the bookshelves, the fireplace, the corner, he could hear her breathing, the sweet rustle of her skirts. In the streets he followed women with his eyes, to see if there were any like her. . . .

He began to feel an overwhelming desire to share his memories with someone. But he could not speak of his love at home, and outside his home who was there for him to confide in? Not the tenants living in his house, and certainly not his colleagues at the bank. And what was there to tell? Was it love that he had felt? Had there been anything exquisite, poetic, anything instructive or even amusing about his relations with Anna Sergeyevna? He had to content himself with uttering vague generalizations about love and women, and nobody guessed what he meant, though his wife's dark eyebrows twitched as she said:

"The role of a coxcomb doesn't suit you a bit, Dimitry."

One evening, leaving the Medical Club with one of his card-partners, a government official, he could not refrain from remarking:

"If you only knew what a charming woman I met in Yalta!"

The official got into his sleigh, and just before driving off, turned and called out:

"Dmitry Dmitrich!"

"Yes?"

"You were quite right, you know—the sturgeon was just a *leetle* off."

These words, in themselves so commonplace, for some reason infuriated Gurov, seemed to him humiliating, gross. What savage manners, what people! What wasted evenings, what tedious, empty days! Frantic card-playing, gluttony, drunkenness, perpetual talk always about the same thing. The greater part of one's time and energy went on business that was no use to anyone, and on discussing the same thing over and over again, and there was nothing to show for it all but a stunted, earth-bound existence and a round of trivialities, and there was nowhere to escape to, you might as well be in a madhouse or a convict settlement.

Gurov lay awake all night, raging, and went about the whole of the next day with a headache. He slept badly on the succeeding nights, too, sitting up in bed, thinking, or pacing the floor of his room. He was sick of his children, sick of the bank, felt not the slightest desire to go anywhere or talk about anything.

When the Christmas holidays came, he packed his things, telling his wife he had to go to Petersburg in the interests of a certain young man, and set off for the town of S. To what end? He hardly knew himself. He only knew that he must see Anna Sergeyevna, must speak to her, arrange a meeting, if possible.

He arrived at S. in the morning and engaged the best suite in the hotel, which had a carpet of gray military frieze, and a dusty ink-pot on the table, surmounted by a headless rider, holding his hat in his raised hand. The hall porter told him what he wanted to know: von Diederitz had a house of his own in Staro-Goncharnaya Street. It wasn't far from the hotel, he lived on a grand scale, luxuriously, kept carriage-horses, the whole town knew him. The hall porter pronounced the name "Drideritz."

Gurov strolled over to Staro-Goncharnaya Street and discovered the house. In front of it was a long gray fence with inverted nails hammered into the tops of the palings.

"A fence like that is enough to make anyone want to run away," thought Gurov, looking at the windows of the house and the fence.

He reasoned that since it was a holiday, Anna's husband would probably be at home. In any case it would be tactless to embarrass her by calling at the house. And a note might fall into the hands of the husband, and bring about catastrophe. The best thing would be to wait about on the chance of seeing her. And he walked up and down the street, hovering in the vicinity of the fence, watching for his chance. A beggar entered the gate, only to be attacked by dogs, then, an hour later, the faint, vague sounds of a piano reached his ears. That would be Anna Sergeyevna playing. Suddenly the front door opened and an old woman came out, followed by a familiar white Pomeranian. Gurov tried to call to it, but his heart beat violently, and in his agitation he could not remember its name.

He walked on, hating the gray fence more and more, and now ready to tell himself irately that Anna Sergeyevna had forgotten him, had already, perhaps, found distraction in another—what could be more natural in a young woman who had to look at this accursed fence from morning to night? He went back to his hotel and sat on the sofa in his suite for some time, not knowing what to do, then he ordered dinner, and after dinner, had a long sleep.

"What a foolish, restless business," he thought, waking up and looking towards the dark windowpanes. It was evening by now. "Well, I've had my sleep out. And what am I to do in the night?"

He sat up in bed, covered by the cheap gray quilt, which reminded him of a hospital blanket, and in his vexation he fell to taunting himself.

"You and your lady with a dog . . . there's adventure for you! See what you get for your pains."

On his arrival at the station that morning he had noticed a poster announcing in enormous letters the first performance at the local theatre of *The Geisha*.[3] Remembering this, he got up and made for the theatre.

"It's highly probable that she goes to first nights," he told himself.

The theatre was full. It was a typical provincial theatre, with a mist collecting over the chandeliers, and the crowd in the gallery fidgeting noisily. In the first row of the stalls the local dandies stood waiting for the curtain to go up, their hands clasped behind them. There, in the front seat of the governor's box, sat the governor's daughter, wearing a boa, the governor himself hiding modestly behind the drapes, so that only his hands were visible. The curtain stirred, the orchestra took a long time tuning up their instruments. Gurov's eyes roamed eagerly over the audience as they filed in and occupied their seats.

Anna Sergeyevna came in, too. She seated herself in the third row of the stalls, and when Gurov's glance fell on her, his heart seemed to stop, and he knew in a flash that the whole world contained no one nearer or dearer to him, no one more important to his happiness. This little woman, lost in the provincial crowd, in no way remarkable, holding a silly lorgnette in her hand, now filled his whole life, was his grief, his joy, all that he desired. Lulled by the sounds coming from the wretched orchestra, with its feeble, amateurish violinists, he thought how beautiful she was . . . thought and dreamed. . . .

Anna Sergeyevna was accompanied by a tall, round-shouldered young man with small whiskers, who nodded at every step before taking the seat beside her and seemed to be continually bowing to someone. This must be her husband, whom, in a fit of bitterness, at Yalta, she had called a "flunky." And there really was something of a lackey's servility in his lanky figure, his side-whiskers, and the little bald spot on the top of his head. And he smiled sweetly, and the badge of some scientific society gleaming in his buttonhole was like the number on a footman's livery.

The husband went out to smoke in the first interval, and she was left alone in her seat. Gurov, who had taken a seat in the stalls, went up to her and said in a trembling voice, with a forced smile: "How d'you do?"

She glanced up at him and turned pale, then looked at him again in alarm, unable to believe her eyes, squeezing her fan and lorgnette in one hand, evidently struggling to overcome a feeling of faintness. Neither of them said a word. She sat there, and he stood beside her, disconcerted by her embar-

---

3. An operetta (1896) by the English composer Sidney Jones.

rassment, and not daring to sit down. The violins and flutes sang out as they were tuned, and there was a tense sensation in the atmosphere, as if they were being watched from all the boxes. At last she got up and moved rapidly towards one of the exits. He followed her and they wandered aimlessly along corridors, up and down stairs; figures flashed by in the uniforms of legal officials, high-school teachers and civil servants, all wearing badges; ladies, coats hanging from pegs flashed by; there was a sharp draft, bringing with it an odor of cigarette butts. And Gurov, whose heart was beating violently, thought:

"What on earth are all these people, this orchestra for? . . ."

The next minute he suddenly remembered how, after seeing Anna Sergeyevna off that evening at the station, he had told himself that all was over, and they would never meet again. And how far away the end seemed to be now!

She stopped on a dark narrow staircase over which was a notice bearing the inscription "To the upper circle."[4]

"How you frightened me!" she said, breathing heavily, still pale and half-stunned. "Oh, how you frightened me! I'm almost dead! Why did you come? Oh, why?"

"But, Anna," he said, in low, hasty tones. "But, Anna. . . . Try to understand . . . do try. . . ."

She cast him a glance of fear, entreaty, love, and then gazed at him steadily, as if to fix his features firmly in her memory.

"I've been so unhappy," she continued, taking no notice of his words. "I could think of nothing but you the whole time, I lived on the thoughts of you. I tried to forget—why, oh, why did you come?"

On the landing above them were two schoolboys, smoking and looking down, but Gurov did not care, and, drawing Anna Sergeyevna towards him, began kissing her face, her lips, her hands.

"What are you doing, oh, what are you doing?" she said in horror, drawing back. "We have both gone mad. Go away this very night, this moment. . . . By all that is sacred, I implore you. . . . Somebody is coming."

Someone was ascending the stairs.

"You must go away," went on Anna Sergeyevna in a whisper. "D'you hear me, Dmitry Dmitrich? I'll come to you in Moscow. I have never been happy, I am unhappy now, and I shall never be happy—never! Do not make me suffer still more! I will come to you in Moscow, I swear it! And now we must part! My dear one, my kind one, my darling, we must part."

She pressed his hand and hurried down the stairs, looking back at him continually, and her eyes showed that she was in truth unhappy. Gurov stood where he was for a short time, listening, and when all was quiet, went to look for his coat, and left the theatre.

IV

And Anna Sergeyevna began going to Moscow to see him. Every two or three months she left the town of S., telling her husband that she was going

---

4. The stalls or back rows; a medium-priced area behind the orchestra seats on the main floor.

to consult a specialist on female diseases, and her husband believed her and did not believe her. In Moscow she always stayed at the Slavyanski Bazaar,[5] sending a man in a red cap to Gurov the moment she arrived. Gurov went to her, and no one in Moscow knew anything about it.

One winter morning he went to see her as usual (the messenger had been to him the evening before, but had not found him at home). His daughter was with him, for her school was on the way and he thought he might as well see her to it.

"It is forty degrees," said Gurov to his daughter, "and yet it is snowing. You see it is only above freezing close to the ground, the temperature in the upper layers of the atmosphere is quite different."

"Why doesn't it ever thunder in winter, Papa?"

He explained this, too. As he was speaking, he kept reminding himself that he was going to a rendezvous and that not a living soul knew about it, or, probably, ever would. He led a double life—one in public, in the sight of all whom it concerned, full of conventional truth and conventional deception, exactly like the lives of his friends and acquaintances, and another which flowed in secret. And, owing to some strange, possibly quite accidental chain of circumstances, everything that was important, interesting, essential, everything about which he was sincere and never deceived himself, everything that composed the kernel of his life, went on in secret, while everything that was false in him, everything that composed the husk in which he hid himself and the truth which was in him—his work at the bank, discussions at the club, his "lower race," his attendance at anniversary celebrations with his wife—was on the surface. He began to judge others by himself, no longer believing what he saw, and always assuming that the real, the only interesting life of every individual goes on as under cover of night, secretly. Every individual existence revolves around mystery, and perhaps that is the chief reason that all cultivated individuals insisted so strongly on the respect due to personal secrets.

After leaving his daughter at the door of her school Gurov set off for the Slavyanski Bazaar. Taking off his overcoat in the lobby, he went upstairs and knocked softly on the door. Anna Sergeyevna, wearing the gray dress he liked most, exhausted by her journey and by suspense, had been expecting him since the evening before. She was pale and looked at him without smiling, but was in his arms almost before he was fairly in the room. Their kiss was lingering, prolonged, as if they had not met for years.

"Well, how are you?" he asked. "Anything new?"

"Wait, I'll tell you in a minute. . . . I can't. . . ."

She could not speak, because she was crying. Turning away, she held her handkerchief to her eyes.

"I'll wait till she's had her cry out," he thought, and sank into a chair.

He rang for tea, and a little later, while he was drinking it, she was still standing there, her face to the window. She wept from emotion, from her bitter consciousness of the sadness of their life; they could only see one another in secret, hiding from people, as if they were thieves. Was not their life a broken one?

"Don't cry," he said.

5. A luxurious hotel in Moscow.

It was quite obvious to him that this love of theirs would not soon come to an end, and that no one could say when this end would be. Anna Sergeyevna loved him ever more fondly, worshipped him, and there would have been no point in telling her that one day it must end. Indeed, she would not have believed him.

He moved over and took her by the shoulders, intending to fondle her with light words, but suddenly he caught sight of himself in the looking-glass.

His hair was already beginning to turn gray. It struck him as strange that he should have aged so much in the last few years. The shoulders on which his hands lay were warm and quivering. He felt a pity for this life, still so warm and exquisite, but probably soon to fade and droop like his own. Why did she love him so? Women had always believed him different from what he really was, had loved in him not himself but the man their imagination pictured him, a man they had sought for eagerly all their lives. And afterwards when they discovered their mistake, they went on loving him just the same. And not one of them had ever been happy with him. Time had passed, he had met one woman after another, become intimate with each, parted with each, but had never loved. There had been all sorts of things between them, but never love.

And only now, when he was gray-haired, had he fallen in love properly, thoroughly, for the first time in his life.

He and Anna Sergeyevna loved one another as people who are very close and intimate, as husband and wife, as dear friends love one another. It seemed to them that fate had intended them for one another, and they could not understand why she should have a husband, and he a wife. They were like two migrating birds, the male and the female, who had been caught and put into separate cages. They forgave one another all that they were ashamed of in the past and in the present, and felt that this love of theirs had changed them both.

Formerly, in moments of melancholy, he had consoled himself by the first argument that came into his head, but now arguments were nothing to him, he felt profound pity, desired to be sincere, tender.

"Stop crying, my dearest," he said. "You've had your cry, now stop. . . . Now let us have a talk, let us try and think what we are to do."

Then they discussed their situation for a long time, trying to think how they could get rid of the necessity for hiding, deception, living in different towns, being so long without meeting. How were they to shake off these intolerable fetters?

"How? How?" he repeated, clutching his head. "How?"

And it seemed to them that they were within an inch of arriving at a decision, and that then a new, beautiful life would begin. And they both realized that the end was still far, far away, and that the hardest, the most complicated part was only just beginning.

The Cherry Orchard[1]

CHARACTERS

LUBOV ANDREYEVNA RANEVSKAYA, *a landowner*
ANYA, *her seventeen-year-old daughter*
VARYA, *her adopted daughter, twenty-four years old*
LEONID ANDREYEVICH GAYEV, *Mme. Ranevskaya's brother*
YERMOLAY ALEXEYEVICH LOPAHIN, *a merchant*
PYOTR SERGEYEVICH TROFIMOV, *a student*
SIMEONOV-PISHCHIK, *a landowner*

CHARLOTTA IVANOVNA, *a governess*
SEMYON YEPIHODOV, *a clerk*
DUNYASHA, *a maid*
FIRS, *a manservant, aged eighty-seven*
YASHA, *a young valet*
A TRAMP
STATIONMASTER
POST OFFICE CLERK
GUESTS
SERVANTS

The action takes place on MME. RANEVSKAYA's *estate.*

Act I

A room that is still called the nursery. One of the doors leads into ANYA's *room. Dawn, the sun will soon rise. It is May, the cherry trees are in blossom, but it is cold in the orchard; there is a morning frost. The windows are shut. Enter* DUNYASHA *with a candle, and* LOPAHIN *with a book in his hand.*

LOPAHIN   The train is in, thank God. What time is it?

DUNYASHA   Nearly two. [*Puts out the candle.*] It's light already.

LOPAHIN   How late is the train, anyway? Two hours at least. [*Yawns and stretches.*] I'm a fine one! What a fool I've made of myself! I came here on purpose to meet them at the station, and then I went and overslept. I fell asleep in my chair. How annoying! You might have waked me . . .

DUNYASHA   I thought you'd left. [*Listens.*] I think they're coming!

LOPAHIN [*Listens.*]   No, they've got to get the luggage, and one thing and another . . . [*Pause.*] Lubov Andreyevna spent five years abroad, I don't know what she's like now. . . . She's a fine person—lighthearted, simple. I remember when I was a boy of fifteen, my poor father—he had a shop here in the village then—punched me in the face with his fist and made my nose bleed. We'd come into the yard, I don't know what for, and he'd had a drop too much. Lubov Andreyevna, I remember her as if it were yesterday—she was still young and so slim—led me to the washbasin, in this very room . . . in the nursery. "Don't cry, little peasant," she said, "it'll heal in time for your wedding . . ." [*Pause.*] Little peasant . . . my father was a peasant, it's true, and here I am in a white waistcoat and yellow shoes. A pig in a pastry shop, you might say. It's true I'm rich. I've got a lot of money. . . . But when you look at it closely, I'm a peasant through and through. [*Pages the book.*] Here I've been reading this book and I didn't understand a word of it. . . . I was reading it and fell asleep . . . [*Pause.*]

1. Translated by Avrahm Yarmolinsky.

DUNYASHA   And the dogs were awake all night, they feel that their masters are coming.

LOPAHIN   Dunyasha, why are you so—

DUNYASHA   My hands are trembling. I'm going to faint.

LOPAHIN   You're too soft, Dunyasha. You dress like a lady, and look at the way you do your hair. That's not right. One should remember one's place.

[Enter YEPIHODOV *with a bouquet; he wears a jacket and highly polished boots that squeak badly. He drops the bouquet as he comes in.*]

YEPIHODOV [*Picking up the bouquet.*]   Here, the gardener sent these, said you're to put them in the dining room. [*Hands the bouquet to* DUNYASHA.]

LOPAHIN   And bring me some kvass.[2]

DUNYASHA   Yes, sir. [*Exits.*]

YEPIHODOV   There's a frost this morning—three degrees below—and yet the cherries are all in blossom. I cannot approve of our climate. [*Sighs.*] I cannot. Our climate does not activate properly. And, Yermolay Alexeyevich, allow me to make a further remark. The other day I bought myself a pair of boots, and I make bold to assure you, they squeak so that it is really intolerable. What should I grease them with?

LOPAHIN   Oh, get out! I'm fed up with you.

YEPIHODOV   Every day I meet with misfortune. And I don't complain, I've got used to it, I even smile.

[DUNYASHA *enters, hands* LOPAHIN *the kvass.*]

YEPIHODOV   I am leaving. [*Stumbles against a chair, which falls over.*] There! [*Triumphantly, as it were.*] There again, you see what sort of circumstance, pardon the expression. . . . It is absolutely phenomenal! [*Exits.*]

DUNYASHA   You know, Yermolay Alexeyevich, I must tell you, Yepihodov has proposed to me.

LOPAHIN   Ah!

DUNYASHA   I simply don't know . . . he's a quiet man, but sometimes when he starts talking, you can't make out what he means. He speaks nicely— and it's touching—but you can't understand it. I sort of like him though, and he is crazy about me. He's an unlucky man . . . every day something happens to him. They tease him about it here . . . they call him, Two and-Twenty Troubles.

LOPAHIN [*Listening.*]   There! I think they're coming.

DUNYASHA   They *are* coming! What's the matter with me? I feel cold all over.

LOPAHIN   They really are coming. Let's go and meet them. Will she recognize me? We haven't seen each other for five years.

DUNYASHA [*In a flutter.*]   I'm going to faint this minute. . . . Oh, I'm going to faint!

[*Two carriages are heard driving up to the house.* LOPAHIN *and* DUNYASHA *go out quickly. The stage is left empty. There is a noise in the adjoining rooms.* FIRS, *who had driven to the station to meet* LUBOV ANDREYEVNA RANEVSKAYA, *crosses the stage hurriedly, leaning on a stick. He is wearing an old-fashioned livery and a tall hat. He mutters to himself indistinctly. The hubbub offstage increases. A* VOICE:

2. Russian beer, made from rye or barley.

"Come, let's go this way." Enter LUBOV ANDREYEVNA, ANYA, *and* CHARLOTTA IVANOVNA *with a pet dog on a leash, all in traveling dresses;* VARYA, *wearing a coat and kerchief;* GAYEV, SIMEONOV-PISHCHIK, LOPAHIN, DUNYASHA, *with a bag and an umbrella, servants with luggage. All walk across the room.*]

ANYA Let's go this way. Do you remember what room this is, Mamma?

MME. RANEVSKAYA [*Joyfully, through her tears.*] The nursery!

VARYA How cold it is! My hands are numb. [*To* MME. RANEVSKAYA.] Your rooms are just the same as they were, Mamma, the white one and the violet.

MME. RANEVSKAYA The nursery! My darling, lovely room! I slept here when I was a child . . . [*Cries.*] And here I am, like a child again! [*Kisses her brother and* VARYA, *and then her brother again.*] Varya's just the same as ever, like a nun. And I recognized Dunyasha. [*Kisses* DUNYASHA.]

GAYEV The train was two hours late. What do you think of that? What a way to manage things!

CHARLOTTA [*To* PISHCHIK.] My dog eats nuts, too.

PISHCHIK [*In amazement.*] You don't say!

[*All go out, except* ANYA *and* DUNYASHA.]

DUNYASHA We've been waiting for you for hours. [*Takes* ANYA's *hat and coat.*]

ANYA I didn't sleep on the train for four nights and now I'm frozen . . .

DUNYASHA It was Lent when you left; there was snow and frost, and now . . . My darling! [*Laughs and kisses her.*] I have been waiting for you, my sweet, my darling! But I must tell you something . . . I can't put it off another minute . . .

ANYA [*Listlessly.*] What now?

DUNYASHA The clerk, Yepihodov, proposed to me, just after Easter.

ANYA There you are, at it again . . . [*Straightening her hair.*] I've lost all my hairpins . . . [*She is staggering with exhaustion.*]

DUNYASHA Really, I don't know what to think. He loves me—he loves me so!

ANYA [*Looking toward the door of her room, tenderly.*] My own room, my windows, just as though I'd never been away. I'm home! Tomorrow morning I'll get up and run into the orchard. Oh, if I could only get some sleep. I didn't close my eyes during the whole journey—I was so anxious.

DUNYASHA Pyotr Sergeyevich came the day before yesterday.

ANYA [*Joyfully.*] Petya!

DUNYASHA He's asleep in the bathhouse. He has settled there. He said he was afraid of being in the way. [*Looks at her watch.*] I should wake him, but Miss Varya told me not to. "Don't you wake him," she said.

[*Enter* VARYA *with a bunch of keys at her belt.*]

VARYA Dunyasha, coffee, and be quick. . . . Mamma's asking for coffee.

DUNYASHA In a minute. [*Exits.*]

VARYA Well, thank God, you've come. You're home again. [*Fondling* ANYA.] My darling is here again. My pretty one is back.

ANYA Oh, what I've been through!

VARYA I can imagine.

ANYA When we left, it was Holy Week, it was cold then, and all the way Charlotta chattered and did her tricks. Why did you have to saddle me with Charlotta?

VARYA   You couldn't have travelled all alone, darling—at seventeen!

ANYA   We got to Paris, it was cold there, snowing. My French is dreadful. Mamma lived on the fifth floor; I went up there, and found all kinds of Frenchmen, ladies, an old priest with a book. The place was full of tobacco smoke, and so bleak. Suddenly I felt sorry for Mamma, so sorry, I took her head in my arms and hugged her and couldn't let go of her. Afterward Mamma kept fondling me and crying. . . .

VARYA   [Through tears.]   Don't speak of it . . . don't.

ANYA   She had already sold her villa at Mentone, she had nothing left, nothing. I hadn't a kopeck left either, we had only just enough to get home. And Mamma wouldn't understand! When we had dinner at the stations, she always ordered the most expensive dishes, and tipped the waiters a whole ruble. Charlotta, too. And Yasha kept ordering, too—it was simply awful. You know Yasha's Mamma's footman now, we brought him here with us.

VARYA   Yes, I've seen the blackguard.

ANYA   Well, tell me—have you paid the interest?

VARYA   How could we?

ANYA   Good heavens, good heavens!

VARYA   In August the estate will be put up for sale.

ANYA   My God!

LOPAHIN   [Peeps in at the door and bleats.]   Meh-h-h. [Disappears.]

VARYA   [Through tears.]   What I couldn't do to him! [Shakes her fist threateningly.]

ANYA   [Embracing VARYA gently.]   Varya, has he proposed to you? [VARYA shakes her head.] But he loves you. Why don't you come to an understanding? What are you waiting for?

VARYA   Oh, I don't think anything will ever come of it. He's too busy, he has no time for me . . . pays no attention to me. I've washed my hands of him—I can't bear the sight of him. They all talk abut our getting married, they all congratulate me—and all the time there's really nothing to it—it's all like a dream. [In another tone.] You have a new brooch—like a bee.

ANYA   [Sadly.]   Mamma bought it. [She goes into her own room and speaks gaily like a child.] And you know, in Paris I went up in a balloon.

VARYA   My darling's home, my pretty one is back. [DUNYASHA returns with the coffeepot and prepares coffee. VARYA stands at the door of ANYA's room.] All day long, darling, as I go about the house, I keep dreaming. If only we could marry you off to a rich man, I should feel at ease. Then I would go into a convent, and afterward to Kiev, to Moscow . . . I would spend my life going from one holy place to another . . . I'd go on and on. . . . What a blessing that would be!

ANYA   The birds are singing in the orchard. What time is it?

VARYA   It must be after two. Time you were asleep, darling. [Goes into ANYA's room.] What a blessing that would be!

      [YASHA enters with a plaid and a traveling bag, crosses the stage.]

YASHA   [Finically.]   May I pass this way, please?

DUNYASHA   A person could hardly recognize you, Yasha. Your stay abroad has certainly done wonders for you.

YASHA   Hm-m . . . and who are you?

DUNYASHA   When you went away I was that high—[Indicating with her hand.] I'm Dunyasha—Fyodor Kozoyedev's daughter. Don't you remember?

YASHA Hm! What a peach!

[He looks round and embraces her. She cries out and drops a saucer. YASHA leaves quickly.]

VARYA [In the doorway, in a tone of annoyance.] What's going on here?

DUNYASHA [Through tears.] I've broken a saucer.

VARYA Well, that's good luck.

ANYA [Coming out of her room.] We ought to warn Mamma that Petya's here.

VARYA I left orders not to wake him.

ANYA [Musingly.] Six years ago father died. A month later brother Grisha was drowned in the river. . . . Such a pretty little boy he was—only seven. It was more than Mamma could bear, so she went away, went away without looking back . . . [Shudders.] How well I understand her, if she only knew! [Pause.] And Petya Trofimov was Grisha's tutor, he may remind her of it all . . .

[Enter FIRS, wearing a jacket and a white waistcoat. He goes up to the coffeepot.]

FIRS [Anxiously.] The mistress will have her coffee here. [Puts on white gloves.] Is the coffee ready? [Sternly, to DUNYASHA.] Here, you! And where's the cream?

DUNYASHA Oh, my God! [Exits quickly.]

FIRS [Fussing over the coffeepot.] Hah! the addlehead! [Mutters to himself.] Home from Paris. And the old master used to go to Paris too . . . by carriage. [Laughs.]

VARYA What is it, Firs?

FIRS What is your pleasure, Miss? [Joyfully.] My mistress has come home, and I've seen her at last! Now I can die. [Weeps with joy.]

[Enters RANEVSKAYA, GAYEV, and SIMEONOV-PISHCHIK: The latter is wearing a tight-waisted, pleated coat of fine cloth, and full trousers. GAYEV, as he comes in, goes through the motions of a billiard player with his arms and body.]

MME. RANEVSKAYA Let's see, how does it go? Yellow ball in the corner! Bank shot in the side pocket!

GAYEV I'll tip it in the corner! There was a time, Sister, when you and I used to sleep in this very room and now I'm fifty-one, strange as it may seem.

LOPAHIN Yes, time flies.

GAYEV Who?

LOPAHIN I say, time flies.

GAYEV It smells of patchouli here.

ANYA I'm going to bed. Good night, Mamma. [Kisses her mother.]

MME. RANEVSKAYA My darling child! [Kisses her hands.] Are you happy to be home? I can't come to my senses.

ANYA Good night, Uncle.

GAYEV [Kissing her face and hands.] God bless you, how like your mother you are! [To his sister.] At her age, Luba, you were just like her.

[ANYA shakes hands with LOPAHIN and PISHCHIK, then goes out, shutting the door behind her.]

MME. RANEVSKAYA She's very tired.

PISHCHIK Well, it was a long journey.

VARYA [*To* LOPAHIN *and* PISHCHIK.] How about it, gentlemen? It's past two o'clock—isn't it time for you to go?

MME. RANEVSKAYA [*Laughs.*] You're just the same as ever, Varya. [*Draws her close and kisses her.*] I'll have my coffee and then we'll all go. [FIRS *puts a small cushion under her feet.*] Thank you, my dear. I've got used to coffee. I drink it day and night. Thanks, my dear old man. [*Kisses him.*]

VARYA I'd better see if all the luggage has been brought in. [*Exits.*]

MME. RANEVSKAYA Can it really be I sitting here? [*Laughs.*] I feel like dancing, waving my arms about. [*Covers her face with her hands.*] But maybe I am dreaming! God knows I love my country, I love it tenderly; I couldn't look out of the window in the train, I kept crying so. [*Through tears.*] But I must have my coffee. Thank you, Firs, thank you, dear old man. I'm so happy that you're still alive.

FIRS Day before yesterday.

GAYEV He's hard of hearing.

LOPAHIN I must go soon, I'm leaving for Kharkov about five o'clock. How annoying! I'd like to have a good look at you, talk to you. . . . You're just as splendid as ever.

PISHCHIK [*Breathing heavily.*] She's even better-looking. . . . Dressed in the latest Paris fashion. . . . Perish my carriage and all its four wheels. . . .

LOPAHIN Your brother, Leonid Andreyevich, says I'm a vulgarian and an exploiter. But it's all the same to me—let him talk. I only want you to trust me as you used to. I want you to look at me with your touching, wonderful eyes, as you used to. Dear God! My father was a serf of your father's and grandfather's, but you, you yourself, did so much for me once . . . so much . . . that I've forgotten all about that; I love you as though you were my sister—even more.

MME. RANESVSKAYA I can't sit still, I simply can't. [*Jumps up and walks about in violent agitation.*] This joy is too much for me. . . . Laugh at me, I'm silly! My own darling bookcase! My darling table! [*Kisses it.*]

GAYEV While you were away, nurse died.

MME. RANEVSKAYA [*Sits down and takes her coffee.*] Yes, God rest her soul; they wrote me about it.

GAYEV And Anastasy is dead. Petrushka Kossoy has left me and has gone into town to work for the police inspector. [*Takes a box of sweets out of his pocket and begins to suck one.*]

PISHCHIK My daughter Dashenka sends her regards.

LOPAHIN I'd like to tell you something very pleasant—cheering. [*Glancing at his watch.*] I am leaving directly. There isn't much time to talk. But I will put it in a few words. As you know, your cherry orchard is to be sold to pay your debts. The sale is to be on the twenty-second of August; but don't you worry, my dear, you may sleep in peace; there is a way out. Here is my plan. Give me your attention! Your estate is only fifteen miles from the town; the railway runs close by it; and if the cherry orchard and the land along the riverbank were cut up into lots and these leased for summer cottages, you would have an income of at least 25,000 rubles a year out of it.

GAYEV   Excuse me. . . . What nonsense.

MME. RANEVSKAYA   I don't quite understand you, Yermolay Alexeyevich.

LOPAHIN   You will get an annual rent of at least ten rubles per acre, and if you advertise at once, I'll give you any guarantee you like that you won't have a square foot of ground left by autumn, all the lots will be snapped up. In short, congratulations, you're saved. The location is splendid—by that deep river. . . . Only, of course, the ground must be cleared . . . all the old buildings, for instance, must be torn down, and this house, too, which is useless, and, of course, the old cherry orchard must be cut down.

MME. RANEVSKAYA   Cut down? My dear, forgive me, but you don't know what you're talking about. If there's one thing that's interesting—indeed, remarkable—in the whole province, it's precisely our cherry orchard.

LOPAHIN   The only remarkable thing about this orchard is that it's a very large one. There's a crop of cherries every other year, and you can't do anything with them; no one buys them.

GAYEV   This orchard is even mentioned in the encyclopedia.

LOPAHIN [Glancing at his watch.]   If we can't think of a way out, if we don't come to a decision, on the twenty-second of August the cherry orchard and the whole estate will be sold at auction. Make up your minds! There's no other way out—I swear. None, none.

FIRS   In the old days, forty or fifty years ago, the cherries were dried, soaked, pickled, and made into jam, and we used to—

GAYEV   Keep still, Firs.

FIRS   And the dried cherries would be shipped by the cartload. It meant a lot of money! And in those days the dried cherries were soft and juicy, sweet, fragrant. . . . They knew the way to do it, then.

MME. RANEVSKAYA   And why don't they do it that way now?

FIRS   They've forgotten. Nobody remembers it.

PISHCHIK [To MME. RANEVSKAYA.]   What's doing in Paris? Eh? Did you eat frogs there?

MME. RANEVSKAYA   I ate crocodiles.

PISHCHIK   Just imagine!

LOPAHIN   There used to be only landowners and peasants in the country, but now these summer people have appeared on the scene. . . . All the towns, even the small ones, are surrounded by these summer cottages; and in another twenty years, no doubt, the summer population will have grown enormously. Now the summer resident only drinks tea on his porch, but maybe he'll take to working his acre, too, and then your cherry orchard will be a rich, happy, luxuriant place.

GAYEV [Indignantly.]   Poppycock!
   [Enter VARYA and YASHA.]

VARYA   There are two telegrams for you, Mamma dear. [Picks a key from the bunch at her belt and noisily opens an old-fashioned bookcase.] Here they are.

MME. RANEVSKAYA   They're from Paris. [Tears them up without reading them.] I'm through with Paris.

GAYEV   Do you know, Luba, how old this bookcase is? Last week I pulled out the bottom drawer and there I found the date burnt in it. It was made exactly a hundred years ago. Think of that! We could celebrate its centenary. True, it's an inanimate object, but nevertheless, a bookcase . . .

PISHCHIK [*Amazed.*]   A hundred years! Just imagine!

GAYEV   Yes. [*Tapping it.*] That's something. . . . Dear, honored bookcase, hail to you who for more than a century have served the glorious ideals of goodness and justice! Your silent summons to fruitful toil has never weakened in all those hundred years [*through tears*], sustaining, through successive generations of our family, courage and faith in a better future, and fostering in us ideals of goodness and social consciousness. [*Pauses.*]

LOPAHIN   Yes . . .

MME. RANEVSKAYA   You haven't changed a bit, Leonid.

GAYEV [*Somewhat embarrassed.*]   I'll play it off the red in the corner! Tip it in the side pocket!

LOPAHIN [*Looking at his watch.*]   Well, it's time for me to go . . .

YASHA [*Handing pillbox to* MME. RANEVSKAYA.]   Perhaps you'll take your pills now.

PISHCHIK   One shouldn't take medicines, dearest lady, they do neither harm nor good. . . . Give them here, my valued friend. [*Takes the pillbox, pours the pills into his palm, blows on them, puts them in his mouth, and washes them down with some kvass.*] There!

MME. RANEVSKAYA [*Frightened.*]   You must be mad!

PISHCHIK   I've taken all the pills.

LOPAHIN   What a glutton!
     [*All laugh.*]

FIRS   The gentleman visited us in Easter week, ate half a bucket of pickles, he did . . . [*Mumbles.*]

MME. RANEVSKAYA   What's he saying?

VARYA   He's been mumbling like that for the last three years—we're used to it.

YASHA   His declining years!
     [CHARLOTTA IVANOVNA, *very thin, tightly laced, dressed in white, a lorgnette at her waist, crosses the stage.*]

LOPAHIN   Forgive me, Charlotta Ivanovna, I've not had time to greet you. [*Tries to kiss her hand.*]

CHARLOTTA [*Pulling away her hand.*]   If I let you kiss my hand, you'll be wanting to kiss my elbow next, and then my shoulder.

LOPAHIN   I've no luck today. [*All laugh.*] Charlotta Ivanovna, show us a trick.

MME. RANEVSKAYA   Yes, Charlotta, do a trick for us.

CHARLOTTA   I don't see the need. I want to sleep. [*Exits.*]

LOPAHIN   In three weeks we'll meet again. [*Kisses* MME. RANEVSKAYA's *hand.*] Good-bye till then. Time's up. [*To* GAYEV.] Bye-bye. [*Kisses* PISH-CHIK.] Bye-bye. [*Shakes hands with* VARYA, *then with* FIRS *and* YASHA.] I hate to leave. [*To* MME. RANEVSKAYA.] If you make up your mind about the cottages, let me know; I'll get you a loan of 50,000 rubles.[3] Think it over seriously.

VARYA [*Crossly.*]   Will you never go!

LOPAHIN   I'm going, I'm going. [*Exits.*]

---

3. The basic unit of currency. One ruble is equal to one hundred kopecks.

GAYEV   The vulgarian. But, excuse me . . . Varya's going to marry him, he's Varya's fiancé.

VARYA   You talk too much, Uncle.

MME. RANEVSKAYA   Well, Varya, it would make me happy. He's a good man.

PISHCHIK   Yes, one must admit, he's a most estimable man. And my Dashenka . . . she too says that . . . she says . . . lots of things. [*Snores; but wakes up at once.*] All the same, my valued friend, could you oblige me . . . with a loan of 240 rubles? I must pay the interest on the mortgage tomorrow.

VARYA [*Alarmed.*]   We can't, we can't!

MME. RANEVSKAYA   I really haven't any money.

PISHCHIK   It'll turn up. [*Laughs.*] I never lose hope, I thought everything was lost, that I was done for, when lo and behold, the railway ran through my land . . . and I was paid for it. . . . And something else will turn up again, if not today, then tomorrow . . . Dashenka will win two hundred thousand . . . she's got a lottery ticket.

MME. RANEVSKAYA   I've had my coffee, now let's go to bed.

FIRS [*Brushes off* GAYEV; *admonishingly.*]   You've got the wrong trousers on again. What am I to do with you?

VARYA [*Softly.*]   Anya's asleep. [*Gently opens the window.*] The sun's up now, it's not a bit cold. Look, Mamma dear, what wonderful trees. And heavens, what air! The starlings are singing!

GAYEV [*Opens the other window.*]   The orchard is all white. You've not forgotten it? Luba? That's the long alley that runs straight, straight as an arrow; how it shines on moonlight nights, do you remember? You've not forgotten?

MME. RANEVSKAYA [*Looking out of the window into the orchard.*]   Oh, my childhood, my innocent childhood. I used to sleep in this nursery—I used to look out into the orchard, happiness waked with me every morning, the orchard was just the same then . . . nothing has changed. [*Laughs with joy.*] All, all white! Oh, my orchard! After the dark, rainy autumn and the cold winter, you are young again, and full of happiness, the heavenly angels have not left you. . . . If I could free my chest and my shoulders from this rock that weighs on me, if I could only forget the past!

GAYEV   Yes, and the orchard will be sold to pay our debts, strange as it may seem.

MME. RANEVSKAYA   Look! There is our poor mother walking in the orchard . . . all in white . . . [*Laughs with joy.*] It is she!

GAYEV   Where?

VARYA   What are you saying, Mamma dear!

MME. RANEVSKAYA   There's no one there, I just imagined it. To the right, where the path turns toward the arbor, there's a little white tree, leaning over, that looks like a woman . . .

[TROFIMOV *enters, wearing a shabby student's uniform and spectacles.*]

MME. RANEVSKAYA   What an amazing orchard! White masses of blossom, the blue sky . . .

TROFIMOV   Lubov Andreyevna! [*She looks round at him.*] I just want to

pay my respects to you, then I'll leave at once. [*Kisses her hand ardently.*]
I was told to wait until morning, but I hadn't the patience . . .

[MME. RANEVSKAYA *looks at him, perplexed.*]

VARYA [*Through tears.*]   This is Petya Trofimov.

TROFIMOV   Petya Trofimov, formerly your Grisha's tutor. . . . Can I have
changed so much?

[MME. RANEVSKAYA *embraces him and weeps quietly.*]

GAYEV [*Embarrassed.*]   Don't, don't, Luba.

VARYA [*Crying.*]   I told you, Petya, to wait until tomorrow.

MME. RANEVSKAYA   My Grisha . . . my little boy . . . Grisha . . . my son.

VARYA   What can one do, Mamma dear, it's God's will.

TROFIMOV [*Softly, through tears.*]   There . . . there.

MME. RANEVSKAYA [*Weeping quietly.*]   My little boy was lost . . . drowned.
Why? Why, my friend? [*More quietly.*] Anya's asleep in there, and here
I am talking so loudly . . . making all this noise. . . . But tell me, Petya,
why do you look so badly? Why have you aged so?

TROFIMOV   A mangy master, a peasant woman in the train called me.

MME. RANEVSKAYA   You were just a boy then, a dear little student, and
now your hair's thin—and you're wearing glasses! Is it possible you're
still a student? [*Goes toward the door.*]

TROFIMOV   I suppose I'm a perpetual student.

MME. RANEVSKAYA [*Kisses her brother, then* VARYA.]   Now, go to bed. . . .
You have aged, too, Leonid.

PISHCHIK [*Follows her.*]   So now we turn in. Oh, my gout! I'm staying the
night here . . . Lubov Andreyevna, my angel, tomorrow morning . . . I do
need 240 rubles.

GAYEV   He keeps at it.

PISHCHIK   I'll pay it back, dear . . . it's a trifling sum.

MME. RANEVSKAYA   All right, Leonid will give it to you. Give it to him,
Leonid.

GAYEV   Me give it to him! That's a good one!

MME. RANEVSKAYA   It can't be helped. Give it to him! He needs it. He'll
pay it back.

[MME. RANEVSKAYA, TROFIMOV, PISHCHIK, *and* FIRS *go out;* GAYEV,
VARYA, *and* YASHA *remain.*]

GAYEV   Sister hasn't got out of the habit of throwing money around. [*To*
YASHA.] Go away, my good fellow, you smell of the barnyard.

YASHA [*With a grin.*]   And you, Leonid Andreyevich, are just the same as
ever.

GAYEV   Who? [*To* VARYA.] What did he say?

VARYA [*To* YASHA.]   Your mother's come from the village; she's been sitting
in the servants' room since yesterday, waiting to see you.

YASHA   Botheration!

VARYA   You should be ashamed of yourself!

YASHA   She's all I needed! She could have come tomorrow. [*Exits.*]

VARYA   Mamma is just the same as ever; she hasn't changed a bit. If she
had her own way, she'd keep nothing for herself.

GAYEV   Yes . . . [*Pauses.*] If a great many remedies are offered for some
disease, it means it is incurable; I keep thinking and racking my brains;
I have many remedies, ever so many, and that really means none. It would

be fine if we came in for a legacy; it would be fine if we married off our Anya to a very rich man; or we might go to Yaroslavl and try our luck with our aunt, the Countess. She's very rich, you know . . .

VARYA [*Weeping.*]   If only God would help us!

GAYEV   Stop bawling. Aunt's very rich, but she doesn't like us. In the first place, Sister married a lawyer who was no nobleman . . . [ANYA *appears in the doorway.*] She married beneath her, and it can't be said that her behavior has been very exemplary. She's good, kind, sweet, and I love her, but no matter what extenuating circumstances you may adduce, there's no denying that she has no morals. You sense it in her least gesture.

VARYA [*In a whisper.*]   Anya's in the doorway.

GAYEV   Who? [*Pauses.*] It's queer, something got into my right eye—my eyes are going back on me. . . . And on Thursday, when I was in the circuit court—

[*Enter* ANYA.]

VARYA   Why aren't you asleep, Anya?

ANYA   I can't get to sleep, I just can't.

GAYEV   My little pet! [*Kisses* ANYA'S *face and hands.*] My child! [*Weeps.*] You are not my niece, you're my angel! You're everything to me. Believe me, believe—

ANYA   I believe you, Uncle. Everyone loves you and respects you . . . but, Uncle dear, you must keep still. . . . You must. What were you saying just now about my mother? Your own sister? What made you say that?

GAYEV   Yes, yes . . . [*Covers his face with her hand.*] Really, that was awful! Good God! Heaven help me! Just now I made a speech to the bookcase . . . so stupid! And only after I was through, I saw how stupid it was.

VARYA   It's true, Uncle dear, you ought to keep still. Just don't talk, that's all.

ANYA   If you could only keep still, it would make things easier for you, too.

GAYEV   I'll keep still. [*Kisses* ANYA'S *and* VARYA'S *hands.*] I will. But now about business. On Thursday I was in court; well, there were a number of us there, and we began talking of one thing and another, and this and that, and do you know, I believe it will be possible to raise a loan on a promissory note to pay the interest at the bank.

VARYA   If only God would help us!

GAYEV   On Tuesday I'll go and see about it again. [*To* VARYA.] Stop bawling. [*To* ANYA.] Your mamma will talk to Lopahin, and he, of course, will not refuse her . . . and as soon as you're rested, you'll go to Yaroslavl to the Countess, your great-aunt. So we'll be working in three directions at once, and the thing is in the bag. We'll pay the interest— I'm sure of it. [*Puts a candy in his mouth.*] I swear on my honor, I swear by anything you like, the estate shan't be sold. [*Excitedly.*] I swear by my own happiness! Here's my hand on it, you can call me a swindler and a scoundrel if I let it come to an auction! I swear by my whole being.

ANYA [*Relieved and quite happy again.*]   How good you are, Uncle, and how clever! [*Embraces him.*] Now I'm at peace, quite at peace, I'm happy.

[*Enter* FIRS.]

FIRS [*Reproachfully.*]   Leonid Andreyevich, have you no fear of God? When are you going to bed?

GAYEV   Directly, directly. Go away, Firs, I'll . . . yes, I will undress myself. Now, children, 'nightie-'nightie. We'll consider details tomorrow, but now go to sleep. [*Kisses* ANYA *and* VARYA.] I am a man of the eighties; they have nothing good to say of that period nowadays. Nevertheless, in the course of my life, I have suffered not a little for my convictions. It's not for nothing that the peasant loves me; one should know the peasant; one should know from which—

ANYA   There you go again, Uncle.

VARYA   Uncle dear, be quiet.

FIRS [*Angrily.*]   Leonid Andreyevich!

GAYEV   I'm coming, I'm coming! Go to bed! Double bank shot in the side pocket! Here goes a clean shot . . .
         [*Exits,* FIRS *hobbling after him.*]

ANYA   I am at peace now. I don't want to go to Yaroslavl—I don't like my great-aunt, but still, I am at peace, thanks to Uncle. [*Sits down.*]

VARYA   We must get some sleep. I'm going now. While you were away, something unpleasant happened. In the old servants' quarters, there are only the old people as you know; Yefim, Polya, Yevstigney, and Karp, too. They began letting all sorts of rascals in to spend the night. . . . I didn't say anything. Then I heard they'd been spreading a report that I gave them nothing but dried peas to eat—out of stinginess, you know . . . and it was all Yevstigney's doing. . . . All right, I thought, if that's how it is, I thought, just wait. I sent for Yevstigney . . . [*Yawns.*] He comes. . . . "How's this, Yevstigney?" I say, "You fool . . ." [*Looking at* ANYA.] Anichka! [*Pauses.*] She's asleep. [*Puts her arm around* ANYA.] Come to your little bed. . . . Come . . . [*Leads her.*] My darling has fallen asleep. . . . Come.
         [*They go out. Far away beyond the orchard, a shepherd is piping.* TROFIMOV *crosses the stage and, seeing* VARYA *and* ANYA, *stands still.*]

VARYA   Sh! She's asleep . . . asleep. . . . Come, darling.

ANYA [*Softly, half-asleep.*]   I'm so tired. Those bells . . . Uncle . . . dear . . . Mamma and Uncle . . .

VARYA   Come, my precious, come along. [*They go into* ANYA's *room.*]

TROFIMOV [*With emotion.*]   My sunshine, my spring!

Act II

A meadow. An old, long-abandoned, lopsided little chapel; near it a well, large slabs, which had apparently once served as tombstones, and an old bench. In the background the road to the Gayev estate. To one side poplars loom darkly, where the cherry orchard begins. In the distance a row of telegraph poles, and far off, on the horizon, the faint outline of a large city which is seen only in fine, clear weather. The sun will soon be setting. CHARLOTTA, YASHA, *and* DUNYASHA *are seated on the bench.* YEPIHODOV *stands near and plays a guitar. All are pensive.* CHARLOTTA *wears an old peaked cap. She has taken a gun from her shoulder and is straightening the buckle on the strap.*

CHARLOTTA [*Musingly.*]   I haven't a real passport, I don't know how old I am, and I always feel that I am very young. When I was a little girl, my father and mother used to go from fair to fair and give performances, very good ones. And I used to do the *salto mortale*,[4] and all sorts of other tricks. And when papa and mamma died, a German lady adopted me and began to educate me. Very good. I grew up and became a governess. But where I come from and who am I, I don't know. . . . Who were my parents? Perhaps they weren't even married. . . . I don't know . . . [*Takes a cucumber out of her pocket and eats it.*] I don't know a thing. [*Pause.*] One wants so much to talk, and there isn't anyone to talk to. . . . I haven't anybody.

YEPIHODOV [*Plays the guitar and sings.*]   "What care I for the jarring world? What's friend or foe to me? . . ." How agreeable it is to play the mandolin.

DUNYASHA   That's a guitar, not a mandolin. [*Looks in a hand mirror and powders her face.*]

YEPIHODOV   To a madman in love it's a mandolin. [*Sings.*] "Would that the heart were warmed by the fire of mutual love!"

[YASHA *joins in.*]

CHARLOTTA   How abominably these people sing. Pfui! Like jackals!

DUNYASHA [*To* YASHA.]   How wonderful it must be though to have stayed abroad!

YASHA   Ah, yes, of course, I cannot but agree with you there. [*Yawns and lights a cigar.*]

YEPIHODOV   Naturally. Abroad, everything has long since achieved full perfection.

YASHA   That goes without saying.

YEPIHODOV   I'm a cultivated man, I read all kinds of remarkable books. And yet I can never make out what direction I should take, what is it that I want, properly speaking. Should I live, or should I shoot myself, properly speaking? Nevertheless, I always carry a revolver about me. . . . Here it is . . . [*Shows revolver.*]

CHARLOTTA   I've finished. I'm going. [*Puts the gun over her shoulder.*] You are a very clever man, Yepihodov, and a very terrible one; women must be crazy about you. Br-r-r! [*Starts to go.*] These clever men are all so stupid; there's no one for me to talk to . . . always alone, alone, I haven't a soul . . . and who I am, and why I am, nobody knows. [*Exits unhurriedly.*]

YEPIHODOV   Properly speaking and letting other subjects alone, I must say regarding myself, among other things, that fate treats me mercilessly, like a storm treats a small boat. If I am mistaken, let us say, why then do I wake up this morning, and there on my chest is a spider of enormous dimensions . . . like this . . . [*Indicates with both hands.*] Again, I take up a pitcher of kvass to have a drink, and in it there is something unseemly to the highest degree, something like a cockroach. [*Pause.*] Have you read Buckle?[5] [*Pause.*] I wish to have a word with you, Avdotya Fyodorovna, if I may trouble you.

DUNYASHA   Well, go ahead.

YEPIHODOV   I wish to speak with you alone. [*Sighs.*]

DUNYASHA [*Embarrassed.*]   Very well. Only first bring me my little cape. You'll find it near the wardrobe. It's rather damp here.

YEPIHODOV   Certainly, ma'am; I will fetch it, ma'am. Now I know what to do with my revolver. [*Takes the guitar and goes off playing it.*]

---

4. Somersault (Italian).   **5.** Henry Thomas Buckle (1821–1862) wrote a *History of Civilization in England* (1857–61), which was considered daringly materialistic and freethinking.

YASHA   Two-and-Twenty Troubles! An awful fool, between you and me. [*Yawns.*]

DUNYASHA   I hope to God he doesn't shoot himself! [*Pause.*] I've become so nervous, I'm always fretting. I was still a little girl when I was taken into the big house, I am quite unused to the simple life now, and my hands are white, as white as a lady's. I've become so soft, so delicate, so refined, I'm afraid of everything. It's so terrifying; and if you deceive me, Yasha, I don't know what will happen to my nerves. [YASHA *kisses her.*]

YASHA   You're a peach! Of course, a girl should never forget herself; and what I dislike more than anything is when a girl doesn't behave properly.

DUNYASHA   I've fallen passionately in love with you; you're educated—you have something to say about everything. [*Pause.*]

YASHA [*Yawns.*]   Yes, ma'am. Now the way I look at it, if a girl loves someone, it means she is immoral. [*Pause.*] It's agreeable smoking a cigar in the fresh air. [*Listens.*] Someone's coming this way. . . . It's our madam and the others. [DUNYASHA *embraces him impulsively.*] You go home, as though you'd been to the river to bathe; go to the little path, or else they'll run into you and suspect me of having arranged to meet you here. I can't stand that sort of thing.

DUNYASHA [*Coughing softly.*]   Your cigar's made my head ache.

[*Exits.* YASHA *remains standing near the chapel. Enter* MME. RANEVSKAYA, GAYEV, *and* LOPAHIN.]

LOPAHIN   You must make up your mind once and for all—there's no time to lose. It's quite a simple question, you know. Do you agree to lease your land for summer cottages or not? Answer in one word, yes or no; only one word!

MME. RANEVSKAYA   Who's been smoking such abominable cigars here? [*Sits down.*]

GAYEV   Now that the railway line is so near, it's made things very convenient. [*Sits down.*] Here we've been able to have lunch in town. Yellow ball in the side pocket! I feel like going into the house and playing just one game.

MME. RANEVSKAYA   You can do that later.

LOPAHIN   Only one word! [*Imploringly.*] Do give me an answer!

GAYEV [*Yawning.*]   Who?

MME. RANEVSKAYA [*Looks into her purse.*]   Yesterday I had a lot of money and now my purse is almost empty. My poor Varya tries to economize by feeding us just milk soup; in the kitchen the old people get nothing but dried peas to eat, while I squander money thoughtlessly. [*Drops the purse, scattering gold pieces.*] You see, there they go . . . [*Shows vexation.*]

YASHA   Allow me—I'll pick them up. [*Picks up the money.*]

MME. RANEVSKAYA   Be so kind. Yasha. And why did I go to lunch in town? That nasty restaurant, with its music and the tablecloth smelling of soap. . . . Why drink so much, Leonid? Why eat so much? Why talk so much? Today again you talked a lot, and all so inappropriately about the seventies, about the decadents.[6] And to whom? Talking to waiters about decadents!

LOPAHIN   Yes.

---

6. A group of French poets of the 1880s (Mallarmé is today the most famous) were labeled "decadents" by their enemies and sometimes adopted the name themselves, proud of their refinement and sensitivity.

GAYEV [*Waving his hand.*] I'm incorrigible; that's obvious. [*Irritably, to* YASHA.] Why do you keep dancing about in front of me?

YASHA [*Laughs.*] I can't hear your voice without laughing—

GAYEV Either he or I—

MME. RANEVSKAYA Go away, Yasha; run along.

YASHA [*Handing* MME. RANEVSKAYA *her purse.*] I'm going at once. [*Hardly able to suppress his laughter.*] This minute. [*Exits.*]

LOPAHIN That rich man, Deriganov, wants to buy your estate. They say he's coming to the auction himself.

MME. RANEVSKAYA Where did you hear that?

LOPAHIN That's what they are saying in town.

GAYEV Our aunt in Yaroslavl has promised to help, but when she will send the money, and how much, no one knows.

LOPAHIN How much will she send? A hundred thousand? Two hundred?

MME. RANEVSKAYA Oh, well, ten or fifteen thousand; and we'll have to be grateful for that.

LOPAHIN Forgive me, but such frivolous people as you are, so queer and unbusinesslike—I never met in my life. One tells you in plain language that your estate is up for sale, and you don't seem to take it in.

MME. RANEVSKAYA What are we to do? Tell us what to do.

LOPAHIN I do tell you, every day; every day I say the same thing! You must lease the cherry orchard and the land for summer cottages, you must do it and as soon as possible—right away. The auction is close at hand. Please understand! Once you've decided to have the cottages, you can raise as much money as you like, and you're saved.

MME. RANEVSKAYA Cottages—summer people—forgive me, but it's all so vulgar.

GAYEV I agree with you absolutely.

LOPAHIN I shall either burst into tears or scream or faint! I can't stand it! You've worn me out! [*To* GAYEV.] You're an old woman!

GAYEV Who?

LOPAHIN An old woman! [*Gets up to go.*]

MME. RANEVSKAYA [*Alarmed.*] No, don't go! Please stay, I beg you, my dear. Perhaps we shall think of something.

LOPAHIN What is there to think of?

MME. RANEVSKAYA Don't go, I beg you. With you here it's more cheerful anyway. [*Pause.*] I keep expecting something to happen, it's as though the house were going to crash about our ears.

GAYEV [*In deep thought.*] Bank shot in the corner. . . . Three cushions in the side pocket. . . .

MME. RANEVSKAYA We have been great sinners . . .

LOPAHIN What sins could you have committed?

GAYEV [*Putting a candy in his mouth.*] They say I've eaten up my fortune in candy! [*Laughs.*]

MME. RANEVSKAYA Oh, my sins! I've squandered money away recklessly, like a lunatic, and I married a man who made nothing but debts. My husband drank himself to death on champagne, he was a terrific drinker. And then, to my sorrow, I fell in love with another man, and I lived with him. And just then—that was my first punishment—a blow on the head: my little boy was drowned here in the river. And I went abroad, went away forever . . . never to come back, never to see this river again . . . I closed my eyes and ran, out of my mind. . . . But he followed me, pitiless, brutal. I bought a villa near Mentone, because he fell ill there; and for three years, day and night, I knew no peace, no rest. The sick man wore me out, he sucked my soul dry. Then last year, when the villa was sold to pay my debts, I went to Paris, and there he robbed me, abandoned me, took up with another woman, I tried to poison myself—it was stupid, so shameful—and then suddenly I felt drawn back to Russia, back, to my own country, to my little girl. [*Wipes her tears away.*] Lord, Lord! Be merciful, forgive me my sins—don't punish me anymore! [*Takes a telegram out of her pocket.*] This came today from Paris—he begs me to forgive him, implores me to go back . . . [*Tears up the telegram.*] Do I hear music? [*Listens.*]

GAYEV   That's our famous Jewish band, you remember? Four violins, a flute, and a double bass.

MME. RANEVSKAYA   Does it still exist? We ought to send for them some evening and have a party.

LOPAHIN [*Listens.*]   I don't hear anything. [*Hums softly.*] "The Germans for a fee will Frenchify a Russian."[7] [*Laughs.*] I saw a play at the theater yesterday—awfully funny.

MME. RANEVSKAYA   There was probably nothing funny about it. You shouldn't go to see plays, you should look at yourselves more often. How drab your lives are—how full of unnecessary talk.

LOPAHIN   That's true; come to think of it, we do live like fools. [*Pause.*] My pop was a peasant, an idiot; he understood nothing, never taught me anything, all he did was beat me when he was drunk, and always with a stick. Fundamentally, I'm just the same kind of blockhead and idiot. I was never taught anything—I have a terrible handwriting. I write so that I feel ashamed before people, like a pig.

MME. RANEVSKAYA   You should get married, my friend.

LOPAHIN   Yes . . . that's true.

MME. RANEVSKAYA   To our Varya, she's a good girl.

LOPAHIN   Yes.

MME. RANEVSKAYA   She's a girl who comes of simple people, she works all day long; and above all, she loves you. Besides, you've liked her for a long time now.

LOPAHIN   Well, I've nothing against it. She's a good girl. [*Pause.*]

GAYEV   I've been offered a place in the bank—6,000 a year. Have you heard?

MME. RANEVSKAYA   You're not up to it. Stay where you are.

[FIRS *enters, carrying an overcoat.*]

FIRS [*To* GAYEV.]   Please put this on, sir, it's damp.

GAYEV [*Putting it on.*]   I'm fed up with you, brother.

FIRS   Never mind. This morning you drove off without saying a word. [*Looks him over.*]

MME. RANEVSKAYA   How you've aged, Firs.

FIRS   I beg your pardon?

7. Satirical reference to Russian efforts, from the time of Peter the Great (1672–1725), to imitate Western Europe and particularly Parisian culture.

LOPAHIN   The lady says you've aged.

FIRS   I've lived a long time; they were arranging my wedding and your papa wasn't born yet. [*Laughs.*] When freedom came[8] I was already head footman. I wouldn't consent to be set free then; I stayed on with the master ... [*Pause.*] I remember they were all very happy, but why they were happy, they didn't know themselves.

LOPAHIN   It was fine in the old days! At least there was flogging!

FIRS [*Not hearing.*]   Of course. The peasants kept to the masters, the masters kept to the peasants; but now they've all gone their own ways, and there's no making out anything.

GAYEV   Be quiet, Firs. I must go to town tomorrow. They've promised to introduce me to a general who might let us have a loan.

LOPAHIN   Nothing will come of that. You won't even be able to pay the interest, you can be certain of that.

MME. RANEVSKAYA   He's raving, there isn't any general.

[*Enter* TROFIMOV, ANYA, *and* VARYA.]

GAYEV   Here come our young people.

ANYA   There's Mamma, on the bench.

MME. RANEVSKAYA [*Tenderly.*]   Come here, come along, my darlings. [*Embraces* ANYA *and* VARYA.] If you only knew how I love you both! Sit beside me—there, like that. [*All sit down.*]

LOPAHIN   Our perpetual student is always with the young ladies.

TROFIMOV   That's not any of your business.

LOPAHIN   He'll soon be fifty, and he's still a student!

TROFIMOV   Stop your silly jokes.

LOPAHIN   What are you so cross about, you queer bird?

TROFIMOV   Oh, leave me alone.

LOPAHIN [*Laughs.*]   Allow me to ask you, what do you think of me?

TROFIMOV   What I think of you, Yermolay Alexeyevich, is this: you are a rich man who will soon be a millionaire. Well, just as a beast of prey, which devours everything that comes in its way, is necessary for the process of metabolism to go on, so you, too, are necessary. [*All laugh.*]

VARYA   Better tell us something about the planets, Petya.

MME. RANEVSKAYA   No, let's go on with yesterday's conversation.

TROFIMOV   What was it about?

GAYEV   About man's pride.

TROFIMOV   Yesterday we talked a long time, but we came to no conclusion. There is something mystical about man's pride in your sense of the word. Perhaps you're right, from your own point of view. But if you reason simply, without going into subtleties, then what call is there for pride? Is there any sense in it, if man is so poor a thing physiologically, and if, in the great majority of cases, he is coarse, stupid, profoundly unhappy? We should stop admiring ourselves. We should work, and that's all.

GAYEV   You die, anyway.

TROFIMOV   Who knows? And what does it mean—to die? Perhaps man has a hundred senses, and at his death only the five we know perish, while the other ninety-five remain alive.

---

8. Czar Alexander II (ruled 1855–81) emancipated the serfs in 1861.

MME. RANEVSKAYA How clever you are, Petya!

LOPAHIN [*Ironically.*] Awfully clever!

TROFIMOV Mankind goes forward, developing its powers. Everything that is now unattainable for it will one day come within man's reach and be clear to him; only we must work, helping with all our might those who seek the truth. Here among us in Russia only the very few work as yet. The great majority of the intelligentsia, as far as I can see, seek nothing, do nothing, are totally unfit for work of any kind. They call themselves the intelligentsia, yet they are uncivil to their servants, treat the peasants like animals, are poor students, never read anything serious, do absolutely nothing at all, only talk about science, and have little appreciation of the arts. They are all solemn, have grim faces, they all philosophize and talk of weighty matters. And meanwhile the vast majority of us, ninety-nine out of a hundred, live like savages. At the least provocation— a punch in the jaw, and curses. They eat disgustingly, sleep in filth and stuffiness, bedbugs everywhere, stench and damp and moral slovenliness. And obviously, the only purpose of all our fine talk is to hoodwink ourselves and others. Show me where the public nurseries are that we've heard so much about, and the libraries. We read about them in novels, but in reality they don't exist, there is nothing but dirt, vulgarity, and Asiatic backwardness. I don't like very solemn faces, I'm afraid of them, I'm afraid of serious conversations. We'd do better to keep quiet for a while.

LOPAHIN Do you know, I get up at five o'clock in the morning, and I work from morning till night; and I'm always handling money, my own and other people's, and I see what people around me are really like. You've only to start doing anything to see how few honest, decent people there are. Sometimes when I lie awake at night, I think: "Oh, Lord, thou hast given us immense forests, boundless fields, the widest horizons, and living in their midst, we ourselves ought really to be giants."

MME. RANEVSKAYA Now you want giants! They're only good in fairy tales; otherwise they're frightening.

[YEPIHODOV *crosses the stage at the rear, playing the guitar.*]

MME. RANEVSKAYA [*Pensively.*] There goes Yepihodov.

GAYEV Ladies and gentlemen, the sun has set.

TROFIMOV Yes.

GAYEV [*In a low voice, declaiming as it were.*] Oh, Nature, wondrous Nature, you shine with eternal radiance, beautiful and indifferent! You, whom we call our mother, unite within yourself life and death! You animate and destroy!

VARYA [*Pleadingly.*] Uncle dear!

ANYA Uncle, again!

TROFIMOV You'd better bank the yellow ball in the side pocket.

GAYEV I'm silent, I'm silent . . .

[*All sit plunged in thought. Stillness reigns. Only* FIRS's *muttering is audible. Suddenly a distant sound is heard, coming from the sky as it were, the sound of a snapping string, mournfully dying away.*]

MME. RANEVSKAYA What was that?

LOPAHIN I don't know. Somewhere far away, in the pits, a bucket's broken loose; but somewhere very far away.

GAYEV Or it might be some sort of bird, perhaps a heron.

TROFIMOV Or an owl . . .

MME. RANEVSKAYA [*Shudders.*] It's weird, somehow. [*Pause.*]

FIRS Before the calamity the same thing happened—the owl screeched, and the samovar hummed all the time.

GAYEV Before what calamity?

FIRS Before the Freedom. [*Pause.*]

MME. RANEVSKAYA Come, my friends, let's be going. It's getting dark. [*To* ANYA.] You have tears in your eyes. What is it, my little one? [*Embraces her.*]

ANYA I don't know, Mamma; it's nothing.

TROFIMOV Somebody's coming.

[*A* TRAMP *appears, wearing a shabby white cap and an overcoat. He is slightly drunk.*]

TRAMP Allow me to inquire, will this short cut take me to the station?

GAYEV It will. Just follow that road.

TRAMP My heartfelt thanks. [*Coughing.*] The weather is glorious. [*Recites.*] "My brother, my suffering brother. . . . Go down to the Volga![9] Whose groans . . . ?" [*To* VARYA.] Mademoiselle, won't you spare 30 kopecks for a hungry Russian?

[VARYA, *frightened, cries out.*]

LOPAHIN [*Angrily.*] Even panhandling has its proprieties.

MME. RANEVSKAYA [*Scared.*] Here, take this. [*Fumbles in her purse.*] I haven't any silver . . . never mind, here's a gold piece.

TRAMP My heartfelt thanks. [*Exits. Laughter.*]

VARYA [*Frightened.*] I'm leaving. I'm leaving. . . . Oh, Mamma dearest, at home the servants have nothing to eat, and you gave him a gold piece!

MME. RANEVSKAYA What are you going to do with me? I'm such a fool. When we get home, I'll give you everything I have. Yermolay Alexeyevich, you'll lend me some more . . .

LOPAHIN Yes, ma'am.

MME. RANEVSKAYA Come, ladies and gentlemen, it's time to be going. Oh! Varya, we've settled all about your marriage. Congratulations!

VARYA [*Through tears.*] Really, Mamma, that's not a joking matter.

LOPAHIN "Aurelia, get thee to a nunnery, go . . ."

GAYEV And do you know, my hands are trembling: I haven't played billiards in a long time.

LOPAHIN "Aurelia, nymph, in your orisons, remember me!"[1]

MME. RANEVSKAYA Let's go, it's almost suppertime.

VARYA He frightened me! My heart's pounding.

LOPAHIN Let me remind you, ladies and gentlemen, on the twenty-second of August the cherry orchard will be up for sale. Think about that! Think!

[*All except* TROFIMOV *and* ANYA *go out.*]

ANYA [*Laughs.*] I'm grateful to that tramp, he frightened Varya and so we're alone.

TROFIMOV Varya's afraid we'll fall in love with each other all of a sudden.

9. Lines from poems by Semyon Nadson (1826–1878) and Nikolay Nekrasov (1821–1878). 1. Lopahin makes comic use of Hamlet's meeting with Ophelia. (Here *Aurelia* conveys the Russian text's distortion of "Ophelia" as "Okhmelia.") Hamlet, seeing her approaching, says: "Nymph, in thy orisons / Be all my sins remembered" (3.1.91–92), and later, suspecting her of spying for her father, sends her off with "Get thee to a nunnery" (3.1.122).

She hasn't left us alone for days. Her narrow mind can't grasp that we're above love. To avoid the petty and illusory, everything that prevents us from being free and happy—that is the goal and meaning of our life. Forward! Do not fall behind, friends!

ANYA [*Strikes her hands together.*]   How well you speak! [*Pause.*] It's wonderful here today.

TROFIMOV   Yes, the weather's glorious.

ANYA   What have you done to me, Petya? Why don't I love the cherry orchard as I used to? I loved it so tenderly. It seemed to me there was no spot on earth lovelier than our orchard.

TROFIMOV   All Russia is our orchard. Our land is vast and beautiful, there are many wonderful places in it. [*Pause.*] Think of it, Anya, your grandfather, your great-grandfather and all your ancestors were serf owners, owners of living souls, and aren't human beings looking at you from every tree in the orchard, from every leaf, from every trunk? Don't you hear voices? Oh, it's terrifying! Your orchard is a fearful place, and when you pass through it in the evening or at night, the old bark on the trees gleams faintly, and the cherry trees seem to be dreaming of things that happened a hundred, two hundred years ago and to be tormented by painful visions. What is there to say? We're at least two hundred years behind, we've really achieved nothing yet, we have no definite attitude to the past, we only philosophize, complain of the blues, or drink vodka. It's all so clear: in order to live in the present, we should first redeem our past, finish with it, and we can expiate it only by suffering, only by extraordinary, unceasing labor. Realize that, Anya.

ANYA   The house in which we live has long ceased to be our own, and I will leave it, I give you my word.

TROFIMOV   If you have the keys, fling them into the well and go away. Be free as the wind.

ANYA [*In ecstasy.*]   How well you put that!

TROFIMOV   Believe me, Anya, believe me! I'm not yet thirty, I'm young, I'm still a student—but I've already suffered so much. In winter I'm hungry, sick, harassed, poor as a beggar, and where hasn't Fate driven me? Where haven't I been? And yet always, every moment of the day and night, my soul is filled with inexplicable premonitions. . . . I have a premonition of happiness, Anya. . . . I see it already!

ANYA [*Pensively.*]   The moon is rising.

[YEPIHODOV *is heard playing the same mournful tune on the guitar. The moon rises. Somewhere near the poplars* VARYA *is looking for* ANYA *and calling,* "Anya, where are you?"]

TROFIMOV   Yes, the moon is rising. [*Pause.*] There it is, happiness, it's approaching, it's coming nearer and nearer, I can already hear its footsteps. And if we don't see it, if we don't know it, what does it matter? Others will!

VARYA'S VOICE   Anya! Where are you?

TROFIMOV   That Varya again! [*Angrily.*] It's revolting!

ANYA   Never mind, let's go down to the river. It's lovely there.

TROFIMOV   Come on. [*They go.*]

VARYA'S VOICE   Anya! Anya!

Act III

A drawing room separated by an arch from a ballroom. Evening. Chandelier burning. The Jewish band is heard playing in the anteroom. In the ballroom they are dancing the Grand Rond. PISHCHIK *is heard calling,* "Promenade à une paire!"[2] PISHCHIK *and* CHARLOTTA, TROFIMOV *and* MME. RANEVSKAYA, ANYA *and the* POST OFFICE CLERK, VARYA *and the* STATIONMASTER, *and others enter the drawing room in couples.* DUNYASHA *is in the last couple.* VARYA *weeps quietly, wiping her tears as she dances. All parade through drawing room,* PISHCHIK *calling,* "Grand rond, balancez!"[3] *and* "Les cavaliers à genoux et remerciez vos dames!"[4] FIRS, *wearing a dress coat, brings in soda water on a tray.* PISHCHIK *and* TROFIMOV *enter the drawing room.*

PISHCHIK   I have high blood pressure; I've already had two strokes. Dancing's hard work for me; but as they say, "If you run with the pack, you can bark or not, but at least wag your tail." Still, I'm as strong as a horse. My late lamented father, who would have his joke, God rest his soul, used to say, talking about our origin, that the ancient line of the Simeonov-Pishchiks was descended from the very horse that Caligula had made a senator.[5] [*Sits down.*] But the trouble is, I have no money. A hungry dog believes in nothing but meat. [*Snores, and wakes up at once.*] It's the same with me—I can think of nothing but money.

TROFIMOV   You know, there *is* something equine about your figure.

PISHCHIK   Well, a horse is a fine animal—one can sell a horse.

    [*Sound of billiards being played in an adjoining room.* VARYA *appears in the archway.*]

TROFIMOV [*Teasing her.*]   Madam Lopahina! Madam Lopahina!

VARYA [*Angrily.*]   Mangy master!

TROFIMOV   Yes, I am a mangy master and I'm proud of it.

VARYA [*Reflecting bitterly.*]   Here we've hired musicians, and what shall we pay them with? [*Exits.*]

TROFIMOV [*To* PISHCHIK.]   If the energy you have spent during your lifetime looking for money to pay interest had gone into something else, in the end you could have turned the world upside down.

PISHCHIK   Nietzsche,[6] the philosopher, the greatest, most famous of men, that colossal intellect, says in his works that it is permissible to forge banknotes.

TROFIMOV   Have you read Nietzsche?

PISHCHIK   Well . . . Dashenka told me. . . . And now I've got to the point where forging banknotes is the only way out for me. . . . The day after tomorrow I have to pay 310 rubles—I already have 130 . . . [*Feels in his pockets. In alarm.*] The money's gone! I've lost my money! [*Through tears.*] Where's my money? [*Joyfully.*] Here it is! Inside the lining . . . I'm all in a sweat . . .

    [*Enter* MME. RANEVSKAYA *and* CHARLOTTA.]

---

2. Promenade with your partner! (French). *Grand Rond:* a ring dance.   3. Make a large circle, get set! (French).   4. Gentlemen, on your knees and thank your ladies! (French).   5. The mad emperor Caligula (A.D. 12–41) brought his favorite horse into the Roman senate to make it a senator.   6. Friedrich W. Nietzsche (1844–1900), German philosopher.

MME. RANEVSKAYA [*Hums the "Lezginka."*[7]]   Why isn't Leonid back yet? What is he doing in town? [*To* DUNYASHA.] Dunyasha, offer the musicians tea.

TROFIMOV   The auction hasn't taken place, most likely.

MME. RANEVSKAYA   It's the wrong time to have the band, and the wrong time to give a dance. Well, never mind. [*Sits down and hums softly.*]

CHARLOTTA. [*Hands* PISHCHIK *a pack of cards.*]   Here is a pack of cards. Think of any card you like.

PISHCHIK   I've thought of one.

CHARLOTTA   Shuffle the pack now. That's right. Give it here, my dear Mr. Pishchik. *Eins, zwei, drei!*[8] Now look for it—it's in your side pocket.

PISHCHIK [*Taking the card out of his pocket.*]   The eight of spades! Perfectly right! Just imagine!

CHARLOTTA [*Holding the pack of cards in her hands. To* TROFIMOV.] Quickly, name the top card.

TROFIMOV   Well, let's see—the queen of spades.

CHARLOTTA   Right! [*To* PISHCHIK.] Now name the top card.

PISHCHIK   The ace of hearts.

CHARLOTTA   Right! [*Claps her hands and the pack of cards disappears.*] Ah, what lovely weather it is today! [*A mysterious feminine* VOICE, *which seems to come from under the floor, answers her:* "Oh, yes, it's magnificent weather, madam."] You are my best ideal. [VOICE: "And I find you pleasing too, madam."]

STATIONMASTER [*Applauding.*]   The lady ventriloquist, bravo!

PISHCHIK [*Amazed.*]   Just imagine! Enchanting Charlotta Ivanovna, I'm simply in love with you.

CHARLOTTA   In love? [*Shrugs her shoulders.*] Are you capable of love? *Guter Mensch, aber schlechter Musikant!*[9]

TROFIMOV [*Claps* PISHCHIK *on the shoulder.*]   You old horse, you!

CHARLOTTA   Attention please! One more trick! [*Takes a plaid*[1] *from a chair.*] Here is a very good plaid; I want to sell it. [*Shaking it out.*] Does anyone want to buy it?

PISHCHIK [*In amazement.*]   Just imagine!

CHARLOTTA   *Eins, zwei, drei!* [*Raises the plaid quickly, behind it stands* ANYA. *She curtsies, runs to her mother, embraces her, and runs back into the ballroom, amid general enthusiasm.*]

MME. RANEVSKAYA [*Applauds.*]   Bravo! Bravo!

CHARLOTTA   Now again! *Eins, zwei, drei!* [*Lifts the plaid; behind it stands* VARYA, *bowing.*]

PISHCHIK [*In amazement.*]   Just imagine!

[CHARLOTTA *throws the plaid at* PISHCHIK, *curtsies, and runs into the ballroom.*]

PISHCHIK [*Running after her.*]   The rascal! What a woman, what a woman! [*Exits.*]

---

7. The music that in the Caucasus mountains accompanies a courtship dance in which the man dances with abandon around the woman, who moves with grace and ease.   8. One, two, three (German).
9. "A good man, but a bad musician" (German), usually quoted in the plural: "*Gute Leute, schlechte Musikanten.*" It comes from *Das Buch le Grand* (1826) by the German poet Heinrich Heine (1799–1856). Here it suggests that Pishchik may be a good man but a bad lover.   1. A small plaid blanket, or lap robe.

MME. RANEVSKAYA And Leonid still isn't here. What is he doing in town so long? I don't understand. It must be all over by now. Either the estate has been sold, or the auction hasn't taken place. Why keep us in suspense so long?

VARYA [*Trying to console her.*] Uncle's bought it, I feel sure of that.

TROFIMOV [*Mockingly.*] Oh, yes!

VARYA Great-aunt sent him an authorization to buy it in her name, and to transfer the debt. She's doing it for Anya's sake. And I'm sure that God will help us, and Uncle will buy it.

MME. RANEVSKAYA Great-aunt sent fifteen thousand to buy the estate in her name, she doesn't trust us, but that's not even enough to pay the interest. [*Covers her face with her hands.*] Today my fate will be decided, my fate—

TROFIMOV [*Teasing* VARYA.] Madam Lopahina!

VARYA [*Angrily.*] Perpetual student! Twice already you've been expelled from the university.

MME. RANEVSKAYA Why are you so cross, Varya? He's teasing you about Lopahin. Well, what of it? If you want to marry Lopahin, go ahead. He's a good man, and interesting; if you don't want to, don't. Nobody's compelling you, my pet!

VARYA Frankly, Mamma dear, I take this thing seriously; he's a good man and I like him.

MME. RANEVSKAYA All right then, marry him. I don't know what you're waiting for.

VARYA But, Mamma, I can't propose to him myself. For the last two years, everyone's been talking to me about him—talking. But he either keeps silent, or else cracks jokes. I understand; he's growing rich, he's absorbed in business—he has no time for me. If I had money, even a little, say, 100 rubles, I'd throw everything up and go far away—I'd go into a nunnery.

TROFIMOV What a blessing . . .

VARYA A student ought to be intelligent. [*Softly, with tears in her voice.*] How homely you've grown, Petya! How old you look! [*To* MME. RANEVSKAYA, *with dry eyes.*] But I can't live without work, Mamma dear; I must keep busy every minute.
      [*Enter* YASHA.]

YASHA [*Hardly restraining his laughter.*] Yepihodov has broken a billiard cue! [*Exits.*]

VARYA Why is Yepihodov here? Who allowed him to play billiards? I don't understand these people! [*Exits.*]

MME. RANEVSKAYA Don't tease her, Petya. She's unhappy enough without that.

TROFIMOV She bustles so—and meddles in other people's business. All summer long she's given Anya and me no peace. She's afraid of a love affair between us. What business is it of hers? Besides, I've given no grounds for it, and I'm far from such vulgarity. We are above love.

MME. RANEVSKAYA And I suppose I'm beneath love? [*Anxiously.*] What can be keeping Leonid? If I only knew whether the estate has been sold or not. Such a calamity seems so incredible to me that I don't know what

to think—I feel lost. . . . I could scream. . . . I could do something stupid.
. . . Save me, Petya, tell me something, talk to me!

TROFIMOV   Whether the estate is sold today or not, isn't it all one? That's
all done with long ago—there's no turning back, the path is overgrown.
Calm yourself, my dear. You mustn't deceive yourself. For once in your
life you must face the truth.

MME. RANEVSKAYA   What truth? You can see the truth, you can tell it from
falsehood, but I seem to have lost my eyesight, I see nothing. You settle
every great problem so boldly, but tell me, my dear boy, isn't it because
you're young, because you don't yet know what one of your problems
means in terms of suffering? You look ahead fearlessly, but isn't it
because you don't see and don't expect anything dreadful, because life
is still hidden from your young eyes? You're bolder, more honest, more
profound than we are, but think hard, show just a bit of magnanimity,
spare me. After all, I was born here, my father and mother lived here,
and my grandfather; I love this house. Without the cherry orchard, my
life has no meaning for me, and if it really must be sold, then sell me
with the orchard. [*Embraces* TROFIMOV, *kisses him on the forehead.*] My
son was drowned here. [*Weeps.*] Pity me, you good, kind fellow!

TROFIMOV   You know, I feel for you with all my heart.

MME. RANEVSKAYA   But that should have been said differently, so differently! [*Takes out her handkerchief—a telegram falls on the floor.*] My
heart is so heavy today—you can't imagine! The noise here upsets me—
my inmost being trembles at every sound—I'm shaking all over. But I
can't go into my own room; I'm afraid to be alone. Don't condemn me,
Petya. . . . I love you as though you were one of us, I would gladly let you
marry Anya—I swear I would—only, my dear boy, you must study—you
must take your degree—you do nothing, you let yourself be tossed by
Fate from place to place—it's so strange. It's true, isn't it? And you should
do something about your beard, to make it grow somehow! [*Laughs.*]
You're so funny!

TROFIMOV [*Picks up the telegram.*]   I've no wish to be a dandy.

MME. RANEVSKAYA   That's a telegram from Paris. I get one every day. One
yesterday and one today. That savage is ill again—he's in trouble again.
He begs forgiveness, implores me to go to him, and really I ought to go
to Paris to be near him. Your face is stern, Petya; but what is there to
do, my dear boy? What am I to do? He's ill, he's alone and unhappy, and
who is to look after him, who is to keep him from doing the wrong thing,
who is to give him his medicine on time? And why hide it or keep still
about it—I love him! That's clear. I love him, love him! He's a millstone
round my neck, he'll drag me to the bottom, but I love that stone, I can't
live without it. [*Presses* TROFIMOV's *hand.*] Don't think badly of me. Petya,
and don't say anything, don't say . . .

TROFIMOV [*Through tears.*]   Forgive me my frankness in heaven's name;
but, you know, he robbed you!

MME. RANEVSKAYA   No, no, no, you mustn't say such things! [*Covers her
ears.*]

TROFIMOV   But he's a scoundrel! You're the only one who doesn't know it.
He's a petty scoundrel—a nonentity!

MME. RANEVSKAYA [*Controlling her anger.*]   You are twenty-six or twenty-seven years old, but you're still a schoolboy.

TROFIMOV   That may be.

MME. RANEVSKAYA   You should be a man at your age. You should understand people who love—and ought to be in love yourself. You ought to fall in love! [*Angrily.*] Yes, yes! And it's not purity in you, it's prudishness, you're simply a queer fish, a comical freak!

TROFIMOV [*Horrified.*]   What is she saying?

MME. RANEVSKAYA   "I am above love!" You're not above love, but simple, as our Firs says, you're an addlehead. At your age not to have a mistress!

TROFIMOV [*Horrified.*]   This is frightful! What is she saying! [*Goes rapidly into the ballroom, clutching his head.*] It's frightful—I can't stand it, I won't stay! [*Exits, but returns at once.*] All is over between us! [*Exits into anteroom.*]

MME. RANEVSKAYA [*Shouts after him.*]   Petya! Wait! You absurd fellow, I was joking. Petya!

[*Sound of somebody running quickly downstairs and suddenly falling down with a crash. ANYA and VARYA scream. Sound of laughter a moment later.*]

MME. RANEVSKAYA   What's happened?

[*ANYA runs in.*]

ANYA [*Laughing.*]   Petya's fallen downstairs! [*Runs out.*]

MME. RANEVSKAYA   What a queer bird that Petya is!

[*STATIONMASTER, standing in the middle of the ballroom, recites Alexey Tolstoy's "Magdalene,"[2] to which all listen, but after a few lines, the sound of a waltz is heard from the anteroom and the reading breaks off. All dance. TROFIMOV, ANYA, VARYA and MME. RANEVSKAYA enter from the anteroom.*]

MME. RANEVSKAYA   Petya, you pure soul, please forgive me. . . . Let's dance.

[*Dances with PETYA, ANYA and VARYA dance. FIRS enters, puts his stick down by the side door. YASHA enters from the drawing room and watches the dancers.*]

YASHA   Well, Grandfather?

FIRS   I'm not feeling well. In the old days it was generals, barons, and admirals that were dancing at our balls, and now we have to send for the Post Office Clerk and the Stationmaster, and even they aren't too glad to come. I feel kind of shaky. The old master that's gone, their grandfather, dosed everyone with sealing wax, whatever ailed 'em. I've been taking sealing wax every day for twenty years or more. Perhaps that's what's kept me alive.

YASHA   I'm fed up with you, Grandpop. [*Yawns.*] It's time you croaked.

FIRS   Oh, you addlehead! [*Mumbles.*]

[*TROFIMOV and MME. RANEVSKAYA dance from the ballroom into the drawing room.*]

MME. RANEVSKAYA   Merci. I'll sit down a while. [*Sits down.*] I'm tired.

[*Enter ANYA.*]

2. Called *The Sinning Woman* in Russian, it begins: "A bustling crowd with happy laughter, / with twanging lutes and clashing cymbals / with flowers and foliage all around / the colonnaded portico." Alexey Tolstoy (1817–1875), popular in his time as a dramatist and poet, was a distant relative of Leo Tolstoy.

ANYA [*Excitedly.*]   There was a man in the kitchen just now who said the cherry orchard was sold today.

MME. RANEVSKAYA   Sold to whom?

ANYA   He didn't say. He's gone. [*Dances off with* TROFIMOV.]

YASHA   It was some old man gabbing, a stranger.

FIRS   And Leonid Andreyevich isn't back yet, he hasn't come. And he's wearing his lightweight between-season overcoat; like enough, he'll catch cold. Ah, when they're young they're green.

MME. RANEVSKAYA   This is killing me. Go, Yasha, find out to whom it has been sold.

YASHA   But the old man left long ago. [*Laughs.*]

MME RANEVSKAYA   What are you laughing at? What are you pleased about?

YASHA   That Yepihodov is such a funny one. A funny fellow, Two-and-Twenty Troubles!

MME. RANEVSKAYA   Firs, if the estate is sold, where will you go?

FIRS   I'll go where you tell me.

MME. RANEVSKAYA   Why do you look like that? Are you ill? You ought to go to bed.

FIRS   Yes! [*With a snigger.*] Me go to bed, and who's to hand things round? Who's to see to things? I'm the only one in the whole house.

YASHA [*To* MME. RANEVSKAYA.]   Lubov Andreyevna, allow me to ask a favor of you, be so kind! If you go back to Paris, take me with you, I beg you. It's positively impossible for me to stay here. [*Looking around; sotto voce.*] What's the use of talking? You see for yourself, it's an uncivilized country, the people have no morals, and then the boredom! The food in the kitchen's revolting, and besides there's this Firs wanders about mumbling all sorts of inappropriate words. Take me with you, be so kind!

[*Enter* PISHCHIK.]

PISHCHIK   May I have the pleasure of a waltz with you, charming lady? [MME. RANEVSKAYA *accepts.*] All the same, enchanting lady, you must let me have 180 rubles. . . . You must let me have [*dancing*] just one hundred and eighty rubles. [*They pass into the ballroom.*]

YASHA [*Hums softly.*]   "Oh, wilt thou understand the tumult in my soul?" [*In the ballroom a figure in a gray top hat and checked trousers is jumping about and waving its arms; shouts:* "Bravo, Charlotta Ivanovna!"]

DUNYASHA [*Stopping to powder her face; to* FIRS.]   The young miss has ordered me to dance. There are so many gentlemen and not enough ladies. But dancing makes me dizzy, my heart begins to beat fast, Firs Nikolayevich. The Post Office Clerk said something to me just now that quite took my breath away.

[*Music stops.*]

FIRS   What did he say?

DUNYASHA   "You're like a flower," he said.

YASHA [*Yawns.*]   What ignorance. [*Exits.*]

DUNYASHA   "Like a flower!" I'm such a delicate girl. I simply adore pretty speeches.

FIRS   You'll come to a bad end.

[*Enter* YEPIHODOV.]

YEPIHODOV [*To* DUNYASHA.]   You have no wish to see me, Avdotya Fyodor-ovna . . . as though I was some sort of insect. [*Sighs.*] Ah, life!

DUNYASHA   What is it you want?

YEPIHODOV   Indubitably you may be right. [*Sighs.*] But of course, if one looks at it from the point of view, if I may be allowed to say so, and apologizing for my frankness, you have completely reduced me to a state of mind. I know my fate. Every day some calamity befalls me, and I grew used to it long ago, so that I look upon my fate with a smile. You gave me your word, and though I—

DUNYASHA   Let's talk about it later, please. But just now leave me alone, I am daydreaming. [*Plays with a fan.*]

YEPIHODOV   A misfortune befalls me every day; and if I may be allowed to say so, I merely smile, I even laugh.

[*Enter* VARYA.]

VARYA [*To* YEPIHODOV.]   Are you still here? What an impertinent fellow you are really! Run along, Dunyasha. [*To* YEPIHODOV.] Either you're play-ing billiards and breaking a cue, or you're wandering about the drawing room as though you were a guest.

YEPIHODOV   You cannot, permit me to remark, penalize me.

VARYA   I'm not penalizing you; I'm just telling you. You merely wander from place to place, and don't do your work. We keep you as a clerk, but heaven knows what for.

YEPIHODOV [*Offended.*]   Whether I work or whether I walk, whether I eat or whether I play billiards, is a matter to be discussed only by persons of understanding and of mature years.

VARYA [*Enraged.*]   You dare say that to me—you dare? You mean to say I've no understanding? Get out of here at once! This minute!

YEPIHODOV [*Scared.*]   I beg you to express yourself delicately.

VARYA [*Beside herself.*]   Clear out this minute! Out with you!

[YEPIHODOV *goes toward the door,* VARYA *following.*]

VARYA   Two-and-Twenty Troubles! Get out—don't let me set eyes on you again!

[*Exit* YEPIHODOV. *His voice is heard behind the door:* "I shall lodge a complaint against you!"]

VARYA   Oh, you're coming back? [*She seizes the stick left near door by* FIRS.] Well, come then . . . come . . . I'll show you. . . . Ah, you're coming? You're coming? . . . Come . . . [*Swings the stick just as* LOPAHIN *enters.*]

LOPAHIN   Thank you kindly.

VARYA [*Angrily and mockingly.*]   I'm sorry.

LOPAHIN   It's nothing. Thank you kindly for your charming reception.

VARYA   Don't mention it. [*Walks away, looks back and asks softly.*] I didn't hurt you, did I?

LOPAHIN   Oh, no, not at all. I shall have a large bump, though.

[*Voices from the ballroom:* "Lopahin is here! Lopahin!" *Enter* PISHCHIK.]

PISHCHIK   My eyes do see, my ears do hear! [*Kisses* LOPAHIN.] You smell of cognac, my dear friend. And we've been celebrating here, too.

[*Enter* MME. RANEVSKAYA.]

MME. RANEVSKAYA   Is that you, Yermolay Alexeyevich? What kept you so long? Where's Leonid?

LOPAHIN Leonid Andreyevich arrived with me. He's coming.

MME. RANEVSKAYA Well, what happened? Did the sale take place? Speak!

LOPAHIN [*Embarrassed, fearful of revealing his joy.*] The sale was over at four o'clock. We missed the train—had to wait till half-past nine. [*Sighing heavily.*] Ugh. I'm a little dizzy.

> [*Enter* GAYEV. *In his right hand he holds parcels, with his left he is wiping away his tears.*]

MME. RANEVSKAYA Well, Leonid? What news? [*Impatiently, through tears.*] Be quick, for God's sake!

GAYEV [*Not answering, simply waves his hand. Weeping, to* FIRS.] Here, take these; anchovies, Kerch herrings . . . I haven't eaten all day. What I've been through! [*The click of billiard balls comes through the open door of the billiard room and* YASHA's *voice is heard:* "Seven and eighteen!" GAYEV's *expression changes, he no longer weeps.*] I'm terribly tired. Firs, help me change. [*Exits, followed by* FIRS.]

PISHCHIK How about the sale? Tell us what happened.

MME. RANEVSKAYA Is the cherry orchard sold?

LOPAHIN Sold.

MME. RANEVSKAYA Who bought it?

LOPAHIN I bought it.

> [*Pause.* MME. RANEVSKAYA *is overcome. She would fall to the floor, were it not for the chair and table near which she stands.* VARYA *takes the keys from her belt, flings them on the floor in the middle of the drawing room and goes out.*]

LOPAHIN I bought it. Wait a bit, ladies and gentlemen, please, my head is swimming, I can't talk. [*Laughs.*] We got to the auction and Deriganov was there already. Leonid Andreyevich had only 15,000 and straight off Deriganov bid 30,000 over and above the mortgage. I saw how the land lay, got into the fight, bid 40,000. He bid 45,000. I bid fifty-five. He kept adding five thousands, I ten. Well . . . it came to an end. I bid ninety above the mortgage and the estate was knocked down to me. Now the cherry orchard's mine! Mine! [*Laughs uproariously.*] Lord! God in Heaven! The cherry orchard's mine! Tell me that I'm drunk—out of my mind—that it's all a dream. [*Stamps his feet.*] Don't laugh at me! If my father and my grandfather could rise from their graves and see all that has happened—how their Yermolay, who used to be flogged, their half-literate Yermolay, who used to run about barefoot in winter, how that very Yermolay has bought the most magnificent estate in the world. I bought the estate where my father and grandfather were slaves, where they weren't even allowed to enter the kitchen. I am asleep—it's only a dream—I only imagine it. . . . It's the fruit of your imagination, wrapped in the darkness of the unknown! [*Picks up the keys, smiling genially.*] She threw down the keys, wants to show she's no longer mistress here. [*Jingles keys.*] Well, no matter. [*The band is warming up.*] Hey, musicians! Strike up! I want to hear you! Come, everybody, and see how Yermolay Lopahin will lay the ax to the cherry orchard and how the trees will fall to the ground. We will build summer cottages there, and our grandsons and great grandsons will see a new life here. Music! Strike up!

> [*The band starts to play.* MME. RANEVSKAYA *has sunk into a chair and is weeping bitterly.*]

LOPAHIN [*Reproachfully.*]   Why, why didn't you listen to me? My dear friend, my poor friend, you can't bring it back now. [*Tearfully.*] Oh, if only this were over quickly! Oh, if only our wretched, disordered life were changed!

PISHCHIK [*Takes him by the arm; sotto voce.*]   She's crying. Let's go into the ballroom. Let her be alone. Come. [*Takes his arm and leads him into the ballroom.*]

LOPAHIN   What's the matter? Musicians, play so I can hear you! Let me have things the way I want them. [*Ironically.*] Here comes the new master, the owner of the cherry orchard. [*Accidentally he trips over a little table, almost upsetting the candelabra.*] I can pay for everything. [*Exits with* PISHCHIK.]

> [MME. RANEVSKAYA, *alone, sits huddled up, weeping bitterly. Music plays softly. Enter* ANYA *and* TROFIMOV *quickly.* ANYA *goes to her mother and falls on her knees before her.* TROFIMOV *stands in the doorway.*]

ANYA   Mamma, Mamma, you're crying! Dear, kind, good Mamma, my precious, I love you, I bless you! The cherry orchard is sold, it's gone, that's true, quite true. But don't cry, Mamma, life is still before you, you still have your kind, pure heart. Let us go, let us go away from here, darling. We will plant a new orchard, even more luxuriant than this one. You will see it, you will understand, and like the sun at evening, joy—deep, tranquil joy—will sink into your soul, and you will smile, Mamma. Come, darling, let us go.

Act IV

Scene as in Act I. No window curtains or pictures, only a little furniture, piled up in a corner, as if for sale. A sense of emptiness. Near the outer door and at the back, suitcases, bundles, etc., are piled up. A door open on the left and the voices of VARYA *and* ANYA *are heard.* LOPAHIN *stands waiting.* YASHA *holds a tray with glasses full of champagne.* YEPIHODOV *in the anteroom is tying up a box. Behind the scene a hum of voices: peasants have come to say good-bye. Voice of* GAYEV: "Thanks, brothers, thank you."

YASHA   The country folk have come to say good-bye. In my opinion, Yermolay Alexeyevich, they are kindly souls, but there's nothing in their heads.

> [*The hum dies away. Enter* MME. RANEVSKAYA *and* GAYEV: *She is not crying, but is pale, her face twitches and she cannot speak.*]

GAYEV   You gave them your purse, Luba. That won't do! That won't do!

MME. RANEVSKAYA   I couldn't help it! I couldn't! [*They go out.*]

LOPAHIN [*Calls after them.*]   Please, I beg you, have a glass at parting. I didn't think of bringing any champagne from town and at the station I could find only one bottle. Please, won't you? [*Pause.*] What's the matter, ladies and gentlemen, don't you want any? [*Moves away from the door.*] If I'd known, I wouldn't have bought it. Well, then I won't drink any, either. [YASHA *carefully sets the tray down on a chair.*] At least you have a glass, Yasha.

YASHA   Here's to the travelers! And good luck to those that stay! [*Drinks.*] This champagne isn't the real stuff, I can assure you.

LOPAHIN   Eight rubles a bottle. [*Pause.*] It's devilishly cold here.

YASHA   They didn't light the stoves today—it wasn't worth it, since we're leaving. [*Laughs.*]

LOPAHIN   Why are you laughing?

YASHA   It's just that I'm pleased.

LOPAHIN   It's October, yet it's as still and sunny as though it were summer. Good weather for building. [*Looks at his watch, and speaks off.*] Bear in mind, ladies and gentlemen, the train goes in forty-seven minutes, so you ought to start for the station in twenty minutes. Better hurry up!

[*Enter* TROFIMOV, *wearing an overcoat.*]

TROFIMOV   I think it's time to start. The carriages are at the door. The devil only knows what's become of my rubbers; they've disappeared. [*Calling off.*] Anya! My rubbers are gone. I can't find them.

LOPAHIN   I've got to go to Kharkov. I'll take the same train you do. I'll spend the winter in Kharkov. I've been hanging round here with you, till I'm worn out with loafing. I can't live without work—I don't know what to do with my hands, they dangle as if they didn't belong to me.

TROFIMOV   Well, we'll soon be gone, then you can go on with your useful labors again.

LOPAHIN   Have a glass.

TROFIMOV   No, I won't.

LOPAHIN   So you're going to Moscow now?

TROFIMOV   Yes, I'll see them into town, and tomorrow I'll go on to Moscow.

LOPAHIN   Well, I'll wager the professors aren't giving any lectures, they're waiting for you to come.

TROFIMOV   That's none of your business.

LOPAHIN   Just how many years have you been at the university?

TROFIMOV   Can't you think of something new? Your joke's stale and flat. [*Looking for his rubbers.*] We'll probably never see each other again, so allow me to give you a piece of advice at parting: don't wave your hands about! Get out of the habit. And another thing: building bungalows, figuring that summer residents will eventually become small farmers, figuring like that is just another form of waving your hands about. . . . Never mind, I love you anyway; you have fine, delicate fingers, like an artist; you have a fine delicate soul.

LOPAHIN   [*Embracing him.*]   Good-bye, my dear fellow. Thank you for everything. Let me give you some money for the journey, if you need it.

TROFIMOV   What for? I don't need it.

LOPAHIN   But you haven't any.

TROFIMOV   Yes, I have, thank you. I got some money for a translation here it is in my pocket. [*Anxiously.*] But where are my rubbers?

VARYA   [*From the next room.*]   Here! Take the nasty things. [*Flings a pair of rubbers onto the stage.*]

TROFIMOV   What are you so cross about, Varya? Hm . . . and these are not my rubbers.

LOPAHIN   I sowed three thousand acres of poppies in the spring, and now I've made 40,000 on them, clear profit; and when my poppies were in bloom, what a picture it was! So, as I say, I made 40,000; and I am offering you a loan because I can afford it. Why turn up your nose at it? I am a peasant—I speak bluntly.

TROFIMOV   Your father was a peasant, mine was a druggist—that proves absolutely nothing whatever. [LOPAHIN *takes out his wallet.*] Don't, put that away! If you were to offer me two hundred thousand, I wouldn't take it. I'm a free man. And everything that all of you, rich and poor alike, value so highly and hold so dear hasn't the slightest power over me. It's like so much fluff floating in the air. I can get on without you, I can pass you by, I'm strong and proud. Mankind is moving toward the highest truth, toward the highest happiness possible on earth, and I am in the front ranks.

LOPAHIN   Will you get there?

TROFIMOV   I will. [*Pause.*] I will get there, or I will show others the way to get there.

[*The sound of axes chopping down trees is heard in the distance.*]

LOPAHIN   Well, good-bye, my dear fellow. It's time to leave. We turn up our noses at one another, but life goes on just the same. When I'm working hard, without resting, my mind is easier, and it seems to me that I, too, know why I exist. But how many people are there in Russia, brother, who exist nobody knows why? Well, it doesn't matter. That's not what makes the wheels go round. They say Leonid Andreyevich has taken a position in the bank, 6,000 rubles a year. Only, of course, he won't stick to it, he's too lazy. . . .

ANYA [*In the doorway.*]   Mamma begs you not to start cutting down the cherry trees until she's gone.

TROFIMOV   Really, you should have more tact! [*Exits.*]

LOPAHIN   Right away—right away! Those men . . . [*Exits.*]

ANYA   Has Firs been taken to the hospital?

YASHA   I told them this morning. They must have taken him.

ANYA [*To* YEPIHODOV, *who crosses the room.*]   Yepihodov, please find out if Firs has been taken to the hospital.

YASHA [*Offended.*]   I told Yegor this morning. Why ask a dozen times?

YEPIHODOV   The aged Firs, in my definitive opinion, is beyond mending. It's time he was gathered to his fathers. And I can only envy him. [*Puts a suitcase down on a hat box and crushes it.*] There now, of course, I knew it! [*Exits.*]

YASHA [*Mockingly.*]   Two-and-Twenty Troubles!

VARYA [*Through the door.*]   Has Firs been taken to the hospital?

ANYA   Yes.

VARYA   Then why wasn't the note for the doctor taken too?

ANYA   Oh! Then someone must take it to him. [*Exits.*]

VARYA [*From adjoining room.*]   Where's Yasha? Tell him his mother's come and wants to say good-bye.

YASHA [*Waves his hand.*]   She tries my patience.

[DUNYASHA *has been occupied with the luggage. Seeing* YASHA *alone, she goes up to him.*]

DUNYASHA   You might just give me one little look, Yasha. You're going away. . . . You're leaving me . . . [*Weeps and throws herself on his neck.*]

YASHA What's there to cry about? [*Drinks champagne.*] In six days I shall
be in Paris again. Tomorrow we get into an express train and off we go,
that's the last you'll see of us. . . . I can scarcely believe it. *Vive la France!*[3]
It don't suit me here, I just can't live here. That's all there is to it. I'm
fed up with the ignorance here, I've had enough of it. [*Drinks champagne.*] What's there to cry about? Behave yourself properly, and you'll
have no cause to cry.

DUNYASHA [*Powders her face, looking in pocket mirror.*] Do send me a
letter from Paris. You know I loved you, Yasha, how I loved you! I'm a
delicate creature, Yasha.

YASHA Somebody's coming! [*Busies himself with the luggage; hums softly.*]
[Enter MME. RANEVSKAYA, GAYEV, ANYA, *and* CHARLOTTA.]

GAYEV We ought to be leaving. We haven't much time. [*Looks at* YASHA.]
Who smells of herring?

MME. RANEVSKAYA In about ten minutes we should be getting into the
carriages. [*Looks around the room.*] Good-bye, dear old home, good-bye,
grandfather. Winter will pass, spring will come, you will no longer be
here, they will have torn you down. How much these walls have seen!
[*Kisses* ANYA *warmly.*] My treasure, how radiant you look! Your eyes are
sparkling like diamonds. Are you glad? Very?

ANYA [*Gaily.*] Very glad. A new life is beginning, Mamma.

GAYEV Well, really, everything is all right now. Before the cherry orchard
was sold, we all fretted and suffered; but afterward, when the question
was settled finally and irrevocably, we all calmed down, and even felt
quite cheerful. I'm a bank employee now, a financier. The yellow ball in
the side pocket! And anyhow, you are looking better, Luba, there's no
doubt of that.

MME. RANEVSKAYA Yes, my nerves are better, that's true. [*She is handed
her hat and coat.*] I sleep well. Carry out my things, Yasha. It's time.
[*To* ANYA.] We shall soon see each other again, my little girl. I'm going
to Paris, I'll live there on the money your great-aunt sent us to buy the
estate with—long live Auntie! But that money won't last long.

ANYA You'll come back soon, soon, Mamma, won't you? Meanwhile I'll
study. I'll pass my high school examination, and then I'll go to work
and help you. We'll read all kinds of books together, Mamma, won't
we? [*Kisses her mother's hands.*] We'll read in the autumn evenings,
we'll read lots of books, and a new wonderful world will open up
before us. [*Falls into a revery.*] Mamma, do come back.

MME. RANEVSKAYA I will come back, my precious.
[*Embraces her daughter. Enter* LOPAHIN *and* CHARLOTTA, *who is
humming softly.*]

GAYEV Charlotta's happy: she's singing.

CHARLOTTA [*Picks up a bundle and holds it like a baby in swaddling
clothes.*] Bye, baby, bye. [*A baby is heard crying:* "Wah! Wah!"] Hush,
hush, my pet, my little one. ["Wah! Wah!"] I'm so sorry for you! [*Throws
the bundle down.*] You will find me a position, won't you? I can't go on
like this.

LOPAHIN We'll find one for you, Charlotta Ivanovna, don't worry.

---

3. Long live France! (French).

GAYEV Everyone's leaving us. Varya's going away. We've suddenly become of no use.

CHARLOTTA There's no place for me to live in town, I must go away. [*Hums.*]

[*Enter* PISHCHIK.]

LOPAHIN There's nature's masterpiece!

PISHCHIK [*Gasping.*] Oh . . . let me get my breath . . . I'm in agony. . . . Esteemed friends . . . Give me a drink of water. . . .

GAYEV Wants some money, I suppose. No, thank you . . . I'll keep out of harm's way. [*Exits.*]

PISHCHIK It's a long while since I've been to see you, most charming lady. [*To* LOPAHIN.] So you are here . . . glad to see you, you intellectual giant . . . There . . . [*Gives* LOPAHIN *money.*] Here's 400 rubles, and I still owe you 840.

LOPAHIN [*Shrugging his shoulders in bewilderment.*] I must be dreaming. . . . Where did you get it?

PISHCHIK Wait a minute . . . it's hot. . . . A most extraordinary event! Some Englishmen came to my place and found some sort of white clay on my land . . . [*To* MME. RANEVSKAYA.] And 400 for you . . . most lovely . . . most wonderful . . . [*Hands her the money.*] The rest later. [*Drinks water.*] A young man in the train was telling me just now that a great philosopher recommends jumping off roofs. "Jump!" says he; "that's the long and the short of it!" [*In amazement.*] Just imagine! Some more water!

LOPAHIN What Englishmen?

PISHCHIK I leased them the tract with the clay on it for twenty-four years. . . . And now, forgive me, I can't stay. . . . I must be dashing on. . . . I'm going over to Znoikov . . . to Kardamanov . . . I owe them all money . . . [*Drinks water.*] Good-bye, everybody . . . I'll look in on Thursday . . .

MME. RANEVSKAYA We're just moving into town; and tomorrow I go abroad.

PISHCHIK [*Upset.*] What? Why into town? That's why the furniture is like that . . . and the suitcases. . . . Well, never mind! [*Through tears.*] Never mind . . . men of colossal intellect, these Englishmen. . . . Never mind . . . Be happy. God will come to your help. . . . Never mind . . . everything in this world comes to an end. [*Kisses* MME. RANEVSKAYA's *hand.*] If the rumor reaches you that it's all up with me, remember this old . . . horse, and say: "Once there lived a certain . . . Simeonov-Pishchik . . . the kingdom of Heaven be his. . . ." Glorious weather! . . . Yes . . . [*Exits, in great confusion, but at once returns and says in the doorway.*] My daughter Dashenka sends her regards. [*Exits.*]

MME. RANEVSKAYA Now we can go. I leave with two cares weighing on me. The first is poor old Firs. [*Glancing at her watch.*] We still have about five minutes.

ANYA Mamma, Firs has already been taken to the hospital. Yasha sent him there this morning.

MME. RANEVSKAYA My other worry is Varya. She's used to getting up early and working; and now, with no work to do, she is like a fish out of water. She has grown thin and pale, and keeps crying, poor soul. [*Pause.*] You know this very well, Yermolay Alexeyevich; I dreamed of seeing her married to you, and it looked as though that's how it would be. [*Whispers to*

ANYA, *who nods to* CHARLOTTA *and both go out.*] She loves you. You find her attractive. I don't know, I don't know why it is you seem to avoid each other; I can't understand it.

LOPAHIN   To tell you the truth, I don't understand it myself. It's all a puzzle. If there's still time, I'm ready now, at once. Let's settle it straight off, and have done with it! Without you, I feel I'll never be able to propose.

MME. RANEVSKAYA   That's splendid. After all, it will only take a minute. I'll call her at once. . . .

LOPAHIN   And luckily, here's champagne, too. [*Looks at the glasses.*] Empty! Somebody's drunk it all. [*Yasha coughs.*] That's what you might call guzzling . . .

MME. RANEVSKAYA [*Animatedly.*]   Excellent! We'll go and leave you alone. Yasha, *allez!*[4] I'll call her. [*At the door.*] Varya, leave everything and come here. Come! [*Exits with* YASHA.]

LOPAHIN [*Looking at his watch.*]   Yes . . . [*Pause behind the door, smothered laughter and whispering; at last, enter* VARYA.]

VARYA [*Looking over the luggage in leisurely fashion.*]   Strange, I can't find it . . .

LOPAHIN   What are you looking for?

VARYA   Packed it myself, and I don't remember . . . [*Pause.*]

LOPAHIN   Where are you going now, Varya?

VARYA   I? To the Ragulins'. I've arranged to take charge there—as housekeeper, if you like.

LOPAHIN   At Yashnevo? About fifty miles from here. [*Pause.*] Well, life in this house is ended!

VARYA [*Examining luggage.*]   Where is it? Perhaps I put it in the chest. Yes, life in this house is ended. . . . There will be no more of it.

LOPAHIN   And I'm just off to Kharkov—by this next train. I've a lot to do there. I'm leaving Yepihodov here . . . I've taken him on.

VARYA   Oh!

LOPAHIN   Last year at this time, it was snowing, if you remember, but now it's sunny and there's no wind. It's cold, though. . . . It must be three below.

VARYA   I didn't look. [*Pause.*] And besides, our thermometer's broken. [*Pause.* VOICE *from the yard:* "Yermolay Alexeyevich!"]

LOPAHIN [*As if he had been waiting for the call.*]   This minute! [*Exits quickly.*]

> [VARYA *sits on the floor and sobs quietly, her head on a bundle of clothes. Enter* MME. RANEVSKAYA *cautiously.*]

MME. RANEVSKAYA   Well? [*Pause.*] We must be going.

VARYA [*Wiping her eyes.*]   Yes, it's time, Mamma dear. I'll be able to get to the Ragulins' today, if only we don't miss the train.

MME. RANEVSKAYA [*At the door.*]   Anya, put your things on.

> [*Enter* ANYA, GAYEV, CHARLOTTA. GAYEV *wears a heavy overcoat with a hood. Enter servants and coachmen.* YEPIHODOV *bustles about the luggage.*]

MME. RANEVSKAYA   Now we can start on our journey.

---

4. Go on! (French).

ANYA [*Joyfully.*]   On our journey!

GAYEV   My friends, my dear, cherished friends, leaving this house forever, can I be silent? Can I, at leave-taking, refrain from giving utterance to those emotions that now fill my being?

ANYA [*Imploringly.*]   Uncle!

VARYA   Uncle, Uncle dear, don't.

GAYEV [*Forlornly.*]   I'll bank the yellow in the side pocket . . . I'll be silent . . .

> [*Enter* TROFIMOV, *then* LOPAHIN.]

TROFIMOV   Well, ladies and gentlemen, it's time to leave.

LOPAHIN   Yepihodov, my coat.

MME. RANEVSKAYA   I'll sit down just a minute. It seems as though I'd never before seen what the walls of this house were like, the ceilings, and now I look at them hungrily, with such tender affection.

GAYEV   I remember when I was six years old sitting on that window sill on Whitsunday,[5] watching my father going to church.

MME. RANEVSKAYA   Has everything been taken?

LOPAHIN   I think so. [*Putting on his overcoat.*] Yepihodov, see that everything's in order.

YEPIHODOV [*In a husky voice.*]   You needn't worry, Yermolay Alexeyevich.

LOPAHIN   What's the matter with your voice?

YEPIHODOV   I just had a drink of water. I must have swallowed something.

YASHA [*Contemptuously.*]   What ignorance!

MME. RANEVSKAYA   When we're gone, not a soul will be left here.

LOPAHIN   Until the spring.

> [VARYA *pulls an umbrella out of a bundle, as though about to hit someone with it.* LOPAHIN *pretends to be frightened.*]

VARYA   Come, come, I had no such idea!

TROFIMOV   Ladies and gentlemen, let's get into the carriages—it's time. The train will be in directly.

VARYA   Petya, there they are, your rubbers, by that trunk. [*Tearfully.*] And what dirty old things, they are!

TROFIMOV [*Puts on rubbers.*]   Let's go, ladies and gentlemen.

GAYEV [*Greatly upset, afraid of breaking down.*]   The train . . . the station. . . . Three cushions in the side pocket, I'll bank this one in the corner . . .

MME. RANEVSKAYA   Let's go.

LOPAHIN   Are we all here? No one in there? [*Locks the side door on the left.*] There are some things stored here, better lock up. Let us go!

ANYA   Good-bye, old house! Good-bye, old life!

TROFIMOV   Hail to you, new life!

> [*Exits with* ANYA. VARYA *looks round the room and goes out slowly.* YASHA *and* CHARLOTTA *with her dog go out.*]

LOPAHIN   And so, until the spring. Go along, friends . . . Bye-bye! [*Exits.*]

> [MME. RANEVSKAYA *and* GAYEV *remain alone. As though they had been waiting for this, they throw themselves on each other's necks, and break into subdued, restrained sobs, afraid of being overheard.*]

GAYEV [*In despair.*]   My sister! My sister!

---

5. Or Pentecost, a Christian festival occurring on the seventh Sunday after Easter.

MME. RANEVSKAYA   Oh, my orchard—my dear, sweet, beautiful orchard! My life, my youth, my happiness—good-bye! Good-bye!

[*Voice of* ANYA: *gay and summoning:* "Mamma!" *Voice of* TROFIMOV: *gay and excited:* "Halloo!"]

MME. RANEVSKAYA   One last look at the walls, at the windows. . . . Our poor mother loved to walk about this room . . .

GAYEV   My sister, my sister!

[*Voice of* ANYA: "Mamma!" *Voice of* TROFIMOV: "Halloo!"]

MME. RANEVSKAYA   We're coming.

[*They go out. The stage is empty. The sound of doors being locked, of carriages driving away. Then silence. In the stillness is heard the muffled sound of the ax striking a tree, a mournful, lonely sound.*

Footsteps are heard. FIRS *appears in the doorway on the right. He is dressed as usual in a jacket and white waistcoat and wears slippers. He is ill.*]

FIRS [*Goes to the door, tries the handle.*]   Locked! They've gone . . . [*Sits down on the sofa.*] They've forgotten me. . . . Never mind . . . I'll sit here a bit . . . I'll wager Leonid Andreyevich hasn't put his fur coat on, he's gone off in his light overcoat . . . [*Sighs anxiously.*] I didn't keep an eye on him. . . . Ah, when they're young, they're green . . . [*Mumbles something indistinguishable.*] Life has gone by as if I had never lived. [*Lies down.*] I'll lie down a while . . . There's no strength left in you, old fellow; nothing is left, nothing. Ah, you addlehead!

[*Lies motionless. A distant sound is heard coming from the sky, as it were, the sound of a snapping string mournfully dying away. All is still again, and nothing is heard but the strokes of the ax against a tree far away in the orchard.*]

A Note on Translation

Reading literature in translation is a pleasure on which it is fruitless to frown. The purist may insist that we ought always read in the original languages, and we know ideally that this is true. But it is a counsel of perfection, quite impractical even for the purist, since no one in a lifetime can master all the languages whose literatures it would be a joy to explore. Master languages as fast as we may, we shall always have to read to some extent in translation, and this means we must be alert to what we are about: if in reading a work of literature in translation we are not reading the "original," what precisely are we reading? This is a question of great complexity, to which justice cannot be done in a brief note, but the following sketch of some of the considerations may be helpful.

One of the memorable scenes of ancient literature is the meeting of Hector and Andromache in Book VI of Homer's *Iliad*. Hector, leader and mainstay of the armies defending Troy, is implored by his wife Andromache to withdraw within the city walls and carry on the defense from there, where his life will not be con stantly at hazard. In Homer's text her opening words to him are these: δαιμόνιε, φθίσει σε τὸ σὸν μένος (daimonie, phthisei se to son menos). How should they be translated into English?

Here is how they have actually been translated into English by capable translators, at various periods, in verse and prose:

1. George Chapman, 1598:

> O noblest in desire,
> Thy mind, inflamed with others' good, will set thy self on fire.

2. John Dryden, 1693:

> Thy dauntless heart (which I foresee too late),
> Too daring man, will urge thee to thy fate.

3. Alexander Pope, 1715:

> Too daring Prince! . . .
> For sure such courage length of life denies,
> And thou must fall, thy virtue's sacrifice.

4. William Cowper, 1791:

> Thy own great courage will cut short thy days,
> My noble Hector. . .

5. Lang, Leaf, and Myers, 1883 (prose):

> Dear my lord, this thy hardihood will undo thee. . . .

6. A. T. Murray, 1924 (prose):

> Ah, my husband, this prowess of thine will be thy doom. . . .

7. E. V. Rieu, 1950 (prose):

"Hector," she said, "you are possessed. This bravery of yours will be your end."

8. I. A. Richards, 1950 (prose):

"Strange man," she said, "your courage will be your destruction."

9. Richmond Lattimore, 1951:

Dearest,
Your own great strength will be your death. . . .

10. Robert Fitzgerald, 1979:

O my wild one, your bravery will be
Your own undoing!

11. Robert Fagles, 1990:

reckless one,
Your own fiery courage will destroy you!

From these strikingly different renderings of the same six words, certain facts about the nature of translation begin to emerge. We notice, for one thing, that Homer's word μένος (menos) is diversified by the translators into "mind," "dauntless heart," "such courage," "great courage," "hardihood," "prowess," "bravery," "courage," "great strength," "bravery," and "fiery courage." The word has in fact all these possibilities. Used of things, it normally means "force"; of animals, "fierceness" or "brute strength" or (in the case of horses) "mettle"; of men and women, "passion" or "spirit" or even "purpose." Homer's application of it in the present case points our attention equally— whatever particular sense we may imagine Andromache to have uppermost—to Hector's force, strength, fierceness in battle, spirited heart and mind. But since English has no matching term of like inclusiveness, the passage as the translators give it to us reflects this lack and we find one attribute singled out to the exclusion of the rest.

Here then is the first and most crucial fact about any work of literature read in translation. It cannot escape the linguistic characteristics of the language into which it is turned: the grammatical, syntactical, lexical, and phonetic boundaries that constitute collectively the individuality or "genius" of that language. A Greek play or a Russian novel in English will be governed first of all by the resources of the English language, resources that are certain to be in every instance very different, as the efforts with μένος show, from those of the original.

Turning from μένος to δαιμόνιε (daimonie) in Homer's clause, we encounter a second crucial fact about translations. Nobody knows exactly what shade of meaning δαιμόνιε had for Homer. In later writers the word normally suggests divinity, something miraculous, wondrous; but in Homer it appears as a vocative of address for both chieftain and commoner, man and wife. The coloring one gives it must therefore be determined either by the way one thinks a Greek wife of Homer's era might actually address her husband (a subject on which we have no information whatever) or in the way one thinks it suitable for a hero's wife to address her husband in an epic poem, that is to say, a highly stylized and formal work. In general, the translators of our century will be seen to have abandoned formality to stress the intimacy; the wifeliness; and, especially in Lattimore's case, a certain chiding tenderness, in Andromache's appeal: (6) "Ah, my husband," (7) "Hector" (with perhaps a hint, in "you are possessed," of the alarmed distaste with which wives have so often viewed their husbands' bellicose moods), (8) "Strange man," (9) "Dearest," (10) "O my wild one" (mixing an almost motherly admiration with reproach and concern), and (11) "reckless one." On the other hand, the older translators have obviously removed Andromache to an epic or heroic distance from her beloved, whence she sees and kindles to his selfless courage, acknowledging, even in the moment of pleading with him to be otherwise, his moral grandeur and the tragic destiny this too certainly implies: (1) "O noblest in desire, . . . inflamed by others' good"; (2) "Thy dauntless heart (which I foresee too late), / Too daring man"; (3) "Too daring Prince! . . . / And thou must fall, thy virtue's sacrifice"; (4) "My noble Hector." Even the less specific "Dear my lord" of Lang, Leaf, and Myers looks in the same direction because of its echo of the speech of countless Shakespearean men and women who have shared this powerful moral sense: "Dear my lord, make me acquainted with your cause of grief"; "Perseverance, dear my lord, keeps honor bright"; etc.

The fact about translation that emerges from all this is that just as the translated work reflects the individuality of the language it is turned into, so it reflects the individuality of the age in which it is made, and the age will permeate it everywhere like yeast in dough. We think of one kind of permeation when we think of the governing verse forms and attitudes toward verse at a given epoch. In Chapman's time, experiments seeking an "heroic" verse form for English were widespread, and accordingly he tries a "fourteener" couplet (two rhymed lines of seven stresses each) in his *Iliad* and a pentameter couplet in his *Odyssey*. When Dryden and Pope wrote, a closed pentameter couplet had become established as the heroic form par excellence. By Cowper's day, thanks largely to the prestige of *Paradise Lost*, the couplet had gone out of fashion for narrative poetry in favor of blank verse. Our age, inclining to prose and in verse to proselike informalities and relaxations, has, predictably, produced half a dozen excellent prose translations of the *Iliad* but only three in verse (by Fagles, Lattimore, and Fitzgerald), all relying on rhythms that are much of the time closer to the verse of William Carlos Williams and some of the prose of novelists like Faulkner than to the swift firm tread of Homer's Greek. For if it is true that what we translate from a given work is what, wearing the spectacles of our time, we see in it, it is also true that we see in it what we have the power to translate.

Of course, there are other effects of the translator's epoch on a translation besides those exercised by contemporary taste in verse and verse forms. Chapman writes in a great age of poetic metaphor and, therefore, almost instinctively translates his understanding of Homer's verb $\phi\theta\iota\sigma\epsilon\iota$ (phthisei, "to cause to wane, consume, waste, pine") into metaphorical terms of flame, presenting his Hector to us as a man of burning generosity who will be consumed by his very ardor. This is a conception rooted in large part in the psychology of the Elizabethans, who had the habit of speaking of the soul as "fire," of one of the four temperaments as "fiery," of even the more material bodily processes, like digestion, as if they were carried on by the heat of fire ("concoction," "decoction"). It is rooted too in that characteristic Renaissance élan so unforgettably expressed in characters such as Tamburlaine and Dr. Faustus, the former of whom exclaims to the stars above:

> . . . I, the chiefest lamp of all the earth,
> First rising in the East with mild aspect,
> But fixèd now in the meridian line,
> Will send up fire to your turning spheres,
> And cause the sun to borrow light of you. . . .

Pope and Dryden, by contrast, write to audiences for whom strong metaphor has become suspect. They therefore reject the fire image (which we must recall is not present in the Greek) in favor of a form of speech more congenial to their age, the *sententia* or aphorism, and give it extra vitality by making it the scene of a miniature drama: in Dryden's case, the hero's dauntless heart "urges" him (in the double sense of physical as well as moral pressure) to his fate; in Pope's, the hero's courage, like a judge, "denies" continuance of life, with the consequence that he "falls"—and here Pope's second line suggests analogy to the sacrificial animal—the victim of his own essential nature, of what he is.

To pose even more graphically the pressures that a translator's period brings, consider the following lines from Hector's reply to Andromache's appeal that he with-draw, first in Chapman's Elizabethan version, then in Lattimore's twentieth-century one:

Chapman, 1598:

> The spirit I did first breathe
> Did never teach me that—much less since the contempt of death
> Was settled in me, and my mind knew what a Worthy was,
> Whose office is to lead in fight and give no danger pass
> Without improvement. In this fire must Hector's trial shine.
> Here must his country, father, friends be in him made divine.

Lattimore, 1951:

> and the spirit will not let me, since I have learned to be valiant
> and to fight always among the foremost ranks of the Trojans,
> winning for my own self great glory, and for my father.

If one may exaggerate to make a necessary point, the world of Henry V and Othello suddenly gives way here to our own, a world whose discomfort with any form of heroic self-assertion is remarkably mirrored in the burial of Homer's key terms (*spirit, valiant, fight, foremost, glory*)—five out of twenty-two words in the original, five out of thirty-six in the translation—in a cushioning huddle of harmless sounds.

Besides the two factors so far mentioned (language and period) as affecting the character of a translation, there is inevitably a third—the translator, with a particular degree of talent; a personal way of regarding the work to be translated; a special hierarchy of values, moral, aesthetic, metaphysical (which may or may not be summed up in a "worldview"); and a unique style or lack of it. But this influence all readers are likely to bear in mind, and it needs no laboring here. That, for example, two translators of Hamlet, one a Freudian, the other a Jungian, will produce impressively different translations is obvious from the fact that when Freudian and Jungian argue about the play in English they often seem to have different plays in mind.

We can now return to the question from which we started. After all allowances have been made for language, age, and individual translator, is anything of the original left? What, in short, does the reader of translations read? Let it be said at once that in utility prose—prose whose function is mainly referential—the reader who reads a translation reads everything that matters. "Nicht Rauchen," "Défense de Fumer," and "No Smoking," posted in a railway car, make their point, and the differences between them in sound and form have no significance for us in that context. Since the prose of a treatise and of most fiction is preponderantly referential, we rightly feel, when we have paid close attention to Cervantes or Montaigne or Machiavelli or Tolstoy in a good English translation, that we have had roughly the same experience as a native Spaniard, Frenchman, Italian, or Russian. But *roughly* is the correct word; for good prose points iconically *to* itself as well as referentially beyond itself, and everything that it points to in itself in the original (rhythms, sounds, idioms, wordplay, etc.) must alter radically in being translated. The best analogy is to imagine a Van Gogh painting reproduced in the medium of tempera, etching, or engraving: the "picture" remains, but the intricate interanimation of volumes with colorings with brushstrokes has disappeared.

When we move on to poetry, even in its longer narrative and dramatic forms—plays like *Oedipus,* poems like the *Iliad* or the *Divine Comedy*—our situation as English readers worsens appreciably, as the many unlike versions of Andromache's appeal to Hector make very clear. But, again, only appreciably. True, this is the point at which the fact that a translation is *always* an interpretation explodes irresistibly on our attention; but if it is the best translation of its time, like John Ciardi's translation of the *Divine Comedy* for our time, the result will be not only a sensitive interpretation but also a work with intrinsic interest in its own right—at very best, a true work of art, a new poem. In these longer works, moreover, even if the translation is uninspired, many distinctive structural features—plot, setting, characters, meetings, partings, confrontations, and specific episodes generally—survive virtually unchanged. Hence even in translation it remains both possible and instructive to compare, say, concepts of the heroic or attitudes toward women or uses of religious ritual among civilizations as various as those reflected in the *Iliad*, the *Mahābhārata*, *Beowulf*, and the epic of *Son-Jara*. It is only when the shorter, primarily lyrical forms of poetry are presented that the reader of translations faces insuperable disadvantage. In these forms, the referential aspect of language has a tendency to disappear into, or, more often, draw its real meaning and accreditation from, the iconic aspect. Let us look for just a moment at a brief poem by Federico García Lorca and its English translation (by Stephen Spender and J. L. Gili):

> ¡Alto pinar!
> Cuatro palomas por el aire van.
>
> Cuatro palomas
> vuelan y tornan.
> Llevan heridas
> sus cuatro sombras.
>
> ¡Bajo pinar!
> Cuatro palomas en la tierra están.

> Above the pine trees:
> Four pigeons go through the air.
>
> Four pigeons
> fly and turn round.
> They carry wounded
> their four shadows.
>
> Below the pine trees:
> Four pigeons lie on the earth.

In this translation the referential sense of the English words follows with remarkable exactness the referential sense of the Spanish words they replace. But the life of Lorca's poem does not lie in that sense. It lies in such matters as the abruptness, like an intake of breath at a sudden revelation, of the two exclamatory lines (1 and 7), which then exhale musically in images of flight and death; or as the echoings of *palomas* in *heridas* and *sombras*, bringing together (as in fact the hunter's gun has done) these unrelated nouns and the unrelated experiences they stand for in a sequence that seems, momentarily, to have all the logic of a tragic action, in which *doves* become *wounds* become *shadows*, or as the external and internal rhyming among the five verbs, as though all motion must (as in fact it must) end with *están*.

Since none of this can be brought over into another tongue (least of all Lorca's rhythms), the translator must decide between leaving a reader to wonder why Lorca is a poet to be bothered about at all and making a new but true poem, whose merit will almost certainly be in inverse ratio to its likeness to the original. Samuel Johnson made such a poem in translating Horace's famous *Diffugere nives*, and so did A. E. Housman. If we juxtapose the last two stanzas of each translation, and the corresponding Latin, we can see at a glance that each has the consistency and inner life of a genuine poem and that neither of them (even if we consider only what is obvious to the eye, the line-lengths) is very close to Horace:

> Cum semel occideris, et de te splendida Minos
> fecerit arbitria,

> *non, Torquate, genus, non te facundia, non te*
> *restituet pietas.*
>
> *Infernis neque enim tenebris Diana pudicum*
> *liberat Hippolytum*
> *nec Lethaea valet Theseus abrumpere caro*
> *vincula Pirithoo.*

Johnson:

> Not you, Torquatus, boast of Rome,
> When Minos once has fixed your doom,
> Or eloquence, or splendid birth,
> Or virtue, shall restore to earth.
> Hippolytus, unjustly slain,
> Diana calls to life in vain;
> Nor can the might of Theseus rend
> The chains of hell that hold his friend.

Housman:

> When thou descendest once the shades among,
>   The stern assize and equal judgment o'er,
> Not thy long lineage nor thy golden tongue,
>   No, nor thy righteousness, shall friend thee more.
>
> Night holds Hippolytus the pure of stain,
>   Diana steads him nothing, he must stay;
> And Theseus leaves Pirithous in the chain
>   The love of comrades cannot take away.

The truth of the matter is that when the translator of short poems chooses to be literal, most or all of the poetry is lost; and when the translator succeeds in forging a new poetry, most or all of the original author is lost. Since there is no way out of this dilemma, we have always been sparing, in this anthology, in our use of short poems in translation.

In this Expanded Edition, we have adjusted our policy to take account of the two great non-Western literatures in which the short lyric or "song" has been the principal and by far most cherished expression of the national genius. During much of its history from earliest times, the Japanese imagination has cheerfully exercised itself, with all the delicacy and grace of an Olympic figure skater, inside a rigorous verse pattern of five lines and thirty-one syllables: the *tanka.* Chinese poetry, while somewhat more liberal to itself in line length, has been equally fertile in the fine art of compression and has only occasionally, even in its earliest, most experimental phase, indulged in verse lines of more than seven characters, often just four, or in poems of more than fifty lines, usually fewer than twenty. What makes the Chinese and Japanese lyric more difficult than most other lyrics to translate satisfactorily into English is that these compressions combine with a flexibility of syntax (Japanese) or a degree of freedom from it (Chinese) not available in our language. They also combine with a poetic sensibility that shrinks from exposition in favor of sequences and juxtapositions of images: images grasped and recorded in, or *as if in,* a moment of pure perception unencumbered by the explanatory linkages, background scenarios, and other forms of contextualization that the Western mind is instinctively driven to establish.

Whole books, almost whole libraries, have been written recently on the contrast of East and West in worldviews and value systems as well as on the need of each for the other if there is ever to be a community of understanding adequate to the realities both face. Put baldly, much too simply, and without the many exceptions and qualifications that rightly spring to mind, it may be said that a central and characteristic Western impulse, from the Greeks on down, has been to see the world around us as something to be *acted on*: weighed, measured, managed, used, even (when economic interests prevail over all others) fouled. Likewise, put oversimply, it may be said that a central and characteristic Eastern counterpart to this over many centuries (witness Taoism, Buddhism, and Hinduism, among others) has been to see that same world as something to be *received*: contemplated, touched, tasted, smelled, heard, and most especially, immersed in until observer and observed are one. To paint a bamboo, a stone, a butterfly, a person—so runs a classical Chinese admonition for painters— you must *become* that bamboo, that stone, that butterfly, that person, then paint from the inside. No one need be ashamed of being poor, says Confucius, putting a similar emphasis on *receiving* experience, "only of not being cultivated in the perception of beauty."

The problem that these differences in linguistic freedom and philosophical outlook pose for the English translator of classical Chinese and Japanese poetry may be glimpsed, even if not fully grasped, by considering for a moment in some detail a typical Japanese *tanka* (*Kokinshu*, 9) and a typical Chinese "song" (*Book of Songs*, 23). In its own language but transliterated in the Latin alphabet of the West, the *tanka* looks like this:

> *kasumi tachi*
> *ko no me mo haru no*
> *yuki fureba*
> *hana naki sato mo*
> *hana zo chirikeru*

In a literal word-by-word translation (so far as this is possible in Japanese, since the language uses many particles without English equivalents and without dictionary meaning in modifying and qualifying functions—for example, *no, mo,* and *no* in line 2), the poem looks like this:

> haze rises
> tree-buds swell
> when snow falls
> village(s) without flower(s)
> flower(s) fall(s)

The three best-known English renderings of this *tanka* look like this:

1. Helen Craig McCullough:

> When snow comes in spring—
> fair season of layered haze
> and burgeoning buds—
> flowers fall in villages
> where flowers have yet to bloom.

2. Laurel Rasplica Rodd and Mary Catherine Henkenius:

> When the warm mists veil
> all the buds swell while yet the
> spring snows drift downward
> even in the hibernal
> village crystal blossoms fall.

3. Robert H. Brower and Earl Miner:

> With the spreading mists
> The tree buds swell in early spring
> And wet snow petals fall—

> So even my flowerless country village
> Already lies beneath its fallen flowers.

The reader will notice at once how much the three translators have felt it desirable or necessary to add, alter, rearrange, and explain. In McCullough's version the time of year is affirmed twice, both as "spring" and as "fair season of . . . haze"; the haze is now "layered"; the five coordinate perceptions of the original (haze, swelling buds, a snowfall, villages without flowers, flowers drifting down) have been structured into a single sentence with one main verb and two subordinate clauses spelling out "when" and "where"; and the original poem's climax, in a scene of drifting petallike snow-flakes, has been shifted to a bleak scenery of absence: "flowers have yet to bloom." The final stress, in other words, is not on the fulfilled moment in which snow flowers replace the cherry blossoms, but on the cherry blossoms not yet arrived.

Similar additions and explanations occur in Rodd and Henkenius's version. This time the mist is "warm" and "veil[s] all" to clarify its connection with "buds." Though implicit already in "warm" and "burgeoning," spring is invoked again in "spring snows," and the snows are given confirmation in the following line by the insistently Latinate "hibernal," chosen, we may reasonably guess, along with "veil," "all," "swell," "while," "crystal," and "fall" to replace some of the chiming internal rhyme in the Japanese: *ko, no, mo, no, sato, mo, zo.* To leave no *i* undotted, "crystal" is imported to assure us that the falling "blossoms" of line 5 are really snowflakes, and the scene of flowerlessness that in the original (line 4) accounts for a special joy in the "flowering" of the snowflakes (line 5) vanishes without trace.

Brower and Miner's also fills in the causative links between "spreading mists" and swelling buds; makes sure that we do not fail to see the falling snow in flower terms ("wet snow petals"), thus losing, alas, the element of surprise, even magic, in the transfor-mation of snowflakes into flowers that the original poem holds in store in its last two lines; and tells us (somewhat redundantly) that villages are a "country" phenomenon and (somewhat surprisingly) that this one is the speaker's home. In this version, as in the original and Rodd and Henkenius's, the poem closes with the snow scene, but here it is a one-time affair and "already" complete (lines 4 and 5), not a recurrent phenome-non that may appear under certain conditions anywhere at any time.

Some of the differences in these translations arise inevitably from different trade-offs, as in the first version, where the final vision of falling snow blossoms is let go presumably to achieve the lovely lilting echo and rhetorical turn of "flowers fall in villages / where flowers have yet to bloom." Or as in Rodd and Henkenius's version, where preoccupations with internal rhyme have obviously influenced word choices, not always for the better. Or as in all three versions, where different efforts to remind the reader of the wordplay on *haru* (in the Japanese poem both a noun meaning "spring" and a verb meaning "swell") have had dissimilar but perhaps equally indif-ferent results. Meantime, the immense force compacted into that small word in the original as both noun and verb, season of springtime and principal of growth, cause and effect (and thus in a sense the whole mighty process of earth's renewal, in which an interruption by snow only foretells a greater loveliness to come) fizzles away unfelt. A few differences do seem to arise from insufficient command of the nerves and sinews of English poetry, but most spring from the staggering difficulties of respond-ing in any uniform way to the minimal clues proffered by the original text. The five perceptions—haze, buds, snowfall, flowerless villages, flowers falling—do not as they stand in the Japanese or any literal translation quite compose for readers accustomed to Western poetic traditions an adequate poetic whole. This is plainly seen in the irresistible urge each of the translators has felt to catch up the individual perceptions, as English tends to require, in a tighter overall grammatical and syntactical structure than the original insists on. In this way they provide a clarifying network of principal and subordinate, time when, place where, and cause why. Yet the inevitable result is a disassembling, a spinning out, spelling out, thinning out of what in the Japanese is an as yet unraveled imagistic excitement, creating (or memorializing) in the poet's mind, and then in the mind of the Japanese readers, the original thrill of consciousness when these images, complete with the magical transformation of snow into the longed-for cherry blossoms, first flashed on the inward eye.

What is comforting for us who must read this and other Japanese poems in translation is that each of the versions given here retains in some form or other all or most of the five images intact. What is less comforting is that the simplicity and suddenness, the explosion in the mind, have been diffused and defused.

When we turn to the Chinese song, we find similarly contesting forces at work. In one respect, the Chinese language comes over into English more readily than Japanese, being like English comparatively uninflected and heavily dependent on word order for its meanings. But in other respects, since Chinese like Japanese lacks distinctions of gender, of singular and plural, of *a* and *the*, and in the classical mode in which the poems in this anthology are composed, also of tenses, the pressure of the English translator to rearrange, straighten out, and fill in to "make sense" for his or her readers remains strong.

Let us examine song no. 23 of the *Shijing*. In its own Chinese characters, it looks like this:

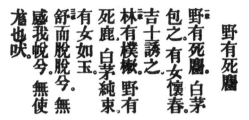

Eleven lines in all, each line having four characters as its norm, the poem seemingly takes shape around an implicit parallel between a doe in the forest, possibly killed by stealth and hidden under long grass or rushes (though on this point as on all others the poem refuses to take us wholly into confidence), and a young girl possibly "ruined" (as she certainly would have been in the post-Confucian society in which the *Shijing* was prized and circulated, though here again the poem keeps its own counsel) by loss of her virginity before marriage.

In its bare bones, with each character given an approximate English equivalent, a translation might look like this:

wild(s)	is	dead	deer	
white	grass(es)	wrap/cover	(it).	
is	girl	feel	spring.	
fine	man	tempt	(her).	
woods	is(are)	bush(es),	underbrush.	5
wild(s)	is	dead	deer.	
white	grass(es)	bind	bundle.	
is	girl	like	jade.	
slow	———	slow	slow.	
not	move	my	sash.	10
not	cause	dog	bark.	

Lines 1 to 4, it seems plain, propose the parallel of slain doe and girl, whatever that parallel may be intended to mean. Lines 5 to 8 restate the parallel, adding that the girl is as beautiful as jade and (apparently) that the doe lies where the "wild" gives way to smaller growth. If we allow ourselves to account for the repetition (here again is a Western mind-set in search of explanatory clues) by supposing that lines 1 to 4 signal at some subliminal level the initiation of the seduction and lines 5 to 8, again subliminally, its progress or possibly its completion, lines 9 to 11 fall easily into place as a miniature drama enacting in direct speech the man's advances and the girl's gradually crumbling resistance. They also imply, it seems, that the seduction takes place not in the forest, as we might have been led to suppose by lines 1 to 8, but in a dwelling with a vigilant guard dog.

Interpreted just far enough to accommodate English syntax, the poem reads as follows:

1. Wai-lim Yip:

> In the wilds, a dead doe.
> White reeds to wrap it.
> A girl, spring-touched.
> A fine man to seduce her.
> In the woods, bushes.   5
> In the wilds, a dead deer.
> White reeds in bundles.
> A girl like jade.
> Slowly. Take it easy.
> Don't feel my sash!   10
> Don't make the dog bark!

Interpreted a stage further in a format some have thought better suited to English poetic traditions, the poem reads:

2. Arthur Waley:

> In the wilds there is a dead doe,
> With white rushes we cover her.
> There was a lady longing for spring,
> A fair knight seduced her.
>
> In the woods there is a clump of oaks,   5
> And in the wilds a dead deer
> With white rushes well bound.
> There was a lady fair as jade.
>
> "Heigh, not so hasty, not so rough.
> "Heigh, do not touch my handkerchief.   10
> "Take care or the dog will bark."

Like the original and the literal translation, this version leaves the relationship between the doe's death and the girl's seduction unspecified and problematic. It holds the doe story in present tenses, assigning the girl story to the past. Still, much has been changed to give the English poem an explanatory scenario. The particular past assigned to the girl story, indeterminate in the Chinese original, is here fixed as the age of knights and ladies; and the seduction itself, which in the Chinese hovers as an eternal possibility within the timeless situation of man and maid ("A fine man *to* seduce her"), is established as completed long ago: "A fair knight seduced her." A teasing oddity in this version is the mysterious "we" who "cover" the slain doe, never to be heard from again.

Take interpretation toward its outer limits and we reach what is perhaps best called a "variation" on this theme:

3. Ezra Pound:

> Lies a dead doe on yonder plain
> whom white grass covers,
> A melancholy maid in spring

```
              is luck
              for                                        5
              lovers
Where the scrub elm skirts the wood
be it not in white mat bound,
As a jewel flawless found
              dead as a doe is maidenhood.            10
Hark!
Unhand my girdle knot.
              Stay, stay, stay
              or the dog
              may                                       15
              bark.
```

Here too the present is pushed back to a past by the language the translator uses: not a specific past, as with the era of knights and ladies, but any past in which contemporary speech still features such (to us) archaic formalisms as "Unhand" or "Hark," and in which the term "maid" still signifies a virgin and in which virginity is prized to an extent that equates its loss with the doe's loss of life. But these evocations of time past are so effectively countered by the obtrusively present tense throughout (lines 1, 2, 4, 7, 8, 10, 11, 12, 13, and 15) that the freewheeling "variation" remains in this important respect closer to the spirit of the original than Waley's translation. On the other hand, it departs from the original and the two other versions by brushing aside the reticence that they carefully preserve as to the precise implications of the girl-deer parallel, choosing instead to place the seduction in the explanatory framework of the oldest story in the world: the way of a man with a maid in the springtime of life.

What both these examples make plain is that the Chinese and Japanese lyric, however contrasting in some ways, have in common at their center a complex of highly charged images generating something very like a magnetic field of potential meanings that cannot be got at in English without bleeding away much of the voltage. In view of this, the best practical advice for those of us who must read these marvelous poems in English translations is to focus intently on these images and ask ourselves what there is in them or in their effect on each other that produces the electricity. To that extent, we can compensate for a part of our losses, learn something positive about the immense explosive powers of imagery, and rest easy in the secure knowledge that translation even in the mode of the short poem brings us (despite losses) closer to the work itself than not reading it at all. "To a thousand cavils," said Samuel Johnson, "one answer is sufficient; the purpose of a writer is to be read, and the criticism which would destroy the power of pleasing must be blown aside." Johnson was defending Pope's Homer for those marks of its own time and place that make it the great interpretation it is, but Johnson's exhilarating common sense applies equally to the problem we are considering here. Literature is to be read, and the criticism that would destroy the reader's power to make some form of contact with much of the world's great writing must indeed be blown aside.

MAYNARD MACK

Sources

Brower, Robert H., and Earl Miner. *Japanese Court Poetry*. Stanford: Stanford University Press, 1961.

The Classic Anthology Defined by Confucius. Tr. Ezra Pound. New Directions, 1954.

Kokinshū: A Collection of Poems Ancient and Modern. Tr. Laurel Rasplica Rodd and Mary Catherine Henkenius. Princeton: Princeton University Press, 1984.

Kokin Wakashū: The First Imperial Anthology of Japanese Poetry. Tr. and ed. Helen Craig McCullough. Stanford: Stanford University Press, 1985.

Legge, James. *The Chinese Classics.* Hong Kong: Hong Kong University Press, 1960.

Waley, Arthur. *170 Chinese Poems.* New York, 1919.

PERMISSIONS ACKNOWLEDGMENTS

Charles Baudelaire: *To the Reader* from IMITATION by Robert Lowell. Copyright © 1959 by Robert Lowell. Copyright renewed 1987 by Harriet, Sheridan and Caroline Lowell. Reprinted by permission of Farrar, Straus & Giroux, LLC. *Spleen LXXVIII, Spleen LXXIX, Correspondences ("Correspondence IV"),* and *Spleen LXXXI* by Charles Baudelaire, from THE FLOWERS OF EVIL, copyright © 1965 by New Directions Publishing Corporation. Reprinted by permission of New Directions Corporation. *Her Hair* by Charles Baudelaire, translated by Doreen Bell, from THE FLOWERS OF EVIL, copyright © 1965 by New Directions Publishing Corporation. Reprinted by permission of New Directions Publishing Corporation. *A Carcass* from THE FLOWERS OF EVIL, translated by James D. McGowan. Originally printed in 66 TRANSLATIONS FROM "LES FLEURS DU MAL" (Spoon River Poetry Press, 1985). Copyright © 1993. Reprinted by permission of Oxford University Press, UK. *Invitation to the Voyage,* translated by Richard Wilbur, from THINGS OF THIS WORLD, copyright © 1956 and renewed 1984 by Richard Wilbur. Reprinted by permission of Harcourt, Inc. *Song of Autumn I* from ONE HUNDRED POEMS FROM "LES FLEURS DU MAL," edited/translated by C. F. McIntyre. Copyright © 1947 C. F. MacIntyre. Reprinted by permission of the University of California Press. *The Voyage* from THE MIRROR OF BAUDELAIRE, edited and translated by Charles Henri Ford. Reprinted by permission of the editor. *One o'Clock in the Morning, Crowds, Windows, Anywhere out of the World* by Charles Baudelaire, translated by Louis Varèse, from PARIS SPLEEN, copyright © 1947 by New Directions Publishing Corporation. Reprinted by permission of New Directions Publishing Corporation.

Gustavo Adolfo Bécquer: Poems from THE RIMAS OF GUSTAVO ADOLFO BÉCQUER, translated by Bruce Phenix. Copyright © 1985. Reprinted by permission of the translator.

Anna Petrovna Bunina: *From the Seashore* from THE BURDEN OF SUFFERANCE, translated by Pamela Perkins and Albert Cook. Reprinted by permission of Garland Books.

Rosalía de Castro: Poems from BESIDE THE RIVER SAR: SELECTED POEMS, edited/translated by S. Griswold Morley. Copyright © 1937 by the Regents of the University of California. Reprinted by permission of the University of California Press.

Anton Chekhov: *The Lady with the Dog* from A. P. Chekhov, SHORT STORIES AND NOVELS. Translated by Ivy Litvinov. Reprinted by permission of the Ivy Litvinov Estate. *The Cherry Orchard,* translated by Avrahm Yarmolinsky, from THE PORTABLE CHEKHOV. Copyright © 1947, 1968 by Viking Penguin, Inc. Copyright © renewed 1975 by Avrahm Yarmolinsky. Reprinted by permission of Viking Penguin, a division of Penguin Books USA, Inc.

Emily Dickinson: Poems 216, 303, 341, 435, 465, 519, 585, 632, 657, 712, 754, 1084, 1129, 1207, and 1593 reprinted by permission of the publisher and the Trustees of Amherst College from THE POEMS OF EMILY DICKINSON, edited by Thomas H. Johnson, Cambridge, Mass.: The Belknap Press of Harvard University Press. Copyright © 1951, 1955, 1979 by the President and Fellows of Harvard College. Poem 1564 from LIFE AND LETTERS OF EMILY DICKINSON, edited by Martha Dickinson Bianchi. Copyright © 1924 by Martha Dickinson Bianchi, renewed 1952 by Alfred Leete Hampson. Reprinted by permission of Houghton Mifflin Company. All rights reserved.

Fyodor Dostoevsky: *Notes from Underground* from NOTES FROM UNDERGROUND: A NORTON CRITICAL EDITION by Fyodor Dostoevsky, translated by Michael R. Katz. Copyright © 1989 by W. W. Norton & Company, Inc. Used by permission of W. W. Norton & Company, Inc.

Gustave Flaubert: MADAME BOVARY by Gustave Flaubert, translated by Francis Steegmuller. Copyright © 1957 by Francis Steegmuller. Used by permission of Random House, Inc.

Asadulla Khan Ghalib: *Ghazal V* translated by Thomas Fitzsimmons; *Ghazal XIV* translated by W. S. Merwin; *Ghazals VIII, XIII,* and *XXI* translated by William Stafford; *Ghazal XIX* translated by Mark Strand; *Ghazals X* and *XII* translated by Adrienne Rich—from GHAZALS OF GHALIB: VERSIONS FROM THE URDU, copyright © 1971 by Columbia University Press. Reprinted by permission of Columbia University Press.

Johann Wolfgang von Goethe: Excerpts from FAUST by Johann Wolfgang Goethe, translated by Walter Kaufmann. Copyright © 1961 by Walter Kaufmann. Used by permission of Doubleday, a division of Random House, Inc.

Heinrich Heine: *The Silesian Weavers, A Pine Is Standing Lonely, A Young Man Loves a Maiden,* and *Ah, Death Is Like the Long Cool Night,* translated by Hal Draper, from THE COMPLETE POEMS OF HEINRICH HEINE. Reprinted by permission of the Center for Socialist History, Alameda, California.

Friedrich Hölderlin: Poems from FRIEDRICH HÖLDERLIN/EDUARD MORIKE: SELECTED POEMS, translated by Christopher Middleton. Copyright © 1972. Reprinted by permission of the University of Chicago Press.

Victor Hugo: *Et nox facta est,* translated by Mary Ann Caws. Copyright © 1990 by Mary Ann Caws. Reprinted by permission of the translator.

Henrik Ibsen: *Hedda Gabler* from HEDDA GABLER AND THREE OTHER PLAYS, translated by Michael Meyer. Copyright © 1962 and 1974 by Michael Meyer. Copyright © renewed 1989 by Michael Meyer. Reprinted by permission of Harold Ober Associates. CAUTION: These plays are fully protected, in whole, in part, or in any form under the copyright laws of the United States of America, the British Empire including the Dominion of Canada, and all other countries of the Copyright Union, and are subject to royalty. All rights, including motion picture, radio, television, recitation, and public reading, are strictly reserved. For professional rights and amateur rights, all inquiries should be addressed to the Author's Agent: Robert A. Freeman Dramatic Agency, Inc., 1501 Broadway, New York NY 10036.

Alphonse de Lamartine: *The Lake,* translated by Andrea Moorhead. Reprinted by permission of the translator.

Giacomo Leopardi: Poems from A LEOPARDI READER, translated and edited by Ottavio M. Casale. Copyright © 1981 by the Board of Trustees of the University of Illinois. Used by permission of the Estate of Giacomo Leopardi.

A13

Stéphane Mallarmé: Poems from COLLECTED POEMS, BILINGUAL EDITION, edited/translated by Henry Weinfeld. Copyright © 1994 by the Regents of the University of California. Reprinted by permission of the publisher, the University of California Press.

Herman Melville: BILLY BUDD, SAILOR, copyright © 1962 by the University of Chicago Press. Reprinted by permission of the University of Chicago Press.

Novalis (Friedrich von Hardenberg): *Yearning for Death* from HYMNS TO THE NIGHT AND OTHER WRITINGS, translated by Charles E. Passage. Copyright © 1960 by the Liberal Arts Press, Inc.

Alexander Sergeyevich Pushkin: *The Queen of Spades,* translated by Gillon R. Aitken, from THE COMPLETE PROSE OF ALEXANDER SERGEYEVICH PUSHKIN. Copyright © 1966 by Barrie and Rockcliff (Barrie Books Ltd). Reprinted by permission of W. W. Norton & Company, Inc., and Georges Borchardt, Inc.

Arthur Rimbaud: *The Drunken Boat,* translated by Stephen Stepanchev. Reprinted by permission of the translator. All other poems from A SEASON IN HELL/THE ILLUMINATIONS by Arthur Rimbaud, translated by Enid Rhodes Peschel. Translation copyright © 1973 by Oxford University Press, Inc. Used by permission of Oxford University Press, Inc.

Paul Verlaine: Poems from PAUL VERLAINE: SELECTED POEMS, translated/edited by C. F. MacIntyre. Copyright © 1948 by the Regents of the University of California. Reprinted by permission of the University of California Press.

Dorothy Wordsworth: Excerpts from *The Grasmere Journals,* from Dorothy Wordsworth, THE GRASMERE JOURNALS, edited by Pamela Woolf. Copyright © 1991. Reprinted by permission of Oxford University Press.

Index